Introduction to Psychology

3rd edition

Under the general editorship of

Claude E. Buxton

YALE UNIVERSITY

Introduction

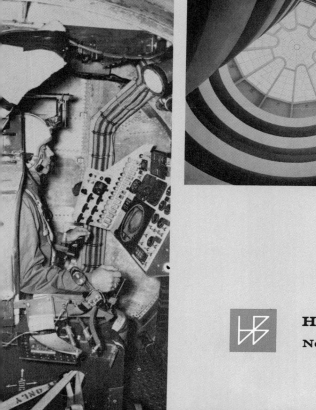

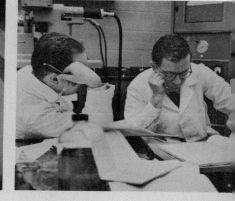

Harcourt, Brace & World, Inc.

New York & Burlingame

Ernest R. Hilgard

STANFORD UNIVERSITY

to Psychology

3rd edition

YELLOW · BLUE · RED · GREEN

Photographs not accompanied by a credit line are from the following sources:

page   1   University of Wisconsin, Primate Laboratory
      63   Photo Researchers, Inc.
    123   United Press International
    185   Ezra Stoller Associates
    251   Cities Service Company
    369   Harbrace Photo
    497   Ralph Buchsbaum
    551   Marc Riboud-Magnum Photographs

Charts by Harry Lazarus; physiology drawings by Lorelle Raboni.

Library of Congress Catalog Card Number: 62-11180

Printed in the United States of America

Preface

Recent advances in physical sciences and technology make urgent the need for social controls of the power that man has unleashed. A growing number of students, puzzled by man's place in the world, and wondering about his capacity for intelligent planning, are turning to the sciences concerned with human conduct. Psychology is one of these sciences of behavior, and courses in psychology show the effects of this growing interest year after year. This serious new interest in what is known and in what is relevant places psychology courses and psychology textbooks under strain, for students are not interested in everything psychologists do just because it is being done: they want to know *why* it is being done.

In developing the third edition of this book, I have relied heavily on the experience of many instructors who used the earlier editions and who reported their sense of the strengths and weaknesses of those editions. But the record of experience with previous editions, valuable as it is, does not suffice to solve many of the problems that arise in trying to prepare a textbook that will be representative of contemporary psychology. With the growth of the psychological profession and the increasing financial support for research, the amount of new research bulks large indeed, with over 10,000 new titles reported annually in *Psychological Abstracts*. The problem of selecting from this vast body of material becomes a staggering one. The rapid growth in the field and the importance of new findings are perhaps best indicated by the fact that about one-third of the references in this edition have appeared since the second edition went to press early in 1957.

Although this version is clearly the outgrowth of earlier editions, the entire book has been rewritten. Users of the previous editions will recognize certain changes in the sequence of presentation, the consolidation or even omission of certain topics, and the addition of a number of totally new topics. No introductory text could do justice to contemporary psychology if it avoided the issues raised by the newer knowledge of the brain (the reticular formation, brain biochemistry, **gating** mechanisms), advances in genetics (changes in chromosome numbers in man, a known basis for mongolism), mathematical models, cognitive simulation by computers, detection methods as against conventional psychophysics, and person perception as an exciting new approach to social psychology. It is hoped that the student who completes the book will have some feeling of the freshness and liveliness of these and other new issues, and of their potential significance for the understanding of man.

In order to incorporate new material without lengthening the book unduly, some curtailing has been necessary. The two chapters on motivation have been reduced to one, with a sharp revision of content reflecting the decline in the position of the need-drive-incentive theory and the rise of competing theories. Two chapters on individual differences and intelligence have also been reduced to one. A single chapter on personality has become two, one dealing with appraisal, the other with theories of personality; personality is today too central a topic to permit adequate treatment in a short chapter. Social psychology is now treated in a single chapter instead of two, as before. There are two significant changes in chapter order: the material on perception precedes that on learning (although person perception is reserved for the social psychology chapter), and the treatment of conflict and adjustment and of psychotherapy comes much later than in the previous edition.

A recurrent theme in the presentation is the idea that psychological explanations often take one of two modes: developmental or interactive. The developmental mode of explanation emphasizes the historical roots of present behavior; this mode of analysis stems in part from association psychology as brought up to date through modern learning theory, and in part from maturational-growth-genetic theories that also see the child as father to the man. By emphasizing what is going on here and now, the interactive mode contrasts with, but does not contradict, the developmental mode. Much of the study of motivation and conflict is naturally cast in interactive terms. This distinction helps orient the student when a transition is made, for example, from the study of perception, in which the interactive mode is uppermost, to the study of learning, in which a developmental approach is more generally adopted. Hopefully, the developmental-interactive distinction will provide an opportunity for the instructor to bring out the relationships among various topics but without tying these topics together so tightly that he will no longer feel free to rearrange chapters to suit his purposes.

Just as the previous editions benefited from the advice of numerous colleagues whose names appeared in the respective prefaces, this edition has been aided by many teachers, too numerous to list here, who communicated their experiences either personally or through a detailed questionnaire circulated to many users of the second edition. I am grateful for their help and interest. Of particular value were the careful readings and comments, either on the second edition or on the revised manuscript, provided by the following: Ernest S. Barratt of Texas Christian University; A. W. Bendig of the University of Pittsburgh; R. N. Berry of Indiana University; John M. Coyne of the Life Sciences Department, General Dynamics/Astronautics; Robert S. Feldman of the University of Massachusetts; Winfred Hill of Northwestern University; Raymond J. McCall of Marquette University; and Herbert F. Wright of the University of Kansas. My gratitude again must be expressed to Claude E. Buxton of Yale University, who as editorial adviser gave his help throughout the revision, even when it interrupted a precious working period while he was on leave in England.

The influence of those who helped in the earlier editions continues, even though I do not repeat their names. As before, I am particularly grateful to my wife, Josephine R. Hilgard, whose case materials have given heightened reality to many parts of the text.

Ernest R. Hilgard

Stanford University
Stanford, California
March 1962

Contents

Growth and Development

Motivated and Emotional Behavior

Conflict, Adjustment, and Mental Health

Social Behavior

21 Vocational and Professional Applications of Psychology

The Science of Psychology

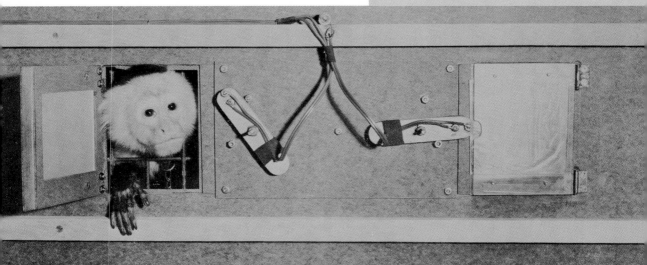

In seeking to understand man and the lower animals, psychology falls among the behavioral sciences that include sociology, anthropology, and those aspects of social science concerned with the individual in relation to his environment. Man's interest in himself began before recorded history, but psychology as a science is a product of the last hundred years. The natural science approach to psychology lays heavy emphasis upon the flesh-and-blood organism—its anatomical equipment, its growth, its processes of integration and interaction. The comparative method, as in other biological sciences, studies the interrelationships among organisms at different stages in evolutionary development.

CHAPTER 1

Psychology as a Behavioral Science

Because he can reflect upon the past, take account of present experiences, and make plans for the future, man has always sought to understand himself and the world about him. When he found occurrences beyond his comprehension, he at first tended to attribute them to divine intervention or to some sort of magic, perhaps practiced upon him by his enemies. The roots of science began when he started to find some sort of order in natural occurrences that made them comprehensible; when, for example, he found that he could control his food supply by domesticating animals or by planting crops.

Science leads to understanding of natural events; it leads to predictions about their course and therefore to some control over what takes place. Psychology is like other sciences in seeking to comprehend, to predict, and to control, taking as its special subject matter the behavior of man and the lower animals. Psychology is interested in the ways in which behavior develops in the evolution of the species and in the growth of the individual, in learning and problem-solving, in the motives that initiate, sustain, and guide behavior. As in the case of other sciences, psychology has its "pure" and its "applied" aspects; as an applied science it proposes ways in which psychological knowledge can be used in child rearing, in education, in industrial production, in government, and in international relations.

The student will naturally ask whether a course in psychology will help him in his human relationships and personality difficulties. Will he be able to form better judgments of other people? Will he be able to plan more wisely for himself? Will he make friends more easily? Will he be less likely to lose his temper when he becomes angry?

The answer to these questions is both "Yes" and "No." The "Yes" part of the answer is that, after studying psychology, you should be better able to understand human motives, better able to appraise your own and others' interests and abilities, better prepared to get along with those about you. The "No" part of the answer is that it is not easy to apply psychological knowledge to the solving of your personal problems. If you have had difficulties in getting along up to now, a single course in psychology is not going to teach you suddenly to overcome all your difficulties. A course in psychology is not a course in self-help, and a psychology textbook is not a manual on the art of handling people.

Psychological science, furthermore, is in an early stage of development. Many of its facts are not yet firmly established, and theoretical interpretations are often controversial. Sometimes we shall be studying more about how psychologists seek answers than about the results they have found.

If, however, you do not expect one course in psychology to teach you all there is to know about human behavior, you may properly look forward to learning many things that will be useful to you in your ordinary life. In fact, you will gain more from your study of psychology if you make an effort throughout to apply what you are learning to yourself and to those about you. Psychology is not to be thought of as something mysterious and remote.

The Definition of Psychology

Psychology may be defined as *the science that studies the behavior of man and other* _animals._ For this definition to be useful, it is necessary to specify more clearly what psychologists mean by behavior. We can get some idea of what _behavior_ means to the psychologist if we look briefly at the organization of this book, pausing occasionally to glance at an illustration of what it is that psychologists do. Later we can return to a more detailed definition of behavior and a consideration of the relationship of psychology to other sciences.

The topics covered in this book

1. _The Behaving Organism._ As a science rooted in biology, psychology is interested in the bodily processes that make activity possible. Thus psychologists often refer to the _stimuli_ (singular: _stimulus_) that impinge upon sense organs, and to the _responses_ that occur because of the way the organism operates. Stimuli include the lights, sounds, odors, pinpricks, and other physical energy sources that are the external (and sometimes internal) occasions for what the organism does, goading it to action, interrupting what it is doing, directing its choices. The responses (in man) are what he does when his brain is active, his muscles move, and his glands secrete. We therefore touch briefly on the operation of the _skeleton_ and the _muscles,_ moving on to glance at the varied functioning of the _endocrine_ (ductless) glands, such as the thyroid or the sex glands. But psychologists are particularly interested in the _nervous system_ and especially in the _central nervous system,_ whose most complex portion is the _brain._

It has been found, for example, that there are centers deep in the brain (in a part of the brain, old from an evolutionary standpoint, called the hypothalamus) that appear to produce the equivalent of pleasure or of pain when these centers are electrically stimulated (Olds and Milner, 1954; Delgado, Roberts, and Miller, 1954).[1] Psychologists

not only participated in the original experiments that made this discovery, but also have since carried out a number of further experiments to determine how similar the responses to electrical stimulation of the brain are to the effects of external pain or food reward. For example, studies have been made of the reaction to conflict when a thirsty rat receives an electric shock as it attempts to drink. The rat at once approaches the water and withdraws from it in fear, assuming a characteristic posture. When the shock is received through an implanted electrode in the brain, the rat behaves just as if a shock had been received on its snout (Figure 1-1). Thus it appears plausible that the shock through the electrode is equivalent to painful stimulation.

2. _Growth and Development._ The child is indeed "father to the man." We can understand much of adult behavior only through a knowledge of the course of its development in the child. Two principles stand out as we study human development. One is that the growth of the body and the nervous system follows certain patterns rooted in biology. These are reflected in the concept of _maturation_ of the organism along built-in (inherited) lines. The other is that a mature organism is also a product of _learning._ In man, this learning is in part a product of _social living,_ a product of his _culture._ Hence in studying human development, we are interested in the processes of socialization, that is, the ways in which the infant turns into a civilized person.

3. _Motivation and Emotion._ The newborn infant is aroused to activity by his bodily needs—the needs for air, food, elimination, a comfortable temperature, sleep. All such needs are the physiological roots of what psychologists call _motivation._ But motives become complex as the individual grows up, and psychologists study how they are acquired, how strong they are, and how people differ in their motives. Some indi-

[1] Throughout this book you will find references to studies which document or expand on the statements made here. Detailed bibliographical information on these studies appears in the list at the end of the book.

viduals conform readily to their cultures, while others rebel: some develop good work habits and have high motives to achieve, while others are more shiftless; some are competitive and aggressive, others self-effacing. Emotions and motives are closely related, for the excitement of highly motivated activity has its emotional coloring, as in the relationship between anger and aggressive action or between fear and fleeing from danger.

4. *Perception.* We perceive the world through our eyes or ears or by way of our other senses. But what is perception? How is it that we recognize a given color as red, or hear one sound as music and another as noise, or "sense" that one facial expression is friendly and another hostile? From its earliest days psychology has devoted a great deal of attention to such questions. It is clear that perception depends not only on our equipment of sense organs, but also upon the structures in our nervous system which enable us to say "This is hot" or "That is ugly." We shall meet a number of the problems posed by perception in this book.

5. *Learning and Thinking.* Because of its importance learning is a topic of special interest to psychologists, both in its theoretical aspects and in its practical aspects. The theoretical problems of learning include the answers to such puzzling questions as how rewards and punishments operate; what goes on when we remember and when we forget, or when we acquire skills; how learning one thing affects the learning of others. The answers to these questions have important practical consequences, for much social effort goes into learning and teaching—of the young by parents and teachers, of apprentices on the job, of members of industrial and business organizations as they face new tasks.

A new interest in "programed" learning, often using so-called teaching machines, illustrates the practical consequences of experimental studies of learning. A *program* is an attempt to apply what we know about the essential features of learning to the task of individual instruction, using a technique in which each step of the process is carefully planned to provide the best conditions for learning. We shall consider later on the detailed ways in which such programs make use of learning theory; for the present we may merely indicate that there have been promising successes in their use. For example, it has been reported that elementary school children who studied their spelling by using a program in a teaching machine did much better than those who learned it in the conventional way (Porter, 1959).

Thinking and problem-solving make use of what we have learned, and thereby provide the occasions for new learning. The interrelations between learning and thinking, including the role of language, furnish plenty of problems for investigation.

6. *Individuality and Personality.* Individual uniqueness is a product of the hereditary and environmental influences that have shaped the person: the accidents of his birth and upbringing, what he has perceived and learned, what he has thought about. Psychologists have developed various ways of assessing or measuring many kinds of differences among people. Perhaps the most familiar of these devices is the intelligence test.

But intelligence is only one aspect of individuality. All of us know people of whom we say "He's a real person" (or, regrettably, "He's got quite a personality"). What is personality? What is it that conclusively distinguishes one individual from another? And what do we mean when we speak of the "self"? These are questions of much concern to psychology.

7. *Conflict, Adjustment, and Mental Health.* For many readers, this aspect of psychology may seem the most important. How does a person meet frustration and conflict? What happens when he can no longer cope with his problems in ordinary ways? Is "adjustment" an ideal, or not? What, indeed, is mental health? While psychology has no final answers to these ques-

tions, it has at least been able to shed some light on them. There have been some successes in applying the methods of the experimental laboratory to these fields, but much has also been done in the interpretation of case histories. The following is one example.

Cadet J was attempting to learn to fly. For some reason that he did not understand he was having difficulty in following the commands of his instructor. The instructor would tell him to practice making right turns. He would make one turn, then forget that he was supposed to make any more. Even though he wanted to follow the commands, he was unable to do so.

When he talked over his problem with a psychological counselor, he showed that he was baffled by his own behavior. It finally became clear to him that the instructor strongly reminded him of his father, whose authority over him as a child he had very much resented. His resistance to the commands of the instructor was similar to the resistance he had offered his father, as well as an expression of resentment against his

1-1

Conflict between thirst and pain in the rat

A rat that has learned to drink from the spout (*left*) is given an unpleasant stimulation through the electrode implanted in his brain when he approaches the spout.

This produces the typical conflict position shown: the rat's neck is stretched out toward the water, but he is ready to back away because of the threatened shock. The conflict between thirst and the pain produced by brain stimulation is indistinguishable from that between thirst and the pain produced by an external electric shock.

Martin Iger

father. This discovery of his own unconscious motives came as a considerable surprise to him (Muench and Rogers, 1946).

8. *Social Aspects of Psychology.* The old saw "Two's company and three's a crowd," familiar as it may seem in one context, illustrates a number of basic psychological questions. What is the difference between one person's response to his physical environment and his response to another person in that environment? What do we mean by a group, and how does group behavior differ from and affect individual behavior? The final section of this book tackles these questions, concluding with a discussion of the ways in which psychologists as professionals address themselves to these and all the other aspects of human behavior touched on in this introductory text.

Behavior as defined by psychology

With the preceding illustrations of psychology before us, we are now prepared to state more precisely what the psychologist means when he says that psychology is the study of the behavior of man and other animals.

Behavior. By *behavior* we mean those activities of an organism that can be observed by another person or by an experimenter's instruments. A child eats breakfast, rides a bicycle, talks, blushes, laughs, and cries. All these verbs describe forms of behavior. Observations of behavior may be made unaided, as in watching a child at play, or they may be aided with instruments, as in giving a lie-detection test.

Though our primary interest in this book is the understanding of man, we shall have something to say, too, about the behavior of lower animals, because what we learn from studying the lower animals often helps us to understand man. We can control the lives of lower organisms in the laboratory from the moment of their birth. In those of short life span we can study inheritance through several generations. We can do brain surgery on animals (as in the illustration of implanted electrodes, Figure 1-1), while such experiments are possible with human beings only under special conditions of illness or injury. Sometimes the fact that animals learn less rapidly than human beings is an advantage in that the details of the process are spaced out for study. While caution is always needed in applying the results of animal experimentation to man, study of lower animals contributes to knowledge in psychology just as it does in biology and medicine.

A point of disagreement among some psychologists exists over the relative emphasis to be placed upon lower organisms and man in a science of psychology. The disagreement leads to two interpretations of *comparative psychology,* the name given to the study of the behavior of lower organisms in their interrelationships with each other and to man. One interpretation is that any specimen of behavior is worth studying in its own right, yielding such generalizations as it may, without regard to its relationship to man. Thus a comparative psychologist studying why salmon return to lay their eggs in the river in which they were hatched does not want to be asked what this has to do with human behavior. The other interpretation is that we seek to understand man, and in order to do so we study the evolution of the processes that we find at work in him. This kind of interest is similar to that of the medical investigator who works with animals in order to find the drugs or other treatment procedures that may prove useful in treating human disease. For a strong defense of the interpretation that the comparative psychologist should not be concerned primarily with man, see Beach (1960). As long as one remains within the framework of natural science, the issue is not a divisive one, for there is plenty of investigatory work to be done by those who accept either one of the alternatives.

---

[2] Critical discussions are introduced from time to time, especially to point up controversial issues in contemporary psychology. They may be omitted at the discretion of the instructor.

Another form of the issue with regard to emphasis upon man is a more important one. Some psychologists hold that man is so different from the lower organisms that human psychology is something entirely different from animal psychology, and the behavior of lower animals can therefore be disregarded. This point of view finds its expression in forms of psychology more prevalent in Europe than in America, going by such names as "understanding"-psychology, character-psychology, phenomenology, existentialism. These psychologies make much of man's ability to foresee the future, of his knowledge that he will die, of his ability to understand directly the feelings of another human being and to find meaning in human suffering. These intuitive, moral qualities are said to be distinctly human, without parallels in animal psychology. Such a point of view deserves acknowledgment, and is not to be lightly dismissed. While it is affiliated more with philosophy and religion than with a naturalistic psychology, it has become influential in psychiatry, that is, in the treatment of human emotional and mental illness (e.g., May and others, 1958).

The emphasis in this book will reflect the general orientation of American psychology today, which seeks to place the study of behavior in the context of natural science, recognizing man's affiliation with other biological organisms, and hence tracing continuities between man and other animals. Such an orientation need not deny man's uniqueness where such uniqueness is demonstrable.

Conscious Processes. Each of us knows what it feels like to be hungry, to have a headache, to burn a finger. Each of us knows what it feels like to be praised or reproved. Each of us is aware of his own anger and fear, excitement and fatigue; no one else has full access to this awareness. An individual's perception of his world, his memories, his flights of imagination, his dreams, his pleasures and pains, belong to a private world, the world of his own *consciousness.* By conscious experiences we mean simply these events of which only the person himself is fully aware. Psychology is interested in this world, even though access to it is necessarily

by way of *inference.*[3] We may learn by external signs that a man is suffering pain and we may even arrive at a satisfactory judgment of its intensity, but the conscious process—the actual awareness of the pain—is his alone.

Psychologists are by no means unanimous as to the place of private experience (conscious processes) in a science of psychology. Some extremists believe that private experiences have no place in science; a consistent science, they say, must be built with objective data open to observation by any unbiased observer. Most psychologists, however, hold that private experiences are just as much a part of the real world as more observable activities, and, while insisting that data must be objective, they accept the *verbal report* of these experiences as data for science. Suppose, for example, you tell me that you had a dream of flying with wings. Then what you have told me about your dream is part of your observable behavior. I can record it on tape and play it back to anyone who wishes to know exactly what you said when you reported your dream. I do not have full access to your dream, although I may be able to make some inferences about its meaning from other things that I know about you and your behavior. By including verbal reports in the study of behavior, psychologists can restrict their data to overt activities, but include in their *inferences* statements about conscious processes.

Unconscious Processes. An even more difficult problem is raised when we infer the presence of *unconscious processes.* This term

[3] Our observations almost always include inferences that go beyond the data given. If I see a man waving his hand on a street corner in New York, I *observe* merely the hand-waving, though I may *infer* that he is trying to hail a taxicab. I may be wrong; he may be trying to catch a friend's attention or he may be making a meaningless drunken gesture. Inferences are thus always somewhat uncertain; the scientific task is to see that our inferences from data are made in such a manner as to have a high probability that the inferences are correct.

is not usually applied to the nonconscious processes such as the circulation of the blood or the reflex constriction of the pupil of the eye. Rather, by unconscious processes we mean processes similar to conscious ones such as wishes or fears, but processes which the subject is not aware of, that is, which he cannot report, such as those controlling the behavior of the aviation cadet (pp. 5-6). Can the existence of such processes legitimately be inferred, and can they be classified as behavior? The answer is yes: most psychologists grant that we can infer unconscious motives from verbal behavior, gestures, and other behavioral signs. For example, if a person acts in a conceited manner it may be that he is actually boasting in order to conceal an *unconscious* fear of being thought inferior. There is no sharp distinction between conscious and unconscious; it would perhaps be better to speak of degrees of awareness. For example, we may be only dimly aware of the clock's striking, yet be able later to count the strokes; we may catch ourselves humming a tune we did not know we had started to hum. The conceited person is not wholly unaware of his need to hide his fears; he may simply be unaware of the extent to which he goes to "cover up." By making inferences from observations, we are then able to include unconscious as well as conscious processes within our science of behavior.

Psychology and other sciences

The family of sciences to which psychology belongs is coming to be known as the *behavioral sciences.* Other members of the family are *anthropology,* which deals largely with nonliterate ("primitive") human societies, and *sociology,* which is concerned with man's social life and the institutions he creates. Other social sciences (e.g., economics, history, political science) are classifiable as behavioral sciences to the extent that they are committed to the study of man by the methods of science.

Psychology, as a behavioral science, touches and overlaps the other behavioral sciences. But psychology leans also toward physiology and toward the physical sciences. Some of these relationships are worth examining.

Psychology in relation to *physical science* is chiefly a borrower. Many of the instruments used in the psychological laboratory, such as galvanometers, amplifiers, and time-measuring instruments, come out of physics or engineering laboratories. The methods of chemical analysis are borrowed when waste products in the blood are studied in fatigue, or when the effects of hormone injection are analyzed.

During World War II, with the elaboration of many new observational devices such as direction finders and radar screens, the importance of man's relation to his instruments came into focus. There developed a branch of applied science known as *human factors research.* This new study is only one illustration of the blending of sciences— here engineering and psychology.

The affiliation between psychology and *physiology* has always been very close. Much of early experimental psychology was concerned with sensory problems and hence with the sense organs and related nervous structures. Many of the developments in the study of animal psychology depended upon correlations between brain damage and learning. Studies of the effects of drugs and hormones also cross the border between psychology and physiology or pharmacology. Other aspects of biology, such as embryology, genetics, and ecology, have their significance for psychology because of the psychologist's interest in growth, in heredity, and in the adaptation of the organism to its environment.

Within medicine, psychology finds its closest affiliation with *psychiatry.* Psychiatry, in its broadest sense, can be defined as a medical psychology. The new field of *psychosomatic medicine* recognizes the part that emotional and other psychological disturbances play in organic ailments such as ulcers and asthma. The interests of psychology and medical science overlap in studying the effects of diet and drugs on behavior or in studying special conditions such as aphasia (loss of speech or language), amnesia (loss of memory), hallucinations, or hypnosis.

These brief suggestions of the interplay between psychology and other fields of study open up fascinating possibilities for collaboration between those whose expertness lies in one or another of these studies and those whose expertness lies within psychology. An interesting question arises as to how much the related expertnesses can be combined in the same person, or whether the collaboration can be better achieved through joint efforts. That is, it may be that a good legal psychology will be forthcoming only when a lawyer trains himself in psychology, or when a psychologist trains himself in the law, rather than when a lawyer and a psychologist get together. Perhaps a compromise is possible; the collaborators may need to know something of the other person's specialty, but they may not need to be equally expert in both specialties.

The Methods
of Psychological Science

The aim of science above all else is to discover new and useful information in the form of verifiable data, that is, of data obtained under conditions such that other qualified people can make similar observations and obtain the same results. This calls for orderliness and precision in uncovering relationships and communicating them to others. The scientific ideal is not always reached, but as a science becomes better established it rests upon a large body of relationships that can be taken for granted because they have been so often validated.

Methods of the experimental laboratory

The term *experimental psychology* was once applied only to a particular subject matter of general psychology inherited from the earliest nineteenth-century laboratories, chiefly sensory processes, reaction time, and associative learning. While there are still some psychologists who define experimental psychology in this limited way (usually adding today physiological studies and studies with lower animals), it is preferable to think of experimental psychology as psychology grounded in the laboratory method, whatever the content of the experiment may be. The distinguishing characteristics are those of the laboratory, not of the subjects used or the topics covered. Thus child psychology and social psychology may be amenable to experimental study, and to the extent that they are they belong within experimental psychology.

The relationships the psychologist seeks to discover are *regular* ("lawful") *relationships among variables*. By a variable is meant something that can occur with different values; if learning ability increases with age, both learning ability and age are variables. Both can take on different values, learning being either slower or faster, and the learner being younger or older. To the extent that learning changes systematically with increasing age, we can discover a lawful relationship between them.

We distinguish the methods of the experimental laboratory from other forms of observation and description by the degree to which the experimenter is able to *control the variables* that determine the experimental outcome. If he seeks to discover whether learning depends upon age, he can control the age variable by selecting groups of children of different ages. If he then sets for each group the same learning task, such as memorizing a sequence of numbers, he can determine whether the older children do indeed master the task more rapidly than the younger ones. In this situation the various age levels reached are the _antecedent_ conditions; the learning performance is the *result* of these conditions (among others, presumably). We call the antecedent condi-

A dynamometer

Lafayette Instrument Co.

This version of the instrument measures strength of grip.

tion the *independent variable;* the variable that changes as a result of change in the antecedent condition is called the *dependent variable.*

The experimenter controls the value of the independent variable; the circumstances of the experiment determine the value of the dependent variable. These terms may be confusing, but the distinction can best be remembered if it is noted that the value of the *dependent* variable *depends* upon what happens in the experiment—it is the outcome variable.[4] The distinction between the two kinds of variable will become clearer if we follow an actual illustrative experiment.

[4] Confusion may arise because the value of the independent variable "depends" upon the experimenter. As in the relation between parent and child (at least in theory!), the one in *control* is more *independent;* the one subject to circumstances beyond his control is *dependent.*

Experiments often begin with hunches coming from ordinary experience. Students typically report that they can get more out of study if they sit upright and are alert rather than relaxed, but they also report that if they are too keyed up they do not profit from study. Not all agree; some prefer to study lying down, some with the radio on. These reports suggest that there may be a relationship between tension in the learner's muscles and his ease of learning. There is uncertainty about the relationship, but we can reduce the uncertainty by studying the relationship in the laboratory.

The following experiment by Courts (1939) illustrates how variables are controlled and measured in the attempt to reduce uncertainty. Sixty college students learned nonsense syllables (consisting of two consonants with a vowel between, such as *geb*) while exerting muscular effort by squeezing an instrument known as a *dynamometer* (Figure 1-2). Each subject participating in the experiment was first asked to squeeze the dynamometer as hard as he could for 30 seconds. The reading at the end of this time was used to assign his maximum grip. He then learned different lists of syllables both under normal conditions (without the dynamometer) and while squeezing with a grip representing various fractions of the maximum grip. The amount learned under each tension condition was tested by the number of syllables recalled after five trials through the list. Meaningless combinations were used so that the several lists could all be made alike in difficulty. The results show that learning increased with the strength of grip up to ¼ the maximum grip; greater tensions were accompanied by reduced learning, until at ¾ the maximum grip the learning was below normal (Figure 1-3).

Note that the experimenter had worked out a careful *plan* before he brought the subjects to the laboratory. First of all, he had planned to hold many conditions constant: the general setting for the experiment, the measuring instruments used, the nature of the materials to be learned, the length of each list, the number of trials allowed for learning, and the method of testing learning. Then he carefully established *tension* as the *independent variable* by assigning a maximum value according to the subject's strength of grip. He obtained this value by having the subject squeeze as hard as he could. Then he set the lower values as fractions of the maximum value. The *dependent variable* became the amount of *learning* associated with each step of tension. To do a quantitative experiment the experimenter had to have scales of measurement for both kinds of variables. The *tension* was measured by the units of the dynamometer (kilograms) and then converted to fractions of the maximum. The *learning* was measured by the number of nonsense syllables recalled. Hence the experimenter could plot the results as a relationship between two variables, in the form of Figure 1-3. Finally, he used enough subjects (60 students) so that he could count on similar results if he repeated the experiment with other subjects.

Psychological laboratories, like other scientific laboratories, are specially equipped places in which experimentation is carried on. Precision instruments are usually necessary to control the experiment and obtain exact data. We may need to produce colors of known wave lengths in studies of vision, or sounds of known frequency for studies of audition. Or we may wish to expose a pattern in the aperture of a viewing screen for a fraction of a second. Control of stimuli thus often requires apparatus. In measuring response, we may also need precision instruments. We may wish to have an accurate measure of time in thousandths of a second, or we may wish to amplify slight electrical currents from the muscles or from the brain. The psychological laboratory has its audiometers, photometers, oscilloscopes, mazes, precision timers, and many other instru-

1-3

Effects of tension on learning

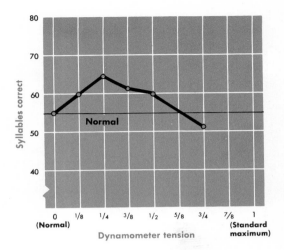

Muscular tension improves learning of nonsense syllables up to one-fourth of the maximum tension possible; greater tension decreases learning. (From Courts, 1939)

ments for presenting controlled stimuli and for accurate registration of response.

The value of an experiment is not determined, however, by the amount of apparatus used. Fundamentally, arrangements for experimentation are a matter of logic. Experiments have to be carefully designed if their results are to be informative. If the logic of experimentation requires precision apparatus, then such apparatus is used; if it does not, then good experimentation may be done by means of pencil and paper procedures.

The degree of control possible in the laboratory makes a controlled experiment the preferred scientific method when it can be used appropriately. However, for psychology to develop as a science, it is not essential that all its problems be brought into the laboratory. Some other sciences, such as geology and astronomy, are experimental only to a very limited extent. Recognizing the great value of the laboratory approach, we shall now turn to some of the other methods used in psychological investigations.

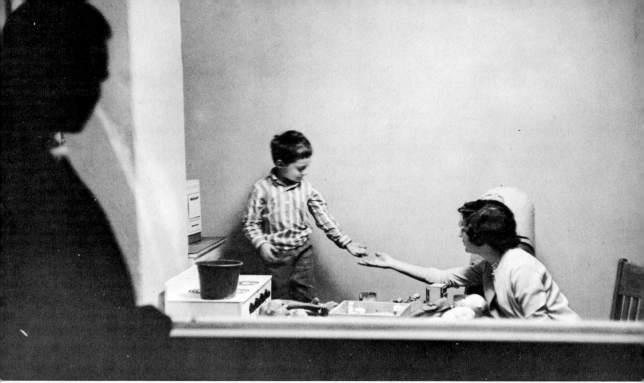

1-4

Observing a child's behavior

When made under controlled conditions, naturalistic observations merge into experimental, as, for example, in this observational room used both in training psychologists and in studying child behavior.

Naturalistic observation

In the early stages of a science it is necessary to explore the ground, to become familiar with the relationships that will later become the subject of more precise study. Careful observation of animal and human behavior (including the study of our own conscious processes) is the starting point for psychology. A study of gibbons in their native environment of Thailand may tell us things about their social organization that will help us to direct our laboratory investigations. Nonliterate tribes will help us to see ranges of variation in human institutions that would go unrecognized if we confined our study to men and women in our own culture. We learn from observing a mother cat caring for her kittens something about the uniformities of innate animal behavior. Motion pictures of a newborn baby can reveal the details of movement patterns shortly after birth. Such observations of natural phenomena gradually merge into experiments as the conditions of observation are standardized through laboratory control (Figure 1-4).

The value of naturalistic observations is limited by the fact that anecdotes may be substituted for genuine observations and that interpretation may be substituted for description. Thus we might be tempted to say that a hungry animal is "looking for food" when all we have observed is heightened activity. Investigators must therefore be trained to observe and record accurately in order to avoid reading their own wishes or biases into what they report. With proper precautions, however, naturalistic observations can be important not only in the early stages of a science but later on, as correctives to incomplete theories.

Case histories

Psychologists are often interested in the individual. For that reason scientific biographies of individuals become important sources of data. A scientific biography is known as a *case history*. Case histories originally were developed largely in connection with social work. The workers found it helpful in making recommendations about the individual to know something of his family background, circumstances of the mother's pregnancy, ease or difficulty of childbirth, health history, school history, social history, any unusual emotional episodes, and circumstances surrounding the present complaint. When case histories are organized for purposes of scientific study, items have to be included which are relevant to the theories being tested. If, for example, someone is studying the difference between bottle-fed and breast-fed children, it is important to have additional details about how the child was fed, who did the feeding, the nature of the weaning, and so on.

Two methods can be used for constructing the case history. One method is that of *the diary of development,* in which the case history is constructed as the individual grows up. Some long-term studies have selected groups of children at birth or in early childhood and then followed their development for years. The second method is to prepare the case history by *reconstructing the biography* according to data from the past as recalled by the individual, his parents, or others who knew him in his earlier days. This method is, of course, the usual way of obtaining a case history when a juvenile gets into trouble or an adult enters a mental hospital. There are disadvantages in this retrospective method because of distortions or oversights, but it is often the only method available.

The interview

The interview as a means of obtaining the data that go into the case history has itself become a research device. The hazards of the interview are many; accurate replies depend upon questions that are clear and unambiguous and upon a good relationship between the interviewer and the person interviewed. The interview is now widely used in studies of voting behavior, opinions on public issues, and market research. With advances in techniques of interviewing, selecting the sample, and treating the data, the interview has become an important tool.

Test methods

The *test* as an instrument of research has an important place in contemporary psychology. We use it to measure all manner of abilities, interests, attitudes, and accomplishments. By means of tests, large quantities of data can be obtained from people in factories or hospitals or schools, with a minimum of disturbance of their living routines and without elaborate laboratory equipment. Test construction and use are no simple matters; later chapters will explore the problems of testing in some detail.

The Roots of Modern Psychology

Although psychology is a young science, thoughtful men of all periods of history have attempted to find solutions to their problems. Books on the history of psychology discuss the views of early Greek philosophers, especially those of Plato and Aristotle. After the Greeks, St. Augustine (354-430 A.D.) is considered the next great precursor of the modern psychologist because of his skill in introspection [5] and his great curiosity about psychological phenomena,

[5] Introspection is a term used in psychology to refer to the description of one's own conscious processes. It is not to be confused with morbid introspection, in which one is preoccupied with one's inner life in an unhealthy way.

including the behavior of young infants and of crowds at chariot races. Descartes (1596-1650) left his mark on the history of psychology through his theory that animals are machines that can be studied much as other machines are studied. He introduced the concept of reflex action, which has had a significant place in both physiology and psychology. Many prominent philosophers of the seventeenth and eighteenth centuries—Leibnitz, Hobbes, Locke, Hume, to name only four—grappled with questions of concern to psychologists today. Thus psychology grew out of philosophy, and its history is intermingled with the history of philosophy and of other sciences.

Two early approaches

In the nineteenth century, before experimental psychology proper began, two theories of the mind competed for psychologists' support. The one, known as *faculty psychology,* was a doctrine of mental powers. According to this theory, the mind had a few principal faculties such as thinking, feeling, and willing, that accounted for its activities. These faculties were further broken down into a couple of dozen mental subfaculties, such that we remembered through the subfaculty of memory, imagined through the subfaculty of imagination, and so on. It was faculty psychology that encouraged early nineteenth-century phrenologists such as Gall to try to localize special faculties in parts of the brain. Careful students were dissatisfied with the doctrine of faculties because it explained nothing but merely classified mental activities.

The *association psychologists* held a second, opposing theory. They denied inborn faculties of the mind; instead, they limited the mind's content to ideas coming by way of the senses, which then became associated through principles such as similarity, contrast, and contiguity. They explained all mental activity through this *association of ideas.* Both faculty psychology and association psychology have their counterparts at the present time, but with notable differences between the old and the new. The search for primary abilities underlying scores on psychological tests, which we will meet later, is related to faculty psychology, but it differs in its careful quantitative approach. Much of learning theory, especially the theory of conditioned responses, is similar to earlier association theory, except that now we believe that stimuli and responses rather than ideas are associated. Very often, thinking men of earlier centuries anticipated later developments.

Wundt's laboratory

Wilhelm Wundt (1832-1920) is commonly called the founder of modern experimental psychology, for it was he who opened the first formal psychological laboratory, in Leipzig in 1879. The largest part of his work was devoted to the senses, especially to vision. But Wundt and his co-workers also did a good deal of work on measuring the time of mental processes through the study of reaction time. In addition, they studied attention, emotional processes, and associative processes in memory.

Wundt's psychology was *introspective* (that is, relying heavily on the subject's report of his own experiences) but it was at the same time devoted to laboratory methods, including the use of various kinds of precision instruments. We may take as an illustration one of the early experiments from Wundt's laboratory, an experiment on *reaction time,* performed in 1888. Reaction time is the time that elapses between a stimulus and the response to the stimulus. Wundt found that if a subject who is prepared to lift a finger from a telegraph key when a light comes on pays careful attention to *seeing the light,* it takes him longer to respond than if he directs his attention to *moving his finger.* This seems a little strange, especially since he reacts very promptly in any case, but the difference, as reported somewhat inexactly in the early experiment, was about 0.1 second. To what was it attributed?

Wundt distinguished between *perception* and *apperception,* a distinction that is now chiefly of historical interest. He said that when the attention was on the movement, there was simple perception, and the light triggered the movement very promptly. When, however, the attention was on the stimulus, there was an additional activity of apperception, which we may think of as a richer perception of the light. Wundt decided that this apperception required about 0.1 second. His interpretations are no longer accepted, for the processes intervening between the stimulus and the response are organized in more complex ways than he proposed. But such experiments helped to tie theory to observations, familiarized psychologists with the use of laboratory instruments, and introduced quantitative measurements.

(Wundt's laboratory is important to us in America because so many pioneers in American psychology went there to study.) Although William James had a small demonstration laboratory at Harvard as early as 1875, the first formal laboratory in America was that established in (1883 at Johns Hopkins University by G. Stanley Hall,) one of those who went to study with Wundt. Hall also founded the first American psychological journal, the *American Journal of Psychology,* in 1887. The first man to be called professor of psychology in America was J. McKeen Cattell, another Wundt student, who took that title at the University of Pennsylvania in 1888. Before the end of the 1890's, Wundt's students were to be found at such universities as California, Catholic University, Clark, Cornell, Harvard, Iowa, Minnesota, Princeton, Stanford, and Yale. It is not surprising that the new laboratories in America were founded largely on the pattern of Wundt's laboratory.

Other roots of contemporary psychology

Although the impetus for the founding of laboratories, and the problems initially dealt with, came largely from Germany, espe-

1-5

Wilhelm Wundt

Bettmann

The founder of modern experimental psychology.

cially from Wundt, other influences soon began to be felt.

One set of influences came from England, especially from Francis Galton (1822-1911). Galton pioneered in an experimental psychology in Great Britain which was devoted mainly to a study of the problem of individual differences, including inherited abilities. Hence he had an important influence on the development of intelligence tests and other kinds of tests that have become prominent in American psychology. He also had his influence upon the laboratory (Figure 1-6). It was he who invented the statistical technique of correlation and developed the index later to be named the *coefficient of correlation.* We shall meet that coefficient often in the pages of this book.

From England also came the influence of the theory of evolution, as propounded by Charles Darwin (1809-82). Because Darwin's theory established the continuity between animal and man, it made *comparative psychology* important. American psycholo-

An early psychological instrument

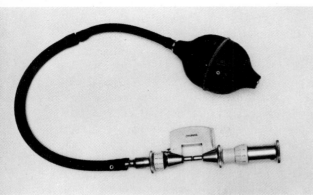

David Linton, *courtesy* N.Y.U.

This Galton whistle, used to measure sensitivity to tones of high pitch, was one of Sir Francis Galton's contributions to the psychological laboratory. It has a modern counterpart in the dog-calling whistles that make use of tones too high for the human ear to hear.

gists have closely studied lower animals, especially white rats, monkeys, and chimpanzees, not only in order to understand their behavior, but also to learn principles important in the understanding of man. The notion of adaptation to environment, inherent in the evolutionary theory, led also to a psychology of adjustment. That is, following Darwin, some psychologists believed that we could understand consciousness, emotions, and other psychological processes if we knew how they served the adjustment of man to his environment.

Another body of influence upon psychology came from medicine and psychiatry, especially from the treatment of the mentally ill. We need think only of the long history of hypnotism, dating especially from Anton Mesmer (1734-1815). And at every turn today we meet the influence of another Viennese physician, Sigmund Freud (1856-1939), the founder of that branch of psychology known as *psychoanalysis.*

Once the laboratories of psychology were in operation and trained psychologists became available to man them, new problems

in increasing numbers were made the subject of experimental attack. Animal psychology, child psychology, social psychology —all have provided material for experimental study. As new problems have entered psychology, they have been studied in the spirit of scientific inquiry. Since the establishment of their first laboratories, psychologists have been intent upon making the methods of psychology conform to those of science in general.

The Role of Theory in Psychology

It was once thought that a science would emerge if facts were simply carefully collected, and generalizations were arrived at from these facts by induction. Few people now hold this simple a view. Sciences are often helped to take form when the search for facts is guided by *theories,* and when the theories are modified or expanded to encompass the range of newly discovered facts.

Three systematic positions

When psychology broke off from philosophy and began to establish itself as an independent science, some of the thought patterns of the philosophers persisted, and psychologists soon found themselves developing competing *systems* or *schools* of psychology. The period of schools in psychology is passing, but these systematic schools have served their purposes in providing rallying points for enthusiastic workers, in correcting faulty emphases within opposing schools, and in giving some measure of unity to the complex fragments of psychology, even though the unity achieved may in some instances have been ill-founded. Without reviewing the many systematic positions that have flourished for a time and then faded away, it is worth our while to consider three systematic positions which are recent enough to help us to understand some contemporary controversies within psychology.

Behaviorism and S-R Psychology. A system known as *behaviorism* has been very influential, especially in America. Its founder, John B. Watson (1878-1958), reacted against the tradition of his time that the introspective study of conscious experience was the province of psychology, and he boldly proposed a psychology that would get along *without* introspection. He felt no need to make assertions about consciousness when he studied the adjustive processes, the various muscular movements and glandular secretions of animals and infants. He decided that the results of animal psychology and child psychology could not only stand on their own as science, but that they set a pattern that adult psychology might well follow (Watson, 1913, 1925).

In order to make psychology a science, Watson said, its data must be open to public inspection like the data of any other science. When a rat runs a maze you can take a motion picture of its movements and any competent person can check your statement about the order in which it entered the blind alleys. So long as you study what the animal or the person *does,* or what he *accomplishes* (his behavior or the products of his behavior), then you can have an *objective science* distinct from the *subjective science* to which introspection limits you. Behavior is public; consciousness is private. Science should deal with public facts.

Watson had to meet many objections. How about a man buried in thought? If he is not moving, is he not thinking? Watson had his reply: he is moving if you make careful enough measurements. Particularly, his vocal cords may be active. One of Watson's favorite theories was that silent thinking consists essentially in talking to yourself. So he made the distinction between *explicit* movements (the kind easily open to observation and measurement) and *implicit* movements (the kind to be detected only by sensitive instruments). Whatever the circumstances, all that the psychologist as behaviorist is interested in is responses of the muscles and of the glands. And, according to Watson, this limitation of interest will prove to be no limitation whatever to the progress of psychology as a science.

How about the richness of emotional experiences? Here again Watson had his answer. The chief characteristic of emotions (for purposes of science) is not their conscious coloring but the stirred-up state of the organism. Nobody doubts that a dog has emotions such as fear or anger or dejection; yet nobody has ever examined a dog's consciousness. Visceral responses, prominent in emotion, can be studied as such. Many of the processes involved in emotion are unconscious or unverbalized—to the behaviorist they are visceral tension states for which we have no words.

Because many psychologists were growing impatient with introspection, the new behaviorism caught on very rapidly in America, particularly in the 1920's, and for a time most of the younger psychologists liked to think of themselves as behaviorists. As enthusiastic supporters of such systems tend to do, they went to extremes, but gradually the excitement about behaviorism has subsided. There are still a few ardent behaviorists, but most contemporary psychologists are not extreme about it.

The heir to behaviorism in contemporary psychology is the *stimulus-response psychologist,* or S-R psychologist, as the position is often abbreviated. Many contemporary psychologists, particularly in America, find it congenial to discuss psychological events as beginning with a *stimulus* and ending with a *response.* For example, if a light is flashed in your eye and your pupil constricts, the light is a stimulus and the pupillary constriction is a response. Stimulus-response theory (or S-R theory, as it is commonly called) asserts that all behavior is in response to stimuli, whether the behavior is overt and explicit (as in running or

Entrance

1-7

A laboratory maze and data processing room

Behaviorism produced many experimental studies of animals, similar to this one. Here the rat in the "Y" maze, *above*, is learning a behavior pattern which results in a reward of food, delivered by the mechanism at the end of the arm of the "Y." His maze is connected electronically to the control room, *below*, where his behavior is automatically recorded. The use of modern automation equipment allows massive quantities of data to be processed in such studies. (After D'Amato and Jagoda, 1960)

David Linton, courtesy N.Y.U.

shouting) or covert and implicit (as in thinking and dreaming).

The advantage of the S-R formulation is that it repeatedly reminds the psychologist that he must anchor his explanations of behavior in the real world—in the world of stimuli, at the beginning of the causal chain, and in the world of responses, at the end of the chain. He thus shares with behaviorism the desire to relate psychological principles to the same sorts of events that are studied in other sciences. The present S-R psychologist goes beyond the earlier behaviorist, however, in his willingness to infer all sorts of processes between the stimulus and the response, processes which he calls *intervening variables*. The nature of the organism, its aroused motives, its previous experiences —all help to determine the response. Because various S-R psychologists prefer and deal with different kinds of intervening variables, not all S-R psychologists have the same theory. They agree only in viewing a psychological event as something that always involves a stimulus-response relationship.

The men who had most to do with establishing a stimulus-response psychology in America were Robert S. Woodworth (1869-1962) and Edward L. Thorndike (1874-1949), both professors at Columbia University. Neither of them was ever a behaviorist, strictly speaking, though they can of course be thought of as behavioral scientists.

CRITICAL DISCUSSION
Some problems of S-R psychology

The more precise meaning of stimulus is that of a restricted source of energy impinging upon a sense organ, and the more precise meaning of a response is the activation of a muscle or a gland. Both Thorndike and Woodworth broadened the concepts of stimulus and response beyond their original meanings, so that a stimulus often became a total situation and a response could mean an outcome made up of fairly complex movements. The problems of how to delimit the stimulus and the response have not yet been fully resolved in S-R theory. If very broad definitions are used, so that stimulus refers to a whole class of antecedent conditions, and response to a whole class of outcomes in the way of movements and products of behavior, then S-R psychology becomes merely a psychology of independent and dependent variables. That is, we can remain within the general logic of S-R psychology if we can clearly specify (and measure) the antecedents of behavior (the independent variables) and then study the results or outcomes associated with these conditions as consequents (the dependent variables). The mediating processes that go on between the specified antecedents and the measured consequents may also be studied, or they may simply be inferred. Viewed in this way, S-R psychology is not a particular set of theory, but rather a *language* which can be used to make psychological information clear and communicable (e.g., Mandler and Kessen, 1959). As such, the S-R outlook is widely prevalent in American psychology today.

Gestalt Psychology and Field Theory. At about the same time that Watson announced behaviorism in America a "new" psychology going by the name of Gestalt psychology was appearing in Germany. The word *Gestalt* is sometimes translated from the German as *form* or *configuration,* and the psychology announced by Max Wertheimer in 1912 was a psychology concerned with the organization of mental processes. The position came to be identified most closely with Wertheimer and his colleagues Kurt Koffka (1886-1941) and Wolfgang Köhler (1887-   ), all of whom migrated to America. An influential variation of Gestalt psychology was developed by Kurt Lewin (1890-1947). His version, often known as *field theory,* laid greater stress than did other Gestalt psychologies upon motivation and social psychology.

The earliest Gestalt experiments dealt with perceived motion, the *phi phenomenon* (Wertheimer, 1912). When two separated lights are flashed in succession, provided the

1-8

The vase and the faces

A reversible figure-ground effect.

timing is proper, what one sees is a single light moving from the position of the first light to that of the second. This illusion of motion is familiar in lighted signs, and of course lies at the basis of the motion picture. The phenomenon of such motion was familiar (a child's toy, known as a stroboscope, has a long history), but the Gestalt psychologists sensed the theoretical importance of the patterning of stimuli in producing the effect. Another illustration of patterning or organization is that of *figure-and-ground,* a tendency to see part of pattern as an object in the foreground, against an unstructured background. The tendency is clear in reversible figure-ground patterns (Figure 1-8).

According to the Gestalt psychologists, then, our experiences depend on the *patterns* that stimuli form, on the *organization* of experience. What we see is relative to background, to other aspects of the whole. The whole is different from the sum of its parts: the whole consists of parts in relationship.

While the Gestalt psychologists did not like the typical introspective psychology of their day any more than Watson did, they were vigorous opponents of behaviorism. They did not wish to give up a kind of free introspection that goes by the name of *phenomenology.* They wanted to be free to ask a child what something looked like, what it meant to him. They were interested in seen movement, in judged sizes, in the appearance of colors under changes in illumination.[6]

[6] While early behaviorists would have thought of such phenomenology as improper science, the

1-9

Pioneers in psycho-analysis

Sigmund Freud with other contemporary pioneers in psychoanalysis on the occasion of his only trip to America, September, 1909. Standing: *left to right,* A. A. Brill, Ernest Jones, Sandor Ferenczi; seated, *left to right,* Sigmund Freud, G. Stanley Hall (psychologist host), Carl G. Jung.

Support for the new position came in part from analogies with modern field physics. The word "field" is used in physics for such things as a magnetic field that describes a pattern of lines of attraction and repulsion. The patterned character of physical fields provided a useful analogy with patterns of organization of psychological events. Hence derivatives of Gestalt psychology, particularly the version stemming from Lewin, sometimes go by the name of *field theory* to contrast them with the more analytical views of the other theories, including S-R theories, that tend to be grouped as derivatives of association theory.

The importance of perception in all psychological events has led those influenced by Gestalt psychology to a number of perception-centered interpretations of learning, memory, and problem-solving. These interpretations are spoken of as forms of *cognitive theory* [7] and are contrasted with S-R interpretations. Contemporary cognitive theorists combine influences from sources other than those of Gestalt psychology, just as S-R theorists have in their background influences other than that from behaviorism. A psychologist influential upon current cognitive theorists was Edward C. Tolman (1886-1959), who called himself a purposive behaviorist, but incorporated a number of notions from Gestalt psychology.

Psychoanalysis. The psychoanalytic psychology of Sigmund Freud (1856-1939) was presented in lectures before leading American psychologists as early as 1909, before behaviorism and Gestalt psychology came on the scene. The lectures were given at Clark University upon the invitation of the psychologist G. Stanley Hall. Thus the first scholarly and scientific recognition of the importance of Freud's work came from professional psychologists, although for many years any recognition of Freud was grudging if not hostile. Freud's influence, direct and indirect, is now so pervasive that those who know nothing else about psychology have at least a nodding acquaintance with Freud.

later incorporation of *verbal report* as a legitimate source of data makes the issue no longer a real one. For historical reasons, however, an ardent behaviorist is less likely to interest himself in these problems.

[7] Cognitive theories are concerned more with "knowing" than with "movement-responses." This will become clearer later on.

If we are to single out any one of Freud's theories for consideration along with behaviorism and Gestalt psychology it is his interpretation of the *unconscious*. Basic to Freud's theory of the unconscious is the conception that the unacceptable (forbidden, punished) wishes of childhood get driven out of awareness. They become part of the active unconscious where, while out of awareness, they remain influential. The active unconscious presses to find expression, which it does in numerous ways, among them dreams, slips of speech, unconscious mannerisms, as well as through such socially approved behavior as artistic, literary, or scientific activity. The method of psychoanalysis—free association under the guidance of the analyst—is itself a way of helping unconscious wishes find verbal expression. In classical Freudian theory the unconscious wishes were almost exclusively sexual. This emphasis upon childhood sexuality was one of the barriers to the acceptance of Freud's theories by the medical and psychological professions when they were first announced. But a consequence of his emphasis upon early childhood has been the encouragement of numerous studies of the effects of child-rearing practices, and a new emphasis upon the motives or drives that initiate or regulate behavior. On the whole, the greater freedom now given to the discussion of sex is a gain for mental health.

The development of child psychology and of clinical psychology has brought Freud's views increasingly to the fore in psychology. Today academic psychologists are friendlier to his teachings than they were earlier, but this does not mean that they are disciples. The general position is that there is much to be learned from psychoanalysis, but that its concepts need to be translated into those of general psychology and experimentally verified where possible.

Scientific models

One can be interested in psychological theories without subscribing to any one of the major psychological systems or schools. Many psychologists refuse to give their loyalty to any closed or final system while the data of their science are being constantly revised, and while many relationships have not yet been satisfactorily studied. Some psychologists have turned their backs upon theory, saying in effect that theory can wait until more facts are known. What is needed first, they say, are the kinds of lawful relationships that are pictured in our graphs or described by our equations summarizing the results of experiments done under standardized conditions. Others prefer to go at theory construction just as they go at the planning of experiments. That is, they build theories appropriate to the limited topics upon which they are working, just as they design experiments appropriate to these topics. So, instead of proposing major systems of psychology, they propose theories of forgetting, or theories of attitude formation, or theories of hearing. These much more limited theories lead to smaller systems that take into account a restricted set of facts and relationships. Such systems we may call *miniature systems* to distinguish them from the more ambitious systems that lead to schools of psychology.

A miniature system attempts to explain a set of facts about a particular subject according to principles designed to account for these facts. The history of the physical and biological sciences is full of many systems of limited scope. In chemistry or physics, you learn about the gas laws relating volume, pressure, and temperature. These laws deal with a limited range of facts which have become important (by way of Gay-Lussac's law of combining volumes) in relation to atomic theory. In biology, the laws of Mendelian inheritance represent an important set of systematic relationships, much more limited in scope, for example, than the theory of evolution. In the later stages of Mendelian theory, however, the principles of mutation become important in relation to evolution. Thus, miniature systems do not remain isolated if the relationships they express are important ones. But they begin modestly and tentatively, seeking to place in order only a few topics within the whole of the science of which they are a part.

Miniature systems are often built around a logical, mathematical, or physical *model*. For instance, the method of Euclidean geometry taught in high school begins with definitions and axioms and leads to theorems to be proved. To prove a theorem you deduce it from what is given, by logical steps on the basis of acceptable assumptions. Once you have proved a theorem, you can discover some corollaries, that is, other theorems that must also be true. The method can be adapted to science, with the additional step that the theorems or corollaries have to be verified by experiment. If the results conform to the predictions, then the assumptions made are possible ones; if the results do not agree, either the assumptions have to be changed or some additional assumptions must be made.

Because the physical sciences have made more progress than psychology, they have often provided models for psychological theorizing. Thus atomic chemistry led psychologists to look for mental atoms (or, more recently, for a basic unit of behavior in the reflex). Field physics provides many analogies for the kinds of relationships of wholes to parts essential to Gestalt psychology.

It would take us too far afield to examine in any detail the models of contemporary psychology. We mention them here to emphasize our previous statement that an interest in psychological theory does not require adherence to a general system or school. The miniature system or more limited model saves science from becoming an unwieldy mass of scattered facts without forcing it prematurely into a mold that might warp its development. Until many smaller systems are securely established, a final comprehensive system of psychology is some distance away.

Developmental and interactive explanations

The foregoing discussion of the points of view of behaviorism and S-R theory, of Gestalt psychology and cognitive theory, and of psychoanalysis, with a mention also of scientific models, is enough to make the beginner in psychology wonder how psychologists are able to communicate with each other. The problem does not turn out to be very great, particularly when attention is turned to the results of experimental investigations. Then everyone understands everyone else, regardless of preferences for one kind of explanation over another. We shall be able to get along with a minimum of system in this book because so many of the references will be to concrete, factual relationships. When there are important alternative ways of formulating an explanation, particularly if the alternatives are a source of controversy, these will be pointed out, for only so will the student appreciate how psychology develops.

There are, however, two modes of explanation that will recur enough for attention to be called to them at this point. One of them is *developmental,* the other *interactive*.

A developmental explanation stresses the historical roots of present behavior, focusing on individual experiences as the individual grows and learns. This mode of explanation has its origins in association psychology, which generally tried to explain what happened in the present according to associations built up in the past. Modern S-R psychology, because of its strong emphasis upon learning, is also very largely a developmental psychology. Psychoanalysis, with its emphasis upon early childhood, also favors such explanations.

An interactive explanation deals with the arousal and control of behavior in the present, according to motives and needs that are active, stimuli that are perceived, and possibilities of action that are open. Gestalt theory and the forms of cognitive theory derived from it have been emphatic in stressing present "configurations" as determiners of behavior. All psychological positions, however, including S-R theory and psychoanalysis, are concerned with present behavior as well as with residues from the past. All must deal, for example, with the way individuals resolve conflicts, since the conflicting tendencies are simultaneously present no matter what their origins may have been in the past. The two explanations, developmental and interactive, belong together, because development always provides the potential that is capitalized on in the present. It is a matter of convenience at some points to stress explanations that are largely developmental, at other points explanations that are largely interactive. This never means that one explanation excludes the other.

An example may make the distinction clearer. Suppose we are studying how a chimpanzee retrieves a stick from outside its cage to be used in scraping in a banana. We can find out, first of all, his prior experience with using sticks as tools. We will learn that if he has had previous experience, he will do much better. This is to take a *developmental* approach, that is, explaining the present in terms of earlier behavior. We can also find out what difference it makes how we present the problem. For example, we may find that if the stick is on the same side of the cage as the banana, he will use the stick as a tool much more promptly than if the stick is out of view on the other side of the cage, though equally accessible to him. In that case we become interested in the *interactive* aspects of his problem-solving behavior. The interaction is important, because sufficient past experience does not lead to prompt solution unless the present display of the problem is appropriate and makes the past experience accessible in the present.

It is important to keep both aspects in mind in order to avoid explaining too much according to the past or too much according

to the present. Thus we may learn that delinquent youths have alcoholic fathers more frequently than nondelinquent youths, and so become tempted to say that this youth is delinquent *because* he had an alcoholic father. He does not become delinquent because he had an alcoholic father but because he shows some inadequacy *at the present time* in relation to specific temptation and opportunities for delinquent acts. It is this inadequacy that must be understood for what it is now, if it is to be corrected. It may help us to understand this present inadequacy if we know both the kind of early history that produces delinquent boys and what the boy's reaction was to his alcoholic father. There is nothing illogical about accepting at once a developmental explanation and an interactive one.

Measurement in Psychology

Whatever methods psychologists use, sooner or later they find it necessary to make statements about *amounts* or *quantities*. Variables have to be assessed in some clear manner, so that investigations can be repeated and confirmed by others and so that the results can be appropriately applied. Occasionally variables can be grouped into *classes* or *categories*, as in separating boys and girls for the study of sex differences. Sometimes the variables are subject to ordinary *physical measurement*: height, weight, age, illumination. Sometimes they have to be *scaled* in a manner that places the values of the variables in some sort of order: for example, from least preferred to most preferred. Usually, for purposes of precise communication, *numbers* are assigned to measures or scale values; then we can say that we are dealing with *quantitative* values. There are a number of problems that arise in using quantities in psychology, but we may speak of *measurement* in a somewhat general sense whenever we mean that we have assigned numerical values to independent and dependent variables or indeed to any variables entering into some sort of systematically studied relationship.

Experimental design

When an experimenter plans his experiments, he has in mind the ways in which he will gather his data and how he will treat the data in order to discover the relationships involved and make inferences from what he finds. The expression *experimental design* has come to be used for any of the more formal patterns according to which experiments are planned. The same design might be used for an experiment in vision, one in audition, and perhaps one in learning. The total plan includes more than the design, for it involves the substance of the particular experiment.

The designs that are most easily understood are those in which one variable at a time is controlled (as the independent variable), and its effects on another variable (the dependent variable) studied. The ideal

1-10

Shock as independent variable; latency as dependent variable

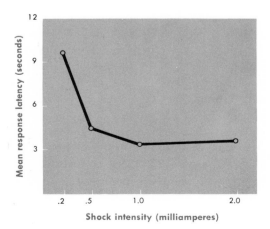

Rats could avoid an electric shock by turning a wheel. The latency of the rat's response gets shorter (that is, the response is prompter) as the shock increases. (After Kimble, 1955)

1-11

Experimental and control groups

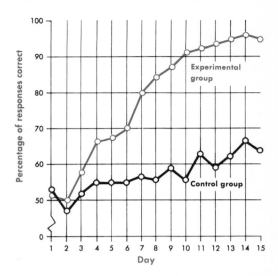

The response called for was a discrimination between a circle and a triangle; the experimental animals had seen circles and triangles in their living cages, the control animals had not. (After Gibson and Walk, 1956)

is to hold everything else constant, so that one comes out with an assertion of the form: "With everything else constant, when X increases, Y also increases." (Or, in other cases, "When X increases, Y decreases," etc.) This form of statement implies *concomitant variation,* the two variables being linked together by some demonstrable relationship. Note that almost any content can be fitted into this kind of study: the amount of change in illumination that can be perceived in relation to the standard illumination with which you start, the rate of learning as related to the age of the learner, the fear of snakes as related to prior experience with snakes. In Figure 1-10 the latency of response (the delay between the stimulus and the start of the response) is related to the intensity of a shock that the response can prevent. Note that the method of *graphical presentation* of the results is a very convenient one to use, with the independent variable plotted along the baseline (the horizontal axis) and the dependent variable plotted on the vertical axis.

Sometimes we are interested only in the influence of a single condition, which can be either present or absent. (Such a condition is simply a variable with only two values, one representing its presence and the other its absence.) In such a case the experimental design commonly calls for an *experimental* group in which the condition is present and a *control* group in which the condition is absent. The results of an experiment designed in this way are presented in Figure 1-11. It is clear that the experimental group made a higher percentage of correct responses than the control group, the differences being more marked as the experiment proceeded. What accounts for the difference? From the point of view of experimental design we can infer that *something* has been related to the difference; from the point of view of a particular experiment we are of course interested in the content. In this case the something was prior experience with the stimuli to be responded to. Laboratory rats were tested on their ability to discriminate (i.e., distinguish) between a circle and a triangle, one or the other being a "sign" on a door that the door was the way to food. The experimental group was already familiar with circles and triangles from having had them on the walls of their living cages; the control group lacked this experience. Apparently familiarity with the forms made it easier for the rats to use them in the later portions of the experiment.

Sometimes it is necessary to study the simultaneous effects of several variables at once. Suppose, for example, that we are studying plant growth and wish to study the effects of moisture, temperature, and illumination. We could hold two of these variables constant and study the effect of one, but a little reflection would show us how limited this design would be: unless *favorable* levels of the other variables were chosen, the plant would not live, and the experiment could not be performed at all.

But *how* favorable would they have to be? A better procedure would be some way of varying at once, in different combinations, moisture, temperature, and illumination. Then the effect of one variable would be studied not against a *constant* value of other variables, but against a *randomized* set of values of the other variable. The statistical problems of such a design are more complex than a design involving changes in only one independent variable at a time, but the yield in information is much greater for the same amount of investment of experimental effort, and hence such designs are increasingly popular in psychology.[8]

The use and interpretation of correlation coefficients

Although the experimental ideal is to have things so under control that one can specify the variables under study and produce changes in them as called for in the experimental design, there are circumstances under which this is not possible. For example, the experimenter who is interested in the human brain is not free to remove portions at will, as he does with lower animals, but can only take advantage of naturally occurring brain damage through disease, injury, or gunshot wounds. He can still use the method of *concomitant variation,* but now the related variables are *correlated* rather than experimentally controlled. For example a relationship may be reported between the amount of damage in some region of the brain and the amount of difficulty in seeing. This is not very different from producing the damage in an experimental animal and noting the changes, except that other factors cannot be as well controlled; that is, other kinds of damage may also be present, kinds of treatment may have varied following the accident,

[8] The statistical methods appropriate to such designs involve *analysis of variance,* now met very frequently in the reports of psychological investigations. The details need not concern us at this point.

the intellectual level prior to the accident may be important in interpreting the results, and so on. Because of its greater precision of control, experimentation is preferred where it is applicable, but where it is not applicable, the general logic of experimentation can still be approximated through the use of correlation.

When large masses of data are available, the method of correlation is often the best available for discovering relationships. For example, we have records of the high school grades of students entering college. The best way to get at the relationship between high school and college grades is to *correlate* them, that is, to find if those who did well in high school generally do well in college, and vice versa.

While in some cases (as in the brain illustration above) a correlational study approximates an experimental investigation with independent and dependent variables, it is not necessary to think of a correlation in these terms. When two measures are made on all members of the population tested, scores can be grouped in either way; that is, you can ask about the average high school grade of those who make C's in college as well as you can ask how B students in high school do when they get to college.

The unit of measurement in correlation is the *coefficient of correlation,* signified by the letter *r*. (Psychologists often omit the word "coefficient" and speak only of "the correlation.") The methods of calculating the coefficient of correlation are described in Chapter 13; at this point we can set forth only some rules of thumb which will help you interpret the coefficients of correlation used in some of the tables and graphs in this book.

1. A correlation of $r = +1.00$ means a perfect *direct* relationship, a one-to-one correspondence between two measures. If weight corresponded exactly to height, so that you could state a person's weight pre-

cisely if you knew his height, then height and weight would be perfectly correlated. (The circumference of a circle and its radius are perfectly correlated, but the perimeter of a triangle and its height are not.) When the correlation is positive, the plus sign is often omitted.

2. A correlation of $r = -1.00$ means a perfect *inverse* relationship. For example, if the number of days of illness during the academic year depressed the course grades earned (the more illness the poorer the grades) and this relationship was one-to-one, it could be expressed by a correlation of $r = -1.00$.

3. A correlation near $r = .00$ signifies no relationship. Thus one would expect a zero correlation between the number of freckles and the score on an intelligence test.

4. A correlation lying between $r = .00$ and *either* $+1.00$ or -1.00 indicates an imperfect relationship; but negative and positive correlations of the same size represent the same *degree* of relationship, other things being equal.[9]

5. A correlation is *not* a per cent, so that a correlation of $r = .25$ cannot be interpreted as being half as great as one of $r = .50$. We shall have some rules later for interpreting correlations. Some typical correlations found by researchers include the following:

> (1) a correlation of $r = .50$ between the height of a parent and the adult height of a child of that parent; (2) correlations of .30–.60 between scholastic aptitude tests and freshman grades in college; (3) correlations of about .70–.80 between grades in the first semester of the freshman year and those in the second semester.

[9] The *sign* of a correlation is often arbitrary. If for days of sickness we substituted days of health, we would obtain a positive correlation between health and grades of the same magnitude as the negative one between sickness and grades. The change of sign would not change the meaning of the relationship.

1-12

A scatter diagram illustrating correlation

Each tally indicates the combined scores of one subject on two separate days of testing hypnotic susceptibility. Tallies in the shaded area indicate identical scores on both tests; those between the solid lines indicate a difference of no more than 1 point between the two scores. The correlation of $r = +.86$ means that the performances were fairly consistent on the two days. (After Hilgard, 1961)

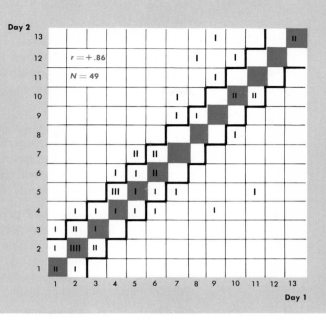

6. Some supplementary information is needed to indicate whether or not a given correlation is *significant,* that is, whether or not the implied relationship is to be counted upon. This depends both upon the size of the coefficient of correlation and upon the number of cases entering into the computation of the coefficient of correlation. Most dependable, of course, is a high correlation (either positive or negative) based on many cases; least dependable, as an indication of relationship or direction of relationship, is a low correlation based on a few cases. Even a high correlation based on few cases is not to be trusted, because it might arise even though no true relationship exists.

The correlations just described correspond to the experimental design in which there is one independent variable and one dependent variable. For the more complex cases there are also more complex correlational methods, but we can wait to meet these later.

The relationships brought out by a coefficient of correlation will become clearer if we look at a diagram of actual results (Figure 1-12). Forty-nine subjects were given a test of their susceptibility to hypnosis on two separate days. Each tally in the diagram represents the *combined* score of one subject on the two tests. Thus two subjects made scores of 1 on both days, and two other subjects made scores of 13 on both days. But one subject (see the lower right-hand portion of the diagram) made a score of 11 on the first test but only 5 on the second one.

If all the subjects had repeated their original scores on the second test, all the plotted tallies would have fallen in the shaded area indicated. The majority of tallies are reasonably close to this area, however; all the tallies within the solid lines represent scores in which one day's score differed from the other by no more than 1 point. This indicates a high degree of correlation between the two pairs of test results; the coefficient of correlation as actually calculated was $+.86$, which is considered to show a substantial relationship.

SUMMARY

1. <u>Psychology is defined as the science that studies the *behavior* of man and other animals.</u>

2. In practice, the definition of behavior implied by psychology is a very broad one. By including within the science the *inferences* that are made from verbal behavior, it is possible to study both *conscious* and *unconscious* processes without sacrificing the objectivity of the data on which these inferences rest.

3. Psychology, like other *behavioral sciences,* has overlapping interests with many neighboring sciences, chiefly with biology on the one hand, and with social sciences on the other. There are affiliations with the physical sciences as well. Many promising opportunities for studies lie ahead in areas where psychology blends with other sciences.

4. Among the methods of psychology as a science the *methods of the experimental laboratory* are preferred where they are applicable. These methods have the advantage that variables can be brought under control and subjected to measurement, both the *independent variables,* whose values the experimenter sets, and the *dependent variables* that take on different values depending on the outcome of the experiment.

5. Other methods of psychology include *naturalistic observations, case histories, the interview,* and *test methods.*

6. Psychology inherited from the pre-experimental period the opposing viewpoints of *faculty psychology* (proposing that the mind consisted of separate mental powers that accounted for mental activity) and of *association psychology* (proposing that everything could be explained through the association of ideas, ideas coming originally by way of sensory experience). The association theory really set the background for the new psychology, and the first experiments were concerned with sensory processes.

7. The first formal laboratory was established by Wundt at Leipzig in 1879. The spurt in experimental psychology in America can be attributed largely to his influence, for many of his students came to hold important positions in American universities. Other important figures were Galton and Darwin in England.

8. Efforts to provide a theoretical orientation for modern psychology have led to the formulation of a number of competing systems, of which three have important residual influence in contemporary psychology. The first of these, *behaviorism,* a psychology that got along without *introspection,* is now represented by *stimulus-response* (S-R) psychology, a somewhat broader position. The second, *Gestalt psychology* or *field theory,* lies behind an increasing prominence given to perception, sometimes called the *cognitive viewpoint* in contemporary psychology. The third influence, that of *psychoanalysis,* has made psychology more dynamic, that is, more concerned with motivational problems, especially with *unconscious motivation* and with motivational conflicts.

9. An alternative to all-inclusive systems is the more modest miniature system or *model,* often based on analogies with physics and chemistry.

10. Two modes of explanation occur frequently within psychology, modes that are related to some of the past systematic emphases but are not in themselves controversial. These are *developmental* explanations and *interactive* explanations. Developmental explanations attempt to account for present behavior on the basis of what has gone before, relying on the *history* of the present behavior. Interactive explanations are contemporary and nonhistorical, trying to account for behavior on the basis of what is currently going on in the way of stimuli, bodily condition, aroused conflicting tendencies, and so on. The two kinds of explanation are not contradictory, because the past provides the potentiality for response in the present. However, it is occasionally convenient to emphasize one kind of explanation over the other; often a full account of behavior requires propositions reflecting both varieties of explanation.

SUGGESTIONS
FOR
FURTHER
READING

To follow up on the early history of psychology or to find the history of a particular topic, the two most useful books are Boring, *A history of experimental psychology* (2nd Ed., 1950), and Murphy, *Historical introduction to modern psychology* (Rev. Ed., 1949).

A number of books describe the larger systems of psychology that have influenced contemporary developments. To the standard older ones, Heidbreder, *Seven psychologies* (1933), and Woodworth, *Contemporary schools of psychology* (Rev. Ed., 1948), have been added Chaplin and Krawiec, *Systems and theories of psychology* (1960), and Wolman, *Contemporary theories and systems in psychology* (1960).

For the methods of psychology, see Andrews, *Methods of psychology* (1948), Underwood, *Psychological research* (1957), and Andreas, *Experimental psychology* (1960). A strong case for bringing psychological investigations under experimental control (rather than relying upon statistics) is made by Sidman in his *Tactics of scientific research* (1960). For methods particularly applicable in social psychology, Festinger and Katz, *Research methods in the behavioral sciences* (1953) is a useful multiple-author volume.

CHAPTER 2

The Behaving Organism

The individual organism grows, learns, and interacts with the physical environment and the social environment. We use the word "organism" rather than "person" because organisms other than man can teach us many lessons applicable to man. A human being is an organism; his habits, thoughts, and aspirations are centered in his brain and nervous system, and whenever we study him we study something he does or expresses through his bodily processes. In this chapter, then, we shall examine man as a flesh-and-blood organism related to other organisms.

We shall also examine him as a vertebrate, a mammal, and a primate, who shares an evolutionary history with the rest of the biological world. Our emphasis here will be on the evolution of man's nervous system; by discovering how the nervous system in the lower animals has evolved, we will learn a good deal about the significance of the various nervous structures for the behavior of man. The nervous system and the related structures of sense organs, muscles, and glands provide for man's responsiveness to the environment and his immediate adjustments to it; they provide also, however, for the storing up of experiences, the development of habits and attitudes that make the past serve the present and the future. Again we confront the distinction between present interactions and developmental history; the nervous system is important in whichever viewpoint we are emphasizing.

Integration Within the Organism

The word "organism" implies organization. The body is not only a collection of cells but an arrangement of cells as organs and organ systems. The character of the body as a unitary organism is determined by the manner in which the parts fit together so that the whole operates with reasonable smoothness.

Integration through skeleton and muscles

What does the psychologist need to know about the skeleton and the related structures of muscles and tendons that tie it together and make it operate? The answer depends upon his purposes. If, for example, the psychologist becomes interested in the limits of possible human performance, he may wish to know about the maximum weight a muscle can support, or about the maximum speed with which it can contract, or the effects of practice upon it. If he is interested in muscular fatigue, he may wish to learn something of the chemical by-products of muscular action. Of course, we cannot go into such details here; we will merely call attention to the importance of the skeleton and the muscles as mechanical integrators of the body.

The body operates as an effective machine partly because of the way in which it is fitted together around a jointed skeleton of rigid bones. This *mechanical integration* makes possible the maintenance of posture, locomotion, skilled action, facial expression, and speech.

Although the bony structure and the arrangements of joints are important, muscular action tends to be of more direct interest to the psychologist because it is the muscles that control the movements.

The body contains three kinds of muscles: *striate (striped) muscles,* the muscles of the arms and legs, the typical muscles visible beneath the skin; *smooth muscles,* which control the action of the digestive organs and other internal organs and of the blood vessels; and *cardiac muscles,* found only in the heart. The striate muscles are bundles of fibers adapted to rapidly changing actions. Smooth muscles are more sluggish in action, but their movements may be powerful, and they are highly resistant to fatigue.

When a muscle contracts, it commonly produces a movement at the joints, as in walking or lifting. But if the joint is prevented from moving, the muscle may still contract. In an alert but quiet state the muscles are bombarded by an irregular barrage of nervous impulses that maintain a normal amount of contraction called *muscle tone.* The tone of muscles varies with the condition of the individual: an energetic, athletic person tends to have high tone, a fatigued and listless person low tone. If tone is reduced too far, the person collapses, as in a faint; if his tone is too high, his movements are interfered with, as in the condition known as *spastic paralysis.* Spastic paralysis, with muscle tone so high that smooth movement is impossible, is not infrequently a result of birth injury.

Although muscle tone is maintained automatically through reflex mechanisms, we can increase the tension in our muscles voluntarily, as in "making a muscle" without moving the arm. Some people habitually tense their muscles, and are unable to relax. Such a high tension state is fatiguing, and may carry with it signs of mild personality disturbance. The voluntary increase of muscular tension, without movement, comes about through increasing the tension of *antagonistic muscles.* Such muscles are arranged in pairs; the contraction of one member of

2-1

Antagonistic muscular action

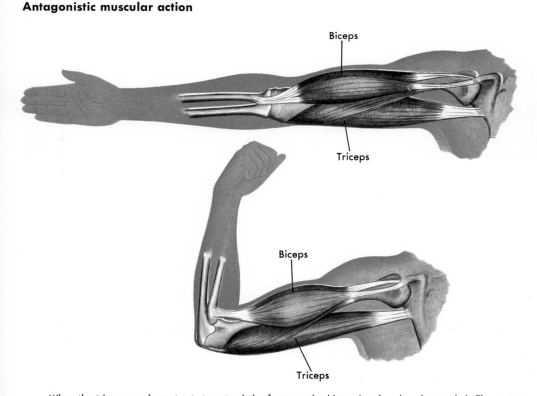

Biceps

Triceps

Biceps

Triceps

When the triceps muscle contracts to extend the forearm, the biceps is relaxed and extended. The pattern is reversed when the forearm is pulled toward the body.

the pair tends to stretch the other member of the pair. Thus the *biceps* of the upper arm is a *flexor* muscle, bending the arm at the elbow, while the *triceps* is an *extensor* muscle, antagonistic to the biceps and tending by contraction to straighten the arm at the elbow (Figure 2-1). The nervous control of muscles is such that when one of a pair of antagonists contracts the other ordinarily relaxes. This principle is known as *reciprocal innervation,* and is very important in the free movements of, say, walking along and swinging the arms. When we move muscles voluntarily, we can either take advantage of this reciprocal relationship to produce free movement or contract both antagonists at once and raise tension.

Integration via the blood stream

A second system that maintains the body as a smoothly operating machine is the circulatory system: the heart, the blood vessels, and the other closely related structures that feed into the system. Because the system contributes to integration by sending chemical substances throughout the body,

we may think of it as *chemical* in its action, supplementing the mechanical integration of muscles and joints. We shall pass over the normal metabolic role of the circulatory system, and turn instead to certain special substances the blood stream carries, the substances called *hormones,* a word derived from the Greek root meaning "activators."

The glands of internal secretion (the *endocrine* or *ductless* glands) discharge their secretions (hormones) directly into the blood stream, with effects upon growth, behavior, and personality. These glands are distinguished from the *duct* glands, such as tear glands or salivary glands, which secrete their products on the surface of the body or into the body cavities but not into the blood stream. Six endocrine glands produce hormones whose actions are fairly well understood, although new evidence about their activity is still being collected: (1) the thyroid gland, (2) the parathyroids, (3) the pancreas, (4) the adrenal glands, (5) the sex glands or gonads (ovaries in the female and testes in the male), and (6) the pituitary gland. In Figure 2-2 their locations are pic-

---

TABLE 2-1

Some typical functions of the endocrine glands

Gland	Activities regulated
Pituitary—anterior	Growth (dwarfism, giantism); as "master gland" influences secretions of thyroids, pancreas, adrenal glands, and gonads.
—posterior	Water metabolism, etc.
Thyroid	Metabolic rate; hence activity and fatigue; body weight.
Parathyroid	Calcium metabolism; maintenance of normal excitability of the nervous system.
Pancreas	Via insulin controls sugar metabolism; excess insulin leads to state of shock.
Adrenal—cortex	Secretes life-maintaining regulators; control of salt and carbohydrate metabolism; may be important in mental illness.
—medulla	Active in emotion through the effects of adrenalin and noradrenalin.
Gonads *	Secondary sex characteristics distinguishing the male and female at maturity; maintenance of a functional condition in male and female reproductive apparatuses.

* As glands of internal secretion; to be distinguished from their reproductive functions.

2-2

The endocrine glands

The location of the endocrine glands in the body.

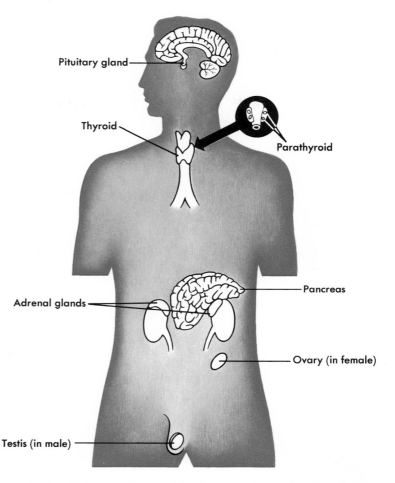

Pituitary gland

Thyroid

Parathyroid

Adrenal glands

Pancreas

Ovary (in female)

Testis (in male)

tured in a schematized human body; their functions are summarized briefly in Table 2-1.

As one illustration of the psychological relevance of the endocrine glands we may consider the role of the *adrenal* glands.

The adrenal glands have two major parts, each secreting its own hormones. The *medulla* of the gland secretes *adrenalin* and *noradrenalin*. The *cortex* of the gland secretes a number of hormonal products collectively called *adrenocortical* hormones.

The adrenal medulla is active in emotion. Secretion of the hormone adrenalin produces many of the symptoms found in excited emotion: tremor in the striate muscles increases; smooth muscles relax; the blood distribution of the body changes; the liver releases blood sugar into the blood and thereby makes available a ready supply of energy; blood pressure increases; the blood clots more quickly in case of injury. Recent discovery of noradrenalin, another secretion of the adrenal medulla, has furthered knowledge of the action of the adrenal glands. Adrenalin and noradrenalin occasionally act alike and occasionally act in opposite ways. Whereas adrenalin may dilate blood vessels, noradrenalin constricts them. There is as yet no simple formula by which to describe their interrelated actions.

The products of the adrenal cortex are so important to the maintenance of life that destruction of the adrenal cortex invariably produces death unless the missing products are continuously replaced from out-

2-3

Evolution of the human hand

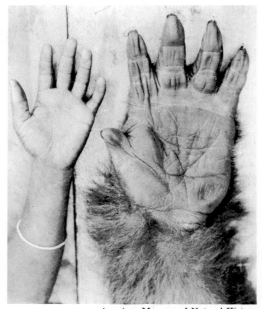

American Museum of Natural History

A human hand compared with that of a gorilla. Note development of the human thumb.

side—a very difficult process. These life-maintaining regulators, which are concerned with salt and carbohydrate metabolism, have been identified as complex chemical substances known as *steroids.* The steroids have become useful agents for the treatment of many health disturbances, such as shock, allergy, and arthritis. Their possible role in mental disturbance is suggested by the occasional appearance of symptoms similar to those of mental illness among mentally normal patients being treated with adrenal steroids such as cortisone.

Neural integration

The nervous system controls the muscles as they make use of the skeletal apparatus; it controls the beating of the heart, respiration, and circulation of the blood; it regulates the secretions of the glands. Therefore this third system, the *neural mechanism,* rules over the mechanical and chemical integrators that we

have just considered. The great gain to the organism through possessing a nervous system is that this system provides the basis for complex and modifiable action, for learning as a result of experience, and for increased adaptability to variety in the environment. So important is the nervous system that most of the remainder of this chapter will be devoted to it.

Evolution of the Nervous System

We need not concern ourselves here with the details of evolutionary theory, which belong to the science of biology. The basic assumptions, since Darwin, are that living organisms vary, and that some of these variations are more adaptive than others. An adaptive variation gives the organism a competitive advantage in the environment in which it finds itself (or perhaps helps it to seek a more favorable environment). Both adaptive and maladaptive (unfavorable) variations are transmitted by heredity, and differences become accentuated through time as organisms continue to vary and to adapt to their special environments, the successful ones surviving, the unsuccessful ones dying off. Modern genetic theory has helped show how variation and selection can occur, not only by way of mutations, but by way of shifts in the available hereditary determiners (genes) as populations of individuals become isolated from each other. In time, species develop that can no longer mate successfully with each other, and then families of organisms develop along these branching lines. The branching lines along which man has developed include, far back, the earliest vertebrate, but specialization continued through the mammalian line and the primate line until now the genus to which man belongs contains only one species: *Homo sapiens sapiens.* The so-called races of man are all variants of the one species.

Because of our interest in behavior, the aspect of evolution that is of primary importance for us is the evolution of the brain and nervous system, those parts of the body that interpret the sensory inputs from the environment, coordinate the organism's responses, and, in general, serve memory and thought.

Nerve net and synaptic nervous system

One-celled animals, such as the amoeba, get along without a nervous system. The cell body is responsive to stimulation, so that the amoeba moves about, avoids noxious stimuli, engulfs food. There must be some sort of conduction within the cell body, for movement often takes place at a distance from the point of stimulation. The sponge is a multicellular organism without a nervous system; its cells conduct individually. Muscle fibers have already evolved in the sponge, so that we have here the beginning of muscular contraction but without a nerve supply to the muscles. Some coordination is provided by one cell influencing a neighboring cell, but the influence is not by way of any connecting nerve fibers.

The real beginning of a nervous system is in the *nerve net* as found in the coelenterates, such as the polyps (Figure 2-4). Here individual specialized cells, called *neurons,* are spread rather evenly through the outer layers of the body. When any part of the nerve net is stimulated, impulses diffuse from that point and produce local contraction of muscles in the areas where the neurons are activated. Nothing very complex is controlled by such a nervous system.

In certain jellyfishes, such as the umbrella-shaped medusa, some of the fibers of the nerve net are concentrated in a ring at the margin of the umbrella (Figure 2-5). This led to some interesting experiments years ago (e.g., Harvey, 1922). He cut from a medusa a doughnut-shaped ring of tissue including the nerve ring. Then he started an impulse around the ring, its course being mapped by the contractions of the muscles around the ring as the impulse passed along. The impulse kept traveling for 11 days, until

2-4

Nerve net in coelenterates

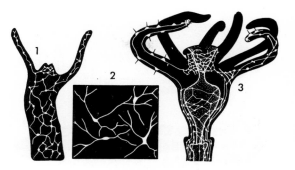

The nerve net in *Hydra* (1) is enlarged in (2) to show the arrangement of neurons. The nerve net of the polyp *Obelia* (3) shows a concentration in the mouth region. (After Simpson and others, 1957)

2-5

Nerve ring of a medusa

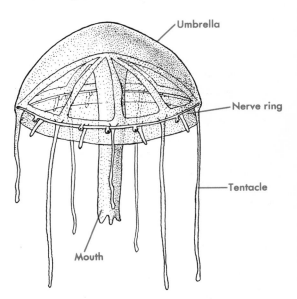

This jellyfish also **has** a diffuse nerve net on the under surface, but its details are not shown. The nerve ring provides an integration of movement in response to impulses originating in the sensitive tentacles. The swimming movement (pulsations of the whole body) may be set off by a stimulus applied to a single tentacle. (From Herrick, *Neurological foundations of animal behavior,* 1924, p. 93)

2-6

Nerve net and ladder nervous system in flatworms

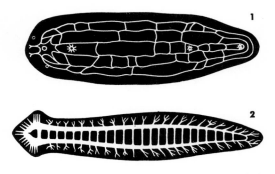

In some flatworms (1) the nervous system is still of the simple net type, while others (2) show the beginning of a central nervous system in the ladder-like structure of cords with a concentration of cell bodies at the head end, constituting a primitive brain. (After Simpson and others, 1957)

the growth of new tissue replacing that cut away produced antagonistic impulses. One by-product of the observation was that the muscle fatigued much earlier than the nerve net.

A characteristic of the nerve net is that the impulses can travel in either direction, although, as the foregoing experiment shows, they may occasionally continue only in the direction in which they get started. Modern research on coelenterates has shown that there is some differential responsiveness based on the number of nervous impulses per second reaching a particular muscle, and that there is some facilitation when impulses converge at a junction between nerve cell and nerve cell (Pantin, 1952). Even with these additions, the processes are relatively simple.

The flatworms, planaria, show a further stage in the evolution of the nervous system, in which the nerve net is combined with a nervous system much more like that of man's. In its ladder-type nervous system, neurons are arranged in bundles called nerve cords (a kind of primitive spinal cord); moreover, the cell bodies of the neurons

concentrate in the head to form something similar to a brain (Figure 2-6). This nervous system is of the *polarized synaptic* variety. A *synapse* is a junction between neurons. A polarized synapse is a junction in which there is conduction of the impulse in only one direction; it is characteristic of all higher nervous systems.[1] The cells making up the eyes at the front end of the flatworm are connected to the collection of neurons that we may call a brain; this pattern is continued in higher forms.

As we move beyond the primitive synaptic nervous system of the flatworms, the lines of evolution divide between invertebrates, such as insects, and vertebrates. Since man is a vertebrate, it is the development of the vertebrate nervous system, and particularly the vertebrate brain, that is of primary interest to us here.

Evolution of the vertebrate brain

The general characteristics of the brain reveal a common pattern throughout the vertebrate series, beginning with primitive fishes and moving through the reptiles; the brains of birds and mammals follow somewhat different directions from this common background. The basic pattern is that of a single hollow cord made up of partially interconnected neurons running along the back of the body, with various more complicated areas of interconnections forming enlargements at the forward (head) end. There are, in most primitive brains, three such enlargements, known as the *forebrain, midbrain,* and *hindbrain,* and these three are still identifiable in man.

The main parts of a primitive vertebrate brain help us to understand the pattern upon which the much more complex human brain is built. A schematic representation of a dogfish brain is shown in Figure 2-7. At this stage the *forebrain* consists of the *olfactory bulb* (connected with the sense organs of

[1] Higher organisms may display residues of earlier forms. The human intestine, for example, contains a nerve net in its wall.

A primitive vertebrate brain

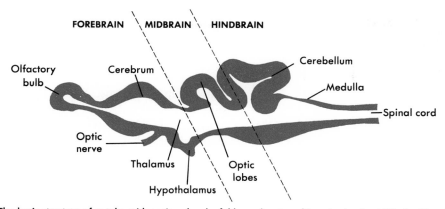

FOREBRAIN / MIDBRAIN / HINDBRAIN

Olfactory bulb

Cerebrum

Cerebellum

Medulla

Spinal cord

Optic nerve

Thalamus

Hypothalamus

Optic lobes

The basic structure of a tube with various bends, folds, and outpouchings is clearly visible in this schematic drawing of the dogfish brain. The three main portions (forebrain, midbrain, hindbrain) are distinguishable, but a "between-brain" (thalamus and hypothalamus) is also present, and the hindbrain has developed a cerebellum distinguishable from the medulla. The forebrain and midbrain are paired structures (see Fig. 2-8).

smell), the *cerebrum* (chiefly at this stage a "nose brain," using the information coming from the sense of smell to guide the behavior of the fish), the *thalamus* (a way-station for impulses coming up from the spinal cord and down from the cerebrum), and the *hypothalamus* (concerned with many of the internal regulatory processes). The *midbrain* consists chiefly of the *optic lobes,* connected with the eyes and regulating behavior by way of stimuli affecting the eyes. The *hindbrain* includes the *cerebellum* (controlling balance, among other things) and the *medulla,* the enlargement of the spinal cord that is important in maintaining the vital functions, such as respiration and circulation of the blood.

While various other changes took place in the evolution of the mammalian brain, the most striking one was the development of an outpouching or cover over the cerebrum, which has come to be called the neocortex ("new cortex") or simply the *cerebral cortex,* as we know it in higher forms, including man.

The gradual changes in proportionate size of the cerebrum and midbrain are shown in Figure 2-8. The cerebral cortex becomes highly wrinkled or *convoluted,* so that its actual surface area is far greater than it would be were it a smooth covering of the surface of the brain.

The organization of the human brain

Among the vertebrates the brain achieves its greatest complexity in man. Before we examine the organization of the human brain, however, we can usefully note five methods psychologists, in conjunction with neurophysiologists and neuroanatomists, use to study the brain.

1. *Study of the Evolution of the Brain.* By comparative study we find that parts of man's brain are very similar to the brains of lower animals. These parts constitute his "old brain." In the course of evolution new parts of the brain have become superimposed on these older structures. They constitute man's "new brain," and give him what advantages in nervous equipment he has over lower animals. The parallels in structure between man's brain and simpler brains lead us to infer similar functions, which

Development of the forebrain in vertebrate evolution

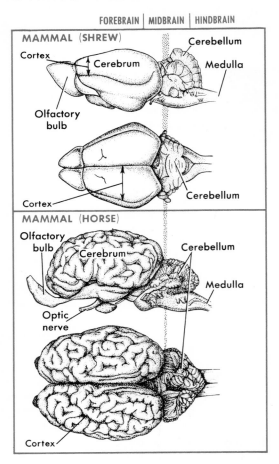

FOREBRAIN | MIDBRAIN | HINDBRAIN

MAMMAL (SHREW)

Cortex
Cerebrum
Cerebellum
Medulla
Olfactory bulb

Cortex
Cerebellum

MAMMAL (HORSE)

Olfactory bulb
Cerebrum
Cerebellum
Medulla
Optic nerve

Cortex

The cortex is still small and unconvoluted in the shrew, a primitive mammal; the convoluted surface of the horse cerebrum is made up entirely of cortex. Top and side views are shown. (After Simpson and others, 1957)

tissue. Similarly, gunshot wounds and other accidents may injure specific parts of the brain or spinal cord. By noting the symptoms produced by the injury (paralysis, loss of sensation, or other disturbances), it is often possible to infer what role a given part of the brain serves. Conversely, when these symptoms appear as a result of a tumor, it is possible to locate the tumor that causes the symptoms. When the tumor is surgically removed, the symptoms may disappear, thus adding evidence of a relationship between that brain location and those symptoms.

Instead of waiting for disease or accidents, it is possible to perform systematic *extirpation* experiments to determine by surgical removal of parts of the brain what kinds of defects are produced by their loss. Surgery of this kind is done primarily upon animals, although surgeons have performed extirpations of parts of the brains of human beings when they expected the operation to benefit the patient.

3. *Study of Nerve Degeneration.* When an area of the brain is destroyed, nerves connecting with the area may degenerate. The pathways of these connecting fibers, which in a normal brain would be lost in a mass of other fibers, can therefore be traced through microscopic study. Related methods use stains that affect some kinds of nervous tissue but not others. With the help of such stains it is also possible to follow the course of nerve pathways.

4. *Study Through Stimulation.* Stimulating parts of the brain with mild electrical currents produces effects on behavior. Surgical patients with their brain surfaces exposed under local anesthetics have assisted in such studies by reporting their experiences when different points are stimulated. Some rather satisfactory "maps" of the cortex have resulted from these studies.

More recently, animal investigators have used permanently implanted electrodes to produce repeated stimulation in a local part of the brain (Figure 2-9). Studies done with

need to be verified by further investigation. Another way to study the evolution of the brain is through embryological development, for in its early stages of development the brain of the human embryo reveals its relation to the brain of organisms lower in the evolutionary scale.

2. *Study Through Disease, Injury, or Extirpation.* Some forms of tumor and disease injure circumscribed areas of brain

the aid of such electrodes are proving very illuminating. For some purposes, stimulation by locally applied drugs has also proved useful.

5. *Study of Action Currents.* When neural action goes on, slight currents are always produced. By inserting electrodes at appropriate places, connected in turn to measuring devices, one can detect whether impulses starting at, say, the ear, reach the part of the brain where the electrodes are inserted.

The brain as a whole also produces rhythmical electrical discharges. The record of these total brain discharges, known as an *electroencephalogram* (EEG), plays its part in the study of central nervous activity. For example, if a particular kind of stimulation gives rise to changes in the rhythmic discharges picked up from one part of the brain and not those from another, we can assume that the stimulation affected that particular region (see Figure 2-10).

Our knowledge of the brain and its action is being greatly enhanced by these and other methods. Even though the goal of understanding the brain is far off, the areas of mystery are being gradually reduced.

The human brain studied by these methods consists essentially of the structures of the primitive vertebrate brain, preserved in somewhat their same anatomical relations but of course modified in detail, plus the enormously developed cerebral cortex built upon the older brain. It helps to think of the mammalian brain as composed of three concentric layers: a primitive core, an older brain evolved upon this core, and an outer layer of new brain evolved in turn upon the second layer (Figure 2-11). All three layers are, of course, interconnected in a complex fashion, and a new layer cannot evolve without changing the conduction of impulses to and from the earlier and more central layers. This particular way of interpreting the action of the brain we owe to Pribram (1960).

The central core, which includes parts of

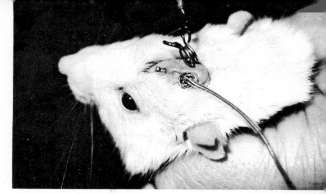

2-9

Electrodes implanted in the brain

Courtesy N. E. Miller; photos by Martin Iger.

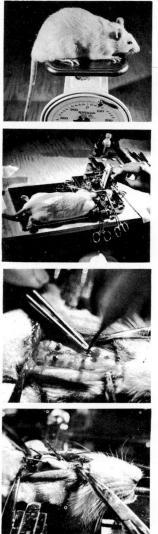

Rat being weighed before operation to determine the proper dose of anesthetic.

Anesthetized rat under the stereotaxic instrument which implants the electrodes through tiny holes in the skull.

Insertion of screws which help to anchor dental cement to skull.

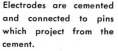

Electrodes are cemented and connected to pins which project from the cement.

2-10

Electrical action of the brain

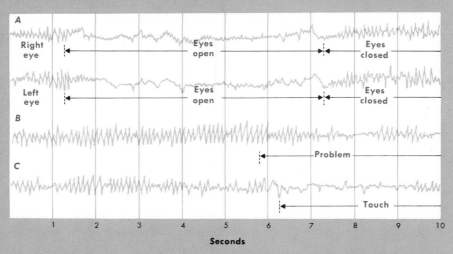

Through electrodes attached to the outside of the skull, the electroencephalograph measures the pattern of electrical activity within the brain. When the brain is at rest, the basic pattern is a large-amplitude "alpha" wave of about 10 cycles per second, as shown in the extreme left column. When the brain responds to sensory inputs, such as vision or touch, or when it is engaged by a mental problem, the alpha waves give way to irregular waves which are higher in frequency and lower in amplitude. (After Eccles, 1958)

the hindbrain, midbrain, thalamus, and hypothalamus, that is, much of the *brain stem,* or stalk upon which the other brain structures are attached, functions in such life-maintaining processes as respiration and metabolism, in the regulation of endocrine gland activity, and in maintaining *homeostasis.* The term homeostasis refers to the general level of functioning characteristic of the healthy organism, such as a normal body temperature, a standard concentration of salt in the blood, a typical heart rate and blood pressure. Under stress the usual equilibrium is disturbed, and processes are set under way to correct the disequilibrium and return the body to the normal level of functioning. Thus if we are too warm we perspire and if we are too cool we shiver—both processes tending to restore the more usual temperature. If we think of temperature control by a thermostat as providing a convenient analogy, we may say that the body has its own *homeostats* for detecting changes in various systems that can get out of balance. These homeostats are located in the hypothalamus, near the midline of the ventricles (hollow portions) at the center of the brain. The homeostats are conceived as structures sensitive to chemical and other changes that represent a feedback from the rest of the body. Their action is closely related to that of the neighboring *reticular formation,* a collection of neurons with short connections to other neurons lying in the brain stem, forming a structure about the size of the little finger. The reticular formation has to do with maintaining an aroused state of the organism, as in changing from sleep to waking, or from diffuse awareness to alert attention. It may have other regulatory functions as well (Magoun, 1958; Samuels, 1959). We thus see how this anatomical core of the brain provides for very important life-maintaining functions.

Much of the information about the homeostats and about the reticular formation is quite recent, and the developments provide an exciting field of inquiry in contemporary neurophysiology and physiological psychology. We may take as one illustration the control of perspiration as a result of temperature change in the region of the hypothalamus (Benzinger, 1961).

The investigator placed a thermocouple (a heat-measuring instrument) on the eardrum, in order to measure temperature as near as possible to the hypothalamus where the "thermostat" or "homeostat" is located. He then placed the subject in a calorimeter, where heat loss from the body could be

2-11

The human brain

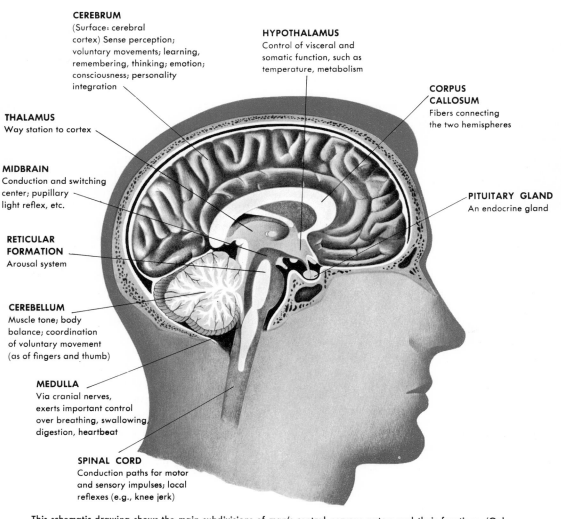

CEREBRUM
(Surface: cerebral cortex) Sense perception; voluntary movements; learning, remembering, thinking; emotion; consciousness; personality integration

HYPOTHALAMUS
Control of visceral and somatic function, such as temperature, metabolism

CORPUS CALLOSUM
Fibers connecting the two hemispheres

THALAMUS
Way station to cortex

MIDBRAIN
Conduction and switching center; pupillary light reflex, etc.

PITUITARY GLAND
An endocrine gland

RETICULAR FORMATION
Arousal system

CEREBELLUM
Muscle tone; body balance; coordination of voluntary movement (as of fingers and thumb)

MEDULLA
Via cranial nerves, exerts important control over breathing, swallowing, digestion, heartbeat

SPINAL CORD
Conduction paths for motor and sensory impulses; local reflexes (e.g., knee jerk)

This schematic drawing shows the main subdivisions of man's central nervous system and their functions. (Only the upper portion of the spinal cord, which is also part of the central nervous system, is shown here; for further detail see Fig. 2-16.)

measured, as an indication of the amount of perspiring. The subject's body (internal) temperature was changed by control of the external temperature and by the subject's exertion. A very clear relationship was found between the internal temperature and the rate of sweating (Figure 2-12). The sharp breakpoint in the curve is at 36.9° C (98.4° F). It is as if the thermostat was set for this temperature. Below it no sweating occurred; above it sweating began. A change in temperature of .01 C° was enough to increase the dissipation of heat through sweating by a measurable amount.

Around this central core we have additional older parts of the brain that serve somewhat more complex functions. These lie along the innermost edge of the cerebral hemispheres, i.e., the earlier evolved parts of the cerebrum. These structures are now commonly referred to as the *limbic system.*

2-12

The hypothalamus as a thermostat

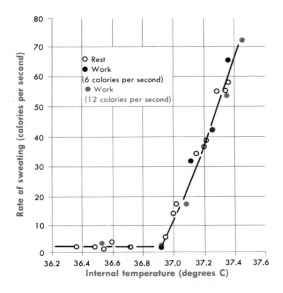

The graph shows the relation between internal head temperature and heat dissipation by sweating. A thermocouple giving a precise temperature measurement was placed on the eardrum to be near the hypothalamus; heat loss was measured by a calorimeter in which the subject worked or rested. (After Benzinger, 1961)

The system is related to some of the internal controls that occur in digestion and circulation, so that the system has sometimes been called the *visceral brain* (McLean, 1950). But it has other "higher" functions also, as in some aspects of memory. Pribram (1958) suggests that if all the data are taken together, we find that the limbic system is concerned with *sequential activities,* that is, with activities that proceed for some time and involve a number of movements before they are completed. These include the activities of feeding, of attacking, of fleeing from danger, of mating—the kinds of activities that have often been called "instinctive" because they are so characteristic of the members of a species. Milner (1958) has shown dramatically that human patients with lesions in parts of the limbic system are particularly helpless in carrying out an intended sequence of actions. That is, a small distraction makes them forget what they have set out to do. The evidence from both lower animals and human studies thus suggests that the limbic system builds upon the homeostatic mechanisms, regulating the dispositions of the organism to engage in sequences of activities related to the basic adaptive functions mentioned above.

Finally, as the outer core is reached, we come to the cerebral cortex. This portion of the brain is so important in behavior that it deserves special emphasis.

The cerebral cortex

The two large hemispheres at the top of the human brain represent man's "new brain." The convoluted layer of gray matter—the cerebral cortex—that covers them controls man's most distinctively human behavior.

Our clearest knowledge of the cortex has to do with those functions that are related to specific areas of the brain. We speak of these as the *localized functions,* the ones that can be mapped; the places where they appear on a map of the cortex are called

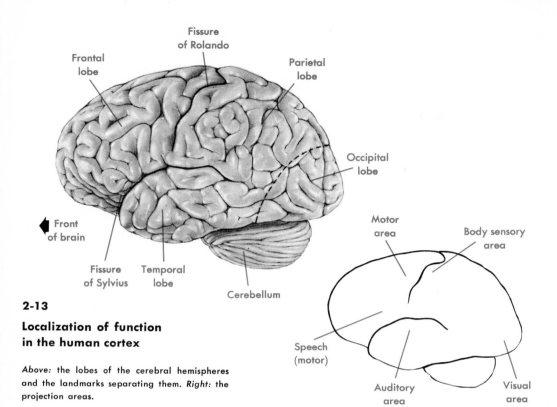

2-13

Localization of function in the human cortex

Above: the lobes of the cerebral hemispheres and the landmarks separating them. *Right:* the projection areas.

projection areas. It can be shown that some areas of the cortex when stimulated electrically will produce known and specifiable kinds of *motor responses* (those involving motion or activity in parts of the body) or *sensory effects* (those involving sensation, feeling, awareness, etc.). When tumors exert pressure on these areas, there are disturbances in the responses. When, through disease or injury, these areas are destroyed, the same functions are altered or obliterated. Yet we would be making an error in logic if we assumed that these functions are *controlled* by these areas alone. Even though an area is *essential* to a function, it may not be *sufficient* to control that function. With this warning, let us turn to some illustrations of localization of function.

Before beginning with the illustrations of localization, we need a few landmarks by which to describe areas of the *cerebral hemispheres.* The two hemispheres are symmetrical, one on the right and one on the left, with

a deep division between them, running from front to rear. So our first classification is into *right* and *left hemispheres.* For the most part, functions of the right side of the body are controlled by the left hemisphere, functions of the left side by the right hemisphere. Each hemisphere is divided into four *lobes:* the *frontal* lobe, the *parietal* lobe, the *occipital* lobe, and the *temporal* lobe. The landmarks dividing these lobes are shown on Figure 2-13. The frontal lobes are separated from the parietal lobes by the *central fissure* or *fissure of Rolando,* running down from the part of the cerebrum near the top of the head sideways toward the ears. The division between the parietal lobe and the occipital lobe is not as clear-cut; it suffices for our purpose to know that the parietal lobe is at the top of the brain, behind the fissure of Rolando, while the occipital lobe is at the very rear of the brain. The temporal lobe is well set off by a deep fissure at the side of the brain, the *fissure of Sylvius.* The tem-

Localization of function within the motor and sensory areas

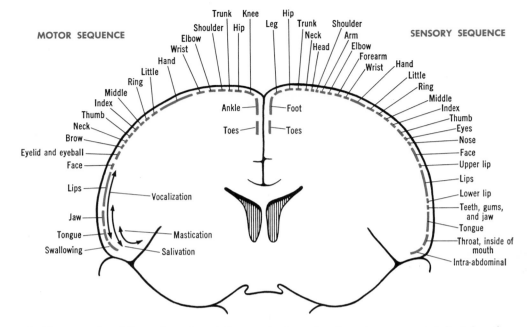

In this cross section of the cerebrum through the sensorimotor region, the motor sequence is indicated on the left and the sensory sequence on the right. Both hemispheres have both functions (see Fig. 2-13). (After Penfield and Rasmussen, 1950)

poral lobes lie below and beside the rest of the hemispheres.

1. *The Motor Area.* The motor area lies just in front of the fissure of Rolando, half of the body being represented on each side. When stimulated electrically, parts of the motor area cause movements in the extremities, and when these areas are injured the same parts are paralyzed. The body is represented in approximately upside-down form, movement of the toes being mediated by the part near the top of the head, and tongue and mouth movements by the part near the bottom of the area toward the side of the brain (Figure 2-14). Movements on the right side of the body originate through stimulation of the motor area of the left hemisphere, movements on the left side through stimulation of the right hemisphere.

2. *The Body-Sense Area.* In the parietal lobes, separated from the motor area by the fissure of Rolando, lies an area which if stimulated electrically gives rise to sensory experiences, as though a part of the body were being touched or moved. Again the lower extremities are represented high on the area of the opposite hemisphere, the face represented low on the area.

Disease or injury in the body-sense area produces disturbances of sensory processes, but seldom produces complete absence of sensation (anesthesia). The injured person may lose the ability to tell the positions of his arms or hands when his eyes are closed, or to recognize objects by touch. While he may still be able to detect extremes of temperature, he may be at a loss to judge finer gradations of warmth and coolness.

3. *The Visual Area.* At the very back

of each cerebral hemisphere, in the part of the occipital lobe known as the *striate area,* lie centers important in vision.

The right halves of the retinas of each eye are connected with the right visual area, the left halves with the left area. If the striate area on one side is destroyed, the person is made blind in the half of each retina lying on the same side as the injury. Because of the reversal of the image through the lens of the eye, the person cannot see objects on the *opposite* side of the midline of the field of vision. Thus the functional loss of vision is consistent with motor and sensory losses of other kinds. Since smaller damage in the visual areas may result in small blind areas in the visual fields, correspondences have been established between parts of the retina and parts of the visual areas.

4. *The Auditory Area.* An area for audition is found on the surface of the temporal lobes at the sides of the hemispheres. There is some spatial distribution (a part sensitive to high tones being different from that sensitive to low tones), but the organization of the auditory areas is unlike that of the visual areas at least in one respect. In the auditory areas, both ears are totally represented on both sides, so that loss of one temporal lobe has little effect upon hearing, while the loss of one striate area causes blindness in half of each eye.

5. *The Speech Area.* One of the very earliest findings in localization is still under dispute. As early as 1861 the neurologist Broca examined the brain of a patient with speech loss and found damage in an area on the side of the left hemisphere. This area has since been known as Broca's speech area, and it has been assigned the functions of motor speech, that is, the control of the tongue and jaws in speaking. The conventional interpretation is that the area is located in the left hemisphere of right-handed people (those whose left hemisphere is dominant), while it is found in the right hemisphere of left-handed people (those whose right hemisphere is dominant).

Speech is far too complex to be localized in this simple manner, and psychological disorders of speech and language (*aphasias*) have defied simple classification and therefore precise localization. In a careful study of ten left-handed people, half with lesions on the right sides of their brains and half with lesions on the left sides, all but one showed disturbances of speech; this one had a lesion on the right side, which, according to convention, should be more severe for a left-handed person (Humphrey and Zangwill, 1952).

6. *The Association Areas.* The many large areas of the cerebrum not accounted for when maps of localized areas are assembled have often been called *association areas* (as distinguished from the primary projection areas), on the assumption that they must serve to bring together phenomena involving more than one sense and must also be involved in learning, memory, and thinking.

The evidence for this assumption is, in fact, quite fragmentary and, such as it is, very puzzling. Electrical stimulation of various parts of these association areas will produce disturbances of speech. Epileptic patients (but not nonepileptic ones) produce hallucinatory experiences and occasionally recount specific memories under electrical stimulation, especially of areas near certain points that produce convulsions when stimulated. For example, when a given point is stimulated, the patient may report a phonograph playing a recognizable and remembered tune. The record can be "turned on" or "turned off" through electrical stimuuation (Penfield and Jasper, 1954; Penfield, 1958). These results are interesting, but their interpretation is baffling. Why should they be limited to epileptic patients? Is the memory of this experience really localized in this small spot? When the spot is surgically excised (as part of an operation to relieve epilepsy), it is of course no longer possible to secure the effect formerly produced by stimulating that spot. But the excision does not destroy the subject's ability to tell what the record sounded like when that spot was earlier stimulated. Evidently other parts of the brain are involved in the total memory experience.

Evidence from extirpation experiments and other studies makes clear that the areas of the brain not concerned with sensory projection are not "silent" or nonfunctional. Such areas may serve distinguishable functions. Thus the frontal lobes appear to be especially important in *sequential tasks,* in which events must be kept in order. In this they supplement the limbic system (p. 42). Other areas appear to cooperate with the primary projection areas whenever complex tasks are involved.

While we do not yet know in detail how the association areas serve, modern methods, both surgical and electrical, are telling us a number of things about the gross functions of these parts that were once described as "silent" because their functions were unknown. Pribram believes that the so-called association areas have their own specialized functions, even though their specializations are of a different order from those of the projection areas. For example, the primary visual projection area (at the rear of the brain) is inadequate for discrimination unless another area (in the temporal lobes) is intact. This secondary area is thus specialized for discrimination. Other parts, such as the forebrain, may serve kinds of memory that the limbic system does not serve. Still other parts serve for learning and problem-solving and, in man, for language. Because each of the brain regions appears to have some special function of its own that is independent of learning, Pribram (1960) would substitute the term "intrinsic system" for "association area" because the latter term smacks too much of the association psychology and does not suggest the specialized ways in which the various areas contribute to integration.

The Autonomic Nervous System

The outgoing nerves, running from the central nervous system to the response mechanisms, can be classified into two groups: those running to the striate muscles and those running to smooth muscles and glands. Those going to the striate muscles are usually grouped with the central nervous system, while those going to smooth muscles and glands are grouped together as the *autonomic nervous system.* An anatomical basis for the distinction is that the nerve fibers of the autonomic system always have a junction with another neuron (i.e., a synapse) *outside* the brain or spinal cord on the way to a muscle or gland, while such outside synapses are not found for nerves running to striate muscle. The autonomic nervous system derives its name from the fact that many of the activities it controls are "autonomous" or "self-regulating," activities such as digestion and circulation that go on even when a person is asleep or unconscious.

There are two divisions of the autonomic system, often antagonistic in their action. These are the *sympathetic* and the *parasympathetic* divisions.

The sympathetic division

On either side of the spinal column, closely connected with it through the spinal nerves, lie chains of nerve fibers and masses of cell bodies (*ganglia*) from which fibers extend to the various visceral organs. These are known as the *sympathetic chains.* The fibers coming from the spinal cord to the sympathetic chain arise in the thoracic and lumbar portion of the spine, between the cervical (neck) and the sacral (lower spine) regions. All the fibers and ganglia together constitute the *sympathetic division* of the autonomic system (Figure 2-15).

The sympathetic division tends to act as a unit. In emotional excitement it simultaneously speeds up the heart and dilates the arteries of the muscles and heart, while

The autonomic nervous system

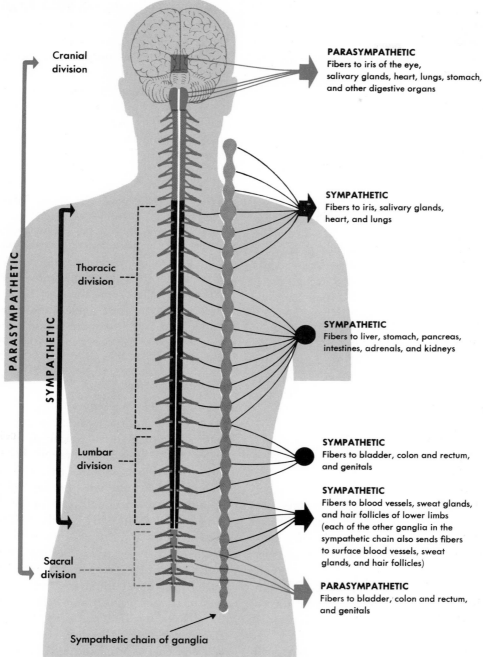

PARASYMPATHETIC
Fibers to iris of the eye,
salivary glands, heart, lungs, stomach,
and other digestive organs

Cranial
division

SYMPATHETIC
Fibers to iris, salivary glands,
heart, and lungs

Thoracic
division

SYMPATHETIC
Fibers to liver, stomach, pancreas,
intestines, adrenals, and kidneys

Lumbar
division

SYMPATHETIC
Fibers to bladder, colon and rectum,
and genitals

SYMPATHETIC
Fibers to blood vessels, sweat glands,
and hair follicles of lower limbs
(each of the other ganglia in the
sympathetic chain also sends fibers
to surface blood vessels, sweat
glands, and hair follicles)

Sacral
division

PARASYMPATHETIC
Fibers to bladder, colon and rectum,
and genitals

Sympathetic chain of ganglia

The diagram represents only one-half of the system, which is duplicated on the other side of the spinal cord. The *sympathetic* system (in black) is characterized by chains of ganglia on either side of the cord and by other large ganglia (represented by large circles). The *parasympathetic* system (in color) has its ganglia (not shown) nearer the organs stimulated so that it acts in a more piecemeal fashion.

constricting those of the skin and digestive organs; its action leads also to perspiring and to secretion of adrenalin. In fact, the responses to adrenalin (see p. 33) and to the action of the sympathetic system are very much alike, and these chemical and neural actions support each other in strong emotion.

The parasympathetic division

The parasympathetic division falls into two parts, some of its fibers originating in the cranial region, above those of the sympathetic system, and others originating in the sacral region, below those of the sympathetic system (Figure 2-15).

Unlike the sympathetic system, the parasympathetic system tends to act in a more piecemeal fashion, affecting one organ at a time. If the sympathetic system is thought of as dominant in violent and excited activity, the parasympathetic system may be thought of as dominant in quiescence. It participates in digestion and, in general, maintains the functions that conserve and protect bodily resources. (It is worth noting that there is no parasympathetic connection to the adrenal gland, which is dominant in excitement.)

Competition and cooperation between the sympathetic and parasympathetic divisions

When both sympathetic and parasympathetic fibers are connected to the same muscle or gland, the usual rule is that they act in opposite manner. Thus the sympathetic system speeds the heart rate, the parasympathetic system slows it; the sympathetic system inhibits digestive processes, the parasympathetic system facilitates them. A list of the functions of the two systems is given in Table 2-2.

There are some exceptions to the principle that the two systems are antagonistic. Both divisions may be active at once, and in some cases they act together in sequence.

While the sympathetic system is usually dominant in fear and excitement, a not uncommon parasympathetic symptom in extreme emotion is the involuntary discharge of the bladder or bowels. The complete sex act in the male requires erection (parasympathetic) followed by ejaculation (sympathetic). One must be careful not to let a generalization misguide one into overstating a case. The two divisions, often antagonistic, interact in more complex ways, and their interaction is even today not fully understood.

How the Nervous System Works

Thus far we have considered the gross features of the nervous system, and the major functions of its parts, without attention to the basic problems of the structure of the neuron and the propagation of the nervous impulse. If we are to understand behavior, we have to know what we can about these finer aspects of the operation of the nervous system.

The reflex pattern

Just as the anatomy of the vertebrate brain is built upon a simple pattern of a tube containing three swellings that has evolved into the intricate brain of the higher animals and man, so the basic pattern of stimulation by the environment and response to stimulation is that of the *reflex circuit*. Irritability and contractibility are primitive properties of protoplasm, as found in single-celled organisms, but when nervous systems develop, response to stimulation becomes divided into the processes of *reception of stimuli, transmission and integration of nervous impulses,* and *activation of muscles and glands.* Specialized *receptors* convert the energy from the environment into nervous impulses; the nerves and central nervous system provide the *connectors;* the nervous impulses are converted back into

TABLE 2-2

Functions of the two divisions of the autonomic nervous system

Organ	Sympathetic function	Parasympathetic function
Heart	Acceleration	Inhibition
Blood vessels		
In skin	Constriction	None
In striate muscle	Dilation, constriction	None
In heart	Dilation	Constriction
In abdominal viscera	Constriction	None
Pupil of eye	Dilation	Constriction
Tear glands	(Possibly a secretory function)	Secretion
Sweat glands	Secretion	None
Hair on skin	Hairs erected	None
Adrenal glands	Secretion	None
Liver	Sugar liberated	None
Salivary glands	Secretion (?)	Secretion
Stomach	Inhibition of secretion and peristalsis (some excitation)	Secretion, peristalsis (some inhibition)
Intestines	Inhibition	Increased tone and motility
Rectum	Inhibition	Feces expelled
Bladder	Inhibition	Urine expelled
Genital organs (male)	Ejaculation	Erection

SOURCE: Data from Best and Taylor (1955), p. 1097, and other sources.

action by the *effectors*. The reflex circuit provides the terminology for S-R psychology, as discussed in Chapter 1.

The truly simple reflex is a convenient fiction. It would represent a simple receptor which, when activated, transmits impulses through a single neuron to a waiting muscle. Actual reflexes consist in the stimulation of numerous nerve fibers, which in turn make junctions with other neurons, often supplemented by bursts of impulses coming from other sources, and resulting in impulses transmitted out along numerous fibers before reaching a muscle or gland, or several muscles and glands, as the effectors. Some reflexes operate relatively mechanically, despite these complications of the simple re-

flex circuit. Thus a tap on the patellar tendon will ordinarily produce a knee jerk; light flashed into the eye will be followed by constriction of the pupil. Even in these cases, however, other processes may accentuate (facilitate) or diminish (inhibit) the response. For example, one way of obtaining a more pronounced knee jerk is to grip the hands together just before the tendon is tapped. Evidently what is happening in the leg is affected by what is happening elsewhere. When we consider more complex processes, such as memory and imagination, the notion of a reflex is continued with greater difficulty, yet it is convenient to assume that the same principles can be applied.

Man's equipment of *receptors* is very inadequately indicated by the traditional five senses. Not only do some of these (e.g., touch) break down into several senses, but receptors related to bodily position and to muscular movements are totally unaccounted for in the traditional scheme. A catalogue of receptors is given in Table 2-3.

A receptor is an energy-converter, what the engineer calls a transducer. That is, it converts energy from the environment into chemical processes that in turn produce electrochemical nervous impulses (Loewenstein, 1960).

The *effectors* which carry out the responses to stimuli are the muscles and the glands. Whether one regards perceptions and ideas as responses depends upon one's theoretical position. It may be that a class of *intracerebral processes* has to be postulated to account for dreams and other thought processes that do not result in movement. This is a matter of some uncertainty, however, and the objective psychologist conveniently gets around this by always using as his *data* responses that have resulted in movement (perhaps only in speech). The processes in the brain that take place between input and output are then inferences, often called *intervening variables,* but they are not considered to be responses in the usual sense unless they actually involve

TABLE 2-3
Man's receptors

Bodily organ or tissue	Location of sensitive portion	Sensory experience or discrimination
Eye	Retina	Black, white, color; visual perception of objects, space, motion
Inner ear	Cochlea	Tones, noises; speech, music, location of sounds in space
	Saccule, utricle	Static position of the body in reference to gravity; accelerated motion
	Semicircular canals	Rotation of the head
Nose	Olfactory epithelium (in upper part of right and left nasal cavities)	Smell
	Sensitive nerve endings (in membranes of nose)	Irritation
Tongue, mouth, and throat	Taste buds (on surface and edges of tongue; in lesser numbers in other tissues of mouth and throat)	Sweet, salt, sour, bitter
Skin	Various end organs (organs and nerve endings of differential sensitivity, distributed unevenly through the superficial and deeper layers of the skin)	Light touch, deep pressure, warmth, coolness pain
Internal organs	Various	Pain from distention (also, in some parts of some organs, touch, warmth, coolness, pressure)
Muscles, tendons, and joints	Muscle spindles (stimulated by stretching of muscle)	Position and movement of parts of the body
	Endings in tendons (stimulated when muscles contract)	
	Pressure-sensitive end organs in tissues around joints	

Spinal cord and spinal roots

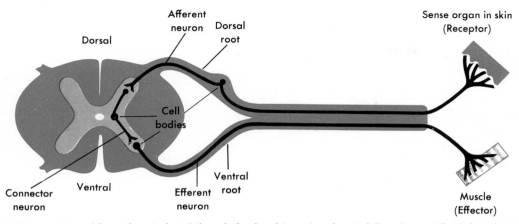

Nerves enter and leave the spinal cord through the dorsal (upper) and ventral (lower) roots. The H-shaped portion is gray matter at the center of the cord, consisting largely of cell bodies and their interconnections. An oversimplified three-neuron reflex circuit is illustrated. The cell bodies (greatly enlarged) for each of the three kinds of neurons are shown. The efferent fibers are not, however, all motor fibers; see text. Note that this is a cross section; much of the cord (the matter surrounding the central gray, called "white matter" though shown in color in the diagram) consists of ascending and descending fibers connecting the various segments with each other and with the brain.

muscles or glands, as when one screws up one's forehead in thinking.

Between the receptors and the effectors lie the *connectors,* or what we call "the nervous system." These may be grouped into three classes:

1. Incoming or *afferent* nerves. The receptors all over the body are connected to nerve fibers over which impulses come into the *central nervous system.* A nerve is a bundle of individual nerve fibers.
2. *Centers.* The internal connections and interconnections of nerve cells, made across their endings at *synapses,* occur chiefly within the brain and spinal cord, although there are some junctions between neurons (synapses) outside the brain and spinal cord in collections of nerve cells called *ganglia* (plural for *ganglion*). We may group all these complex switching places together as *central processes,* or, simply, *centers.*
3. Outgoing or *efferent* nerves. From the centers, nerve fibers lead out, again

through bundles called nerves, to connect with effectors. (It is easy to recall which nerves are called *af*ferent and which *ef*ferent by remembering that *ef*ferent nerves are connected with *ef*fectors.)

This simple picture of afferent and efferent nerves, supported both by the anatomy of nerves and by the physiology of reflex action, is another one of the oversimplifications that has recently been corrected. The oversimplification lies not in the direction of movement of impulses, but in their purposes. It has been assumed that afferent nerves were sensory nerves, and efferent nerves motor nerves, that is, that afferent nerves served purposes of signaling changes at the sense organ, and motor nerves purposes of movement and secretion (Figure 2-16). It is now known, however, that the efferent fibers also regulate the amount of sensory input, through what has been called a "gating" mechanism (Bruner, 1957), thereby selectively allowing more or fewer afferent im-

The many synapses at the cell body of a neuron

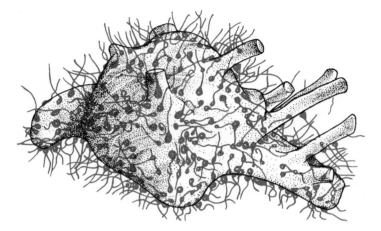

This diagram of a neuron of the cerebral cortex suggests the multiple interconnections with other neurons. Axon fibers from other neurons (in color) connect with the cell body and its dendrites via synaptic knobs (indicated by the enlarged areas at the ends of the axons). The stumps of the neuron's dendrites are shown at the right, the stump of its axon at the left. (After Eccles, 1958)

pulses to be transmitted. As many as one-third of the fibers in the *efferent* ventral roots to muscles serves this purpose of regulating the *afferent* impulses from muscle receptors (Livingston, 1958). Similar efferent modification of afferent processes has been reported for the visual and auditory mechanisms in the brain.

Parts of the neuron

As we have seen, the specialized cells called neurons are the basic units of the nervous system. Each neuron is a living cell with a nucleus and other parts common to all cells. Its specialized structure has three main parts: the *cell body,* containing the nucleus; the *dendrites;* and the *axon.* The dendrites and the cell body *receive* impulses from receptors or from other neurons; the axon *transmits* impulses to other neurons or to effectors.

A nerve is really a bundle and may contain hundreds of nerve fibers, originating from as many neurons. The axons from a great many neurons (perhaps of the order of 1000) may make synaptic junctions with the dendrites and cell body of another neuron. The synapse is not a direct connection; there is always a slight physical separation across which the nervous impulse travels. A

neuron of the cerebral cortex, with the axons of other neurons making synapses with it, is pictured schematically in Figure 2-17.

Transmission of neural impulses

While a nerve impulse moves along a nerve fairly rapidly, its motion should not be strictly compared to that of an electrical current through a wire. Electricity travels at the speed of light, while a nerve impulse moves along at about 60 to 100 feet per second in a frog's motor nerve and perhaps at 300 feet per second in the fastest fibers of warm-blooded animals. The analogy to a fuse has sometimes been used: when a fuse is lighted, one part of the fuse lights the next part, the impulse being regenerated along the way. The details are much more complex than this, though they are now fairly well understood. The action is electrochemical: when a nerve fiber is stimulated, there is an interchange between potassium (K) ions and sodium (Na) ions through the surface of the fiber, thereby changing its electrical characteristics so as to produce a small electrical current that can be recorded with a sensitive instrument (see Figure 2-18).

Some nerve fibers have an insulating sheath called a *myelin* sheath; such fibers are known as *myelinated* fibers. The sheath has gaps at regular intervals, called *nodes*. It is now known that in such myelinated fibers the impulses are relayed at each node, with the result that the impulse travels ten times faster and with much less energy expenditure than in a nonmyelinated fiber. It is not surprising to learn that the myelin sheath was a late development in evolution and is characteristic of the nervous systems of higher animals.

Synaptic transmission

The synaptic junction between neurons is of tremendous importance because it is here that switching of impulses takes place, making possible facilitation, inhibition, coordination, and integration of impulses through the way in which groups of neurons act together. A single neuron transmits an impulse, or "fires," when the impulses reaching it become strong enough. Because its axon does not transmit at all prior to this, the neuron has been said to follow an "all-or-nothing" principle of action. The neuron fires in a single transient burst and then is temporarily inactive (in what is called a *refractory phase*) for a few thousandths of a second. This is not, however, the complete story of neuron action. Recent work has shown much longer enduring activity in dendrites, lasting 15 to 30 thousandths of a second and probably accounting for electrical effects of varying intensity which show up in the EEG (Bishop and Clare, 1952; Li, Cullen, and Jasper, 1956). Thus there has come about a new interest in graduated activity, as distinct from all-or-nothing activity, but the work is very recent and its implications have not yet been fully understood.

It is now believed that some kind of chemical substance is released when the impulse reaches the end of the axon, and that it is this substance that activates the next neuron. Convergence of many impulses (at least more than one!) is necessary to cause a neuron to fire; this complexity may ac-

2-18

Electrochemical basis of the nervous impulse

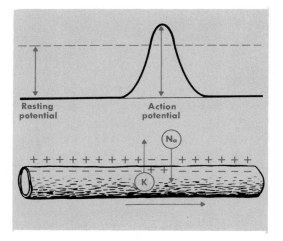

Transmission of the nervous impulse is made possible by an interchange of charged particles, or ions, through the membrane of the nerve fiber. (Katz, 1952)

count for the fine adjustments that must occur in learning, memory, and thought. These chemical processes go on at a minute scale. The energy involved in firing a neuron is something like a billionth of a watt; with 10 billion neurons in the human brain, this means that the whole brain can operate on a power supply of about 10 watts, assuming every neuron to be active simultaneously (which is hardly likely).

CRITICAL DISCUSSION
The physiology of memory

We really know so little about what happens in the brain when we learn, and thus store information, or when we recall, and thus make use of what we have learned, that our knowledge based on the facts of behavior is much firmer than our knowledge based on the operation of the brain. There have been many conjectures, however, and some of these are worth examining.

A special problem is what happens when learning takes place and memory is "stored" in

The reverberating circuit as a holding mechanism

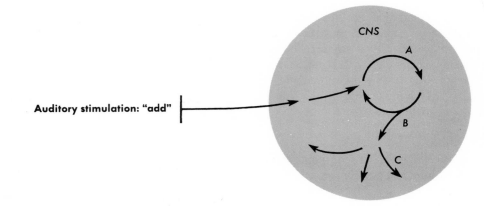

An instruction (say, to "add"), received as auditory stimulation, excites A which excites B. To complete the adding operation, B must excite other paths, such as C, but at the same time it re-excites A. Therefore when other stimuli (for example, mention of specific numbers) enter by other paths, the continuing activity in A and B will facilitate the adding operation, presumably by way of some path such as C. The point is that the activity in the closed pathway continues long after the instruction to add. (From Hebb, 1958, p. 55)

some part of the brain. Some theorists believe that a change takes place at the synapse—perhaps in the growth of the endings of the neuron itself, or perhaps growth in the surrounding tissue, or perhaps some chemical change; another possibility is the setting up of loops of linked neurons that continue to operate even when all stimulation is withdrawn.

This is a most important problem, but at present we do not have any clear answer. Some of the leads have developed in the following ways:

1. The possibility of reverberating circuits (loops of neurons) that continue to be active after stimulation is withdrawn is supported by experiments showing that electrical changes in isolated brain tissue continue for several seconds after brief stimulation (e.g., Burns, 1951). Such a "holding mechanism" is postulated by Hebb (1955) to make possible the delays characteristic of thought processes; perhaps, with some elaboration, such mechanisms might also serve learning and memory (Figure 2-19).

The facts that the brain is always active, even in sleep, and that the pulsations of electrical activity during rest are at the rate of about 10 per second suggest the possibility that this may be a sign of reverberating circuits firing at this rate. The EEG (electroencephalograph) records show a disruption of this rhythm when the brain is active on a specific problem, which might be expected if the reverberating circuits were storage systems that simply kept activity going until something happened to mesh with this stored material; then the already active neurons would be ready to facilitate or inhibit the specific impulses reaching this reverberating circuit (Figure 2-19).

Against this view of memory is the fact that under some conditions brain waves, as shown by the EEG measurements, can be reduced virtually to nothing, with no impairment of memory. For example, the hamster, a hibernating animal, can be brought to a state of inactivity by chilling it to a body temperature of 40° F. The brain waves then virtually disappear, as EEG measurements show. But the hamster, when warmed up, has not forgotten how to run a maze it earlier learned (Gerard, 1953).

2. Even though neurons do not divide and regenerate as other cells do, they readily grow new axons and dendrites after injury, and these new portions seem to have some way of making appropriate connections to receptors or effectors or other neurons. It is not therefore a

"wild" conjecture that there might be some sort of growth taking place to establish closer connections between neurons that repeatedly fire together. The growth might consist of an amoeboid shift in the cell body or the growth of new portions of the neuron. This view is not as popular as it once was, but it is still considered as possible (e.g., Hebb, 1958, p. 147).

3. Because of the tendency for units of the nervous system to fire as a whole and then to have a period of inactivity (refractory phase), there is a temptation to use the analogy of modern electronic digital computers whose units are either "on" or "off." The brain might work like such a computer, an assembly of neurons being "on" or "off" in a pattern that would store information for future use. There are plenty of neurons to provide the necessary storage capacity, but the details, though intriguing, are still conjectural.

It should be noted that on-off, dot-dash mechanisms are by now very familiar in ordinary life. The fact that the television screen works in this way is what makes possible the "taping" of programs for later transmission. Because the brain has on-off mechanisms, it might conceivably manage something that corresponds to taping of patterned stimuli.

4. The possibility of some sort of "chemical memory" has also been explored. The simplest analogy is that of a storage battery, in which "electricity" is stored by the deposition of chemical substances. For such a memory to be specific, some form of "coding" must take place; and analogies can be drawn from certain developments in modern computers and from modern chemical genetics.[2] Experimental evidence indicates that there are important chemical interchanges between the neuron and the surrounding proteins in the supporting cell structure (the *glia cells*) (Galambos, 1961). The glia cells comprise some 80 per cent of the cells of the brain, yet heretofore

they have been assigned merely supporting or nutritive roles, because they apparently do not participate directly in the fiber conduction of impulses. It was recently found, however, that when stimulated the glia cells give rise to electrical response and mechanical contraction (Hild, Chang, and Tasaki, 1958). The possibility that these cells provide some kind of accessory system for the coding of memory is now raised, and it may be that memory is coded chemically, ready to be aroused when an appropriate enzyme is released by the activation of a particular set of neurons whose actions are related to the stored material (Hydén, 1961).

Additional interest in brain biochemistry has arisen because of experiments showing certain differences in brain chemistry (specifically, the amounts of substances known as acetylcholine and cholinesterase) in the brains of brighter and duller strains of rats (Rosenzweig, Krech, and Bennett, 1960).

While it is probable that memory somehow takes place at synapses, the storage points for memory of a single event may be widely scattered over different parts of the brain. The concept of memory stored chemically does not require that there be some precise localization of the memory. We might think of a system in which references are cross-filed. Then the loss of one filing card will not make the information on that card inaccessible. There is no one "memory center" in the brain.

Levels of Functioning

We have completed a survey of the major bodily systems that are provided for integration within the organism and for interaction with the environment. We are now ready to consider some general problems of level of functioning in *adaptive behavior,* that is, behavior that brings the organism into adjustment with its variable environment.

Understimulation

It was pointed out earlier that the body tends to preserve a normal state of equilibrium, or *homeostasis,* from which behavior

---

[2] The analogy from genetics is that the whole pattern of the mature organism is transmitted at birth by way of the complex molecules of DNA (deoxyribonucleic acid), a self-duplicating substance that is rigid in its structure and serves well as a fixed code for the development of the organism. Actual development takes place by the combination of amino acids into proteins, a process presumably guided by the interaction between DNA and RNA (ribonucleic acid) (Lederberg, 1960).

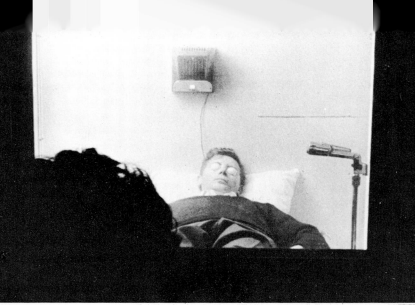

David Linton, courtesy N.Y.U.

2-20

An experimental isolation chamber

The observer views the subject through the window in the isolation chamber. Stimulation is reduced to a minimum by means of the soundproofing, heat control, and vibrationless surroundings of the room. Subjects wear eye covers consisting of half ping-pong balls which show the subject only a continuous gray field of vision. Subjects stay in this chamber up to 36 hours in this experiment.

in response to stimulation departs. Once there is effort or change of any sort, homeostasis is temporarily disturbed, and mechanisms are aroused that tend to restore it. Despite the importance of homeostasis and the stresses that are implied when it is upset, the normal life of the organism is not one of quiescence, but one of action.

The fact that a healthy organism seeks stimulation and activity is evident to anyone who has watched children and animals at play. As adults we know that solitary confinement is the cruelest form of punishment, reducing as it does opportunities for physical stimulation and eliminating social stimulation and response.

Our level of activity can vacillate between complete quiescence and an overactive, stressful level. In the normal cycle of sleep and wakefulness, the vacillation is between moderate limits of quiet and action. The harmful effects of extreme overactivity are obvious (exhaustion, collapse), but extreme inactivity can also have serious consequences.

Experiments have shown that even a relatively short period of inactivity will disturb the adaptive responses of a person. In one such experiment, college students were paid to remain in bed in isolated cubicles for two to three days under conditions of very restricted stimulation. Not only were the rooms free of pictures and other centers of interest, but the students wore special cuffs to reduce the stimulation from their own movements as they lay quietly in bed. They were interrupted occasionally for psychological testing. During the isolation period scores on a number of intelligence test items decreased markedly. Some disturbances in perception were noted as the students left the cubicles. Occasionally during the period of isolation hallucinations appeared, not dissimilar to those found in some cases of mental illness (Bexton, Heron, and Scott, 1954; Heron, Doane, and Scott, 1956; Doane, Mahatoo, Heron, and Scott, 1959).

These experiments show in rather striking fashion that the normal level of psychological functioning depends upon active participation with the environment. Workers in mental hospitals have found that some gains are produced merely by keeping patients active, as in sports and hobbies. This fact has led to the development of the special techniques known as *occupational therapy*. Some minimum level of active stimulation and response is necessary to keep us operating as human beings.

Overstimulation: stress

When conditions place the organism under great strain, the homeostatic mechanisms no longer operate smoothly; if the stresses continue, the organism may suffer injury, even as a consequence of its own efforts to meet the stress. Many kinds of agents and events can place the organism under stress. These include infections, nervous strain, physical injury, excessive heat or cold, muscular fatigue. Conditions of modern life place some people under stress for long periods of time. The physiological mechanisms of adaptation to stress become significant as we try to understand what is happening to such people.

Dr. Hans Selye, a professor of medicine at the University of Montreal, has conducted a number of investigations of what happens under extreme and long-continued stress. He proposes that there is a stereotyped bodily response to general systemic stress, a pattern of response that he has named the "general adaptation syndrome." This pattern moves through three stages:

1. An *alarm-reaction,* in which adaptation has not yet been acquired. This commonly includes a stage of reduced activity (a state of shock), followed by excessive mobilization of forces within the organism to meet the threat (counter-shock).
2. The stage of *resistance,* in which adaptation to threat is adequate.
3. The stage of *exhaustion,* in which the acquired adaptation is again lost (Selye, 1956).

These stages are supported in the experimental findings in rats, as illustrated in the left-hand portion of Figure 2-21, leading to the generalized concept of what happens, as illustrated in the right-hand portion.

The organism's attempts to meet continued stress may lead, according to Selye, to "diseases of adaptation." Of particular interest psychologically are the *psychosomatic disorders,* in which psychological stress in the form of worry or anxiety may produce tension states resulting, for example, in

2-21

General adaptation syndrome

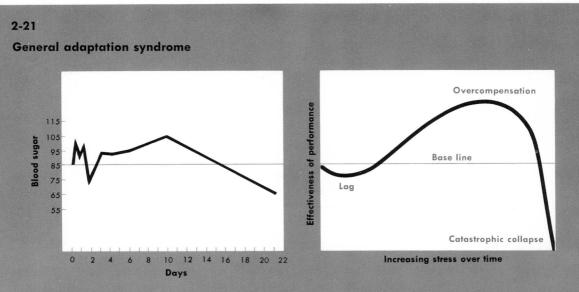

Blood sugar changes in rats chronically exposed to cold. (Modified from Selye, 1950, p. 117)

Schematicized course of a general adaptation syndrome. (From Miller, 1955, after Selye)

stomach ulcers. Such a condition would fit Selye's idea of diseases of adaptation.

Optimal levels of functioning

Between the understimulation that produces less than human functioning and the stress conditions that produce disease and exhaustion, there is a wide range within which normal functioning goes on. Man can live an active life or a sedentary life and still be healthy.

W. B. Cannon, who introduced the notion of homeostasis, is often misunderstood as proposing that the condition of homeostasis represents the optimal level of activity. On the contrary, he stated the position that homeostasis merely protects the body so that a person can go about his enterprises, motivated by goals unrelated to maintaining the equilibrium of processes within the body. He said, in part, that bodily homeostasis liberates the nervous system from the necessity of paying routine attention to the management of the details of bare existence. Without homeostatic devices we should be in constant danger of disaster, unless we were always on the alert to correct voluntarily what normally is corrected automatically. With homeostatic devices, however, that keep essential bodily processes steady, we as individuals are free from such slavery—free to enter into agreeable relations with our fellows, free to enjoy beautiful things, to explore and understand the wonders of the world about us, to develop new ideas and interests, and to work and play, untrammeled by anxieties concerning our bodily affairs.[3]

Cannon is saying here that homeostasis does not define the appropriate level of human functioning; it is merely a protective device. The activities beyond homeostasis carried on without any thought about the condition of the body include man's highest attainments.

[3] Cannon (1939), p. 323.

SUMMARY   1. The human body is a complex sensitive and responding organism, capable of functioning harmoniously because of its mechanical structure of bones and muscles, its blood stream that carries hormones throughout its body, and its nervous system that rules over all the rest.

2. Among the mechanisms that permit fine muscular coordination are those of *reciprocal innervation* whereby the interaction of *antagonistic muscles* is provided for, and the slight but constant action in resting muscles that yields *muscle tone.*

3. The *endocrine glands* by way of the *hormones* secreted into the blood stream are important for aspects of behavior concerned with emotion, motivation, and personality. Among those most relevant to behavior are the *pituitary, thyroid,* and *adrenal glands* and the *gonads,* but the *parathyroids* and the *pancreas* are also important.

4. Because of its intimate relationship to behavior, the evolution of the *brain* and *nervous system* is of primary interest. One-celled animals react directly to the environment, without a specialized nervous system; even a multicellular animal such as a sponge has no nerves. The beginning of the nervous system is seen in the *nerve net* found in coelenterates such as jellyfishes. This is a network of nerve cells called *neurons.* Muscles contract locally where the nerves are stimulated; conduction spreads in all directions from the point of stimulation. One form of coelenterate, the jellyfish *medusa,* achieves some coordination of its swimming movements by having

some of the nerves concentrated in a ring at the margin of its "umbrella," but there is no central coordination, nothing corresponding to a "brain." In the flatworms, planaria, we have the beginnings of the kind of nervous system found in higher forms. The nerve net is combined with a *polarized synaptic* nervous system, in which conduction is in one direction only across the junction between neurons, this junction being called the *synapse*. In some flatworms there is a ladder-type nervous system with nerve cords and a primitive brain.

5. The vertebrate brain evolves about a single hollow cord of nerves running along the back of the body, with some enlargements at the forward (head) end. The three enlargements become the *forebrain, midbrain,* and *hindbrain,* connecting in turn with the *spinal cord*. This basic pattern is preserved in man's brain.

6. Even a primitive vertebrate such as the dogfish has developed more specialized parts of the forebrain such as *olfactory lobes, cerebrum, thalamus,* and *hypothalamus.* The midbrain consists at this stage chiefly of *optic lobes,* connected with the visual apparatus. The hindbrain includes *cerebellum* and *medulla.*

7. While other changes of course occur, the most notable change in the brain in higher vertebrate forms is the development of the new brain, the *cerebral cortex,* the large convoluted portion of the brain that is about all one sees when he looks at the brain of a higher animal such as a horse or dog or at a human brain. The midbrain has decreased a great deal in relative size.

8. The organization of the human brain can be comprehended as composed of three concentric layers: a *primitive core,* an *older brain* evolved upon this core, and a third or outer layer of *new brain* evolved in turn upon the second layer. The primitive core within the *brain stem* serves life-maintaining processes such as respiration and metabolism and keeps the level of body functioning near a steady equilibrium state through *homeostatic* processes. These homeostatic processes operate by way of *homeostats* within the hypothalamus, analogous to thermostats in maintaining constant temperature. An activating system, the *reticular formation,* lies within the brain stem and helps control waking and sleeping, alertness and attention. At the next level are structures lying along the innermost edge of the cerebral hemispheres, the older or more primitive cortex, now referred to as the *limbic system.* These regulate the *sequential activities* such as feeding, attacking, fleeing from danger, mating—essential activities that include interaction with the environment and take place in sequences somewhat spread out in time. Finally, the outer core of new brain, the cerebral cortex, controls discrimination, choice, learning, and thinking—the "higher mental processes," the most flexible, least stereotyped aspects of behavior. The *projection areas* represent specific sensory inputs or centers for control of specific movements; the remainder of the brain consists of *association areas* or *intrinsic systems.*

9. The *autonomic nervous system* is made up of two parts, a *sympathetic* and a *parasympathetic* division. Its fibers mediate the action of the viscera and of the glands, and hence the autonomic system is particularly important in emotional reactions. The sympathetic division is usually involved in excited action and the parasympathetic in quiescent states, but the antagonism between the two divisions is not universal, and they cooperate in complex fashion.

10. In considering the way in which the nervous system works, psychologists find it convenient to build upon the notion of the *reflex circuit,* beginning with the stimulation of a sensitive organ (*receptor*) where the energy of the stimulus is converted into a *nervous impulse* (or a train of such impulses) which travels to the spinal cord and brain via incoming (*afferent*) nerves; switching and integration take place in *centers* of the nervous system; then impulses are propagated along outgoing (*efferent*) nerves to the responding organs, muscles, and glands (*effectors*). While a simple reflex is a convenient fiction, the pattern of the reflex circuit permits discussion of action in terms of input from the environment, central coordination and elaboration, and output in the form of response.

11. The nervous system is composed of cells called *neurons.* They receive stimulation by way of their *dendrites* and *cell body* and transmit impulses via their *axons.* Two types of propagation of the nerve impulse are of importance: that along nerve fibers; that across the junction between neurons, called a *synapse.* Propagation along fibers is by way of an electrochemical process involving the interchange of sodium and potassium ions across the fiber membrane; the conduction is much more rapid for myelinated fibers, reaching a rate of about 300 feet per second in some mammalian nerves. The activation of a neuron across a synapse is also by way of a chemical intermediary; any one axon discharge does not provide enough of the activating substance to fire the neuron, so that several impulses must arrive close together to produce a response. This makes possible a kind of complex switching at the synapse, undoubtedly important in the integration of behavior. The neuron tends to fire in all-or-nothing fashion, followed by a brief *refractory phase.* However, longer-lasting and graduated reactions within the dendrites probably influence the electrical activity of the brain in some manner other than by the axon-discharge of the neuron.

12. The problem of accounting for the neural basis for memory is a very puzzling one. Among present conjectures are: (1) reverberating circuits (loops of neurons that continue to fire after stimulation ceases), (2) some kind of growth process taking place at the synapse, (3) some kind of on-off registration, similar to the storage mechanisms of digital computers, and (4) some kind of chemical memory, in which the supporting tissue, composed of *glia cells,* may play a role. (These cells, abundant in the brain, play no direct role in the fiber conduction of impulses.) There is at present no firm physiological knowledge about the storage of memory in the brain; what we know comes from studies of behavior.

13. Studies of the consequences of under- and overstimulation show the radical effects of extreme departure from the equilibrium state of homeostasis. Understimulation may produce in adult human beings extreme symptoms of loss of adaptive response and the development of hallucinations. The *general adaptation syndrome,* found under conditions of extreme stress, may lead to disease. But the normally functioning organism has enough protective devices to engage in widely varied activities without threatening its survival.

SUGGESTIONS FOR FURTHER READING

For a general introduction to neurology and neuroanatomy, Gardner, *Fundamentals of neurology* (3rd Ed., 1958) is useful; a recent interpretation of brain function, including the concentric patterning described in the text, can be found in Pribram, "A review of theory in physiological psychology," *Ann. Rev. Psychol.,* 1960, Vol. 11. A speculative account, giving various possibilities for accounting for behavior on the basis of brain action, can be found in Hebb, *The organization of behavior* (1949). Another account, with a good deal of physiology but also a good deal of speculation, is Eccles, *The neurophysiological basis of mind* (1953).

A careful account of the methods and results of electrostimulation as a means of studying brain function is that of Sheer, *Electrical stimulation of the brain* (1961).

For a summary on stress see Selye, *The stress of life* (1956). On the effects of sensory deprivation (understimulation) see Solomon and others, *Sensory deprivation* (1961).

Growth
and
Development

The developmental point of view within psychology suggests that present behavior can often best be understood if we know something of its history, for the child is indeed "father to the man." The human infant, like other animals, is born with a wide range of possible behavior. His maturation depends upon his physiological growth potential and the characteristics of his species. He becomes an individual through his experiences as he grows up—experiences in interacting with both the physical and the social environment. The process of socialization—the training for group living given by the cultural environment in which an individual happens to be born—has much to do with adult behavior.

CHAPTER 3

Infancy
and
Childhood

We are now prepared to look at the functioning of the individual from the point of view of his development. The human infant is helpless for a relatively longer time than any other mammal. If we consider only man's nearest relatives in the animal world, we find that we can make a scale of dependency from the more primitive lemur through the more highly evolved primates to man. The lemur can move himself from place to place within a few hours, or at most a few days; the monkey is dependent for a few days or weeks; the infant chimpanzee remains with his mother three to six months. The human infant is dependent for a far longer period; despite (or because of!) this long slow start he has had a highly diversified career by the time he becomes adult.

Some Aspects of Growth
and Development

Before turning to the development of the human infant, we first need to consider some aspects of growth and development applicable to other organisms as well. We shall be concerned with two main principles— *maturation* and *learning*—in accounting for the way in which the individual organism comes to behave as other members of his species. We shall take for granted a third principle—*heredity*—and return to it later on (in Chapter 15).

Maturation refers to growth processes that result in orderly and predictable changes in behavior. The timing and patterning of these changes are relatively independent of exercise or experience, and they go on despite wide variations in the amount of exercise. If birds whose wings have been restrained from birth learn to fly as quickly as birds that have fluttered their wings many days before they fly, we may reasonably say that flying is controlled more largely by maturation than by learning. Whenever we use the word "maturation" to describe the development of neuromuscular processes underlying behavior, we imply that behavior is the result primarily of growth rather than of learning.

By *learning* we mean the shaping of individual behavior through the training that contact with the physical environment and that life among a species' own kind provide. The learning that takes place through social contact is particularly important in man, because he must learn to live in a complex culture. For him the parents are, of course, the most important agents of the social environment; that is, they are the people who influence him early and teach him the ways of the society in which he is to live. But animals are also subject to many social influences; their behavior is not all "inborn" any more than all human behavior is determined at birth.

Embryological development as maturation

In all the higher forms of life a good deal of development takes place before birth, so that much of the hereditary potential has already manifested itself by the time the infant is born. To understand the nature of development it is necessary to note what has happened before birth. The orderly stages of prenatal development help us to grasp what is meant by maturation.

In its earliest stages the human embryo resembles that of other animals, but by the eighth week of existence it has acquired rudimentary human characteristics; from then until birth it is known as a *fetus*. Fetal development goes on in the uniform environment of the mother's body according to a relatively fixed time schedule. Fetal behavior, such as turning and kicking, also follows an orderly sequence, depending on the growth stages of the fetus. Studies have been made of the responsiveness to outside stimulation of the human fetus born prematurely, and more systematic studies have been made of fetal behavior in animals such as the guinea pig and cat. When the fetus is surgically removed from the mother in animal studies, the circulation of the blood in the fetus is maintained through the umbilical cord, which is not severed. Then the fetus is placed in a salt solution at body temperature. Now the response of the fetus to stimulation can be studied at successive stages, with the physiological condition of the fetus essentially normal (Figure 3-1). Such studies show the appearance of behavior patterns in a developmental sequence depending upon growth (i.e., fetal age) rather than upon prior external stimulation (Carmichael, 1954*a*).

Transplantation experiments with simpler forms of life, such as sea urchins and salamanders, have helped biologists to understand the nature of the developmental processes in the embryo. At an early stage of the salamander's development a small group of cells known as "the organizer" becomes very important. The *organizer* determines which will be the head end and which the tail end of the growing embryo. Previously undifferentiated cells begin to differentiate appropriately to their location, so that the embryonic salamander develops properly.

As development proceeds, subregions, such as the mouth region or eye region, are also "organized" by the environment of cells around them. That is, tissue from the belly region, if transplanted to the eye region or the mouth region at the appropriate stages, will conform to the new environment of cells and form an eye or a mouth.

The transplantation experiments help to define what is meant by a normal environment so far as it sustains growth. A normal *external* environment is one that does not distort the *cellular* environment of the grow-

3-1

Maturation prior to birth

Since the guinea pig fetus has just been removed from the mother's body, it has not previously experienced stimulation from external stimuli. With light stimulation above the eye the only response is closing of the eye (*left*), but with stronger stimulation the forepaw is raised to the stimulated spot. Fetal age, 51 days; birth is normally at 68 days. (After Carmichael and Smith, 1939, p. 432)

3-2

A transplantation experiment

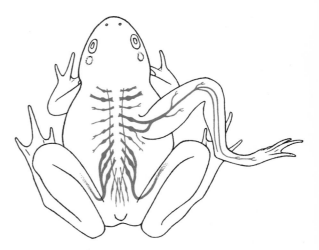

Plasticity has its limits, as shown by an experiment in which a hindlimb bud is grafted onto the back of a tadpole. An extra limb is grown as the tadpole develops, and the limb is invaded by sensory nerves destined for the back, flank, and belly. But no motor nerves appear; when the grafted limb is stimulated, the muscles of the normal right hindlimb respond. (After Sperry, 1959)

ing tissue. If the cellular environment is distorted by physical injury or by chemical means, normal development is interfered with. These experiments also define the *limits* of environmental influence. If we judge from the transplantation experiments, the transplanted tissue to some extent controls what happens when it becomes part of another embryo. For example, when transplanted belly tissue from one donor species is made to form a mouth in a different host species, the tissue will form a mouth characteristic of its own species (the donor species) even if the host species has a differently shaped mouth (Willier, Weiss, and Hamburger, 1955).

These experiments suggest considerable *plasticity* in growth, development being in all cases a result of both the intrinsic properties of the growing tissue and the cellular environment. Because the extent of plasticity is a very important problem for a developmental psychology, we need to examine it further.

Plasticity and its limits

It is well known that lower forms of life readily regenerate missing parts. A flatworm can be cut in two, and soon new heads and tails will grow so that there are two complete flatworms; a lizard may lose its tail and grow a new one. Such observations, together with the transplantation experiments referred to above, led several years ago to a kind of optimism about plasticity, so that, for example, surgeons dealing with injuries of the facial nerves confidently attached motor nerves from the shoulder to a muscle in the face, expecting normal function to be restored. In the last few years there has been an about-face, and it is now recognized that plasticity in most levels of the nervous system is very limited, despite the enormous capacity for learning, memory, and problem-solving shared by higher animals and man.

In an interesting series of experiments with frogs, Miner (reported in Sperry, 1959)

showed that even in an organism in which transplantation and regeneration occur with relative ease, there is a basic pattern of relationships between types of sensory input and muscle output that is unchangeable. She grafted an extra hindlimb to the back of tadpoles, as shown in Figure 3-2. Sensory nerves from the spine that would not ordinarily reach the leg grew into the extra member, making the skin sensitive to stimulation. These belly and trunk nerves took on a hindlimb "flavor," however, so that when the extra grafted limb was stimulated, the animal moved not that limb but the normal hindlimb on the same side. Thus plasticity went so far as to convert belly and trunk sensory nerves into limb nerves, but not so far as to have the motor connections serve the grafted leg.

In corresponding experiments with the white rat, Sperry (1959) crossed the sensory nerves to the hind legs, so that the nerves that normally served the left leg now served the right, and vice versa. Now when the right leg was stimulated by shock, the left leg was withdrawn; a sore on the right foot caused the animal to limp about on three legs, but with the wrong leg lifted up and with the wrong foot being licked. Similar experiments with monkeys showed very little correction of the movement of improperly innervated muscles.

These experiments, taken together, suggest that there is a basic pattern of development within the organism that is laid down at conception, and that later development is modifiable and plastic only within limits. Maturation does not imply total lack of plasticity, but only that development is orderly.

Imprinting

The manner in which inborn readiness affects what is later learned is well illustrated by the process of *imprinting,* a kind of learning that capitalizes upon an "instinctive" tendency when the time is ripe. The clearest example is given by the tend-

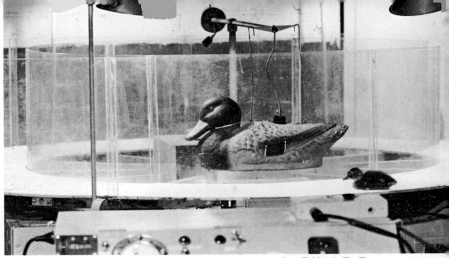

3-3

Imprinting in ducklings

The newly hatched duckling learns to follow the model duck around a circular track.

Dr. Eckhard H. Hess

ency of a young duckling to start following its mother shortly after it is hatched, and then to follow only this particular female duck. Incubator-hatched ducklings can be imprinted upon artificial models. For example, mallard ducklings exposed to a moving model for 10 minutes between 12 and 17 hours after hatching will continue to treat that model as though it were the "mother" and will remain with it against the attraction of live mallard ducks (Figure 3-3). Once imprinting has occurred, the response of following will be elicited only by the imprinted object (Ramsay and Hess, 1954; Hess, 1959).

> ### CRITICAL DISCUSSION
> #### The problem of instinctive behavior

The word "instinct" was formerly used to account for much of the behavior now discussed under the concept of "maturation." Instinct referred to unlearned, patterned, goal-directed behavior characteristic of a species, such as nest-building in birds or the complex hive behavior of bees. The word was often used in reference to human behavior as well, a mother's love illustrating a parental instinct, warfare an aggressive instinct, social behavior a gregarious or herd instinct.

The presence or absence of instincts in man was a source of intense controversy in the 1920's. The controversy became part of an argument over the relative contribution of heredity and of environment, those believing in instincts attributing the major developmental influence to heredity. Those who did not believe in them won the victory, because the believers failed to agree with each other on either the number or the kinds of instincts man possessed. Because of man's prolonged infancy and the great importance of learning in all that he does, the concept of instinct has not proved helpful in studying or understanding human behavior.

The problems raised by the study of instincts are genuine ones and have taken on renewed interest under the influence of a group of European zoologists who call themselves *ethologists* (e.g., Tinbergen, 1951; Hinde, 1959). While at first they used the term "instinct," they now prefer to speak of *species-specific behavior* in order to avoid the controversies to which the notion of instinct leads. By pointing out the richness of species-specific behavior, whether innate or learned, they show the result of the interplay of maturation and the environment (as in imprinting, which is one of the fields of study they initiated).

Effects of early experiences

Regardless of certain fixed relationships within the nervous system, there is little doubt that early experiences with the environment have something to do with later behavior. There are many kinds of evidence, of which the following experiments are representative.

Infant chimpanzees were reared in the dark for seven months. When removed from the dark, they failed to show the normal blinking response to an object moving toward their eyes. Even when a large yellow- and black-striped disk was connected repeatedly with electric shock, they showed no signs of recognizing (and avoiding) it, although normal animals develop avoidance responses after one or two mild shocks. Three such animals were used in this part of the experiment; a fourth, of the same age, had been in the light for 1½ hours each day. His reactions to light after seven months were entirely normal. Being raised in the dark may cause some injury to the eyes, but in addition there are behavioral defects that are gradually removed by practice, such as the inability to converge the eyes upon an object. These results led to more careful study of normal chimpanzee infants, and it was found that their visual development was rather slow, with blinking in response to moving objects in the visual field not appearing until the age of two months. The animals raised in the dark took about two weeks to acquire the response after they had been brought into the light. Thus fully adequate use of vision in the chimpanzee depends both upon internal growth factors continuing after birth and upon practice in the use of vision (Riesen, 1950).

In another experiment, dogs reared in confined quarters so that they did not have the opportunity to explore the environment were perfectly healthy, but in some respects appeared stupid (Melzack and Scott, 1957). For one thing, they appeared quite insensitive to pain. They did not respond to a pinprick or to having their tails stepped on. They would investigate a lighted match by putting a nose into the flame; this would be repeated time after time, without any of the avoidance reaction expected from a normal dog. Whatever the felt experience may have been to the dog, certainly the pain stimulus did not evoke the compelling responses found in the normal dog. Similar results were found for an infant chimpanzee raised with its arms and legs bandaged in cylinders that prevented normal exploration with the hands and feet (Nissen, Chow, and Semmes, 1951).

A curious effect of early experience upon emotional responsiveness has been reported, based on experiments with white rats. The experimenter subjected one group of young rats to mild electric shocks, expecting to produce some abnormalities in behavior later on. As controls he had two other groups of young rats, one handled as the shocked rats were, but without shocks, the other merely left in the nest and not handled at all. The result of the experiment was unexpected: the shocked rats after they grew up were not distinguishable from those handled but not shocked; it was the nonhandled rats that showed the abnormalities! They were particularly timid when placed in a new environment, crouching in the corner rather than exploring the open cage as normal rats do. Other lines of evidence showed that the handled rats developed more rapidly in many respects, opening their eyes sooner, gaining weight more rapidly. Later, under stress, the handled animals were found to have a more rapid response from the adrenal glands than the nonhandled ones. Thus the handling produced profound changes in development, reflected in changes of the regulatory systems within the body as well as in overt behavior (Levine, 1958).

These experiments, taken together, suggest that early experiences are very important to higher animals in providing the background for coping with the environment when they are older. The implications for child-rearing practices are not firm, but they suggest that the early fondling (or neglect) of the infant may have important consequences. In the spirit of comparative psychology, they at least tell us some of the things to look for when we study infants.

Maturation of the Human Individual

As we have seen, the orderly development of the organism begins long before birth. The regulation of fetal development lies within the organism's own tissues, although normal development requires the continuing protection and sustenance provided by the mother's body. Evidence that the timing of development is internally regulated can be found in prematurely born infants who, kept alive in an incubator that simulates the intrauterine environment, develop at much the same rate as infants remaining in the uterus full term.

The regularity of development before birth provides a clear picture of what is meant by maturation, for growth goes on in regular and predictable ways, as earlier indicated (p. 64).

Postnatal maturation is regulated much like growth before birth. That is, many kinds of behavior follow orderly sequences little changed by environmental influences, provided only that the environment is sufficiently favorable to support the necessary growth. Such sequences are found in standing, walking, using hands and fingers, and talking. For example, every infant goes through such regular sequences of crawling and creeping before he walks upright that a uniform growth pattern is evidently responsible for the behavior.

Maturation of structure continues into adult life. Some of the growth changes at adolescence are internally regulated in a sequence not unlike the regulation of fetal development. To the extent that adolescent behavior corresponds to bodily changes, maturational principles apply. The changes associated with aging also go on at their own rates. While maturation is thus a lifelong process, its nature is most readily understood through observing infants and young children, in whom behavioral changes dependent upon growth are rapid and apparent.

Orderly behavior patterns

In the process of learning to walk, the infant goes through the movement stages illustrated in Figure 3-4. Again, this regularity of sequence suggests that a growth process determines the order of behavior. The alternative conclusion would be that all parents go through a uniform training ritual which leads to this uniformity of performance from child to child. We know, of course, that *all* parents do nothing of the sort. Not all children go through the sequence at the same rate; in general, the *order* in which they go from one stage to the next is more alike from infant to infant than the *age* at which they reach each stage. An idea of the range of variation from child to child is given in Figure 3-5, showing the age zones within which 95 per cent of a group of infants reached a stated level of performance. Some of the zones spread over four or five months, indicating that some infants are four or five months ahead of others in reaching the stage of standing alone or walking alone.

A study made by two psychologists, man and wife, shows clearly how the rate of growth influences the development of behavior. The psychologists "adopted" a chimpanzee infant. At the time, their son Donald was nine and one-half months old; the adopted chimpanzee daughter, Gua, was seven months old. Gua and Donald were fed, dressed, spoken to, punished, and caressed alike. Gua was far superior to Donald in her rate of development of skipping, obeying commands, opening of doors, eating with a spoon, drinking from a glass. She revealed a more rapid rate of maturation than Donald did. However, at the end of the nine months of the experiment, Donald, with a slower rate but a higher eventual level of maturation, had caught up with Gua and was superior to her in every respect except in muscular strength (Kellogg and Kellogg, 1933).

Another psychologist couple considerably later did all they could to produce human

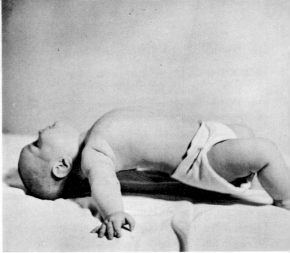

3-4

**Muscular activity of babies
at the rolling stage**

This six-month-old baby discovers for itself movements that prepare it for further development and lead to its ability to walk later on.

responses in a chimpanzee (Hayes, 1951). They even succeeded in obtaining a few simple speech sounds, but the differences between a young chimpanzee and a human child were nevertheless clearly evident. By one year of age the chimpanzee falls well behind the normal performances of a human infant.

The sequences of normal behavior lead to the conviction that growth lies beneath the development of behavior, and further evidence of the influence of maturation comes from experiments in which the environment is either restricted or enriched. If environmental variations produce little change in the rate of change of behavior, then it becomes clearer that the process is determined by growth *within* rather than by influence from *without*.

Observations of the effects of restricted movements have been made on human infants. Hopi Indians, for example, have traditionally kept their infants bound to a board carried on the mother's back. Some Hopi mothers continue to follow the custom, while, through contact with white American culture, others do not. Although the cradleboard markedly restricts movements of the infant's arms and legs during the early months, children raised on it began (on the average) to walk at the same age as those who were never bound on it (Dennis and Dennis, 1940).

A similar study, made with fraternal twins (twins developed from separate eggs), provided similar results. A pair of fraternal twin girls were kept in their cribs from the age of one month until the age of nine months. They were given no training of any kind and only a minimum of handling. They spent most of the time lying on their backs, their hands and feet under the bedclothes. Despite this marked restriction of activity, they developed normally in such behavior as putting their hands to their mouths, grasping objects, playing with their hands, and sitting up when propped. They did, however, fall slightly behind the norms for other children in the age at which they were able to walk holding onto furniture and that at which they were able to stand alone. There was no report of any permanent effect upon the ability to walk or upon other muscular skills (Dennis, 1935). Maturation thus appears to be an important influence, but too severe restrictions may cause some delay in development.

Maturation and training

The practical (and theoretical) importance of recognizing the influence of maturation lies in the relation of maturation to the results of training at different ages. Most behavior is developed by *both* maturation and learning. Language provides a useful illustration. The child learns to talk only

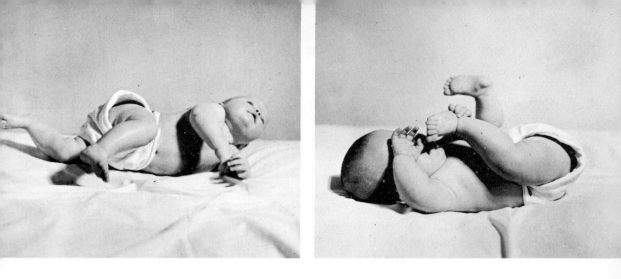

when he has *grown* old enough to learn (maturation), but the language he learns to talk is the one he *hears* (learning).

From many experiments like those just cited psychologists have drawn a number of generalizations about the relationship of maturation to proficiency through training.

1. *Skills that build upon developing behavior patterns are most easily learned.* In almost all languages there are words for mother and father with sound patterns similar to *pa-pa* and *ma-ma*. The words which the infant usually acquires first are words like these which fit in most readily with his natural babbling. He can be taught words like *ma-ma, pa-pa, da-da, ba-ba, bye-bye,* because these words are like the sounds that he makes spontaneously.

2. *The rate of development remains uni-*

3-5

Babies develop at differing rates

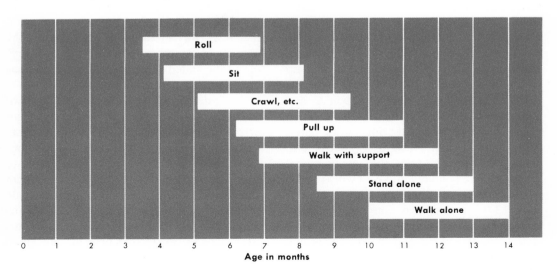

Although development is orderly, some infants reach each stage ahead of others. The bars show the zones of age within which 95 per cent of infants in a well-baby clinic achieved the stated performances. (After Aldrich and Norval, 1946)

form within wide ranges of stimulation. The maturation of performance often requires environmental support, since growth alone is not enough to account for the resulting behavior. But maturation may still be fundamental in accounting for the *rate* of development. A study of stair climbing by a pair of twins bears this out.

Twins T and C were identical twins, that is, twins developed from a single egg and with identical heredity. Because of their common heredity and similarity in development, they made an ideal pair for purposes of study. At the age of 46 weeks, the two twins showed no discernible difference in their behavior when placed at the bottom of a small staircase consisting of four treads and a platform that formed the fifth tread. As an initial test, the experimenter placed each twin before the staircase, while holding both hands. Each twin stepped forward and lifted one foot, but neither was able to place a foot or knee on the first tread.

Twin T was then given a daily 10-minute practice period in stair climbing, while twin C (the "control" twin) was given no practice on stairs. At the end of six weeks, T could climb the steps in a little over 25 seconds, while C had not progressed further than putting the left knee on the first tread. Now T's training was discontinued, and a week later C began a two-week period of training. In these two weeks she caught up with and surpassed T's performance at the end of six weeks of training. Twin C had the advantage because she was older when she began her practice. One week later, when both T and C were 56 weeks old, their performances on the experimental stairs were essentially alike. Twin T took 13.8 seconds to climb the stairs; twin C took 13.9 seconds. The time measurements were made from motion-picture records. It did not matter at the end that one twin had had three times the specific training of the other (Gesell and Thompson, 1941).

Within very wide limits of encouragement and exercise (i.e., environment), the child learns to walk and talk only when old enough and continues to improve at his own rate (i.e., maturation).

3. *The more mature the organism, the less training is needed to reach a given level of proficiency.* Many experiments point to the faster gains of older children over younger, with the same amount of directed practice. Maturation thus produces a certain *readiness* for specific kinds of learning. The generalization applies only within the period of growth; after adult status is achieved, a decline in learning rate may set in.

An experiment on typing was conducted in the first five grades of a school. After one year of practice, children in the second grade were typing at an average rate of less than five words per minute, while those in the fifth grade were typing at an average rate of ten words per minute. In each grade the average gain with one year's practice was greater than in any lower grade.

The experiment went on for two years. It was then found that children who had had two years of typing experience were typing no faster than children in the same grade who had but one year of experience (Wood and Freeman, 1932).

The results of this experiment show that the final rate of typing depends more upon the level of maturation than upon the amount of typing experience, thus conforming to the stated principle that the more mature organism learns more readily.

4. *Training given before maturational readiness may bring either no improvement or only temporary improvement.* In an experiment on training in bladder control, conducted with two pairs of twins, an effort to train *one* member of each pair was begun shortly after birth, while no effort was made to train the other member of each pair. Training was ineffective until the infants were old enough; at that time the other two babies, previously untrained, learned very promptly. Although the two pairs of twins differed by some months in the time at which control was achieved, the trained and

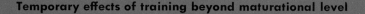

3-6

Temporary effects of training beyond maturational level

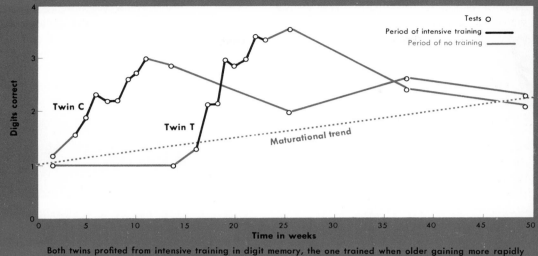

Both twins profited from intensive training in digit memory, the one trained when older gaining more rapidly than the one trained when younger. Without continued training, both fell back to the maturational trend level. (After J. R. Hilgard, 1933)

untrained member of each pair acquired control at the same time (McGraw, 1940). The necessary understanding awaited maturational readiness, and premature training was wasted. Any gains made under premature training are short-lived.

The temporary nature of improvements made beyond the natural maturational level is shown in some additional experiments done with the pair of identical twins who participated in the stair-climbing experiment.

When twins T and C were four years old, they participated in a number of experiments in which one was trained while the other received no training. The experiments included learning to cut with scissors, reciting digits, learning a ring-toss game, and maintaining balance while walking on boards of various widths. The experiments were so arranged that after a pretest of both twins only one was trained. Then there was a retest of both twins, followed by a period in which the second twin was trained. After

discontinuance of training, both twins were retested three additional times at approximately 10-week intervals.

The typical result was that both twins profited by training, but that the one trained second gained more than the one trained first. After training was discontinued, there was loss in skill in both twins, as the performance dropped back to the level typical for children of their maturational development. One of the tasks, digit memory, called for repeating numbers of several digits, spoken slowly by the experimenter. Results for digit memory are plotted in Figure 3-6 (J. R. Hilgard, 1933).

There was thus no evidence of permanent gain from training which had taken place too near the ceiling of ability for these twins.

5. *Premature training, if frustrating, may do more harm than good.* Although lack of training delays development, the lack appears to do no harm, for the retardation is overcome when practice begins. What is the effect of overstimulation, that is, pre-

mature training, before maturational readiness? May it also retard development?

The child who has been exposed too early to an activity for which he is not ready may lose his natural enthusiasm for the activity when he reaches the stage of development appropriate for it. This loss was noted in an experiment in which there was a daily effort to teach a one-year-old to ride a tricycle. The experimenter observed, after the experiment was over, that the child's seven months of futile effort to ride the tricycle curtailed the interest that he would have shown later had the training been delayed (McGraw, 1943).

Experiments concerned with methods of drilling in arithmetic suggest that pressure for speed before the child is ready may actually interfere with learning. Children who were able to master arithmetic in the first grade when taught without pressure for speed did less well on a test, after two years of speed drill, than they had in the first grade (Myers, 1928). Readiness is a complex phenomenon, as this experiment indicates.

These five generalizations suggest a need to understand maturation if one is to understand the relationship between growth and learning. Educational psychologists, impressed by the possible importance of maturation, have proposed the *pacing* of tasks with which the child is confronted. Pacing means presenting activities at a rate commensurate with the development of the individual child. Experiments in pacing, which involve letting the child select his own reading and arithmetic materials, have been tried with promising results (Olson, 1949). Children who are ready read many more books and solve many more arithmetic problems than those less ready; their progress in reading and arithmetic is probably due more to maturation than to specific practice in arithmetic and reading. That is, exposure to books is not the sole condition for reading, and forcing an immature child to attempt to read a large number of books will not produce a good reader. There is, of course, no magic in maturation, and pacing is not a substitute for teaching. Readiness for reading and for arithmetic is not solely a matter of maturation; motivation and previous training are important. The principle of pacing merely warns against wasteful methods of teaching, in which more is expected of the child than he is ready to do.

It is extremely difficult to unravel the relative importance of maturation and training in most human performances. For one thing, it is almost impossible to distinguish between certain behavioral changes due to underlying growth processes and those due to *nonspecific* practice. For example, an older child requires less practice than a younger one in cutting a straight line with scissors, even though both have had no experience with scissors. Does this mean that the ability underlying cutting with scissors has matured? The possibility exists that other kinds of practice in eye-hand coordination, rather than underlying growth, may be the determinant for learning the skill (J. R. Hilgard, 1933). The experiments on restricted environment cited earlier show how stimulation is needed for vision and pain sensitivity. Whether stimulation merely helps maturation or provides training is hard to ascertain.

More recent experiments show that in monkeys inadequate experience with other monkeys in early life makes mating almost impossible when they become adult; females, eventually impregnated, make very poor mothers (Harlow, 1961). Because young monkeys cannot mate, some of their practice must qualify as nonspecific, yet necessary for normal development.

Socialization in Early Infancy

We turn now from maturation, the regulation of development by factors internal to the organism, to *socialization,* the controls external to the infant and characteristic of the culture in which he is born. Different peoples use different child-care practices, and even within our own country the many social groups raise their children in various ways. We wish to discover, if we can, how these practices mold the child's personality and how they prepare him for life in the society of other people. Cultural influences begin at birth; from the first day of life we begin to civilize the child.

Psychological accompaniments of feeding

What goals does the civilized mother have in mind when she begins to feed her baby? She wishes to do two things: (1) to nourish him, and (2) to train him to eat properly. Good nourishment is primarily a matter of physiology, although cultural standards may enter—some cultures insist on fat babies, while others prefer them sturdy. "Proper" eating, then, depends upon practices within the culture. For example, in American middle-class culture, the mother looks forward to raising a three-meal-a-day child who will eat noiselessly and without spilling, who will consume everything on his plate, and who will use knife, fork, and spoon correctly. The expectations of the mother may cause a great many difficulties both for her and for the child before these ends are accomplished.

The infant-feeding practices of the last few decades in America give us an instructive example of the way in which cultural expectations determine what we ask of the infant. Between 1920 and 1940, nearly all pediatricians (physicians specializing in child care) recommended for the newborn child a regular feeding schedule which had the goal of a three-meal-a-day child distantly in view. The infant wards in most hospitals adopted the four-hour schedule: 6 A.M., 10 A.M., 2 P.M., 6 P.M., 10 P.M., and 2 A.M. Parents wished their child to learn to eat at mealtimes normal to the usual routine of adult life (and to disturb

that routine as little as possible!), and so they tried to eliminate the 2 A.M. feeding as soon as they could. The four-hour feeding schedule thus represented a compromise between the needs of the child and parental desires in our middle-class culture. Of course, culture cannot jeopardize the infant's survival by demanding of him what he cannot do, and the four-hour schedule would not have become standard if practice had not proved it safe. However, not all babies conformed well to this schedule, and in the attempt to hold to it many parents found it necessary to tolerate an inordinate amount of crying before feeding their infants.

In the early 1940's the pendulum began to swing away from a fixed feeding schedule to a "self-demand schedule." According to this practice, whenever the infant cried the nurse picked him up, patted him to expel air, changed his diaper, and replaced him in his crib. If he did not stop crying, the nurse fed him. In one experiment using this method the only restriction imposed was that the feedings could not occur at intervals of less than one hour (D. P. Marquis, 1941). The natural feeding rhythm, as judged from this study, appears to be somewhat variable, usually three hours or more between feedings, but seldom as long as four hours within the first week after birth. Even during these first days the length of time between feedings at night was longer (3.6 hours) than during the day (2.9 hours). The preferred schedule is subject to fluctuation as the infant grows older.

The enthusiastic adoption of the self-demand schedule perhaps went too far, and there is now a tendency to return to a schedule without being a slave to it. That is, a schedule adapted to the infant achieves the advantages of both regularity and respect for the individuality of the infant.

While the effort to make the child a three-meal-a-day individual who eats properly is one of the ways in which the infant

3-7

Breast-feeding and increased vigor of sucking

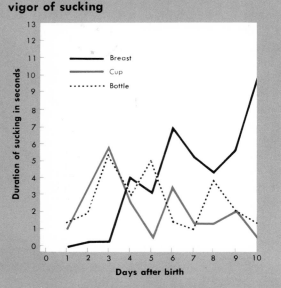

Sucking on a finger guard shows an increase following breast-feeding, but no corresponding increase with cup- and bottle-feeding. Twenty infants in each group. (After Davis, Sears, Miller, and Brodbeck, 1948)

is civilized in our culture, eating habits have other consequences for development. For example, an infant who is troubled about eating may develop forms of insecurity that will trouble him later in other ways, while one who has reassuring eating experiences may become a more secure person.

It has been conjectured that in order to have satisfying feeding experiences an infant needs to suck; that is, an infant can be emotionally "starved" from too little sucking just as he can be nutritionally starved from too little food. Those who receive their food supply too rapidly and easily through large holes in the bottles' nipples are said to make up for the lack of sucking during eating by sucking their hands or bedclothes or other objects accessible to their lips. According to one study, from the first week until the fourth month of life infants seem to require two hours of sucking per day, either during the eating period or at other times (Ribble, 1943).

Another possibility exists, however—that the need to suck is derived from the experience of sucking. Infants fed from a cup from birth show much less evidence of a need to suck than those who are breast-fed from birth (Davis, Sears, Miller, and Brodbeck, 1948). The increased vigor of sucking by those breast-fed over those fed from a bottle or a cup is shown in Figure 3-7. A later study has shown that infants whose sucking was much encouraged showed resistance to weaning. When they were four or five years old, if given a choice between a suckable food (lollipop) and a nonsuckable one (a piece of chocolate), they more often chose the lollipop (Bernstein, 1955).

The emotional consequences of weaning, like those of bottle-feeding, are harsh only if weaning is harshly handled. If the child suddenly loses the comfort of his mother's caresses, if he ends the mealtime hungry because of his dislike for new food or his lack of skill with new eating instruments, he will be physically unsatisfied and emotionally disturbed. The result may well be feelings of insecurity which will have later psychological consequences.

Affection toward and dependency upon the mother

It has been indicated that the psychological accompaniments of feeding may be as important as nourishment in making for a comfortable infant. It is quite possible that these accompaniments are independently satisfying, that is, that there is a reassurance in the bodily contact between the infant and the mother that has nothing particularly to do with the fact that the mother is the source of food. This suggestion is borne out very strongly by certain experiments with animals.

Some species of animals, such as young ducklings, feed themselves from birth, yet they follow their mothers around closely and spend a great deal of their time in con-

Gordon Coster from *Scientific American*

3-8

A monkey's response to an artificial mother

Left: Although fed via the wire "mother," the infant spends more time with the terry-cloth mother. *Right:* The inert "mother" is a safe base from which to explore the world. Experiments of Harlow (1958); Harlow and Zimmerman (1959).

tact with the mother. (This is a consequence of imprinting, covered on p. 66.) The point here is that the comfort from dependency on the mother cannot come from the mother's role in feeding.

More dramatic are some experiments with young monkeys reared in isolation from their true mothers, but permitted to feed from and cling to artificial mothers (Harlow and Zimmerman, 1959). Two "laboratory mothers" were provided with arrangements permitting the young monkeys to obtain milk by sucking. Both "mothers" were immobile and, although they had torsos, heads, and faces, they did not much resemble monkey mothers (see Figure 3-8). One of the laboratory mothers was constructed of wire, so that, while the young monkey could cling to it, it could scarcely be described as "cuddly." The other, covered with terry cloth (of Turkish towel type) over the wire frame, was more "cuddly" than the wire model.

The experiment consisted in seeing whether, if one "mother" was always the source of food, that mother would be the one to which the young monkey would cling. The ·results were dramatic: no matter which mother was the source of food, the infant monkey spent his time clinging to the terry-cloth "cuddly" mother. This purely passive but soft-contact mother served as a source of security for the monkey. For example, when the infant monkey was placed in a strange environment in which he showed great signs of fear, the fear was allayed if the infant could make contact with the cloth mother. While holding to her with one hand he was willing to explore objects that were otherwise too terrifying to approach (Figure 3-8).[1]

These results suggest that through evolutionary processes the helpless young have

[1] The findings are not negated by the fact that the terry-cloth mother was also in some ways inadequate (p. 74).

developed need for contact with adults, this need showing itself in human infants in pleasurable responses to being carried, held, fondled, or being close to a mother or mother substitute (Bowlby, 1958).

Cleanliness training

Training for cleanliness, like that for feeding, has first of all a hygienic purpose. By teaching the infant to keep his diapers dry and clean, the mother protects him from skin irritation, produced by waste products from his body, and from the dangers of infection. In addition, the training leads to conduct which in our culture is considered proper and admirable. A mother in our culture is proud when her baby achieves the ability to stay dry and unsoiled and when he confines elimination to the places provided for it.

It may be that the child experiences primitive emotional satisfactions from the relief of tension in the bladder or the bowels, corresponding to the satisfactions he gets from the relief of hunger tension when he eats. He may experience annoyance and conflict if there is excessive pressure to make him conform to adult demands. Control comes slowly, and, as we saw earlier (p. 72), experiments show that efforts to train yield little success if they are begun too soon. Instead of learning to control his bladder and bowels, the child is perhaps dimly aware of not coming up to expectations, and the parent, too, has a sense of disappointment and of failure which may be communicated to the child. Generally a child is not ready for control until he can take the initiative in indicating his desires by means of word or gesture.

Closely related to remaining dry and unsoiled are the proprieties we know as modesty. (Modesty has sexual connotations as well, but in the beginning the distinctions between toilet functions and sexual functions are either not made or are unclear.) The toilet functions are private; they go on behind closed doors and are not talked about to strangers. Similarly, the parts of the body involved in these performances are private, not to be exposed to view, not to be played with. It is in connection with these parts of the body that the child becomes sensitive to taboos.

Highly conventionalized ways of acting are so familiar by the time we become adults that they appear to be "natural." But the child often is unable to meet the standards expected of him because these "natural" ways are in part artificial—and sometimes contradictory. After he begins to learn about modesty and privacy at home, he may go to a nursery school where the bathroom doors remain open. He is usually told not to undress before other people, yet he is expected to let the new maid give him a bath or to strip for examination by a nurse or physician. If he undresses before the doctor, he is a good boy; if he undresses in the front yard, he is a bad boy. If he goes to the bathroom "all by himself," he is praised and told that he is really a big boy now; but if he urinates against a tree in pleased imitation of a dog, he is scolded, perhaps spanked. Modesty, as our society interprets the word, is not at all "natural," and long and patient training is needed before it can seem so to a child. Those discriminations between what is permitted (and where) and what is not permitted are hard for a child to understand.

Aftereffects of Infantile Insecurity

The accepted methods of infant feeding and cleanliness training are designed to maximize the child's sense of comfort, well-being, and security, and to minimize his feelings of annoyance and anxiety. Conversely, harsh training methods can sometimes produce feelings of anxiety and insecurity which may have an adverse effect on the later personality of the child. But harsh treatment by parents may be no more damaging than an attitude of rejection. Not all children are wanted, and, quite unknowingly, one parent or both parents may emotionally reject an unwanted child. They may provide conscientious physical care for the child, but they cannot successfully pretend the warmth and tenderness of true parental love. On the other hand, when the infant cries at night and a parent comes to comfort him, the very handling and fondling communicate something to the infant. The parents' attitude toward the child is more important than specific training methods.

Early consequences of insecurity in infancy

There is evidence that lack of mothering sometimes actually weakens a baby physically and retards his behavioral development. Though he eats, he does not gain weight; he seems dull and sluggish. This condition is known as *infant debility*. For it some hospitals prescribe increased handling and mothering, often with beneficial results.

Beyond infancy, when parents treat a child without affection, he may show signs of retardation. The following case illustrates this fact; here the supplying of affection proved to be restorative.

George was brought by his mother to the child guidance clinic in a Midwestern city at the age of two and one-half years because he could not talk, could not comprehend simple commands, paid no attention to people, and had developed no habits of bladder and bowel control. His only speech was "ga-ga" to denote pleasure. His mother thought he was hopelessly retarded in intelligence and probably ought to be placed in an institution for backward children.

George had been unexpected and unwanted. The family routine had been built around a plan which provided for no more children, and George's coming interfered with his mother's career. After his birth she continued her work on a part-time basis. He was bottle-fed because the thought of nursing him was repulsive to her. She took care of him dutifully, with part-time help, and yet resented his interference with her freedom. She thought George was receiving adequate care and did not realize until later how much her social and professional interests took her away from him.

When the psychologist at the clinic attempted to give George an intelligence test, she was impressed by his negative reaction to the slightest influence or suggestion. When she asked him to bring a chair, he turned it toward the wall. When forced to yield ever so little, he threw himself on the floor and scattered in all directions whatever objects were in reach. His negativism and contrariness showed on the test items as well as in the general behavior. The psychologist felt that he had more understanding of what was expected than his performances showed. She refused to accept the test scores as valid and reported that he might not be nearly as backward as his lack of development indicated. It was decided that remedial measures rather than commitment to an institution be tried.

George's grandmother, a warm-hearted person with a genuine interest in children, was asked to take over his care. She came to live in the house with George. After she had devoted herself exclusively to him for three months, he returned to the clinic for testing.

An excerpt from the mother's account shows the progress he had made:

> Toilet training occurred practically overnight about two weeks after grandmother took charge. He is now playing with other children and is friendly with strangers. He participates in ball games and delights in hide-and-seek. He can build high towers with blocks, throw rings over a post, scribble with a pencil, lace his shoes, and understand directions. He uses words such as "hi," "bye-bye" and "mama." He shows affection not only to his grandmother, but to his brother, and sometimes to me.[2]

Test results indicated that except on tests depending on speech, he was at a level of development normal for his age.

[2] Case courtesy of Josephine R. Hilgard.

What an infant will tolerate may depend upon what he has become accustomed to. This was shown by a study of the rearing of Albanian children, who during their first year were bound securely to a wooden cradle which was customarily placed in the darkest corner of the room. A cloth was often thrown over their heads to exclude the light. Despite some early muscular incoordination, they recovered, and on standardized tests scored as well as Viennese children (Danzinger and Frankl, 1934). Perhaps the main point is that these Albanian infants never knew any other kind of handling so that, in a psychological sense, they were not actually insecure. Having been "mothered" very little, they did not miss mothering.

The importance of familiarity with handling is shown in other studies in cradling practices. Navaho and Hopi Indian babies, once accustomed to their cradle-boards, have been known to cry when they were removed from them. On the other hand, a Hopi infant's mother gave up an attempt to cradle a daughter who had been raised in freedom for the first five months, so strenuous were the struggles of the child (Dennis, 1940). It is obvious, then, that what is thwarting to one child may not be thwarting to another; the reaction of the child depends upon what he has previously experienced.

Effects of separation from the mother

During the air raids of World War II in England, many young children became separated from their parents, and a series of studies were made as to the consequences of such separation. Children whose parents were alive and available were often sent to residential nurseries because of the conditions under which the parents were forced to live—for example, spending their nights crowded in an underground shelter.

The case of Patrick, a boy of three years and two months, is illustrative (Freud and Burlingham, 1943). He was first evacuated to a country home but "fretted" so much

that he was returned, and —after hospitalization for measles—came to live at the Hampstead Nursery, a residential center for children. He gradually developed a kind of ritual in which he would nod his head compulsively and repeat over and over again: "My mother will put on my overcoat and take me home again." Every effort to reach him with understanding words, affection, and sympathy failed; a visit from his father did not help. Only having his mother come and stay in the house helped; he clung to her much as the baby monkeys clung to the terry-cloth mother. An interesting feature of the case was that after this restoration he came gradually to accept his mother's absence, although the transition required three or four weeks. The authors of this account believe that the suddenness of the separation was often the cause of the most serious reactions by the children.

Residential treatment in such nurseries, as contrasted with life in a single-family home, has varying effects upon the various aspects of development. Such adjustments as good eating habits and the development of muscular control seem to favor the residential children, while those adjustments of more emotional significance, such as the social responsiveness to people (in the ages of five months to twelve months), cleanliness training, and acquiring language, place the residential child at a disadvantage (Freud and Burlingham, 1944).

Remote effects of early insecurity

The hypothesis that unfortunate early experiences adversely affect the child's development is sometimes broadened to include the idea that adult personality traits are not only determined by experiences in infancy but are actually predictable from them. Some psychologists believe that the emotional wounds of infancy never entirely heal and that, even though the intervening childhood years are entirely healthy and happy, during adolescence or adult life some strain may open those very early wounds again. The following case history illustrates the kind of experience on which this conjecture is based.

Lillian Page was adopted at the age of three after a harrowing experience following the death of her parents. She was so terrified at first that she hid under her bed, and to feed her it was necessary to place the food on the floor beside her bed and leave the room.

Patient handling by her foster parents overcame her terror, and she developed into a normal, outgoing girl. In a private boarding school she did well in her studies, and in a summer camp she won prizes for swimming and diving.

Suddenly, upon entering high school, she became seriously disturbed. The girls thought her queer; her teachers reported her inattentive, uncooperative, and failing in her work. The change was inexplicable until the school psychologist, reviewing the circumstances under which she was entering high school, found that for the first time she was being placed in direct social and scholastic competition with an older sister, Sarah, who was born into the home, not adopted as Lillian had been. Sarah had grown to resemble her mother and so became an increasing threat to the adopted sister. The insecurity of Lillian's position in the family at this time was interpreted as re-arousing the insecurity of early childhood, so that she now overreacted to the competition.

While adolescents often need greater independence, Lillian required instead emotional reassurance and support. These were given her by her understanding foster father, and the crisis passed successfully (Smithies, 1933).

This interpretation of Lillian's case history is not the only possible one. More evidence of an experimental nature is needed to test the hypothesis that early experiences have remote consequences. Some such evidence is provided by experiments with white rats, which have shown that irregular feeding in early life may affect adult hoarding of food, even though the rats have eaten regularly in the meantime.

At the age of twenty-four days, shortly after weaning, seven young rats were put on a schedule of irregular and limited feeding for a period of eight days. Seven other rats from the same litters were treated as controls and were not deprived of food. Following the eight-day period, both groups were fed on a normal and adequate diet until adulthood. Tests of hoarding five months after the deprivation experience, when both groups were well fed, showed no differences between the groups. When, however, both experimental and control animals were fed irregularly, so that they had occasional periods of extreme hunger, and then tested after food was plentiful, those deprived in infancy hoarded two and a half times as many food pellets as those not deprived in infancy. The excessive hoarding by those deprived in infancy conforms to the hypothesis that some aftereffects of the infantile deprivation persisted and were re-activated at a time of stress in adult life (Hunt, 1941).

Another experiment raised the question whether hoarding depended solely on deprivation or might depend also on frustration (a situation in which goal-directed activity is blocked or thwarted). A frustrating situation was established by placing food behind a wire screen where hungry rats could see it but not reach it. Such thwarted rats, when tested shortly after the frustrating experience, hoarded nearly twice as many pellets as other deprived rats which had not known the frustrating experience of visible but inaccessible food (McCord, 1941). Thus hoarding, while presumably due to a number of influences, seems to reflect the influence of both deprivation and frustration (Morgan, 1947).

Conjectures have been made that adult human attributes such as greediness and acquisitiveness may be the result of infantile frustrations. These conjectures receive some support from observations of nonliterate peoples. The Arapesh of New Guinea and the Pitchentera of Central Australia are generous and optimistic and do not hoard food, even though they live in lands where food is never ample and where there is occasional famine—in lands, that is, where hoarding would be justified. In these societies infants receive affectionate and indulgent handling. Other societies, for example the Normanby Islanders, are dominated by a tendency to hoard food, even though it is abundant. Among the Normanby Islanders, infants are treated harshly. The Mundugumor, of the same racial stock as the Arapesh, raise their infants with little affectionate handling, and the adults are arrogant, aggressive, impatient, and quarrelsome (Mead, 1940; Roheim, 1943).

Dramatic as such evidence is, there are many exceptions to the hypothesis that the adult culture can be predicted from the methods of infant handling. Though the Navaho Indians are indulged as infants, they grow up insecure (Leighton and Kluckhohn, 1947). Negro children of St. Thomas in the Virgin Islands, also treated affectionately in infancy, grow up insecure and suspicious (Campbell, 1943).

An anthropologist and a psychologist, Whiting and Child (1953), have made a related but somewhat different approach to the adult consequences of child-training practices. They conjecture that harsh training in a specific area of socialization (feeding, toilet training, management of sex and aggression, or dependency, for example) may produce anxiety in that specific area, and they look for residues in adult behavior related to that specific area. For example, some cultures may be harsh with respect to eating but lenient with respect to toilet training, some may overstress making the child independent of adults, some may control sex severely. Whiting and Child tested their theory by sorting out cultures according to their child-rearing practices and then comparing aspects of adult behavior in those cultures. They were careful to secure independent ratings of child training and adult behavior. To find evidence they went to the cross-cultural files located at Yale University, where anthropological reports of researches on some 200 cultures are summarized in relation to a great many special topics. The following summary indicates how they made their comparisons.

Nonliterate societies have many interpretations of illness: possession by evil spirits, punishment for violation of taboos, poisoning by invisible darts from an enemy, food poisoning. The investigators classified cultures according to the interpretation that predominated in each culture.

One such interpretation is that illness is caused by something passing through the mouth, such as poisoned food. Through symbolic extension of the importance of the mouth arises the related interpretation that illness is caused by verbal spells or incantations performed by other people. These two causes of illness (food poisoning and verbal spells) are grouped together as "oral" interpretations. The investigators theorized that cultures suffering food anxiety in infancy and early childhood would tend to use these oral interpretations of illness.

In the files they found data on 39 cultures which they could classify as producing high or low food anxiety in childhood. They could also determine for these cultures whether or not the adult interpretation of illness was oral. The results can be stated as follows:

Of 20 cultures producing high food anxiety in childhood, 17 (85 per cent) used oral interpretations of illness.

Of 19 cultures with low food anxiety in childhood, only 6 (32 per cent) used oral interpretations of illness.

Because the preponderance of cultures agrees with the predictions, the results support the hypothesis, even though there are many exceptions. Whiting and Child found that they could also predict adult interpretations of illness in cultures that were high in producing anxiety over being dependent on adults and anxiety over control of childhood aggression. For toilet training and sexual anxiety, however, the evidence did not establish relationships between childhood rearing and adult belief.

Although it seems justifiable to conclude that handling in infancy may affect both early childhood development and later personality, we must make two reservations: (1) Experiences of insecurity, anxiety, and tension are more important than specific feeding or training methods. The latter should be judged according to their contribution to such experiences, since children can be satisfactorily raised by quite dissimilar methods. (2) Formative influences upon personality do not end in infancy but *continue throughout life.* Early experiences may have persistent aftereffects, but later experiences may be corrective (as in the case of George, p. 79) or may continue the frustration and thwarting. Thus in a

culture that shows both affectionate handling of infants and adult kindness, it does not follow that adult kindness is *caused by* the early affectionate handling. Later experiences are important, too, and it is quite likely that a sense of personal security is engendered through many experiences beyond those of infancy. The older child also lives among loving adults. Similarly, in a culture in which harsh treatment of infants may influence adult aggressiveness and quarrelsomeness, it should be noted that the children grow to maturity among such adults. The controlling influences of the culture do not cease in infancy.

CRITICAL DISCUSSION
Issues in aftereffects of insecurity

The aftereffects of infantile insecurity do not yield results predictable from any simple theory. The somewhat conflicting evidence has

3-9

In-between age of weaning associated with maximum emotional disturbance in later childhood

If the Kansas City results alone were at hand (black line), the conclusion would be justified that less emotional disturbance occurs following very early weaning; if the cross-cultural results alone were known (colored line), the opposite conclusion would be reached. The graph shows the importance of having available the whole range of information. (After Whiting, 1954)

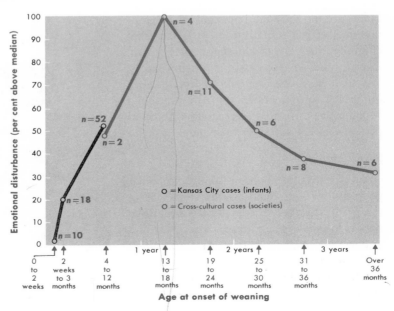

been reviewed by Orlansky (1949), Slotkin (1952), Stone (1954), and Yarrow (1961).

Whiting (1954) has pointed out an important problem in method. He shows that it is possible to harmonize conflicting results obtained with a sample of Kansas City children and a sample of evidence from the cross-cultural files mentioned earlier. Both studies tested the hypothesis that early weaning would result in emotional disturbances later in childhood. The Kansas City study (Sears and Wise, 1950) showed that *late* weaning was associated with emotional disturbance, while the cross-cultural study (Whiting and Child, 1953) showed that *early* weaning was associated with emotional disturbance. When, however, Whiting plotted the results of both studies on a common graph (see Figure 3-9), it became clear that *late* weaning for the Kansas City sample was actually *early* weaning for the cross-cultural study. Where the two studies overlapped, results were consistent. The lesson is that we need to have a total range of influences before we can be confident in our interpretations.

The Course of Social Development

Development is a continuous process. Whether or not the earliest months of infancy are of unusual importance, we cannot neglect the socialization processes that continue throughout childhood and youth. Growth and development have many facets. We shall here consider only a few that are important for understanding how the child becomes a personality interacting with other persons in his social environment.

Social smiling

As a baby grows, his responses to other people show a gradual development. One of the first evidences of his social responsiveness is his smile when he sees a face. At first it does not matter whether the face is that of a familiar person or of a stranger, or whether the face is smiling or threatening. Even a mask will evoke the smile. The young infant will smile as long as the face is directed toward him and bobs around in the manner of a solicitous adult. There is some distinction between a face pattern and other patterns, for the infant will cease to smile if the face (or mask) is turned in profile. This kind of smiling appears between the ages of two and six months in children of unlike cultural and racial groups. The trait appears to be one of the products of growth or maturation, relatively independent of training. Here biology prepares for social response (Figure 3-10).

Smiling at a strange face ceases almost completely after the age of six months (Table 3-1). The child continues to smile,

3-10

Smiling

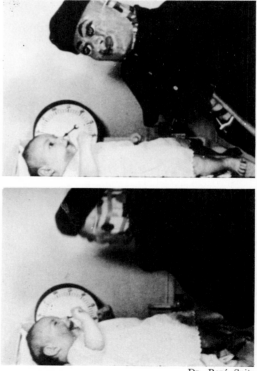

Dr. René Spitz

Up to the age of six months the baby may give a smiling response to anyone's face, even to a mask, provided it is presented full face and bobs about. The profile of the mask does not elicit smiling.

TABLE 3-1

Smiling at a strange human face at different ages

Age of children	Number of children	Per cent smiling at a strange face
0 to 20 days	54	0
21 days to 2 months	144	2
2 months to 6 months	145	98
6 months to 12 months	147	3

SOURCE: Spitz, 1946.

but now only at the face of a familiar person. The distinction between familiar people and strangers is somehow recognized; social discrimination has begun.

Language

Learning to talk reveals another aspect of development that can be understood only in the light of the interplay of biological potentialities and the molding effect of culture. Biological development (i.e., maturation) accounts for the ability to talk; the culture (i.e., the language heard) accounts for what the child actually says.

The infant's babbling is a kind of phonetic play that only gradually becomes transformed into the speech sounds of the language he hears. While some responsiveness to adult verbal intonation begins as early as six weeks, the child's mastery of language comes slowly. A few words are spoken between one and two years, but the child's language is usually very fragmentary before the age of two, when a rapid development begins.

By the age of three most children have enough of the sounds of the language to give a very presentable version of it, though they usually still do not know many of the grammatical forms. Between three and six these deficiencies are corrected and everywhere in the world and for all languages, the normal child of six has acquired all the sounds and all the grammatical forms of his native language, though of course he does not have all the adult vocabulary.[3]

Although words alone are a somewhat ambiguous index of language usage, word counts provide one way of studying the growth of language ability in the child. At first the child acquires new words slowly, but later his vocabulary increases at an astonishing rate. Figure 3-11 shows how the spoken vocabulary increases from birth to six years of age. The data in this figure are based on the records of words used in the child's spontaneous speech. From three words at one year of age this spoken vocabulary increases to 2500 words at six.

The child is able to understand the meaning of many words he does not use—words which he hears others use and words which he meets in his reading. One study suggests that the recognition vocabulary for children in the first grade may be nearly ten times as large as the spoken vocabulary. The increase in recognition vocabulary through grade school and high school is plotted in Figure 3-12.

It is not enough for the child to know the meaning of words, to understand sentences, and to make himself understood. He must conform to what society expects of him; he must not only make himself understood, but he must speak *properly*. In many languages, speaking properly means that he must learn to address those of a different status with different words or a different phraseology. The German child learns to say *Sie* (deferential form of the word meaning *you*) when addressing superiors and strangers, and to say *du* (familiar form of *you*) to those with whom he is intimate or to those of inferior status. The Japanese child has to learn several degrees of deferential expression.

The child born in an English-language culture escapes a good many difficulties, because the language is relatively free of many

[3] Trager, 1957.

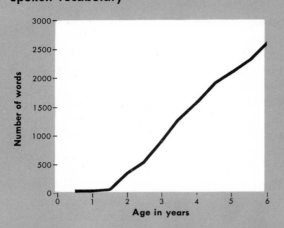

Within the first six years the child gradually learns to use over 2500 words. (After M. E. Smith, 1926)

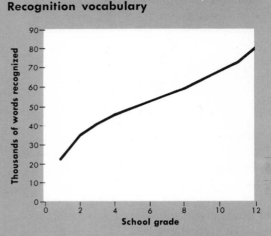

The total number of words recognized (basic plus derivative words) is much higher than the number of words that the child uses in speech. It reaches some 80,000 words by the twelfth grade. (After M. K. Smith, 1941)

changes in word forms, such as are found in the declensions of the more inflected languages. But he must learn to speak properly, just as he has to learn to eat properly. He has problems of irregularities in grammar and of courtesy words such as "please" and "thank you," which have little to do with literal meanings. Once he knows these expressions, he uses them when he wishes to conform, and he may refuse to use them when he wishes to defy. They become a way for him to exercise power. Then there are the forbidden words, some of which he may use in the privacy of the family, some of which he may not use at all—even though father or mother occasionally does in emotional moments. Thus the child learns about certain prohibitions, social taboos. While he is learning to talk *properly,* he is also learning the ways of his culture.

Adherence to or deviation from the proprieties in language is one standard on which social class distinctions are based. The choice of words or of pronunciation is often a give-away as to one's social position. The "cockney" speech of the lower-class Londoner is but an extreme example. In America certain grammatical errors are associated with the uneducated ("them things"; "I come home" for "I came home"). Distinctions are also made on the basis of troublesome variations in usage, as between "I feel bad" and "I feel badly" (sometimes deliberately avoided by the more elegant "I do not feel well"). Those who have risen in social position and attempt to improve their language may reveal the lack of early training in good usage by such efforts at refinement as "between you and I." Students of language call such occurrences "hyperurbanisms"—an exaggerated effort at upper-class urban speech.

As the child learns the language, he learns much more than the words and grammar. He learns to control other people through words, he learns courtesy, he learns taboos, and he learns social distinctions. He also acquires an instrument that permits him to think and reflect.

Sex roles

The child has to establish his place in the society of people about him, eventually to take his place as a man or a woman. Very important to him in finding his place are the members of his own family: mother, father, brothers, and sisters.

Because parents are the dominant figures and the primary sources of both satisfactions and prohibitions, the child's attitudes toward them are mixtures of wishes to please and wishes to protest. In our culture there is often between the ages of two and three a period characterized by defiant or _negativistic_ behavior. It may be that with his new-found freedom of locomotion and with the increase of manipulative skills, the child asserts his individuality and tests his powers by his refusals to respond to parental requests. His favorite word becomes "No!" The negativistic stage is not an inevitable one; it is not found in all children. It is common, however, and parents and nursery school teachers must be prepared for it.

Although a kind of tug-of-war between children and parents goes on, with occasional negativism and defiance, the long-run influence of parents is that of models, or _identification figures,_ for the children to copy. The _role_ that the boy will eventually play in society is that of a man, and the man he knows best is his father. Similarly, the girl learns the woman's role from her mother. Both mother and father, through their attitudes to each other, help the children of either sex to acquire an appropriate role.

The play activities of boys and girls gradually diverge, especially after the age of five years. By that age they are aware that their roles in society are unlike ones, and they begin to try out in play the roles that they will act some day in fact. Sometimes they would like to begin playing the adult role immediately, for they are jealous of the advantages that adults have over them.

Sex differences in behavior have many features much more subtle than the girl's interest in dolls and the boy's interest in electric trains. Aggressive behavior is a case in point. Healthy children are active, and active children on occasion become aggressive. In a moment of aggressiveness the child may strike an adult, may attack another child, may hurt a pet, or may destroy property. Parents differ in the severity with which they restrict aggressiveness in children, but in one way or another they have to teach restraint. A study of aggressive behavior in boys and girls of kindergarten age (approximately age five) was followed seven years later by a study of their attitudes toward aggression. It was already clear at age five that boys were permitted (and even encouraged) to be more aggressive than girls; it was not surprising to find that these same children and their classmates at age twelve showed sex differences in approving antisocial aggression, the figures being for the 261 boys a mean (average) of 6.09 on a 9-point scale, for the 264 girls a mean of 4.75 on the same scale—a difference highly significant statistically.

The boys and girls also differed in their anxiety over aggression at age twelve. It is not surprising, in view of the discouragement of aggression in girls, that they are more disturbed over aggressive behavior than boys are. On the same 9-point scale they averaged 6.11 in aggression anxiety as compared with 4.82 for the boys, a difference just as significant as the opposite difference in approval of antisocial aggression.

It seems clear that boys are permitted by age five to be more aggressive than girls, and that at twelve they approve more of aggressive behavior and are not as anxious about it as twelve-year-old girls are. But aggression anxiety at age twelve in girls and in boys proved to be differently related to child-rearing practices prior to age five. For example, the higher a girl's "conscience rating" at age five, the *higher* her aggression anxiety at age twelve, while for boys the higher the conscience rating at age five, the *lower* the aggression anxiety at age twelve. This is somewhat paradoxical until other relationships are taken into account. Using an analysis that considered a number of relationships between the data at age five and those at age twelve, the author of this study concluded that aggression anxiety has a different history for boys than for girls, which fact accounts for such apparently paradoxical correlations as those just stated. He believes that for boys the results are consistent with a straightforward socialization process in which the boy learns to conform to social standards, limiting his aggression to acceptable levels and not being anxious about it. In the case of the girl, however, even minor acts of aggression are not "feminine," so that if she is permitted to act like a boy, later on her anxiety over aggression mounts. Thus in a home that permits aggression at age five, the girl tends to develop enhanced aggression anxiety by age twelve, while the boy's aggression anxiety is reduced at age twelve (Sears, 1961).[4]

Aggression is not only encouraged by parents under some circumstances and discouraged under others, but the *techniques* of aggressive behavior are taught by the adult models whom the child copies. In an experiment with nursery school children, a motion film showed an adult acting aggressively toward a large-sized clown made of inflated plastic material. When the children who had watched the film were permitted to

[4] Sex typing is here related to socialization rather than to biological sex differences. Both aspects are, of course, important. That a kind of "socialization" experience is important in the lower animals has been shown in the failure of isolated male monkeys to make satisfactory sexual contacts with receptive females when they matured (Mason, 1960).

play alone with the clown afterwards, they copied the adult aggressive behavior in great detail (Bandura, Ross, and Ross, 1961). Some photographs of a boy and a girl imitating the adult are shown in Figure 3-13.

Aggressive behavior is but one illustration of the "role expectations" that differ for boys and for girls. Its complexities warn us that socialization is a process in which many strands are interwoven, and unraveling them poses many unsolved problems for research.

Sibling rivalry

In trying to maintain a favorable position in the eyes of his parents, the child often shows jealousy of brothers and sisters. The phrase *sibling rivalry* is used to describe the competitive struggles between two brothers or two sisters or a brother and a sister (i.e., between siblings).

Rivalry is often shown after the birth of a brother or sister. The child of two or three who was the center of parental affection and attention now sees parental interest shifted to the new baby. As a result he may express dislike for the baby in words or he may act aggressively toward it. Often he is forced to tell visitors how happy he is to have the new baby, how proud he is. He may then show his jealousy indirectly, even though publicly he may conform to the role of the loving brother or sister. Sometimes rivalry is expressed in *regressive* behavior, that is, behavior characteristic of a younger child. The older child who has been sleeping dry through the night for several months may begin to wet his bed. The following case illustrates how the birth of a sibling may affect a child.

Before her baby brother was born, two-and-a-half-year-old Jane fitted her mother's ideal of a "good baby," seldom crying, requiring little attention, playing happily alone in her play pen. After his birth, she was very nervous and apprehensive and full of questions about the new baby. For the first time she began having temper tantrums.

A   B   C

3-13

The imitation of adult aggression by children

Nursery school children observed a motion picture in which an adult expressed various forms of aggressive behavior toward a clown figure. Both boys and girls who had watched the film behaved aggressively toward the figure, using many of the detailed acts of aggression copied from the adult in the film, as in lifting and throwing (A), striking with hammer (B), and kicking (C).

Although she wanted to be around the baby, she gleefully suggested cutting his hands and taking him down to the creek to drown.

Presently she decided that she wanted to be a boy. She began to call herself David and refused to play with the neighborhood children who called her Jane. She began to dress herself as a boy and changed the clothes of her Teddy bear, also dressing it as a boy. When she saw the attention and affection her little brother was getting, it somehow seemed to her that if only she were a boy she, too, might get the affection she needed. Her disturbed behavior continued

3-14

Symbolic expression of sibling rivalry

C. Bernstein from Black Star

Steve has an older brother, and a new baby brother has just arrived in the family. In the **permissive atmosphere** of the playroom he lets off steam, expressing his pent-up hostility in violent action. Squeezing the two dolls together is a better way of handling his sibling rivalry than fighting with his brothers.

for a year until her mother took her to a child guidance clinic, and then her problems began to clear up.[5]

Parents may minimize rivalry by preparing the older child for the birth of the baby and by taking care that the new baby does not completely absorb their affection. However, some signs of sibling rivalry are almost inevitable in our competitive culture. Parents may unwittingly produce rivalries among their children, based on rivalry problems persisting from their own childhoods (J. R. Hilgard, 1951). The solution is to

[5] Case courtesy of Josephine R. Hilgard.

handle the relationships among children so that these relationships will induce maturing rather than become causes of insecurity and ill-will. Sibling rivalry, properly handled, need not be damaging to either the older or the younger child.

Birth order and personality

The relation of one child to another in the family may produce lasting effects on personality. One study of personality roles in large families identified eight different roles, three of which showed some relationship to birth order. These three were (1) the responsible child (often the first-born), (2) the sociable, well-liked child (often the second), and (3) the spoiled child (often the youngest). Other roles that made for individuality in large families were (4) the social butterfly, who places a high value on social activities, (5) the studious child, (6) the isolate, who minds his own business, (7) the irresponsible child, and (8) the sickly child (Bossard and Ball, 1955).

While many circumstances lead to individual variations in these roles, other studies point to some consistent effects of birth order, especially for the older and younger child in the two-child family. In general, the older child of two tends to be *serious, shy,* and *adult-oriented,* while the younger of two tends to be *cheerful, placid, easygoing,* and *not studious* (McArthur, 1956). These findings are not to be interpreted as a biological effect of order of birth, but rather as a consequence of the differences in circumstances under which the first child and the second child are socialized.

Following conjectures of this kind, Schachter (1959) has gathered a good deal of evidence showing that when confronted by the threat of pain, first-born and only girl children seek the company of fellow-sufferers more than later-born girls do. It is as though misery loves the company of other miserable people—and the first-born appear more miserable than later-born subjects in these experiments. His interpretation is that first-born children receive more attention from parents when they are small than do later-born children, and that under threat the tendency to find support from other people is stronger in these individuals.

Disciplinary practices and their consequences

In order to produce a child who obeys the demands of the society in which he grows up and who internalizes these values so that he becomes a self-controlling person, parents find it necessary to exert control in the form of discipline, approving some kinds of behavior, disapproving others. Discipline may take various forms. These have been classified by Sears, Maccoby, and Levin (1957) as follows: *positive sanctions* (praise, tangible reward); *negative sanctions* (physical punishment, deprivation of privileges, withdrawal of love, isolation); and *directing behavior* (use of positive models, use of negative models, and reasoning).

Classifying these forms in a somewhat different way, the same authors group together the *love-oriented techniques* (praise as reward, isolation and withdrawal of love as punishment) and the *object-oriented techniques* (tangible rewards, deprivation of privileges, physical punishment). Which of these is favored in child-training makes a difference in the kind of child that results.

If we think first of effectiveness in producing socially conforming behavior, such as good eating habits, we find that those mothers who report the regular use of physical punishment have more feeding problems with their young children than those who use punishment rarely or occasionally; by contrast, those mothers who show affectionate warmth toward their children have fewer feeding problems than the mothers who tend to be cold and hostile. Some of the findings are shown in Table 3-2.

If, instead of looking at the behavior itself, we think of self-control or a developed

TABLE 3-2 Children's feeding problems and the training practices of their parents	Number of cases	Children having feeding problems (per cent)
Extent of use of physical punishment:		
Rarely or never used	58	17
Occasionally to fairly often	293	20
Regularly used	25	36
Mother's affectional warmth toward child:		
Exceptionally warm	36	11
Warm and quite warm	233	19
Matter-of-fact	63	22
Cold, some hostility	46	35

SOURCE: Sears, Maccoby, and Levin (1957), p. 521.

conscience, we also find a relationship to the kind of training the parents have given. The children rated highest on conscience were those whose mothers were not only relatively warm but used withdrawal of love as a means of control (Table 3-3).

Evidence of the effect of childhood discipline on later behavior comes very strikingly from a follow-up study of boys from rather poor neighborhoods, many of whom were later convicted of crimes or sentenced to penal institutions (Table 3-4). In addition to the punitive or love-oriented techniques, another dimension enters here: the matter of consistency and laxity. Apparently the worst form of discipline is that classified as Erratic C (punitive-lax), with 56 per cent of the boys coming from such homes later being convicted of crimes, and 30 per cent serving sentences in penal institutions.

It is evident that home training is an important factor in the socialization of the child. The subtleties are such that it is difficult to give cook-book recommendations as to how parents should treat children, but

TABLE 3-3

Conscience as related to mother's warmth and use of withdrawal of love *

	Children rated high on conscience
Mother relatively warm and uses withdrawal of love fairly often	42%
Mother relatively warm and uses little or no withdrawal of love	24
Mother relatively cold and uses little or no withdrawal of love	25
Mother relatively cold and uses withdrawal of love fairly often	18

SOURCE: Sears, Maccoby, and Levin (1957), p. 388.
* Number of cases not stated in original table. Total cases in four groups 188.

some of the perferred directions appear clear enough from the results of research. Whatever the method used, it should be used with consistency and firmness. Punitive methods, harshly or erratically used, appear notably unsuccessful, whereas love-oriented techniques, including affectional warmth but also withdrawal of love to enforce conformity, appear to be successful in producing not only desirable behavior but the kind of conscience that internalizes control.

Social relationships outside the home

While the patterns of the child's social relationships begin in the home, people outside the home, especially his own age-mates, soon become important to him. Neighborhood play groups are important, but the conditions of modern urban life have led increasingly to dependence upon schools to provide social life for children.

The nursery school takes the place of the large family and of the back yard for many young children. In the nursery school the child learns to overcome his shyness, to play with others, and to conform to a routine in which he is not the center of attention. He must be aggressive enough to keep others from interfering with his rights, yet he must learn to share with others and to play cooperatively. The nursery school provides a transitional experience through which the child detaches himself from home and becomes prepared for more formal schooling.

TABLE 3-4

Parental discipline and later crime convictions and incarcerations

Type of discipline	Number of cases	Convicted of crimes	Sentenced to penal institutions
Punitive	14	21%	7%
Love-oriented	60	27	5
Erratic A (love-lax)	40	35	5
Erratic B (love-lax-punitive)	41	49	19
Lax	52	50	19
Erratic C (punitive-lax)	43	56	30
TOTAL GROUP OF BOYS	250	41	15

SOURCE: McCord, McCord, and Zola (1959), p. 77.

The school continues the process of preparing the child for life in our kind of society. It gives him the necessary tools (such as the three R's) and it also teaches him how to live within the school discipline, how to maintain standards of work, how to set goals and strive toward them. He learns to share the attitudes and ideals of the community. He learns his own strengths and limitations. In the long view, he is preparing himself to earn a livelihood, to manage his life in a family, and to take on the responsibilities of citizenship.

What his playmates expect of him becomes very important to the child of school age. He must dress as they do and must be good at the games they play. If he is teased for awkwardness or called a "sissy," he will feel deeply hurt. So important is the opinion of the age-mates that parents whose standards for their children differ from those of other parents may find their authority lessening or their child emotionally upset.

Influences outside the home, like influences within the home, gradually mold the child's personality. The personality that we find expressed in adult life is no simple thing. It is a complex product based on the capacities for growth in an energetic organism learning to satisfy its needs amid the pressures and opportunities of the social environment.

SUMMARY

1. The course of development in man, as in other organisms, is shaped by *maturation* and by *learning*. The study of maturation shows that development goes on at its own rate, relatively independent of the environment, although an essential minimum of environmental stimulation and support is needed. Embryological development clearly illustrates the meaning of maturation within a relatively uniform environment. Studies of transplantation in lower forms reveal some plasticity, but this is quite limited, indicating that the basic pattern of the development of the organism is laid down in its tissues.

2. Imprinting, whereby at the right time the young duckling follows whatever appropriately moving object is nearest, shows the interplay between maturational readiness and environmental opportunity.

3. Other studies of the development of young animals show the need for adequate stimulation if appropriate reaction to the environment of things and other organisms is to be achieved.

4. Studies of the human infant and child suggest a number of relationships between maturation and training: (1) Skills that build upon developing behavior patterns are most easily learned. (2) The rate of development remains uniform within wide ranges of stimulation. (3) The more mature the organism, the less training is needed to reach a given level of proficiency. (4) Training given before maturational readiness may bring either no improvement or only a temporary improvement. (5) Premature training, if frustrating, may do more harm than good.

5. The process of *socialization* begins at birth. Even though the demands upon the infant must be limited to what he can do, his feeding schedules move in the direction of the three-meal-a-day person he is expected to become. The accompaniments of feeding may be psychologically as important as nutrition. The need for appropriate body contact has been

dramatically illustrated by experiments using monkeys with artificial mothers. They support the results obtained in studies of human children separated too early from their mothers, in whom there were many signs of disturbance.

6. Insecurity in infancy, whether through irregularities in feeding or through other kinds of frustration, may have consequences in later life, even though the intervening years are without signs of disturbance. Studies of nonliterate cultures, experimental studies of animals, and case histories within our own culture bear out this possibility.

7. Illustrations of social development are provided in the study of social smiling and the use of language. The further socialization of the child takes place pre-eminently through interactions with other people inside and outside the home. Sex roles, according to which the boy comes to act like a man and the girl like a woman, are early prepared for. One illustration is provided by the handling of aggression, leading to higher aggressiveness and approval of antisocial aggression by the boy, less aggression and more anxiety about aggression in the girl. Negativism and sibling rivalry are aspects of adjustment to interpersonal relationships within the home. Order of birth also has its impact.

8. Disciplinary practices are important not only in the control of specific behavior, but in the development of conscience and in later social conduct.

9. The age-mate cultures of the neighborhood and of the school are important socializing influences.

SUGGESTIONS FOR FURTHER READING

For the embryological basis of development a useful source is Willier, Weiss, and Hamburger, *Analysis of development* (1955). The general problems of maturation in animals and man are discussed in chapters by Carmichael and by Gesell in Carmichael, *Manual of child psychology* (2nd Ed., 1954). Birney and Teevan, *Instinct* (1961) is a collection of readings, available in paperback edition, that includes material on imprinting and the early development of behavior. A number of chapters concerned with the consequences of early environmental stimulation can be found in Fiske and Maddi, *Functions of early experience* (1961).

A useful review of studies of socialization can be found in the chapter by that title, written by Child, in Lindzey, *Handbook of social psychology* (1954).

There are many books on child development, of which the following are representative: Martin and Stendler, *Child behavior and development* (2nd Ed., 1959); Mussen and Conger, *Child development and personality* (1956); and Sears, Maccoby, and Levin, *Patterns of child rearing* (1957). The special problems of language development in children have been the occasion for a number of studies, such as Piaget, *The language and thought of the child* (1926), and Church, *Language and the discovery of reality* (1961).

The methods of investigation are summarized by a number of experts in Mussen, *Handbook of research methods in child development* (1960).

CHAPTER 4

Adolescence and Adulthood

Adolescents have a bad reputation. Parents feel that troubles double when their children enter adolescence; policemen are caustic about the mischief adolescents get into. Someone is always talking about the "youth problem" and the prevalence of juvenile delinquency. When a "hot rod" goes by, packed full of noisy youngsters, its horn blowing and the tires squealing as it turns the corner, one adult turns to another and says with disdain or disgust, "A bunch of teen-agers."

The foregoing picture is, of course, incomplete and unfair to youth, but there is some truth in it. The transition from childhood to adult life is not always smooth. As the youth breaks his emotional dependence upon his parents, he may embrace his newfound freedom with excessive exuberance. But he may also be shy and sensitive. He has many adjustments to make within the next few years: he faces the choice of his lifework and preparation for it; he finds ways to manage his new interest in members of the opposite sex; he looks ahead to selecting a mate and establishing a home of his own. And he faces these social problems and decisions at the very time that striking changes in his physical appearance and physiological functioning may often make it hard for him to understand and accept himself.

The importance of puberty (the transition to sexual maturity, which is the chief physical development in adolescence) is signalized in many nonliterate societies by initiation ceremonies through which the adolescent is inducted into adulthood. Anthropologists have described such ceremonies in societies all over the world, in places as remote from each other as Africa, Indonesia, Polynesia, and North and South America. However, the rites are not universal among nonliterate groups; some groups in each area mentioned above have no such ceremonies.

While rites of initiation often force the adolescent boy of nonliterate cultures to undergo ordeals of starvation, sleeplessness, and pain, once the initiation is over he is honored by new status and responsibilities. The more gradual transition to adult life in other nonliterate societies and in our own has some advantages, but it also produces in the adolescent a period of conflict and vacillation between dependence and independence. Such vestigial remains of ceremonial introduction into adult life as are seen in the confirmation ceremonies of some religious groups, the "coming out" parties of debutantes, and the fraternity initiation form no sharp break with the past, nor do they confer the privileges and responsibilities of full adulthood.

The adolescent period is only a phase in the stream of growth, and it is a mistake to emphasize too sharply its discontinuities with other phases. A number of recent studies (e.g., Elkin and Westley, 1955; Bandura and Walters, 1959) have pointed out that there is a certain amount of mythology about adolescence, so that parents wait in fear and trembling for their teen-age children to show the expected defiance and rebellion; when some issue comes up, they say to themselves "Here it is!" and perhaps make more of the incident than they should. For many adolescents the transition to adult life runs smoothly; for others, the problems and conflicts have a long history, and troubles in adolescence are but further manifestations of earlier troubles. To be sure, the adolescent is stronger and more powerful when he becomes defiant; hence a problem that once could have been handled easily may get out of hand.

Bodily Changes During Adolescence

Everyone is aware of the striking changes that take place in the body during adolescence. Changes take place in *primary sex characteristics,* that is, in the reproductive organs, both internal and external, which make possible sexual union and reproduction. Modifications also occur in the *secondary sex characteristics,* those physical features distinguishing a mature man from a mature woman in ways not directly related to the sexual apparatus. Some of these modifications, such as the development of the breasts, appear only in girls; some, such as the marked change in voice and the growth of a beard, appear only in boys; others, such as the appearance of pubic hair, are common to both boys and girls. These physical changes are of psycho-

4-1

The puberal period

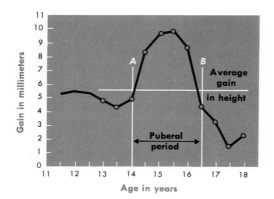

The puberal period is defined according to rate of growth in height. Data from a single subject. (Stolz and Stolz, 1951)

4-2

Measuring stem length

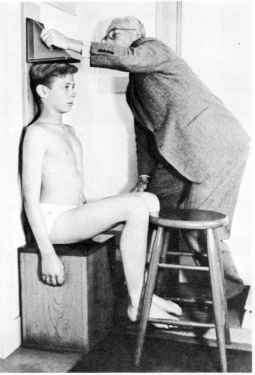

Wilson D. Ellis

The scientist makes his measurements according to carefully standardized procedures to get accurate data on the details of growth rhythms. (From Stolz and Stolz, 1951)

logical interest because of the behavioral changes that accompany them—changes in attitudes, in emotional responsiveness, and in social behavior.

The definition of adolescence

The developments of adolescence take place over several years. Students of adolescence have found it difficult to demarcate both the whole period and its phases exactly, because the first signs of puberty appear very gradually, and bodily changes continue after the sexual apparatus has matured. The onset of pubescence (or puberty) has commonly been assigned to that stage of development in which pig-

4-3

Growth in height

The average height of American boys and girls has increased several inches in the 50-year period separating these two studies, but the differences in height between boys and girls remain much the same. The beginning of puberty at an earlier age for girls is reflected in the years between 11 and 15, when their height exceeds that of boys. (Data from Hastings, 1902, and Boyd, 1952, reproduced by Hathaway, 1957)

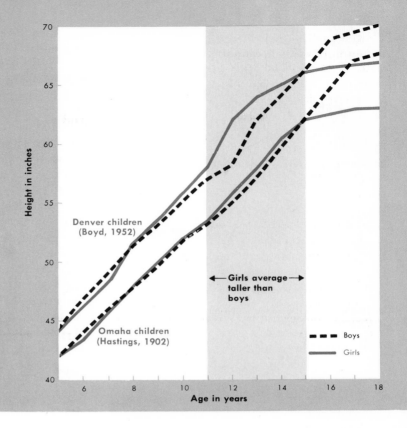

Denver children (Boyd, 1952)

Omaha children (Hastings, 1902)

← Girls average taller than boys →

- - - Boys
—— Girls

Height in inches

Age in years

mented hairs appear in the pubic region. The period of *prepubescence* is then all of life before this, and *postpubescence* is the period marked by the development of more advanced sexual characteristics. Later workers, however, have sought to refine the scale of development in order that more precise statements could be made about the stages of adolescence and about the studies made of personality changes in relation to these stages. These later workers have proposed a division of the adolescent period into four phases: prepuberal, puberal, postpuberal, and late adolescent (Stolz and Stolz, 1951).

The *prepuberal phase* begins a year or two before the puberal phase. The changes are not very striking or very uniform. Some two-thirds of boys enter an early adolescent fat period during the prepuberal phase. The excessive fat usually disappears by the midpoint of the puberal period. There may be a temporary slowing up of growth in height during this period.

In the *puberal phase* the most marked and rapid changes occur. Height and weight increase most rapidly, and the sex organs mature. Not all boys and girls enter the puberal period at the same ages. Girls tend to have their puberal growth earlier than boys, and any one boy or any one girl may mature as much as five years earlier or later than another boy or girl. The puberal period varies in length also, but extends typically between 2.5 and 3.5 years.

The *postpuberal phase* shows less striking changes. Most of the puberal growth is over, but a few features of it are still continuing (e.g., increase in muscular strength, increase in subcutaneous tissue, spread of pigmented hair). It lasts from one to two years.

The *late adolescent phase* continues the development of the final signs of maturity.

Annual increments in height

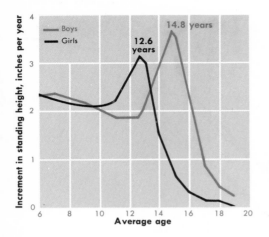

The peak growth period comes earlier for girls than boys. (After Shuttleworth, 1939)

4-5

Age of maximum growth rates

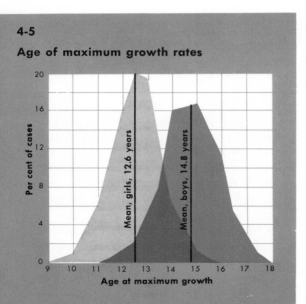

The age at which growth increment was most rapid (see Figure 4-4) was determined for each boy and for each girl, and these results were then plotted to make this figure. Note that a very few boys and a very few girls developed very early and very late, the largest numbers falling around the average of 12.6 years for girls and 14.8 years for boys. (After Shuttleworth, 1939)

In males there is a continuation of the development of the pigmented hair on the face, and for many the development of pigmented hair on the chest and thighs.

The whole cycle of changes from childhood to maturity may cover as much as nine or ten years, starting before the teens (for girls) and not ending (for boys) until the early twenties.

The many aspects of adolescent development have led investigators to seek reference points by which to define its phases as precisely as possible. It is now generally agreed that the period of maximum physical growth (e.g., in height) is a convenient point from which to study adolescent development. It has been found that, for girls, the *menarche* (first menstruation) usually occurs within the year following the period of maximum growth. With boys, mature spermatozoa tend to appear shortly after the peak of growth. Thus the maximum growth period serves as a convenient index to the level of maturity (Shuttleworth, 1939).

In their study of adolescent boys, Stolz and Stolz (1951) arrived at an objective method of defining the duration of the puberal phase. They chose the following definition: *The puberal growth period is that period during which the growth rate exceeds the average rate as measured within a five-year period around the peak of maximum growth.* This sounds rather confusing, but is easily understood with the help of Figure 4-1. The curve plots the rate of growth at half-year intervals, as shown by the dots on the graph. The line marked "average gain in height" is an average for five years around the maximum measurement. By drawing the lines marked *A* and *B* to the measurements nearest the points where the average gain intersects the growth curve, we have the beginning and the end of the above-average growth. This is the puberal period, which in Figure 4-1 extends from age 14 to age 16.5.

The growth pattern as reflected in height

In infancy the child grows very rapidly in height, so that half the adult height is reached between the ages of two and three. Then the rate of growth slows until the new spurt in the prepuberal period. Figure 4-3 shows the rate of growth from age 5 to age 18.

Annual gains in height (growth increments) for boys and for girls are plotted in Figure 4-4. The curves are constructed by plotting the average annual increment for each year before and after the age at which the maximum growth occurs. The maximum growth rate is achieved by girls at an average age of 12.6 years, and for boys at an average age of 14.8 years. The patterns of growth in height for boys and girls are very similar, both showing a striking spurt in the prepuberal period and a gradual decline as adult stature is approached.

Some kind of plot other than that used in Figure 4-4 is needed to show the variations from one boy or girl to another in the age of maximum growth. While the general pattern of growth is common to all individuals, some individuals mature early, some late. How the ages of maximum growth spread out over the years from 10 to 18 is shown in Figure 4-5. The girls as a group mature earlier than the boys as a group, but the graph shows that there is considerable overlap. Two-thirds of the girls achieve their maximum growth within a year before or after the average of 12.6 years; two-thirds of the boys achieve their maximum growth within a year before or after the average age of 14.8 years. The differences between the averages (2.2 years) correspond to the differences in ages of maturing. But the overlap cannot be ignored. For example, at age 13.5 about one-sixth of the girls have not reached their maximum growth rates, while about one-sixth of the boys have already reached theirs. For these particular boys and girls of age 13.5, the usual differences are reversed: the boys are ahead and the girls are behind. Some of the contrasts in appearance at these ages may be seen in Figure 4-6. It is not surprising that adults expect different behavior from these two girls; they might well view age-appropriate behavior from the larger to be excessively childish.

The question is often asked whether the early maturer tends to grow taller than the late maturer. The answer is that there is very little relationship between time of onset of puberal changes and adult height. In the study by the Stolzes, the two shortest and the two tallest boys were all early developers. There is, however, a positive correlation between prepubescent height and ultimate adult height at all ages.

4-6

Variations in adolescent growth

These girls are the same chronological age and the same mental age; they are in the same school grade and have very similar home backgrounds. Yet one is physically mature, and the other obviously immature. (From Barker and others, 1953)

During the period of rapid growth, when there are often wide differences between children of the same age, there is frequently some interest in predicting ultimate height.

One formula for predicting height is based upon the heights of parents (Gray, 1948). To estimate a boy's ultimate height, the rule is add to the father's height in inches the mother's height multiplied by 1.08 and then divide by 2. For a girl, add to the mother's height the father's height multiplied by .923 and divide by 2. The hitch in this rule is that children of this generation tend to be taller than predicted from their parents' heights, so that today an inch or more may have to be added to the prediction following the mid-parent rule (Bayley, 1954).

Another formula takes into account the child's own height prior to the more striking adolescent changes. For greatest accuracy, however, it is necessary to estimate the skeletal age as well as the chronological age; this is done from x-rays of the wrist (Bayley, 1946).

Changes in growth levels that have taken place over the years are well summarized in two government publications, Hathaway (1957) and Hathaway and Ford (1960).

While the time of maximum growth rate has come to be accepted as a convenient index of maturing, reaching adulthood is much more complex than this. For example, the fact that a girl has menstruated does not necessarily indicate that she has become fertile. In fact, most girls menstruate before their ovaries can produce ripe eggs (Ford and Beach, 1951). One major study of child-bearing showed that of 700 women who married between the ages of 15-19, 44 per cent bore children within two years of marriage, while of 1835 who married between the ages of 20-24, 91 per cent bore children within the next two years (Duncan, as reported by Montagu, 1946). The inference is that many of the younger women may not yet have been mature enough to bear children at the time of their marriage. A period of sterility in early adolescence is very common among many mammals, including primates (Ford and Beach, 1951). For the male the best index of sexual maturity is the ability to produce fertile spermatozoa, but this index is difficult to apply.

Sexual maturity is not the whole story of becoming adult, and merely because a man or woman has become fertile does not mean that the maturing process has been completed. With these reservations, we may still take the maximum growth rate as a convenient milestone by which to compare different individuals as to their relative levels of maturity.

Some out-of-step adolescent changes

Growth curves for height during adolescence (e.g., Figure 4-5) show that not all adolescents follow the same pattern of growth. A boy once relatively tall may find himself short by comparison with his friends; a girl once considered small may later find herself unusually large for her age. Too much may be expected of those who mature early; anxiety may be created among those who mature late and are left behind by their companions. Among the adolescents in one study, the *early-maturing girls* and the *late-maturing boys* suffered most from their out-of-step growth (Bayley and Tuddenham, 1944).

There is another way in which adolescent growth may be out of step: the body does not grow as a unit, and one part may be out of step with another. Metabolism has to be adjusted to a rapidly growing skeleton and musculature, and a new glandular balance reached. The relative sizes of different bodily tissues at different periods, plotted in Figure 4-7, show most rapid fluctuation during the early teens. No wonder there are occasional disturbances in the balance of physiological processes within the body as these shifts take place. Adolescent acne is a commonly occurring symptom of these internal disharmonies.

Uneven growth rates of different body tissues

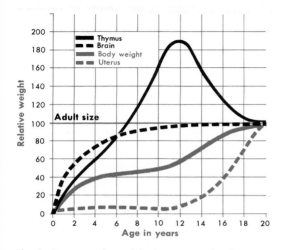

The brain approaches adult size very early; tissues related to reproduction (e.g., uterus) wait until later for rapid growth. (After Jackson, 1928)

Adolescent awkwardness

The idea is common that during adolescence boys and girls go through an "awkward stage." Such awkwardness might conceivably result from the out-of-step growth just described. But to some extent the "awkward stage" is more illusion than fact.

If adolescents are genuinely awkward, they ought to show muscular incoordination or loss of athletic prowess. Careful studies indicate that adolescents improve steadily at athletics; at no point is there loss of skill. Figure 4-8 shows the results of such a study. The Brace Motor Skills Test, named after its originator, consists of a set of tasks measuring the kinds of muscular coordinations characteristic of good athletes. While boys, according to the tests used, surpass girls athletically, both boys and girls improve throughout the teen years, when awkwardness might be expected.

In another study designed to relate these results to individual development, 200 boys between the ages of 12 and 16 were sep-

arated by age and then classified into three groups on the basis of developmental signs (prepubescent, pubescent, and postpubescent). Each group was then tested on the Brace test over a two-year period. There were gains at all ages, regardless of stage of development. While there was some indication that the rate of increase of motor ability slowed somewhat at the advent of puberty, this slowing down preceded the period of most rapid growth in height and weight and therefore could not have been the result of rapid growth (Dimock, 1937).

If we accept this evidence that adolescents are not *in fact* awkward, how can we account for the general *impression* that they are?

The first reason for the false impression of awkwardness is the *size-age confusion* during adolescence. Because of the out-of-step nature of some growth, muscular skill and size do not keep pace, and muscular skill depends more on age than on size. A twelve-year-old boy who looks like a fourteen-year-old is expected to act like a four-

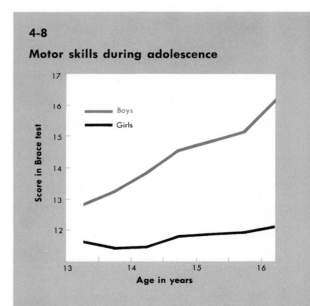

Motor skills during adolescence

Both boys and girls show steady improvement in motor skills during adolescence. (After Espenschade, 1940)

teen-year-old, but he has the movement patterns characteristic of a twelve-year-old. He therefore looks awkward, although he has not really *become* so; he has not yet outgrown whatever awkwardness younger boys have.

It should be noted that we are considering averages. A few boys are genuinely awkward during the period of most rapid growth, and they show loss of skill on motor tests. Loss of skill may occur at any age, but it appears to be somewhat more frequent during the year in which puberty is reached (Dimock, 1937). This may be due to a real awkwardness produced by a sudden shift in body proportions (Ausubel, 1954).

The size-age confusion is not limited to adolescence. Even in nursery school, the two-year-old who looks like a three-year-old will be considered awkward. The confusion is emphasized in adolescence because of the rapidity of growth over short periods of time.

The second source of the impression of muscular awkwardness is the very real *social* awkwardness of some adolescents. Self-consciousness is often intensified during the adolescent years, and an adolescent boy who is highly skilled on the tennis court may spill the punch at an afternoon party. Even for a poised adult, it isn't easy to acknowledge an introduction while holding a teacup in one hand and a sandwich in the other. For the inexperienced adolescent, the teacup and the sandwich become unsolvable problems when he is expected to shake hands. He certainly looks awkward—and he is awkward, *socially awkward,* but not necessarily physically awkward. He may be able to dance in perfect rhythm or swim with a smooth, sure stroke.

Problems of the Adolescent

The adolescent commonly becomes a problem to his parents or to the community because he is a problem to himself. The transition from childhood to adulthood brings with it both the strains accompanying physical growth and physiological change and the conflicts associated with achieving the social behavior characteristic of adults in our culture.

It has been pointed out by Barker (Barker and others, 1953) that adolescent problems can be classified as those arising from *new situations* and those arising from *overlapping situations.* Such problems are found at other ages as well, but the adolescent meets new situations somewhat more frequently because his larger size and greater age provide many adult opportunities previously denied him. He confronts overlapping situations because some demands for adult behavior are not accompanied by adult freedom: he is in some respects both a child and an adult.

What happens when the adolescent faces a new situation? He finds it ambiguous, because the signs telling him what to do are not familiar to him; he is unsure about the direction in which to move, for he does not know what actions will produce the desired effect. Whatever he does is likely to be at once inviting and threatening. Under such circumstances some disorganization of behavior is inevitable; it is as though one is walking on thin ice, with danger lurking in any move. The adolescent will then be in a state of conflict, will vacillate in action, will be easily influenced by those who offer confident resolutions of his difficulties. The new situations that lead to these problems are those "for grown-ups only," to which the adolescent now has access: the use of the car, public dance halls, adult clothing, cosmetics, work opportunities, new kinds of athletic participation.

In some respects the overlapping situations provide the more characteristic problems, because they imply the vacillation between childhood and adult status. Partly this is the nature of growth itself: the boy's voice may not yet have deepened when his beard begins to grow; the girl's figure may be more mature than her behavior. Partly this is a matter of the way in which adolescents are viewed. Barker suggests that adults treat adolescents a little as if they were semi-independent colonial people, subject to two authorities: some of their behavior is governed by their own rules and customs, some by the laws and edicts of the higher power.

If we grant that adolescents are often placed in marginal situations, in which their behavior is determined both by what is expected of a child and by what is expected of an adult, some consequences follow. Barker gives a number of theoretical derivations, followed by examples. In the following his theoretical statements are paraphrased, but the examples are quoted:

1. When the situations call out childish and adult behavior approximately equally, both childish and adult characteristics will be manifested.

   Examples:

   A 13-year-old girl dressed in her first "grown-up" evening dress claps her hands and skips about the room in delight.

   A boy with a man's job that is too difficult for him does barely satisfactory work with great fatigue, boyish pranks, and unreliability; the conflict between the satisfaction of being accepted as an adult, and the fun and freedom of a child may be very great.

2. When the relative appeal of childish and adult behavior is continually shifting due to changing social pressures and fluctuating physiological conditions, great changes from childish to adult behavior will occur.

   Example:

   Boys' club meeting begins with great seriousness and dignity, but ends with a roughhouse.

3. Although the adolescent at times is supposed to act as a child and at times as an adult, his choice as to how to act is not always appropriate; sometimes, when adult behavior is called for, it will be so unattractive to him that he responds instead with exaggerated childish behavior.

   Examples:

   Boy avoids shaving even when the need is apparent to others; girl refuses to have inappropriate, childish hairdress changed; student prolongs school career, and thus avoids facing problems of choosing a vocation.

4. For children who have early had to fend for themselves, adult activities may be attractive, childish activities unattractive; in this case adult behavior will be exaggerated, childish behavior avoided.

   Examples:

   The adolescent who strives to pass as an adult, before he is easily able to do so, by exaggerating any behavioral symptoms of adulthood he can exhibit—girls who wear adult clothes and cosmetics and go with older boys; boys who engage in "masculine" conversation, and who get jobs and have money of their own.

With these suggestions as to why problems are created by new and overlapping situations, we are prepared to turn to some of the specific problems faced by adolescents.

a Sexual development as a source of problems

Adolescents are keenly aware of changes in their bodies—changes that are at once a source of pride and of embarrassment. The boy, secretly proud of his budding mustache, may find teasing about his "lip fuzz" or "pinfeathers" humiliating. The girl, pleased with the development of a more womanly figure, may feel overly conspicuous in her bathing suit. But adolescent self-consciousness is due to invisible changes as well as visible ones. There are new wishes, desires, and fantasies stirred by sexual maturing. Because of the taboos on sexual matters in our culture, the new intense awareness of sex can become a source of embarrassment.

That physiological changes do bring with them distinct changes in outlook is shown by a study of girls of the same age, some of whom had reached sexual maturity and some of whom were still in the prepuberal period. Of two groups of 175 girls, matched for age and socioeconomic status, the postmenarcheal girls (those who had begun to menstruate) were found to differ significantly from the premenarcheal girls in their responses to the questions of a personality inventory. They reported more interest in boys, more interest in their own physical appearance, less desire for vigorous physical exercise, a stronger tendency to daydreaming, and greater concern over conflicts in family life (Stone and Barker, 1937).

Sexual emotions are not an experience new to the adolescent, but his intensified sexual motivation makes the taboos against sexual expression more frustrating than in childhood. Our culture imposes taboos on sexual relationships before marriage, and the circumstances of modern life lead to the postponement of marriage for several years beyond the attainment of sexual maturity. There is a theory that the "storm and stress" of adolescence is due more to cultural conflicts arising from sexual restrictions than to biological development. This theory receives support from studies of nonliterate cultures in which greater sexual freedom is permitted. Some of these cultures may be called *permissive* in contrast to cultures, like ours, that are *restrictive*. In permissive cultures adolescence is relatively uneventful, and the transition from childhood to adulthood is reported to be smoother than in ours.

The Trobriand Islanders, for instance, are tolerant of premarital sexual relationships. Sexual experimentation goes on freely among preadolescents. An easy transition from childhood to adulthood ensues (Malinowski, 1929). Anthropological studies of several New Guinea and Samoan groups indicate that the period of adolescence is less trying in the tribes which have the less restrictive sex taboos (Mead, 1935).

It is always unwise, however, to examine one aspect of a culture apart from other aspects of that culture. It may be that cultures which permit greater sexual freedom than ours may also permit greater freedom for the adolescent in many other ways, so that he is relieved of "stress and strain" in problems of wider scope as well as in sexual problems.

Just as sexual restrictions vary from one culture to another, they also vary in the subcultures of a complex society such as ours. Studies suggest that in American society young men from lower educational and occupational levels are more likely to find sexual outlets in actual intercourse than are those from upper educational and social levels, who are more likely to find their outlets in masturbation and petting to climax (Kinsey, Pomeroy, and Martin, 1948). Among those who accept the cultural taboos, any form of sexual interest (even sexual fantasy) brings with it feelings of apprehension, of experimentation with the forbidden. Under these circumstances sex becomes a source of adolescent conflict, even though biological demands alone would not make such conflict inevitable.

b **Emancipation from home**

Emancipation from parental authority and from emotional dependence upon parents begins in childhood, but the process of emancipation is greatly accelerated during adolescence. Some independence is achieved in the nursery school years, and the child's spheres of independence and responsibility are extended throughout his childhood. The ease of transition to fuller independence in later adolescence depends largely upon the attitudes parents take during the preceding years. Some parents who have insisted upon close supervision of the child in his early years attempt to continue their control through his adolescence. One result for the child is likely to be the continuance through adolescence of childish dependence and obedience, which may make him an adult who never becomes fully mature.

The "parent problem" as seen by teenagers has been the subject of inquiry among girls and boys of high school age (grades 9 through 12) by the Purdue Opinion Poll, a survey receiving replies from several thousand students representative of the nation at large (Remmers and Radler, 1957). Apparently there is little ground for alarm in their findings, for in no case do more than 1 in 5 high school students voice a specific complaint about parents (Table 4-1). On the whole, there is no evidence of a very high parent-child conflict. Even so, the areas of conflict reported are of interest. Many of the problems revolve around restrictions on grown-up behavior (dates, use of the family car, use of money); in these, as in other ways, the teen-ager sees the parents as treating him (or her) too much like a child. The differences in replies of boys and girls represent in part a sex-typing in our culture, so that the boy is troubled more about having the car and about spending the money he earns, while the girl is more troubled about her freedom in choosing her friends, about strictness concerning dates, and about favoritism (which, one may guess, she feels is demonstrated in her brother's greater freedom). Concealed in the figures may be the fact of the girl's maturing earlier, so that her desire for dates in the ninth grade may produce parental opposition, while a ninth-grade boy may not yet care very much about dating.

Resentment of parental control is not limited to adolescence. The negativism of the preschool child has already been referred to. Defiance of parental authority is not something that appears at only one

TABLE 4-1

"The parent problem" as seen by high school students

Problem	Per cent of replies acknowledging this problem *		
	BOYS	GIRLS	TOTAL
Afraid to tell parents what I've done wrong	18	19	19
Parents too strict about my going out at night	16	19	18
Parents too strict about family car	24	9	16
Family always worried about money	15	15	15
Parents too strict about dating	8	17	13
Parents interfere in my choice of friends	10	15	13
Parents nag about studying	16	10	13
Parents hate to admit I'm sometimes right	13	13	13
Parents too strict about dates on school nights	10	13	12
Wish parents would treat me like a grown-up	10	14	12
Parents interfere with spending money I earn	15	7	11
Parents play favorites	8	12	10

SOURCE: Remmers and Radler (1957), pp. 117-18.

* The percentages are not additive, because one student may make several complaints.

stage of growth, but may increase during adolescence, as shown by the data of Figure 4-9. In this study, done in Europe, girls of ages nine to seventeen reported poor, moderate, and good social relations with other members of their own family. The number of reports of bad relations increased gradually until a peak was reached near age thirteen, and then it declined. While the exact ages would undoubtedly vary from one culture to another, the close relationship between the peak of family difficulties and the puberal period suggests an important connection between the two.

The relationships of parents to adolescent children can create problems for both.

Adolescent difficulties with social relations

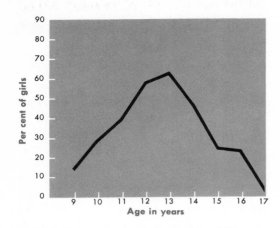

Percentage of girls at each age between 9 and 17 reporting poor social relations with members of their families. (After Buseman, reported by Bühler, 1933)

The differences in age and the circumstances of the parents' remembered youth are likely to make the parents seem "old-fashioned" to their children. The adolescent's vacillation between childish dependence and the desire for independence and privacy makes it hard for the parent to know how he should treat his child at any given time. Emancipation from home and parents does not come all at once, and the unevennness of the transition may baffle both the parents and the adolescent youth.

Relations with age-mates

If the adolescent can find secure relations with others of his own age, he is freer to emancipate himself from home ties. Adolescents place great importance on being accepted by their own group. Ample evidence of this need is offered by the emphasis they place upon conformity. If the fashion in junior high school is to wear blue jeans with the cuffs turned up, almost all the boys will insist that they have to wear blue jeans with the cuffs turned up. To differ would be to risk criticism and rejection.

The need for the security that comes from the group leads to the formation of in-groups, such as "gangs" among boys and "cliques" among girls. Members of an in-group feel especially close to others within the group and are very much aware of the distinction between "in" and "out," between those who belong and those who do not. The nature of these closely knit groups depends very much upon the opportunities which the neighborhood provides. Close friendship with a few of his fellows is important to the adolescent, and the isolated child does suffer.

Attempts have been made to study the nature of the mutual attractions among adolescents.

What do children and adolescents consider desirable characteristics among those of their own group? In order to find out, two age groups were chosen for study: twelve-year-olds (most of them prepubescent), in the sixth and seventh grades, and fifteen-year-olds (many postpubescent), in the ninth grade. Of the 350 individuals studied at each age (half of each group boys, half girls), 260 participated in both studies. Children assigned traits to each other by a modified form of the "Guess Who" test, described below. It was then possible to see which traits tended to be assigned to those voted as popular, friendly, or leaders. Because the children knew each other well, it was assumed that the characterizations were fairly accurate. It was also assumed that traits assigned popular children were those considered desirable.

The modified "Guess Who" test was composed of paragraphs describing behavior of selected kinds. Each child wrote down the names of one or more classmates who seemed to fit the description. Restlessness and its opposite, for example, were portrayed as follows:

1. Here is someone who finds it hard to sit still in class; he (or she) moves around in his (or her) seat or gets up and walks around.

2. Here is someone who can work quietly without moving around in his (or her) seat.

The test is scored by counting the number of times each child is mentioned by his fellows. A child classified as restless by 25 other children scores higher on "restlessness" than one so classified by 15 or 20 other children. Traits considered desirable by fifteen-year-olds varied somewhat from those considered desirable by twelve-year-olds. The following summaries show these variations for boys and girls. '

1. Boys and girls of twelve tend strongly to emphasize for *boys* of this age the desirability of activity of any sort; to prefer in the boy aggressiveness, boisterousness, and unkemptness as opposed to submissiveness, reserve, and tidiness; to respect above all competence in group games.
2. Boys and girls of fifteen continue to value in *boys* of their age attributes considered "masculine," such as skill in games, fearlessness, and self-assertion. However, equal emphasis is placed on personableness and social ease and poise with girls. Cheerfulness and a sense of humor are important, but boisterousness and hyperactivity are regarded as rather childish and unimportant.

While there is thus continuity between the traits considered desirable for boys of age twelve and those for boys of age fifteen, two changes may be noted. At fifteen there is more emphasis upon maturity and success with girls, and there is a rejection of "little-boy" antics.

The changes in traits considered desirable for girls between the ages of twelve and fifteen are indicated in the summaries which follow. The changes appear to be somewhat greater for girls than they are for boys.

3. The qualities most indicative of prestige for the *girl* of twelve, as seen by her age-mates, are a neat, attractive appearance; a friendly but rather demure and docile social manner; quiet good humor; and controlled behavior conforming to adult standards. A certain amount of tomboy-ishness is acceptable, but raucous, noisy activity is not.
4. For *girls* of fifteen, prestige is achieved through two major channels: either a buoyant, rather aggressive good-fellowship with both boys and girls or through sophisticated, glamorous qualities which attract boys (Tryon, 1943, pp. 558-65).

One finding of the study, not evident from the brief summaries, is that the boys of fifteen who were admired by the girls were also admired by the boys; that is, desirable fifteen-year-old male qualities were alike as viewed by boys and girls. But the girls of fifteen who were admired by boys might be liked, disliked, or regarded with indifference by their own sex.

The values which youth places upon personality characteristics are not always those with which adults agree. Thus the lack of concern for neatness shown by twelve-year-old boys and the value they place upon boisterousness may be the despair of their mothers. The glamor admired by fifteen-year-old girls often leads them to dress and act in a fashion that makes their mothers fear they have been getting into bad company. If adolescents are to be understood, it is important that parents know what adolescents expect of each other.

Juvenile delinquency

Enough adolescents engage in antisocial behavior to make juvenile delinquency a serious social problem. The circumstances that lead adolescents into antisocial behavior, if understood, can throw light on the more general problem of adolescent development.

We can distinguish between two kinds of delinquency: *social delinquency* and *individual delinquency*. Social delinquency expresses itself in gang behavior, in which

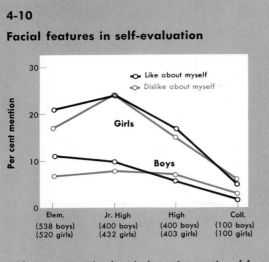

4-10

Facial features in self-evaluation

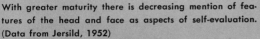

Per cent mention (y-axis)

- ● Like about myself
- ○ Dislike about myself

Girls

Boys

Elem. (538 boys) (520 girls)
Jr. High (400 boys) (432 girls)
High (400 boys) (403 girls)
Coll. (100 boys) (100 girls)

With greater maturity there is decreasing mention of features of the head and face as aspects of self-evaluation. (Data from Jersild, 1952)

large numbers of young people conform to a neighborhood pattern that may include car stealing, fighting, sexual indulgences, or other forms of behavior frowned upon by the adult culture. Individual delinquency, by contrast, crops up anywhere, in "good" families and neighborhoods as well as "bad" ones, and can be best understood as an attempt by the young person to solve some sort of problem of his own.

The circumstances that lead to social or gang delinquency and the kind of subculture that leads the gang members to conform to its standards have been well stated by Cohen (1955). One explanation he offers is that children from lower-class homes meet a great deal of frustration and humiliation in schools, which all tend to value middle-class standards. Hence those who suffer together tend to draw together in little groups, and they express their defiance by attacking or assaulting the middle-class status system. The problem is a complex one, accentuated by poverty, broken homes, cruelty, and rejection. The main point, however, is that youth with common back-

grounds find in the gang and its rewards a basis for mutual support.

Individual delinquency, not associated primarily with bad neighborhoods or cultural conflict, is in some ways more puzzling. That it has something to do with the subtle influences of child-rearing practices is indicated by the data presented in the preceding chapter with respect to the influence of childhood discipline on later aggression and crime. The fact that the tendency toward delinquent careers starts early has been pointed out in several studies in which delinquent or criminal careers have been foreshadowed between the ages of six and ten (Glueck, 1956; McCord, McCord, and Zola 1959).[1]

Self-perception, ideals, and values

If the adolescent is to achieve any consistency in his social behavior, he has to arrive at standards of conduct. He must decide for himself the kind of person he wishes to be and ascertain for himself what things are worthwhile. Such standards are known as *ideals* or *values*. When he becomes independent of home, shall he continue to accept the standards that his parents approve? In making himself acceptable to his age-mates, does he have to do everything they urge or dare him to do? He has to choose whether to conform or to defy, whether to respect conventional taboos or to see what he can "get by" with, whether to seek immediate pleasures or to set his sights on distant goals. He arrives at some sort of image of the ideal self he would like to become, and then judges himself according to this ideal.

In this process of self-appraisal the adolescent is often quite self-conscious, finding much to admire in himself, but also much to criticize. In an effort to find out about the changing self-perceptions during these years, Jersild (1952) asked a large number of boys and girls from the late elementary

[1] We shall return to consider some of the explanatory theories later on.

grades through college to indicate what they liked best about themselves and what they disliked. Some mentioned appearance, others social qualities, others abilities and special skills. The concern over features of the face and head, during these years of change, becomes especially great during the junior high years, but falls off rapidly as other aspects of self-evaluation take over (Figure 4-10). Other aspects of social relationships and personality become more important as the boy or girl becomes more mature.

The adolescent does not always find it easy to attain stable standards and guiding values. His parents are the most natural source for his standards, but he does not always agree with his parents. The younger generation faces certain problems the older generation did not have to face. Today television or the drive-in theater presents problems to the young that differ somewhat from the problems their parents faced when they were young. New rules have to be made, and debate with parents over the rules may become a source of conflict.

Despite the conflict between generations, adolescents turn to parents or other adults for advice on matters of greater long-range importance, relying on their peers more for matters having to do with present social participation (Table 4-2).

The problem of finding a set of values by which to regulate conduct is made difficult because the values of society itself are in a state of flux. Furthermore, the adolescent's own values change as he grows older. Some indication of changing standards between older and younger contemporaries over a 30-year period are given by a study of the attitudes of adolescents, a study which also shows how the standards of society itself changed during the period. The time span of the study was from 1923 to 1953.

Eighth-grade, high school, and university students checked a set of 375 behavior items in 1923. Each item could be marked as "disapproved," "worried about," or "liked." The study was repeated at 10-year intervals. The present account is based on the replies of 1734 students in 1923, 1706

TABLE 4-2

Peer group versus adults as source of advice on various matters, as reported by high school students

	Peers	Parents (or other adults)	Equally important
Peers more important:			
What to wear to a party	72%	17%	11%
The clubs you join	64	22	14
Personal grooming (how to comb your hair, dress, etc.)	58	21	21
How to act when out with the gang	57	29	14
Adults more important:			
Advice on personal problems or troubles	16	75	9
Your political feelings	21	54	25
How you spend your money	31	49	20
How you feel about people of other races or nationalities	30	32	38

SOURCE: Remmers and Radler (1957), pp. 234–35.

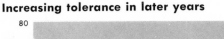

4-11

Increasing tolerance in later years

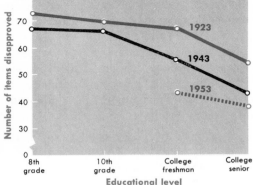

Shifts in attitude between the eighth grade and the senior year in college, and between 1923, 1943, and 1953. (After Pressey and Jones, 1955)

in 1943, and 842 (college freshmen and seniors only) in 1953.

Results for items disapproved (thought "wrong") are charted in Figure 4-11. Two trends can be noted: (1) In both 1923 and 1943 college students disapproved of fewer items than did contemporary eighth-grade pupils or high school sophomores. (2) Between 1923 and 1943 and again between 1943 and 1953, there was a decrease in the number of items disapproved, at least by college students.

Most of the items which fewer of the students tested in 1953 thought wrong than did comparable students in 1923 were "borderline" failings: flirting, toughness, disgrace, sportiness, smoking, overeating, extravagance, betting, shooting craps, slang, chewing, talking back (Pressey and Jones, 1955; Kuhlen and Arnold, 1944).

While many of the items included in the above study were somewhat trivial, the over-all trend is toward a relaxing of standards, both with increasing age at any one time and in our society generally as the years go by. Similar age trends have been found in the attitude toward religion. With increasing age (from 12 years to 18 years)

those studied showed increasing tolerance toward others' religious beliefs and practices and more doubt about such beliefs as the infallibility of the Bible or the sure existence of God (Kuhlen and Arnold, 1944).

Whether he abides by parental values or makes fresh choices for himself, the adolescent has the inescapable task of selecting standards, ideals, and values.

The Adult Years

The adolescent years shade imperceptibly into adult life. The physical changes of adolescence may not be completed until the age of twenty or beyond, although the more dramatic changes have occurred several years earlier. Problems of psychological adjustment continue, for the years of early adult life are highly competitive in our culture.

The problems of young men and young women differ. The man must establish himself in his occupation and prepare for marriage and a family. The woman, while usually also interested in self-support, is run-

TABLE 4-3

Years which appeared happiest in retrospect

Years which appeared happiest	Resident in New York *	Resident in Iowa †
Childhood (5-15 years)	15%	11%
Youth (15-25 years)	19	19
Young adulthood (25-45 years)	49	51
Middle age (45-60 years)	12	6
Later life (60 and up)	5	5
Undecided or no data	—	8
TOTAL	100	100
Number of persons reporting	370	450

* SOURCE: C. M. Morgan (1937). Subjects from ages 70 to the 90's.

† SOURCE: J. T. Landis (1942), as reported by Kuhlen (1945). Subjects from ages 65 to 98.

ning a risk of remaining unmarried if she does not find a husband by the time she is thirty. If she does find a husband, the problems of home and family become hers; if she does not, she faces the difficulties of the unmarried woman in our culture.

No period of life is free of problems. However, despite the problems it brings, the period of young adulthood is looked back upon by most older people as their time of greatest happiness (Table 4-3). In the study cited, women often reported their satisfaction in housekeeping and raising their children; men, while also referring to happy family life, mentioned prominently their interest in their work during those years. It is worth noting that in the Iowa group studied, two-thirds of those who had not been married selected the childhood years as the time of greatest happiness, while only a third of the married ones chose the years of childhood and youth in preference to the years of early adult life (Landis, 1942).

Masculine and feminine roles

In the adult years we find a culmination of the differences between the sexes that have resulted in part from biological differentiation and in part from the roles assigned the sexes in our culture.

Because the sexes are physiologically unlike, it would be easy to infer that as adults the differences in behavior between them correspond simply to their different biological organizations. Actually the situation is much more complex. Whether it is the man or the woman who wears lace or highly colored clothes depends upon the styles current at the time. A series of historical accidents determined that until recently men became bank clerks and women cashiers in stores; men telegraph operators and women telephone operators; women are increasingly taking over some of the jobs men alone formerly held. Therefore the problem becomes one of determining whether the behavioral differences between men and women are to be attributed to biological differences or to cultural influences.

Masculinity and Femininity in Nonliterate Societies. Studies of cultures very unlike our own dramatically reveal the wide range of possibilities in the behavior of the two sexes. Reports on sex roles in three New Guinea tribes illustrate well how those roles differ in various cultures.

1. A mountain-dwelling tribe, known as the Arapesh, was predominantly "feminine" from our point of view. That is, men and women were more alike than in our culture. Their similarity lay in their passivity, gentleness, mildness, and domesticity. Men and women shared the care of the children and other home duties with less division of labor than that with which we are familiar.

2. Among a river-dwelling people, called the Mundugumor, men and women also were more nearly alike than in our culture. But the Mundugumor similarity was "masculine." Both sexes tended to be ruthless, aggressive, and violent. In our culture such behavior is more often expected of a man than of a woman.

3. The lake-dwelling Tchambuli offer the most dramatic contrast to our culture. While the sexes had dissimilar roles, as ours do, the pattern was largely reversed. The Tchambuli woman was the aggressive partner, the manager of business affairs. The man was emotionally responsive to the feelings of his children, more like a mother than a father in our culture, and he was subordinate to and dependent upon his mate. The psychological reversal was so real that the Tchambuli interpreted it as biologically natural—even to the extent that the man went into confinement and suffered while his wife had a baby! (Mead, 1935, 1949.)

What these contrasting cultures tell us is that sex roles are subject to a variety of different patternings. This difference does not mean that anatomical and physiological differences between the sexes have nothing to do with behavior, but it does mean that culture has to be taken into account.

It is certainly true that the common division of labor between the sexes in nonliterate cultures is determined in part by physical differences between men and women. Study of 224 tribes throughout the world shows that, in general, men gravitate toward work requiring muscular strength (warfare, metal-working, hunting, mining and quarrying, boat-building). Women tend toward occupations centering on home and children (basket-making, gathering fruits and nuts, water-carrying, grain-grinding, pottery-making, and clothes manufacture and repair) (Murdock, 1937). Bearing and nursing children provide a biological reason for keeping women at home; man's greater muscular strength makes possible his participation in more strenuous activities. Once the division of labor is established, however, complex regulation by social pressure sets in, and familiar ways of doing things are enforced by taboo, ritual, superstition, prejudice, and other forms of social control. After the patterns have been set, members of one sex may do exclusively what members of the other sex could do equally well.

Masculinity and Femininity in American Culture. The differences between men and women on ability tests are slight. Yet on the basis of recognized achievements, women tend to fall far behind men. An early list of the thousand most eminent persons in the world included only 32 women (Cattell, 1903). Lehman's list of 116 noteworthy young creative workers, those in all fields who did significant work before age 22, included but three women, and no woman appeared on his list of older achievers. In a few fields, however, women workers represent a substantial proportion of the recognized experts (i.e., those whose names appear in biographical dictionaries or in chronological lists of important achievements). Leaving aside the acting profession, where feminine roles are required, we note that the most striking field is that of children's literature: 46 per cent of the recognized authors are women. Women represent a fifth or more of American authors in other literary fields and a fifth of the recognized sculptors, but women do not represent even 5 per cent of the eminent people in any of the scientific fields (Lehman, 1953).

How can we explain the relatively poor showing of women? One reason may be that our culture offers men greater opportunities for achievement, so that, for equal ability, the man tends to be encouraged more than the woman. There is also greater social pressure motivating men toward achievement. All men, for example, are expected to earn a living, and for them marriage provides an added incentive to earn it; women, on the other hand, often expect a professional career to be ended by marriage. What our culture expects of men and women may be more important than any differences in abilities.

Ability tests are designed to be "fair" to men and to women. Thus tests of general muscular ability do not use knitting or crocheting, which would give advantage to the women, or the assembling of electrical devices, which would give advantage to the men. It is possible to reverse this approach by selecting tests which seek to discover exactly those items within our culture on which men and women are most likely to differ, and thereby to arrive at a *social* definition of masculinity and femininity. Such a test has been devised (Terman and Miles, 1936). Items have been retained in the test if men and women tend to answer them differently; items are discarded if both men and women tend to give the same answer. When any one person takes the test, it therefore can be determined whether he answers the questions predominantly as men do or as women do. He thus receives a score characterizing the masculinity or femininity of his interests.

By *social masculinity* and *social femininity* we mean only the tendencies for men in general and for women in general to differ in the relative frequencies with which they answer questions one way or another. Social masculinity and femininity so defined must be distinguished from certain other concepts of maleness and femaleness.

The extremes of social masculinity and social femininity do not yield pictures of the personalities most generally *admired* in men and women. For example, chewing tobacco, spitting on the floor, and hanging around pool halls are extremely masculine characteristics as judged by the fact that those activities are engaged in by many more males than females in our culture. Men who engage in such activities are not necessarily more admired merely because they are socially more masculine.

One ideal of masculinity and femininity is based on sexual attractiveness, with attendant considerations of youthfulness and vigor. This ideal also is not identical with social masculinity and femininity. The young woman at the height of her sexual attractiveness is likely to have many socially masculine interests, such as an interest in sports or politics. This fact accounts for the somewhat unexpected ranking of the twenty-year-old woman in Table 4-4. By the criteria of social femininity she is only moderately feminine; women over sixty are more feminine in their interests because they tend to be more domestic than twenty-year-olds, and domestic interests are associated in our culture with social femininity.

The kinds of items yielding differences between men and women help us to see the importance of cultural roles in the determination of interests. Men tend to express interest more frequently than women in science, mechanics, and sports; women more often than men express interest in religion, art, domestic arts, and music. Tests of information bear out these differences in interests. Men are able to give the correct answers more frequently when the subject matter is science, mechanics, or sports; women give the correct answers more often when the subject matter is flowers, dress fabrics, color combinations, precious stones, or household furnishings.

The results of such a test show us that masculine and feminine interests are largely determined by custom and that they are only moderately influenced by the native endowments of men and women.

TABLE 4-4 Social masculinity and femininity of interests of representative groups of men and women	
Groups of men	*Groups of women*
Most socially masculine: Male college athletes Engineers and architects	**Most socially feminine:** Domestic employees Stenographers Dressmakers and hairdressers Women over sixty
Moderately socially masculine: Men in *Who's Who* Farmers Policemen and firemen	**Moderately socially feminine:** Twenty-year-old women Teachers Nurses
Less socially masculine: Journalists, artists, clergymen Men over sixty	**Less socially feminine:** *Who's Who* women Women with Ph.D.'s and M.D.'s Superior women athletes

SOURCE: Terman and Miles (1936), pp. 160, 181.

CRITICAL DISCUSSION

Alternatives to a social definition of masculinity and femininity

While it is convenient to determine how men and women differ in a given culture by the ways in which they characteristically act, this may tell us more about the culture than it does about the masculinity or femininity of a given man or woman within that culture. By cultural standards a young woman may be much too interested in sports and politics to score high on the Terman-Miles femininity test; yet in terms of her femininity as judged by appearance, dress, attractiveness to the opposite sex, she might be rated highly feminine. Similarly, a young man interested in music and religion will by these interests lower his score on a social masculinity test, yet he, too, might rate highly masculine by physical appearance, strength, interest in and attractiveness to women. It would evidently be possible to construct a masculinity-femininity scale that would not exaggerate the differences in answers by men and women, but would use other criteria, such as prominence of the appropriate secondary sex characteristics or interest in and capacity to elicit favorable responses from the opposite sex.

Other interesting pencil-and-paper tests of masculinity and femininity tend to resemble the Terman-Miles test in construction, although at least one of these, a scale on the California Psychological Inventory (Gough, 1957), has attempted to eliminate extreme items (such as attendance at pool halls or beauty parlors) as *too* social to deserve inclusion in a test based purely on the differences in the way most men and women answer.

A radically different kind of test, devised by Franck and Rosen (1949), is based on the assumption that men and women differ in their fantasies and hence in their imaginative productions. They prepared a test consisting of simple arrangements of lines or geometrical forms. The subject is then asked to draw a picture to complete the form in any way he wishes. Because men and women tend to complete the forms somewhat differently, it is possible to score the productions of any one subject with respect to the agreement or disagreement with the productions typical of his sex. The scores on this test, while meeting satisfactory standards of consistency, do not correlate with scores on the previously described question-and-answer tests. The presumption is that the Franck scores test certain latent or "unconscious" aspects of masculinity and femininity not revealed in the more superficial social type of tests (Miller and Swanson, 1959). While more evidence is needed, the point is clear enough that masculinity and femininity as de-

fined by a test such as that of Terman and Miles, or that of Gough, are incomplete measures of what is meant by masculinity and femininity.

Marital happiness

As we follow the development of the child through adolescence and into adult life, we may naturally inquire as to his or her suitability for marriage and likelihood of making a happy marriage. The increasing divorce rate (now about one divorce for every five marriages) is only one indication of the amount of unhappiness in marriage, for many unhappy marriages do not end in divorce. We may well investigate the factors in early life that make one person better suited for marriage than another.

Two large-scale studies, carried on at about the same time and with somewhat similar techniques, provided useful information which has been followed up by later investigators. One study was based on the replies of 792 couples, primarily from the Los Angeles area (Terman and others, 1938), the other on the replies of 526 couples located in the Chicago area (Burgess and Cottrell, 1939).

The logic of both studies was similar. First the investigators tried to establish a reasonably satisfactory index of happiness in marriage; then they examined the background of each person to find certain factors, present before marriage, from which a scale predictive of happiness could be made. Hence each couple was asked to supply information of two sorts: (1) information about the happiness of the present marriage, and (2) information about his or her experiences before marriage. By relating the two sorts of information, something can be said as to the kind of person likely to make a happy marriage and the kind of person likely to make an unhappy marriage. There are some difficulties about obtaining both kinds of information because of the deceptiveness of memories, which may be colored by the present state. Thus a person now happy may be more likely to recall his childhood as happy than one now unhappy, even if their childhoods were similar.

Later studies have shown that the original investigations were valid by taking the essential next step: testing engaged couples *before* marriage and then studying their happiness *after* marriage. Kelly (1939) tested 82 couples before marriage on background-personality items and then tested them on marital-happiness items after they had been married for two years. He found correlations of +.26 for husbands and +.30 for wives, showing a low but positive relationship.

Burgess and Wallin (1953) report a study in which they tested 1000 engaged couples and followed up 666 of them after they had been married three to five years. They found correlations of +.31 for husbands and +.27 for wives, values similar to those found by Kelly. The significance of these studies is that they show some people to be better marital risks than others. Whether or not a person is a good risk can perhaps be determined from the kind of person he is and the kinds of experiences he has had before marriage. The correlations are too low for much weight to be given to these tests, however, for purposes of individual guidance.

The continuity of personality is well illustrated by the fact that characteristics most predictive of happiness have their origins in early childhood: the happiness of the parents' marriage, lack of conflict with the mother or father, attachment to the parents and to brothers and sisters, attractiveness of the opposite-sexed parent. Any of these increases the likelihood of a happy marriage when this child grows up.

One item found in the California study to be related to marital happiness scores was happiness in childhood. Those who re-

4-12

Childhood discipline and marital happiness

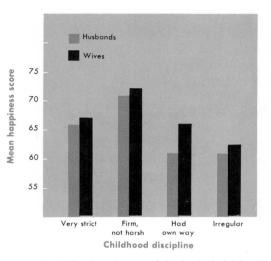

Reports by husbands and wives of the kind of childhood discipline they experienced show its effects on marital happiness. (After Terman and others, 1938)

membered their childhoods as being generally happy made higher marital happiness scores than those whose childhoods were remembered as less happy.

> It is a favorable omen for the success of a marriage if husband and wife had a happy childhood. According to our data, no other item of information relating to background is more significant. . . . It far outweighs such items as adequacy of sex instruction, religious education, adolescent "petting," or even premarital intercourse.[2]

Discipline in the home is another item predictive of later happiness or unhappiness. As we might have expected from the discussion in Chapter 3, the favorable type of discipline is that which is *firm but not harsh* (Figure 4-12). The most unfavorable kind is that which is irregular and unpredictable. The relationships hold equally well for men and for women. It will be noted that the kind of discipline leading to happy marriage is the kind associated with nondelinquency (p. 92).

[2] Terman and others (1938), p. 228.

The productive years

During the working years of adult life, careers reach their climax and then taper off toward retirement. From which years can we expect man's best work? How long is he likely to remain productive? The answers to these questions are important for a society in which life expectancy is increasing and in which there will be more and more older people.

Performers who depend upon strength, speed, or precision of movement tend to reach their peaks of skill in the years from twenty-five to twenty-nine. It may be assumed that champion performers are always well trained and eager to do their best, so that a study of the ages at which the championship is reached furnishes useful evidence of age as an element in skill. The ages at which championships were won in a number of sports are plotted in Figure 4-13. The sports which make less demand upon stamina and more upon precision (rifle and pistol shooting, billiards) do not show the rapid falling off with age characteristic of the more strenuous sports such as tennis and boxing. The leisure-time interests of adults correspond in part to these age changes in skill: as adults grow older, they turn to sports, such as golf, which can be played at a pace suited to the age of the participant.

4-13

How old are champions?

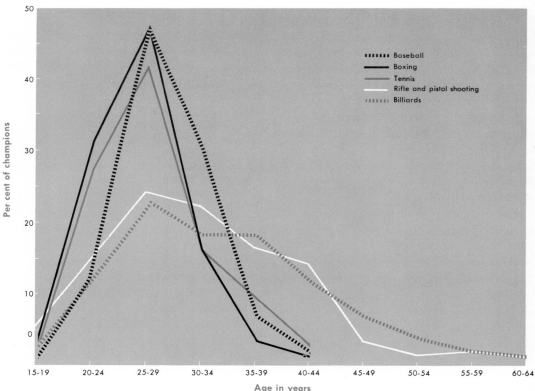

Ages at which championships have been won in sports. (After Lehman, 1938)

° TABLE 4-5

Age of maximum rate of very superior contributions

General field of creative work	Age at time of maximum rate of contribution			
	25-30	30-35	35-40	40-45
Physical sciences, mathematics, inventions	Chemistry	Mathematics Physics Electronics Practical inventions Surgical techniques	Geology Astronomy	
Biological sciences and medicine		Botany Classical descriptions of disease	Bacteriology Physiology Pathology Medical discoveries	
		Genetics Entomology Psychology		
Philosophy, education, and social sciences		Economics and political science		
			Logic Ethics Esthetics "General philosophy" Educational theory and practice	Metaphysics
			Social philosophy	
Musical compositions	Instrumental selections	Vocal solos Symphonies	Chamber music Nonsymphonic orchestral music Grand opera	Cantatas Light opera and musical comedy
Literary compositions	Lyrics and ballads (German) Odes Elegies Pastoral poetry Narrative poetry Sonnets Lyric poetry	Satiric poetry Short stories Religious poetry (hymns) Comedies	Tragedies "Most influential books" Hymns by women	Novels "Best books" Best sellers Miscellaneous prose writings
Painting and sculpture		Oil paintings	American sculpture	Modern architecture Oil paintings (contemporary artists)

SOURCE: Lehman, 1953.

4-14

Age at which superior works were produced

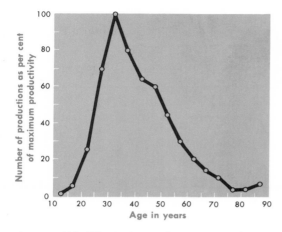

Ages at which 933 scientists, mathematicians, and inventors produced 1359 superior contributions. (After Lehman, 1953)

How about productive efforts in science, literature, and the arts? When are men at their best in creative work?

The results of a prodigious amount of work by Lehman (1953) are summarized in Table 4-5. Here we find the ages at which men tend most frequently to make superior contributions to the fields specified in the table. Lehman produced the data by going to bibliographies and historical summaries of the various fields and by getting the cooperation of experts in sorting out the superior from the pedestrian performance. By then finding out the age of each man at the time of his discovery or creative work, Lehman was able to chart the most productive years in each of the fields. In this way he avoided the bias that comes from looking either for very young producers or very aged ones. For most of the fields the age of maximum productivity is between 30 and 40; for a few it is earlier, for a few later. Within each field productivity begins before 30 and continues after 40; a generalized curve for the

fields of science, mathematics, and invention is plotted in Figure 4-14. Although distinguished contributions are made throughout life, the rapid rise to the peak and the gradual decline thereafter are striking.

The previous data have all been concerned with superior performances. Do scientists and writers who do *good* work early tend to do *better* as they mature, or is their best work done early? Lehman has chosen to answer this question by finding the ages at which distinguished men in various fields produced their one "best work," as judged by other competent men in the same field. If the ages at which the "best works" were produced are compared with the ages at which the total works were produced, we get an answer to our question. One such answer, typical of a number obtained by Lehman, is given in Figure 4-15. The one "best work" of each of a number of distinguished philosophers tends to be published at the height of the period of general productivity. While philosophers continue to produce until late in life, the distinguished contributions made late represent a progressively smaller fraction of the total output. The same general conclusion applies in other fields: when the very best works only are plotted, the peak of maximum productivity remains early, and the decline with

TABLE 4-6

Predictability of later productivity based on productivity in earlier decades

Decade from which prediction is made	Coefficient of correlation between scientific productivity in earlier and later decade			
	30-39	40-49	50-59	60-69
20-29	.58	.31	.51	.53
30-39		.80	.73	.68
40-49			.71	.65
50-59				.82

SOURCE: Dennis, 1954b. Based on study of 43 psychologists born between 1850 and 1860 and living until 70.

Age at which best work was produced

Age of best work and general productivity of 182 deceased philosophers. The colored line indicates the one best treatise (as determined by consensus); the black line, ages at which 1593 other books by these same men were first published. (After Lehman, 1953)

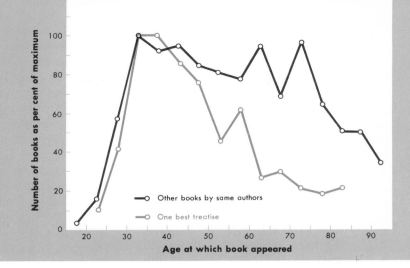

Legend:
- Other books by same authors
- One best treatise

Number of books as per cent of maximum

Age at which book appeared

age is more striking than for generally superior productivity.

Eminent scientists, whether they achieve eminence early or late, continue to be productive throughout their lives, so that a relationship can be established between eminence and productivity (Dennis, 1954a). Not only in the sciences but in other fields as well (e.g., music, general books, linguistics), the upper tenth of productive writers produces between one-third and two-thirds of the material (Dennis, 1955). These data raise fascinating but elusive problems. Do very productive people have a better chance to hit upon something important? Do people who happen to attract prominence early become motivated to remain productive? We need further research to give answers to these questions. We do know that people who are productive early are more likely than the less productive to continue to create in their later years. This is true whether or not they attain eminence (Table 4-6).

The data in Table 4-6 are based solely on psychologists, but Dennis also studied the publication lists of 41 nonpsychologist members of the National Academy of Sciences. These men were more highly selected than the psychologists (whose names were taken from a general register of psychologists, regardless of eminence). The average number of publications for the National Academy members was much higher than for the psychologists. The correlations between early decades and later ones were similar for those of the psychologists, except that the decade of the 20's was somewhat less predictive for nonpsychologists. In general, productivity during the 30's is a good predictor of what will happen in succeeding decades (Dennis, 1954b).

CRITICAL DISCUSSION

Life-history data vs. laboratory data; advantages and hazards

The work of both Lehman and Dennis calls attention to the possibility of using existing historical data for quantitative purposes. Hypotheses can be tested with such data as well as with data freshly gathered in the laboratory, and (as in these studies) can provide information which could not be obtained in the laboratory. Historical data have some other advantages over laboratory data, in that the people studied represent an ability level that could not be matched in the laboratory and are more highly motivated in their work than laboratory subjects generally are. The laboratory has the advantage of more stringent control, but the disadvantage of more restricted subjects.

Dennis (1958) points out certain hazards in the use of historical data. He has argued that one reason Lehman's scientists seem more eminent when they are younger than when they are older is that the number of scientists increases very rapidly, so that on the basis of numbers alone scientists are losing their competitive advantage. That is, if the same famous man had been a young man 25 years later, his chances of fame, with the same amount of creativity, would have been much less. Perhaps, therefore, Lehman has been plotting an increase in competition rather than a decrease in productivity with age. This is an interesting point, but Lehman (1960) appears to have shown that the amount of this effect as a distortion of his findings would not be very great.

Retirement

The problem of how to occupy one's day in a manner which makes one feel needed and useful is a severe one for older people, particularly for those who reach an arbitrary retirement age (often at 65) while they are still energetic and in good health. Increasing longevity has produced a great many more older people in our society than there once were, and their problems hence take on more social importance (Figure 4-16). A man receives emotional support from his work and from the people associated with it; those who reach retirement age are often unprepared for the loss of this support.

One method of cushioning the psychological shock of retirement is that of tapering off, or partial retirement. Such partial retirement provides greater leisure while the person is vigorous enough to develop new interests appropriate to his mature years. He is not suddenly pushed off the crowded dock of work into an endless sea of leisure. The president of a corporation often becomes chairman of the board in his later years. The emeritus-professor plan in most of our universities permits the retired professor to continue his research and writing, even though he no longer conducts classes. Such a method of tapering off has genuine psychological advantages, and related plans are being developed within other lines of work (Breckinridge, 1953).

The problems of the later years of life have many other facets. The person who has suffered a heart attack or other debilitating illness is often demoralized by the experience and requires a period of psychological as well as physical rehabilitation. The problems of loneliness due to death of family members, children moving away, inability to travel, have to be met. Various kinds of activity centers for older people are being developed to meet these needs. The present scale of the problem of the later years is such as to direct a good deal of attention to it, and undoubtedly more adequate research will be conducted, on the basis of which sound policies can be proposed.

4-16

The aged in the United States

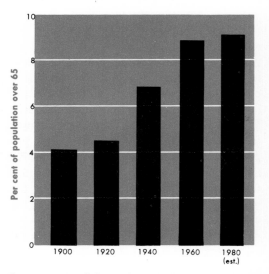

The percentage of the total population aged 65 or over has more than doubled in the last half-century, though the trend shows signs of slackening. (U.S. Bureau of Census)

SUMMARY 1. Puberal changes **bring the** greatest modifications in physiological processes during the lifetime of the individual. These changes differ between boys and girls, but there are similarities in the pattern of changes both undergo. Girls enter upon the puberal changes earlier and on the average reach maturity about two years before boys do, but because of individual differences some boys go through puberal changes earlier than some girls.

2. The out-of-step character of adolescent changes aggravates some of the social and emotional problems of adolescence. These out-of-step changes are responsible for the idea that adolescence is an awkward age, which is true enough of some adolescent social behavior but not of physical coordination.

3. Many adolescent problems can be understood in terms of the *new* situations the adolescent faces and the *overlapping* situations that confront him. The new situations arise when he is large enough and old enough to be permitted to do things that smaller and younger children are not allowed to do. The overlapping situations come about because entering adulthood is a gradual process and the adolescent is in some sense at once a child and an adult.

4. Specific problems arise in the areas of sex, emancipation from home, relation to age-mates, and arriving at standards of value.

5. Adolescent conflicts may result in juvenile delinquency. *Individual delinquency,* based on personal problems, is distinguished from *social delinquency,* expressed in gang behavior.

6. The problems familiar in adolescence do not end with the attainment of adulthood. Problems of adjustment in early adult life are continuous with those in adolescence except for the lesser importance of growth changes.

7. Sex roles become differentiated in adult life. Study of nonliterate cultures (as well as our own) shows that the differences depend only in part upon the biological roles of the two sexes. Cultural arrangements determine many of the differences that we find.

8. Studies of marital happiness point up the fact of continuity of development, for the most important predictors of marital happiness go back to childhood: the happiness of parents, a happy childhood, affectionate relations with parents and siblings, and a firm but not harsh discipline.

9. The years of greatest proficiency and productivity center in the ages between 20 and 40. Although productivity may continue until late in life, the later rate can generally be predicted from productivity in the 30's.

10. Increased longevity creates new problems for those who pass the retirement age.

The physical and physiological changes in adolescence, along with their correlates in social behavior, are dealt with in Henry (Ed.), *Adolescence* (1944), and in Stolz and Stolz, *Somatic development of adolescent boys* (1951). There are a number of textbooks on adolescent psychology, such as Jersild, *The psychology of adolescence* (1957), Strang, *The adolescent views himself* (1957), and Wattenberg, *The adolescent years* (1955).

The nature of sex differences and the cultural roles assigned to men and women in different cultures are treated by Mead, *Male and female* (1949), and Scheinfeld, *Women and men* (1943).

The problem of the most productive years is dealt with in great detail in Lehman, *Age and achievement* (1953).

For a general overview of development, including the problems of the older years, see Pressey and Kuhlen, *Psychological development through the life span* (1957).

For some of the problems of aging, see Kleemeier, *Aging and leisure* (1961).

Motivated and Emotional Behavior

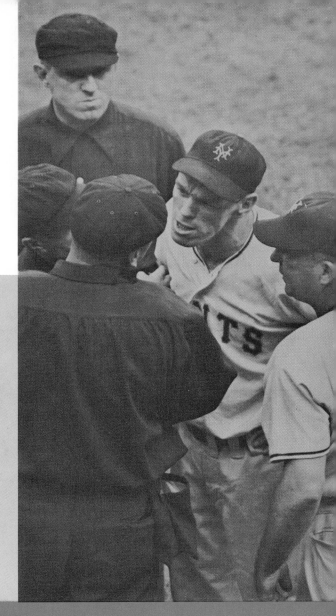

To understand behavior we must know how it is aroused and directed; these aspects of energetic and goal-directed behavior fall within the province of motivational psychology. Because pleasures and pains, hopes and fears, satisfactions and annoyances are closely related to the successes and failures of motivated behavior, there is an intimate connection between motivation and emotion.

CHAPTER 5

Motivation

We may well ask whether or not *all* behavior is motivated. The answer is not easy, for even such reflex behaviors as the heartbeat and digestion serve purposes in the life of the organism, and are responsive to various kinds of motivational activation. Simple reflex behavior is not usually thought of as motivated, although there is no simple rule by which it is excluded, but all more complex behavior, especially all learned behavior, is clearly responsive to motivational activation and control.

Although organisms are occasionally quiescent—as in sleep or hibernation—it is much more characteristic of them to be active. In order to understand the active organism—why it does what it does when it does it—we search for motives, for springs of action. By a *motive* we mean something that incites the organism to action or that sustains and gives direction to action once the organism has been aroused. A dog buries a bone, a child practices on the piano, a task force sends a rocket to the moon. When we ask "why" these actions take place, we are inquiring about motives.

There are two main aspects of motivated behavior: first the *activating* or *energizing* aspect, and second the *directional* aspect. By activation we mean the difference between being asleep or awake, between being relaxed and being tense, between "taking it easy" and putting forth effort. Motivational activation produces a state of readiness for behavior, as in the difference between the horse standing quietly in the stall and champing at the bit when ready for the race. The same act engaged in by a less activated organism will be done less vigorously than by an aroused one. In addition to producing a state of readiness for behavior, an activated motive also tends to set off behavior in a particular direction. The hungry animal is ready to run to food and to eat, the thirsty one to drink, the one in pain to escape the painful stimulus.

The Range and Classification of Motives

Motivational dispositions vs. aroused motives

Not all the motives which can incite an organism to action are likely to be operative at the same time. A student who spends long hours studying during the week because of his motivation to make good grades may be seen howling with excitement at the Saturday afternoon football game for quite different motives. He carries many motives with him, even when they are not being expressed; these are called *motivational dispositions,* persistent characteristics deriving from inheritance or prior experience or both. We may speak of *aroused motives* when these dispositions find expression in behavior actually taking place. This distinction reflects the idea, repeatedly noted in the text, that the explanation of behavior has both its developmental (historical) and its interactive (contemporary) aspects. Motivational dispositions reflect the organism's past; aroused motives are a consequence of present interactions among internal and external circumstances.

Even though they belong to the same species, individuals differ in their motivational dispositions. One person may be a voracious eater, while another may have a moderate appetite. Moreover, at any one

Soibelman Syndicate

5-1

An attempt to use motivational arousal

This Kentish merchant has learned by experience and tradition what it is that will motivate a donkey to move.

time the voracious eater may be well-fed and not ready to eat more, while the person with a moderate appetite may at times be very hungry indeed. In making these statements, we are distinguishing between the persistent motivational disposition and the aroused motive.

A large part of the experimental work on motivation is concerned with easily identified motives such as hunger, thirst, sex, and pain, and most of this work is concerned with the manifestations of these motives when they are aroused. Most *classifications* of motives deal, however, with motivational dispositions. That is, the classification seeks to provide a catalogue of the motives that will be found in an activated state when the circumstances of arousal become appropriate. It turns out that such classification is highly arbitrary, a fact that becomes clear when we see how different are the various attempts to classify human motives. Thomas (1923) reduced human motives to four "wishes": for security, for recognition, for response from one's fellows, and for new experience. Maslow (1954) listed the basic "needs" (i.e., motivational dispositions) as

physiological needs, safety needs, belongingness and love needs, esteem needs, and the need for self-actualization. Others have preferred much longer lists. Murray (1938) listed 12 "viscerogenic" (i.e., physiological) and 28 "psychogenic" needs (Table 5-1). The following considerations help to account for the differences in lists that various writers propose:

1. The expression of human motives differs from culture to culture and from person to person within a culture. This difference arises because many motives are learned as a result of specific experiences and in any case are expressed through learned behavior.
2. Similar motives may be manifested through unlike behavior. A motive to assert antagonism to another person may be expressed either by an attack upon him or by withdrawal from his presence.
3. Unlike motives may be expressed through similar behavior. Thus two people may take up oil painting, one to please a parent, the other to annoy a parent.
4. Motives often appear in disguised form.

TABLE 5-1

A list of psychogenic needs

A. Needs associated chiefly with inanimate objects

1. **Acquisition:** the need to gain possessions and property.
2. **Conservation:** the need to collect, repair, clean, and preserve things.
3. **Orderliness:** the need to arrange, organize, put away objects, to be tidy and clean; to be precise.
4. **Retention:** the need to retain possession of things; to hoard; to be frugal, economical, and miserly.
5. **Construction:** the need to organize and build.

B. Needs expressing ambition, will power, desire for accomplishment, and prestige

6. **Superiority:** the need to excel, a composite of achievement and recognition.
7. **Achievement:** the need to overcome obstacles, to exercise power, to strive to do something difficult as well and as quickly as possible.
8. **Recognition:** the need to excite praise and commendation; to demand respect.
9. **Exhibition:** the need for self-dramatization; to excite, amuse, stir, shock, thrill others.
10. **Inviolacy:** the need to remain inviolate, to prevent a depreciation of self-respect, to preserve one's "good name."
11. **Avoidance of inferiority:** the need to avoid failure, shame, humiliation, ridicule.
12. **Defensiveness:** the need to defend oneself against blame or belittlement; to justify one's actions.
13. **Counteraction:** the need to overcome defeat by restriving and retaliating.

C. Needs having to do with human power exerted, resisted, or yielded to

14. **Dominance:** the need to influence or control others.
15. **Deference:** the need to admire and willingly follow a superior; to serve gladly.
16. **Similance:** the need to imitate or emulate others; to agree and believe.
17. **Autonomy:** the need to resist influence, to strive for independence.
18. **Contrariness:** the need to act differently from others, to be unique, to take the opposite side.

D. Needs having to do with injuring others or oneself

19. **Aggression:** the need to assault or injure another; to belittle, harm, or maliciously ridicule a person.
20. **Abasement:** the need to comply and accept punishment; self-depreciation.
21. **Avoidance of blame:** the need to avoid blame, ostracism, or punishment by inhibiting unconventional impulses; to be well behaved and obey the law.

E. Needs having to do with affection between people

22. **Affiliation:** the need to form friendships and associations.
23. **Rejection:** the need to be discriminating, to snub, ignore, or exclude another.
24. **Nurturance:** the need to nourish, aid, or protect another.
25. **Succorance:** the need to seek aid, protection, or sympathy; to be dependent.

F. Additional socially relevant needs

26. **Play:** the need to relax, amuse oneself, seek diversion and entertainment.
27. **Cognizance:** the need to explore, to ask questions, to satisfy curiosity.
28. **Exposition:** the need to point and demonstrate; to give information, explain, interpret, lecture.

SOURCE: Murray, 1938. The psychogenic needs are distinguished from viscerogenic, or physiological, ones. In the listing, changes of wording have been made to avoid some of the neologisms coined by Murray.

Boys have been known to steal because of sexual conflicts. Here the motive for stealing was not a "motive to acquire" (recognized by some psychologists as one of the basic motives) but a disguised sexual drive.

5. Any single act of behavior may express several motives. A scientist at work in

his laboratory may be motivated by a yearning to search for truth, by a desire for fame, by the necessity of increasing his earning power to support his family. All these as well as other motives may be active at the same time. The principle of multiple determination of behavior is an important one, but it makes difficult the description of the motives active at any given time.

These five considerations mean that we cannot arrive at a definitive list of motives simply by classifying the activities in which men engage. Instead, we must infer basic motives underlying these activities. Even though we know a great deal about human motives and even though our inferences are accurate, we still have to decide how detailed our list shall be. Perhaps the desire for status may be treated as a single motive. Or, if we wish, we may treat the various aspects of status—domination, prestige, power, and security—as separate motives. Hence the fact that experts choose lists of different lengths does not necessarily imply contradiction.

While there appears to be less arbitrariness in listing motives (such as hunger and thirst) which have clear physiological bases, these motives too display complications that make classification somewhat arbitrary. There are specific hungers that are motivating, such as the salt-hunger that sends animals to the salt-lick. There are perversions of appetite in which the desire for particular kinds of food is quite out of proportion to bodily needs. There are specific cultivated thirsts, as is well known. Thus hunger and thirst are by no means simple and unitary motives.

A provisional classification

A classification of motivational dispositions and of the aroused motives to which they give rise serves primarily as a reminder of the complexity of motivation. It should not be taken as a final listing and should not be permitted to distract attention from the subtle interrelationships, equivalences, and transformations that occur among motives.

We may take as a rough basis of classification those motives most closely related to maintaining the organism in its environment (the *survival* motives); those that provide for group life, particularly the interaction with other organisms of the same species, although sometimes involving other species (the *social* motives); and, finally, the motives built around the self, which are particularly important in man (the *ego-integrative* motives).

The *survival motives* are often identified with bodily needs, such as the need for food, for water, or for moderate ranges of temperature. We therefore speak of the motives of hunger or thirst or avoidance of extremes of heat or cold. Related to these are the motives dealing with activity and rest, with elimination of waste products, with escape from bodily injury and pain. It is, however, difficult to specify as needs certain motives that belong in this group. These include the desire for an optimum level of activity (seen, for example, in the play of animals and children), and the satisfying of curiosity, a motive which provides an alertness to environmental danger, but which goes much farther. Because they are so closely related to bodily deficiencies, the survival motives when aroused display a persistence that gives them a "driven" quality—a fact which has led to their being called *drives*.

The *social motives* all involve other organisms. The survival of the species may depend upon these motives, but they do not have the same urgency for the individual as the motives previously listed. Thus the sex motive is essential for reproducing the species, but an individual can live out his life even though this motive is frustrated. Also closely related to survival are the parental motives that lead to the care of the helpless young, and the other affiliative motives that make group life possible. More complex, but found through much of the animal world as well as in man, are motives having to do with dominance and submission, with aggression and abasement. Not all social motives are affiliative; some lead us to seek the company of others, some lead us to avoid others, some lead us to attack others. What social motives have in common is their reference to other organisms, usually, but not always, of the same species.

The *ego-integrative motives* have to do with self-respect and mastery in ways that are insufficiently described in terms of survival and affiliation. They include mastery of the environment, as in the desire to grow things, to construct or invent, or to exert power in destruction. They also include the desire for prestige in the eyes of other individuals or for power over them. The negative aspect of these personal motives is the desire to avoid a sense of inferiority and self-depreciation; the positive aspect is to have a sense of attainment, self-actualization, or self-fulfillment.

This threefold classification (survival, social, and ego-integrative motives) will serve as a useful indication of the territory a theory of motivation must cover, provided we do not consider it a final or definitive list.

Survival Motives: Drives

Some motives are more readily studied in the laboratory than others, particularly those that have clear physiological correlates. We can begin our detailed study of motives by examining hunger, thirst, and pain drives, all obviously important in permitting the organism to survive in the environment. The concept of *drive* usually implies a state of deprivation or injury, giving the related behavior a certain urgency, but as we shall see, certain other kinds of motives may also be called drives.

Drives are usually studied as aroused motives. Whatever the motivational disposi-

tion, behavior does not occur unless there is some kind of activation or arousal. From a physiological standpoint, arousal may be by way of (1) incoming nervous impulses from stimuli either in the environment or within the organism, (2) chemical or hormonal changes reaching a nerve center or a homeostatic mechanism, or (3) processes generated within the central nervous system itself. Many sensory stimuli are motivationally relevant as arousers, e.g., the odor of a female in heat sexually arouses a male animal, a thorn in the foot arouses the hiker. The stimuli may be internal, as when stomach contractions produce hunger pangs. There is abundant experimental evidence on the importance of hormones in behavioral arousal, particularly behavior related to sexual activity. The spontaneous activity of the brain has been indicated earlier (Chapter 2), but how the brain may spontaneously determine some of the rhythms of motivational arousal is still a matter of conjecture. The importance of the reticular formation as an arousal mechanism has already been indicated, and the specific regulatory features of the hypothalamus have also been noted.

Hunger drive

Studies of hunger permit us to understand some of the components of motivation. The need for food rests upon the depletion of food substances in the blood. This condition leads to restless activity in animals and, in man, to the awareness of a craving for food. When food substances are depleted in the blood, the need to replenish them causes an increase in stomach contractions. These stomach contractions produce internal stimuli that are part of the aroused state: they make the organism active and they are the source of hunger pangs.

A person who has gone without food for some hours does not feel hungry all the time. The aching or gnawing feelings described as hunger pangs occur irregularly.

Hunger pangs and stomach contractions

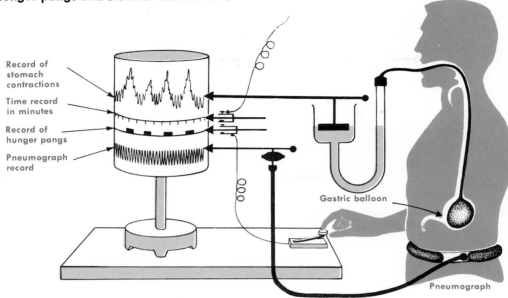

Record of
stomach
contractions

Time record
in minutes

Record of
hunger pangs

Pneumograph
record

Gastric balloon

Pneumograph

Note that the reported hunger pangs correspond closely to the periods when stomach contractions are at their maximum. (After Cannon, 1934)

In experiments designed to discover the basis for these pangs, the food-deprived subject swallowed a rubber balloon, which was then inflated until it was firm against the walls of the stomach. A small tube from the balloon was connected to a recording instrument, so that a pointer moved whenever the walls of the stomach contracted (see Figure 5-2). The subject, who could not see the pointer, was given a telegraph key to press whenever he felt the pangs of hunger. It was found that his pressing of the key was almost simultaneous with the contractions of his stomach.

The relationship of food deprivation to stomach contractions suggests that the hunger drive may be identified with stimuli from the contracting stomach. The explanation is not so simple, however, for hunger can occur in the absence of stomach contractions. The hunger drive to which food deprivation gives rise is dependent on more than these contractions. For ex-

ample, a man whose stomach had been removed surgically and whose esophagus was then connected directly to his intestine reported periodic desires for food much the same as those of persons with stomachs (Hoelzel, 1927). And rats whose stomachs were removed for experimental purposes showed hunger behavior like that of normal rats, except that they tended to show it more frequently. The more frequent hunger may have been due to the reduced food-storage capacity (Tsang, 1938).

Hunger stirs a rat to activity. If we assume that its hunger is due to stomach contractions, we must also assume that its activity is the result of sensory messages from the stomach to the brain; but the fact is that, when the sensory nerves from the stomach to the brain are cut, a rat's hunger behavior remains normal (C. T. Morgan and J. D. Morgan, 1940).

We have sufficient evidence to indicate that the chemical state of the body influ-

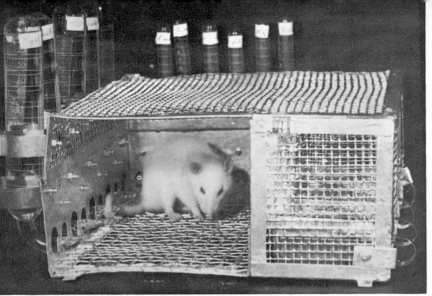

5-3

Self-selection of diet

Cage showing the apparatus used in studies in which rats are allowed to select their own diet from fifteen to eighteen different substances. Under these conditions rats select a healthful, nutritious diet.

ences the hunger drive in ways other than by stomach contractions. The complexity of hunger is further indicated by the presence not only of a general hunger drive but of specific hungers, that is, drives toward specific food incentives.

Specific hungers

A child who is no longer hungry for spinach may still be hungry for ice cream. Foods differ in their attractiveness to different people. Differences in food preferences are sometimes due to cultivated tastes. They may, however, arise from specific bodily needs. A diet that is deficient in some essentials causes special drives. Experiments with animals have shown that such specific drives are satisfied only by the foods appropriate to them.

Rats on a fat-free diet, when offered a choice among fat, sugar, and wheat, exhibit a marked preference for fat. Similarly, rats deprived of either sugar or wheat will prefer the food of which they have been deprived. Other experiments have shown that rats have specific hungers for sugar, fat, protein, thiamine, riboflavin, salt, phosphorus, sodium, and calcium. (See Figure 5-3.)

Still other experiments have shown that

barnyard animals as well as laboratory animals will commonly select a well-balanced diet if given a wide range of foods from which to choose. Experiments on the self-regulation of diet have been carried out on pigs, dairy cows, and chickens as well as on laboratory rats and mice. The results of these experiments show that animals demand in their food something more than the requisite number of calories; they hunger for the necessary chemical constituents of a balanced diet.

It is not clear how specific hungers are regulated, but it is assumed that the needed foods must taste better to the animal or child choosing from among a variety of foods. That taste does indeed influence choosing is indicated by the fact that rats with their taste nerves cut failed to select a balanced diet (Richter, 1943).

Whatever may be the origin of appetite and food preference, it is evident from ordinary observation that the preferences can be distorted by learning. The deficiency disease beriberi is found among peoples whose diet consists largely of polished rice. This preference for polished rice instead of whole-grain rice is contrary to needs of the body. Animal experiments have also shown that preference can be established for poor diets, so that the animal may continue for some time to choose the poor food to which it has become accustomed, even though a more balanced food is accessible. We need neither carry "naturalness" too far nor be alarmed by the harmful results of learning. Modern dietitians can provide more nutritious diets for both animals and human beings, and organisms can learn to like better diets as well as poorer ones.

Thirst drive

Dryness of the mouth and throat contributes to thirst; when the tissues are relatively dry, we are aware of being thirsty. But the craving for water can be satisfied only in part by relieving the sense of dryness in the mouth through stimulating salivation by chewing gum, wetting the mouth, or anesthetizing the skin of mouth and throat. Just as stomach contractions provide only one component of the hunger drive, so dryness in the mouth and throat provides only one component of the thirst drive. Experiments with dogs bear out the fact that water intake is regulated by the amount of water that the body needs, not merely by the dryness of the mouth.

Dogs whose normal daily intake of water had been computed were placed on a schedule limiting the amount of water they were given, so that the water deficit could be known and systematically varied. When later tested, the dogs showed an accurate "ability to estimate" the amount of water needed to make up the deficit; that is, they drank the amount of water of which they had been deprived (Adolph, 1939).

In another experiment, water equal to the deficit was placed directly in the dog's stomach either through a surgical opening or by means of a tube. Thus the water entered the stomach without affecting the dryness of the mouth and throat tissues. If allowed to drink before the water had been assimilated, the dog drank as much as he would have if no water had been artificially placed in his stomach. If, however, a 15-minute wait was introduced, so that the water could be assimilated into his system, the dog did not drink at all, showing that thirst had been relieved without any direct wetting of the mouth and throat tissues (Adolph, 1941).

How can we explain results such as these? There must be some regulator within the nervous system that acts to control the thirst drive much as a thermostat regulates the temperature of a room. Experiments have located a region in or near the hypothalamus where such regulation may occur. The first experiments testing this theory were done with goats, although the results have since been confirmed with other animals. If a slight amount of salt solution is injected into the third ventricle (a fluid-filled cavity inside the brain in the region of the hypothalamus), the goat drinks an excessive amount of water. Injection of pure water does not lead to such drinking (Andersson, 1953). The conclusion is that there must be some "brain center," sensitive to the body's need for liquid, which controls thirst, and the speculation arises that there may be such "centers" for other drives. Specific desires may be cultivated for other liquids such as coffee or tea or alcoholic beverages. The thirst drive, like the hunger drive, can be modified by experience.

An ingenious suggestion has been made by Deutsch (1960) that the act of drinking (and tasting) sends some sort of "thirst-quenching" messages to the brain, thereby regulating the amount drunk. A thirsty animal requires more such "messages" and hence drinks more. As a specific test of this theory he studied the drinking of saline solution by rats. The assumption is that one unit of saline solution will not be as thirst-quenching as one unit of ordinary water: it is as though the salt "dilutes" the water. If a thirsty animal is permitted to drink all it wishes of both salty water and ordinary water, it will actually drink more of the water with salt in it (Deutsch and Jones,

1959). However, if the amount is limited, so that it can drink only a given amount, it will prefer to drink ordinary water, as the theory would predict.[1]

Pain as drive

The drive to avoid pain arises from the organism's need to escape damage through tissue injury, and is created by the discomfort and intolerability of the painful state. It thus illustrates the usual circumstance that physiological drives are aversive, that they are states from which the organism is led to escape. Just as the hunger drive leads to escape from hunger pangs and the thirst drive leads to escape from a parched throat, so the pain-avoidance drive leads to whatever behavioral sequence will reduce the organism's discomfort—running off a charged grid, taking off a shoe that pinches, placing an ice pack on a feverish brow, or escaping to a safe place.

Pain differs from hunger and thirst in that it is not a result of deprivation, but is based on a readiness that is always present though inactive unless a painful stimulus is encountered. Thus pain is *episodic*, while other drives tend to be *cyclical*, depending as they do upon the body's metabolism.

Other drives with physiological bases

Many other conditions serve as drives. We have a drive to avoid extremes of temperature; a drive to avoid suffocation; a drive against accumulating waste products in the body; a drive against excessive fatigue and exhaustion.

Sometimes the physiological basis of a drive is acquired. Drug addiction provides an example, for a person who habitually takes morphine originally had no need for it. Continued use, however, creates an imperative need; morphine then becomes necessary for him. He has become an addict and, deprived of the drug, is driven by his craving for it; without it he becomes restless and develops symptoms of acute illness that are relieved only by the drug.

Drives with unspecified physiological correlates

Among the motives readily studied with animals are three whose physiological correlates are not readily specified, though they operate very much as if they were "drives" in the same sense as the motives just considered. These are *activity, manipulation,* and *curiosity* drives. An animal that has been deprived of the opportunity for movement will seek to engage in activity for its own sake (Hill, 1956); monkeys given the opportunity to take mechanical equipment apart will do it without any evident reward other than the satisfaction of some sort of manipulation drive (Harlow, Harlow, and Meyer, 1950) (see Figure 5-4); and much animal behavior can be shown to be motivated by curiosity (Butler, 1953; Berlyne, 1955).

Berlyne (1960) has recently summarized the work on exploration and curiosity. He finds it convenient to classify exploratory behavior into three kinds: *orienting responses, locomotor exploration,* and *investigatory responses.*

The orienting reaction has been given particular attention by Russian investigators, e.g., Sokolov (1960). When a novel or striking stimulus appears, the organism responds by changes in posture and by sense-organ adjustments that have widespread physiological consequences permeating the organism. The reaction tends to disappear gradually if the novel stimulus is presented repeatedly at intervals of a few seconds or a few minutes.

The determinants of the orienting reaction are those we associate with attention: intensity, color, novelty, surprisingness, complexity. For example, when Berlyne (1958) showed the patterns of Figure 5-5 to 3- to 9-months-old infants, the eyes were

[1] If salt "dilutes" water, can anything "concentrate" it? Yes: water is more thirst-quenching per unit amount if it is cold or slightly acid (Deutsch).

much more likely to be turned first to the patterns on the right.

Locomotor exploration refers to the tendency for animals when in a new place to run about, investigating and inspecting the environment: the kind of behavior folklore attributes to the housecat when taken to a new house. Such behavior is readily demonstrated in the laboratory. For example, hungry rats well-trained through 80 trials to select an arm of a Y-shaped maze for food reward selected a new arm on the 81st trial when this opportunity for exploration was opened to them (Thiessen and McGaugh, 1958). When the rear walls of otherwise empty goal boxes at the end of a runway contained either familiar or novel visual figures, rats spent more of the time in the goal box exploring the novel figures rather than the familiar ones (Berlyne and Slater, 1957).

By investigatory responses, Berlyne means those that involve some sort of manipulation that changes the unfamiliar object: picking it up, tearing it apart, and so on. A laboratory equivalent is provided by experiments in which one response gives the organism information about something else, as in the following experiment with chimpanzees (Kelleher, 1958). By pressing one key, the chimpanzee could find out if a second key would deliver food. If pressing the first key resulted in a red light, then the second key would lead to food. If a blue light resulted, then the second key would not produce food. The chimpanzee learned to use the investigatory information from the first key to determine whether or not to press the second one.

Piaget has made a number of observations on children, bearing on investigatory responses early in life. Thus within the first few months of life the human infant learns to pull a string to activate a hanging rattle— a form of manipulation that must be considered merely entertaining. Between five and seven months the infant will remove a cloth covering its face, anticipating the

H. F. Harlow

5-4

Manipulation drive

The monkey takes the latches apart, even though there is no "incentive" or "reward" except that deriving from the manipulation itself.

5-5

Complexity and curiosity

Three- to nine-month-old infants looked first at the right-hand figures, presumably because they were more complex. (Berlyne, 1958, as reproduced in Berlyne, 1960, p. 100)

5-6

Activity measurement

Lafayette Instrument Co.

In the activity cage the distance that the rat runs is recorded by a revolving drum.

peekaboo game. At eight to ten months the infant will begin to look for things behind or beneath other things. By eleven months he will "experiment" with things, varying the reaction each time (Piaget, 1952). Thus inquisitive behavior is a dependable characteristic of the growing child.

The explanation of the kinds of behavior discussed here that is most coherent with that used in describing hunger and thirst is that the lack of activity, and the limitation of opportunity to explore, produces a kind of boredom, that is, a sort of deficiency which the organism seeks to overcome. The deficiency must not be simply a state of understimulation, however, or we would expect the organism to be quiescent or to sleep; apparently the restriction of activity leads eventually to a state of arousal that induces the organism to do something about it, just as the polar bear, restricted to his cage, engages in his endless march back and forth in the cage.

Measuring drives

A good deal of ingenuity has been used in finding ways of measuring drives, since psychologists often want to know the "drive level" in order to relate it to other behavior, such as learning.

We may consider four such methods: measures of general activity level, the rate of performing learned acts, the obstruction method, and the choice method.

5-7

Obstruction box (floor plan)

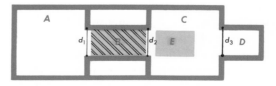

A, entrance compartment; B, charged grill giving access to C and D, the incentive compartment. A release plate E opens a door (d_3) which permits access to an incentive in D. Other doors (d_1 and d_2) are manually operated. (After Warden, 1931)

1. *Measures of general activity level.* It is assumed that heightened drive leads to restlessness, so that restless behavior will increase as drive increases. Thus speed of running in an activity cage (Figure 5-6) can be related to hours of food deprivation. Another form of activity measurement is that of the living cage suspended on springs with markers, so that amount of restless activity is recorded.

It has been found that these measures, while useful, have to be used with some sophistication. For example, the home cage activity of unfed rats is not higher than that of well-fed rats *unless* some external source of stimulation is provided, in which case the differences become marked (Campbell and Sheffield, 1953).

2. *Rate of performing learned acts.* If a rat has learned to press a lever in order to receive a food pellet, but the pellets come only occasionally, the rat will press the lever more rapidly when hungry. Thus rate of lever-pressing may be used as a measure of drive (Skinner, 1938). Alternate behavior measures are the delay of starting a run down an alley (latency of response) or the running speed itself (Fredenburg, 1956). Care has to be taken not to depend upon one measure only. Thus rate of lever-pressing and amount of water ingested may not be equivalent as measures of the thirst drive (Miller, 1961).

3. *Overcoming an obstruction.* A number of years ago a method of drive measurement was devised in which drive strength could be assessed by seeing how much punishment the organism would take in order to satisfy the drive. An *obstruction box* (Figure 5-7) provided a passageway with a grid floor through which the animal received a shock in crossing. The aroused animal was placed at the starting point and allowed to run across the uncharged grid to the chamber in which the goal-object (food, water, etc.) was placed. Then, with the shock turned on, a record was kept of the number of crossings that the animal would make in a given 20-minute period.

4. *The choice method.* Occasionally more than one drive is active at a time. In the case of two simultaneously aroused drives the relative strengths of the drives may be determined by permitting the animal to choose one goal-object if he turns in one direction, another goal-object if he turns in the other direction. This method, also developed a number of years ago (Tsai, 1925), has had little recent use.

Of the four methods, the most used today are the first two, in one or another variation. The first method relies on the general restlessness associated with heightened drive; the second depends upon the intensification of a well-learned act under appropriate drive.

Social Motives: Drives and Dispositions

Some of the motives that are the basis of social life are just as "physiological" or "biological" in origins as hunger and thirst. We shall see this in relation to sex and maternal behavior particularly, although innate bases may exist for other motives as well. The social motives as we see them in man, however, are so strongly affected by learning that the vocabulary of drive becomes somewhat forced in application to them. In order not to prejudge the issue of origins, we shall use the more neutral expression "motivational disposition" to refer to persistent motives when their origin in specific drives is remote or unclear; when these motivational dispositions are aroused, we shall speak of "aroused motives" rather than of drives.

Maternal drive

A mother rat is strongly motivated to care for her newborn offspring. She will return them to the nest if they are placed out-

Estrus cycle and activity

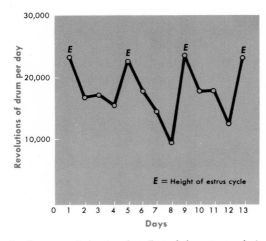

Specimen record showing the effect of the estrus cycle in the female rat. Note that activity tends to be at its maximum near the peak of estrus. (After Wang, 1923)

side it. If she is separated from them, she will overcome barriers and suffer pain in order to reach them.

The physiological states that activate this maternal behavior are complex. The hormone *prolactin,* associated with milk secretion, is one influence, for if it is injected into virgin female rats or even into males, they begin to build nests and take care of young rats as a mother does. Nest-building among rats appears to be in part regulated by temperature. The hormonal condition may reduce the body temperature, and the mother rat perhaps builds a nest not so much because of the needs of her young as to make herself comfortable.

Although the human mother shares with the lower animals the bodily changes associated with pregnancy and lactation as well as some aspects of maternal drive, her care of children differs from culture to culture and is largely regulated by learning. It is a general rule that human motives can never be fully explained on the basis of physiological influences alone.

Sex

Sex as a Drive. The cycle of sexual receptivity in female animals, known as the *estrus* cycle, demonstrates the influence of sex hormones upon sex drive. The estrus cycle in the rat is between four and five days in length. Every fourth or fifth day of her life the mature female rat is in the receptive state known as *estrus,* or, as we say colloquially, she is *in heat.*

The sexually aroused state in the female rat leads to tension and restless activity, just as do hunger and thirst drives. An illustration of the increase in rate of a female rat's running in an activity cage during estrus is given in Figure 5-8. At the height of estrus the female rat is sexually receptive as well as physically active; when placed with a male rat, she actively seeks copulation by presenting herself appropriately.

Sexual receptivity and appropriate mating behavior can be made to appear (or reappear) in female rats through the injection of ovarian hormones. If young female rats receive injections of ovarian hormones, they develop mature mating patterns well in advance of the time when such patterns would normally appear. Mature female rats whose sexual activity has ceased after removal of the ovaries will again engage in normal sexual behavior if treated with ovarian hormones. Mating patterns appear whether the ovaries were removed before or after sexual maturity had been reached.

Immature male rats engage in incomplete sexual behavior while they are still incapable of complete copulation. In this they differ from young female rats, which do not indulge in sexual behavior until they are sexually mature. Castration does not completely abolish mating behavior in the male as it does in the female. This persistence of sexual behavior of the castrated adult male contrasts with the immediate cessation of sexual responsiveness in the female after loss of the ovaries (Beach, 1944).

These studies suffice to indicate the important role played by hormones in the sexual behavior of lower animals. There is a hint, however, in the conduct of the castrated adult male rat, of controls other than hormones. Hormonal control, although significant, is less central in sexual behavior among higher animals, including primates and man (Beach, 1956).

The results of castration on human beings are variable. In a high proportion of women whose ovaries have been surgically removed sexual desire and capacity are little changed. While castration of the male may result in gradual diminution of sexual interest, sex drive and the capacity for sexual intercourse may persist undiminished for several decades.

Sex as a Motivational Disposition. To treat sex merely as a physiological drive, capable of giving pleasure or releasing tension, would be to ignore its pervasive influence in relation to the institutions of culture. The fundamental social institution, the family, is based upon a sexual union in which, under ideal conditions, an enduring relationship of affection binds the mates together and gives them both a feeling of security. The sexual partner becomes highly prized, and jealousy of rivals (in cultures like ours) becomes motivationally important. The triangle theme is one of the powerful themes in literature. In the social aspects of sex we have a clear illustration of a motive with a physiological basis in sex drive, yet with a central role in the development of acquired social behavior.

The pervasive nature of sexual motivation has been dramatized in the theories of Sigmund Freud. His theories have emphasized the many derivatives of sex in dream symbols, in art, in religion, and in many forms of social behavior not manifestly sexual. While these theories have been subject to criticism in detail, the general import of their teaching—that sexual motivation may appear in various disguises—can scarcely be questioned.

Dependency and affiliation

A number of motivational dispositions clearly involve relationships with other members of the species. All animals display a sex drive, and mammals a maternal drive. But not all animals band together in groups, and their aggressive reactions to each other and to animals of other species differ. Thus the *affiliative motives* form an important group within the larger grouping of social motives. Affiliative behavior takes various forms from the extreme dependency of the infant on the mother, through ordinary companionship and friendship, to the loyalty and devotion of happily married couples.

As representative of attempts to measure affiliative motives we may consider two studies, one of young children and one of college students under experimental arousal.

1. *Sources of dependent behavior in young children.* Some theorists have held that the mother's rewarding role in feeding causes the infant to depend on her and thereby gives rise to the dependency motive. In an attempt to test this assumption, 40 preschool children were studied. First an attempt was made to determine their present disposition to show dependent behavior when the opportunity presented itself.

TABLE **5-2**

Correlations between infancy experiences and dependent behavior in preschool

Infancy experiences	Correlations with total dependency measures *	
	GIRLS	BOYS
Self-demand feeding	−.38	−.08
Weaning severity	.54	.40

SOURCE: Sears and others, 1953.

* With the number of children (*N*) between 18 and 21 in the different comparisons, correlations must reach at least .35 to approach significance.

TABLE 5-3

Relationship between anxiety and the affiliative tendency among college women *

Experimental manipulation	Waiting conditions chosen			
	TOGETHER	DON'T CARE	ALONE	TOTAL
High anxiety	20	9	3	32
Low anxiety	10	18	2	30

SOURCE: Schachter (1959), p. 18.

* The probability, *P*, is .05 that the obtained differences might have been found even though no differences existed. This convention will be followed with other probability statements throughout the text. For explanation see Chapter 13.

Teachers rated their dependency, and research workers derived dependency scores based on observing the reactions of the children to other children and to the teacher in the nursery school, and under controlled conditions in which the child played with dolls representing his family. A single dependency score was arrived at, best characterizing the child at the nursery school age.

These same children received separate ratings on infancy experiences, based upon interviews with their mothers. Scales were designed to get at *nurturance* (i.e., the mother's care in feeding), and *frustration* (i.e., the infant's helplessness in the face of insoluble problems). The feeding practices of the mothers who used the self-demand schedule were scored as high nurturance, those based on rigidly scheduled feeding as low nurturance. The abruptness and harshness of weaning determined the score on feeding frustration. The resulting correlations between infant experiences and later dependent behavior are given in Table 5-2.

Contrary to initial expectations, the most carefully nurtured children (on the self-demand schedule) showed *less* dependent behavior than those strictly scheduled. Apparently feeding frustration is the variable that results in later dependent behavior, if we interpret rigid scheduling as well as severe weaning as being frustrating (Sears and others, 1953, 1957).

In view of the theory that the mother's rewarding role in feeding causes the infant to depend on her, thereby giving rise to the dependency motive, the somewhat unexpected result of the foregoing experiment calls for explanation. In order to survive at all, the infant must have his basic needs met. Hence *all* infants have their hunger drives satisfied in a social context, and they all develop a normal amount of dependency motive. If the mother's behavior in scheduling or weaning produces frustration, something happens in addition to this normal drive satisfaction. The infant's troubled and helpless protests are eventually responded to by the mother, so that she probably gives *additional* satisfaction to dependent forms of behavior. In any case, the infant who has experienced a great deal of frustration with accompanying feelings of helplessness is the one who later on turns to others for support.

2. Affiliative behavior when anxiety is aroused. Schachter (1959) placed college students in a situation that they saw as threatening. They were then asked to wait for a later stage in the experiment. The experimental problem was to find background factors in the individuals that would predict whether or not they would prefer to wait alone or with others. It was assumed that those who wished to have company in the threatening situation had stronger affiliative tendencies.

In one of these studies, university women were shown, as part of an experiment, some forbidding-looking apparatus which they were allowed to believe could deliver severe electric shocks. Another group, similarly reporting for an experiment, were shown nothing threatening and were assured that the experimental procedures were mild and nonpainful. When both groups were given

the choice of waiting alone or waiting together, a larger proportion of the threatened
group preferred to wait together (Table
5-3). The general interpretation is that
the more threatened ones turned to company
because affiliative needs were aroused. (In
the end, neither group had to undergo any
painful experiences.)

Another analysis of the same kind of behavior showed that some individuals, under
threat of pain, were more eager to have
company than others. If only children and
first-born children were separated from the
later-born ones, it was found that the only
and first-born children showed the higher
tendencies toward affiliation in this situation. Schachter interprets this to mean that
the first-born child probably experienced
more adult responsiveness to his uneasiness
in early childhood than later-born children,
whom parents may take more for granted.
This explanation is, however, conjectural.

These studies illustrate two things about
the affiliative motive. First, its expression
may be influenced by early childhood experiences (and thus may be related to birth
order). Second, its expression is enhanced
under threat, so that those who do very well
alone under ordinary circumstances will
seek companionship when their anxieties
are raised.

These illustrations of attempts to bring
dependent or affiliative tendencies under
experimental observation do not, of course,
exhaust the kinds of things men do in seeking companionship of other people or in
participating in group life. They indicate,
however, that it is possible to make some
measurements even in a field as complex
as this, with the kinds of results that will
eventually add up to a science of human
motives.

Dominance and submission

Dominance status among animals has
been much studied. Barnyard hens establish
a "pecking order," so that one hen has peck-

ing rights over most of the others. Hens
of lower rank have pecking rights over those
beneath them, while the least dominant may
be pecked by all the rest (Schjelderup-
Ebbe, 1935). Administration of male hormone raises the status of low-ranking hens,
which become more aggressive. Once they
have established a new status, that status
is maintained even though the hormones are
no longer provided (Allee, Collias, and
Lutherman, 1939). Here we see an interplay between hormones and acquired motives even in the barnyard.

Social hierarchies are common among
many animal groups. A herd of cows establishes a standard status order, and they return from the pasture to the barn in that
order. It is not only at diplomatic banquets
that rank is respected! If social animals generally establish hierarchies, it is evident that
either innate tendencies or the requirements
of group life (or both) make such systems
arise naturally.

When the animal pairs are male and female, the male is usually the dominant
member. Such observations give plausibility
to the naturalness of the aggressive role for
the male and the naturalness of the submissive role for the female. It does not follow
that one role is originally more need-satisfying than the other; rather, when the pattern of dominance and submission has been
established, each knows his role and may
derive satisfaction from playing the appropriate part. However, male dominance is not
invariable among animals; even in the species in which the male usually dominates,
the female may become dominant when
sexually receptive or when caring for young.
For example, a normally dominant male
chimpanzee permits a sexually receptive female to control a food-getting situation. He
sits idly by, with saliva dripping from his
lips, waiting until she has finished before he
begins to eat what remains (Yerkes, 1940).

Dominance relationships between two female chimpanzees, one normally dominant
and the other submissive, may change when

5-9

Natural enemies at peace

These cats and rats live in the same cage and eat from the same dish. This raises the question of the nature of instinctive behavior.

one is in estrus. The normally dominant one when in estrus may grant food rights to the submissive one. The normally submissive one when in estrus may become dominant. Estrus reverses the pattern for both members of the pair (Nowlis, 1942).

Because of the usual predictability of the male-female dominance pattern, as well as its change with hormonal control, one senses its continuity with other forms of physiologically controlled behavior. Whether or not this is sufficient to provide a biological basis for man's usually dominant relation to woman in Western culture is, of course, a matter of speculation. At least some parallels can be found in nature.

Aggression

The problem of human cruelty is a baffling one, but the history of human behavior abounds with man-imposed suffering upon other men. In a search for biological origins, one looks for the nature of aggression in animals. **By** *aggression* we mean violent, attacking, destructive behavior that results in pain to the victim.

It is sometimes difficult to distinguish between aggressive behavior that is merely behavior in the service of another motive and aggressive behavior that serves the motive of aggression, that is, the intent to injure or pain another. Normal food-gathering on the part of a meat-eating animal is necessarily aggressive (unless the animal is a carrion-eater), but this does not necessarily serve an aggressive motive. When a cat appears to have satisfaction in playing with a half-dead bird or mouse, one is more inclined to assign some motive other than hunger, or when animals kill food that they do not eat there seems to be some sort of aggressive tendency operating. Animals that appear to enjoy fighting each other (e.g., fighting cocks) seem to exhibit nearly pure aggression, though in nature this behavior probably serves other motives, such as sex rights over the females.

In any case, through the evolutionary process, some animals are better equipped for aggression than others. This includes not only such aggressive equipment as claws and fangs, but internal hormones that favor anger over fear (see distinction between adrenalin and noradrenalin in the next chapter). Thus the lion is by nature aggressive and the rabbit is by nature timid. Even a fighting animal such as the Siamese fighting fish can be made gentle by the administering of appropriate drugs (Abramson and Evans, 1954).

The fact that nature is "red in tooth and claw" gives an evolutionary basis for man's potential aggressiveness, and it may explain why he is capable of cruel and destructive behavior. Such an evolutionary history is no more a *justification* for his aggressiveness, however, than hunger is a justification for stealing just because a fox steals chickens when hungry. The study of motivated behavior in lower animals often helps us to understand man's behavior, but it does not in itself tell us how man can control what he does.

We may appropriately look for the origins of human aggression in infancy. It is partly related, no doubt, to the need for activity. A growing child is active, and activity will sooner or later lead the child to destroy something or to injure someone. At that point adults will judge his behavior as aggressive, although it may not yet have any hostile quality in it. In the same study referred to in relation to dependency, Sears and others (1953) also studied aggression. They found, as one might expect, a high correlation between the general activity level and aggression as rated by teachers: .86 for boys and .66 for girls. From these figures alone it is not possible to tell which is cause and which is effect. An active child may stumble into aggressive acts; an aggressive child may become active in expressing his aggression.

A suggestion, deriving from Freud and widely accepted by others, is that aggression is one of the consequences of frustration (Dollard and others, 1939). The measures used by Sears and others (1953) of experienced frustration in early infancy did not correlate significantly with rated or observed aggressive activity in preschool. These authors suggest that the learning involved in true hostile aggression (making another person experience pain) develops slowly. The kinds of aggression shown by the very young infant are mere obstacle-removing activities, often violent or strenuous, but not really oriented toward a goal response of inflicting pain upon another. If this suggestion is correct, the true motive for aggression develops late and is not directly correlated with the experiences of very early infancy.

If we accept a slow development of the aggressive motive, we might expect a correlation with later parental encouragement of, or punishment of, aggression. Davis and

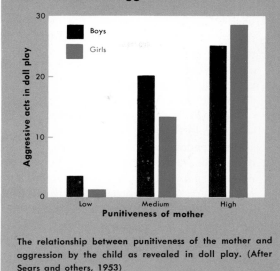

5-10

Punishment and aggression

The relationship between punitiveness of the mother and aggression by the child as revealed in doll play. (After Sears and others, 1953)

Dollard (1940) studied the behavior of Negro children raised in different social classes. It was very clear that among most of these children aggressive behavior was often rewarded by the parents, and that where the behavior was rewarded, the amount of aggression increased.

Punishment of aggression also has its consequences. A parent who punishes a child excessively tends to set up in the child some sort of wish to punish in return. This is clearly revealed in the doll play of children grouped according to the punitiveness of their mothers (Figure 5-10). The more punitive the mother, the more aggressive are the acts shown in doll play.

In later studies, aggression was measured in 5-year-old children and again when they were 12 (Sears, 1961). Among the findings was a difference in the *anxiety about aggression* shown by the 12-year-old boys compared with the girls. Boys who have conformed to parental demands in a love-oriented home, with a tight control of aggression, tend to develop anxiety over their own tendencies toward aggressive behavior. Most girls show less tendency toward aggression than boys, but even so they show more anxiety about aggression. As noted on p. 88, Sears believes that aggression anxiety in girls mounts when they are permitted unladylike aggression in childhood, and are thrown into conflicts over aggressive behavior as they grow older and adopt the feminine role.

However the aggression comes about, some children and some adults develop strong tendencies to injure themselves or others. The extreme forms have been given names: *sadism* for the extreme motive to pain others, and *masochism* for the extreme motive to inflict pain upon oneself. In some forms of sadism and masochism the satisfaction to the aggressive person appears to be sexual in nature. This fact merely illustrates how the strands from different motivational dispositions become intertwined.

Measuring motivational dispositions

If we say that one person acts as he does because he has high achievement motive, another because his need for affiliation is high, a third because he seeks power, these statements can have scientific validity only if the motives can be scaled in some way that specifies the intensity in which they are aroused for this person compared to another, when the circumstances of arousal are as alike as possible. A number of methods have been developed for estimating how the motives operate for the individual; some of these have been illustrated in the foregoing account. Now we are ready for a summary of methods.

1. *Behavioral observation and case study.* By studying how the individual confronts the variety of situations that face him in real life, an observer or interviewer can make certain inferences about the various motives operating and their importance to the individual. This method was used in an extensive study by Frenkel-Brunswik (1942). Selecting eight of the psychogenic needs proposed by Murray (1938), and adding a ninth,[2] she had three adults, familiar with the 40 adolescent boys and 46 adolescent girls in the study, rate each of them on each of the motives. The resulting ratings were then compared, and motive interrelationships studied. She found, for example, a negative correlation between ratings of abasement and ratings on recognition and dominance.

2. *Self-reports.* Self-reports can take various forms. One method used is that of the personality inventory, in which the subject replies to questions about himself. Edwards (1954) constructed a test called the Edwards Personal Preference Schedule, in which the items composing the test were selected to represent 16 of Murray's needs. The subject has to make a choice between two statements, one representing one need, the other representing another; he thus indicates which of the needs have higher priority for him. The scores on each of the 16 needs can be intercorrelated, just as the ratings were in the Frenkel-Brunswik study. Edwards found, for example, a positive correlation ($r = .46$) between the need for affiliation and the need for nurturance (to take care of someone), and a negative correlation ($r = -.36$) between the need for nurturance and the need for autonomy. These results, which were to be expected, serve merely to indicate how such an instrument can be used.

3. *Imaginative productions.* What one wants is often expressed in one's daydreams and in fantasy productions of other kinds. It is possible to secure specimens of imaginative productions in various ways: through "doodles," stories told in response to pictures, story-completion tests, and so

[2] The nine needs rated were (1) autonomy, (2) social acceptance, (3) achievement, (4) recognition, (5) abasement, (6) aggression, (7) succorance (to be taken care of), (8) dominance, and (9) escape.

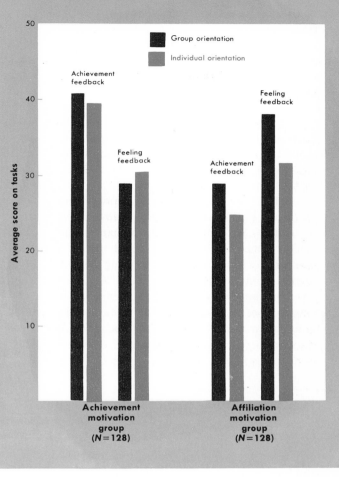

5-11

Effect of appropriate motivation on performance

For the groups high in achievement motivation, arousal of this motive ("achievement feedback") leads to superior performance; for those high in affiliation, its arousal ("feeling feedback") leads to superior performance. The pattern holds regardless of whether the task orientation is group or individual. (Plotted from the data of French, 1958)

on. As we shall see in the later discussion of achievement motives (pp. 144-46), the analysis of imaginative productions has proved to be a fertile method.

4. *Experimental arousal of motives.* The assumptions of the preceding methods are that the circumstances under which the observations are made are arousal situations. That is, observation of actual behavior in a club meeting of adolescents should presumably reveal motives in action; a subject making choices of statements of preference presumably pictures himself making some such choices in reality; when stories are told in response to pictures, the pictures themselves arouse fantasies of real opportunities for motivated action. These assumptions are, however, simply implied, and it

is no doubt advantageous to observe motivated behavior when the conditions of arousal are better known.

As one example of such studies, French (1958) selected two groups of subjects, 128 found to be high in achievement motivation but low in affiliation and 128 high in affiliation motivation but low in achievement motivation on the basis of a test she had earlier devised. Both groups were set the same task, in which a story had to be assembled from phrases or short sentences printed on separate cards. The subjects had to get information from others to complete the story, but were not permitted to show each other their cards. The members of each group worked in teams of four, with each team given either a "group" orientation, focused on achieving the one best solution, or an "individual" orientation, which encouraged individual versions of the story. The experimenter interrupted the task twice to record scores and also to give a progress report, or "feedback," on how well the subject was doing. One kind of feedback emphasized achievement: "This team is working very efficiently." The other feedback was one of "feeling": "This team works very well together." The results (Figure 5-11) were in the direction predicted, the group performance of the achievement-motivated subjects being higher with achievement feedback than with feeling feedback, while the affiliation group scored higher with feeling feedback. This held whether the orientation of the teams was "group" or "individual." Thus when conditions of arousal fit with the motivational disposition, the task performance is superior.

Ego-Integrative Motives

Motives built around the self

The problems of human motivation pervade all of psychology, so that they cannot all be dealt with adequately in a single chapter. We need to consider a good deal more about emotion, perception, learning, and individuality before we are prepared to deal with the concept of the self and all that it implies; this treatment will be found in later chapters.

Here, however, we must note that various writers find some master motive related to the self as of primary importance in understanding human conduct. This master motive goes by various names, such as self-actualization (Goldstein, 1939; Maslow, 1954), self-expansion (Angyal, 1941), self-consistency (Lecky, 1945), competence (White, 1960). Because these theorists disagree among themselves as to the one master motive, we are on safer grounds to think

of a group of *ego-integrative* motives, that is, motives with some sort of self-reference. Included in a catalogue of the ego-integrative motives would be the values by which a man guides his choices, including his esthetic and religious preferences, and, in some sense, his philosophy of life. Rather than deal with these larger issues at this time, we shall use achievement motivation as an illustration of how one aspect of self-related motives lends itself to study. The desire to achieve and to avoid failure is one avenue toward self-respect in our culture. While its importance will vary from one culture to another, some mastery over the environment, beyond the needs for survival, probably characterizes all human cultures. The presence of artistic creations, even in the caves of early man, shows that some form of self-expression, beyond mere sustenance and group survival, has had an age-old appeal to man.

Achievement motivation

If man is a social animal (and therefore affiliative), he is also a doer, and all observers have found a place for some sort of achievement motive, whether in the form of an "instinct of workmanship" or in the desire to master nature and other men. While achievement has social aspects, it has so much to do with the way in which a person sees himself that we have classed it among the ego-integrative motives.

McClelland and his associates (1953) have developed a method by which fantasy productions are used for measuring achievement motivation. The following account illustrates the method.

The experimenter showed male college students three pictures with the instructions to write brief 5-minute stories about each. The pictures suggested a work situation (two men working at a machine), a study situation (a boy seated at a desk with a book in front of him), and a father-son situation. The stories were written around the following four questions printed on the answer sheet: "What is happening?" "What has led up to this situation?" "What is being thought?" "What will happen?"

The stories were examined for notions emphasizing the importance of achievement, of getting things done, of success. Subjects who wrote into their stories many such ideas were scored as having a high motive for achievement, those with few such ideas a low one. There were 19 in the high group and 21 in the low group.

Following this test the experimenter asked the subjects to work on a 20-minute scrambled-words test, in which they had to rearrange an anagram such as WTSE into a meaningful word such as WEST. Results for those high and low in achievement motive are given in Figure 5-12. Similar results were found for problems in addition, with output higher for those with strong achievement motivation. Evidently the results in the test of fantasy did measure a motive having to do with success in these laboratory tasks (Lowell, 1950, as reported by McClelland, 1955).

Having shown their success in measuring at least some aspects of the achievement motive through this and related experiments, McClelland and his associates attempted to discover the origins of the motive in childhood. The following statements are typical of their results:

1. In those American Indian cultures whose folklore lays stress on achievement, great emphasis is placed in childhood on independence training (McClelland and Friedman, 1952). While their results are questioned by Child, Storm, and Veroff (1958), these later investigators found a positive relationship between emphasis on achievement in early training and the achievement-orientation of the adult culture.

2. American college men scoring high on achievement motive tend to rate their parents (especially their fathers) as un-

5-12

Achievement motivation and performance

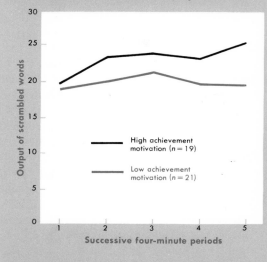

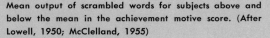

Mean output of scrambled words for subjects above and below the mean in the achievement motive score. (After Lowell, 1950; McClelland, 1955)

friendly, unhelpful, and unsuccessful (McClelland, 1951).

3. Mothers of high-achievement children tend to make demands for achievement at earlier ages than do mothers of low-achievement children (Winterbottom, 1953).

In summary, it appears that high achievement motivation in adults is related to the severity of independence training in childhood. The child who is forced to be on his own early develops a high motivation toward accomplishment.

What is the meaning of a moderately low score on achievement motivation as revealed in fantasy? Is it laziness, laxness, a desire to loaf? There is some evidence that a low score does not negate a concern for success, but rather that the fear of failure is so great as to inhibit the risk of raising sights too high. That is, by not aiming very high, the individual reduces the chance of failure. Some children who have experienced repeated failure in school tend to stop trying, thereby avoiding the experience of defeat (P. S. Sears, 1940).

Evidence on the different orientation of those with moderate achievement motivation from those with high achievement motivation came from an experiment by Atkinson (1953) on the memory for completed and incompleted tasks, the latter having been interrupted while the subject was still working at them. Eighty-three male students participated in the experiments. It had been found in other experiments that the more important such tasks are to the subject, the more likely he is to remember the *incompleted* tasks beyond those completed. (Memory for completed and incompleted tasks will be considered again in the text in Chapter 10.) Subjects with high achievement motivation were especially prone to remember the interrupted tasks, as though the tasks represented a challenge to them and were therefore easy to recall. For the subjects of moderate achievement motivation (those in the middle third of the group), the results were reversed: as the tasks increased in importance they tended to remember more of the *completed* tasks than the incompleted ones. For them the incompleted tasks appeared to be a threat and were therefore forgotten. While this evidence is somewhat indirect, the interpretation that those with moderate achievement scores are security-oriented and fearful of failure conforms to the interpretation of related experiments (McClelland and Liberman, 1949).

The achievement motive is deeply rooted in our culture. To say that a person is productive and successful is to give him high praise. It is no wonder that we find thoughts of accomplishment and success in the fantasies of American college students.

Goals, purposes, and plans

When an individual knows what he wants, knows the effort that will be involved in overcoming obstacles along the way, and knows what satisfaction the end state will bring, he can put his goals into words. If there are risks, he is prepared to face them. Such behavior is clearly *purposeful,* in that an intention is carried out according to an announced goal. The student who enters college to train himself to become an engineer knows in general what the profession of engineering is and what courses he must pursue in order to achieve his goal. He may see mathematics as an obstacle to overcome, but he assumes the risk.

For many years psychologists have avoided the term *will* to refer to such purposeful action to which the person is committed, although nonpsychologists have continued to use the word and seem to feel that they know what it stands for. The objections to the concept of will by psychologists are three: (1) it implies some entity or thing that controls action, (2) it has philosophical implications with respect to the old issue of freedom versus determinism, and (3) it gets involved in certain legal problems concerned with responsibility for criminal acts. In order not to get entangled in these problems, psychologists have usually treated the notions covered by "will" under other names, such as motivation, decision-making, and conflict-resolution. As psychologists have become less timid about the scientific status of psychology, some of these older terms have found their way back into psychology, because something was lost in rejecting them.[3] The term "will" has been used freely in a recent book (Miller, Galanter, and Pribram, 1960), though the treatment is largely in terms of "plans," a word without the historical quarrels associated with "will."

There is no doubt that an individual can make *plans* and carry them out. He knows what he wants to do, where he wants to be at a particular time, and he arranges things

[3] Another such term is "self," long avoided by psychologists but now again in use.

so that he gets there.[4] He can leave word where he can be found, and (except for unforeseeable circumstances) there is often a high probability that the plan will materialize. By a person of "strong will" we mean one who can adopt a plan and commit himself so firmly to it that he will show resistance to distractions and resourcefulness in finding ways to continue toward the intended goal. A person of "weak will" is one who is unable to stick to a plan, no matter how clearly he may be able to formulate it; he gives up easily in the face of obstacles or distractions. There is no deep philosophical issue here; the matter is complicated, but does not lie outside of empirical science. People differ in their capacities to announce and fulfill plans just as they differ in their capacities to solve intellectual problems or to perform acts of skill.

Plans are of various kinds and lengths, including not only the seeking of certain goals but also *stop-plans* to avoid fatigue or danger. A stop-plan, for example, is not taking too many cups of coffee before retiring, or determining to leave the card game in order to have enough sleep. The more that a person is able to formulate plans, even short-term ones, and carry them out, the more sense of self-control he develops. Thus plan-behavior is relevant to ego-integration.

CRITICAL DISCUSSION
Freedom vs. determinism

When the concept of will is reintroduced into psychology, the issue of freedom versus determinism has to be faced whether or not it is resolved. The deterministic position is that all events are caused by energy configurations operating upon structures, just as the movements of the sun, stars, and planets are not capricious but are regulated by the immutable laws of universal gravitation. While causes are very complex and not fully knowable, we can always detect causal strands that make the theory of determinism plausible. When John "chooses" to buy a cigar and Bob "chooses" not to smoke, the real "choice" was determined long ago in the way they were brought up, the fact that John's father, with whom he identifies, smokes, while Bob's father does not, and so on. According to the determinist, neither could have behaved any differently from the way he actually behaved. The believer in freedom, on the other hand, thinks that human choices really matter and that things would be different had not a human will intervened. This is a very subtle problem. An individual may have been an agent in the course of events without necessarily having been a free agent. For example, he might have been walking along as a baby fell out of a window and, simply by his presence, have broken the baby's fall so that he saved the baby's life without any initiative on his part. If he had seen the baby about to fall and had run to catch it, he would have taken some initiative, but the determinist asks: "Could he have done otherwise?" Not everyone would have been as alert and quick, to be sure, so it is to his credit that he was, but could *this* individual, given all the influences that have affected him up to this moment, have done anything other than what he did? Was his "alertness" as determined as his "presence" at the time? It is quite clear that we can never get a scientific answer to that question; all we can know is what he *did* do, not what he *might* have done. The difficulty of this example shows how a determinist can hold to his position that all acts are a result of the play of forces at the time, without any real influence from the subject's intentions. Such intentions as exist, according to the determinist, also reflect the play of inevitable forces.

This is an old problem within philosophy, and the fact that a determinist cannot be challenged on empirical grounds, since the past can never be repeated, does not settle the problem. However, the determinist *can* be challenged on the prediction of the future. If the future were strictly predictable, then

---

[4] Miller, Galanter, and Pribram (1960) use the word "Image" to refer to the organized knowledge and values that serve as the occasion for a "Plan." Thus the intended goal is part of the Image, while the steps along the way are part of the Plan. We shall not follow their interesting theoretical treatment further.

determinism would be clearly established. Since the predictability of the future is limited, however, any assertion that determinism is true must be as much an act of faith as an assertion to the contrary. Because a psychologist, as such, is not concerned with such acts of faith, he does well to leave the issue of freedom versus determinism an open one.

The problems of human intentions and their fulfillment according to plans, of decision-making on the basis of adequate (or inadequate) information, of the capacity to resist distractions once a plan is embarked upon—these are problems of human willing and effort that are genuine, realistic, and empirical, and do not depend upon a resolution of the freedom-determinism problem.

One difficulty of the freedom-determinism issue is that it suggests an absolute choice: man is either free or not. The choice is not that simple. There are surely areas in which human behavior is determined very largely by the interaction of physiological processes and environmental factors (such as food, water, air), by prior learning, by socialization in childhood. Psychology seeks to find lawfulness in behavior wherever it can be found; such lawfulness implies some measure of determinism, but not necessarily an absolute determinism. Science does not require such absolutes.

Unconscious motives

The belief that man is a rational animal who makes his plans with foresight is appealing and to some degree true, but it is an incomplete statement of man's nature. Man is also irrational; he is often driven by impulses of which he is unaware or that he would prefer to deny, and he often does things that in his more rational moments he would prefer not to have done. Yet these controls are part of his "nature," and in that sense part of his "self." We cannot give a full account of ego-integrative motives without attention to unconscious motives.

While literary men long recognized some unconscious controls over human conduct, it remained for Freud to call to the attention of the public the powerful role of unconscious motives in human behavior. He pointed to several forms of behavior through which unconscious motives express themselves:

1. The dreamer often expresses in his dreams wishes of which he is unaware.
2. Unconscious mannerisms and slips of speech "let the cat out of the bag" and reveal hidden motives.
3. Symptoms of illness (especially the symptoms of neurotic illnesses) often can be shown to serve the unconscious needs of the person.

Following Freud's lead, most psychologists now accept the existence of unconscious motives, although they differ from one another in their ways of talking about them.

Under ordinary circumstances no sharp line divides conscious from unconscious motives; perhaps it would be wisest to say that all motives have both a conscious and an unconscious component. A young man may fall in love with a young woman partly because she is in reality the attractive person he believes her to be (the conscious aspect) and partly because something about her, unknown to him, reminds him of his mother (the unconscious aspect). Sometimes a person is aware of certain motives in himself but unaware of how important they are. He may know that he works hard and likes to succeed, but he may not realize how overweening his ambition is and how incapable he is of accepting defeat.

Calling attention to the irrational and unconscious aspects of human motivation need not lead to pessimism about human nature. On the contrary, the only hope of rational control of conduct lies in the frank facing of the unconscious springs of action. It is a triumph of rationality that we have been able to discover how much of our behavior is irrational. If we are to behave reasonably, we must be ready to unmask our own unreasonableness.

Theories of Motivation

We have sketched some of the physiological correlates of drives and studied some representative motivational dispositions, without much concern for the manner in which the motivational concepts have fitted in with other psychological concepts, such as learning and perception. We shall now turn to some theoretical problems that arise in the systematic treatment of motivation and to some ways in which these problems have been dealt with by theorists.

The need-drive-incentive theory

Making use of the general notion that deprivation states are the basis of drive, a prevalent theory takes the position that bodily *needs* give rise to *drives* as their psychological representation, and that these drives then spur *activity* until a *goal-object* or *incentive* is reached which can *reduce* the drive through satisfying the need. The familiar example is hunger. Depletion gives rise to the hunger drive, which goads the organism to activity until food (the incentive) is reached and the drive is reduced by eating. Drive and need are to be distinguished, because the food-deprived animal may not be hungry at all times, and sometimes the drive can be reduced when the need is not satisfied, as when a hungry animal is rewarded with nonnutritive saccharin. The need-drive-incentive theory has been particularly influential because drive-reduction has been proposed as one basis for the function of rewards in enhancing learning. (We shall meet this concept in Chapter 9.)

Within the need-drive-incentive theory there are some unresolved issues, one of the more important of which is whether there is but *one* drive, to which all drive conditions contribute, or a *number* of drives. The one-drive interpretation (e.g., Hull, 1943; Brown, 1961) is that any active drive contributes to a general state of activation that facilitates ongoing activity,

whether or not it is relevant to the drive. When, for example, the activity wheel is used as an indicator of drive level, it is perhaps immaterial whether the drive arousal is by way of sex hormones or hunger. This interpretation, which has a good deal of support, depends upon a somewhat limited interpretation of drive, namely that it is concerned only with the activation or energetic aspect of behavior and not at all with its direction. As soon as the direction of behavior enters in, then specific drive conditions become important. The one-drive theory accepts the fact that drive conditions also have "steering" functions, as when an animal turns one way for water when thirsty, another way for food when hungry. Thus the issue is not whether there are specific drive conditions, but whether there is a general activity level to which all drives contribute. The nonspecific arousal action of the reticular formation in the brain can be cited in support of the one-drive interpretation.

If goal-direction (e.g., toward a preferred incentive, away from an unpreferred one) is accepted as one of the aspects of drive, however, one is forced to a multiple-drive interpretation. Those who take this position distinguish, for example, between appetitive drives and aversive drives, such as the seeking of food (appetitive) and the avoidance of pain (aversive).

In the classical form of the drive-incentive theory, drive is a push from within leading to energetic action, and the role of the incentive is to relieve the tension created by the drive. It is recognized, however, that the drive-incentive relationship is more complex than this. Some incentives become preferred over others, and the incentive appears under some circumstances to enhance the drive (as when the smell of freshly baked bread makes us wish to eat, even though we were not previously hungry).

Drive theorists commonly accept a list of primary or basic drives, for which the physiological states are readily identified (usually hunger, thirst, sex, pain), and then add other "learned" or "acquired" drives to account for motivated behavior not based directly upon these primary conditions. The many difficulties encountered in attempting to apply the need-drive-incentive theory to all behavior have caused a number of theorists to question it, and the theory is not held as confidently as it once was.

Cue-stimulus (nondrive) theory

If one turns away from the drive aspect of the need-drive-incentive theory and pays attention instead to the incentive (and other conditions of stimulation), it is possible to account for motivated behavior without recourse to the concept of an energizing drive. This point of view has evolved gradually—from the position that as motivated behavior is repeated, the drive gradually becomes "externalized" so that the incentive takes on drive properties (Anderson, 1941)—through the conception that incentive has a role somewhat comparable to drive, either multiplying the effectiveness of drive (Hull, 1952) or adding to drive as though it were a component of it (Spence, 1956)—to the position that the concept of a general energizing drive is superfluous (Estes, 1958).

In essence, the cue-stimulus theory substitutes the notion of *habit* for that of drive. When the doorbell rings, we answer it: we do not require a "doorbell-answering" drive, or a "curiosity-about-who's-at-the-door" drive. Our habits are called forth when stimulus conditions are appropriate. These may, to be sure, include stimuli from a contracting stomach as well as the call to dinner, but if we identify the stimuli that call forth our responses we can get along without a special class of stimuli called drives. The main idea is that all behavior is under the control of stimuli.

While a theory of this kind is not proposed without good reason, and must therefore be considered as a possible alternative to drive theory, those who refuse to accept it believe that there is some importance in distinguishing between the *energizing* of behavior and the *directing* of behavior. In some cases these two roles can be performed by a single stimulus, as in the case of a painful burn that both intensifies excitement and directs the withdrawal from the source of the heat. In other cases, as in the intensification of learned activity under increased hunger, the two functions appear separable.

Affective arousal theory

It has long been recognized that the kinds of behavior that organisms seek tend to have satisfying or pleasurable connotations, while the kinds of behavior that are avoided have annoying or unpleasant connotations. Hence emotion (or *affect,* an alternative word for emotional quality; see Chapter 6) may enter either as a determinant of motivated behavior or at least an important accompaniment to it. The affective arousal theory takes the position that affective (emotional) consequences are inherent features of motivated behavior, that an aspect of the goal-behavior in appetitive motives is indeed the positive affect (pleasure) and an aspect of avoidance behavior is indeed the negative affect (pain or displeasure).

McClelland (1955), a proponent of the affective-arousal interpretation, defines a motive as a strong affective association, *characterized by an anticipatory goal reaction and based on past association of certain cues with pleasure or pain.* Thus the expectation of pleasure (or pain), based on what has happened in the past, is said to "control motivated action."

Cognitive theories

A cognitive theory (the word comes from the Latin for "knowing") emphasizes some sort of understanding or anticipation of events, through perception or thought or judgment, as in the estimation of probabilities or in making a choice on the basis of relative value. The cognitive interpretation, as we shall see in several contexts in this book, tends to be an alternative to a stimulus-response interpretation, although the two kinds of interpretations are not necessarily contradictory.

Any organism with memory is capable of recognizing some similarities between the present and the past and hence is able to form some sort of expectancies with regard to the consequences of its behavior. According to a cognitive theory, motivated, goal-seeking behavior comes to be regulated by these cognitions, which are based on the past, modified by circumstances of the present, and include expectations about the future. We can illustrate cognitive theories by calling attention to three representative formulations of some cognitive aspects of motivation.

Level of Aspiration. Goal-setting has been studied in experiments on the *level of aspiration*. In these experiments level of aspiration refers to a fairly immediate goal, that is, something almost within reach, a possible success near at hand. The goal-setting in the experiments parallels what the high jumper does when he sets the bar between the posts. Where he sets it is his momentary goal, a measure of his level of aspiration. He expects to succeed, but he sets it high enough that he might fail. He would take no satisfaction in setting it so low that he could jump successfully every time. Satisfaction comes when he is able to clear the bar at a new height.

Experiments on level of aspiration help to define a person's goals, because in these experiments (as in the high jump illustration) success is determined by what the person himself is trying to do.

In the first experiment definitely concerned with these problems (Hoppe, 1930) it was revealed that the experiencing person's feeling of success or failure depends upon the difficulty of the task. As shown in Figure 5-13, a task may be "much too easy." Then the person experiences no sense of success, even though he accomplishes the

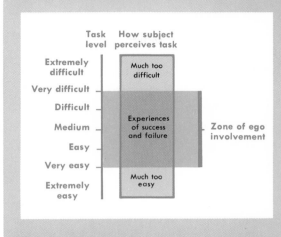

5-13

Level of aspiration

The subject tends to set his own goal (level of aspiration) within the shaded area in which he can experience success or failure. (After Hoppe, 1930)

task. A person who can play chess is not satisfied to win at dominoes. Or a task may be "much too difficult." Because he has no *ego involvement,* a person who makes no pretense of knowing Russian grammar will not have a sense of failure if he is unable to answer questions about it; he does not expect himself to know the answers. Success and failure experiences come in the in-between range: between the point at which success is highly probable, but failure possible, and that at which failure is highly probable, but success possible. This is the range in which the high jumper in the example will set his bar.

Experiments on level of aspiration have been concerned with a number of problems, among them the effect of group standards on individual behavior.

In one experiment, by Hilgard, Sait, and Magaret (1940), college students worked together in small groups (usually four students at a time). The task set was simple arithmetic problems, the score being the time required to complete a page. Public

5-14

Effect of prestige of reference groups on level of aspiration

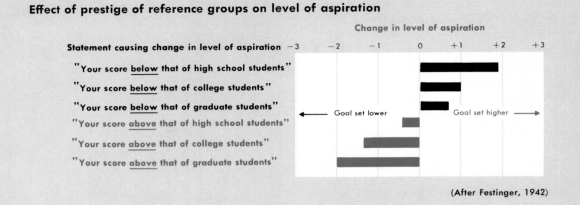

(After Festinger, 1942)

announcement of the finishing time was made, so that each student knew what the others were doing. Each student recorded privately his level of aspiration, that is, the score he expected to make on the next test. It was found that these private expectations were modified by the group performances: those whose groups had scores above average tended to lower their estimates; those with scores below average tended to expect to gain. The same tendency was found whether the score differences were due to differences in arithmetic ability on tests of equal difficulty or due to hidden differences in test difficulty for students of equal ability.

In another experiment with college students, by Festinger (1942), shifts in aspiration level were studied when all the student knew was his own previous scores and when he was told that his score was above or below that of one of three reference groups: high school, college, and graduate students. The results are shown in Figure 5-14. If the score was below that of the low prestige group (high school students), the aspiration level increased most; if it was above that of the high prestige group (graduate students), aspiration level decreased most.

Thus individual goal-setting is modified by prestige-seeking, self-protection, and other goals that reflect the setting in which motivated behavior occurs.

Cognitive Dissonance and Dissonance Reduction. A somewhat related theory has been proposed by Festinger (1957), in which certain kinds of unbalanced cognitions are described as *dissonant,* and the subject is under stress to remove this dissonance. The kind of disagreement or disharmony with which Festinger is chiefly concerned is that which occurs after a decision has been made; under such circumstances there is often some lack of harmony between what one does and what one believes, and there is thus pressure either to change one's behavior or to change one's belief. For example, if a regular smoker reads about the relationship between smoking and lung cancer, the habitual action and the new information are dissonant. If the decision is made to continue smoking, the dissonance will be reduced by disbelieving the information about the relationship between smoking and lung cancer; if the decision is made to give up smoking, the information on the linkage between smoking and lung cancer will be stoutly defended. (See Figure 5-15.) Parallels can be found in the behavior of lower organisms as well (Festinger, 1961).

Expectation-Value Theories. There are many kinds of theories relevant to motivation that are not always regarded as being

5-15

Cognitive dissonance reduced by change in belief

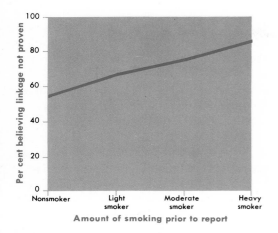

Belief in lack of linkage between smoking and lung cancer on the part of those who smoke. (Data from Minneapolis *Sunday Tribune,* March 21, 1954, as reported by Festinger, 1957)

psychological theories. Among these are certain types of decision theory that have had their origins chiefly within economics. In simplest terms, these economic theories assume that the individual can assign *value* or *utility* to possible incentives, and that he makes his decision according to the *risk* involved. He is willing to take more risk for something that he values more. Such a theory can be expressed in mathematical terms, for example, in simplest form:

Choice = f(Value $\times$ Probability of attainment) [5]

A somewhat similar type of formulation, made by Atkinson (1957), has been put in motivation terms. His formula, modified somewhat to conform with the vocabulary of this book, is as follows:

Motive arousal = f(Motivational disposition $\times$ Incentive $\times$ Expectation)

[5] The f in an equation of the form $y = f(x)$ means "function of" or "depends upon."

This formula is very much like the preceding one, substituting incentive for value and expectation for probability of attainment. The "motivational disposition" term recognizes the existence of individual differences—something the economists have occasionally overlooked in their concept of "economic man."

Atkinson's own experimental tests of his formula were based on two main conjectures derived from it. These conjectures were (1) the subject should work hardest at a given task when the expectation of success is most uncertain, that is, when the probability of success or failure is 50:50, and thus can be most influenced by what he does, and (2) subjects in whom the achievement motive is stronger than the motive to avoid failure should prefer intermediate risks, while those whose motive to avoid

5-16

Heightened performance at probability of 50:50

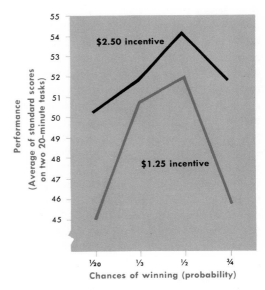

Different groups of subjects were offered different rewards for solving arithmetic problems. Regardless of the size of incentive, scores were highest at a 50:50 chance of success, where individual effort appears to make most difference in the outcome. The size of the incentive also influences the outcome. (From J. W. Atkinson, 1958, p. 294)

failure is stronger should avoid intermediate risks and prefer either "safe" or "risky" undertakings. In a "safe" undertaking there is little likelihood of failure; in a "risky" undertaking you are not "blamed" if you fail. Atkinson performed several experiments testing these implications. In an experiment with 124 female college students, their performance scores on arithmetic problems were indeed highest, as predicted, when their chances of winning and of losing were $50:50$ (that is, $\frac{1}{2}$) (see Figure 5-16). The second conjecture was not borne out directly in these experiments, although some evidence exists for it in other connections (e.g., McClelland, 1958).

Psychoanalytic theory of motivation

Among the motivational dispositions discussed in this chapter, two—sex and aggression—are particularly prominent in the system of psychoanalysis (based upon the writings of Sigmund Freud). Freud originally conceived of sex as the primary driving force; in his view the psychic energy that drives men, called the *libido,* was entirely sexual in its origin. Later, as he contemplated man's cruelty, aggression was also assigned the role of a primitive, "instinctual" drive. At one stage Freud contrasted the two drives as a life instinct and a death instinct, but contemporary followers of Freud are now usually satisfied to speak of the two drives of sex and aggression as accounting for instinctively driven behavior in man.

According to the Freudian view, the unfolding of sexual behavior follows a developmental pattern from primitive self-love (narcissism) through various other attachments until adult sexuality is achieved. In the process there is attachment to the parents, particularly to the parent of the opposite sex. This attachment is said to give rise to motivational conflicts because in loving one parent the child becomes a rival to the other parent. The love by the child for the parent of the opposite sex is known

as the *Oedipus complex,* the name deriving from the Greek tragedy in which Oedipus unwittingly marries his mother. Although the interpretation of the Oedipus complex has been much criticized (Fromm, 1949), the attachment of the child to the parent may be recognized as an important stage in the development of affectionate responses to people. Later on there is a stage of like-sexed attachments, represented in childhood by gangs or cliques, or in the "crushes" of a child on a heroic figure of the same sex. A like-sexed affiliation is called *homosexual.* It is a normal stage of development and represents deviation from the norm only if it is not outgrown as sexual functions mature. The final stage of sexual development culminates in attraction to a partner of the opposite sex, representing normal *heterosexual* interest. Whether or not all the successive affectionate attachments should be called sexual is a matter of debate; that such affectionate attachments exist as the child grows into adulthood is common knowledge.

It is significant that these stages are described according to the person for whom the affection is felt. The normal pattern is for the object of affection to shift as the child grows. There may, however, be arrested development at any one stage. That is, some adults are narcissistic, some are dependent upon parents, and some are homosexual. Even in normal development there are usually fragmentary residues of earlier attachments, so that the shift from one stage to another is not necessarily clear-cut. When the arrested development is extreme, we need to know why the normal development did not occur in order to help the individual attain the more usual adult relationships.

The foregoing account shows the stages of development of the sex drive as it becomes directed toward different objects. These objects do not all satisfy the physiological drive, in the sense of culminating in the sex act, but they provide some derivative satisfaction in the affiliation between persons.

The earlier Freudian theory found sexual motivation behind nearly all of human behavior, though later psychoanalysts have tended to reduce somewhat the emphasis upon the instinctual drives by paying more attention to what they call the ego—the part of the person concerned with the wider aspects of reality. Like other motive systems, the sexual drive leads to varied activity, in part through its satisfaction, in part through the anxiety that arises from attempts to suppress it.

Psychoanalytic theories changed somewhat during Freud's life. The notion that aggression arises as one of the consequences of frustration, mentioned on p. 140, derives from an earlier Freudian interpretation. The suggestion that aggression has to be viewed as an expression of a primary drive, along with sex, came later.

SUMMARY   1. A *motive* is something that incites the organism to action or that sustains and gives direction to action once the organism has been aroused. Hence motives have both an *activating* or *energizing* aspect and a *directing* aspect.

2. A *motivational disposition* is a persistent tendency for behavior to be influenced by a given kind of motive; such a disposition derives from inheritance, prior experience, or both. When such a disposition finds expression in behavior actually taking place, we have evidence for an *aroused motive*.

3. The *classification* of motives is somewhat arbitrary, because motives may be expressed through learned behavior that differs from culture to culture and from person to person within a culture, and because similar motives may be manifested through unlike behavior and unlike motives through similar behavior. Furthermore, motives may appear in disguised form, and several motives may be active at once.

4. A provisional classification groups motives into *survival motives, social motives,* and *ego-integrative motives.*

5. The survival motives, especially hunger, thirst, and avoidance of pain, are commonly treated as *drives* because of their strong influence upon behavior. Other drives include avoidance of extremes of temperature, avoidance of suffocation, a drive against accumulating waste products in the body, and a drive against excessive fatigue and exhaustion. There are also some acquired drives, as when the drug addict comes to require his drug.

6. Some drives, such as *activity, manipulation*, and *curiosity,* lack specified physiological correlates, yet they operate much as the survival drives do, and hence are here treated with them.

7. Four methods have been used to *measure* drives: general activity level, rate of performing learned acts, overcoming an obstruction, and the choice method. The first two of these are in more common use.

8. Some social motives can be treated as drives in the same sense as the drives treated under survival motives. These include *maternal drive* and

sex drive. However, the learned aspects of social motives are so important that the more neutral expression "motivational disposition" is often more appropriate than drive. This applies to the many indirect expressions of sexual motivation, especially as we observe these expressions in man. Other motivational dispositions such as *dependency* and *affiliation, dominance* and *submission,* and *aggression* are pervasive and can be studied among lower animals as well as among man.

9. Motivational dispositions in man have been studied by several methods, including behavioral observation and case study, self-reports, imaginative productions, and experimental arousal.

10. *Ego-integrative motives* are peculiarly human and are built about a concept of the self. While some theorists favor a single master motive, such as self-actualization, self-expansion, self-consistency, or competence, the failure to agree on a single designation suggests that there may be a group of ego-integrative motives, all with some sort of self-reference. The *achievement motive* is used to illustrate such motives, because in American culture to see oneself as productive and successful is one aspect of a favorable self-image.

11. Purposeful activity and planning have led to a reconsideration of the problem of "will" in psychology. Although "will" has been a word avoided in psychology for a number of years, planning behavior is so relevant to ego-integration that it cannot be overlooked.

12. Man is often driven by impulses of which he is unaware or which are at least unclear to him; such motivation is called *unconscious.* Unconscious motives express themselves in dreams, in mannerisms and slips of speech, and in symptoms of neurotic illness. Recognizing that man is in part irrational does not degrade man; it is in fact a triumph of rationality that man is able to discover his own irrationality.

13. *Theories of motivation* include the *need-drive-incentive* theory with emphasis either upon a single energizing drive, to which several circumstances contribute, or several distinguishable drives which also give direction to behavior; a *cue-stimulus* (nondrive) theory, which assigns drive value to stimuli; an *affective-arousal* theory, which states that the emotional consequences of an act determine its motivational significance; *cognitive* theories, based on how the individual perceives or represents the situation before him; and *psychoanalytic* theories, based largely upon unconscious motives and their derivatives.

14. The cognitive theories include *level of aspiration* (concerned with individual goal-setting), *cognitive dissonance* (concerned with the impulses to change associated with the disharmonies that often persist after a decision has been made), and *expectation-value* theories (which treat of decision-making when both probabilities and costs, or risks, are taken into account).

15. According to psychoanalytic theory, the primary drives are sex and aggression. The unfolding of sexual behavior follows a developmental pat-

tern involving various object-choices until a mature sexual attachment is achieved. Modern psychoanalytic interpretations find more place for ego-processes than did the earlier ones.

SUGGESTIONS FOR FURTHER READING

For the need-drive-incentive theory in its various forms, see Bindra, *Motivation* (1959), Brown, *The motivation of behavior* (1961), Hall, *Psychology of motivation* (1961), or Young, *Motivation and emotion* (1961). The drives with unspecified physiological bases are treated particularly in Berlyne, *Conflict, arousal, and curiosity* (1960).

For the affective arousal theory, see McClelland and others, *The achievement motive* (1953), and Young, *Motivation and emotion* (1961).

For human motives as revealed through fantasy, the best sources are McClelland (Ed.), *Studies in motivation* (1955), and Atkinson (Ed.), *Motives in fantasy, action, and society* (1958). Other approaches to human motives, including psychoanalytic approaches, are treated in Lindzey (Ed.), *Assessment of human motives* (1958), and Stacey and DeMartino (Eds.), *Understanding human motivation* (1958). A general discussion of the social role of achievement motivation can be found in McClelland, *The achieving society* (1961).

Representative of cognitive approaches are the books by Festinger, *A theory of cognitive dissonance* (1957), and Heider, *The psychology of interpersonal relations* (1958). The literature on decision theory is difficult for the beginner. Bross, *Design for decision* (1953) is more accessible than Thrall, Coombs, and Davis (Eds.), *Decision processes* (1954), and Chernoff and Moses, *Elementary decision theory* (1959).

CHAPTER 6

Emotion

Life without emotion would be drab. If there were no joys and sorrows, no hopes and dismays, no thrills or triumphs, the warmth and color would go out of human experience.

Men prefer to have pleasurable states endure and do things to make them recur; men also prefer to have unpleasant, painful, or annoying states end promptly and do what they can to avoid them. But is this a sufficient statement of the relation between emotion and motivation? We need to look more closely into pleasant and disturbing emotional states to see how they are related to goal-directed behavior.

Emotional States

The range of affectively toned experience

The *mild* states of feeling that accompany many of our activities can be described as states of pleasantness or unpleasantness. We may find a warm test tube pleasant to touch and a piece of sandpaper unpleasant to touch. In a restaurant at breakfast we may find the hot cup of coffee pleasant, but waiting for it unpleasant. When we call attention to the pleasantness or unpleasantness of experiences, we are referring to their *affective tone*. When psychologists were more given to making fine introspective distinctions than they are today, they called these mild affective states *feelings* and reserved the term *emotion* for the more profound, widespread, and

stirred-up states suggested by such words as terror, grief, rage, or exultation. However, the stirred-up character is not enough to distinguish between emotions and other states, for the body is stirred up when we chop wood or saw a board; it is really the intensity of the affective toning that makes the state emotional. To be sure, such a full-fledged emotion will be reflected in characteristic behavior and diffuse changes in body physiology—the kinds of behavior that permit us to detect emotions in others or in animals. We may recognize, however, many states intermediate between the very mild experiences of pleasantness and unpleasantness and the violent, intense emotions: states of excitement and quiescence, of appreciation of beauty or of dislike of ugliness. We shall therefore not attempt to define "an emotion," but instead will be concerned with a variety of emotional states.

Once we recognize the gradation from the less intense to the more intense experiences, the old distinction between feeling and emotion loses its force. In discussing the emotional aspects of behavior and experience, we shall include all our affectively colored activity regardless of intensity. In summary, we shall define as an *emotional state* the condition of the organism during affectively toned experiencing, whether the affective toning is mild or intense.

Virtually all psychologists who have classified emotions divide them into those that are *pleasant* (e.g., joy, love) and those that are *unpleasant* (e.g., anger, sadness). This classification suggests the primacy of pleasantness and unpleasantness, of acceptance and rejection, of approach and avoidance as the very basis of emotion. Beyond the classification into pleasant and unpleasant states, many of our emotional terms express the *intensity* of the experience. The differences in intensity are carried by word pairs such as the following: anger-rage, fear-horror, pain-agony, sadness-grief. By grouping together the whole family of experiences from mild satisfactions and annoyances at one end of the scale through weak emotional states up to the most intense emotions at the other end, we emphasize the continuities among these emotional states.

The variety of bodily changes in emotion

The symptoms of fear reported by army fliers on missions in World War II (Table 6-1) well illustrate the complexity of the bodily processes in an emotional state. The symptoms at the top of the list, the ones most frequently mentioned, are the milder ones (pounding heart, tense muscles), while the less frequent symptoms, near the bottom of the list, are more severe (confusion, faintness, loss of memory, nausea).

The symptoms of emotion, especially of intense emotion, include profound changes throughout the body, changes regulated in a complex way by the central nervous system, by both divisions of the autonomic system, and by the endocrine glands. Out of the mass of these physical changes, psychologists have studied a number of selected indicators, some of which follow.

1. *Galvanic Skin Response.* Whenever emotions are aroused, detectable electrical changes take place on the skin. Electrodes attached to the skin (e.g., on the palms of the hands) are connected with a recording galvanometer. The *galvanic skin response* (GSR) is a sensitive indicator of changes in emotional state. Demonstrations such as the following are commonly used in psychology classes: A male student, with the electrodes attached to his palms, recites the alphabet aloud slowly while thinking of the name of his girl friend. The class tries to judge from the swing of the galvanometer needle when he has come to her initial. His slight embarrassment or excitement or concern about being detected is commonly revealed through an unusually wide swing of the needle.

2. *Blood Distribution.* Changes in blood pressure and changes in the distribution of the blood between the surface and the in-

TABLE 6-1			
Symptoms of fear in combat flying			
"During combat missions did you feel"	*"Often"* (per cent)	*"Sometimes"* (per cent)	*Total* (per cent)
A pounding heart and rapid pulse	30	56	86
That your muscles were very tense	30	53	83
Easily irritated, angry, or "sore"	22	58	80
Dryness of the throat or mouth	30	50	80
"Nervous perspiration" or "cold sweat"	26	53	79
"Butterflies" in the stomach	23	53	76
Sense of unreality that this couldn't be happening to you	20	49	69
Need to urinate very frequently	25	40	65
Trembling	11	53	64
Confused or rattled	3	50	53
Weak or faint	4	37	41
Right after a mission, unable to remember details of what happened	5	34	39
Sick to the stomach	5	33	38
Unable to concentrate	3	32	35
That you have wet or soiled your pants	1	4	5

SOURCE: Based on reports of 1985 flying officers and 2519 enlisted fliers of World War II. After Shaffer (1947).

terior of the body occur in emotion. We are familiar with blushing in embarrassment or a flushed face and neck in anger ("hot under the collar"). These changes occur because blood vessels in the skin dilate, and more blood is found near the surface of the skin. The opposite symptom is the blanching of

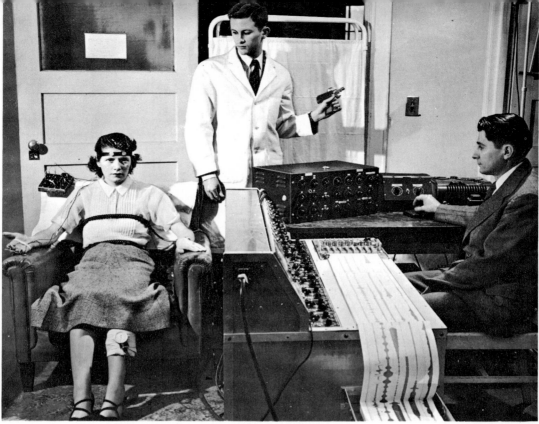

6-1

Graphic recording of bodily changes in emotion

By means of appropriate instruments, simultaneous records can be secured of changes in breathing, heart rate, blood pressure, blood volume in the arms, electrical changes on the skin surface—correlated with the presentation of emotion-arousing stimuli. An enlargement of the tape is seen below. (After Ax, 1953)

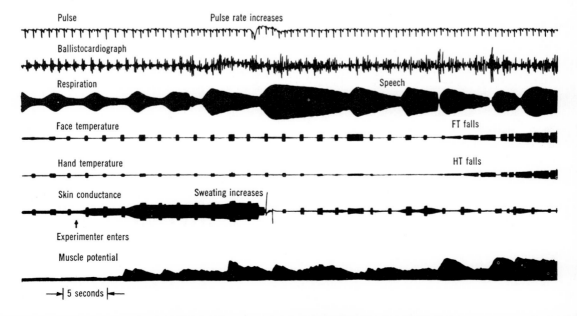

the face under some conditions of fright. In this case the blood vessels constrict.

3. *Heart Rate.* The pounding of the heart in emotional excitement is so familiar that the heart has long been a symbol of emotion.

4. *Respiration.* The rate and depth of breathing as well as the relative amount of time spent in inspiration compared to expiration provide useful indicators, especially in emotional conflict. The relative times determine the "inspiration-expiration ratio" (I/E ratio). Gasping for breath and sighing are the kinds of changes that affect the I/E ratio.

5. *Pupillary Response.* The pupil of the eye tends to dilate in moments of anger and pain or in emotional excitement generally, and to constrict in quiescence.

6. *Salivary Secretion.* Experimental evidence supports the common observation that emotional excitement often produces a dryness of the mouth because of a decrease in saliva or of a change in its consistency.

7. *Pilomotor Response.* This is the technical name for "goose pimples," which appear when the hairs of the skin stand on end.

8. *Gastrointestinal Motility.* Investigators have used x-ray methods and the stomach-balloon technique (the method described in connection with the study of hunger, p. 129) to determine that the movements of stomach and intestine are affected by strong emotion. Emotional excitement may lead to nausea or diarrhea. Persistent emotional or mood states may be responsible, through the tensions set up in the walls of the stomach or intestines, for the ulcers that some people get when under stress.

9. *Muscle Tension and Tremor.* We sometimes say of a person, "If only he could relax. He's too tense." Muscular tension is a symptom of emotion. Tensed muscles may also tremble when opposing muscles are contracted simultaneously. (See Chapter 2, p. 31.) The tremor may also

occur when a person experiences a conflict of desires, as, for example, a powerful desire to slap an irritating smart aleck conflicting with an equally powerful desire to retain one's dignity and self-respect.

10. *Blood Composition.* Because the endocrine glands are active during emotion and pour hormones into the blood stream, chemical analysis reveals actual changes in blood composition. There are changes in blood sugar, acid-base balance, and adrenalin content. In Chapter 2, adrenalin and noradrenalin were described as hormones of the adrenal medulla, important agents in emotional excitement.

These ten emotional indicators suffice to dramatize the profound and widespread changes that go on in the body when one is emotionally aroused.

Physiological mechanisms in emotion

The many bodily changes that occur during emotion are not unrelated phenomena; they fit together into patterns organized under the influence of the nervous system and the endocrine glands. W. B. Cannon, the physiologist, noted that one large group of symptoms prominent in anger and rage prepare the organism to face emergencies, to defend it against attack and injury.

If a cat, quietly digesting its meal, is confronted suddenly by a barking dog, the following physiological changes (among others) take place: (1) digestive movements of the stomach cease; (2) blood pressure increases; (3) heart rate is accelerated; (4) adrenalin is secreted into the blood stream.

Each of these reactions is regulated through the sympathetic division of the autonomic nervous system. The secretion of adrenalin has the effect of: (1) raising the blood pressure; (2) increasing the sugar in the blood, making it available for energetic action and to counteract fatigue; (3) making the blood clot more quickly.

The **cat arches its back** and hisses (these

particular activities are *not* mediated by the sympathetic system, although they are part of the emotional activity). Its hair stands on end. It is now ready to fight. The additional sugar in its blood gives it energy and increased endurance. If it is wounded, its blood will clot more quickly. If the cat is bitten, the dog is likely to get a mouthful of hair instead of a chunk of flesh.

Because these physical responses fit together and prepare the organism for action, Cannon called them *emergency reactions.* He therefore interpreted intense emotional excitement as a method of preparing the organism to meet emergencies. Reactions that at first seemed independent and unrelated, he found, form a pattern serving the common purposes of protection.

Most of the reactions demonstrated in the cat are found in man also. When we get angry we may have stomach-aches due to changes in stomach movements; our hearts beat faster, our adrenalin flows, and our blood, like the cat's, clots more quickly. The bloody nose of the basketball player disturbs him less than it would if he were not excited, and the blood flow stops more quickly because he is excited.

The sympathetic and parasympathetic divisions often have nerve connections to the same organs, but, as we learned in Chapter 2 (p. 48), they usually produce opposite effects. Stimulation over the sympathetic system accelerates the heart rate; stimulation over the parasympathetic system slows the heart rate. Stimulation over the sympathetic system inhibits the muscular contractions of the stomach in digestion, while stimulation over the parasympathetic system enhances contractions.

The antagonism between the two systems suggests that the sympathetic system is active in excited emotional states, the parasympathetic in quiescent emotional states. This idea is true to some extent; for example, pleasant tastes and smells stimulate the gastric secretions, which are under parasympathetic control. But the parasympa-

thetic system participates in unpleasant and excited states as well. It is responsible for vomiting in disgust as well as for salivation in anticipation of pleasure. The parasympathetic system may excite discharge of the bladder and the bowels in moments of extreme fright. One series of studies of emotionality in rats used amount of defecation as an index of emotionality, so highly correlated was the increase in amount with other evidences of emotional excitement (Hall, 1934).

The central nervous system is also active in emotion. Through its control of skeletal muscles, it is responsible for frowning, grimacing, muscular tension, trembling, moaning, whining, purring, snarling. The central and autonomic systems thus cooperate in producing organized patterns of emotional expression such as laughing, weeping, and sexual excitement, patterns which are incomplete without this cooperation. The tears in laughter and weeping are controlled by the autonomic system, the vocal and facial muscles by the central nervous system, the changes in breathing by both systems.

How are these patterned states regulated? There are many theories and much fragmentary evidence, but we need to know more before we fully understand the physiological patterning of emotional expression.

There is evidence that the hypothalamus plays a central role in the organization and activation of many types of emotional and motivational behavior (Stellar, 1954). For example, it exerts some sort of control over the pattern described as "rage." A restricted surgical lesion in part of the hypothalamus may make a cat that formerly welcomed friendly petting and caressing turn savagely upon the person who tries to handle it in a gentle manner (Wheatley, 1944).

Some emotional expressions clearly involve the cerebral cortex, the highest centers of the brain. For example, after cortical injury, one side of a patient's face may be affected. He may be unable to laugh voluntarily except with the "good" side of his face, though an involuntary laugh will spread over both sides. Another line of evidence comes from patients who have undergone brain surgery in order to relieve or reduce the intractable pain suffered in the last stages of cancer. The frontal lobe operation, even when it is successful in relieving suffering, does not produce total insensitivity to pain. A pinprick still feels painful. The pain that disappears is the overwhelming one that most disturbed the patient, best described as a kind of anguish (Landis, Zubin, and Mettler, 1950).

What we do know with assurance is that intense emotions involve profound changes throughout the body, which are regulated in a complex way by the central nervous system, by both divisions of the autonomic system, and by the endocrine glands.

Distinguishing among emotions

Psychologists and physiologists have tried unsuccessfully for many years to differentiate among human emotional states according to characteristics of the bodily indicators of emotion. The reasons for the difficulty are not hard to find:

1. Intense emotions (such as anger and fear) are highly activated, disturbed states, and have many bodily responses in common. The specific responses do not serve to define a particular emotion: one may turn pale in either anger or fear, and one may start to run when either afraid or angry.

2. A person can express any one emotion in a variety of ways. In fear, he may freeze to the spot or he may run away from danger. In anger, he may bite his lip, turn on his heel, or attack the person who has aroused him.

3. The *name* of the emotion depends commonly on supplementary information about the stimuli that aroused the emotion or about the nature of the goal-directed activity that follows the stimuli. That is, the emotional response to a dangerous animal will be called *fear,* especially if the person tries to escape; an emotional response to an insult will be called *anger,* especially if the person retaliates against the one who insulted him. The bodily state might be alike in the two cases, even though the emotions have different names.

4. The *conscious* or *introspective* differentiation of the emotions is not free of influence by external circumstances. A classical theory of emotions, called the *James-Lange theory* after the two men who originated it, stressed the importance in felt emotion of the repercussion ("feedback") of the bodily responses. William James stated this in the form of seeming paradoxes which apparently put the cart before the horse: "We are afraid because we run," "We are angry because we strike." What gives the theory some plausibility is that our awareness of bodily states involves not only a judgment of the situation (e.g., as a dangerous or frightening one), but also what today we call a *feedback* from the bodily responses released in emotion. Thus if I stumble on the stairs, I automatically grasp the handrail before I have time to recognize my emotional state; my felt emotion, after the crisis is over, includes the perception of my pounding heart and exaggerated breathing. Because this recognition comes after the bodily responses, the theory has some plausibility; at the same time, in view of the fact that recognition comes after the circumstances have already been judged (as dangerous, etc.), it is doubtful if the felt bodily responses are entirely responsible for the quality that differentiates one emotion from another.

Physiological psychologists have not permitted these difficulties to prevent their search for some response differences underlying the major emotional states.

Ax (1953) attached various devices to his subjects so that he could record at once seven different physiological indicators of

Differential reactions in anger and fear

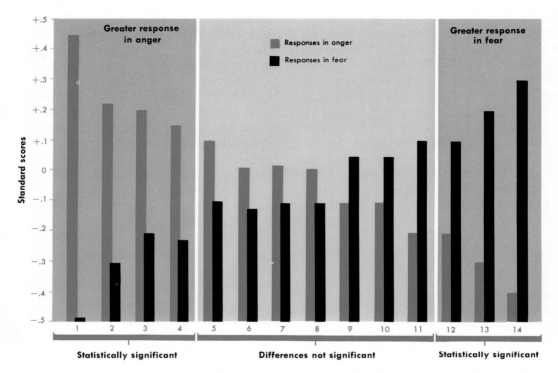

Physiological responses in anger and fear. The chart plots changes from the normal (zero) level for 14 indicators all simultaneously recorded. The indicators are numbered to correspond to the numbers at the base of the chart. (After Ax, 1953)

More responses in anger

1 Galvanic skin responses (increases in number).
2 Heart rate decreases.
3 Muscle tension increases.
4 Diastolic blood pressure rises.

Responses not significantly different

5 Face temperature decreases.
6 Heart-stroke volume decreases.
7 Heart-stroke volume increases.
8 Hand temperature decreases.
9 Systolic blood pressure increases.
10 Face temperature increases.
11 Heart rate increases.

More responses in fear

12 Muscle tension peaks.
13 Skin conductance increases.
14 Respiration rate increases.

emotional response (pulse rate, heart stroke, breathing, face temperature, hand temperature, galvanic skin response, and muscle action currents just over the eyes). He then on some occasions frightened his subjects and on others angered them. In doing this, he made very clever use of technicians in his laboratory, whose clumsiness invoked fear and whose remarks induced anger; the emotional arousal was thus more natural than is usually the case when a person is strapped up with instruments. Each of the 43 subjects was angered once and frightened once (about half in one order, half in the reverse) and then questioned about the reality of the emotion as experienced.

The experimenter developed fourteen indexes or scores, based on the seven physiological indicators, to use in describing the emotional responses of the subjects. Half of these were common to both fear and anger. But the other half (seven of the indexes) showed significant differences in the degree to which they were displayed in anger and in fear (Figure 6-2). The differences more prominent in fear correspond to the action of adrenalin; those more prominent in anger correspond to the action of both adrenalin and noradrenalin (see p. 33).

These findings on the differences between fear and anger gain support from studies of the adrenal medullas of wild animals. Rabbits, which depend for survival on running away (as in fear), show a predominance of adrenalin; lions and other aggressive animals (whose responses resemble behavior in anger) show a relatively high amount of noradrenalin (Funkenstein, 1955).

Funkenstein and his collaborators have extended the type of study done by Ax to include heart responses and chemical studies of the blood (Funkenstein, King, and Drolette, 1957). Under experimental circumstances designed to arouse anger or apprehension, some subjects openly expressed their anger, others felt angry but turned the anger inward against themselves, while still others became severely anxious. The open expression of anger and the anxiety reaction were associated with the secretion of noradrenalin in the blood; the controlled, inward-directed anger was associated with the secretion of adrenalin.

It is difficult to differentiate human emotions on the basis of bodily changes and easier to differentiate them by the conventionalized expressions humans learn to use to convey emotional meanings. (These are superimposed upon the "natural" expressions resulting from maturation, which will be discussed shortly.) Psychologists have photographed the faces of actors portraying various emotions and have then asked subjects to try to identify the emotions from the photographs. While there are some confusions, identification is well above chance. If six broad classes are used, subjects can assign the posed emotions reasonably well (Table 6-2). The percentage of correspondence between the posed and judged emotion varies from a high of 93 per cent for love, happiness, and mirth to

---

TABLE 6-2

Success in judging posed emotions from photographs

Emotions as judged from the photographs	Emotions intended in the posed photographs					
	(1) Love, happiness, mirth	(2) Surprise	(3) Fear, suffering	(4) Anger, determination	(5) Disgust	(6) Contempt
(1) Love, happiness, mirth	93	5	1	2	0	0
(2) Surprise	1	77	3	4	0	0
(3) Fear, suffering	0	7	79	24	3	1
(4) Anger, determination	0	1	10	60	22	4
(5) Disgust	0	0	2	1	63	7
(6) Contempt	0	0	0	3	12	86
Other	6	10	5	6	0	2
	100	100	100	100	100	100

SOURCE: Woodworth (1938), p. 251. Data from Feleky (1922). Results with 100 subjects.

A simplified version of Schlosberg's surface of emotions

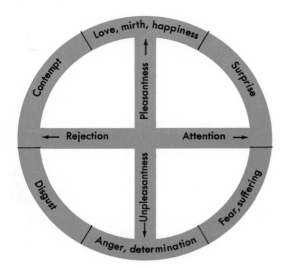

a low of 60 per cent for anger or determination. The list of six classes can be arranged in a scale; that is, items often confused are placed nearer together; those less often confused are placed farther apart. Such an arrangement (used in Table 6-2) works only because there is some systematic relationship among the pictured emotions.

Subjects asked to name the emotions represented in unposed candid camera shots do quite well also, even when the facial expression is presented alone, with the background masked out. They do better, of course, when they know the whole context of the picture (Munn, 1940).

Schlosberg (1952, 1954) has attempted to refine the scaling of posed emotions. When a very large number of pictures were used, showing all manner of expressions (he used 72 pictures of the same face expressing various emotions), he noted that in some sortings the ends of the scale were confused; that is, some subjects interchanged pictures intended as mirth with pictures intended to show contempt. This result led him to arrange his scale into a circular sur-

face, upon which all of the pictured emotions can be made to fit. A simplified version of his arrangement is presented in Figure 6-3. Note that there are two main axes, the familiar *pleasantness-unpleasantness* one, and another at right angles to it, which he calls *rejection-attention*. Any pictured emotion can be placed on this surface, depending upon how it is judged in accordance with these two dimensions.

Other studies have shown some success in judging emotions from gestures of the hands alone (Carmichael, Roberts, and Wessel, 1937) or from the recorded speaking voice (Dusenbury and Knower, 1939). We do not know how successful such judgments would be if the materials came from an alien culture. Success in recognizing emotions from face, gesture, and voice probably depends greatly upon the conventions of the society in which one has been reared.

A somewhat different approach to a study of the organization and description of emotional states has been taken by Block (1957), who investigated how men and women tended to interpret emotional states from the *names* of these states. He asked 40 male and 48 female college students to rate each emotion according to 20 scales based on pairs of adjectives, such as weak-strong, active-passive, tense-relaxed, happy-sad, loud-soft. This method is an application of the "semantic differential" of Osgood (1952), which we shall meet again later (Chapter 12). Block arrived at a series of typical connotations for the different emotions and was thus able to determine by correlational methods which emotions grouped together. It turned out that the three main dimensions of emotion, as revealed by this method, bore a family resemblance to those found by Schlosberg's study of facial expression, although they are not exactly equivalent. Block named the dimensions *pleasantness-unpleasantness,* a *level of activation* factor, and an *interpersonal relatedness* factor. Men and women within American culture appraised the emotions very similarly; an intercorrelation of the whole set of correlations between pairs of emotional descriptions, known as a matrix intercorrelation, yielded an $r = .93$, which shows the two sets of correlations, for men and for women, to be essentially equivalent.

The effort to find a physiological basis on which to differentiate the emotions, to state just how many emotions there are and what their bodily responses are, has not proved to be a very fruitful quest. With shifts in the nature of the problems that interest psychologists, the question has tended to decrease in importance.

More attention is now being paid to the general state of emotional excitement rather than to the fine distinctions between the several emotions. A favorite theory today goes by the name of the *activation theory* (Lindsley, 1951; Schlosberg, 1954). It suggests that there is an intensity scale or dimension in emotion, from sleep at the one end to diffuse excitement at the other. This theory, stressing energy mobilization (Duffy, 1951), makes it difficult to distinguish between drive and emotion; but drive and emotion are in fact closely related, no matter how we try to define them. There are certain to be difficult borderline cases; behavioral phenomena always resist tight compartmentalization, and perhaps emotion and drive need not be differentiated at all.

Present interest in psychosomatic medicine has, however, led to renewed effort to distinguish among the physiological *consequences* of fear, anger, and anxiety. For example, a patient was found with a gastric fistula (an artificial passage to the surface of the abdomen) through which food could be placed directly into his stomach. Direct observation of his stomach showed differences in reactions associated with fear and hostility, thus indicating a physiological differentiation of these states (Wolf and Wolff, 1942). But psychosomatic medicine is concerned more with chronic, persistent, or recurrent emotional states than with the emotional crises that have been the usual subject matter of psychological studies of emotional expression.

Emotional Development

Emotional expression, like other complex behavior, develops through maturation and learning. The infant cries at birth; as he grows older, his laughter is as spontaneous as his crying. He is born with the capacity to cry, and the capacity to laugh comes through maturation. However, some aspects of his emotional behavior are acquired. As the child grows older, he learns to cry for a purpose—to gain parental attention or sympathy—and he learns to withhold his tears sometimes when he feels like crying. He learns, too, that there are times when it is proper to laugh and times when laughter is frowned upon. The child has to learn not only the occasions for emotion, but how to control emotional expression according to the patterns considered proper in his culture. He may laugh and cry softly or loudly, with or without restraint. He learns to distinguish between a pleasant smile, a gentle laugh, and a loud guffaw.

The maturation of emotional patterns

The newborn infant has a very limited repertory of emotional responsiveness. Most contemporary students of infant behavior agree that at birth the only distinguishable emotion is excitement. Besides this emotion there is only quiescence, probably not an emotional state at all. The state of excitement (crying, straining, thrashing about) appears to the observer to be an emotionally unpleasant one. The resting or quiet state of the newborn child is emotionally neutral, without the positive qualities of the later cheerful, cooing, delighted state. Thus, in the beginning, the one emotional state is a rather unpleasant departure from quiescence. How then does emotional responsiveness develop? The following study suggests the course of development typical during the first year of life.

An observer kept careful daily records of the emotional expression of some 60 infants in a Montreal hospital. While the experiment covered only a period of four months, ages of the infants ranged from birth to two years. The study found the following typical stages for the children under one year old:

1. *Diffuse excitement.* This is the only emotion distinguishable at birth.
2. *Distress and delight.* By three months of age the infant's excited state has become differentiated into two distinguishable states, described as distress and delight. Distress corresponds closely to the original excited emotion; delight takes on positive qualities absent at birth.
3. *Anger, disgust, fear, elation, affection.* Anger and disgust usually become distinguishable from distress by the fifth month. Fear becomes identifiable at about the seventh month. Between the tenth and twelfth months elation and affection become distinguishable from delight (Bridges, 1932).

The regularities of pattern suggest that the first year's development can be attributed at least in part to maturation. Opportunities for learning increase as the child grows older, so that it becomes harder to determine how much, if any, later emotional differentiation can be assigned to maturation.

That the process of differentiation through maturation goes on beyond early infancy is supported by a study of emotional expression in a 10-year-old child, deaf and blind from birth, whose opportunities to learn from others were greatly restricted. This child had had scarcely any opportunity to observe the expression of emotions by other children, since her only observations came through touch. Yet under conditions that would tend to provoke fear, anger, or pleasure, her facial expressions of crying or laughter and her accompanying postures and gestures all accorded very well with the classical descriptions of emotional behavior (Goodenough, 1932).

It appears that characteristic forms of emotion as well as many of the actions which indicate emotion to us develop through maturation.

Learning how to express emotion

Learning modifies the manner in which emotion is expressed. Anger, for example, may be expressed by fighting, by using abusive language, or by leaving the room. Unlike crying, leaving the room is not an expression of emotion that is known at birth; and certainly the abusive language has to be learned.

Studies of emotional expression in different cultures demonstrate impressively how much of that expression is developed by learning. One psychologist reviewed several Chinese novels in order to determine how a Chinese writer conveyed to his readers pictures of various human emotions. He found many of the bodily changes in emotion (flushing, paling, cold perspiration, trembling, goose pimples) used as symptoms of emotion in Chinese fiction much as they are in Western writings. There are, however, among the Chinese many other and quite different ways of expressing emotion.

The following quotations from Chinese novels would surely be misinterpreted by an American reader unfamiliar with the Chinese:

> "Her eyes grew round and opened wide." (This means that she became angry.)
> "They stretched out their tongues." (They showed signs of surprise.)
> "He clapped his hands." (He was worried or disappointed.)
> "He scratched his ears and cheeks." (Now we know that he was happy.) (Klineberg, 1938.)

Such evidence indicates that cultures teach conventionalized or stereotyped forms of expression which become a kind of "language of emotion" recognized by others within the culture. Thus skilled actors are able to convey to their audiences any intended emotion by using facial expression, tone of voice, and gesture according to the patterns an audience recognizes. In simulating emotion, those of us who are less skilled actors can convey our intent deliberately by exaggerating the conventional expressions: gritting our teeth and clenching our fists to indicate anger, turning down the corners of our mouths to look sad, raising our eyebrows to express doubt or disapproval.

The child growing up in a culture gradually learns to interpret the signs of emotion used by those about him, just as he learns also to express his feelings as they do. Experiments have shown that the ability to judge emotions from posed pictures increases with age (Gates, 1923).

Learning the occasions for emotion

Emotional behavior occurs in response to objects or situations which are the *occasions* for emotion. We fear something, are angry at someone, are worried about some possible turn of events. Though we may not have to learn how to fear, we learn what to be afraid of.

Ordinary observation shows many learned occasions for emotions. In American culture, for example, men seldom weep, whether the occasion be a wedding, a funeral, or failure to pass an examination in college, although American women commonly weep on such occasions. French men, however, weep much more freely than American men. Sending a loved one off on a trip may be the cause for weeping by the whole French family. How to weep is not learned, but when and where to weep are learned.

As the infant grows he learns to distinguish between what is familiar, and therefore "safe," and what is unfamiliar, and therefore perhaps "dangerous" or "threatening."

In the course of giving psychological tests to 61 infants during their first year of life,

6-4

Infants' reasons for crying change with age

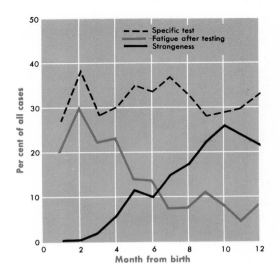

The relative amount of crying to be attributed to strangeness increases as contrasted with other causes of crying. (After Bayley, 1932)

Bayley (1932) noted the occasions on which the infants cried. As the infants grew older the causes of crying shifted, as shown in Figure 6-4 which is plotted as the percentage of total crying to be attributed to the specific tests, to fatigue after testing, and to strangeness. Strangeness of places and persons produces the largest increase in relative frequency of crying as the child gets older. A possible interpretation is that the older the child is, the better he is able to discriminate between the familiar and the strange, and hence the more often he reacts to strangeness by crying (see Figure 6-5).

An experiment was designed by Hebb (1946) to study the kinds of objects which provoked fear in chimpanzees that had been born and reared in captivity, so that the history of their previous experience with objects was known. These chimpanzees tended to show fear of many strange objects seen for the first time: a skull, a painted wax snake, a disembodied chimpanzee head.

6-5

Fear of strangers at eight months

At about eight months, the child's ability to discriminate among people leads to increasing uneasiness with strangers.

Dr. René Spitz

Alone, but calm and attentive.

Apprehension and screaming at approach of stranger.

Stranger turns away; screaming subsides.

Infant reaches for hand of motionless stranger.

They showed marked fear of strangers and were disturbed by slight changes in the clothing of familiar attendants. Thus learning enters, in that it is the unfamiliar that arouses fear.

Learning may enter in other ways. One explanation of the manner in which emotions become associated with new objects or occasions is through *conditioning*. Conditioning (discussed in detail in Chapter 9) is a process of association whereby something present at the time an emotion is experienced takes on the capacity of arousing that emotion. For example, a song heard during an unhappy experience may always thereafter arouse in the hearer an emotion of unhappiness.

A famous experiment in which a child learned to fear a white rat serves as the prototype of emotional conditioning (Watson and Rayner, 1920). The infant boy, Albert, when shown a white rat, reached for it and showed no signs of fear. While he was paying attention to the rat, he was suddenly frightened by a loud sound. Thereafter he was afraid of the rat. The originally neutral rat became a "conditioned stimulus" to fear. Albert now also showed fear of his mother's fur neckpiece and of other soft and furry objects. He showed no such fear of rubber balls or blocks that were entirely un-ratlike in appearance.

It is supposed that many irrational fears are acquired in this relatively automatic way. Because lightning precedes thunderbolts, the child comes to fear the lightning as well as the thunder, although the loud sound of the thunder is the primary reason for fright. But many children (and adults) experience fear when they are aware of impending danger; their fear of lightning is probably less related to its association with thunderclaps than to the real danger of being struck by lightning. One must be careful not to explain too much by conditioning; fear of real danger is rational and arises in part, at least, through understanding.

Preferences, attitudes, prejudices, and complexes as tendencies to experience emotions

study well

As we grow older, we become predisposed to experience emotion in relation to persons, objects, and ideas that have become important to us through our individual experiences. Emotions aroused by our own parents are different from and more intense than emotions aroused in us by parents in general; our country's flag stirs us, while the flag of another country may leave us unmoved. These are learned tendencies to experience emotion, and they are learned with individual discrimination so that one person's emotional attachments are not quite like another's.

The mildest form of affective coloring is aroused by simple *preferences,* such as likes and dislikes for one color over another or for one food over another. Because nearly all our experiences fit into a pattern of likes and dislikes, most of them are affectively colored, if ever so mildly. That people vary markedly in their preferences is indicated by the old adage, "There's no accounting for tastes."

Simple preferences become organized into patterns of preference called *attitudes.* A person may have a favorable or unfavor-able attitude toward labor unions, the Republican Party, coeducation, churchgoing, or smoking. If the attitude is favorable, the person, object, situation, or idea produces pleasant or favorable emotional response; if the attitude is unfavorable, the response is unpleasant, unfavorable, possibly hostile. Thus the attitude is more than a statement or judgment that something is good or bad, desirable or undesirable, for the judgment is accompanied by affective response.

An attitude that is firmly fixed and not open to free discussion is known as a *prejudice.* Some cooks prefer cane sugar to beet sugar. This preference can be called a prejudice if the cook is unwilling to try beet sugar where sugar is required in a recipe. Fixed social beliefs—that members of one race are inferior to another, that women cannot think as keenly as men—are also prejudices, because the people holding them are not capable of change through the examination of evidence bearing on them.

The word *complex* is used to refer to an attitude that is accompanied by excessive emotion, often leading to neurotic types of response. When an individual's attachment to his mother becomes so exaggerated that it interferes with other normal human relationships, we speak of his attitude to-

Erich Locher

6-6

Differing emotional reactions to the same stimulus

These children were shown a closed box and instructed to open it. When it was opened, they discovered a molted snake skin. Note the decided difference in their reactions to the same object.

ward his mother as a "mother complex." An inferiority complex is an attitude of excessive self-depreciation that acts to the detriment of the individual troubled by it.

Whether we speak of preferences, attitudes, prejudices, or complexes, we are calling attention to the fact that through learning, some persons, objects, institutions, and ideas come to arouse in an individual emotional responses different in kind or intensity from those aroused in other persons by the same stimuli.

Emotions and Motivated Behavior

No arguments are needed to establish the close relationship between emotion and motivation. Think of the stirring scenes in drama or literature, in which emotions provoke men to violent or desperate action and in which resolute, heroic, or shameful actions are accompanied by an intensification of emotion. These examples suggest that emotion acts both as a *drive* and as an *accompaniment to motivated action.* The triangle theme of love and jealousy is at once a story of motivation and of emotion. Sex

6-7

Apparatus used in studying fear as an acquired drive

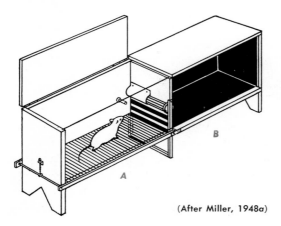

B

A

(After Miller, 1948a)

is not only a powerful motive; it is a source of vivid emotional experience as well. Moreover, the emotional experience itself may become a goal—as is made clear by the lyrics of many popular songs.

Emotion as drive

study well

Emotional states are aroused states. If the emotional state is an unpleasant one, the organism seeks to terminate it. This unpleasant emotional state corresponds to the tension state in aroused drive. The organism, if frightened, tries to escape exactly as it attempts to escape from pain. The person with fear of high places will learn to avoid such places or, if he finds himself on a height, will be restless until he gets away. Reduction of the tension aroused in unpleasant emotion is equivalent to the reduction of drive tension; in this situation emotion *is* drive.

Fear. In order to show how fear may serve as an acquired drive, Miller (1948a) placed rats one at a time in the left compartment of the box shown in Figure 6-7. Each rat received an electric shock in the closed compartment, with no means of escape. All the rats showed the same reactions. Each reacted to the shock with all the signs of pain and fright—jumping about, squealing, defecating. After a few repetitions of shocking in this compartment, each rat became emotionally agitated when placed in it without any shock. All the rats had acquired a conditioned fear of the compartment.

Now each rat learned to use a trap door as a means of escape into the second compartment, where it had never received a shock. For several hundred trials, whenever a conditioned rat was placed in compartment *A*, it went through the trap door to compartment *B*, although it received no additional shocks in compartment *A*. When the trap door was locked and a second escape device substituted, the rat learned to use the new device as a means of escape.

This experiment shows not only that the rats acquired a fear of the compartment in which they were shocked, but that the fear became an acquired drive. The animals went from the compartment in which they were tense and agitated to the one in which they were relaxed and comfortable. The "safe" compartment served as an incentive to relieve the fear. Thus aroused fear and the impulse toward fear reduction are not unlike aroused hunger and the impulse to reduce hunger pangs. Many psychologists believe that such acquired fears and related states of anxiety and apprehension account for much of human motivation.

Once a fear is acquired, it leads to strong avoidance of those situations in which the feared object or event is likely to appear. Fear motivates the organism both to escape from the feared object and to avoid contact with it. Extreme or pathological fears, known as *phobias,* strongly affect the conduct of those who suffer from them. The fears may be of high places, of closed spaces, of open spaces, of animals, of dirt, or of diseases. This list is, of course, not complete; almost anything can become the object of a phobia. A striking case history of such a phobia is given by William Ellery Leonard, poet and professor of English at the University of Wisconsin, in his autobiography, *The Locomotive God.* His fear of a locomotive, based on a childhood incident, led to fear of leaving home, until he virtually imprisoned himself. He dared go only a short distance away. Fear was for him a very powerful motive greatly affecting his movements, and hence the very course of his life.

Anxiety. Anxiety is a state closely related to fear and, like fear, has motivational consequences. The vocabulary of emotion, having come from the language of ordinary life and of literature, lacks scientific precision. Anxiety is a word from this vocabulary, and psychologists are not consistent in the way they use it.

Anxiety is first of all a state of apprehension, of concern, of uneasiness. It is a special kind of fear. While ordinary fear always has an object, anxiety is fear with a vague object or with no object at all. One meaning of anxiety is, then, a *vague fear.* This is perhaps the commonest meaning for psychologists.

A state of anxiety, like that of fear, is an unpleasant state, a tension state from which we yearn to escape. Hence anxiety, too, can be considered a drive. An individual is often made to conform to social expectations by threats to his security; that is, the threats make him anxious if he does not conform. If he breaks the law, he may be punished by a fine or by imprisonment. Society hopes that the punishment will not only control his conduct in the future but also stand as a warning to others, intensifying their anxieties if they violate the code. Some religions use the threat of divine vengeance against those who sin. The appeal to conscience, to a personal sense of guilt, is a more powerful anxiety-producer for some people than threats by external authority. It may be possible to escape the eye of the policeman, but it is impossible to escape your own conscience. Not all nonconformity is serious enough to require punishment, but the nonconformer may find himself teased or ridiculed. Ridicule puts him apart, makes him feel ostracized, and so arouses anxiety about his status and puts pressure upon him to behave like those about him.

Thus the enforcement of many commonly accepted and approved social practices is aided by the threat of anxiety. External controls become internalized in the form of conscience, so that the person feels more comfortable when he behaves in the way he (and society) thinks he should. The thought of behaving otherwise makes him feel guilty and arouses his anxiety. Because anxiety is unpleasant, one tends to avoid it, that is, one tends to behave most often in accordance with the dictates of his conscience.

Jealousy. Jealousy, a special form of anxiety based on insecurity, involves *fear of loss of affection to a rival.* That it has strong drive properties is evident enough from the triangle theme so common in dramatic literature. The husband who is jealous of another man believes that the man is stealing his wife's affection; even when there is no rival, the jealous husband guards his wife lest one appear. The reactions of the jealous person may be violent. If there is a genuine rival, the jealous person may attack him. If there is only the fear of a rival, the jealous person may go to great pains to protect and keep informed about the loved one whose faithfulness he is afraid of losing. Emotions such as jealousy and envy are distinguished more by their motivational aspects than by their feeling tones. A careful effort to distinguish between envy and jealousy as *states* that could be described introspectively or according to bodily responses led to failure (Ankles, 1939). As *motives,* however, useful distinctions can be made between jealousy as fear of a rival and envy as wishing for something possessed by another. For example, a person may *envy* another person his car without bearing any ill will toward that person. In jealousy, however, attitudes toward the rival are always hostile. These illustrations point up the importance of considering emotions as motives and not merely as stirred-up states of the organism.

CRITICAL DISCUSSION

Additional meanings of anxiety

While the definition of anxiety as a vague fear, as in "free-floating" anxiety, covers many instances of anxiety, there are several other conjectures that have found some support.

A second use of anxiety restricts it to a more limited kind of vague fear: the *fear of insecurity.* According to the concept on which this use is based, anxiety is social in its origin, beginning in infancy while the child is dependent upon the adults who care for him. Deprivation, neglect, and loss of affection arouse the feelings of insecurity that the infant comes to fear. (We saw in Chapter 3 some of the consequences of infantile insecurity.) This fear of insecurity is considered the basic anxiety, and it is a fear always associated with other people. What is feared is isolation, lack of affectionate responses by other people. When anxiety is used with this meaning, it is distinguished from fear: *things* can cause fear; only *people* can cause this kind of anxiety (Sullivan, 1949).

Anxiety is used in a third way to mean *concern over our own conduct,* i.e., feelings of guilt. We are uneasy about forbidden impulses or past misdemeanors. We fear that if they come to light, our guilt will be uncovered. Children, for example, have learned to show love and respect for their parents, yet are often resentful of parental authority. Fear of blurting out their hidden resentments may be a source of anxiety. The adolescent may fear to reveal his intensified interest in sex. Fear of being afraid or of showing fear may give rise to anxiety, especially if the accepted code (as in some military groups) is to appear fearless. Concern about our own feelings is undoubtedly one important form anxiety takes.

Modern existentialists, concerned with man's concept of himself, identify other aspects of anxiety, but these are described in half-mystical ways making it difficult to incorporate them in science. Anxiety in this usage is said to arise in part because of the contemplation of the inevitability of death and in part because of a sense of man's unrealized possibilities. These views derive from S. Kierkegaard (1831-55), an early existentialist philosopher (Kierkegaard, 1844, tr. by Walter Lowrie, 1944). While Kierkegaard's translator uses the word "dread," the word "anxiety" can be substituted for it (May, 1950; Tillich, 1952).

Anxiety came to be emphasized as a drive state at the time when the notion of aversive drives was at its height of popularity. Now that there is a tendency to turn to more positive aspects of motivation, a number of authors have begun to introduce the concept of "hope" as a counterpart to anxiety when an uncertain future is faced (e.g., French, 1952; Mowrer, 1960). This position was anticipated by Kierkegaard, who felt that only when one had faced anxiety could he find faith (that is, hope).

It should be evident that easy answers to the problems of anxiety and hope are bound to be superficial ones. More profound answers do not permit brief treatment—nor do they bring ready agreement.

Emotions as goals

Parents and other adults sometimes tear their hair over the seemingly deliberate efforts of eight- or nine-year-old boys to generate and enjoy excitement, trouble, danger. The emotion appears to be a kind of end in itself. Commercial amusements and the entertainment and recreation industries in general play on people's wishes to experience emotion. Some people go to the theater for a good laugh or cry.

While emotions can serve as motives, they can thus also serve as goals. We are reminded again of hedonism, the belief that men *seek* pleasure and *avoid* pain. Can we specify the incentives in these situations? The goals sought are not disembodied emotions, but *activities* that have emotional coloration. If the specific nature of the activity is less important than the excitement, thrill, delight, or joy it provides, the emotion itself can be said to define the goal. But once these emotions have been aroused by particular activities or particular people (e.g., a favorite comedian as a source of laughter), such activities or people become sought-after sources of stimuli and hence positive incentives.

Emotion as an accompaniment of motivated behavior

Motivated behavior tends to be tinged with emotion in all its stages; that is, affective coloration is not confined only to the drive state or to the consummatory response, but also accompanies the intervening activity. It is unpleasant to be hungry and pleasant to eat when hungry, but there is pleasure also in food-seeking, in antici-pating a good meal. We feel elated when we overcome obstacles on the way to a goal, even though we have not yet arrived at the goal. Because we are on the way to the goal, obstacles create a problem, and overcoming them brings the satisfaction of problem-solving. On the other hand, serious blocking or delaying of action on the way to a goal arouses in us annoyance and anger—or anxiety lest the goal not be reached.

The emotional accompaniment of activity toward a goal is a kind of comment on the progress. Words such as "encouragement," "suspense," "surprise," "worry," "hope" indicate the emotional significance of motivated behavior that takes a new turn, that is fraught with uncertainty, that has high or low probability of success. The pleasure of goal achievement is modified or enhanced by the struggle to attain success. When a man goes trout fishing, he enjoys the preparations and anticipation and tolerates getting out of bed at dawn, hiking through underbrush, and struggling against the cold current in the stream. The fish he catches taste much better than fish purchased at the market.

The affective coloration of goal-seeking activity may at times be a by-product, as in the annoyance of working at an inherently unpleasant task no matter how desirable the goal. But the emotional accompaniment is not a *mere* by-product without motivational significance, for it serves to sustain and reinforce (or weaken and disrupt) the ongoing activity.

We consider here two common emotional responses as accompaniments of motivated behavior: laughter and anger.

Laughter. The child who jumps up and down in joyous laughter at the announcement that he is going to the circus well illustrates an emotional accompaniment of motivation. The laughter is not here an end in itself, for laughter as a goal has not been substituted for the desire to go to the circus. While psychologists are by no means in agreement as to all the occasions for laughter, two aspects are commonly recognized:

1. Most occasions arousing laughter are social. One investigator found that in 223 situations in which preschool children laughed, 209 (or 94 per cent) of the laughing episodes occurred in the presence of a second person (Kenderdine, 1931). Another investigator, studying 240 college students, found their laughter attributed to social situations in 98 per cent of the instances (Young, 1937). Even something as physiological as response to tickling has a large social component. The child does not laugh when he tries to tickle himself; there is no tickle. He laughs only when someone else tickles him (Leuba, 1941).

2. Most occasions for laughter have in them an element of surprise. Tickling—one of the most primitive and universal sources of laughter—usually has in it an element of surprise. The tickling is usually threatened before it begins, and the moment of beginning is uncertain. Children's games that call forth laughter, such as "peekaboo," have both social and surprise elements.

The preliminary stages of the laughter-provoking sequences are usually tension-producing, so that the laughter comes as an expression of relief. We may assign as one of the motivational aspects of laughter this relief from certain tension-producing situations in the presence of other people. The excitement of mild tension is not damaging, the social attention is welcome, and the resolution through laughter provides a happy ending. Adults as well as children seek such sequences of events; under such

6-8

Emotion and motivation

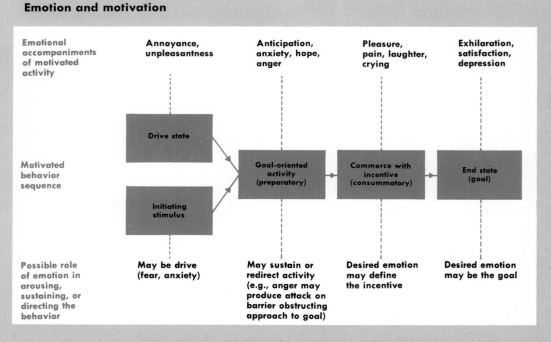

Relation of emotional behavior to the motivated behavior sequence.

circumstances laughter becomes a goal (p. 149). It is these sequences that produce laughter in plays, on radio and television, and in stories; their popularity sufficiently attests to their appeal.

Anger. Just as laughter is representative of pleasant emotional concomitants of motivated behavior, so anger is representative of unpleasant emotional accompaniments.

The primary occasion for anger is the thwarting of goal-seeking activity. Hence anger may be the by-product of any interrupted motivational sequence regardless of the motivational content of that sequence. Although anger may in turn acquire drive properties and lead to retaliatory action against the person or object held responsible for the thwarting, anger *begins* as an emotional accompaniment of something else.

Fifty-one college women kept records of the occasions on which they experienced anger or extreme irritation and of the impulses which resulted (Gates, 1926). The period of observation covered one week. The annoyance which produced anger or irritation included such matters as unjust accusations and insults, contradictions, scoldings, the loss of a fountain pen, the breaking of glasses. The impulses to which the anger or irritation led were reported as follows:

Women !! Impulses following anger	Number of reports
To make a verbal retort	53
To do physical injury to offender (slap, pinch, shake, strike, choke, push, step on, scratch, shoot, beat, throw out of window, kill, tear to pieces, throw something at, spank)	40
To injure inanimate objects	20
To run away, leave the room	12
To cry, scream, swear	10

Both laughter and anger originate as by-products of behavior sequences otherwise motivated. But when occasions for laughter are sought, and when anger, once aroused, starts sequences of retaliatory action, they become translated into goal-seeking behavior as drives and incentives. They then function as motives, not only as motivational accompaniments.

The foregoing discussion of emotion in relation to motivation stresses the three roles: as *drive,* as *goals,* and as *accompaniments of motivated behavior.* Since this is not the way in which emotions are usually characterized in other discussions of the topic by psychologists, some further comments are in order to clarify the position of the text.

Emotion as drive is familiar, and the Miller experiment on acquired fear as a drive (p. 172) nicely fits the conventional discussions by others based on the drive-incentive analysis.

How about emotions as goals and as accompaniments of other behavior? Many writers ignore these problems because they do not fit the standard current theories. For example, the development of laughter in the child may be discussed, or some theories of the humorous presented, but the fact that laughter is a significant part of motivated sequences of behavior is commonly overlooked. The entertainment business would not be one of our leading enterprises were it not for its motivational significance!

The accompanying diagram (Figure 6-8) illustrates the position taken by the text. The motivated behavior sequence, as it is described in terms of events between the arousal and the end state, is pictured in the boxes. Above the boxes are the characteristic emotional accompaniments, serving as a kind of commentary on the progress toward the goal. These accompaniments are not meaningless to the activity, but as commentary they are not its defining features, just as, say, the pounding heart and heavy breathing are accompaniments of a foot race but do not define the activity.

Below the boxes are characterizations of emotional behavior as it intrudes into the activity itself, perhaps redirecting it or defining its outcome.

There must be many borderline cases in which an emotional accompaniment suddenly becomes decisive for the activity. The parallel case would be when the runner, out of breath, drops out of the race. Then breathing is no longer a mere accompaniment of the race, but a decisive factor in it.

The purpose in presenting these distinctions is not to insist upon them as the only possible way of categorizing emotional activity, but to avoid the oversimplification that is so often attempted for the sake of clarity.

Emotional States as Adaptive and Disruptive

What is the role of emotions in civilized life? Do they help organisms to survive or are they chiefly sources of disturbance, of maladjustment? When we consider whether or not emotions hinder living in civilized society, we first have to inquire about the intensity of the emotional experience.

Intensity of emotion and adaptive significance

Emotional responses vary from the mildest satisfaction to the most complete panic. Mild emotions have a tonic influence. We work better when we are interested, when we have some enthusiasm for what we are doing. One consequence of mild emotion is a moderate increase in normal physiological functioning, possibly due to a slight increase in general tension. We know that a moderate increase in tension aids learning. This principle has been demonstrated in experiments in which the subject had to lift a weight or squeeze a dynamometer while memorizing. We noted earlier that the subject memorized best under mild tension, when neither too relaxed nor under too much strain (Courts, 1939; see also text, p. 10). If mild emotion produces similar tensions, it may also aid learning. A second consequence of mild emotion, provided it is relevant to the task, is to make the task more important and meaningful. Without affective coloring, activity becomes dull and

meaningless and soon takes on a monotonous tone. Therefore, a mild emotional state, generated by interest in a task, is serviceable.

Intense emotions play a more ambiguous role. They vary from the unpleasant states of anger, fear, and grief to the pleasant ones of joy and affection. When intense emotions are free to run their course, they may do no harm and may increase one's zest for living. Excitement may be followed by relaxation, fear by relief, despair by satisfaction. But situations may arise in which intense emotions cannot run their course. Then worry, anxiety, and heightened tension develop and become distractions that interfere with smooth performance. In experiments on the role of tension in memorizing, it was found that there was an optimum point beyond which tension interfered with memorization.

The adverse effects of intense emotion on problem-solving have been demonstrated in a number of experiments. In one, grade-school boys participated one at a time in an experiment consisting of three steps. As his first step, each boy took a short form of the Stanford-Binet Intelligence Test. Then he engaged in a problem-solving task for which success led to reward, failure to no reward. As a possible reward, he selected one of several attractive packages containing candy or money or a model airplane. The task was so arranged that half the boys succeeded and half failed. Those who succeeded were jubilant over their rewards; those who failed were downcast. As the third step, each boy repeated the intelligence test. The experiment showed very definite loss of score on the second test by those boys who had experienced the upset of failure in the intervening problem-solving situation (Lantz, 1945).[1]

[1] That such changes in score can occur as a result of frustration indicates the need of skill on the part of those who do intelligence testing. See Chapter 14.

Consequences of enduring emotional states

Some individuals react more strongly to mild emotional stimuli than do others; we consider such people "emotional." The characteristic level of emotional reactivity of a person is called his *temperament*. A more temporary state of emotional reactivity is called a *mood*. When we find a person who is usually cheerful, we say that he is of cheerful temperament; when we find a person of unpredictable temperament who is in a cheerful state, we say that he is in a cheerful mood. Either temperament or mood tends to arouse emotions congruent with it; that is, events otherwise more or less neutral became affectively colored according to the prevailing mood. If a person is in a gay mood, he may see minor setbacks as amusing challenges and take them in his stride; if he is in a troubled mood, he may see the same minor setbacks as occasions for anger or despair.

Moods sometimes represent the aftereffects of an emotional shock, as when a person goes around somewhat depressed for a time after having received bad news. The mood may linger on, even if the emotion has been overtly expressed; occasionally the mood continues as a state of tension because the feelings were not freely expressed when the occasion for them arose. Both internal conditions and external events may determine moods. A study of the time of day when children are most likely to show anger revealed that the peak of irascibility was just before meals and just before retiring. Hunger and sleepiness undoubtedly had some influence in arousing the irritable mood (Goodenough, 1931). But many events in daily life—good news, failure in an examination, loss of money—are conducive to moods (Young, 1937).

Medical men today are aware of a group of illnesses which they call *psychosomatic disorders* because the circumstances that give rise to the symptoms appear to lie in the emotional life of the person, although the symptoms themselves are "somatic," that is, symptoms of damage or disturbance in bodily organs or tissues. Prominent among these psychosomatic illnesses are ulcerative disorders of the digestive tract. It is supposed that ulcers of the stomach, for example, may be caused by the changes in muscular tension and in blood distribution in the walls of the stomach resulting from often-repeated or long-continued emotional states. Excessive digestive secretions, which are aroused by intense emotion, may have chemical effects accentuating the damage. Although the details concerning these effects are still somewhat in question, the association of organic ailments with prolonged emotional states of certain kinds appears now to be reasonably well established (Dunbar, 1955).

We have seen, then, that emotional intensity affects the role of emotion in adjustment. Mild emotions are tonic, intense emotions sometimes disruptive. More enduring emotional states, as in temperament and mood, may also make adjustment to life's demands easier or more difficult and may sometimes lead to actual illness.

Emotional suppression and emotional release

If some features of emotional behavior are adaptive and other features disruptive, we need a hygiene of emotions so that mature people can enjoy emotional expression without suffering the damage due to emotional excesses.

The hygiene of emotions largely involves the question of emotional control. Does maturity consist primarily in suppressing emotional expression so that life can be conducted more rationally? Or is emotional expression a kind of safety valve essential to healthy living?

Civilization requires us to suppress much overt emotional expression. To be civilized is to be moderate in behavior, not to "lose

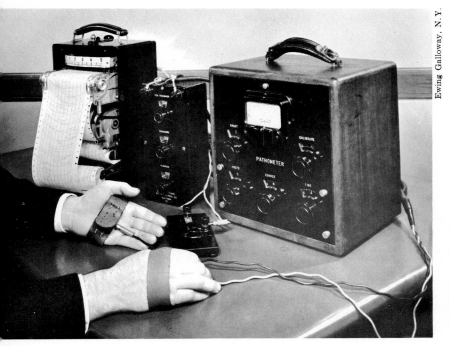

Ewing Galloway, N. Y.

6-9

The lie detector

The galvanic skin response (GSR) is measured by electrodes placed on the palms. The changes in the electrical resistance of the skin are an indication of emotional response as a result of interrogation.

one's head," not to "fly off the handle." We consider imperturbability, the ability "to take it," a virtue. While we admire emotional sensitivity in the form of social warmth and tenderness, we think it should be exercised with restraint. In all things we admire temperance over free indulgence.

Psychologists doubt the desirability of a general suppression of emotional expression. While some emotional control is no doubt essential for adults as well as for children, there are two qualifications concerning the *amount* of control, and these should be kept in mind: (1) Emotional suppression is not always successful; instead of being eliminated, the emotion may express itself in distorted form or in illness. (2) The beneficial results of appropriate emotional release can be demonstrated.

The physiological aspects of emotional expression—muscular tension or blushing, for example—are not under voluntary control. Hence voluntary suppression does not completely suppress, nor does it always succeed in eliminating, the emotional state.

Sometimes, however, the suppression goes on so long and so successfully that one is no longer consciously aware of any need to suppress. Under such circumstances, the emotion is said to be repressed. We will return to the problems of repression and suppression in Chapter 18. But even repressed emotions are not lost; by appropriate means it is possible to find signs that they are still active. Some evidence of the impossibility of fully suppressing emotional expression is found in studies making use of the "lie detector," an instrument designed to determine whether or not an accused person is telling the truth.

The lie detector is based on the principle that a person accused of crime will be apprehensive and therefore will involuntarily make characteristic emotional responses to stimuli related to the crime. When he is asked questions that he can answer without any feeling of guilt, his responses will show his general relief. When he is asked questions which he must answer with a lie in order to conceal his crime, he will usually experience an inner disturbance over which he has little if any control. In the lie-detector test, the person's words are recorded along with his bodily changes, e.g., changes in breathing, blood pressure, and electrical responses from the skin. (See Figure 6-9.)

While there is no magic in the instrument and it has to be used with extreme caution by skilled operators, those who use it report a high proportion of success. Many of the people tested who yield "giveaway" responses confess their guilt when they are shown the machine's recording, and thus validate the findings of the instrument (Inbau, 1942).

The lie detector shows the lack of success a person has in attempting to hide his true feelings. If we accept the interpretation of psychosomatic disorders as evidences of failures in the attempt to conceal emotions, we again see the impossibility of eliminating emotion through suppression.

As we shall learn in Chapter 19 in the discussion of psychotherapy (that is, the treatment of personal maladjustments by psychological means), many patients early in treatment yield an outpouring of statements heavily loaded with pent-up emotion. This outpouring has been called an "emotional catharsis." Such a purging or cleansing is often the first and necessary step toward a reorientation for the disturbed person. In work with children in need of psychological help it has been found useful to permit them great freedom of emotional expression. This "release therapy," as it is called, often results in better emotional control at a more healthful level.

It is not healthful to deny expression to emotional impulses that are genuine or natural. This does not mean that free play should be given to each and every impulse; emotional control is possible without emotional denial. If you lose a student election or fail a course, you may legitimately feel disappointed and unhappy. It is not necessary to toss the failure off as of no consequence or to deny that you feel dejected. But the disappointment need not turn to bitterness, to attacks upon the rival who won the election or upon the teacher who assigned the grade. You have proper control if you accept the naturalness of your own feelings and do not feel guilty because you are emotionally upset, and if at the same time you do not become the victim of your emotions. When a person can experience emotionally charged impulses without anxiety and guilt and can achieve a proper balance between expression and control, he is then emotionally healthy. He finds it possible to accept his emotional impulses as natural and to handle their expression in ways that are socially acceptable. In this way he has achieved emotional control without emotional denial.

We must recognize, however, that while it is easy to make generalizations about emotional expression and emotional control, the generalizations are often difficult to apply. For one thing, their application may depend upon circumstances peculiar to a particular culture or subculture (how would they apply to a Buddhist monk?). For another, in applying them to oneself, one runs up against tendencies to self-deception that make self-regulation of emotion particularly difficult. We shall return to these topics in later chapters (Chapters 18 and 19).

SUMMARY 1. Emotional states range from the mild *affective states* of pleasantness and unpleasantness that accompany virtually all behavior to the more intense affective states usually known as emotions. The more intense states can be classified into those that are pleasant (joy, affection) and those that are unpleasant (anger, fear, grief).

2. Emotional states as experienced in ordinary life are complex, and little is to be gained by trying to distinguish sharply among them. Studies of the bodily processes in emotion show that widespread changes are common to all intense emotions, although some physiological differentiation has proven possible. For example, one study showed responses in *fear* to be those predictable from the action of adrenalin, those in *anger* to be predictable from the action of adrenalin combined with noradrenalin.

3. Interpretation of emotional expression from the face, gesture, and voice is somewhat easier, because added to the natural expressions are the conventional ones the culture uses as its language of emotion.

4. Emotional development takes place through maturation and learning. As the child grows older, the *diffuse excitement* present at birth becomes *differentiated* into a variety of emotional states. That maturation is involved is suggested both by the regular pattern of emotional development in normal infants and by the similarities of expression of emotion in deaf-blind children to those in physically normal children. Learning is involved both in determining the *occasions* upon which emotions can be safely expressed and in shaping the *form of expression* to conform to patterns approved within the culture. Emotional tendencies become associated with persons, objects, and ideas. These tendencies vary from *attitudes* to *prejudices* to *complexes*. Each individual's particular tendencies become important in his behavior.

5. When emotional states are considered in relation to motivation, it is found that emotions may serve as *drives,* as *goals,* or as *accompaniments of motivated behavior.* Emotions such as fear and anxiety function as drives because they are tension states that we seek to relieve by appropriate behavior in relation to an incentive. When the goal of motivated behavior is excitement or thrill, emotion serves as an incentive.

6. Emotions as accompaniments of motivated behavior arise in the course of goal-seeking activity when that activity is blocked or thwarted. The study of *laughter* provides a convenient introduction to the nature of pleasant emotional accompaniments, just as *anger* provides an introduction to unpleasant emotional accompaniments.

7. Emotions may be both useful and harmful: they may serve the purposes of smooth adjustment and problem-solving, but they may also interfere with these purposes. Certain physiological changes accompanying excited emotion energize the organism for action and thereby serve as aids to survival for animals struggling in combat. While these "emergency reactions" may have been useful for primitive man, they are of little use in our culture where violent emotion is frowned upon. The question may be a matter of intensity, *mild* emotional states being tonic and helpful, *strong* emotional states being debilitating and disruptive.

8. More enduring emotional states, known as *mood* and *temperament,* may under some circumstances maintain internal tension with harmful bodily consequences. These difficulties are studied as *psychosomatic disorders.*

9. Modern civilization may have gone too far in the direction of seeking to suppress emotional expression. For one thing, the effort to be rid of emotion through suppression or repression is relatively unsuccessful, as shown by the signs of residual emotional effects registered on a lie detector or manifested in psychosomatic illnesses. Emotional expression may be beneficial to health. Emotional control need not mean emotional denial. It is possible to accept emotions as normal and natural, while directing emotional expression into channels that are socially acceptable.

SUGGESTIONS FOR FURTHER READING

Cannon, *Bodily changes in pain, hunger, fear, and rage* (2nd Ed., 1929) is a classical treatment of the physiological accompaniments of emotional states. A good introduction to psychosomatic concepts is Dunbar, *Emotions and bodily changes* (4th Ed., 1954); the subtitle is "A Survey of Literature on Psychosomatic Interrelationships, 1910-1953." Reymert (Ed.), *Feelings and emotions* (1950) is a symposium, with stress on theoretical interpretations. Chapters 5-7 of Woodworth and Schlosberg, *Experimental psychology* (Rev. Ed., 1954) deal with emotions, particularly their expression and physiological correlates. A survey relating emotion to motivated activity can be found in Young, *Motivation and emotion* (1961).

Perception

All organisms discriminate among stimuli that impinge upon them by way of sensitive tissues which in the higher organisms take the form of sense organs. The senses are thus the channels for information about the world. It is a central fact of behavior that we react not to single stimuli but to patterns of stimuli. For that reason we turn first to some general characteristics of perceiving objects and events before considering in greater detail the role of the specific sense organs in perceiving.

CHAPTER 7

The Perception of Objects and Events

Life goes on in a world of things and other people. Were the individual not sensitive and responsive to his environment, he would be unable to satisfy his needs, communicate with his fellows, or enjoy his surroundings. The individual learns to know his world through the data that come to him by way of his sense organs, but what he perceives depends also on what he brings along with him from his past experiences and what his present needs and wishes are as he faces the world. Thus, as in all the topics of psychology, perception has its developmental as well as its interactive aspects; perception depends upon more than the stimuli now impinging upon sense organs. In order to keep perspective on the total process of perception, some of the more general problems will be treated first, and the special problems of how the sense organs operate in perception will be postponed until the next chapter.

Usually the objects of which we are aware are sources of multiple stimuli and are embedded in surroundings providing additional stimuli. We see signs or pictures instead of spots of light; we hear words or music instead of single pure tones. We react to *patterns* of stimuli, usually with little awareness of the parts composing the pattern. When we put a jigsaw puzzle together, the colors and sizes of figures in the individual pieces often look entirely different from the way they look when embedded in the whole picture. An oil painting, viewed close up, may appear to be a meaningless collection of daubs of paint. The total impression, from organized stimuli, has properties not predictable from the parts in isolation.

All experiences of objects and events take place within a framework of space and time. Vision and audition provide the most complex patterns of these perceptual experiences. Vision is our preferred spatial sense, giving us variegated patterns of form and color in three dimensions, but it is also a good time sense because we see succession, movement, and change. Audition is a spatial sense also, though its spatial patterns are much more limited than those of vision; it is primarily a time sense, for its primary patterns are those of succession, change, and rhythm. Because of vision's pre-eminence as a spatial sense, much discussion of perception goes on in terms of vision. Of course many perceptual experiences depend at once on several senses; then the prominence of one sense over another becomes a matter for study.

Object Perception and Perceptual Constancies

If you look around the room and ask yourself what you see, your answer is likely to be, "A room full of people and things." You may pick out specific people or things instead of making such a general statement, but you are not likely to report that you see a mosaic of light and shadow. Perception is oriented toward things rather than toward the sensory qualities that describe things. Detached sensory qualities ("blueness," "redness") can be perceived, but are usually perceived as the qualities of objects. You see the yellow flowers or the soft pillow or the hot radiator, not "yellowness," "softness," or "hotness."

Our perceptual experiences are not isolated; they build us a world of identifiable things. When you turn your head away, you think of the objects as remaining where you saw them. Objects endure, so that you meet the same object over and over again. This all seems very obvious, but to perceive the world in such a way represents quite an intellectual achievement.

Growth of object perception

We do not know what the world looks like to the newborn infant. If we hazard a guess, we may choose between the world as a "blooming, buzzing confusion" (as William James put it) or as a relatively undifferentiated background on which simple figures begin to emerge. Whatever the infant may see at first, we know that he soon achieves order in the world. The question is: How?

The child achieves order in his perceptual world when he discovers enduring objects in this world, objects he recognizes when they reappear. These recognized identities he establishes through active manipulation. The nipple of the nursing bottle becomes real to him because the child does something with it. The fact that it furnishes milk when sucked on is more important to him than that it has a particular shape or color, though *later* the shape or color becomes an identifying characteristic. He knows an object first by interacting with it; after such interaction it becomes perceptually identifiable to him. He soon recognizes his mother and distinguishes between her and strangers. *Object achievement* in perception is simply the recognition of an object as enduring and recurring (Piaget, 1950).

Object constancy

When an object has been constituted perceptually as a permanent and stable thing, we perceive it as such, regardless of the illumination on it, the position from which it is viewed, or the distance at which it appears. The tendency to see it as of normal color regardless of light and shadow is called *brightness* and *color constancy*. The tendency to see it as of standard shape regardless of the viewing angle is called *shape constancy*. The tendency to see it as its usual measurable size regardless of distance is called *size constancy*. Finally, the fact that objects retain their "same" positions, even as we move about, is known as *location constancy*. The word "constancy" is an exaggeration, but it dramatizes our relatively stable perception of objects. Object constancy is made up, then, of these five constancies of brightness, color, shape, size, and location.

Brightness and color constancy

Black velvet looks just as black to us in bright sunlight as in shadow. We refer to this fact as *brightness constancy*. Although this effect holds under ordinary circumstances, a change in the structure of the surroundings can destroy it. Attach the black velvet to a board and throw a bright light on both it and the board. It still looks black. Now, without changing anything, place an opaque screen between you and the velvet, with the source of light behind the screen (Figure 7-1). The screen has a small opening in it, so that you see only a small patch of the velvet. Such a screen is called a *reduction screen,* for it reduces what you see to the actual light reflected from a surface, independent of the setting. Now the velvet looks *white* because it is reflecting more light than the surrounding screen. In natural settings we somehow take into account the total illumination and are thereby able to maintain constancy.

Constancy is not perfect, and objects seem to fade somewhat when illumination is decreased. In order to measure the actual degree of constancy we may use an arrangement such as that of Figure 7-2. The two disks can be adjusted to yield grays differing in brightness by changing the proportion of white and black in a mixture. The procedure is to present to a subject some fixed brightness value on disk *A* in

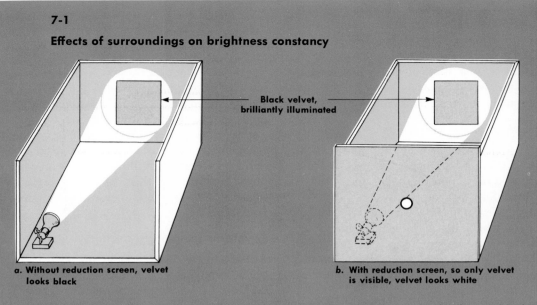

7-1

Effects of surroundings on brightness constancy

Black velvet,
brilliantly illuminated

a. **Without reduction screen, velvet looks black**

b. **With reduction screen, so only velvet is visible, velvet looks white**

Even though the square of velvet is brilliantly illuminated, it still looks black, provided the illuminated background is also visible. However, when only the velvet is visible through the reduction screen, it looks white, even though the illumination on it is the same.

the shadow, then to adjust disk B (in the light) until the subject judges the brightness of the two disks to be alike. If constancy were perfect, he would set the black-white mixture in B equal to that in A; if there were no constancy, he would reduce the whiteness of B to make it reflect the same amount of light as A. What he usually does is to compromise between the two, thereby showing imperfect brightness constancy. Such constancy as he does achieve depends upon his seeing shadows cast by the disks against their backgrounds, so that he can correct for the illumination. Experimenters have shown that the subject's judgment can be changed by using backgrounds designed as artificial shadows, some with the fuzzy edges usual to shadows, others without these. Only with a sharp boundary between the disk and its shadow and with a natural-looking shadow is the usual constancy result found (MacLeod, 1940).

Similar considerations apply for color constancy. Colored objects may be per-

ceived as retaining their original colors not only when the intensity of light changes but even when illuminated by colored light, provided there are sufficient contrasts and shadows (Wallach and Galloway, 1946). There are severe limitations to constancy under colored illumination, however, because of the different ways in which various pigments absorb colored lights. Objects will change their colors when illuminated by a light artificially restricted to narrow bands of the spectrum, even though the light appears white. For example, a white light composed solely of red and blue-green may make a yellow object appear red and a green object gray. Fluorescent objects radiate light at wave lengths other than those that strike them. Objects treated with the dye fluorescein appear yellow in light from which blue has been eliminated, but appear green when illuminated by light containing blue. These effects, often dramatically used in the theater, are possible only because the constancy of the color of objects breaks down under certain circumstances.

One factor in color constancy is the remembered color of familiar objects. When conditions of visibility are such as to make colors somewhat ambiguous, this "memory color" helps determine what we see. For example, a lawn in poor condition may be seen as much greener *in toto* than when viewed through a reduction screen, because we remember grass as green. The following experiment illustrates this tendency to preserve mentally the color of familiar objects.

Several different objects were cut out of the same sheet of orange paper. These two-dimensional objects were identified as a banana and a lemon (normally yellow), a tangerine and a carrot (normally orange), and a cooked lobster claw and a tomato (normally red). The subject was asked to adjust a color wheel so that its color matched that of the paper objects presented one at a time. The subject had to turn his head away from the object to look at the color wheel so that he could not make a direct comparison of color quality.

Under these conditions of experimentation, there was a striking tendency to distort the matching color in the direction of the natural color of the object, even when the subject was fully aware that all the pictures were cut out of the same paper. That is, the match for the normally red objects was redder, and for the normally yellow objects yellower, than the match for the normally orange objects (Bruner, Postman, and Rodrigues, 1951).

Shape constancy

When a door swings open toward us, its rectangular shape goes through a series of

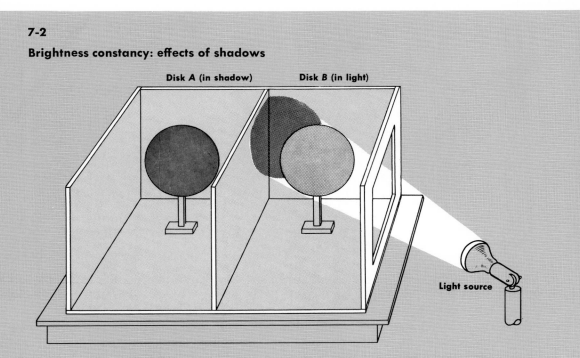

7-2

Brightness constancy: effects of shadows

Disk A (in shadow)   Disk B (in light)

Light source

The subject adjusts the mixture of black and white in Disk B to make it match that in Disk A. Because of the light shining on Disk B, his adjustment is usually imperfect. If B casts a sharp shadow, he is able to achieve more brightness constancy. (After MacLeod, 1932)

Illusion created by rotating trapezoidal window

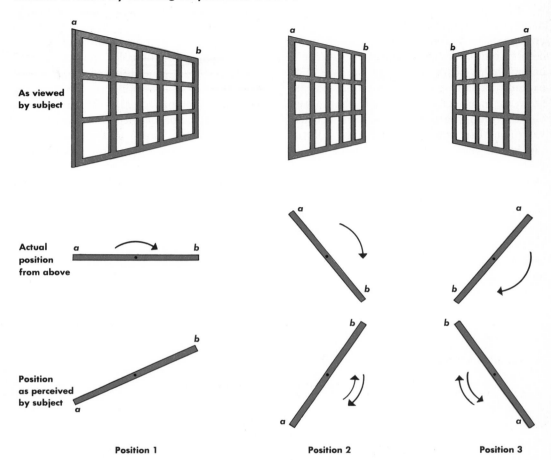

As viewed by subject

Actual position from above

Position as perceived by subject

Position 1   Position 2   Position 3

The window is so constructed that in Position 1 it looks like a rectangular window with the left edge closer to the subject. Actually the left edge (a) and the right edge (b) are equally distant from the observer. As the window rotates clockwise (as viewed from above), the left edge remains larger to the subject than the right edge; hence it still seems nearer, even though it is moving away (Position 2). Even when the window rotates completely—goes through what would be twelve o'clock on a clock and begins to come closer again (Position 3)—a is still seen as closer than b. The viewer then tends to see the window as waving back and forth rather than as going around. (After Ames, 1951)

distortions. It becomes a trapezoid, with the edge toward us looking wider than the hinged edge; then the trapezoid grows thinner, until all we can see is a vertical line the thickness of the door. We can readily distinguish these changes, but what we *perceive* is an unchanging door swinging on its hinges. The fact that the door does not seem to change its shape is called *shape constancy*. We see the top of a milk bottle as round, whether we view it from the side or from the top.

The distortions that occur when a familiar object rotates are used by us as cues to its rotation rather than as indications that the object is changing. This principle is well illustrated by some demonstrations with a rotating trapezoidal window, as pictured in

7-4

Size constancy

> Here there is no difficulty in perceiving that the arches on the right receding in perspective are all of the same size, and that they are the same as the three arches in the background. The conditions are thus good for size constancy. Now measure on this page the reproduced height (perspective size) of the nearest arch and compare it with the reproduced height of the distant arches. You will find that the near arch is more than four times as high (in perspective size) as the distant arch.

Figure 7-3. No matter what the position of the window, our experiences with shape constancy suggest that edge *a* is nearer than edge *b*. Hence as the window rotates in space, to the observer it appears to vacillate back and forth, with edge *a* always in front. Because we continue to see the window as a familiar rectangle, we are led into illusory perception.

Size constancy

When we see an object at a distance, we might conceivably judge its size in one of three ways:

1. *Perspective size.* We might judge it according to the geometry of perspective, seeing it as smaller the farther away it is, the size inversely proportional to distance. This size would correspond to the size of the image on the retina. The retinal projection of an object at 20 feet is half the retinal projection at 10 feet.
2. *Object size.* If object constancy were perfect, we might judge an object by its known (measurable) size and hence not see it any smaller at a distance.
3. *Compromise between perspective size and object size.* We might compromise and see the object somewhat smaller at a distance, but not as much smaller as the geometry of perspective indicates.

Of the three alternatives described, the last one is usually correct. Our size perceptions represent compromises between perspective size and object size. Experiments can tell us more exactly the nature of these compromises.

Although we distort perspective, we do of course see things as smaller the farther they are from us. As we look through a row of arches, each fits inside the preceding one. The farthest arch may look about half the size of the nearest one, even though it is ten times the distance away and ought to look only one-tenth as large. It certainly looks smaller, but, if asked whether or not it *is* a smaller arch, we may unhesitatingly say: "All the arches look the same size." The distant arches look both *smaller than* and *equal to* the near ones! (See Figure 7-4.) When we speak of *size constancy*, we refer to the ability to see the far object as equal in size to a near object of the same size.

The ability to match near objects with far ones of the same size begins early in life. Even the six-month-old child shows some evidence of this ability to maintain the constancy of objects (Cruikshank, 1941), but the six-year-old child is not as adept as an adult. For example, children of six, in their attempts to match a 9-centimeter box placed at a distance of 11 meters with one of several boxes at 1 meter, tended to choose a 7-centimeter box (Beryl, 1926). Adults unhesitatingly choose (correctly)

7-5

Size perception as influenced by conditions of viewing

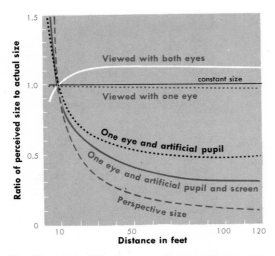

The objects judged for size were circular cardboard disks viewed in dimly illuminated hallways. (After Holway and Boring, 1941)

the 9-centimeter box. A child of three, watching motor cars on a roadway below a lookout point, will see the cars as miniatures and often insist that they cannot be full-size. He may even beg for them as toys. His size constancy is not yet developed for this new viewing angle. Adult size constancy commonly breaks down also when objects are viewed from a height, but the adult makes an intellectual correction that the young child does not make.

We are now ready to consider more carefully the nature of the compromise between perspective size and object size that we make in actual perception. It is safe to say that the more information available, the more the perceived size approaches the object size; to the extent that information is lacking or ambiguous, the more closely perceived size approaches perspective size.

The effect of reducing the number of environmental supports for maintaining size constancy is well demonstrated in Figure 7-5. When we look with both eyes, there is overconstancy, that is, we see the distant object somewhat larger than object size. When we use only one eye, there is nearly perfect object constancy, a relation holding also for observers who have only one eye (Taylor and Boring, 1942). When the surroundings are cut off, first with an artificial pupil (a reduction screen worn near the eye, with a small hole corresponding to the pupil of the eye but of fixed size) and then with an additional screen, the compromise falters and the reported size approaches more nearly perspective size.

The compromise between object size and perspective size thus depends upon the environmental surroundings in which the judgment is made.

Location constancy

Our world has perceptual stability for us because we perceive objects as enduring, as being the same as when we last looked. We also perceive these objects in a setting that remains essentially fixed, despite the fact that we see a kaleidoscopic world which sends us a myriad of changing impressions as we move about in it. We take the general background of perception so for granted that we have difficulty in realizing that there are psychological problems in it.

But why doesn't the world whirl by us in the opposite direction when we move our heads? Why don't we get the same kind of blurred movement that occurs in motion pictures taken by the beginner who moves the camera as he ordinarily moves his head? One reason is the way our eyes move as we look about. They *jump* from one resting spot to another, and we do not perceive whatever registers while they are in motion. When the eyes drift, as they do when we are dizzy from spinning, the world does appear to whirl in front of us. But constancy is not simply a result of the way our eyes operate; it is also learned. In a classical experiment a subject wore reversing lenses so that he saw the world upside down. At first the perceived world swirled by as he looked around. One of his first adaptations to the new way of perceiving the world was a decrease in this movement as constancy of location was regained. Another sign of regained constancy of location was that the fire was again heard to crackle in the fireplace where it was seen, a harmony of location that was at first lost because only the eyes, and not the ears, were perceiving in reverse (Stratton, 1897). The experiments have been repeated, with comparable results (Snyder and Pronko, 1952; I. Kohler, as reviewed in Werner and Wapner, 1955).

The later experiments performed by Kohler (1961) added other dimensions to visual changes introduced by wearing distorting lenses. In one series half the visual field was inverted, while the other remained normal; in another, half the visual field was blue, while the other half was yellow. In every case there was an adjustment to the lenses so that there was less distortion, or occasionally a shift in the kind of distortion, after many days. In some cases it took as long as forty days after ceasing to wear the lenses for the distortions to disappear. In the case of the colored lenses, which distorted only by coloring the world blue when the subject looked to the left and yellow when he looked to the right, there was at first an intensification of the color yellow when he looked from left to right, an effect to be expected in terms of contrast and afterimages (see Chapter 8, p. 230). This effect no longer occurred after he had worn the glasses for some days. When he ceased to wear the glasses, however, the effect returned: he now saw yellow when he looked to the right and blue when he looked to the left. It is as though his experience with seeing yellow and blue when turning his eyes now led him to see these colors when he looked right and left, even though he was no longer wearing the colored lenses.

Organization in Perception

The perceptual constancies imply *organization* within perception. We are now ready to be somewhat more analytical and to see if we can find principles of perception that help us to explain the perception of objects.

Figure and ground

Geometrical patterns are always seen against a background and thus appear object-like, with contours and boundaries. We may think of such *figure-ground* organization as basic to stimulus patterning. Patterns do not have to contain identifiable objects to be structured as figure and ground. Patterns of black and white and many wallpaper designs are perceived as figure-ground relationships, and very often figure and ground are reversible (Figure 7-6). Note that the part seen as *figure* tends to appear as slightly in front of the background, even though you know it is printed on the surface of the page. You seem to look *through*

7-6

Reversible figure and ground

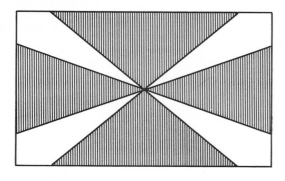

Note that either the light portions or the dark portions can be perceived as figures against a background.

the spaces in and around the figure to a uniform background behind, whether the background is in white (or a light color) or black (or a dark color).

Careful studies of what people see when they suddenly recover from blindness (e.g., when they have cataracts removed) show that the figure-ground organization is found when other features of perception are missing (Senden, 1932; see Hebb, 1949). Adults, seeing for the first time, have no difficulty in seeing *a something* as a figure on a background, although they are unable to identify familiar forms by sight. They are able to point out a black cardboard circle or a black cardboard triangle lying on a white tablecloth, but they do not know which is circle and which is triangle until they handle the objects. The primitive figure-ground organization is there, but what is seen is merely a form, as though some black ink had been spilled on a paper. It often takes several weeks for such patients to learn to *identify* things well from sight. If during recovery the patient is shown un-

der colored light such familiar objects as eggs or pieces of fruit, he may not recognize them.

Perceptual grouping and patterning

Even simple patterns of lines and dots fall into ordered relationships when we look at them. When we look at Figure 7-7, we tend to see three *pairs* of lines, with an *extra* line at the right. But notice that we could have seen three pairs beginning at the right and an extra line at the left. A slight modification (Figure 7-8) causes us to do just that. These tendencies to *structure* what we see are very compelling; what we see in figures seems to be forced upon us by the patterns of stimulation (Wertheimer, 1923).

Gestalt psychologists have been particularly interested in figure-ground relationships and other patterned aspects of stimulation and have suggested a number of principles to explain results such as those found with Figures 7-7 and 7-8. We shall consider four of their principles: (1) proximity, (2) similarity, (3) continuity, and (4) closure.

7-7

Patterning and perceptual structuring

The proximity of the lines that appear to be in pairs leads us to see three pairs and an extra line at the right.

7-8

The same lines as in 7-7, but with extensions, lead to the opposite pairing: three broken squares and an extra line at the left.

Proximity. Look at the dots in Figure 7-9. They appear to be arranged in horizontal rows in *A* and in vertical columns in *B*. Why? Merely because they are *closer together* in rows in *A* and in columns in *B*. It takes effort to counteract proximity and

7-9

Proximity and structuring

· · · · · · · ·   ·   ·   ·   ·
                       ·   ·   ·   ·
· · · · · · · ·   ·   ·   ·   ·
                       ·   ·   ·   ·
· · · · · · · ·   ·   ·   ·   ·
                       ·   ·   ·   ·
· · · · · · · ·   ·   ·   ·   ·

     A   *B*

The dots appear to form rows in A and columns in B; the dots closer together seem to "belong" together.

7-10

Similarity and structuring

o   o   o   o   o   o   o   o

·   ·   ·   ·   ·   ·   ·   ·

o   o   o   o   o   o   o   o

·   ·   ·   ·   ·   ·   ·   ·

o   o   o   o   o   o   o   o

Because the circles, and the dots, appear to "belong" together, we perceive rows instead of columns.

7-11

Continuity and structuring

The wavy line is perceptually continuous, as is the rectangular motif, so that it is easier to see the figures as composed of these two parts (as in B) than as the logically equivalent parts in C.

to see them in columns and rows in the other direction.

The principle of proximity applies also within other senses. Consider a series of tapping sounds, for example, arranged as follows: tap-tap—tap-tap—tap-tap—tap. We hear these as three pairs of taps and an extra tap, again grouping those that lie near each other—but in time rather than in space.

Similarity. In Figure 7-10 all the dots are equally spaced, so that proximity is not an important factor in determining whether we emphasize horizontal or vertical lines. Now the influence of similarity is compelling, and we see rows of dots and rows of small circles, grouping like items together.

Continuity. What does Figure 7-11A appear to be? It is easy to break it into the two parts shown in Figure 7-11B, a wavy line over a rectangular motif. Again if we expend some effort we can break it into the two parts shown in Figure 7-11C, but there is little doubt about the greater "naturalness" of *B*. The explanation is that the parts are more continuous this way, the wavy line continuing as a wavy line and the right-angled figures also following each other continuously.

Closure. If you look back at Figure 7-8, you will remember how you tended to fill in the gaps to complete the rectangles. The tendency for incomplete figures to become complete in perception is called

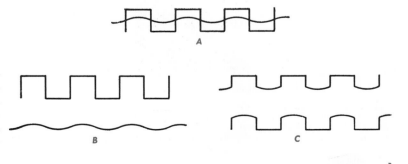

closure. The picture in Figure 7-12 also illustrates this tendency. Closure leads toward a stable organization.

Under some circumstances the tendency toward a stable organization may *destroy*

7-12

Closure

Although very few details are given, it is easy to fill in the blanks perceptually and "organize" the black areas into the picture of a dog. (After Street, 1931)

7-13

How organization conceals parts

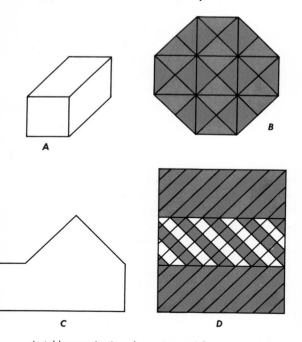

A stable organization of superimposed figures may destroy the organization of an original figure. It is difficult to see that A is contained in B and that C is contained in D. (After Witkin, 1959)

7-14

Effect of the whole on the parts

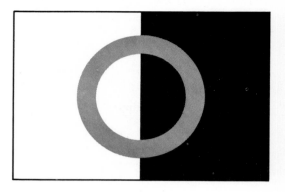

Separating the circle into two parts produces a contrast effect (see text). (After Osgood, 1953)

one figure perceptually in order to favor a more stable one. This principle is capitalized on in *camouflage,* which seeks to hide something by incorporating it into a dominant pattern that destroys the original contours. In Figure 7-13 we see the concealing of originally stable figures by a superimposed organization.

The properties of wholes affect the ways in which parts are perceived. For that reason we may say that the whole is different from the sum of its parts—a favorite slogan of Gestalt psychology.

The gray circle of Figure 7-14 is a stable whole, and hence tends to be seen as a uniform gray. If, however, there had been two circles cut from the same gray, one mounted on black and one on white, they would have appeared very different as a result of contrast with the two backgrounds. The contrast effect can be restored by dividing the gray circle into halves. Placing a pencil across the circle between the black and white areas will do. The left half-circle suddenly looks distinctly darker than the right half. Move the pencil slowly to the right or to the left, and the darker (or lighter) portions of the gray circle will seem to follow it, retaining uniformity within each segment. Thus we see that wholeness characteristics affect the perception of the parts.

Effect of experience on figure-ground perception

Although the features of stimulus organization stressed by the Gestalt psychologists are clearly important in determining what we see, perception is also influenced by previous experience. This can be shown to be true even for the organization of patterns into figure and ground.

Figure 7-15 can be perceived either as an attractive young woman (the wife) or as an old hag (facetiously referred to as her mother-in-law).

An experiment was performed to compare the ways in which the picture would be seen by those who had and had not met it before. Sixty per cent of those seeing it for the first time tended to see the wife; 40 per cent, the mother-in-law.

Two groups were given prior experience before being shown the ambiguous picture. One group saw first the unambiguous picture of the wife shown in Figure 7-15B. The other group saw the picture of the mother-in-law (Figure 7-15C). Now what happened when both of these groups saw the ambiguous picture (Figure 7-15A) for the first time? All of those who had earlier seen the wife (100 per cent) now saw her in the ambiguous picture. Of the others, 95 per cent saw the mother-in-law in the ambiguous picture (Leeper, 1935).

The way we perceive an ambiguous figure can be taught, according to experiments of Solley and Santos (1958). They used the outline cubes (Necker cubes) shown in Figure 7-16. The two "improved" cubes, with one face outlined with a heavier line, favor in the one case a left-to-right perspective and in the other a right-to-left perspective. The "test" cube, without accentuated lines, can of course be interpreted easily in either perspective. The method of training used was that which has come to be known as "verbal conditioning," which we shall meet in Chapter 9. The two training figures were exposed one at a time for two seconds each, and the subject was asked to state the direction of the perspective ("left-to-right" or "right-to-left"). For the improved cubes these judgments were usually in the expected directions. The experimenter planned to favor an interpretation opposite to that of the subject's initial bias when viewing the ambiguous (balanced) test figure. If, for example, he wished to favor the "left-to-right" method, he "rewarded" the subject when

7-15

Ambiguous figure-ground effects

A   B   C

The wife and mother-in-law ambiguity.   Dr. Robert Leeper

Resolving ambiguity through learning

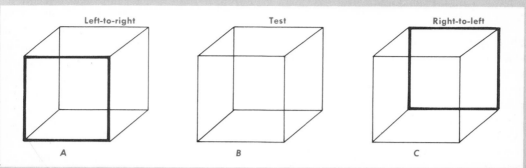

Left-to-right	Test	Right-to-left
A	B	C

Accenting one or the other face of the cube causes it to be perceived in different perspectives. Following the rewarded learning of one way of perceiving the cube, the originally ambiguous cube (B) is perceived in the favored orientation. (After Solley and Santos, 1958)

the subject said "left-to-right" for an improved cube. The reward was merely saying "uh-huh," "good," "you're doing fine," etc. So as not to be too obvious, the experimenter rewarded 70 per cent of the trials in the direction sought and 30 per cent of the trials in the other direction. Test trials with the balanced cube were interspersed; the experimenter said nothing following the subject's response. All 10 subjects gradually came to see the ambiguous, balanced cube as in the perspective that had been most often rewarded.

The main point about figure-ground relationships is that a figure is perceived as "thinglike." In our ordinary commerce with objects, we perceive things against their backgrounds, and these things maintain their identity as they move on the background. Books can be moved on the table top, the pencil can be picked up and put into your pocket, people rise from their chairs and walk down the corridor.

Problems created by visual illusions

For the most part our perceptions serve us very well. Most of the time seeing is be-

lieving. Many problems are raised by the fact that perception is so satisfactory (the constancy tendencies, for example), but it is easy to take the accuracy of perception for granted. Hence in the study of perception psychologists have turned to *illusions,* in which perceptions are obviously misleading, in order to find out how perception works.

Geometrical illusions have been studied for many years, but their explanations have never been fully agreed upon. Sometimes the illusion is due to some feature of *embeddedness,* so that the part being judged is improperly isolated. The familiar arrowhead illusion and its variations (Figure 7-

7-17

Illusions based on embeddedness of lines

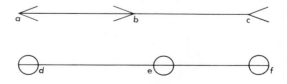

Distances *ab, bc, de,* and *ef* are equal.

Illusions based on size contrasts

The two figures in *A* are identical. The center circles of *B* are the same size.

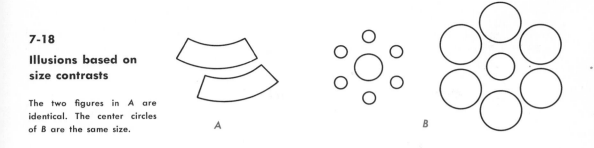

A

B

17) illustrate the difficulty of isolating the lines to be judged from the areas in which the ends are embedded. Other illusions are based on *relative size* due to contrast with surroundings (Figure 7-18). The many illusions depending upon *angles* usually can be explained if we suppose the figures to be projected in the third dimension (Figure 7-19). If the lines in figures *A* and *B* were drawn as they are on the surface of a solid double cone, or on a system of wires meeting at the horizon, they would have to be curved in order to be parallel as viewed. The lines in figure *C* are as though drawn on a set of steps moving off in the distance. If that is what they were, the long lines (drawn parallel) would *not* be parallel in the frontal plane of the stairs. Thus we tend to view these figures as though they were perspective drawings, and the tendency to "constancy" previously discussed is now misleading. Occasionally two factors act together, as in Figure 7-20. Here the line that looks longer appears to be the diagonal of a larger rectangle. This is the influence of embeddedness. But if you think of the picture in perspective, the line would also have to be longer to look as it does.

7-19

Illusions based on intersecting lines

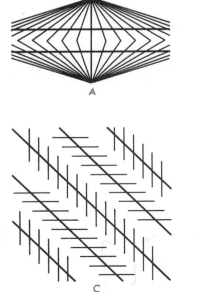

A

B

The horizontal lines in *A* and *B* are parallel. The long diagonal lines in *C* are parallel. The spirals of *D* are actually concentric circles.

C

D

7-20

Illusions based on falsely implied perspective

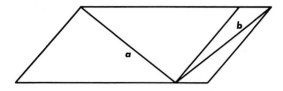

If the figure is seen as a perspective drawing of a rectangle, the diagonal a would have to be longer than b. Check the actual length.

A particularly puzzling illusion has been the subject of study for hundreds of years, as early as the Arab astronomer Alhazen (c. 965?-1039?). This is the *moon illusion,* the fact that the moon looks larger near the horizon than overhead. The French philosopher Malebranche (1638-1715) viewed the moon in both positions through a smoked glass and found no difference in the measurements. He therefore refuted the view that distortion through the atmosphere was the cause.

It remained for more recent experimenters to isolate the actual cause of the moon illusion (Holway and Boring, 1940; Taylor and Boring, 1942). If you stoop over and look between your legs at the moon near the horizon, the illusion disappears. This fact eliminates many of the conjectures about the effects of intervening objects, atmospheric distortion, and so on. The experimenters decided that the illusion must have something to do with the equilibratory apparatus, neck, or eyes of the subject. They prepared a small artificial moon in a darkroom and strapped their subject to a board so that he could view the moon from various body positions. They discovered that the smaller size of the moon at the zenith (overhead) depended upon seeing the moon with the eyes lifted. Just why this should be the case is not understood, but it calls attention to a very important

feature of perception, namely, the relationship of what is perceived to the bodily orientation of the perceiver and to the muscular effort involved in perceiving.

Because the moon illusion depends upon raising the eyes vertically, it is tempting to relate it to other illusions involving the vertical. Note the letter S and the figure 8 printed boldly in Figure 7-21. Are they symmetrical? Turn the page upside down and you will see how unequal they are. This suggests that as we raise our eyes we magnify things, a conclusion opposite to the moon illusion. Apparently we have to be careful to avoid easy explanations; puzzling contradictions of this sort have prevented agreement about the reasons for illusions.

In fact, what appeared to be the definitive experiments on the moon illusion itself have not gone unchallenged. Leibowitz and Hartman (1959, 1960) found that when an "artificial moon" was suspended from an 85-foot building for overhead viewing, and placed at the same horizontal distance for "horizon" viewing, the moon illusion was greater for children than for adults. The results are presented in Figure 7-22. The authors interpret the adults' experience with size constancy as reducing the illusion with age, and they account for the persistence of the illusion as being due to the greater familiarity with objects viewed in the horizontal plane. These results supplement rather than contradict the findings of Holway and Boring and of Taylor and Boring. More recent experiments (Kaufman and Rock, 1960) lend support to an older interpretation holding that the usual cues to dis-

7-21

An illusion of the vertical

8 S

Are the upper and lower halves of the figures equal?

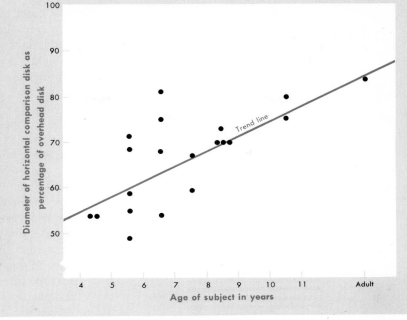

7-22

Age and the moon illusion

Subjects selected a horizontal comparison disk which appeared equal to a 20-inch overhead disk suspended at a distance of 85 feet. The smaller the comparison disk judged equal, the greater the tendency to overestimate the horizontal as compared with the overhead disk. The solid trend line is derived by statistical calculation from the various values indicated by the dots. (After Leibowitz and Hartman, 1959, 1960)

tance that are present in horizontal viewing place the moon farther away and hence make it look larger, while the absence of such cues in the overhead sky makes it appear closer and hence smaller.

Movement perception

Events are organized in time as well as in space; the pattern of a melody is an organization in time, just as a geometrical figure is an organization in space. When we perceive movement, we sense action in space taking place in time. We usually explain the perception of real movement according to the stimulation of successive parts of the sensory surface. Trace a path on the skin and you feel movement as successive "local signs" come into play. Perhaps a similar stimulation takes place on the retina. While these suggestions are a little glib, they are probably in the direction of a true explanation.

Illusions of movement are harder to explain. Some of them depend upon relative motion, as when the train on the next track moves and you believe your own train to be in motion because you see through the

window what you would see if you were moving. If you keep looking at the passing track when your train runs along, and then look at the track when your train stops, the track will seem to be moving in the opposite direction. Two laboratory devices for producing such aftereffects of movement are pictured in Figure 7-23. One of these is the "waterfall illusion," the other the expanding-contracting spiral. After you stop the artificial waterfall, the surrounding field appears to move in the reverse direction. If the revolving spiral is rotated so that it appears to be contracting, whatever you look at after watching it for a while appears to be expanding. While these effects have been known for a great many years, we have no fully satisfactory explanation of them.

Another kind of illusion of motion has been much more thoroughly studied, so that we know its conditions even though its explanation also eludes us. This is *stroboscopic motion,* the illusion of movement created when separated stimuli, not in motion, are presented in succession. Stroboscopic motion is the basis of the motion pic-

Devices for studying the aftereffects of perceived movement

Above: the expanding and contracting spiral; *below:* the waterfall illusion. (After James, 1890)

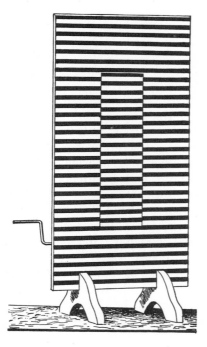

In an attempt to get at the basic conditions for seeing motion, experimenters have devised apparatus such as that of Figure 7-24. Four lights at the ends of the crossbars can be turned on in any order. When one light blinks on and then off, followed shortly by another, there is the illusion of a single light moving from the position of the first to the position of the second. This simple illustration of stroboscopic motion is called the *phi phenomenon,* and its conditions have been much studied. When the four lights of Figure 7-24 flash on and off in proper sequence, you apparently see a rotating circle, but the diameter of the circle is *less* than that of a circle that would actually pass through the four lights. Whatever "attracts" the light to the position of the next light operates also to "attract" it to cut across the diameter of the circle toward the opposite light, thereby making the circle smaller. The two tendencies (to form a circle and to cut across the circle) result in the compromise that is seen as a circle too small to pass through the actual position of the lights. This phenomenon makes the Gestalt psychologists find unsatisfactory an explanation according to familiarity with real motion.

Even though the phi phenomenon is illusory, it tends to preserve the perceptual structure that would be possible in real motion. For example, in Figure 7-25A the perceived motion is through an arc but in the plane of the paper, while in Figure 7-25B the motion is seen in the third dimension, the figure turning over as it moves across.

Depth perception

We cannot conclude our study of the organization of perception without considering the problems of perceiving the third dimension, that is, distance and depth. The retina is essentially a two-dimensional surface. How, then, is it possible for us to perceive things as filling a space of three dimensions?

ture. Pictures blend into smooth motion, with little or no flicker, if the frames occur rapidly enough. Alternating light and dark stimuli give rise to flicker until the rate gets high enough for fusion to take place; the point at which flicker changes to fusion (called the *critical flicker frequency*) varies with light intensity, but for ordinary motion pictures lies at about 15-20 frames per second.

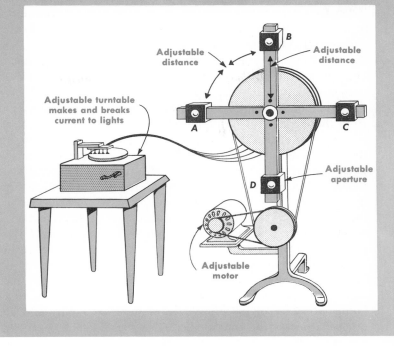

7-24

Producing the phi phenomenon

This apparatus permits comparison between the genuine rotation of a single light and the illusion of motion (the phi phenomenon) that is produced when the lights are stationary but flash on and off in succession. (After Brown and Voth, 1937)

Stereoscopic Vision. Many of the facts of vision in this and the next chapter can be treated by considering only phenomena that can be registered with but one eye. A man with one eye can have most of the visual experiences of a man with two eyes. He sees colors, forms, and space relationships, including third-dimensional configurations. We might suppose that two eyes have evolved merely to give man a "spare"

in case of injury, just as he has two kidneys although one is enough. However, the evolutionary importance of two eyes is suggested by the fact that in more primitive forms of life the two eyes are on either side of the head and take in separate visual fields.

A man with two eyes does have some visual advantages over a man with one eye. The advantages are two: (1) his total vis-

7-25

Special cases of phi movement

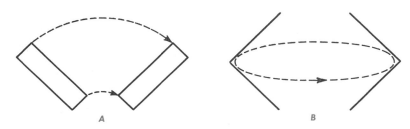

When the bars of *A* are lighted in succession, motion is seen through an arc, but two dimensional as in the plane of the paper. When the halves of *B* are lighted in succession, motion is seen in the third dimension, the figure turning over as it moves across.

ual field is larger, so that he can see more at once, and (2) he has the benefit of stereoscopic vision. In *stereoscopic vision* the two eyes cooperate to yield the experience of solidity and distance. That the experience does indeed depend upon the cooperation of the two eyes is clear enough from the effects that can be produced with a *stereoscope*. In this device two flat pictures, presented one before each eye, combine to yield an experience of depth very different from that received from a single flat picture. The depth appears real, as though the objects pictured were actually set up on a stage or in their true relations of depth and distance.

The difference between the stereoscopic experience and the experience of third dimension in flat pictures is by now rather familiar because of the prevalence of stereoscopic cameras for amateur use. The stereoscopic effect depends on presenting a slightly different picture to the right eye from that presented to the left, thereby duplicating what normally happens when we view objects. Because our eyes are separated in our heads, the left eye does not get exactly the same view as the right eye.

The facts of stereoscopic vision are clear enough, but just how the process works is not so clear. Because of the way in which the nerve fibers from the eyes are separated in passing to the brain, the combination cannot take place in the eyes. Hence the images from the two eyes must somehow be combined in the brain, probably at the level of the visual cortex. It seems reasonable to suppose that the tendency to use our two eyes for stereoscopic vision is inherited. We lack direct evidence, though some studies of the chick indicate strongly that for the chick, at least, stereoscopic vision does not have to be learned (Hess, 1956).

Stereophonic Hearing. A single good ear, like a single good eye, can provide nearly all possible hearing experiences. Having both ears helps, however, because (1) we hear better with two ears than with one, and (2) there is a stereophonic effect in hearing which corresponds in a way to the stereoscopic effect in seeing.

By the *stereophonic effect* we mean the location of sound sources by the use of two ears, much as position is determined visually by the two eyes. How such "auditory perspective" is obtained in stereophonic phonographs or "hi-fi" systems is diagramed in Figure 7-26.

What is the basis of this ability to locate the direction of sounds by the use of the two ears? By testing a blindfolded person, you can easily show the importance of the position of the ears. Using an ordinary "snapper" such as children play with, you can show that your blindfolded subject has no trouble locating sounds at ear level if they are to the right or to the left. If, however, you present the sound in a plane dividing the body vertically, equidistant from the two ears (for example, just over his head), he is helpless in locating the direction of the source. More careful experimentation shows that the differences in stimulation primarily responsible for locating the direction of sounds are (1) *intensity* differences (louder in the nearer ear), and (2) *time* differences (reaching the nearer ear first). In these experiments the subject with his head in a fixed position wears a pair of headphones, so that we know what comes to each ear. If tones alike except for loudness are sent to the two ears, we can move the localization from right to left merely by changing the relative loudnesses. If we send two clicks very close together, one to the right ear and one to the left, the clicks will be heard as one (if they are given at very short intervals, below 0.0025 seconds), but the single click will be heard as coming from the side receiving the first click. These two experiments illustrate intensity differences and time differences in localization.

The localization on the basis of time dif-

Producing stereophonic sound effects

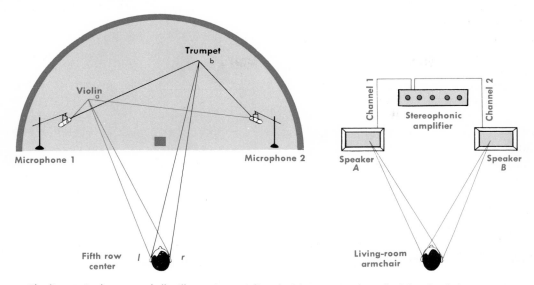

The listener in the concert hall will perceive a violin solo (a) as coming from the left side of the stage, a passage on the trumpet (b) as coming from the right. Microphone 1 will pick up more from the violin than it will from the trumpet; for microphone 2 the reverse will be true. If the recordings from the two microphones are channeled via the stereo amplifier to speakers A and B, the armchair listener will hear the violin from speaker A, the trumpet from B.

ferences turns out to be remarkably accurate, for an interval between clicks of 0.00003 to 0.0003 seconds (for different subjects) is all that is needed to permit localization of the apparent single sound on one side or the other (Woodworth and Schlosberg, 1954, p. 355). When the interval is extremely short, the sound is placed just slightly off center, but when the differences reach about 0.001 seconds, the single sound that is heard is localized well to one side or the other.

We may ask, as we did for stereoscopic vision, where this interaction takes place. It cannot take place in the ears, for it depends on their separate stimulation. Hence it must take place at some common point in the nervous system reached by the impulses from the two ears, probably in the auditory cortex.

One experimenter has shown, for example, that there is more electrical activity in a cat's *left* auditory cortex when time differences would favor placing the sound on the *right,* and more activity in the *right* cortex when time differences would favor placing the sound on the *left.* These are the results we would expect if analysis of stereophonic effects does occur at the cortical level (M. R. Rosenzweig, 1954).

Monocular Cues to Distance. Although having two eyes and two ears helps us to perceive depth and distance, we are by no means limited to these binocular and binaural effects. If you close one eye the world does not suddenly collapse, and if you close one ear the origins of sounds do not become completely ambiguous. Some precision is lost, but there is much left to go on.

An artist is able to give depth to his picture because he can make use of the many *monocular cues* that tell us the distance of objects. Except for those cues that depend

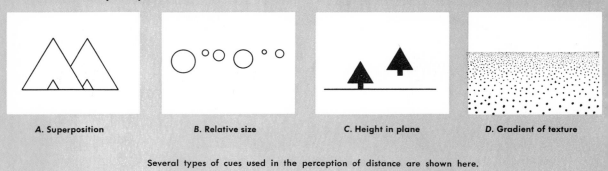

| A. Superposition | B. Relative size | C. Height in plane | D. Gradient of texture |

Several types of cues used in the perception of distance are shown here.

upon movement, the artist can use all the following cues:

1. *Superposition of objects.* If one object appears to cut off the view of another, the presumption is strong that the first object is nearer (Figure 7-27A).

2. *Perspective.* When you look down a railroad track, the rails appear to converge in the distance. Most of us have been taught how to prepare perspective drawings making use of the fact that parallel lines apparently come together at the horizon. This geometry of perspective, or linear perspective, is one of the familiar signs of distance. The facts of perspective are carried in many subtle ways, however, not all immediately evident. *Decreasing size* with distance is, of course, related to the geometry of perspective, so that the telegraph poles alongside the railroad track appear to grow smaller in the distance, just as the track becomes narrower. Even a series of scattered circles of different sizes are viewed as spheres of common size at varying distances (Figure 7-27B). Another hint of perspective is *height in the horizontal plane.* As we look along a flat plane, objects farther away appear to be higher, so that we can create the impression of depth for objects of the same size by placing them at different heights (Figure 7-27C). (If the plane is above us, e.g., a ceiling, some-

thing higher in the field of vision appears closer.) Even for irregular surfaces, such as the waving surface of the ocean or a rocky desert, there is a *gradient of texture* with distance, so that the "grain" becomes finer as distance becomes greater. This is also a form of perspective (Figure 7-27D). Finally, there is an *aerial perspective* ("the purple of distance") that produces changes in brightness and saturation of distant objects, some changes in hue, and a blurring of detail.

3. *Light and shadow.* Light and shadow help to define the contours of three-dimensional objects. One curious consequence of the prevalence of light sources from above is that convex and concave surfaces are sometimes reversed when a photograph is turned upside down. It is difficult to believe that Figure 7-28A is 7-28B upside down.

4. *Movement.* If you move in one direction, distant objects at the side appear to move with you, while near objects appear to move in the opposite direction. Thus the relative movement provides a basis for judging distance. In attempting to judge distance, a person will often move his head back and forth even though he is unaware of the reason for doing so.

Resolving Ambiguity. Usually the various cues to distance harmonize, so that we

7-28

Effect of light and shadow

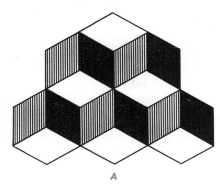

A

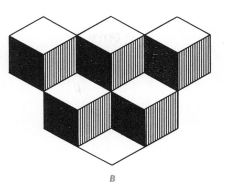

B

Turn the book upside down. Note the transformation when the pictures are reversed. (After Kahn, 1943)

look out upon the world with assurance. Sometimes, however, the environment presents too few cues for accurate depth perception, and sometimes the cues are actually misleading. What, then, does the perceiver do? It is possible to set up experimental arrangements in which cues are controlled and in which using the normal cues to distance leads the subject into error. We shall consider four demonstration experiments in which the perceiver is led to make faulty perceptions of the distance of objects. The following demonstrations are described in detail by M. Lawrence (1949):

1. If an object of familiar size is magnified or reduced in size and presented without other cues to distance, perceived distance is influenced by the misjudged size of the familiar object.

Playing cards are of standard and known size. If a subject looks at an oversized playing card in an alleyway uniformly illuminated and screened so that cues to depth are lacking, he will see it as at a place *nearer* than it actually is. He will see a small-sized replica of a playing card, at the same distance, as *farther* away than its true position.

2. If two similar objects of unknown size are placed at the same distance in an

environment lacking cues to distance, the larger object appears to be closer.

Two white balloons are uniformly illuminated so that they appear as white circles at indeterminate distance in an otherwise dark room. The balloons are mounted on tubes through which their sizes can be changed by inflation and deflation (Figure 7-29). If the experimenter alternately inflates and deflates them, the subject perceives the one growing larger as moving toward him, the one growing smaller as moving away from him. Actually, of course, they remain at the constant original distance (except for the small and unimportant displacement of their near surfaces due to the changing diameters of the balloons).

3. Of similar objects of unknown but equal size, the brighter appears to be closer.

The two balloons are arranged as in the demonstration above. With both balloons inflated to equal size, the amount of illumination on each is varied. The subject sees the balloon that grows brighter as moving toward him and the one that grows darker as moving away from him, although neither balloon moves.

4. If two objects at indeterminate distance are changed both in size and brightness, apparent motion toward or away from

Producing illusions of distance and movement

Dr. Franklin P. Kilpatrick

The experimenter can change the relative sizes of the balloons by moving one of the two levers, and can change the relative illumination on them by moving the other lever. A subject who views the balloons in an otherwise dark room sees them moving either closer to him or farther away with changes in size and brightness, although the balloons remain at a constant distance.

the subject will be enhanced if the cues cooperate and will be reduced if the cues conflict. Hence the apparent motion depends upon a weighing of available cues.

The experimenter can change the appearance of the two balloons either by inflating

or deflating them or by changing the illumination on them. If the experimenter makes one balloon both larger and brighter, the subject will see it moving nearer to him than if the experimenter makes it larger at the same brightness or brighter at the same size.

If as the experimenter makes a balloon larger he makes it darker, or if as he makes it brighter he makes it smaller, the subject will see it move less from its original position than he did under the other changes.

The study of perception in ambiguous situations like these leads to interpretations such as the following:

1. Perceptions are based not only on information provided by the stimuli but also on presumptions as to the objects perceived. (Recall the familiar-sized playing cards.)
2. These presumptions arise through many past experiences with objects.
3. In arriving at the perception of objects at rest and in motion, a number of cues are weighed, and if some of them are contradictory a compromise perception results. This weighing goes on swiftly and unconsciously.

According to these interpretations, a perception is a kind of statistical average or computed probability. It might be called a prediction or wager concerning the environment. Ordinarily the result is a useful guide to action; in fact, it is only because cues are so often dependable that we trust them on occasions when they cannot be trusted and so we therefore may be led into error.

CRITICAL DISCUSSION
Nativism vs. empiricism in space perception

The phenomena of perceptual organization, depth perception, and the various constancies lend themselves to simple and convincing ex-

7-30

The "visual cliff"

Infants and young animals show an ability to perceive depth as soon as they can move about. The visual cliff consists of two surfaces, both displaying the same pattern, which are covered by a sheet of thick glass. One surface is directly under the glass; the other is dropped a foot or more. This one-day-old goat, as well as the other experimental infants and animals, prefers the shallow side and avoids the deep side. Further study showed that this was true even of animals reared in the dark and having no opportunity to learn. Photos show kid walking freely on shallow side (top) and leaping across "chasm" to safety (center and bottom). (After Gibson and Walk, 1960)

perimental demonstration, so that by now there is general agreement over what the subject perceives. There are many disagreements, however, over how to *explain* what happens.

The two main sides in the argument favor a *nativist* explanation ("we are born to perceive the way we do") or an *empiricist* or *learning* explanation ("we come to perceive as we do through experience with objects in the world about us").

The nativist position is supported by the nature of our inherited sensory equipment, for example, our eyes arranged for stereoscopic vision and our ears for stereophonic hearing. Experimental support comes from such experiments as those of Hess (1956), already referred to, in which it was shown that chicks, even though raised with blinders, were able to demonstrate stereoscopic vision. Some later experiments with a "visual cliff" (Figure 7-30) have shown that inexperienced animals are guided by visual cues (Walk, Gibson, and Tighe, 1957).

The empiricist position is made plausible by much common experience: that we identify the roar that we hear as jet planes flying overhead because we have earlier seen them as well as heard them; the red poker *looks* hot, even though it does not affect our temperature receptors, and there is no unlearned visual cue for hot. There is experimental evidence, too, as previously cited (pp. 197, 208). The experimental evidence for the role of learning in perception has been reviewed by Solley and Murphy (1960).

The constancies furnish a particularly interesting but confusing set of evidence. The constancies of size, shape, and location appear to be most simply accounted for by experience, for they depend upon familiarity of both the object and its surroundings. But brightness and color constancy are not so easy to explain. The empiricist of course draws upon such learned features as memory color and experience with shadows. But the nativist (on this issue) deals with subtle effects in the laboratory, where the explanation on the basis of experience is more difficult to apply. For example, in an experiment by Wallach (1948) lights were projected in the form of two circular areas on the wall of a darkened room. Additional projectors superimposed smaller circles of light on the two larger circles, thereby producing within each circle an inner circle of light with a gray band around it. He found that if the surrounding bands were of unequal brightness, the central circles were judged of equal brightness if their brightnesses were *a constant ratio* of the surrounding brightness. This is exactly what happens when a shadow passes over a black-and-white drawing: the ratios of brightness of figure and ground remain constant, although the total illumination changes. The nativist will argue from such evidence that the tendency to see equal ratios as constant is a "given" in perception, while the empiricist will argue that this is learned from the experience of enduring objects under changing illumination.

Many contemporary psychologists believe that a fruitful integration of these two traditions is possible. That perception depends partly on the sensory apparatus seems self-evident. We need only consider stereoscopic vision. That some learning is involved seems evident also, if only through the size judgments dependent upon the recognition of familiar objects at a distance. Hebb (1949) has developed a physiological account, accepting a kind of compromise between the Gestalt and learning explanations.

A third position has recently been set forth (J. J. Gibson, 1959). Everything that we perceive, he says, is given in stimulation; in vision, all we see is what is recorded on the retina. Our perceptions improve as we become more discriminating and make better use of stimuli. Hence our perceptions, instead of supplementing sense data, come to show *greater* correspondence with stimuli. As its author admits, the theory accounts only for accurate perceptions and not for illusions, so that this theory is in any case incomplete.

Influences upon Perception

Attention

Our perceptions are selective. We do not react equally to all the stimuli impinging upon us; instead we focus upon a few. This perceptual focusing is called *attention*. Through attentive processes we keep in focus selected stimuli and resist distracting stimuli.

Even as you sit reading this, stop for a moment, close your eyes, and attend to the

7-31

Apparatus for producing brief visual exposures

David Linton, courtesy N.Y.U.

Left: The New York University model of the Dodge mirror tachistoscope in use. *Right:* As seen from above. When light is on at *A,* subject sees the picture presented at the back of the box at *A.* When the light is on at *B,* the diagonal smoked glass acts as a mirror and the subject sees the picture presented on the wall of *B.*

various stimuli affecting you. Notice, for example, the tightness of the heel of your left shoe, the pressure of clothing on your neck or shoulders, the sounds coming from outside the room. We are bombarded all the while by stimuli to which we do not attend. While reading a book, we may be unaware of the music on the radio and we may not notice the ticking of the clock. As the following experiment shows, even while attending to a given source of stimulation, we may note only certain details.

Cards containing pictures of a number of objects differing in color and in size were exposed briefly in an instrument known as a tachistoscope (Figure 7-31). When asked to report what they saw, some subjects reported the number of things, some the colors of things, some their sizes. When questioned about the other details of the stimuli, they were often relatively helpless.

If they were prepared in advance to report one detail or another, their success in reporting the specified detail was greater (Chapman, 1932).

There is competition among stimuli; therefore when we select for attention one detail or pattern rather than another, we have resolved a conflict. The direction in which the conflict is resolved depends upon *factors of advantage* favoring one organization of stimuli over another. It is one of the tasks of the advertiser to discover these characteristics so that he can direct attention to his product. Among competing stimulus patterns, advantage rests with the one of greatest *size,* strongest *intensity,* most frequent *repetition,* and most *vivid* because of contour, contrast, or color. The attention-getting qualities of stimuli depend in part upon other stimuli which the observer has lately experienced. It is exciting to come upon a green lawn after riding through the Arizona desert, but who notices a particular lawn in the lush green of a New England village? Yet in any given place and at any

Influence of preparatory set on interpretation of ambiguous stimuli

Stimulus as presented	Common interpretation as animal or bird	Common interpretation as travel or transportation
chack	chick	check
sael	seal	sail
wharl	whale	wharf
pasrort	parrot	passport
dack	duck	deck
pengion	penguin	pension

SOURCE: Siipola (1935).

given time, the compelling quality of a stimulus pattern may be fairly well predicted. The advertiser counts on this fact.

Among the individual conditions that cause one person to attend to something differently from another, the most important are habitual or momentary interests that prepare him for certain kinds of stimuli. The naturalist will hear sounds in the woods that the ordinary picknicker would miss because of his different habits of attention. A mother will hear her baby's cry above the conversation of a living room full of people. These two illustrations represent abiding interests. Sometimes momentary interest controls attention. When you page through a book looking for a map or diagram that you know to be there, what you see depends on what you are looking for. Only pages with illustrations cause you to hesitate; others you ignore. Emotional states, especially moods, may affect the ways in which attention is directed. In a hostile mood, personal comments are noticed that might go unremarked in a more friendly mood.

Preparatory set

Some of the selectivity in perception is present before the stimulus appears. We can prepare ourselves to perceive, and to act upon, stimuli that we expect to appear. Such a preparation goes by the name of *set,* and it has the same meaning here as in the situation of a runner who gets *set* to run at the sound of the gun. His set includes both the readiness to hear the gun and the readiness to leap forward into the race. When a person is set, the actual stimulus that initiates his action is, like the sound of the shot for the runner, merely an occasion for action that was largely prepared in advance.

Momentary set is an anticipatory adjustment holding certain kinds of responses in readiness. How such a set influences what we perceive may be illustrated by an experiment in which, because of readiness, the subject perceives nonsense words as meaningful.

By means of a projection tachistoscope short words were flashed on a screen. Among the words presented were six nonsense words, as listed in Table 7-1. Each word appeared for 0.10 second, followed by a pause long enough for the subject to write down what he thought the word was. The 160 subjects of the experiment were divided into two groups, one of which received the information that the words to appear would have to do with animals or birds, the other that they would have to do with travel or transportation.

The group instructed to expect animals or birds gave animal or bird responses to the nonsense words 63 per cent of the time, travel or transportation responses only 14 per cent of the time. The remaining responses were in other categories. By contrast, the second group gave travel or transportation responses 74 per cent of the time and animal or bird responses only 11 per cent of the time. Thus the subjects interpreted the ambiguous stimuli according to their preparatory sets (Siipola, 1935).

Perceptual readiness may be created by instructions (as in the foregoing experiment), by immediately prior experience (as in the perceived young woman or her mother-in-law in the picture on p. 197), or by a general tendency to assimilate unclear or novel experience to the familiar. The following experiment illustrates the influence of the familiar upon what we perceive.

Playing cards were exposed briefly in a tachistoscope, and the subject was asked to name the card exposed. Among the cards exposed were some unusual ones, such as a black six of hearts or a red four of spades.

1. On first meeting an incongruous card, the subjects assimilated it into their prior knowledge of playing cards. That is, 27 of 28 subjects called the red four of spades either a red four of hearts or a black four of spades (ignoring either the incongruous color or the incongruous form).
2. Once the subjects had identified a card as incongruous, their perceptual readiness changed so that they expected incongruous cards. After that, they made fewer false identifications (Bruner and Postman, 1949).

What a person perceives depends in part upon what he is ready for. This is the meaning of preparatory set as it affects perceiving.

Needs and values

When the objects of perception are ambiguous—things seen through a haze, sounds heard through masking noises—the perceiver tends to give them more meaning than the stimulating conditions alone demand. What he perceives may be determined to some extent by his needs and his personal values. He perceives the environment to be what he wishes it to be or perhaps what he fears it to be.

Needs as Influencing Perception. We have already noted how habitual or momentary interests may affect attention. Closely related is the influence of aroused needs upon perception, especially under conditions of stimulus ambiguity.

Of 108 sailors, candidates for submarine training, who participated in an experiment to determine the influence of hunger on perception, 44 took the perception test 1 hour after eating, 24 took it 4 hours after eating, and 40 took it 16 hours after eating. The purpose was to see whether or not those longer deprived of food would give evidence of increased food interest in their perceptual responses.

Each subject saw very ambiguous stimuli projected on a screen. He was told what to look for ("Three objects on a table." "All the people in this picture are enjoying themselves. What are they doing?"). Actually no pictures were shown. The screens were either dimly illuminated or clouded with a smudge. Under the general set to see objects, the hungrier subjects saw more food-related objects than the less hungry ones. One comparison showed 15 per cent food responses for the 1-hour group, 21 per cent for the 4-hour group, and 23 per cent for the 16-hour group. The differences in number of food responses between the 1-hour and 16-hour groups were statistically significant.

In another comparison, the subjects gave size estimates. Questions such as this were put to them: "Here is an ashtray and a hamburger. Which is the larger?" (Actually, as before, no picture was shown.) Under these circumstances, food objects were estimated as larger more often by those who were hungrier. The percentages for which food objects were larger were as follows: 1-hour group, 50 per cent; 4-hour group, 61 per cent; 16-hour group, 75 per cent (McClelland and Atkinson, 1948).

The foregoing experiment illustrates that when the perceived objects are ambiguous, need tends not only toward an increase in frequency of need-related perceptions but also toward an exaggeration in size attributed to need-related objects.

Values as Influencing Perception. Social values accrue to objects as part of their perceptual enrichment. Once accrued, they may affect such direct impressions as those of size. For example, children from poorer homes when matching sizes from memory tend to overestimate the sizes of coins more than do children from well-to-do homes (Bruner and Goodman, 1947; Carter and Schooler, 1949). The following experiment attempted to subject this process to direct laboratory control.

The experiment was performed with nursery school children, a total of 54 in the experimental group and 17 in the control group. The experimental subjects learned to turn a crank in order to receive a poker chip. When the subject inserted the poker chip in a slot, he automatically received a piece of candy. The conjecture was that the candy would enhance the value of the poker chip and that this increased value would result in overestimation of size, as in the coin experiments. Both control and experimental subjects overestimated the size by 5 or 6 per cent in a pretest, but after 10 days of rewarded learning with poker chips the experimental group increased its overestimation to 13 per cent, a statistically significant gain. During the same period the overestimation of the control group had not increased significantly.

As further evidence of the importance of learning, the values of the experimental group underwent extinction through nonreward. Then the size estimation returned to normal. After reinstatement of the value of the poker chip through reconditioning, the size was again overestimated (Lambert, Solomon, and Watson, 1949).

Personality Characteristics as Influencing Perceptual Distortion. While all people seek to perceive things clearly and definitely, there are individual differences in the needs for clarity and definiteness. Interestingly, there seems to be a definite relationship between social attitudes and perception of ambiguous stimuli. To some people, all things must be either white or black. People who cannot tolerate ambiguity show it not only in their social attitudes but also in their perceptual responses in the laboratory.

On the basis of attitude and personality studies, the experimenters picked out individuals who were markedly prejudiced in their dealing with minority groups. These individuals were found to be fixed and rigid in their behavior in several situations, including perceptual ones. Their reactions were compared with those of another group made up of relatively unprejudiced people.

In one experiment, a picture of a dog was followed by several other pictures, which by gradual stages made a transition to the picture of a cat. The prejudiced group held to the first object (that is, they interpreted the transitional pictures as a dog) longer than the unprejudiced group. They were reluctant to let go of what was once clear. A corresponding finding was obtained when, instead of animal pictures, the subjects saw a gradually changing series of numbers. The prejudiced group, here regarded as intolerant of ambiguity, held longer to the original numbers (Frenkel-Brunswik, 1949).

Investigators have found that people differ in the ways in which they maintain their orientation in space. The following experiment illustrates the kind of test situation that can be used.

A subject is strapped to a chair so that his body will remain perpendicular to the chair seat if the chair is tilted. He views a luminous frame in a darkened room against a dark background. He is given the task of adjusting the rod in the center of the frame to a vertical position. If the frame is in normal position and he is seated normally, he succeeds in setting the bar vertically with a minimum of error. If the frame only is tilted, as in Figure 7-32A, and his position is normal, he places the supposed upright at a slant in the direction of *b* instead of the true vertical (*a*). In the experiment cited, the average error from the vertical when the frame was tipped 28° was 7° for men and 11° for women. If the chair is also tilted, as in Figure 7-32B, so that his body axis corresponds more nearly to that of the frame, he misses the true vertical still more (c), with an average error of 12° for men and 17° for women (Witkin and others, 1954).

Individuals differ greatly in the degree to which they respond to these distortions of the environment. Witkin and his associates classified them as *field-dependent* if their judgments were based very largely on the visual surroundings, and *field-independent* if they accepted the cues from their own bodies (e.g., gravitational cues) and hence were not led astray by the distortions of the visual field. Field-dependence and field-independence were found to be related to personality characteristics and to childhood upbringing, the field-dependent people being in general more anxious, the field-independent ones less anxious and more sure of themselves.

We note again the artificiality of any sharp distinctions among the various topics

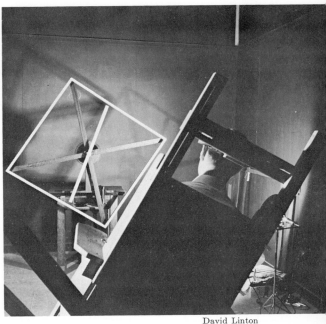

David Linton

7-32

Orientation of the body and the perceived vertical

Tilting the chair increases the error in placing a bar in a vertical position. The photo shows the actual experimental setup that was used. (After Witkin and others, 1954)

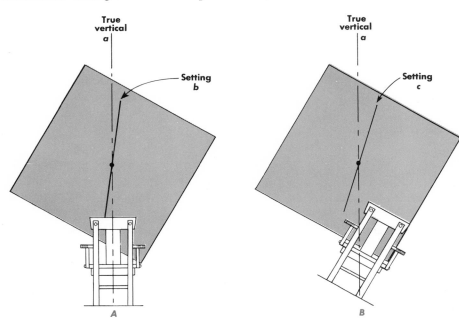

in a psychology textbook. We cannot understand perception satisfactorily unless we recognize its interrelationships with motivation, learning, and personality.

Objections to foregoing experiments and extension of the meaning of perception

The experiments here cited on the influence on perception of needs, values, and personality have been very much criticized. The criticisms have chiefly taken two directions. Some of them are directed at technical imperfections in the experiments. In the Navy experiments of McClelland and Atkinson, for example, the subjects must have known that their period of starvation had something to do with the experiment. Therefore they may have been "set" for seeing an object related to food. This fact might place a somewhat different interpretation upon the results, for control through induced "set" is not quite the same as control by enhanced "drive." Another technical criticism of related kind is that the experiments deal very largely with verbal behavior, and that perhaps some of the responses could be elicited from blindfolded subjects without the aid of visual stimuli. For example, if you ask hungry people their thoughts, they might tell you more often than less hungry people that they were thinking about food.

The second criticism of the experiments is that they imply an improper definition of perception. The experiments work only when stimuli are ambiguous, when direct comparisons cannot be made, when *memory* for stimulus patterns and sizes is tested instead of direct perception. The critics argue that the experiments test *supplements* to perception, not perception itself. For example, when a subject interprets an ink blot, they say, you are studying his fantasy life, not his perception. If you asked him to copy the ink blot, he might show you that he *perceived* it quite accurately.

The first criticism can be met, and is being met, by better-designed experiments. The second is more difficult to meet, for the argument is partly over the definition of perception. If the better-designed experiments continue to add to our knowledge of how behavior is determined in the presence of discriminable

stimuli, however, it does not matter too much what the process is called (McCurdy, 1956).

In line with the extension of the meaning of perception, considerable interest has developed in recent years in person perception. The skill in "sizing-up" a person is a complex skill, surely not unrelated to the perception of objects. The difference lies in that a person represents to us far more than the patterns of sensory qualities available to the senses; we use our observations to infer his "intentions, attitudes, emotions, ideas, abilities, purposes, traits" (Tagiuri and Petrullo, 1958, p. x). However, there are transitional situations in which the motion of geometrical figures in relation to each other gives an immediate impression of causality—not too different from person perception (Heider and Simmel, 1944; Michotte, 1946). Thus, there is here a legitimate field of inquiry, to which we shall return in another context (Chapter 20).

Extrasensory Perception

If there are so many influences upon perception other than those coming from the presented stimuli, are there perhaps perceptions that require no sense-organ stimulation whatsoever? The answer to this question is the source of a major controversy within contemporary psychology over the status of *extrasensory perception* (ESP). A minority of psychologists believe that the evidence for the existence of certain forms of ESP is now incontrovertible (e.g., Murphy, 1949b; Rhine and Pratt, 1957; Soal and Bateman, 1954; Thouless, 1950). Despite these contentions, most psychologists remain unconvinced.

The phenomena under discussion are of four main kinds:

I. Extrasensory perception (ESP)
　1. Telepathy, or thought transference from one person to another.
　2. Clairvoyance, or the perception of objects or events not influencing the senses.
　3. Precognition, or the perception of a future event.

II. Psychokinesis (PK), whereby a mental operation affects a material body or an energy system (e.g., wishing for a number affects what number comes up in the throw of dice).

The experimenters go at their work in accordance with the usual rules of science and generally disavow the connection between this work and spiritualism, supernaturalism, mediumistic phenomena, and other occult effects. Yet the phenomena with which they deal are so extraordinary, and so similar to the superstitious beliefs of nonliterate people, that many scientists disavow even the legitimacy of their inquiries. Such a priori judgments are out of place in science, however, and the real question is whether or not the empirical evidence is acceptable by ordinary scientific standards. Many psychologists who are not convinced would find it congenial to accept evidence that they found satisfactory. For example, the possibility of some sort of influence from one brain to another, other than by way of the sense organs, would not be inconceivable within the present framework of science, were the facts of telepathy to be established in some orderly fashion. Some of the other phenomena are more difficult to find believable (precognition, for example), but if the evidence were firm, previous thought patterns would have to yield to the facts.

The case for ESP is based largely on experiments in card-guessing, in which, under various conditions, the subject attempts to guess the symbols on cards randomly arranged in packs. The usual pack consists of 25 cards with five symbols, so that a chance performance would be 5 hits per pack. Even very successful subjects seldom reach as high a level as 7 hits, but they may score above 5 often enough to meet acceptable standards of statistical significance. If the experimenter or "sender" thinks of the symbol at the time the subject makes his record, the experiment is one on telepathy; if the experimenter does not perceive the card at all (it may be face down on the table before him or sealed in an envelope), then the experiment is one on clairvoyance. The kind of evidence used in support of the nonchance nature of the findings can be illustrated by the successive runs of one "sensitive" subject, Mrs. Gloria Stewart, studied in England over a long period (Table 7-2). If the evidence is viewed in the same spirit as that from any other experiment, it is clear that Mrs. Stewart responded above chance on the telepathy trials, but not on the clairvoyance ones. This fact also meets certain objections about

TABLE 7-2

Results of interspersed telepathy and clairvoyance trials with one subject *

Chronological order of successive groups of 200 trials	Hits per 200 trials (Expected = 40)	
	TELEPATHY TRIALS	CLAIRVOYANCE TRIALS
1945	65	51
	58	42
	62	29
	58	47
	60	38
1947	54	35
	55	36
	65	31
1948	39	38
	56	43
1949	49	40
	51	37
	33	42
Total hits	707	509
Expected hits	520	520
Difference	+187	−11
Hits per 25 trials	6.8	4.9

SOURCE: Soal and Bateman (1954), p. 352.

* Each group of 200 trials consisted of alternating blocks of 50 telepathy and 50 clairvoyance trials.

card arrangements sometimes used against such experiments, for her chance performance on the clairvoyance trials shows that above-chance scores are not an inevitable result of something having to do with the shuffling of the cards. The telepathy results are above the expected level in 11 of the 13 runs of 200, and the average scoring level of 6.8 hits (instead of 5) per pack of 25 is well above chance.

The complaint has been voiced that ESP results are not subject to systematic variation through ordinary experimental control. This also is not entirely fair to the findings. For example, there are some order effects reported, in which early trials are more successful than later ones (Rhine and Humphrey, 1944; McConnell, Snowdon, and Powell, 1955), and there is reported evidence that an attitude favorable to ESP, noted in advance, leads to positive results, while an unfavorable attitude leads to scoring below chance levels (Schmeidler and McConnell, 1958).

Thus empirical findings are offered in support of ESP and PK, which meet ordinary statistical standards. Why, then, do not the results become a part of established psychological science? Many arguments have been used against the work, but they usually boil down to a few such as the following: (1) the fact that many claims of extraordinary phenomena in the past have turned out to be false when investigated; (2) certain problems in statistical inference that arise when very large numbers of trials are used to establish the significance of small differences; (3) the failure of improved methods to yield better results than crude methods; and (4) general lack of orderliness in the phenomena, without which rational theorizing cannot replace the highly irrational theories now used to account for what occurs.

These arguments are not, in fact, decisive, and it is desirable to keep an open mind about issues that permit empirical demonstration, as the ESP phenomena do. At the same time it should be clear that the reservations of the majority of psychologists are based on more than stubborn prejudice.

The following critical discussion is provided for those who might care to look a little further into these issues.

We may expand a little upon the objections that psychologists have to the ESP and PK experiments and to *psi*, the special ability attributed to the "sensitive" subject.

1. *General scepticism about extraordinary phenomena.* Throughout history there have always been reports of strange happenings, of ghosts, little men, poltergeists (noisy spirits who engage in throwing things about), dreams foretelling the future. The continuing appearance of these stories does not make them true, any more than reported flying saucers establish the visits of men from Mars. Painstaking investigation by the U.S. Air Force yields no "flying saucers"; nobody ever traps the Loch Ness monster. A famous mediumistic case (still mentioned favorably by Soal and Bateman, 1954, p. xiv) is a case in point. Eusapia Palladino was a medium who was able to make a table move and produce other effects, such as tapping sounds, by the aid of a "spirit" called John King. Investigated repeatedly between 1893 and 1910, she convinced many distinguished scientists of her powers, including the distinguished Italian criminologist Lombroso and the British physicist Sir Oliver Lodge. She was caught in deceptive trickery as early as 1895, and the results were published. Yet believers continued to support her genuineness, as some do today, even though in an American investigation in 1910, her trickery was abundantly exposed (Jastrow, 1935; Rawcliffe, 1959). Two investigators, dressed in black, crawled under the table unobserved and were able to see exactly how she used her foot to create the "supernatural" phenomena. When, therefore, those most convinced about ESP are also convinced about already disproven phenomena, their testimony carries less

weight than if they were more critical. A similar case in point is Rhine's belief in an ESP interpretation of "water-witching" or "dowsing," in which water is discovered by means of a divining rod (Rhine and Pratt, 1957, p. 104). (See Figure 7-33.) Careful study of this bit of primitive magic shows that success in water-witching requires no such explanation (Vogt and Hyman, 1959).[1] While attacking ESP experiments on the basis of the belief systems of the investigators is a kind of *argumentum ad hominem*, and hence somewhat unfair, it is understandable that one is less likely to trust the observations of a person known to be gullible than one known to be critical.

2. *Problems of statistical inference with large numbers and small effects.* One of the major contributions of ESP research to scientific psychology may turn out to be the attention it has drawn to the circumstances that make a scientific finding believable. It is commonly supposed that tests of statistical significance are sufficient guarantees of objectivity, and hence a satisfactory statistical outcome should lead to acceptance of a hypothesis as plausible. This turns out not to be the case in ESP experiments, and it is probably not the case in other experiments either. Statistical tests merely tell us how well measurement seems to establish something that is already plausible; if it is not plausible, we search for some source of error that has produced the nonchance result. For example, in a major attempt to produce random digits by an electronic roulette wheel (The RAND Corporation, 1955), it proved very difficult to eliminate bias; in fact, a sample of 125,000 digits tested after the machine had been running a month departed from a random distribution by an amount that was statistically significant. One does not argue that some devilish scientist was using PK to foul the machine; one assumes that the machine somehow ran down with continuous use.

Let us compare this example with an experiment performed in Rhine's Duke University laboratory (Rhine, 1942). He was trying to detect whether or not a subject might, through some combination of ESP and PK, influence the positions of cards in a mechanical shuffler. In all, 51 persons wrote down their predictions of the orders in which cards would come out of a mechanical shuffler 2 to 10 days later, the order of cards emerging from the shuffler being further complicated by having the cards cut by hand at a random trial. The experiment was carefully performed, and in a total of 57,-550 trials the results were at chance level—just 11 hits in excess of expectation. But was this plausible result accepted? No; further statistical analyses were made. Two more of these, based on the division of the trials into segments, failed to yield nonchance results. Finally, a fourth analysis, based on a complex effect called a "covariance of salience ratio," gave a nonchance effect, with odds of 625 to 1

7-33

Attempting to locate underground water by means of a divining rod

David DeHarport, © University of Chicago Press

Human gullibility continues in an age of science. Here the principle of long-distance dowsing is illustrated. The divining rod is held over a hand-drawn map in order to tell the owner where to dig for water.

[1] It may come as something of a surprise that there are estimated to be some 25,000 water-witchers in America—more than all the psychologists who are members of the American Psychological Association (Vogt and Hyman, 1959, p. 3).

in its favor. When belief in bizarre effects is carried this far, it is no wonder that the unconvinced begins to suspect the statistics, even though the rules are followed and all computations are accurate.

There is a scientific problem here. A phenomenon may be rare and still important; hence large numbers of subjects or experiments may be needed if its existence is to be established. But the "good" or "sensitive" ESP subjects are rare. Soal and Bateman (1954, p. 49), state that no such subject has turned up in America since 1938, despite the continuing research in the field, and in England they have had but three who maintained the ESP ability for a considerable time. These unusually sensitive subjects tend to reach a level of about 7 of 25 hits, instead of the 5 expected; such an ability is not very significant from a social point of view, no matter how established it may be statistically. The possibility of some undetected bias, as was found in the electronic roulette wheel, is real enough to temper belief.

3. *Failure of improved methods to increase the yield.* In most scientific fields, the assay from the ore becomes richer as the methods become more refined. But the reverse trend is found in ESP experiments; it is almost a truism in research in the field of telepathy and clairvoyance that the poorer the conditions the better the results. In the early days of the Duke experiments subjects yielding high ESP scores were rather common, one virtuoso averaging, in the course of 650 trials, 10.7 hits in 25 instead of the 5 expected. As the experiments have become better controlled, however, these high-scoring subjects have disappeared.

4. *Lack of systematic consistency in the phenomena.* Sensitive subjects in the Rhine laboratory appear to be about equally successful at clairvoyance and telepathy; but the English subjects appear to be good at telepathy and not at clairvoyance. Other peculiarities emerge. In a famous series of experiments in England, Mr. Basil Shackleton (one of the three good subjects mentioned above) gave no evidence of either telepathy or clairvoyance when scored in the usual way against the target card. Instead he was shown to be successful in *precognition telepathy,* that is, in guessing what was *going to be* on the experimenter's mind in the next trial. He was unsuccessful in clairvoyance, no matter how scored (Soal and Bateman, 1954). Why, the sceptic asks, does the direct telepathy fail with Mr. Shackleton in favor of something far more mysterious than the telepathic success of Mrs. Stewart? [2]

Because the *psi* ability does not follow the ordinary rules, explanations of its operation can be produced with the greatest of freedom. It need not be affected in any ordinary way by space or time, so that success over great distances is accepted as a sign of its extraordinary power rather than something to cause a search for artifacts. Similarly, the precognition experiments are merely evidence that it is as easy to read what is *about* to be on someone else's mind as what is on it now. The PK effects, which require the sorting of cards or the rolling of dice by mental effort ("mind over matter"), are nevertheless said to occur without any transfer of physical energy, thus presumably violating the usual belief in the conservation of energy. But in any experimental work *some* aspects of time and space have to be respected, such as spatial form and color and order of succession in time. Unless some restraint is shown, one might invent such hypotheses as that the subject was sometimes perceiving the cards in reverse order, sometimes in a place-skipping order, and so on; any significance test that depends upon coincidences requires some respect for order.

The believer in *psi* is impatient with this kind of criticism. He says that we ask more of him than we do of other experimenters. In fact, we do ask more. To demonstrate something highly implausible requires better evidence than to demonstrate something plausible. The reason is that supporting evidence for the plausible finding comes from many directions, while the implausible one must hang upon the slender thread of nonrandomness until certain systematic relationships are found that tie it firmly to what is known.

---

[2] Mrs. Stewart, who failed in clairvoyance also, was above chance in hits on the target card, but *also* on the preceding card and the following card.

SUMMARY   1. We mainly perceive *things,* and we perceive environmental objects as "thinglike," that is, as stable and enduring. The stability of perceived objects depends on various *constancies:* color and brightness constancy, shape constancy, size constancy, and location constancy. In the choice between perspective size and object size, perception usually tends to conform more nearly to object size unless the contextual cues are greatly reduced. When they are, perception comes close to perspective size (that is, it corresponds to the size suggested by the image on the retina).

2. The basic organization of visual perception appears to be that of *figure and ground,* so that we recognize patterns as figures against a background whether or not the patterns are familiar. Something of the same organization is found in hearing, with groupings in time rather than space.

3. Stimuli that are not highly organized tend to be perceived as structures according to a number of principles, such as *proximity* of parts, *similarity* of components, *continuity* of patterned parts, and *closure,* the tendency to form a complete and stable whole.

4. Geometrical visual illusions present problems for interpretation. The results can in part be explained by the failure to isolate clearly lines that are *embedded* in compelling areas, by *size contrasts* with the surroundings, and by the misleading interpretation of lines intersecting at *angles.* The old puzzle of the size of the moon has been partly solved by experiments showing that an artificial moon looks smaller when seen with the eyes elevated than when viewed straight ahead. The *phi phenomenon,* an illusion of movement, illustrates *stroboscopic motion,* the principle underlying the motion picture.

5. Visual depth is perceived binocularly with the help of *stereoscopic vision,* the fusion of slightly unlike images of the two eyes. A somewhat comparable effect within audition is *stereophonic hearing,* the localization of sounds depending on the intensity and time relations of sounds reaching the two ears.

6. Visual depth is perceived monocularly with the aid of a number of *cues: superposition* of objects, *perspective* (whether geometric or given through relative size, height in the frontal plane, gradients of texture, or aerial perspective), *light* and *shadow,* and *movement.* If the cues are ambiguous, the subject weighs them (without being aware that he does so), and the resulting perception is a compromise.

7. Perception is *selective,* so that we *attend* at once to only part of the influx of sensory stimulation. Factors of advantage, favoring attention to one pattern of stimuli over another, reside partly in the stimuli themselves but also on both the habitual and momentary interests of the individual. *Preparatory set* is one condition for perception.

8. The satisfying of individual *needs* and *values* may lead to perceptual distortion. Personality characteristics, such as rigidity and intolerance of ambiguity, may also determine how the individual perceives.

9. *Extrasensory perception* (ESP) in its various forms (telepathy, clairvoyance, precognition) and *psychokinesis* (PK), the influencing of physical events by mental operations, are the sources of controversy in contemporary psychology. There are many reasons for reserving judgment, but an a priori condemnation of the experiments is unjustified. The experiments raise interesting issues about the criteria by which scientific credibility is established.

SUGGESTIONS FOR FURTHER READING

Allport, *Theories of perception and the concept of structure* (1955) is valuable for its review and critical analysis of the major theories of perception. A collection of original articles, many translated from German sources, can be found in Beardslee and Wertheimer, *Readings in perception* (1958). Dember, *The psychology of perception* (1960) is a clearly written textbook on perception as a psychological topic, with little reference to physics and physiology.

The viewpoint that learning is important in perception is well represented in Solley and Murphy, *Development of the perceptual world* (1960), and in Kilpatrick, *Explorations in transactional psychology* (1961).

CHAPTER 8

The Sensory Basis of Perceiving

No Test on eight

Questions for test from this page

At one time the study of sensory psychology was the chief preoccupation of experimental psychologists. Even early in the development of their new science psychologists could arrange laboratory investigations of the senses, in which they achieved precise control of the stimulating conditions and could measure changes in the stimuli and record the responses of the subjects to them. Scientific interests show swings of the pendulum just as do other human pursuits, and with the upsurge of interest in learning and adjustment there has been a decline in the interest of psychologists in the sensory mechanisms.

There are some signs that this trend is reversing itself and that interest in sensory and perceptual phenomena is being renewed, not to the exclusion of the other topics, but in better balance with them. Such readjustments of interest are never merely returns to an earlier period; the renewed emphases always come with differences.

The earlier studies of the sensory processes were predominantly of the "pure science" variety; that is, they were efforts to understand the details of the relationships among stimuli, the sense organs, the nerve tracts, and the brain areas, as well as the conscious processes associated with the stimulation of the sense organs and their connections. More recent sensory studies have continued in this direction but have moved also into the area of applied psychology. During World War II there was much interest in what was at first called *human engineering,* now known as the study of *human factors* in relation to machine operation. As modern military equipment becomes more precise and automatic, it depends more and more on the accurate discriminations of the human operator. An operator picks up visual signals on the radar screen and discriminates auditory signals from underwater sound detection devices. The pilot has to watch the dials of his countless instruments and make appropriate adjustments. Instructions coming over earphones have to be heard above the surrounding noise and, sometimes, against intentional "jamming." After the war, sensory psychology began to find uses in industry as well as in the military services—and, of course, in dealing with the problems of the jet and rocket age.

Some General Characteristics of the Senses

Thresholds

A certain minimum of sense-organ stimulation is required before any sensory experience will be evoked. This minimum is called the *absolute threshold.* For example, a spot of light appearing in a dark room must reach some measurable intensity before it can be distinguished from darkness, and a sound emitted in a soundproof room must reach a certain intensity before it can be heard.

There must also be a certain amount of difference among stimuli before one can be distinguished from another. The minimum amount necessary to tell stimuli apart is known as the *difference threshold.* Two reds must differ in wave length by some finite amount before they can be discriminated from each other; two tones must differ in a measurable amount before one is heard as higher than the other. Thus thresholds are identified at the transitions between no experience and some experience (the absolute threshold) and between no difference and some difference (the difference threshold).

Threshold measurement requires appropriate methods for detecting the results of very small changes in stimuli. To measure thresholds we need reliable equipment for presenting controlled stimuli, a plan for recording responses, and appropriate methods for treating the data in order to compute the thresholds. We discover that thresholds vary with individuals and fluctuate within one individual, so that a threshold measurement is always a statistical average of some sort. The standard procedures by which these averages are reached are known as *psychophysical methods*. The name comes from the fact that we are determining a "psychological" (*psycho-*) equivalent of a "physical" quantity (*physics*).

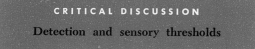

CRITICAL DISCUSSION
Detection and sensory thresholds

Those working in human factors research tend to distinguish between *detecting* a change in the environment and *identifying* it. These are evidently two different kinds of thresholds. Detection, which corresponds closely to the absolute threshold, occurs always against interfering processes. Even under good conditions, a soundproof room cannot eliminate the faint sounds made by the subject's circulating blood, and a darkened room cannot eliminate the slight visual impressions ("intrinsic light") always present in our eyes. Such considerations have led human factors research workers to propose that our mathematical treatments of thresholds should include the interfering stimuli, and they have worked out formulas for computing the stimulus level needed for detection under specified conditions. This is quite clear and not controversial; however, those who are very enthusiastic about these newer developments are inclined to believe that older efforts to find a "true" threshold were misguided, and they doubt if indeed there is any such thing as a "true" sensory threshold (Swets, 1961).

Others, not denying the significance of detection against noise, believe that with good methods we can come very close to a "true" threshold. In part this conviction comes about because of the very low amounts of energy in the stimuli that can be perceived under favorable circumstances. Thus Hecht, Shlaer, and Pirenne (1941) computed that at the threshold of vision something could be detected when each of 5 to 14 rods in the eye received but a single quantum of light. A sensitivity of this order cannot be very much distorted. Another line of evidence is that under certain carefully controlled conditions changes in stimulation are reacted to in a step-like manner that implies a true threshold for differences (Stevens, 1961).

A related problem is that of the effects of stimuli *below* threshold, i.e., *subliminal* effects. This is an area of controversy. For some of the issues see Ericksen (1960) and Klein (1959).

Sensory adaptation

While thresholds are always changing, their changes are not entirely haphazard. One consistent kind of change, found within several senses, is called *sensory adaptation*. It refers to the reduction in sensitivity to stimulation (i.e., the raising of thresholds) as stimulation persists through time. It is familiar within vision, smell, and temperature, though not limited to these senses. When we have been in sunlight, our eyes become much less sensitive, so that if we enter a dimly lighted room we cannot see the objects about us until our eyes have become dark-adapted. The person working in a fish store or a paint store soon becomes unaware of the odors about him. A room hot to someone coming in from the cold may feel cool to one emerging from a bath.

The Visual Sense

In the course of evolution, a number of mechanisms have evolved to permit the organism to respond to light or to visual patterns. The "eyes" thus developed often bear little resemblance to the human eye. The invertebrate eye (as in the octopus) is constructed on a pattern very different from the vertebrate eye; if viewed from the way the eye develops in the embryo, it is as though one kind of eye was based on a pattern turned inside-out as compared with the others. Insects display both simple (one-lens) and compound eyes. Many fish and other aquatic animals have light-sensitive skin, as well as eyes. A third eye on the top of the head (a "parietal eye") is found in certain lizards and in other reptiles and fish. What these evolutionary "experiments" signify is that sensitivity to changes in illumination has had important adaptive usefulness; hence the organisms that have evolved various kinds of light-sensitive mechanisms tend to be among those that have survived.

The human eye

The main features of the human eye are shown in cross section in Figure 8-1. Light enters the eye through the *cornea,* the amount of light being regulated by the *pupil,* which is an opening in the *iris;* then the *lens* focuses the light on the sensitive surface, the *retina.* The space between the cornea and the lens is filled with the *aqueous humor,* and the eye cavity inside the lens is filled with the *vitreous humor.*

The most sensitive portion of the eye in normal daylight vision is a small part of the retina called the *fovea,* on which is focused light that comes from the center of the *visual field.* (By the visual field we mean what the subject looks at.) Since the single con-

8-1

A cross section of the left human eye

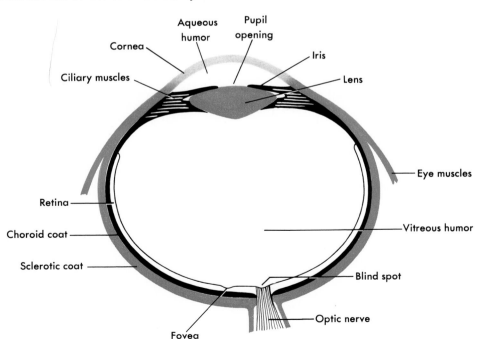

The size of the pupil is regulated by the iris, the diaphragm that gives the eye its color. The shape of the lens is regulated by the ciliary muscles. The external muscles that move the eye are not shown. (After Ranke, 1894)

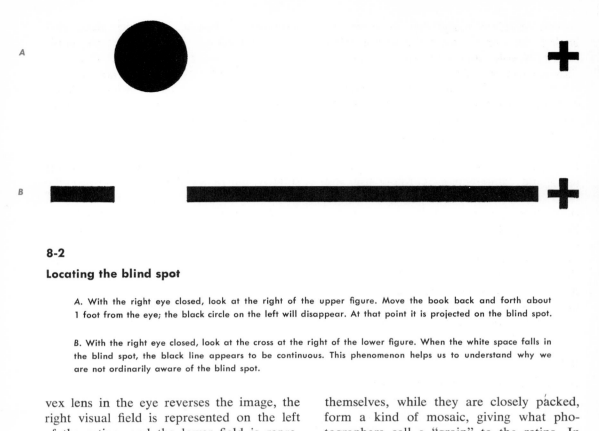

8-2

Locating the blind spot

A. With the right eye closed, look at the right of the upper figure. Move the book back and forth about 1 foot from the eye; the black circle on the left will disappear. At that point it is projected on the blind spot.

B. With the right eye closed, look at the cross at the right of the lower figure. When the white space falls in the blind spot, the black line appears to be continuous. This phenomenon helps us to understand why we are not ordinarily aware of the blind spot.

vex lens in the eye reverses the image, the right visual field is represented on the left of the retina, and the lower field is represented at the top of the retina.

Also on the retina and not far from the fovea is an insensitive area, the *blind spot,* where the nerve fibers from the cells in the retina come together to form the bundle making up the *optic nerve.* In the left eye the blind spot falls to the right of the fovea, so that the area of blindness is in the left visual field; in the right eye it is on the opposite side. You can easily find the blind spot in your own eye (Figure 8-2).

The eye is a very imperfect optical system. The light waves not only have to pass through the humors and the lens, none of which is a perfect transmitter of light, but they have to penetrate the network of blood vessels and nerve fibers that lie on the *inside* of the eye before they reach the sensitive cells—the *rods* and *cones* in the retina —where the light is converted into nervous impulses (Figure 8-3). The rods and cones

themselves, while they are closely packed, form a kind of mosaic, giving what photographers call a "grain" to the retina. In spite of these imperfections, the eye does remarkably well. The fovea, equivalent in area to a photographic film of 1 square millimeter, is able to detect a telephone wire at a distance of a quarter of a mile. At its best the eye can detect a wire whose thickness covers but 0.5 seconds of arc, about 1 two-millionth of the arc of a circle. This discrimination is all the more remarkable because a single cone fills an angular part of the retina 60 times as large as the thickness represented by the image of the wire. The fine discrimination takes place while the eye is in constant motion through an arc larger than the size of the minimum visible object (Ratliff and Riggs, 1950). In fact, such fine *visual acuity* is probably possible only *because* the eye is constantly in motion, and it may be the result of stimulating many neighboring cones as the eye moves back and forth over the object. (We may note in passing that the temptation to press the analogy between the eye and a photographic camera breaks down when we consider the finer aspects of seeing.)

The sensitive cells of the retina—the rods and the cones—are not uniformly distributed. The fovea contains only *cones,* some 50,000 of them packed closely together in its small area. Outside the fovea there are both rods and cones, with the cones decreasing in number from the center of the retina to the periphery. As we shall find out in more detail later, the cones are active in daylight vision. They permit us to see both *achromatic* colors (white, black, and the intermediate grays) and *chromatic* colors (red, green, blue, etc.). The rods, by contrast with the cones, function especially during vision under reduced illumination (night vision), and they permit us to see only achromatic colors.

Adaptation to illumination

When you go from daylight into a darkened motion picture theater, the usher may use a flashlight to escort you to your seat. You are unable to locate an empty seat unaided because your eyes are unaccustomed

8-3

Rods and cones and their connections

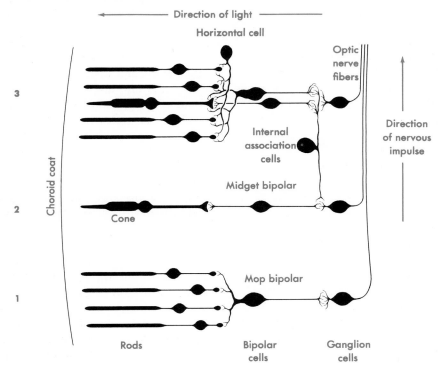

Shown here are the main layers of the retina: rods and cones, bipolar cells, and ganglion cells. The bipolar cells receive impulses from one or more rods or cones and transmit the impulses to the nerve fibers, whose cell bodies are shown as the ganglion cells. In (1) is a typical arrangement of several rods connected by one "mop" bipolar cell, in (2) an arrangement of one cone attached to a single "midget" bipolar cell, while in (3) some (but not all) of the more complex patterns are shown. Integration across the retina is accomplished by horizontal cells connecting rods and cones, and by internal association cells at the ganglion cell level, as well as by the mop bipolar cells. (Simplified, after Polyak, 1941)

to the darkness. After a while you can see people around you even though the lighting has not changed, for you have undergone *dark adaptation*. The sensitivity of the dark-adapted eye compared with the light-adapted is about 100,000 to 1.

The course of dark adaptation (Figure 8-4) provides indirect support for the difference in action between the rods and the cones. The first part of the curve shows that the *cones* gradually become sensitive to fainter lights, but after 5 minutes in the dark their sensitivity has increased as much as it will, as measured by the absolute threshold. Then the *rods* continue to adapt and become appreciably more sensitive for about half an hour.

The difference in function between rods and cones was discovered in part by studies on limited areas of the retina. As mentioned earlier, the center of the retina (the fovea) is rod-free. This means that in this area we can study the cones alone, which adapt according to the first part of Figure 8-4. When

8-4

The course of dark adaptation

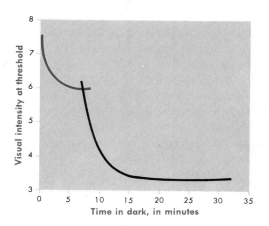

The subject stares at a bright light until the retina has become light-adapted. When he is then placed in darkness, he becomes increasingly sensitive to fainter lights as the retina becomes dark-adapted. The first part of the curve is for cones, the second for rods. The units of visual intensity are logarithms of micromicrolamberts (a very small unit of visual intensity). (After Hecht and Shlaer, 1938)

we realize that the cones are not very sensitive in the dark, we can understand why at night we detect a faint stimulus, such as a dim star, better if we do not look directly at it. Our rods, in the peripheral parts of the retina, are more sensitive in the dark-adapted eye than are the cones.

Color

When sunlight is sent through a prism, it breaks into a band of varicolored light, such as is familiar to us in the rainbow. The colors correspond to wave lengths, the *red* end of the rainbow produced by the *long* waves, the *violet* end by the *short* waves. A band produced by sending sunlight through a prism of known characteristics is described as a *solar spectrum* (Figure 8-5). The wave lengths corresponding to the various portions of the spectrum are indicated below the chart. They are expressed in millionths of a millimeter—a unit called the millimicron and abbreviated mμ. The spectrum fades into invisibility at the red end at about 780 mμ, and at the other end extends through the violets at about 380 mμ. We are able to see some vivid colors that do not exist in the spectrum at all, although they can be produced by mixing spectral lights. These are the purples redder than the violet end of the spectrum, and the red that looks "purest" to most normal eyes. The reddest part of the solar spectrum looks a little yellowish.

An interesting relationship among colors was discovered by Sir Isaac Newton. He found that the spectral colors can be wrapped in their natural order around the circumference of a circle, allowing room between the red and violet ends of the spectrum for the purples not found on the spectrum. If properly spaced, colors opposite each other on the circle will be *complementary*, that is, if lights of these colors are mixed in proper proportions, they disappear to a neutral gray. Such a color circle is presented in Figure 8-5, with specimen complementary colors pictured. For con-

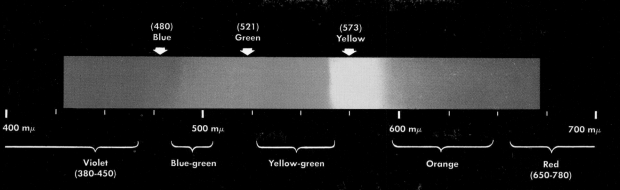

(480) Blue (521) Green (573) Yellow

400 mμ   500 mμ   600 mμ   700 mμ

Violet (380-450)   Blue-green   Yellow-green   Orange   Red (650-780)

8-5 The solar spectrum

The colors are in the order of the rainbow, as seen when sunlight is sent through a prism.

A color circle showing complementary colors

The colors opposite each other, if in proper proportions, will mix on a color wheel to yield the neutral gray at the center. Wave-lengths are indicated around the circle in mμ. Note that the spectral colors lie in their natural order on the circle, but their spacing is not uniform by wave-length and the circle includes the non-spectral reds, purples, and violets.

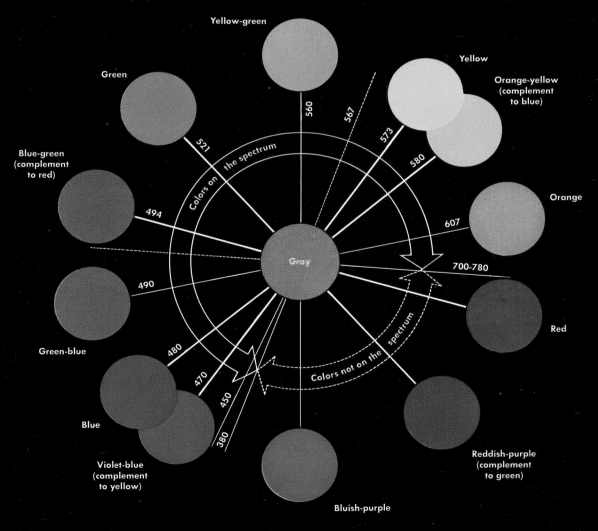

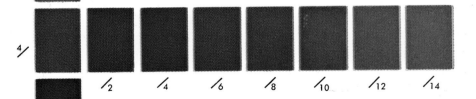

8-6 Additive and subtractive color mixtures

Additive color mixture takes place when lights are mixed or when sectors of colored papers are mixed by rotation on a color wheel. If the color mixture primaries red, green, and blue are so mixed, the red and green combine to produce yellow, and the yellow and blue combine to yield a neutral gray. Mixture of any two of the three colors produces the complement of the third, as shown in the triangular portions. Subtractive mixture takes place when light is transmitted through colored filters placed one over another, or when pigments are mixed. Usually, blue-green and yellow will mix to green, and complementary colors will reduce to black, as in the example given. Unlike additive mixture, one cannot tell from the colors of the components what color will result. For example, blue and green will commonly yield blue-green by subtractive mixture, but with some filters they may yield red. Note that in the diagram the triangular portions are the original complementary colors used in the additive mixtures, but here they appear as a result of subtractive mixture.

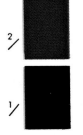

White

9/

8/

7/

6/

5/

4/   /2   /4   /6   /8   /10   /12   /14

3/

8-7 The brightness dimension of achromatic color

(*Vertical*) The brightness range is from black to white. The steps are numbered according to the Munsell system of notation.

2/

The dimension of saturation in red

(*Horizontal*) The saturation ranges from the "pure" red to a hue approaching pure gray as a limit. The numbers follow the Munsell system.

1/

Black

8-8 A color mixer

Disks with sectors of different colors are fastened to the metal plate. When the plate rotates, the colors fuse, yielding an additive mixture.

8-9 Tests for color blindness

Two plates from the Dvorine Pseudo-Isochromatic series of color-blindness tests. In the plate to the left, individuals with certain kinds of red-green blindness see only the number 5; others see only the 9; still others, no number at all. Those with normal vision see 95. Similarly, in the plate to the right, the person with normal vision sees the number 28, whereas those with red-green blindness see no number at all. (From I. Dvorine, *Dvorine Pseudo-Isochromatic Plates,* 1953, reproduced by permission of the author)

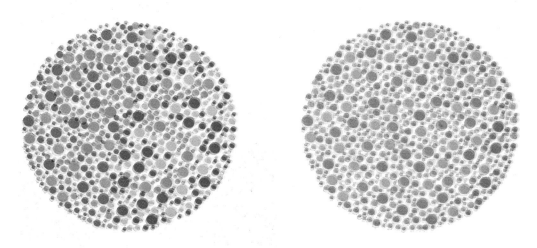

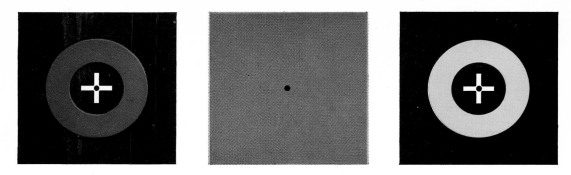

8-10 Negative afterimages

Look steadily for about 20 seconds at the dot inside the blue circle; then transfer your gaze to the dot inside the gray rectangle. Now do the same with the dot inside the yellow circle. What do you see? (After Evans, 1948)

8-11 Simultaneous contrast

Note the darkening effect on the gray patch when it is against white; the same patch of gray against black looks much lighter. A gray patch against a colored background tends to take on the complementary hue; the effect is much increased if a piece of thin tissue paper is placed over the colors. With colors that are approximately complementary (as in the red and green patches), there is an enhancement through contrast. Pennants are often red and green or yellow and blue.

8-12 The spreading effect

The same red is used throughout the strip. But the red with black looks darker than the red with white. (After Evans, 1948)

venience in remembering the positions, we usually name the main complementary pairs as blue-yellow and red-green, although the yellow complementary to blue is slightly orange and the green complementary to red is really a blue-green (see Figure 8-6).

Those familiar with painting will object to the naming of yellow and blue as complementaries because those pigments when mixed give green, not gray. We are here talking about mixing *lights,* not pigments. The principles of mixture in the two cases are not contradictory, though the explanation of the difference is somewhat involved. Without going into detail, it is worth noting that the mixture of lights is an *additive* mixture, while the mixture of pigments is in part a *subtractive* mixture because of the way in which pigments selectively absorb some of the light. (It is never possible to be sure from the color of the components what the result of subtractive mixture will be.) See Figure 8-6.

While the order of colors is alike, there are differences between the spectrum and the color circle. First is, of course, that the circle includes reds and purples not on the spectrum. Second is the stretching and shrinking of portions of the spectrum. The violets between 380 mμ and 450 mμ are almost indistinguishable on the color circle, as are the reds from 700 mμ to 780 mμ. Between the blue at 480 mμ and the green at 510 mμ the various wave lengths are widely spaced. After some narrowing of spacing of wave lengths in the yellow-greens, there is some stretching out of the yellows and another shortening in the oranges and reds. The stretching and shortening are not arbitrary, but are based upon the ease with which the eye can discriminate steps of color difference at various parts of the spectrum.

Some of the colors appear to us to be more elementary than others; that is, they appear to be composed of a single hue. These elementary colors are called *psychological primaries,* and usually four are named: *red, yellow, green,* and *blue,* as shown on Figure 8-6. Between them are "secondary" colors in which the components are still identifiable: orange between red and yellow, the yellow-greens between yellow and green, the blue-greens between green and blue, and the purples and violets between blue and red. Another set of primaries is called *color-mixture primaries.* Any three widely spaced colors on the spectrum can be used to provide all the other colors by additive mixture. The three usually chosen are a *red,* a *green,* and a *blue.* For this purpose, the red and green are so chosen that mixing them will yield yellow.

Hue, brightness, and saturation

The circumference of the color circle describes one *dimension* of color experience, *hue*—the technical term for the quality of redness, blueness, yellowness, or greenness that differentiates one color from another. (By a *dimension* we mean simply some characteristic according to which items can be placed in an order, along some sort of scale. Thus hues are placed in the order in which they are found along the circumference of the color circle.)

The achromatic colors have only the dimension of *brightness* from very dark (black) through the scale of gray to very bright (white); see Figure 8-7. Chromatic colors also have a brightness dimension, by which we mean their similarity to gray in lightness or darkness. A pure yellow is brighter than a pure blue, and one shade of blue can be brighter than another.

Many chromatic colors look as though they are mixed with gray. Near the extreme are grays with a mere touch of color; the limit is pure gray. We need a third dimension to describe such colors, since they can have any hue or any brightness. This third dimension is called *saturation* and refers to the apparent purity of the color (Figure 8-7). Highly saturated colors appear to be pure hue, without any gray, while colors of low saturation appear close to gray. Saturation is a matter of appearance, whatever the composition of the color may be. Although saturation can be reduced by mixing gray with a hue, it can also be reduced by increasing (or decreasing) the brightness of a pure color. This follows because all extremely bright colors merge in white and all extremely dark colors merge in black, thus reducing their saturation as they lose their hues.

One way to become familiar with saturation is to mix on a *color wheel* a vivid (near-spectral) color with a gray of equal brightness (Figure 8-8). The exposed area of a color on the color wheel is expressed in degrees, the sum of all exposed colors being 360°. If two colors are used, one can be increased from 0° to 360° of the wheel, while the other decreases from 360° to 0°. If one of these colors is a gray of brightness equal to the chromatic color, a saturation series will be created varying from pure hue to pure gray. Another way is to consider the colors that would be needed to fill the area of the color circle between the gray at the center and the colors on the circumference (see Figure 8-5). The reds and purples would become pink as light gray is added; the oranges and yellows would become variations of brown.

Afterimages and color contrast

If you stare at a *red* circle and then look at a plain gray rectangle, you are likely to see a *green* circle on it; that is, you experience a *negative afterimage,* negative because green is the complementary color of red. Not all afterimages are in the complementary color—after staring at a very bright light you are likely to see a whole succession of colors—but seeing the complementary color is very common.

The complementary color pairs are also found in *simultaneous contrast.* The shadow cast by chromatic light upon a surface dimly illuminated by achromatic light is vividly colored in the hue complementary to that of the chromatic light. It is hard to convince yourself that the shadow is not actually tinted, but you can prove this by viewing it through a tube that cuts off the chromatic light from your vision. Then the shadow will be seen as gray. This contrast effect enhances the borders between complementary colors, and is one reason for making pennants of such complementary pairs as red and green and yellow and blue.

The facts of vision are enormously complex, and until our knowledge is more precise we must be prepared for exceptions to many of our generalizations. It was mentioned above that the afterimage need not always be in the complementary color. Another exception is worth noting. Usually dark surroundings make a light area seem lighter, and light surroundings make the enclosed area seem darker. But under some conditions there is what is called a *spreading effect* so that dark areas make neighboring portions appear darker, and light areas make neighboring portions appear lighter. We lack explanations of these seemingly contradictory effects, and they set problems for future investigators.

Afterimage and contrast phenomena and spreading effect are illustrated in Figures 8-10 to 8-12.

Color blindness

We may conveniently think of the normal eye as discriminating three pairs of colors: light-dark and the complementaries yellow-blue and red-green. All other combinations can be derived from these. Color blindness may show as a deficiency in one or two of these systems, the light-dark system remaining if the person can see at all. The normal eye sees all three, and the person with such vision is called a *trichromat.* If a person lacks one system but has use of the two others, he is called a *dichromat.* A dichromat is partially color-blind. Finally, if only the light-dark system remains, the person is a *monochromat* and totally color-blind.

By far the commonest form of color

blindness is red-green blindness, with the blue-yellow and light-dark systems intact. It is much more common among men than among women, affecting some 7 per cent of men (if we count color weakness along with the more extreme deficiencies), but affecting less than 1 per cent of women. There are different forms of red-green blindness, named red blindness and green blindness; but these names are inaccurate, for both the red-blind form and the green-blind form lack both red and green; their differences lie in the regions where they see gray instead of blue and yellow. Total color blindness, in which the person sees merely black, white, and gray, is extremely rare, and yellow-blue blindness, in which red-green discrimination is preserved, is rarer still.

Many color-blind persons are unaware of their defect because they are able to make such skillful use of their remaining color discrimination, combining it with the learned colors of familiar objects. Because our color vocabulary is unclear for unsaturated colors, the color-blind person can make some mistakes on these most troublesome colors without being noticed.

Many tests are available for the detection of color blindness. They usually require the subject to read a figure composed of colored dots on a background of other colored dots (Figure 8-9). The colors are chosen so as to confuse subjects who have the various forms of color deficiency.

Is there any way of telling what color the color-blind person actually sees? We can be sure of the colors that look alike to him, because he will confuse them when, for example, he attempts to sort out colored yarns. But we can go farther than that, thanks to a few cases of people who are color-blind in only one eye (Sloan and Wollach, 1948; Graham and Hsia, 1958). We know that for the red-green blind, blues and yellows (as hues) look very much the same as they do to those with normal eyes, and these, in combinations with gray, are all that he sees.

There are other words in his color vocabulary, however, so that he will call "green" the yellow of low saturation (that is, a grayish yellow) that he sees when he looks at a lawn, and will call "red" the grayish yellow that he sees when he looks at a fire engine.

Nothing can be done to cure congenital color blindness, although such aids as colored filters can be provided to help the color-blind person make more accurate color discriminations. Some forms of color blindness are the result of disease or injury (poisoning by carbon disulfide, lead poisoning, optic neuritis, etc.). Recovery from color blindness may be possible in some such cases.

The physiology of vision

The distinction between rod function and cone function noted in the differences between foveal vision and peripheral vision and in the nature of dark adaptation has been well confirmed in the physiological laboratory. At least for the *rods* the distinction of function seems to be clearly established. A light-sensitive substance called *visual purple* or *rhodopsin* can be extracted from the rods and its properties studied. It is found to be bleached by lights of different wave lengths in a manner that corresponds to the sensitivity of the dark-adapted eye to these wave lengths (Figure 8-13). Furthermore its bleaching *rate* corresponds to the rate of adaptation to light (Wald, 1951).

These correspondences strongly suggest that visual purple is an intermediary between the light entering the eye and the activation of the sensory nerves that leads to seeing. The search for corresponding substances in the cones goes on, but so far without definite results (Wald, 1954).

Each attempt to explain how the eye sees color has taken as its starting point one of the three bodies of facts about color that we have just discussed: color mixture, color contrast and afterimages, and color blindness.

The classical theory starting with the facts

The chemical basis for rod vision

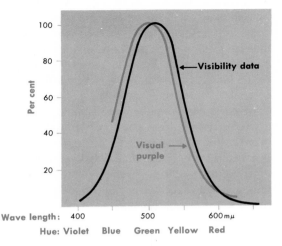

Wave length: 400   500   600 mμ
Hue: Violet   Blue   Green Yellow   Red

The black line represents the relative visibility of the different wave lengths to the dark-adapted human eye; the colored line represents the rate at which visual purple (rhodopsin) is bleached by light of different wave lengths. The two curves are superimposed by using arbitrary units so that the maximum of each curve is at 100 per cent. Because the curves so nearly coincide, it is plausible to suppose that visual purple (which is obtained from rods) is the chemical substance that mediates rod vision. (After Hecht and Williams, 1922-23)

of *color mixture* goes by the name of the Young-Helmholtz theory, after the physicist Young and the physiologist Helmholtz. Being impressed by the fact that three colors were enough to produce all combinations, they proposed that three kinds of sensitive elements in the eye might serve to explain color phenomena. The modern form of the theory attempts to search out three kinds of cones or three kinds of cone substance.

A second theory, which starts with the facts of *contrast* and *afterimages,* is attributed to Hering, another physiologist. He was impressed by the appearance of color pairs under so many circumstances. Hence a black-white pair, a red-green pair, and a blue-yellow pair seemed to him the fundamental units of visual activity. He proposed three processes that in their building-up phase (anabolic) would yield one member

of the pair, and in their tearing-down phase (catabolic) would yield the other. Hence when stimulation is withdrawn, as in the afterimage experiment, the contrasting color appears because the anabolic-catabolic process is reversed.

A third theory was proposed by the psychologist Ladd-Franklin, who was impressed by the facts of *color blindness* and had an evolutionary theory to account for them. She assumed that monochromatism was the most primitive form of seeing, followed by the addition of blue and yellow (equivalent to red-green color blindness), and this in turn followed by trichromatism. Hence the red-green color-blind person has regressed one step; blue-yellow blindness would require a second regressive step, only one step removed from complete color blindness. The fact that blue-yellow blindness is rarer than total color blindness makes her theory less plausible than it otherwise would be.

Even this brief sketch shows how theorists tend to build their theories around a limited set of facts. Of course they go on to try to explain the other facts as well, but the nature of the theory often shows its origin in a specific starting point. Actually, no one of the theories is yet satisfactory, and newer theories have been proposed.

CRITICAL DISCUSSION
Color theories

Great advances have been made in the specifications of color and in reference standards, necessitated in part by such developments as color photography and colored motion pictures and television. The use of color in mass-produced objects such as automobiles and radios, to say nothing of its use in interior decoration, calls for precise designation of colors. Theories of the Young-Helmholtz type have remained popular because three colors are enough to serve the purposes of precise specification. Hence a three-color theory is called *parsimonious,* that is, it gets along with as few variables as possible. But the fact that three colors can produce all combinations does not prove that the eye is constructed on a three-color system. It proves only that this is the *minimum* required. It may be that there are more than three kinds of cones in the eye, perhaps more than four (Granit, 1947).

While certain features of Hering's theory have kept psychologists interested in it, the development of theories related to it has not kept pace with those deriving from Young and Helmholtz. A serious attempt has recently been made, however, to restate Hering's type of theory in quantitative form (Hurvich and Jameson, 1955).

Considerable interest was aroused in 1959 by Land (1959), the developer of the Land Polaroid camera, who, in seeking to develop color photography for his camera, fell upon an interesting method of producing a variety of colors by mixing only two wave lengths (instead of the usually required three). He found that he could photograph any array of colored objects in black and white using colored filters so that the resulting black-and-white transparencies would differ according to the filters used. Now, regardless of the filters used, he could project *two other colors* through these transparencies, and by their overlap reproduce a colored scene rather like the one originally photographed. While this finding apparently calls for a new theory of color vision, critics have shown how the effects can be harmonized with existing theories if sufficient play is given to contrast effects (as in Hering's theory) (Walls, 1960). However the discussion turns out, the complexity and richness of contrast effects can no longer be ignored in considering how we actually perceive a colored display.

The Auditory Sense

The human ear

Like the eye, the ear has "focusing" equipment as well as specifically sensitive portions (Figure 8-14). The *external ear* is an evolutionary remnant, now giving little service as an "ear trumpet" but showing its similarity to the larger movable ears of lower animals which still serve well as sound receivers. The muscles that control man's external ear are still there, and some people learn to use them; for the most part, however, man's external ear is a degenerate organ.

The external ear connects with an auditory canal leading to the *eardrum,* a movable diaphragm activated by sound entering the ear. On the inner side of the diaphragm is a cavity housing the bony transmitters of the *middle ear* (hammer, anvil, and stirrup). The pressure inside and outside the eardrum is equalized by way of the *Eustachian tube* that leads into the mouth cavity. When pressure changes rapidly, as in an airplane, yawning or coughing or chewing gum employs the Eustachian tube in making the pressure inside the ear change to correspond with the pressure outside. The hammer is attached firmly to the eardrum, and the stirrup to the *oval window* that conducts the sounds to the cochlea, the auditory portion of the *inner ear*. Small movements at the eardrum are condensed into a magnified pressure on the oval window, an increase in pressure per unit area of about 30 to 1.

Pressure at the oval window sets into motion the fluid inside the cochlea. Pressure at the oval window is relieved at the *round window* that also lies between the cochlea and the inner ear, at the other end of the fluid-filled channel through the cochlea. The pressure on the fluid in the cochlea stimulates the true auditory receptors lying in the *organ of Corti,* the portion of the cochlea that contains the auditory equivalent of the retina (Figure 8-15). Pressure changes in the fluid displace the *basilar membrane* upon which the organ of Corti rests, and this displacement stimulates the sensitive elements in the *hair cells* of the organ of Corti, connected with the auditory nerve. The inner ear also contains other sensitive (nonauditory) portions that we shall consider later.

Pitch and loudness

The stimuli for pure tones are sound waves—physical vibrations in the air (or

A cross section of the ear

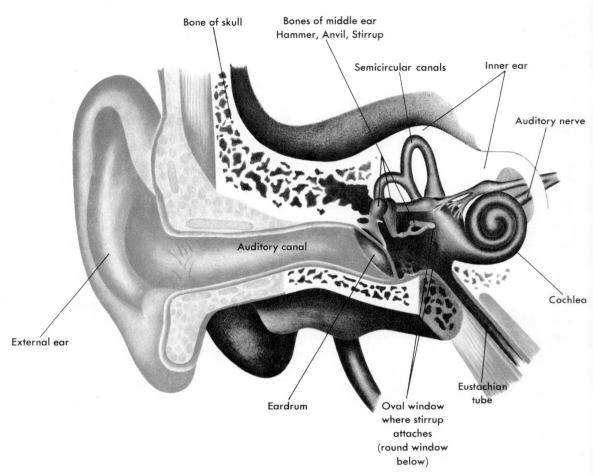

Bone of skull

Bones of middle ear
Hammer, Anvil, Stirrup

Semicircular canals

Inner ear

Auditory nerve

Auditory canal

External ear

Cochlea

Eardrum

Oval window
where stirrup
attaches
(round window
below)

Eustachian
tube

This drawing shows the general structure of the ear. For the detailed neural connections see Fig. 8-15. (Drawn in part after Sabatta, 1909, and Spalteholz, 1918)

in other substances such as water or metal). For example, at one end of a speaking tube, the vibrations compress the air molecules in front; this "push" is transmitted from air molecule to air molecule, alternately causing compressions and expansions of the air; these compressions and expansions cause "sound" to be heard at the other end of the tube when the ear is placed against it.

Sound waves can be graphically represented as transverse *sine waves* (Figure 8-

16). The figure shows how a single complete cycle represents the successive compression and expansion of the air as the sound wave moves along. The two main characteristics of such a wave are its *frequency* and its *amplitude*. Frequency refers to number of vibrations per second, that is, the number of times per second that the whole wave is repeated. Amplitude refers to the amount of compression and expansion, as represented by the amount by which the curve is displaced above or below the base line. The psychological correlate of frequency is *pitch:* the higher the vibration frequency, the higher the pitch we hear. The corresponding correlate of amplitude is *loudness:* the greater the amplitude, the louder the tone (provided pitch remains constant).

The range of frequencies that we hear as pitch runs from about 20 to 20,000 cycles per second. The piano produces frequencies up to a high of 4096, and the piccolo goes somewhat higher (Figure 8-17).

As for amplitude, while we all know the difference between a loud sound and a soft one, assigning scale values to loudness is not so easy. Engineers from the Bell Telephone Laboratories have contributed to the measurement of sound intensity by formulating a convenient unit by which to convert the physical pressures at the eardrum into an understandable scale. The unit is called a *decibel* (one-tenth of a *bel,* named in honor of Alexander Graham Bell, who invented the telephone). The rough meaning of a decibel is indicated in the scale of familiar sounds given in Figure 8-18.

Sensitivity to differences in frequency

How much change in vibration frequency is necessary in order for us to hear a difference in pitch? When we tune two instruments so that the same intended notes sound alike, how much leeway is there? The answer depends on the frequency at which we are working. The most convenient way in which to plot this is to represent the

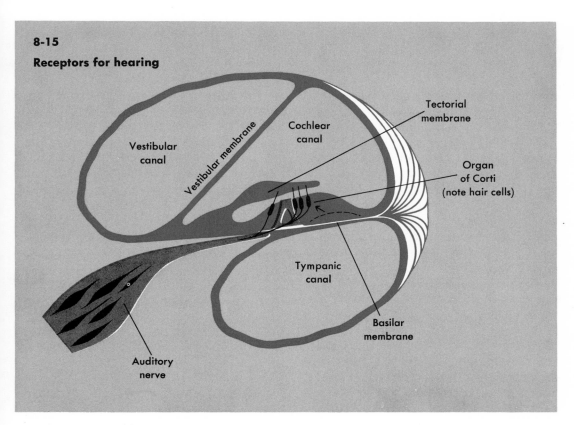

8-15

Receptors for hearing

Vestibular canal

Vestibular membrane

Cochlear canal

Tectorial membrane

Organ of Corti (note hair cells)

Tympanic canal

Basilar membrane

Auditory nerve

A section through the snail-shaped cochlea. The true auditory receptors lie in the organ of Corti, which rests upon the basilar membrane. Deflection of the basilar membrane activates the hair cells and produces impulses in the auditory nerve.

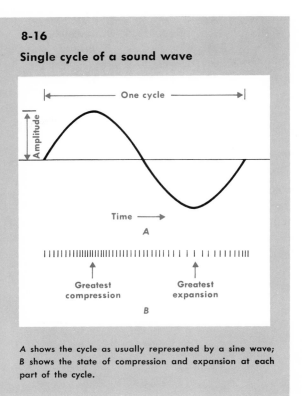

8-16

Single cycle of a sound wave

One cycle

Amplitude

Time →

A

Greatest
compression

Greatest
expansion

B

A shows the cycle as usually represented by a sine wave;
B shows the state of compression and expansion at each
part of the cycle.

most sensitive at about 2000 cycles per second.

Above threshold the same relationships hold. That is, with equal amplitudes well above threshold, tones in the middle ranges continue to sound louder than either very low or very high tones. This fact explains why high-fidelity amplifiers provide adjustments for increasing the amplitude of the "bass" and "treble" sounds on a recording. (In fact, it has long been standard practice for recording engineers to incorporate such an adjustment in the recording itself.)

Complex tones and noises

In addition to its fundamental tone of one frequency, a musical tone has additional tones, known as *overtones,* which are multiples of that frequency. Doubling the frequency of a tone creates a second tone *one octave* higher than the first; therefore we say that the first overtone is at the octave. Other overtones have a more complex relation to the fundamental.

The tones of one musical instrument differ from those of another in characteristic quality, or *timbre.* The reeds, strings, and brasses in an orchestra have identifying differences that go beyond pitch and loudness. Timbre depends upon the overtones and other impurities in the tone typical of the instrument. Instead of the regular sound wave pictured at the top of Figure 8-21, a tone from any instrument has a complex wave form, preserving only the peaks and troughs that help to define the fundamental pitch.

If one compares the dimensions of tone with those of color, the following correspondences hold approximately:

Dimensions of color	Dimensions of tone
Hue	Pitch
Brightness	Loudness
Saturation	Timbre

Hue and pitch are functions of wave frequency; brightness and loudness are func-

change necessary as a ratio to the frequency itself. Suppose that at a frequency of 200 cycles it takes a change of 4 cycles before a second tone is heard as higher than the first. Then the ratio would be 4:200 or .02. If at 2000 cycles 10 cycles are required, the ratio drops to 10:2000, or .005. The ratios depend also upon the amplitude of the tone, becoming lower at greater amplitudes. Some representative ratios for a loudness level of 10 decibels and for a loudness level of 40 decibels are given in Figure 8-19.

Sensitivity to amplitude

Sensitivity to amplitude also varies with the frequency of the source (Figure 8-20). Tones between 800 and 4000 cycles require less than 10 decibels to reach threshold, but a low tone of 40 cycles requires over 70 decibels, and one of 10,000 cycles requires nearly 30 decibels. Our ears are

236

Range of frequencies of the piano and other musical instruments

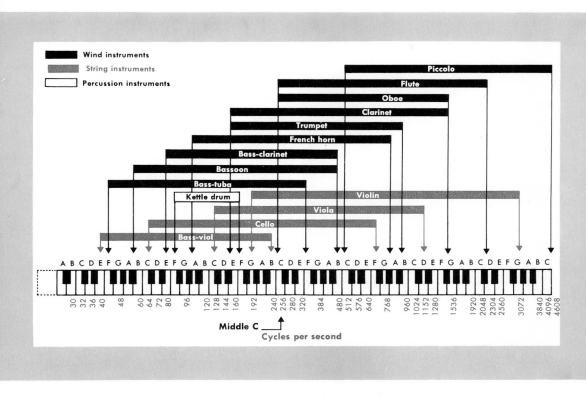

Note that each octave represents a doubling in frequency. (After Henney, 1938)

tions of amplitude (or other measure of intensity); and saturation may be a result of mixture, just as timbre is. But these are analogies only and are limited as all analogies are.

What happens when two tones are sounded together? They do not lose their identity as colors do when mixed, although they may lead to a fusion that is heard as *consonant* (pleasant) or as *dissonant* (unpleasant). One reason some combinations of tones are preferred to others is that the two tones create a third tone based on the difference in their frequencies. This *difference tone* may or may not harmonize with the fundamental tones that are sounded. If the two tones are close together in frequency, *beats* are heard (instead of a dif-

ference tone), at a rate per second equal to the number of cycles per second difference between them. For example, if a tone of 256 cycles is sounded along with one of 260 cycles, we hear a single pulsating tone beating 4 times per second (260 minus 256 is 4). Musical harmony depends in part on the complex interaction between fundamental tones, their overtones, and the beats and difference tones that combine to make up the complex tonal stimulus.

A *noise* is a very complex sound, composed of many frequencies not in harmonious relation to each other. Acoustical experts sometimes speak of "white noise" when referring to a noise composed of all frequencies in the sound spectrum, by analogy to white light as composed of all fre-

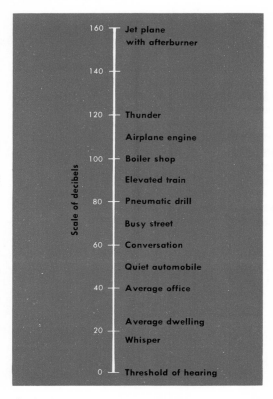

The loudness of various common sounds is indicated. (After Stevens and Davis, 1938; jet plane added)

ing. Under the organ of Corti lies the *basilar membrane* that somehow detects the changes transmitted through the oval window and converts them into appropriate auditory signals.

Helmholtz, whose theory of color vision we studied, made the brilliant suggestion that the basilar membrane acts like a series of resonators, responding at its narrow end to high tones and at its wide end to low tones, just as the strings of a piano or a harp will vibrate in resonance with tones that are sounded at the natural resonant frequency of the instrument. The nerve fibers connected with the different parts of the membrane signal to the brain whether the tone is high or low, each fiber (or group of fibers) transmitting stimuli of a specific frequency. This type of hearing theory has come to be called a *place theory,* because it associates pitch with the *place* on the basilar membrane where auditory stimulation occurs.

The opposite type of theory interprets the membrane more nearly as though it were the diaphragm of a microphone, vibrating as a whole at the frequency of the incoming sound. This second theory is called a *frequency theory,* because it assumes that nervous impulses are initiated by the basilar membrane in accordance with the frequency at which tonal vibrations reach it. There are many compromises between these two theories, and the final theory, as in vision, has not yet been agreed upon.

Some aspects of the *place theory* are by now so well established that any final theory will surely incorporate them. We know from several lines of evidence that tones of given frequencies have their maximum influence on the basilar membrane at well-defined places. The evidence comes from electrical and mechanical measurements made within the normal-functioning ear, and from the tonal gaps that are produced when portions of the basilar membrane are

quencies in the light spectrum. The sound of a hissing steam radiator approximates the sound of white noise.

A noise may have a characteristic pitch. For example, we may legitimately use the musical term *bass* to characterize a drum, even though a drum is more noisy than tonal. Speech sounds make use at once of tonal qualities and of noise qualities; *vowels* are tonal, and *consonants* are noisy.

The physiology of hearing

We know that the organ of Corti within the cochlea contains the sensitive cells that connect with the fibers of the auditory nerve, over which the impulses travel to the brain and lead to our experiences of hear-

damaged or when the ear is injured by prolonged exposure to loud tones of a given frequency. This evidence agrees sufficiently to permit a map of the basilar membrane such as that in Figure 8-22.

Evidence for some kind of *frequency theory* comes from the representation within the auditory nerve of the actual frequencies of sounds sent into the ear, particularly for sounds not over 4000 or 5000 cycles. The early experiments on frequency were faulty in that the electrical impulses picked up from the nerve were not true signs of activity within the auditory nerve, but were effects from the cochlea as a whole acting as a microphone. Later experiments have sought to correct these defects, however, and there does appear to be some representation of frequency in the auditory nerve.

Perhaps some kind of compromise between the place theory and the frequency theory will account for all the facts.

CRITICAL DISCUSSION
Auditory theories

Modern *place* theories have moved far from the theory that the basilar membrane is composed of fibers that resonate like piano strings. The ear is filled with a viscous fluid, and the membrane is not free to vibrate in that way. The most promising theory, worked out by Békésy along hydrostatic lines, is known as the *traveling wave theory*. When a sound of a given frequency enters the ear, a wave travels along the basilar membrane and displaces it a maximum amount at a certain point, depending on the frequency of the wave. Békésy's beautifully precise experiments on both animal and human ears strongly support his interpretations (Békésy, 1960).

Similarly, earlier *frequency* theories have undergone changes. The strongest contender today is the *volley theory*, which proposes that the frequency may be represented in a bundle of fibers firing in turn, even though no single fiber carries impulses at that rate (Wever, 1949).

Frequency theories are kept alive in part

8-19

Sensitivity to differences in frequency

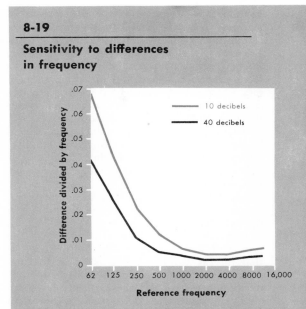

The figure plots the difference threshold as a ratio of the frequency for two loudness levels, 10 and 40 decibels above threshold. (After Shower and Biddulph, 1931)

8-20

Sensitivity to differences in amplitude

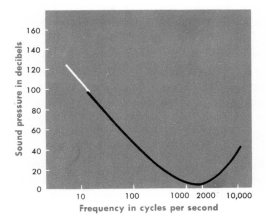

The threshold for loudness decreases up to about 2000 cycles, then increases. (Approximate, from various determinations)

by the need to account for some kinds of analysis that take place in the brain when sounds are sent separately to the two ears. For example, if tones differing slightly in frequency are sent separately to the ears, a *binaural beat* may result. Unless the frequencies are somehow represented where the paths from the two ears meet in the brain, it is difficult to understand how the beat arises.

Another complexity thus far unmentioned is the problem of accounting for loudness while also accounting for pitch. Loudness is usually explained by the number of impulses produced, either through the increase in the number of fibers stimulated as loudness increases or through more frequent impulses in the same fibers.

Licklider (1959) finds that many of the prevailing theories are too limited in scope so that, in his words, "There is no systematic, overall theory of hearing." He then proceeds to consider three part theories: (1) a theory of signal detection, more sophisticated than the classical work on thresholds, (2) a theory of speech intelligibility, going beyond considerations treated in this chapter, and (3) a theory of pitch perception, which accepts Békésy's findings but adds other considerations based on correlations of excitations arising in the two ears.

Other Senses

Man's senses other than vision and audition are very important for him, but they lack the richness of patterning and organization which have led men to call vision and audition the "higher senses." Our symbolic experiences are expressed largely in visual and auditory terms. Our spoken language is to be *heard,* and our written language is to be *seen.* Musical notation permits music to be read or played on an instrument. Except for Braille (the raised form of printing that permits the blind to read) we do not have any comparable symbolic coding of odors, tastes, or touches. These so-called "lower senses" are important so far as survival is concerned, but they are lower in the richness and variety of experiences they mediate.

Smell

From an evolutionary point of view, smell is one of the most primitive and most important of the senses. The sense organ for smell has a position of prominence in the head appropriate to a sense intended to guide behavior. The receptors high in the nose, in the *olfactory epithelium* of each nasal cavity, are connected without synapse directly to the olfactory bulbs of the brain, lying just below the frontal lobes. (See Chapter 2.) Thus smell has a more direct route to the brain than any other sense. The olfactory bulbs are in turn connected with the olfactory cortex on the inside of the temporal lobes, and extend to the neighboring cortex. The exact connections are a matter of some uncertainty (Pfaffmann, 1951).

In fish, the olfactory cortex makes up the entire cerebral hemispheres. In the dog, the olfactory cortex represents about one-third of the area of the side of the brain, as contrasted with one-twentieth of this area in man. The dog's well-known abilities to make discriminations on the basis of odor have been demonstrated under controlled conditions (Kalmus, 1955). In man, odor has become of relatively little adaptive significance, playing its part, however, in warning of danger by fire or of being overcome by gas, in the discrimination of foods, and in the enjoyment of pleasant odors.

Progress in the scientific study of odors has been delayed by three obstacles: (1) there is little agreement upon "primary" odors; (2) chemistry and physics have given us no satisfactory ordering of the stimulus aspects of odors, which would provide fixed reference points corresponding to the wave lengths of light or the frequencies of sounds; and (3) accurate threshold determinations are difficult because of the inaccessibility of the receptors.

Because of the commercial importance of odors, especially in the perfume industry but also in the wine and liquor industries,

8-21

The wave forms of complex tones

Dr. Hugh Linebach

some standardization of odor terminology and measurement would be desirable. An industrial chemist proposed a classification of odors into four groups: fragrant (musk), acid (vinegar), burnt (roast coffee), and caprylic (goaty) (Crocker, 1945). But his classification does not appear to hold up any better than earlier ones, as shown by the following investigation.

The 32 odors of the commercially available Crocker-Henderson Odor-Classification set were used in this test. Each of the 15 subjects tried to sort these odors into as few groups as possible on the basis of their similarities. Only one subject was satisfied to sort them into four groups. The rest used more groups, up to as many as 19 (Figure 8-23). The effort to scale odors within any one class on the basis of intensity was also unsuccessful (Ross and Harriman, 1949).

The nature of the olfactory stimulus has been the source of a great deal of speculation. Some theorists assume that smell is due to a chemical reaction between the odorous substance and the receptor, while some assume a kind of radiation activity, such as the differential absorption of infrared radiant energy corresponding to the gas being smelled (Beck, 1950). But the whole matter is far from settled, and remains a promising field for research (Jones and Jones, 1953).

Taste

We are at least clear about the primary taste qualities. They are *sweet, salt, sour,* and *bitter,* as shown on the taste tetrahedron (Figure 8-24). Everything else in taste experience is contributed by fusions of these qualities and other senses. When we taste lemonade, we enjoy its odor and its coolness by senses other than taste; the taste sense provides only for its sweet-sour-bit-

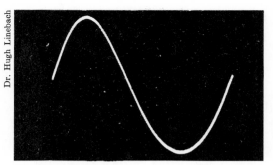

Pure tone—fundamental

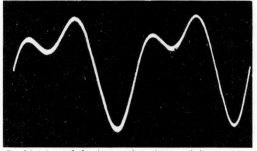

Combination of fundamental and second harmonic

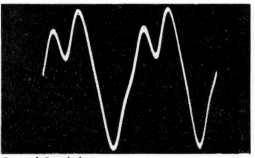

Tone of French horn

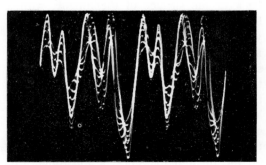

Tone of trumpet

Each illustration is of the tone of A above middle C (440 cycles per second). All the tones were actually played on a Hammond organ.

8-22

Sound map of the basilar membrane

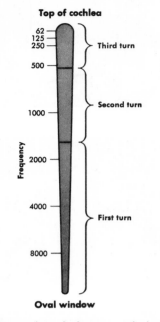

Top of cochlea

Frequency

62
125
250 — Third turn

500

1000 — Second turn

2000

4000 — First turn

8000

Oval window

This diagram shows the location on the basilar membrane, within the coils of the cochlea, of maximum sensitivity to sounds of different frequency. (After Stevens, Davis, and Lurie, 1935)

ter components. With our nostrils clamped tight, we cannot distinguish between the taste of a raw apple and a raw potato.

The taste receptors are found in the *taste buds* on the edges and toward the back of the surface of the tongue, with a few elsewhere in the soft palate, the pharynx, and the larynx. It is known that the number of taste buds decreases with age, so that older people are less sensitive to taste than children. Some taste buds at the tip of the tongue react only to sweet, salt, and sour, while others react to some or all of these in combination. In general, sensitivity to *sweet* is greatest at the tip, to *salt* on the tip and the sides of the tongue, to *sour* on the sides, and to *bitter* on the back of the tongue.

Despite the much greater specificity of our knowledge of stimulus-receptor corre-

lation in taste as compared with smell, we are quite unclear about just what happens at the receptor, or even if there are four kinds of processes related to the four primary tastes. We are also uncertain about the area of the cortex in which taste is represented. It was formerly supposed that the cortical area for taste was closely associated with the area for smell, but recently it has appeared that taste is more closely related to the sensitivity of the skin on the face, which is represented cortically behind the central fissure at the lower part of the side of the brain (Patton and Ruch, 1946).

CRITICAL DISCUSSION
Physiology and sensory quality

The general agreement that taste qualities include only sweet, salt, sour, and bitter led to a search for taste buds that mediated these qualities. This rather simple notion that the experienced quality would be closely related to underlying physiology goes back to the doctrine of *specific nerve energies* formulated early in the nineteenth century by Sir Charles Bell and Johannes Müller (Carmichael, 1926). This doctrine states that we are aware of the state of our nerves, rather than of external stimuli: that is, that stimulation of the eye gives rise to experiences of light, and of the taste buds to experiences of taste. It was thus simple to infer that some taste buds should produce the experience of sweet, others of salt, sour, or bitter.

Advances in electrophysiology have made it possible for our knowledge of what happens upon stimulation to become much more precise. The records shown in Figure 8-25 indicate that an increasing concentration of salt solution gives rise to an increasing number of impulses in a single taste nerve fiber. A nerve is of course a bundle of fibers, but modern techniques make possible this isolation of a single one. When such a single fiber is stimulated by other substances, it will also yield impulses. In terms of thresholds, based on the minimum concentration of the substance that can be detected, various basic stimuli can be arranged in order from low to high as follows: quinine, hydrochloric acid, sodium chloride, potassium

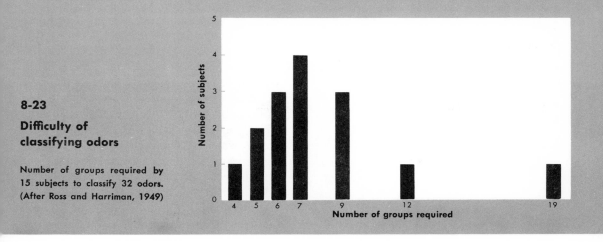

8-23

Difficulty of classifying odors

Number of groups required by 15 subjects to classify 32 odors. (After Ross and Harriman, 1949)

chloride, and sucrose. That is, the taste mechanism reacts most readily to quinine (bitter) and is least sensitive to sucrose (sweet).

How, then, are we to account for the fact that different substances do taste differently? The answer must lie in some sort of "code," which includes the frequency of stimulation in neighboring fibers and the relative amounts of parallel activity in units that happen to be more sensitive to one kind of stimulation than to another (Pfaffmann, 1959). While something like the doctrine of specific nerve energies is still appropriate, the doctrine must not misguide us into oversimple theories of the relationship of phenomenal experience to what goes on in our nervous systems.

The skin senses

It turns out that the familiar sense of touch is not one sense but at least four: *touch, pain, warm,* and *cold,* which are felt through four distinct kinds of sensitive spots on the skin surface. If the skin is explored with appropriate instruments (fine hairs, needle points, warmed or cooled pointed hammers), it is found that these sensitive spots are unevenly distributed. This *punctiform distribution* is also not alike for the four qualities; the separate sensitive spots are not equally numerous nor are they found at the same locations. On most parts

of the skin the relative frequencies are, in descending order: pain spots, touch spots, cold spots, and warm spots.

The precise receptors for the various skin senses have been the subject of much study and dispute. The firm knowledge is so slight that we can ignore it here (Jenkins, 1951).

A number of fascinating problems emerge in the study of the skin senses. We can illustrate them by taking a look at temperature perception, local signs, and the two-point threshold.

Temperature. The thermometer scale is continuous; it is not divided into a part called "cold" and another part called "warm." Yet our skin senses are so divided. The experiences of "warm" and "cold" depend upon a *level of adaptation,* this level providing a kind of zero point. A very old experiment demonstrates this. You prepare three pails of water, one containing ice water, one containing hot water, and one containing water at room temperature. Then you place your right hand in the hot water and your left hand in the cold water, and leave them there for a few minutes. Now plunge both hands into the water at room temperature. To the left hand the water feels warm, to the right hand, cool.

This experience is familiar. Another fact, however, is unlikely to be discovered without special experimentation. The experience of "hot" is distinct from the experience of "warm"; it results from the stimulation *at once* of "warm" and "cold" spots. With a device consisting of intertwined coils so that two streams of water can be passed through alternate coils, this fact can be easily demonstrated. Pass cold water through both coils; of course they feel cold when you grasp them with one hand. Pass warm water through both and they feel warm. Now pass cold water through one set of coils and warm water through the other. When you grasp the coils they now feel hot! This is not the way the experience of "hot" is usually produced, but it is the way the receptors respond. Cold spots have two thresholds. They respond to stimuli of low temperature, do not respond to stimuli of intermediate temperature, but respond again to stimuli of high temperature. Hence with high temperatures there is an activa-

8-24

The taste tetrahedron

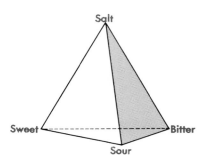

The four basic taste qualities can be plotted on a surface such as this.

8-25

Data from electrical stimulation of nerve fiber in rat

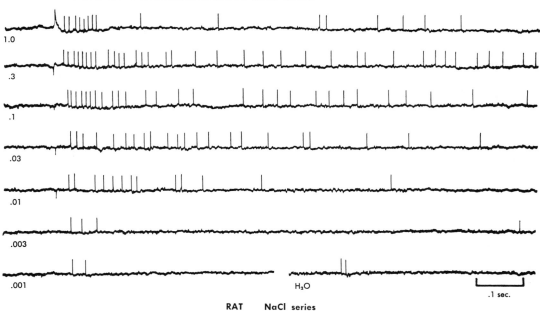

A series of oscillograph tracings obtained from a single taste nerve fiber when different concentrations of salt solution are placed on the tongue. Note that water as well as .001M NaCl will elicit two impulses. A concentration of .003M NaCl will elicit three impulses and may be considered as threshold. (From Pfaffmann, 1959)

tion of *both* warm and cold spots, and the felt experience of "hot" depends upon this double effect.

Local Signs. If someone touches your arm while your eyes are closed, you can tell whether he touched your right or left arm and approximately where he touched it. Thus the sensory effect is accompanied by some sort of sign of location, known as a *local sign*.

The problem of what is inborn and what is acquired runs through all the topics concerned with capacity for discrimination and response. This is also true with local signs. It has been argued that local signs arise through learning. When you prick yourself on your right hand, you make a reflex withdrawal and look for the sharp object that caused the pain. Through many experiences of this kind, you learn to know when (and where) something touches your right hand; by then the touch has acquired a local sign. The argument is used to explain, for example, why it is so hard to guide someone to scratch an itch located high on your back. As the argument runs, localization is poor on the back, because there are few opportunities to learn the necessary discriminations.

The other side of the argument is supported by skin transplants in animals, as illustrated in the following experiment done with frogs. Frogs are quite accurate in localizing disturbing stimuli on their skin; when they wipe off an irritant from their skin, they aim very well with their feet. If skin flaps from a tadpole are transplanted across the midline (Figure 8-26) before any localization of touch has developed, the tadpole will develop unharmed into a frog. Now, however, if the frog is stimulated at *A* it will try to wipe off something at *B* (Sperry, 1951).

This experiment shows that, at least for the frog, the local signs are laid down in the nervous system without any necessary learning.

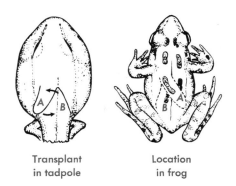

Transplant   Location
in tadpole   in frog

Transplantation of skin in a frog made in study of localization of stimuli. (After Sperry, 1951)

Two-Point Threshold. If the skin is stimulated at once with two points very slightly separated, the impression will be that of a single stimulus. As the points are placed wider apart, there comes a time when the impression is distinctly that of two stimuli with intervening space. The transition point from one to two is called the *two-point threshold*. Were we unable to make such discriminations, our use of touch would be clumsy, and the blind could not learn to read with their fingers. It comes as something of a surprise, however, to find how wide the separation of points must be to be discriminated on different parts of the body. An old rule of thumb is that the more mobile the bodily part, the smaller the two-point threshold. Thus the tip of the tongue and the finger tips do better than the back or forearm. (See Figures 8-27, 8-28.) As in the case of local sign, the possibility exists that there is more practice in discrimination at these places. The error of localization (that is, the degree of accuracy of local signs) is closely correlated with the size of the two-point threshold.

Kinesthesis

Our ordinary vocabulary lacks a word for the sensory system that informs us of

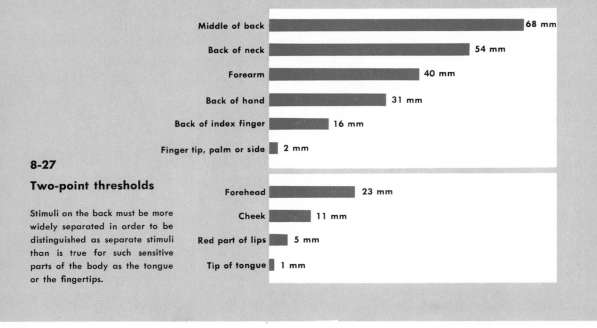

8-27

Two-point thresholds

Stimuli on the back must be more widely separated in order to be distinguished as separate stimuli than is true for such sensitive parts of the body as the tongue or the fingertips.

Middle of back	68 mm
Back of neck	54 mm
Forearm	40 mm
Back of hand	31 mm
Back of index finger	16 mm
Finger tip, palm or side	2 mm
Forehead	23 mm
Cheek	11 mm
Red part of lips	5 mm
Tip of tongue	1 mm

the position and movement of parts of the body. In technical language this is *kinesthesis*—the muscle, tendon, and joint sense. Position and movement are detected by sense organs in the joints, while sense organs in the muscles and tendons tell us whether a muscle is stretched or contracted and help to adjust muscular tension to the load upon it.

Without kinesthesis we would have great difficulty in maintaining posture, in walking and climbing, and in controlling voluntary movements such as reaching, grasping, manipulating. Whenever we act, we make somewhat tentative movements and then adjust them according to their environmental effects. If something turns out to be heavier than expected, we brace ourselves and lift with greater effort. If we slip or stumble as we walk, we make prompt corrective movements. The kinesthetic sense gives us a "feedback" from the environment that keeps telling us how things are going. We take this for granted until a foot "goes to sleep" and we realize how strange it is to walk without information as to the foot's contact with the floor.

The joints are surprisingly sensitive to position and movement. If the arm is strapped to a tilting board so that the experimenter can move it through a very small angle, the threshold for perception of movement turns out to be less than 0.5 degree of arc (Laidlaw and Hamilton, 1937). In an arm that stretches 2 feet from the shoulder to the finger tip, this represents a movement of about $\frac{1}{5}$ of an inch at the finger tip. Some systems of handwriting once required control of the pen by the shoulder joint, a demand which would not be possible if it were not for the high degree of discrimination at the joint.

Equilibratory senses

Cooperating with kinesthesis are the *equilibratory senses* dealing with total body position in relation to gravity, and with motion of the body as a whole. The relation of bodily parts to each other and to external objects is the responsibility of kinesthesis; the orientation of the body in space is the responsibility of the equilibratory senses.

The sense organs for equilibrium are located in the bony labyrinth of the inner ear, in the parts other than the cochlea. There are two systems: the semicircular canals and the vestibular sacs (Figure 8-29).

The *semicircular canals* of each labyrinth lie in three planes, so that bodily rotation in any one of the planes will have maximum effect on one of the canals, and rotation at an angle to the planes will affect more than one. The canals are filled with a liquid called *endolymph*, which is displaced when the body rotates. The nerve elements connect with hair cells embedded in a gelatinous mass known as the *cupula*. When the endolymph brings pressure on the cupula, it bends the hair cells and produces the nervous impulses that lead to the responses to rotation.

When rotation is slow and of moderate amount, the chief consequence is information that we are moving. When it is more extreme, the responses are also more extreme. Most of us as children played games in which we whirled our bodies until we lost balance, were dizzy, and watched the visual world spin around us. The eye movements following rotation, which are responsible for the spinning world, are known as *nystagmus*. They show how complex, yet orderly, some of our reflex processes are. Adults find getting dizzy less amusing than children, because they tend to become nauseated as well. Motion sickness is brought about, in part at least, through sensations from the semicircular canals (Wendt, 1951).

The *vestibular sacs* (the utricle and saccule) lie in the vestibule proper, between the base of the semicircular canals and the cochlea. They provide for our perceptions of bodily position when the body is at rest. The sensitive portion is again a gelatinous mass with hair cells and with granules known as *otoliths* (literally, "ear stones") embedded in it. The normal pressure of the otoliths on the hair cells gives us the sense of upright position, and any distortion tells us that the head is tilted.

How the otoliths can control reflexes of

8-28

Determining two-point thresholds

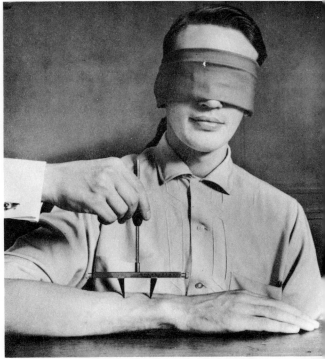

David Linton, courtesy N.Y.U.

The two compass points of the esthesiometer are adjusted until the subject perceives two separate stimuli.

position is illustrated by an old experiment done with lobsters. The lobster's equilibratory organ lies in a cavity open to the outside. When the lobster outgrows its shell, it loses its equilibrium until it has collected a new batch of small stones in the cavity serving the equilibratory organ in its new shell. Iron filings substituted for the stones work as well until a strong magnet is placed above the lobster. Now the lobster turns over on its back, because the attraction of the magnet has substituted for gravity. While the lobster is on its back, the iron filings press against the equilibratory organ as the stones ordinarily would when the animal is upright.

The equilibratory senses also signal accelerated motion in a straight line, but

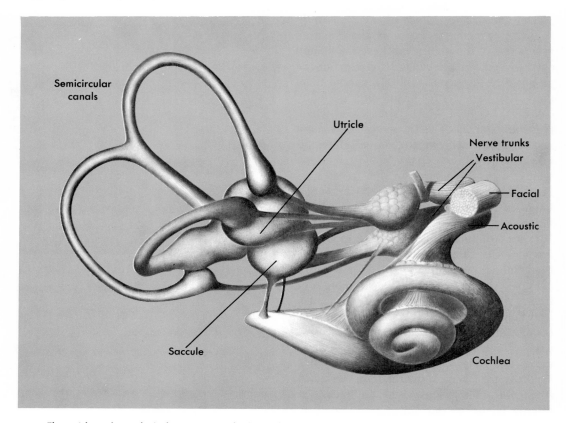

The utricle and saccule (enlargements at the base of the semicircular canals) are shown in their relation to the cochlea, which contains the receptors for hearing. The diagram is schematic. (After Hardy, 1934)

sometimes they produce illusions that distort the true path of motion. These illusions occur in flying because of changes in speed and the banking and climbing of the plane, occasionally under conditions of poor visibility. For example, when a plane is increasing its speed gradually, a blindfolded subject may feel sure that the plane is climbing; if its speed is decreasing gradually, he may feel equally sure that it is diving (Clark and Graybiel, 1949). Under conditions of poor visibility a flyer does better to trust his instruments than his equilibratory senses! Other illusions beset him also. There are, for example, visual illusions of movement as a consequence of involuntary eye movements (nystagmus) while a plane is banking. These can easily produce trouble in night maneuvers, when the movement of another plane in formation is misjudged.

SUMMARY   1. All sense experiences have their *thresholds* (both *absolute* and *difference* thresholds). Thresholds fluctuate, as illustrated by *sensory adaptation*—the reduced sensitivity (raised threshold) after prolonged exposure to a stimulus.

2. Some of the main features of the *visual sense* are:

A. The eye receives light waves by way of the *cornea, pupil, lens,* and *retina*. The receptors proper are the *rods* and *cones* of the retina. The cones, concentrated in the *fovea* but scattered throughout the retina, mediate experiences of both black and white and hue (*chromatic* colors). The rods, in the periphery of the eye, mediate experiences only of black and white (the *achromatic* colors). In night vision the rods are more sensitive than the cones.

B. The distinctive roles of the rods and the cones can be inferred from *dark adaptation,* in which the cones reach their maximum sensitivity in about 5 minutes, while the rods continue to become more sensitive for about half an hour.

C. The *chromatic colors* can be arranged in the form of a *color circle,* following the order of wave lengths (i.e., the order seen in the rainbow or solar spectrum) but allowing space for the nonspectral purples. When properly spaced, the colors opposite each other are *complementaries*. When complementary colors are mixed as lights (additive mixture), they cancel each other and result in a neutral gray. Although four *psychological primaries* can be identified (red, yellow, green, blue), three *color primaries* are enough to produce the range of hues by additive mixture (red, green, and blue). The chief dimensions of color are *hue, brightness,* and *saturation*.

D. *Afterimage* and *contrast effects* further emphasize the pairing of colors, for very often (though not always) the withdrawal of stimulation produces the complementary hue, and the contrast effect is maximum between complementaries.

E. *Color blindness* also calls attention to color pairs as well as to the primacy of certain colors. The most common form, red-green blindness (a form of *dichromatism*), is much more frequently found among men than among women. Total color blindness (*monochromatism*) is rare, while yellow-blue blindness, the alternate form of dichromatism, is rarer still.

F. *Color theories* take these facts as their starting point and attempt to give them physiological explanation. The Young-Helmholtz theory begins with color mixture; the Hering theory starts with afterimages and contrast; the Ladd-Franklin theory proposes an evolutionary explanation, stressing evidence from color blindness.

3. Some of the facts and principles arising from study of the *auditory sense* are:

A. The auditory apparatus consists of the *external ear,* leading by way of the auditory canal to the *eardrum,* giving access to the *middle ear*. The bones of the middle ear transmit the sound waves to the *oval window,* leading to the *inner ear*. The *cochlea* houses the receptors of the inner ear, found in the *organ of Corti*. The *basilar membrane* has played a special role in auditory theories. The auditory nerve leads off from the organ of Corti.

B. The chief dimensions of auditory experience are *pitch,* correlated with the *frequency* of vibration of the sound waves that constitute the stimulus, and *loudness,* correlated with the *amplitude* of these waves. Sensitivity to frequency differences depends on loudness and on the frequency region in which the measurements are made. In the most sensitive region, a difference of about 5 cycles can be detected as a change in pitch from a tone of 2000 cycles. To reach threshold or to sound equally loud, greater amplitude is needed for low and for high tones than for intermediate tones, the ear being most sensitive to tones of about 2000 cycles per second.

C. Many tones are not pure. The distinguishing quality of musical instruments, while sounding a tone of given pitch and loudness, is called *timbre,* and depends upon the *overtones* and other impurities differing from one instrument to another. The most impure sounds are called *noises.*

D. Theories attempting to give a physiological explanation of pitch fall into two groups: the *place theories,* which emphasize the place on the basilar membrane where a particular frequency produces its effect; and *frequency theories,* which assume that the effect on the basilar membrane corresponds in some direct fashion to the frequency of the stimulus. While the clearest present evidence favors some form of place theory, because of the agreement between various methods of "mapping" the basilar membrane, some compromise between the two types of theory may be necessary in order to explain all the facts of hearing.

4. The other senses, important as they are, do not enter as much into man's symbolic behavior and so are thought of as "lower senses." They include *smell, taste,* the four *skin senses* (touch, pain, warm, cold), *kinesthesis* (muscle, tendon, and joint sense), and the *equilibratory senses.*

SUGGESTIONS
FOR
FURTHER
READING

For a general introduction to the various senses, see Geldard, *The human senses* (1953). A useful reference work is Stevens, *Handbook of experimental psychology* (1951) with twelve chapters on the sensory mechanisms and sensory processes written by experts. An interesting set of papers on a variety of topics related to the role of the senses can be found in Rosenblith, *Sensory communication* (1961).

There are many sources on visual perception, including Bartley, *Vision: a study of its basis* (1941), Evans, *An introduction to color* (1948), and Judd, *Color in business, science, and industry* (1952). An authoritative volume on color and color standards is that by the Optical Society of America, *The science of color* (1953). Teevan and Birney, *Color vision* (1961) provides a convenient source of readings.

On audition there are Békésy, *Experiments in hearing* (1960), by the leading contemporary investigator of the physiological basis of hearing, awarded a Nobel prize in 1961 for his contributions; Davis, *Hearing and deafness* (1947), a more general book for the nonspecialist; Hirsh, *The measurement of hearing* (1952). The history of the several theories of hearing, and a defense of the author's own volley theory, can be found in Wever, *Theory of hearing* (1949).

Learning and Thinking

While modification through learning is a rule throughout the animal kingdom, the higher organisms, with prolonged infancy, depend more upon learning for their adjustment to the environment than do those lower in the evolutionary scale. Man is a learner par excellence. *He not only learns muscular habits and skills but also acquires and remembers information coming to him in various forms. He is also a thinker and a problem-solver, often inventing tools and methods that help him overcome the obstacles in the way of getting the answers that he seeks.*

CHAPTER 9

The Nature of Learning

Illustrations of learning occur throughout the preceding chapters, and we have thus far taken the details of the learning process for granted. We have noted how children learn food preferences, increase their vocabularies, acquire social motives, and learn to perceive the environment.

We may define *learning* as *the process by which an activity originates or is changed through responding to a situation,* provided the changes cannot be attributed to growth or to the temporary state of the organism (as in fatigue or under drugs). Learning could be defined more simply as profiting by experience, were it not that some learning does not "profit" the learner: useless or inappropriate habits are learned as well as useful ones. Not all changes in behavior can be explained as learning, and hence our definition has to be qualified to exclude them.

The task before an *applied* psychology of learning is clear. If psychologists can offer suggestions for improving the efficiency of learning, they may help us avoid wasteful methods in our own learning and in directing the learning of others. These applications of psychological principles go on in the home, in the school, on the playground, in the factory, at the military training station. In time of war we are confronted with large-scale problems of learning: how to teach women to replace men in the factories; how to teach men to fly airplanes, navigate ships, send and receive code messages, and do the countless tasks that war demands. The urgencies of war call these problems strongly to our attention, but they exist in peacetime as well. Efficient methods of teaching and learning can lead to enormous savings in time and effort and can reduce waste.

The task before *general* and *systematic* psychology in the study of learning is related to that of applied psychology, because the more we know about the fundamentals of learning, the more soundly we can make recommendations for practice. But the scientific understanding of learning has a wider scope. Not only does it help us to understand the most evident kinds of learning, such as memorizing a poem or learning to type; it also bears upon the most fundamental problems of individual development, motivation, social behavior, and personality.

Learning can be seen from the point of view of *development,* in that our knowledge and skills accumulate throughout our lives; what we are able to do today depends not only upon our natural capacities and maturational level but also upon what we have learned in the past. Learning is also *interactive,* in that it comes about through active interchange with the environment (either in movement and manipulation or in observation and discrimination), and the manner in which we are able to use our past learnings depends upon circumstances active in the present. We shall find the developmental-interactive distinction useful if we think of the accumulation of habits and knowledge as a developmental problem and their utilization in recall, in new settings, and in problem-solving, as an interactive problem.

Because learning is basic, a number of controversies within theoretical psychology revolve about it. Most psychologists who prefer to emphasize stimulus-response relationships interpret learning as *habit formation,* by which they mean *associative learning*—that is, acquiring a connection between a stimulus and a response that did not exist before. Thus the naming of objects in English depends upon a set of *verbal habits* according to which, for example, certain objects made of wood and graphite serve as stimuli for the associated response of "pencil." Riding a bicycle illustrates a set of *sensorimotor habits* appropriate to that complex stimulus. It is possible to go beyond these obvious habits and interpret *all* learned behavior as of essentially the same kind, including habitual attitudes, habitual ways of thinking, habitual emotional expression. According to this interpretation all our learning is associative learning: we learn only habits.

We shall distinguish three sources of data about habits and the principles governing them: *classical conditioning, operant conditioning,* and *multiple-response learning,* waiting to define these until they are under discussion. They all fit within the concept of associative learning.

Other psychologists are not convinced that it is most profitable to treat all learning as habit formation. They are impressed by the role of *understanding* in learning or, in more technical vocabulary, the role of *cognitive processes.* Examples of cognitive processes are our ability to follow maps over routes we have never taken before and to reason our way to conclusions previously unfamiliar to us. At the end we have surely learned something new. Have we merely exercised old habits? To be sure, we have *used* old habits, and herein arises disagreement among psychologists. Some psychologists are satisfied that the results of cognitive learning, or learning with understanding, can be *predicted* from knowledge of earlier habits and the principles of habit formation, while others believe that some new principles have to be added to account for what the learner does when he makes sophisticated use of his earlier habits in novel situations. We shall return to this problem after considering the case for learning as

habit formation; it is worth noting here, however, that the issue between associative learning and learning with understanding has been the source of lively controversy within contemporary psychology.

Classical Conditioning

Pavlov's experiments

The study of associative learning can be carried on in the *conditioned response* experiment. This experiment was originated by the Russian physiologist and Nobel Prize winner Ivan Pavlov (1849-1936). While studying the relatively automatic reflexes associated with digestion, Pavlov noticed that the flow of saliva in the mouth and of gastric juice in the stomach of the dog was influenced not only by food placed in the dog's mouth but also by the sight of food. He interpreted the flow of saliva and gastric juice to food in the mouth as an unlearned response or, as he called it, an *unconditioned response.* But surely, he thought, the influence of the *sight* of food has to be learned. Hence this is a learned or conditioned response. Pavlov experimented to find out how conditioned responses are formed. He taught the dog to salivate to various signals, such as rotating disks or the sound of a metronome, thereby proving to his satisfaction that a new stimulus-response association could be formed in the laboratory.

When Pavlov's method is used, a dog is prepared for experimentation by performing a minor operation on its cheek, so that some of the salivary gland is exposed to the surface. A capsule is attached into which saliva flows, so that accurate registration of salivary flow is possible. The dog is brought to the soundproof laboratory on several occasions and is placed in a harness on the table where the experiment is to be conducted. This preliminary training is needed so that the animal will stand quietly

Classical conditioning apparatus

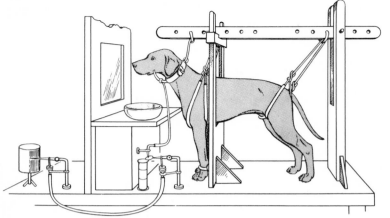

Arrangements used by Pavlov in classical salivary conditioning. Mechanical arrangements (not shown) permit the light as a conditioned stimulus to appear in the window, and the meat powder (as the unconditioned stimulus) to appear in the food bowl. (After Yerkes and Morgulis, 1909)

in the harness as the experiment proceeds. The laboratory is so arranged that meat powder can be delivered to a pan in front of the dog by remote control. Salivation is recorded automatically. The experimenter can view the animal through a glass panel, but the dog is alone in the experimental room. (See Figure 9-1.)

A light (the *conditioned stimulus*) is turned on. The dog may make some exploratory movements, but does not salivate. After a few seconds, the meat powder (*unconditioned stimulus*) is delivered. The dog is hungry and eats. The recording device registers copious salivation. A few more trials are given in which the light is always followed by the meat, the meat by salivation. (This following of the conditioned stimulus by the unconditioned stimulus and response is called *reinforcement*.) After several reinforcements, the dog salivates when the light is turned on, even though food does not follow. When this happens, a *conditioned response* has been established. The usual order of events (conditioned stimulus—unconditioned stimulus —response) can best be remembered if the conditioned stimulus is thought of as a *signal* that the unconditioned stimulus is about to appear; in the foregoing example

the light is a signal that food (the unconditioned stimulus) is coming.

The conditioned response may be considered a simple habit because (1) an association is demonstrated to exist between a stimulus and a response, and (2) this association is a learned one.

With this introduction we are ready for a definition of the process of *classical contioning* as it is represented by the model of Pavlov's experiment. (We shall presently meet another variety of conditioning, called *operant conditioning;* hence the adjective "classical" is applied to Pavlov's model.)

Classical conditioning may be defined as the formation (or strengthening) of an association between a conditioned stimulus and a response through the repeated presentation of the conditioned stimulus in a controlled relationship with an unconditioned stimulus that originally elicits that response. The original response to the *unconditioned stimulus* is called an *unconditioned response;* the learned response to the *conditioned stimulus* is called a *conditioned response.*

The arrangement described in this definition is diagramed in Figure 9-2. Because the conditioned response resembles the unconditioned response, classical condition-

A diagram of classical conditioning

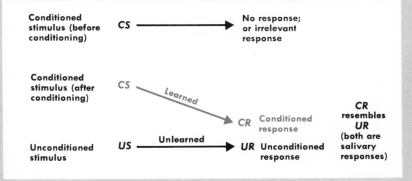

The association between the unconditioned stimulus and the unconditioned response exists at the start of the experiment and does not have to be learned. The association between the conditioned stimulus and the conditioned response is a learned one. It arises through the pairing of the conditioned and unconditioned stimuli followed by the unconditioned response (i.e., reinforcement). The conditioned response resembles the unconditioned one (though they need not be identical).

ing is sometimes referred to as learning through *stimulus substitution,* the conditioned stimulus eventually "substituting" for the unconditioned one in eliciting the response.

Reinforcement, extinction, and spontaneous recovery

Psychologists have followed Pavlov's lead in experimenting with conditioned responses, using many different organisms (including human subjects) and many responses other than salivation. The investigation of classical conditioning has proved important, because the relations between stimuli and responses are under experimental control and the results show a certain regularity and lawfulness. We will now consider some of these regularities within classical conditioning.

When the conditioned stimulus is regularly followed by the unconditioned stimulus and unconditioned response, conditioned responses to the conditioned stimulus appear at greater strength and with

greater regularity as this paired stimulation is repeated. The pairing of the conditioned and unconditioned stimuli is called *reinforcement,* because any tendency for the conditioned response to appear is facilitated by the presence of the unconditioned stimulus and the response to it. The appearance of the conditioned response can be detected on test trials in which the unconditioned stimulus is omitted, or within reinforced trials if there is a sufficient time interval between the conditioned and unconditioned stimuli so that the conditioned response begins before the unconditioned one. To refer again to Pavlov's experiment, after conditioning has begun there may be a little conditioned mouth-watering to the light as a conditioned stimulus just before the copius unconditioned salivation to the food when it comes.

The conditioning experiment is a *quantitative* one, and measures of response are needed. The following measures can be used to demonstrate that one method of conditioning is more successful than another or

9-3

Extinction

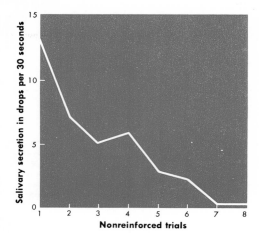

The conditioned salivary response gradually decreases when food reinforcement no longer accompanies the conditioned stimulus. (After Pavlov, 1927)

that one subject conditions more readily than another. They may also be used to plot the course of conditioning:

1. Amplitude of conditioned response. (Drops of saliva, extent of muscular movement, etc.)
2. Latency of conditioned response. (Promptness with which the conditioned response follows the appearance of the conditioned stimulus.)
3. Trials to a criterion of conditioning. (How many reinforcements are needed before the first measurable conditioned response appears or before some other criterion is met, e.g., before the first five conditioned responses have been given.)
4. Probability of conditioned responses. (Percentage of trials in which a detectable conditioned response appears. Even after considerable conditioning has been demonstrated, conditioned responses are not necessarily elicited on every presentation of the conditioned stimulus.)

We shall find that these measures, possible within classical conditioning, are not equally applicable to operant conditioning, and therefore they help to provide a distinction between the two classes of conditioning.

Once formed, the conditioned response undergoes systematic changes in strength, depending upon the experimental arrangements. If the unconditioned stimulus is repeatedly omitted, so that there is no reinforcement, the amount of conditioned response gradually diminishes, as shown in Figure 9-3. Repetition of the conditioned stimulus without reinforcement is called *extinction*. Further studies show that the decrease in response during extinction is not a mere passive disappearance of response, but is instead an active *inhibition,* that is, a tendency against responding that may spread to other responses not included in the original conditioning. Thus extinction of a conditioned response to a bell may also weaken the conditioned response to a flickering light.

Extinction does not actually *destroy* the

9-4

Generalization gradient

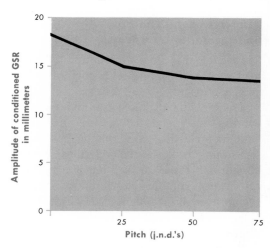

Conditioned stimuli: tones, expressed in j.n.d.'s ("just noticeable differences") of pitch from the one originally serving as the conditioned stimulus. Unconditioned stimulus: shock. Response: galvanic skin response (GSR). (After Hovland, 1937)

The course of conditioned discrimination in man

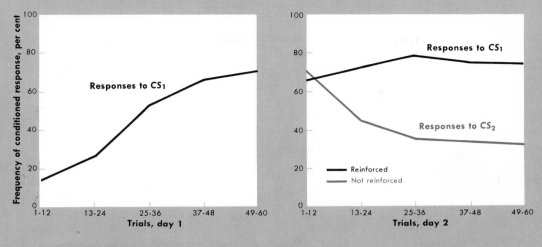

Conditioned stimuli: lights. Unconditioned stimulus: air-puff to the cornea. Response: blinking. (Hilgard, Campbell, and Sears, 1938)

conditioned response, for following a period of rest by the subject the conditioned response returns, even though no reinforcements have intervened. This return without reinforcement is called *spontaneous recovery,* and it lends support to the interpretation of the consequences of extinction as some sort of active inhibition or suppression of the conditioned response, not to be confused with a forgetting or permanent disappearance of the response.

Generalization

When a conditioned response to a stimulus S_1 has been acquired, other similar stimuli S_2 or S_3 will also evoke the response. If the dog learns to salivate to the sound of a tuning fork producing a tone of middle C (S_1), he will also salivate to higher or lower tones (S_2 or S_3) without further conditioning. The more nearly alike the new stimuli are to the original, the more completely they will substitute for it. This principle, called *generalization,* lies behind our ability to react to novel situations in accordance with their similarities to familiar ones.

Careful study shows that the amount of generalization falls off in a systematic manner as the second stimulus (S_2) becomes more and more dissimilar to the original conditioned stimulus (S_1). The plotted relationship is that of a *gradient of generalization* (Figure 9-4).

Inhibition also generalizes. That is, if a stimulus has become inhibitory as a result of extinction, other similar stimuli will also be inhibitory, the amount of inhibition showing a gradient with remoteness from the primary stimulus.

Discrimination

A process complementary to that of generalization is discrimination. Generalization is reaction to similarities, and discrimination is reaction to differences. Conditioned discrimination is brought about through selective reinforcement and extinction, as illustrated in Figure 9-5. In the experiment illustrated, lights on adjacent windows served as conditioned stimuli CS_1 and CS_2, leading to conditioned blinking to that light which was followed by an air puff to the eye as an unconditioned stimulus. Although on the first day only CS_1 was presented and reinforced, a conditioned response developed, by generalization, to CS_2 as well. When, on the second day, trials with CS_1 and with CS_2 were intermingled, and only CS_1 was reinforced, conditioned blinking continued to CS_1 but was gradually extinguished to CS_2. Thus conditioned discrimination between CS_1 and CS_2 was demonstrated.

Classical conditioning and other instances of habit formation

The precise relationships studied in the Pavlov kind of experiment require careful restrictions of ways in which the subject can react and careful recording of both stimuli and responses. Since such restrictions cannot be used outside the laboratory, there appears to be a certain artificiality about conditioning. However, it is not necessary to reproduce the conditioning *experiment* in order to make use of *principles* derived from conditioning. We have already illustrated, for example, how conditioning principles help us to understand one form of acquired emotional behavior—conditioned fear (p. 170). It is not difficult to make inferences from generalization and discrimination to ordinary behavior. When a young child has learned to say "bow-wow" to a dog, it is understandable that a similar stimulus, such as a sheep, will elicit the response "bow-wow." When the child first learns the name "Daddy," he uses it for all men. By differential reinforcement and extinction the response is finally narrowed to the single appropriate stimulus or class of stimuli.

We shall postpone further discussion of the extension of conditioning principles until we have considered operant conditioning.

Operant Conditioning

We now turn to *operant conditioning* as a second approach to the study of habit formation. When you teach a dog a trick, such as playing dead or rolling over, it is very difficult to specify the unconditioned stimuli that could produce such behavior before conditioning. Actually you "got him to do it" as best you could and *afterwards* rewarded him either with food or approval. The food or approval did not *produce* the behavior in the first place.

In Pavlov's experiment the conditioned salivation resembles the response elicited by the unconditioned (reinforcing) stimulus, but in operant training the "trick" that is reinforced bears no resemblance to the behavior in the presence of the reinforcing stimulus. Still, the learning that takes place corresponds in some respects to classical conditioning: it can be shown to exhibit such principles as extinction and spontaneous recovery, generalization and discrimination.

Skinner's experiments

To provide a better model for this kind of conditioning, B. F. Skinner introduced the concepts of *operant behavior* and *operant conditioning*. Operant conditioning supplements classical conditioning, and many of the same principles apply to both kinds of conditioning. The arrangements for the experiments differ, however, and some of the measures of strength of conditioning differ also.

Skinner proposed a distinction between two kinds of behavior that he called *respondent* and *operant* behavior. Respondent behavior is directly under the control of the stimulus, as in the unconditioned reflexes of classical conditioning: the flow of saliva to food in the mouth, the constriction of the pupil to a flash of light on the eye, the knee jerk to a tap on the patellar tendon. The relation of operant behavior to

9-6

Apparatus for operant conditioning

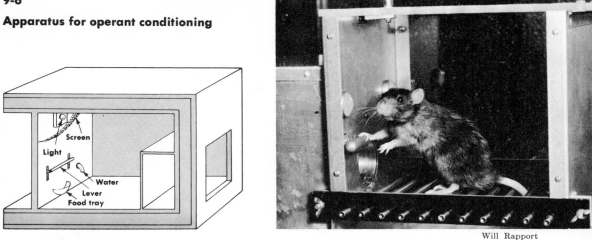

Will Rapport

The diagram shows the interior arrangement of the box used in operant conditioning of the rat. The space behind the panel at the left contains additional apparatus. This box has been named a "Skinner-box" after its developer. (From Skinner, 1938) Photo shows an actual box in operation.

stimulation is somewhat different. The behavior often appears to be *emitted,* that is, it appears to be *spontaneous* rather than a response to stimulation. The gross movement of the limbs of a newborn baby can be classified as emitted behavior in this sense; most so-called voluntary behavior is emitted rather than respondent. When operant behavior becomes related to a stimulus (as when I answer the ringing telephone), the ringing telephone is a *discriminated* stimulus, telling me that the telephone is answerable, but it does not force me to answer. Even though the ringing telephone is compelling, the response to it is operant and not respondent behavior.

The word operant derives from the fact that operant behavior "operates" on the environment to produce some effect.[1] Thus going to where the telephone is and raising the telephone from the hook are *operant* acts that lead to the telephone conversation.

To produce operant conditioning, a hungry rat is placed in the box diagramed in

[1] For the same reason such behavior is sometimes called *instrumental* behavior, because it produces effects, just as a tool or other instrument does. Hence operant conditioning is also known as instrumental conditioning (Kimble, 1961).

Figure 9-6. The inside of the box is plain, except for the protruding bar with the food dish beneath it. A small light bulb above the bar can be lighted at the experimenter's discretion.

Left alone in the box, the rat moves about restlessly and occasionally presses its paws upon the bar. The rate at which it pushes on the bar defines its preconditioning *operant level* of bar-pressing.

Now the experimenter attaches the food magazine, so that every time the rat presses the bar a pellet of food falls into the dish. The rat eats, and soon presses the bar again. The food *reinforces* bar-pressing, and a record of the rate of bar-pressing plotted against time furnishes a record of the course of operant conditioning.

If the food magazine is disconnected, so that pressing the bar no longer delivers food, the rate of bar-pressing will fall off. That is, the operant response undergoes *extinction* with nonreinforcement, just as a classical conditioned response does.

The experimenter can set up a *discrimination* by presenting food only if the bar is pressed while the light is on. Thus the response is reinforced if the light is on, not

A diagram of operant conditioning

In operant conditioning the main emphasis is upon the strengthening of the response (R_1) by the reinforcing stimulus (S_2). The unconditioned response (R_2) does not determine the form of the conditioned response (R_1), as it does in classical conditioning.

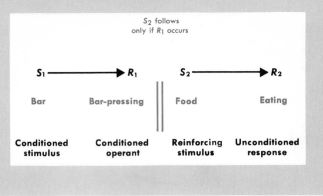

reinforced if the response is made in the dark. This selective reinforcement leads to the rat's pressing the bar only in the presence of the light.

With this illustration before us, we are ready to consider the meaning of conditioned *operant* behavior. As indicated above, it is called operant because it "operates" on the environment: the rat's bar-pressing *produces* or *gains access to* the food. In classical conditioning the animal is passive; it merely waits until the conditioned stimulus is presented and is followed by the unconditioned stimulus. In operant conditioning the animal has to be active; its behavior cannot be reinforced unless it does something.

Now for a definition. *Operant conditioning* refers to the strengthening of a stimulus-response association by following the response with a reinforcing stimulus. Usually the reinforcing stimulus is the kind that can satisfy a drive, but it need not be. *It is reinforcing if it strengthens the response that precedes it.* Operant conditioning is diagramed in Figure 9-7.

A large part of human behavior may be classified as operant—turning a key in a lock, driving a car, writing a letter, carrying on a conversation. How many of these activities can be produced by way of an unconditioned stimulus of the Pavlovian variety? Yet once the behavior occurs, it can be reinforced according to the principles of the conditioned operant.

Measures of operant strength

Because the bar is always present in the Skinner box, the rat can respond to it as frequently or infrequently as he chooses. Hence *rate of response* becomes a useful measure of operant strength. The more frequently the operant occurs over a given interval of time, the stronger it is. This measure cannot be used for classical conditioning, because the rate there depends upon how often the experimenter presents the conditioned stimulus. Another measure of operant strength is *total responses until extinction.* As Figure 9-8 illustrates, a single reinforcement can produce considerable strength, according to this measure.

Intermittent reinforcement

Operant conditioning shows a high degree of orderliness or lawfulness. One illustration of this orderliness is the behavior controlled by *intermittent reinforcement,* that is, behavior taking place when the response is reinforced only a fraction of the times it occurs.

A pigeon learns to peck at a spot and receives access to a small quantity of grain as its reinforcement. Once this conditioned operant is established, the pigeon will continue to peck at a high and relatively uniform rate, even if it receives only a few reinforcements. The pigeon whose remarkably regular pecking is illustrated in Figure 9-9 was reinforced on the average of once every 5 minutes, that is, 12 times an hour, and yet it pecked at a rate of some 6000 responses per hour.

The practical significance of intermittent reinforcement is very great. A child's mother is not always present to reward him for looking both ways before crossing the street. But the influences of reinforcements are such that they persist against many non-reinforcements. A long drive will keep a golfer at his game despite many balls lost in the rough. (See Figure 9-10.)

Secondary reinforcement

Pavlov noted that, once a dog had learned to respond to a conditioned stimulus in a dependable way, the conditioned stimulus could be used to reinforce a conditioned response to a new stimulus. Suppose the animal learns to salivate to bubbling water as a conditioned stimulus. This is a first-order conditioned response. If a flashing light is then presented along with the bubbling water, the flashing light when presented alone will come to give the conditioned response. Pavlov called this process *second-order conditioning*. The conditioned stimulus of first-order conditioning (bubbling water) has become a *secondary reinforcer*. While second-order conditioning can thus be established within classical conditioning, it is much more easily demonstrated within operant conditioning, and for that reason its consideration has been postponed until now. The general principle, holding within both classical and operant conditioning, can be stated as follows: *any stimulus can be made reinforcing through association with a reinforcing stimulus*. Higher-order responses (third-order, fourth-order) are possible, but tend to be established with greater difficulty the more remote they are from primary reinforcement.

When a rat in a Skinner box presses a lever, a light comes on, followed shortly by a pellet of food in the tray. After several groups of animals are conditioned in this way, some receiving more reinforcements

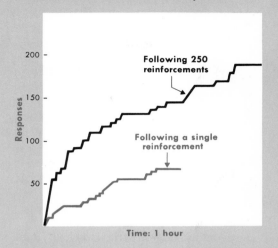

9-8

Extinction of a conditioned operant

Curves of extinction of operant responses in the rat are plotted following a single reinforcement and following 250 reinforcements. The response is that of bar-pressing to obtain food. The plot shows the cumulative number of responses; every response raises the height of the curve, and the curve levels off when responses cease. (After Skinner, 1938)

than others, the response is extinguished in the dark. That is, when the rat presses the lever, neither the light nor the food appears, and presently the animal almost ceases to press the lever.

Now the light is connected again, but without the food. When it is discovered that pressing the lever turns on the light, the rate of pressing increases, overcoming the extinction, even though no food follows. Hence the light has acquired secondary reinforcing qualities. The number of responses in a 45-minute period corresponded to the prior number of light-and-food trials, showing that the strength of secondary reinforcement depended upon the frequency with which the light had been associated with the primary reinforcer, food (Bersh, 1951).

Another arrangement of the secondary reinforcement experiment brings second-or-

9-9

Operant responses sustained by intermittent reinforcement

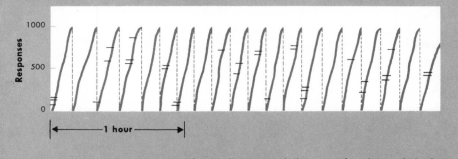

The curves are of the pecking responses of a single pigeon which are reinforced irregularly, but at an average interval of 5 minutes. The reinforcements are represented by horizontal dashes. Each of the sloping lines represents 1000 responses; the pen resets after each 1000. (After Skinner, 1950)

der conditioning a little closer to familiar habitual behavior. In this arrangement, known as *token learning,* the secondary reinforcer is a token to be substituted later for a primary reinforcer, just as money is exchanged for food. A well-known experiment on chimpanzee learning illustrates the acquisition of reinforcing power by a token (Figure 9-11).

Chimpanzees were taught to work for poker chips as rewards instead of food. The chimpanzees could use the poker chip to obtain food from a vending machine called a "Chimp-o-mat." Thus poker chips became secondary reinforcers. After learning, the animal would work as hard for a poker chip as for the food itself, saving up a few poker chips occasionally before converting them to food.

After the chimpanzees had learned to use the Chimp-o-mat, they were introduced to another device, which consisted of a lever attached by strong springs so that the chimpanzees could move it forward only by great exertion. The effort was rewarded by a grape attached to the end of the lever. After the chimpanzees had learned to obtain grapes in this manner, a poker chip was substituted for the grape. Three of four chimpanzees would strain as hard at the

instrument for the poker chip as for the grape, using the chip later on to get grapes from the vending machine (Wolfe, 1936; Cowles, 1937).

The value of secondary reinforcement derives originally from association with the primary reinforcer. In token learning the secondary reinforcer is a subgoal, a sort of milestone along the road to drive satisfaction, for it *assures* such satisfaction even if it does not itself *provide* it.

A feature of secondary reinforcement that is very important for human social behavior is its wide degree of *generalization.*[2] The principle can be stated: *Once established, a secondary reinforcer can strengthen other responses than the response used during its original establishment, and can do so with motives other than the motive prevailing during the original training* (Keller and Schoenfeld, 1950). We know from ordinary observation that such reinforcers as social approval can be effective over a wide range of behavior, but there is also *experimental* evidence in support of the principle that secondary reinforcers have

[2] Note that this generalized power to reinforce is analogous to but not the same as the generalization of conditioned responses from one stimulus to another (p. 257).

FPG

9-10

Intermittent reinforcement

The occasional small reward—and less frequent jackpot—keep hopeful gamblers playing the slot machines at Reno.

wide generality. In an experiment demonstrating this principle, Estes (1949), using water-deprived rats, associated an auditory stimulus with bar-pressing reinforced by water. When the rats were deprived of food rather than water, the same auditory stimulus evoked bar-pressing. If enough drive of any kind is present to instigate activity, a secondary reinforcer is effective, even though it derived its strength while another drive prevailed.

Secondary reinforcement greatly increases the range of possible conditioning. If everything we learned had to be reinforced in unlearned stimulus-response sequences, the occasions for learning would be very much restricted. As it is, however, any habit once learned can have other habits built upon it. A verbal promise of food can reinforce behavior that would otherwise require the food itself; mere praise (without the promise of a primary reinforcer) itself becomes rein-

forcing. Long chains of responses can be sustained by a single reinforcement at the end, because the signposts along the way, as secondary reinforcers, sustain the learned movements in the approach to the goal.

The method of approximations

As we noted earlier, classical conditioning is sometimes called the method of *stimulus substitution,* because the conditioned stimulus substitutes for the unconditioned stimulus in evoking the response appropriate to the unconditioned stimulus. The substitution principle fails, however, to account for *novelty* in behavior—for the learning of totally new movement patterns. Operant conditioning, however, can be studied in such situations.

How is novel behavior produced by operant conditioning? The experimenter takes advantage of random variations in the operant response, reinforcing only those

The Chimp-o-mat

Yerkes Laboratories of Primate Biology

The poker chips which can be used to obtain food are secondary reinforcers.

responses that move in the desired direction. For example, he can make a pigeon hold her head ever so high as she walks around, by reinforcing with grain, at first only when her head is at average height, then when slightly above average, and finally only when her neck is stretched high. He can teach quite elaborate routines of behavior by using this *method of approximations,* reinforcing only responses that meet his specifications and extinguishing all others. (See Figure 9-12.) This is sometimes called "shaping" the operant behavior through appropriate reinforcement.

This method has been successfully used to teach many amusing stunts to barnyard fowls, pigs, and calves for use in county fairs in the Midwest. One popular number was a pig show called "Priscilla, the Fastidious Pig." Priscilla turned on the radio, ate breakfast at a table, picked up dirty clothes and put them in a hamper, ran a vacuum cleaner over the floor, picked out her favorite food (from among foods competing with that of her sponsor!), and took part in a quiz program, answering questions from the audience by flashing lights indicating "Yes" or "No." She was not an unusually bright pig; because pigs grow so fast, a new "Priscilla" was trained every 3 to 5 months (Breland and Breland, 1951). The ingenuity was not the pig's but the experimenters', who used operant conditioning and shaped the behavior to produce the desired behavior.

Operant conditioning of human behavior

Analogies between operant conditioning of animals and human learning are easy to find. For example, a child's spontaneous babbling is differentially reinforced so that he begins to "talk," that is, to yield operant utterances recognizable to the parents. Though plausible, such an analogy should be supported by experimental evidence that the laws of learning we find in our animal experiments also apply to human behavior.

In the following experiment the subject did not know that he was being experimented upon, and the experimenter thereby avoided the artificiality of many conditioning experiments. The experimenter carried on an informal conversation with the subject, but behaved according to a plan, kept his eye on the clock, and tallied responses inconspicuously in the "doodles" that he drew while the two were talking together.

The experimenter determined in advance to reinforce, by means of agreeing with the subject, all statements of opinion, such as sentences beginning "I think," "I believe," "It seems to me," and the like. *Reinforcement* through agreement was expressed by saying, "You're right," "I agree," "That's so." *Extinction* was carried out in another portion of the experiment by mere nonreinforcement, silence, following a statement of opinion. Other conditions of the experiment included extinction by disagreement. Following verbal reinforcement, statements of opinion increased in frequency; following extinction, they decreased (Verplanck, 1955).

A review of 46 such experiments by Krasner (1958) showed 34 (74 per cent) of them to be successful, indicating that the laws of operant conditioning are applicable to human behavior and that it is possible to demonstrate them without the restrictions imposed by more formal laboratory conditions.

CRITICAL DISCUSSION
Disagreements over fundamentals of conditioning

Operant conditioning illustrates a kind of behavior under control of its consequences, that is, under control of reward and punishment. A distinguished psychologist, Edward L. Thorndike (1874-1949), studied similar behavior, but instead of talking about operant conditioning he talked about selective learning under the *law of effect* (Thorndike, 1911). In its later forms, the law of effect stated that a stimulus-response sequence (an S-R connection) could be strengthened by a reward that followed it. This is virtually a statement of operant conditioning. We have adopted the language of reinforcement rather than that of the law of effect as better representing contemporary usage.

The distinction between *classical* conditioning and *operant* conditioning, with their related interpretations, has led to a number of conjectures about the fundamentals of learning. Some writers, such as Guthrie and Estes, believe that all learning is essentially *substitutive* in character, thus following more nearly the principles derived from classical conditioning; others, such as Hull and N. E. Miller, accept the principles from operant conditioning and the law of effect as fundamental, thus placing more emphasis on reward and punish-

9-12

A result of the method of approximations

Yale Joel, © Life Magazine

By reinforcing only the desired responses, the experimenter taught the pigeon to tap the correct sign when light of a certain color was turned on. (Skinner, 1950)

ment. Still others accept some variety of two-process theory, acknowledging that we learn something from both types of conditioning. Among those who have proposed a two-process theory are Thorndike, Skinner, Schlosberg, Mowrer, and Spence. The theoretical issues are too complex to be discussed here. (For some of the issues, see Hilgard [1956].)

A new development in laboratory studies of learning may force a modification of some of our basic concepts of associative learning. In the past it has been assumed that repetition and reinforcement increase associative strength gradually, so that with more practice an associative connection will be longer retained; the evidence for this "fact" has appeared to be irrefutable, regardless of slight differences among theorists as to how associative strength should be characterized. Now this view is challenged by another: the idea that in its most elementary form an association is formed in all-or-none fashion, like the throwing of a switch, and is *not* increased by further reinforcements (Estes, 1960).[3] While a number of earlier experiments had proposed a somewhat similar concept (e.g., Voeks, 1955; Kimble and Dufort, 1956), the new position was given dramatic impetus by the experiments of Rock (1957). He set up a situation in which a number of paired items were to be memorized; any pair not memorized in a single trial was replaced by a new pair, so that nothing but one-trial learning was possible. He found that it took the same number of trials to learn a list calling for one-trial learning (substituting new items each trial for those missed) as for a list in which the subjects had repeated reinforcements with the same pairs (no substituted items). Most of those who repeated Rock's experiments set out to show that his results were due to the design of his experiment and were thus not "typical." There is a flaw in the experiment, in that the items dropped out tend to be those difficult to learn, so those subjects who worked with the substituted items (demonstrating one-trial learning) had somewhat easier tasks. But this flaw does not necessarily discredit the general significance of the results: others who have improved on the experiment have appeared to confirm the all-or-none aspect of learning (Clark, Lansford, and Dallenbach, 1960; Estes, Hopkins, and Crothers, 1960).[4]

The argument has sometimes been advanced that in choosing artificial laboratory tasks the experimental students of learning have moved too far away from real life learning. On the basis of these new developments, Estes (1960) argues that, if anything, we have made the mistake of choosing laboratory tasks that are too complex and have thus missed the true essence of associative learning that these newer experiments reveal. In any case, much remains to be done before associative learning is fully understood.

[3] If this view is upheld, it might conceivably have an important bearing on the neurology of learning, strengthening the analogy with the digital computer that works by on-off effects (p. 55).
[4] Any novel development of this kind initiates efforts to assign the new phenomena their proper place. It already appears that one-trial incremental learning is more limited than at first supposed; it is most convincingly demonstrated when the material to be learned is very familiar and all that has to be learned is new "connections" (Bower, 1961).

The extension of conditioning principles

There are two main ways in which the principles from conditioning have been extended to explain more complex habit formation: by *direct analogy* and by the *deductive use of conditioning principles*.

The *direct analogies* are clear. We may interpret conditioned emotion as a direct illustration of classical conditioning. The flag waves while the noise of the crowd and the martial music arouse deep feelings within us. Later the flag alone comes to arouse these feelings. Or we can interpret language behavior as directly illustrative of operant conditioning, as in Verplanck's experiment. We can simply observe conditioning going on under the circumstances of ordinary life.

The *deductive use of conditioning principles* is more complex. Some behavior will exhibit relationships that have no direct analogy within conditioning experiments. For example, there is nothing in conditioning experiments that explains why rats eliminate errors in a maze in backward order, eliminating first the alley nearest the goal, or why in memorizing a poem we learn the first and last stanzas more readily than those in the middle. Yet it is possible, by using at once several principles from conditioning, to *derive* some of these consequences in a manner similar to that used for proofs in geometry.

This method was used very skillfully by Clark L. Hull of Yale University (e.g., Hull, 1932, 1952). His approach can be illustrated by a derivation of the fact that in maze learning a blind alley near a goal tends to be eliminated more rapidly than one more remote from the goal. For illustrative purposes consider the simple mazes pictured in Figure 9-13. We wish to show that it is easier to learn the true path (i.e., the shorter path) in Maze *A* than in Maze *B*. We begin with an initial assumption that an event taking place near the goal is "reinforced" more strongly than one farther away from the goal. This is not only plausible, but is supported by evidence that animals running down a long alley run faster when they get closer to the place where they have been fed in the past. Therefore, in a choice between a shorter path and a longer one, we assume that the shorter one will be preferred (once the animal has had a chance to explore both paths and discriminate between them), because its initial segments are more strongly conditioned due to their proximity to the goal. A further assumption is required that the degree to which a shorter path is preferred to a longer one will depend upon the ratio of their lengths. Thus if the paths are nearly equal, the choice will be more nearly 50:50; if the differences between the paths are extreme, one will be preferred in more trials. (This assumption is supported by countless experiments which show that animals can indeed discriminate between quantities or magnitudes—the length of a bar, the loudness of a sound, etc.)

Now we go back to the mazes in the figure. If the animal is at choice-point b in Maze A, the ratio of the path with the blind alley to the true path (without the blind alley) will be:

$$\frac{bb' + b'b + bg}{bg} = \frac{3}{1} = 3.0$$

At choice-point a in Maze B, the corresponding ratio will be:

$$\frac{aa' + a'a + ab + bg}{ab + bg} = \frac{4}{2} = 2.0$$

Under these circumstances the choice of the true path over the blind-alley path will be more strongly reinforced in Maze A than the path in Maze B—which is what we set out to deduce. It is not assumed, of course, that this is all that happens in a maze, or that the deduction could be tested in a maze as simple as those pictured. The deductive procedure is illustrated, however, and it is clear that it goes beyond the simple assertion that maze behavior is conditioned. No single analogy from conditioning could be found to make just this prediction, without

9-13

Conditioning principles applied to maze behavior

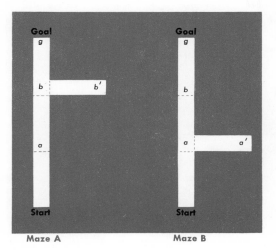

The problem is to deduce that the blind alley nearer the goal (*bb'* of Maze A) will be eliminated more readily than the blind farther from the goal (*aa'* of Maze B). For explanation see text. (After Hull, 1932; Hilgard and Marquis, 1940, p. 218)

some intervening steps or supplementary principles.[5]

Multiple-Response Learning

Thus far (except for the maze illustration) we have considered the strengthening or weakening of single identifiable responses. Although some of these are complex (such as a statement of opinion), they are still identifiable as unitary acts. But much of our learning consists in acquiring patterns or sequences of movements or words, as in learning skills or in memorizing a poem. These patterns illustrate *multiple-response learning,* a kind of learning involving more than one identifiable act, with the order of events usually fixed by the demands of the situation. Psychologists have designed a number of laboratory tasks by which to

[5] The illustration has been adapted from Hilgard and Marquis (1940), p. 218.

Mirror drawing

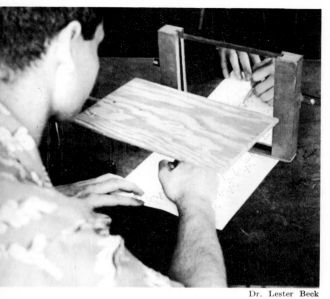

Dr. Lester Beck

The subject attempts to follow with his pencil the out-lines of the stars on the paper shielded from direct view. Because in the mirror the usual right-left relationships are reversed, he has to learn a new eye-hand coordination.

study this kind of learning. Among them are maze learning (used with both animals and men), mirror drawing, pursuit learning, and rote memorization. The first three tasks are forms of *sensorimotor skill,* while the last is largely verbal. Tasks such as these approximate the learning of common skills with the tools and language of our physical and social environment. We shall discuss sensorimotor skills and rote memorization as illustrative of multiple-response learning. It is assumed, to be sure, that such principles as reinforcement, extinction, and generalization will apply, but perhaps new principles will emerge because of the complex patternings involved.

Sensorimotor skills

By a *sensorimotor skill* we mean one in which muscular movement is prominent, but

under sensory control. Riding a bicycle, turning a flip from a springboard, playing a piano, and operating a lathe are sensorimotor skills. They are not simply a pattern of skilled movements. The bicycle rider has to watch the traffic and the bumps in the road, and be guided by them; the diver must adjust his timing to the height of the platform; the musician reads notes and attempts to play with feeling; the lathe operator must follow a blueprint and stay within the tolerances allowed. These considerations call attention to the *sensory control* of skill, and are the reason for the somewhat awkward name of sensorimotor skill.

In studying skills, psychologists have not limited themselves to laboratory tasks; the pioneer study was, in fact, a practical one on learning to send and receive telegraphic messages, done by Bryan and Harter in 1897. Many of the best-established principles are first worked out on laboratory skills, however, and later validated in more complex practical situations. A convenient laboratory illustration is given by the mirror-drawing experiment. We learn something of the importance of eye-hand coordination in developing skills by studying what happens when our usual eye-hand coordinations are inappropriate, and we have to reorient accordingly:

In a typical mirror-drawing experiment, the subject is required to trace a path around a geometrical figure, such as a six-pointed star, while viewing it in a mirror. The subject knows what the correct performance is—a smoothly traced line within the path around the figure.

The subject starts out by using familiar habits. These of course get him into trouble, for if he uses the visual cues of a mirror as he uses cues in direct vision, his pencil will not go where he wishes it to go. He therefore attempts to correct and so gradually approximates a good performance, although he draws at first a very jagged line. He may have special trouble at the corners, where again old and new habits interfere. With practice, however, his lines smooth out, and he can achieve a rapid tracing of the figure (Figure 9-14).

Learning Curves for Skill. Experimenters typically keep track of progress in skill learning by plotting a learning curve. We have met learning curves earlier in this chapter, without naming them, in the plots of the course of conditioning, such as Figure 9-5. Stated in its most general terms, a learning curve is a plot of *proficiency* against *practice.* The *independent variable,* under the control of the experimenter, is the kind and amount of practice, plotted on the base line, or abscissa. The *dependent variable,* a measure of what the subject accomplishes, is plotted on the vertical axis, or ordinate. Two learning curves for mirror drawing are plotted in Figure 9-15, one with practice trials following each other consecutively within one period (*massed practice*), and one with practice

9-15

Learning curves for mirror drawing

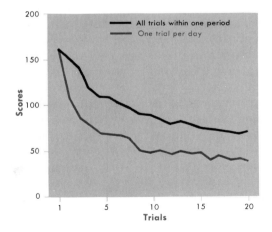

The scores that constitute the curves are related to the amount of time required to trace a figure in the mirror, and hence decrease as skill goes up. The top curve is for massed practice, all trials within one period. The bottom curve is for trials spaced one trial per day. (After Lorge, 1930)

9-16

Subject following the target of a pursuit-rotor

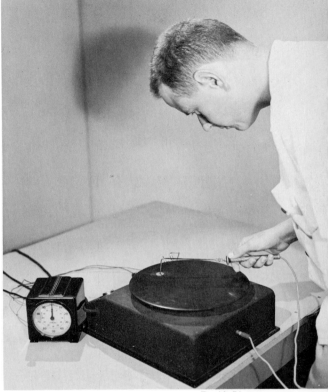

David Linton

The task is to keep the stylus on the small target as the turntable revolves.

trials spaced at one trial per day (*distributed practice*). Note that distributed practice is more efficient. We shall return to the problem of distributed practice later, but this comparison shows how learning curves can be used to display a relationship.

The general form of a learning curve depends upon the units of measurement. In Figure 9-15 the measure of proficiency is a score related to the time required to trace a figure seen in the mirror. Hence improvement shows a *decrease* in time required, and yields a falling curve.

If the measure of proficiency is a score

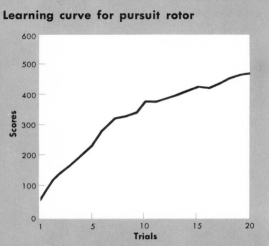

9-17

Learning curve for pursuit rotor

The scores that make up the curve are for successive trials and represent the time on the target per 1-minute rest with a maximum possible score of 600; i.e., a possible score of 10 per second if the stylus remains on the target. (After Bell, 1950)

that *increases* with practice, then the learning curve rises. Scores on *pursuit-rotor* learning are of this kind. For instance, the subject attempts to hold the tip of a metal stylus on a small spot revolving on a turntable similar to that of an ordinary phonograph (Figure 9-16). His score depends on the amount of time his stylus remains in contact with the spot. Proficiency gain will in this case be represented by a rising curve, for the longer the subject stays on the target, the better his score (Figure 9-17).

Whether the curve falls or rises, we can describe its curvature according to the way in which the amount of gain varies with successive trials. The curves of both Figure 9-15 and Figure 9-17 are curves of *decreasing gains*. Such curves are by all odds the most common in studies of sensorimotor skill. They tell us one reason why the learning of skill is often discouraging to the learner, for gains are visible and satisfying at first, but the slowing down of improve-

ment after the first few trials may easily become disappointing.

Occasionally learning begins slowly, rises rapidly, and then slows down, yielding curves of roughly S-shape (Figure 9-18). There is some reason to believe that this S-shape may be the most generalized form for learning curves, provided we were able to catch the learning at its very early stages and carry through the whole process. Most learning tasks capitalize on much prior practice in related skills, so that the learning curve studied is only that later part of the total curve which shows decreasing gains with practice.

Qualitative Changes with Practice. A learning curve plots proficiency as though the subject followed the same pattern of activity at the end as at the beginning and improved only in efficiency. But it is quite possible that in the course of improvement he has changed his task. For example, in studying the learning of typewriting, some investigators have detected a shift from a *letter habit* (learning the location of the individual keys associated with each letter) to a *word habit* (learning to write familiar words with a single burst of movement, imbedding the letters in a total pattern). Occasionally these higher-order learnings and the lower-order learnings conflict, and there is a period of no improvement in the learning curve, described as a *plateau*. The period is called a plateau because it has been preceded by improvement and will be followed by improvement when the higher-order learning wins out. The plateau is not universally found in skill learning, and other explanations than the one given here have been offered for it. One, for example, is that it is caused by a temporary decrease in motivation related to discouragement with the decreasing gains in the typical learning curve.

Achieving a smooth performance always takes time. At first the learner responds in varied fashion, making corrective move-

Some S-shaped learning curves

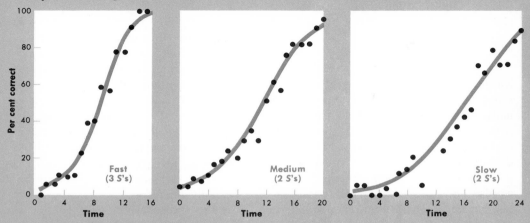

The data for the curves were obtained from the learning of three-place symbols. Results are plotted separately for fast, medium, and slow learners. The phase of increasing gains, absent from many learning curves, is prominent here. (After Culler and Girden, 1951)

ments as necessary. The first successful movements are often only crude approximations of the final skilled acts. Characteristically, excess movements accompany them, as, for example, the movements of the eyebrows or forehead that accompany your first attempts to wiggle your ears, or the movements of the other hand when you are learning a one-handed skill. With practice the excess movements decrease. If we really understood the process by which the excess movements disappear, we would probably discover a pattern of differential reinforcement, corresponding to operant conditioning. The correct responses are more consistently reinforced than the excess ones.

The smoothing of response patterns, after bare mastery is attained, goes on in many ways. We do as much short-cutting as is consistent with success, e.g., we learn economical ways of typing such familiar words as "the" and "that," but we have to be careful in gaining speed not to skip letters or to run words together. As long as a short

cut is consistent with success, it leads to economical and smooth-running action; if it leads to errors, it has to be counteracted through discrimination. In addition, acts are smoothed according to principles of rhythmic and graceful action, based in part upon the ways in which our muscles and joints operate as levers obeying physical principles of acceleration and momentum. Highly skilled acts conform to the laws of mechanics as well as to the laws of habit formation.

A useful skill is actually a family of habits, so that adjustments are involved in adapting to the variety of conditions under which the skill is called forth. Nailing with a hammer requires smooth adjustment to large nails as well as to tacks, to nailing on the floor as well as on the ceiling. The activities of the skilled nailer do not represent a single associative habit between nail and hammer, but a multitude of such habits. The basketball player must shoot the ball toward the basket from a variety of positions, with a guard menacing him and with different speeds of approach. Time is required to learn the multitude of habits belonging to one skill family, and to discriminate among the stimuli that guide the selective use of all these habits.

Rote memorization

By *rote memorization* we mean verbatim learning by repetition, as contrasted with substance memorizing. Hermann Ebbinghaus, a distinguished German psychologist, performed a pioneer study of memorization in 1885. He used nonsense syllables in order to avoid the influence of previous learning that would be found in using ordinary words. The nonsense syllables consisted of two consonants with a vowel between, such as *pov* or *juk*. Other materials have also been used in rote memorization, such as meaningful words or lists of numerals.

Experiments on rote memorizing take one of two chief forms, corresponding to the kinds of things learned verbatim in ordinary experience. One form is *serial memorization,* as in the memorizing of poetry or lines of a play. In the laboratory, a series of words is memorized from beginning to end, so that each word is in some sense the stimulus for the word to follow. The second form is *paired-associates* learning, comparable to the method sometimes used in learning the words of a foreign language. That is, the words are learned in pairs, such as *prepared-afraid, careless-vacant, hungry-quiet;* a stimulus word is presented, and the response word has to be learned. The pairs are not learned in any special order and may or may not be meaningfully related.

The experimenter usually presents the material to the subject by means of an exposure device called a *memory drum* (Figure 9-19). The items to be learned (nonsense syllables, words) appear one at a time in the aperture of the memory drum. After the first presentation of the items, the sub-

9-19

A memory drum

The material to be memorized appears in the aperture as the drum revolves.

Lafayette Instrument Co.

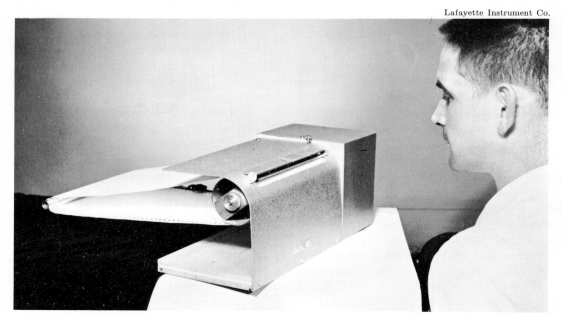

9-20

Rote memorization of nonsense syllables

Serial learning of nonsense syllables was of a 12-item list, with a 2-second exposure of each item. Paired-associates learning was of a 9-item list, with a 2-second exposure of the cue item followed by a 2-second exposure of the cue and response items together. The plotting is somewhat unusual in that instead of presenting trial-by-trial averages, we have the average number of trials required to yield the stated number of correct responses. (After Hovland, 1939)

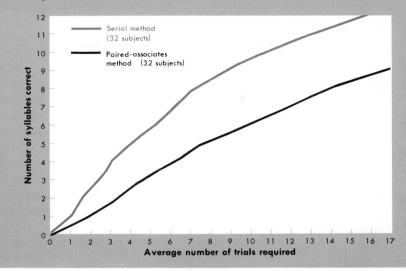

ject tries to state in advance the next item to appear in the aperture. By keeping score of the subject's hits and misses throughout memorizing, the experimenter can plot a learning curve from his record.

Because the subject tries to state what lies immediately ahead, the method is called the *anticipation method*. It can be used for either serial memorization or paired-associates memorization. In the serial method the item anticipated, once it appears in the aperture, becomes the stimulus for the next anticipation. Therefore it is both a response item and a stimulus item. In the paired-associates method the stimulus item is used only as a stimulus, not as a response. When the experimenter uses the anticipation method in paired-associates learning, he presents the stimulus alone and then presents the response item beside it for an equal time before the next stimulus item appears. The paired-associates method is closely analogous to conditioning, the stimulus word corresponding to the conditioned stimulus to which a response is to be learned. When the response word appears

in the aperture, it "reinforces" what the subject has just said (if his anticipation was correct) or "extinguishes" a faulty anticipation. It can be shown that paired-associates learning does in fact exhibit principles in common with conditioning, such as the modifying effects of reinforcement and extinction (Peak and Deese, 1937).

Learning curves for rote memorization, like those for sensorimotor skills, call attention to significant relationships (Figure 9-20). We learn from Figure 9-20 that serial learning is easier than paired-associates learning, for a 12-item serial list was memorized in 16 trials while a 9-item paired-associates list required 17 trials, despite the fact that longer lists are generally harder than shorter ones. This greater difficulty of paired-associates learning has often been demonstrated. The explanation probably can be found in the overlapping anticipatory tendencies that bind the serial list together into a whole. The paired items of the paired-associates list are always presented in scrambled order to prevent these serial effects and to assure that the learning is of separate and distinct pairs. Some theorists (Gibson, 1940; Hull and others, 1940) have attempted to explain many of the findings in rote memorization on the basis of conditioning.

Learning as the Achievement of Understanding

The kinds of learning that we have thus far emphasized (classical conditioning, operant conditioning, and multiple-response learning) all stress the organization of behavior

9-21

A monkey solving a multiple-stick problem

Dr. Harry F. Harlow, Univ. of Wisconsin

In order to obtain the incentive (food on a string), the monkey has to use a shorter stick to obtain one long enough to reach the incentive. Once having succeeded, he demonstrates his insight by readily solving variations of the problem.

into *habits* or *associations,* learned stimulus-response sequences of greater or less complexity. Those who treat learning as habit formation do not deny the role of understanding; they recognize, for example, the effects of meaningfulness of materials and the significance of knowledge of results.[6] But they emphasize features other than understanding—a kind of fumbling trial and error until success is reached. Some psychologists prefer to place the emphasis elsewhere, with more attention to the roles of perception and knowledge, or *cognitive processes.* They fear that emphasis upon habit formation may lead to too much concern for piecemeal activities, and too little attention to organized relationships and meaning. In school, for example, the teacher impressed by habit formation may use rote memorization and drill excessively, without caring enough about the child's understanding of what he learns.

Köhler's insight experiments

Partly in protest against too much study of the kinds of learning that result in a gradual improvement by trial and error, Wolfgang Köhler, a German psychologist who later came to America, performed some dramatic experiments with chimpanzees. At some point in working on a problem, chimpanzees appeared to grasp its inner relationships in the form of "insight." By *insight* we mean the solving of a problem through perceiving the relationships essential to solution. The chimpanzees did not seem to acquire right responses gradually and eliminate wrong ones gradually; in other words, their method did not seem to be mere trial and error. The following experiment by Köhler is typical.

Sultan [Köhler's most intelligent chimpanzee] is squatting at the bars but cannot reach the fruit which lies outside by means of his only available short stick. A longer stick is deposited outside the bars, about two meters on one side of the objective and

[6] To be discussed in Chapter 11.

274

The bird and the locomotives: an insight problem

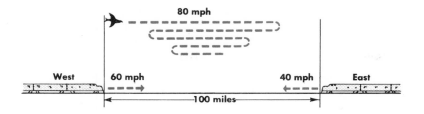

Two locomotives, now 100 miles apart, are moving toward each other. The east-bound locomotive is travel-ing at the rate of 60 mph. The west-bound one is traveling at the rate of 40 mph. An energetic bird, start-ing from the east-bound locomotive, flies back and forth between the two locomotives, without stopping or losing any speed on the turns. The bird flies at the uniform rate of 80 mph. Problem: How far does the bird fly from the start to the moment that the two trains meet? The problem can be solved by those without mathematical training. (See text.)

parallel with the grating. It cannot be grasped with the hand, but it can be pulled within reach by means of the small stick [see Figure 9-21 for an illustration of a similar multiple-stick problem]. Sultan tries to reach the fruit with the smaller of the two sticks. Not succeeding, he tears at a piece of wire that projects from the netting of his cage, but that, too, is in vain. Then he gazes about him (there are always in the course of these tests some long pauses, dur-ing which the animals scrutinize the whole visible area). He suddenly picks up the little stick once more, goes up to the bars directly opposite to the long stick, scratches it to-wards him with the "auxiliary," seizes it, and goes with it to the point opposite the objective (the fruit), which he secures. From the moment that his eyes fall upon the long stick, his procedure forms one con-secutive whole, without hiatus, and, al-though the angling of the bigger stick by means of the smaller is an action that could be complete and distinct in itself, yet ob-servation shows that it follows, quite sud-denly, on an interval of hesitation and doubt —staring about—which undoubtedly has a relation to the final objective, and is imme-diately merged in the final action of the attainment of the end goal.[7]

A moderate degree of insight is so com-mon in human learning that we tend to take it for granted. We know how to insert the battery into a flashlight, how to fill our

[7] Köhler (1925), pp. 174-75.

fountain pens, with various degrees of un-derstanding about what we are doing. Oc-casionally insight comes dramatically, and then we have what has been appropriately called an "Aha"-experience. The solution of a problem becomes suddenly clear, as though a light had been turned on in the darkness. This experience usually comes with types of puzzles (or riddles) that make good parlor tricks, precisely because people enjoy the experience of insight when (and if) it comes. One illustration is furnished by the problem presented in Figure 9-22.

If we use the ordinary methods of prob-lem-solving to solve the problem of Figure 9-22 and rely heavily on past experience, we may set up some sort of algebraic equa-tion to determine, step by step, how far the bird flies on each trip. For example, we know that on the first trip the bird flies east at 80 mph while the train coming west toward it is running at 40 mph. It can be determined without too much difficulty that the bird will go twice as far as the train by the time they meet. Hence when they meet, the train will have gone 33⅓ miles from its starting point while the bird has flown 66⅔ miles. For the bird's return flight it will be necessary to take account of the movement of the first train during the time the bird flew the 66⅔ miles. Then, knowing the rate of flight of the bird and of the train coming to meet it, the second trip can be computed just as the first one was. We continue these computations until the trains have met.

What is meant by solving this kind of problem with insight? Instead of trying to determine, first of all, how far the bird flies on each of its trips, we can make a different try. The clue comes from the question: How long will the bird have been flying by the time the trains meet? When this question is answered, the rest of the solution comes quickly. If you now have the answer, having first been puzzled and then suddenly having "caught on," you know what the experience of insight means.

In many respects insightful learning takes place in much the same way as all other multiple-response learning. Insight, like other learning, depends upon the capacity of the learner. Older children, for example, can learn things that younger children cannot learn. Insight is also influenced by past experience. A chimpanzee who has retrieved food with one stick is better able to learn to retrieve food with a second stick. The student who has solved many mathematical problems does better on similar new problems. Also, the moment at which the first success will occur is unpredictable, because it comes about partly as a result of varied activity. But, in spite of what it has in common with all other learning, there are several characteristics of the insight experiment that suggest that it can be explained on the basis of the understanding of relationships.

1. *Insight depends upon the arrangement of the problematical situation.* Appropriate past experience, while necessary, does not guarantee problem solution. Insight will come easily only if the essentials for solution are arranged so that their relationships can be perceived. For example, a chimpanzee solves the stick problem more readily if the stick is on the same side of the cage

as the food. He has more difficulty if he must turn away from the food to see the stick (Jackson, 1942).

2. *Once a solution occurs with insight, it can be repeated promptly.* Gradual solution appears to be the rule in trial-and-error learning. Sudden solution is the rule in insightful learning. Once the chimpanzee has used a stick for pulling in a banana, he will seek out a stick on the next occasion.

3. *A solution achieved with insight can be applied in new situations.* What is learned in the insight experiment is not a specific movement habit, but a cognitive relationship between a means and an end. Hence one tool may be substituted for another, or one lure substituted for another. In Figure 9-22 boats could replace trains without confusing the problem.

A good learner is a resourceful, adaptable person, one who is able to use what he knows in new situations, and one who is able to discover for himself solutions to problems that he has never before faced. Emphasis upon insightful learning, rather than upon rote learning or mechanized skills, encourages such problem-solving behavior.

Can the Capacity for Insight Be Learned? Because insightful solution of problems occurs promptly when the essentials for solution are open to observation and the learner is bright enough, insight appears to be a capacity that the learner is born with and that matures like other capacities. A chimpanzee is capable of insight into relationships forever closed to a guinea pig. An older child can solve problems which leave a younger child helpless (Richardson, 1932).

Insight is not, however, independent of experience. The learner must have prior familiarity with the essentials of the problem. No one can solve a novel algebra problem without knowing the meaning of the symbols and the operations for which they stand. Such experience, however, does not in itself produce the solution, as any algebra teacher knows. Insight requires the learner to see facts in relation, to understand the essentials as they bear upon the problem.

Monkeys that have had training on successive discrimination problems can finally learn in a single trial. This single-trial learning has all the earmarks of insight; yet it is a final stage reached only with practice. Here we have the clearest indication of an acquired insight.

The following method is used to teach a monkey one-trial learning. While shielded from view, the experimenter hides a peanut under one of two objects on a tray in front of a monkey's cage. The objects may differ in shape, size, or color. Suppose, for example, that the peanut is hidden under a green triangular piece of wood, and that the other object on the tray is a round red piece.

On the first trial, the monkey has to "guess" where the peanut is. If he picks up the green triangle, he will find the peanut and eat it. If he picks up the red circular piece, he will find nothing and will have to wait for the next trial. After each trial the experimenter replaces the screen. The experimenter again presents the same triangle and circular object, either in the same position or reversed, but with the peanut still under the green triangle. After a number of trials, the monkey will learn where to find the peanut and will always pick up the green triangle no matter where it is placed. This is typical discrimination learning, selectively reinforced or nonreinforced with the peanut or lack of it.

There is a variation of the experiment, known as discrimination reversal. Having learned that the green triangle is positive (reinforced) and the red circle negative (nonreinforced), the monkey suddenly finds that the peanut is not under the green triangle, but under the red circle. If he has "insight" he will thereafter choose the red instead of the green, overcoming his pre-

vious habits. He does not make this change all at once. Instead he looks first under the previously rewarded green or becomes disturbed and for a time looks under both. But eventually he learns the reversed habit and invariably chooses the red circle as the one now positive.

When the monkey has later learned to select the positive member of a new pair of stimuli and then suddenly finds the positive stimulus unrewarded, he much more promptly switches to the other stimulus. With practice, he learns to make the change after a single trial. That is, when the first positive stimulus is once unrewarded, on the next trial he invariably chooses the other stimulus as positive. He no longer needs to fall back on trial and error; he knows the rules of the game; he shows the behavioral signs of insight (Harlow, 1949).

Such experiments may help to explain how trial-and-error learning and insightful learning are related. We have all learned by insight often enough to know that the process occurs. The scientific question now raised is whether or not insight can be accounted for on the basis of principles of habit formation. A definite answer awaits further research.

Tolman's sign learning

It is possible that some learning classified as conditioned response may actually be instead a learning of the signs of what-leads-to-what. This was the contention of Edward C. Tolman (1886-1959), who believed that much learning is *sign learning* (Tolman, 1948). A rat running through a maze may be learning a kind of map of the maze instead of merely a set of running and turning habits. If a familiar path is blocked, he can adopt another route based on this understanding of spatial relationships.

Sign learning may be defined as an acquired expectation that one stimulus will be followed by another provided a familiar behavior route is followed. Note that what is acquired is an *expectation* (i.e., a cognition, knowledge, prediction) rather than a *movement response*. Although the expectation may lead to movement, the movement is variable, not as fixed as in conditioning; that is, one movement may be readily substituted for another, provided both movements lead to the same end point where the expected stimulus can be encountered. Because what is learned is expectation rather than response, sign learning classifies as learning with understanding rather than as conditioning.

Three kinds of experiments are pointed to by Tolman as showing how sign learning may characterize animal learning.

1. *Reward Expectancy.* In an experiment with monkeys, the experimenter placed food under one of two containers in order to study how well the monkey could "remember" under which container it had been placed. Some observations made during the course of the experiment indicated reward expectancy by the monkey.

A female monkey has learned to find food under one of two cups. After she sees food placed under one of the cups, the experi-

Place learning

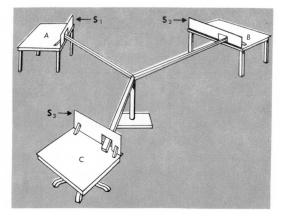

Arrangement used by Maier in studying place learning in rats. (After Maier and Schneirla, 1935)

menter screens them from view. The monkey's choice is made after a delay.

The experimenter now displays a piece of banana, removes the screen, and places the banana under one of the cups. The screen is then replaced, and working behind it the experimenter takes the banana out and deposits a piece of lettuce in its place. After the delay the monkey is told to "come and get the food." She jumps down from the chair, rushes to the proper container and picks it up. She extends her hand to seize the food. But her hand drops to the floor without touching the lettuce. . . . She looks around the cup and behind the board. She stands up and looks under and around her. . . . After several seconds spent in searching, she glances toward the other cup, which she has been taught not to look under, and then walks off to a nearby window. The lettuce is left untouched on the floor (Tinklepaugh, 1928).

If reward is to be understood merely as something that satisfies an active drive, one food ought to be as useful as another for the purpose, provided it is acceptable food. But these experiments show that a given kind of food is anticipated, and palatable food (in this experiment, lettuce) which is not expected may even be rejected.

2. *Place Learning.* Habit-formation theories assume that what the organism learns is movements or responses to stimuli. Sign learning proposes that under some circumstances the organism, instead of learning movement habits, learns the *location* of paths or places.

Place learning can be demonstrated in a number of experiments of which the following is typical. A white rat has run on the various parts of a system of trestles and tables (Figure 9-23) and has been fed on the table at the end of each run. Any one table may be used as a starting point, and any one as a feeding station. The screens S_1, S_2, and S_3 keep the rat from seeing which table is being used as a feeding station. If

Latent learning in rats

Note that after reward is introduced, on the eleventh day, the rats represented by the solid line perform as well as, or even a little better than, those regularly rewarded (dotted line). (After Tolman and Honzik, 1930)

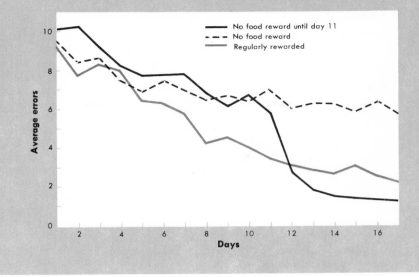

the rat is fed for a short time on one of the tables (say table *A*) and then carried by hand to either of the other tables *B* or *C*, it will choose the appropriate path back to the table with food, even though it has never before taken this path in this order. That is, the rat appears to be guided by spatial relationships rather than by reinforced movement sequences (Maier, 1932; Oakes, 1956).

3. *Latent Learning.* Another experiment, that on latent learning, supports the theory that spatial orientation rather than movement is learned. Latent learning, broadly conceived, refers to any learning that is not demonstrated by behavior at the time of the learning. Typically, such learning goes on under low levels of drive or, if drive is active, when incentives are lacking. When drive is heightened or appropriate incentives appear, there is a sudden use of what has been learned.

Although at present there is a controversy over the exact circumstances under which latent learning occurs, the fact of latent learning is a familiar one in human experience. Through mild curiosity we note the location of a store selling goods in which we are not interested at the moment. When, however, we want something that

the store sells, we can head directly for the store even though it was never before a goal situation. The "reinforcement" which comes through a purchase is not necessary to evoke the approach behavior, once the appropriate motive is aroused. This familiar experience has been duplicated in rat behavior by experiments in which the animal ran a maze without reward. When a reward was later introduced, the rat quickly took the short path to the food. Some typical results are charted in Figure 9-24.

The three kinds of experiment (reward expectancy, place learning, and latent learning) all favor an explanation of learning that goes beyond mere habitual movement sequences. All require some recognition of what-leads-to-what and hence favor a sign-learning explanation.

CRITICAL DISCUSSION

Learning responses vs. learning cognitive structures

Suppose that an animal learns a discriminated operant by usual conditioning methods, so that he presses a bar only when a light is on.

Automatic vs. insightful learning

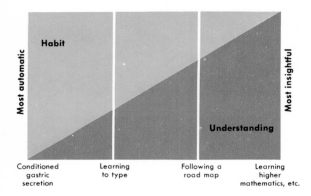

The scaling of learning tasks according to degree of understanding involved. Most learning involves a mixture of habit and insight.

He then reacts to the light as a "sign" that the bar will be reinforced, i.e., will produce food. Why make a distinction between operant conditioning and sign learning? For many purposes the distinction is unimportant, but, as was pointed out at the beginning of the chapter, there is a controversy over the question whether the subject learns *responses* (which conditioning theories imply) or *cognitive structures* (which sign-learning theories imply). By cognitive structure psychologists mean an idea or knowledge, the root meaning of *cognition* being "knowledge." Does the rat learn a chain of movements in running from the start of an alley to the food box at the end, or does it learn the location of the food? Response learning emphasizes the movement patterns; sign learning emphasizes the knowledge of location. If the rat learns a maplike representation of the environment, so that it can take new paths and short cuts, then it has acquired a cognitive structure. Those psychologists who favor sign learning do experiments in place learning and latent learning, both of which are critical of theories that treat learning as the reinforcement of specific responses.

Those who favor response interpretations have met this challenge in several ways. They no longer question the results of latent-learning experiments, except that they insist upon careful specification of the conditions under which these results hold. When the conditions are thus specified, sign-learning explanations

are shown to have their limitations also. The critics show how the equivalent of "ideas" or of "knowledge" can be inferred from responses, and end up by giving a response interpretation to what the sign-learning theorist calls cognitive structure (Seward, 1956). Thus the outcome is scarcely a victory for one side or the other, though both groups have contributed new knowledge about behavior, and the excitement engendered by the controversy has had a tonic effect upon investigators.

The conflicting theories are too abstract for further discussion here. For our purposes, it is possible to look on habit formation (associative learning) and understanding (cognitive learning) as complementary, neither complete in itself as an explanation of learning, but each helping to explain some features of learning that the other neglects or explains with greater difficulty.

A provisionally satisfactory position is that any given illustration of learning can be graded on a crude scale, with the most automatic kind of learning (explained best as conditioning) at the one end, and the most insightful and rational at the other (explained best according to principles of understanding). We may picture such a scale by the diagram of Figure 9-25. At the left are the habits learned automatically, without awareness and with a minimum of understanding, by conditioning mechanisms. Perhaps learning to secrete gastric juice in our stomachs when we see food before us would illustrate such conditioning. Toward the right of the diagram are the tasks learned with full awareness, but still in a somewhat conventional manner, as when we use a map to select the route to be followed in a motor trip. At the extreme right fall tasks that require reasoning about many facts in complex relationships. Most learnings fall somewhere between, as a kind of mixture between habit formation and understanding. Learning to operate a typewriter competently, for example, includes the automatic habits of finger action, but it also includes the insights involved in inserting bond paper and carbon paper or in changing a ribbon.

This kind of "mixture" theory is considered too eclectic for many psychologists who would rather commit themselves to one or the other position and then attempt to "derive" the behavior that the opposing theorists find critical of the adopted position. Through such efforts at consistency uniform theories arise.

Mathematical Models of Learning [8]

The experimental study of learning has progressed far enough that a number of psychologists have attempted to formulate the lawful relationships within learning in the language of mathematics. In this, psychology repeats the history of other sciences that have become more mathematical as they have become more advanced in their theories and more precise in their measurements. While the details of mathematical theories of learning must be left for more advanced study, the student is not fully aware of the contemporary developments within psychology if he does not know something of the direction of these developments. A knowledge of high school algebra will enable the student to follow the thread of the description which follows, though the mathematical techniques used in developing the models were of course considerably more complex.

The Hull-Spence theory

While there were earlier attempts to fit mathematics to the course of learning and forgetting, going back at least to Ebbinghaus (1885), one of the most thorough attempts at systematizing was undertaken by Clark L. Hull (1884-1952), working at Yale University. A number of younger psychologists were influenced by him, among whom Kenneth W. Spence, at the State University of Iowa, is considered to be in some sense Hull's intellectual heir. Hence the theory that Hull proposed and that Spence and his students have moved forward has come to be known as the Hull-Spence theory (Logan, 1959).

Hull recognized two sets of components in any learned performance—first, habit strength ($_sH_R$), a result of *associative learn-*

ing under reinforcement, as in operant conditioning, and, second, *non-associative* components, of which drive (D) is the most important. He set up the fundamental formula (Hull, 1951, p. 35): [9]

$_sE_R$ (excitatory potential)
     $= D$ (drive) $\times$ $_sH_R$ (habit strength)

What this equation states is that the tendency to make a response ($_sE_R$) depends upon habit strength ($_sH_R$) acquired from prior learning, with the actual amount of responding depending also upon the level of drive (D) operating at the time the response is evoked. Thus a hungry rat, having learned its way through the maze, will run the maze faster than a well-fed rat equally experienced in the maze. This fundamental formula becomes complicated with other nonassociative factors in addition to drive —factors such as the intensity of the stimuli which evoke responses and the size of the incentive used in reinforcement. The basic idea of the system can be learned, however, from the fundamental equation in its uncomplicated form.

To move from the very simple equation to something that fits the data from experiments, Hull had first to develop a formula to express the *law of habit formation,* that is, the most typical form of the learning curve for the acquisition of a simple response reinforced on each trial. This equation he expressed as follows (Hull, 1951, p. 32):

$$_sH_R = 1 - 10^{-aN}$$

where N is the number of evenly distributed reinforced trials, and a is a constant.

This law states that, other things being

---

[8] This section may be regarded as optional by instructors, depending upon the mathematical preparation of their students.

[9] Hull used the subscripts S and R in symbolizing habit strength ($_sH_R$) and excitatory potential ($_sE_R$) to serve as reminders that what was symbolized was an association between a particular stimulus and response (in the case of habit) and a tendency for a particular stimulus to evoke that response (in the case of excitatory potential). The subscripts serve no mathematical purpose; they are merely descriptive labels on the symbols.

equal, habit strength increases regularly with reinforcement to a maximum of strength 1.00 (in arbitrary units). The resulting curve is one of decreasing gains.

Let us see how this *law of habit formation* combines with the fundamental formula under consideration. Hull selected data from experiments by Perin (1942), in which rats acquired the habit of lever pressing under two conditions of hunger (Figure 9-26). Curves were then derived according to standard mathematical conventions (in this case, the least-squares method) in order to assign numerical values to the exponent *a,* and to provide other constants so that the mathematical formulas, when used for plotting, would come close to the points found experimentally.

The resulting two equations were:

$$_sE_R = 66(1 - 10^{-.02N}) - 4$$
$$\text{for 22 hours of hunger}$$

and

$$_sE_R = 25(1 - 10^{-.02N}) - 4$$
$$\text{for 3 hours of hunger}$$

While there were minor differences in the exponents (here reported as −.02), the portions of the equations representing the acquiring of $_sH_R$ are essentially alike (as they should be according to the theory); but the multiplying parameters [10] (66 and 26), reflecting the contribution of drive, differ in size (as they should according to the theory), higher drive being associated with greater food deprivation.

If the ratio of 66:25 represents the drive contributions from 22 hours of hunger and from 3 hours of hunger, we already have some hint as to how hunger varies with hours of food deprivation, and we are ready then to test this relationship in new situations. The advantage of having a strictly quantitative system is that there eventually develops a network of relationships that

[10] A parameter is a variable that has taken a fixed value, i.e., become a constant.

must be self-consistent if the theory is to be considered satisfactory.

Hull and his followers have been both painstaking and ingenious in adding more and more data to the system. They have, of course, found it necessary to revise the system when inconsistencies were found. This is no sign of weakness, but is of the very nature of quantitative science. All science is unfinished, and to the extent that it is self-correcting it is good science. The details of Hull's system (Hull, 1952) and the changes that Spence (1956) made in it, are beyond the scope of this book.

The Estes statistical model

Some psychologists have developed mathematical models of learning starting with assumptions somewhat unlike those of Hull and Spence, but often arriving at expressions not so different from theirs. As an illustration we shall use a model developed by Estes (1959).

The statistical theory begins with some assumptions about the nature of the stimulus and the nature of associative learning. Any stimulus is said to be composed of a large number of elements, only a fraction of which are effective at any one time. In common sense terms, we might think of paying attention to but part of what is present, or of having some stimulus components near threshold so that they are sometimes above threshold, sometimes below it. Hence only those parts of the stimulus that are effective can enter into associative learning. The theory assumes that *all* the stimulus components that are effective at the time a response occurs become attached to that response. (This can be considered a form of classical conditioning.) The theory further assumes that circumstances usually allow only a given fraction of the unattached stimuli to become effective at any one time. This fraction is represented by a constant θ (Greek letter Theta), which has some value less than one, say .05. This is a kind of index of the learning rate of the learner,

9-26

Mathematical expression of influence of drive on excitatory strength

In the experiment from which the plotted dots were derived, rats were reinforced for varying numbers of trials in a bar-pressing apparatus under two levels of drive (22 hours hunger and 3 hours hunger), and then tested for the number of unreinforced responses required to produce extinction, a value that served as an estimate of the excitatory potential ($_SE_R$). The hungrier animals proved more resistant to extinction at all levels of learning (Perin, 1942). According to Hull's theory the difference in drive level should multiply the effects due to number of reinforcements. If the expression $(1 - 10^{-.02N})$ is taken as a measure of $_SH_{R'}$ it is seen that the curves (derived mathematically from the plotted data) do indeed conform to the formula $_SE_R = D \times _SH_{R'}$ with the values of D represented by 66 and 25 for 22 and

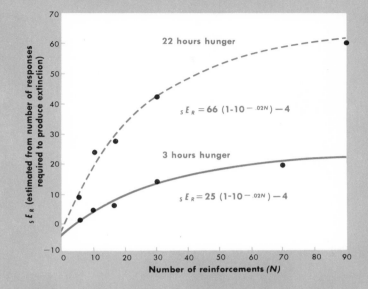

3 hours, respectively. The -4 is a constant that reflects the fact that the fitted curves start below zero, suggesting that a few reinforcements are needed before excitatory strength reaches the threshold of response. The curves using Perin's data are reproduced by Hull, 1943, p. 228, and the equations are given in Hull, 1943, p. 254.

a subject with higher θ making more rapid improvement. If θ has a value of .05, this means that on any one trial there will be added to the components of the stimulus already associated with the response .05, or 1/20th, of the remaining portions of the stimulus complex. Now the likelihood that a response will occur is directly proportional to the per cent of stimulus components attached to it through association. If none is attached, the stimulus complex will not evoke the response at all; if all components are attached through association, the response will occur inevitably on every trial. It is clear that we have a probability theory here: the probability of the response follows from the proportion of the stimulus components that have become attached to it. This is the theoretical background for the acquisition of responses.

For the extinction of responses, it is necessary for fractions of the stimulus complex to become separated from the response by becoming attached to something else (or, what is the same thing, to "nonresponding"). Thus when the response fails to occur (as in extinction), the *decrease* in degree of association can be defined as θ times the stimulus components that have previously become associated with the response. By degree of association is always meant, in this model, the probability that the response will occur.

Although learning is defined by probability of response to the stimulus complex, it does not follow that probability is the only experimental measure that can be used to test the theory. Mathematical expressions can be found relating probability to rate of responding, to latency of response, and so

Mathematical transformations of theoretical curves

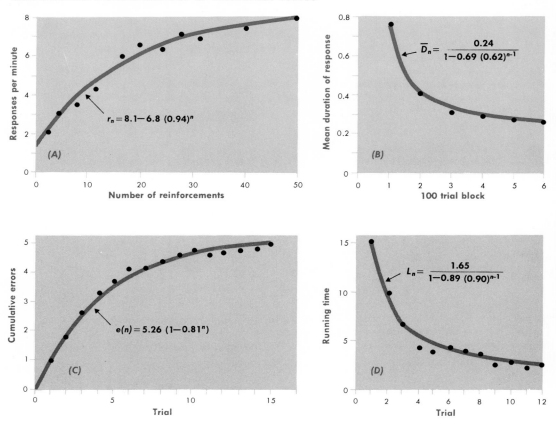

The same general curve, derived according to Estes' statistical learning theory, has been transformed to a form allowing it to be tested empirically according to four measures: (1) responses per minute, (2) mean duration of a response, (3) cumulative errors, and (4) running time. The first two curves (A and B) are from a bar-pressing experiment, the last two (C and D) from a T-maze experiment. The solid line represents the theoretical curve in each case, while the black dots represent the data from experiments. (The precise meaning of the formulas for each curve, and the way they were derived, are beyond the scope of this text.) To the extent that the curves "fit" the data, the theory is meeting with success. (From Estes, 1959, p. 402)

on, so that the theory can be tested with the use of any of the standard measurements that one made in the learning laboratory.

Beginning with these assumptions, the mathematics is straightforward, although the expressions in terms of probability are somewhat unfamiliar to those who have studied only conventional algebra and geometry.

The basic equation for the change in probability of response between trial n and trial $n + 1$ is (Estes, 1959, p. 398):

$$p_{n+1} = p_n + \theta(1 - p_n)$$

Put into words, this says that the probability of response on the next trial (p_{n+1}) will equal the probability on the given trial (p_n) plus a fraction (θ) of the remaining probability required to reach 1.00, that is $(1 - p_n)$. Hence this merely writes in mathematical form the assumptions described in the preceding discussion. An equation of this kind is known as a *difference equation,* because it expresses the change in probability from one step to the next.

It is possible by mathematical operations which need not concern us to develop a mathematical expression of what must happen when the difference equation is applied over and over again, beginning with the probability at trial one (i.e., p_1) and ending at any given trial n (i.e., at probability p_n). The expression that results is (Estes, 1959, p. 401):

$$p_n = 1 - (1 - p_1)(1 - \theta)^{n-1}$$

This is a generalized learning curve equation, serving the same purpose as Hull's *law of habit formation* (p. 281). In fact, the two expressions are really very much alike. Because p_1 and θ are constants, both equations state that the progress of learning can be stated according to the limit of learning (1.00) minus a constant which is raised to a power in which n, the number of trials, is the number that varies. Both equations imply that the gain per trial is some constant fraction of the amount remaining to be learned. (The fact that one exponent carries a minus sign and the other does not results merely from the fact that in the Hull equation the number raised to a power is *greater* than one, while in the other case the number raised to a power is *less* than one. Hence the differences in sign are a result of mathematical conventions, and do not represent any real differences in the equations in this respect.)

In Figure 9-26 we saw how Hull used his

theory in relation to data. Let us now examine some simple applications of Estes' equation. In Figure 9-27 we have four illustrations of equations fitted to actual data. The forms of the equation differ slightly from the one given because transformations have been made to convert probability to responses per minute, to duration of response, to cumulative errors, and to running time. It is evident from inspection that the theoretical curve (the solid line in each case) fits quite well the points that represent the data from experiments.

Conclusions on mathematical models

Only the early steps in model-building have been described for the Hull-Spence model and the Estes model. In both cases many further steps have been taken in order to account in similar fashion for what happens in extinction, in discrimination learning, in generalization, and in various forms of multiple-response learning. Estes has introduced additional considerations to take care of time-dependent phenomena, such as spontaneous recovery and forgetting. Others, too, have entered the field with models of various degrees of applicability and generality (e.g., Bush and Mosteller, 1955; Suppes and Atkinson, 1960).

As Estes points out, the general notion of learning as a probabilistic or statistical process has been taken up by so many investigators that it is likely to be one of the dominant features of future theoretical development in psychology. This does not mean that there will not continue to be other lines of inquiry and theorizing, but the serious student of learning theory cannot now ignore these mathematical developments.

SUMMARY   1. Pavlov's experiments on *classical conditioning* in the dog brought to light several principles useful in the understanding of habit formation. These include reinforcement, extinction, spontaneous recovery, generalization, and discrimination.

2. Skinner's experiments on *operant conditioning* have extended conditioning principles to kinds of responses that cannot be elicited by recognized unconditioned stimuli. Operant behavior acts upon the environment to produce or gain access to reinforcement and becomes strengthened by reinforcement.

3. Rate of responding is a useful measure of operant strength, with applicability to practical behavior. *Intermittent reinforcement* illustrates the orderliness of operant behavior, since long and regular runs of responses can be sustained by occasional reinforcement.

4. An animal trainer can use the *method of approximations,* under which he reinforces those variations in the operant response that move in the desired direction and extinguishes those that do not, in this way *shaping* the response. Thus operant conditioning can account for the learning of novel movements. Recent experiments have shown that ordinary verbal behavior can be brought under control through operant conditioning.

5. Conditioning is most directly applicable to single identifiable responses, but much habit formation is more complex than this. These more complex instances are classified as *multiple-response learning.* Two examples are sensorimotor skills (such as mirror drawing and pursuit learning) and rote memorization (including serial learning and paired-associates learning).

6. The experimenter plots the results of multiple-response learning in the form of *learning curves,* indicating changes in proficiency with practice. These curves usually show decreasing gains per trial, but there is the possibility that an S-shape is the most general form of a complete learning curve. Such a curve shows increasing gains at first, followed later by decreasing gains.

7. Emphasis within conditioning and multiple-response learning is upon the acquiring of movements or verbal habits. Some psychologists warn against an overemphasis on the automatic nature of learning which comes from exclusive concern with movements. They stress instead situations in which understanding comes to the fore. Köhler's *insight* experiments pointed out how the arrangements of the problem make the solution easy or hard, and how a solution once achieved with insight can be repeated or applied to novel situations.

8. Tolman's *sign-learning* experiments also emphasize the role of knowledge or understanding. Three kinds of experiment (reward expectancy, place learning, and latent learning) are critical of theories that lay stress upon the reinforcement of particular movements without taking into account the subject's understanding of the relationships involved.

9. Something can be learned from each of these emphases. Learning goes on in part through automatic processes with little rational direction from the learner, and in part through processes in which the learner perceives relationships and acts with knowledge.

10. As learning experimentation has become more precise, theorists have begun to develop mathematical models in which equations derived on the basis of various assumptions are fitted to the data from experiments, so that a curve plotted mathematically looks very much like one that connects the points which plot experimentally obtained values. If the curves fit the data, the assumptions have greater plausibility than if they do not fit. Starting with rather simple relationships, the theories are gradually extended to cover more complex instances of learning. The Hull-Spence and the Estes models illustrate some of these developments.

SUGGESTIONS FOR FURTHER READING

Pavlov, *Conditioned reflexes* (1927) is the classical work on conditioned salivary reflexes in dogs. Skinner, *The behavior of organisms* (1938) is the corresponding statement of operant conditioning. The later developments in conditioning theory and experiment are summarized in Kimble, *Hilgard and Marquis' Conditioning and learning* (1961).

Cognitive theories also have their classics. Köhler, *The mentality of apes* (1925) describes the famous insight experiments with chimpanzees. Tolman, *Purposive behavior in animals and men* (1932) is the major statement of his cognitive (sign learning) position.

The major points of view toward learning, in their historical settings and with some typical experiments to which they have led, are summarized in Hilgard, *Theories of learning* (2nd Ed., 1956). Some useful original papers dealing with various approaches to learning theory have been collected by Birney and Teevan (Eds.), *Reinforcement* (1961).

For substantive approaches, emphasizing the contributions of the learning laboratory, there are a number of textbooks on learning such as McGeoch and Irion, *The psychology of human learning* (2nd Ed., 1952), Bugelski, *The psychology of learning* (1956), Deese, *The psychology of learning* (2nd Ed., 1958), Lawson, *Learning and behavior* (1960).

The literature on mathematical models is growing rapidly. In addition to the references cited in the text, mention should be made of Bush and Estes, *Studies in mathematical learning theory* (1959).

CHAPTER 10

Remembering and Forgetting

All learning implies retaining, for if nothing were left over from previous experience, nothing would be learned. When we have studied the nature of learning, we have already begun to study remembering, because many of the same principles apply. But remembering and forgetting are far too important to dismiss merely as continuous with learning. We think and reason largely with remembered facts; the very continuity of our self-perceptions depends upon the continuity of our memories. We are able to deal with the concept of time as no other animal can, relating the present to the past and making predictions about the future, because of the strength, flexibility, and availability of our memories.

Kinds of Remembering

To remember means to show in present responses some signs of earlier learned responses. We need a set of words to distinguish among several ways in which our memories appear.

One way of remembering is to *recollect* or *redintegrate* an event and the circumstances surrounding it, as when you remember going with a "date" to your first dance. The word *recollect* is from the ordinary vocabulary; *redintegrate* is a technical word meaning to reintegrate or to reestablish an earlier experience on the basis of partial

cues. For example, you redintegrate that first date only if something "reminds" you of it. The stimuli to redintegration are in a literal sense *souvenirs,* remembrances or reminders of a total, personal experience, which occurred at a given time in the past. In your recollection you conjure up the orchestra seated before the potted palms, the dance music that was then popular, the cool breeze on the terrace, perhaps your aching feet when you finally got home after the dance was over. While such redintegrative memories are often quite detailed and complete, they need not be. They are distinguished from other kinds of remembering because they reconstruct a past occasion from your personal autobiography with its setting in time and place.

Many signs of earlier experience lack this reconstruction of the past. For example, you may *recall* a poem by reciting it, even if you do not remember the circumstances under which you learned it. You can remember how to climb stairs or ride a bicycle or sing a song without any direct reference to the past. This kind of remembering, shown through recall, is easier to measure than the redintegration of earlier experiences, and it is the kind usually studied in the laboratory.

A third kind of remembering is the indication of memory merely by *recognizing* someone or something as familiar. "That tune is familiar. What is it?" "Someone I used to know had a copy of that picture on the wall, but I can't place it now."

Finally, you may show that you once learned something by now *relearning* it more rapidly than you could if there were no retention of the earlier learning.

Redintegration, recall, recognition, and relearning all give evidence of memory, but each of these terms implies a different aspect of remembering.

Redintegrative memory

Experimental psychologists have paid relatively little attention to redintegrative memory, partly because it is difficult to check details of the recovery of events in the personal past of the subject. A few studies have been done under hypnosis; one of these, for example, has shown that memories of schoolroom experiences at ages 7 and 10 can be more accurately recovered by adults under hypnosis than in the waking state (Reiff and Scheerer, 1959). These memories, of other pupils in the class, of the teacher's name, were subject to confirmation.

Studies of testimony are concerned with the reinstatement of scenes witnessed in the past. A class may unexpectedly witness a staged crime and then report what happened. The reports are often distorted, even when a student insists his recollections are vivid and dependable. The author once engaged in a staged argument with a workman who interrupted his lecture. The workman spoke with a German accent. Although the assistant who acted the part of the workman in this little drama had blond hair and dark brown eyes, a substantial proportion of the students reported confidently that they had seen his *blue* eyes—the color falsely inferred from his Nordic appearance and German accent. Such experiments have bearing on the reliability of witnesses in courtrooms.

Studies of personal memories have been carried on more by those engaged in psychotherapy than by experimental psychologists. In psychoanalysis the recall of childhood memories is one of the bases of treatment and cure. A curious problem, not yet fully understood, is created by the paucity of very early memories, from the very time that the child is having many exciting new experiences. This is the problem of "childhood amnesia," early noted by Freud. One conjecture is that the child perceives the world so differently from an adult that the adult's effort to recall what registered for the child fails because of this difference (Schachtel, 1959).

Recall

The kind of remembering most easily tested in the laboratory is active *recall* of some performance learned in the past. You may show that you remember how to ride a bicycle by climbing on one and riding away. You may show that you know Hamlet's soliloquy on death by reciting it. What you are demonstrating is that present performance is different from what it would be if there were no residue from the past. You ride the bicycle. If there were no residue from the past, you could not ride it.

To get a quantitative measure of recall in the laboratory, the investigator allows time to elapse after a subject has memorized some material, usually by the serial method or the paired-associates method described in Chapter 9 (pp. 272-73). Then the subject returns to the laboratory and attempts to anticipate the items *the first time* the stimulus item appears in the aperture of the memory drum, that is, before there is any new learning. The percentage correct is the *recall score*.

Recognition

When we recognize something, we mean that it is familiar, that we have met it before. Recognition is a common experience, but it is a rather complex and, in a sense, mysterious process. The entire process takes place quite automatically. We meet someone and say, "I'm sure we have met before, though I cannot recall your name or just where or when it was."

We learn a little about recognition from faulty recognition, from a deceiving sense of familiarity. The French expression *déjà vu* ("previously seen") is often used to describe the sense of familiarity that is sometimes aroused in otherwise strange surroundings. So important and convincing was this experience that Plato, the Greek philosopher, made it part of the basis for his belief in a previous existence. What may happen is that a pattern of buildings along a street is actually somewhat like one seen in earlier experience, or that in a strangely familiar garden the scent of a flower permeating the air is one met on an earlier occasion but since forgotten. Then the present, though actually strange, seems vaguely familiar. This is a form of generalization from past experience; it merely happens to be inappropriate.

To study recognition in the laboratory we have to distinguish between correct and faulty recognition. We do this by presenting to the subject a series of items, such as a set of 25 photographs, with which he then becomes familiar. Now we test his recognition by mixing these 25 with 25 additional ones of the same general kind, and have him sort out those he saw before. We can obtain a score as we do for a true-false examination corrected for guessing. The formula is:

$$\text{Recognition score} = 100 \frac{\text{Right} - \text{Wrong}}{\text{Total}}$$

That is, if all the original pictures are sorted in the "familiar" pile and all the new or misleading ones in the "unfamiliar" pile, the subject gets a score of 100 per cent. If he sorts by chance, getting half right and half wrong, his score drops to 0 per cent, as it should.

Relearning

Another way to show that there is some residue from the past is to demonstrate that previously familiar material can be learned more rapidly than it could be learned if it were unfamiliar. Even though something may seem to be completely "forgotten," it may be easier to learn a second time because it was once learned in the past. A dramatic illustration of how this may occur is given by an experiment in which a child was read selections from Greek and then learned those same selections years later.

The experimenter read three Greek selections a day to a boy of fifteen months, repeating the same selections daily for three months. Each selection consisted of 20 lines of iambic hexameter material. At the end of three months another set of three selections was repeated daily for three months. The procedure was continued until the subject was three years old and 21 selections had been read.

The residual influence of this early experience was studied through memorization experiments conducted with the boy at the ages of $8\frac{1}{2}$, 14, and 18. He had not studied Greek in the meantime. At each of these ages he learned selected passages from the early experience along with equivalent but unfamiliar passages. The results indicated a substantial saving in learning the familiar material at the age of $8\frac{1}{2}$. About 30 per cent fewer repetitions were required than for equivalent new material. By the age of 14, however, the saving was only 8 per cent, and by 18 years no saving could be demonstrated. The main point is that there was demonstrable saving in learning five years after the original reading took place, even though the material to which the child had listened was classical Greek, a language that to him was without meaning (Burtt, 1941).

To use the relearning method in the laboratory, the experimenter proceeds as for the study of recall; after the first learning he allows time over which retention is to be tested in a second learning. The subject, having previously learned by one of the standard methods well enough to meet some *criterion of mastery* (e.g., one perfect recitation), learns the material again *to the same criterion*. If the second learning requires fewer trials than the first, we may assume that there has been a saving due to the prior learning.[1] We may express this saving as a percentage by using the formula:

[1] We have to assure ourselves through appropriate controls that there has not been in the meantime a "learning how to learn," or we must introduce a necessary correction for this variable.

Saving score

$$= 100 \frac{\text{Original trials} - \text{Relearning trials}}{\text{Original trials}}$$

If the relearning criterion is reached on the first trial, then the saving is 100 per cent; if it takes as much time as original learning, there is 0 per cent saving.

When standard learning and relearning methods are used, it is possible to secure recall and saving scores at the same time. The recall score is computed from the degree of success on the first relearning trial, and the saving score from the number of trials required to reach the criterion.

The processes underlying redintegration, recall, recognition, and relearning are not distinct. Each kind of memory, however, makes a somewhat different demand upon the subject, so that his retention of earlier learning might be detected by one method and not by another. For example, the retention of a past experience completely unavailable to redintegrative memory or to direct recall might be detected by recognition or relearning. The response to stimuli is easier for recognition than for recall: with the stimuli of a face before you, you are asked only to *recognize* these stimuli as familiar, while you are expected to *recall* a name from the stimuli the face provides.

While it is assumed that there are many overlaps among the kinds of processes underlying redintegration, recall, recognition, and relearning, it must not be supposed that these are merely arbitrary methods of measuring the same thing. There are differences in process as well as similarities, and these differences show up in a number of ways.

The major distinction is between a memory dated in one's personal past, here called *recollection* or *redintegration*, and the kind of undated memory shown in, say, the memory for familiar words of the ordinary vocabulary. This latter we have termed *recall*. If one remembers having looked up an unusual word, then that memory is a recollection of a concrete experience, but most words are not tied in such a way to a personal history. In a recent book concerned with the nature of memory, Reiff and Scheerer (1959) have elaborated the same distinction, calling the personal memories *remembrances,* and the undated, habitual kind *memoria.* They make a number of additional distinctions that need not concern us here. In cases of amnesia, it is usually the personal memories that are lost, while the victim of amnesia is able to talk his familiar language, buy bus tickets, count his change, and do many other things that show that his *memoria* (in the Reiff and Scheerer sense) have not been lost.

It cannot be assumed that recall and recognition will follow the same quantitative laws either, for recognition has in it some features of remembrance (having been experienced before) while recall can be automatic, without any personal reference whatever.

These distinctions become more important when problems of motivated forgetting are under consideration, as in repression, hypnotic amnesia, and the like. (See pp. 301-04.)

The Course of Forgetting

We know that our memories are not perfect. There are songs we once sang whose words we have now forgotten. There are childhood playmates whose names we no longer remember. There are skills that have diminished or grown "rusty." These processes of fading of memories or loss of skill with disuse are open to study.

Curves of retention

The effects of an interval of no practice after learning can be plotted in the form of *curves of retention,* based upon tests introduced at set periods following learning. A typical curve falls rapidly at first and then gradually tapers off. This pattern was discovered by Ebbinghaus, a pioneer investigator in the study of retention, who first published a curve showing the course of

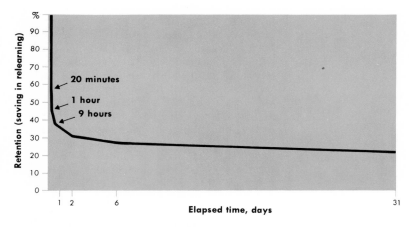

10-1

A retention curve

Curve of retention for lists
of nonsense syllables. (After
Ebbinghaus, 1885)

forgetting (Figure 10-1). Ebbinghaus invented the nonsense syllable (see p. 272) in order to have a quantity of equivalent materials in constructing lists to be memorized. His curves were for the retention of such nonsense syllables after they had been barely memorized, as tested by the relearning method.

Later investigators have found that the course of forgetting is usually similar to that found by Ebbinghaus, but that the rate at which forgetting occurs varies enormously with the materials used and with the circumstances under which memorization occurs. Studies of the rote memory of materials learned in high school and college courses have yielded results shown in Table 10-1.

More is forgotten in the first year after memorizing than in the second year; this is the same trend as in the Ebbinghaus curve, but with the time axis enormously stretched out. About as much forgetting of nonsense syllables occurs in a day as occurs in a year with the materials of an academic course. There are two limitations to the interpretation of the data of Table 10-1. We do not know what the scoring level was before the course. Some students might have made nearly as good scores before taking the course as they did two years after taking it. We also do not know what additional learning or relearning took place in related courses during the two-year interval. A medical student who remembers his anatomy did not learn all of it in his anatomy course; he relearned some old facts and learned some new facts in later work on the body, in physiology, in neurology, in surgery.

The testing of rote memory for course work raises the question of what should be retained. Many examination items are scarcely worth remembering after the course is over. As we shall see later, the meaningful generalizations from the course are re-

TABLE 10-1

Retention of content of high school and college courses

	Per cent of perfect score on examination		
	End of course	After 1 year	After 2 years
College courses:			
Botany	68	21	16
Psychology	70	24	19
Zoology	78	39	30
High school courses:			
Algebra	87	56	Not tested
Chemistry	63	47	33
Latin	82	60	Not tested

SOURCE: Based on several investigations, as summarized by English (1943).

membered better than rote items such as terminology.

Retention as measured by recognition, recall, and relearning

Our everyday experiences tell us that recognition is usually easier than recall. And we can easily see that relearning is a very sensitive measure of retention, because it can show some residue of past learning even when there is no evidence from either recognition or recall. A frequently quoted study by Luh (1922) tested these separate aspects following nonsense syllable memorization, under circumstances as closely comparable as he could make them (Figure 10-2). Over a two-day period of testing he found highest scores for recognition, next highest for relearning, and lowest scores for recall. The flattening of the curve for relearning suggests the possibility that in the long run relearning scores might exceed those for recognition, but the retention intervals were not long enough to find this out. In exceptional circumstances these relationships may be reversed. For example, we sometimes correctly recall the

10-2

Three measures of retention

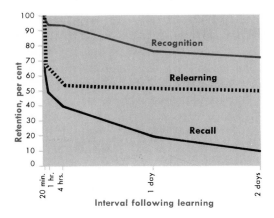

Retention curves for nonsense syllables by three methods of measurement. Luh actually used five methods, but the other two are not standard and need not concern us. (After Luh, 1922)

10-3

A reminiscence curve

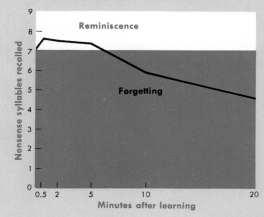

Reminiscence curve following rote memorization. This retention curve shows an initial rise before it begins to fall, though this pattern does not always appear in studies of forgetting. (After Ward, 1937)

spelling of a word, only to fail to recognize that it is correct. Then recall is better than recognition.

Reminiscence

Sometimes the retention curve does not fall rapidly at first, as we have learned to expect from the results of Ebbinghaus and later experimenters. In other words, instead of a fall there is an initial *rise* (that is, greater retention after an interval than immediately after learning). This phenomenon has come to be known as *reminiscence*. The name came from an early attempt at an explanation, which suggested some kind of review or mulling over between learning and the test of retention, but it has now come to mean simply a rise in the curve of retention, without implying any particular theory. One such *reminiscence curve* is that of Ward (1937), reproduced in Figure 10-3. This curve was obtained with nonsense syllables. Retention at 5 minutes after learning is higher than immediately

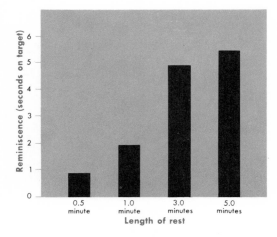

In motor-skill learning, the reminiscence pattern is more apparent. (After Irion, 1949)

after learning; by 10 minutes the usual fall has set in; and by 20 minutes the curve is where it is expected on the basis of results such as those of Ebbinghaus and Luh. A number of later experimenters have found it difficult to reproduce the reminiscence effect following verbal memorization (e.g., Underwood, 1957c), so that its conditions are somewhat uncertain.

Reminiscence curves are typical with motor skill learning. Irion (1949) found, for example, that following 25 seconds of massed practice on a pursuit rotor, longer rests improved the scores on the next five trials more than did shorter ones. In fact, the amount of improvement increased almost directly with the length of rest, up to 5 minutes (Figure 10-4).

A number of theories have been proposed to account for reminiscence. While none is fully satisfactory, among the more plausible theories is one that may be called the *recovery-from-work* theory. This theory assumes that continuous practice is fatiguing, so that the subject cannot show all that he has learned and his scores are lower than they

would be if he were rested. With rest, all the learning that occurred has a chance to show itself in the actual scoring (Hovland and Kurtz, 1951).

The Nature of Forgetting

At the present time, there are four different explanations of forgetting, and each plausibly accounts for some of the known facts. Because the explanations are not contradictory, each may help us to understand the nature of what we remember and why we forget. The four are: (1) passive decay through disuse, (2) systematic distortions of the memory trace, (3) retroactive and proactive inhibition, and (4) motivated forgetting.

Passive decay through disuse

Forgetting is sometimes thought to be due to the fading or decay of *memory traces* in the brain (i.e., the inferred physical basis of memory) with the passage of time. Such fading or decay could be the result of the normal metabolic processes of the brain. As time passes, these processes might cause the traces of material once learned to disintegrate gradually and eventually to disappear altogether.

The experience of rapid fading of barely learned material lends credence to this view of forgetting. Even as you try to write down verbatim a definition given in a lecture, you may find it fading away.

Our forgetting of pictures or stories also suggests a process of fading with the passage of time. When first perceived, a story or picture may reveal a wealth of detail. But with the passage of time, the details are rapidly forgotten and only the main outlines are remembered.

Plausible as is the disuse, or organic decay, theory of forgetting there is no direct evidence for it; and there is much evidence that it is a dubious or at least incomplete theory. The form of the retention curve can be accounted for on other grounds.

One of the arguments against the passive decay theory rests on the recovery of memories supposedly lost. People approaching senility often recall vividly events of their youth when they can barely remember the events of the day. Occasionally in delirium a patient speaks a language unused since childhood. Unavailable memories have not necessarily "decayed." It cannot be denied, however, that some forgetting may occur through the organic changes taking place in the nervous system with the passing of time. All we can be sure of is that this explanation does not account for all the facts about forgetting.

Systematic distortions of the memory trace

The theory of forgetting through disuse suggests that the change with time is chiefly a blurring of memories, a fading, a falling away of items. But this is only one aspect of forgetting. Later recollections differ from earlier ones in other ways. Experiments on testimony have shown that many things are remembered that never happened at all or that actually happened in ways very different from those recalled. Forgetting through *distortion* has to be accounted for.

The theory of systematic distortion of the memory trace, like the theory of passive decay, attributes the changes in recall to changes in the brain tissue. Whereas the decay theory emphasizes fading and loss, the theory of systematic distortion attempts to account for orderly changes other than memory loss. These orderly changes are attributed to spontaneous changes taking place in the memory trace.

Evidence for spontaneous change comes chiefly from experiments on memory for visually perceived forms. When forms such as those in Figure 10-5 are presented, later reproductions are said to move in the directions shown. According to Wulf (1922), changes tend to fall into one of three main patterns:

10-5

Systematic distortion of memory: leveling and sharpening

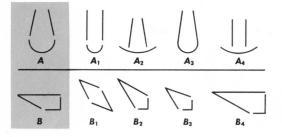

Several figures, such as A and B, are shown to the subject, who then draws what he remembers having seen. Some typical reproductions are shown. Two of Wulf's three tendencies are illustrated: leveling (making more symmetrical, closing in gaps) in A_1, A_3, B_1, B_2; and sharpening (accentuating spaces and parts) in A_2, A_4, B_3, B_4. (From Gibson, 1929)

1. *Leveling.* Figures move toward greater symmetry, smoothing out irregularities.
2. *Sharpening.* Sometimes an irregularity is the most impressive feature in a figure. If so, in successive reproductions there may be an accentuation of the irregularity, a process contrasting with that of leveling.
3. *Assimilating.* The figure tends to be assimilated to something it resembles so that it becomes a more "normal" representative of that object. These changes are well illustrated in Figure 10-6.

Later experiments have been unable to demonstrate that these progressive changes go on with the mere passing of time; that is, a reproduction made after greater elapsed time does not show a more striking distortion than one made almost immediately after the figure has been perceived (Hebb and Foord, 1945). Such distortions do take place, but it appears that they may take place at the time the figure is seen and first reproduced (Bruner, Busiek, and Minturn, 1952). Progressive changes take place with successive reproductions of the figure, but such changes

Systematic distortion of memory: assimilation

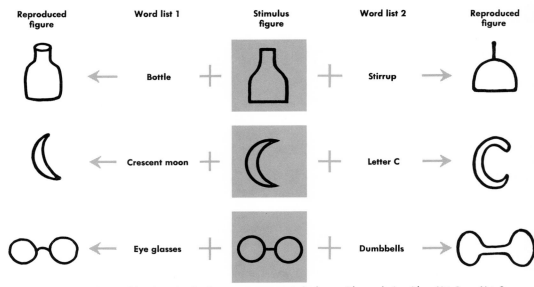

| Reproduced figure | Word list 1 | Stimulus figure | Word list 2 | Reproduced figure |

When stimulus figures like those in the boxes were presented along with words in either List 1 or List 2, the reproduced figure tended to be distorted in the direction of the object named, as shown. (After Carmichael, Hogan, and Walter, 1932)

may occur only because the later reproduction reflects distortions made in the earlier one. The following simple experiment, using a group of subjects, demonstrates this point: One of the subjects reproduces a figure and passes his reproduction on to his neighbor; the neighbor in turn makes his reproduction from the reproduction, and so on. One such chain of reproductions is shown in Figure 10-7.

In everyday life, we often have occasion to recall an experience over and over again so that opportunity for progressive distortion arises in the retelling. Experiments paralleling those on memory for form have been made with the retelling of short tales. The instructions specified that the tales be told in as nearly verbatim form as possible. One such experiment, extending over several years, revealed the following forms of distortion (among others):

[1] With infrequent reproduction, omission of detail, simplification of events and structure, and transformation of items into more familiar detail, may go on almost indefinitely, or so long as unaided recall is possible.

[2] . . . in long-distance remembering, elaboration becomes rather more common in some cases; and there may be increasing importation, or invention. . . .

[3] Detail is outstanding when it fits in with a subject's preformed interests and tendencies. It is then remembered, though often transformed, and it tends to take a progressively earlier place in successive reproductions.

[4] In all successive remembering, rationalization, the reduction of material to a form that can be readily and "satisfyingly" dealt with, is very prominent.

[5] There is evidence of delay in manifest changes, transformations being foreshadowed weeks, or perhaps months, before they actually appear.[2]

There is no doubt that the activity of recalling is productive as well as reproductive. Bartlett's experimental results do not

[2] Bartlett (1932).

10-7

Systematic distortion: changing reproductions

Each person sees the reproduction by the person who precedes him, and then shows his reproduction to the next person. The selected reproductions were chosen from a series of 18 that began with the original figure. (From Bartlett, 1932, pp. 180-81, by permission of the Cambridge University Press, England, and The Macmillan Company, Publishers, New York)

necessarily mean that the distortions must be due merely to the passing of time. The theory of systematic changes in the trace, like the theory of decay, calls attention to important features of forgetting. As explanations of these features, both theories lack convincing positive evidence, though neither may yet be said to be completely disproved.

The use of the expression *memory trace* in connection with the two foregoing theories requires a word of explanation. The memory trace is purely hypothetical; it is not something known or understood or something we can point to in the brain. It refers to whatever representation persists in our brains or nervous systems of an experience that is subject to recall. We must somehow carry a representation of the experience around with us when we are not recalling it, for someone who has not had the experience cannot recall it as we can. When we say that a memory trace fades or that something else happens to it, all we are really saying is that what emerges when we attempt to recall is something different from the experience that was originally registered. When the psychologist assumes the existence of something as a basis for his experiments and theories, he makes what is known as a *hypothetical construct*. This particular hypothetical construct suggests that the memory trace does exist and that we may some day discover its nature and perhaps learn thereby the physical processes responsible for remembering and forgetting (Gerard, 1953). Some psychologists object to such constructs on the grounds that they make *things* out of mere *conjectures.* If, however, the psychologist is aware of this danger, such abuses can be avoided, and constructs can prove to be convenient. See earlier discussion, p. 53.

Retroactive and proactive inhibition

A story told about Stanford University's first president illustrates a third theory of forgetting. David Starr Jordan was an authority on fishes. As the president of a new university, he began to call the students by name; but every time he learned the name of a student he forgot the name of a fish. Hence, it is said, he gave up learning the names of the students. Although the story lacks foundation in fact, it illustrates how new learning may interfere with the recall of old learning. This theory of interference with retention of the *old* by the *new* is known as *retroactive inhibition.*

A companion interference theory, based on the same principles, is that prior learning can also interfere with the learning and recall of new material. This aspect of the theory is called *proactive inhibition.* We shall postpone consideration of it until the discussion of retroactive inhibition is completed.

Retroactive inhibition can easily be demonstrated by experiment. The subject learns one list of items (list *A*) and then learns another list (list *B*). After an interval he attempts to recall list *A*. If a control group that has not learned list *B* recalls list *A* better than the group that has learned the new list, we infer that this new learning interferes with the recall of list *A*. The experimental arrangement can be diagrammed very simply as follows:

Arrangement for testing retroactive inhibition

Experimental group	Learn *A*	Learn *B*	Recall *A*
Control group	Learn *A*	(Rest)	Recall *A*

If the control group's recall of *A* is significantly better than the experimental group's recall of *A*, we infer that the ex-

perimental group's recall has been interfered with by the intervening learning of *B*. This is *retroactive* inhibition, because the *later* learning of *B* interfered with the recall of the *earlier* learning of *A*.

By varying the amount or nature of the interpolated activity (corresponding to list *B*), the experimenter can control the amount of forgetting of list *A* which will occur over a given interval of time. This effect is illustrated by the results shown in Table 10-2, in which the interpolated material most similar in meaning to the original list produced the most interference at recall, that is, the most retroactive inhibition. The following word pairs illustrate degrees of meaningful similarity: most similar—perfect-faultless; moderate similarity—skillful-expert; slight similarity—idle-unused. (Had the material been made even more similar, perhaps identical with the original, then the intervening trials would have given additional practice and there would have been no retroactive inhibition.)

If recall is tested after an interval of rest, without any interpolated activity corresponding to list *B*, some forgetting of course occurs. Can this, too, be accounted for according to the theory of retroactive inhibition? Perhaps, but only if we think of the ordinary processes of waking life as corresponding in some respects to active learning between original learning and recall. This extension of the theory of retroactive inhibition can be tested by comparing retention after periods of sleep and waking. If waking activity interferes with recall, then retention should be better after sleep, when less intervening activity has occurred. It is found, as shown in Figure 10-8, that you do forget more when awake than when asleep. You lose a little during the first hour or two of sleep, but after that you forget very little more during the night. These results have been confirmed by other experimenters. Newman (1939) found that the results of Figure 10-8 can be confirmed for rote materials but do not hold as well for

TABLE 10-2

Retroactive inhibition as increased by similarity of interpolated and original material

Degree of similarity	Interpolated material	Recall after standard interval, mean
Least	Control (rest)	5.42
Slight	Synonyms (degree 3)	2.04
More	Synonyms (degree 2)	1.33
Most	Synonyms (degree 1)	0.83

SOURCE: McGeoch and McDonald (1931).

organized materials. A subject who read a story before going to sleep could remember both the plot and many nonessential details when he was awakened. When he remained awake after reading the story he remembered the plot as well as he did after sleep, but he forgot more of the details.

We may therefore accept the demonstration that retroactive inhibition occurs, not only when formal learning occurs between initial learning and recall but also when ordinary waking life intervenes. Hence retroactive inhibition has a secure place as one phenomenon of forgetting. Can we go further and say that it is a *sufficient* theory of forgetting and that the disuse, or passive decay, theory is disproved?

It would be very difficult indeed to disprove a disuse theory. The nearest we can come is to look for a state close to suspended animation, and then try to show that no forgetting occurs while the learner is in that state. One of the more successful experimental attempts has been made with cockroaches.

The cockroach in this experiment learned to avoid a given corner of the cage; if it went there, it received an electric shock. The experimenters sought to find out whether it would remember what it had learned, and how its retention would be affected by its activity between the original learning and the test of retention. A very satisfactory rest condition was discovered. If the cockroach was placed in a dark, damp passageway, it would remain immobile for as long as 24 hours. Placed in the dry, lighted cage, it was fairly active; activity was increased by placing it on a small treadmill. Results were like those of sleep experiments with humans. When moderate activity intervened, forgetting occurred, with an increase in forgetting as the length of time since learning increased. (Forgetting was measured by the trials required to relearn the avoidance of the corner where shocks were received.) When the roach was immobilized, its retention lessened over the first hour or two, and then there was little further drop over 24 hours (Minami and Dallenbach, 1946).

The experiment gives additional support to the retroactive-inhibition theory of forgetting, but it does not, of course, disprove the possibility of some passive decay.

Proactive Inhibition. Another kind of interference between related learnings is

10-8

Retroactive inhibition

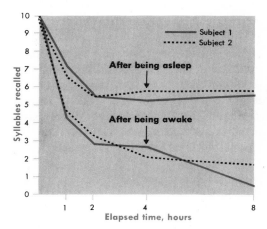

Forgetting during waking and sleeping. (After Jenkins and Dallenbach, 1924)

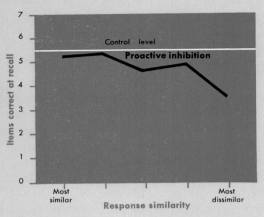

10-9

Proactive inhibition

Proactive inhibition as related to response similarity in paired-associates learning. (After Morgan and Underwood, 1950)

that between old learning and new learning. We may think of the following experimental arrangement for comparison with that used in the study of retroactive inhibition:

Arrangement for testing proactive inhibition

Experimental group	Learn *A*	Learn *B*	Recall *B*
Control group	(Rest)	Learn *B*	Recall *B*

If the recall by the experimental group is less satisfactory than that by the control group, we may infer that there has been *proactive inhibition*. It is *proactive* because it affects the recall of *later* learned material.

As an illustration we may cite an experiment of Morgan and Underwood (1950). Twenty-four subjects learned lists of paired adjectives, using the anticipation method with the paired associates, as described on p. 273. They followed the arrangement diagramed above, learning first one list and then a second list. After a 20-minute rest, during which they were kept occupied with puzzles, they relearned the second list. The

stimulus adjectives were identical in the first and second lists, but the response adjectives differed. Five degrees of response similarity were used, from very unlike responses (pairs such as *noiseless-sincere* in the first list and *noiseless-latent* in the second list) to very similar responses (pairs such as *willing-dirty* in the first list and *willing-unclean* in the second). The experimenters found that the amount of proactive inhibition increased from the most similar responses to the most dissimilar. That is, the most proactive inhibition was found with the most dissimilar response items (Figure 10-9).

While in most experimental arrangements retroactive inhibition appears more impressive than proactive inhibition, it may be that proactive inhibition produces effects that are commonly overlooked. Underwood (1957a), reviewing many previous studies of retention, showed that the use of experienced subjects tended to lessen the amount the subjects could retain. There is something of a paradox here, for it has been shown (e.g., Ward, 1937) that the more lists a subject has learned in the laboratory, the more readily he learns; now Underwood's summary indicates that the more lists he has learned the less well he retains. The failure of retention is interpreted as a result of interference due to prior learning, hence a form of proactive inhibition. When the subject is asked to recall the nonsense syllables that he learned yesterday, the more nonsense syllables he knows from the past, the harder it will be for him to select those he recently learned. The effect is so great that Underwood finds that a typical practiced subject after 24 hours will recall 25 per cent and forget 75 per cent, while if the subject has learned only the list he is now asked to recall, the figures are reversed, and he will recall 75 per cent and forget 25 per cent. In Figure 10-10 are plotted means from a number of studies showing how recall after 24 hours is related to

10-10

Interference of previous learning with recall

Each dot represents an average from one study of learning. In those studies in which the subject had less previous practice, the amount retained after an interval of a day was greater than in those studies in which the subject had learned many prior lists. Thus a proactive inhibition is demonstrated. (After Underwood, 1957a, p. 53)

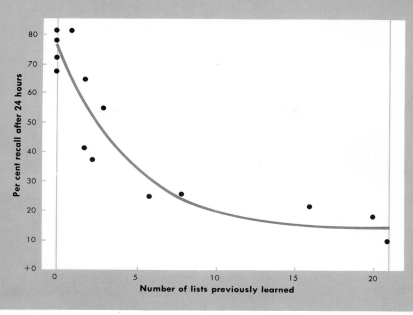

the number of previous lists memorized. The effect of prior learning upon recall is impressive.

CRITICAL DISCUSSION

Explaining retroactive and proactive inhibition

Although retroactive and proactive inhibition are explanations of forgetting, they are themselves in need of explanation. Two lines of theorizing have proved helpful, but incomplete:

1. *Intrusion of interfering items.* When the effort is being made to recall a list, say list *A*, some of the items from list *B* intrude, thus reducing the score. Some of these intruding items can, in fact, be detected, but they are not frequent enough to account for the total effect.

2. *Unlearning.* It can be assumed that when something new is being learned, something old is being unlearned. (This is the kind of assumption made in the Estes mathematical model, pp. 282-85.) In that case, learning of list *B* produces some unlearning of list *A*, and hence accounts for the poorer recall of list *A* in the retroactive inhibition experiment. Such unlearning should be less effective in proactive inhi-

bition, because it is the new learning that is later tested for recall. Hence according to this theory, retroactive inhibition should be more disruptive than proactive inhibition, as indeed it is found to be (McGeoch and Irion, 1952, pp. 432-47).

Motivated forgetting

The preceding theories of forgetting emphasize forgetting as a matter either of physiological processes affecting the memory trace or of interference between new and old material. Neither theory gives much attention to the person whose memories are under consideration or to the motives which his memories satisfy. This omission is a serious one; a complete theory of forgetting cannot ignore what the person is trying to do—both when he remembers and when he forgets.

Repression. According to the principle of repression, certain of our memories become inaccessible to recall because of the way in which they relate to our personal problems. The inaccessibility is due neither to faded traces nor to disruptive learnings, for the memories are still there and can be revealed under appropriate conditions. The theory of repression holds that the memories are not recalled because their recall would in some way be unacceptable to the person —because of the anxiety that they would produce or the guilt that they might activate. While psychologists are not fully agreed upon the nature of repression, the facts are as acceptable as, and no more obscure than, those cited in other discussions of remembering and forgetting.

The nature of the forgetting which takes place in dramatic instances of amnesia aids in the understanding of repression. The amnesia victim does not forget everything. He evidently uses a rich store of memories and habits as he conducts his present social life. What he forgets are items of personal reference—his name, his family, his home address, his personal biography. The beginning of the amnesia is often to be traced to some severe emotional shock which the individual suffered and from which the amnesia provides an escape.

Occasionally cases in psychotherapy give rather convincing evidence of repressed memories and recovery from the repression, of which the following is a dramatic, if unusual, illustration, for the memory is recovered in a dream.

Richard C., a skilled worker 40 years old, came to a mental hospital with serious depression and haunting ideas about death. As a child he had lost his mother under traumatic circumstances. About the actual death he could remember only being wakened from sleep in order to be taken to the hospital some distance away. When he and his sisters arrived there, his mother was dead. The mother's death had been very disturbing to him, and it was evident to the psychiatrist who treated him that some of his present symptoms dated from it. In order to help him recall specific events of that period, the psychiatrist asked, among other questions, whether he recalled the time of night in which the events happened. He

could not remember. That these memories were repressed is suggested by the information that came in a dream the night following this interview.

The patient dreamt that he saw two clocks. One was running and one had stopped. The one that was running said twenty minutes to three, and the one that had stopped said twenty minutes to five. He was mystified by the dream.

Because of the possibility that those clocks represented the repressed childhood memories, the man's older sister was located and asked about the circumstances of the mother's death. She said that they had been roused from sleep in their farmhouse about 2:30 A.M. and had driven to the distant hospital. When they arrived there about 4:30, their mother had just died.

Whether we accept the sister's version or the patient's, it is quite convincing that the times dreamed of were close to reality. Yet this memory was not consciously accessible to the patient, even when the psychiatrist pressed him for it. But the probing by the supportive therapist in the midst of treatment may have facilitated the recall in the dream.[3]

A number of experimental attempts have been made to determine whether or not repression can be demonstrated in the ordinary experiences of people who do not show dramatic symptoms of memory disturbance. Psychoanalytic studies of normal people suggest that repression is a very general phenomenon, but laboratory studies are not yet very satisfactory.

One study by Aborn (1953) may be selected to represent the kind of investigation that may be carried on in the laboratory. The portion of his experiment to be described concerned the incidental memory for the numbers used in a color-blindness test. (Incidental memory means unintentional memory, that is, the memory for something that one does not try to memo-

[3] Case courtesy of Josephine R. Hilgard.

rize and that one does not expect to have to recall.) Color-blindness tests are often arranged so that the color-blind person reads one number and the person with normal color vision sees another, or the color-blind person may see no number at all. To test the theory of repression, the subjects who were taking the color-blindness test were subjected to "ego-threat" by being shown a number of cards without numbers, with the implication that numbers should be seen by those with normal color vision. The threat was enhanced by having the subject fail on some presumably related perceptual tasks consisting of stencil designs. As an unexpected test of memory the subject wrote down the numbers from the color test cards. A control group of subjects went through the same procedure, except that the threatening experiences were not included. In the memory test the control subjects remembered more of the numbers than the experimental ("threatened") subjects. This was the first evidence that there might have been some repression. Another unexpected test was given two days later. The control subjects showed forgetting, as expected, but still did better than the experimental subjects, who remembered approximately what they had on the first test. Now the threat was removed, and the experimental subjects learned the true nature of the experiment. Without any further opportunity to learn, the experimental subjects recovered some of their forgotten numbers, and on unexpected tests two and three days later scored even better than the control subjects (Figure 10-12).

Motivation to Complete Unfinished Work. Another set of experiments dealing with motivational aspects of forgetting has been devised to test the memory for finished and unfinished tasks. A number of simple tasks are presented—making clay models, solving Chinese puzzles, doing arithmetic problems. Some of the tasks are carried to com-

10-11

Recovery from amnesia

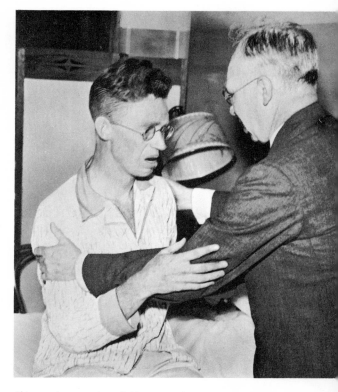

This man's memories of his personal connections begin to revive when his father walks into the hospital room. His memory is recovered without relearning by this dramatic reunion.

C. S. Borjes

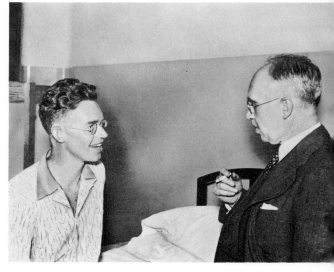

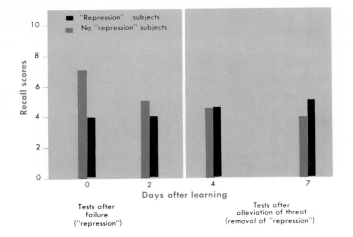

The recall scores are for numbers learned incidentally while taking a color-blindness test which was so arranged as to be threatening (through failure) for some subjects, nonthreatening for others. Those threatened are plotted as the "repression" subjects. (From Hilgard, 1956, p. 317; plotted from the data of Aborn, 1953)

pletion; others are interrupted by the experimenter after the subject has become absorbed in them but before he has completed them. After some twenty such tasks have been attempted and the materials are out of sight, the experimenter asks the subject to list everything he has worked on. There is a tendency to name more of the unfinished than of the finished tasks (Zeigarnik, 1927).

The results show that absorption in a task sets up a motivation toward completion. The unresolved motive to complete heightens memory for the uncompleted task.

The importance of motivation is shown by reversal of results when the experiment is somewhat modified (Marrow, 1938). The task was so set up that the subject thought he was helping to standardize materials for an intelligence test. The experimenter explained that if he saw the subject was getting along well he would stop him and give him a new task. Only if the subject took unusually long or was having trouble would the experimenter let him continue, so that he could be sure how long such a task would take. Under these conditions, interruption became a mark of success and noninterruption a mark of failure. When the subject had completed several of these tasks, he was asked to list what he had done. Now he

remembered best those tasks which were completed!

These contradictory results are best reconciled if we think of the selective retention as fitting in with the motives of the subject. In both cases the tasks remembered were unsuccessful, so that an achievement-motivated subject might wish to have another chance at them. This conclusion suggests that with high achievement motivation more incompleted tasks would be remembered than with lower motivation. A later experimenter found this to be true. Atkinson (1953) tested subjects with high drive for achievement and with low drive for achievement in an experiment similar to Zeigarnik's. Under conditions favoring involvement in the tasks, those with high drive for achievement remembered more of the incompleted tasks than those with low drive for achievement.

It is evident that a theory of remembering and forgetting must take account of motivation.

Concluding comments on theories of forgetting

Now that we have examined four theories of forgetting, what can we conclude? Each theory highlights something important about forgetting, but each is incomplete in itself. There may be some forgetting due to passive decay; at least it is well-nigh impossible to prove that there is not. However, passive decay is assuredly an incomplete theory. There may be some memory distortion due to spontaneous and progressive changes in the memory trace, but again the direct evidence is very thin, the objections many, and the theory (to the extent that it is true) incomplete. We can assert with confidence that some forgetting takes place through the interferences of new learning interpolated between original learning and recall. In other words, forgetting through retroactive inhibition is well authenticated. Similar results are found with proactive inhibition. Finally, motivational-emotional features, as implied in the theories of repression and goal tension, have to be taken into account as genuine influences upon forgetting. Beyond this we cannot go at the present time. We do not know the nature of the memory trace.

Circumstances Affecting Recall

We may arbitrarily divide the whole course of learning and memory into the three major steps: *fixating* the material, *retaining* it over a period of disuse, and *reinstating* it at the time of recall. Where is memory improvement most likely to come? Improving general retentivity—the capacity to remember something for a long time—seems the least likely. In any case, it is extremely difficult to find any evidence for changes in general retentivity with practice. But the other phases—fixation and recall—can certainly be affected. Of these, the act of fixation, of memorization, seems to be the more important. (We shall return to this topic when we consider efficiency in learning in Chapter 11.) As we think of improvement at recall, we shall also consider things that are done at the time of fixating the material—for example, recalls during practice as well as after, and practicing beyond bare mastery.

Recalls during practice

Recall within practice usually takes the form of reciting to oneself. Such self-recitation increases the retention of the material learned. Suppose, for example, a student has 2 hours to devote to the study of an assignment which he can read through once in 30 minutes. Rereading the assignment four times is likely to be much less effective than reading it once and asking himself questions about the material he has read. He can then use rereading to clear up points which were unclear as he attempted to recall them. The generalization that it is efficient to spend a good fraction of study time in attempting recall is supported by experiments with laboratory learning as well as by experiments with school learning.

A well-known laboratory experiment dramatized the value of self-recitation by showing greatest efficiency in recall when as much as 80 per cent of the study time was devoted to active self-recitation. The materials used consisted of nonsense syllables and short biographies. The results for nonsense syllables are given in Table 10-3. The results for biographies were similar but not as striking (Gates, 1917).

When the same kind of experiment was conducted with the learning of French

TABLE 10-3

The value of self-recitation in memorizing nonsense syllables

Per cent of time devoted to self-recitation (remainder to reading)	Per cent of 16 nonsense syllables recalled	
	Immediately	After 4 hours
0	35	15
20	50	26
40	54	28
60	57	37
80	74	48

SOURCE: Gates (1917).

vocabulary, the kind of task often met with in school, the self-recitation method was found much superior to merely reading over the words and their definitions (Seibert, 1932). Similar results have been found for spelling and arithmetic (Forlano, 1936).

One reason for the advantage of the self-recitation method in ordinary learning is that it forces the reader to define and select for himself what it is that he wishes to remember. In memorizing lists of nonsense syllables or any other material in which what is to be learned is already clear, the recitation method offers two other advantages. One is that recitation demands more active participation from the learner and helps to sustain both his attention and his motivation. In addition, recitation represents practice in recall of the material in the form likely to be demanded later on. That is, the learner sees if he can outline a history chapter or find illustrations of a defense mechanism, as he may have to do on an examination. The rule is to begin an active process of recall early in a study period. Time spent in active recall, with the book closed, is time well spent.

Effects of overlearning on retention

Something to be long retained must be overlearned, that is, learned beyond the point of bare recall. This fact is well illustrated by the rapid forgetting of rote items that can be learned in a single exposure. In testing the *immediate memory span,* items are presented once only. An item of the Stanford-Binet intelligence test measures memory span for digits read to the child one at a time. The task is to see how many digits can be correctly recited. For adults, the span is usually seven or eight digits. If the list is read but once and is near to the limit of the memory span, it is very quickly forgotten, for it is barely learned in the single exposure.

When you ask the information operator for a telephone number not in the directory, you have to learn the number in a sin-

gle exposure unless you ask her to repeat it for you. Unless you write the number down or say it over several times, it is hard to remember even long enough to make use of it in dialing. While it can be learned in a single exposure, it is better retained if it is overlearned through repetition.[4]

Overlearning also aids retention in serial learning, in which many trials are required to learn. In a study of memorization of lists of 12 monosyllabic nouns, learning was continued for half again as many trials as were required to learn, and also for twice as many trials as were required to learn. (If a subject needed 10 repetitions to learn a list of nouns, he continued first for 15 repetitions, then for 20.) Bare mastery was described as 100 per cent learning, adding half the number of trials as 150 per cent overlearning, and twice the number of trials as 200 per cent overlearning. The results for retention after different intervals of time are shown in Table 10-4. There is a great advantage for retention in a moderate amount of overlearning (150 per cent), with less added advantage from again as much overlearning (200 per cent) (Krueger, 1929).

The retention of skills learned in childhood, even after years of disuse, is not so surprising when we consider the amount of overlearning involved in such skills as swimming, skating, riding a bicycle. The skill is not learned only to bare mastery, but is repeated far beyond the point of original learning. Overlearning may not suffice to account for all the difference in retention between skills and information, but it is assuredly a strong contributing influence.

Periodic reviews

The advantages of periodic reviews are similar to those of self-recitation, for self-

---

[4] The one-trial ("all-or-none") learning to which Estes (1960) calls attention (see Chapter 9) does not necessarily negate the effects of overlearning. The theory states that there is no evidence of learning through repetition *before* mastery is achieved. What happens *after* mastery is unsettled in the theory.

recitation is in fact an early review. Experiments have been made on both the most effective spacing of reviews and the advantages of one kind of review over another.

In one extensive study of learning of sixth-grade children, one group of students was tested on its recall of a selection immediately after learning, while other groups had their first recalls (i.e., tests) after 1, 7, 14, 21, 28, or 63 days. In most cases a second test was given later on. The first recalls showed the decrease of remembered material with passing of time, a phenomenon that was expected from our knowledge of curves of retention. But the main point of the experiment was that active recall slowed the forgetting process, as measured by the second recall some days or weeks later (Spitzer, 1939).

The ones who did best on the second test were those who had reviewed the material (by means of the first test) *shortly after* they first learned it. For example, among those whose second test came three weeks after original learning, those who had had their first test immediately after learning did best, followed in order by those first tested after 1 day, 7 days, and 14 days. The suggested explanation is that the pupils had overlearned the material they recalled on this early test so that they could recall it again later on. When the first recall came too late, so much was already forgotten that the recall did not provide much overlearning. Hence those whose first recall was late did not do as well on the second test as those whose first recall came early.

Another experiment provides added evidence on the relationship between active recall, rereading, and ultimate retention. In this experiment, seventh-grade children read an article about making paper. They had one review, either a few days after learning or a week or two later. The effectiveness of the original reading and review was tested six weeks after the original reading. Reviews were of two types. One consisted of a test on what had been read, serving as a review

TABLE 10-4 Effects of two degrees of overlearning on retention			
	Mean number of words recalled		
Interval between learning and retention	After bare mastery (100% learning)	First degree of overlearning (150% learning)	Second degree of overlearning (200% learning)
1 day	3.10	4.60	5.83
1 week	.20	1.30	1.65
2 weeks	.15	.65	.90
4 weeks	.00	.25	.40

SOURCE: Krueger (1929). Subjects memorized lists of 12 monosyllabic nouns.

through recall or recitation. The other consisted of a rereading of the selection. If the review came early, the *testing review* was more beneficial than the rereading. If the review was delayed, however, the *rereading review* was more beneficial than the testing (Sones and Stroud, 1940).

The results of the foregoing experiment are consistent with what might be expected. Once material has been forgotten, it is better reinstated through relearning. If, however, it is still fresh, it is better fixed by recall than by rereading.

Rote vs. logical memory

In the earlier discussion of curves of retention, the implication was that forgetting consists in the mere dropping out of items, so that retention was scored as the percentage of original material retained. But memory is not merely a collection of items, some of which escape with time. Memories are of *patterns of items,* woven together with varying degrees of organization, and the success in retention depends upon how much organization is present. Meaningful materials, even though arranged in random lists, are

TABLE 10-5

Retention of number sequences learned with understanding and learned by rote

	Subjects * who reproduced correctly		Subjects * who made 19 or more errors	
	Class I "under-standing" (per cent)	Class II "rote" (per cent)	Class I "under-standing" (per cent)	Class II "rote" (per cent)
Half-hour after learning	38	33	10	7
Three weeks later	23	0	15	74

SOURCE: Katona (1940), p. 189.
* There were 29 subjects in Class I and 30 subjects in Class II for the original tests. Of these, 26 and 23, respectively, were available for the retests.

retained better than nonsense materials because of their greater richness of associative organization. When meaningful materials are tied together in logically related patterns, retention is further improved.

A simple memorization and retention experiment illustrates how understanding a principle of organization may aid in the reproduction of the material after several weeks have elapsed.

For Class I, a group of 29 subjects who were to learn with understanding, the experimenter wrote the following numbers on the blackboard:

581215192226
293336404347

Then he gave these instructions: "The numbers are not in random order. They have a principle. Try to find it. I shall give you one clue: both rows have the same principle." Most of the subjects soon discovered that the principle consisted of alternately adding 3 and then 4:

$$5 + 3 = 8, \ 8 + 4 = 12, \ 12 + 3 = 15$$

For Class II, a group of 30 subjects who were to learn by rote, the experimenter placed on the blackboard:

581 215 192 226
293 336 404 347

Then he gave these instructions: "In memorizing, the best method to use is rhythmical grouping. Therefore you should learn: two nine three, three three six, and so forth." He read the numbers aloud five times.

The results with the two groups are given in Table 10-5. The groups differed little on the test given shortly after learning. But three weeks later the differences were striking. While 23 per cent of Class I, who had learned with understanding, gave entirely correct reproductions after three weeks, not one of the rote memorization group was able to give a correct reproduction. The number of subjects making excessive errors in reproduction likewise shows the superiority of the understanding group (Katona, 1940).

It is obvious that a relationship or rule is easier to remember than the detailed illustrations of that rule. It is certainly easier to remember that the square of a number is the number multiplied by itself than it is to remember the table of squares. The student who understands his courses needs to rely less on rote memory than the one who sees the course as merely a collection of unrelated facts.

Learning with understanding has two advantages over rote learning: (1) it is more permanent, and (2) it is more applicable to new problems. Experiments have shown that groups learning with understanding have been able to master new tasks more readily than groups that have learned by rote.

Most of the memorization and retention experiments described in this chapter and the preceding one have dealt with *rote* or *verbatim* memory. If instead we consider substance memorizing, the role of meaning becomes even more pertinent. Results from a study on residual learning in college biology are given in Table 10-6. Terminology is forgotten in accordance with what we expect from our knowledge of the curve of retention, but the application of principles and the interpreting of new experiments show no such loss. Instead, there is a slight gain. This gain may be due to the influence of other courses, but then it must be noted that the other courses did not keep the terminology alive. The practical implication is certainly that efficient teaching will lay stress upon the understanding of principles and the application of what is learned to new situations, for such learning is the kind likely to remain more permanently available.

TABLE 10-6

Permanence of gains in three types of learning in college biology

	End of course *	One year later
Naming terminology		
Biology	100%	23%
Zoology	100	23
Applying principles		
Biology	100	101
Zoology	100	127
Interpreting new experiments		
Biology	100	125
Zoology	100	111

SOURCE: Tyler (1934).

* The gain during the course is set arbitrarily at 100 per cent. The scores a year later indicate what percentage of this gain persists. Scores above 100 indicate improvement beyond that at the end of the course.

SUMMARY

1. When we remember something we may show the marks of earlier memory in several ways. *Redintegrative memory,* or the recollection of a personal event, reconstructs a past occasion not only in terms of its content but also of its setting in time and place. Such rich memories have been little studied in the psychological laboratory. Much easier to test are *recognition,* requiring only a sense of familiarity, and *recall,* requiring a reinstatement of something learned in the past. *Saving in relearning* is another test for the influence of prior learning.

2. The course of forgetting has been studied chiefly for material learned by rote, or, as we say, committed to memory. The most usual form of the *curve of retention* is that of rapid forgetting at first, followed by decreasing losses. The form holds true for different sorts of materials, but the time axis differs. About as much forgetting of nonsense syllables may occur in a day as occurs in a year from the more meaningful substance of a college course.

3. Under some circumstances there is an initial rise in the curve of retention. A retention curve of this form—the rise before the curve begins to

fall—is called a *reminiscence curve,* without implying an explanation of "reminiscence."

4. Four theories that seek to account for forgetting have been proposed: (1) the theory of *passive decay* through disuse, (2) the theory of *systematic distortions of the memory trace,* (3) the theory of *retroactive* and *proactive inhibition,* and (4) *motivated forgetting,* illustrated by repression and the effect of goal-seeking (i.e., motivation to complete unfinished work) on retention. These four theories are supplementary rather than contradictory, and each calls attention to important features of forgetting. The memory trace is purely hypothetical, and has not been identified in the nervous system.

5. Most of the improvement in retention comes about through improved methods of *fixating* the material in the first place, and in part through *practice in recall.* It is doubtful if there is any change in basic retentivity, though little is known with any assurance about the nature of this underlying basis for memory.

6. The rapidity of memory loss is lessened by *active recall* during learning, by *overlearning* beyond bare mastery, and by *periodic reviews.* Logically understood material is retained much better than material learned by rote.

SUGGESTIONS FOR FURTHER READING

The classical study that introduced the experimental study of memory is Ebbinghaus, *Memory* (1885, tr., 1913), still readable today. The experiments carried out in the tradition of Ebbinghaus are well summarized in McGeoch and Irion, *The psychology of human learning* (2nd Ed., 1952). Many pertinent sections can be found in Osgood, *Method and theory in experimental psychology* (1953), and in Woodworth and Schlosberg, *Experimental psychology* (Rev. Ed., 1954).

Less conventional treatments are those of Bartlett, *Remembering* (1932), in which productive as well as reproductive memory is considered; Katona, *Organizing and memorizing* (1940), emphasizing the distinction between rote memorizing and learning with understanding; and Rapaport, *Emotions and memory* (1942; reprinted 1950), dealing with what in the text is called motivated forgetting.

CHAPTER 11

The Management of Learning

Most of the principles of learning and retention suggest practical applications, but it is never possible to move directly from general principles to applications. It is always necessary to take account of the setting, to try out the principles in practical contexts, and to make adjustments to fit the demands of special conditions. A drug may be found to kill the bacteria causing a given disease, but before this knowledge can be put to use, the dosage of the drug must be decided upon as well as the most appropriate way to administer it. In this chapter we shall examine the laboratory findings that bear most directly upon the problems of efficient learning, and that yield suggestions for the management of learning.

Economy in Acquiring Skill and in Rote Memorization

The many experiments on multiple-response learning have led to the discovery of circumstances favorable to rapid learning. When these laboratory findings are confirmed in more practical situations, they help the teacher to teach and the student to learn with maximum efficiency.

Massed vs. distributed practice

By massed practice is meant the crowding of trials or practice sessions close together; distributed practice implies rest intervals between trials or sessions. Abundant evidence exists that learned performances are better (for a given amount of practice) when practice is distributed rather than massed, although there are a number of exceptions to this generalization. Let us first examine the evidence that distribution is advantageous.

We have already seen this principle demonstrated in the experiment on mirror drawing (Figure 9-14, p. 268), where greater gains were made with one trial per day than with all trials in one day. The generalization holds for the intertrial intervals within a single session as well (Figure 11-1). In this experiment, the frequency of eyelid responses yielded in 100 trials varied directly with the interval of time between trials (Spence and Norris, 1950).

There is evidently a relationship between the advantages of distributed practice and the circumstances under which reminiscence

11-1

Distributed practice in eyelid conditioning

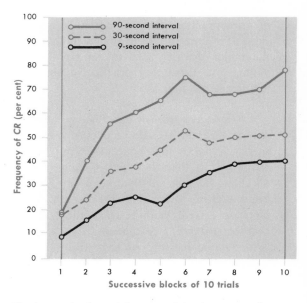

The longer the interval between trials, the greater the frequency of conditioned eyelid responses for a given number of reinforced trials. (After Spence and Norris, 1950)

11-2

Inefficiency of massed practice

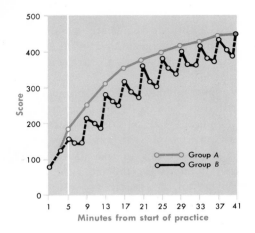

The first three one-minute trials (1st, 3rd, and 5th minutes) were alike for both groups. Thereafter Group A practiced one minute and rested three minutes. Group B practiced three minutes and rested one minute. Note that scores at each minute for Group B fell off within practice (solid lines) but increased after rest (dashed lines). (After Doré and Hilgard, 1937)

is found (p. 294); the two phenomena are alike in that they show an increased effect of prior practice after an interval of elapsed time. It is appropriate to review at this time the major theories used to explain the advantage of distributed practice, when such advantage is found.

1. *Recovery-from-Work Theory.* As we saw in Chapter 10, the recovery-from-work theory assumes that continuous practice is fatiguing, so that the subject cannot show all that he has learned and his scores are therefore lower than they would be if he were rested. With rest, all the learning that occurred has a chance to show itself in the actual scoring. An experimental illustration of this possibility is shown in Figure 11-2. Note that with continuous practice there is an actual decrease in scores, with recovery during the rest intervals. The theory does not cover all the significant facts, however; note that the subjects with

massed practice had more actual practice than those with distributed practice and yet made identical scores at the end of the experiment. Apparently there is some additional inefficiency in the massed practice, something other than the generation of a fatigue which can be recovered from.

2. *Differential Forgetting Theory.* This theory assumes that the subject learns both the correct performance and some irrelevant performances that interfere with it. But the irrelevant performances are likely to be less well practiced and so may be forgotten more rapidly than the correct and better-learned performances. If the interfering performances fall off rapidly enough, so that the original learning shows up before much of it has been forgotten, then there will be a rise in the performance curve (reminiscence) between trials. Plausible as this theory sounds, most of the evidence for it is very indirect and unsatisfactory (Buxton and Ross, 1949).

3. *Consolidation Theory.* This theory assumes that the full effect of whatever underlies learning takes time, so that allowing time between trials permits this consolidation or "setting" process to take place. The neurophysiological theories which assume that some sort of growth at synapses accompanies learning (p. 55) would find some support were this consolidation period demonstrable. The results of Doré and Hilgard (Figure 11-2) would be consistent with the notion that elapsed time was determining the course of improvement rather than the number of trials. Recent experiments by McGaugh and Hostetter (1961) have again opened consideration of this theory, which heretofore has found only scattered support and has faced a number of objections. McGaugh and Hostetter argue that if the interferences of waking activity prevent the consolidation of what was learned, then material tested after a period of sleep should be better retained than material tested after waking, as had been found by earlier investigators (see p. 298). But

11-3

Evidence for a consolidation period in learning

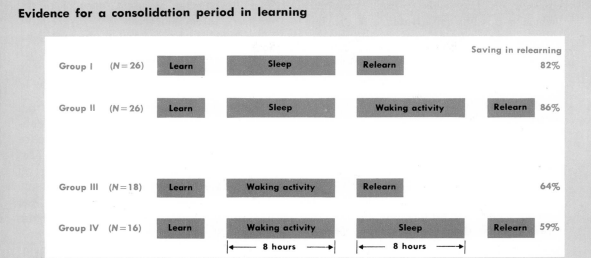

When sleep follows immediately after learning, retention is high (82-86 per cent), regardless of whether the sleep is followed by waking activity before relearning. When learning is followed by waking activity, retention is less (64-59 per cent), regardless of whether sleep intervenes before the test of retention. The results show Group I to have higher savings (i.e., retention) than Group III, and Group II to have higher savings than Group IV, with equal elapsed time in each comparison. These results are statistically significant. (After McGaugh and Hostetter, 1961)

they add another step to the argument: if sleep comes only after a period of new waking activity which is long enough to interrupt consolidation, it should not be of any benefit in retention; conversely, if waking activity follows a sleep period which is long enough to consolidate learning, then the waking activity should no longer be disruptive. Their results are entirely in line with their predictions (Figure 11-3), thus giving support to a consolidation theory.

The above theories all assume that distributed practice is advantageous over massed practice; if they were fully satisfactory, they would also have to account for the exceptions. The puzzling questions raised by massed and distributed practice have been studied in a long series of investigations by Underwood and his students (e.g., Underwood, 1961, and references cited there). Most of the experiments are on rote memorizing, sometimes using the serial anticipation method, sometimes the method of paired associates. Usually (but not always) distributed practice led to more rapid learning, but seldom, in these experiments, did it lead to better retention. Hence the generalization that distributed practice is a favorable condition of learning has to be stated with extreme caution, especially if it cannot be shown to have advantages for retention.

Other reservations over distribution of practice arise when more difficult materials are learned. In some kinds of hard puzzles or other "thought" problems there seems to be an advantage in staying with the problem for a few massed trials at first, rather than spending a day or more between trials (Cook, 1934; Garrett, 1940; Ericksen, 1942). This kind of learning calls for a varied attack, rather than a smooth-running skill or rote performance. It may be that massed practice leads to such variability, which is possibly an advantage in problem-solving but a disadvantage in serial learning.

Learning by wholes and by parts

Suppose you have a long poem to memorize. Is it better to learn one stanza at a time or to learn the poem as a whole? Early studies of this problem favored the generalization that it is better to learn by the *whole method* rather than by the *part method*. Later studies have usually turned out ambiguously, with neither method uniformly better than the other. The problem remains an important one, at least for those people who have to memorize the lines of a play or a musical selection.

One analysis of the whole-part problem proposes that all the following factors have to be considered, because they have all proved important in one or more experiments:

1. The more intelligent the subject, the more likely that the whole method will prove advantageous.
2. The advantage of the whole method increases with practice in using it.
3. When practice is distributed rather than massed, the whole method becomes increasingly favorable.
4. Material that is meaningful and unified tends to favor the whole method.
5. The total length of the material, the actual sizes of the parts, and the number of parts making up the whole must be considered. (There is no simple rule here, for it is quite possible that very short and very long passages will profit from the whole method, with in-between ones favoring the part method.)
6. A disadvantage of the part method is the time required to connect the separately learned parts. Methods that get around this difficulty will reduce the advantages of the whole method.
7. Following the separate learning of the parts, attempted recall may reveal more mutual interference among the parts with some materials than with others. Hence the disadvantage of the part method may depend upon the material to be learned.[1]

What general conclusion emerges from this? In general, the whole method is probably advantageous, but slavish adherence to it cannot be recommended. In the learning of rote material there is a well-known *serial position effect,* which means that the ends are learned most readily and that the hardest part to learn is the middle (Figure 11-4). Slavish following of the whole method leads to overlearning of the beginning and end material in order to achieve bare mastery of the material in the middle. It seems only sensible, therefore, for the learner to select for special practice the parts that are most difficult to learn. Remembering that the recombining of parts is a disadvantage of the part method, the learner should make a running start in practicing the more troublesome parts; that is, he should start *just before* a transition to the difficult material and should run *beyond the next transition.* Thus he will have practice in maintaining the whole while giving special attention to the part.

If the part is naturally separable from the whole, there is no reason why part learning should be disadvantageous. For example, in the game of golf, driving and putting are such separable activities that it makes good sense to practice them separately. But in swimming, the arm and leg movements and the breathing represent such a closely interrelated whole that one would expect a gain from the whole method. Thus the advantage of the whole method over the part method depends somewhat on how we define wholes and parts. In one study in

[1] These seven points are paraphrased from McGeoch and Irion (1952), pp. 501-07.

11-4

The serial position effect in memorization

In the memorization of syllables, it takes much longer to bring the middle of a list up to a high level of mastery than either the beginning or the end. The curves are for the levels of mastery indicated: 3 syllables correct out of a list of 12 syllables; 5 syllables correct; and 7 syllables correct. (After Ward, 1937)

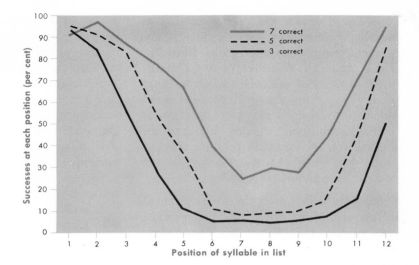

which the whole was defined as a unified pattern and the parts were unnatural subdivisions, the advantages of the whole method were easily demonstrated (Seagoe, 1936).

Effect of meaningfulness

In general, one can learn meaningful materials more readily than nonsense. But we need to say more than that a task is meaningful if we are to understand the influence of meaning upon acquisition. We may distinguish four kinds of meaningfulness that affect learning:

1. *Meaningful items vs. nonsense items.* As the results given in Table 11-1 indicate, haphazard lists of real words are learned more easily than haphazard lists of nonsense syllables, and nonsense syllables that suggest words are learned more easily than nonsense syllables that do not suggest words. The beginner who is learning to receive telegraphic messages does far better with letters that make words than with letters in nonsense order (Taylor, 1943).

2. *Patterned material vs. unorganized material.* If for random lists of words we substitute words that connect to make intelligible prose or poetry, ease of learning is further increased (Reed, 1938).

3. *Logical meanings and understood relationships.* Substance learning or logical learning involves ideas in relationship—such as the causes of the Civil War, or how to derive a formula for the area of a circle. Experiments show that memory for the basic ideas of a passage that is understood is more permanent than rote learning (Briggs and Reed, 1943).

TABLE **11-1**

The effect of meaningfulness on memorization

Material memorized	*Number of items recalled after 2 minutes' study of 10-item lists*
Three-letter words	9.1
Nonsense syllables	
High association value (100%) *	7.4
Medium association value (53%)	6.4
Low association value (0%)	5.1

SOURCE: McGeoch (1930).

* "Association value" refers to the tendency for the nonsense syllable to elicit an associated word in a verbal association test. All syllables in the 100% list, but none of the 0% syllables, call forth words under the conditions of the test.

4. *Knowledge of use.* Another kind of meaning is the "what-for" meaning, helpful in the learning of many skills, formulas, and procedures. Something may be meaningful in terms of use even though its inner workings are not understood. Many licensed automobile drivers know very litttle about internal-combustion engines, clutches, or fluid drives. A statistical formula may be used if you know what it is for even though you may not know how it is derived.

Each of the four preceding kinds of meaningfulness affects learning and has practical consequences for efficient learning. Learning can be facilitated by making all tasks as meaningful as possible.

Knowledge of results

We learn many things by paying attention to outcomes. When we shoot at a target, we try to aim a little higher if the last shot went too low. But learning is not quite as rational as this; we do not always use all the information available to us, and sometimes we use it without being aware of it. In one experiment, for example, subjects were asked to say words. If they gave plural nouns they were rewarded, while other responses were ignored. They learned to give plural nouns, but without knowing what it was they had learned (Greenspoon, 1955).

In the pursuit-rotor task the subject knows fairly well when his stylus is on the target, because he watches the target as it goes around and makes corrective movements when he loses it. Hence he is constantly influenced by knowledge of results. Even so, if he hears an audible click when he has succesfully remained on the target for an appreciable time, he improves more rapidly (Reynolds and Adams, 1953). When errors as well as successes are signaled, learning is speeded if the subject is told both the size and the direction of the errors.

These results can be applied to industrial tasks and classroom learning. The beneficial effects of knowledge of results have been shown in the industrial training of disk cutters (Lindahl, 1945). In this process the operator has to use his right foot and both hands in cutting small disks from tungsten rods. When trained subjects saw records of their own performances, they were able to correct their work accordingly. The group trained with this knowledge, as compared with a group trained without this advantage, cut more disks per wheel and broke fewer cutting wheels in the process.

Students in a freshman chemistry class who learned their right and wrong answers immediately after they took their hour quizzes during the term did significantly better on the final examination than students in a matched group who waited until the next meeting of the class to find out their results (Angell, 1949). Apparently, promptness of knowledge of results is important.

Knowledge of results does two things: (1) It furnishes information according to which mistakes can be corrected and performances improved. (2) It makes a task more interesting to the learner, and thus has incentive value.

Transfer of Training

One problem of economy in learning is the extent to which the learning of one thing helps in the learning of something else. This spread of learning is usually called *transfer of training.*

Formal discipline

An older view of the nature of transfer of training was often stated as the *theory of formal discipline.* This theory held that the mind is made up of faculties that can be strengthened through exercise much as muscles are strengthened. It was advanced in support of keeping in the high school curriculum such studies as Latin and Greek whose content is little used in everyday life.

In educational writings of a half-century ago, the argument that these subjects provide the discipline necessary to strengthen the mental faculties was advanced in such statements as: "Study of Latin trains the reason, the powers of observation, comparison, and synthesis."

The doctrine of formal discipline has been largely discredited by experiments. Some transfer takes place, but it depends much more on learning to use for another purpose the specific thing learned than on formal mental training. For example, the study of Latin does indeed improve the understanding of English words, but only those with Latin roots. It does not improve the understanding of words of Anglo-Saxon origin (Thorndike and Ruger, 1923).

Thorndike carried out an investigation with 13,500 senior high school students to determine the effect on reasoning ability of studying various subjects (Thorndike, 1924). By studying the reasoning abilities of students who had taken different combinations of courses, he found that those who had taken courses in mathematics and languages reasoned somewhat better than those who were taking cooking and stenography. But he came to the conclusion that the results were due not to what the courses taught but to the fact that brighter students chose the abstract courses. The differences in the results were slight, whatever the reasons for them, so that the experiment gave no support to the idea that certain studies provided mental discipline.

Classical theories of transfer

Two classical theories of transfer of training find support in experimental data: the theory of transfer through identical components, and the theory of transfer through principles.

Transfer Through Identical Components. This theory, identified with Edward L. Thorndike and Robert S. Woodworth, suggests that in a new situation the learner takes advantage of what the new situation has in common with earlier experiences. For example, the student who has had botany is helped in zoology because he knows how to use the microscope. These common components are carried over so directly from one task to another that the theory of transfer through identical components scarcely classifies as a theory of "transfer" at all.

Transfer Through Principles. The learner need not be aware of identical components for these to mediate transfer. But sometimes he can use a previously learned *principle* in a new application, with full awareness of what he is doing. The principles that the Wright brothers learned in flying kites were applied by them in building an airplane. Principles of reasoning learned in mathematics are equally applicable in logic. Transfer through principles was emphasized by Charles H. Judd, a prominent psychologist of the early twentieth century. He proposed that what makes transfer possible is not the objective identities between the two learning tasks but the appropriate application in the new situation of principles or generalizations learned in the old. The following experiment by Hendrickson and Schroeder (1941) (similar to one Judd had earlier conducted) gives support to his theory.

Two groups of boys shot with rifles at a target submerged under water. After they had become reasonably proficient when the water was at a certain depth, the depth of the water was changed. For one group, learning to hit the target at the new depth was a matter of trial and error. But the other group studied the principles of refraction so that they understood the displacement of the target under water. The group that knew the generalization made better scores when the depth of the water was changed, for their prior learning was now adaptable to the new arrangement.

To these classical theories we may now add a more contemporary theory, based on stimulus-response analysis.

Suppose that a subject has learned a stimulus-response sequence, S_1-R_1. Two clear cases of related new learning arise: learning a new response to the familiar stimulus (S_1-R_2), or learning to give the familiar response to a new stimulus (S_2-R_1). It becomes a matter of experimental study to find out whether the effect of old learning will be a help (*positive transfer*) or a hindrance (*negative transfer*). The next step in the analysis is to consider what will happen if the subject attempts new learning with stimuli or responses (or both) showing some resemblance to the original stimuli and responses, rather than with totally novel stimuli or responses. Then we would expect gradients of generalization to apply, similar to those studied in simple conditioning.

A well-known experiment performed a number of years ago was designed to investigate these possibilities (Bruce, 1933). The experimenter chose to work with paired-associates learning, because the stimulus material and the response material are of the same kind, and stimuli and responses can be made more or less similar at the discretion of the experimenter. The subject first learned a list with one set of paired items. The transfer effects were then studied as he learned a second list with specified changes. The main conclusions from Bruce's experiment are as follows:

1. If the new stimuli are similar to the original ones and responses remain identical, *high positive transfer* results. That is, learning S_1-R_1 makes it easy to learn $S_1'R_1$, where S_1 and S_1' are similar. This is the result that would be predicted from knowledge of generalization in conditioning.

2. If the new stimuli are dissimilar from the original ones but responses remain identical, *slight positive transfer* results. That is, learning S_1-R_1 helps in the learning of S_2-R_1, even though S_1 and S_2 are dissimilar. The practical meaning of this is that, if we already have a response in our repertory of learned responses, it is a little easier to attach it to a new stimulus than to learn both a new response and a new stimulus.

3. If the stimuli are identical and the responses are similar but not identical, there is *negligible transfer*. Learning S_1-R_1 does not help very much in the learning of S_1-R_1', even though R_1 and R_1' are similar. One suspects that there must be some interference due to conflicting response tendencies when the two responses are made to the same stimulus.

4. If the stimuli are identical but the responses are dissimilar, *negative transfer* is found. Learning S_1-R_1 interferes with the learning of S_1-R_2 when R_1 and R_2 are dissimilar. This result confirms the suspicion above; learning a new response to a stimulus that already has a response attached to it produces conflict, and hence negative rather than positive transfer.

Bruce's results have led to a number of further efforts to specify in greater detail the circumstances under which tasks will interfere with each other and those under which they will be mutually facilitating. Osgood (1949), on the basis of some additional experimental evidence, developed a three-dimensional model summarizing the relationships to be expected with various combinations of stimulus and response similarity. He did not attempt to assign quantitative values, but indicated the direction of results to be expected. In a test of his model, Bugelski and Cadwallader (1956) failed to confirm some of his conjectures. Apparently the matter is complex enough to require careful control of the set of the learner, the nature of the experimental materials, and the definition of similarity, before assertions can be made with assurance. Osgood assumed that a common model could be used to show the results for transfer and for retroactive inhibition, an assumption that Lindsay (1959) has shown to be faulty.

While these efforts have therefore not yet led to definitive conclusions, they show the advantage of a careful analysis as against broad statements about the nature of transfer.

Concluding remarks on transfer

The foregoing discussion of transfer gives some hints as to the circumstances under which transfer may occur—when it will be positive and when negative—but it does not tell us very much about the size of the effects to be expected under ordinary circumstances. Under ordinary circumstances the stimulus and response changes upon which similarities and differences rest are not usually clearly specified.

The experiments on transfer in practical situations permit the following summary:

1. Transfer tends to be less than the traditionalists commonly believed and often less than the learner himself expects. For example, gain in learning high school geometry from a prior study of high school algebra is so negligible that it matters very little whether a student joins a geometry class with or without the algebra prerequisite. In general, it is more economical to attack directly any activity to be learned rather than to approach it indirectly via expected transfer. That is, if the aim is to learn French, it is more economical to begin by learning French than to begin by learning Latin in order that Latin may be an aid in learning French. (This does not deny, of course, that knowledge of Latin is an aid in learning French.)

2. Conversely, the possibilities of transfer are somewhat greater than were implied by the early critics of formal discipline. How much transfer there is depends in part on the method of teaching and, hence, the method of learning. Good study habits and good attitudes toward school work transfer readily, for they are relatively independent of the content of courses. But transfer is not automatic, even when good possibilities for transfer exist. These possibilities have to be made use of skillfully by the teacher and the learner, as the following experiment shows.

College students served in an experiment to test how well they could retain six kinds of memory materials: poetry, prose, miscellaneous facts, Turkish-English vocabulary, history dates, and orally presented consonants. The 108 subjects were divided into three groups. One group (practice) spent 177 minutes in memorizing similar material between each test. A second group (training) spent 177 minutes partly in practice in memorizing similar material and partly in being taught certain principles of efficient learning, such as favoring wholes, self-testing, and attention to meaning. A third group (control) took the memory tests before and after a time period equivalent to the practice time of the other groups.

Results of the final test showed that the group that had merely practiced memorizing similar material did little better than the control group that had had no intervening practice. The training group, however, averaged 30 to 40 per cent better than the other two groups (Woodrow, 1927).

Improvement in learning how to learn, which is certainly part of transfer, came about in the foregoing experiment only when the practice period was used for training directed toward such improvement. If Latin, for example, is to be taught in order to increase English vocabulary, special attention must be given to word derivation. In one investigation it was found that special work in a Latin class on the derivations of English words resulted in a gain in English vocabulary twice that made by students in a conventional Latin class (Haskell, 1923).

Teaching Machines and Programed Learning

A great deal of society's energy is spent upon learning, that is, upon instruction in schools, upon teaching workers their jobs, and upon persuading people to adopt one or another point of view toward the solution of social problems. The aim of an applied psychology of learning is to produce as high a quality of learning as possible with the greatest possible efficiency. In recent years there have been many public discussions of the issues involved in the preferred methods of teaching reading, arithmetic, and social behavior. All of these concern the

Pressey's multiple-choice self-scoring machine

Ohio State Univ. Photo

The problem appears in the window, with one answer to be selected from four presented. When the subject has pressed the correct key, the problem moves on and a new one appears. The machine counts the erroneous answers. (From Pressey, 1927)

appropriate applications of the principles of learning in the arts of practice.

In the course of promoting learning there have been developed throughout history a number of teaching aids, in the form of both methods and materials. Among the time-honored methods is the recitation, whether in rote fashion by the group or in individual question-and-answer sessions. Among the traditional aids are the blackboard, the slate, the notebook, charts and maps, the textbook, the workbook. With the development of more modern technology, the motion picture, the radio, and, more recently, the closed-circuit TV have become important adjuncts to instruction. Many investigations have been conducted to determine the effectiveness of these aids. The usual finding is that there is instructional benefit from the appropriate use of each of them, but the benefit is not as great as enthusiasts would wish it to be.

Three kinds of teaching machine

A relative newcomer on the scene is the so-called *teaching machine* (Galanter, 1959; Lumsdaine and Glaser, 1960). Although still largely in the developmental stage, such devices are worth considering because of the way in which they illustrate principles of the management of learning.

Let us first consider three devices typical of the many that are now being developed.

The first of these (Figure 11-5) was developed over thirty years ago by S. L. Pressey at Ohio State University (Pressey, 1926). While originally developed as a self-scoring machine for giving examinations, it was soon applied as a self-instructional device. The student reads the question and chooses the correct answer; then he presses the button corresponding to this answer. If he is correct, the next question appears in the slot; if he is incorrect, the original question remains until he presses the right button. Because he knows he is right when the question moves, he has immediate information that tells him which answer was correct, and he learns this while testing himself. The machine counts the number of errors that he makes, so that his total score on the test can be read off as soon as he is finished.

Pressey's machine did not catch on, although a number of studies by him and his students showed it to be effective as a teaching device. A new forward push was given to the idea of automatic self-instruction by the publication of an important paper in 1954 by B. F. Skinner of Harvard University (Skinner, 1954), whose experiments on operant conditioning we studied earlier (pp. 258-65). Skinner and his students have prepared several different models of machines; one inspired by Skinner's work is shown in Figure 11-6. The items to which the student makes his responses are presented in the form of statements with a fill-in blank (see the space at the left of the machine). The student writes the appropriate word in the answer space at the right of the machine, then moves a lever which covers his answer with a transparent window and simultaneously exposes the correct answer for him to compare. He now decides whether he is right or wrong, and then moves the knob at the left to present the next item in the sequence.

Not all automatic instruction devices depend on the simple question-and-answer method. A quite different device was developed in the U.S. Air Force (Lumsdaine, 1959). Step-by-step film projection is used to teach a technician how to operate a piece of electronic equipment. A single demonstrational segment appears on the screen until the learner has mastered it. He then presses a button to bring on the next illustration, and so on until he has learned the complete operation.

Programing

The essence of learning by means of a teaching machine lies of course in the material to be learned, arranged in such a form as to be most readily mastered. Such a body of arranged material is called a *program,* and the advantages of a program can be obtained without a machine. The program is not intended as a review or testing device, as in some older forms of testing machines or workbooks; it is intended to do the teaching, that is, to do the sorts of things textbooks and teachers do prior to an examination. Hence a program must present information and must make it possible for the learner to participate by supplying answers that are at first *hinted at* or *prompted* before they are overlearned in further use. Hence the person who constructs a program has to have in mind the *organization of knowledge,* both its *logical* organization (what has to be known before

A Skinner-inspired machine

Will Rapport

A statement with a fill-in blank is presented in the open space at the left of the machine. The student writes the appropriate answer in the right-hand space.

something else can be understood) and its *psychological* organization (how attention can be directed to significant parts, generalizations made from prior information, and so on). Because these tasks are elusive, actual programers try their programs out on intended learners, correcting them as they go. A successful program is one that can be mastered by its intended learners with very few errors; if the material is well arranged, the correct learning takes place in orderly progression.

Some of the kinds of techniques used to furnish cues are illustrated in Table 11-2. They show how the student can be led to give the correct answer by the form in

A response is made to a *stimulus* (plural: stimuli). For the response "4," the stimulus might be "How much is 2 + 2?" Similarly, if the response is "Paris," then "What is the capital city of France?" would be called the _____. 5	stimulus
To the stimulus "hand," the student of Russian responds "ruka." To "city," he responds "gorod"; to "table," "stol." He makes Russian responses to the English words which serve as _____. 6	stimuli
In these pages the statements you are reading are the stimuli, whereas the words you are writing in the blanks are your _____. 7	responses
You are accustomed to think in terms of an "answer" being given to a "question." We can generalize more conveniently if we say, instead, that a response has been made to a _____. 8	stimulus
We learn what responses go with what stimuli through the process of forming "associations." Thus, the learner is said to associate "4" with "2 + 2"; to associate "Paris" with "capital city of France"; to _____ "H_2O" with "water." 9	associate
It appears that much of learning throughout life is based upon the formation of *associations* between stimuli and _____. 10	responses
Carefully conducted studies have shown that certain conditions aid the formation of _____ between stimuli and responses. 11	associations
Skillful teaching is not a mysterious art. Fundamentally, it consists of employing those conditions which are known to aid the formation of _____ between _____ and _____. 12	associations stimuli, responses (either order)

Here are the opening steps of a short program designed to introduce programed instruction to the general public. In the printed version the steps appear on successive right-hand pages with the correct responses on the following left-hand page. The sequence presented here begins with Item 5; the preceding four items have identified *learning* as the subject of the program and have shown that learning involves making *responses*. (By permission from Milton and West, 1961)

TABLE **11-2**

Some techniques of prompting used in teaching machine programs

1. Partial presentation of a word, with omitted letters to be filled in.
2. Similarity of ideas, calling for a response that is provided in a similar context, e.g.:
    Just as smoke rises, warm air will also _____.
3. Similarity of grammatical construction, e.g.:
    The higher the temperature, the faster the molecules move; the lower the temperature, the
    _____ they move.
4. Constriction of the range of response by grammatical construction, e.g.:
    The throttle is advanced just _____ the ignition is turned on. (Requires a temporal word
    such as before or after.)
5. Similarity of word roots with similar meaning used in a preceding "frame" or earlier part of the same
    frame, e.g.:
    A candle flame is hot; it is a(n) _____ source of light. (Desired response "incandescent,"
    same root as candle.)
6. Obvious transpositions, e.g.:
    Gross profit less overhead equals net profit; so to get net profit you subtract _____ from
    _____ .

SOURCE: Lumsdaine, in Lumsdaine and Glaser (1960), p. 535.

which a statement is made. A sample of an actual teaching program is given in Figure 11-7. The unit of a program has come to be called a *frame,* for it is the material that is exposed at one time; it may be a question, a statement, a problem to be solved, but in any case it has a definite answer or outcome if it is mastered.

As just indicated, the essence of the new self-instruction approach lies in the programing of materials, not in the mechanical form of presentation. Careful studies comparing programs learned in book form and by teaching machine have shown the two methods to yield essentially similar results. In one study, subjects closely matched according to intelligence and preknowledge of basic electricity (the content of the course) were assigned either to the programed book or to the teaching machine. They learned the course in the same average number of hours, gave essentially similar results on a factual examination at the end, and showed equal facility in applying the concepts learned to new problems (Table 11-3). This does not mean that the teaching machine has no advantages. Especially for research purposes

it is important to have the record that it provides. In the end the machine might prove more economical, insofar as the answers are written in the programed book and it is therefore destroyed in a single use, while the program can be used over and over again in a machine, only the answer tape being replaced. (However, it appears

TABLE **11-3**

Comparison of programed book with teaching machine

	Pro-gramed book (N = 28)	Teaching machine (N = 35)
Predictors		
1. Aptitude (Otis) *	49.3	50.8
2. Preknowledge	21.1	17.6
Criteria		
1. Time (hours to complete)	51.0	51.0
2. Facts (items in test)	54.0	52.3
3. Concepts (problems solved)	57.7	56.9

SOURCE: Holt and Hammock (1961).
* Standardized with mean of 50.0.

that some publishers have anticipated this problem by providing separate answer sheets and eliminating the answer spaces in the printed book.) For some subjects the movement of the machine and the supplementary clicks may have motivational significance. Many related issues are now the subject of investigation.

There are many possibilities within programing, and machines can be designed to handle various kinds of programs. Not all programs follow a single track through the material; another possibility is *branching,* depending upon what the learner does. For example, he may be given alternative answers to select, where he goes next depending on the alternative selected; if he chooses a wrong answer, his error is pointed out to him, and he is given help to avoid making that error again. If he has done very well on a number of questions, he may be given an opportunity to jump ahead, or, if he has made a number of mistakes, he may retrace his steps or take an alternative route to clear up his difficulties. These aspects are built into the program, and machines are then designed to make it easier to do what the program intends.

Principles illustrated by teaching machines

What principles of the management of learning do these machines illustrate? Lumsdaine (1959) has called attention to the following three features:

1. The learner is actively responding, practicing and testing each step of what is to be learned. The old adage of "learning by doing" is well exemplified, in contrast to the passive learning that sometimes takes place in the lecture hall.

2. The learner finds out with a minimal delay whether or not his response is correct, leading him either directly or indirectly to correct his errors. This we know to be important whether we refer to the importance of immediate reinforcement of operant responses or to the importance of knowledge of results in learning. In most of the devices the last response made to the question is the correct one, a condition that is also favorable to learning.

3. The learner moves ahead on an individual basis at his own rate. The rapid learner can bounce through the steps, while the slower learner can plod his way until he too completes the right answers.

There are a number of unsolved problems about teaching machines. Skinner believes that there is real advantage in having the learner provide his own responses (as in the machine of Figure 11-6), because this simulates more nearly the manner in which problem-solving occurs in real life, where recall has to be made appropriately with minimal cues rather than with the aid of alternatives of which one has to be recognized as correct. (This is the distinction between the short-answer question on a course examination and the multiple-choice question.) An advantage of the multiple-choice arrangement is, however, that the student has the right answer before he moves on, and this may be a help to learning. This kind of issue is resolved only by experiment, and of course it may turn out that one kind of program is better for one purpose and another kind for another purpose.

Dogmatism is out of place in applying principles of laboratory learning to a practical device such as a teaching machine. For example, the principle that we learn by doing is a good one, but whether this "doing" can be done symbolically or requires overt movements is a matter for testing. Several experiments have indicated that *writing* answers in a teaching machine may be a waste of time and may slow up mastery; in fact, in some cases the advantage can be shown to lie entirely in orderly programing, so that with the answers provided in the blanks of the frame, merely underlined for emphasis, learning is as efficient as with arrangements in which the student has to supply the answers (Goldbeck, 1960; Goldbeck, Campbell, and Llewellyn, 1960).

Another problem is that of size of step in learning. Whoever prepares the material for a program has to decide how fast to move. Smaller steps tend to take more time but to lead to fewer errors (Evans, Glaser, and Homme, 1959; Coulson and Silberman, 1959). In fact, the very small size of step that may be required for efficient learning is one of the "findings" of teaching machine studies; few teachers (or tutors) would have the patience to proceed at such a slow rate, and textbook writers often assume that once an assertion has been made it has registered with the student. In practice, the size of step to be used in a program will undoubtedly depend on many complex factors related to the specific learning situation, involving the kinds of learners as well as the kinds of materials.

We will undoubtedly see an increase in the use of programs to aid learning. The phonograph in music appreciation courses, the lantern-slide in art courses, the tape-recorder in language and speech courses are so common that we do not think of them as mechanized teaching aids. Programs, whether or not they are used with self-instructional machines, are innovations only in that they are being used in courses where heretofore they would not have been thought appropriate, as in teaching high school courses in grammar (Blumenthal, 1960) or college courses in psychology (Harvard), logic (Hamilton College), or interpretation of the Old Testament (Earlham College).

There is a gain to be expected from the programed learning devices beyond their practical utility: that is their contribution to psychological theory. There are already suggestions that individual differences between slow learners and rapid learners (as shown by other criteria) are reduced when they use these devices; if this should turn out to be the case, it will make a contribution to our understanding of individual differences. Many principles from the theoretical analysis of learning in the laboratory are put to the test in programing; time interval in reinforcement, intermittent reinforcement, distribution of practice, reward vs. punishment, stimulus and response generalization, and so on. Because most of the teaching devices provide an item-by-item measure of choices by the subject (whether correct or incorrect), the research possibilities are very great. Many laboratory learning devices have deliberately slowed up learning by using unfamiliar material (nonsense syllables, for example), and by using time pressure (e.g., two seconds between exposures in a memory drum). Heretofore we have been little concerned about the amount of frustration that these devices have engendered. The teaching machine, by contrast, seeks a high level of success, and by reducing frustration may enhance learning by those very pupils who have had the greatest tendency to give up in the earlier kind of laboratory study. It may be that new interpretations of learning will arise because of changes in the situation brought about by programed learning.

Motivational Control of Learning

Learning and motivation are inseparable. Any arrangement designed to encourage learning must provide for motivation as well.

Reward and punishment in the control of learning

Parents are responsible for training their children, teachers their pupils. Anyone who finds himself responsible for training or instruction, whether in home, school, army camp, or factory, has to make decisions about the motives to rely upon. Through

11-8

Intrinsic motivation   Building huts—and enjoying them—require no added incentives.

his position of responsibility he usually has access to rewards and punishments, and part of his success will depend upon his skill in using them to encourage the learning he wishes, with a minimum of the by-products that he prefers to avoid.

Intrinsic and Extrinsic Relations Between Tasks and Goals. In choosing goals to set before the learner, it may be possible to select those *intrinsically* related to the task rather than those *extrinsically* related. The relation is *intrinsic* if it is natural or inevitable. For example, the boy who assembles a radio in order to communicate with a friend across town derives a satisfaction inherent in the task when he completes the instrument and finds that it works. The relation between a task and a goal is *extrinsic* if the relationship is arbitrarily or artificially established. For example, a father may promise to *buy* his son a radio if he cuts the grass each week. The radio is an incentive extrinsically related to grass-cut-

ting because there is no natural relationship between grass-cutting and radio ownership or operation. As we go on to consider the use of rewards and punishments in the control of learning, we shall note that they are often extrinsically related to the learning tasks leading up to them, and that their disadvantages derive from the conflicts produced because the incentives are arbitrary.

The advantages of intrinsic motivation are evident from everyday experience. No special rewards for good behavior or punishments for errors are needed to teach a boy to ride his new bicycle. The learning and the end result have an intrinsic relationship. It is not always possible, of course, to make use of intrinsic motivations. A child taking piano lessons may not find the satisfactions of making music great enough to hold him to the task, so that he must be controlled extrinsically by rewards or threats of punishment. But if the individual responsible for learning can capitalize on intrinsic motives, his battle is half won.

Controlling Learning Through Reward. The rewards used to regulate human learning beyond earliest infancy are almost all learned incentives; that is, the goal objects are secondary reinforcers. In school such objects as gold stars, marks, and rank orders derive their reward values from such learned motives as the desire for status.

While all that we know about the role of reinforcement in learning tells us that rewards are effective, extrinsic rewards—such as prizes for excellence—may have some objectionable by-products, two of which are worth specifying:

1. A reward planned by an adult (parent or teacher) and arbitrarily related to the activity is a kind of bribe. It leads to docility and deference to authority rather than to originality and self-initiated activity. It engenders in the child an attitude of "What do I get out of this?" That is, the activity becomes worth while only for the remuneration it brings in praise, attention, or financial gain. Some of the problems of cheating on examinations arise when desire for the external reward outweighs regard for the processes by which the reward is achieved.

2. Rewards are often competitive, so that while one or a few learners may be encouraged by the reward, many are doomed to frustration. If there is only one prize and many contestants, the problems of the losers must be faced. Is the gain to the winner worth the price in disappointment to the losers?

It was suggested above that controlling through extrinsic reward puts the learner in conflict. That is, a learning task which has to be controlled by the promise of reward lacks sufficient intrinsic motivation to be carried through, or, in fact, the task may be one that is disliked and would be avoided were it not for the reward. One way of dia-

Barriers that prevent easy access to reward

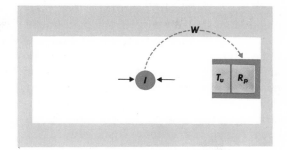

The individual *I* is not closed in by barriers as in the case of punishment, but the reward R_p is protected in order to prevent access from a path such as W which does not go by way of the unpleasant task T_u. The solid arrows show that *I* is in conflict because he is repelled by T_u while he is attracted by R_p. (Modified from Lewin, 1946)

graming this conflict is shown in Figure 11-9. The individual *I* is shown as attracted by the positive incentive value of the pleasant reward R_p, and repelled by the negative incentive value of the unpleasant task T_u. Here we have what is called an approach-avoidance conflict. (Conflict is discussed at length in Chapter 18.) Because the reward is extrinsically related to the task, the learner will prefer to take an easier road to the reward if possible. Hence the one in authority must place a barrier around the reward (shown as a solid line in the drawing), so that the learner can reach it only by way of performing the task. Mother must keep the candy out of reach until Mary sweeps the walk. The teacher proctors the examination to see that the answers are not found in an easy way.

Controlling Learning Through Punishment. Our folklore leads us to believe that punishment is an effective way of controlling learning. "Spare the rod and spoil the child" is not an isolated epigram. Social control by way of fines and imprisonment is sanctioned by all governments. Arguments have gone on for many years over the relative advantages and disadvantages of kind treatment (emphasizing reward for good behavior) and stern treatment (emphasizing punishment for error). The preference has shifted slowly from punishment to reward, so that the paddle is used less today than formerly in home and school, and the whipping post has disappeared from penal institutions. It is worth asking whether this shift has come about solely on humanitarian grounds or whether punishment has been found less effective than reward.

Evidence from psychological experiments suggests that punishment is indeed less effective than reward. Many such experiments were conducted by Thorndike, who came to the conclusion that reward directly strengthens the rewarded behavior, while punishment works only indirectly and does not universally weaken the behavior punished. The kinds of experiments on which Thorndike's conclusions were based are illustrated by the following experiment with chicks.

A simple maze gave the chick the choice of three pathways. One of these led to reward, to "freedom, food, and company"— an open compartment where other chicks were eating. Either of the other pathways led to punishment, in the form of 30 seconds' confinement. Records were kept of the tendencies to return to the preceding choice when it had led to reward and to avoid the preceding choice when it had led to punishment. The results showed that there was a distinct tendency to return to the rewarded path, but little evidence that punishment led to any tendency to avoid the punished path (Thorndike, 1932).

No single investigation of this kind can be conclusive, for there is no way of knowing whether the punishment was as punishing as the reward was rewarding. But many other experiments, with human subjects as well as with animals, lead to the same conclusions. Testimony going back many years from the biographies of schoolmasters and others, as reviewed by Thorndike and his staff (1935), gives nearly universal support to the contention that punishment is less effective than reward.

The argument against punishment in the control of learning rests on a number of reasons specific to the punishing situation. Some of the objections to punishment are as follows:

1. As the Thorndike experiment with the chicks shows, the results of punishment, although they may include altered behavior, are not as predictable as the results of reward. Reward says: Repeat what you have done. Punishment says: Stop it! Punishment fails to tell what to do and may simply result in emotional upset.

2. The results of punishment are said to be less permanent than the results of reward. Evidence from animal experiments suggests that the effects of punishment are sometimes primarily emotional, disrupting performance but not changing the learning that underlies the performance (Estes, 1944). That is, once the emotional state wears off, the old tendencies will be as strong as ever unless new rewarded learning has taken place in the meantime. This finding that punishment merely suppresses behavior through emotion but does not cause its unlearning may prove to be of fundamental importance. It is possible that a great deal of abnormal behavior is due to the repressive nature of punishment, so that response tendencies are inhibited but remain active in indirect or disguised ways because they are not unlearned.

3. Punishment under some circumstances tends to fix the behavior rather than to eliminate it, perhaps as a consequence of the complex acquired motives (fear, anxiety, and so on) based on punishment. Experimental evidence for this conclusion will be cited later.

4. The by-products of punishment may be unfortunate. Punishment often leads to dislike of the punishing person, whether parent or teacher, and to dislike of the ac-

tivity that led to punishment. This conclusion applies also to punished adults and accounts in part for the reputation of top sergeants.

There are many hazards in an excessive use of punishment. The parent or teacher who relies often upon punishment may be emotionally upset and may be expressing aggression by victimizing a helpless child. Children frequently act in provocative ways which exasperate adults, but the danger of injustice in punishment is great, and children are very sensitive to injustice.

The conflict in threatened punishment is diagramed in Figure 11-10. The individual I is caught between two aversive situations, an unpleasant task T_u and an unpleasant punishment P_u. In a conflict between two aversive possible outcomes the learner tries to do something else. This reaction is shown in the diagram by the broken arrow. The person in charge has to provide barriers to force the learner to face the conflict and not leave the field. We create these barriers in animal experiments by walls and roofs on the runways so that the animal cannot escape; we use high walls and barred windows for human prisoners, too. For children, however, the parent or the teacher usually provides the barrier. The parent sees to it that the child stays in his chair and eats or is punished. Punishment will control the child's behavior if the aversive value of the punishment is sufficiently greater than the aversive value of the disliked food. But before the conflict is resolved, the child may attack the barrier by whatever devices he thinks may be effective —stubbornness, nagging, crying, delay. The barriers in punishment are stronger and more pervasive than in reward, and the nature of the conflict differs in the two settings. Activities controlled by the threat of punishment may become increasingly hated, while those controlled by reward may become interesting and liked. Both reward and punishment may lead to resent-

11-10

Barriers that enforce the threat of punishment

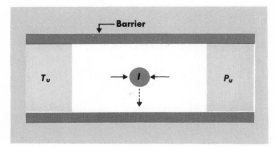

The individual I is between two negative incentives: an unpleasant task T_u and an unpleasant punishment P_u. He would escape the choice if it were not for the barrier. (Modified from Lewin, 1942)

ment of authority; without authority neither the threat of punishment nor the promise of reward can be effective.

The cautions in the foregoing discussion about the use of punishment do not mean that punishment is never serviceable in learning and teaching. It may be for the following reasons:

1. *Escape* from an unpleasant (or punishing) situation can be rewarding, so that the principles of rewarded learning apply; that is, the learner does then learn the technique of escape. People learn to come in out of the rain, to seek shade when the sun is too hot, and so on. Such learning by punishment is not, however, the kind of punishment we usually refer to. Punishment is usually something threatened, not present unless it is "deserved."

2. *Avoiding* a threatened punishment is also rewarding. The policeman is seldom a punishing person; he is much more usually a symbol of *threatened* punishment. How does a policeman control us if he has never struck us with his stick or placed us under arrest? We can explain his control over us by anxiety. If we drive too fast on the boulevard and see a motorcycle policeman in the rear-view mirror, we become anxious

Avoidance learning

FPG (Keystone)

A single strand of wire, lightly charged with electricity, keeps the cows in their pasture. The wire is a negative incentive; because the avoidance gradient is steep (see Figure 18-3) the cows are quite relaxed a short distance away from the wire.

lest we get a ticket, and we feel reassured when we have slowed down and he has driven past without stopping us. This reduction in anxiety is rewarding, for by conforming to the law we reduce our apprehension. The threat of punishment is increased by occasional punishment; we drive more slowly on roads where we have been arrested or where we have seen others stopped by policemen.

Experiments show that intermittent punishment (which parallels intermittent reinforcement) controls behavior more effectively than regular punishment (Estes, 1944). The reasons are not clear; perhaps occasional punishment makes even the nonpunished situation threatening and so regulates behavior through fear and anxiety. Fear and anxiety conceivably may control behavior more effectively than direct punishment.

3. Punishment may be *informative*. If the child handles electrical appliances and gets shocked, he may learn which connections are safe, which hazardous. A teacher's corrections on a student's paper are

punishing (because they reduce the grade received), but they are also informative about erroneous answers and thereby provide an occasion for learning if the student understands and corrects his errors. When punishment is an informative cue, mild punishment is as effective as (or even more effective than) intense punishment. Informative punishment can redirect behavior so that the new behavior can be rewarded. In the language of conditioning, mild punishment provides discriminatory stimuli rather than arousing a drive state such as anxiety. When the teacher says, "No, not that way," the student may be directed into doing the work correctly and receive a reward, "Yes, that's it."

Parents are often puzzled about how much they should punish their children, and yet most of them find that they resort to some sorts of deprivation if not to the actual inflicting of pain. The most effective use of punishment is the informative one, so that the child will know what is and is not allowed. Children occasionally "test the limits" to see what degree of unpermitted behavior they will be able to get by with. When they do, it is advisable to use discipline that is firm but not harsh, and to administer it promptly and consistently. Nagging at the child for his nonconforming behavior may in the end be less humane than an immediate spanking. The child who is threatened with some kind of vague but postponed punishment ("What kind of person do you think you will grow up to be?") may be punished more severely than one who is taught what is expected, who pays a consistent penalty for infringement, but who then is welcomed back into the family circle as a good citizen.

CRITICAL DISCUSSION
Influencing performance vs. influencing learning

A troublesome issue in interpreting the practical significance of motivation in learning is the distinction between *performance* and *learning*. A change in motivation may affect the way learning is revealed in behavior without affecting the actual learning. We met this problem in the discussion of latent learning (p. 279). A change in performance is not necessarily a change in learning. For example, under the influence of a drug a person's performance might be very poor, but this does not mean that he has forgotten what he has learned. When the drug wears off, he will know what he knew before. This issue arises particularly in the contrast between reward and punishment. It appears from experimental results that positive incentives lead not only to better performances but to better learning as well. Negative incentives, used as punishers, tend to reduce performance but not to reduce learning. Only careful experiments can determine the different influences of these incentives on performance and on learning. In most practical situations we do not bother about the distinction, because circumstances that lead to favorable performances usually provide for favorable learning. But the negative cases are more serious, for circumstances that inhibit unwanted performances may lead to troublesome repressions rather than to the desired elimination of undesirable learning.

Emotions and Learning

Emotional preoccupations as obstacles to learning

Remedial teachers who look on learning as an activity of the whole child and seek to help him satisfy his needs and understand his environment, often find that their diagnostic work must go beyond the specific difficulties in learning. The teacher may find the child to be generally immature, so that the tasks set him are actually too difficult. Or he may find that the child is jealous of brothers and sisters and that these jealousies affect his learning. The child may resent authority and thus find it hard to conform to the rigid and arbitrary requirements of spelling correctly. Sometimes the treatment of a child in a child guidance clinic gives little or no attention to direct remedial work. After certain problems such as parent-child relationships are cleared away, the school work may improve without any special attention to the school deficiency.

The following case illustrates how personal experience may interfere with learning to read.

Thomas was an eleven-year-old boy failing the fifth grade for the second time. Although intelligence test scores showed that he had the ability to do satisfactory school work, his reading disability held him back not only in reading but in other work as well.

His trouble started at the time his third-grade teacher went to the hospital for an operation. When she did not come back, he assumed that she had died, and his obsession with these thoughts interfered with his work. It was discovered that when he was five he had been very much disturbed when his mother went to the hospital.

In the course of interviews with a therapist he did some reading aloud. In reading a story about a dog, Thomas began making errors and continued to do so until he paused to talk about a dog he had once owned. He had loved his dog very much, he said, but had not been permitted to keep it. "I was afraid my dog might die without my knowing about it," he explained. "It is awful to be wondering whether someone you love is alive or dead."

His unconscious conflicts over problems connected with death and loss, occasioned by his mother's hospitalization and the renewal of these conflicts when the teacher went to the hospital, accounted for part of his trouble. Even the word "dog" appearing in his reading material was enough to activate a train of thoughts interfering with his reading. Once these problems were dealt with in treatment, he could read naturally, and his school work progressed satisfactorily (Blanchard, 1946).

Any learning activity has many meanings besides those specific to it. It may satisfy a need for orderly and precise work; it may be an activity carried on competitively with someone else; it may be entered upon as a submission to authority or in defiance of authority; its content may start fantasies or stir up memories quite remote from it. Unless these supplementary features of motivation are understood, failures to learn are often baffling. Unless they are understood, successful learners may achieve less than they otherwise could.

Anxiety and learning

The apprehensiveness and uneasiness raised by school tasks are familiar to most of us. Examinations are threatening, and often a student does less well than he might have done had he not panicked during the examination. Young children occasionally develop school phobias; they may become nauseated every school morning yet escape all symptoms on Saturdays and Sundays (Johnson and others, 1941). While these are extreme cases, most people in Western culture carry some burden of anxiety. What can we say about the effect of the individ-

ual's general anxiety level on his learning?

College students were chosen for a high-anxious group and a low-anxious group on the basis of a questionnaire given to a larger number of students (S. B. Sarason, Mandler, and Craighill, 1952). The 36 subjects in each group represented extremes on the questionnaire, which asked the student about his subjective experiences in testing situations: uneasiness, accelerated heartbeat, perspiration, "worry" before and during a test session.

Subjects received two types of instructions. Half of each group received "expected-to-finish" instructions. That is, they were told the task would be easy enough to finish in the time allowed, and the instructions put some pressure on them to finish. The other half, given "not-expected-to-finish" instructions, were told that the test was too long to finish (as it was, for no one finished in the time allowed). Hence the "expected-to-finish" subjects fell behind what they thought they ought to be doing, while the "not-expected-to-finish" subjects were reminded (after failing to finish) that they need not worry because nobody could finish.

The results for one of the tests, requiring the subjects to substitute digits for geometrical symbols, are plotted in Figure 11-12.

The conclusions that can be drawn from this experiment are (1) that low-anxious subjects do better in general than high-anxious subjects, and (2) pressure to finish results in improved scores for low-anxious subjects but not for high-anxious subjects.

The study reported above is but one of a number showing that anxiety level affects performance in learning tasks. These studies are so numerous that they have been the subject of several reviews (e.g., Child, 1954; Farber, 1955). Some of the major findings are:

1. High-anxious subjects condition more rapidly than low-anxious subjects.

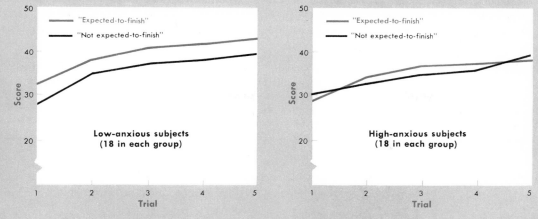

11-12

Anxiety and learning

Left: Digit-symbol learning by low-anxious subjects under two sets of instructions. *Right:* Digit-symbol learning by high-anxious subjects under two sets of instructions. (After S. B. Sarason, Mandler, and Craighill, 1952)

2. Results for conditioned discrimination are somewhat contradictory, some studies having found better discrimination among the more anxious subjects, others no difference.

3. With more complex tasks, high-anxious subjects do less well than low-anxious subjects.

Complications in the relation between anxiety and learning

While the foregoing account summarizes the main results of the anxiety studies in relation to learning, there are some further complications. For example, interrupting the learning with reports of either success or failure tends to depress the scores for high-anxious subjects but to raise the scores for the low-anxious ones (Mandler and S. B. Sarason, 1952). Also, high motivation conditions result in *poorer scores* for high-anxious subjects than for the same subjects under low motivation conditions (I. Sara-

son, 1956). There is a thread of coherence through all these studies: high-anxious subjects cannot tolerate any pressure at all, even interruption, without losing ground on complex learning tasks.

The studies relating anxiety to laboratory learning prove important not only because of their practical significance for the management of learning but because of the testing ground they provide for theories of learning.

Three interpretations have been offered for the relationship between anxiety and performance on learning tasks.

The first of these is *enhanced drive*. High anxiety is interpreted as high drive level, corresponding to hunger or thirst, and thus results in high performance levels on simple tasks such as conditioning where output varies directly with drive level (Spence, 1954; Farber, 1954).

The second interpretation is based on *irrelevant learning*. Under high anxiety, subjects certainly learn, but they learn some distracting things (e.g., worries) that interfere with their making good scores on the complex task. The overt signs of emotional activity while under pressure may be indicators of such irrelevant learning, which conflicts with high scores (Mandler and S. B. Sarason, 1952; Child, 1954).

The third interpretation calls upon *inferior perceptual discrimination.* Perceptual discrimination may be poorer under threat, as implied in the expression "blind with rage" (Hilgard, Jones, and Kaplan, 1951). Some support is given to this interpretation by the breakdown of both auditory and visual discrimination in schizophrenics under threat of punishment (Garmezy, 1952; Dunn, 1954).

The second and third interpretations may overlap if it can be shown that the irrelevant learning is what interferes with discrimination. However these issues may eventually be resolved, the studies point up significant relationships for further investigation.

SUMMARY

1. Experiments on sensorimotor learning and rote memorization suggest a number of arrangements leading to more economical learning.

2. *Distributed practice* is usually to be favored over *massed practice,* except for certain difficult problem-solving tasks.

3. The *whole method* cannot be said to be universally better than the *part method* because of the puzzling problems of defining wholes and parts in relation to each other. A satisfactory compromise is to favor the whole method but to use the part method on portions of the task that cause special difficulty.

4. *Meaningful material* is mastered more readily than meaningless material. *Knowledge of results* is beneficial.

5. Learning usually leads to *transfer of training;* that is, appropriate learning makes it easier to learn new tasks. The older theory of formal discipline (strengthening the mind through the exercise of its faculties) is largely discredited, but this does not mean that no transfer occurs.

6. Two classical theories of transfer find some support: transfer through *identical components,* and transfer through *principles.*

7. The circumstances under which transfer is occasionally positive, occasionally negative, can be understood by making an appropriate stimulus-response analysis.

8. Transfer occurs best in actual learning situations when there is a clearly designed effort on the part of teachers to make transfer one of the goals of learning.

9. While there are many mechanical teaching aids, the automatic self-instructional device ("teaching machine") is a relative newcomer. Combined with proper programing, it is an important aid to learning. Programing makes use of three learning principles: (1) active participation, (2) knowledge of results (or immediate reinforcement), and (3) rate of learning adjusted to individual differences.

10. In the control of the learning of another person, reward is to be favored over punishment. Reward strengthens the rewarded behavior, whereas punishment may not lead to unlearning of the punished behavior;

instead, the behavior may be merely inhibited, reappearing again when the threat of punishment is removed or perhaps appearing in disguised form. Arbitrary rewards and punishments both have some unfavorable consequences because of the authoritarian control they often imply. Under some circumstances, however, punishment as well as reward may aid learning.

11. Subtle emotional factors, based on the personal experiences of the individual, play a role in learning; these become especially evident when otherwise bright children find difficulty in learning special school subjects. When college students are separated into high-anxious and low-anxious groups, the high-anxious ones often do less well on complex learning tasks than do the low-anxious ones; pressure on them to do better may actually impede their performances, while such pressure spurs the low-anxious students to improve.

SUGGESTIONS FOR FURTHER READING

Many of the standard experiments on economy in learning and on transfer of training are treated in McGeoch and Irion, *The psychology of human learning* (2nd Ed., 1952), and in Woodworth and Schlosberg, *Experimental psychology* (Rev. Ed., 1954).

The teaching machine is a newcomer, but its literature is mounting rapidly. The two leading surveys are Galanter (Ed.), *Automatic teaching: the state of the art* (1959), and Lumsdaine and Glaser (Eds.), *Teaching machines and programmed learning* (1960). Teaching machines are discussed along with films, TV, and other aids in Schramm (Ed.), *New teaching aids for the American classroom* (1960).

The best single summary of anxiety in relation to learning is now S. B. Sarason and others, *Anxiety in elementary school children* (1961). Some interesting observations on obstacles to learning, chiefly in the age range of seven to sixteen, but with a few cases at college level as well, are reported in Harris, *Emotional blocks to learning* (1961).

CHAPTER 12

Thinking, Language, and Problem-Solving

Thinking is of many kinds. We think as we woolgather while waiting for a bus. We think as we solve a problem in mathematics or write a poem or plan a trip. Much of our thinking is highly practical, and we are more likely to think when we cannot operate by old habits alone, when thinking helps us to get where we want to go and do what we want to do. While thinking represents man's most complex form of behavior, his highest form of "mental activity," it is not so different from the other activities he engages in that we must stand in awe of it. We proceed to study it as we do any other behavior, according to its antecedents, the conditions that facilitate and impede it, and its outcomes.

The Nature of Thinking

The varieties of thinking

Thinking is any behavior that uses *ideas,* that is, *representational* or *symbolic* processes. When you eat an apple or walk across the room, you do not necessarily engage in thought (although of course you may), but if you try to make reference to the eating of something that is *not* present or to walking that is not now going on, then you have to use some sort of *symbolic* reference. Such symbolic reference characterizes thought. Thought can deal with remem-

bered, absent, or imagined things and events (as well as with those that are present); because it is symbolic, it can range more widely in its content than other kinds of activity. It incorporates present perceptions and activities into its topics, but deals with their *meanings* in a way that goes beyond the given present; hence thought reflects upon and elaborates what is given in perception and movement.

Though familiar, such a complex and wide-ranging activity is not easily characterized, for it penetrates all other forms of activity. Although we may picture thinking as the kind of process that goes on while the philosopher sits in meditation with his eyes closed and his hands folded, most thinking occurs in the course of active manipulation and exploration of the environment: it goes on in the shop, in the field, in the business office, as well as at the study desk, in the library, and in the laboratory.

If we try to sort out the kinds of thinking, we note first two major groupings: the relatively undirected and uncontrolled thinking that goes on in reverie and dreams, and the goal-directed thinking that goes on in reasoning about a problem. We may call the first *associative thinking* to emphasize the way in which one thing leads to another, in what William James called the "stream of thought." Although associative thinking often seems to be purposeless and uncontrolled, there are often directions (perhaps unconscious) in it. We may call the more obviously goal-pointing thinking *directed thinking,* because it reaches a sort of end point when its task is fulfilled. If we break down these classes, we get a further classification of kinds of thinking:

Associative thinking

FREE ASSOCIATION: sequences of words in which one word leads to another freely, without the usual restraints of grammatical or meaningful organization. Used in psychoanalytic therapy.

CONTROLLED ASSOCIATION: sequences of words in which one word leads to another, but with some restrictions imposed by instructions. The instructions may call for words that are *opposites* of the stimulus, *parts* of the whole named as the stimulus, etc.

REVERIE OR DAYDREAMING: free fantasy, wool-gathering, building castles in the air.

NIGHT DREAMING: scenes or episodes occurring involuntarily during sleep, remembered by the person when he awakes.

AUTISTIC THINKING: subjectivity of interpretation; the process in which belief and judgment are colored by the personal needs of the thinker more than by external reality. Includes rationalization.

Directed thinking

CRITICAL THINKING: the kind of thinking that goes on in forming judgments about propositions, whether this or that is true, whether or not this is the cause of that, whether this or that is the more probable. It may deal with other values than truth: whether this is morally preferable to that, whether this is more beautiful than that.

CREATIVE THINKING: the kind of thinking that discovers new relationships, achieves new solutions to problems, invents methods or devices, produces new artistic objects or forms.

The table helps us to sense the range of the topics within thinking. Otherwise the table must not be taken too seriously, for the boundary lines will turn out not to be sharp, and the classification system is therefore somewhat arbitrary.

Associative thinking

The thinker solving a problem has a goal toward which he is moving. But what of the person who is engaged in fanciful musing, whose mind is idling? What of night dreams, with their kaleidoscopic shifts of scene and bizarre actions? Day and night dreams illustrate what we have called *associative thinking*.

Daydreaming is a form of associative thinking, often rich in imagery. One thought serves as a stimulus to another. William James has given this account of a chain of thoughts, with his interpretations:

Thus, for instance, after looking at my clock just now (1879), I found myself thinking of a recent resolution in the senate about our legal-tender notes.

The clock called up the image of the man who had repaired the gong. He suggested the jeweler's shop where I had last seen him; that shop, some shirt studs which I had bought there; they, the value of gold and its recent decline; the latter, the equal value of greenbacks, and this, naturally, the question of how long they were to last, and of the Bayard proposition.

Each of these images offered various points of interest. Those which formed the turning points of my thoughts are easily assigned. The gong was momentarily the most interesting part of the clock, because, from having begun with a beautiful tone, it had become discordant and aroused disappointment. But for this the clock might have suggested the friend who gave it to me, or any one of a thousand circumstances connected with clocks. The jeweler's shop suggested the studs, because they alone of all its contents were tinged with the egoistic interest of possession. This interest in the studs, their value, made me single out the materials of its chief source, etc., to the end.[1]

James detected that even in the somewhat rambling thought sequence there was a hidden theme that gave it order, a theme built around the "egoistic interest of possession."

Some associative thinking, as in daydreams, appears chaotic, because topics shift and thought progresses in a seemingly disorderly manner; but, as James noted, underlying this surface disorganization are drives and desires being fulfilled in fantasy. When such thinking is highly personal, it is called *autistic,* from the Greek word *autos,* meaning "self."

Occasionally what seems to be rational thinking is actually guided by personal desires rather than by external reality. Such thinking sometimes goes by the name of *rationalization.* For example, the self-made man, in writing his autobiography, may recall how hard he worked and how carefully he saved his money, attributing his success to his own efforts and discounting the chance opportunities that may have been crucial. Whenever personal motives are strongly involved, we must be prepared to

[1] James (1892), p. 263.

suspect irrationality in a man's arguments. The discovery that so much of our thinking is colored by personal habits, preferences, and unconscious wishes has been a blow to the rationality man assumed for himself. He formerly supposed the normal mind to be rational and only the diseased mind to be irrational. Now he has learned to look for irrationality in what on the surface appears to be the most rational conduct.

Modern psychology does not deny the old distinction between the rational and the irrational, nor does it deny that much of man's conduct is genuinely rational. Man reasons constantly about himself and his environment, but he has to be on guard for behavior that reveals his self-deceptive mechanisms.

Dreams as associative thinking

The thought processes that go on in the dreams of sleep are usually primitive and uncritical. The dreamer tolerates animals that talk and people who fly without mechanical assistance. Dreams that clearly solve problems upon which the dreamer has been working do occur, but they are rare.

One of the primitive mechanisms of the dream is the play on words, or the dream pun. For example, a sister named Katherine, called Kitty, may appear in the dream in the form of a kitten. To take another example, a college student reported a dream in which he was driving in a car, trying to keep an appointment. He was disturbed to find that he was driving in a circle, forever returning to a bridge that he had crossed before. His immediate association, shamefacedly admitted, was that he was worried because he had been playing so much bridge that it was interfering with his studies.

As in other instances of uncontrolled association, much of the content of dreams reflects simple associative learning. It

comes from the previous day, from what the individual was thinking about before retiring. Some of it comes from immediate sensory stimulation. The sense impression may be incorporated into a story: if his hair is pulled, the dreamer may dream he is being scalped; if the covers are disturbed, he may dream that he is freezing in mountain snow; if the alarm rings but does not awaken him, he may hear a fire engine on its way to a fire.

Freud opened a new era of dream interpretation by pointing out that dreams were not as aimless and senseless as they appeared but were usually (if not always) wish-fulfilling. Because the wishes of the dream come from the sleeper's unconscious, he said, and may not be acceptable to him, they are disguised. Hence Freud distinguished between the *manifest* content of the dream and its *latent* content. The manifest content is what actually goes on in the dream—its characters and what they say and do. The latent content is what the dream implies about the wishes of the dreamer.

The source of the manifest content of a dream can often be traced to events of the day prior to the dream. The important events may have been "registered" even though their perception was not fully conscious, as the following experimental report illustrates.

A psychiatrist lecturing to a group of other psychiatrists about experiments on the relationship between perception and dreams illustrated his lecture by presenting with a tachistoscope a brief exposure of the picture labeled "The Three Kings" (Figure 12-1A). (He had used the picture to elicit dreams from patients.) The exposure of 1/100 of a second was not sufficient for a clear perception of the picture. One of the physicians present at the lecture later reported his own experiences as follows.

When the picture was exposed, he saw something that looked to him like Cam-

12-1

Perceptual source and resulting dream picture

A. The picture exposed for 1/100 second—"The Three Kings."

B. What the subject saw—three Cambodian temples.

C. The subject's dream—a desert scene, shooting a movie.

D. The perception and dream combined.

Courtesy Dr. Charles Fisher

bodian temple ruins in a jungle. Figure 12-1B is a drawing of what he saw.

The night following the lecture he had a dream, described in his own words as follows:

> There was an outcropping of rock, a little hill about 20 feet high, in a desert area. The hill was fairly level, but on the left one particular rock was standing detached and a little higher than the others. The people were standing on the sloping area; they were wearing blue shorts and blue short-sleeved shirts.[2] A sequence of film was being made and characters were fleeing across the desert, running up over the hill while being shot at. One of the people, myself, is aware that the bullet is a real one and not a blank. The bullet struck in the middle of the hill, between the two people. I am one of the two people on the slope. A whole camera crew was behind us shooting the picture.[3]

The subject illustrated this dream by drawing a picture (Figure 12-1C). The dot between the two men shows where the bullet struck. Without attempting to interpret the latent content of the dream, we can find sources of the *manifest* content in the picture that he had seen at the lecture and in the circumstances of the lecture. If his two drawings (immediate recall and dream, Figures B and C) are combined, the whole (Figure 12-1D) bears a strong resemblance to the original picture (A).

Some of the other details, such as the cameramen, may well reflect the fact that in the lecture the picture was projected from behind. The sudden brief projection of the picture may have become translated into the gunshot in the dream. When shown the original picture, the subject was able to confirm many of the relationships that had been inferred from his pictures and the accounts of what he saw.

The following dream and a typical Freudian interpretation suggest the complex processes that go on in the kind of thinking we call dreaming.

A middle-aged German businessman sought treatment for a severe depression accompanied by suicidal impulses. The depression developed a year and a half after his return from military service as an officer in the first World War, when he was confronted with the task of assuming civilian responsibilities. Early in his treatment he reported the following dream:

> I am taking a walk with one of the ranking officers of the Russian army and become aware that it is the Czar. Suddenly a stranger appears with a sword and wants to kill the Czar. I wish to intervene to save the Czar, but it is too late. The Czar is killed.

The patient associated the Czar with the fact that in Russian the Czar is called "little father." He connected the officer in the dream with one of his war experiences. During a lull in operations the opposing forces agreed for a period not to shoot at each other from the closely adjoining trenches. The soldiers could see each other, even knew each other by name and sight. On one occasion the patient violated the agreement, which appeared to him "strange" because in normal life "he wouldn't kill a fly." He vindicated his cruelty by the thought that the Russians were prepared to kill the wives and children of their enemies.

When asked to associate with the word "strange," he hesitated. Nothing came to his mind, and he stated with annoyance that he did not know who the stranger was. He was then told that the stranger probably meant the strange part of his own personality which had committed the murder. It was pointed out to him that he used the word "strange" when he described how unlike his naturally kind character it was to shoot at the Russians. The patient protested energetically and said, "How could it be myself when in the dream I try to save the Czar?" It was then explained to him that he was the author of the dream and if he had wanted to, he could have saved the Czar. Intellectually the point became clear, and he later produced memories in which hostile feelings to his father were recalled.[4]

The manifest content of the dream is the story of the dream: the threat on the Czar's

---

[2] The original picture of "The Three Kings" was in color, with blue sky, clay-colored rocks, and the men dressed in blue shirts and trousers.

[3] Fisher (1954).

[4] Alexander (1948), pp. 161-62.

life and the unsuccessful rescue attempt. But the dreamer has built into this disguised manifest content a great many thoughts and impulses from his past and his present. The Czar may be a disguise not only for the Russian soldier he once shot but also for his own father, as well as for the analyst who is now in a father's role toward him. These additional interpretations are not, of course, evident from the brief sketch just quoted. Dreams tend to have themes and, when the themes are understood, they tell the trained analyst something of the dreamer's motives.

The experimental study of dreaming, a field that was slow in opening up, has been given new impetus by the discovery that the moment of dreaming can be detected while the dreamer sleeps. Two main indicators are used: (1) the *electroencephalogram* (EEG), an electrical record obtained from the scalp, from which depth of sleep can be inferred, and (2) *eye movements* occurring under the closed eyelids, also detectible electrically (Dement and Kleitman, 1957). When these indicators show light sleep accompanied by eye movements, and the person is awakened, he almost invariably reports he has just been dreaming. Thus interesting new information has been forthcoming on the amount of dreaming that occurs and on the length of dreams. For example, it has been found that dreaming occurs during about 20 per cent of sleeping time. Most of this dreaming is unremembered upon waking. An interesting suggestion, bearing indirectly on the Freudian theory that dreams serve a purpose, is that if a person is *deprived* of dreams by being wakened when he begins to dream, he makes up\ for it by dreaming more on the following nights. It is, of course, necessary to do controlled experimentation by waking the same number of times *between* dreams. If one is wakened between dreams, there is none of the build-up of dreams on the next night (Dement, 1960).

Directed thinking

In contrast to the associative type of thinking, in which one thing leads to another without any specific goal or end point of thinking, we have *directed thinking,* in which we seek an answer, try to solve a problem, or create something that meets acceptable standards. Although any classification in this field is somewhat arbitrary, it is convenient to distinguish between critical thinking and creative thinking.

Critical thinking is the kind that is used to scrutinize an argument to determine whether or not it is sound. We look for erroneous thinking, as in logical fallacies. Formal logic is a special discipline concerned with the rules of critical thinking. Logic and psychology differ in that logic deals with formal rules (as a special kind of mathematics), while psychology deals with the foibles of the thinker, who may not follow the rules even though he understands them. But the logician is, of course, also aware of the thinker, and when he speaks of an *argumentum ad hominem* ("argument to the man") he recognizes the psychological tendency to evaluate an argument in terms of the estimate of the person who makes it rather than in terms of its intrinsic soundness.

The manner in which a psychologist can contribute to the study of logical thinking, and the fallacies into which the thinker falls, can be illustrated by studies of what have been called *atmosphere effects,* that is, the context in which a proposition occurs (Woodworth and Sells, 1935). Consider the following set of statements set up in the form of a syllogism:

All Mongolians have slant eyes.
The Chinese have slant eyes.
Therefore, the Chinese are Mongolians.

Is this logically true or false? Many subjects are trapped into calling it logically true because it is substantively true, i.e., they know that Chinese are called Mongolians. The absurdity of the argument can easily be pointed out by using other ingredients fitted into the same pattern:

> All women have eyes.
> American men have eyes.
> Therefore, American men are women.

An interesting question concerns the possibility of overcoming the misleading atmosphere effect by using abstract symbols:

> All x's are y's.
> All z's are y's.
> Therefore, all z's are x's.

Under some circumstances converting the statements into an abstract form is more advantageous, while at other times the concrete material helps.

For example, consider the form:

> Some x's are y's.
> All z's are x's.
> Therefore, some z's are y's.

In the abstract form, Woodworth and Sells found that there is a tendency to assert that this is a true argument, although in concrete form the fallacy is immediately detected:

> Some boats on the river are sailboats.
> All of Bob's boats are on the river.
> Therefore, some of Bob's boats are sailboats.

The abstract form has the advantage of overcoming the atmosphere effect of knowledge that may be true but inconsistent with the logic form, while the concrete form has the advantage of providing a way to test conclusions that may be incompatible with reality, and hence identifying the source of the difficulty.

Creative thinking uses the skills of critical thinking, not to review an argument but to produce something that is both novel and valuable. The creative act involves the discovery of something previously unknown, the invention of something that serves a purpose, or the creation of something satisfying in the field of literature, art, or music. We shall return to its problems later in this chapter.

Symbols, Language, and Thought

Symbols and meaning

When we said that thought was symbolic (p. 336), we did not try to define a symbol but merely indicated that symbolic thought could range widely in its reference to things present, absent, or imagined. The main point was that thought could refer to something by means of a *symbol* that *stands for* something. The word *book* is a symbol that stands for printed pages within a firm cover —the object called a book—but of course the symbol is not the book. When we say what the word *book* means or signifies, we imply that it refers to something not itself. We can think about the real books on the shelves, and talk about them through the use of language symbols, among which the word *book* is one. Words are thus very important components of our *symbol system*. When something has a name, it is much easier to refer to it in language. Language symbols can refer to all manner of things, with various degrees of concreteness; but they always refer to something else, even though the something else may not be a thing, such as a book, but perhaps an action, such as *rising,* or an evaluation, such as *beautiful.*

Symbols are not limited to the familiar language of words. There are other symbolic languages, such as those of modern logic or of mathematics. There are also many concrete symbols: a stop sign, a cross on a church, a musical note, a red flag, a paper dollar. Symbols always convey meanings through reference beyond themselves; that is, as symbols, they stand for something else. Of course we can talk about the symbols themselves. We can talk about the spelling of a word or the painting of a sign. When we do, we use symbols to refer to other symbols.

It is not surprising, in view of the power of symbols in communication, that there is an intimacy between language and thought.

We think in symbols; because language is a rich symbolic process, much thinking goes on in terms of language.

A symbol conveys *meaning*. It provides information about some object or event to which it refers and thereby suggests appropriate action to the person who perceives it. Symbolic stimuli thus differ from stimuli in general in that the symbolic stimuli produce reactions appropriate to some stimulus *other than themselves*. The sign POISON alerts to danger, but the danger does not reside in the sign itself. A sign STOP arrests movement, without itself being a barricade or hazard. The fact that signs and words carry meaning is so familiar that it is a little surprising to find many theoretical disputes over what constitutes meaning and over the relationship between the symbol and its meaning.

The problem of meaning would not be very difficult if all symbols pointed only to specific things or actions, such as names of objects ("table," "pencil") or specific directions ("turn right," "no parking"). Such meanings are called *denotative*. They specify something to which you can point and are alike to all who can comprehend them. But there are other kinds of meaning, called *connotative*, which accompany the denotative meanings of many words; connotations are emotional, usually expressing some kind of evaluation or preference and varying from one person to another. A word such as "beatnik" may refer to a specific group of nonconformists in our culture, but it adds the connotative meanings of "beaten down" and "alien." The problems of connotative meaning are harder to get at than those of denotative meaning and are more interesting psychologically. Many quarrels and misunderstandings arise because the words people use have different connotations for one person than for another.

In order to pin down connotative meanings somewhat more precisely, Osgood (1952, 1954) developed a method of measurement that he called the *semantic differential*. He called it "semantic" because it has to do with meaning, and "differential" because the method provides several different dimensions of meaning.

Despite individual differences in connotations, a fairly homogeneous group of people tends to have similar connotations for familiar words. For example, what distinctions in connotation do the words *good* and *nice* have for American college students? By using his method, Osgood found that "good" had slightly male overtones and "nice" female ones. To express simple approval the nearly equivalent statements for the two sexes would be: "He's a good man," "She's a nice girl." It does not seem rational to assign sex overtones to simple words such as "good" and "nice," but connotative meanings are not strictly rational.

To go about finding the connotations of a word, Osgood asked the subject to rate the word according to a number of adjective pairs; one example is the pair strong-weak. One member of the adjective pair was placed at one end of a 7-point scale, the other member at the opposite end. Then the subject indicated the direction and intensity of his judgment by rating the word under study at some point along this scale. In Figure 12-2 are illustrations of the way such scale values were assigned by students judging the word "polite." Pooled judgments of two groups appear on the plot, and their interpretations of the meaning of "polite" turn out to be very much alike, even though the adjectives used have little to do with the denotative meaning of politeness.

The next step in arriving at the semantic differential is to simplify the scales into more basic dimensions. In his preliminary work, Osgood found three main dimensions of connotative meaning: (1) an *evaluative* dimension (good-bad, clean-dirty, etc.), (2) a *strength* dimension (strong-weak, large-small, etc.), and (3) an *activity* dimension

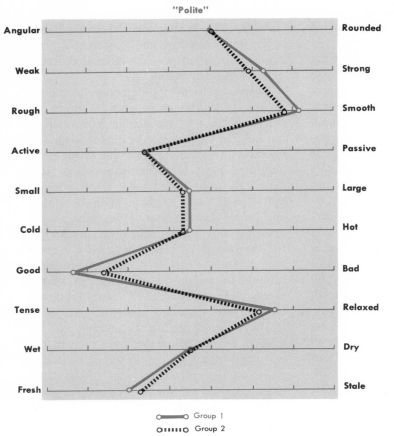

"Polite"

Angular		Rounded
Weak		Strong
Rough		Smooth
Active		Passive
Small		Large
Cold		Hot
Good		Bad
Tense		Relaxed
Wet		Dry
Fresh		Stale

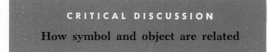

○———○ Group 1
○ıııııı○ Group 2

12-2

Osgood's semantic differential

Profiles of ratings used in arriving at a semantic differential for measuring the connotative meaning of the word "polite." Median responses from two groups of 20 subjects each. (After Osgood, 1952)

(fast-slow, active-passive, etc.). These three dimensions account for a good share of connotative meanings, with the evaluative factor carrying the most weight.

CRITICAL DISCUSSION

How symbol and object are related

A symbol somehow relates to or stands for something else—the object of the symbol. There are various ways in which we may think of the relationship between the symbol and its object (Osgood, 1953; Brown, 1958).

1. *A natural or magical relation between the symbol and the object.* Freud and Jung give a great deal of attention to symbols in myths and dreams and tend toward an interpretation that there is a natural (perhaps uni-

versal?) tendency for certain symbolic representations. For example, the snake as a sexual symbol is found in many primitive myths and is also found in the dreams of individuals today. Satisfactory evidence on the origins of such symbols is lacking, and they therefore have not played much part in theories of meaning.

The magical view that symbols and their objects are very intimately related is often found in childhood, among nonliterate peoples, and occasionally among adults. It leads to a kind of "sign magic," in which doing something to the "sign" is believed to affect the "object."

It is not surprising that a child growing up in a culture in which he hears only one language comes to assume a natural relationship between the name and the object, so that he believes that a pig is called a pig because it is dirty.

2. *Symbol and object related through a common "image."* If the word "book" arouses in the mind of the listener an "image" of a book, this "image" carries the meaning. This interpretation of meaning is adequate as a common-sense statement and seems to apply naturally enough to something concrete. But it is much more difficult to see how the image can carry the meaning in the case of abstract concepts. For example, the concept of "justice" may give rise to an image of a blind goddess, but this image is merely another symbol, and its meaning remains to be explained. The part that images play in thought has been the subject of an old controversy in psychology; in any case the image theory has not proved to be a satisfactory explanation of the relation between a symbol and its meaning (Brown, 1958).

3. *Symbol and object related through a common response.* When Pavlov's dog salivates to light followed by food, his response to the light is the one appropriate to food. Hence we may say that the light is for him a sign that the food is coming, or that the light *means* food. Actually the dog does not act to the light as if it were food (he does not eat it!), so the theory, if it is to be useful, must have further refinement.

The behavioral orientation of contemporary psychologists has led them to suggest various ways in which to refine this third (response) interpretation of meaning. One attempt to modify it is to suggest that the substitute behavior can be only partial. The dog's salivation to the light is a mere *fraction* of the behavior of eating. According to Osgood (1953) this fractional response is a *mediation process,* stimulating the subject to respond to the symbol as he would to the object. Thus the sign DANGER must arouse some slight form of the emotional or alarm (autonomic?) reactions that encountered danger would produce; these responses, as mediators, then lead to responses appropriate to the avoidance of actual dangers. It may be noted that the mediation process is a kind of behavioral substitute for an "idea" or "image" of danger.

4. *Meaning as a behavior disposition.* According to Morris (1946) the fractional response to the symbol, which has something in common with the appropriate response to the object symbolized, is a mere *disposition* to make the response; it is this disposition that carries the meaning. The disposition theory has been extended by Brown (1958), as an alternative to theories that seek particular forms of behavior as carrying the meaning. A disposition is a more general tendency to behave in certain ways, controlling a variety of particular behaviors, just as an attitude toward an ethnic group will determine many different kinds of behavior toward representatives of that group. Because words carry both denotative and connotative meanings, the *dispositions* they evoke are complex; one is "at home" in a language when a word evokes for him many dispositions that are evoked by that word in other members of the community who use that same language. The shades of difference between the meaning of "nude" and "naked" in English are carried by these somewhat different dispositions that they suggest; a dictionary definition might not reveal them.

A finally agreed-upon interpretation of meaning has not yet been reached; some writers attribute this lack of agreement to an attempt to make meaning some one thing, when in fact it refers to all kinds of behavior (Humphrey, 1951, p. 229).

Concepts and their attainment

When a symbol stands for a class of objects or events with common properties, we say that it refers to a *concept.* Words and signs both stand for concepts of varying degrees of generality. The concept "mammal" is more general than the concept "dog," which in turn is more general than the concept "Irish setter." As concepts become more general, they also become more abstract; that is, they lose the "thing-character" that ordinary objects possess. The thinker uses concepts of all degrees of concreteness and abstractness. He deals with concrete things when he chooses the key that fits the lock; he deals with abstractions when he discusses Hegel's philosophy.

What kinds of concepts are attained most readily? A series of experiments led to the conclusion that "thinglike" characteristics are easier to conceive than more abstract relationships of form and number. In one such experiment, materials were constructed similar to those in Figure 12-3. Each series consisted of nine sets of drawings, each set reproducing identical figures

12-3

Concept formation

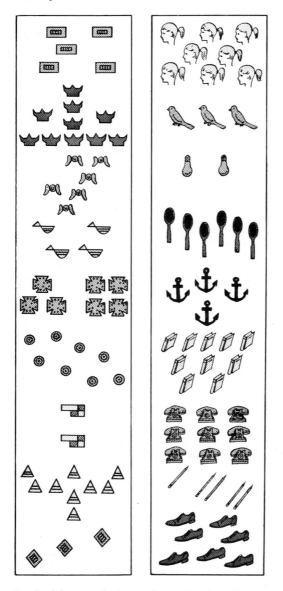

On the left: sets of abstract forms. On the right: sets of representations of concrete objects. The sets varied in color (not shown) and in number of items. See text for further discussion. (After Heidbreder, Bensley, and Ivy, 1948)

all of one color and form but varying in number. Some figures represented familiar objects (books, shoes, pencils); others were abstract geometrical forms. The figures on the right in Figure 12-3 represent concrete objects, and those on the left represent forms.

To each set of objects or forms, whether abstract or concrete, the experimenter assigned a nonsense name, such as *lorb, dwin,* or *telf.* The materials were presented as in the paired-associates form of a memorization experiment, and the subject attempted to speak the name of the set as it appeared. If the concept labeled by the name was understood (e.g., if *lorb* was known to stand for any *shoe*), the response to the set was of course much easier than if the concept was not yet attained. Memorization was carried to two perfect repetitions, and then the subject was questioned to find if she had discovered the concept or had simply learned the pairs by rote. Usually the concept had been attained, but the first correct pairing of a name with a particular card tended to appear a few trials before the concept itself was reached.

The results of the experiment showed clearly that the concept most easily attained was that of an object (shoe, bird, book), next that of spatial forms, then colors (red, yellow, blue), then numbers (two, four, five) (Heidbreder, Bensley, and Ivy, 1948). The results have been confirmed, but interpreted somewhat differently, by Grant (1951).

Although there are some qualifications that have to be made, it appears that our thinking tends to run to *things,* rather than to *abstractions.* Hence objects are more readily comprehended as belonging together than spatial forms, because the forms are less "thinglike." Numbers are even less "thinglike" than forms, so that the concept of fourness or sixness is harder to arrive at, in an experiment such as that described, than the concept of triangularity. Higher thinking, exemplified by mathematics, requires the more abstract kind of concept.

In a later but related study, Hunt and Hovland (1960) distinguished among *conjunctive, disjunctive,* and *relational* concepts. A *conjunctive* concept is of the type in which all objects of a class share common characteristics; their example is rubies, all of which are hard, translucent, and red. A *disjunctive* concept is one in which two members belong to the same class because of possessing either of two quite different characteristics. The typical example is that of the "strike" in American baseball, which means either (1) a pitch that the batter attempts to hit, but misses, or (2) a pitched ball that crosses the plate between the batter's knees and shoulders, even though he does not attempt to hit it. A *relational* type of concept is one in which instances of the concept do not share fixed characteristics, but do share fixed relationships. An isosceles triangle has two sides equal, but they can be of any length, and there can be any size of angle between them. Experimentation with such concepts showed that subjects tended to search first for conjunctive and relational concepts, arriving at disjunctive concepts much later. The earlier studies are thus extended to show that there are levels of difficulty among the various types of more abstract concept.

Language in children's thinking

Social communication requires that speaker and listener share a common meaning of words. A child can learn to obey verbal signals before he can say words that have the same meaning to him that they have to the person he addresses. It is only when he communicates these common meanings that he really uses language.

The close correspondence between the child's use of language and his ability to deal with a problem of relationships is illustrated by an experiment performed with children while they were at an age when language was becoming for them a tool of thought.

The experimenter taught the children (of preschool and kindergarten age) to select the smaller of a pair of squares, each mounted on the lid of a box. If the child chose the smaller square, he found the box open and an attractive toy inside. If he mistakenly chose the larger square, he found the box locked. The child began by learning to choose a 6-inch square in preference to an 8-inch one. When he had learned to choose the 6-inch square regularly, he was ready for the crucial tests with smaller squares.

He was now confronted with two test pairs, all pairs being smaller than the original ones. Of these smaller pairs, one (known as the near pair) was close to the original squares in size (4.5 inches and 6 inches), the other (known as the remote pair) was much smaller (1.4 and 1.9 inches). If the child had learned to "transpose," that is, to choose the smaller square regardless of absolute size, he should succeed in choosing the smaller square for both the near and the remote pairs. The results are plotted in Figure 12-4. While all children did well with the near pair, on the remote pair there was a striking increase in success with age (Kuenne, 1946).

The reason that the older children did better with the far pair was quite clearly related to their use of language. If a child could say the equivalent of "The smaller one is always right," he could succeed with the far pair. Of the 13 children who failed to express in words the principle of correct choice, none transposed on the test with the remote pair; of the 31 children who stated the correct solution in words either spontaneously or upon questioning, 73 per cent transposed successfully with the remote pair.

Of course the older children were more developed as problem-solvers, whether or not they relied upon language; the younger children, although able to use language to some extent, were not able to use it well enough to serve as a tool for thinking in the transposition. We can recognize that

12-4

Language and the perception of relationships

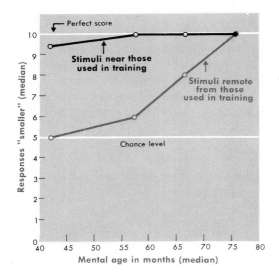

The older children, who were better able to state a test relationship in the form "The smaller one is always right," were able to transpose what they had learned from one pair to another remote pair, while the younger children could transpose only pairs close to those used in training. (After Kuenne, 1946)

language and thought are related, without making the assumption that they are identical.

Language and forms of thought

Most of us assume that reality as we know it exists independently of the ways in which we talk about it. We believe, for example, that any idea expressed in one language can be translated into another language. This statement seems so obvious that to question it is rather startling. But a student of American Indian languages, Whorf (1950, 1956), found such direct translation often impossible: one of the languages he studied has no clear distinction between nouns and verbs, another blurs the distinctions of past, present, and future, a third uses the same name for the colors gray and brown. These differences led Whorf to two conclusions:

1. The world is conceived very differently by those whose languages are of completely unlike structure.
2. The structure of the language is a cause of these different ways of conceiving the world.

Whorf's thesis is the subject of active debate among anthropologists and experts in the study of language structure. Most of them accept a correspondence between the language and the ways of conceiving the world, but they tend to turn things around and try to show that the experiences significant to the people affect the way things are expressed in language. Thus some Eskimos have different words for different kinds of snow, and some groups have a whole vocabulary to describe different kinds of reindeer hides that we would scarcely be able to tell apart.

For us, the important part of Whorf's conjecture is that there is this close correspondence between language and thinking. Experimenters interested in his theory have tested it, for example, in an experiment on the recognizing and naming of colors by English-speaking college students.

The color names most common in English are red, orange, yellow, green, blue, purple, pink, and brown. Preliminary to the experiment, five judges picked from 240 color patches the ones best representing these names. They agreed remarkably well. To these 8 colors the experimenters added 16 more to provide a fairly even representation of all colors. The 24 subjects who served in the next part of the experiment first saw all 24 colors mounted on a chart in random order. Then they saw the colors one at a time and were asked to name them.

The experimenters called the ease with which a color was named its codability. The easiest-to-code colors were those described by a single word of a single syllable (e.g., "red"), given with short reaction time and with high consistency by all subjects. The hardest to code were colors that were described with many words, after hesitation, and with little agreement among the subjects. These measures were converted to quantities, so that each of the 24 colors had a *codability score*.

The *recognition* part of the experiment was carried out with new subjects. Each saw only 4 of the original 24 colors, but by dividing the colors among the subjects all colors were used. The new subject then had as his task picking out these 4 colors among 120 mounted on a chart. Most subjects said that they were able to keep the colors in mind by naming them and then "storing" the names while doing the recognition task. Based on the success of these subjects, a recognition score was assigned to each of the original colors.

The hypothesis that ease of naming and ease of recognition have something in common could be tested by correlating the codability score with the recognition score. This correlation turned out to be .42, thus agreeing with the hypothesis (Brown and Lenneberg, 1954).

This experiment has been satisfactorily repeated with Zuni Indians, with somewhat different colors emerging as the most readily codable or recognizable. The general implication is that the regions of experience in which a society makes careful discriminations are likely also to be represented in linguistic discriminations. These differences among cultures will show up in the ease or difficulty of particular intellectual tasks, of which recognition is a rather simple variety.

Thought and the brain

While no one doubts that we use our brains when we think, beyond that we can say very little with confidence. There is no localized "thought center" in the brain, as there are localized centers for muscular action or vision.

Two main approaches to thinking pose somewhat different problems for students of brain physiology. Those who take the *peripheralist position* that all thinking goes

12-5

Muscular movements in thinking

Although the subject's arms and hands were resting quietly, the thought of hammering twice with the right arm resulted in the two bursts of electrical impulses shown in the record. (After Jacobson, 1932)

on in action (speech or other movements) see the problems of thinking as essentially the same as those dealing with other aspects of movement control. According to this position all that psychology requires is a stimulus-response analysis of thinking; then a physiology of conditioned responses would also provide a physiology of thinking. The *centralists* believe that thinking goes on inside the brain and nervous system, with the muscular movements merely accompaniments (or facilitators) of the "central" process. For a centralist, a physiological explanation of thinking requires a theory of what goes on in the brain when we think; a stimulus-response analysis does not suffice.

CRITICAL DISCUSSION

Peripheralist vs. centralist theories

The extreme form of the peripheralist position on thought was advocated by John B. Watson, usually regarded as the founder of behaviorism. His main point was that *movements* were the substance of thought, chiefly the movements that we make in talking to ourselves. To put it another way, thought consists merely in *implicit language habits*, including within language not only speech but also such other movements as may be involved in gesture, writing, or other language accompaniments. The habits are *implicit* because they cannot be observed without the aid of instruments. Young children, having just learned to talk, often talk aloud as they solve their problems. As they grow older, they learn to talk silently to themselves. Then, according to Watson, they have learned to think. You can try an old demonstration of this theory on yourself. Try to think the word "bubble" with your mouth open. You may feel a catch in your throat while you are thinking.

When you think, you make other muscular movements besides those of speech. Suppose you permit an experimenter to attach electrodes to your arms so that he can measure electrical response (action currents) from your muscles. Now while your arms are quiet, he tells you to think of hammering twice with your right hand. His instrument will often show two bursts of impulses from your right arm muscles, corresponding to your imagined hammering (Figure 12-5). When you imagined hammering, you moved your muscle slightly, even though your arms remained in resting position (Jacobson, 1932). Deaf-mutes, who use their arm muscles in talking a sign language, show more activity in these muscles when they dream than normal subjects do (Max, 1935). The presence of eye movements in dreaming is also consonant with the importance of muscular movement in thinking (Dement and Kleitman, 1957).

While these peripheral indicators of thought make plausible a theory such as Watson's, the centralist answers that a movement *accompaniment* of thinking is not the thinking itself. Thus the slight muscular movements in the arms result from the subject's *thinking about* hammering, just as the movements themselves might result if he had decided actually to hammer. The crux of the issue is that the decision to hammer need not have been made in the muscles.

The desire to hold to the stimulus-response interpretation of behavior lies behind the peripheralist position. Thus one thought in a chain of associations is a stimulus to the following thought, but to be a stimulus it must have physical attributes. Hull (1931), for example, considered some thoughts to be what he called *pure-stimulus acts*, that is, acts whose sole purpose was to furnish stimuli for other acts. Although there was little evidence, he made a purely conjectural transformation of the *idea* into an *act*, so that the stimulus would be tangible.

The centralist argues that the stimulus-response analysis is not essential. Groups of nerve cells, and even the brain as a whole, appear to be spontaneously active, and there is nothing in the physiology of the brain to re-

quire that everything that happens must be a stimulus-response circuit from sense organs to muscles or glands.

Some evidence of the role of the brain in thinking comes through studies of the results of injury. Brain injury often produces serious disturbance of the speech processes, with symptoms described as *aphasia*. Various classes of aphasia have been proposed from time to time, but that of Head (1926) calls clearest attention to the relation between language defect and thought. He distinguished four classes of aphasia: (1) *verbal defects,* defective forming of words or using one number instead of another without awareness of the error; (2) *syntactical defects,* in which the correct naming of objects may persist, but a formulated sentence becomes unintelligible jargon; (3) *nominal defects,* in which the operations of naming are interfered with; and (4) *semantic defects,* in which verbal meanings and rote memory are unimpaired, but fuller understanding of meaning is lost. Thus a patient can name the cards but cannot understand the rules of a card game.

Other experiments with brain-injured patients tell us that they may lose the ability to deal with the abstract, even though they get along very well when dealing with concrete things.

1. A patient could not be induced to repeat the sentence, "The sun is shining," on a rainy day.
2. A patient is well able to throw balls into three boxes which are located at different distances from him. He never misses. Asked which box is further and which is nearer, he is unable to give any account or to make a statement concerning his procedure in aiming.
3. A patient can count on his fingers and by various roundabout methods; in this fashion he can even obtain results which look like subtraction and addition, but he is entirely unable to state whether 7 or 4 is more and has no concept of the values of numbers whatever.
4. The patient can use a key to open a door, but he is unable to demonstrate how to use the key unless the door is present.
5. Another patient cannot demonstrate how to drink out of an empty glass, whereas he can drink out of a full glass (Goldstein and Scheerer, 1941).

Electrical stimulation of portions of the sensorimotor area of the human cortex, exposed under local anesthetic, results in spontaneous vocalization—speech sounds without words. If the patient is talking at the time of the stimulation, his speech is interrupted. Surgical removal of the tissue in these areas is likely to produce a form of aphasia (Penfield and Roberts, 1959).

While these studies show us the importance of the brain in thinking and give us some hints about the processes of thought, they do not resolve the issue between the peripheralist and the centralist.

Problem-Solving

What is a problem? Whenever goal-oriented activity is blocked, whenever a need remains unfulfilled, a question unanswered, perplexity unresolved, the subject faces a problem. We turn now to a consideration of realistic problem-solving, in which evidence is marshaled, reasoning goes on, and a satisfactory solution is reached.[5]

Strategies in problem-solving

A subject trying to solve a problem seeks some strategy, some systematic mode of attack, and unless the problem is a very arbitrary one, he usually finds this to his advantage.

One experiment sharply contrasts two strategies, described as *wholist* and *partist* (Bruner, Goodnow, and Austin, 1956). The task in the experiment was to abstract a concept from a series of cards. The subjects in this experiment were given more knowledge about the task than is usual in concept-formation experiments. They were taught that each card was an *instance* either representing the sought-for concept (a positive instance) or not representing it (a negative instance). They were also taught the relevant *attributes* of the cards and how many *values* each attribute could take, selected from the following table:

[5] Some unrealistic attempts at problem-solving will be considered later (Chapter 18).

Attributes	Values
1. Number of figures	One, two, or three
2. Kind of figures	Square, circle, or cross
3. Color of figures	Red, blue, or green
4. Number of borders	One, two, or three
5. Kind of borders	Solid, dotted, or wavy
6. Color of borders	Red, blue, or green

The subjects, 46 Harvard and Wellesley undergraduates, were each given 14 problems to solve. The number of possibly relevant attributes varied in each problem from three to six, and the number of attributes that actually defined the solution from one to five. The subject knew for each problem which attributes were possibly relevant, and also which attributes remained constant throughout the series of cards. Cards were presented one at a time; the experimenter stated whether the card was a positive or negative instance, and the subject wrote down his best guess of the concept. Thus the subject's strategy could be inferred from the way in which he moved from one concept to the next.

The two main strategies can be described as follows:

1. In the *wholist* strategy the subject assumes that *all* relevant attributes of the first instance (which in the test is always a positive instance) must be necessary to define the concept. Thus if the relevant attributes in the particular experiment are number, kind, and color of figures (with borders irrelevant and constant), the subject will state the concept for the first positive instance as "three red squares" if those are the values of the attributes that are present, even though he knows that the correct concept could be "all cards containing squares." The next card can be either a positive or a negative instance of the concept. If it is a negative instance, the subject holds to his original concept, for he can learn nothing from it; unless his first hypothesis is wrong, no negative instances are relevant. For example, if "three blue squares" is wrong, "three red squares" might still be right, and

12-6

Strategies in problem-solving

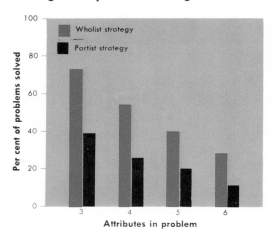

Relative success of wholist vs. partist strategy in solving problems. (After Bruner, Goodnow, and Austin, 1956)

so on. But a positive instance that contains fewer attributes than or different attributes from his original concept will make him simplify his concept accordingly, accepting only what the original card and the new one have in common. If the new positive instance is "three blue squares," he will now correct the concept to "three squares" because the blue has contradicted the red. Thus the correct concept is finally arrived at by reducing the original total concept to those parts that are common to all instances. Information comes from positive instances that cause modification of the original guess.

2. In the *partist* strategy, the subject begins by guessing that a *part* of the original positive instance defines the concept. Thus when presented with three red squares, he guesses that the correct concept is "three squares." Now he can learn from either positive *or* negative instances. If this subject encounters a *negative* instance consisting of three blue squares, for example, then he knows his "three squares" hypothesis is wrong, and he tries a new one. Similarly, he may have a positive instance inconsist-

ent with his guess. If he finds a positive instance of "two red squares," he must also change his original hypothesis of "three squares." In the partist strategy the fact that the subject has to remember which hypotheses he has used and rejected puts him at some disadvantage by comparison with the wholist strategy.

What happens in practice? While subjects are not entirely consistent, there is a marked tendency for a subject to use one or the other of the strategies on a majority of the problems. Hence the relative successes with the two types of initial approach (Figure 12-6) represent in part the successes of different subjects. The superiority of the *wholist* approach over the *partist* one is evident under the circumstances of this experiment. The results were obtained under time pressure. When there was plenty of time, the partists were not at any disadvantage (Austin, Bruner, and Seymour, 1953). The main disadvantage of the partist method is its reliance upon memory, which proves difficult when the subject is hurried.

The half-split technique in the use of information

The most practical approach to problems of concept formation is in studies of "trouble-shooting." This is an expression used by technical workers to describe the detection of the fault in some form of mechanical failure, as when a television or radar set stops working. Studies made by the U.S. Air Force have compared two methods of attack: (1) on the basis of tables of probabilities that a given operational fault or symptom will be due to a given mechanical failure, and (2) the half-split technique, in which half the hypotheses are eliminated at each step (as when, in guessing a number between 1 and 100, we first ask, "Is it between 1 and 50?"). According to their experiments (and on theoretical grounds also),

TABLE 12-1

Reduction of uncertainty through information in a modified "Twenty Questions" game

Number of response	Theoretical uncertainty remaining	Actual uncertainty (mean, 3 games)	Information used from prior trial *
	bits †	bits	bits
1	4	3.60	
2	3	2.77	0.83
3	2	1.86	0.91
4	1	1.65	0.21
5	0	0.87	0.78

SOURCE: Bendig (1953). Results from 127 subjects.

* Obtained by subtracting actual uncertainty in one trial from that of preceding trial. The theoretical gain would be 1.00 bit per trial.

† The "bit" is a unit from technical information theory (an abbreviation for "binary digit"); whenever uncertainty is reduced by half, one "bit" of information has been received.

the second of these methods is to be preferred (Miller, Folley, and Smith, 1953).

For an analogy to the half-split technique in trouble-shooting we may turn to the parlor game of "twenty questions." In this game, familiar from radio and television, the audience attempts to "guess" what the leader has in mind by asking questions to which he replies simply "yes" or "no." The best questions divide the answers into two equal halves, so that a "yes" reply says that the correct concept lies in one half and a "no" answer says that it lies in the other. Then "yes" and "no" will be equally informative. In the usual game, if the correct answer comes in 20 questions or less, the audience "wins"; if not, it "loses." For laboratory purposes a somewhat simplified version has proved more satisfactory.

A class of 127 college students were given sheets listing 16 topics (all animal, including human) and sheets on which to record their responses. The problem was to find which one of the 16 had been selected as "correct." The class participated by observing one trained subject who asked the experimenter questions. The experimenter answered "yes" or "no," helping the students to narrow their choices. Each student first made and recorded one blind guess. Then after each question and reply he wrote down the topic that seemed to him most likely to be correct. The following questions were asked and answered appropriately, the answer to each question logically eliminating half the remaining possibilities: "Is the subject a whole animal?" "Is the subject human?" "Is there more than one of this subject?" "Is the subject fictional?"

The recorded answers provided an opportunity to find out whether the subjects used all the information available at each step (Bendig, 1953).

The results in Table 12-1 show that reduction in uncertainty proceeded as expected for the first three steps, that is, for the blind guess and the replies to the first two questions. But the information transmitted by the reply to the third question was much less, with a gain of only 0.21 bit recorded on trial 4. Except for this question, the subjects used most of the information available. The actual gains were from 80 to 90 per cent of what was possible.

The relationship between this experiment and trouble-shooting is fairly obvious. Only so many things can go wrong. If you can devise tests for locating the defect, each of which reduces the alternatives by half, you will make the maximum progress in putting your finger on the trouble.

The use of the notion of information (in a technical sense) and its unit of measurement (the bit, in Table 12-1) calls for comment on both the nature of information theory and its place in psychology.

Communication engineers have been concerned not only with the instruments required to transmit electrical impulses but with the ways in which to transmit *signals* that will communicate the maximum amount of information against the disruptive influence of *noise* (static, etc.). In dealing with the kind of knowledge that is coded in words or numbers, they have adopted as their unit of information the *bit* (an abbreviation for "binary digit"). The *bit*, as we have seen, is *the amount of information that reduces the uncertainty (the number of remaining alternatives) by one-half.*

Suppose I am thinking of a number from 1 to 8, and you try to guess it systematically. You ask, "Is it 4 or less, or more than 4?" I answer, "4 or less." Now you have eliminated the numbers 5, 6, 7, and 8—half the original alternatives. You have thus received one "bit" of information. Now you ask, "Is it 2 or less, or more than 2?" "2 or less." You have now eliminated 3 and 4, and thus have a second bit of information. You need only one more bit, and you have your answer. You can guess now, "Is it 2?" Whether I reply "yes" or "no," you receive the information you need. It took three bits of information to reduce 8 alternatives to 1. In mathematical terms, the amount of information required to reduce uncertainty increases as the logarithm of the alternatives, according to the formula:

$$\text{bits} = \log_2 \text{number of alternatives}$$

Here $\log_2$ means "logarithm to the base 2," which is a logarithm in the binary system, whereas familiar logarithms, in the decimal system, can be written $\log_{10}$ (or simply log). The value of $\log_2$ of 8 is 3, corresponding to the example given above.

Psychological applications of the quantitative estimation of information have taken several tacks. We have already seen an application in problem-solving in the Bendig example. Another application has been within the study of meaningfulness in memorizing. Meaningful materials may transmit information more easily than nonsense materials because of the way in which information is *coded;* that is, whether it has system or pattern. For example, the number 14916253649 is hard to remember with a single reading, but it can be remembered more easily if it is *coded* as consisting of the successive squares of 1, 2, 3, 4, 5, 6, and 7.

The greatest usefulness of information measurement thus far has been in providing a new way of measuring verbal stimuli. It is too early to say just what its ultimate range of usefulness within psychology may be (Miller, 1953, 1956; Attneave, 1959).

Obstacles to problem-solving

The skills involved in problem-solving are so complex that we have made somewhat greater advances in identifying obstacles to good problem-solving than we have in locating the essential features of an efficient approach to varied tasks.

Two related but dissimilar impediments to efficient problem-solving have turned up in many experiments. These are (1) the *persistence of a habitual set* toward a solution that may once have been efficient but is no longer efficient, and (2) *functional fixedness,* or the inability to see alternative uses for a tool or object whose familiar use-meaning has become entrenched.

Thinking requires alertness to new possibilities and to the possibility of doing things differently from the ways in which they were done before. Overlearned habits may so firmly fix routine ways of doing things that the habitual set interferes with thinking. An experiment illustrates this possibility.

TABLE 12-2

Comparing habitual solution with thoughtful search

Problem	Given the following empty jars as measures			Measure the required amount of water	Habitual solution	Easier solution to be discovered
	A	*B*	*C*	*D*		
1	21	127	3	100	$D = B - A - 2C$	
2	14	163	25	99	$D = B - A - 2C$	
3	18	43	10	5	$D = B - A - 2C$	
4	9	42	6	21	$D = B - A - 2C$	
5	20	59	4	31	$D = B - A - 2C$	
	Subjects are told "Don't be blind"					
6	23	49	3	20	$D = B - A - 2C$	$D = A - C$
7	15	39	3	18	$D = B - A - 2C$	$D = A + C$

SOURCE: Modified from Luchins (1942).

Fifteen members of a graduate seminar took part in a problem-solving experiment. All the problems were devoted to measuring a given amount of water through the use of jars of different sizes. For example, with a 29-quart jar and a 3-quart jar, it is possible to measure 20 quarts by first filling the 29-quart jar and then filling the smaller jar from the larger jar three times. This illustration was shown the group as an explanation of how their answers were to be written. Then they were given the 7 problems listed in Table 12-2. The first 5 of these problems can be most simply solved in one way—first by filling the middle jar *B*, then by subtracting the first jar *A*, then by subtracting the last jar *C* twice. In abstract form, we may write the solution as $D = B - A - 2C$. Because all these solutions are alike, the students developed a set to use that formula.

Eleven subjects, without special instructions, went through the 7 problems using the standard solution throughout. Because they followed the habitual set, they did not notice that there was an easier way of solving problems 6 and 7.

After the fifth problem, four subjects were instructed to write the words "Don't be blind," as indicated in the table. These subjects were the only ones who used the easier methods. They were not entirely consistent, but they used the easier method for five of their eight answers to problems 6 and 7 (Luchins, 1942).

One of the problems faced by mathematics (and statistics) teachers is that of teaching students to avoid overdependence upon memorized proofs and formulas and to understand the essence of what they are trying to do. Overdependence upon habitual solutions may be an enemy of understanding.

Habitual set, as interfering with problem-solving, turns out to have two components: susceptibility to set and the ability to overcome a set once established. Guetzkow (1951) found a sex difference in the ability to overcome set, favoring men over women, but he found no sex difference in susceptibility to set as measured by the jar problem.

Many objects have clearly defined uses, but they may also serve in other ways. A hammer is normally used to drive nails, but it may be used as a weapon as well. A knife is designed to cut, but it will also serve as a screw driver or as a pry to lift the lid of a jar. The use-meaning of an object, while it often appears to inhere in the object as perceived, is determined by the relationship between the object and the other objects, and so is subject to change. The following experiment bears upon the problem of the use-meaning of an object in problem-solving.

Five tasks were arranged, each in two versions. One version of the task required that a tool be used first in its normal way and then in some new way. The second version required only the novel use. The conjecture being tested was that use of the tool in a normal way would then make it more difficult to perceive the meaning-use of the tool in the new way required for

12-7

Overcoming functional fixedness

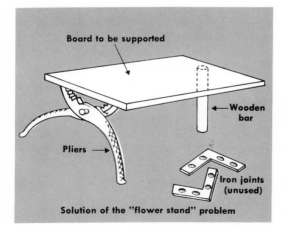

Presented with the object shown, the problem is to construct a flower stand using any of the items given, not necessarily all. The best result is obtained by using the pliers in an unusual way, as shown.

problem-solving. The five problems were as follows:

Tool	Normal use	Novel use
Gimlet	To bore holes	To support a hanging cord
Box	As a container	As a platform
Pliers	To unfasten wire	To support a board
Weight	As a pendulum bob	As a hammer
Paper clip	To fasten papers	As a hook (unbent)

The two versions of the pliers problem will help to show how the experiment was arranged. The task was to make a board firm on two supports (as a "flower stand or the like") (Figure 12-7). In front of the subject were two iron joints, a wooden bar, and the crucial object: the pliers. The problem was to be solved by using the wooden bar as one support and the pliers as the other. In one version, the bar to be used as a support was nailed to the board. It had to be freed by using the pliers. Hence the pliers were used first in their normal function. In the other version, the bar was tied to the board so that it was easily removed without the use of the pliers.

From 7 to 15 subjects worked on each of the problems, each subject having some tasks in one version, other tasks in the second version. Those working on tasks in which they first used the tool in its normal way found more difficulty in perceiving a novel use for the tool than did those who used the tool only for a novel purpose. Success was easy when the only use required was the new one. There were 50 successes out of 51 tries (98 per cent success) when the tool entered the novel solution without having first been used normally. But, following normal use, successes fell down to 30 out of 49 tries (61 per cent success) (Duncker, 1945).

This same kind of experiment has been repeated by other experimenters with similar results, e.g., Birch and Rabinowitz

(1951), Adamson (1952), Adamson and Taylor (1954).

This tendency for normal use to make new use more difficult is known as *functional fixedness*. That the effects of such normal use may persist for some time is shown by Figure 12-8, in which the effects last for at least a day but are gone in a week. These results imply an advantage in leaving a task for a while and then coming back to it for a fresh attack. The necessity of overcoming functional fixedness may be one of the background conditions for the observation that after turning away from a problem for a while we return to it with a fresh approach and achieve a solution.

How are we to avoid getting into the ruts of either persistent set or functional fixedness? One way is to train for flexibility. Schroder and Rotter (1952) trained four groups of 20 subjects each on a card-grouping task, similar to the typical concept-formation experiments. The groups received varying amounts of experience with changed concepts, so that the group with most experience of change came most to expect change. When tested in a novel problem-solving situation where change leads to easier solution, the groups trained for flexibility adopted the changed solutions earlier.

Group or individual?

Much thinking these days goes on in groups—in conferences, among teams of research workers—and the question naturally arises as to whether the group is better at problem-solving than the individual, or vice versa.

The question is not a simple one, for any one group, say, of five people, is likely to get an answer to a problem sooner than any one individual of equal ability and background. But this might be due merely to the fact that the group capitalizes on the best thinker in the group. Thus if the group were split into five groups of one man each and results compared, the group

12-8

Persistence of functional fixedness

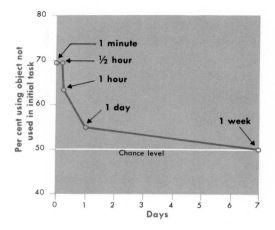

Using an object in its normal way lessens the probability of finding a novel use for it. This effect disappears over time. (After Adamson and Taylor, 1954)

might not do better than the best man working alone. In analogy with fishing, the more lines there are in the water, the more likely that a fish will be caught, even though the group process contributes nothing to the art of fishing. This line of thinking has been developed by Taylor and McNemar (1955). We therefore must really ask whether or not the group is *more effective* than the best person in the group. Experiments lead to rather ambiguous results.

Earlier experimenters tended to find group solution superior, but they did not generally make the corrections needed to allow for the advantage the group has in using its most superior members, while an average performance for one-man groups counts everybody. More recent experiments (e.g., Taylor and Faust, 1952) have shown little superiority for randomly chosen groups, although this does not, of course, deny the effectiveness of groups composed of experts bringing different information to bear on the problem.

Group solutions will be superior to individual solutions under the following conditions:

1. One or more members of the group must possess the essential information needed for solution, such as relevant knowledge and past experience.
2. The more varied these requirements are, so that no one member possesses all the relevant background, the more advantage the group will have over an individual.
3. The group requires leadership, so that its deliberations are focused on the objective.

It is not always easy to establish these conditions in artificially created groups. Hence a general answer can scarcely be given to the question whether or not groups "think better" than individuals: the answer can be given only if one specifies what kind of group, composed of what kinds of people, working on what kinds of problems.

A technique of group thinking known as "brainstorming" (not brainwashing!) was widely used by business and industrial establishments in the 1950's (Osborn, 1953). The main principle was that in a first session the group members should produce ideas in rapid succession, not considering their worth and thinking "wildly and freely." The point was that the members, through relinquishing criticism, might overcome functional fixedness (pp. 356-57) and bring fresh light upon the solution of the problem under consideration. Then the ideas could be sorted out soberly in a later session, and the valuable ones retained. William James had earlier recommended that an author write in haste and revise at leisure, and the modern brainstorming appeared to be based on some sound psychological advice.

Careful test of the brainstorming method in the laboratory failed to show, however, that any more original ideas were created than if individuals sat alone thinking up new ideas (Taylor and others, 1958). These results do not necessarily condemn the brainstorming method under some circumstances, but they show that dramatic expectations from it are unwarranted.

Computer simulation of thinking

Modern high-speed electronic computers are often referred to as "giant brains." Their importance to modern science, technology, and management can scarcely be overestimated, but another question is asked: Can they think? An immediate answer in the negative—that they can do only what they have been taught (programed) to do—is too glib. Perhaps a human thinker can do only what he has been programed to do also, either by inheritance or by his training. Without language and the symbols of mathematics there are many things the human thinker could not do. But of course the human thinker *can* make programs for machines. Perhaps we should ask: Can a machine ever program itself? Within limits the answer is "yes," and we therefore need to look at the matter more closely (Newell and Simon, 1961).

There are two chief ways in which a computation takes place. One is by way of an *algorithm*, which is a fixed routine for finding a solution provided one exists. The word "algorithm" is not very familiar, but what it stands for is much more familiar. Any simple mathematical rule used in solving problems is an algorithm: "to divide by a fraction, invert and multiply"; "to transpose a term from one side of the equation to the other, change its sign." Most of us learned a more complex algorithm in order to extract the square root of a number. If we follow the steps exactly, we will come out with an integral number, assuming the number we started with was a perfect square. It is easy to build such rules into a machine, and this is probably the most familiar use of the high-speed computer. The second method of computation is not as rigorous, because it uses various short cuts and rules of thumb; there is no guarantee that the solution will be found, but it *may* be found much more quickly than if the painstaking method of the algorithm is used. This method goes by the name of *heuristic*, a method of tentative search rather than of exhaustive trying out of all appropriate algorithms. Human thinking is particularly skilled in the use of heuristic methods. A good chess player solves his problems heuristically;

he could not possibly see the consequences of every possible move. In solving a geometrical problem, we often add a line here or there, hoping that by forming a new triangle we may perceive relationships that were previously not evident. This new construction may help, but, unlike an algorithm, there are no guarantees implied.

The main point is that machines can be programed so that they, too, can solve problems heuristically. They can simulate what a human learner does in concept attainment (Hovland and Hunt, 1960; Cahill and Hovland, 1960); they can derive theorems if they are programed to do so. The most elaborate such effort to date has been the development of a General Problem Solver by Newell, Shaw, and Simon (1958a). They have succeeded, for example, in developing a program for theorems in symbolic logic. After building into the program the definitions, axioms, and rules used by Whitehead and Russell in their famous *Principia Mathematica* (1925), they set a computer to work to attempt to derive the 52 theorems of the second chapter of that work. It succeeded in giving adequate proofs for 38 of the theorems, using heuristic searching methods. At least one of the proofs was considered more elegant than that which Whitehead and Russell had been able to provide (Newell, Shaw, and Simon, 1958b).

These rather exciting developments are of great importance in unraveling the problems of human thinking. The process is clearly a two-way street. That is, one has to know something about how creative problem-solving goes on in order to make a program for a machine. The analysis of heuristic thinking in mathematics by Polya has been a contributor in this respect (Polya, 1945, 1954). Because the machine will do only what it is instructed to do, the steps have to be specified very clearly in "computer language." If any error has been made in the interpretation of the steps in problem-solving, the machine will not succeed. Thus the machine serves as a check on the theory. The chief advantage that the machine has over a human thinker is its perfect memory and its attention to all detail that it is programed to attend to. If a man teaches the machine to play a checker game, for example, the machine will eventually win over its teacher, because it never overlooks anything that it has been taught to attend to and it never forgets the past consequences of a particular

move in a particular context. If, however, there is some strategy not available to the machine, because it is not derivable from what has been programed, then the man will have an advantage.

The modern high-speed computer is therefore more than an elaborate machine for carrying out arithmetical and other mathematical operations; it is an important instrument for discovering and verifying principles of human problem-solving and creativity.

Creative Thinking

Scientific discovery

Knowledge verified by the methods of science has made possible many of man's most conspicuous achievements. We dam rivers; irrigate and fertilize land; improve seed; harvest, store, and ship food; extract minerals; prevent and cure diseases; illuminate dwellings and factories; print books and newspapers; send and receive telephone, radio, and television messages; and travel on land and sea, through the air, and even into space. Through science we not only have achieved these practical ends but also have obtained many answers to our questions and speculations about the universe—about the nature of matter, energy, and electricity; about distant stars and subatomic particles. Because scientific activity is problem-solving organized according to the best rules that man has so far been able to invent or discover, we will do well to study the behavior of scientists as they work at their problems.

The testimony of scientists about their own work is hard to interpret, for the distinguished scientist can tell little more about how he arrives at his insights than can anyone else. However, the particular insight which leads to a notable advance is a striking experience and can therefore often be identified and dated. It is a unique event marking a turning point in thought, and we can look for the circumstances surrounding it.

One student of creative thought has suggested that thinkers, whether scientists or artists, reach their solutions through four steps: *preparation, incubation, illumination,* and *verification* (Wallas, 1921). These are not the formal steps of orderly scientific method; they are, instead, the steps in the germination of the ideas we call original, inventive, or, occasionally, revolutionary. Let us examine in more detail some of the testimony of scientists to see whether or not this analysis is justified.

Preparation. Even though an idea may seem to come to us suddenly in final form, we usually can discover that we have made a great deal of preparation for it. Einstein as a student of sixteen began to be troubled by certain basic problems in physics, centering around the meaning of the speed of light, and he grappled with these problems for seven years. When he saw that his problem could be solved by questioning the ordinary concept of time, it took him only five weeks to write his famous paper on relativity, even though he was then employed full time in the Swiss patent office. We cannot ignore the years of preparation when we marvel at the speed with which he produced his remarkable paper.

The scientist prepares himself for discoveries by his study of what has gone before, by willingness to disagree with what he has been taught, and by readiness to follow leads directed by observation or conjecture, whether his own or those of other scientists. Sometimes an inquiry is started by what is called a stroke of "luck." For example, A. H. Becquerel discovered radioactivity when he found that a uranium compound had affected a covered photographic plate on which he had left it. Would we say, however, that his discovery was complete luck and that there was no preparation for it? We would have to ask ourselves how he happened to be working with uranium compounds, how he happened to have photographic plates lying around, and what

prior knowledge made him ready to infer the process of radioactivity. Alexander Fleming discovered the usefulness of penicillin by accident. He was working with staphylococci (pus-forming bacteria) on a culture plate on which penicillin mold was present as a troublesome impurity. He noticed that the staphylococci were dissolving near the penicillin mold. He asked himself why, and the experiments he made to find an answer led eventually to the use of penicillin in the treatment of disease. But without Fleming's training as a bacteriologist, this discovery, so important for mankind, could not have been made.

Incubation and Illumination. The stage of scientific discovery or invention in which things suddenly become clear is prepared for, as we saw with Einstein, by understanding of the problem, a strong orientation toward its solution, and an acquaintance with the relevant facts. When the solution will come, if it comes, is unpredictable. This uncertainty has led to the notion of some sort of *incubation* process that goes on after the preparation has taken place, even though the thinker may not be actively engrossed with the problem.

Something of the sort happened with the formulation of the emergency theory of emotions, a theory which served to clarify a number of apparently unrelated physiological processes found present in strong emotion (see Chapter 6, p. 161). The account is by Walter B. Cannon, who proposed the emergency theory:

> These changes [bodily changes which occur in great emotional excitement]—the more rapid pulse, the deeper breathing, the increase of sugar in the blood, the secretion from the adrenal glands—were very diverse and seemed unrelated. Then, one wakeful night . . . the idea flashed through my mind that they could be nicely integrated if conceived as bodily preparations for supreme effort in flight or in fighting. . . .[6]

[6] Cannon (1945).

What is the nature of the incubation process which goes on before such an integrating idea? One possibility is that it is *unconscious thinking*. The number of acceptable reports of conclusions appearing in dreams or immediately upon awakening is very small, but some of these reports are sufficiently striking to have some claim as evidence.

Descartes reported that he first encountered the basic notions of analytic geometry in two dreams, but he did not clearly describe the circumstances. Friedrich Kekule solved the problem of the arrangement of carbon and hydrogen in benzene through a dream (among a number of similar dreams) in which he saw the atoms dancing in a ring. The dreams led him to the concept of the benzene ring, one of the most important steps in organic chemistry.

> In 1865 Kekule, then professor of chemistry at Ghent, was engaged one evening in writing his textbook, but his thoughts were elsewhere.
>
> > I turned my chair to the fire and dozed. . . . Again the atoms were gamboling before my eyes. This time the smaller groups kept modestly in the background. My mental eye, rendered more acute by repeated visions of this kind, could now distinguish larger structures, of manifold conformation; long rows, sometimes more closely fitted together; all twining and twisting in snakelike motion. But look! What was that? One of the snakes had seized hold of its own tail, and the form whirled mockingly before my eyes. As if by a flash of lightning I awoke. . . .
>
> The picture Kekule had seen of the snake which had seized its own tail gave him the clue to the most puzzling of molecular structures, the structure of the benzene molecule, for which Kekule suggested a closed ring of six carbon atoms, to each of which a hydrogen atom is attached.[7]

Another well-known experience is that of Hermann Hilprecht, the archeologist who solved a Babylonian inscription in a dream. In each of these experiences the dream work was of the kind for which the expert was prepared. The fact that the solution appeared in a dream is dramatic, but actually no more mysterious than if it had appeared suddenly in a waking state.

Henri Poincaré, the distinguished French mathematician, tells how the solution to a difficult mathematical problem came to him while he was traveling and giving no thought to mathematics. As he put his foot on the step of a bus, the idea came to him with perfect certainty. He went on with the conversation already begun before he entered the bus, and waited for his return to Caen to verify the solution at his leisure (Poincaré, 1913).

Sudden solutions in dreams or in waking states are not necessarily the results of unconscious thinking. Rest from strenuous attention to the problem, as in reminiscence, provides a fresh look, and rejected alternatives are seen in a new light. Some thinkers have insisted that the suddenly occurring solution was one completely different from any previously entertained (Hadamard, 1945). The tricks of memory are such, however, that even competent testimony has to be accepted with caution. We need more evidence for safe conclusions.

Verification. After the illuminating idea has come, the scientist must verify it. Modern scientific method always ends in such steps of verification. Poincaré went home and wrote down the proof that verified the solution for him and for other mathematicians. Einstein finally presented his theory as a formal argument from certain basic principles or axioms. According to his testimony, the theory came about by a different process. The presentation was a form of verification. Einstein has been quoted as follows:

> The way the triple set of axioms are contrasted in the Einstein-Infeld book is not at all the way things happened in the process of actual thinking. This was merely a later formulation of the subject matter, just

[7] Findlay (1948), pp. 36-38.

a question of how the thing could afterwards best be written. The axioms express essentials in a condensed form. Once one has found such things one enjoys formulating them in that way; but in this process they did not grow out of any manipulation of axioms.

These thoughts did not come in any verbal formulation. I very rarely think in words at all. A thought comes, and I may try to express it in words afterward. . . . During all these years there was a feeling of direction, of going straight toward something concrete. It is, of course, very hard to express that feeling in words; but it was decidedly the case, and clearly to be distinguished from later considerations about the rational form of the solution. Of course, behind such direction there is always something logical; but I have it in a kind of survey, in a way visually.[8]

Einstein went on through the formal steps of hypotheses and prediction, incorporating the special theory of relativity (to which references have just been made) into his general theory. The general theory dramatically predicted that rays of light would be bent in the gravitational field of a large object. The prediction was precisely verified during the solar eclipse of 1919. This kind of physical verification indicated enough agreement between Einstein's theory and the known facts of the universe that the theory could no longer be dismissed as a mathematical fantasy.

We know a great deal about techniques of verification and about the logic of proof. What we know least about is how preparation starts the processes that ripen through incubation to culminate in an illumination that can be verified. We need to guard against the kind of preparation that will stultify thinking and destroy creativity, leading instead to routine, pedantic, and unimaginative approaches to problems. Creative, inventive insights often mark the steps in scientific advance; we need to discover,

[8] Wertheimer (1959), pp. 183-84.

if we can, how best to prepare a mental climate for them.

Creative thinking in the arts

Creative thinking goes on both in artistic production and in scientific discovery. Whereas the scientist is bent upon the discovery of facts and principles (and the invention and applications of theories), the artist seeks to interpret imaginatively things, relationships, or values as he perceives them. Scientific knowledge is factual and can be stated in the form of the proposition, "Thus and so are true under specified conditions," which can be verified by any competent person with the proper equipment. The "truth" of a work of art is felt intuitively as well as intellectually and can be verified only by reference to one's personal experience. Both artist and scientist may have the thrill of discovery or of invention; both may have a period of incubation before their thoughts are clarified through a "hunch" or inspiration.

We have examined the analysis of creative thought in science that suggests four stages in achieving the final solution: preparation, incubation, illumination, and verification. An experimental study of the creative activity of artists and poets showed that they went through these same stages in creating.

Fifty-five poets consented to serve in an experiment in which they would create poetry and help the experimenter to understand the processes employed. A control group of 58 nonpoets also participated. The experimenter followed a standard procedure. She showed each poet the same picture and asked him to write a poem suggested by it. The picture was a mountain scene, with waterfalls in the background— a kind of imaginary Yosemite Park. The experimenter kept a record of all the comments made by the poets and of the successive versions of their poems. The task was taken seriously, and some excellent poems were produced. (Those by the poets, as might be expected, turned out better than those by the nonpoets.) Subsequently, two of the authors sold their poems for publication without further revision.

That a kind of problem-solving was going on appeared from the analysis of the data. It took the subjects a while to isolate a theme, which gave a kind of goal direction to the poem. This was the stage of preparation and incubation, cut short by the limited time allowed. The theme often came suddenly with accompanying emotion. This was the stage of illumination. Then words had to be chosen to fit both this theme and the formal arrangement of line and meter preferred by the poet. Often the first draft did not satisfy, and fresh starts, or corrected approximations, were made. These activities were similar to the scientist's steps in verification. Because of their greater skill, the poets spent less time in revising than did the nonpoets. At some point, each poet felt satisfied that he had reached a solution: the poem expressed the intended theme in a finished way (Patrick, 1935).

Patrick's results with artists and poets have been summarized by Johnson (1955) in graphic form (Figure 12-9). Because the whole process took place in one sitting, the incubation-illumination stages of Wallas are represented by "formulation," into which these processes are condensed.

Thus it appears that the chief differences are not in the processes of thinking used by scientist and artist but in the tasks they choose. The end result for the scientist is a conclusion stated clearly, communicating information that other scientists can verify for themselves. The end result for the artist is a production that can be judged or appreciated, but not proved as scientific statements can be proved. Intellectual demands do not differentiate artists and scientists. The kinds of facts and values dealt with, the emotions involved, and the kinds of critical judgments called for are probably sufficiently different to attract different

12-9

Problem-solving during creative activity

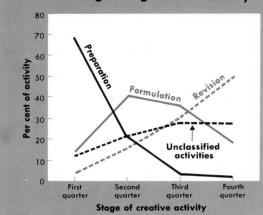

The artists and poets completed their task in one sitting. Hence the incubation-illumination stages of Wallas are represented by the stage of formulation. (Data from Patrick, 1935, 1937, as plotted by Johnson, 1955)

sorts of people, although some rare individuals, such as Leonardo da Vinci, have excelled at both.

Wallas' four stages in thinking are suggestive, but not a final scientific analysis. Eindhoven and Vinacke (1952), repeating an experimental study of artists along the line of the work by Patrick (1937), found it necessary to add a good many intervening steps and asides other than Wallas' four, if they were to describe accurately what the artists did and the differences between experienced artists and novices. Many other schemes for defining the steps in problem-solving have been proposed from time to time. A widely used one, which originated with Dewey (1910), divides the problem-solving process into five steps: (1) a felt difficulty, (2) location and definition of the problem, (3) suggestion of possible solutions, (4) reasoning about these suggestions, and (5) testing the solution by tryout and experiment. Johnson (1955) finds it more convenient to think in terms of three major stages: (1) preparation, (2) production, and (3) judgment.

The creative person

Some people are more original, inventive, and creative than others, and it is pertinent to inquire whether there are common characteristics among such people. While this means that we shall have to anticipate somewhat our discussion of personality appraisal (Chapter 16), some of the major approaches to this problem are worth citing at this point.

One approach is to study the characteristics of outstandingly creative people. Roe (1952), for example, studied scientists nominated by their own colleagues as among the more distinguished within their own branches of science. On the whole, they were highly intelligent people, but there were some differences from one field to another in other respects. For example, the laboratory scientists tended to rely more on visual imagery than the theoreticians, who seemed to lay particular emphasis upon thinking in words. A number of superior groups have been studied in the Institute for Personality Assessment Research at the University of California in Berkeley, under the general direction of MacKinnon (e.g., MacKinnon, 1960). The groups have included writers, artists, mathematicians, and research scientists. One of their findings has been that these more creative groups have all scored high on *both* theoretical and esthetic values on the Allport-Vernon-Lindzey test of values (Allport and others, 1960), irrespective of their fields of endeavor.

Another approach is to study a more general population by the usual methods of psychological testing in order to determine what kinds of abilities or personal characteristics seem to appear among those who score high in creativity or problem-solving. Masculinity appears to be one of the general traits associated with a high order of problem-solving ability (Sweeney, 1953;

Milton, 1957); social nonconformers also appear to be somewhat better problem-solvers (Nakamura, 1958). When the methods of factor analysis (see Chapter 14) are used, such traits as fluency, flexibility, and ability to elaborate emerge as important aspects of creative ability and planning (Guilford, 1959b).

The issue is often raised about the relationship of emotional instability and neuroticism to creative ability. It is easy to think of distinguished artists and writers who were tormented by personal problems and whose creative abilities may therefore have sprung from their internal conflicts. There is a division of opinion on this topic, even among psychoanalysts who have had considerable experience in dealing as physicians with disturbed artists and other creative people. Kris (1952) sees some contribution of neuroticism to art, while Kubie (1958) believes that neuroticism, while it can be found among artists as among all people, is essentially a handicap to their artistic fulfillment.

Several observations are appropriate in this connection:

1. For some artists and writers, the themes that form the content of their creative efforts are in a large measure autobiographical, and in that sense may reflect their own unresolved conflicts. This was apparently the case with Eugene O'Neill, whose "conscious" autobiography appears in the play *Long Day's Journey Into Night,* whereas his "unconscious" autobiography is perhaps revealed in *Desire Under the Elms* (Weissman, 1957).

2. A writer who makes use of his own experiences does not necessarily write just for himself, out of inner compulsion; he generalizes his own experiences so that they have a message for a larger audience. In such a case, the purposes served and the satisfactions achieved are not all of the kind which might be elimi-

nated were the individual to undergo psychotherapy.

3. A writer, artist, or other creative person who presents himself for psychotherapy usually does so because the suffering caused by his conflicts, far from serving creativity, makes it impossible for him to create. For him, successful therapy permits him to *return* to his typewriter or his canvas.

There are some definitely neurotic people who are very creative, and there may be some neurotic traits among many others. Many creative persons show some immature or childlike qualities, such as (1) *dependency* on others, with refusal to accept (or to carry out) the ordinary social responsibilities of adult life; (2) *defiance* of authority or convention; (3) a sense of *omnipotence,* or what has been called a sense of destiny (Gough, 1957; McCurdy, 1957); (4) *gullibility,* or uncritical acceptance in some intellectual sphere, no matter how critical in others. That these traits are coherent with flexibility, nonconformity, and imaginative elaboration, as found in quantitative studies, is not too surprising. The most puzzling of these is the last one, gullibility, but a good case for it has been made by Jones (1957). He gives biographical references to Copernicus, Darwin, Goethe, and Newton to illustrate his point. Each of these great thinkers displayed surprising areas of credulousness, Copernicus in his fascination with the Aristotelian notion that the perfection of the Divine Creator required circular motion, Darwin in a curious notion of "pangenesis" that has since been ignored, Newton in some fantastic conclusions about the symbolism of the Book of Daniel and the Book of Revelations. Concerning Goethe, Jones quotes Thomas Mann, who referred to him as "The union in one human being of the greatest intellectual gifts with the most amazing naïveté." Jones interprets these cases to mean that there is in men of genius a characteristic receptivity to novel ideas, and the fact that some of these are uncritically accepted may have been a small price to pay for the creative ideas that have stood up under criticism.

There are undoubtedly many facets to creative activity; some creative efforts must have simply followed Carlyle's dictum that "genius . . . means the transcendent capacity for taking trouble" or Edison's "genius is one per cent inspiration and ninety-nine per cent perspiration."

SUMMARY   1. Thinking is behavior that uses *ideas* or *symbolic* representations of things and events. It thus can go beyond perceptual solution of problems, or solution through manipulation, by having reference to events not present, that is, to remembered, absent, or imagined things.

2. Thinking may be subdivided into *associative thinking* and *directed thinking.* Associative thinking includes *free* and *controlled* association, reverie or daydreaming, night dreaming, and autistic thinking, of which rationalization is one variety. Directed thinking includes both *critical* and *creative* thinking.

3. Thinking of a less controlled sort, known as *associative thinking,* goes on in reverie, daydreaming, and in the dreams of sleep. In both daydreams and night dreams, free association accounts for much of the content, but both are governed by drives which determine the direction of association and some of the content. Both are influenced by the needs of the individual and hence in the extreme represent autistic thinking, of which rationaliza-

tion is another example. We distinguish between the *manifest* content of a dream (its superficial characters and plot) and its *latent* content (its meaning in terms of the motives of the dreamer).

4. *Critical thinking* attempts to find erroneous conclusions and logical fallacies. Stating propositions in abstract form may help to remove *atmosphere effects,* in which the fact that parts of a statement are substantively true may lead to conclusions that are logically false. Stating propositions in concrete form provides a way of testing conclusions against reality.

5. A symbol *stands for* something else. Some symbols are concrete objects, e.g., a stop sign; *words* are especially powerful symbols, and language is thus an important agent in the thinking process. A symbol conveys *meaning;* but the precise relation between the symbol and the object it stands for (i.e., its meaning) is a subject on which psychologists are not agreed.

6. A useful distinction can be made between *denotative* meanings, which are fixed and specific, and *connotative* meanings, which express evaluation or preference. One attempt to measure connotations is by the *semantic differential.*

7. Studies of *concept formation* show that concepts tend to be attained in the following order: concrete things, spatial forms, color, and number. One formulation distinguishes between *conjunctive, disjunctive,* and *relational* concepts; the first and third of these are more easily arrived at than the second.

8. Language and thought are intimately related. Thus children are able to solve some kinds of transposition problems only when they are old enough to state the solution in words. Even man's way of conceiving the world is reflected in the language forms he uses. The cause-and-effect relationships here are confusing, but are now becoming the subject of experimental study.

9. The way in which we use our brains in thinking is still a matter of conjecture. Two theories of thinking suggest differing functions of the brain: the *peripheralists* hold that all thinking goes on in muscular movements, and the *centralists* hold that thinking goes on inside the brain and nervous system and that muscular movements merely accompany the "central process."

10. Subjects in problem-solving experiments adopt systematic modes of solution, such as the half-split technique, which are often a help to them. Such systematic solutions help in trouble-shooting because they lead to an efficient use of information.

11. Two obstacles to problem-solving crop up in many experiments: *persistence of habitual set* and *functional fixedness,* based on the normal use-meaning of a tool or other object. These obstacles can best be overcome through training that stresses flexibility in approach to problems.

12. There are difficulties in stating a generalization about group thinking compared with individual thinking. The group has advantages only under specified circumstances, such as the possession of more relevant information by the group as a whole than by any one member.

13. Scientific discovery is a complex process illustrating the best rules man has so far devised for problem-solving. Scientists report in their own work a period of *preparation,* followed occasionally by sudden *illumination* after a period of *incubation.* They finally *verify* their work by making logical deductions from accepted principles and by checking their predictions through experiment.

14. The work of creative artists, so far as the steps in thinking are concerned, is not very different from that of scientists, although the goals of scientific and artistic work differ. While the end result for the scientist is an objective, factual statement, the end result for the artist is a product that communicates values or emotions.

15. Studies of creative people, whether based on samples of unusually creative individuals or on general population studies, show a number of characteristics, such as flexibility, fluency, and capacity to elaborate, along with some social nonconformity. No easy statement can be made about the relationship between neurotic symptoms and creativity; sometimes neurotic conflicts may provide the themes for creative efforts, sometimes these conflicts may hamper creativity. There is a suggestion that some creative people may display childlike traits of dependency upon others, defiance of authority and convention, a sense of omnipotence, and gullibility (in certain limited areas).

SUGGESTIONS FOR FURTHER READING

Two textbooks cover the kinds of problems dealt with in this chapter: Johnson, *The psychology of thought and judgment* (1955), and Vinacke, *The psychology of thinking* (1952). A very useful summary of contemporary views held by a number of authors who participated in a conference on thinking can be found in Harms (Ed.), *Fundamentals of psychology: the psychology of thinking* (1960).

The relation between language and thought is considered in Miller, *Language and communication* (1951), and Brown, *Words and things* (1958). Meaning and the semantic differential are the topics of Osgood, Suci, and Tannenbaum, *The measurement of meaning* (1957). The development of thinking in the child is reported by Inhelder and Piaget, *The growth of logical thinking from childhood to adolescence* (1958).

The opposite of flexibility is, of course, rigidity, reported more extensively in Luchins and Luchins, *Rigidity of behavior* (1959), and Rokeach, *The open and closed mind* (1960).

A number of authors have contributed their views on creativity in Anderson (Ed.), *Creativity and its cultivation* (1959).

For a psychoanalytic view of thinking, Rapaport, *Organization and pathology of thought* (1951) is a good but difficult source.

Individuality and Personality

While there are general principles of psychology that apply to all men everywhere, the individual differences among men (and among other organisms) are of great interest—not only because of the desire to understand individual uniqueness, but also because a complex society demands specialized roles for its members, and problems arise in finding those individuals most suited for the various requirements of a differentiated community. The introduction of statistical methods into psychology came very largely through the attempts to measure individuality and to find interrelationships among individual characteristics. Among the aspects of individuality that we need to understand are basic abilities, such as intelligence, the influence of heredity and of environment upon such abilities, and, in general, the unique personality as an end product of all the influences within and upon the individual.

CHAPTER 13

Statistical Methods and Measurement

Before we turn to the problems of human differences and their measurement, we shall digress a little to consider the tools used in such measurement. The basic tools come from *statistics*—the science that deals with collecting and handling numerical data, and with making inferences from such data. In preceding chapters we have met many statistical statements, such as statements of correlation and statements that were statistically significant. We are now ready to consider more fully what such statements mean.

The procedure of this chapter

Because many students who study introductory psychology are poorly trained in mathematics and timid about using the mathematics they know, the concepts of statistics are often considered inaccessible to them. This chapter is written on the assumption that the problems of statistics are essentially logical, that is, problems of clear thinking about data, and that an *introductory* acquaintance with both descriptive statistics and statistical inference is *not* beyond the student who can use a little arithmetic and understands only enough algebra to use plus and minus signs and to substitute numbers for letters in equations.

Even a little acquaintance with statistics requires time and exercise in applying what has been learned. Because in a beginning psychology course the amount of time that can be devoted to these problems is limited,

the treatment that follows states the essential relationships first in words and in simple numerical examples that require little computation. For understanding the more complex processes there follows, in a separate section that can be omitted if necessary, a specimen computation illustrating the particular statistical measure under consideration. These illustrations use a minimum of data, artificially selected to make the operations clear even to the student who is unskilled in arithmetic. Because of the scantiness and artificiality of the data, these specimen computations violate an important principle in the use of statistics, namely, that a formula should be used only on appropriate data. But this violation can be justified, because the purpose is to provide examples easy to master, and because the knowledge necessary to judge the appropriate uses and limitations of the formulas requires advanced study.

Averages and Measures of Variation

Statistics can serve, first of all, to provide us with a shorthand description of a mass of data. Suppose that we wish to study the ages of 5000 students recorded on cards in the registrar's office. These ages are *raw data*. If we thumb through the cards, we will get some idea of the ages of the students, but it will be impossible to keep all of them in mind. So we make some kind of statistical summary, counting the number of students of each age, and from this summary we find it easier to talk about the ages of the students. It will be still easier if we find the average age and also the age of the youngest and the oldest student. Such simplifying or summarizing statements are known as *descriptive statistics*.

Frequency distributions

Items of raw data become comprehensible if they are ranked in numerical order or grouped in a *frequency distribution*. To group the data, we first divide into portions the scale along which they rank, and then we count the items of data (cases) that fall into each interval. To go back to our example, if we group together all students of ages 16 and 17, those of 18 and 19, and those of 20 and 21, we have combined the data into orderly groups. The two-year interval in which the students are grouped is called a *class interval* and represents a portion of our scale. The choice of interval and its scope depend upon the matter we are studying.

A simple set of artificial data is given in Table 13-1, and the data are accumulated into a frequency distribution in Table 13-2. The class intervals are chosen so as to include ten scores (10-19, 20-29, etc.). It is much easier to see what is happening by looking at Table 13-2 than Table 13-1. We

A frequency diagram

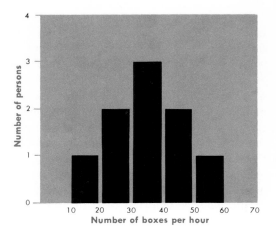

The data plotted are those from Table 13-2.

can easily pick out the more extreme performances and those that are more nearly representative of the group.

A frequency distribution is commonly plotted as a *frequency diagram*. Such diagrams are merely graphical methods of presenting the same data found in the frequency table. One form of frequency diagram is illustrated in Figure 13-1, based on the data of Table 13-2.

In practice one would want far more cases than those plotted, but all our illustrations use a minimum of data so that the student can easily check all the steps in tabulating and plotting.

Averages

By an average we mean merely some representative point on our scale, a central point with scores scattering on either side.[1] Three such measures are in common use:

The *mean* is the familiar arithmetic average, obtained by adding the scores and dividing by the number of scores. The sum of the raw scores of Table 13-1 is 309.

[1] An average has been called a *measure of central tendency,* but there is little point in using the more cumbersome expression when the single word *average* will do.

TABLE 13-1

Raw scores

Number of boxes packed in one hour by 9 beginners in a factory

12	53	24
27	48	32
41	38	34

TABLE 13-2

Frequency distribution

Raw scores of Table 13-1, accumulated with class intervals of 10

Boxes packed in one hour	*Number of persons achieving this score*
10-19	1
20-29	2
30-39	3
40-49	2
50-59	1

Divide this by 9 (the number of scores), and the mean turns out to be 34.3 boxes per hour.

The *median* is the score of the middle case, obtained by arranging the scores in order and then counting in to the middle from either end. The median case in Table 13-1 is the fifth from either end of a group of nine, that is, 34 boxes per hour. If the number of cases is even, some compromise is necessary. A simple one is to average the two cases on either side of the middle. For instance, in a group of 10 cases, the median can be taken as the mean of cases 5 and 6.

The *mode* is that part of the scale where most cases occur. It is the score equivalent to the high point of the frequency diagram in Figure 13-1. In this example the mode falls in the interval of 30-39 boxes per hour.

In a *symmetrical distribution,* in which the cases distribute evenly on either side of the middle (as in the example of Table 13-2 and Figure 13-1), the mean, median, and mode all fall together. This is not true for distributions that are *skewed,* that is, un-balanced. Suppose one were analyzing the starting times of a morning commuting train. The train is usually on time in leaving; occasionally it starts late, but it never starts early. For a train with a correct starting time of 8:00 A.M., one week's record might be:

M	8:00	Mean starting time:	8:07
T	8:05	Median starting time:	8:00
W	8:00	Modal starting time:	8:00
Th	8:30		
F	8:00		

The distribution of starting times in this example is *skewed* because of the two late departures; they raise the mean departure time, but do not raise either the median or the mode. Skewed distributions are named by the direction in which the *tail* of the distribution falls—the direction of the most extreme scores (Figure 13-2). In our example, the skew is toward the late departure.

Skewness is important because, unless it is understood, the differences between the median and mean may sometimes prove misleading. Suppose that two political parties are arguing about the prosperity of the country. It is quite possible (though not common) for the mean and median incomes to move in opposite directions. Suppose, for example, that a round of wage increases was combined with a reduction in extremely high incomes. Then the median might go up while the mean went down. The party wanting to show that incomes were getting higher would choose the median; the one that wished to show that incomes were getting lower would choose the mean.

The mean is the most widely used of the measures of central tendency. It can always be computed from raw scores by adding them and dividing by their number. Sometimes it is convenient to compute the mean from grouped data. This produces a slight distortion because of the use of class intervals, but the distortion is usually negligible.

Specimen computation of the mean from grouped data. When the mean is computed

TABLE **13-3**

Computation of mean from grouped data of Table 13-2

Boxes per hour	(1) Midpoint of class interval *	(2) Number of persons	Product (1) × (2)
10-19	14.5	1	14.5
20-29	24.5	2	49.0
30-39	34.5	3	103.5
40-49	44.5	2	89.0
50-59	54.5	1	54.5
		$N = 9$	Sum 310.5
			Mean $= \dfrac{310.5}{9} = 34.5$

* The midpoint is determined by averaging the highest and lowest case that can fall in the interval. Thus $(10 + 19)/2 = 14.5$.

13-2

Skewed distribution curves

Note that skewed distributions are named by the direction in which the tail is found.

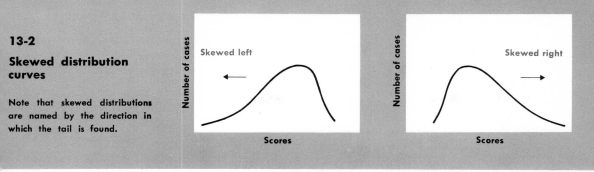

from grouped data, it is **assumed that all scores fall at the midpoint of the class interval in which they lie**. The data from Table 13-2 are used as a basis for the computation illustrated in Table 13-3. Because of the symmetry of the distribution the mean falls at 34.5, the midpoint of the middle interval, very close to the mean of 34.3 obtained from the raw scores.

Measures of variation [2]

Usually we need more information about a distribution than we can get from an average. For example, we need a measure to tell us whether scores cluster closely around their average or whether they scatter widely.

[2] Also called measures of dispersion.

A measure of the spread or dispersion of scores around the average is called a *measure of variation*.

Measures of variation help us in at least two ways. First, they tell us how representative the average is. If the variation is small, we know that individual cases are close to it. If the variation is large, we can make use of the mean as a representative value with less assurance. Suppose, for example, we are designing clothing for a distant people, e.g., Eskimos. Knowing their average size would help us, but it would be very important to know also the spread of sizes. The second thing the measure of variation gives us is a "yardstick" by which we decide how

13-3

Distributions differing in variation

It is easy to see by inspection that the scores of Class I cluster closer to the mean than those of Class II, even though the means for the two classes are alike. Computations (by the methods to be discussed in this chapter) show these comparisons of measures of variation for the two classes: range, 20 and 30; mean deviation, 3.0 and 5.5; standard deviation, 4.5 and 7.2. Class II thus has the larger variation no matter how variation is measured.

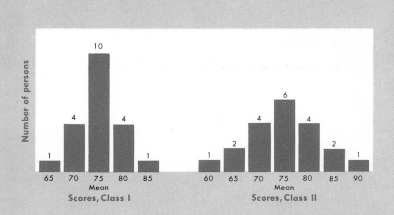

far a single score is above or below the mean. For example, if you have a grade of 85 on an examination, you want to know not only what the mean was, but how high the scores went. Without some measure of variation you do not know *how far* 85 is from the mean.

Distributions of scores from two classes of 20 students showing the same mean but with different variation are pictured in Figure 13-3. It is evident that some sort of measures are required to specify more exactly how these two classes differ. Three measures will be considered: the *range,* the *mean deviation,* and the *standard deviation.*

Why so many measures? The choice is in part a matter of convenience. We shall see that the range is the easiest to compute, that the mean deviation is easily understood, and that the standard deviation, even though it is the most complex, has some mathematical advantages that make it a preferred measure.

In order to simplify our example still further for ease in arithmetical computation, let us suppose that five students from each of these classes seek entrance to college, and that the entrance examinations of these students reflect (and exaggerate) the differences between the classes from which they come. Their entrance examination scores are as follows:

Students from
Class I: 73, 74, 75, 76, 77 (mean = 75)

Students from
Class II: 60, 65, 75, 85, 90 (mean = 75)

Let us now compute the measures of variation for these two small samples, one from Class I, the other from Class II.

The *range* is the spread between the highest and the lowest score. The range for the five students from Class I is 4 (from 73 to 77); for those from Class II it is 30 (from 60 to 90).

The *mean deviation* is the average amount by which each score departs from the mean of all scores. For this purpose we disregard the sign of the difference, that is, whether the score is above or below the mean. Then our formula for the mean deviation becomes:

$$\text{Mean deviation} = \frac{\text{Sum of } D}{N}$$

where D is the deviation from the mean, and N the number of cases entering into the determination.

The advantage of the mean deviation is that it is so easily understood: anyone who can understand a mean can comprehend a mean deviation from the mean. It is not much used because of certain advantages of the standard deviation, but it is included here, along with a specimen computation, in order to show the rough similarity between it and a standard deviation.

Specimen computation of mean deviation. In Table 13-4 the scores from the samples from the two classes are arranged for a separate computation of the mean deviation for each class. In order to avoid minus signs, the mean (75) is subtracted from all scores equal to or above it; scores below the mean are subtracted from it. The deviations from the mean are then added, and divided by the number of cases (5) in order to obtain the mean devia-

TABLE **13-4**	
Computation of mean deviation	
From Class I *(mean = 75)*	*From Class II* *(mean = 75)*
77 − 75 = 2	90 − 75 = 15
76 − 75 = 1	85 − 75 = 10
75 − 75 = 0	75 − 75 = 0
75 − 74 = 1	75 − 65 = 10
75 − 73 = 2	75 − 60 = 15
—	—
Sum of deviations = 6	Sum of deviations = 50
Mean deviation = 6/5 = 1.2	Mean deviation = 50/5 = 10.0

TABLE **13-5**

Computation of standard deviation

	From Class I (mean = 75)			From Class II (mean = 75)	
	D (deviation from mean)	D^2 (deviation squared)		D (deviation from mean)	D^2 (deviation squared)
$77 - 75 =$	2	4	$90 - 75 =$	15	225
$76 - 75 =$	1	1	$85 - 75 =$	10	100
$75 - 75 =$	0	0	$75 - 75 =$	0	0
$74 - 75 =$	-1	1	$65 - 75 =$	-10	100
$73 - 75 =$	-2	4	$60 - 75 =$	-15	225
Sum of $D^2 = 10$		10	Sum of $D^2 = 650$		650
Mean of $D^2 = 10/5 = 2.0$			Mean of $D^2 = 650/5 = 130$		
Standard deviation $(\sigma) = \sqrt{2.0} = 1.4$			Standard deviation $(\sigma) = \sqrt{130} = 11.4$		

tion. Class I's mean deviation of 1.2 is much less than Class II's 10.0, as we determined from our inspection of the raw data.

The *standard deviation,* for which we use either the initials (S.D.) or the lower-case [3] Greek letter *sigma* (σ), is also based upon the deviation from the mean. However, instead of averaging the deviations directly, as in the mean deviation, each deviation is first squared; then the average of these squares is obtained. The standard deviation is the square root of this result, according to the formula:

$$\text{Standard deviation } (\sigma) = \sqrt{\frac{\text{Sum of } D^2}{N}}$$

There are complex mathematical reasons for the advantage that is derived in squaring the deviations, having to do with the stability of the measure as compared with the mean deviation, but there is also a matter of convenience in that the algebraic sign of the deviation disappears in the squaring. With the mean deviation the sign of the difference has to be ignored.

[3] The lower-case letter *s* is also in use, especially when dealing with standard deviations of small samples. For this introductory treatment we shall use sigma (σ) throughout.

Specimen computation of the standard deviation. The data used in Table 13-4 for the computation of the mean deviation are arranged (Table 13-5) for the computation of the standard deviation. In Table 13-5 we subtract the mean from the score regardless of the size of score. We therefore get minus scores, but these disappear when we square the deviations. Note that the two standard deviations show the same order of difference as the mean deviations. For this example, the two measures tell much the same story, although we note that they are not mathematically equivalent.

The reasons for a general preference for the standard deviation over other measures lie, first, in the fact that it shows a greater stability than other measures when new samples of data are gathered, and, second, in certain characteristics that make it useful in the scaling of data and in further computations, such as the product-moment coefficient of correlation. We shall meet both these topics later in the chapter.

The three measures of variation (range, mean deviation, and standard deviation) all show that the variabilities of the scores from the sample of Class I are smaller than those from Class II. While these values therefore agree with what is obvious from inspection of the original data, the statistical statements are more precise.

Statistical Inference

Now that we have become familiar with averages and measures of variation as ways of describing collections of data, we are ready to turn to the processes of interpretation, to the making of inferences from data.

Populations and samples

We need first of all to distinguish between a *population* and a *sample* drawn from the population. The U.S. Census Bureau attempts to reach everyone in the country, to describe the whole population, obtaining descriptive material on age, marital status, and so on. The word "population" is appropriate to the Census, because it represents *all* the people living in the United States.

The word "population" in statistics is not limited to people or animals or things. The "population" may be all the temperatures registered on a thermometer, all the words in the English language, or all of any other specified supply of data.[4] Usually we do not have access to the total population, and so we try to represent it by a *sample* drawn in some *random* (unbiased) fashion. We may ask some questions of a random fraction of the people, as the U.S. Census has done as part of recent censuses; we may derive average temperatures by reading the thermometer at specified times, without taking a continuous record; we may estimate the words in the encyclopedia by counting the words on a random number of pages. These illustrations all represent the selection of a *sample* from a larger population. If we repeat any of these processes, we will

come out with slightly different results, owing to the fact that a sample does not fully represent the whole population, and hence has within it *errors of sampling*. This is where statistical considerations enter.

We gather data from samples and study them in order to make inferences. Thus we examine the census data to see if the population is getting older, if the trend of migration away from the center of the city to the suburbs is continuing, and so on. Similarly, we study our experimental results to find out what effects our conditions of practice have had upon ultimate performance, whether or not the threshold for pitch is affected by loudness, whether child-rearing practices have detectable effects later on. In order to make *statistical inferences* from data we have to study the relationships revealed by our data, and make appropriate comparisons showing one condition to be more favorable than another, or the size of one variable related to the presence or absence or size of another. These inferences are always made under circumstances where there is some degree of uncertainty because of sampling errors and measurement errors (to be discussed below). If our statistical tests show us that the magnitude of the effects we find in our comparisons are great relative to the estimates of error, then we can have confidence in what we have found.

As an introduction to statistical inference we shall first consider the normal distribution and its use in interpreting standard deviations. Then we shall turn to problems of sampling errors and the significance of differences. *Study Well*

The normal distribution

Thus far we have mentioned symmetrical and skewed distributions that result when we gather data into frequency distributions. When large masses of data are collected, tabulated, and plotted on a graph, they often fall into a symmetrical distribution of roughly bell shape, known as the *normal distribution* and plotted as the *normal curve*

[4] Sometimes the supply of data (the total population) is not so easily specified, as when we sample a subject's speed of reaction by taking 100 measurements among all those he might possibly yield if we continued the experiment endlessly. As long as the total supply of data is several times that of the sample (whether finite, e.g., all students studying Latin at College *X*, or indeterminate, as in the case of all possible reaction times), we are able to use statistical sampling theory in treating the results.

(Figures 13-4 and 13-6). Most cases fall near the mean, thus giving the high point of the bell, and the bell tapers off sharply with very high or very low scores. This form of curve is of special interest because it also arises when we plot *chance* events—hence our assertion that it is the "normal" curve.

What do we mean by "chance" events? We mean only that the causal factors are very complex and numerous, yielding results of the sort found in tossing dice or spinning a roulette wheel. Long ago Sir Francis Galton (1889) devised a machine consisting of rows of nails over which a stream of shot was poured through a funnel into partitioned compartments below (Figure 13-5). The "chance" factors of the interaction of the shot particles with the nails and with each other result in a symmetrical distribution, more shot falling straight down, but an occasional one reaching the end compartments. This is a useful way of visualizing what is meant by a chance distribution that conforms closely to the "normal" curve.

13-4

A curve approaching the normal distribution

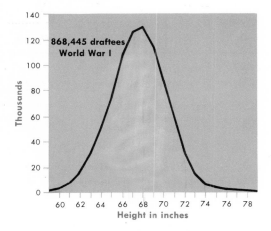

Distribution of height of 868,445 American men drafted in World War I. The lower end of the curve is curtailed through rejection of men of very short stature. (After Davenport and Love, 1921)

13-5

A machine to illustrate a chance distribution

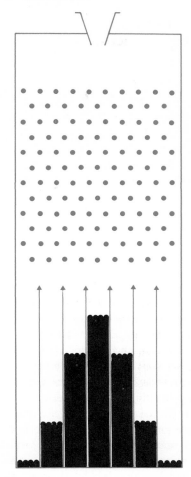

With the board tilted slightly backward, shot is poured through the funnel at the top. It then bounces down through the nails, to form the distribution shown in the compartments below. Because the amount of shot in each compartment (approximating a normal distribution) can be computed from the coefficients of a binomial distribution, Galton, who designed such a machine, called it a "binomial machine." (After Galton, 1889, p. 63)

The normal curve (Figure 13-6) can be defined mathematically to represent the pure case of the distribution approximated by the machine described in Figure 13-5. It shows the likelihood that cases within a normally

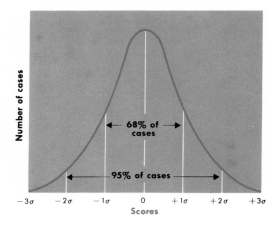

The normal distribution curve can be constructed provided we know the number of cases, the mean, and the standard deviation.

distributed population will depart from the mean by any stated amount. It is convenient to remember that roughly two-thirds of the cases (68 per cent) will tend to fall within 1σ of the mean, and 95 per cent within 2σ. Thus if we understand the properties of the normal curve, we can interpret any statistic expressed in units of the standard deviation, provided the cases on which the statistic is based are normally distributed. The percentages marked on Figure 13-6 represent the *percentage of the area* lying under the curve between the indicated scale values, with the total area representing the whole population. A more detailed listing of areas under portions of the normal curve is given in Table 13-6.

We shall have a number of uses for the values in Table 13-6.

First let us see where the 68 per cent and 95 per cent values of Figure 13-6 come from. We find from column 3 of Table 13-6 that between -1σ and the mean there lies .341 of the total area, and between $+1\sigma$ and the mean also .341. Adding these, we get .682, which has been expressed in Figure 13-6 as 68 per cent. Similarly we can

find the area between -2σ and $+2\sigma$ to be $2 \times .477 = .954$, which has been expressed as 95 per cent.

We shall have two uses for these percentages in this chapter. One of them is in connection with the interpretation of standard scores, to which we next turn. The other is in connection with tests of significance of the differences between means and other statistical measures.

Both these uses make an important assumption, namely, that the scores being interpreted, when plotted as a frequency diagram, fit the normal curve. It is fortunate that a great many score distributions do fit the normal curve or come very close to it, so that this basic assumption does not cause us much trouble. Since we are aware, of course, of skewed distributions, we know the normal distribution is not always found. Fortunately, some skewness in the data does not prevent applying most of the ordinary statistical formulas.

TABLE 13-6

Area under normal curve as ratio of total area

Standard deviation *	(1) Area below this value	(2) Area above this value	(3) Area between this value and mean
-3.0σ	.001	.999	.499
-2.5σ	.006	.994	.494
-2.0σ	.023	.977	.477
-1.5σ	.067	.933	.433
-1.0σ	.159	.841	.341
-0.5σ	.309	.691	.191
0.0σ	.500	.500	.000
$+0.5\sigma$	.691	.309	.191
$+1.0\sigma$	.841	.159	.341
$+1.5\sigma$	.933	.067	.433
$+2.0\sigma$	.977	.023	.477
$+2.5\sigma$	.994	.006	.494
$+3.0\sigma$	.999	.001	.499

* Measured from the mean (0.08).

Scaling of data

In order to interpret a score we often want to know whether it is high or low relative to other scores. If I take a practical driver's test and find that I need 0.500 seconds to put my foot on the brake after a danger signal, how can I tell whether my performance is fast or slow? If I make a 60 in my physics examination, do I pass the course? To answer questions of this kind we have to derive some sort of *scale* against which we can compare the scores.

Ranked Data. By placing scores in rank order from high to low we derive one kind of scale. We interpret an individual score by telling where it ranks among the group of scores. Thus the graduates of West Point know where they stand—perhaps 35th or 125th among a class of 400.

Centile Scale. If ranks are converted to positions between 0 and 100, then a rank can be interpreted according to our knowledge of percentages. Such a ranking yields a *centile scale.* A person at the 90th centile in a large group knows that only 10 per cent of the group score higher than he; one at the 50th centile knows that he is halfway between the top and the bottom of his group.[5]

Specimen computation of centiles from ranks. When computing centiles, one usually begins with ranks. That is, the scores are first placed in order. The usual convention is that the highest score receives a rank of 1, and we shall follow this in the example. It should be noted, however, that centiles run the other way, the highest score being near 100 and the lowest near 0. Our formula, taking these conventions into account, is:

$$\text{Centile position} = 100 - \frac{100(R - .5)}{N}$$

where R = rank (with 1 high), and N = number of cases ranked.

Suppose we now wish to find the centile po-

[5] The *centile* scale is often improperly called a *percentile* scale.

sition of a student who ranks tenth in a class of 50 students. The computation becomes:

$$\text{Centile position} = 100 - \frac{100(10 - .5)}{50}$$

$$= 100 - 19 = 81$$

It is a little puzzling to understand why we do not use simple percentages, and call the centile position of rank 10 simply 80 (i.e., there are 40 scores below this, and they represent 80 per cent of the sample). The reasoning becomes a little clearer when we consider the two middle scores, that is, ranks 25 and 26. They lie on either side of the middle of the scale, and so one should fall slightly above 50, the other slightly below. That is what the formula makes them do. Computation will show their centiles to be 51 and 49, respectively.

Standard Scores. The standard deviation is a very convenient unit for scaling because we know how to interpret how far away 1σ or 2σ is from the mean (Table 13-6). A score based on some multiple of the standard deviation is known as a *standard score.*

Many scales used in psychological measurement are based on the principle of standard scores, although modifications are often made to eliminate negative signs and decimals. The negative signs are eliminated by using some arbitrary number as the mean instead of 0, and the decimals are eliminated by using values of 10 or more for the standard deviation instead of 1. The principle holds, however, that, when such a scale is used, scores are assigned a common mean and a common standard deviation. Some of these scales, related to standard scores in this way, are given in Table 13-7.

Specimen computations of standard scores and transformation to arbitrary scales. In Table 13-5 we had ten scores on an entrance examination, five each from two classes. Without more information we do not know whether these are representative of applicants from other classes or not. Let us make an assumption that the Class I and Class II students have a mean score corresponding to an assumed na-

TABLE 13-7

Some representative scales derived from standard scores *

Standard score	Graduate Record Examination	Army General Classification Test	Navy General Classification Test	Air Force Stanine †
-3σ	200	40	20	—
-2σ	300	60	30	1
-1σ	400	80	40	3
0σ	500	100	50	5
$+1\sigma$	600	120	60	7
$+2\sigma$	700	140	70	9
$+3\sigma$	800	160	80	—
Mean 0	500	100	50	5
Standard deviation 1.0	100	20	10	2

* After many scores are accumulated, the actual means and standard deviations sometimes depart widely from the intended ones. For example, the Army General Classification Test (AGCT) proved to have a mean of 97.0 and a standard deviation of 24.0 after many thousands of inductees had been tested. The norms of the Graduate Record Examination also depart from the intended scale.

† The word "stanine" was coined by the Air Force to refer to a scale known originally as "standard nine," a type of standard score with mean of 5 and standard deviation of 2, with scores ranging from 1 to 9.

tional average of 75 on the examination and that the national standard deviation is 10.

What is the *standard score* for the student from Class II who made 90 on the examination? We must express how far this score lies above the mean in multiples of the standard deviation.

$$\text{Standard score for grade of } 90 = \frac{90 - 75}{10}$$

$$= \frac{15}{10} = 1.5\sigma$$

Suppose we wish to convert the standard score computed above to a score on the scale used in the Navy General Classification Test, as shown in Table 13-7. This scale has a mean of 50 and a standard deviation of 10. Therefore the standard score of 1.5σ for our student from Class II becomes $50 + (10 \times 1.5) = 50 + 15 = 65$.

Using column 1 of Table 13-6, we find beside the value for a standard score of $+1.5\sigma$ the figure .933. This means that 93 per cent of the scores of a normal distribution will lie *below* the score of a person whose score is $+1.5\sigma$ above the mean on any score based on standard deviation. Thus

a score of 65 on the Navy General Classification Test, 650 on a Graduate Record Examination, or 8 on the Air Force Stanine (each score being equivalent) is above that achieved by 93 per cent of those on whom the test was calibrated. In other words, the standard score of $+1.5$ of our student with the grade of 90 lies at the 93rd centile. Scores representing any other multiple of the standard deviation can be similarly interpreted.

CRITICAL DISCUSSION

Ratio scales, interval scales, ordinal scales

An aspect of scaling not discussed above is very important in the theory of measurement. Problems arise over *equality of units* at different parts of the scale and over an *absolute zero* of measurement. Measures of length (inches, centimeters) have both equal units and a genuine zero. Such scales are called *ratio scales* because their numerical values can be used as ratios. For example, a pipe 8 feet long is *twice* as long as one 4 feet long, and a pipe weighing 6 pounds is *three times* as heavy as one weighing 2 pounds. Some physical scales have equal units but an arbitrary zero. The Fahrenheit and centigrade scales are examples. They are called *interval scales*. A temperature of 40° C is as much above one of 30° C as 30° C is above 20° C. That is, the 10-degree *intervals* are equal at all parts of the scale. But 40° C is *not* twice as hot as 20° C, because the scale begins at an arbitrary zero (the freezing temperature of water).[6]

Most psychological scales do not achieve the status of either interval scales or ratio scales. They are *ordinal scales*, scales that merely place items in order of size. One example of an ordinal scale is the centile scale. A centile scale does not have a true (absolute) zero, because its zero is merely the score of the lowest ranking individual included. Also, its intervals are unequal because a greater increase in proficiency is needed to move from the 90th to the 95th centile than from the 40th to the 45th centile. Scores based on the standard deviation come nearer to meeting the requirements of an interval scale, but it is very difficult to determine whether or not the scale units are really equal. Standard scores are not ratio scores, for they have no absolute zero.

Advances are continually being made in the theory of psychological scaling, and recognizing the limitations of present scales is merely to acknowledge some of the difficulties in handling the data with which psychology necessarily deals. The present scales permit great advances in a quantitative psychology, even though they fall short of some of the desirable features of physical measurement.

How representative is a mean?

When we ask about the representativeness of a mean, we are really implying two questions. First, what are the *errors of measurement?* Second, what are the *errors of sampling?* Two people measuring the same

[6] Those familiar with the gas laws from chemistry or physics will recall that the centigrade temperature scale can be converted to a ratio scale (the so-called absolute or Kelvin scale) by adding 273° (absolute zero is −273°) to ordinary centigrade readings.

length with a ruler may not get exactly the same result, and if they time an event with a stopwatch they may differ slightly in what they report. These differences are errors of measurement, which we may assume to be small. The slight errors that come from grouping data, as in computing the mean in Table 13-3, belong with errors of measurement. The second kind of error, the sampling error, interests us now. Suppose we were to select another random sample of the same size, make the necessary measurements, and compute the mean, what differences between the first and the second mean could be expected by chance?

Successive random samples drawn from the same normally distributed population will have different means, forming a distribution of *sampled means* around the *true mean* of the population. These sample means are themselves measures with a mean and standard deviation of their own. We call the standard deviation of a mean a *standard error,* and can make an estimate of it even though we have drawn only one sample and hence have only one mean:

$$\text{Standard error of the mean, } \sigma_M = \frac{\sigma}{\sqrt{N}}$$

where σ is the standard deviation of the distribution of scores, and N is the number of cases from which the mean is computed.

Because, according to the formula, the size of the standard error of the mean decreases with increase in the number of cases, a mean based on a large sample is more trustworthy (i.e., more likely to be close to the actual population mean) than one based on a smaller sample. This agrees with what common sense would lead us to expect. Computation of the standard error of the mean permits us to make clear assertions about the degree of uncertainty in our computed mean. The more cases in the sample, the more we have reduced uncertainty.

Specimen computation of the standard error of a mean. In order to compute the standard error of a mean, all we need is the number of cases in the *sample* and the standard deviation of the *sample*. (We do not have to know how large the original population is, as long as it is a fairly large multiple of the sample, say 5 to 10 times as large.) Suppose we take the mean and standard deviation computed in Table 13-5 for Class II, but assume that the sample was larger. The mean is 75, and the standard deviation is 11.4. Let us assume samples of 25, 100, and 900. Then the three standard errors of the mean would be:

For a sample of

$$25: \sigma_M = 11.4/\sqrt{25}$$
$$= 11.4/5 = 2.28$$
$$100: \sigma_M = 11.4/\sqrt{100}$$
$$= 11.4/10 = 1.14$$
$$900: \sigma_M = 11.4/\sqrt{900}$$
$$= 11.4/30 = 0.38$$

We can see that the standard error of the mean goes down as the sample size goes up. How can we interpret these differences? We can again go back to Table 13-6, for the standard error can be interpreted as any other standard deviation. Now we may ask, how much variation can we expect among newly obtained means if we repeat measurements on samples of 25, 100, and 900? We know from Table 13-6 that 68 per cent of the cases in a normal distribution lie between -1σ and $+1\sigma$ of the mean. Our obtained mean of 75 is our best estimate of the population mean. We know the size of σ_M, so we may infer that the probability is .68 that the population mean lies between these limits:

For samples of

25 each: 75 $\pm$ 2.28, or between 72.72 and 77.28

100 each: 75 $\pm$ 1.14, or between 73.86 and 76.14

900 each: 75 $\pm$ 0.38, or between 74.62 and 75.38.

Significance of a difference between means

The conclusions of many psychological experiments are drawn from the difference or lack of difference between two means, obtained from measurements taken under two conditions. The standard error of the mean therefore poses an important problem for the experimenter: Does the differ-

ence in means reflect a true difference in the population from which the samples were drawn, or is it simply the result of sampling and measurement errors?

Although we can never be sure that error has been eliminated entirely, we can test the significance of the difference and we can state with some confidence, if there were no difference in population means, the likelihood that the obtained difference might occur between sample means. The computation will obviously depend on two sets of facts: (1) how precise the means themselves are (standard error of the mean), and (2) how great the difference is between them. When put in this way, the statistical problem is clear enough. If the sample means are highly variable and the difference between them is small, we have little reason to expect the population means to differ; if the sample means show little variability and are widely separated, we have more confidence that the population means differ.

Let us consider some examples. In a reaction-time experiment the subject lifts his finger from a key when a stimulus signal comes on, and the time between the stimulus and his response is measured. His responses constitute a *sample* of his reaction times, for he does not respond with equal promptness at every trial. If the stimulus is a *light* instead of a *sound,* most of the reaction times are longer, but the times of the two responses overlap. Now we have an opportunity to test whether the excess of the mean reaction time to light over the mean reaction time to sound is *statistically significant.* Obviously we need to take into account both the spread of scores to light and sound, and the size of the difference between the two means.

As a second example, let us consider the scores of Spanish-American children in Los Angeles on reading tests, compared with the scores of the other school children in Los Angeles. The Spanish-American children score lower than the others, as far as mean differences are concerned, but again there is a great deal of overlap, some Spanish-American children doing very well, and some of the others doing very poorly. Hence we cannot accept the obtained differences in mean scores without making a test of significance. Only then can we tell whether the population means differ by an amount that is statistically significant.

Suppose that in an experiment to determine whether right-handed men are stronger than left-handed men, the results shown in the first table had been obtained.

Strength of grip in kilograms, right-handed men	Strength of grip in kilograms, left-handed men
40	40
45	45
50	50
55	55
100	60
Sum 290	Sum 250
Mean 58	Mean 50

The right-handed men averaged 8 kilograms stronger than the left-handed men. Is the result to be trusted? Obviously not, for averages derived from most of the right-handed men would not differ from averages derived from the left-handed men; the one very deviant case tells us we are dealing with an uncertain situation.

Suppose that, instead, the results had been those shown in the second table.

Strength of grip in kilograms, right-handed men	Strength of grip in kilograms, left-handed men
56	48
57	49
58	50
59	51
60	52
Sum 290	Sum 250
Mean 58	Mean 50

Again the same mean difference of 8 kilograms is found, but now we are inclined

to have greater confidence in the results because the left-handed men were consistently lower than the right-handed men. What we ask of statistics is that it furnish us a more precise way of taking into account the dependability of the mean differences, so that we do not have to rely solely on intuition and hunch that one difference is more reliable than another.

As already noted, the significance of the difference will depend both on the size of the obtained difference and upon the variability of the means being compared. We shall find below that from the standard errors of the means we can compute a *standard error of the difference between the means* (σ_{D_M}). We can then evaluate the obtained difference by using a *critical ratio,* which is the ratio between the obtained difference between the means and the standard error of the difference:

$$\text{Critical ratio} = \frac{\text{Obtained difference}}{\text{Standard error}} = \frac{D_M}{\sigma_{D_M}}$$

This ratio helps us to evaluate the significance of the difference between the means. As a rule of thumb, a critical ratio should be at least 2.0 in order for the difference between means to be accepted as significant. Earlier statements, accompanying tables in this book, that the difference between means was "statistically significant" meant that the critical ratio was at least that high.

Why is a critical ratio of 2.0 selected as significant? Simply because it can be reached by chance only 5 in 100 times. When we do a single experiment, we are willing to gamble that it will not happen to be one of the 5 in 100 chance instances. Where do we get the 5 in 100? We can treat the critical ratio as a standard score, for it is merely the difference expressed as a multiple of its standard error. Referring to Table 13-6, column 2, we ascertain that the likelihood of a standard deviation as high as +2.0 occurring by chance is .023. Because the chance of deviating in the opposite direction is also

.023, the total probability is .046. This is 46 times in 1000, or about 5 in 100, that a critical ratio as large as 2.0 would be found by chance if population means were alike.

Specimen computation of standard error of a difference and critical ratio. The computation of the critical ratio calls for finding the *standard error of the difference* between the means. Let us consider first the case in which the data are *uncorrelated.* If we are comparing the mean height of Korean girls with that of Chinese girls, the data would be uncorrelated. There is no reason for pairing one Chinese girl with one Korean girl in determining the two means.

The formula for uncorrelated data is:

Standard error of difference between means =

$$\sigma_{D_M} = \sqrt{(\sigma_{M_1})^2 + (\sigma_{M_2})^2}$$

In this formula, σ_{M_1} and σ_{M_2} are the standard errors of the two means being compared.

As an illustration of uncorrelated data, suppose we were to compare the school achievement test scores in two cities with scores on an arbitrary scale. Scores in city A have a mean of 70 and a standard error of the mean of 0.40. Scores in city B have a mean of 72 and a standard error of 0.30. We want to know if the mean of 72 of city B is significantly higher than the mean of 70 of city A.

$$\sigma_{D_M} = \sqrt{(\sigma_{M_1})^2 + (\sigma_{M_2})^2}$$
$$= \sqrt{.16 + .09} = \sqrt{.25}$$
$$= .5$$

Critical ratio $= \dfrac{D_M}{\sigma_{D_M}} = \dfrac{72 - 70}{.5} = \dfrac{2.0}{.5} = 4.0$

Because 4.0 is above 2.0, we may assert that the mean difference between the two schools meets our test of significance.

When the measurements whose means we are testing occur in pairs and are *correlated* (if, for example, we were comparing the strength of right and left hands of the same right-handed men, or studying the differences in mean height of pairs of brothers and sisters), the procedure for obtaining the standard error of the difference has to be modified to take the correlation into account. Once the standard error of the difference has been computed, taking the correlation into account by

a formula that need not concern us, the same procedure is followed as above for obtaining the critical ratio and for testing the significance; that is, the difference between the means is divided by the standard error of the difference to obtain the critical ratio, which must meet acceptable standards of significance if the difference between the means is to be accepted.

Statements about statistical significance

The rule of thumb which says that a critical ratio should be at least 2.0 is just that —an arbitrary but convenient rule. Instead of relying on this one arbitrary figure, our knowledge of the normal curve permits us to make other probability statements from our data.

Confidence Limits. We know that an interval extending from two standard deviations below to two standard deviations above the mean will include about 95 per cent of the cases (Figure 13-6, Table 13-6, column 3). Hence, with these values in mind, we can state *confidence limits* within which a mean will fall. For example, if we assume as values for right-hand strength a mean of 50.0 and a standard error of 1.0, as determined from a single sample, we can say that the chances are 95 in 100 that the population mean for right-handed strength will fall between 48, i.e., $(50 - 2 \times 1)$ and 52, i.e., $(50 + 2 \times 1)$. (We earlier used this form of expression in discussing the mean score of Class II, p. 382.) Another way of putting this is as follows: Were we to repeat the experiment a number of times, each time we would get a different mean and a different set of confidence limits. But of these sets of confidence limits, 95 per cent would include the population mean.[7] With the aid of Table 13-6 we can set other confidence limits if we prefer to.

[7] This statement has to be read with care. It does *not* say that if the experiment were repeated 100 times, the means of the samples would fall within the stated confidence limits 95 per cent of the time.

Probability Values. We used the critical ratio in order to prove that the hypothesis that the differences tested arose by chance was *not* plausible. The higher the critical ratio, the less plausible the hypothesis that *no* difference exists between the population means. Because the critical ratio has to be interpreted by a table, it is customary to give the probability values of a finding directly in the form of a statement. Instead of saying that the critical ratio is 2.0, we say, "the probability (P) is .05 that the difference might have occurred, even though the population means were the same." Or a statement might be made: "Only those differences are considered significant for which P is .05 or less." In later tables of this book, P-values will be presented on the assumption that they can now be appropriately interpreted.

The Coefficient of Correlation and Its Interpretation

We have already met the *coefficient of correlation* in several places. Correlation refers to the concomitant variation of paired measures, so that when one of the paired measures rises, so does the other, or (in negative correlation) as one rises, the other falls.

We meet correlation very often in the study of psychological tests. Suppose that a test is designed to predict success in college. If it is a good test, high scores on it will be related to high performance in college, and low scores will be related to poorer performance. The coefficient of correlation gives us a way of stating more precisely the *degree* of relationship.

Product-moment correlation (r)

The most frequently used method of determining the coefficient of correlation is the *product-moment* method, which yields the index conventionally designated r. Such an r varies between perfect positive correlation ($r = +1.00$) and perfect negative correla-

tion ($r = -1.00$). Lack of relationship is designated $r = .00$.

The formula for computing r is:

$$\text{Coefficient of correlation, } r = \frac{\text{Sum }(dx)(dy)}{N\sigma_x\sigma_y}$$

Here dx and dy refer to the deviations of each score from its mean, σ_x and σ_y are the standard deviations of the two distributions, and N is the number of paired values being studied. The name "product-moment" comes from the fact that for each pair of values dx is multiplied by $dy,$ and these products are then summed in the computation of the coefficient. It is evident that the higher the sum of the $(dx)(dy)$ products, the higher will be the correlation.

The computation of the coefficient of correlation requires the determination of the sum of the products of the deviation of each of the two scores (x and y) from its respective mean, that is, the sum of the $(dx)(dy)$ products for all of the subjects entering into the correlation. This sum, in addition to the computed standard deviations for the x-scores and y-scores, can then be entered into the formula. When there are only a few cases, the formula can be used directly; however, r is commonly computed for test scores or other data obtained from large groups of subjects, and the computation is cumbersome unless specially devised procedures are followed, some of them adapted for modern machine computation. These methods are too complex to be discussed here.

Rank-difference correlation (ρ)

A simpler method for determining correlation when there are relatively few cases (usually less than 50) makes use of ranked scores. While the resulting correlation is an estimate of r, it is not an exact equivalent of r, so that the coefficient obtained by the rank-difference method is designated by the lower-case Greek letter *rho* (ρ).

TABLE 13-8

Computation of rank-difference coefficient (ρ)

Subject	Entrance test	Freshman grades	Rank, entrance test	Rank, freshman grades	Difference in rank (D)	Squared difference (D^2)
Adam	79	79	1	1	0	0
Bill	77	73	2	4	−2	4
Charles	75	77	3	2	+1	1
David	73	75	4	3	+1	1
Edward	71	71	5	5	0	0
	$N = 5$					Sum $D^2 = 6$

$$\rho = 1 - \frac{6(\text{Sum } D^2)}{N(N^2 - 1)} = 1 - \frac{6 \times 6}{5 \times 24} = 1 - \frac{36}{120} = +.70$$

The formula is: [8]

$$\rho = 1 - \frac{6(\text{Sum } D^2)}{N(N^2 - 1)}$$

where D is the difference in ranks for the scores of any one subject, and N is the number of subjects whose scores are being correlated.

Specimen computation of rank-difference coefficient. Suppose that we had the following pairs of scores, the first being a score on a college entrance test, the second being freshman grades:

Name of student	Entrance test	Freshman grades
Adam	79	79
Bill	77	73
Charles	75	77
David	73	75
Edward	71	71

Looking at this little table, we can easily detect that there is some positive correlation. Adam makes the highest score on the entrance test and also the highest freshman grades; Edward makes the lowest score on both. The others are a little irregular, so we know that the correlation is not perfect; hence it is less

[8] The formula for *rho* is derived as an approximation of r by a method that need not concern us. Those interested can find a derivation in Siegel (1956), pp. 202-04.

than 1.00. We shall proceed to compute the correlation to illustrate the method, though no statistician would consent, in practice, to determine a correlation from so few cases.

All the details are given in Table 13-8. The procedure is to rank both sets of scores, obtain the differences in ranks for each subject on the two tests, square and sum these differences, and enter them into the formula. The value of ρ turns out to be +.70. Both r and ρ have similar properties, and ρ may be thought of as an estimate of r.

CRITICAL DISCUSSION

Nonparametric statistics

The differences between r and ρ illustrate a difference between two kinds of statistics that have been called *parametric* and *nonparametric* statistics. The word "parametric" is the adjective form of the noun "parameter," which means a variable that has taken a fixed value—in this context, some implied distribution such as an implied normal distribution with a fixed mean and standard deviation. Another name for nonparametric statistics is "distribution-free" statistics (Moses, 1952; Siegel, 1956). The product-moment correlation is a parametric statistic, implying various assumptions about the underlying distributions of x and y. The rank-difference correlation is nonparametric, because in converting everything to ranks it implies nothing about measurement other than ordinal scaling. There is some tendency to reverse the earlier preference for the product-moment correlation in favor of various rank correlations, of which that given in the foregoing account (ρ) is but one of several. The issues are complex, however, and are a source of some controversy. For example, the rank-difference method is actually derived as an approximation of r, and it is usually interpreted in that way. Hence there is a logical question whether it is in any fundamental sense a truly "nonparametric" statistic (McNemar, 1960).

When is a coefficient of correlation significant?

A coefficient of correlation, like other statistical measures, has a standard error. That is, if new samples were taken, the correlations computed from them would not be just the same as that obtained from the first samples. The *standard error of r*, to be used to determine whether or not r differs significantly from zero, is given by the following formula:

$$\text{Standard error of } r, \sigma_r = \frac{1}{\sqrt{N-1}}$$

where N is the number of pairs entering into the correlation.

If we then divide r by σ_r, we get a critical ratio, which can be interpreted just like the critical ratios given above. If the value of r/σ_r is greater than 2.0, we may be fairly confident that the "true" value of r is greater than 0; in other words, that there is a real correlation between the scores in the population from which the samples were drawn.

Specimen computation of the significance of a coefficient of correlation. In the study of Brown and Lenneberg (1954), cited on p. 349, a correlation of $r = .42$ between codability of colors and their ease of recognition was mentioned as supporting a contention of the authors. The study was done with 24 subjects. How significant, we may ask, was the correlation of .42?

$$\text{Standard error of } r, \sigma_r = \frac{1}{\sqrt{N-1}} = \frac{1}{\sqrt{24-1}}$$

$$= \frac{1}{\sqrt{23}} = \frac{1}{4.8} = 0.21$$

$$\text{Critical ratio, } \frac{r}{\sigma_r} = \frac{.42}{.21} = 2.00, P = .05$$

This critical ratio meets our arbitrary value of 2.0, corresponding to $P = .05$. Hence a correlation as high as .42 (either positive or negative) would be expected to occur by chance with 24 subjects only 5 times in 100.

Interpreting a coefficient of correlation

It is not always enough to know that a correlation is significantly greater than zero. Sometimes we wish to make use of correlations in prediction. For example, if we have an entrance test that we know from past experience correlates with freshman grades, we can predict the freshman grades for beginning college students who have taken the test. If correlation were perfect, we could predict their grades without error. Because correlations tend to be less than 1.00, we make errors in prediction; the lower the correlation, the greater the sizes of the errors in prediction based on it.

While we cannot go into the technical problems of computing freshman grades from entrance examinations, or of making other similar precise predictions, we can consider the meanings of coefficients of different sizes. There are several ways of interpreting correlations. For our purposes we may select one interpretation, based on the predictive efficiency of coefficients of correlation of different sizes.

It is evident that with a correlation of zero between x and y, knowledge of x will not help us to predict y. Thus, if eye color is unrelated to intelligence, it does us no good to know eye color when we are trying to estimate intelligence. At the other extreme, a perfect correlation would mean 100 per cent predictive efficiency—knowing x we can predict y without error. What of in-between values of r?

TABLE **13-9**

Predictive efficiency of r:
ȳ predicted from x

Coefficient of correlation (r_{xy})	Predictive efficiency * (E_r) (%)
.10	0.5
.20	2
.30	5
.40	8
.50	13
.60	20
.70	29
.80	40
.866	50
.90	56
.95	69
.98	80
1.00	100

* Efficiency of prediction refers to the percentage reduction in the standard error of estimate.

We need some measure of errors in prediction. An error in prediction for a single score is the amount by which a value of y, which we may designate $\bar{y}$, predicted from x, differs from the obtained value y, that is $(\bar{y} - y)$. The *standard error of estimate* is the standard error of all such differences, and can be computed from the standard deviation of the score to be predicted (σ_y) and the coefficient of correlation (r_{xy}) by the formula:

Standard error of estimated $\bar{y}$,

$$\sigma_{\bar{y}} = \sigma_y \sqrt{1 - r_{xy}^2}$$

It can be seen that when r is zero, the standard error of estimate is equal to the standard deviation of y, and when r is 1.00, the standard error of estimate is zero. Hence we may find a way of describing the predictive efficiency of an r of given size by stating the per cent by which it *reduces* the standard error of estimate. The formula, easily derived from that just given, becomes:

Predictive efficiency of r,

$$E_r = 100(1 - \sqrt{1 - r^2})$$

The predictive efficiencies of r's of different sizes are given in Table 13-9. It is clear from Table 13-9 that correlations cannot be interpreted as simple per cents, because the predictive efficiency goes up very rapidly as correlations become high. The low correlations often found in psychological measurements (often between .30 and .70) are not very powerful in prediction. It takes a correlation of .866 to reduce the standard error of estimate by half. Note also the great gain in prediction as correlations approach 1.00: a 20 per cent gain in predictive efficiency between .98 and 1.00.

Some appreciation of the meaning of correlations of various sizes can be gained from a careful study of the *scatter diagrams* of Figure 13-7. Note that each dot represents the scores on two tests (an x-score and a y-score) for the same individual. If the scores are alike, they fall on the diagonal; if not, they fall away from it. The closer all scores are to the diagonal, the higher the correlation. (The fact that the axes do not have conventional scales does not change the interpretation, as can easily be demonstrated by labeling the lower left-hand corner of each graph as 0 and assigning the values 1 through 5 to the left-hand and bottom coordinates.)

Correlation Does Not Yield Cause. When two sets of scores are correlated, we may assume that they have some causal factors in common, but we have to be careful not to state that *one* of them causes the *other*. For example, the softness of the asphalt in the streets of a city may correlate with the number of heat prostrations, but this does not mean that the asphalt when soft gives off some kind of poison that sends people to hospitals. We understand the cause in this example—a hot sun both softens the asphalt and produces sunstroke. Hence a correlation may lead us to *search* for a cause, but alone it does not *explain* the relationship it *describes*.

Correlations sometimes appear paradoxical. For example, the correlation between time in study and college grades often has been found to be slightly negative (perhaps −.20). If a causal interpretation were assumed, one might suppose that the best way to raise grades would be to stop studying! The negative correlation arises because some

13-7

Scatter diagrams illustrating correlations of various sizes

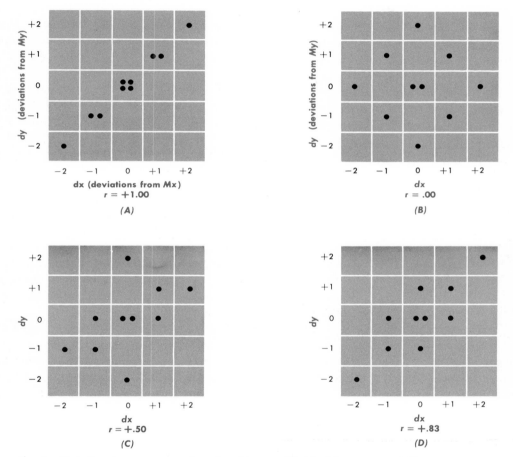

The simplified diagrams are presented to show how score distributions, alike on each of two tests, can differ in their correlation with each other. Each dot represents one individual's score on two tests, x and y. In A, all cases fall on the diagonal; the correlation is perfect (r = +1.00). If you know a subject's score on x, you know that it will be the same on y. In B, the correlation is zero. When you know a subject's score on x, you cannot predict whether it will be at, above, or below the mean on y. For example, of the 4 subjects who score at the mean of x (dx = 0), one makes a very high score on y (dy = +2), one a very low score (dy = −2), and two remain average. In both C and D, there is a diagonal trend to the scores, so that a high score on x is associated with a high score on y, and a low score on x with a low score on y, but the relation is imperfect. The interested student will discover that it is possible to check the value of the correlations by using the formulas given in the text for standard deviation (p. 375) and the coefficient of correlation (p. 385). The computation has been very much simplified by presenting the scores in the deviation form that permits entering them directly into the formulas.

students have advantages over others in grade-making (possibly because of native ability or better preparation), so that often the students who study the hardest are those having a difficult time earning barely passing grades. Many students make moderately good grades with a slight amount of time spent in study. This example provides sufficient warning against giving a causal interpretation to a coefficient of correlation.

However, when two sets of data are correlated, the first set may *possibly* be the cause of the other. The search for causes is a logical one, and correlations can help. Alone they do not tell us whether one variable is the cause of another, or whether what they have in common is a result of some third variable.

Statistics in Psychology

Statistical methods are becoming increasingly important in all sciences, but they are particularly important in psychology because of the complexity and variability of the phenomena with which psychology deals.

The earliest demand upon statistics was made when psychologists began to use the psychophysical methods for *threshold measurement*. One weight slightly heavier than another is not always judged as heavier, even though the judgment "heavier" is made more frequently than judgments of "lighter" and "equal." Hence the threshold requires a statistical definition. It has both an average value and a standard deviation.

The most widespread development of statistical methods came in connection with *tests of individual differences*. This chapter on statistics has been introduced at this point, because we shall make references to statistical concepts in the following chapters on individuality.

More recently (especially since 1935) statistical considerations have entered increasingly into the *design of experiments* in all branches of psychology. While some statistical considerations have long been important (e.g., in computing the significances of differences between performances of *experimental* and *control* groups), newer methods permit the economical treatment of a number of variables at once. These methods not only save in the time and costs of experimentation, but yield kinds of information that earlier experimental comparisons could not produce.

Another field, that of *attitude and opinion surveys* (of which election polls are but one illustration), relies very largely upon sampling methods to determine how many people and which people to interview. The results must meet acceptable statistical standards if they are to be appropriately interpreted.

Modern computational aids, including statistical tables, machines (from simple hand-operated computers to electronic "brains"), punched-card methods, and test-scoring machines, permit the rapid handling of masses of data.

Modern psychology as we know it would be impossible without these developments in statistical methods.

SUMMARY 1. Statistics is the science that deals with the collection and handling of numerical data and with making inferences from such data.

2. *Descriptive statistics* provide shorthand descriptions of large numbers of observations.

3. *Averages* include the *mean,* the *median,* and the *mode.* Because of its many arithmetical and other advantages, the mean is the most favored

of these measures; fortunately it is familiar as the ordinary arithmetical average.

4. The *measures of variation* include the *range,* the *mean deviation,* and the *standard deviation.* The standard deviation, although the hardest to understand, is the measure favored by statisticians.

5. *Statistical inferences* are made from a *sample* of a *population* whose unknown characteristics are estimated from the sample, always with a margin of uncertainty. It is widely assumed that statistics derived from samples fit a *normal distribution.* While this assumption has important exceptions known to statisticians, it usually causes little distortion.

6. In the *scaling* of data, raw scores may be converted into *ranks, centiles,* or *standard scores.* Standard scores, based on distance from the mean expressed as multiples of the standard deviation, have many advantages and are widely used. Some of the better-known scales based on the assumptions of standard scores are the scale used in the Graduate Record Examination and the scales used in classification tests by the Army, Navy, and Air Force.

7. The mean of a sample has a *standard error* that is smaller than the standard deviation of the sample, its size decreasing as the number of cases in the sample increases.

8. It is possible to compute a *standard error of a difference* (σ_{D_M}) between two means from the standard error of each mean. The *critical ratio* (D_M/σ_{D_M}) expresses the obtained difference in multiples of the standard error of the difference. If the critical ratio is 2.0 or above, we have confidence that a true difference between the means exists, i.e., that the difference is unlikely to be the result of uncontrolled chance factors.

9. Ways of stating statistical significance include *confidence limits* derived from standard deviations and *probability values.* A critical ratio can be converted to a probability (P) by a table descriptive of the normal distribution. For a critical ratio of 2.0, P is about .05; this means that the difference tested might arise in 5 out of 100 repetitions of the sampling method employed, even though no difference exists. For smaller critical ratios P is larger (and therefore less significant), and for larger critical ratios P is smaller.

10. The *coefficient of correlation* is a convenient method of expressing a relationship between two variables. The *product-moment correlation* (r) is the one favored in psychological measurements. A convenient approximation is provided by the *rank-difference coefficient* (ρ). A coefficient of correlation (r) is significant if the critical ratio between r and the standard error of r is 2.0 or more and P is .05 or less.

11. The coefficient of correlation can be interpreted according to its efficiency in prediction. The predictive efficiency (E_r) may be stated as the percentage reduction in the *standard error of estimate* made possible by an r of stated size. That r is not a per cent is clear when it is noted that r

must reach .866 for its predictive efficiency to reach 50 per cent. In predicting from correlation coefficients, it must be kept clear that y can be predicted from x without x's being the *cause* of y.

12. Statistics as an important tool has found its place in all branches of psychology, beginning with threshold measurement. It is especially important in tests of individual differences, and more recently it has found a place in the design of experiments and in attitude and opinion surveys.

SUGGESTIONS FOR FURTHER READING

Because of the importance of statistical methods in psychology, a number of textbooks are available for the teaching of statistics specifically to students of psychology, of which McNemar, *Psychological statistics* (3rd Ed., 1962), is a representative one. The nonparametric methods are treated extensively by Siegel, *Nonparametric statistics* (1956).

Quantitative methods in general, including the fitting of curves to data and the computation of thresholds, are included in Guilford, *Psychometric methods* (2nd Ed., 1954), and Lewis, *Quantitative methods in psychology* (1960).

The role of statistics in the design of experiments is explained in Edwards, *Experimental design in psychological research* (Rev. Ed., 1960).

For the general notion that statistics helps in the making of decisions in an uncertain situation, see Bross, *Design for decision* (1953), and Wallis and Roberts, *Statistics: a new approach* (1956). An entertaining little book on the dangers in the misuse of statistics is Huff, *How to lie with statistics* (1954).

CHAPTER 14

Ability Testing and Intelligence

The statement that men are both alike and different seems to be a mere cliché. Yet one of psychology's most difficult problems is to describe and understand precisely the ways in which men are alike (what is consistent in human nature) and the ways in which men differ (how each individual is unique).

We know from our study of growth, motivation, and learning that one man will differ from another because he inherits individual characteristics and also because he experiences his culture through home, school, and community in unique ways, and thus acquires habits, attitudes, and understandings that are distinctively his own. We are now interested in the individual as a unique person, the product of all these influences. We wish to know in what ways men are unlike, the extent of their differences, and how to appraise these differences.

This is not a task of idle curiosity, for our society requires individuals to be appraised, classified, and given responsibilities on the assumptions both that they differ and that their differences will suit them better for one social role than for another. We decide by examination to send some boys into active military service and others to college. Within a college we try to assess individual differences in order to help students choose their majors or their vocational objectives. In offices and factories we test adults in order to place them in the jobs best suited to them.

Testing Aptitudes and Achievements

While there are other ways in which men differ, we shall be concerned in this chapter with *ability testing,* that is, with the study of individual differences in knowledge and skills, in aptitudes and achievements in the area of general competency.

When we are confronted with the problem of appraising a person's abilities, we make a distinction between what he can do now and what he might do if he were trained. For example, John is an excellent premedical student and some day he will make a fine physician, but we would not ask him to remove an appendix before he has had his medical training. James is a young recruit who will become a good aviator, but we do not trust him with an airplane before he has learned to fly. This distinction between a *capacity to learn* and an *accomplished skill* is important in our appraisal devices. Tests designed to measure capacities, that is, to *predict* what one can accomplish with training, are known as *aptitude tests.* Tests that tell what one can do now are *achievement tests.* Intelligence tests that predict how well you will do in college are aptitude tests; end-of-the-term tests on how much you have learned are achievement tests. Both are ability tests.

The relation between aptitude and achievement tests

Whenever you measure what a person can do, you obtain samples or specimens of his present behavior. Hence the *items* composing all ability tests are necessarily samples of achievements—samples of what the person can do here and now.

Aptitude tests, by definition, predict performances not yet attained. But the *items* in the tests must consist of samples of achievements, that is, of what can be accomplished *now.* How, then, is it possible to construct anything but achievement tests? This diffi-

Testing mechanical aptitude

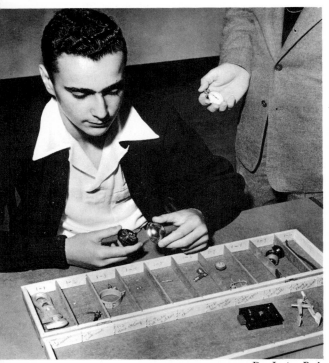

Dr. Lester Beck

The results of this test will be helpful in predicting success in specific kinds of work.

culty does not become an impasse, because it is possible to *sample* abilities from performances other than those being predicted. Typing can furnish us an example. One of the abilities entering into success in typing is good spelling. Spelling is something that can be tested before experience with typewriters. Therefore a test of spelling may enter into the typing *aptitude* test, even though from another point of view the spelling test is an achievement test. The distinction between an aptitude test and an achievement test is not based on the content of the items, but upon the *purposes* of the two kinds of test, namely, upon what the tests are designed to do. Aptitude tests predict future performance; achievement tests measure present attainment.

Aptitude tests

Aptitude tests are sometimes classified according to the breadth or generality of the abilities they predict. Thus there are tests of abilities used in a wide range of performances. The best known of these tests of *general aptitude* are tests of *general intelligence,* to be treated more fully later in this chapter. A number of tests are for *mechanical aptitude,* because so much of the work of the world is done either by hand or with mechanical devices (Figure 14-1).

Many tests are given to discover *special aptitudes.* For example, there are tests of *musical aptitude*—tests based on discrimination of pitch, rhythm, and other aspects of musical sensitivity that might be predictive of musical performance with training. *Clerical aptitude* is another kind of special aptitude. A test in simple number checking, for example, proves predictive of an individual's later achievement as an office clerk. A great many aptitude tests have been constructed for the purpose of predicting success in specific jobs or vocations. World War II led to the devising of many tests designed to select aviators, torpedomen, radio technicians, submarine crews, and other specialists for the countless skilled jobs within the armed services.

In attempting to measure aptitude, it is usually necessary to use a number of different tests in combination. Earlier we used the illustration of present ability in spelling as a test for predicting typing ability. But spelling is not the only ingredient in typing skill; a good typing aptitude test must also include tests of finger dexterity and other kinds of items. A combination of tests used for prediction is known as a *test battery.* A well-planned battery is composed only of tests that contribute to the final prediction, and scores from the individual tests are *weighted* in such a way as to get the best possible prediction. That is, scores on the tests that predict well count more in the prediction than scores on the tests that predict less well. For instance, if a finger-dexterity test predicts typing success better than a spelling test, scores in finger dexterity will count more than scores in spelling.

A useful test battery was developed during World War II for the selection of air-crew specialists for the Army Air Forces. Many tests were tried, and only those found by experience to aid in the prediction of success were kept. By making use of the weights appropriate to each of the specialties, officials could assign a candidate to the duty in which he was most likely to succeed. The battery of tests that remained in June, 1945, is listed in Table 14-1, with an X marked for those tests that received weights

for predicting success as bombardier, navigator, bomber pilot, fighter pilot, and flight engineer.

This set of tests classifies as an aptitude battery, because its aim was to *predict* success in the different specialties. Look at the individual tests of Table 14-1. Some reflect basic capacities, such as speed of identification, judgment, or finger dexterity, while others seem to reflect training, such as instrument comprehension, general information, reading comprehension, and knowledge of mechanical principles. But all these capacities can be assessed *before* the candidate has had his training in any one of the air-crew specialties. Therefore the tests classify

TABLE 14-1

Tests composing classification battery for air-crew specialists

| | Specialties for which tests predicted success * | | | | |
	Bombardier	Navigator	Bomber pilot	Fighter pilot	Flight engineer
Printed tests					
Dial and table reading	X	X	X		X
Biographical data		X	X	X	
Spatial orientation I	X	X	X		
Spatial orientation II	X	X	X	X	
Reading comprehension	X	X	X		X
Instrument comprehension			X	X	
Mechanical principles			X	X	X
Speed of identification				X	
Numerical operations	X	X			
Mechanical information					X
General information			X	X	
Judgment			X		
Arithmetic reasoning	X	X			X
Apparatus tests					
Rotary pursuit with divided attention			X		
Rudder control			X	X	
Finger dexterity	X				
Complex coordination	X		X	X	
Two-hand pursuit	X	X		X	
Discrimination reaction time	X	X		X	X

SOURCE: Adapted from DuBois (1947), p. 109.

* Two additional tests were included in the battery, applicable only to other specialties. These were a printed test of coordinate reading, used only in the battery for radar operators, and an apparatus test of pedestal sight manipulation, weighted only for the aerial gunner. For the sake of simplicity, not all the specialties are shown in this table.

as aptitude tests. We shall return a little later to the question of how successful this battery was in predicting success.

Achievement tests

The most widespread use of achievement tests is in the schools. Any examination covering what has been studied, whether in elementary school, high school, or college, can be considered an achievement test. Even when one's school days are past, one sometimes has to take examinations. They are required of prospective lawyers, physicians, certified public accountants, and others. Because these examinations are tests of what has been learned in preparation for the practice of a specialty, they are achievement examinations. The many civil service examinations are also tests of achievement. The consequences of all these achievement tests are highly important to the candidate who takes them. If he succeeds, he will receive a degree or a license to practice or an opportunity to enter the diplomatic service. If he fails, many paths may be blocked for him. Therefore it is crucial that examinations be well conceived, so that they measure what they are intended to measure and so that their scores represent fairly the relative abilities of the candidates who take the tests.

Two reasons have led psychologists to interest themselves in achievement tests. Practical demand provides the first reason; tests are needed, especially in education and civil service. The second reason is this: *achievement tests furnish the standard on which aptitude tests are based.* If you wish to prepare and try out an aptitude test for typing, you have to have a standard of good typing against which to measure the aptitude. Otherwise you have no way of checking your predictions. Achievement tests, then, furnish the standard, or *criterion,* that is being predicted. If professors assigned college grades whimsically instead of on the basis of what the student has learned in the course, it would be futile to try to predict grades from an aptitude battery. Only with improved achievement examinations can predictions be made most efficient.

Standardized achievement tests have been widely used in the elementary schools. A number of useful test batteries are available; one such battery, the Stanford Achievement Test, is described in Table 14-2. Representative scores or *norms* in tests designed for the elementary school are commonly stated for each grade level; that is, the score made by a child in the third grade can be compared with the scores made by all the other third-grade children who have taken the test. Scores are commonly stated as *centiles* (see p. 379).

If Susan is at the 75th centile, she falls in the upper fourth of her grade; if Charles is at the 40th centile, he falls below the average for his grade.

Although standardized achievement tests are desirable and their usefulness has been substantiated in practice, they have their

---

TABLE 14-2

Composition of Stanford Achievement Test

Primary battery (Grades 2 and 3)
Test 1 Reading: Paragraph meaning
Test 2 Reading: Word meaning
Test 3 Spelling
Test 4 Arithmetic reasoning
Test 5 Arithmetic computation

**Intermediate battery (Grades 4, 5, and 6)
  and advanced battery (Grades 7, 8, and 9)**
Test 1 Reading: Paragraph meaning
Test 2 Reading: Word meaning
Test 3 Language usage
Test 4 Arithmetic reasoning
Test 5 Arithmetic computation
Test 6 Literature
Test 7 Social studies I
Test 8 Social studies II
Test 9 Elementary science
Test 10 Spelling

SOURCE: Kelley and others (1953).

limitations. In the first place, achievement tests tend to be subject-oriented, so that they tend to stress the subject matter emphasized in more conventional schools. Second, local conditions make it important to obtain local, as well as national norms. What is to be expected from the children of one community is not always to be expected from those of another. Third, other ways of determining individual progress can be used to supplement the purely competitive results of standardized test scores. Some children below their grade levels are doing all that should be expected of them; others, above their grade levels, are not achieving what they might.

This acquaintance with some of the problems of aptitude testing and of achievement testing prepares us now to inquire more carefully into the nature of test scores and their use in prediction.

Prediction from standardized tests

To a certain extent all tests are instruments of prediction. Aptitude tests are entirely predictive, of course, but achievement tests, although assessing present attainment, may also be partially predictive. Those who pass the medical examination are judged qualified to accept patients for treatment; those who pass the bar examination are judged to know enough to serve clients competently in legal matters.

In order to make predictions we have to know how to interpret test scores, and we have to understand how to relate these scores to the likelihood of success in whatever it is we are predicting.

Reliability and validity

In order that test scores may be used for scientific purposes, they must be trustworthy. In the terms used by psychologists, this means that they must meet two requirements: *reliability* and *validity*.

By *reliability* we mean that the scores are dependable and reproducible, that they measure *consistently* whatever it is they measure. Test items can be so confusing, misleading, unclear, or tricky that they mean different things to different subjects, or even to the same subject at different times. Hence good items are the first essential of reliability. But tests may also be too short to be reliable, or scoring may be too subjective. Our first question is, then, how good a yardstick we have; if it is inconsistent in its results when measurements are repeated, or when the same test is scored by two people, it is unreliable. A simple analogy is a rubber yardstick; if one never knew how much it was stretched when a measurement was made, the results would be unreliable, no matter how carefully it had been marked to begin with. We need stable and consistent tests if we are to use the results with confidence.

In order to measure *reliability,* we must secure two independent scores for the same individual from the same test, either by treating halves of the test separately, by repeating the test, by giving it in two forms, or by deriving some sort of statistical measure equivalent to having two such scores. We can then compare the first and second set of scores. If the same relative ranks are preserved on the two scores, the test is reliable. Some departures from identity of score are to be expected, owing to errors of measurement and sampling errors, so that a measure of *degree of relationship* between the two sets of scores is needed. This relationship is provided by the *coefficient of correlation,* already familiar to us as a measure of degree of correspondence between two sets of scores. The coefficient of correlation between the two series of scores, adjusted according to statistical conventions, is called a *reliability coefficient.* Well-constructed psychological tests of ability usually have *reliability* coefficients of $r = .90$ or above.

By *validity* we mean that the test scores represent what they are supposed to represent. A college examination in economics full of clever questions might turn out to be a

TABLE 14-3

Validity coefficients for prediction of success in pilot training

Tests among those in classification battery	Validity for completed pilot training (N = 1275) Validity coefficient * (r)(bis)
Printed tests with highest validity coefficients	
General information	.49
Instrument comprehension	.46
Mechanical principles	.42
Dial and table reading	.40
Spatial orientation II	.38
Apparatus tests with highest validity coefficients	
Complex coordination	.42
Discrimination reaction time	.41
Rudder control	.36
Two-hand pursuit	.35
Rotary pursuit	.31
Pilot stanine (a composite score)	.64

SOURCE: Modified from DuBois (1947), p. 190.

* In the group studies, pilot selection was not based upon test scores, because the success of the tests was still under study. Because the criterion was simply that of passing or failing in pilot training, a special kind of correlation coefficient (called biserial *r*) was computed; the usual *r* requires scaled values for both variables.

measure of what it is that the test is supposed to be measuring. This measure is called a *criterion*. Suppose that a test is designed to predict success in learning to receive telegraphic code. To determine whether or not the test is valid, it is given to a group of men beginning to study code. Later on, each man is tested on the number of words per minute he can receive. This later measure furnishes an additional set of scores which can serve as a criterion. Now we can obtain a coefficient of correlation between the early test scores and the scores on the criterion. This correlation coefficient is known as a *validity coefficient*. A validity coefficient tells something about how valuable a given test is for a given purpose. The higher the coefficient, the better the prediction that can be made from an aptitude test, and the greater the confidence that can be placed in an achievement test.

High validity coefficients are essential if test scores are to be used to help an individual with such choices as those of vocation. But even relatively low validity coefficients may prove useful when large numbers of people are tested. For example, the battery of tests for the selection of air-crew specialists (Table 14-1) proved effective in predicting job success, even though some of the validity coefficients were of very moderate size. Some illustrative validity coefficients from this battery are shown in Table 14-3. No single test shows a validity above .49, but a battery of tests is better than any single test. In these tests the "stanine" score (see Chapter 13) derived from the battery correlates .64 with the criterion.

test of student intelligence rather than of the economics that was learned in the course. Such an examination might be reliable, but it would not be a valid test of achievement for the course. A test of sense of humor, for example, might be made up of jokes whose points were very hard to catch unless one were both very bright and very well-read. Hence it might turn out to be a *reliable* test of something (intelligence? educational achievement?) but still not be *valid* for what was intended as a test of the sense of humor.

To measure *validity,* we must also have two scores for each person. One of these is the test score, the reliability of which we have just been discussing. The other is some

CRITICAL DISCUSSION

The criterion problem and alternate forms of validation

Whenever validity is to be determined, the criterion problem becomes very important. If a good measure of achievement exists, then the validity of an aptitude test is simply a matter of how well it predicts. It is this *predictive validity* that is most readily understood and most easily assessed through correlation. Other kinds of validity exist. The achievement test is assigned its validity through comparing it with an alternative estimate of achievement; if, for example, a multiple-choice portion of a college examination correlates high with an essay portion, the teacher has confidence that the multiple-choice portion is valid (because the validity of the essay portion is assumed). This can be called *concurrent validation,* as distinct from predictive. Validity often depends in the first instance upon judgment, for example, the judgment that an essay examination really reflects the contents of a course, or that a psychiatrist's diagnosis correctly appraises a patient's symptoms. Such judgments are fallible, and the question arises whether a test can have any higher validity than the criterion on which it is based. The answer is "yes," but it depends on types of validity other than predictive and concurrent validity.

If content is carefully scrutinized to be sure that it is related to what is being measured, then the logic of the test can suggest its validity without relating it to a criterion outside itself. This is known as *content validity* and can be used to characterize achievement tests, such as those in mathematics or grammar, where the content to be tested is clear. In this case all that is required is reliability, the validity being inferred from the contents. (Our example of the test of sense of humor shows that caution is needed; a test made up entirely of jokes may not be a good test of humor.) If the criterion is itself not very good, it may still serve as a check on content. For example, even if teachers are not very good judges of the exact intelligence of their pupils, they know in a general way those who are backward and those who are bright. An intelligence test must have at least some correspondence with these judgments, but it may build upon its own contents to produce a measure that is more valid than these teacher judgments that served as an initial check on its validity. An improved clock could be validated against an hourglass by showing that it measured what the hourglass measured, but that it did so more consistently than two hourglasses. (The improvement here is in re-

liability; the definition of "one hour," upon which validity depends, would be weak if there were nothing but hourglasses to define it!) Internal consistency, given appropriate content, is related to both reliability and validity.

A final kind of validity, *construct validity,* is determined by a more complex process of inference. A test may be used in relation to some kind of hypothesis. We earlier met an anxiety test, used in relation to learning (p. 332). The hypothesis might go something like this: "If this is a measure of anxiety, and anxiety acts as a drive, those who score high on this test will yield a higher percentage of conditioned eyelid reactions in a given number of trials than those who score lower." The experimental test provides an indirect validation of the psychological principles involved and permits an interpretation of the test scores as measures of anxiety.

These four kinds of validity have been distinguished by Cronbach (1960, p. 106), who gives a good discussion of them.

Test scores as a basis for prediction

With high enough reliability and validity coefficients, we know that we have satisfactory tests, but there still remains the problem of using the tests in prediction.

The method of prediction most easily understood is the one based on *critical scores.* By this method, a critical point on the scale is selected after experience with the tests. Then only those candidates with scores above the critical scores are accepted —for training, for admission to college, or for whatever purpose the testing may serve.

The pilot-selection program of the air forces illustrates this use of critical scores. The pilot stanines gave each candidate a pilot-prediction rating from 1 to 9. Figure 14-2 shows that during the experimental period those with low stanines were eliminated much more frequently than those with high stanines. Hence after experience with the tests, the examiners rejected those with low stanines from further training. In November, 1943, for example, a candidate had to receive a stanine score of 5 or better in order to be accepted for pilot training. Thus a stanine of 5 became a critical score.

What is accomplished by adopting a critical score may be judged by examining the data, presented in Table 14-4, upon which Figure 14-2 is based. Suppose that from the beginning of the pilot training program all those with stanines below 5 had been eliminated. We can see from the table that we would have eliminated a group of which 44 per cent failed in training. Of the group retained (with stanines of 5 and above), only 17 per cent failed.

The data of Figure 14-2 and Table 14-4, expressed in correlational terms, represent a correlation between stanine and completion of training of $r = .51$, for this total group of 166,507 trainees. People trained in statistics are able to estimate from the size of a validity coefficient just how successful their predictions are likely to be by making use of the predictive efficiency formula given on p. 388. For our present purposes it suffices to know that with a validity coefficient of about .50 we can have the degree of success represented in Figure 14-2 and Table 14-4. This is appreciable success and represents substantial savings when the costs of training are considered.

14-2

The basis for a critical score

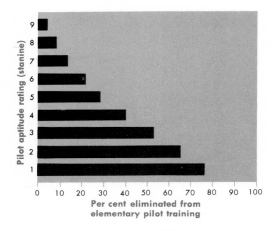

The graph shows the percentage of failures in pilot training at each stanine level. At one point the Air Forces established a stanine score of 5 as a requirement for further pilot training. (After DuBois, 1947)

TABLE 14-4

Success and failure in pilot training at each stanine level

Pilot stanine	Total receiving this score *	Elementary pilot training		
		Graduated	Eliminated	Per cent eliminated
9	20,127	19,304	823	4.1
8	17,935	16,316	1,619	9.0
7	29,762	25,672	4,090	13.7
6	36,129	28,421	7,708	21.4
5	31,048	22,132	8,916	28.7
5-9	*135,001*	*111,845*	*23,156*	*17.1*
4	20,439	12,589	7,850	38.5
3	9,109	4,364	4,745	52.0
2	1,415	486	929	65.5
1	543	130	413	76.0
1-4	*31,506*	*17,569*	*13,937*	*44.3*

SOURCE: Computed from data in DuBois (1947), p. 118.

* Stanine credit was given for previous flying experience. This raised the proportion of candidates receiving the higher stanine scores. In the later stages of training, those with low pilot stanines were no longer accepted for pilot training. This reduced the relative numbers with low stanine scores.

Tests of General Intelligence

Intelligence tests are designed to measure the abilities that distinguish the bright from the dull. Because brightness and dullness are important in school success, in vocational success, and in social adjustment generally, the intelligence test is one of the major tools psychology has developed. In our study of individuality, we will therefore do well to scrutinize more carefully the nature of intelligence tests and the findings that have resulted from them.

Alfred Binet, a French psychologist, invented the intelligence test as we now know it. In 1904 the French government asked him to devise a test to detect those children who were too dull to profit from ordinary schooling. He published (with Théodore Simon) a scale in 1905, and revised it in 1908 and again in 1911. These Binet scales are the direct ancestors of contemporary intelligence tests.

Binet's method: a mental-age scale

Binet assumed that a dull child was like a normal child but retarded in his mental growth; that is, he assumed that the dull child would behave on tests like a normal child of younger age. This assumption need not have turned out to be so. For example, subnormal children might have excelled at rote memorizing, while being incapable of reasoning or of abstract behavior. But Binet's original conjecture, while not entirely correct, has proved serviceable as a guide in test construction. Binet decided to scale intelligence as the kind of change which ordinarily comes with growing older. The behavior studied in Binet's and related intelligence tests is that which distinguishes those obviously bright from those obviously dull by ordinary social standards. Accordingly, Binet devised a scale of units of *mental age*. Average *mental-age* (M.A.) scores correspond to *chronological age* (C.A.), that

14-3

Totally novel items used in intelligence tests

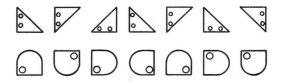

The following instructions accompany the test: "Here are some cards for you to mark. In each row mark every card that is like the first card in the row." (After Thurstone and Thurstone, 1941)

is, to the age determined from the date of birth. A bright child's M.A. is above his C.A.; a retarded child has an M.A. below his C.A. The mental-age scale is thus easily interpreted by teachers and others who deal with children differing in mental ability.

Item selection

Because the intelligence test is designed to measure brightness rather than the results of special training, it is necessary to find test items that can be passed without specific preparation. In other words, the intelligence test is designed to be an *aptitude* test rather than an *achievement* test, and it must be constructed accordingly.

There are two chief ways to find items on which success is uninfluenced by special training. One way is to choose *totally novel items* upon which an unschooled child has as good a chance to succeed as one who has gone to school. Figure 14-3 illustrates a totally novel item. In this particular case the child is asked to choose figures which are just alike; the assumption is that the designs as such are unfamiliar to all children.

The second way is to choose *assuredly familiar items,* so that all those for whom the test is designed will have had the requisite prior experience to deal with the item. The following problem provides an example of an assuredly familiar item:

Mark F if the sentence is foolish; mark S if it is sensible.

S   F   *Mrs. Smith has had no children, and I understand that the same was true of her mother.*[1]

This item is "fair" only for children who know the English language, who can read, and who understand all the words in the sentence. *For such children,* detection of the fallacy in the statement becomes a valid test of intellectual ability.

Many of the items on an intelligence test of the Binet type are of the second sort, that requiring the assumption of general familiarity. A vocabulary test, for example, appears in almost all the scales. Familiarity with the language is necessarily assumed.

The intelligence test is in some respects a crude instrument, for its assumptions cannot be strictly met. The language environment of one home is never exactly that of another, the reading matter available to the subjects differs, in different homes the stress upon intellectual goals varies. Despite the difficulties, items can be chosen that work reasonably well in practice. The items of contemporary intelligence tests are those that have survived in practice after many others have been tried and found defective.

CRITICAL DISCUSSION
Culture-fair intelligence tests

As indicated, items for an intelligence test are often selected on the assumption that the substance is assuredly familiar to all those being tested. This assumption is extremely difficult to satisfy, because rural and urban children lack some common experiences, the vocabulary levels of homes of different social strata vary, and accuracy of discrimination may be rewarded in some environments and ignored in others. Because of these difficulties, serious efforts have been made to construct tests that will be less dependent on the specific culture than the more familiar tests of the Binet type.

[1] From L. L. Thurstone and T. G. Thurstone (1941), p. 47.

Among these are the test constructed by Cattell (1949), called a "culture-free" test, and that by Davis and Eells (1953), called a "culture-fair" test. Both attempt to provide tests that will not penalize the child from a lower-class home.

Consider the following question:

Pick out ONE WORD *which does not belong with the others*

cello   harp   drum   violin   guitar

This question is used by Eells and others (1951, p. 306) to illustrate how experience can bias vocabulary. Eighty-five per cent of children from homes of high socioeconomic status underlined "drum," the correct answer, while only 45 per cent of the children from homes of low socioeconomic status answered correctly. The low-status children most commonly made the mistake of answering "cello," the word on the list least likely to be familiar to them, and hence likely to be the word not belonging in the list. Children in homes of high socioeconomic status are more likely to become acquainted with cellos or at least are more likely to hear the word than children from poorer homes.

There were, however, many other questions in this study showing class differences for which the effects of differing experience would be hard to demonstrate. For example, the following question was also answered correctly more often by those from higher than by those from homes of lower socioeconomic status:

Find the THREE THINGS *which are alike in each list*

store   banana   basket   apple   seed   plum

This question (Eells and others, 1951, p. 316) requires noting that banana, apple, and plum are fruits, and that store and basket are nonfruits. It is hard to believe that nine- and ten-year-old children, even from underprivileged homes, would be unacquainted with the six words or would lack acquaintance with the fruits. Such an item is culture-fair, even though it shows class differences in its answer; the classes may actually differ in intelligence as measured by items that are "fair."

While high hopes were expressed for such tests by those who developed them, the subsequent results have not been very encouraging. In some cases class differences in scores have been reduced, but for the most part the class differences found with these tests are very similar to the differences found with the more usual tests (Coleman and Ward, 1955; Hess, 1955; Marquart and Bailey, 1955; Knief and Stroud, 1959). Moreover, as predictors of scholastic achievement the newer tests are inferior to the more conventional ones; this may be due to a middle-class bias in the schools, but it is still the case (Stroud, 1942). Hence, with all their difficulties, the ordinary Binet-type tests serve their predictive purposes as well or better than these substitute tests.

Item testing

How did Binet know that he had hit upon a good item? He, and those who have come after him, developed ways of testing the individual items to be sure that they serve their intended purposes. It is not enough to look at an item and to decide that it requires intelligence to reply successfully to it. Some "tricky" or "clever" items, which seem to put the test taker on his mettle, turn out to be poor because of chance successes or failures. Somewhat "pedestrian" items,

such as matters of common information, sometimes turn out to be most useful. These are items that are "fair," because all have had a chance to learn the answers.

How can the assertion be made with assurance that one item is better than another? One method of testing an item is to study the *changes in proportions of children answering it correctly at different ages.* Unless older children are more successful than younger ones in answering the item, the item is unsatisfactory in a test based on the concept of mental growth. The curves in Figures 14-4A and 14-4B show increases in the percentage of children passing some representative items at different ages. These data were obtained in a later revision of a Binet-type scale.

A second method of testing an item is to find out whether or not the results for it *correspond to the results on the test as a whole.* This can be found out by correlating success and failure on the item with the score made on the remaining items. If all items measure something in common, then

14-4

Intelligence test items: per cent passing should increase with age

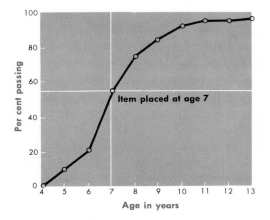

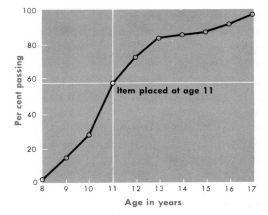

A. This item, Opposite Analogies 1, comes from the Revised Stanford-Binet. At age 7 just over half the subjects are successful. The question is of the form: "Brother is a boy; sister is a _____." (After McNemar, 1942)

B. Placed at age 11 on the scale, this item is **more** difficult than the one shown in A. The item is Abstract Words 1. The question asked is: "What do we mean by _____?" (After McNemar, 1942)

every single item ought to contribute a score that correlates with the total score. The two items charted in Figure 14-4 met the first test of increase in percentage passing with age. They also met the second test of correlating with total score. The correlation between the Opposite Analogies Item (14-4A) and the total score at age 7 was $r = .65$; that for the Abstract Words Item (14-4B) and the total score at age 11 was $r = .89$.[2]

These two requirements for an acceptable item (change in per cent passing with age, and correlation with total score) reflect both validity and reliability. The first of these requirements is an indirect way of guaranteeing validity (based on the inference that what we mean by intelligence should distinguish an older child from a younger one), while the second requirement is a guarantee of reliability through internal consistency of the measures.

By choosing items that meet these requirements, and by arranging them in a convenient form for the person giving the test, a self-consistent and useful test of intelligence results.

The definition of intelligence

The definition of intelligence has been postponed until we learned how intelligence tests are made. Now that the processes and purposes of making the tests have been explained, we can give the following practical definition of intelligence: *Intelligence is that which an intelligence test measures*. Although the statement sounds empty, it is not, for it implies all the careful steps that have gone into the construction of the tests. All the tests constructed by different workers distinguish the dull from the bright and lead to scores with high intercorrelations; therefore they are measuring something in common. What they measure in common defines intelligence.

Of course the testers had something in

mind as they constructed the tests. Suppose the tests did not exist. What kind of definition of intelligence could we give someone to furnish specifications for the test he should construct? Although Binet did not give a formal definition of intelligence, he made many detailed studies of the processes that appeared to distinguish between the bright and the dull. He emphasized the active nature of intelligence: making attempts, groping one's way, choosing between alternatives. Three characteristics of the thought processes impressed him: (1) the tendency to take and maintain a direction, without becoming distracted or sidetracked, (2) the capacity to adapt means to ends, and (3) the capacity for self-criticism, dissatisfaction with a partial solution that does not really solve the problem. It is such a definition that we imply when we say that intelligence is what an intelligence test measures.

Contemporary Binet tests

The tests originally developed by Alfred Binet underwent several revisions in this country, the first by Goddard in 1911. For many years the best known and most widely used revision was that made by Terman in 1916, commonly referred to as the Stanford-Binet. The test was later revised by Terman and Merrill in 1937 and again in 1960.

The Stanford-Binet revisions followed Binet's practice of arranging the tests in the form of an age scale. The procedure was to select items appropriate for a wide range of ages and abilities, and then to give the tests to a large and representative sample of the population for whom the test was intended. Only those items were retained that increasing proportions of children passed at older age levels and that significantly correlated with their total scores. A final and difficult step required the selection of items that could be usefully combined into a scale containing items appropriate to all ages.

An item is age-graded at the level at which a substantial majority of the children

[2] These are biserial correlations, as presented by McNemar (1942), pp. 178, 179.

pass it, as we saw in connection with the items of Figure 14-4. In the present Stanford-Binet there are usually six tests assigned to each year, each test when passed earning a score of two months of mental age.

The procedure for testing is first to establish the *basal mental age,* the mental age level at which (and below which) all tests are passed. Two months of mental age are then added for each test passed at higher ages. Consider, for example, the child who passes all tests at the six-year mental age level. If he then passes two tests at the seven-year level, four months are added to his mental age; if he passes an additional test at the eight-year level, two more months are added. The earned mental age for this particular child will be six years and six months, whatever his chronological age. The test allows for some unevenness in development, so that two children can earn the same mental age by passing different items on the test.

The giving of an individual intelligence test is a professional responsibility requiring special training. The test is a kind of standardized interview, and the skilled tester must be trained in interviewing as well as in the principles of testing. A test of this kind cannot be given satisfactorily by following printed instructions. Our discussion here is to acquaint us with the nature and the purposes of the test; to become trained to use the test a great deal more study would be essential.

The intelligence quotient (I.Q.)

Terman adopted a convenient index of brightness (suggested by the German psychologist Stern), the *intelligence quotient,* commonly known by its initials I.Q. It expresses intelligence as a ratio of the mental age to the chronological age:

$$I.Q. = 100 \frac{\text{Mental age (M.A.)}}{\text{Chronological age (C.A.)}}$$

14-5

A normal distribution curve of I.Q.'s

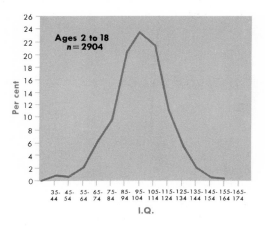

Distribution of I.Q.'s for 2904 children and youths, ages 2 to 18. This is the group upon which the Revised Stanford-Binet was standardized. (After Terman and Merrill, 1937)

The 100 is used as a multiplier to remove the decimal point and to make the average I.Q. (when M.A. = C.A.) have a value of 100. It is evident that if the M.A. lags behind the C.A., the resulting I.Q. will be less than 100; if the M.A. is above the C.A., the I.Q. will be above 100. Thus the brightness scale has about the same meaning from one age to another.

How is an I.Q. to be interpreted? The distribution of I.Q.'s follows the normal curve rather closely (Figure 14-5). For the group upon which the Stanford-Binet was standardized (after adjustment for sampling), the I.Q. had a mean of 100 and a standard deviation (σ) of 16. From our knowledge of the normal distribution, we know that we may expect about 68 per cent of the I.Q.'s to fall between 100 ± 16, or between 84 and 116, and 95 per cent between 68 and 136. The adjectives commonly used to describe the various I.Q. levels are given in Table 14-5, along with a frequency distribution of I.Q.'s for those tested in the standardization of the 1937 revision of the Stanford-Binet.

14-6

Testing adult intelligence

New York University Testing and Advisement Center

Subject taking one phase of the Wechsler-Bellevue Intelligence Test for Adults.

It is well also to have some reference points by which to judge the general level of competence of children and adults with various I.Q.'s. While general intelligence is by no means the only ability, it is of sufficient importance to limit the individual's activity. However, even persons with low I.Q.'s can succeed at many socially useful tasks. Some typical levels of competence represented by I.Q.'s of various levels are given in Table 14-6.

In the 1960 revision of the Stanford-Binet the authors have introduced a method of computing the I.Q. from tables. The meaning of an I.Q. remains essentially the same as before, but the tables permit some corrections so that at any age the I.Q. can be interpreted somewhat more exactly. It is

now arranged so that for each age the I.Q. averages 100 and has a standard deviation of 16. The I.Q. is thus a kind of *standard score* (see p. 379), with a fixed mean and standard deviation. This kind of I.Q. is known as a *deviation I.Q.,* and was earlier used in the Wechsler Adult Intelligence Scale, to be considered presently. The Stanford-Binet tables run only through age 18, and the test is no longer recommended for use with adults.

Diagnostic Tests of Intelligence

Tests following the pattern originated by Binet use a great assortment of items to test intelligence, and a pass or a fail on one kind of item is scored the same as a pass or a fail on another item. But those who are skilled in the use and scoring of the tests learn much more from them than appears in the final I.Q. They may note special strengths and weaknesses; tests of vocabulary, for example, may be passed at a higher level

TABLE 14-5

Interpretation of intelligence quotients on the Stanford-Binet

I.Q.	Verbal description	Per cent falling in each group (among 2904 subjects, ages 2 to 18)
140 and above	Very superior	1
120-139	Superior	11
110-119	High average	18
90-109	Average	46
80-89	Low average	15
70-79	Borderline	6
Below 70	Mentally retarded or defective	3
		——
		100

SOURCE: Merrill (1938).

than tests of manipulating form boards. These observations lead to the conjecture that what is being measured is not one simple ability, but a composite of abilities.

Tests with more than one scale

If it is desired to obtain information on specific kinds of abilities, rather than a single mental-age score, one way is to separate the items into more than one group and to score the groups separately. The Wechsler Adult Intelligence Scale and the Wechsler Intelligence Scale for Children are composed of items similar to those in the familiar Binet tests, but the total test is divided into two parts according to the content of the items, and two scales result—a *verbal scale* and a *performance scale*. By a *performance* item is meant one that requires manipulation or arrangement of blocks,

TABLE **14-7**

Tests comprising the Wechsler Adult Intelligence Scale and the Wechsler Intelligence Scale for Children

Verbal	*Performance*
Information	Digit Symbol *
Comprehension	Picture Completion
Arithmetic	Block Design
Similarities	Picture Arrangement
Digit Span †	Object Assembly
Vocabulary	Coding ‡
	Mazes §

SOURCE: Wechsler (1949, 1958).
* Adult scale only.
† Adult scale; alternate test for children.
‡ Scale for children only.
§ Alternate test for children.

beads, pictures, or other materials in which both stimuli and responses are nonverbal. Both kinds of items also appear in Binet tests, but the separate scaling of the items within one test is a convenience for diagnostic purposes. The tests comprising the two scales are listed in Table 14-7.

The names of the tests in most cases suggest their natures, though some of them require a word of explanation. The *digit span* test calls for reciting back to the tester a series of numerical digits that he repeats aloud, such as 7-5-8-3-6, first in a forward direction, and then other series in a backward direction. The score depends upon the length of the series that the subject gets correct. The *digit symbol* test requires following a sample in which various-shaped marks appear in squares under other squares containing numerals. The subject then fills in blank squares below other numerals according to the code provided. The *object assembly* test calls for putting together parts to complete a figure such as a manikin, human profile, hand, and elephant. The block design and object assembly tests are pictured in Figures 14-6 and 14-7.

In general, the full scale and the verbal

TABLE **14-6**

Interpretation of intelligence quotients according to level of social competence

I.Q.	*Competence represented*
130	Mean of persons receiving Ph.D.
120	Mean of college graduates
115	Mean of freshmen in typical four-year college
	Mean of children from white-collar and skilled-labor homes
110	Mean of high-school graduates
	Has 50-50 chance of graduating from college
105	About 50-50 chance of passing in academic high-school curriculum
100	Average for total population
90	Mean of children from low-income city homes or rural homes
	Adult can perform jobs requiring some judgment (operate sewing machine, assemble parts)
75	About 50-50 chance of reaching high school
	Adult can keep small store, perform in orchestra
60	Adult can repair furniture, harvest vegetables, assist electrician
50	Adult can do simple carpentry, domestic work
40	Adult can mow lawns, do simple laundry

Summarized by Cronbach (1960), p. 174, from various sources.

An intelligence test requiring nonverbal performance

Harbrace Photo

An item in the Wechsler object assembly test.

scale of the Wechsler Scale yield scores most nearly corresponding to those of the Stanford-Binet. In one study of 52 young adults (Wechsler, 1955), the following correlations were obtained between scores on the Stanford-Binet and the Wechsler Adult Intelligence Scale: with the full scale, .85; with the verbal scale, .86; with the performance scale, .69.

The two types of item-sorting are really intended to serve two different purposes. Sorting verbal and mathematical items in college aptitude tests attempts to locate *different* dimensions of intelligence; that is, one set of items may predict some kinds of college grades better than the other. Sorting into verbal and performance tests, on the other hand, is intended to find *equivalent* items for convenience in test administration. Some subjects handicapped by lack of knowledge of the language, or with special difficulties in the use of words, can be tested only with performance items; they are "fairer" items in the same sense as attempted in "culture-fair" tests.

Unfortunately, neither kind of item-sorting accomplishes its purpose very well. The results of the subtests overlap, so that both parts test abilities that have much in common. But the correlations between subtests are lower than the self-correlations between tests of similar items, so that the subtests appraise slightly different abilities. The two subscales of the Wechsler Adult Intelligence Scale correlated .77 for the 300 subjects at ages 25-34 in the standardization groups. For those same subjects the self-correlation (i.e., the reliability coefficient) for the verbal scale is .96, and for the performance scale .93. To make an analysis of the separate abilities whose composite we call intelligence calls for a more refined approach than item classification gives us.

Tests based upon factor analysis

Statistical methods have been devised that give much more precise information about the component parts of intelligence. These methods, known collectively as *factor analysis,* make it possible to construct tests which detect patterns of underlying abilities. Factor analysis as a tool of test construction is still in a developmental stage, even though the first steps were taken as early as 1904 (by Charles Spearman) before Binet's test appeared.

The method of multiple factor analysis developed by L. L. Thurstone (1947), although but one of several similar methods, is until recently the one most widely used, and our discussion will be based upon it.

As an illustration of tests constructed with the aid of factor analysis, let us consider a battery of intelligence tests developed by Thurstone. This battery is known as tests for Primary Mental Abilities (L. L. Thurstone, 1938). Thurstone set himself to find a few clusters of abilities that made up the composite tested by familiar intelligence tests. In other words, he wished to find some reliable method of grouping items that earlier item-sorting had grouped crudely.

Thurstone's method is to give a large number of tests to the same children. As many as sixty have been used (L. L. Thurstone and T. G. Thurstone, 1941). Each single test is composed of items very much alike, so that the test content is easily described. One test is for verbal comprehension, another for arithmetical computations, etc. Then the scores of all the tests are intercorrelated. Obviously those tests whose scores show high correlations with one another have much in common; those tests whose scores yield low correlations with one another have little in common. The method of factor analysis is merely a systematic way of finding what few common factors may account for the many obtained correlations.

In order to show what this means, let us consider a simple example, based on the intercorrelations of four hypothetical tests (Table 14-8). Without knowing anything at all about the tests, we can see that tests A and B have more in common than any two other tests, and tests C and D represent another pair with considerable in common. Lacking any method of factor analysis, we can still infer that there are two different abilities represented among these tests; a formal factor analysis would tell us how much each of the tests is influenced by ("loaded with") each of the two factors. Thus the correlation of .40 between B and D shows

TABLE 14-8

Intercorrelations of scores on four tests *

	A	B	C	D
A		.80	.20	.10
B	.80		.30	.40
C	.20	.30		.60
D	.10	.40	.60	

* Note that the same correlations appear above and below the diagonals. Often in a table such as this only the correlations above the diagonal will be shown.

that they have something in common from both factors, and mere inspection does not permit us to say how much. Having completed the factor analysis and determined the factor composition of each test, we can "explain" Table 14-8, in the sense that we could reconstruct it from what we know of the underlying factors.

The factors discovered are purely mathematical, explaining in mathematical terms what the test correlations show. But the presumption is that the factors represent some underlying "traits" or "unitary abilities" that produce the test results. Thus the name assigned a factor is really an educated guess as to the kind of trait that would reasonably yield the scores obtained.

The result of a number of studies of this kind led Thurstone to identify seven factors as the *primary abilities* revealed by the items on intelligence tests. These seven are:

1. Verbal comprehension (V). Vocabulary tests represent this factor.

2. Word fluency (W). This factor calls for the ability to think of words rapidly, as in solving anagrams, or in thinking of words that rhyme.

3. Number (N). Simple arithmetic tests, especially those calling for computations, represent this factor.

4. Space (S). Tests of this factor deal with visual form relationships, as in drawing a design from memory.

5. Memory (M). This factor is found in tests requiring memory for pairs of items.

6. Perceptual (P). Calls for the grasping of visual details and of the similarities and differences between pictured objects. (Tests for P are omitted from some forms of the Primary Mental Abilities batteries.)

7. Reasoning (R). Best represented by tests that call for finding a general rule on the basis of presented instances, as in finding how a number series is constructed from a portion of that series.

Once the several factors have been identified, it is possible to construct tests that are truly diagnostic for each factor, so that a test profile for the individual will indicate how well he performs on tests that demand each of the several abilities.

The practical question remains whether or not primary abilities tests are more efficient predictive instruments than the earlier general intelligence tests. At present, one is about as successful as the other. But the possibility of gaining more fundamental information on patterns of ability through tests of known structure is so great that tests constructed with the aid of factor analysis will undoubtedly become more and more widely used.

CRITICAL DISCUSSION
How "primary" are primary abilities?

The development of factor analysis methods gave promise that we might become much more precise in specifying the nature of intelligence through isolating basic components of intellectual abilities. Have we succeeded in breaking intelligence into its basic elements? The answer is clearly "No," because it turns out that the primary abilities are themselves interrelated. But we are much farther along in identifying the abilities that underlie scores on tests, and we know what we are about when we give a profile based on subtests in the battery. The primary abilities are not completely independent, but they sum-

marize a great deal of information under a few headings. Some six or seven primary abilities can account for the 1770 correlations between the 60 tests of a long battery.[3] In shortening such a battery for convenience in use, there is obviously an advantage in including tests that best represent the primary abilities common to the whole battery.

The primary abilities isolated by the Thurstones are themselves not completely independent. When used on eighth-grade pupils, they show intercorrelations with r's ranging from .15 to .55. Each of the subtests is also correlated with a "general factor" which the subtests have in common. For the same group of eighth-grade pupils, the individual factors correlate with this general factor with r's between .34 and .84. The Thurstones conclude that "each of the primary factors can be regarded as a composite of an independent primary factor and a general factor which it shares with other primary factors" (L. L. Thurstone and T. G. Thurstone, 1941, p. 38).

Many fascinating possibilities for continuing investigation exist in factor analysis. For example, the interpretation of the more general factors and the unique factors in tests remains a source of controversy, because the logic of factors is only partially understood. The possibility that factors are "culture-bound" rather than universal among men has to be considered; perhaps some aspects of behavior are differentially reinforced in one culture and not in another, thereby leading to different factors. The possibility that the specific factors emerge in this way is hinted at by the differences in results from childhood to adulthood in our culture. Studies done with children show higher intercorrelations among the factors than studies with adults. Does this difference mean that a general factor operates more strongly in childhood than in later life and that specific factors arise as a result of experience? At present we do not have a satisfactory answer.

Recent work has tended to multiply rather than reduce the number of factors making up intelligence. Guilford, for example, reports that some 40 intellectual factors have been isolated, and, according to a scheme he has proposed, the number may run as high as 120 (Guilford, 1960).

[3] The number of correlations between pairs of tests is $[N(N-1)]/2$, where N is the number of tests in the battery.

Adult Intelligence

Adult mental age and I.Q.

During World War I (and again during World War II) psychological tests were used in appraising the abilities of millions of men. Nothing like so many scores from a single testing program had ever been available before.

Two major intelligence tests were developed in World War I. These were known as the Army Alpha, a test for those who could read and write English, and the Army Beta, a test for illiterates and those handicapped in the English language. They differ from the Binet tests in that they are *group tests,* while Binet tests are *individual tests.* A group test can be given to many subjects at once, like an ordinary written examination. The Army tests were modeled to some extent upon the Binet tests, and the experts who designed them had had experience with earlier revisions of the Binet.

The psychologists decided to compare the scores on the Army Alpha with Stanford-Binet M.A.'s. This comparison was obtained by giving the Stanford-Binet as an individual test to a representative sample of 653 men who had also taken the Army Alpha. When Army Alpha scores were converted according to this comparison, it turned out that the average M.A. of the white draftees in World War I was close to 13 years (Yerkes, 1921). The apparent conclusion—that ours was a nation of thirteen-year-old mentality—led to a further question: If the average mental age at any chronological age is simply that chronological age, then the average adult (as represented by World War I soldiers) has a *below-average adult mental age.*[4] How can this be?

The fact is that the mental-age concept is not a very useful one above the age of 13. Up to that age, it is not difficult to find

tests that can be passed by a higher age group while being failed by those one year younger. But after age 13 the gain in scores per year is so little that good mental-age scales cannot be constructed. That is, we cannot find satisfactory tests that 18-year-olds will pass and 17-year-olds fail. Without such tests, we cannot continue our mental-age scale. In order to maintain the M.A. concept (and the I.Q.) above age 13, we have to use arbitrary scoring devices, such as deviation I.Q.'s.

When it is seen from this point of view, the Army M.A. of 13 years should be interpreted not as meaning that adults score at childish levels, but rather as reflecting the fact that the 13-year-old is near to his adult level of scoring on an intelligence test. That the Army mean was below the expected adult average is not surprising in view of the fact that those of high intelligence were excused from the draft in order to perform essential civilian services, and that conditions of testing were far from ideal.

Other measures of adult intelligence

If the mental-age concept is inappropriate for adults, so also is the I.Q., unless some method is used to produce an I.Q. score for adults that can be interpreted in a way comparable to that for a child. The simplest method is to adopt a mean of 100 and a standard deviation similar to that of I.Q.'s obtained in the earlier years. This is just what has been done in the Wechsler Adult Intelligence Scale.[5] The average score for any one adult age is interpreted as an I.Q. of 100, regardless of any change that may be taking place with age. Then the I.Q. is computed on the basis of the obtained standard deviation of scores near this mean value, one standard deviation being interpreted as 15 I.Q. points.

[4] For evidence on the level of intelligence of World War II enlisted men, see p. 439.

[5] This "deviation I.Q." has now been adopted for children in the new revised Stanford-Binet. Note, however, that the Wechsler test uses a standard deviation of 15 instead of the 16 used in the Stanford-Binet.

Changes during adult years

Although it is desirable for comparative purposes to assign a mean of 100 to the I.Q. at all ages, there is, in fact, some decline over the years in intelligence as measured by the ordinary tests. By using the mean scores for the years 25-34 as a reference point, and scoring subjects at other ages as though they were from the same age population, the curves of Figure 14-8 result. The peak for verbal intelligence comes in the 25-34 age range and falls off slowly, while the peak for performance scores comes a little earlier, and the performance scores fall off more rapidly with age. The greater handicap of older people on the performance tests may be a result of the emphasis on speed of performance in those tests.

The differences in rate of decline of the actual verbal and performance scores with age correspond to earlier findings that not all adult abilities decline at the same rate (Jones and Conrad, 1933). In general, *information-type* items hold up best, while *cleverness-type* and *speed-type* items show the greatest decline. Thus some arbitrariness enters into using any one score as an index of the intelligence of an adult.

The decline of measured intelligence in one's fourth decade does not signify that the mature adult is less competent to play his role in life. He may be accumulating new experiences less rapidly than he once did, but he has not forgotten all that he has accumulated in the past. If we think of *wisdom* as an accumulation from past experience and of intelligence as the ability to apply that experience to problems in the present, we may see how an older person may be much *wiser* than a brighter younger person who lacks his experience. Intelligence tests are heavily loaded with items demanding cleverness, alertness, and adaptability to novel situations. They do not weight the background of experience which permits the older person to meet wisely the familiar situations in his own life and work.

The Extremes of Intelligence

We can learn something further about the meaning of intelligence by looking at extreme groups—the mentally subnormal and the gifted.

The mentally subnormal

Intelligence tests were developed, first of all, to discover those children least likely to profit from ordinary schooling. There is no sharp break between the subnormal and the normal, and there are many borderline cases. Furthermore, when a child is classified as subnormal, the classification tells us very little about him. There are many kinds and degrees of retarded children. Not all subnormal children are alike, and, because they are not alike, calling them by a common name such as "feeble-minded" is misleading.

CRITICAL DISCUSSION

Some rejected labels for the subnormal

The mentally subnormal child suffers a number of handicaps, but is able to overcome many of them and live a useful and satisfying life. One of the most difficult handicaps to overcome is the stigma of being classified as subnormal. The terms that society uses sooner or later become terms with negative connotations. Such terms as "half-wit" and "simpleton," familiar to an earlier generation, became replaced by the then less offensive term "feeble-minded," but this has since come to have unfavorable connotations. The classification of the retarded into a high group (moron), intermediate group (imbecile), and low group (idiot) has also outlived its usefulness, as the adjectives "moronic," "imbecilic," and "idiotic" have become terms of reproach.

The more modern approach recognizes that there are mentally subnormal children with

14-8

Decline of adult intelligence over the years

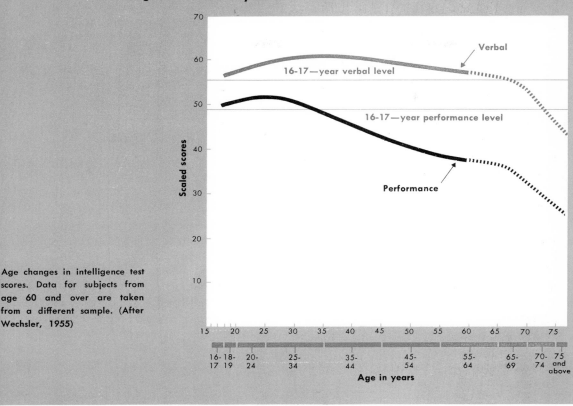

Age changes in intelligence test scores. Data for subjects from age 60 and over are taken from a different sample. (After Wechsler, 1955)

a variety of handicaps, and general terms of classification are avoided. Descriptive expressions such as more severely defective, or less severely retarded, or trainable, or educable have come into use to avoid the stigma of harsh labels.

The one main distinction, supported by the World Health Organization and encouraged by the National Association for Retarded Children, is that between the organically damaged, classified as *"mentally defective,"* and the individual whose problems lie in a learning disability, classified as *"mentally retarded"* (Masland, Sarason, and Gladwin, 1958). This distinction is followed here.

The Prevalence of Retardation. The classification of a child as mentally subnormal or retarded depends primarily upon social com-

petence, and a child can be classified by what he can do without recourse to an intelligence test. Any classification runs into difficulty with borderline cases. The distinction between dull normal and subnormal depends on an interpretation of "marginal social success under favorable conditions." The farm hand who was unable to finish school but lives his own life as a hired man on the farm, spending his free time in the neighboring village, is economically independent and is normal in his environment, even though recognizably dull; the same man might find difficulty in living independently in the city. Hence the distinction between the dull normal and the subnormal depends upon the complexity of the social conditions under which independence must

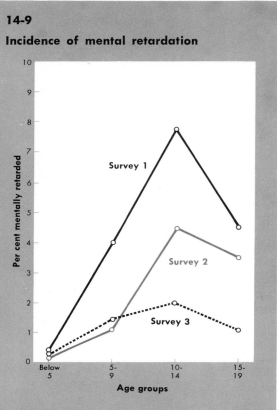

14-9

Incidence of mental retardation

Survey 1

Survey 2

Survey 3

Per cent mentally retarded

Age groups

Below 5 | 5-9 | 10-14 | 15-19

Three different surveys disagree on the total incidence, but agree in finding a larger proportion of children classified as retarded when in the 10-14-year age bracket. (After Masland, Sarason, and Gladwin, 1958, p. 140)

of this kind of change in the proportion of retarded individuals with age.

Examination of the distribution curve of I.Q.'s (Figure 14-5, p. 405) shows that the slope is very steep in the region of 70 to 80, where the borderline cases tend to fall. Hence any change in the criterion of subnormality will readily produce a change in the proportion of individuals estimated to be retarded.

Because of these uncertainties, it is hard to state a firm figure about the prevalence of mental subnormality. It is usually asserted that about 1 or 2 per cent of the population can be classified as subnormal, but as indicated in Table 14-9, the potentially retarded may constitute as much as 3 per cent of the population. Because of favorable circumstances, many of these "potentially retarded" are not recognized as retarded; on the other hand, some individuals with higher intellectual potential, through unfavorable aspects of health or experience, may become classified as subnormal. It is easier to count the more severely retarded, because a larger fraction of them are found in institutions.

Causes of Subnormality. A useful distinction is now made between the individual who is *mentally retarded* and the one who is *mentally defective* (see p. 413). A child is classified as belonging to the *mentally retarded* group if he is essentially sound phys-

be maintained. By social criteria, an individual might change his classification by moving from one place to another, even though his tested intelligence has not changed in the meantime.

The importance of social demands in determining retardation is well illustrated by the detection of retardation as related to age. When surveys have been conducted of the number of children retarded at each age, the highest per cent of retardation is found at the ages of 10-14, when the competitive demands of academic performance become emphasized in judging retardation (Figure 14-9). There is no other good explanation

TABLE 14-9

Estimated prevalence of retardation in the total population

Potentially retarded, but educable (ultimate M.A. under 12)	3 per cent
Moderately severe retardation, trainable (ultimate M.A. 4 to 7)	0.3 per cent
Most severely retarded, helpless (ultimate M.A. under 4)	0.1 per cent

SOURCE: Masland, Sarason, and Gladwin (1958), p. 3.

ically and if there is no history of disease or injury that might have caused intellectual impairment. He suffers from a general deficiency rather than an identifiable specific defect. With such a child there is often a history of retardation in the family, so that the possibility of inherited mental weakness is not ruled out. A child is classified as belonging to the *mentally defective* group if his mental impairment is due to brain injury, disease, or accidents of development that preclude normal intellectual growth. The causes may occur at any time during fetal life, childhood, or even adult life. Such individuals crop up in any family, in any socioeconomic group, regardless of any history of retardation in the family.

The brain-injured child shows kinds of intellectual impairment that differ from those of the merely retarded child. Among the differences that show on tests is defective perception of pictures with confusion between figure and ground. When presented with pictures like that of Figure 14-10, the brain-injured but not the retarded child has difficulty in picking out the figure from the background.

The differences between the perceptual responses of normal children and those of two groups of subnormal children are shown in Table 14-10. There is so little difference

14-10

Distinguishing the mentally defective

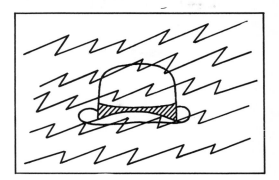

This figure-ground problem is difficult for brain-injured but not for retarded children. (After Werner and Strauss, 1941)

between the perceptual responses of the normal children and of the mentally retarded ones that the test would not be useful in an ordinary intelligence test battery. Yet it proved to have real value in distinguishing between those children with brain damage, as a group, and those children with similarly low I.Q.'s but without evidence of brain damage.

Now and then we come upon a child who is apparently subnormal but actually is not. He reacts emotionally to his environment by withdrawal and negativism, so that his learn-

TABLE 14-10						
Reactions to a picture test from three groups of children						
Group	*Number*	*Mean I.Q.*	*Responses to figure*	*Responses to background*	*Vague responses*	*Total*
Normal	30	Normal	63%	9%	28%	100%
Subnormal *						
Retarded						
(non-brain-injured)	25	64	58	14	28	100
Defective						
(brain-injured)	25	63	12	75	13	100

SOURCE: Werner and Strauss (1941). Ages of the children ranged from 7 to 10.

* In the original source, the mental retardation is called "endogenous," mental defect "exogenous."

14-11

Aid for the subnormal child

Cornell Capa—Magnum

Training in a workshop for retarded children. Today many such children become self-supporting members of their communities. (Capa and Pines, 1957)

ing of language is delayed and his test performances are poor. Only a skilled test administrator can discover that the test score is misleading. Such a child can be aided by psychotherapy.

Treatment of the Subnormal. From time to time there appear dramatic reports of remarkable achievements in the raising of the I.Q.'s of subnormal children. Headlines in newspapers and articles in magazines raise hopes of countless parents who have retarded children. This is unfortunate, because such evidence as we have today is not encouraging. It gives little promise of dramatic improvement in the mentally subnormal (e.g., Kirk, 1948). But this does not mean that the retarded or defective child cannot be helped. There is a difference between doing all that we can to provide a favorable opportunity for the backward child to develop and giving optimistic promises of change that are unlikely to be fulfilled.

A great deal can be done for the backward child. He can be taught social habits; he can learn vocational skills appropriate to his intellectual level; and in some instances he may learn to take his place in the community outside an institution. Social aid for the mentally defective must not be confused, however, with raising the I.Q. In many subnormal individuals a small increase in I.Q. comes with better social adjustment, but there is little reason to expect striking changes as a result of bettered environment.

Many persons of low intelligence get along satisfactorily in the community. Several follow-up studies have been made of children whose I.Q.'s during school age rated them as mentally retarded. All the investigators found a substantial proportion of these individuals maintaining themselves vocationally in the community when they became adults.

Even institutionalized subnormal persons are frequently paroled to the community and many make adequate adjustments there. In one report, the work histories of 177 higher-grade retarded paroled from the Wayne County (Michigan) Training School were studied. Because the study was made at a time of favorable employment opportunities during World War II, these workers were able to find jobs for themselves, usually above the unskilled level, and to hold the jobs for months (Hegge, 1944).

Society has a responsibility toward all its

members, not only to provide for their physical needs but also to make use of their abilities in socially productive ways. This responsibility extends to the subnormal who, despite their limitations, are able to do useful things. Suitable opportunities for employment make their lives more satisfying, and at the same time their labors contribute to the general welfare.

The mentally gifted

At the other end of the scale from the mentally defective lie those who are gifted intellectually. With the development of intelligence tests it has become possible to select for study large groups of superior children, and then to follow their careers. One of the best-known of these studies, started in September, 1921, by Terman and his associates, covers more than 1500 gifted children from their early school years through the middle years of adult life, the latest report having appeared in 1959 (Terman and Oden, 1959).

The group was chosen on the basis of I.Q. of 140 or above. About 10 or 11 of 1000 children in the public schools have I.Q.'s that high. Less than 1 in 1000 has an I.Q. above 160.

What do Terman's findings reveal about the gifted child? So far as parental backgrounds were concerned, the children came mostly from the homes of professional people (about ⅓ of the group) and of higher business classes (about ½). Less than 7 per cent came from semiskilled or unskilled laboring classes, despite the fact that these classes constitute a higher proportion of the population. The home environment probably contributed to the gifted children by way of both heredity and environment. The brighter parents are found for the most part in superior occupational groups, and they provide more stimulating environments for their children.

Although the ratio of gifted boys to gifted girls was only 7:6 in the grade school groups, the boys with I.Q.'s of 140 and over outnumbered the girls 2:1 in high school. This larger percentage of boys at this level is not to be interpreted as a sign that boys become brighter than girls as they grow older. At the time the study was begun, there was still more encouragement to the boy than to the girl to go on with his education.

Terman's gifted children were better than average physical specimens. They averaged more than an inch taller than others of the same age in elementary school. Their birth weights were above normal. They talked early and walked early. When the tests started, seven out of eight were in grades ahead of their age group in school; none was retarded. They were unusual in the kind and number of books they read, but reading did not interfere with their superiority in leadership and social adaptability.

These characteristics of the gifted children gave the lie to the notion that the very bright child is a weakling and a social misfit. The evidence is all to the contrary. Superior intelligence turned out to be associated with good health, social adaptability, and leadership.

Gifted Children as Young Adults. The extent to which early promise was fulfilled by the gifted children of Terman's group can be estimated from their performances in early adult life.

While the group on the whole gave a superior account of itself, it should be noted, first of all, that not all the subjects had a history of success. Some failed in college, some were vocational misfits, some ran afoul of the law. But the less successful differed little in their adult intelligence test scores from the more successful. The comparative scores are given in Table 14-11. The average I.Q. difference between the most and least successful is only 6 points. The slight difference in intellectual level as measured cannot account for the differences in achievement. We must therefore conclude

TABLE 14-11

Adult intelligence of most successful and least successful men among a group with high I.Q.'s as children

Group	N	Mean score on concept mastery test	Estimated equivalent I.Q. as adults
A Most success as adults	79	112	139
B Intermediate success	322	99	134
C Least success as adults	116	94	133

SOURCE: Terman and Oden (1947), pp. 132, 144, 323.

that nonintellectual qualities are very important in success.

What does "successful" and "unsuccessful" mean in these comparisons? The subjects whose test scores are reported in Table 14-11 were all men from the gifted group selected many years earlier on the basis of a childhood I.Q. of 140 or higher. These were classified into three success groups: *A*, the most successful; *B*, the intermediately successful; and *C*, the least successful. The criterion of success was primarily "the extent to which a subject made use of his intellectual ability." Listing in *Who's Who* or *American Men of Science,* representation in literary or scholarly publications, responsible managerial positions, outstanding achievement in any intellectual or professional calling—all entered into the judgments. Earned income was taken into account but was given relatively little weight.

The *A* and *C* groups differed significantly on many of the 200 items in the case histories, trait ratings, and test records. Among the most important of these were social and mental adjustment, family background, and ratings previously made on three traits: perseverance, self-confidence, and integration toward goals. In other words, the *A*'s differ from the *C*'s most of all in general adjustment and in motivation to achieve. These are personality and motiva-

tional traits rather than intellectual ones. The *A* and *C* groups began to diverge educationally in high school. Fewer of the *C* group went to college; of those who did, 31 per cent averaged grades of C or lower, compared with but 7 per cent of the *A* group.

To illustrate the extreme contrasts sometimes found between the most and least successful, the authors have summarized briefly the achievement records of two of the men to 1950.

A SUCCESSFUL SUBJECT

Subject A792 graduated from high school at 16, from college at 20, with Phi Beta Kappa honors, and received his Ph.D. in science at 23. In his undergraduate college years he earned a quarter of his expenses and in his graduate years supported himself entirely. He was then awarded a National Research Fellowship for postdoctorate study, after which he was appointed to a position in a leading university. By the age of 40 he was nationally eminent and director of a great scientific laboratory. He is listed both in *American Men of Science* and in *Who's Who.*

AN UNSUCCESSFUL SUBJECT

Subject C49 had almost exactly the same I.Q. rating as A792, like him had a superior record through high school, and in college earned about the same proportion of his expenses. There the similarity ends, for C graduated from college well below the average of his class. After graduation he drifted for several years, then returned to college and managed to complete his work for a master's degree. His occupations since then have ranged from semiskilled labor and clerical jobs to positions of minor responsibility in business organizations. His chief handicaps have been inferior social adjustment, uncertainty with respect to life goals, and lack of drive or persistence. As a result he has accomplished less than the average college graduate.[6]

Men of the *A* group who have attained national or near-national eminence are found in a great variety of work, including law, medicine, surgery, pharmacology, physiology, physics, astrophysics, oceanography, engineering, psychology, psychiatry, literature, business management, and government service. Men in the *C* group are more commonly found in semiprofessional pursuits or in the upper clerical and ordinary business levels. In the ten years after the *A* and *C* ratings were made, the success of a few of the *A* men was lessened by physical or mental illness, and the success of a few of the *C*'s changed for the better. For the most part, however, the two groups remained about as widely separated as ever.

The later follow-up (Terman and Oden, 1959) showed that the distinctive abilities of the gifted were becoming more fully recognized as they grew older. The 1955 edition of *American Men of Science* listed 70 men and 7 women, while the 1944 edition listed but 19 of the men. Listings in *Who's Who in America* grew from 5 in 1946 to 33 in 1958. It takes time to achieve recognition, and this group, picked in childhood, has given a good account of itself.

Our social responsibility to make good use of those of high ability is no less pressing than our responsibility to provide for those handicapped by low ability. The need for highly trained specialists already comes close to tapping our available talent (Wolfle, 1954). If much of this talent is dissipated

through poor social and personal adjustment or through inadequate motivation, as the *C* group in Terman's study suggests, one place to begin increasing our supply is with promising youth in their early years. We need to do what we can to create the atmosphere in which they will be stimulated to use their creative abilities in socially productive ways.

Present Status of Intelligence Tests

Despite their limitations, intelligence tests provide what is perhaps the most useful quantitative tool that psychology has developed. Their usefulness will continue, provided they are kept in perspective and neither overvalued as telling more about a person than they actually measure, nor undervalued because of their obvious defects. The following assertions provide a balanced evaluation of where we now stand in the measurement of intelligence.

1. General intelligence tests measuring a composite of abilities are serviceable instruments. The best of these are individual tests, such as the Stanford-Binet and Wechsler scales, rather than group tests. Individual tests are somewhat inconvenient, because they require trained testers and take a long time to administer. But these requirements are also an advantage: a trained person can detect when the test is or is not appropriate; moreover, being trained, he secures a great deal of specific information from the test, information that goes beyond the intelligence score he obtains. Good group tests are convenient and timesaving, but are subject to larger errors for individuals than are individual tests. When crucial decisions are to be made on the basis of intelligence test scores, supplementary individual tests should be given.

2. The common ability that accounts for the intercorrelations of the test items of

[6] Private communication, courtesy of the late Lewis M. Terman and Melita H. Oden.

general intelligence tests appears to be largely verbal. General intelligence tests, because of this stress on words, tend to handicap children from impoverished environments where the necessary verbal stimulation is not provided.

3. Despite the appearance of performance scales depending less on words than do the obviously verbal tests, most of the performance scales are not free of dependence on verbal abilities. For example, the directions for taking the test are usually given in words, not in pantomime. For most predictive purposes performance scales have not shown as high validity as verbal scales. Perhaps more inventiveness needs to be directed toward performance tests.

4. Factor analysis provides a tool that may help intelligence tests of the future to become more truly diagnostic. If with the aid of factor analysis some stable primary abilities are defined and verified experimentally, many of the generalizations made from general intelligence tests will have to be reviewed in the light of these findings. For example, such problems as twin resemblance, sex differences, age effects, and environmental influences will require restudy with respect to the special abilities represented, for it is unlikely that all abilities will be found equally influenced by growth or environmental opportunities. The multiplication of factors in recent research makes this kind of research less simple than it appeared to be a few years ago, but makes such investigations all the more necessary.

SUMMARY   1. Men differ in all sorts of ways, and any one of these differences may affect how well they succeed in their work and in society.

2. The psychologist uses ability testing to study individual differences. *Aptitude tests* attempt to predict the success in some kind of performance net yet attained, as in judging how much an individual will profit by training before training is undertaken. *Achievement tests* measure present attainment, or what the subject has learned after the completion of training. Both tests can use similar items. The difference lies in their purposes.

3. Achievement tests are very widely used. Most educational examinations, whether in elementary school, high school, or college, are of this kind, as are also most civil service examinations.

4. In order to make predictions from tests, tests must meet certain specifications. Studies of *reliability* tell us whether or not the test scores are self-consistent. Studies of *validity* tell us how well the tests measure what they are supposed to measure, how well they predict according to an acceptable criterion.

5. When tests meet the specifications, they can be applied in schools, in industry, in civil service, or in the armed forces. The pilot-selection program of the U.S. Army Air Forces during World War II illustrates the nature of a *test battery* and how the results of tests are used in prediction.

6. The simplest application of the results of studies in prediction is the *critical score,* so set that those who score below this point are disqualified, while those above it are accepted or permitted to continue.

7. Intelligence tests are useful aptitude tests because they measure abilities important in school, in vocational success, and in other aspects of social adjustment.

8. The first successful intelligence tests were developed by Alfred Binet in France in 1905. To him we owe the concept of *mental age,* according to which we regard dull children as slow in their development, their responses being like those of children younger in chronological age. Conversely, bright children are advanced beyond their years. This concept has been followed in later revisions of Binet's scales, the most widely used of which has been the Stanford-Binet. Terman, who was responsible for the Stanford-Binet, introduced the *intelligence quotient* (I.Q.) as an index of mental development, following a suggestion of Stern. The I.Q. is obtained by expressing intelligence as a ratio of mental age (M.A.) to chronological age (C.A.). The *deviation I.Q.* adopted in the most recent Stanford-Binet adjusts the obtained I.Q.'s so that at each chronological age they have a mean of 100 and a standard deviation of 16.

9. Efforts to improve the diagnostic value of intelligence tests have taken two chief forms. One is to divide the items of the test into more than one scale. This attempt is illustrated by the verbal and performance scales of the Wechsler Adult Intelligence Scale and the Wechsler Intelligence Scale for Children. The second method of improving the diagnostic value of intelligence tests is to arrange subtests according to the findings of *factor analysis.* The individual tests can then represent the factors found to determine the test intercorrelations. One such battery, the tests for Primary Mental Abilities developed by Thurstone, is proving to be a promising tool of research and prediction.

10. The Wechsler Adult Intelligence Scale uses a somewhat arbitrary procedure, thereby making it possible to use the concept of intelligence quotient (I.Q.) with adults, and to interpret such an I.Q. approximately as it is interpreted earlier in life. The I.Q. is assigned an average of 100 for each adult age group, and the standard deviation is set arbitrarily at 15. When intelligence test scores are not adjusted in this way, it is found that verbal intelligence reaches its peak at the age of 25-34, performance intelligence somewhat earlier. Intelligence test scores decline slowly thereafter, with the performance scores falling off more rapidly than the verbal ones.

11. The extremes of intelligence are represented by the *mentally subnormal* at one end of the scale and the *intellectually gifted* at the other. A final decision that a child is or is not subnormal depends on more than intelligence test scores; for example, with the same score one child may be classed as subnormal, another as normal. The subnormal are further classified as *mentally retarded* or *mentally defective.* Mental retardation is a deficiency present from birth, with no obvious brain damage. Mental defectiveness results from illness, injury, or a physical defect. Subnormal children can learn, and thus many of them can do socially useful work under supervision or even achieve a measure of social independence. The fact that the impairment in intelligence level persists throughout life means only that this condition imposes a special responsibility upon society to make provision for adequate care and training.

12. The mentally gifted as a group show superior attainments throughout childhood and early adult life. Their histories belie the notion that very highly intelligent people are sickly or poorly adjusted. Superior intelligence is of itself no assurance of success; some gifted children are misfits in adult life even though their intelligence scores remain high.

13. The intelligence test, cautiously used, is an important predictive device, though it gives undue weight to verbal ability. Factor analysis may help intelligence tests become more truly diagnostic.

SUGGESTIONS FOR FURTHER READING

For general summaries of the present status of knowledge about individual differences, two useful books are Anastasi and Foley, *Differential psychology* (3rd Ed., 1958), Tyler, *The psychology of human differences* (2nd Ed., 1956), and Thorndike and Hagen, *Measurement and evaluation in psychology and education* (1961).

The general principles of test construction, problems of reliability and validity, and appropriate use of tests can be found in Cronbach, *Essentials of psychological testing* (2nd Ed., 1960). The latest revision of the Stanford-Binet is Terman and Merrill, *Stanford-Binet intelligence scale: manual for the third revision* (1960); of the Wechsler Adult Intelligence Scale, Wechsler, *The measurement and appraisal of adult intelligence* (4th Ed., 1958).

The problems of subnormality are treated in an extensive review of the literature sponsored by the National Association for Retarded Children: Masland, Sarason, and Gladwin, *Mental subnormality* (1958). The last of several volumes on a group selected for high intelligence as children, and now studied 35 years later, is Terman and Oden, *The gifted group at mid-life* (1959).

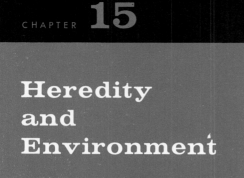

CHAPTER 15

Heredity and Environment

In the effort to understand individual differences a persistent question requires answer: Is a person *born* that way, or does he *become* what he is as a result of learning? The question runs throughout psychology, and we have met it already in the discussion of instinct (p. 67), and space perception (pp. 208-10). The concept of evolution, which assumes the survival of those best fit to survive and the transmission of adaptive qualities through inheritance, suggests a strong hereditary component in the differences between species and hence also in the individual differences within a species.

There is no point in arguing an extreme view that all that matters is heredity, or all that matters is environment. A little reflection will point immediately to an interaction, for an organism cannot grow without the sustenance that the environment provides. Hence while there may be a hereditary component to height, the actually attained height will depend upon the variety and adequacy of the diet; so, too, a behavioral characteristic such as intelligence may have a hereditary component, but the actually attained intellectual level will depend upon various kinds of stimulation during growth. The problem is not to decide between heredity and environment, but to learn what we can of the limitations imposed by heredity on individual potential, and the range of change that can be produced by favorable and unfavorable environments.

Behavior Genetics

Modern genetics, the science of heredity, shows how the physical characteristics of offspring derive from the characteristics of the parents. Behavior genetics is a newer branch of genetics concerned with the inheritance of behavior rather than of physical structure. There is an interesting question here, whether or not anything is added by studying behavior, for surely behavior (if inherited) must depend upon physical structures. That is, if intelligence is inherited, it is because the brighter person inherits a nervous system that is superior to the one inherited by the less bright person. While this sounds logical enough, even inherited structure is not observed directly; what is observed, even in such features as size and coloration, reflects the interaction of heredity and environment. Viewed in this way, a rat's ability to run a maze may be just as useful an indicator of heredity as the weight of its brain. Thus the inheritance of behavior can be studied in its own right, just as the inheritance of physical structure can be studied. Before examining the evidence for the inheritance of behavior, we shall review briefly the major principles of hereditary transmission.

Phenotypes and genotypes

While heredity in general produces resemblances between parents and offspring, the science of genetics teaches us to search beneath superficial resemblances; in fact, certain *lacks* of resemblance between parents and offspring give us our chief clues to the mechanism of heredity. For example, the black guinea pigs whose offspring are in the proportion of 3 black to 1 white illustrate a fundamental principle of heredity; so also the fact that half the sons of parents who see colors normally may be color-blind illustrates another principle. To understand these illustrations we have to distinguish between the *phenotype*—the actual individual as we can describe him (e.g., the black guinea pig or the parent who sees color normally), and the *genotype*—the individual as a carrier of genetic qualities that may or may not be manifested by him (e.g., a mother who may transmit color blindness to her sons).

Chromosomes and Genes. An individual's *genotype* consists of the hereditary units that he has received from his parents and that he will transmit to his offspring. These units are carried by microscopic particles found within each cell of the body, known as *chromosomes*. A chromosome is composed of many individual determiners of heredity called *genes*. Each body cell has 46 chromosomes. At conception the human being receives 23 chromosomes from the father's sperm and 23 chromosomes from the mother's ovum. These 46 chromosomes form 23 pairs, which are duplicated in every cell of the body as the individual develops. (It was thought until recently that man had 24 pairs of chromosomes, but the lower number is now established as typical, although there are some abnormal cases; Tjio and Levan, 1956.)

Genes also occur in pairs—one gene of each pair comes from the sperm chromosomes and one gene from the ovum. We have no exact way of counting the genes as we can count the chromosomes, for they do not show up under the microscope as separate particles. But we may be sure from what we know of other organisms that the total number in each human chromosome is of the order of 1000 and perhaps much higher. Because the numbers of genes and chromosomes are so high, it is extremely unlikely that two human beings would have the same heredity, even with the same parents. One exception, however, is identical twins.

An important attribute of the gene is *dominance* or *recessiveness*. If both members of a gene pair are dominant, the individual will show the trait determined by the genes. If one is dominant and the other recessive, he will show the trait of the dominant gene, but he will also carry the recessive gene, which may show up as a trait in his offspring. A recessive trait shows up only if both genes are recessive.

One pair of chromosomes proves to be of particular interest, the pair that is associated with the sex of the individual, and with the genes of certain traits that are "sex-linked." A normal female has two X-chromosomes, a normal male one X-chromosome and one Y-chromosome. The female inherits one X-chromosome from the mother, one from the father; the male inherits his X-chromosome from his mother, his Y-chromosome from his father. Because the Y-chromosome is a defective chromosome, it acts in heredity as though it carries only recessive genes. The X-chromosome may carry either dominant or recessive genes. Hence a recessive characteristic in the male, such as color blindness, comes about only when the male inherits a recessive color-blindness gene from his mother; females are less often color-blind, because to be so they would have to have both a color-blind father and a mother who was either color-blind or carried a recessive gene for color blindness. Thus the X-chromosomes and Y-chromosomes have helped to unravel some of the puzzling problems of human hereditary traits.

New Knowledge Concerning Human Chromosomes. The techniques that led to correcting the number of human chromosomes from 48 to 46 have also made possible other advances in human genetics, particularly the discovery of a chromosomal basis for some puzzling developmental difficulties.

A male developmental difficulty, known as Klinefelter's syndrome, is one in which the male genitals fail to develop normally. A test of skin tissue cells in normal males yields a test known as chromatin negative, but cases of Klinefelter's syndrome are chromatin positive, as in normal females.

It turns out that this sexual ambiguity in development is associated with an *extra* sex chromosome, the person having two *X*-chromosomes *and* a *Y*-chromosome, making 47 chromosomes altogether (Jacobs and Strong, 1959).

A related difficulty in the female, a condition known as Turner's syndrome, shows lack of development of secondary sex characteristics at the age when pubertal changes are expected. In a reported case of this kind, the young woman was chromatin negative, as usual with males. It turned out that she had 45 chromosomes, lacking one *X*-chromosome (Ford and others, 1959*b*).

A condition *not* associated with sex is a form of mental subnormality known as mongolism. It turns out that the mongoloid individual has an extra small chromosome, probably one of his chromosomes reduplicated (Lejeune, Gautier, and Turpin, 1959).

A beautiful illustration of the precision with which the extra chromosomes can be identified is given by a case in which a patient showed *both* mongolism *and* Klinefelter's syndrome, and had the appropriate *two* extra chromosomes (Ford and others, 1959*a*).[1]

Population Genetics. The basic characteristics of a population of animals or of human beings depend upon the genes extant in that population. Because of various selective factors that occur through inbreeding, the death of the unfit, and the like, there is a "drift" in the genes available, so that, for example, some human groups differ markedly in their blood groups, although all share the same basic blood types. The study of the gene distribution throughout groups of individuals that mate with each other, and its consequences for these groups, is known as *population genetics.*

The principles that have been developed in connection with population genetics have an

[1] New chromosomal anomalies are frequently being reported as these newer techniques have become more widely used (Miles, 1961).

15-1

Chromosomes

Dr. J. H. Tjio

A photo of all the human chromosomes; based on skin tissue, male (enlarged 1500 $\times$).

important consequence for the study of human genetics: since evidence can be obtained simultaneously on the characteristics of parents and children, it can be gathered in the lifetime of a single scientist, without requiring the gathering of family histories over several generations. The application of the method to problems of psychological interest has thus far been slight, but it is to be hoped that eventually more ways may be found to use this method in the study of psychological inheritance.

One interesting study of population genetics resulted in the discovery of a curious kind of taste deficiency in about 30 per cent of the population. A substance with the chemical name of phenyl-thio-carbamide, when taken into the mouth at low concentrations, tastes very bitter to 70 per cent of the population. It is insipid or tasteless to the rest. There are some differences in

TABLE 15-1		
Inheritance of taste deficiency to phenyl-thio-carbamide		
	Children with taste deficiency	
Matings of parents	Predicted	Observed
Taster × Taster (N = 425) *	12.4%	12.3%
Taster × Nontaster (N = 289)	35.4	36.6
Nontaster × Nontaster (N = 86)	100.00	97.9

SOURCE: Snyder (1932).

* N = number of families tested.

tasters. The results of a study of the inheritance of taste deficiency are given in Table 15-1. The data show how successful the prediction is: the phenotypes occur in the proportions expected from the inferred genotypes.

Most psychological characteristics do not lend themselves to as straightforward a study as that of tasting and nontasting of phenyl-thio-carbamide. The greater complexity is in part due to the fact that psychological characteristics enter into the choice of mates, and hence a random distribution of genetic determiners cannot be assumed. In addition, it is unlikely that many psychological characteristics are determined by single gene pairs.

Heredity in animal behavior

Animal breeding experiments tell us something about the influence of heredity on behavior. Some strains of mice, for example, go into convulsions when they are exposed to high-pitched sounds, while others do not. When these strains are crossed, the susceptibility to seizures follows genetic rules as though the seizures were inherited as a dominant trait (Witt and Hall, 1949). Wildness and tameness in rats are hereditary. According to some authorities, change in a single gene pair will convert a wild strain into a tame one (Keeler and King, 1943).

Several experiments have been directed to a study of the inheritance of learning ability in rats. By mating those that did poorly in maze learning with others that did poorly, a "dull" strain was produced; by mating those that did well with others that did well, a "bright" strain was produced (Heron, 1935, 1941; Tryon, 1940). Although separation of "bright" and "dull" strains was successfully achieved, the experiments were somewhat unsatisfactory on two counts: (1) the "brightness" and "dullness" were specific to maze learning (Searle, 1949), and (2) the strains were not genetically pure, so that it was difficult to infer the genetic determiners involved (Hall, 1951). A more recent ex-

threshold, but the resulting distribution has two modes,[2] as expected from a distribution composed of two "types" (Figure 15-2). Because taste is not a characteristic by which people choose their mates, the genetic determiners for phenyl-thio-carbamide tasting are distributed at random throughout the population. That is, in any 100 people tested from a given intermarrying population, the proportion of tasters to nontasters will be relatively constant. Because the ratio is constant, it is possible to predict the taste deficiencies of the offspring of marriages of tasters and nontasters, according to the principles of genetic determination. The prediction is based on the assumption that nontasting is a simple recessive trait, determined by one gene pair, and that tasting is dominant. Since all nontasters are assumed to be pure recessives (having two recessive genes), all the children of two nontasters should be nontasters. When both parents carry a dominant and a recessive gene, the offspring, according to the Mendelian ratio, should be in the proportion of 3 tasters to 1 nontaster. Whenever one parent is pure dominant, all children should be

[2] A distribution that has two modes, or two points of high frequency, is called a *bimodal distribution*. It tends to arise when there are two major types among the population. For a discussion of mode, see Chapter 13.

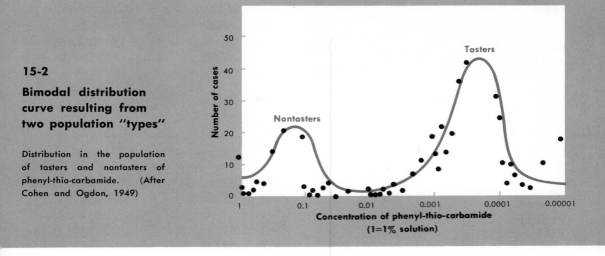

15-2

Bimodal distribution curve resulting from two population "types"

Distribution in the population of tasters and nontasters of phenyl-thio-carbamide. (After Cohen and Ogdon, 1949)

periment has tended to meet these two objections by using a type of maze more analogous to a general intelligence test, and by attempted control of the genotypes through brother-sister matings (Thompson, 1954). The experiment succeeded in a separation of bright and dull strains within a few generations (Figure 15-3).

Experiments quite satisfactory from the point of view of genetics have been done with the fruit fly, Drosophila. The behavior selected was phototaxis, that is, the tendency to be attracted to a source of light. By mating those with a strong tendency with others showing the strong tendency, and mating those with a weak tendency with others with weak tendency, a segregation of types was attempted. The results over successive generations led to the same kind of separation as earlier found in the rat (Figure 15-4). The fruit fly has two advantages over the rat for this kind of experiment: (1) successive generations take far less time to breed, and (2) the detailed mapping of genes and chromosomes has gone much farther.

The carefully controlled breeding experiments carried out with animals are not possible with human beings for a number of reasons. Social obstacles prevent our making marriages to suit the convenience of the

geneticist. Even if marriages could be planned, the long life span of human beings would make it difficult to follow several generations except by going back to old records, which are often incomplete. The difficulties do not, however, prevent our obtaining satisfactory evidence that the human inheritance of some characteristics does in fact follow the genetic principles established by studying other animal forms. The evidence is fairly satisfactory for eye color, hair color,

15-3

Inheritance of maze-learning in rats

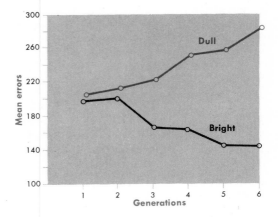

Mean error scores of "bright" and "dull" rats selectively bred for performance on the Hebb-Williams maze. (After Thompson, 1954)

Selective breeding for phototaxis in the fruit fly

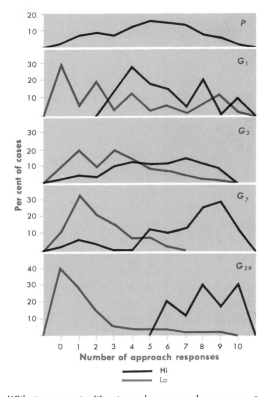

With ten opportunities to make approach responses to light, the offspring of parents selected for a high number of approaches average much higher in successive generations than the offspring of those selected for a low number of approaches. Vertical axis, per cent of cases yielding each number of approaches. The original parent generation (P) is shown with the first (G_1), second (G_2), seventh (G_7), and twenty-ninth (G_{29}) offspring generation. (From Hirsch and Boudreau, 1958)

and many parts of the body. The evidence regarding the inheritance of psychological characteristics is much harder to evaluate.

Heredity in Human Behavior

The familiar rules of genetics are stated in terms of unitary traits determined by single gene pairs, but actually most traits for which the determiners are known are not so simple. The usual red eye color in the fruit fly is known to depend on the combined action of at least 50 genes. Traits that vary along a dimension, as height does in man, tend to be determined by more than one gene. If there were only one pair, we would have one height for dominant men and one height for recessive men, just as the tasters and nontasters form separable groups. Intelligence varies, as height does, on a scale from subnormality to great brilliance, without the sharp break that would let us classify men into two groups—the bright and the stupid. Hence to the extent that intelligence (or any other complex trait) may be inherited, we would expect it to be controlled by a number of genes.

The hereditary component in intelligence

To study the possibility of hereditary determiners of a complex trait, we examine *resemblances* between parents and offspring or of the offspring to each other. A convenient index of resemblance is the familiar coefficient of correlation. We turn now to some studies that use the coefficient of correlation to determine evidence for the inheritance of intelligence.

Parents and Children. If parents contribute to the intelligence of their children through heredity, we would expect a correlation between the intelligence of parents and children. The earlier in the child's life this correlation was found, the more evidence it would give for heredity; for after the child has lived in a home for several years, the influence of environment cannot be ruled out. But the discovery of a correlation early in life depends upon the possibility that intelligence can be measured early.

A number of scales have been prepared for measuring the psychological development of infants. We know now, however, from studies such as the following, that these scales do not adequately predict the scores the child will later make on intelligence tests.

Fifty-nine mothers of infants born in Berkeley, California, in 1928 and 1929 cooperated in a long-term study of their children. Because the original population included two pairs of twins, it consisted of 61 infants, 31 males and 30 females. The group was studied for 18 years, with 40 of the children remaining throughout most of the study.

The infants were tested monthly through the first 15 months with the California First-Year Mental Scale. Up to age 3 they were tested every 3 months with the California Pre-school Scale. The same scale was used at 6-month intervals through age 5. At age 6 began yearly tests using the Stanford-Binet, the Terman-McNemar Group Test, and the Wechsler-Bellevue (an earlier form of the Wechsler Intelligence Scale for Children). The different forms were staggered to avoid too much test familiarity.

The results with these repeatedly tested children give us a basis on which to judge the stability of intelligence scores, and the ages at which resemblance between children and parents is found (Bayley, 1933, 1949).

Because the Berkeley Growth Study (the name by which this investigation has been known) tested infants at frequent intervals within the early months of life, we may inquire how early the later scores could be predicted. For the present, we shall take as a later score the I.Q. at age 6 as measured by the Stanford-Binet. Two sets of correlations are given in Table 15-2, one between intelligence test scores before the age of 6 and the 6-year I.Q., the other a set of correlations between the parents' years of schooling and the child's intelligence test scores at the several ages. We see that during the first year the correlations with 6-year I.Q. are negligible, so that we may guess the 6-year I.Q. as well without the test as with it. Not until the age of 2 years does the correlation with 6-year I.Q. exceed .50. Also at about 2 years an appreciable correlation with pa-

TABLE 15-2

Correlations between intelligence test scores in preschool years, I.Q. at age 6, and mean of parents' education

Age at which intelligence was tested	Correlations with I.Q. at age 6 *		Correlations with mean of parents' education †	
	Number of children	r	Number of children	r
1-3 months	48	−.13	61	−.14
4-6 months	48	−.07	60	−.29
7-9 months	45	.02	59	−.08
10-12 months	48	.20	58	.02
13-15 months	45	.30	56	−.01
18-24 months	48	.50	53	.29
2 years	48	.59	48	.50
3 years	48	.63	49	.47
4 years	45	.77	45	.50
5 years	47	.85	47	.58
6 years			48	.57

SOURCE: Based on the Berkeley Growth Study (Bayley, 1940a, 1940b).

* For scores up to the age of 2, the correlations are between the averages of three monthly tests and the averages of the three yearly tests at ages 5, 6, and 7.

† For scores up to the age of 2, the correlations are between the averaged amount of parental schooling and the test score of the middle month.

rental education begins, rising to .57 at age 6. Because we know the parents' educational level before we test the child at all, we see that during the first 2 years we can estimate the child's I.Q. at 6 better by studying the parents than by studying the child! When the child is about 2 years old, testing him begins to tell us more than we can learn from testing the parents.

This instability of the scores during the first years prevents us from obtaining an early estimate of intelligence free of the influence of home environment. Part of the reason for the low correlations between early and later tests lies in the shift in test content. Tests of very young infants are necessarily nonverbal, while verbal tests become very important later on. Not until the child becomes verbal (beginning at the age of 2, so far as our test results indicate), is the I.Q. predictive of later I.Q. Within the school years, the I.Q. is relatively stable; immediate retests tend to correlate about .89, tests separated by 20 months about .84, and tests separated by 5 years, about .70 (Bradway, 1945; Bayley, 1949).

If we wait until the school years, when the I.Q. can be satisfactorily measured, we find a positive correlation between the parents' and the child's I.Q. With a large parent-child sample (428 father-child scores and 534 mother-child scores) the score of either parent alone correlated .49 with that of the school-age offspring (Conrad and Jones, 1940). This correlation is about the same size as that obtained between parent and child for a physical characteristic such as height, and gives some presumption of hereditary influence, although, of course, environment has now become a factor.

Foster Parents. One way to isolate the influences of inheritance and environment is to study children raised by foster parents. A great many children are placed for adoption each year. Because adoptions are handled by social agencies, tests are usually given and records are kept so that the possibilities of follow-up studies are good.

Two main questions require answer:

1. Does the ultimate I.Q. of children adopted within the first few months of life *correlate* more highly with that of their *true* parents or with that of their *foster* parents? Does the I.Q. of foster children also correspond to the educational and occupational levels of their *foster* parents?
2. Does the generally favorable atmosphere of homes into which children are adopted raise the general *level* of intelligence, whether or not the correlation changes?

In answer to the two questions, we shall use the data from three studies.

1. A study done at Stanford University compared the relationships between legally adopted children and their foster parents with similar relationships between children and their true parents. The group studied included 214 foster children and 105 control children living with their true parents. The average age of adoption of the foster children was 3 months; all were adopted before the age of 12 months (Burks, 1928).

2. A study done at the University of Minnesota after the California study repeated many of the same comparisons. The foster-child group consisted of 194 legally adopted children, all of illegitimate birth and all placed in the adoptive home before the age of 6 months. A like number of control children, living with their own parents, furnished comparative data (Leahy, 1935).

3. A third study was made at the State University of Iowa, in which foster children were given repeated tests as they grew up, and their ultimate intelligence level was compared with the low intelligence level of their true mothers. All the children had been placed for adoption before the age of 6 months. Several reports were published earlier, but a final report gives the test results for the foster children when they reached a mean age of 13 years (final test at ages 11 to 18) (Skodak and Skeels, 1949).

How do these studies answer the two questions that were posed? First we may consider the *correlational* data. Does the intellectual status of the child resemble that of the true parents or that of the foster parents? Here the Iowa data are the most pertinent, because test scores are available from the true mothers, and some evidence is also available on the educational levels of the true fathers. The data are given in Table 15-3. If parental education affects the child through environment, then we would expect a correlation with the education of the foster parents, *with whom the child lives.* On the contrary, however, the correlations

Correlations between true-parent I.Q. and education, foster-parent education, and I.Q. of foster child

	Correlation with Stanford-Binet I.Q. of child tested at ages 10-18 (mean age, 13) *	
	N	r
True parents, with whom child has not lived		
True mother's I.Q. and child's I.Q.	63	.44
True mother's education in years, and child's I.Q.	92	.32
True father's education in years, and child's I.Q. †	60	.40
Foster parents, with whom child has lived at least 10 years		
Foster mother's education and child's I.Q.	100	.02
Foster father's education and child's I.Q.	100	.00

SOURCE: Skodak and Skeels (1949).

* All children were placed for adoption before the age of 6 months.

† Not given in the report, but computed from the data given there. The true father's education was unknown for the other 40 cases in the sample of 100.

in Table 15-3 are significant only with the true parent, with whom the child has *not* lived. The complete lack of correlation with foster-parent education is surprising. A small correlation between foster parent and foster child would be expected on the basis of selective placement, that is, on the basis of the fact that social agencies place children as often as possible in homes matching the anticipated ability level of the child. For example, in the Iowa study under discussion, the true mother's I.Q. and the foster father's occupational status correlated .35 as a result of selective placement (McNemar, 1940).

In the Stanford and Minnesota studies we have the possibility of comparing parent-child resemblances of children living with their own parents and of children living with foster parents. For those living with their own parents we have, of course, the joint influence of heredity and environment. The main comparisons are in Table 15-4.

Parent-child resemblances: correlations between parents and true and foster children

	Parent-child correlation	
	I.Q. of foster children	I.Q. of true children
Mother's I.Q.		
Stanford study *	.19	.46
Minnesota study †	.24	.51
Father's I.Q.		
Stanford study	.07	.45
Minnesota study	.19	.51
Cultural index of home		
Stanford study	.25	.41
Minnesota study	.26	.41

* SOURCE: Burks (1928).

† SOURCE: Leahy (1935).

TABLE 15-5

I.Q.'s of foster children compared with those of true children in families of similar status

	Foster child		True child	
	N	I.Q.	N	I.Q.
Stanford study *	214	107	105	115
Minnesota study †	194	111	194	110

* SOURCE: Burks (1928).

† SOURCE: Leahy (1935).

In every comparison true children resemble parents far more than foster children do.

Our first question is now ready for answer. Parent-child resemblances are greater with true parents than with foster parents, *whether or not* the child has grown up with his true parents.

The answer to the second question requires other kinds of data, for now we are concerned with the *level* of intelligence rather than with the relative ranks reflected in correlation coefficients. Here two of the three studies agree that the intelligence level of foster children is *higher* than would be predicted from their hereditary backgrounds. How much higher is not too clear, but an average gain of 10 or more I.Q. points over predictions based on the true mother's intelligence level is suggested by these two studies. This gain is to be attributed to the fact that homes selected for placement are above the average not only in socioeconomic level but also in general stability. An infant raised in a warmly affectionate and stable home where he is definitely welcomed, and often the only child, has an excellent opportunity for developing his capacities to the fullest—beyond the development of the unselected children on whom test norms are based. This increase is a general pattern regardless of the attributes of the particular foster home, as is shown by the fact that the child's I.Q. bears little relation to the degree of intelligence of foster parents.

The most striking increases were reported by the Iowa study, in which mothers averaging low normal (I.Q. 91) produced children who scored at an average level of 109 or 117 I.Q.[3] at the average age of 13, after living in superior homes from early infancy. The Stanford study showed the foster children doing well, but found the true children in such homes to be superior to the foster children (Table 15-5).

No significant difference between true children and foster children was found, however, in the Minnesota study (Table 15-5). One difference between the studies, leading to the higher I.Q. of the Minnesota foster children, was that the Minnesota foster children were all of unmarried mothers. Illegitimate children placed for adoption early in life tend to have more intelligent mothers than children placed for adoption from broken or destitute homes.

As the Iowa and Stanford studies indicate, we are justified in the broad conclusion that a good home environment beginning early in life has central importance for the development of the child, intellectually as well as socially. A good environment will not make all children alike, but it will give each a chance to develop fully his biological potentialities.

CRITICAL DISCUSSION

Correlations vs. means

Heated controversies have flared up from time to time among psychologists over the interpretation of data on heredity and environment, particularly some of the data from foster homes that have just been reviewed. It turns out, in retrospect, that one source of disagreement arose through a failure to see that

---

[3] The average was 109 on the 1916 Stanford-Binet, using divisors recommended in 1937, and 117 on the 1937 Stanford-Binet.

Is musical talent inherited?

Veit Bach — Hans — Christoph — Johann Ambrosius — **Johann Sebastian**

Johann
- Johann Christian
  - Johann Jacob
  - **Johann Christoph**
    - **Johann Samuel**
    - **Johann Christian**
    - **Johann Günther**
- Johann Aegidius
  - **Johann Bernhard**
    - Johann Ernst
  - **Johann Christoph**
    - **Johann Friedrich**
    - Johann Aegidius
    - **Wilhelm Hieronymus**
- **Johann Nicolaus**
  - **Johann Nicolaus**

Georg Christoph
- **Johann Valentin**
  - **Johann Lorenz**
  - **Johann Elias**
  - **Johann Heinrich**
- Johann Christian
- Johann Georg

Christoph — Johann Ambrosius
- **Johann Christoph**
  - **Tobias Friedrich**
  - **Johann Bernhard**
  - **Johann Christoph**
  - **Johann Heinrich**
  - **Johann Andreas**
- **Johann Jacob**

Johann Sebastian (First wife)
- **Wilhelm Friedmann**
- Johann Christoph
- J. Christoph's twin sister
- **Carl Philipp Emmanuel**
- **J. Gottfried Bernhard**
- Leopold August

Johann Christoph
- **Johann Ernst**
- Johann Christoph

Heinrich
- **Johann Christoph**
  - **Johann Nicolaus**
  - **Johann Christoph**
  - **Johann Friedrich**
  - **Johann Michael**
- **Johann Michael**
  - **Johann Ludwig**
  - Maria Barbara, first wife of J. Sebastian
- **Johann Günther**

Johann Sebastian (Second wife)
- Gottfried Heinrich
- Christian Gottlieb
- Ernst Andreas
- **J. Christoph-Friedrich**
- Johann August Abraham
- **Johann Christian**
- and eight daughters

The unusually high percentage of musicians in the Bach family seems to point to the inheritance of musical talent, although there was also environmental encouragement. All those listed in black type are known to have been competent musicians, and all but two of them gained their livelihood in music. (After Sandiford, 1938)

for a given body of data interpretations based on *correlation coefficients* might lead to one result, and interpretations based on *mean scores* might lead to another. As a general rule, correlation coefficients lead to results favoring the hereditary interpretation, while mean changes favor the environmentalist interpretation. Therefore those engaged in the debate have in the past tended to emphasize the kinds of data that supported their own preferences.

That correlations and means consider different aspects of the data is clear from a comparison of the Burks (1928) and Leahy (1935) studies. The results from the two studies, considering correlations only, are as much alike as would be expected if either study had simply been repeated (Table 15-4). The correlations thus seem to support the heredity argument. But the results for means are quite different (Table 15-5) and can be interpreted to support the environment argument.

While the difference between correlational results and mean results is at first puzzling, another example takes away some of the mystery. Consider the heights of children as related to the heights of parents. Within the last several decades there has been a remarkable increase of height, owing to improved diet and control of disease, so that children now tend to be taller than their parents. Thus if one were in a debate, he could argue that height is a matter of environment (nurture) and he could point to the increase in the stature of Italians in New York City over their counterparts in Italy, the increase in height

of the Japanese since World War II, as well as the gradual increase in height of American college students. If, however, he were taking the other side in the debate (i.e., the importance of nature) he would turn to correlation coefficients, and he would then show that taller parents still have taller children than shorter parents do, and that the correlation between parent and child height is now just what it was a century ago.

We shall see in the remainder of this chapter that the same general conclusions will emerge again and again: if attention is paid to correlation coefficients, great weight will be given to heredity, while if attention is paid to changes in mean scoring level, weight will be given to environment. We shall consider again (p. 444) some attempts to find a solution to the relative importance of heredity and environment.

Twin Studies. Study of heredity and environment in man is greatly furthered by the presence of *identical twins* among pairs of children born to the same parents. Consider, for example, family resemblances in height (Table 15-6). Ordinary brothers and sisters (known as *siblings*) show a moderate degree of resemblance, as represented by a correlation of $r = +.60$. *Fraternal twins* are no more alike genetically than ordinary siblings, for they develop from separate ova. It is possible that the effects of a common intrauterine environment and common diet after birth might make fraternal twins slightly more alike than ordinary siblings, but the greater similarity, if any, is not fully proved by the correlations of Table 15-6. The highest degree of similarity is found for identical twins ($r = .93$). *Identical twins* are so named because they are genetically identical, that is, they develop from the same egg or ovum. Identical twins are always of the same sex and usually resemble each other very closely. Fraternal twins need not be of the same sex and need not resemble each other.

What can correlation coefficients tell us about the inheritance of intelligence? Again

TABLE 15-6

Resemblance in height of children of the same parents

Pairs of children	Number of pairs	Coefficient of correlation (r)
Ordinary siblings (like-sexed)	52	.60
Fraternal twins (like-sexed)	52	.64
Identical twins	50	.93

SOURCE: Newman, Freeman, and Holzinger (1937), p. 75.

the study of twins provides us with the most illuminating data (Table 15-7). We find the resemblances in the same order as those for height: ordinary siblings are least alike, fraternal twins more alike but close to siblings, and identical twins most alike.

The question was raised earlier (p. 420) whether or not the discovery of several factors making up intelligence might modify interpretations of the role of heredity. Two studies have tested identical- and fraternal-twin pairs with Thurstone's tests for Primary Mental Abilities (Blewett, 1954; Strandskov, 1954). Both found higher correlations for the identical-twin pairs than for the fraternal-twin pairs, but the differences were more marked for some tests than for others. In both studies space, verbal, and fluency factors showed large differences between the two kinds of twins, thereby indicating a relatively high hereditary component. Number showed little dependence on heredity in either study; results for reasoning disagreed, Blewett finding a difference between the two types of twins, Strandskov finding none.

Most identical twins are reared in very similar environments. Hence further evidence on the contributions of both heredity and environment is provided by a study of identical twins reared apart.

After careful search, 19 pairs of identical twins were located, all of whom had been separated from each other early in life. Study of their characteristics permitted a partial answer to the question of the influence of environment on the similarity of twins genetically alike. The two chief findings so far as intelligence is concerned were as follows:

1. Despite the subjects' being raised apart, the resemblance in intelligence of identical-twin pairs remained higher than for fraternal twins raised together. The coefficient of correlation between Binet intelligence quotients for separated identical twins was .77, compared with .63 for fraternal

TABLE 15-7		
Resemblance in Binet intelligence quotients of children of the same parents		
Pairs of children	*Number of pairs*	*Coefficient of correlation (r)*
Ordinary siblings *	384	.53
Fraternal twins (like-sexed) †	52	.63
Identical twins †	50	.88

* SOURCE: McNemar (1942), p. 40.
† SOURCE: Newman, Freeman, and Holzinger (1937), p. 77.

twins reared together (Table 15-7). This persistent similarity of identical twins, despite their separation, suggests the importance of heredity.

2. The lower correlation for pairs of identical twins reared apart as against that for pairs reared together (a reduction from .88, in Table 15-7, to .77), was produced chiefly by four pairs who were reared apart in the most highly contrasting environments. It follows therefore that extremes of environment can influence intelligence test performance, even of identical twins (Newman, Freeman, and Holzinger, 1937; McNemar, 1938).

Putting all these findings on siblings and twins together, we are led to the following conclusions with regard to the contributions of heredity and environment to measured intelligence.

1. Since *identical twins* are more alike in intelligence than *fraternal twins,* inheritance appears to play a part in the determination of intelligence. This conclusion is plausible, because the resemblance in intelligence corresponds to the known correspondence of identical twins in heredity.

This greater resemblance in test scores of identical-twin pairs as compared with fraternal-twin pairs persists until late in life. This has been confirmed for 51 pairs of female twins, all of whom were over sixty years of age. The 30 identical pairs showed significantly less difference from each other than did the 21 fraternal pairs on four of six tests (vocabulary, block designs, digit span, and digit-symbol substitution). Differences between the two types of twins were not significant on tests of recognition of similarities and on motor coordination, although here too the direction of difference favored greater similarity between the identical pairs (Kallmann and Sander, 1949).

We cannot be sure, however, that the greater resemblance of identical twins as compared with fraternal twins is due entirely to heredity. The environment of identical twins may be more alike than that of fraternal twins, because they look alike and hence tend to be dressed alike and otherwise treated as a pair. Fraternal twins may diverge from each other in physical characteristics and hence provide unlike environments for each other.

Yet the additional finding that identical twins reared apart still resemble each other in intelligence more than fraternal twins reared together is a potent argument for the hereditary contribution.

2. Since *fraternal twins* are more alike in intelligence than *ordinary siblings,* we know that environment must also play a part in the determination of intelligence. The influence must be environmental, because from a genetic standpoint fraternal twins are no more alike than ordinary siblings. They do, however, share a common intra-uterine environment and are subjected in common to any congenital effect due to the mother's nutritive or glandular condition during pregnancy. This prenatal condition is a potential environmental influence upon their development. They also share an environment after birth which is more alike than that for ordinary siblings. Brothers and sisters born singly are necessarily born into families of unlike size and to parents of un-like age and experience, and these differences in family pattern are undoubtedly an important environmental influence in the shaping of many psychological characteristics. Children born in pairs (i.e., as twins) have the same number of brothers and sisters, have parents of the same age and socioeconomic status, and are (usually) brought up under identical theories of diet and of child care. Thus while the social environments of the two members of a pair of fraternal twins are unlike in any way the twins happen to be unlike, their environments tend to be more alike than those of ordinary siblings and somewhat less similar than those of identical twins.

Again the fact that the mean differences between the identical-twin pairs reared apart were greater for those with most dissimilar environments supports the importance of the environment.

If we accept the correlations of Table 15-7 at their face value, along with the evidence from identical twins reared apart, we arrive at a compromise position on the nature-nurture issue. We are led to the conclusion that there is some contribution to psychological characteristics from heredity, some from environment. Knowing that evidence from correlations and from means may differ, we do not make brash statements about the *relative* contributions of heredity and environment.

Only careful study and better theoretical models will tell us how much environmental modification to expect of the various characteristics determined jointly by heredity and environment. In the study of identical twins above, the authors came to the conclusion that physical characteristics are least modified by the environment, intellectual characteristics somewhat more, and personality characteristics most of all.

Heredity and mental illness

Because, as we shall see later (Chapter 19), mental illness is a social problem of great magnitude, a number of studies have been directed to determine the hereditary component in such illness. Particular attention has been given to the illness known as *schizophrenia.*

Here again the studies of twins have proved to be illuminating. If one member of a twin pair is diagnosed as schizophrenic, what are the chances that his co-twin will also be schizophrenic? If there is a hereditary component to the illness, it will be expected that among identical twins the chances will be much higher than among fraternal twins. This is indeed found to be the case in a number of studies, as summarized by Kallman (1953) (Table 15-8). The results for childhood schizophrenia (onset before age 15) are similar (Kallman and Roth, 1956).

These studies have been subjected to a number of criticisms, but the conclusion appears to be justified that there is a large hereditary component in the susceptibility to at least some forms of schizophrenia. The complexity of the issues involved is well illustrated by Rosenthal's reanalysis of some of Slater's data (Rosenthal, 1959; Slater, 1953). Rosenthal selected for careful case study those identical-twin pairs in which both members had schizophrenia (concordant pairs) and those in which only

TABLE 15-9

Schizophrenic twins and family background of schizophrenic illness *

	Schizophrenic illness in family reported	No reported schizophrenic illness
Concordant pairs (both twins schizophrenic)	13	9
Discordant pairs (only one twin schizophrenic)	1	12

SOURCE: Rosenthal (1959).
* $P = .01$.

one was affected (discordant pairs). On a number of indexes he was able to show a greater likelihood that the illness was hereditary when both twins were affected, and essentially nonhereditary when only one was affected. For example, 60 per cent of the 22 concordant pairs showed some schizophrenic illness in the family background, while only 1 of the 13 discordant pairs showed any family background of schizophrenia (Table 15-9). Rosenthal concludes that there may well be two broad classes of schizophrenia, one with a substantial hereditary component, one with the hereditary component absent or very slight.

The Interaction of Heredity and Environment

Even the clearest studies (for example, those involving twin pairs) leave us with some uncertainty about the extent of the role to assign to heredity, the extent to environment. In those aspects of ordinary social living such as securing an education and entering upon a job, the interactions of heredity and environment become very significant, and their independent roles even

TABLE 15-8

Schizophrenic illness in co-twins of fraternal and identical twin pairs

Investigator	Fraternal twins		Identical twins	
	No. of pairs	Per cent of affected co-twins	No. of pairs	Per cent of affected co-twins
Luxenburger	60	3.3	21	66.6
Rosanoff	101	14.9	41	68.3
Essen-Möller	24	16.7	7	71.4
Slater	115	14.0	41	76.0
Kallman	685	14.5	268	86.2

SOURCE: Kallman (1953).

harder to assign. We shall now examine some of these areas of human life in which the two forces are most difficult to disentangle.

Intelligence and education

If we classify adults according to the years of education they have completed, we have also come close to classifying them according to levels of intelligence. For example, in a sampling of 4330 men in World War II, a correlation of .73 was found between the Army General Classification Test score and the highest year completed in school (Staff, Personnel Research Section, Adjutant General's Office, 1945).

Again we face a problem of interpretation. Those who cannot profit from schooling tend to drop out early. Because there is a relationship between intelligence and success in school, only those who are sufficiently intelligent will continue through high school and college. This educational survival of the more intelligent would result in a significant correlation between intelligence and education. The correlation would be found even though the extent of education had no influence whatever upon intelligence test scores. The possibility exists, however, that increasing experience in school does in fact contribute to measured intelligence. An additional and related possibility is that influences in home and community that keep children in school longer may have an effect upon intelligence scores, even though the schooling itself does not.

Many studies have sought to determine whether or not schooling affects intelligence. Studies of nursery school children show that for the most part, such children make slight gains, averaging about 5 I.Q. points, above the gains of control groups of nonschool children (Wellman, 1945). These studies have provoked a great deal of controversy, because the ones that have shown the most striking changes are by no means free of technical errors (McNemar, 1940, 1945). The difficulties in such studies are many: the selective factors that lead parents to send children to nursery school; the unsatisfactory predictions from tests given in the first years of life, which we have met above; the importance of social adjustment leading to rapport with testers; seasonal changes in score; and lack of equivalence between different test batteries.

The effectiveness of the nursery schools is, of course, not dependent upon their success in raising I.Q.'s. The advantages of nursery schools are many, especially in helping the young child to make social adjustments with other children and adults. Those psychologists who interpret the evidence as showing only slight, if any, increase in I.Q. through nursery school attendance may still be as favorable toward nursery schools as those who believe they raise intelligence levels.

How about the effects of later schooling? One illustration of a change in the level of intelligence over a period of years comes from tests given in Hawaii, first in 1924 and again in 1938. While many of the national and ethnic subgroups studied maintained their relative standings on the two tests, the scores in 1924 averaged far below the mainland (Seattle) norms, but in 1938 compared favorably with mainland norms (Smith, 1942). The most plausible explanation is that better educational opportunities, improvement in the use of English (which permits the children to profit more from English-language schools), and related environmental changes produced the increases in Hawaii over the 14-year interval.

In the United States between the two world wars there occurred changes in intelligence level that perhaps can also be attributed to education.

In one study, a sample of 768 soldiers, representative of the white nonofficer servicemen of World War II, was selected. These men took both the AGCT of World War II and a revised form of the Army Alpha used in World War I. While it was necessary to use a revised Army Alpha,

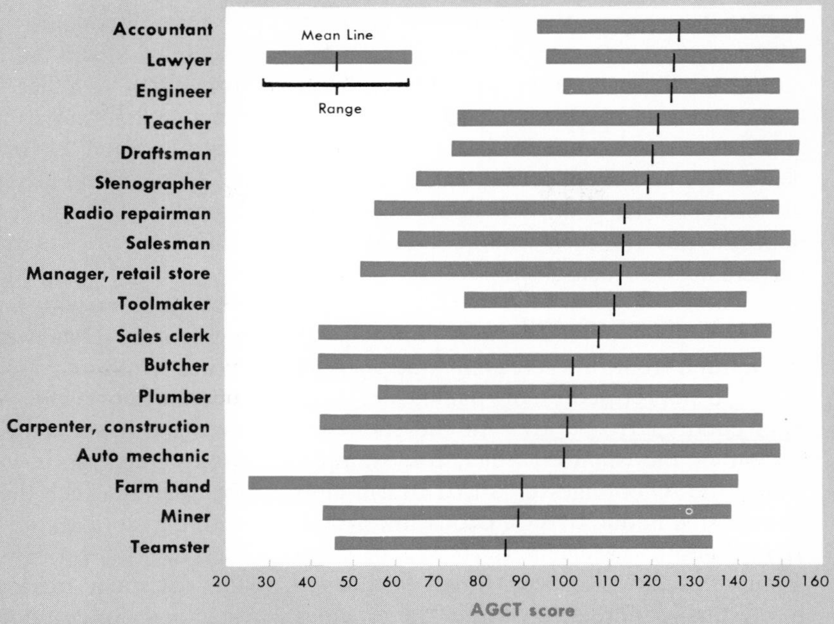
Accountant
Lawyer
Engineer
Teacher
Draftsman
Stenographer
Radio repairman
Salesman
Manager, retail store
Toolmaker
Sales clerk
Butcher
Plumber
Carpenter, construction
Auto mechanic
Farm hand
Miner
Teamster
Mean Line
Range
20 30 40 50 60 70 80 90 100 110 120 130 140 150 160
AGCT score

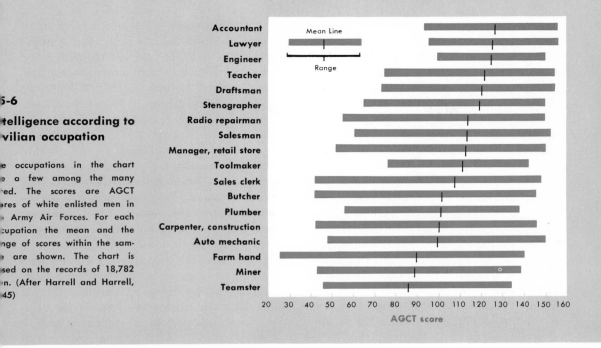

5-6

telligence according to vilian occupation

e occupations in the chart e a few among the many ed. The scores are AGCT res of white enlisted men in Army Air Forces. For each cupation the mean and the nge of scores within the sam- e are shown. The chart is sed on the records of 18,782 n. (After Harrell and Harrell, 45)

there was good reason to suppose that its difficulty was essentially the same as it had been in 1918.

The result showed a marked improvement in scoring level between the two wars. The median score obtained by the World War II group on the Army Alpha was 104, contrasting with the median of 62 received in World War I. The score of 104 was at the 83rd centile of scores of World War I. That is, in the second war 50 per cent of the scores fell at or above the level reached by only 17 per cent of the scores in the first war (Tuddenham, 1948).

This general rise in scoring level probably results from higher educational level, greater familiarity with tests, better conditions of testing, and perhaps greater motivation to do well on the tests. The average educational level in World War I was the eighth grade, while the average for World War II was two years of high school. A group test, such as the Army Alpha or the AGCT, is a written examination. Scores for such tests tend to run higher for those familiar with the taking of examinations; it is difficult to know exactly how to interpret the increase in score between the two wars, but surely the higher educational experience had something to do with it.

Occupational level

If we group individuals according to their occupations, we find again that we have grouped them according to intelligence. This correspondence is a result in part of the interrelationships among intelligence, education, and occupation level. Representative results from World War II tests are charted in Figure 15-6. The rankings of occupations remained much the same as in World War I. For the occupations that could appropriately be compared, results for World War I correlated .84 with those for World War II (Stewart, 1947).

It should be noted that the general increase in educational level has changed the mean level in the various occupations, without changing their relative ranks. Here is another evidence of the differences that result when either correlations or means are studied.

Both heredity and environment undoubtedly operate to produce the correlation between intelligence and occupation. Selection occurs because people of higher intelligence enter the occupations that make more demands upon intelligence. But such people also provide good education and other opportunities for their children, tending to perpetuate the relationship.

Living in city or country

Children from rural areas in America tend to make poorer scores on intelligence tests than children from cities. In the standardization of the Stanford-Binet, for example, within the school ages of 6 to 18 farm children scored about 10 I.Q. points lower than city children (McNemar, 1942, p. 37). Similar results have been found in Europe by testing children in several large cities and in rural areas (Klineberg, 1931). The difference has not been found, however, in Scotland (Rusk, 1940).

We have two main theories to explain the differences in scores obtained in farm and city. One is *selective migration*. People who are attracted to the cities may represent a disproportionate number of those who score high on intelligence tests. They may go to cities because they have the kinds of numerical and verbal abilities that are of special value in cities. The second conjecture is that city life provides *environmental stimulation* in educational and other opportunities. Some evidence supports each of these conjectures. The migration hypothesis is supported by evidence that in more remote rural areas, where the pull of the city is less directly felt, intelligence scores remain high (Thomson, 1921; Jones, Conrad, and Blanchard, 1932). If the tests favored city dwellers, such isolated people would seem to be at unusual disadvantage, but they are not.

The stimulation hypothesis is supported by the well-known poverty of rural schools in many parts of America. In Scotland, where rural teachers are as well trained as city ones, the differences are not found.

A more conclusive test of the stimulating effects of life in the city is to ask the question directly: What happens to intelligence when a child moves from a less favored to a more favored environment?

Negro children born in Philadelphia took repeated intelligence tests at intervals of a year or more. The mean I.Q. did not change significantly between Grade 1A and 9A for 424 children who took the tests each time.

Identical tests were given each year to Negro children who had moved to Philadelphia from the South. These children averaged lower than Philadelphia-born children on entrance to school, regardless of the year at which they entered. The number entering at each level studied varied from 109 to 219, providing an adequate sample for statistical treatment. Between entrance time and Grade 9A their intelligence tended to rise, and, in general, the improvement in their mean scores at Grade 9A corresponded with the number of years they had lived in Philadelphia (Figure 15-7) (Lee, 1951).

While the data are clear, we again face a problem of interpretation. The effects can hardly be attributed to schooling, for the Philadelphia-born were superior to the Southern-born even in the first grade.[4] Also, the local-born did not improve materially during their years in the Philadelphia schools. Apparently the ultimate level of intelligence was affected by the general increase in environmental stimulation that came with the move to the large city.

National and racial origin

The analysis of national or racial differences in intelligence is fraught with many difficulties.

Three problems make the determination of differences between such groups difficult: (1) the problem of obtaining an adequate sample, (2) the problem of assuring that

---

[4] Those Philadelphia-born who had been to kindergarten had been eliminated in the tabulations from which Figure 15-7 was constructed.

15-7

Increase in mean I.Q. with years in a large city

The mean scores are for Negro children born in Philadelphia and Southern-born Negro children reaching the Philadelphia schools at the grades indicated. Scores at the time of initial testing shortly after coming to the city are compared with scores at Grade 9A. (After Lee, 1951)

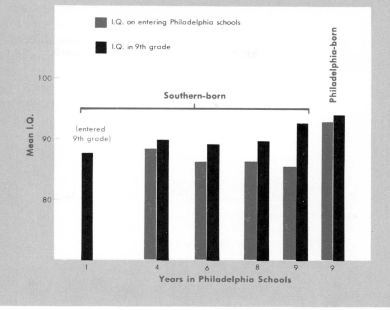

■ I.Q. on entering Philadelphia schools

■ I.Q. in 9th grade

Southern-born

Philadelphia-born

(entered 9th grade)

Mean I.Q.

100 —

90 —

80 —

Years in Philadelphia Schools

1   4   6   8   9   9

test items are fair, and (3) the problem of rapport in testing. When immigrant groups are tested, each group may represent a different fraction of its own native stock. It is generally conceded that in the period of most rapid immigration the northern European immigrant into the United States represented a higher level of socioeconomic status within his native land than most of the immigrants from southern Europe. Again, successive waves of immigration, as from Russia and Poland, came from different fractions of the native stock. When, therefore, a small group of Swedish-Americans or Italian-Americans or Russian-Americans is tested for purposes of determining national differences, selective migration becomes important as a possible cause of the results. The same difficulties appear in the study of racial differences. We have no way of knowing, for example, how representative the American Negro is of African Negroes.

The test items in today's intelligence tests represent primarily the language and culture of American public schools. Children from unassimilated cultural groups, even though they are attending these schools, may be handicapped by bilingualism at home. Or they may see the need for schooling differently, so that they do not use opportunities which the school offers in the same way as do native children. The assumption of a common exposure to the substance of the test items may be faulty.

Finally there is the problem of *rapport*. When an urban white experimenter tries to test a rural Negro in the South or visits an Indian school in the West, he may not be able to get representative results. Psychologists have used various methods to get around these difficulties, including training as psychological examiners some who belong to the groups being tested, but the difficulties continue to confuse efforts to establish intellectual differences among various groups of people.

National and Ethnic Groups from Europe. The common characteristics of groups of people arise in part from their racial stock and in part from the cultural practices that they share. We use the word *national* to refer to people according to their political

TABLE 15-10

Intelligence of American school children of foreign parentage in Massachusetts

Number of cases	Nationality or ethnic group of parents	Intelligence quotient of children	
		Mean	Standard deviation
75	Polish Jews	102.8	14.6
232	Swedish	102.1	15.5
213	English	100.7	14.9
627	Russian Jews	99.5	14.6
190	Germans	98.5	15.1
1030	Americans	98.3	15.9
468	Lithuanians	97.4	13.9
214	Irish	95.9	16.1
155	British Canadians	93.8	14.7
90	Russians	90.9	12.9
227	Poles	89.6	13.0
270	Greeks	87.8	15.1
350	Italians	85.8	11.9
243	French Canadians	85.3	14.6
671	Portuguese	82.7	13.5

SOURCE: Hirsch (1926), p. 287. The children were in grades 1 through 9.

grouping (Italian, French), and *ethnic* to refer to groups defined by common cultural or racial traits that may cut across national boundaries (Mediterranean, Nordic, Jewish).

The difficulties of drawing inferences from studies done in America are illustrated by the results of a large sampling of various national and ethnic groups in Massachusetts. The children tested were all in school (1st-9th grade) in small manufacturing communities. The I.Q.'s fell in the order shown in Table 15-10. The samples were large enough for many of the differences to be statistically significant (Hirsch, 1926).

Why do we distrust the results of a careful study of this kind, with significant differences? We do not distrust the study itself or its data, but we must guard against drawing from it general conclusions about Italians or Swedes or other nationalities as a whole. Another experiment makes plain

why we must be cautious. In this experiment, an investigator (Franzblau, 1935) studied Danish-American girls and Italian-American girls in this country, using a non-language test known as the International Intelligence Test. She found the same order of difference between Danish origins and Italian origins that we see between Swedish and Italian origins in Table 15-10. The investigator then tested Danish girls and Italian girls in their native lands, equating socioeconomic levels as best she could. On their home soil there were no significant differences between the mean scores of the Danish and Italian girls. The study points to the strong possibility that differences found in this country are a result of the fraction of the native populations that migrated here.

Racial Groups. There has been so much intermixture of peoples that human races are not "pure." Nevertheless, some gross differences in *trait distributions* exist, not only in external features such as skin color, hair, and facial configuration, but also in blood groups. On the basis of blood reactions, it is possible to sort out six human varieties differing in their distributions of the components of the blood: early European, European (Caucasoid), African (Negroid), Asiatic (Mongoloid), American Indian, and Australoid (Boyd, 1950). Note that geography enters strongly into these classifications.

We may ask whether or not the members of these different human varieties differ in intelligence. Summarizing the results of numerous tests made in the United States, we discover that the rank order for the different varieties most studied with verbal intelligence tests is:

White (Caucasoid)
Oriental (Mongoloid)
Negro (African)
American Indian

On performance tests the Chinese-Americans and Japanese-Americans have sometimes shown up as superior to the white Americans, and the American Indian as equal to the whites.

Again we face problems of interpreting the findings. Let us examine some evidence in more detail, using studies of the Negro as the source of data.

Even under somewhat favorable circumstances the Negro intelligence mean tends to remain below that of whites. Evidence for this conclusion comes, for example, from a settlement of Negroes in Kent County, Ontario, Canada, which dates back to 1812. Many escaped Negro slaves found their way there before the Civil War, where they were accepted, went to good schools, and were treated on terms of equality. Still, over a hundred years later, the mean intelligence of the Negroes in Kent County remained below that of the whites (Figure 15-8). As usual in such group comparisons, the two distributions overlap, and a number of Negro children score above the mean of the white children. The means, however, are different beyond chance expectation, suggesting a difference between the Negro stock and the white stock. These results were also influenced by socioeconomic differences. In rural areas of Kent County, where the circumstances of the Negroes are more nearly similar to those of the whites, the mean difference in I.Q. between Negroes and whites is 6 points, while in the cities, where their circumstances are less alike, the difference is 16 points.

The many difficulties in making a causal analysis of racial differences appear in the results of tests made during World War I. In some Southern states, the scores on the Army Alpha test obtained by members of the white draft were no higher than the scores obtained by Negro draftees in some Northern states. In every state, however, the scores of the Negro draftees averaged below those of the white draftees. If we consider the two circumstances of being either

15-8

Distribution of I.Q. in one investigation of racial differences

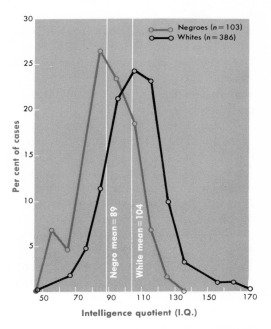

Distribution of I.Q. for Negro and white school children in Kent County, Ontario, Canada. (After Tanser, 1939)

white or Negro and being either from the North or from the South, the circumstances favorable to higher intelligence scores were being white and from the North; those unfavorable were being a Negro and from the South. Therefore, we ask whether the unfavored position of both the Northern and Southern Negro, rather than any inherent racial difference, may not have been responsible for his poor showing on the tests (Alper and Boring, 1944).

The study of rising mean I.Q.'s of Southern-born Negroes who migrated to Philadelphia (p. 441) shows that gains can be expected with improved environment. The results of other studies have led to similar conclusions (e.g., Klineberg, 1935). But a difference in mean I.Q. still remains, though of course the distribution of I.Q.'s is such that racial membership alone can never tell us whether a given individual is bright or stupid. Even though according to intelligence tests very bright Negroes are fewer proportionately than very bright whites, there are, of course, many Negroes with high I.Q.'s. Research in seven Chicago public schools led to the identification of 103 Negroes possessing a Stanford-Binet I.Q. of 120 or above, and one girl who achieved an I.Q. of 200 (Witty and Jenkins, 1934).

Is there any consensus among psychologists on racial differences in intelligence? Results with other races lead to the same conclusions as do the studies of the Negro. Although some racial groups score consistently below whites on the tests, many of the differences are probably due to inadequacies in measurements or to inequalities in environmental opportunity, and many authorities believe that no racial differences have been demonstrated. Even if the obtained differences are taken at their face value, the results show so much overlap that membership in one or another group is no index of an individual's brightness.

CRITICAL DISCUSSION

The possibility of determining the relative contribution of heredity and environment

The foregoing discussion has indicated some of the difficulties in making clear assertions about the relative contributions of heredity and environment, yet the fact that some kinds of behavior are more hereditary than others makes the possibility of assigning some kind of numerical value to heritability intriguing.

The statistical models that have been developed for assigning relative values to heredity and environment are all based on the contributions to variation in the traits studied, and ignore means. Thus they tend to over-emphasize the hereditary contribution relative to what it would be were changes in means taken into consideration (pp. 432-34).

A convenient measure of variation used in these models is *variance*, the square of the standard deviation. Then the variance of the phenotypes in a population is made up of the variances of the genotype, the environment, and their interaction, as follows:

$$\sigma_p{}^2 = \sigma_g{}^2 + \sigma_e{}^2 + r_{ge}\sigma_g\sigma_e$$

where $\sigma_p{}^2$ = variance of the phenotypes in the population, $\sigma_g{}^2$ = variance due to differences in the genotype, $\sigma_e{}^2$ = variance due to environmental influences, and r_{ge} = correlation between hereditary and environmental effects.

In practice, this basic formula is either simplified or made more complex before algebraic manipulations are made to solve the equation. In some animal experimentation it is possible to assume that the third term is negligible, and then the formula becomes:

$$\sigma_p{}^2 = \sigma_g{}^2 + \sigma_e{}^2$$

From this a measure of heritability, called h^2, is derived, representing the proportion of the genetic variance to the total variance:

$$h^2 = \sigma_g{}^2/\sigma_p{}^2$$

Complexities within the formula arise when special kinds of matings are introduced (e.g., sibling matings), or when, in human studies, one has to recognize the various environments of family and community. A variety of models has been constructed, and the models are finding some uses in empirical studies (Lerner, 1950; Cattell, Kristy, and Stice, 1957; Cattell, 1960).

The possibility exists of stating with greater precision than we now can the relative contribution of heredity and of environment, but some arbitrariness enters into the determinations as they can be made at the present time. When such determinations are made on the basis of correlations such as those in Table 15-7, the hereditary component in intelligence is found to be substantially greater than the environmental component (e.g., Woodworth, 1941; Burt and Howard, 1957).

SUMMARY   1. The methods of the science of genetics are proving to be as applicable to behavior as to structure. The same distinctions are needed between the *phenotype* (that is, the expressed characteristic) and the *genotype* (the underlying hereditary determiners that will be transmitted to the offspring) as are made when physical characteristics are under consideration. The *chromosomes* and *genes* must be responsible for hereditary components of behavior, as they are for inherited structures. Because some genes are *dominant,* some *recessive,* some *sex-linked,* various statistical predictions can be made about the traits of the offspring of particular kinds of matings. When these studies are conducted on whole populations, the methods become those of *population genetics,* a form likely to prove important in the study of the heredity of human behavior.

2. Selective breeding experiments in animals have resulted in convincing evidence that forms of behavior can be inherited. Illustrations include maze-brightness in rats and phototaxis in fruit flies.

3. Because selective breeding is out of the question for human studies, and many human characteristics are complexly determined, we are led to depend upon studies of resemblance as a function of blood relationship.

4. Studies of parent-child resemblance in intelligence are limited because the I.Q. of a child cannot be determined accurately before the age of 2, when the influence of the home environment is already considerable. At later ages, parent-child resemblances in intelligence are of the same order of size as resemblances in height.

5. The study of foster children provides an opportunity to isolate the effect of home environment on intelligence. Three studies reviewed led to similar conclusions: (1) the *correlation* between the true parents' intelligence and the child's intelligence remains higher than that between the foster parents' intelligence and the child's, even though the child moves into the adopted home within the first few months of life; (2) intelligence develops within the favorable environment of the foster homes to a *level* above that predicted from the true mother's intelligence and, on the average, to a level corresponding closely to that of children born into homes of the same general characteristics.

6. In studying resemblances of brothers and sisters, twins provide much useful information, because there are two types of twins (*identical* and *fraternal*) with unlike degrees of genetic similarity. Studies based on the correlations between the intelligence tests scores of ordinary siblings, fraternal twins, and identical twins (including identical twins reared apart), lead to the conclusion that both heredity and environment are important as determiners of individual differences in intelligence.

7. Studies of schizophrenia in fraternal and identical twins have found so much more correspondence for identical twin pairs that a strong hereditary component is very plausible. However, careful analysis of identical twin data indicates that there may be two types of schizophrenia, one with a strong hereditary component, one with scarcely any contribution from heredity.

8. Those with more education score higher on intelligence tests, partly because brighter children continue longer in school. However, more schooling may actually raise scores.

9. Higher-ranking occupational groups also score higher in average intelligence.

10. Rural-urban comparisons commonly (although not universally) favor the city child. Two interpretations of this fact are possible: (1) that various influences have pulled the brighter people from the farms to the city; (2) that life in the city provides the kind of stimulation that raises scoring levels.

11. Studies of national and racial differences in intelligence show how difficult it is to construct tests that will lead to valid conclusions. Results indicating national and racial differences, commonly found on the tests, do not justify propositions about fundamental differences between races. Three difficulties are hard to overcome: (1) representativeness of the population tested, (2) fairness of the tests to all groups, and (3) rapport with those being tested. Overlap in I.Q. among the groups is so great that an individual's intelligence can never be judged on the basis of his membership in a given national or racial group.

SUGGESTIONS FOR FURTHER READING

There are many good sources of information on genetics, of which an authoritative one is Stern, *Principles of human genetics* (2nd Ed., 1960). There is now for the first time a good book on the genetic aspects of psychological characteristics in animals and man, Fuller and Thompson, *Behavior genetics* (1960).

For differences based on race, nationality, and class, useful summaries can be found in Anastasi and Foley, *Differential psychology* (3rd Ed., 1958), and Tyler, *The psychology of human differences* (2nd Ed., 1956).

CHAPTER 16

Personality Appraisal

"Personality" is one of the most difficult concepts in psychology. All of us use the term in our everyday conversation, but most of us would be hard put to provide an accurate statement of its meaning. Yet the psychologist, for whom the concept is of central importance, cannot escape the necessity of attempting a precise statement. We begin, then, with a formal definition of personality, adding to our definition by a discussion (in this chapter) of the attributes that psychologists look at when they study personality and by an examination (in Chapter 17) of a number of attempts to construct a theory of personality.

In this text the term *personality* is used to mean the configuration of individual characteristics and ways of behaving which determines an individual's unique adjustments to his environment. We stress particularly those personal traits that affect the individual's getting along with other people and with himself. Hence personality includes any characteristics that are important in the individual's personal adjustment, in his maintenance of self-respect. Any description of the individual personality must take into account appearance, abilities, motives, emotional reactivity, and the residues from experiences that have shaped the person as we find him. The term "personality" is thus a very inclusive one. It is saved from being synonymous with all of psychology, because its reference is to the single individual and to the unique organization of the traits that characterize him and his activities.

Personality Structure as a Unique Attainment

Because each individual is unique, the scientific description of a personality is bound to be difficult. We need to find some way to understand the enduring features of a person's behavior as they follow naturally from his developmental history, his goals, and the real-life problems that confront him. Our aim is to discover and describe, if we can, his *personality structure*. If we succeed in this, we can understand superficial inconsistencies in his behavior. What he does will be consistent with his total personality structure, even though his actions may appear self-contradictory to those who do not understand him. He may be tender toward his family and cruel to his employees; of strong physique yet overly concerned about his health; sentimental about music and hard-boiled in politics. Even personal peculiarities and mannerisms (idiosyncrasies) can be seen as significant expressions of the deeper unity that is the total personality structure.

The possibility that we may comprehend personality in this way is opened up by clinical case studies. The clinical psychologist, as he tries to understand the conduct of his client, attempts to fit all aspects of the individual's behavior, including symptoms of disturbance, into a consistent pattern. Then what the client does is seen to follow from the kind of person he is. Once we understand his personality organization, we begin to understand him as a unique individual.

To understand personality structure we need to know, first, how it comes about.

The shaping of personality structure

The broad outlines of personality formation are clear enough. We have already noted the importance of heredity, of maturation, of training in infancy, of social motives acquired through learning, and of ways of perceiving. What we are attempting now is a kind of summary of these many factors in development and socialization *as they have shaped the particular individual before us,* and as they affect our understanding of him. As he stands before us now, he is an end product of his potentialities as they have been realized in the course of growing up. The problem that remains is for us to understand the patterning of these consequences of experience that gives the individual his uniqueness. From our point of view this is his *personality;* from his point of view this is his *self*.

In surveying the origin of the personality structure we can begin with the infant's potentialities as established by his specific heredity and by whatever influences impinged upon him prior to birth. One infant does not start on equal terms with another. One may be born sturdy, another a weakling. One may be born more talented than another because of the kind of sense-organ equipment and nervous system he inherits. These potentialities are developed by the individual's experiences as he matures. Although all experiences are of course individual, we may distinguish between two broad classes: first, the *common experiences* shared by most individuals growing up in a given culture; and, second, *unique* or *individual experiences,* not predictable from the roles that the culture assigns the individual.

Experiences common to the culture

The process of growing up includes learning to behave in ways expected by our society. We accept group values without much reflection and without awareness that peoples of other cultures may not share these values. If our culture values cleanliness, promptness, and hard work, then we also try to be clean, prompt, and industrious; and we tend to think people admirable who exhibit these qualities.

Conspicuous among the influences of the culture upon the individual are the *roles* that it assigns to him. He is born into some of these, e.g., the boy is born into a masculine sex role and the girl into a feminine sex role. The demands of these roles vary from culture to culture, as we learned earlier (Chapter 4), but it is considered "natural" in any culture for boys and girls to have predictable differences in personality structure merely because they belong to one or the other sex.

Some roles are of our own choosing, but still patterned by the culture. The occupation is a conspicuous role of this kind. Occupational training is not merely a matter of learning the technical skills associated with the job. Success and comfort in an occupation or profession require also that one behave as others do in that occupation, and that one be prepared to accept the status that his occupation brings. Sometimes the occupation has its visible sign. The artist's smock is not unlike the military uniform. Both are signs of a social role. Occupations may develop special attitudes and special speech forms as well as special types of dress. The counterman at the soda fountain dons not only a white jacket but also a special vocabulary that enables him to communicate swiftly and efficiently with his co-workers. An expression such as "combo wheat, hold the butter" cannot be defined from the dictionary, but it is perfectly clear in its context.

Because adult behavior largely conforms to social roles, to some extent it is predictable. You know what behavior to expect of people at a formal tea or reception or at a football rally or at a national political convention. A naturally dignified or reserved man when at his Rotary Club meeting may act like his fellows, calling each by his first name, sharing the mood of open friendliness. When the meeting is over, he becomes again his usual self.

Because culture molds the individual, the suggestion has been made that each culture develops a somewhat characteristic personality structure; individuals then ring changes on this typical personality (Kardiner, 1939). Thus one culture may be typically more aggressive or passive than another. This theory fits in with popular notions of "national character," whereby Italians differ in characteristic ways from Germans or the Irish, though caution is needed lest the basic truths be exaggerated (Inkeles and Levinson, 1954).

Even though cultural pressures impose some personality similarities, individual personality is not completely predictable from a knowledge of the culture in which the individual is raised, for two reasons: first, the cultural impacts upon the person are not actually uniform, because they come to him by way of particular people—parents and others—who are not all alike in their values and practices, and, second, the individual has some kinds of experiences that are distinctly his own.

Unique experiences

Each person reacts in his own way to the social pressures upon him. As Allport has so effectively put it: "The same fire that melts the butter hardens the egg" (Allport, 1937, p. 102).

Personal differences in response may result from the biological equipment of the individual. As we noted earlier, no two individuals (except identical twins) are alike from a hereditary point of view; in addition to differences in size and intelligence, individuals may inherit all manner of subtle differences in sensitivity, reactivity, and endurance, which bear upon ultimate personality development. When an individual is notably deviant (e.g., born with a club foot, a birthmark, or a hearing defect), we expect him to face problems out of the ordinary; but every individual, if we could only know everything about his inheritance, would appear "out of the ordinary" in his own way.

The biological potentialities of the individual are soon socialized under the influence of significant persons: parents, nurses, brothers and sisters, and others. It is these significant perons who transmit the culture in the precise form in which it makes its impact upon the individual. It is they who impose the social roles and provide the models which show how the roles are played. They give and withhold satisfaction of primitive impulses: they give food to satisfy hunger and use force to prevent biting. They approve and disapprove the child's behavior.

As the child comes to seek approval and to avoid disapproval, he becomes capable of hindsight and foresight and begins to see himself as a responsible agent. He develops a *conscience* whereby he judges his own conduct according to ideals he has acquired.

In the process of cultural transmission not all parents (or parent-substitutes in the form of other significant persons) are equally successful. Some are incapable of providing the affection that the child needs in order to grow up a secure person (see pp. 78-84). Others have themselves so resisted adopting conventional social roles that they transmit the roles badly to the new generation.

A child always shows the influences of his parents, though he need not resemble his parents. The contrasting possibilities are well described by two brothers in Sinclair Lewis' novel *Work of Art*. Each of them ascribes his personality to his home surroundings.

My father [said Oral] was a sloppy, lazy, booze-hoisting old bum, and my mother didn't know much besides cooking, and she was too busy to give me much attention, and the kids I knew were a bunch of foul-mouthed loafers that used to hang around the hoboes up near the water tank, and I never had a chance to get any formal schooling, and I got thrown on my own as just a brat. So naturally I've become a sort of vagabond that can't be bored by thinking about his "debts" to a lot of little shopkeeping lice, and I suppose I'm inclined to be lazy, and not too scrupulous about the dames and the liquor. But my early rearing did have one swell result. Brought up so unconventionally, I'll always be an Anti-Puritan. I'll never deny the joys of the flesh and the sanctity of Beauty.

My father [said Myron] was pretty easy-going and always did like drinking and swapping stories with the boys, and my mother was hard-driven taking care of us, and I heard a lot of filth from the hoboes up near the water tank. Maybe just sort of as a reaction I've become almost too much of a crank about paying debts, and fussing over my work, and being scared of liquor and women. But my rearing did have one swell result. Just by way of contrast, it made me a good, sound, old-fashioned New England Puritan.[1]

Beyond his unique biological inheritance and the specific ways in which the culture is transmitted to him, the individual is shaped by particular experiences. An illness with a long convalescence may provide satisfactions in being cared for and waited upon that profoundly affect the personality structure. Death of a parent may disrupt the usual identifications. Unusual successes or failures, accidents, opportunities for heroism, winning a contest, moving to another part of the country: countless such experiences relevant for development are not predictable from the culture, although of course their effects are partly determined by the culture. It is no wonder that by the time the individual grows up there are both common and unique elements in his make-up.

Identity formation

The diverse influences of the common culture and experiences specific to the individual must become unified or *integrated* before the person has a recognizable personality structure. We need to take a further look into the integrating processes before turning to the problems of personality measurement.

[1] Lewis (1934), as quoted by Allport (1937), p. 102.

Erikson has described the process of achieving adult personality integration as *identity formation* (Erikson, 1959). What are the steps through which the final adult identity comes about? An important series of steps results in the *identifications* of the child with significant people in his environment—with mother and with father, with a brother or sister, with a favorite neighbor or teacher. As long as these separate identifications remain, the personality is made up of parts, often not self-consistent. To be at once a mother and a father, an older brother and a favored music teacher, is to be torn into a variety of roles—to experience what Erikson calls *role diffusion*. Such role diffusion, unless outgrown, may result in serious personality disturbance, as the following case illustrates.

Mr. Orchard, an advertising layout man for a department store, came to a mental hospital at the age of 35 because of increasing irritability and headaches which were associated with delusions that people were trying to take his job away from him and were trying to injure his 12-year-old son. He also had some religious preoccupations, and thought he was walking with God. He came to the hospital voluntarily.

In the course of growing up, Mr. Orchard had developed imperfect identifications with several people important to him, and he had been unable to achieve that kind of integration we describe as identity. His close attachment to his mother had been interrupted by her death when he was 12; he longed for closeness to his father, but his father was away from home a great deal until his early adult life. The third influence upon him was an aged, religious grandfather who took much responsibility for him after his mother's death, but who was too old to be a good identification figure. Who did Orchard think himself to be? He was like his mother in her hard-working, gentle ways. He was like his father in caring for artistic work, but with a certain debonair irresponsibility. His religious conflicts derived in part from his grandfather. Sometimes Orchard was a steady worker (like his mother), but at times, for no apparent reason, he would leave his job out of sheer restlessness (reminiscent of his picture of his father); at times he was full of religious devotion (like his grandfather), but occasionally he became religiously indifferent. Even when he was functioning at his best he showed a certain immaturity; with the increasing demands of parenthood, he was unequal to the crises that eventually brought him to the hospital. His identifications conflicted too greatly, and he could not settle upon a fixed image of himself.

Therapy was directed first toward a more realistic appraisal of his childhood. He had to give up being his mother's little boy; she had not deserted him, nor could any magic bring her back. His father had gone away to work as a salesman when work was hard to find; he had not deliberately failed his son, nor had he been as irresponsible as the son pictured him. As Mr. Orchard became clearer about his relationships with mother, father, and grandfather, his present problems came into sharper focus. After two months in the hospital he was well enough to return to home and job, and appeared to have achieved a more satisfactory level of integration.[2]

Role diffusion is normally characteristic of early adolescence, when the youth has not yet "found himself" (not yet achieved identity), when he is both dependent and independent, loyal and defiant, daring and timid. He must master these divergent trends, give up being a carbon copy of other people (his identifications), and become himself (achieve identity).

The processes by which identity is finally achieved are various, but they all imply some experimentation with various experiences and roles. The adolescent characteristically seeks a range of subjective experiences, examines a number of philosophies

[2] Case courtesy of Dr. Josephine R. Hilgard.

of life (whether religious or political ideologies or both), commits himself temporarily (seriously or playfully) to occupational and other choices. Most societies allow a certain amount of freedom during the transition from childhood to adulthood, a period Erikson describes as a kind of *moratorium* (literally, a delay period during which debts do not have to be paid, i.e., a period during which the adolescent does not have to assume full social obligations). If all goes well, the young adult emerges from that period prepared to make lifelong commitments. He has then achieved identity.

The items that have to be brought together into some sort of unified pattern include, according to Erikson, constitutional gifts, individual needs, favored capacities, significant identifications, effective defenses, and consistent roles. The individual's sense of identity is bolstered by what others think of him. In the end, according to Erikson, "society (often through subsocieties) identifies the young individual, recognizing him as somebody who had to become the way he is, and who, being the way he is, is taken for granted" (Erikson, 1956, p. 68).

If we are to appraise or measure personality we must first of all be aware of the complex history of each personality formation.

The question has been raised as to whether or not a conception of personality structure as *unique* permits a scientific study of personality. An extreme view would be to abandon the attempt to describe the rich uniqueness of the individual, leaving it to the artist rather than to the scientist. To accept this position would be to give up a psychology of personality, a step many psychologists would be reluctant to take.

The problem of uniqueness in personality is in essence no more difficult than the prob-

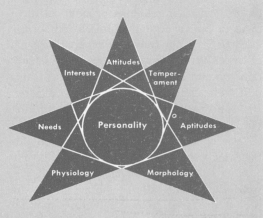

16-1

Modalities of traits representing different aspects of personality

In this diagram, personality is shown as an integrated whole, which can be viewed from different directions: from one direction we see one kind of trait, from another we see another kind of trait. (From Guilford, 1959a)

---

lem of biological uniqueness. Whenever the consequences of a very large number of antecedent variables (whether these variables are "genes" or "individual experiences") produce a composite effect, the result is unique chiefly because a repetition of any one combination is mathematically improbable. It is not *unlawful* in relation to antecedent events; it is merely *unlikely* because of the many possible combinations. An example is provided by the uniqueness of individual fingerprints. Despite this uniqueness, it is possible to find a number of signs by which to classify fingerprints, so that an individual can be identified according to a code. Thus the lawfulness of fingerprint design does not conflict with uniqueness.

Granted this uniqueness, we are free to make our analysis as we will, according to single variables, according to multiple variables, or according to some complex type of patterning. When we deal with single variables, we deal with *traits;* when we deal with larger concatenations of variables, we deal with *types* or *syndromes.* We shall meet these terms as we study attempts to measure personality. The point is that these approaches do not conflict with the conception of the individual as unique.

Personality Characteristics Subject to Appraisal

The present personality is of course a product of its development, but it is appraised or characterized by the way in which it is now expressed. Following the distinction we have made from time to time between the developmental and interactive viewpoints, we may say that the present personality can be *understood* according to its developmental history, but can be *assessed* according to its contemporary interactions. Thus we are interested in how well a person gets along with others *now,* even though there may be various routes over which he could have traveled in becoming the person he now is.

Personality expression is so diverse that there are many ways of talking about it and many ways of characterizing an individual. Allport (1960) has listed ten kinds of units used in describing personality, ranging from "ideational schemes" to unconscious motives; Guilford (1959a) writes of seven "modalities of traits," indicating that the kind of trait we see depends upon the direction from which we view personality (Figure 16-1). There are many overlapping terms in their lists, but the lack of agreement shows that some arbitrariness enters. Common properties that appear in various descriptive characterizations of personality can be summarized as follows:

1. *Physique and temperament.* A person's physical endowments of bodily size, strength, grace, and appearance become aspects of his personality, because of the manner in which he affects other people and because these interactions shape his image of himself as worthy or unworthy. *Temperament,* the name given to a person's characteristic mood, is thought to be influenced by certain inherited physiological patterns, as, for example, by the general responsiveness of the autonomic nervous system or the activity levels of the various endocrine glands. Physique and temperament thus em-

phasize the physiological correlates of personality.

2. *Intellectual and other abilities.* Personality really covers the whole field of individual differences, and it is important to bear in mind that intellectual abilities are also a part of personality, even though for convenience we may sometimes distinguish between "intelligence tests" and "personality tests." Other abilities, such as the skills involved in musical performance, are also relevant to personality. A developed sense of humor requires a quick appreciation of literary allusions; the detection of similarities and incongruities depends upon a high order of intelligence. It is evident that "personality" and abilities are intertwined in many ways.

3. *Interests and values.* Personality is in part reflected in the kinds of things one likes to do, what one enjoys, what one appreciates.

4. *Social attitudes.* A person necessarily adopts attitudes toward features of his contemporary culture (e.g., labor unions or Communist China); these attitudes reveal aspects of his individual personality such as authoritarianism, equalitarianism, or dogmatism.

5. *Motivational dispositions.* We have already met attempts to assess individuals according to their achievement motives or their affiliative motives (Chapter 5). Other motivational dispositions have served in the description of individual personalities. Some of the motives implied may be unconscious.

6. *Expressive and stylistic traits.* Very often when we characterize a person we tell something about his style: politeness, talkativeness, consistency, hesitancy, sociability, criticalness. There are a great many such "personality traits" that seem somewhat independent of the content being expressed; that is, the traits will show themselves at home and at the office, in social groups and in professional meetings. These expressive and stylistic traits are commonly revealed in interaction with other people.

7. *Pathological trends.* Sometimes it is easier to characterize illness than health; one way of describing the normal person is to say that he differs from others in the direction of one or another mental illness.[3] Thus an overexcited form of mental disturbance is known as a *manic* form, and a generally excited and vivacious person (not really in any danger of mental illness) may be called *hypomanic,* which means "under-manic" and which suggests that he resembles the manic but doesn't go that far. Similarly, a form of illness that is characterized by emotional withdrawal is known as *schizophrenia;* a person who is withdrawn and introverted (again, not at all mentally ill) may be described as *schizoid.* Because these terms tend to take on value connotations, they are probably not to be encouraged; yet their convenience, in some instances, is not to be denied.

This listing of descriptive terms referring to personality may suggest why it is difficult to find satisfactory brief descriptions of individual persons, and why some sort of theory is needed to bring order into the characterization of personality. By treating personality measurement before personality theory, we are in some sense putting the cart before the horse, yet there is good reason for seeing how psychologists go about personality appraisal before we attempt to understand the nature of their theories. In a field as elusive as personality, there are advantages in beginning with the concrete efforts at assessment, and then examining what has happened when an effort has been made to bring order by way of theory.

Personality Inventories

Among the most important instruments for assessing personality is the *personality inventory,* a self-rating device which typically consists of 100 to 500 questions similar to

[3] Mental illness is discussed in Chapter 19.

the following, taken from the Thurstone Neurotic Inventory:

Yes No ? Do you take responsibility for introducing people?
Yes No ? Are your feelings easily hurt?
Yes No ? Do you like to be with other people a great deal?
Yes No ? Do your interests change quickly?

The person taking the test checks whether his answer to each question is yes, no, or uncertain.

The personality inventory has been developed on the model of the intelligence test and is often called a personality test. It should conform to the rules of reliability (self-consistency) and validity (correlation with a criterion) (pp. 397-399). Those constructing personality inventories commonly choose groups of well-adjusted and groups of poorly adjusted persons whose scores serve as criteria for validating the test; that is, the test is tried out on both groups, and only those questions which the two groups answer differently are retained. The "purified" test (consisting of the best items) will then supposedly discriminate between well-adjusted and poorly adjusted. But it is difficult to be sure that the groups really represent the qualities that the test proposes to distinguish.

A personality inventory may be designed to measure a single trait, a dimension of personality. Thus we have tests of ascendance-submission and tests of introversion-extroversion. Or the test may provide an over-all estimate of personal adjustment in an attempt to distinguish between the adjusted and the neurotic. When a test seeks to measure at once several aspects of personality, it may come out with a *profile* of scores rather than a single score. Some illustrative personality inventories are described below.

Minnesota Multiphasic Personality Inventory

The Minnesota Multiphasic Personality Inventory (MMPI) illustrates a self-rating instrument following the seventh category cited above (pathological trends). The test is arranged in the form of 495 statements, sometimes with each printed on a separate card. The subject sorts the cards into three piles: the statements that he judges to be true, those that he judges to be false, and those about which he "cannot say." [4] Some of the items are:

I have never done anything dangerous for the thrill of it.
I daydream very little.
My mother or father often made me obey even when I thought it was unreasonable.
At times my thoughts have raced ahead faster than I could speak them.
I like to read newspaper editorials.

Responses are scored according to the correspondence between the answers of the subject and the answers given by patients with different kinds of psychological disturbances. The result is a profile of nine scores, each arranged as a standard score (see p. 380). Typical profiles are shown in Figure 16-2. One is for "normal" persons, the other for those classified as "neurotic."

In addition to the scales originally provided for the test, a great many new ones have been developed. The number of items is so large and the range of questions asked is so great, that it is possible to construct scales that reflect many dimensions of personality other than those for which the test was originally intended. At least 100 such scales have been constructed (Welsh and Dahlstrom, 1956).

Built into the scoring of the MMPI are a number of "control keys" to correct for types of responding that make the results invalid. For example, one control key counts the number of items skipped, or interpreted as "cannot say." If the subject has failed to reply to too many questions, his answers obviously cannot be compared with

---

[4] In the booklet form he indicates merely whether each statement does or does not apply to himself; the "cannot say" is indicated only by omitting a reply.

the statistical norms of those who answer many more of the questions. Another key provides an L ("lie") score by detecting those who give many improbable answers, such as replying "false" to "I sometimes put off until tomorrow what I ought to do today." Another scale counts up the number of very rare answers that the subject gives, again a sign of falsification or carelessness if too many are given, while still another corrects for a tendency to deny symptoms. Thus various degrees of subtlety have been employed in improving the value of the test.

Edwards Personal Preference Schedule

Another approach to personality description, which employs a different technique for obtaining self-report, is illustrated by the Edwards Personal Preference Schedule. The unit of measurement, instead of being a pathological symptom as in the case of the MMPI, is one of 16 basic motives or needs, following Murray (1938). This approach illustrates our fifth descriptive category, for it appraises motivational dispositions. The method is that of forced choice among pairs of items considered equally desirable socially; by the nature of his choices the subject gives evidence of his controlling motivational patterns. Edwards (1954) has built into his scale some of the features that the control keys of the MMPI are designed to correct. The forced-choice method has a disadvantage, however, in that it gives the *relative* preferences for one pattern of motive over another but does not reveal anything about the *absolute* level of that motive. It is assumed that a motive that is chosen consistently against others in the paired situation must be a strong one.

Cattell's 16 PF Questionnaire

Cattell's use of 16 PF ("personality factors") scales illustrates another approach to the construction of a personality inventory. The MMPI was based empirically on

16-2

Personality profiles

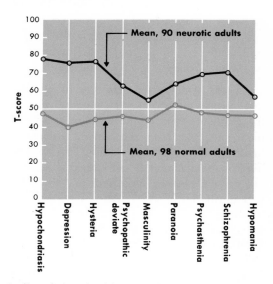

Profiles of normal adults and adults with neurotic tendencies on the Minnesota Multiphasic Personality Inventory. Each of the nine scores is arranged as a standard score, with mean of 50 and standard deviation of 10. The nine scales are based on scores of groups of patients showing the symptoms indicated. The beginning student need not attempt to understand the individual scales in order to understand what the test attempts to do. (After Schmidt, 1945)

the scores of groups of diagnosed patients; the Edwards PPS used the motivational classification of one psychologist (Murray) as a basis for selecting items. Cattell began with a very large number of ratings of personal characteristics and behavior, found their clusters by factor analysis, then developed inventory items to fit the lines of cleavage suggested by the prior factor analyses. The result of an enormous amount of work has been condensed into a relatively short test that yields a set of 16 relatively independent measures, such as dominance, emotional stability, radicalism, and will control (Cattell, 1957b). While in principle the test has certain advantages, the individual scales or subtests are too short to be very reliable, so that the test is not very useful in studying a single subject.

The validity of personality inventories

The success of the intelligence test led to great hopes for similar success with personality inventories. The problems of the two kinds of test turn out, however, to be quite different. Two major differences are worth mentioning:

1. Any single item on an intelligence test always has a correct answer. Hence, the main problem of the test constructor is to arrange the items according to their difficulty or representative quality. But a single item of the personality test has *no independent correct answer*. One item may be, "Do you blush frequently?" Who is to say that blushing considered by itself is a desirable or an undesirable quality? Some items may be answered in the affirmative by 80 per cent of neurotic people and by 60 per cent of normal people. Hence an item may be useful as one among many that help to distinguish the neurotic from the normal, but taken by itself it means little. It may have a neurotic *weight* in the test score, but it is scarcely a sign of neuroticism if 60 per cent of non-neurotic people find it applicable to themselves. The single items in the personality inventory thus have different status from those in the intelligence test.

2. A second difficulty is that a subject may deliberately give false answers to items in a personality inventory, thereby producing a score more indicative of either normal or neurotic adjustment than is actually the fact. False answering on an intelligence test leads only to lower scores, ordinarily against the subject's wishes, while false answers on a personality inventory are commonly made in the effort to give a picture of good adjustment.

The consequence of these differences is that personality tests have not been as successful as intelligence tests, although they have been successful enough to be genuinely useful. The personality inventory results in errors of two kinds. The *false positives* classify one as disturbed or neurotic when he is not seriously in need of help. While one is unlikely to report troubles he does not have, the test items do permit exaggerated reporting of minor difficulties. But the *false negatives* are more troublesome—the disturbed individuals who are fighting to conceal their weaknesses and who are intelligent enough to falsify their self-estimates in the direction of social conformity. (This falsification need not be deliberate; the mechanisms of self-deception are sufficient to lead to faulty self-judgments even when the subject is trying to be honest.) Personality inventories, however, can be used successfully to pick out from a larger population those likely to become neuropsychiatric casualties. The tests can then be supplemented by interview.

To establish the validity of a test it is necessary to have some *criterion* against which to measure its predictions. Thus a scholastic aptitude test has school grades as its criterion. It is very difficult to secure appropriate criterion measures for personality tests. One method, mentioned above, is to consider the scores of extremely disturbed individuals as indications of what a disturbed test score would look like. Then a "normal" individual is judged to be maladjusted if his scores resemble those of hospitalized patients. This method is not very satisfactory, however, because personality is more a matter of individual trait patterning than a sum of answers to test items. When the method was turned around and a search made for "sound" individuals, as judged by those who knew them best, these "sound" individuals were found to have a wide range of scores on personality inventories (Barron, 1954). Thus the method of item-sorting ·by correlation with a criterion, which works well for intelligence tests, is not as satisfactory for personality tests.

The fact, pointed out by Cronbach (1960), that we seek in personality tests a *characteristic* performance, rather than one at its *best,* means that valid personality tests are harder to develop than ability tests (which seek the performance at its maximum). Since it is not difficult to falsify a score on a personality inventory, there are always likely to be maladjusted people who score within the normal range on the test.

Personality inventories have provided us with useful information about trait distributions within the population and about the intercorrelations among traits. Nevertheless, these tests remain fallible instruments, and their improvement is one of the pressing tasks facing psychology.

CRITICAL DISCUSSION

Biasing factors in the responses to personality inventories

The interpretation of a personality inventory does not depend upon the accuracy of the answers, provided one subject makes answers that are consistently different from another. Thus if men answer a question consistently one way and women another, the question may be used in a masculinity-femininity scale regardless of its content. However, it is important that the answers do in fact reflect the content of the questions. That is, we hope that those who say "I blush frequently" do actually blush more frequently than those who deny blushing frequently, although for some purposes of interpretation it would not matter how frequently they blushed. Analysis of answers to personality inventories shows two very prevalent kinds of distortion, one of which is based on the general (but not the specific) content of the question, the other of which merely depends upon the way the question is asked.

The first of these, which has been called the *social desirability* variable by Edwards (1957), is a tendency to answer the questions in a manner that would be expected of well-adjusted and acceptable people or of people who wish to deny illness and deviancy. The lower end of the social desirability scale is, of course, the exaggeration of anxiety, symptoms, and nonconformity to social expectations. A straightforward method of estimating social desirability in inventory responses is to count the number of agreements with items that the

majority of a general population answer in a given direction. When Edwards constructed a key in this manner, with a 39-item social desirability scale, he found substantial correlations with many of the MMPI scales—for example, +.61 with Gough's status scale and −.84 with Taylor's manifest anxiety scale (Edwards, 1957, p. 33). Thus the tendency to conform to social expectations is certainly one feature in personality inventories; it is a feature that Edwards attempted to correct in the PPS by forcing choices between items rated equal in social desirability. Other ways of studying social desirability are possible, leading to conclusions slightly different from those of Edwards, but the relevance of social desirability as a biasing variable is unquestioned (Wiggins, 1959; Messick, 1960; Hanley, 1961).

The second tendency found in personality inventories is an *acquiescence tendency* (Cronbach, 1942; Wiggins, 1962). This is a tendency to agree with the test item when no issue is at stake; the opposite extreme is that of caution, even when the issue is innocuous. Studies have shown that items relatively free of a consistently meaningful content may still distinguish between groups with identifiable personality characteristics, one study characterizing the "yea-sayers" as contrasted with the "nay-sayers" (Couch and Keniston, 1960). A factor-analytic study showed that the acquiescence tendency can operate independent of the social desirability tendency (Messick and Jackson, 1961). It should be noted that the acquiescence tendency can be estimated regardless of the content of the test items; while the reply to a statement may therefore tell something about the subject, it does not necessarily describe him according to the content of the test item (Berg, 1959).

These advances in the understanding of response biases in personality inventories do not discredit the inventories, but they indicate that more sophisticated types of test construction and score interpretation are possible.

Projective Tests

If there is a unity of personality which expresses itself directly or indirectly through all that a person does, then there ought to be some way of characterizing this unity,

A picture similar to one in the Thematic Apperception Test

The pictures usually have elements of ambiguity in them, so that the subject can "read into" them something from his own experience or fantasy.

this personality structure lying behind and giving direction to the individual act. Because this individual style of behavior ought to reveal itself most readily when expression is free, psychologists have selected imaginative productions as being perhaps the most revealing of personality. In imagination the individual is free to build his own world and to make himself the hero in whatever drama he chooses to construct. These imaginative productions the psychologists obtain through *projective tests*. The personality inventories already described have fixed alternatives, so that the subject must reply by making a choice among ready-made answers. Projective tests are more ambiguous and less highly structured, and the answers the subject can give are freer. Because the subject puts more of himself into the answers, he is said to *project* his personality through them, as the movie camera projects the image on the screen. Hence the name, projective tests.

Thematic Apperception Test

One kind of projective test consists of a series of pictures about which the subject tells stories. The subject usually becomes absorbed in the imaginative productions he is building around each picture and says things about the characters in his stories which really apply to himself. The somewhat forbidding name of the test, Thematic Apperception Test (abbreviated TAT) (Morgan and Murray, 1935; Stein, 1955) is intended to describe the fact that the test reveals basic "themes" that recur in the imaginative productions of a person. Apperception means a readiness to perceive in certain ways, based on prior individual experience. (Hence the test name implies that a subject interprets an ambiguous stimulus according to his individual readiness to perceive in certain ways (see pp. 212-13) and that he elaborates the stories in terms of preferred plots or themes that reflect his fantasies.

When confronted with a picture similar to that in Figure 16-3, a twenty-one-year-old patient told the story that follows. He had been an Air Force bombardier with thirteen missions before the war ended in Europe. After his discharge, he entered a university and was at the time of testing a sophomore majoring in English. He was taking psychological treatment for some emotional difficulties. Here is his story:

> She has prepared this room for someone's arrival and is opening the door for a last general look over the room. She is probably expecting her son home. She tries to place everything as it was when he left. She seems like a very tyrannical character. She led her son's life for him and is going to take over again as soon as he gets back. This is merely the beginning of her rule, and the son is definitely cowed by this overbearing attitude of hers and will slip back into her well-ordered way of life. He will go through life plodding down the tracks she has laid down for him. All this represents her complete domination of his life until she dies.[5]

Although the original picture shows only an elderly woman opening a door, the subject's readiness to respond with something

[5] Arnold (1949).

about his relationship to his mother led to this story of a woman's domination of her son. The clinician whose patient told this story reports that facts obtained later fully confirmed the interpretation that the story reflected the subject's own problems.

In taking the TAT, the subject tells stories about twenty pictures. If special problems are preoccupying him, they may show up in a number of the stories. For that reason, the TAT in the hands of a skilled interpreter may make possible the discovery of personality patterns unique to the person being tested.

The subtlety of the TAT does not assure that the subject is in fact revealing himself in the stories that he tells. While various kinds of data have tended to support TAT interpretations (e.g., Henry, 1956), some negative evidence also exists. In one study, the relationship to parents represented in TAT stories failed to correspond to known relationships to parents revealed in the course of psychotherapy (Meyer and Tolman, 1955). When special scoring keys are developed, satisfactory results are commonly obtained, as in the earlier reported studies on achievement motivation (p. 144), and in other studies, as on aggression and fear (Mussen and Naylor, 1954).

Rorschach test

The Rorschach ink-blot test is another of the many projective tests. It consists of a series of cards, each displaying a rather complex ink blot (Rorschach, 1942; first published in 1921) (see Figure 16-5). If ink is spilled on a piece of paper that is then creased down the middle, a bilaterally symmetrical blot like that in Figure 16-5 will result. From many such designs, a few standard ones have been selected, and the experienced tester knows something about the responses to be expected from each. The subject tells what he sees on the card. He may see several different things on a single card, or he may see the same ambiguous shape as representing at once several

16-4

Administering a thematic apperception test

David Linton

The subject tells a story suggested by the picture. An effort is made to have the stories as spontaneous as possible. (The photograph here is posed.)

figures. The test capitalizes on our familiar tendency to see imaginary faces, animals, battle scenes, or fairyland figures in cloud formations.

The subject's responses to the ink blot are in some ways more revealing than his replies to a personality inventory. The subject is much less self-conscious about his responses than when replying to questions about himself in a personality inventory, and what appear to him to be very matter-of-fact responses to what he sees in the blots may be revealing of unconscious aspects of his personality. The TAT has a

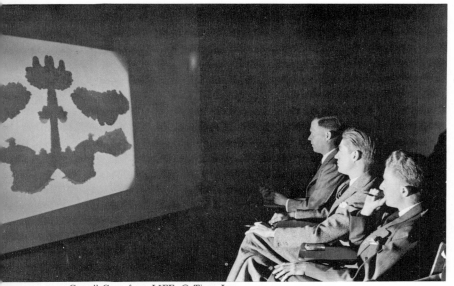

Cornell Capa from LIFE, © Time, Inc.

similar advantage over the personality inventory, but even in it the characters of the stories are often recognizable to the subject. The Rorschach is the more subtle of these tests.

How can Rorschach responses be scored and interpreted? It takes several months of training for a tester to learn to score the test and to interpret the results. Hence we can give here only the briefest hints as to

the directions the scoring and interpretation take (Table 16-1). First, the responses are classified by type according to a conventional system, with a minimum of interpretation, as in the column of Table 16-1 headed "Nature of scored response." The response classes include detail, form, color, movement, and similar objective categories. The frequencies of these categories are then counted and used in interpretation. Some

TABLE 16-1

Nature of interpretations of Rorschach responses

Example of response	Nature of scored response	Direction of interpretation
"Reminds me of a bat, the whole thing."	Location on card of described features	Suggests intellectual aspects of personality
"Two women with high-heeled shoes, trying to pull something apart."	Human movement	Related to creative capacity
"A pair of raccoons climbing."	Animal movement	Related to immaturity-maturity
"Here's a green grasshopper."	Color	Degree of contact with outer reality
"A pair of pliers."	Form	Degree of emotional control
"The darkness there may be clouds."	Shading and color	Expression of anxiety

SOURCE: Table courtesy of Frances G. Orr.

of the directions of interpretation are given in the last column of Table 16-1. The main point of the table is to show how remote the interpretation is from what the subject has reported. If the subject responds predominantly to a few features of the card to the exclusion of others, he presumably tells us something about himself.

Those skilled in the use of the Rorschach claim to obtain from it important information about the subject's personality structure. Because the test is more ambiguous in content than the TAT, it is said to get at deeper unconscious patterns. While the limits of what can be done with the Rorschach are a matter of debate at the present time, it remains popular in clinical practice.

Because the personality picture that results from the Rorschach is largely individual, the problem of validating the conclusions is a difficult one. Among the more appropriate methods of validation is that known as "blind matching." A judge has two sets of data about a group of individuals. One set of data consists of their Rorschach responses. The other set consists of biographical material giving characteristic behavior in life situations. The judge attempts to match the test results with the personality portrait given by the biography. The conditions for an experimental validation of this kind have to be set up very carefully to assure independence of the two sets of material, and few studies fully meet these demands. Unfortunately, satisfactory validation of the Rorschach by such methods is still lacking, and most recent studies are damaging to the test's reputation (Zubin, 1954; Cronbach, 1956).

Why should a test of doubtful validity remain popular? There are several answers. For one thing, the results, while not always dramatic, are usually beyond chance. For another thing, the responses given are judged in a context of other information about the person, and the value of the test does not necessarily reside in it alone. For this second reason, clinicians prefer the test more often than psychologists whose interest is in test construction (Levy and Orr, 1959). A third point is that responses to the test are highly varied, and the test can be rescored for many specific purposes, often with useful results.

One illustration of a special use of the Rorschach test is in connection with studies of body image (Fisher and Cleveland, 1958). It is found that people with different kinds of personality may have quite different concepts of their own bodies, and of the relative significance of parts of the body. Fisher and Cleveland point out that some people have a much greater degree of clarity about the distinction between their bodies and the surroundings than others. They show this in their Rorschach responses by many indicators of definite boundaries or barriers, such as a man with a high collar, or an animal, such as an alligator, with a distinctive or unusual skin. Counting up such responses yields what these researchers call a *barrier score*. While these scores do not correlate with any of the standard Rorschach scores, they prove useful in distinguishing among those with different types of bodily complaint. For example, those with illnesses in which the symptoms lie on or near the surface (rheumatoid arthritis, dermatitis, conversion hysteria) have significantly higher barrier scores than those whose symptoms are internal (stomach disturbances, ulcerative colitis) (Fisher and Cleveland, 1958, p. 77). It is various findings of this kind that keep the Rorschach in use despite frequent criticism. A systematic effort to improve the test has been made by Holtzman and others (1961), who have developed many new ink blots, with variations among them based on conjectures that have arisen in connection with research with Rorschach's original blots.

These two tests, TAT and Rorschach, which we have described in some detail, suffice to introduce us to projective tests. They show in part how test devices can be

16-6 A graphic rating scale

A. How are you and others affected by his appearance and manner?

| Avoided by others | Tolerated by others | Liked by others | Well liked by others | Sought by others | No opportunity to observe |

Please record here instances that support your judgment.

B. Does he need constant prodding or does he go ahead with his work without being told?

| Needs much prodding in doing ordinary assignments | Needs occasional prodding | Does ordinary assignments of his own accord | Completes suggested supplementary work | Seeks and sets for himself additional tasks |

Please record here instances that support your judgment.

C. Does he get others to do what he wishes?

| Probably unable to lead his fellows | Lets others take lead | Sometimes leads in minor affairs | Sometimes leads in important affairs | Displays marked ability to lead his fellows; makes things go |

Please record here instances that support your judgment.

D. How does he control his emotions?

| Too easily moved to anger or fits of depression, etc. | Tends to be over-emotional | Usually well balanced | Well balanced | Unusual balance of responsiveness and control |

| Unresponsive, apathetic | Tends to be unresponsive |

Please record here instances that support your judgment.

E. Has he a program with definite purposes in terms of which he distributes his time and energy?

| Aimless trifler | Aims just to "get by" | Has vaguely formed objectives | Directs energies effectively with fairly definite program | Engrossed in realizing well-formulated objectives |

Please record here instances that support your judgment.

A scale such as this one helps the judge to be specific about the basis for each of his judgments. (American Council on Education; after Fryer and Henry, 1950)

selected (or invented) which are appropriate to analyzing personality as an organized whole, as a "structure."

Other Methods of Personality Assessment

Many appraisals of personality depend upon the judgment of skilled observers. While the foregoing accounts of personality inventories and of projective tests indicate efforts to parallel the successes of intelligence tests, in the end we must always return to observation of the person functioning in his environment if we are to know how successful our tests have been. In this section we shall be concerned with efforts to improve observation and judgment.

Rating scales

Many personality judgments are made by other people. The employer selects his employee; the jury decides the responsibility of the accused; the scholarship committee decides which students deserve aid; each of us decides whose friendship he wishes to cultivate. A rating scale is a device by which a rater can record his judgment of another person according to the traits defined by the scale. The preferred form of rating scale is that known as the *graphic rating scale,* an example of which is shown in Figure 16-6. Each trait is represented by a segmented line; one end indicates one extreme of the trait to be rated, and the other end represents the opposite extreme. The rater places a check mark at an appropriate place on the scale to represent the degree to which the subject possesses the trait. There are a number of other rating-scale devices, such as rankings and man-to-man comparisons (Tiffin, 1959).

The rater must understand the scale; he must be sufficiently acquainted with the person rated to make useful judgments of him; and he must avoid the *halo effect* and other common errors in rating. (The halo effect is the tendency to rate a person high on all traits because he makes a very good impression on one or two or, conversely, to rate him low throughout because he makes a poor impression on one or two traits.) When used with proper care, the rating scale is a very helpful device for recording judgments of other people.

Sociometry

Sociometry deals with one very important aspect of personality: how the person affects others. William James once said that we have as many selves as there are people who recognize us (because our "self" is in large part how we affect others), and a later psychologist, Mark A. May, once defined personality as "social stimulus value."

Sociometry is a word coined by Moreno, a psychiatrist much impressed by the importance of the individual's role among other people. The mutual attractions and rejections among the members of a social group can be plotted, as in Figure 16-7. Such a diagram is a *sociogram,* or sociometric chart of the relations within the

16-7

A sociometric diagram

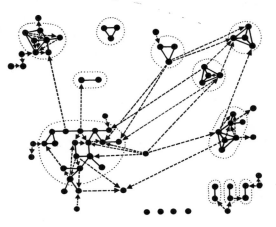

Mutual attractions among 15-year-old girls are shown here. Each dot represents one girl. Solid lines show mutual attractions; broken lines show one-way attraction in the direction of the arrow. Four of the girls are completely isolated from the group. (After Jones, 1943)

group, and tells us something about the more popular and less popular group members.

The method of sociometry is applicable to the study of any group of mutual acquaintances, whether in a club, a classroom, a housing project, or an office. The procedure is simple. There is some sort of vote in which each person expresses choices for or against other members of the group: the one to sit next to in class or to work next to in the laundry or to share a room with in the dormitory. Often a short list is called for, so that a preferential order is established for four or five group members. Preferably, from the standpoint of group morale, these are decisive choices; that is, they result in a shift of seating arrangements, partnerships, and so on. But the ballots also provide the necessary information for a sociometric mapping of the groups, from those with the highest votes who are the most admired or respected, down to those who remain unchosen by anyone. The resulting data can be used to make inferences about the socially significant aspects of personality, which lead on the one hand to individual acceptance and participation, on the other hand to isolation (Jennings, 1950).

Complex observations and judgments

A dissatisfaction with any partial approach to the measurement of personality has led to a number of studies in which very extensive records were kept. Subjects under study were assigned special field tasks to perform, participated in house parties, and were thus under observation for many hours in "naturalistic" settings, as well as having their test responses recorded and analyzed. This kind of procedure has come to be called "assessment," a familiar term that became used in this more specialized sense in the Office of Strategic Services during World War II, when such devices were used to select candidates for various hazardous missions (OSS Assessment Staff, 1948).

The major studies that have been carried on using this method are not very encouraging in their results. The most successful study was one of candidates for the British civil service (Vernon, 1950), in which there had been a careful job analysis and the future occupational tasks of the candidates were therefore clearly identified. Among the tasks assigned the candidates during a three-day "house party" were civil service paper work, committee tasks, and group discussions. Validities for later job performances were in the range of .50 to .65.

On the other hand, elaborate studies of trainees in clinical psychology (Kelly and Fiske, 1951) yielded little beyond what could have been predicted from material in the folders of the candidates before assessment began; similarly, a study of candidates for psychiatric training in the Menninger School of Psychiatry yielded very little (Holt and Luborsky, 1958). One of the most thorough studies was that of Air Force officers, conducted at the Institute for Personality Assessment Research at the University of California in Berkeley (MacKinnon, 1958). Although 100 officers were brought for three-day assignments during which they lived with psychologists under almost continuous observation, and over 600 "scores" were obtained, almost no correlations rose above .30; the whole enterprise must be viewed as a failure of prediction, although there were some useful by-products.

In summarizing the assessment procedures that have shown most promise of success, Cronbach (1960) mentions three:

1. Peer ratings appear to be as useful as those of trained psychologists, probably because the peer knows more about the job requirements than the clinician.
2. Performance tests which are very near to the task to be performed have considerable validity.
3. "The most important criterion for valid assessment is that the assessors have a clear understanding of the psychological

16-8

The wall problem: an assessment situation

The team of candidates under study approaches a wall 10 feet high and 15 feet long. They are told to imagine that it is a barrier miles long (so that they cannot go around it, or even look around), and that between this wall and a far wall is a canyon. Nearby are a heavy log, an old board slightly longer than the log, and some short two-by-fours. The men must get across; the picture shows one solution, in which the log is placed across as a "bridge" with the aid of the board. Observers study how the men organize themselves, who takes leadership, who shows signs of despair, etc. (From OSS Assessment Staff, 1948, p. 94)

Donald W. MacKinnon, Univ. of California

requirements of the criterion task" (Cronbach, 1960, p. 589). This was true of the British civil servant study; it was also true of a study of officer candidates who were judged by recent graduates of Officer Candidate School (Holmen and others, 1956).

To sum up: While personality tests are far from satisfactory, they appear to be as successful as judgments based on complex observations.

People experienced in the judging of other persons can often take advantage of slight clues and specific individual experiences that are lost to the test standardized on groups of people. Their judgments, which can be called *clinical*, are the alternatives to predictive scores arrived at by methods which, in contrast, can be called *statistical*. How does the issue stand as between the relative successes of clinical and statistical predictions?

A careful review by Meehl (1954), who has had abundant clinical and statistical experience, is informative. He found 20 studies that provided competent clinicians with information of a type that could also be expressed in mechanical formulas. With the same type of information available for judgment, in all but one of the studies the statistical predictions based on the formula were equal to or superior to the predictions made by the clinicians. In most cases if the clinician supplemented the statistical information by corrections made on the basis of his judgment, the prediction was weakened rather than improved.

This support for tests (which permit arriving at scores that can be entered into formulas) must not be taken as an indictment of the clinical method, and is not so intended by Meehl, who points out that there are many times when a usable formula is not available (Meehl, 1957). Holt (1958), in a kind of reply and supplement to Meehl, further points out that the clinicians were sometimes denied information and forced to guess in situations in which the statistical evidence was available, e.g., the relation between high school grades and college grades.

An important aspect of clinical practice is that many hypotheses (in the nature of tentative predictions) are tried out and discarded. As long as firm findings result, it does not matter how many false leads have been tried and rejected. The kind of comparison in which clinical prediction is pitted against statistical prediction does not permit this trial-and-error process. While the evidence does not therefore discredit the clinical method, it does at the same time show that the methods of statistical prediction have their place. This is the justification for further efforts at personality test construction.

SUMMARY   1. *Personality* is defined as the configuration of individual characteristics and ways of behaving which describe an individual's unique adjustments to his environment.

2. *Personality structure* refers to the persistent unique features that give coherence to a personality. A man's personality structure arises through the roles that culture assigns to him and through individual experiences.

3. Out of the many experiences of growing up, a person moves through the stages of *identifications* with others toward the achievement of *identity* for himself.

4. There are many ways of characterizing an individual. At least seven classes of units can be used in personality appraisal: *physique and temperament, intellectual and other abilities, interests and values, social attitudes, motivational dispositions, expressive and stylistic traits,* and *pathological trends.*

5. The personality inventory is a device for self-characterization through replies to a large number of questions. Three examples include the Minnesota Multiphasic Personality Inventory (MMPI), basing its scales upon the empirical comparison of responses with those given by various deviant groups; the Edwards Personal Preference Schedule (PPS), based on Murray's theory of needs and using a forced-choice technique; and Cattell's 16 PF Questionnaire, using sixteen categories chosen according to the results of factor analysis.

6. The personality inventory, by contrast with an intelligence test, seeks to determine a characteristic performance rather than one at its best. Various biasing factors enter in to make personality testing by means of inventories difficult and to some extent uncertain.

7. Projective tests are more ambiguous and less highly structured than personality inventories, thus permitting the person to reveal his personality style more freely. Examples are the story-telling picture test, known as the Thematic Apperception Test (TAT), and the Rorschach ink-blot test.

While results with these tests appear to be at above-chance levels, there are many difficulties in the interpreting of test scores derived from them.

8. Other methods of personality appraisal involve judgment by informed observers. Among these methods are *rating scales,* in which traits to be judged are specified, *sociometry,* in which social interaction is appraised, and *assessment,* the result of complex observations and judgments.

9. In comparisons between clinical and statistical predictions greater success has usually been reported for the statistical predictions. In some sense, however, the tasks appropriate to the two methods are different, and the issues between them are not completely settled by appeal to specific prediction.

SUGGESTIONS FOR FURTHER READING

Cronbach, *Essentials of psychological testing* (2nd Ed., 1960) has a number of chapters on personality appraisal; other books, specifically devoted to personality, are Ferguson, *Personality measurement* (1952), and Allen, *Personality assessment procedures* (1958).

The MMPI is probably the most worked-over of the personality inventories. Useful books about it are Welsh and Dahlstrom, *Basic readings on the MMPI in psychology and medicine* (1956), and Dahlstrom and Welsh, *An MMPI handbook: a guide to use in clinical practice and research* (1960). Edwards, *The social desirability variable in personality assessment and research* (1957) shows one of the biasing factors in self-inventories.

For the results of factor analysis in the personality sphere, the best summaries are Cattell, *Personality and motivation structure and measurement* (1957), and Guilford, *Personality* (1959); a British variant, not dealt with in the text, is Eysenck, *The structure of human personality* (1959).

There are a number of books on the TAT, of which Henry, *The analysis of fantasy* (1956), Tomkins, *The Thematic Apperception Test* (1947), and Kagan and Lesser, *Contemporary issues in thematic apperceptive methods* (1961) are fair representatives. Klopfer and others, *Developments in the Rorschach Technique* (1954) and Rickers-Ovsiankina, *Rorschach psychology* (1960) are advanced books on the ink-blot test. The most recent development using more ink blots is Holtzman and others, *Ink blot perception and personality* (1961). For projective tests in general, see Abt and Bellak, *Projective psychology* (1950), and Anderson and Anderson (Eds.), *Introduction to projective techniques* (1951).

For more complex assessment and observational procedures, see OSS Assessment Staff, *Assessment of men* (1948), and Stern, Stein, and Bloom, *Methods in personality assessment* (1956).

CHAPTER 17

Theories of Personality

there are at least *some* people whose personalities revolve about a cardinal or dominant characteristic—ambition, pride, adventure, bodily comfort. Perhaps, then, it might be possible to classify people into a few types if we could arrive at a short list of these central *themes* or *styles of life* that characterize some individuals so well. In the effort to do just this, students of personality have turned for clues to *physique* (body types), to *physiology* (body chemistry), and to *behavior* (psychological types).

Physique: body types

One kind of classification that goes far back in history is the theory of *body types* as determinants of personality. Bodily constitution, health, and vigor undoubtedly determine some manifestations of personality. The plausible relation between body and personality has led to the age-old tendency to assign traits on the basis of features of the body or face. The classification of physique into types has little meaning unless a type classification of psychological characteristics is also accepted. Theories based on body type (or other constitutional givens) usually stress differences in general affective or emotional reactivity. Mothers of several children often report that their children seemed very different from birth: one was always lively, energetic, active, another was always more placid, calm, quiet; one smiled readily, the other was more sober from the start. These general differences in reactivity are often referred to as differences in *temperament;* it is such differences that tend to be related to types of physique.

One theory of this kind, influential in the early part of this century, was that of Kretschmer (1925). He began with the plausible theory that the two major forms of mental breakdown, schizophrenia and manic-depressive psychosis, represented extreme personality types. Normal people, he thought, would show in milder form some of the characteristics of these illnesses. He

Theories of personality are attempts to account in a systematic and orderly way for what in the previous chapter was called personality structure. A successful theory must weave together the various strands descriptive of individuality into a fabric that has enduring, identifiable features, unique for each individual, yet permitting individuals to be compared with one another. There are many theories—partly because personality is so loosely defined that not all theories deal with the same subject matter, partly because the facts upon which a finished theory must rest are not yet well enough known. We shall consider four groups of theories: *type* theories, *trait* theories, *developmental* theories, and theories of personality *dynamics*.

Type Theories

Theories of *personality types* are ancient in origin; they persist today, despite repeated rejections of type classifications by psychologists. The reasons for the prevalence of these theories are not hard to find. They represent a commendable effort to find some order in the midst of human diversity. Classification into *kinds* is the beginning of most sciences—kinds of rocks, kinds of weather, kinds of plants and animals; why not kinds of personalities? Furthermore, type theories build upon the common observation that

further asserted that these two kinds of illness were associated with two body types: schizophrenia with the tall, thin body (*asthenic*), and manic-depressive with the short, fat body (*pyknic*). Normal people would then tend to share temperaments appropriate to their body types, the asthenic body associated with the *schizothyme* temperament, the pyknic body with the *cyclothyme* temperament (manic-depressive symptoms being cyclical in character). Careful measurements of schizophrenic and manic-depressive patients have not confirmed the basis for Kretschmer's theory; manic-depressive patients tend to be older than schizophrenic patients in the same hospital, and all patients share with the general population the tendency toward an enlarged waistline with increasing years (Burchard, 1936).

Among the more serious recent attempts to develop a type theory based on bodily characteristics, that of Sheldon has attracted the most attention from contemporary psychologists. Sheldon and his collaborators (Sheldon, Stevens, and Tucker, 1940; Sheldon and Stevens, 1942; Sheldon, 1954) reject the idea that individuals can be divided into distinct physical types, but instead they classify them according to three components. The terms used to describe the components derive from the names of the cell layers in the embryo from which different bodily tissues originate. The first or *endomorphic* component refers to the prominence of the intestines and other visceral organs. The obese individual is high in this component; his paunch indicates excess viscera. The second or *mesomorphic* component refers to bone and muscle. The athlete is predominantly mesomorphic, wide-shouldered, narrow-hipped, with rippling muscles. The third or *ectomorphic* component is based on delicacy of skin, fine hair, and sensitive nervous system. The ectomorphic person is tall, thin, stoop-shouldered; no one would confuse him with a mesomorph or an endomorph.

In rating a person, the system assigns one digit between 1 and 7 for each component in the order endomorph, mesomorph, and ectomorph, high numbers standing for more of the component. A man rated 3-6-2 might make a football fullback: low in respect to endomorphy, athletically powerful (with a 6 in mesomorphy), low in the delicate features of ectomorphy.

To each of these physical components there is assigned a corresponding temperamental component. The predominantly endomorphic person tends to be classified temperamentally as one who loves to eat, seeks bodily comforts, and is sociable. The predominantly mesomorphic person is energetic, likes exercise, and is direct in manner. The ectomorph is sensitive, given to worry, fears groups, and needs solitude. He may or may not use his sensitive nervous system for artistic or scientific work.

The scheme satisfies all the appeals of a "type" theory of personality: it is biologically plausible because of its emphasis upon embryological origins, it dramatizes familiar extremes in physique, and it plays up familiar correspondences between the body and its activities.

Although they appeared plausible and were bolstered by impressive statistical data, Sheldon's types met the fate of most of the older type systems, once they were subjected to impartial scrutiny. The dimensional scheme by which the three components of the body were selected turns out to be dependent on the statistical methods used; two dimensions would, in fact, cover the data equally well (Ekman, 1951; Lorr and Fields, 1954; Humphreys, 1955). The correlations between body type and temperament seem to reflect the contamination produced when one rater judges both type and temperament. Studies using *ratings* have usually given some small support to Sheldon's claims, but studies using *tests,* in which bias is excluded, have found few, if any, significant correlations between body build and personality (Tyler, 1956, p. 444).

Physiology: types based on body chemistry and endocrine balance

The ancient Greek classification of temperaments into four types was based on what was at that time known about the body chemistry. The four types were *sanguine, phlegmatic, melancholic,* and *choleric,* based on the prominence of one of the four "body fluids": the sanguine person, generally warm-hearted and pleasant, had a prominence of blood; the phlegmatic person, listless and slow, had his qualities attributed to phlegm; the melancholic person, suffering from depression and sadness, had too much black bile; the choleric person, easily angered and quick to react, was influenced by his yellow bile. The modern counterpart of this theory would assign such functions to hormones, and at least one prominent contemporary biochemist has advocated a careful look at the chemistry of the body as a basis for temperament (Williams, 1956). While each of us has the same endocrine glands, they vary greatly in size from one person to another. It is found, for example, that the same gland in one person may weigh three times as much as it does in another (without any enlargement due to disease); hence the relative prominence of one or another gland may give one person an excess of thyroid, another an excess of adrenal tissue. Williams concludes that each person has his own distinctive pattern of endocrine activity; according to this view, individual temperament is a kind of "endocrine symphony."

Some data exist that show a considerable stability in certain indicators of autonomic balance. Thus measures have been devised to determine whether the sympathetic or the parasympathetic responses are more active when stimuli call forth their antagonistic responses; in some individuals the sympathetic responses will be ascendant, in others the parasympathetic. When such measures are taken as much as a year apart, children react very much alike on the two occasions, as indicated by a correlation of .70 in responsiveness from one time to the other (Wenger and Wellington, 1943). Individuals may demonstrate quite specific patterns of autonomic response; these patterns of physiological response have been demonstrated to bear some relationship to personality measures (Lacey and Van Lehn; 1952; Lacey, Bateman, and Van Lehn, 1952). The evidence is good enough that there is a constitutional (perhaps hormonal) basis for differences in temperament, but just how far we can go in appraising an individual in terms of his physiological functioning is not at present known.

It should also be noted that the results of accurate measurement do not actually yield "types" but continuities; individuals differ in their autonomic functioning in many ways, and cannot be grouped into a few "types."

Behavior: psychological types

It is not necessary to turn to body types or to physiological types in order to hold to a theory of personality types. It is possible to look for types based on *behavior* or *psychological characteristics,* without recourse to other correlations. Perhaps the best known of the psychological type theories is the classification into *introverts* and *extroverts* proposed by the Swiss psychologist Carl J. Jung (1875-1961). The introvert, especially in time of emotional stress or conflict, tends to withdraw into himself. Characteristics of introversion include shyness and a preference for working alone, e.g., in libraries and laboratories rather than among people. The introvert may take to the speaking platform, as in the leading of a religious movement, but even there he is impelled from within. The extrovert, by contrast, when under stress tends to lose himself among people. He is likely to be very sociable, a hail-fellow-well-met. He tends to choose occupations such as sales or promotional work, where he deals with people rather than with things. He is likely to be

Distribution of scores on an introversion-extroversion test

The distributions of scores are for 44 medical students and 44 clinic patients showing no mental abnormality. Both distributions follow the nomal curve rather than showing a bimodal distribution, as would be expected if two separate types were being identified. (After Neymann and Yacorzynski, 1942)

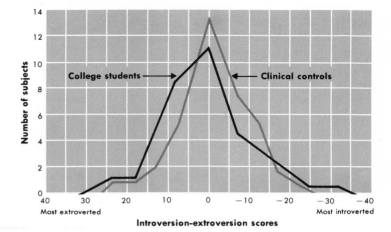

conventional, orthodox, well-dressed, outgoing. It is not difficult for each of us to find among his acquaintances a "typical" introvert or a "typical" extrovert. This gives such a classification plausibility and accounts for its popular appeal (Jung, 1923).

When we select traits that appear to belong to an introvert or an extrovert, however, and construct tests on the basis of these traits, we make two discoveries. First, it develops that a test of general introvertive or extrovertive tendencies leads to a normal distribution of scores with a single mode, rather than to the bimodality that a type theory would call for (Figure 17-1); in other words, we discover that the introvert and extrovert are merely extremes on a scale, not actually two distinct types. They differ as do tall and short by departing in both directions from some middle condition: most people are *ambiverts,* neither introverts nor extroverts, but sometimes one, sometimes the other. The second discovery is that the scale is complex. When tests of introversion-extroversion are analyzed by the method of factor analysis, as many as five factors can be identified (Guilford, 1940). These factors have been described as social introversion, thinking introversion, depression, tendency to mood swings, and happy-

go-lucky disposition. Such results have made psychologists skeptical of otherwise plausible classifications into personality types.

Estimate of type theories

Satisfactory type theories are not impossible. It may be that we shall eventually isolate men into types as distinctive as the blood types that so markedly affect the success of blood transfusions. There are no logical barriers against such theories. The fact is, however, that present theories have not produced the evidence needed to verify them. Even if the evidence were more satisfactory than it is now, two dangers in type theory would remain.

1. *The type description tends to assert too much about the individual.* As soon as a person is tagged according to a type theory, the assumption is that a great many assertions can safely be made about him. That is, he is expected to have all the characteristics belonging to that type; but the determiners of individual personality are too many, and they combine into something both too rich and too unusual to be described with a single general term.

The danger is that of assigning the person

to a *stereotype*. We all too readily come to believe that Negroes are carefree and musical, Italians volatile, Scots thrifty, Swedes stolid. Such characterizations are stereotypes that ignore the individual differences among members of a group. A stereotype is, to be sure, a faulty type classification, but even a better type classification easily lends itself to abuse.

2. *The type description tends to hold to outmoded conceptions of personality and especially neglects cultural influences.* Students of the development of the individual are aware of the enormous importance of childhood experiences and later opportunities in shaping personality. Type theories are sponsored primarily (though not exclusively) by those who see human characteristics as chiefly the result of biological inheritance. That is why many type theories refer to body form. The body is an important locus of personality, but personality is also interpersonal, that is, dependent on relations to other people. When one understands the richness and diversity of cultural influences, he loses faith in type theories.

Trait Theories

A *trait theory* is in some respects at the opposite extreme from a type theory; instead of grouping people according to a few types, it classifies people according to the degree to which they can be characterized in terms of a number of traits. According to trait theory, one can describe a personality by its position on a number of *scales,* each of which represents a trait. Thus we may place the person on a scale of intelligence as indicating one personality trait, on a scale of emotional sensitivity as another trait, on a scale of ascendance-submission as a third. Because our language is very rich in trait names, a mere listing of specific traits is not enough; some sort of order has to be made of the countless ways in which a person can be characterized. We shall consider two sub-

varieties of trait theory: Allport's theory of personal dispositions, and Cattell's theory of surface and source traits.

Allport's theory of functionally autonomous traits

Gordon W. Allport (1937, 1961) accepts a kind of trait theory, but distinguishes between it and the more generally accepted theory of common traits. In order to avoid confusion, he now prefers to speak of *personal dispositions* instead of traits. He makes a number of distinctions among kinds of traits, and his theory cannot be understood without these distinctions.

The first distinction is between *common traits* and *personal dispositions*. Common traits are those that are comparable between people; when we measure people according to trait scales, we are implying common traits. Thus his *Scale of Values* (Allport, Vernon, and Lindzey, 1960) is designed to appraise common traits, comparing one person with another according to preferred values (theoretical, economic, esthetic, social, political, and religious). He prefers, however, to consider true traits as *personal dispositions* that are unique for the person, and hence cannot be used in an exact way in comparing one person with another. Thus two people may both be aggressive, but each will be aggressive in his own way, depending upon his individual experiences and capabilities. When Allport is being strict, he asserts that the common trait is not a true trait at all, but merely a measurable aspect of personal dispositions that differ in complex ways from one person to another.

Another set of distinctions is made by Allport to indicate that dispositions are organized in a kind of hierarchy, some much more important to the individual than others; for this purpose he distinguishes between *cardinal, central,* and *secondary* traits. Some individuals stand out because they are dominated by a single *cardinal* trait; such persons, whether historical or fictional, often become "reference personalities" by which we describe others. If we say that someone is a Beau Brummell or a Don Juan or quixotic or narcissistic, we are classifying him by his resemblance to a reference personality whose characteristics we expect others to know. While few people are dominated by a cardinal trait, many have a *few* traits that centrally describe their personalities. Allport refers to a description of the psychologist William James as having the benign traits of "sensibility, vivacity, humanity, and sociability." These are *central* traits, because a few terms suffice to characterize him. In a pilot study with 93 students, Allport asked each one to characterize someone he knew well in as many words, phrases, or sentences as were required. He found that the characterizations required an average of 7.2 essential characteristics, with a range of from 3 to 10 (Allport, 1960). This is support for the notion of a few central traits. Finally, there are many *secondary traits,* expressing relatively isolated interests or modes of responding; many of these are better characterized as "attitudes" than as "traits."

We shall later consider (pp. 476-83) personality theories that stress the developmental history of the individual. Allport recognizes that development shapes the individual, but he prefers to de-emphasize the history of traits. His views become particularly clear in his belief in the *functional autonomy* of motives, by which he means that a present motive can direct behavior without deriving any support from the tensions that were originally present when the motive system first developed. Thus the miser may have had a deprived youth and thus, out of anxiety, have come to be very saving; yet his present miserliness is now no longer related to any need for money, but rather reflects an interest in money for its own sake. Allport's objection to a developmental approach is not that he is against trying to understand a person in terms of his history, but that he believes an emphasis upon development leads to a doctrine of "pushes" from the past, rather than one of "pulls" toward present or future goals. He believes that normally healthy adults are motivated by their value orientations and their present interest systems, regardless of the past origins of these values and interests (Allport, 1960, p. 28).

The essence of Allport's theory is that patterned individuality constitutes the subject matter of a science of personality. He therefore resists the tendency of others to reduce personality to the traits that are common to all men. Cardinal, central, and secondary traits can be treated as personal dispositions in describing individual uniqueness.

Cattell's theory of surface and source traits

Unless one has some sort of ordering principle, what comes out of a theory of common traits is simply a description of a person's position on a number of scales. If one could arrive at a *short* list of the main *common traits,*[1] then one could characterize a person according to a *trait profile* or *psychograph* (Figure 17-2). The problem is to obtain a short list that is not arbitrary. One method that suggests itself is *factor analysis* (p. 408); by obtaining a great many ratings or scores from the same people, we ought to be able to find those traits that cluster together so that we can use one name for the cluster.

While many investigators have used this approach, we may select the work of Raymond B. Cattell as illustrative, for it has represented a prodigious amount of data collection and analysis. In gathering his data, Cattell has used behavior observations and ratings, laboratory studies, and inventories, working with many different populations and age groups.

Allport and Odbert (1936) listed 17,953 words used in English to distinguish the be-

[1] Note that the short lists which Allport cites are lists of *central personal dispositions,* the lists differing from one person to another; this is not the same as a short list of *common* traits.

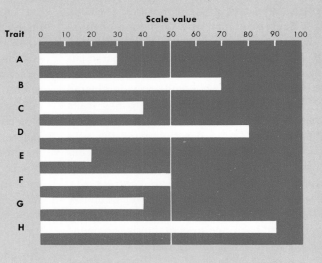

17-2

Trait profile (hypothetical)

If a standard set of common traits (such as A through H) could be agreed upon as giving a satisfactory characterization of a person, then an individual trait profile, such as the one shown here, would be as characteristic of the person as his fingerprints, provided the traits were stable and could be satisfactorily appraised.

havior of one person from another. Cattell began his research with this list of trait names, adding the terms that psychologists have coined in their researches. By eliminating overlap of meanings, he came out with 171 personality or temperament variables describing the whole "personality sphere" (Cattell, 1946, pp. 219-32). Although some traits, such as ability, can be thought of as positions along a scale ranging from zero to a high value, most temperament variables can be expressed as polar opposites (e.g., cheerful-gloomy). Cattell prefers such paired terms wherever possible. If many such variables are used to describe the same group of individuals, the variables can be examined for correlation; that is, it is possible to find out which are closely related to others and which are distinct.

Two main techniques of examining the interrelationships exist, leading to a distinction that Cattell makes between *surface* traits and *source* traits.

Surface traits are found by studying the *clusters* of the actually obtained correlations. For example, all traits that intercorrelate .60 or higher can be assumed to be a manifestation of one cluster or *surface trait*. Thus it is found that people judged on the three trait pairs of thoughtful vs.

unreflective, wise vs. foolish, and austere vs. profligate, tend to fall in similar positions on all three scales, at least to the extent of a correlation of .60; hence these three are clustered together (with others of similar sort) into the surface trait called disciplined thoughtfulness vs. foolishness. This and a few other surface traits are listed in Table 17-1. They are called *surface* traits, because the similarity lies on the "surface," that is, is evident in the actual raw ratings, without any transformation or any process of inference leading to some less obvious underlying uniformity.

Source traits are found by another method, that of *factor analysis,* which is more subtle than *cluster analysis;* while it will reflect the belonging together of traits that correlate highly with each other, it may also assign to one factor some traits that correlate less highly with each other, and it will tell the extent to which each of the traits also reflects other factors. The traits that belong together as a result of factor analysis are called *source traits,* on the assumption that they reveal a deeper-lying unity than that revealed through surface traits. The traits most representative of a source trait will also be highly correlated with each other as surface traits; the point

TABLE 17-1	TABLE 17-2
Some of the chief surface traits	**Some of the chief source traits**

The traits clustered together have all correlated at least $r = .60$ with each other within at least four investigations conducted with adults. The specific traits listed are examples from longer lists, and some liberties have been taken in shortening trait names as stated by Cattell.

Integrity-Altruism vs. Dishonesty, Undependability
Honest vs. Dishonest
Loyal vs. Fickle
Fairminded vs. Partial

Demanding Self-Centeredness vs. Emotional Maturity
Infantile vs. Emotionally Mature
Exhibitionist vs. Self-Effacing
Not Self-Controlled vs. Self-Controlled

Disciplined Thoughtfulness vs. Foolishness
Thoughtful vs. Unreflective
Wise vs. Foolish
Austere vs. Profligate

Heartiness vs. Shyness
Sociable (Forward) vs. Shy
Sociable (Gregarious) vs. Seclusive
Intrusive vs. Reserved

Warmth vs. Aloofness
Responsive vs. Aloof
Affectionate vs. Cold
Even-Tempered vs. Sensitive

Austerity, Stability vs. Playfulness, Changeability
Deliberate vs. Impulsive
Not Playful vs. Mischievous (Playful)
Emotionally Stable vs. Changeable

Thrift, Tidiness, Obstinacy vs. Lability, Curiosity, Intuition
Habit-Bound vs. Labile
Thrifty vs. Careless of Property
Pedantic, Tidy vs. Disorderly

SOURCE: Cattell (1950), pp. 37-41.

A source trait has always been identified through factor analysis, and is said to determine the variability in measured surface traits. The examples are selected from a longer list.

General Mental Capacity vs. Mental Defect
Intelligent vs. Unintelligent
Thoughtful vs. Unreflective
Smart, Assertive vs. Dull, Submissive

Cyclothymia vs. Schizothymia
Adaptable vs. Rigid
Trustful vs. Suspicious
Self-Effacing vs. Egotistical

Adventurous Cyclothymia vs. Withdrawn Schizothymia
Adventurous vs. Shy, Timid
Gregarious vs. Aloof
Frank vs. Secretive

Emotionally Stable Character vs. Neurotic General Emotionality
Emotionally Stable vs. Dissatisfied
Free of Neurotic Symptoms vs. Showing Variety of Neurotic Symptoms
Calm, Patient vs. Excitable, Impatient

Dominance-Ascendance vs. Submissiveness
Self-Assertive vs. Submissive
Boastful, Conceited vs. Modest, Retiring
Aggressive, Pugnacious vs. Complaisant

Surgency vs. Desurgency
Cheerful, Joyous vs. Depressed, Pessimistic
Sociable, Responsive vs. Seclusive, Retiring
Talkative vs. Taciturn, Introspective

Positive Character vs. Dependent Character
Persevering, Determined vs. Quitting, Fickle
Responsible vs. Frivolous, Immature
Attentive to People vs. Neglectful of Social Chores

SOURCE: Cattell (1950), pp. 58-62.

---

is not that surface traits never reveal source traits, but rather that source traits help to explain the clustering of the surface traits, and pick out those that are "purer" examples of a basic trait. Some of the chief source traits reported by Cattell are given in Table 17-2.

The ideal is clear enough: to find the few main source traits that turn up in a number of separate investigations. If these source traits can be identified, tests can be con-

structed to measure them; these test scores can then be weighted for any kind of personality assessment or prediction that may be desired. As we saw in Chapter 16 (p. 455), Cattell has indeed constructed a test, called the 16 PF Questionnaire, which is designed to assess sixteen source traits (Cattell, 1957b).

In general, the promise of the method, as abstractly conceived, is not fulfilled in the results obtained thus far. This comes about because of some difficulties in the procedures by which measures of traits are obtained, and because of some unresolved problems within factor analysis as a method of defining stable source traits. The move toward simplification implied in the concept of source traits is, however, a useful one.

Estimate of trait theories

What can we say about the success of trait theories as alternatives to type theories?

1. The trait approach is a straightforward one, lending itself readily to experimentation. As a starting point there is scarcely any alternative to a trait approach; even contemporary type theories begin with trait appraisal. Hence the methods of trait appraisal are legitimate and merit additional careful investigation.

2. The trait profile that emerges from the scores of an individual is not an adequate description of his personality, even though it may be a true one. When behavior is broken down into traits, we have no way of knowing how the traits are ordered in the goal-seeking behavior of the individual. Thus a person characterized by the trait of compulsiveness may occupy himself merely with useless repetitive rituals, or, on the contrary, he may show dogged determination to stay with a productive task.

Thus the trait profile, while it tells something about personality patterning, is not dynamic enough to show the interrelationships of the traits in the individual. One method proposed for meeting this objection is the use of *profile analysis*. It consists in appraising the trait patterns, stressing interrelationships as well as individual traits (Meehl, 1950).

3. An individual's traits are his ways of behaving under environmental provocation, and their existence depends upon this interaction between person and environment. There is some objection to assigning traits to an individual as though they were something he *possessed*. He does not possess

shyness or forwardness: he acts (and feels) shy under some circumstances and acts forward (and does not feel shy) under other circumstances. Care is needed lest traits, like types, divert attention from the importance of the cultural surroundings in which behavior occurs.

A simple illustration of how environment elicits behavior is given by a study of aggressive behavior of boys in a camping situation. The total amount of aggressive interplay in the dining room so exceeded that observed elsewhere that a boy who might have been judged as lacking in aggression on the playing field might well have been judged aggressive if observed only at the table (Gump and Kounin, 1959).

A theory of traits as characterizations of the person (dispositions that he possesses) lacks something in meaning, for traits will manifest themselves differently depending upon the environmental stresses upon the individual. Some sort of interactive theory is needed, in which what the person possesses is somehow appraised according to a range of situational circumstances in which these dispositions are called into play. We do not know how best to state such a theory, but the developmental theories and theories of dynamics about to be discussed make consideration of interaction a point of departure.

Developmental Theories

Theories which stress the importance of developmental history for personality need not deny the biological potentialities of the individual, as stressed in theories of physique or physiology, but they insist that this potential merely provides a set of limits within which personality takes shape. The relationship is comparable to that between maturation and learning: maturation provides a kind of ground plan of development; learning determines what the individual actually does with his matured capacities. Developmental theories tend to stress continuities; one way of putting this is that one can best predict what a person will do in a given situation by what he has done before in earlier situations that resemble the present. Thus environmental interaction finds a place in these theories, somewhat more firmly than in either type or trait theories. Three varieties of developmental theory will be considered: psychoanalytic, learning, and role theories.

Psychoanalytic theory of development

Psychoanalytic theory has both a developmental and an interactive aspect; that is, it is concerned both with the course of development from earliest childhood and with the motivational conflicts and crises that occur at any given time. At this point we shall be concerned primarily with the developmental aspects of the theory, returning later to the interactive (dynamic) aspects. Psychoanalysis finds a continuity in growth: beginning in earliest childhood, a shaping process goes on that results in a relatively enduring personality structure, one which changes slowly and is therefore characteristic of the mature individual at any given time.

According to classical psychoanalysis, the basic maturational plan of development consists of an unfolding of the sexual impulses (instinct or drive), with certain transformations being considered universal. The steps involved are indicated in Table 17-3, which shows how successive phases are said to be passed through until there is the final mature genital stage of normal sexual relations with the opposite sex. Sex is broadly interpreted; the three earliest stages—oral, anal, and phallic, together called *pregenital*—have no reproductive aims, but merely represent sources of pleasure through stimulation that are in some sense forerunners of mature sexual pleasure. The significance for personality development of each of the stages depends upon a tendency for the earlier experiences to be variously transformed, particularly through *displacement;* for example,

pleasure in retaining feces is said to become pleasure in retaining any possessions of value. This process is called displacement, because one object of gratification "displaces" another.

The statements in Table 17-3 summarize a highly complex theory that has evolved over half a century and is still undergoing changes. In its more classical form, the theory emphasized changes within the individual personality (called *intrapsychic* processes, meaning within the psyche), with a strong flavor of biological maturation and with little attention to social and environmental influences. Some critics have pointed out that the scheme may not be universal at all, but may be plausible for us because of the child-rearing practices within Western culture. A careful look at the stages of development shows that there are developing interpersonal relationships throughout. The first relationship (in the oral stage) is with the mother or mother-substitute, with important social consequences in security and insecurity in relation to other people; the next relationship (in the anal stage) is with those persons responsible for bowel training, and the rewards and punishments of this relationship (including the possibility of defiance) also may have consequences for later social interaction. In both the oral and anal stage, the interaction is always with one other person at a time. The phallic-Oedipal stage is particularly important, because in it the child becomes aware of a fabric of social relations, involving more than two people at a time: at least mother, father, and child, perhaps other siblings. The Oedipal jealousy is said to arise because the child detects the special relationship that the mother and father have to each other, which excludes him; the Oedipal *solution* is to recognize that people can have these several relationships, that the child is not being rejected just because mother and father care for each other. The identification with parents is a complex matter which includes some copying of them, but the young child must

TABLE 17-3

Stages of psychosexual development according to classical psychoanalysis

Age	Stage	Source of pleasure	Significance for personality development
First year	Oral	Pleasure derived through lips and mouth: sucking, eating, thumb-sucking. Later, when teeth erupt, pleasure through biting.	Foundation for dependency upon others. "Oral incorporation" a factor in identification, acquiring knowledge, possessions, belief. "Oral aggressiveness" a basis for sarcasm, argumentativeness, etc.
Second year	Anal	Pleasure derived through retention and expulsion of feces; also through muscular control.	"Anal retentive character": obstinate, stingy, compulsive. "Anal expulsive character": cruel, destructive, disorderly. Under favorable circumstances parental handling of bowel training leads to creativity and productivity.
Third year through fifth year	Phallic; Oedipal	Pleasure derived through genital stimulation and associated fantasies. Oedipus complex: boy's sexual interest in his mother, girl's interest in her father.	Identifications with parents emerge as Oedipus complex is solved. Superego ("conscience") develops. Many important consequences for accepting appropriate age and sex roles.
Sixth year until puberty	Latency	With temporary repression of sexual interests, pleasure derives from external world, curiosity, knowledge, etc. as substitute gratifications.	This period (the elementary school age) is very important for the social development of the child, for acquiring the knowledge and skills needed to get along in the workaday world.
Adolescense to adulthood	Genital	Pleasure derives from mature sexual relations with opposite-sexed partner.	Self-love (narcissism) of the pregenital period turns to the love of others, and includes altruistic motives. Emancipation from dependence upon parents.

SOURCE: Various, e.g., Munroe (1955), Hall (1954).

also recognize that he is *not* his father or his mother. It is easy to see the importance for later life of a good solution of the problems that arise at this period of development. The classical theory was particularly weak in dealing with the problems of latency, where the important learnings of this childhood period were largely passed over, the gratifications being interpreted as mere substitutes for sexual satisfaction at a time when sexual interests were being held in check. There is said to be a temporary resurgence of Oedipal conflicts at puberty, with re-

newed expression of jealousy of parents, followed, if all goes well, by emancipation from the parents and a satisfactory relation with a sex partner appropriate to one's own age.

An attempt within psychoanalysis to correct the lacks within the classical theory and to deal more adequately with the environmental and social adjustments required at each stage of development has been made by Erikson (1959). He sets forth a maturational scheme that recognizes the psychosexual stages (with some modifications), but at each stage he identifies *psychosocial crises* which if successfully met lead to maturity of psychological development, if unsuccessfully met leave neurotic residues. His scheme is outlined in Table 17-4. Note that at each stage the psychosocial crisis is indicated by a pair of terms of which the first indicates a favorable outcome, the second an unfavorable outcome. The theory holds that we carry with us throughout life the consequences of each of the earlier resolutions of a crisis, a kind of problem-solving from which we learn, or perhaps one that we use again when we face later crises. The end result is the unique personality structure as it is shaped by the changes that have been imposed upon this common outline of development.

While Erikson's scheme is a refreshing supplement to the classical psychosexual development pattern, and as such has been influential, the terms used to express the psychosocial crises were not chosen on any consistent basis, and further revision would be very desirable. Some of the terms are polar opposites (e.g., trust vs. mistrust); some are chosen from entirely different spheres of discourse (autonomy vs. shame, doubt). Such a scheme cannot become part of scientific theory until it is better ordered, no matter how much intuitive appeal it may have.

TABLE 17-4

Areas and stages of development

Stage	Psychosexual stages	Psychosocial crises	Radius of significant relations
I **Infancy**	Incorporative: Oral-Respiratory Sensory-Kinesthetic	Trust vs. Mistrust	Maternal person
II **Early Childhood**	Retentive-Eliminative: Anal-Urethral, Muscular	Autonomy vs. Shame, Doubt	Parental persons
III **Play Age**	Intrusive, Inclusive: Infantile Genital, Locomotor	Initiative vs. Guilt	Basic family
IV **School Age**	Latency	Industry vs. Inferiority	"Neighborhood"; School
V **Adolescence**	Puberty	Identity and Repudiation vs. Identity Diffusion	Peer groups and outgroups; Models of leadership
VI **Young Adult**	Genitality	Intimacy and Solidarity vs. Isolation	Partners in friendship, sex; Competition, cooperation
VII **Adulthood**		Generativity vs. Self-Absorption	Divided labor and shared household
VIII **Mature Age**		Integrity vs. Despair	"Mankind"; "My Kind"

SOURCE: Modified from Erikson (1959), p. 166.

The fact that earlier modes of dealing with crises persist in the present is emphasized in the psychoanalytic concept of *fixation,* which refers to arrested development. That is, an individual may in some sense have remained immature by being fixated or caught at one stage of development, so that there are excessive manifestations of that stage in his adult behavior. Such arrested development is partial only; in other respects such a person may be more fully grown up. Fixations lead to forms of character structure or personality structure associated with the stage at which the person is fixated. Two forms of personality structure that have been widely studied may serve to illustrate the psychoanalytic interpretation: the *compulsive* personality and the *authoritarian* personality.

The *compulsive* personality is characterized by excessive cleanliness, orderliness, obstinacy, and stinginess. In extreme cases, behavior becomes repetitive and ritualistic. Psychoanalysts believed that this personality structure arose through excessive cleanliness training in the period of early infancy and therefore called it the "anal" character, after the developmental stage in which it presumably arose. In this view, if the crises associated with the anal stage are not successfully resolved, there will be residual fixations, i.e., excessive residues from this stage operating in adult behavior. Later investigators have questioned this oversimplification of the origin of such a personality pattern, while not denying its existence. It is pointed out that the same parents who are excessive in cleanliness training are likely to make excessive demands for conformity, punctuality, and so on, beyond early infancy, and that the personality structure may very well come about through such continued childhood training.

The existence of the compulsive personality received at least partial confirmation in one experiment, in which thirty-seven men living together in college fraternities rated each other on three traits. The ratings were made on a seven-point scale, and a pooled rating resulted for each of the men on each of the traits of stinginess, obstinacy, and orderliness. The reliabilities of these averaged ratings were found to be satisfactory, and they could thus be interpreted like test scores.

The test of the theory that the three traits form a pattern rests upon a correspondence among the traits. The correlations between trait ratings turned out as follows:

Stinginess and orderliness	.39
Stinginess and obstinacy	.37
Obstinacy and orderliness	.36

The correlations, while low, are all positive and in the expected direction. The results are all the more convincing when we recall that we consider orderliness a desirable trait, but both stinginess and obstinacy undesirable (Sears, 1936, 1943).[2]

The *authoritarian* personality is another personality structure for which there has been a series of studies (Adorno and others, 1950). It is said to arise out of extreme parental rejection or domination in childhood, leading to repressed hostility. This hostility finds expression in adult life in attacks on minority groups, as in anti-Semitism. The authoritarian personality pattern includes highly conventional behavior, superstition, destructiveness and cynicism, desire for power, concern over sex.[3]

Learning theories

Learning theories overlap with the psychoanalytic theories because they also stress the importance of early developmental experiences and the residues of earlier experience in later problem-solving. The differences between the two kinds of theories lie chiefly in the desire of the learning theorist to find specific experiences of reward and

---

[2] It may be noted that one of Cattell's surface traits includes thrift, tidiness, and obstinacy (Table 17-3).

[3] The tests for authoritarian personality have not escaped criticism, e.g., Christie and Jahoda (1954).

punishment that shape development, while the psychoanalyst (particularly of the more classical groups) seeks to explain development in terms of certain universal patterns that are to be found in all cultures. To the extent that both theories describe reality, they necessarily overlap.

Some of the learning theorists have indeed taken the Freudian theories as a starting point, but have translated these theories into learning terms. This is true of both Dollard and Miller (1950), and Whiting and Child (1953), although neither pair is bound by commitment to the psychoanalytic interpretation. For example, the motivational systems studied by Whiting and Child include the consequences of feeding, toilet training, the management of sex and aggression, and dependency. While each of these aspects of behavior is for Whiting and Child an area of socialization, for a psychoanalyst each of them is an area also of psychosexual development. One wonders if, without the influence of psychoanalysis, the same areas would have been chosen; at the same time, the manner in which the development is studied differs greatly from that of the psychoanalyst. Cultural contrasts are studied, for example, where the classical analyst would have looked for similarities; and the later consequences of early experience are interpreted as generalized habits rather than the reflection of unconscious mechanisms.

It is instructive to consider the similarities and differences between the learning viewpoint and the psychoanalytic one. While the classical psychoanalyst considers the basic drives to be those of sex and aggression, the learning theorist adds hunger, thirst, and pain as drives in their own right. There are in psychoanalysis many derivative motives, established by way of some of the transformation mechanisms that we shall meet later (Chapter 18), but these transformations are stated largely in metaphorical terms; the learning theorists have worked out a more careful system of arriving at secondary motives through learning based on primary drives. The stages in development that the psychoanalyst calls psychosexual are recognized by the learning theorists, but are held to depend upon other aspects of maturation than sex, and to be relative to the demands made by parents in a particular culture. In other words, the rewards and punishments administered by significant people in the culture are seen as important in forming habits, including those of anxiety. The mechanisms of fixation, displacement, and the like can be studied as habit phenomena. Fixation is likely to be a result of overlearning, not corrected by new learning; displacement follows principles of generalization by way of similarity. The distinction between conscious and unconscious is essentially that between the labeled and the unlabeled; if one can label and talk about an experience, it is conscious; if one is vague about it, and cannot label it and talk about it, then it has its effects "unconsciously." The learning of labels is itself a habit phenomenon.

What psychoanalysis and learning theories have in common is the explanation of the present in terms of the past. The past provides a residue of experiences and memories (habits, to the learning theorist) that can be tapped when a present problem comes up. We tend to relate new experiences to past ones similar to these new ones, and hence bring to bear the modes of behavior that have worked for us in the past; when past experiences have been unsatisfactory (frightening, anxiety-provoking), similar experiences in the present may give rise to similar responses of alarm or panic. Present personality is somewhat consistent and predictable because of this tendency to draw upon a long past in meeting the problems of the day.

Role theories

Closely related to the learning theories are the *role* theories, which describe personalities according to the manner in which the individual meets the various demands that society makes upon him in his role of child, parent, man, woman, worker, citizen. These theories are close to learning theories in that the assumption is made that the biological individual is adaptable enough to fit a variety of roles; he evidently has to *acquire* his role behavior through experience with his particular culture. The difference in emphasis between the two theories lies chiefly in that the continuity of behavior in learning theory is attributed to habit, while in role theory much of this continuity is contributed by the stability of the roles into which the individual is cast; thus the enduring fabric of society is as important as the enduring fabric of his habits (Newcomb, 1950).

Role *behavior* depends first of all on the role *positions* that society establishes; that is, certain ways of behaving toward others are defined by different positions. According to Linton (1945), there are at least five kinds of positions in even the simplest societies: (1) age-sex positions, (2) occupational positions, (3) prestige positions (e.g., chief, slave), (4) family, clan, or household positions, and (5) positions in association groups based on congeniality or common interests (e.g., an orchestra member). Occupants of a given position are expected to fulfil the role by behaving in certain ways; some kinds of behavior are prescribed, some are permitted, and some are forbidden. A prescribed role makes a few firm demands and a number of permissive ones. Thus a mother, if she is to fulfil her role, must provide her children with enough to eat and should not treat them cruelly or torture them; she has discretion, however, about how much she reads to her children or whether or not she sends them to Sunday school.

The possibility of studying personality through role behavior is a good one, in part because the samples of behavior to be studied are somewhat specified by the role. As a mother, for example, the behavior toward the child is relevant, as a wife the behavior toward the husband, as an employer the behavior toward the employee. To some extent we may consider the results of sociometry (p. 463) to be ways of appraising role behavior, for the judgments about an individual are made according to his participation in some social group.

The role theory of personality development, in summary, is something like this. The infant is born into certain prearranged roles (family, sex, nationality). His freedom is limited by these roles, in that many of his choices have been made for him before he is born: where he will live, what language he will learn, and so on. When he is still dependent, his parents (or other responsible adults) are obligated to teach him the behavior appropriate to these pre-established roles. Depending upon the society in which he is born, he will be able to make a number of role choices of his own: whether or not to take up music or to participate in athletics, what occupation to prepare himself for. There may be great pressures from his social environment that limit his choices even in these areas, but in any case he will begin to put a personal stamp upon the way in which he behaves in the roles. In the end, what we mean by his personality (from this point of view) is the consistent features of his role behaviors.

An interesting study of the changes in personality associated with role behavior was made following World War II, in which the subjects were returned British soldiers who made poor adjustments to home after being several years in prisoner-of-war camps (Curle, 1947). Their habitual role behaviors were first disrupted by entering military life, with its new demands upon them; then they went overseas and had to learn new roles; finally they entered prison camp. At each stage their home ties became more remote and their new ways of life became more real. In the prison camp, where the men were separated from their officers, they had to participate vigorously to create a tolerable culture of their own; this new culture became social reality for them, and they did not do well when transplanted to their homes. When they were helped to make the shift by living for a time in "transitional communities," they adjusted much better than those who were returned directly to their homes (Curle and Trist, 1947). The point here is that some of the continuity of personality as we know it is provided by the continuity of the roles in our familiar communities; old habits are not enough to retain this continuity if circumstances are too drastically changed for too long.

Estimate of developmental theories

A developmental theory is certainly on sound ground in recognizing that man can and does learn and that he grows up in a culture in which he necessarily participates according to the rules and provisions of that culture. Hence any adult personality is a product of its development. This does not solve the problem, however, of selecting any one developmental theory as most cogent.

Some of the unresolved issues are:

1. What is the relative importance of the earliest years compared with the later years of childhood? The psychoanalytic theories (and some of the learning theories as well) place great emphasis upon the very early years in the shaping of personality; we do not know how reversible these influences are.[4]

2. What is the relative importance of the constitutional givens, as compared with learning? The same problem met with in intelligence (Chapter 15) is equally pertinent in the study of personality. If physique and endocrine balance are important, as some claim, just how important are they?

3. Is development a continuous process, in which a gradual maturation interacts with gradually acquired habits, or is development discontinuous, with definite maturational *stages,* as implied in the psychoanalytic the-

[4] Note in this connection the remarks in Chapter 3, p. 83-84.

ory of psychosexual development or as in Erikson's theory of psychosocial crises?

4. To what extent is the continuity of personality maintained by the stability of social structure (role positions) rather than by continuities within the individual habit structure? This is the main issue between learning theories and role theories.

5. How, in a developmental theory, can personality best be appraised? The *case history* appears to be called for; but if this is constructed from a retrospective interview, it may be inaccurate. Perhaps present behavior can be sampled; but in that case our *measurements* conform to other theories, even though our *explanations* may take developmental forms.

Theories of Personality Dynamics

Because we seek a characterization of the enduring aspects of personality, we are led to characterizations according to types or traits, or personality structures of one kind or another as a result of developmental history. There is another way of looking at personality, however, and that is according to various strands that are in unstable equilibrium, so that present behavior is a result of the interplay of various dispositions, often in conflict; these conflicts always take place in the present, no matter what their origins in the past may have been, so that theories of *personality dynamics*—the theories concerned with these present conflicts—are inevitably *interactive* theories rather than developmental ones. This causes something of a problem, because many theories that are from one point of view developmental are from another point of view concerned with personality dynamics; this is certainly true of psychoanalysis and of learning theories. In any case, we need to consider those aspects of several theories that address themselves to personality dynamics.

Psychoanalysis as a theory of personality dynamics

We have already considered psychoanalysis as a developmental theory, concerned with the historical origins of personality. It is also a theory of personality dynamics, concerned as well with features of contemporary personality organization and action.

As one way of approaching the problems of conflicting tendencies within the individual, Freud (1927) introduced the concepts of the *id, ego,* and *superego.* While each of these portions of the personality has its own developmental history, we are here concerned with the interactions that take place in the adult personality. The *id* is the depository of the innate instinctual drives (sexual, aggressive), which in their bald form seek immediate expression when aroused. If unbridled, the id would always seek immediate gratification of primitive, irrational, pleasure-seeking impulses. The id is manifested at an early stage of development, but it is not outgrown; we are all our lives to some extent creatures of impulse, and it is this irrational, impulsive part of ourselves that is used to infer the id as an "institution" or "structure" of the personality. Classical psychoanalytic theory saw the *ego* as developing later out of the id, but modern ego theory within psychoanalysis postulates a primitive ego alongside a primitive id; in any case, the more fully developed ego, as the part of the personality responsible for controlling behavior in socially approved ways, comes into play later in life. The desire for immediate pleasure must be held in check; a long route may be necessary before the pleasure can be obtained in a proper manner. With maturity, the ego rules the id, but there are conflicts between them, and occasionally the id has its way. In dreams, for example, when the ego is relaxed, wish-fulfillment (an id function) may hold sway, and rational controls may be abdicated. The ego thus represents our ordinary social self, going about the work of the world, being realistic and as rational as possible, being in general congenial with other people, and accepting the social roles that are prescribed. If the id is in the service of the "pleasure principle" (implying immediate gratification), the ego is subservient to the "reality principle" (implying postponed gratification). The third portion of the personality, the *superego,* develops out of the ego's experiences with social reality. The inferred superego is most nearly synonymous with *conscience.* It keeps us working according to an ideal of the self arising in early childhood, especially through parental prohibitions.

From the point of view of a dynamic interpretation of personality, the key concept here is that these three inferred parts of the personality are often at odds: the ego postpones the gratifications which the id wants right away; the superego wars with both the id and the ego, because they fall short of the moral code that it represents. There is some danger in thinking of these three inferred parts of the personality as three warring persons within the individual, but the threefold classification, if not overdone, usefully calls attention to discordant trends commonly found within the same person.[5]

If the classification into id, ego, and superego is to become the basis for a personality theory that takes into account individual differences, then many more differentiations have to be made. In recent psychoanalytic writings (Hartmann, 1958; Rapaport, 1959), more of these differentiations have been made in regard to the ego than to the other portions of the personality, although there must be variations in the strength of id impulses as well, and the superego is sometimes characterized as more or less harsh. The system really calls for a separate assessment of each of the three

[5] Cattell believes that he has arrived through factor analysis of motivation at factors representing id, ego, and superego (1957, pp. 457-61), but he has taken such liberties in assigning these correspondences that little support is given in fact to the psychoanalytic classification.

parts (id, ego, and superego), with some consideration of their interactions.

One reason that such an obvious translation from theory to personality measurement has not been made is that other concepts are very important and do not fit the threefold scheme very well. Anxiety, for example, is a pervasive motivating factor; while it is the ego that takes on the problem of controlling anxiety, anxiety may arise when the ego recognizes the intrusion of the id, or when the superego catches the ego at some sort of social improvisation unacceptable to the superego. Hence a study of the id, ego, and superego in isolation would not get us very far. The so-called defense mechanisms, which we shall examine in the next chapter (Chapter 18), are also considered ego functions, but they have many aspects that involve a complex interplay with id and superego.

The efforts at personality appraisal following from the psychoanalytic interpretation of personality dynamics include the interpretations of projective tests (Shafer, 1954; Holt and Havel, 1960); the tests based on needs (Edwards, 1954); a number of tests of ego strength (e.g., Block and Thomas, 1955); and tests and experiments based on the concept of ego defense (e.g., Blum, 1954; Klein, 1954). What is lacking is something that fits Cattell's ideal of the whole "personality sphere." Many sensible things can be said about personality from the point of view of Freudian theory, yet it is not clear just what sort of summary characterization of a person would be the appropriate outcome of an assessment of his personality dynamics. This is a promising field for further research.

Learning theory and role theory in relation to personality dynamics

Conflict also has its place in learning theories and role theories of personality, although in these theories the arena of conflict is not defined by the id, ego, and superego. In learning theory, the structural units are habits and drives, any of which may come into conflict with any other; in role theory, the demands of the various positions that an individual holds may produce conflicts in his role behaviors appropriate to these roles. The conflicts provide learning experiences out of which new habits and new role behaviors emerge. Since conflict is discussed in terms of habits in the next chapter, further consideration will be omitted at this point.

Lewin's field theory

Another approach to personality dynamics, one which also emphasizes what is contemporary rather than what is historical, is the *field theory* associated with the name of Kurt Lewin (Lewin, 1935, 1936). The word "field" (see p. 20) derives from the concept of a force field in physics, in which the behavior of a part within a field is influenced by the total field in which that part is embedded. Lewin, on theoretical grounds, was critical of what he called "class" concepts, which tend to assign characteristics on the basis of the class to which something belongs; these he thought to be a hangover from "Aristotelian" thinking, according to which an object fell rapidly because it belonged to the class "heavy." This he contrasted with "Galilean" thinking, which considered the forces acting upon the object rather than its intrinsic properties. To Lewin, explaining a person's behavior in terms of his "traits" was an example of fallacious "class" thinking; he preferred to study the situation in which the person was embedded.

The momentary situation in which a person finds himself is to Lewin his *life-space,* which is the psychological representation of the individual's environment and the alternatives open to him. The person is sometimes conceived of as a point that moves about in the life-space and is acted upon by the forces operating there. Thus the person is repelled by disliked tasks, attracted by preferred ones, meets barriers, circumvents them, and so on. All these statements refer

17-3

Lewin's representation of the person

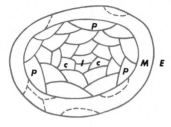

The motor and perceptual regions (M) are in contact with the environment (E), but they are in turn controlled by the underlying personality structure, shown as regions and boundaries. The more peripheral parts (p) cover the more central layers (c), and at the center lies the inner personal region (I). (After Lewin, 1936)

to "locomotions" in life-space, whether or not the solutions of the person's problems take place in thought or in action.

But the person also has a structure, so that what is seen from one point of view as a point moving about in life-space can also be given a geometrical representation of its own (Figure 17-3). In this representation the motor and perceptual regions that interact with the environment are shown at the surface, and the "inner personal region" lies within, divided into the more peripheral parts and the more central parts that are deeply buried. Personality development over time has to do with the *differentiation* or "de-differentiation" of the part regions within the whole. The regions represented in a Lewin personality diagram are interconnected across *boundaries* that vary in the degree to which they are *rigid* or *permeable*. With greater differentiation the boundaries are less permeable, permitting the insulation of one part from another. The personality of the child is little differentiated; that is, the child fails to distinguish very clearly between himself and the environment, and in addition the various regions within his own personality are not as complex as they will be when he grows older. The process of differentiation produces the more complex personality organization that we generally speak of as the personality structure.

Although Lewin's theory is a variant of Gestalt psychology, which tends to emphasize unity and wholeness, Lewin made it clear that in the differentiated personality of the adult there are a number of "tension systems" relatively isolated from each other. These systems have, however, a measure of interdependence, so that energy can flow from one tension system to another; under extreme stress the tension systems are no longer isolated, energy levels become equated, and there is a de-differentiation to the more primitive organization of the younger child.

A dynamic theory such as Lewin's which lays major emphasis upon the present very naturally becomes concerned with problems of conflict and conflict resolution, for these are the ways in which contemporary personality problems manifest themselves. We shall consider his approach to these problems later (Chapter 18).

One can ask of Lewin's theory the same question one asks of psychoanalysis: How is the individual to be characterized according to the theory? If class concepts are to be avoided (so that the individual cannot be assigned traits), are there dispositional concepts that can be used to characterize him? Those who have followed in Lewin's footsteps have done little to convert the theory into a way of appraising personality, although some steps have been made in recognizing the problem of personality rigidity, arising from barriers that are too firm (Kounin, 1941; Rokeach, 1960), and in emphasizing the importance of the total surroundings (ecology) and social interaction in understanding the individual (Barker and Wright, 1954).

Estimate of theories of personality dynamics in relation to developmental theories

Theories of personality dynamics attempt to deal with the present manifestations of

17-4

Relationships studied in developmental theories and in theories of personality dynamics (interactive theories)

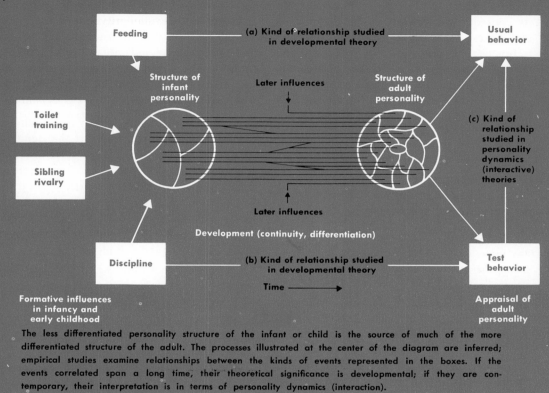

The less differentiated personality structure of the infant or child is the source of much of the more differentiated structure of the adult. The processes illustrated at the center of the diagram are inferred; empirical studies examine relationships between the kinds of events represented in the boxes. If the events correlated span a long time, their theoretical significance is developmental; if they are contemporary, their interpretation is in terms of personality dynamics (interaction).

the results of development in a manner which gives due attention to the different strands of development, recognizes the multiple demands upon the individual, and allows for the fact that personality reveals itself in the interactions among people. The relationship between a developmental theory and a theory of personality dynamics can be conceived of as in Figure 17-4. The central portion of the diagram represents the theories; the outer portion (the boxes and their interconnections) represents the kinds of measurements the theories require. The *developmental* theory stresses the lines of influence from the early years to the later ones, postulating significant continuities, modified to be sure by maturation and new

learning. These developmental continuities can be studied by correlational techniques, in which early influences (such as feeding, toilet training, sibling rivalry, parental discipline) are related to later behavior, either in the usual environment (as indicated by relationship (a) between feeding and typical adult behavior), or in special test situations (as shown in the relationship (b) between a formative influence and a later test). To explain such relationships the course of development is *inferred;* that is why we call it a *theory* of development.

The theory of *personality dynamics* deals with the same set of facts in another way. It is concerned with an inference to the personality structure as it exists at a given time, as, for example, in the circles representing the infant personality structure and the adult personality structure. Consider the adult personality structure. It cannot be studied directly but has to be *inferred* from its consequences, shown in the diagram as two boxes at the right: usual behavior, as a function of ordinary life situations, and special examples of behavior elicited by tests. The kind of relationship commonly studied is that in which behavior in ordinary life situations is predicted from test scores, relationship (c) in the diagram. *If* this prediction is satisfactory, and *if* the test has been constructed in terms of some sort of theory of personality structure, then (and only then) can useful statements be made about the individual's inferred personality structure. In this manner a theory of personality dynamics makes use of personality data.

If one accepts the analysis portrayed in Figure 17-4, it is evident that there is no conflict between developmental theories and theories of personality dynamics. It is understandable that theories such as those of psychoanalysis, learning, and role behavior are almost necessarily concerned both with development and dynamics; a theory such as Lewin's, which tries to be dynamic only, necessarily has its developmental overtones.

There is room for many individual variations of theories stressing developmental and dynamic aspects of personality, but it appears plausible that an advanced personality theory will find some way of eventually combining both aspects into an over-all theory.

Characterizing the Individual: The Personality Syndrome

Having considered a number of theoretical approaches to personality, none of which has provided a generally accepted position, we are led to a provisional way of characterizing the individual according to the *personality syndrome*. The word *syndrome* as used in relation to disease means a set of symptoms commonly found together when a person suffers from that disease; as used in relation to personality, it means a coherent pattern of trait organization. Such a trait organization must be sufficiently integrated to reveal a basic similarity among those who fit the pattern, yet it must permit of a wide variation among individual traits. We may consider the syndrome in relation to the four theories that have been treated (type, trait, developmental, and personality dynamics).

Type theory. A type theory is a syndrome theory, but of an extreme sort that tends to overstate the case for the common traits of those who fit the type. Thus the assertion that one belongs to a type carries with it the implication that the individual has essentially all the traits that characterize that type; a syndrome interpretation allows much more room for individual variation.

Trait theory. The only objection to a trait theory is that it does not carry within itself any theory of trait organization. Allport's notion of a hierarchical structure comes close to a syndrome, but it is not the same because the structure is characteristic merely of one individual; a syndrome must characterize more than one person. Common source traits, in Cattell's scheme, might very well lead to personality syndromes, even though the surface traits differ widely.

Developmental theory. The psychoanalytic theory of development has led to what are essentially prototypes of the personality syndrome in such groupings of traits as those found in the anal character or in the authoritarian personality. Here common childhood experiences, deviating somewhat from the norms for the culture, produce somewhat similar personality characteristics in different people. The cultural patterns by which one nonliterate group of people differs in predictable ways from another, in the Whiting-Child learning analysis, are another illustration of the syndrome type of thinking about personality.

Theories of personality dynamics. One approach to personality syndromes, influenced by the psychoanalytic theory of personality dynamics, is that of *cognitive styles* (Klein, 1958). In this approach, contrasts are drawn between those who deal with the environment in a more rigid and narrow way and those who are more flexible in their perception of the environment—the more constricted person attending, so to speak, to one thing at a time, while the more flexible one "scans" the environment (Klein, 1954). In a related vein, some individuals tend to exaggerate contrasts that they perceive in the environment, and so are labeled "sensitizers," while others minimize perceived differences, and are called "levelers" (Gardner, 1959). These individual styles are essentially dynamic syndromes, but not full-blown personality types because they do not characterize all aspects of personality.

Three comments are appropriate here:

1. The usefulness of the notion of a personality syndrome is not lost if the syndrome explains only some personality manifestations, leaving others unexplained. Anything that simplifies the understanding of a person can be of service, even though it does not lead to an *exhaustive* understanding.

2. A full development of the idea of the personality syndrome would find some place for everyone; at the present time the idea is useful chiefly for a few people who can be characterized by their symptoms of disturbance (as in the case of profiles derived from the MMPI), and for a few who fit such personality syndromes as the compulsive personality or the authoritarian personality. How well syndromes such as cognitive styles will fit the population generally remains to be determined. While the syndrome is thus a conceivably satisfactory way of describing a personality, there does not exist at present any kind of syndrome analysis that finds room for everyone.

3. The somewhat limited description implied in the personality syndrome (in contrast to a type) is consistent with the observation that personality is not in fact completely unified. For some people the personality structure may have greater unity and coherence than for others, but most people can at times adopt different roles and behave very differently in them. The search for some ordering structure within an individual personality must not blind us to the possibility of some personality manifestations that are fragmented and quite independent of the main theme, whatever that may be. A few cases of *multiple personality* dramatize the possibility of substructures within the total personality. We turn now to one such case.

Multiple personality

An extreme case testing the notion of the personality syndrome is that in which several such syndromes exist at once in the same person, so that the individual at one time behaves in accordance with one integrated behavior pattern, at other times in accordance with another. To the classical cases in the literature (e.g., Prince, 1906, Franz, 1933), there has recently been added the case of Eve White, with her alternate personalities known as Eve Black and Jane (Thigpen and Cleckley, 1954, 1957; Lancaster, 1958).

Eve White was a serious-minded and conscientious young mother who came to a therapist for treatment of severe headaches. In the midst of one of her interviews, in which with considerable agitation she reported that she had occasionally been hearing hallucinatory "voices," she suddenly underwent a striking personality change, and became a youthful, buoyant, flirtatious personality who called herself Eve Black. The personality Eve Black was completely aware of the thoughts and activities of Eve White, but Eve White did not even suspect Eve Black's existence, until they became "acquainted" in the therapist's office. Later on a third personality emerged, a more mature one who called herself Jane. The

Eve White and Eve Black personalities had apparently been coexisting since early childhood, when Eve Black would get Eve White into trouble, only to withdraw, with Eve White denying everything and suffering more extreme punishment because she denied what Eve Black had caused her (unknowingly) to do. Some of these childhood incidents were substantiated by interviews with her parents. Recently Eve Black had gone on a clothes-buying spree, and had then hidden the clothes at home. When the irate husband reprimanded Eve White, she could only deny that she had purchased the clothes, and she escaped her husband's further anger by her eagerness to take the clothes back to the store in order to replenish their bank account.

The major differences between Eve White and Eve Black have been summarized as follows:

Eve White	Eve Black
Demure, retiring, in some respects almost saintly.	Obviously a party girl. Shrewd, childishly vain, and egocentric.
Face suggests a quiet sweetness; the expression in repose is predominantly one of contained sadness.	Face is pixie-like; eyes dance with mischief as if Puck peered through the pupils.
Voice always softly modulated, always influenced by a specifically feminine restraint.	Voice a little coarsened, "discultured," with echoes or implications of mirth or teasing.
An industrious and able worker; also a competent housekeeper and a skillful cook. Not colorful or glamorous. Limited in spontaneity.	A devotee of pranks. Her repeated irresponsibilities have cruel results on others. More heedless and unthinking, however, than deeply malicious.
Almost all who know her express admiration and affection for her. She does not provoke envy. Her strength of character is more passive than active. Steadfast on defense but lacking initiative and boldness to formulate strategy of attack.	Is immediately amusing and likeable. Meets the little details of experience with a relish that is catching. Strangely "secure from the contagion of the world's slow stain," and from inner aspects of grief and tragedy.[6]

[6] Quoted, but with some abbreviation, from Thigpen and Cleckley (1954), pp. 141-42.

The distinctiveness of the personalities of Eve White and of Eve Black shows up on projective tests, on electroencephalograms, and in handwriting as studied by experts. A "blind analysis" made from the case material by other workers (Osgood and Luria, 1954) by means of the semantic differential method (Chapter 12) also shows distinctive personalities and gives some cues as to the role diffusions involved. It is fairly evident that Eve White's primary identification is with her mother, who had trouble with her husband when Eve was young, just as Eve now is having trouble with her husband. Eve Black's identification appears to be with her father; it is to be regretted that we do not know more about him. Those who studied the case find no good explanation for Jane. A possibility is that she represents the grandmother with whom Eve lived after her mother was separated from her father and went to earn a living in a distant city. In any case we appear to have here a case of extreme disparity of childhood *identifications* which prevent the achievement of a single *identity* for the various aspects of the one individual (see p. 450).

What can we learn from a case of this kind? First of all, we should hesitate to make any effort to correlate personality strictly with the body, for here we have the quite discordant possibilities of an Eve White or an Eve Black in the same physique. Secondly, we see that the recognizable unity of an individual personality (the personality syndrome) is based solely on its behavioral characteristics, for with the same body, the same physical and social history, personalities as different, yet as individually consistent, as Eve White and Eve Black emerge. Thirdly, what we find here dramatized is also true to a lesser extent of the normal person—that the typical personality integrates a number of strands which at different times and under different occasions may cause us to behave in ways that seem very different, and yet reflect certain basic personality needs. The unity of personality is at best precarious.

Study well

The Self in Contemporary Personality Theory

Because of some philosophical problems connected with the concept of the self, psychology long managed without any such concept. More recently, however, in recognition of the need for some kind of unifying principle or ground for personality, the concept of the self has been coming back into psychology.

Although the terms of the discussion are not yet fully agreed on, many psychologists accept a distinction between two aspects of the self—one inferred by an external observer, one of which the subject himself is aware. The *inferred self,* that is, the personality structure that represents the core of decision-making, planning, and defensiveness, can be understood by an external observer (who may detect unconscious features of which the individual is unaware). This aspect of the self is commonly called the *ego,* the term being borrowed from Freud, though not adhering precisely to the Freudian definition. The ego is, then, a construction from behavior, an inference that can be made by competent and informed observers. The word *self* can then be reserved for the self of which the subject is aware (sometimes called the *phenomenal self*), the self of self-perception.

Self-perception

A newborn child makes no distinction between himself and things outside himself. Self-perception is an achievement that comes through growth and experience. In time the child learns that his fingers are tied onto his body as his clothes are not; he learns that there are other people who treat him in special ways and whom he can influence. He learns to stand off and take a look at himself, to see his behavior in relation to others. The result is the complex awareness of self. Four aspects of self-awareness are worth noting.

Perceiving the self as an agent. We feel responsible for our acts; we pride ourselves on our achievements and blame ourselves for our failures. This feeling of responsibility implies an active someone who does things, an actor behind the activity. Because we tend to think primarily in concrete terms, we often identify this agent with our bodies. The body enters self-awareness because it is sensitive (the pains of the body are *my* pains) and because it is able to do things (it is *I* who chop the wood). Threats to the body are threats to me. But I and my body are not quite one and the same; in one sense the body belongs to me and as an agent I make use of it. The feeling of effort, that I have to force my body to do what I wish it to do, gives a subjective basis for the distinction between my body and me. One source of self-awareness is, then, the feeling of the self as in control of the body, as something that receives impressions and manages the body's affairs.

Perceiving the self as continuous. To the external observer the continuity of the bodily organism suffices to make John the same person today that he was yesterday. But to John himself his identity is maintained by his memories—continuous memories dated in his personal past. Multiple personalities (as in the Eve White case) persist only because some of the memories are not available.

The perception of the self as continuous makes possible a reflective self-evaluation that carries the burdens of the past into the present and projects them into the future. One becomes especially aware of self in uncertainties about the self, in doubts and self-criticism. The continuity of the self makes the self an object of permanent concern for the individual.

Perceiving the self in relation to other people. Just as the personality is largely the result of interpersonal relations, of social interaction with other people, so, too, self-perception is importantly influenced by other people. That is, our self-perceptions are formed largely by the acceptances and rejections of other people, although we may in self-defense deny what they see in us. Good mental health requires that our self-perceptions do in fact correspond in general to the perceptions others have of us; distortion of self-appraisal and of self-evaluation is always found in mental illness.

Perceiving the self as the embodiment of values and goals. Consider what we mean by ambition, jealousy, vanity, prestige, shame, guilt. Self-regard looms large in all of these. Detach them from a perception of the self, and the words have no meaning for the individual. A system of values and attitudes is built up around situations that have goal character, that can stir up feelings of self-enhancement or self-degradation. An *ideal self* (the self I would wish to become) is developed, and a person judges his actual conduct against this ideal. The ideal and the judgments combine to give self-perception a central place in social motivation. There are those who believe the maintenance and enhancement of the self to be the central feature of social motivation (Combs and Snygg, 1959). The self is assuredly an object of primary value to us. Because we perceive the self as an object of value, its successes and failures are important to us.[7]

Measuring self-perception

The self as perceived by the person is a subjective experience, and yet it is not wholly inaccessible to objective study. The personality inventory, previously described, rests on self-ratings, and can be interpreted as one kind of report on self-perception. As ordinarily used, however, the personality inventory is scored against norms obtained from a larger population, and thus loses something of individual uniqueness.

Another promising method for the study of self-perception is finding increasing use. The method, known as the *Q-technique* (Stephenson, 1953), is like the personality inventories in that it depends on statements that the person accepts as applicable or inapplicable to him, but there the similarity ends. The subject, under instructions, sorts a large number of statements, perhaps 100, into a number of piles, so that the statements form a distribution from the few least applicable to him to the ones most applicable. The middle piles, which will be the largest, will contain the statements of ambiguous applicability ("sometimes yes, sometimes no"; "can't say"). Now each statement can be given a score according to the pile in which it is found. The subject is then asked to sort the same statements under different instructions. For example, he can sort statements bearing on introversion and extroversion as they apply to him in different kinds of social situations. "Consider yourself at a formal dinner where the guest of honor is a distinguished musician." "Consider yourself on a picnic with a few of your best friends." "Consider yourself in a committee meeting of a group of experts in a field in which you, too, are an expert." Each statement gets a score for each condition. These scores can be correlated for any two conditions, and the results factor-analyzed or treated by other appropriate statistical methods of analysis. What can be learned from such analyses? It is possible to determine which are the most persistent traits as perceived by the individual, and how they cluster. Some statements will be found to vary more than others in their applicability; that is, a person does not find himself equally introverted or extroverted in all social groups: he may be the life of the party among his intimates, but easily cowed in the presence of strangers (Stephenson,

---

[7] The concept of the self is a difficult one, and not yet fully assimilated within contemporary psychology (e.g., Lowe, 1961).

1939). By the use of this method the inter-personal nature of traits is kept in the fore-ground.

Another aspect of self-perception holding considerable promise has to do with studies of body image (Fisher and Cleveland, 1958), as earlier mentioned in connection with the Rorschach test (p. 461). The way in which one's own body is perceived gives hints as to one's self-concept.

Self-perception and self-evaluation are likely to have an increasing place in the psychology of personality. The individual as a planner and decision-maker, who knows what he is about and how he feels, is too important to ignore.

SUMMARY   1. The tendency to group personalities into a few *types* is a very old one. Some theories stress *body types,* others stress *physiology* (body chemistry and endocrine balance), some are based solely on *behavior* (for example, Jung's classification into introverts and extroverts). Such evidence as exists tends to refute type theories; objective measures of temperament and personality show little relation to Sheldon's body types, and other measures tend to fall into normal distributions rather than into the bimodal distributions that type theories suggest.

2. Allport's theory of personal dispositions is a kind of trait theory that he sets against the notion of common traits shared by all people. He prefers to emphasize the inner organization of motives, traits, and personal styles, thus stressing patterned individuality. Within the individual there is a hierarchy of traits (or dispositions) from *cardinal* through *central* to *secondary* traits. A short list of central dispositions often suffices to describe an individual; the listed dispositions vary from person to person and are not common traits.

3. Cattell bases his trait theory on common traits, holding that sufficient uniqueness can be indicated through combinations of common traits present at different strengths. He distinguishes between *surface traits,* grouped together through cluster analysis (because they all correlate together), and *source traits,* arrived at through factor analysis. The hope is that a limited number of source traits might suffice to be used in the satisfactory appraisal of all personalities, but that day has not yet arrived.

4. The trait principle is an essential starting point for an empirically grounded theory of personality, whatever the nature of that theory, but a *trait profile* is an insufficient characterization of an individual. Some kind of meaningful organization of traits is essential in order to characterize the person in his interaction with the strains of the environment.

5. *Developmental theories* stress the origins of personality in early life, and the continuities of development as growth proceeds.

6. *Psychoanalytic theory* stresses stages in development, called *psychosexual stages* in the classical theory (oral, anal, phallic-Oedipal, latency, genital). Erikson has added *psychosocial crises* as a recognition of the environmental influences at each stage. The significance for personality development is that throughout life there are residues from each of these

stages, especially through *fixation* (arrested development at one or another stage) or *displacement* (one object of gratification substituting for another). Two adult personality structures are representative: the *compulsive* and the *authoritarian* personality.

7. *Learning theories* also recognize the continuities in development, but emphasize the formation of *habits* which are then generalized to new situations.

8. *Role theory* is also a developmental theory, in that *role behavior* has to be acquired appropriate to the *role positions* that are ready-made for the individual, or which he chooses. The stability of personality structure is determined by the stability of social structure as well as by the stability of the individual's system of habits.

9. Theories of *personality dynamics* are concerned with contemporary manifestations of personality in interaction with the physical and social environment, particularly as *conflicts* arise because of discordant trends within the personality, or habit conflicts, or role conflicts.

10. The *psychoanalytic* theory of personality dynamics is given order by the concepts of *id, ego,* and *superego* as the persistent features of the personality that enter into conflict. The id is irrational and impulsive, seeking immediate gratification; the ego postpones gratification, so that it can be achieved realistically and in socially approved ways; the superego ("conscience") imposes a moral code.

11. Lewin's *field theory* describes personality as *regions,* with *boundaries* and *tension systems.* The adult personality is more highly *differentiated* than that of the infant or child; this means that some systems are insulated from each other, and energy does not move easily from one to the other. Often, under stress, the boundaries may be weakened, energy moves more freely, tensions are equalized, and *de-differentiation* results.

12. None of the present theories of personality dynamics has succeeded in formulating a way in which to characterize all personalities according to some common scheme, although the possibility of such a formulation clearly exists.

13. The *personality syndrome* appears to be the most hopeful way of characterizing all individuals according to some common plan, although at present syndromes can be specified only for *some* individuals. A syndrome is a pattern of traits (preferably source traits, in Cattell's sense) which arise through common experiences, so that a number of personalities can be described as similar according to this pattern. Such a syndrome can be useful even though it does not describe a person completely. The syndrome has the advantage over a type in that it does not assert too much; it has the advantage over unsystematic trait theories in that it seeks for a meaningful patterning of traits. It is coherent with developmental approaches and with theories of personality dynamics.

14. The concept of a personality syndrome is clarified by *multiple personalities,* in which several syndromes appear in alternation in the same individual.

15. The concept of the *self* is increasingly being accepted in contemporary psychology, after having long been denied a place. In general, the word *ego* is used for the *inferred* structure of the central core of personality (an inference that can be made by an external observer), while the word *self* is used for the self of awareness, the *phenomenal self,* the self of self-perception. The self so defined is perceived as an agent, as continuous, as reflected by relations with other people, and as the embodiment of goals and values. Methods of measuring self-perception are being developed.

SUGGESTIONS FOR FURTHER READING The best single source on personality theories is the book by Hall and Lindzey, *Theories of personality* (1957), in which a dozen theories are systematically but sympathetically set forth, with temperate criticisms. See also David and von Bracken, *Perspectives in personality theory* (1957) for the views of a number of contemporary American and European psychologists.

There are a number of textbooks of personality, of which a good representative is Stagner, *Psychology of personality* (3rd Ed., 1961). Books with interesting flavors of their own are Leeper and Madison, *Toward understanding human personalities* (1959), McCurdy, *The personal world: an introduction to the study of personality* (1961), and Dalton, *Personality and social interaction* (1961).

An introduction to Allport's theory is his small book, *Becoming* (1955), also available in a paperback edition. Some of his papers have recently been collected in Allport, *Personality and social encounter* (1960); the major statement of his present position is now Allport, *Pattern and growth in personality* (1961).

Cattell, *Personality and motivation structure and measurement* (1957) is a big book devoted largely to his own researches and theories; a convenient shorter introduction can be found in his chapter in Lindzey (Ed.), *Assessment of human motives* (1958), now available in a paperback edition. Guilford, *Personality* (1959) gives an excellent review of personality dimensions, especially those arrived at by factor analysis, which allows his summaries to be compared with those of Cattell.

There is an abundant literature on psychoanalysis, much of it available in paperback. A very useful introduction to the personality theory is Hall, *A primer of Freudian psychology* (1954), available as a paperback; a good selection from Freud's own writings, with an appendix on anxiety and a glossary of psychoanalytic terms, is Rickman (Ed.), *A general selection from the works of Sigmund Freud* (1957), also paperbound.

The best single treatment of learning theory and personality is Dollard and Miller, *Personality and psychotherapy* (1950); role theory is emphasized in Newcomb, *Social psychology* (1950).

Conflict,
Adjustment,
and
Mental Health

We have completed a survey of the growth processes from infancy through
adulthood and have considered the major topics of general psychology,
culminating in the characterization of the individual personality. Now we are
prepared to see what happens when the individual is placed under stress
through conflict and frustration. When the ordinary methods of adjusting to the
problems that arise are not adequate, we face threats to mental health and so
become interested in psychotherapy and other methods of readjustment.

CHAPTER 18

Conflict and Adjustment

The circumstances of life inevitably place the personality under strain, even though we have many resources for coping with our problems. Our motives are not always easily satisfied: there are obstacles to be overcome, deficiencies to be supplied, and choices to be made. Even when our wishes are realizable, there are often long delays before they are fulfilled, and such delays are thwarting; we are faced with conflict and frustration whenever our goal-seeking behavior is hampered by blocking and postponement. Frustrating situations vary from petty annoyances to major defeats and disappointments; it is especially in the face of helplessness and hopelessness that we feel the full impact of frustration.

The Nature of Frustration

A salesman has an appointment with a customer who does not like to be kept waiting. He is delayed by a telephone call and rushes out to his car to make a ten-second "getaway." He tries the starter several times, but the engine will not turn over. He swears loudly, jumps out of the car, and slams the door. We say that he is being frustrated. What do we mean by this?

A *frustrating event* is one in which goal-directed activity is blocked, slowed up, or otherwise interfered with. The salesman whose car will not start is in the midst of a frustrating event. His goal-seeking now takes a turn; there is a new problem—to start the car.

Psychologists and laymen sometimes use the word "frustration" to refer to a state instead of an event. That is, as a consequence of blocked goal-seeking, a man is confused, baffled, annoyed. If we were to ask him how he felt, he might say that he felt "angry and frustrated." His statement implies that frustration is a state of unpleasant emotion. But in this book we shall hold to the meaning of frustration as the *thwarting circumstances* rather than their consequences.

A frustrating or thwarting situation involves problems. A frustrating problem exists whenever goal-seeking behavior has been aroused but there exists some barrier to satisfaction. Such problems arise through *obstacles, deficiencies,* and *conflicts.*

Obstacles and deficiencies

Obstacles to drive satisfaction are present both in the physical and in the social environment. The physical world presents such obstacles as icy weather, rugged mountains, wide oceans, and arid deserts. Many obstacles to satisfaction are raised throughout life by other people or by the customs of social living. Children are thwarted by parental denials, disapprovals, and postponements. Larry has the tricycle that David wants to ride. Father won't let John drive the car until he is seventeen. Alice refuses to "go steady" with Bill. Jane, her parents insist, is not old enough to marry. The boss refuses to raise Jim's salary. The list could be extended endlessly.

Lack of something in the environment prevents need satisfaction quite as effectively as an obstacle. A drought can be as frustrating to a farmer as a blizzard. Something that is lacking has to be provided, just as a barrier has to be surmounted.

Many of the deficiencies found to be frustrating are those within the individual himself. Some people are handicapped by blindness, deafness, or paralysis. Not everyone who wants to can become a distinguished musician or painter or can pass the courses necessary to become an engineer, physician, or certified public accountant. If goals outside of one's ability are set, need satisfaction is prevented through such deficiency, and frustration occurs.

Conflicts

When we say that you cannot have your cake and eat it too, we are acknowledging the fact of conflict. In any individual there are always many motives active at a given time, and the goals to which they lead may be mutually exclusive. Often a student cannot be a major athlete and still earn the grades needed to enter medical school. Even when only one motive is involved, there may be various ways of approaching the goal; in such cases conflict arises at the point where the paths to the goal diverge. You can get an education at any one of a number of colleges, but you have to choose which to enter. Such a conflict situation is frustrating, because smooth-running activity toward the goal tends to be disrupted by the necessity for choice. One method of analysis describes conflicts as of three types: approach-approach, avoidance-avoidance, and approach-avoidance (Lewin, 1935). These are defined as requiring a choice between two (or more) positive incentives, between two negative incentives, or between two aspects of an incentive at once positive and negative.

The conflicts of real life often involve more than two alternatives; classifying the conflicts according to two alternatives is convenient but does not, of course, tell the whole story.

Approach-approach conflict

When a person has two or more desirable but mutually exclusive goals, he is temporarily torn between them. Two interesting classes may be scheduled for the same period. Two attractive positions may become available at the same time. A menu may offer a choice among equally attractive entrees. When such acceptable alternatives occur (all positive incentives), the choice is usually made promptly after a brief period of vacillation. The period of vacillation and indecision is increased, however, as the importance of the outcome is increased and as the alternative goals are made more nearly equal.

Nineteen boys, ages nine to eleven, participated in an experiment in which each was presented with pairs of liquids and asked to indicate which one of each pair he desired to drink. The liquids used were orange juice, tomato juice, water and lemon juice, vinegar, and a saturated solution of salt water. Some of these liquids are attractive, some are mildly repulsive; for the present purpose, however, we may view them as lying along a single dimension of degree of attractiveness. In the experiment each liquid was paired with every other liquid, with the names of the liquids accompanying them in an exposure apparatus. Each boy indicated his choice by moving a lever through an arc until a buzzer sounded; smaller movements were recorded on a tape but did not "count." That is, the boy was free to vacillate until he sounded the buzzer by an extreme movement to one side or the other. The record thus showed the time required for decision and provided a graphic record of conflict behavior. Each boy made both "real" and "hypothetical" choices. After a "real" choice, he drank the liquid; after a "hypothetical" choice, he did not drink it.

By summarizing each boy's choices, the experimenter could arrange the liquids in a preference series for each boy. The time for decision and the amount of vacillation could then be studied for pairs of liquids differing only slightly and for pairs differing more in preference value. The decision time decreased when the chosen items were farther apart in preference (Figure 18-1). Similarly, the amount of vacillation also decreased (Barker, 1942).

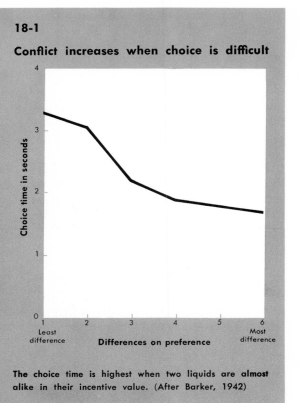

18-1

Conflict increases when choice is difficult

Choice time in seconds

4

3

2

1

0

1 — Least difference   2   3   4   5   6 — Most difference

Differences on preference

The choice time is highest when two liquids are almost alike in their incentive value. (After Barker, 1942)

Avoidance-avoidance conflict

Given a choice between two unattractive alternatives (both incentives negative), there is a strong tendency to escape the dilemma by doing something else. The child who is told to eat his spinach or go right to bed may play with his fork or stare out the window. If his choice is forced, he takes longer to decide and vacillates more than he would in choosing between two attractive alternatives.

The approach-approach and avoidance-avoidance conflicts differ in the choice behavior they call forth, depending upon changes in the attractiveness (or repugnance) of the goal as it is approached. The nearer one gets to a positive incentive, the stronger the approach reactions; the nearer one gets to a negative incentive, the stronger the avoidance reactions. When there are two attractive goal objects (an approach-ap-

proach conflict), starting toward one of them increases the tendency to go toward it, at the same time reducing the tendency to go to the other, so that a return to the state of indecision is unlikely. When there are two unattractive goal objects (an avoidance-avoidance conflict), starting toward one of them increases the tendency to withdraw and hence tends to force the individual back into indecision and vacillation. The spinach becomes more repugnant when it is on the fork than when it is on the plate, but the thought of bed keeps the child at the table.

Approach-avoidance conflict

Many incentives are at once desirable and undesirable, both positive and negative. The girl likes candy, but she does not want to get fat. Skiing is fun, but torn ligaments are not. The attitude toward a goal at once wanted and not wanted, liked and disliked, is called an *ambivalent* attitude. Ambivalent attitudes are very common (Figure 18-2). The child runs away from home to escape parental domination, only to come running back to receive parental protection; his attitude toward his parents is ambivalent. Another child enjoys school but looks forward to vacation; his attitude toward school is ambivalent. The approach-avoidance conflict is one of the most important for us to understand, for many of the conflicts of ordinary life are of this sort.

A person confronted by a goal object that is at once attractive and dangerous vacillates in his approach. The dangers seem less real when the goal is at a distance, so that the inviting character of the incentive leads to approach reactions. But the sense of danger increases as the goal is approached, so that nearer to the incentive one has a tendency to withdraw. This simultaneous tendency "to" and "from" leads to vacillation at some point near enough to the goal for one to be aware of the dangers, but distant enough to be safe from them. When a man is about to ask the boss for a raise, he is drawn near

18-2

A case of ambivalence

The boy wants both to approach the goose and to back away from it. Such an approach-avoidance conflict results in a great amount of vacillation, as the attractiveness of the object keeps the child in the region of conflict, while fear is enhanced as he gets closer.

Camera Clix

the boss's door by the possibility of success, but his anxiety about possible rebuff or even dismissal mounts as he approaches. The result may be several false starts before he either carries through his plan or abandons it.

We may illustrate by two experiments in which hungry rats were taught to run the length of an experimental alley to obtain food at a point made distinctive by the presence of a light. This training established approach reactions. Then the rats were given a brief electric shock while eating. The shock added avoidance tendencies to the approach tendencies and hence produced an approach-avoidance conflict, or ambivalence toward the food.

To test the resulting conflict behavior, the rats were placed at the start of the maze. The characteristic behavior corresponded to that predicted: the rat started in the direction of the food but came to a stop before

reaching it. The place of stopping could be experimentally controlled by modifying the strength of either hunger or shock (Brown, 1942; Miller, 1959).

The behavior of the rats in this experiment can be better understood and explained by using the concept of *gradients* of approach and avoidance. By a gradient we mean a change in the strength of a tendency as related to some other systematic change (in the experiment with the rats, a change of distance from the goal object). The pull of a magnet upon a piece of iron at a distance is an analogous (but simpler) gradient. The pull (or strength of the gradient) increases greatly as the distance between the piece of iron and the magnet is shortened.

The method for determining gradients was devised as follows. The rats wore a light harness so that the experimenter could restrain them briefly along the route. When they were restrained, the amount of pull on

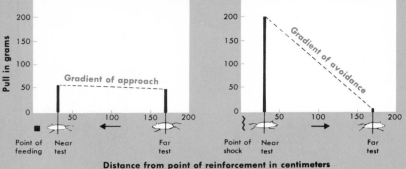

The strength of approach and avoidance is measured by the pull on the restraining harness. Note that the avoidance gradient (*right*) is steeper than the approach gradient (*left*). (After J. S. Brown, 1948)

the harness could be recorded in grams, thus providing a measure of the approach tendency. When restrained near the goal, the rats pulled harder than when restrained farther from the goal. This increase in pull is shown (see Figure 18-3, *left*) by the slight rise in the line representing the gradient of approach between the far and the near test.

Other rats received a brief electric shock at the end of the alley. When placed at that end of the alley, without shock, they tended to run away from the place where the shock had been received. When restrained nearer to the place of shock, the rats pulled away from the place of shock much harder than when restrained farther away from it. The difference between the test near shock and far from shock is shown in the gradient of avoidance (Figure 18-3, *right*).

Note also that the slope of the two lines differs; the line for avoidance is much steeper than the one for approach (Brown, 1948; Miller, 1959).

How do the results of this experiment on gradients of approach and avoidance help us understand the results of the experiment on ambivalence? If we examine the two plotted gradients, the one for approach (Figure 18-3, *left*) represents a pull on the harness to the left, the one for avoidance (Figure

18-3, *right*) represents a pull on the harness to the right. When a rat has been fed and shocked at the same point, both gradients are set up at once. If we imagine the two gradients superimposed, they would cross at a point between 100 and 150 centimeters from the goal. At this point the two opposing tendencies would exactly balance. If the lines represented the true reaction tendencies, the rat in the experiment on ambivalence would be expected to stop at the point where the lines cross, and this is approximately what happened. This point of intersection can be moved either to the right or to the left by changing the strengths of either the approach or the avoidance tendencies. The effect of increasing the shock is to raise the avoidance gradient, thus placing the point of intersection farther from the place of being shocked. These predictions could be made from the experiment on gradients and were confirmed in the experiment on ambivalence.

The two foregoing sets of experiments, taken together, illustrate four principles important in the understanding of ambivalent behavior.

1. The tendency to approach a positive incentive is stronger the nearer the subject is to it.

2. The tendency to go away from a negative incentive is stronger the nearer the subject is to it.
3. The strength of avoidance increases more rapidly with nearness than does that of approach. In other words, the avoidance gradient is steeper than the approach gradient.
4. The strength of the tendency to approach or to avoid varies with the strength of the drive upon which it is based. Increased drive tends to raise the height of the entire gradient of approach or avoidance (Miller, 1959).

In everyday human living the practical consequences of conflicts of the approach-avoidance type are very great. The third principle helps explain how a person is drawn back into an old conflict situation by his own tendencies. He follows the pull, because at a distance the positive aspects seem more inviting than the negative ones seem forbidding. The young swimmer who wants to show off as a diver is led by his positive wishes to climb to the high platform. As he climbs, however, he begins to realize that it is a long way down to the water. His fears mount, and he may suffer the humiliation of climbing down again. He need not have placed himself in the conflict, but at a distance the desire to dive took precedence over the fear. Such conflicts are characteristic of ambivalence. They are not resolved smoothly: even though the conflict situation is avoidable, the approach tendencies draw the individual back into the zone where the avoidance tendencies begin to mount. Everyone knows of couples who go steady, break up, make up again, only to break up once more. Away from each other, their mutual attraction takes precedence because negative feelings are reduced; close to each other, the negative feelings drive them apart. To an outsider it appears irrational that people who get along so poorly attempt reconciliation. Once the ambivalence of their attitudes is recognized, however, their attempts at reconciliation become understandable, even if not reasonable.

18-4

Measuring approach and avoidance gradients

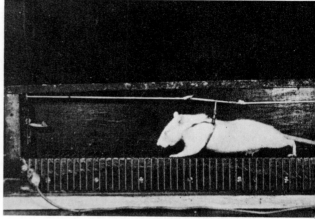

Dr. Neal E. Miller

The harness permits measurement of the amount of pull exerted by the rat, thereby yielding the results plotted in Fig. 18-3.

A person is often aware of his approach-avoidance conflicts and may see them as weakness or vacillation. He forbids himself the pleasure he yearns for; he feels "weak-willed" because he cannot refrain from doing the things he wishes to avoid. The resolution of these conflicts—whether the boy overcomes his fear and dives off the high board or backs down the ladder, whether the alcoholic remains on the wagon or returns to the bar—is a matter both of the individual's position on the approach-avoidance gradients and of the strengths of his other motives.

In addition, some complications result from the fact that the gradients of real life are usually multiple. Alcoholism is not a choice merely between the amount of liking for the taste of alcohol and the amount of dislike for the next morning's headache; the conflict can involve religious scruples, forgetting of troubles, losing of self-control, seeking of companionship, escaping responsibility. Sometimes an approach-avoidance conflict is resolved by refusing to select either alternative and becoming ill or in some other way evading the choice.

Another approach to the problem of conflict resolution has been proposed by economists who try to state the circumstances under which one item of goods is purchased in preference to another when there are limited amounts of money available and the purchaser is attracted to more than one item. For example, the purchaser may have to choose between buying a hamburger and going to the theater or buying a steak dinner and staying at home. The economist's solution recognizes that there are compromise outcomes and substitute goals (hamburger vs. sirloin steak) and that the choice is not just between eating and enjoying the theater. The prior discussion of conflict oversimplified the situation to make it appear that one goal or the other had to be chosen, and the only compromise was frustration (e.g., the rat vacillating along the path, getting neither food nor shock). While the principles of conflict resolution as discussed are valid, they represent an oversimplification, and the economist's solution in terms of some sort of compromise needs to be worked into psychological theories as well (Holzman, 1958).

If the psychologist were able to define an individual's unfulfilled motives as easily as his bank account is defined, the treatment of conflict would be simpler. Many individual choices require a commitment of large amounts of *time* (as in training for law or medicine) so that the choices are exclusive, at least for a number of years; thus available time acts in somewhat the same way as available money to force choices, and hence to produce conflict at the moment of choice. These choices are often among more than two alternatives (i.e., law and medicine are not the only careers open). Social institutions may force choices; in our culture one can have but one wife at a time, so that a single mate must be chosen from among many possible ones.

In addition to many possibilities for satisfying a single motive, choices often involve compromises among many considerations. In choosing a house, one has to consider price, immediate neighborhood, size, distance from work, and perhaps other factors; one may seldom find all of the considerations to be ideal. In choosing a college, one may consider its general reputation (if high, an approach factor), its tuition (if high, an avoidance factor), and a whole host of other aspects (location, social life, athletic emphasis, family tradition, etc.); and presumably more than one college could provide a perfectly acceptable compromise for a given individual.

Immediate Consequences of Frustration

Frustration has both immediate and remote consequences. When blocked in his goal-seeking, the individual may react immediately or may develop attitudes toward uncertainty or risk-taking that have more enduring consequences. We shall first turn to a consideration of some of the immediate consequences of frustration. These consequences might equally well be called *symptoms* or *signs* of frustration.

An experiment on the effects of frustration in young children illustrates several of its immediate consequences. The subjects were 30 young children, ages two to five—that is, of nursery school and kindergarten age. The experiment will be described in the present tense, as though we were observing it.

The children come one at a time into a room which contains several toys, parts of which are missing—a chair without a table, an ironing board but no iron, a telephone receiver without a transmitter, a boat and other water toys but no water. There are also papers and crayons. Some of the children set about playing eagerly and happily. They make up for the missing parts imaginatively. They use paper as water in which to sail a boat or they substitute their fist for the telephone transmitter.

Another group of children behave quite differently. Although they appear to be in the same general physical condition as the first group, and their clothes show that they come from similar social and economic backgrounds, something is the matter. They seem unable to play constructively, unable to fit the toys into meaningful and satisfying activities. They play roughly with the toys, occasionally jumping on one and breaking it. If they draw with the crayons, they scribble like younger children. They whine and nag at the adult present. One of them lies on the floor, stares at the ceiling, and recites nursery rhymes, paying no attention to anyone else.

What accounts for the differences in behavior of these two sets of youngsters? Is the second group suffering from some sort of emotional disturbance? Have some of these children been mistreated at home? Actually, the children in this second group are the same as those in the first group; they are simply in a later stage of the experiment. They are showing the symptoms of frustration—frustration that has been deliberately created in the following way.

After playing happily with the half-toys, as described earlier, the children had been given an added experience. An opaque screen had been removed, allowing them to see that they were in a larger room containing not only the half-toys but other toys much more elaborate and attractive. This part of the room has a table for the chair, a dial and bell for the telephone, a pond of real water for the boat. When we see the children so unhappy, in this later stage of the experiment, a chicken-wire screen has been placed between them and their happy hunting ground. They are denied the "whole" toys; they can use only the "part" ones. They are frustrated (Barker, Dembo, and Lewin, 1941).

Why was the half-toy situation satisfying the first time and frustrating the second? The answer is easy to find. Goal-seeking behavior was satisfied the first time, as the children played happily with the available toys; in the second stage they knew of the existence of the more attractive and satisfying toys, and so a new goal had been set up. The first day the goal was attainable; the second day, it was not. To play now with the half-toys is to be stopped short of a richer possible experience, and hence is frustrating.

This experiment illustrates a number of the immediate consequences of frustration. In discussing some of these consequences, we shall make reference to additional details of the experiment and draw further illustrations from related experiments and from the frustrating experiences of everyday life.

Restlessness and tension

In the toy experiment, one of the first evidences of frustration shown by the children was an excess of movement: fidgeting about and generally restless behavior. Drawings took the form of scribbling, because the muscles were tense and movements were thus jerky. This restlessness was associated with many actions indicating unhappiness: whimpering, sighing, complaining. Unhappy actions were recorded for only 7 of the 30 children in the free-play situation but for 22 of the same 30 in the frustrating situation.

An increase in tension and in the level of excitement also occurs when adults are blocked and thwarted. They blush or tremble or clench their fists. Children under tension fall back upon thumb sucking and nail biting; adults also turn to nail biting, as well as to smoking and gum chewing, as outlets for their restlessness.

Destructiveness

Closely related to increased tension and restless movements are the rage states that lead to destructiveness and hostile attacks. In the frustration experiment, kicking, knocking, breaking, and destroying were greatly increased following frustration. Only 5 children did any kicking or knocking in the original free-play situation, but 18 did so in frustration.

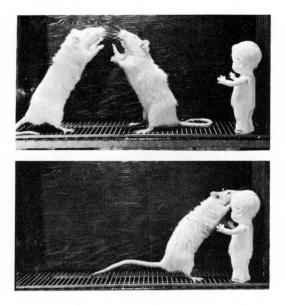

When the rat that has been the object of aggression is not present, the attacking rat displaces his aggression toward the doll. (From Miller, 1948a)

Direct Aggression. <u>Frustration often leads to aggression against the individual or object that is the source of the frustration.</u> In the experiment just described, direct attack on the barrier was not uncommon. In ordinary play situations, when one small child takes a toy from another child, the second is likely to attack the first in an attempt to regain the toy. The victim of a slighting remark usually replies in kind— though for many adults the aggression may be verbal rather than physical. The anger engendered when one is blocked tends to find expression in some kind of direct attack. Because the obstacle or barrier was the source of the blocking in the experiment, the children's first attempt at problem-solving was to get by the barrier or remove it. Aggression of this kind need not be hostile; it may be a learned way of solving a problem. When the obstacle is another person, the first tendency is to attack that person,

treating him as a barrier. But this may not be the only form in which frustration is met through aggression.

Displaced Aggression. Frequently the frustrated individual cannot satisfactorily express his aggression against the source of the frustration. Sometimes the source is vague and intangible. Then he does not know what to attack and yet feels angry and seeks *something* to attack. At other times the person responsible for the frustration is so powerful that to attack him would be dangerous. When circumstances block direct attack on the cause of frustration, the result is what we call "displaced aggression." Displaced aggression is an aggressive action against an innocent person or object rather than against the actual or intangible cause of the frustration. The man who is bawled out by his boss may come home and take out his unexpressed resentment on his wife or children. The tongue-lashing Bill gives his quiet freshman roommate may be related to the poor grade Bill received in the midterm quiz. The child who is not getting along well with his playmates may come home and pull the kitten's tail.

Displaced aggression can be demonstrated experimentally. One rat is taught to strike another by being rewarded for such aggression. An electric current gradually builds up in the grid on which he stands. When he strikes the other rat, the electricity is turned off and he escapes the shock. This rewards the aggressive behavior. When another rat is no longer present, the trained rat directs his aggressive behavior toward the "innocent bystander," a rubber doll previously ignored (Figure 18-5). Thus aggression is transferred from an inaccessible to an accessible object (Miller, 1948a).

There are many interesting problems connected with the processes of displacement. Just what kinds of objects will become attacked in displaced aggression? The more similar they are to the objects of direct aggressive attack, the more likely they are to be attacked. As brought out earlier in the text, when one stimulus is similar to another, the response to the second is said to *generalize* from the first. Thus in the experiment just described, the rubber doll looks more like a rat than do the walls of the compartment, so that when the second rat is absent, the doll is attacked. However, the displacement may come about in another way: when attack on the frustrating object is inhibited through punishment. Thus the child cannot retaliate against the parent who frustrates him. In that case he is likely to displace his aggression, but will he choose another adult, similar to his parent? He is now in a conflict situation, of the kind described earlier: he would like to attack the parent, but that satisfying response is prevented by his fear of punishment. If another adult resembles the parent too closely, the fear of punishment will be aroused by him also, and so the second adult is unlikely to become the object of attack. Some distance is needed; when displacement occurs because of fear of retaliation, the object of displaced aggression must not be *too* similar to the object of direct aggression. It is often easier to blame foreigners for our troubles than to blame our neighbors.

An experiment intended to help explain the choice of object in displaced aggression was performed by Miller and Kraeling (1952). The hypothesis was that displaced aggression was possible because the positive tendencies (to attack) would overcome the inhibiting tendencies (to withhold attack) provided the new stimulus was sufficiently *dissimilar* from the original object of aggression. Were this not the case, aggression restrained against the primary object would be restrained against the secondary one also. In this experiment, an approach-avoidance conflict set up in one situation (an alley-maze problem with rats) was tested later in the same alley and in two different alleys. The prediction was that the inhibiting tendencies would fall off more rapidly than the approach tendencies as the

Generalization of a conflict

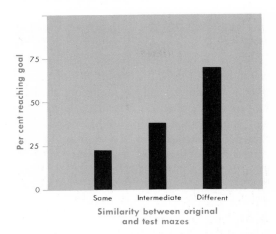

Because of the previously experienced conflict, the rat hesitates to approach the goal in the original maze; the more dissimilar the mazes, the less the old conflict is reinstated. (After Miller and Kraeling, 1952)

new situation became increasingly unlike the original one. The results confirmed the prediction, as shown in Figure 18-6. It is presumed, by analogy, that comparable relations hold for displaced aggression. That is, the new object must be something like the original object of aggression, but enough different so that the inhibitions against attack are overcome.

Apathy

One baffling feature of human behavior is the tendency for similar situations to lead to diametrically opposite behavior by different individuals. While a common response to frustration is active aggression, another response is its opposite—apathy, indifference, withdrawal, inactivity, inattentiveness. A study of fifth- and sixth-grade children showed that disturbed children were more hesitant in turning to direct aggression after frustration than the more "normal" children, that is, those with fewest "neurotic" symptoms (Zander, 1944).

When resistance is futile, the frustrated person may become sullen and detached instead of angry and defiant. Apathy often indicates that aggressive tendencies are being held in check or inhibited, but they may express themselves indirectly.

Fantasy

When problems become too much for us, we sometimes seek the "solution" of escape into a dream world, a solution through *fantasy* rather than on a realistic level. This was the solution of the child who lay on the floor reciting nursery rhymes in the frustration experiment (p. 504), and of other children in the experiment who crossed the barrier by talking about the whole toys on the other side. One little girl fished through the wire, imagining the floor on the other side to be the pond that was actually out of reach.

It will be recalled that one approach to the study of the achievement motive is through fantasy (p. 144). This suggests that the desired level of accomplishment is often not achieved and hence appears as an imagined success.

Unrealistic solutions are not limited to children. The pin-up girls in the soldiers' barracks symbolize a fantasy life that goes on when normal social life with women is frustrated. But experiments have also shown that men on a starvation diet lose their interest in women and instead hang on their walls pictures of prepared food cut from magazines (Guetzkow and Bowman, 1946).

Stereotypy

Another consequency of frustration is *stereotypy* in behavior, that is, a tendency to blind, repetitive, fixated behavior. Ordinary problem-solving requires flexibility, striking out in new directions when the original path to the goal is blocked. When repeated frustration baffles a person, especially if the frustration arises through punishment, some of this flexibility appears to be lost, and he stupidly makes the same effort again and again, though experience has shown its futility.

Stereotypy has been most carefully studied in rats, but parallels can be found in human behavior.

A white rat can be taught to jump to one of a pair of stimulus cards attached to windows by so arranging the cards that the rat finds food behind the positive card but is punished if he jumps to the negative card. The positive card may be one with a black circle on a white background, the negative one a white circle on a black background. The cards are so arranged that the rat knocks over the positive card when he hits it, opening the window that gives access to a platform where there is a food reward. If the rat jumps against the negative card, the card does not give way. Instead, the rat bumps against the card and falls into a net. By varying the positions of the cards, the experimenter can teach the rat to select the positive one and to jump consistently to it.

This discrimination experiment is converted into a frustration experiment by making the problem insoluble. That is, each of the two cards leads half the time to reward (positive reinforcement), half the time to punishment (negative reinforcement), regardless of its position at the left or the right. Hence, whichever choice the animal makes is "correct" only half the time. The result is that the rat, forced to jump, tends to form a stereotyped habit of jumping regularly to one side, either to the right or to the left, no longer paying attention to which card is exposed. The rat is still rewarded half the time and punished half the time after having adopted this stereotyped habit.

Once the stereotyped habit has been adopted, it is very resistant to change, so much so that it has been called an "abnormal fixation." For example, if the rat that has come to jump regularly to the right is now punished every time he jumps, he may continue to jump to the right for as many as 200 trials, even though the left window remains open as an easy and safe alternative. The behavior is so stereotyped that the alternative does not exist for the rat (Figure

18-7) (Maier, Glaser, and Klee, 1940; Maier, 1949).

Further studies must be made before we know just what analogies are permissible between human behavior and these experimental results. It is quite possible, though not proved, that some forms of persistent behavior, such as thumb-sucking in young children or stuttering, have become more firmly fixed (i.e., stereotyped) because punishment and repeated frustration in efforts to get rid of them have intensified the undesirable responses. The persistence of difficulties in arithmetic and reading and spelling among bright children (and some adults) may be explained in part as a consequence of errors similarly stereotyped by early frustration.

CRITICAL DISCUSSION

Controversy over stereotypy experiments

The experiments of Maier and his collaborators have been the source of some controversy. There are those (e.g., Wilcoxon, 1952) who believe that ordinary principles of reward and punishment in learning will account for the behavior of Maier's rats, without calling on any novel principle leading to stereotypy. Maier's students have attempted to answer this argument, however, insisting that something new does occur when punishment is frustrating (e.g., Ellen, 1956; also Maier, 1956).

We may remind ourselves of the related problem raised in connection with the socialization of aggression (p. 141). Why is aggressive behavior in children increased *both* by rewarding aggression and by punishing it? The result of reward is understandable; punishment is more puzzling. In a problem situation which does not lead to a resolution, punishment may engender a state of hopelessness, and in this state the subject's behavior becomes detached from its environmental consequences. Behavior is likely to be repetitive, stereotyped, ritualistic, and perhaps superstitious. We shall have to leave this discussion unsettled, for there is no present agreed-upon answer as to how punishment works.

18-7

Stereotypy

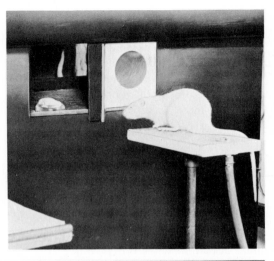

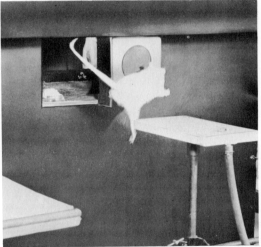

Dr. N. R. F. Maier

Shown here is the apparatus used in Maier's experiment on stereotypy. *Above:* The left window is open, the food exposed, and the frustrated rat seems to pay attention to it. *Below:* The rat's jump, however, remains fixated; that is, despite the open window the rat continues to jump to the right and to bump his nose and fall into the net below.

Regression

Regression is defined as a return to more primitive modes of behavior, that is, to modes of behavior characterizing a younger age. There are two interpretations of regression. One is that in the midst of insecurity the individual attempts to return to a period of past security. The older child seeks the love and affection once bestowed upon him by again behaving as he did when younger: crying, seeking parental caresses, and so on. This type of regression is called *retrogressive* behavior, a return to behavior once engaged in. Such returns to earlier habits, when more recently acquired ones are blocked, have frequently been demonstrated in animal experiments (Mowrer, 1940).

The second interpretation of regression is that the childish behavior following frustration is simply of more primitive quality, but not actually a return to earlier behavior. This kind of regression, in contrast to retrogression, is called *primitivation*. Thus the adult accustomed to the restraints of civilized behavior may become so upset by frustration as to lose control and start a fist-fight, even though he did no fist-fighting as a child. Both forms of regression may, of course, occur together. In the frustration experiment with half-toys and restricted space earlier discussed, regression was shown through decrease in the constructiveness of play. We consider that this decreased constructiveness is a form of primitivation, rather than retrogression, because we do not ask whether the child returns to a mode of play characteristic of *him* at an earlier age. Without careful case studies we have no way of being sure, however, that the behavior was not retrogressive. It is a safe conjecture that it was retrogressive in some instances. Through a careful device of rating, each child's play in both the free and the frustrating situation was appraised as to its degree of constructiveness, that is (1) according to its likeness to the well-thought-out and systematic play of older children, or (2) according to its similarity to the fragmentary play of younger children. As a consequence of frustration the play tended to deteriorate. Drawing became scribbling; instead of pretending to iron clothes on the ironing board, children would knock the board down. The total loss in maturity shown amounted to 17 months of mental age; that is, the play of the children, who were two to five years of age, became like that of children about a year and a half younger. Not all children showed regression; some few showed little change, and a small minority even showed increased constructiveness. The prominence of regression is shown in Figure 18-8, in which the changes in constructiveness of play for individual children are plotted.

The immediate consequences of frustration—the evidence that a person has been thwarted—are themselves ways of fighting the frustration. They are not merely signs of trouble but are also attempts at solution. If the solution is successful, the obstacles are overcome, the needs met, the conflicts resolved, and the frustrating episode is ended. However, some personal problems endure for a long time. They have continuing histories, and ways of dealing with them become habitual. These ways become so typical of the person that they help reveal what he is like. When we say that a person is aggressive or retiring, that he stands up for his rights, that he lets himself get pushed around, that he lives in a dream world, that he has a suspicious nature, we are talking about ways in which he habitually meets frustration.

Defense Mechanisms

The immediate reactions to frustration (restlessness, destructiveness, apathy, fantasy, stereotypy, regression) illustrate general techniques that young children adopt in order to solve their problems. These attempts at solution may become habitual, so that even at the nursery-school age not all children react alike. In adults these habitual modes of meeting repeated or continuing conflict and frustration are highly individual and complex, but a few modes of adjustment occur so frequently that they have

Regression as an immediate consequence of frustration

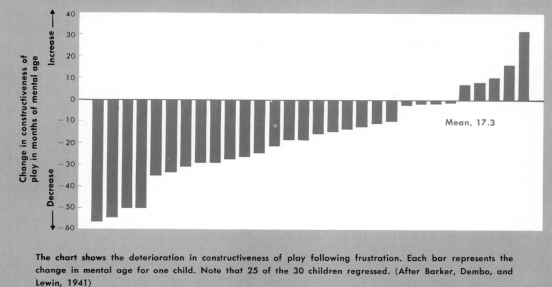

The chart shows the deterioration in constructiveness of play following frustration. Each bar represents the change in mental age for one child. Note that 25 of the 30 children regressed. (After Barker, Dembo, and Lewin, 1941)

been sorted out and given names. They are called *defense mechanisms*[1] because they protect the individual's self-esteem and defend him against excessive anxiety when faced with continuing frustrations.

Purposes served by defense mechanisms

When the fox in Aesop's fable rejected the grapes that he could not reach "because they were sour," he illustrated a defense mechanism known as rationalization. He escaped acknowledging his inability to reach the grapes by asserting that he did not really want them. In the following discussion we shall meet a number of other mechanisms, such as projection, in which we falsely attribute to others the undesirable traits that we possess, and repression, in which we conveniently forget what might otherwise be troublesome. Because nearly all these mechanisms distort reality in one way or another,

[1] The defense mechanisms were first called to the attention of psychologists by Freud and other psychoanalytic writers.

we may well consider what purposes they serve.

We may describe the purposes of defense mechanisms both positively and negatively. Positively, they seek *to maintain or enhance self-esteem;* negatively, they seek *to escape or defend against anxiety*. The goal of seeing ourselves as commendable, admirable, strong makes us enhance our self-respect as best we can, partly by denying any memory, impulse, or action that might be interpreted as self-belittling or self-degrading and, on the other hand, by taking credit for whatever appears fine and noble in our behavior. The goal of reducing anxiety is a closely related one, for a good deal of anxiety has to do with security of status. In any case, a state of anxiety is unpleasant, and we seek to avoid such states and to reduce them when they arise.

Chief methods of defense

All defense mechanisms have in common the quality of *self-deception,* which may be evident in two chief forms—*denial* and *disguise*.

The clearest evidence for *denial* of impulses, memories, or actions that might cause us anxiety or might belittle us comes through *amnesia,* in which memory is temporarily lost. As we noted earlier (p. 301), and as we shall meet again (p. 516), the fact that such memories may be recovered without relearning supports the interpretation that they are not "lost" but merely hidden by repressive mechanisms. That the lost memories tend to be personal, while impersonal memories are not lost, supports the interpretation that the repression in amnesia is often motivated by some form of anxiety or guilt.

Disguise is the second form of self-deception. Whenever impulses are falsified, as in rationalization, or traits inappropriately assigned, as in projection, the person's true motives are being masked. We shall meet other disguises in the mechanisms known as "reaction-formation" and "substitution."

Three precautions should be kept in mind during the discussion of individual defense mechanisms: (1) All of the mechanisms are to be found in the everyday behavior of normal people. Used in moderation, they increase satisfaction in living and are therefore helpful modes of adjustment. It is only when the mechanisms become the dominant modes of problem-solving that they indicate personality maladjustment. (2) The classification of the separate mechanisms is arbitrary, and the borderlines between them are not distinct and clearly marked. Often the reaction of an individual to a particular frustrating event can show characteristics of two or three different mechanisms. (3) Labeling behavior (e.g., as displaced aggression, rationalization, or substitution) may provide useful descriptive information, but it is never an explanation of the behavior involved. A full explanation requires understanding of the needs that make the person rely on mechanisms in his attempt to solve his problems.

1. *Rationalization.* Each of us wishes to act reasonably and on the basis of acceptable motives. If we act impulsively, or for motives that we do not wish to acknowledge even to ourselves, we often interpret what we have done so that we seem to have behaved rationally. Assigning logical reasons or plausible excuses for what we do impulsively is known as *rationalization*. Rationalization does not mean "to act rationally"; it means to so justify conduct according to personally desirable motives that we *seem* to have acted rationally.

In the search for the "good" reason rather than the "true" reason for what we do, we can bring forward a number of excuses. These excuses are usually plausible, and the circumstances they justify may be true ones; they simply do not tell the whole story. A number of brief illustrations may serve to show how common rationalization is. The following classification follows Symonds (1949), and the examples are in part his:

1. Liking or disliking as an excuse: The girl who was not invited to the dance said she would not have gone if asked because she did not like some of the crowd.
2. Blaming circumstances and other people: "Mother failed to wake me." "My tools were dull." (Note that in true rationalization as distinguished from deliberate falsifying, the actual situation would be that the mother had failed to do the waking and the tools were actually dull. But the mother may have expected the speaker to set the alarm clock as usual, and sharpening the tools may have been the responsibility of the one who used them.)
3. Procrastination as an excuse: "I was just going to telephone you about it."
4. Necessity as an excuse: "I bought this new model because the old car would have had a lot of expensive repairs coming up before next summer."
5. Comparison with others as an excuse:

"If Johnny is allowed to do it, I guess I can, too."

While the foregoing examples show the person fooling himself instead of others, the excuses are of the sort that a person conceivably might use consciously to put himself in a favorable light with others. We therefore need a more convincing illustration to show us that rationalization may be used when the person is completely unenlightened about the reason for his conduct —when, in other words, rationalization is unconsciously motivated. Such an illustration is provided by the results of experiments on post-hypnotic suggestion.

A subject under hypnosis is told that when he wakes from the trance he will watch the pocket of the hypnotist. When the hypnotist removes a handkerchief from the pocket, the subject will raise the window. The subject is told that he will not remember the hypnotist's telling him to do this.

Aroused from the trance, the subject feels a little drowsy, but presently circulates among the people in the room and carries on a normal conversation, all the while furtively watching the hypnotist's pocket. When the hypnotist in a casual manner removes his handkerchief, the subject feels an impulse to open the window, takes a step in that direction, but hesitates.

Unconsciously he mobilizes his wishes to be a reasonable person; so, seeking for a reason for his impulse to open the window, he says, "Isn't it a little stuffy in here?" Having found the needed excuse, he opens the window and feels more comfortable.

Rationalizations may later become genuine reasons. When they do, the element of self-deception disappears, and they enter into the realm of thoughtful control of behavior. If at first I do something impulsively and then rationalize about it, I may end by doing it deliberately—for the very reasons that furnished the good rationalizations. Perhaps while preoccupied with something else, or in the interest of variety, I departed from my usual path to the university this morning. On the different street I happened to see in a sports shop an interesting display which I would have missed had I taken my usual route. If asked why I took the new route, I might *rationalize* that I wanted to look at the sports-shop window (which had nothing to do with my choice of routes). But tomorrow I might decide to take the new route again, for the genuine reason that I am interested in what I can see along the way. Today's rationalization may easily become tomorrow's reason.

2. *Projection.* All of us have undesirable traits or qualities that we do not acknowledge even to ourselves. One unconscious mechanism that protects us from acknowledging them we call *projection*. In projection we protect ourselves from recognizing our own undesirable qualities by assigning them in exaggerated amount to other people. Our own tendencies are thereby justified. Thus we remove the stigma from our bad qualities by minimizing them in ourselves and by exaggerating them in others. Suppose I have a tendency to be critical of or unkind to other people, but would dislike myself if I recognized this tendency. If I am convinced that those about me are cruel or unkind, then any harsh treatment I give them is not based upon *my* bad qualities. I am simply giving them what they deserve. If I can assure myself that everybody else cheats in college examinations, my unacknowledged tendency to take some academic short cuts is not so bad. Projection is really a form of rationalization, but the tendency to projection is so pervasive that it merits discussion in its own right.

Two experiments highlight the pervasiveness of projection. The first (Sears, 1936) [2]

[2] We met this same experiment earlier in connection with personality structures (p. 480). Note that orderliness was there used as a trait name instead of disorderliness; this is the same rating with its sign reversed.

deals with a group of American university students, members of three college fraternities. The members of each fraternity were asked to rate the other members on four undesirable traits: stinginess, obstinacy, disorderliness, and bashfulness. The first three of these are strongly disapproved-of traits, while the fourth is mildly disapproved of. Each student was asked also to rate himself on each of these traits. In all, 97 men participated in the experiment.

Some members obviously possessed one or another of the traits to a high degree. Among these, some, as shown by their self-ratings, were aware of their traits; others were unaware of them. Our interest centers chiefly in those students who possessed an undesirable trait in a high degree and yet were unaware of possessing it. Such students tended to assign their own undesirable traits to others to a greater extent than did the rest of the students.

While the correlations on which these interpretations are based were all low, they were consistently in the direction that would be expected if they were interpreted according to a projection mechanism.

The second experiment in projection was done in Vienna, with graduate students with whom the judges in the experiment were very well acquainted. The most striking finding of this study was a tendency on the part of the subjects to go so far in self-ratings as to convert bad traits to their opposite. The person who said of himself that he was "sincere under all conditions" was rated by the judges as lacking in sincerity. This subject, of course, found others full of sham and insincerity as compared with himself (Frenkel-Brunswik, 1939).

3. *Identification.* Just as in projection we assign our own bad qualities to other people, so in *identification* we often take other people's desirable qualities as our own.

Identification and imitation have much in common, but there is a difference. In imitation we model our behavior after that of another person. The child takes the parent as the model, and likes to dress up in adult clothing and copy adult ways. To the extent that we like the person who is our model we might be said to be identifying with him. But in true identification we do not merely copy a model; we become, in fantasy, the very person with whom we identify. We do not become merely *like* him, but we are one with him, experiencing his success and failures, his joys and sorrows.

The mechanism of identification explains in part the appeal of the theater and of novels. We become the hero or heroine, whose adventures are in some sense our own. The standard mystery story plays upon this mechanism. The private detective (with whom the reader identifies himself) is usually made an attractive and clever person. He gives learned discourses on philosophy, Chinese vases, or experimental embryology while fitting together the fragmentary clues. The reader himself is working on the crime as he sees it through the eyes of the detective. The police sergeant is made an amusingly incompetent fellow, to whom the reader feels superior. Thus the writer of the detective story uses the tendency of the reader toward identification as part of the craftsmanship of his writing art. The reader raises his own self-esteem by identifying himself with admirable and heroic characters.

4. *Reaction-Formation.* A person can often conceal a motive from himself by giving strong expression to its opposite. We have met this tendency, called *reaction-formation,* in the foregoing experiment on projection in which self-appraisals were occasionally completely the reverse of fact. The mother of an unwanted child may feel guilty about not welcoming her child and so become overindulgent and overprotective of the child in order to assure the child of her love and also, perhaps, to assure herself that she is a good mother.

Thus one mother who wished to do everything for her daughter could not understand why the child was so unappreciative. At great sacrifice she had the daughter take expensive piano lessons. She sat beside the little girl to assist in the daily practice sessions. While she thought she was being extremely kind to her child, she was actually demanding and, in fact, hostile. She was unaware of her own hostility, but, when confronted with it, she admitted that as a child she had hated piano lessons. Under the conscious guise of being kind, she was actually being unconsciously cruel to her daughter. The daughter, vaguely sensing what was going on, developed symptoms that brought her to the child guidance clinic.

The possibility of reaction-formation is always present among those who engage in "anti" activities, such as censoring salacious literature or preventing cruelty to animals. The censoring individual may actually be fascinated by such literature. He wages a campaign against it in order to fight its fascination for him. Among the ardent antivivisectionists there are some who fear their own tendency toward cruelty so deeply that they become sentimental about protecting animals from the implied cruelty of others.

The existence of reaction-formation in some people does not mean that motives can never be taken at their face values. Not all reformers are moved to action by veiled or hidden impulses. Real abuses need to be corrected; if a polluted water supply is spreading disease, rational men seek to get rid of the source of trouble. It would be a foolhardy exaggeration to say that those who take responsibility for correcting such an abuse are illustrating reaction-formation against their own unconscious desires to poison someone.

5. *Dissociation.* In the normal course of events, actions, feelings, and thoughts belong together. If you realize that someone is hurting you, you feel angry and strike back; your thought, your anger, and your muscular actions are all part of one harmonious whole. But such a unity of thinking, feeling, and doing is easily disrupted by the conflicts that early training produces. Then *dissociation,* or a splitting of the total activity, occurs.

Although dissociation takes many forms, we shall consider here only two of its manifestations: compulsive movements and excessive theorizing.

Compulsive movements, actions that the person feels compelled to repeat over and over again, show the splitting off of movement from the feelings appropriate to them. Most people have a few such mannerisms, gestures, tics, or ritualistic movements (Krout, 1954).

For some people such compulsive movements are very important: one person avoids the lines on the sidewalk, another touches the telephone poles as he walks by, a third counts things. Folklore gives us a hint of what sort of impulse may be dissociated: "Step on a crack and you'll break your mother's back." Why, then, avoid cracks? When you avoid cracks, you avoid the impulse to injure someone. Thus your self-esteem is maintained because, through dissociation, your hostile impulses or fears are concealed (Figure 18-9).

Compulsive routines are carried out quite automatically, usually with little emotion, thus belying the depth of feeling that lies behind them. But the compulsive person may display excessive emotion when, for any reason, his ritualized behavior is interrupted. He thus shows, indirectly, that the behavior is actually strongly motivated. Why? In the first place, the ritualistic activity stands for something else, not recognized by the person himself. A twitching arm may substitute for the act of hitting in anger; blinking eyes may symbolize a wish to look at some forbidden scene, and at the same time express a conflict about looking; avoiding cracks may symbolize avoiding temptation. In the second place, carrying out the ritual, without emotion, unconsciously assures the person that the dangerous or forbidden act for which the movement stands will not be carried out, and possible guilt is successfully warded off.

Excessive theorizing is another form of dissociation, in which talking or thinking

18-9

Compulsive behavior as a defense

LINES AND SQUARES

Whenever I walk in a London street,
I'm ever so careful to watch my feet;
  And I keep in the squares,
  And the masses of bears,
Who wait at the corners all ready to eat
The sillies who tread on the lines of the street,
  Go back to their lairs,
  And I say to them, "Bears,
  Just look how I'm walking
    in all of the squares!"

Compulsive behavior in both children and adults reduces anxiety by a magical, ritualistic protection against a worry or fear. The true basis for the anxiety is often unacknowledged, as indeed it is in the Milne poem. The child's fears are not really "the bears who wait at the corners." (From the book *When We Were Very Young,* by A. A. Milne, illustrated by Ernest H. Shepard. Copyright 1924 by E. P. Dutton Co., Inc. Renewal 1952 by A. A. Milne. Reprinted by permission of E. P. Dutton Co., Inc., and Methuen & Co., Ltd.)

about something becomes a substitute for action, and the person thereby avoids the feelings of self-depreciation which might otherwise result from the incapacity for action. A young psychologist, for example, found participation in group discussion very difficult. He then became interested in the theory of group discussion, took a notebook along to record what people did in discussion groups, and so protected himself from feeling inadequate as a group member. Young people, somewhat confused in their religious feelings as part of their struggle with parental authority, may get into endless arguments about theological matters, thereby protecting themselves by words from strong feelings.

6. *Repression.* By this time we are prepared to see how each new mechanism is a method of protecting a person from full awareness of impulses that he (perhaps unconsciously) would prefer to deny. If the impulse is denied entirely, we have the mechanism of *repression.*

As we learned in the discussion of emotional control in Chapter 6, repression must be distinguished from suppression. The process of suppression is one of self-control—keeping impulses, tendencies, or wishes in check and perhaps holding them privately while denying them publicly. In such an instance, the person is aware of a suppressed impulse. In repression, the person himself is unaware of whatever it is that is repressed. The amount of repression that goes on depends in part upon the culture. Some cultures, such as those of China and Japan, are said to rely much more upon suppression than upon repression. Western cultures, such as those of Germany and the United States, are said to rely much more upon repression (Hsu, 1949). This distinction means that in the Oriental cultures many social controls are external. They lead people to behave in ways that simply "save face" in the presence of others. In Western cultures, the controls are internal: we are supposed to behave according to the dictates of conscience regardless of those about us. The distinction is a relative one only, for there are both suppressive and repressive controls in all cultures.

Another way of stating the social difference between a culture emphasizing suppression and one emphasizing repression is to say that suppressive cultures depend upon *shame* as a means of social control, while repressive cultures depend upon *guilt*. True shame cultures rely on external sanctions for good behavior, not, as true guilt cultures do, on an internalized conviction of sin. Shame is a reaction to other people's criticism. A man is shamed either by being openly ridiculed and rejected or by fantasying that he has been made ridiculous. In either case it is a potent sanction. But it requires an audience or at least a man's fantasy of an audience. Guilt does not. In a nation where honor means living up to one's own picture of oneself, a man may suffer from guilt though no man knows of his misdeed and a man's feeling of guilt may actually be relieved by confessing his sin (Benedict, 1946).

Repression, if completely successful, would mean a total forgetting—a total absence of awareness of the personally unacceptable motive and a total absence of behavior resulting from such a motive. Usually, however, repression is not completely successful, and impulses find indirect expression. Many of the defense mechanisms already discussed serve repression, as they protect the individual (by means of the several disguises) from awareness of his partially repressed impulses.

Cases of *amnesia* (recoverable memory loss) illustrate some aspects of repression.

In one such case, a man was found wandering the streets of Eugene, Oregon, not knowing his name or where he had come from. Study by means of hypnosis and other techniques made it possible to reconstruct his history and to restore most of his memories. Following domestic difficulties he had gone on a drunken spree completely out of

keeping with his earlier social behavior, and he had subsequently suffered deep remorse. His amnesia was motivated, first of all, by the desire to exclude from memory the mortifying experiences that had gone on during this spree. He succeeded in forgetting all the events before and after the spree which might remind him of the spree itself. Hence the amnesia spread, and he completely lost his sense of personal identity. When his memories returned, he could recall events before the drinking episode as well as subsequent happenings, but the deeper repression of the period of which he was most ashamed successfully protected him from recalling its disagreeable events (Beck, 1936).

Experimental studies have succeeded in demonstrating some of the typical characteristics of repression. In most of them, the subject had suffered failure that caused some loss in self-esteem. Later his recall of these self-depreciating events was distorted (e.g., Aborn, 1953).

7. Substitution. The last defense mechanism we shall consider is the one that best succeeds in fulfilling its function, that is, solving a person's problems and reducing his tensions without exposing to him (or to the world) motives or tendencies of which he or his culture disapproves. This is the mechanism of *substitution,* whereby approved goals are substituted for unapproved ones, and activities that have possibilities of success are entered upon instead of activities that are doomed to failure.

Substitution is sometimes divided into two forms: sublimation and compensation. Both are incompletely understood, but the families of behavior to which they refer are familiar and important.

Sublimation is the process whereby socially unacceptable motives find expression in socially acceptable form. The desire for sexual gratification, if frustrated, may be sublimated in the writing of love letters or poetry or in painting. According to psychoanalytic theory, in the sublimation of the sexual impulse the energy of the original impulse finds expression through another means. The expression is disguised, but it is the original impulse that gains expression; hence successful sublimation reduces tension and leads to satisfying behavior. This is the theory, but it has been subjected to criticism. A study of 40 adult males suggests that the sublimation of sex is seldom fully successful; although normal sexual outlets may not be used, some forms of residual sexual expression are usually present (Taylor, 1933). Whether or not direct sublimation takes place, substitute activities undoubtedly occur when a basic drive is thwarted. These may be called attempts at sublimation and, whether or not they are completely successful, they serve in part to reduce tension. Sexual behavior satisfies other motives than those affecting tension in the sex organs—motives such as those centering around companionship, dependency, being mothered, and mothering. Some of these associated motives can be successfully satisfied by activities not satisfying primary sex needs.

Compensation is a strenuous effort to make up for failure or weakness in one activity through excelling in either a different or an allied activity. The boy who fails at games may compensate for the failure by excessive study in order to gain recognition in the classroom. Here, a completely different activity substitutes for the athletic ineffectiveness.

A peculiar form of compensation known as *overcompensation* comes in an attempt to deny a weakness by trying to excel where one is weakest. The weakness thus acts as a goad to superior performance. Such overcompensation was much stressed by Alfred Adler, one of the early psychoanalysts who broke with Freud and set up his own system of individual psychology (Adler, 1917; Ansbacher and Ansbacher, 1956). Illustrations are not hard to find. The power-driven dictators of recent times have been mostly men of short stature, who may have suffered a

sense of physical powerlessness for which they overcompensated by a struggle for political might. Mussolini, Hitler, and Stalin were short, as was Napoleon before them. Theodore Roosevelt, a frail boy with weak eyes, took up boxing at Harvard and later led the Rough Riders during the Spanish-American War. Overcompensation is an energetic and effective (though not necessarily admirable) way of meeting weakness.

Rationality and Irrationality in Adjustment to Personal Problems

Man is capable of rational problem-solving; that is, he can face a problem squarely, weigh the alternatives according to their probable consequences, and take action guided by the results of deliberation. Our knowledge of the defense mechanisms tells us, however, that much behavior that appears to be activated by conscious reasoning is in fact directed by unconscious motives.

Limitations upon direct problem-solving

It is possible to attack and solve a personal problem as we do any other kind of problem—such as one in mathematics or science—by asking clear questions, assembling evidence, judging the possible consequences, and trying to verify in practice what we have concluded from the evidence. There are two chief reasons, however, why we are often not able to solve our personal problems in a straightforward, rational manner.

1. A person's motives or emotions may be so strongly involved that they distort the evidence or the problem itself, so that the person is incapable of direct problem-solving. The self-deceptive mechanisms that we have been considering tend to set up such obstacles. For example, the engineering or medical student who finds himself failing cannot admit to himself that he is not bright enough to pursue these courses at the col-

lege of his choice, and he must therefore find a rationalization instead of solving his academic problem. If he gets sick, he converts an academic problem into a health problem; if he becomes a subject for disciplinary action, he converts an intellectual problem into a moral one. When defense mechanisms hold sway, the person himself sets obstacles in the way of a rational solution to his problems.

2. Sometimes there are too many unknowns in the equation. The world in which we live is not sufficiently orderly to permit fully rational problem-solving. Thus at best a man has to take risks based on his best estimates against the uncertainty of the future; while the most rational solution is to estimate probabilities, this may not satisfy, and so his anxiety may be relieved by adopting a superstitious or fatalistic solution.

Because of these limitations upon purely reasonable conduct—limitations both internal and external—man is often tempted to fall back on irrational mechanisms.

How mechanisms may contribute to satisfactory adjustment

How successfully can a person use defense mechanisms to avoid or reduce anxiety and to maintain self-esteem? If defense mechanisms were not partially successful, they would not persist as they do. They may provide a protective armor while we are learning more mature and realistic ways of solving our problems. When we no longer need the defenses, their importance fades, and we increasingly face our problems according to the demands of the total situation. The defense mechanisms thus help toward satisfactory adjustment in several ways.

1. *They give us time to solve problems that might otherwise overwhelm us.* If we are able to rationalize failures that would otherwise cause us to despair, or if we can find partial justification for conduct that would otherwise make us despise ourselves,

such defense mechanisms sustain us until we can work out better solutions to our conflicts. They provide palliatives comparable to those drugs that reduce symptoms without curing disease. Some of the antihistamines, for example, get rid of the sneezing and itching and watering of eyes of the hay-fever victim until he takes the pollen tests that will get at the causes of those symptoms. The temporary relief helps him to live more comfortably until he is cured. Ultimately, of course, he wants to find a cure so that he will no longer need the drugs. So, too, one should no longer need his defense mechanisms if he attains realistic ways of solving his personal problems.

2. *The mechanisms may permit experimentation with new roles and hence teach new modes of adjustment.* Even when we adopt new roles for faulty reasons, as in reaction-formation, or when we misjudge people, as in projection, we expose ourselves to corrective experiences from which we may learn social techniques. We may judge someone to be unkind, but as we discover his genuine acts of kindness we may learn to correct our error in judgment. What begins as self-deception may provide occasions for modifying the self.

3. *Rationalization, by starting a search for reasons, may lead to rational conduct in the future.* The tendency to justify behavior that we have found satisfying may lead to false reasons, but it may also lead to a more careful analysis of cause-and-effect relationship. If the latter occurs, as pointed out earlier, a present rationalization may become a future reason.

4. *Behavior illustrative of a mechanism may be socially useful and even creative.* Romantic poetry or art, even though it is produced as a substitute for, or sublimation of, unfulfilled desires, may still be valuable art. So, too, compulsive tendencies may lead to concentrated effort on a task. The person who works hard toward well-defined objectives because of an excessive need for achievement may, in fact, achieve a great

deal. Thus the defense mechanisms may get us over rough spots and give a motivational lift leading to more satisfactory adjustments.

Why the defense mechanisms fail to provide satisfactory adjustment

Nearly all the statements just made about the usefulness of the mechanisms can also be reversed to point up their failures. The person who depends upon defense mechanisms for protection may never be forced to learn more mature ways of behaving; the roles adopted through the mechanisms may remain unrealistic, leading to withdrawal from social contacts rather than to improved relationships with people; rationalizations may take the form of useless rituals or wasteful compulsions instead of creative effort.

Even socially useful behavior, if it has its roots in irrational purposes, will not prove completely satisfying to the person himself. Energetic action that is motivated by drives foreign to it will not completely satisfy, for tension reduction is incomplete because the incentives are inappropriate to the drive. Actions based on such defense mechanisms never reach their goals; the drive continues (Hitler and Stalin remain short), and the resulting ambitions may know no bounds.

SUMMARY

1. *Frustration* arises whenever ongoing, goal-seeking activity is obstructed. The chief causes of frustration are obstacles, the opposition furnished by things or other people; deficiencies in the environment or in the person himself; and conflicts. *Conflicts* are of three major types: *approach-approach, avoidance-avoidance,* and *approach-avoidance.*

2. These conflicts and the resulting behavior can be understood according to four principles: the gradient of approach, the gradient of avoidance, the greater steepness of the avoidance gradient, and the heightening of the gradients with increased motivation.

3. Among the immediate consequences of frustration are the following six: (1) restlessness (and tension), (2) destructiveness and aggression, (3) apathy, (4) fantasy, (5) stereotypy, and (6) regression. They show us how important it is to understand the behavior of individuals when their goal-seeking behavior is blocked.

4. The *defense mechanisms* represent habitual efforts to meet more enduring conflicts. Among the defense mechanisms found in everyday behavior are: *rationalization, projection, identification, reaction-formation, dissociation, repression,* and *substitution.* This list is not complete, and there is much overlap. The defense mechanisms have two purposes in common: to protect the individual against excessive anxiety and to maintain his self-esteem. They serve these purposes and effect tension reduction by means of self-deception, the denial of impulses, and the disguise of motives.

5. Many personal problems can be solved rationally, that is, by taking into account the evidence, the alternatives available, and the consequences of each of the alternatives. But clear, logical choice is difficult for two reasons: (1) The person's own emotions and prejudices often get in the way of such a choice. (2) The future is always uncertain, so that there are always unknowns and risks have to be taken. Here defense mech-

anisms often enter. When defense mechanisms are employed in moderation and do not exclude more realistic facing and solving of problems, they may increase the sense of well-being and so serve a useful purpose, sometimes protecting the person until he can reach a realistic solution. But actions based on defense mechanisms can never be genuinely satisfying because they are impelled by motives irrationally related to the defensive behavior.

SUGGESTIONS FOR FURTHER READING

The experimental analysis of conflict has been best formulated by Miller in a chapter entitled "Liberalization of basic S-R concepts; Extensions to conflict behavior, motivation and social learning" in Koch, *Psychology: a study of a science,* Vol. 2 (1959). The original discussion of the three types of conflict appears in Lewin, *A dynamic theory of personality* (1935).

Frustration as a source of aggressive behavior is documented in Dollard and others, *Frustration and aggression* (1939), as a source of stereotypy in Maier, *Frustration: a study of behavior without a goal* (1949). Both are now available in paperbound editions.

The classical account of the defense mechanisms is Anna Freud's *The ego and the mechanisms of defense* (1937); the most thorough outline and discussion of the many mechanisms that have been proposed is Symonds' *Dynamic psychology* (1949). Several experiments relating preferred defenses to various background factors, including socioeconomic class, are reported in Miller and Swanson, *Inner conflict and defense* (1959).

CHAPTER 19

Mental Health and Psychotherapy

In one way or another each of us is inevitably involved in conflict; all people are occasionally placed under strain. The person whose mental health is good is better able to withstand such strains than one whose mental health is faulty, just as the person in better physical health can stand exposure or recover from infection more readily than one in poor health. The branch of psychology that is known as clinical psychology is especially devoted to these problems: it seeks to discover and promote better mental-hygiene practices so that the general level of mental health will be raised, and also to develop and apply methods of psychological readjustment through which those with personality disturbances can be restored to health.

Mental Health

It is always easier to identify illness than health. We might say that a person is healthy if he is not sick, but such a definition does not distinguish between a level of robust health and mere absence of symptoms of disease. We need a positive characterization that tells us more than that a mentally healthy person is not mentally ill. A positive program for mental health goes beyond the prevention of disease and requires many trained people other than physicians to carry it out.

Adjustment vs. maladjustment

A mentally healthy person can be characterized as an adjusted person. This statement means that he is not unduly distressed by the conflicts he faces. He attacks his problems in a realistic manner; he accepts the inevitable; he understands and accepts his own shortcomings and the shortcomings of those with whom he must deal. The maladjusted person, by contrast, is unduly disturbed by his conflicts. He often tries to solve his problems by denying reality. He commonly tends to take issue with other people over matters that cannot be helped, or he may withdraw from other people so that mutually satisfactory solutions are impossible. The gross distinction between adjustment and maladjustment is evident enough, but there are two misunderstandings about adjustment that must be cleared up.

It is, first, a misunderstanding to suppose that an adjusted person is without emotional conflicts. Adjustment refers to the manner of handling conflicts—to the manner of living with them as well as to the manner of resolving them. In a culture such as ours, some conflicts always arise. The adjusted person recognizes this fact and knows when he is making compromises or acting inconsistently. He does not have to defend himself by distorting the situation, nor does he have to feel guilty for failing when he has done the best he can under the circumstances.

A second misunderstanding is that the adjusted person must be a social conformist. Adjustment through conforming may, and often does, result in less conflict than protesting. A person who lives comfortably under the rules of the group with which he associates is saved some of the problems that confront the social reformer. But a reformer can be as well-adjusted as a conformer. The reformer may have a vision of the good society that he seeks, he may associate with others who agree with him, and he may accept on a realistic basis the clashes with those who disagree.

Productivity vs. unproductivity

A mentally healthy person is also a productive person. That is, he has a quality of spontaneity in work and in social relations that we recognize as creative, as using his potentialities and powers (e.g., Fromm, 1947, p. 84). A productive attitude is a quality of relatedness to things and people. There is productiveness in being a good friend, a good roommate, a good homemaker. It is not necessary to be especially talented in order to be creative; a very talented person may, in fact, be uncreative. We think of highly trained musicians or artists who are skilled performers or craftsmen but who lack the spark of originality or productivity. The mentally healthy person is able to use his endowments, whether meager or ample, in productive activity. He may not be brilliant, but he can be adequate.

Zest vs. malaise

A person in good physical health has a high energy level. He can do hard work, endure strain, and go enthusiastically about his business. A person in poor physical health becomes fatigued easily, avoids effort, and lacks enthusiasm. One of the frequent signs of poor mental health, similarly, is a readiness to fatigue, a desire to avoid effort. Indeed, it is often difficult to distinguish between fatigue that is due to organic illness and fatigue that is due to emotional conflict.

A mentally healthy person has zest for living; he does not have to drive himself to meet the demands of the day, but instead seeks out the opportunities for useful activity, for play, and for good fellowship. Such healthful zest has to be distinguished, of course, from an exaggerated restlessness that makes activity an escape from conflict; frenzied overactivity is as unhealthy as overfatigue. A zestful attitude arises from the same condition as that for productive activity in general: freedom from the burden of conflicts that are unrecognized, denied, or badly handled, and a positive orientation toward valued ends.

It is sometimes argued that people who suffer from unresolved emotional conflicts do creative work precisely because they suffer. Artists such as Van Gogh and Gauguin were artistically productive but emotionally disturbed, and one wonders if achieving mental health would have robbed them of creative power. The question is debatable, but it is clear from their lives that these artists achieved their artistic products at the cost of great pain to themselves, their families, and their friends. Although a few people somehow turn their troubles to advantage, many other people are unable to use their creative abilities because their conflicts inhibit their productivity, as in the following illustration.

An engineer neglected his work because he felt that all technical inventions were being misused for warfare. His personal difficulty with controlling his aggressive impulses led him to subject conventional social institutions and other people to intense criticism. His trouble in understanding and controlling his own hostility made it impossible for him to work at his occupation (Fenichel, 1945, p. 178).

One positive goal of mental health is to free the individual to use his abilities to the full. There are enough realistic reasons for productive and creative effort to allow us to question the necessity for neurotic motivation. It may be that neuroticism more often holds back or distorts creativity instead of enhancing it (see pp. 364-65).

Mental Disorders

The normal person's quota of symptoms

The distinction between health and illness is not a sharp one, and a person well within the range of normal health is seldom entirely free of the symptoms of sickness. Consider physical defects: How many people have no cavities in their teeth, no skin blemishes, no colds? Yet most people are healthy. Similarly, people who are well within the range of normal mental health may have occasional outbursts of temper, may get a headache after an unpleasant argument, may lose their appetites or become nauseated because of an emotional crisis, may become suspicious that someone is talking about them. As we go on to consider some of the symptoms of mental disorder, we will do well to acknowledge that each of us has his quota of symptoms, and that to be free of mental illness does not require us to be symptom-free.[1]

Psychoneuroses

The less severe forms of mental disorder, troublesome enough to call for expert help and occasionally requiring hospitalization, are called *psychoneuroses* (plural form of *psychoneurosis*). These disturbances are often merely more extreme forms of normal defense mechanisms; they fall somewhere on a line between normal mental health and severe *psychotic* disorders. In the psychoneuroses we see individuals attempting to cope with their conflicts and anxieties, but suffering because the defenses they use are not adequate.

Some of the *psychoneurotic reactions* are anxiety reaction, conversion reaction, phobic reaction, and obsessive-compulsive reaction.[2]

Anxiety reactions of psychoneurotic intensity commonly represent a diffuse dread, accompanied by tenseness, palpitation, sweating, nausea. The anxiety is like fear without an object, the fear that something dreadful is about to happen, that the individual will no longer be able to cope with

his problems. Such anxiety, sometimes called "free-floating," is very different from the fear of real danger, such as an attack by a wild animal, or from the phobias mentioned below.

Conversion reactions, formerly called hysteria or conversion hysteria, appear in the form of paralyzed limbs, or as insensitive (anesthetic) portions of the body, or in uncontrolled outbursts of laughing or crying. The presumption is that anxiety has been reduced or dispelled by being "converted" into symptoms that serve the unconscious purposes of the patient. For example, if, through conversion reactions, a soldier's legs become paralyzed, he is protected from acknowledging his fear of battle, which would be belittling to him; he is likely to be sent away from the battle front, so that the occasion for his fear will be removed; discharged from the army, he will probably recover the normal use of his legs, for he has no organic or structural injury.

Phobic reactions are excessive fears of certain kinds of situations in the absence of real danger, fears that beset the patient even though he knows there is no danger. His neurotic reaction means that there is an unconscious source of his apprehension. Typical phobias are fear of open places (*agoraphobia*) and fear of closed places (*claustrophobia*). A person suffering from claustrophobia, for example, may find it impossible to ride in an elevator because its walls confine him in an intolerable manner.

Obsessive-compulsive reactions occur in three major forms: obsessive thoughts— thoughts that recur persistently—often unwelcome and disturbing; compulsive acts— irresistible urges to repeat a certain stereotyped or ritualistic act; a combination of obsessive thoughts with compulsive acts, such as thoughts of lurking disease germs, combined with the compulsion of excessive handwashing. We have already met the milder forms of compulsive behavior as one of the common defense mechanisms.

---

[1] A person with any doubts about the severity of his symptoms should not hesitate to consult a mental health counselor.

[2] The terms used to describe mental disorders throughout this chapter are those officially adopted by the American Psychiatric Association (1952).

Psychotic disorders

The person with a *psychotic disorder* (*psychosis,* plural *psychoses*) is more severely disturbed than one with a psychoneurotic disorder. His personality is disorganized, and his normal social functioning is greatly interfered with. Experts are not in agreement about the distinction between psychoneuroses and psychoses. Some believe that the differences are so great that they are two disease entities, differing in kind rather than in degree, just as lobar pneumonia, caused by a pneumococcus, differs from the common cold, caused by a virus, despite some similar symptoms. Others, whose views appear to be gaining in popularity, believe that there is a continuity from normality through psychoneurosis and psychosis, the differences being largely a matter of severity of the symptoms.

The *functional psychoses* (officially, disorders of psychological origin without clearly defined tangible cause or structural change) include the *affective reactions* (manic-depressive reaction and psychotic-depressive reaction), the *schizophrenic reactions,* and *paranoid reactions.*

Manic-depressive reactions are characterized by recurrent and exaggerated changes of mood from the normal to either the *manic phase* of strong excitement and elation, or to the *depressive phase* of extreme fatigue, despondency, and sadness. A few patients exhibit the whole cycle, but more vary between the normal mood state and one of the extreme phases, depression being the more common. Not all depressions of psychotic intensity classify as manic-depressive reactions; some, classified as *psychotic-depressive reactions,* are not cyclical but arise as a consequence of a severe personal crisis.

Schizophrenic reactions, by far the most common disorders among hospitalized mental patients, are so named because they represent a lack of harmony or split between aspects of personality functioning (*schizo*

derives from a Greek root meaning "split or divided").[3] The split is particularly noticeable between emotion and conduct. A once well-groomed and socially acceptable person may become slovenly and lose all emotional interest in home and friends. Very often the patient withdraws from reality into a world of his own. The patient may have *hallucinations,* that is, sense experiences in the absence of appropriate external stimuli, such as imaginary "voices" talking to him in abusive language. Schizophrenic symptoms come in great variety, and there are nine official subclasses of the disorder; the whole family of disturbances given this name is not well understood. The disorder may manifest itself as early as childhood or late in life, though the most common time of incidence is in late adolescence and early adult life.

Paranoid reactions are characterized by persistent systematized delusions. Delusions differ from hallucinations in that they are false beliefs rather than false sense perceptions. The paranoid person may react entirely normally except when his delusions are touched upon. Then he is sure that his inventions have been stolen, that he has been deprived of a great fortune by unscrupulous people, or that someone has given him "the evil eye." Delusions often take the form of either *delusions of grandeur* (the patient believes he is Napoleon) or *delusions of persecution* (the patient has suffered at the hands of his enemies). Paranoid symptoms are common in some types of schizophrenia, and most hospitalized cases with paranoid symptoms are classified as schizophrenics. The "true" paranoid is so intact in respects other than his systematized delusions that he may manage very well outside a hospital. In paranoia we see an extreme of defense mechanisms common to us all: the mechanisms of rationalization and projection. The delusions of grandeur are elaborate ration-

---

[3] Note that the split is *not* usually into multiple personalities, as in the Eve White case (Chapter 17).

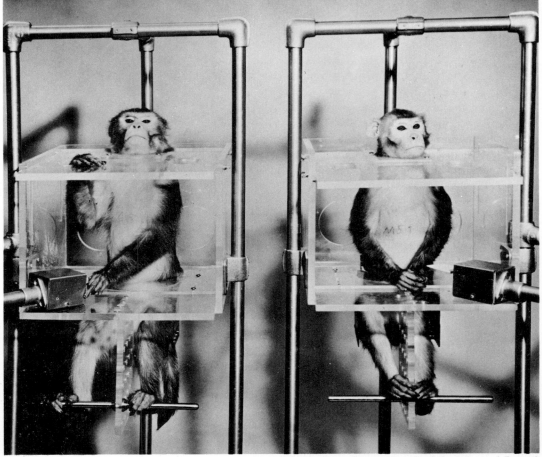

Medical Audio Visual Dept., Walter Reed Army Inst. of Research

Both animals receive brief electric shocks at 20-second intervals. The one at the left (the "executive") has learned to press the lever in its left hand, thus preventing shocks to both animals, provided the lever is pressed at least once every 20 seconds; the lever in the right-hand monkey's box is a dummy. Although both monkeys receive the same number of shocks, only the "executive" monkey develops the ulcers. (After Brady, 1958)

alizations, and the delusions of persecution are clearly projections.

Organic and functional illness

The psychoneuroses and psychoses described in the foregoing sections are classified as "psychogenic," or "functional," meaning that there is no identifiable *organic* change in the brain or nervous system asso-

ciated with them. There are in addition to these reactions many kinds of mental disturbance associated with known organic changes in the brain or nervous system: disorders associated with alcoholism, syphilis, acute infections, tumors, gunshot wounds.

When we call an illness functional or psychogenic, we do not mean that there are no changes in the nervous system associated with it. There may indeed be some hereditary basis for susceptibility to the particular disturbance. We imply, however, that the changes are of the kind that take place in learning and habit formation, rather than the kind associated with bacterial infection or surgical damage. If the changes are of the functional variety, the disorder is more likely to be reversible, that is, more susceptible to cure through a kind of re-education process, than is an organically based illness. The possibility of functional illness was recognized, and treated as such, over 900 years ago by the Arabian physician Avicenna, who died in the year 1037.

> A certain young man of Gurgan, by the Caspian Sea, lay sick of a heart malady which baffled all the local doctors. Avicenna (his identity being then unknown) was invited to give his opinion, and, after examining the patient, requested the collaboration of someone who knew all the districts and towns of the province, and who repeated the names while Avicenna kept his finger on the patient's pulse. At the mention of a certain town he felt a flutter in the pulse. "Now," he said, "I need someone who knows all the houses, streets, and quarters of the town." Again a certain street was mentioned, and the same phenomenon was repeated, and a third time, when the names of the inhabitants of a certain household were enumerated. Then Avicenna said, "It is finished. This lad is in love with such and such a girl who lives at such and such an address; and the girl's face is the patient's cure." They were brought together and married and the cure was completed.[4]

Moreover, functional psychological illness may be associated with organic physical change in parts of the body other than the nervous system. These are the illnesses commonly called *psychosomatic*. A dramatic illustration is provided by experiments on the induction of duodenal ulcers, colitis, and other gastrointestinal disturbances in monkeys through a conditioning procedure (Brady and others, 1958). In one arrangement, monkeys participated in the experi-

[4] Quoted by Miller and McLean (1941), from Whitwell (1936).

ment in pairs, each monkey being confined in a chair-type restraining device (Figure 19-1). An electric shock was delivered at intervals. One of the monkeys (whimsically called the "executive" monkey) had a lever that could be used to turn off or prevent the shock. When he pressed the lever, the shock was turned off for *both* monkeys. Thus both monkeys suffered identical shocks; if their physiological damage were due to shocks, it would affect both equally. What happened was that only the "executive" monkey developed the ulcers; apparently the constant alertness required to turn off or prevent the shock produced a continuing state of tension that resulted in the ulcers. The helpless monkey, who could only take the shocks as they came, was somehow less reactive and less disturbed (Brady, 1958).

While the psychogenic or functional origins of symptoms in psychoneurosis and in some psychotic reactions have been rather firmly established, present knowledge is too fragmentary for us to state dogmatically the relative importance of hereditary susceptibility and psychogenic factors in producing the more severe disturbances.

CRITICAL DISCUSSION
Research on the causes of schizophrenia

Arguments over organic *vs.* functional factors in the causation of mental disease have centered lately around schizophrenia, the most common form of psychotic reaction. The fact that schizophrenia is at present classified as a "functional" psychosis does not mean that it will necessarily remain in that category. Current research on schizophrenia can be classified into four groups, each group having a different point of view about cause:

1. *Research stressing functional causation.* The most prevalent theory of the functional type is that something in the early mother-child relationship predisposes to schizophrenia. The mother may be overdemanding, overtly rejecting, or dominating through the kind of

submissiveness that makes her cooperate to absurd limits (Tietze, 1949); perhaps the main point is that the mother (not the father) dominates the child's life (Kohn and Clausen, 1956). Although psychiatrists agree in their impressions of the mothers of schizophrenics, actual study does not differentiate them from the mothers of neurotics (Block and others, 1959).

An additional line of evidence points to the significance of childhood loss of a parent by death in certain late-appearing schizophrenias (J. R. Hilgard and Newman, 1959, 1961).

2. *Research stressing heredity.* Careful search of the family histories of schizophrenics permits a statement of the probability that other members of the family will also have schizophrenic symptoms. One such study reports that if one *identical* twin has schizophrenia, his twin will tend to have it in 86 per cent of the cases studied, whereas the second twin of a *fraternal* twin pair will have it in but 14 per cent of the cases. Because identical twins are born from a single ovum, they have common heredity; fraternal twins are no more alike than ordinary brothers and sisters. Hence this study as well as related ones lend support to the theory that heredity is a factor in the development of schizophrenia (e.g., Kallmann, 1953, 1959; Kallmann and Roth, 1956).[5]

3. *Research stressing biochemical factors.* It may be that as a result of some hereditary defect (or other causes) schizophrenics metabolize products that cause their mental symptoms. Some investigators (e.g., Hoffer and Osmond, 1959) have therefore searched for products (especially steroids) in the blood or urine that differentiate schizophrenics from other persons.

The logic of the drug studies calls for two additional kinds of evidence to answer the following questions: (1) If the kinds of chemical products found excessively in schizophrenics' blood or urine are injected into a normal person, will he develop symptoms resembling those of schizophrenia? (2) If known chemical antidotes to these products are injected, will the symptoms of schizophrenics be alleviated? While a clear answer cannot be given to these questions, partial evidence is encouraging to those who believe in a chemical basis for the symptoms. A drug that is a derivative of lysergic acid (known as LSD-25) if injected produces hallucinatory symptoms in a normal person which somewhat resemble those in schizophrenia (Hoch, 1955). Drugs known to be antagonistic to LSD-25 sometimes have ameliorative effects in schizophrenia. All these drugs have chemical similarities with adrenalin, with the chemical products that result from its metabolism, or with its neutralizers. The drugs are marketed under many names, two of which are the so-called tranquilizers, chlorpromazine and reserpine (Kolb, 1956). The results of research are not yet sufficiently established to provide a chemical explanation of schizophrenia. For a critique of such studies, see Kety (1959).

4. *Research stressing local brain functions.* Some experimenters explore the electrical activity of the brain by inserting needles into specific portions and studying the responses. Electrical stimulation via electrodes implanted deeply into the brains of schizophrenic patients has in some cases produced increased alertness and clarity of thought (Heath, 1954).

All of these developments are promising, all are controversial, and they are not mutually exclusive. For a review from many vantage points, see Jackson (1960).

Prevalence of mental disorders and the prospect of cure

Severe mental illness is an important social problem. Some 750,000 patients are being cared for at any one time in the mental hospitals of the United States, and they occupy half of all hospital beds. The cost of caring for mental patients with public funds today runs over one billion dollars annually.

The most prevalent diagnosis is *schizophrenic reaction;* individuals classified as having this illness make up about half the state hospital population. The admission rate is 16 per year per 100,000 population, as compared with 4 per 100,000 for the affective reactions (Felix and Kramer, 1953). The number of psychoneurotics admitted to hospitals is only slightly smaller than the affective-reaction group of psychotics, although there are more psychoneurotics

[5] This problem was discussed earlier, Chapter 15, p. 437.

treated as outpatients who therefore do not become entered on hospital records.

Careful estimates based on New York State studies suggest that 1 out of every 10 babies born today will be hospitalized for mental illness at some time during his life (Goldhamer and Marshall, 1953).

Severe mental illness is by no means hopeless. About half the patients admitted to mental hospitals are eventually discharged as improved or recovered, most of these within the first year of entering the hospital. The percentage is higher for well-equipped and well-staffed hospitals using modern treatment methods. At present 55 to 60 per cent of the schizophrenics, who represent the largest group of hospitalized patients, show recovery or improvement sufficient to permit discharge from the hospital. Many of them are not permanently well; some have repeated periods in the hospital. Research is continuing in the hope that better methods of treatment may be found. Promising advances are being made both in *psychotherapy* (treatment by psychological means) and in *somatotherapy* (treatment of the body), the latter with the aid of drugs, electric shock, surgery, and other methods.

The tranquilizing drugs have produced such dramatic results in some cases of severe mental illness that physicians have prescribed them somewhat indiscriminately. As early as 1956 the American Psychiatric Association felt called upon to release a statement cautioning against their casual use.

The prevalence of psychoneuroses, the less severe disorders, is hard to estimate because the disorders are ill-defined and merge with the normal and because psychoneurotics are usually treated outside of hospitals and do not enter into the statistics of disorder. Two careful surveys, one in Maryland (Lemkau, Tietze, and Cooper, 1941) and one in Tennessee (Roth and Luton, 1943), found an incidence of psychoneurosis of 3 or 4 per thousand; more recent studies, by different methods, suggest that these figures are probably too low.

Two community studies, one in a large city (New York) and another in a small town in Nova Scotia, arrived at higher figures on the extent of symptoms of disturbed mental health. The New York study arrived at a figure of 30 per cent of the population as having clinical symptoms sufficient to disturb their everyday lives (Rennie, 1955). That this high figure is not due solely to the strains of urban life is indicated by the figure arrived at for the small town. The second study (Leighton, 1955)

TABLE 19-1

First admissions to mental hospitals, 1885 and 1940: rates per 100,000 for men and women of each age group below 50

Age group	Male			Female		
	Mass. 1885	Mass. 1917-40	Northeast 1940	Mass. 1885	Mass. 1917-40	Northeast 1940
10-19	22	25	35	15	22	25
20-29	96	99	95	75	72	79
30-39	111	115	115	108	90	105
40-49	110	124	132	108	102	111

SOURCE: Goldhamer and Marshall (1953), Tables 6 and 8. The differences in the definitions of "admission rate" are carefully considered in the original source. Admission rates for those above 50 (not shown in the table) have risen substantially but for reasons having little to do with the prevalence of mental illness in those years.

found 37 per cent of the people 18 years and over sufficiently impaired by psychiatric symptoms to be in need of help.

The question arises whether or not the conditions of modern life have increased the amount of mental illness. The most careful study to date yielded the kind of results presented in Table 19-1. The data permit the conclusion that there was no increase in severe mental illness between 1885 and 1940 for women under 50 or men under 40. Additional data and other considerations led the authors of the study to conclude that there was no demonstrable difference in the incidence of psychotic disorders for either men or women over this period.

Techniques of Psychotherapy

Treatment of personality disturbances by psychological means is known as *psychotherapy*. There are several kinds of specialists in this field. Milder problems can be settled with the help of nonprofessional advisers such as parents or friends. Trained advisers, guidance workers, or psychological counselors work in community agencies such as family service associations and child guidance and mental health clinics. Most school systems provide help on academic or vocational problems or give counsel on the personal problems arising at home or in school.

A pattern of cooperation that developed within child guidance clinics has now come to be fairly widespread in other agencies concerned with mental health. In these clinics, a team of workers representing three professions works together on each case: a psychiatrist, a clinical psychologist, and a psychiatric social worker. Together they collect the pertinent facts, discuss a plan for treating the case, and agree on a division of responsibility. In any one clinic the division of labor among the members of the team may vary from case to case, but is determined in part by the special competences of the three professions.

A *psychiatrist* is a medically trained specialist, whose experience covers both cases in mental hospitals and in outpatient clinics. In the team approach he takes medical responsibility in addition to any specific role he may have in an individual case. A *psychoanalyst* is a specialist within psychiatry who uses the methods and theories derived from Sigmund Freud. A psychoanalyst is today almost always a psychiatrist,[6] but a psychiatrist is often not a psychoanalyst.

A *clinical psychologist* has had graduate training in psychology, has usually earned the Ph.D. degree, and has served special internships in the fields of testing and diagnosis, counseling and psychotherapy, and research. He tends to administer and interpret the psychological tests used in the clinic, but uses his other skills as well.

A *psychiatric social worker* usually has earned a master's degree at a graduate school of social work, including an internship, and has special training in interviewing in the home and in carrying treatment procedures into the home and community. Because of this special training, the social worker is likely to be called upon to collect information about the home and to interview relatives, in addition to carrying a share in the therapeutic procedures with the patient.

In mental hospitals a fourth professional person joins the team: the *psychiatric nurse*. Psychiatric nursing is a specialty within the nursing profession and calls for special training in the handling of severely disturbed mental patients as well as those on the way to recovery.

The following discussion of psychotherapeutic techniques does not specify the profession to which the counselor belongs; the assumption is that he is a trained and competent member of any one of these professions.

[6] There are a few "lay" psychoanalysts, that is, analysts without the M.D. degree.

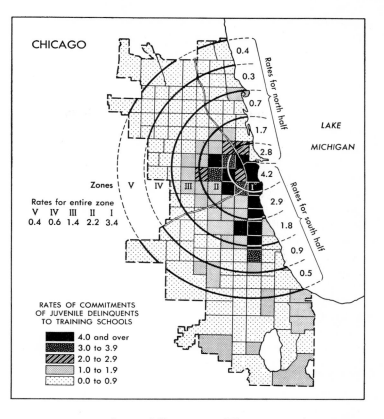

19-2

Environment and delinquency

This map of Chicago shows how the rate of delinquency is related to residential standards. The rate is highest at the center of the city where slums are abundant; it decreases progressively as one moves toward the suburban areas. (From Shaw, McKay, and others, 1942)

CHICAGO

0.4
0.3
0.7
1.7
2.8
4.2

LAKE
MICHIGAN

Zones V   IV   III   II   I

Rates for entire zone
V   IV   III   II   I
0.4 0.6 1.4 2.2 3.4

Rates for north half

2.9
1.8
0.9
0.5

Rates for south half

RATES OF COMMITMENTS
OF JUVENILE DELINQUENTS
TO TRAINING SCHOOLS

4.0 and over
3.0 to 3.9
2.0 to 2.9
1.0 to 1.9
0.0 to 0.9

Social readjustments

Because personality is largely a social product, the readjustment of a disturbed personality often can be achieved by changing his relation to his social environment. Improvement takes place either because the environment changes or because the person is helped to relate himself to it in new ways.

Changing the Environment. When the home addresses of urban youths who come into conflict with the authorities are plotted on a city map, it is generally found that they tend to concentrate in a few areas of the city, usually in transitional areas between the central business sections and the more favored residential sections (Figure 19-2). In these transitional or disintegrating sections (where residences are gradually being replaced by used car lots, temporary warehouses, or other unstable enterprises), both the social and physical environments favor delinquency. When recreation centers are placed in these areas, providing more normal outlets for the energies of youth, the delinquency rate commonly goes down (Shaw, McKay, and others, 1942).

Frequently a delinquent child from a bad home environment shows improvement when placed in a good foster home. Juvenile court authorities usually prefer foster home treatment to institutional care for the delinquent child (Merrill, 1947). Change in environment is useful in other kinds of disturbances than delinquency. Children raised in orphanages, for example, sometimes develop personality difficulties that may be eliminated by good foster home placement.

Training in Social Skills. Social adjustment requires social skill. If a child is to be accepted by other children, he must have something to offer in group activities. He must be a useful member of the ball team, for example; he must know how to play games according to the rules. Occasionally a child who is having adjustment difficulties needs to be taught certain skills. The boy who throws a ball like a girl can be taught to throw like a boy. The child in nursery school who cries when someone gets the toy he wants can be taught to take turns or to assert his rights. Perhaps the girl needs help in how to dress; perhaps the boy needs to learn to dance. The need for training in social skills is not limited to childhood. Adults, especially if they find themselves in a markedly different environment from that in which they were raised, can often improve their adjustment by acquiring the skills the new environment demands. These social skills may be relatively superficial things, but by acquiring these skills, a person can improve his social participation and hence personality adjustment.

Traditional counseling

A person in trouble usually seeks both help in understanding his problems and advice about the next steps to take. The giving of advice or counsel is no doubt the most typical form of psychotherapy, whether by parents and teachers, clergymen and lawyers, or by physicians and psychologists. Professional counseling takes many forms. Among these are vocational counseling, industrial counseling, secondary school and college counseling, marriage counseling, and religious counseling.

Several assumptions ordinarily enter into traditional counseling. One of these is that the counselor is an *expert,* with resources of knowledge and experience superior to those of the client. His role therefore somewhat resembles that of an educator; he imparts information, interprets facts, and widens (or limits) the choices before the client. A second assumption is that the counselor is *wiser* than the client in understanding and interpreting the client's problems. Hence the client relates his life history so that the counselor may gain insight into his problems and help him see his way through them. A third assumption is that the counselor, because he is not caught in the client's conflicts, will be *more objective* and clear-headed in analyzing alternatives that will lead to decisions. The relationship between client and counselor is similar to that between patient and physician. The physician is the expert on disease. When the patient tells his health history and recounts his symptoms, the physician gets leads to follow up with blood tests or other diagnostic methods. When the physician has decided what is wrong, he prescribes the treatment—anything from an aspirin to a major operation. His expertness and authority are accepted.

The counselor who uses traditional methods is often successful, but occasionally runs into difficulty, as does the physician at times. Some patients, for instance, seem to be unable to follow a prescribed diet, though they may know the diet is important to their health. The doctor who tells a man to give up alcohol is likely to be correct in both his diagnosis and his recommendation, but unsuccessful in his cure. Because many people with psychological maladjustments find it hard to accept advice (even good advice), other techniques of readjustment have grown up to supplement traditional counseling.

Client-centered counseling

A method which seeks to escape the limitations of traditional counseling has been developed by Rogers and his associates under the name of *client-centered counseling* (Rogers, 1951; Rogers and Dymond, 1954)—a name which suggests that the method is the opposite of authoritative advice-giving. The method is called "client-centered" to distinguish it from traditional, "counselor-centered" counseling; its purpose is to have the client rather than the counselor arrive at the insights and make the decisions.

Client-centered counseling can be described rather simply, although in practice it requires great skill and is much more subtle than at first appears. The counselor begins by structuring the interview, that is, by explaining the terms of agreement between him and the client: the responsibility for working out his problems is the client's; he is free to leave at any time, and it will be his choice whether or not to return; the relationship is a private and confidential one, as in other counseling relationships; the client is free to speak of intimate matters without fear of reproof or of having the information given to others. Once the interview is structured, the client does most of the talking. Usually he has a good deal to "get off his chest." The counselor is a patient but alert listener. When the client stops, as though expecting the counselor to say something, the counselor usually acknowledges and accepts the feelings the client has been expressing. For example, if the client has been telling about how he is nagged by his mother, the counselor may say: "You feel that your mother tries to control you." His effort is to *clarify* the feelings the client has been expressing, not to judge them or to elaborate on them.

What usually happens is that the client begins with a rather low evaluation of himself, but in the course of facing up to his problems and bringing his own resources to bear on them he turns to the positive. For example, one reported case began with statements such as the following:

> Everything is wrong with me. I feel abnormal. I don't do even the ordinary things of life. I'm sure I will fail on anything I undertake. I'm inferior. When I try to imitate successful people, I'm only acting. I can't go on like this.[7]

By the time of her eleventh and final interview she expressed the following atti-

[7] From the case of Miss Tilden, reported by Snyder and others (1947), pp. 128-203. All names in reported cases have been changed to protect the subjects' privacy.

tudes, contrasting strikingly with those of the first interview:

> I am taking a new course of my own choosing.
> I am really changing.
> I have always tried to live up to others' standards that were beyond my abilities.
> I've come to realize that I'm not so bright, but I can get along anyway.
> I no longer think so much about myself.
> I'm much more comfortable with people.
> I'm getting a feeling of success out of my job.
> I don't feel quite steady yet, and would like to feel that I can come for more help if I need it.

To see whether this kind of progress is typical, experimenters have carefully analyzed recorded interviews. When the client's statements are classified and plotted, the course of therapy turns out to be fairly predictable. For example, in the early interviews the client spends a good deal of time talking about his difficulties, stating his problem, describing his symptoms. In the course of therapy, he increasingly makes statements showing that he understands the meaning for his personality of the topics being discussed, that he foresees a favorable outcome. By classifying all the client's remarks as either problem restatements or statements of understanding and insight, one can see the progressive increase in insight as the counseling proceeds (Figure 19-3).

What does the counselor do to bring about these changes? First and foremost, he creates an atmosphere in which the client feels his own worth and significance. The atmosphere arises not as a consequence of technique but out of the therapist's conviction that every person has the capacity to deal with his psychological situation and with himself, "to deal constructively with all those aspects of his life which can potentially come into conscious awareness" (Rogers, 1951, p. 24; Rogers, 1961).

In accepting this point of view, the counselor is not merely a passive listener, for if he were the client might feel that the

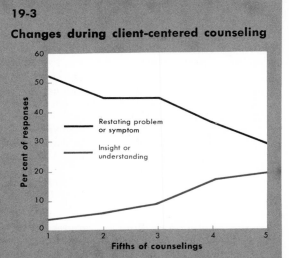

19-3

Changes during client-centered counseling

Per cent of responses (y-axis, 0 to 60)

Restating problem or symptom

Insight or understanding

Fifths of counselings (x-axis, 1 to 5)

Results for 10 subjects and 60 interviews in client-centered counseling are shown here, with three to nine interviews per subject. Stating of the problem gradually gives way to increased frequency of statements indicating understanding. (Drawn from data presented by Seeman, 1949)

counselor was not interested in him. So the counselor listens intently and tries to show in what he says that he can see things as the client sees them. In the beginning, Rogers, as the originator of client-centered counseling, laid great emphasis upon having the counselor try to clarify the feelings expressed by the client. Rogers now believes that method to be too intellectualistic; he currently places the emphasis upon the counselor's trying to adopt the client's own frame of reference, upon his trying to see the problems as the client sees them, although without becoming emotionally involved in them. To have therapeutic value, the change in the client must be a change in feeling, a change in attitude, and not merely a change in intellectual understanding.

A great deal has been learned from those who advocate and practice client-centered counseling. It is too early to know with certainty what its range of usefulness will be and wherein its limitations lie. Its techniques have been applied within play therapy, group therapy, and even in classroom teaching.

Group therapy

The two major threats to mental health are (1) excessive conflict, with feelings of helplessness, tension, and anxiety, and (2) isolation from one's fellows, with feelings of loneliness and rejection. The psychotherapist seeks, on the one hand, to help the client break the deadlock of his conflicts and, on the other hand, to help him achieve more satisfactory interpersonal relations. When we state the aims of therapy in this way, we can foresee that there might be some advantage in *group therapy,* in which conflicts are resolved in the presence of other people, and in which the members of the group achieve mutual respect, support, and affiliation through working on their problems together.

Group therapy, in one form or another, has gone on informally for many years. Camp counselors have been able by group discussions to help children who come to summer camps. They have thereby improved the child's relations to his fellows and raised the child's respect for himself as an accepted member of the group. Children have found help in scout troops and in other clubs under wise and friendly leadership.

More recently, psychologists and psychiatrists have come to recognize group therapy as a scientific psychotherapeutic method to be planned and studied like any other acceptable method (Powdermaker and Frank, 1953; Slavson, 1950). In developing formal group techniques, they have built on a variety of prior experiences with therapeutic methods.

The advantages of group therapy over individual therapy are two: (1) the method saves time, because one therapist can help several people at once, and (2) the group provides experiences of communicating with and interacting with other people not pos-

Monkmeyer

19-4

Release therapy

Here in a clinic a boy harmlessly works off his aggression on a large inflated toy. Also available are life-sized rag dolls that make substitute brothers and sisters.

sible between the client and the therapist alone. The second advantage needs further study, but it may very well be found that some clients respond better to group therapy than to individual therapy. It is also possible that for some individuals a combination of individual and group experience may be desirable.

Therapy with children

It was indicated above that not all psychotherapy is based upon words. With young children a good deal of use is made of their spontaneous self-expression in play. A child's play is more than an outlet for excess energy. It is a natural medium of self-expression; through it he may come to grips with his problems. He may be said to "play out" the solutions to his problems, just as an adult may "talk out" the solutions to his. Making use of the play situation as an aid to solving the child's adjustment problems is called *play therapy*.

The room to which the child comes is well supplied with play materials. It has a sink with running water, so that he can play with clay and paint. A dollhouse with movable partitions provides an opportunity for free expression, possibly in reconstructing the rooms at home. There is ample furniture and dolls in scale, representative of adults and children. Hand puppets, sometimes called mitten dolls, are available. Toy guns, cars, animals, telephones—all make possible a range of expressive play.

In the hands of different therapists, play therapy employs all the practices that are found in other types of counseling. Three chief techniques of play therapy are worth special mention because each calls attention to an important feature of the process of readjustment. These techniques are known as release therapy, relationship therapy, and interpretive therapy.

Release Therapy. Release therapy emphasizes the importance of giving expression to pent-up emotions, especially hostile, aggressive tendencies. In the playroom the child is permitted to throw clay, to smear paint, to break dolls. He thus gets his inhibited feelings out of his system, with beneficial results. Limits are usually set to the amount of destructiveness permitted, so that only expendable things are destroyed. Doll destruction is sometimes limited to the tearing of paper dolls. The child is permitted to accept and give expression to destructive impulses, but at the same time he has to learn to give that expression within socially acceptable limits. Were the child permitted to break things that seemed to him too valuable to break, or to do things he himself considered taboo, his anxiety and guilt would mount, and the beneficial effects of release might be lost.

Relationship Therapy. This type of therapy lays emphasis upon the interchange between the child and the therapist in the playroom. The assumption is that the child's troubles arise through a disturbed relationship to people about him so that he has come to distrust others and perhaps has lost faith in himself. Now the child meets an adult who understands him, who lets him be himself, who is warm and friendly. The child becomes changed through his relationship to the therapist, rather than through anything the therapist explains to him. Because he learns how to achieve a satisfactory relationship to one person (the therapist), the child's attitudes toward himself and toward other people become modified in wholesome ways (Allen, 1942).

Interpretive Therapy. Interpretive therapy goes one step beyond release and relationship therapy. This is the step of communicating the understanding of the therapist to the child. The therapist sees in the child's play the acting out of certain conflicts which are not clear to the child, or which the child cannot put into words. The therapist helps him put these conflicts into words and in so doing helps the child to solve them (Erikson, 1950). For example, the therapist may point out that boys both love and hate their fathers. This generalization of the conflict, which the boy thinks of

as his alone, may make the boy feel less guilty over his ambivalence, and so enables him to establish a better relationship with his father. We shall meet the problems of interpretation again when psychoanalytic interpretations are discussed.

Research on psychotherapy

It is evident from the foregoing discussions that there are several approaches to psychotherapy, and that they involve somewhat different presuppositions. Scientific status will eventually be achieved by that system which is most coherent with some established set of psychological principles and is so worked out that it is a feasible and efficient method of dealing with mental health problems. One summary of current methods lists 36 systems of psychotherapy —enough to show that there is no agreement at present on the best method (Harper, 1959).

The theories that have been most influential in guiding research on psychotherapy are three: (1) psychoanalysis (and its variants), (2) learning theory, and (3) value-oriented personality theories, such as that of Carl Rogers.

Psychoanalysis is a complex body of theory, and research investigations usually narrow their scope to some fraction of the theory. We shall consider some illustrations of such research in the next section, in which psychoanalysis is given separate treatment.

The learning theorists have argued that bad mental health practices must be due essentially to bad habits, and psychotherapy must therefore be concerned with learning to overcome them. One illustration is provided by the work of Wolpe (1958). He showed in experiments with cats that electric shocks received in the feeding cage would make the animals refuse food in other parts of the experimental room. This he took to be similar to the spread (or generalization) of anxiety in a patient. The conditioned anxiety conflicted with the normal eating response. Psychotherapy must

David Linton

19-5 Research in psychotherapy

The therapist attaches GSR electrodes to the patient's finger. The electrodes detect very small changes in skin resistance, indicating emotional reactions; the patient feels no pain or other sensation of any kind from them. With the patient's consent, a microphone concealed in the lamp records the interview. (The photograph here is posed.)

An assistant operates the galvanometer which records the patient's GSR's. A portion of the record is shown below. The GSR is represented by the sharp jump in the curve; the breaks at 1 and 2 are signals which allow this record to be synchronized with the recording of the interview. Research set-up that of Dollard and Auld (1959).

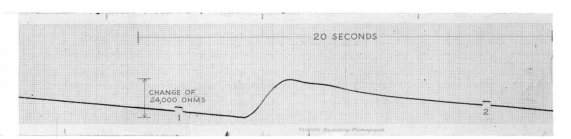

20 SECONDS

CHANGE OF
24,000 OHMS

1   2

therefore consist in some sort of extinction of the anxiety response so that the normal (i.e., eating) response can occur. He found that he could inhibit the anxiety by a gradual process of feeding the animal elsewhere in the laboratory at some distance from the room in which it was shocked. Although there might be incipient anxiety reactions, these were overcome (inhibited) by the successful act of eating. Gradually the feeding was brought closer to the original place, but never at a pace too rapid to upset the eating. When the cat was able to eat in the room where it had become disturbed, it was soon ready to eat also in the cage where it had originally been shocked. Thus it was "cured" of its neurosis. The cure is described by Wolpe as taking place by *reciprocal inhibition*. That is, the strengthening of eating inhibits the anxiety.

With treatment sessions that he designed for human patients according to the same theory, Wolpe reports a high percentage of success. In adapting the theory to human psychotherapy, Wolpe begins with establishing a hierarchy of the circumstances that arouse anxiety in the patient; that is, he finds through interview and discussion those situations that provoke the most violent responses and those that provoke only mild disturbance. Beginning with the least disturbing situations (corresponding to having the cat in a remote room in the laboratory), he overcomes the mild anxiety through having some positive response take its place, usually relaxation or assertive responses. By working up through the hierarchy at the patient's own pace, the patient is eventually able to face what was his most disturbing or terrifying situation with appropriate responses rather than with irrational neurotic ones.

A number of other psychologists have worked out psychotherapies with learning theory as a background (e.g., Dollard and Miller, 1950; Mowrer, 1950; Rotter, 1954). They differ in detail, but all agree that the essence of psychotherapy is relearning.

As for the value-oriented theories, we have already met one illustration of research designed within the pattern of client-centered therapy (Figure 19-3, p. 534), in which changes in the patient's self-evaluations are reflected as he begins to solve his own problems.

Much of the contemporary research work within psychotherapy is addressed to the *process* of psychotherapy rather than to the *outcome*. While, of course, a favorable outcome is the hope of all psychotherapies, it is important from the point of view of science to know how changes come about.

Studies of process imply some theory, since otherwise the investigator would not know what to look for. But the theory need not bias the research; the scientist will accept the changes that occur, regardless of whether they support or refute the theory being tested.

An illustration of a method of studying the process of psychotherapy in detail is provided by the work of Dollard and Auld (1959). Their background includes both psychoanalysis and learning theory, and this background is reflected in the categories they use in studying what happens in psychotherapy.

The procedure can be illustrated as follows:

In the private and informal atmosphere of the therapy room, a patient discusses her problems with the therapist. With the knowledge and consent of the patient, a microphone concealed in a lamp in order to be inconspicuous carries the conversation to an adjoining room where it is recorded on tape. Later it is transcribed for analysis. Simultaneously, electrodes fastened to the patient's left middle finger detect changes in skin resistance (such changes, called galvanic skin responses or GSR's, indicate emotional reactions, as described in Chapter 6). The information from the electrodes is carried to a recording galvanometer in the adjoining room, and the records are retained for analysis (Figure 19-5).

P. It seems almost as though a blanket were over me, a suppression,

a su--a suppression or a stifling agent or... sort of fouling
                                                        101
me up or... tangling me up (sighs)./
        102-110
(44-sec. pause)/

                                                               111
P. I had uh... an argument with the circulation manager./   And

you know that's the uh...
        112-114
(16-sec. pause)/

P. ...that's the first real argument that I can think of and pin
                                            115
down at all with anybody./
        116-117
(10-sec. pause)/

P. I said exactly what I felt instead of the ducking around the
                                        118
issue or coming in the back door or.../
        119-121
(16-sec. pause)/

P. But I wasn't angry... to the extent where I got excited or
                            122
flushed or lost control or.../   I just told the fellow
                    123
exactly the way I felt./   He had agreed to let me inter-
                                124
view some people in the conference room./   And uh I had--
                                125
I had a group of people in the room./   One was a visitor
                126
from New York./   He's a well-known scientist and uh there

was another fellow who is a researcher for a pharmaceutical
        127   128
company./   And we were talking./   And then right in the

middle of uh interviewing them there uh the circulation mana-

ger was having his people bring in charts and maps of different
                                            129
parts of the city and spread them out on the table./   And

uh there was uh---they were bringing in file cases of old circu-

lation records and putting them right on the table we were
        130
sitting at./   And uh my guests were visibly uh wondering I

19-6

Interview analysis

The transcribed interview is divided into units prior to coding. Each sentence and each five-second pause is considered as one unit.

19-7

Interview analysis

The interview units (Fig. 19-6) are coded according to predetermined categories.

CONTENT-ANALYSIS SCORE SHEET

CASE *Mr. A*

HOUR *32*   PAGE *2*

SCORER *Auld*

	P	T
101	H·a	
102	Res 5	
103	"	
104	"	
105	"	
106	"	
107	"	
108	"	
109	"	
110	"	
111	H circulation manager	
112	Res 5	
113	"	
114	"	
115	H·a	
116	Res 5	
117	"	
118	H circ. mgr	
119	Res 5	
120	"	
121	"	
122	H circ. mgr	
123	"	

Changes during therapy as revealed by interview analysis

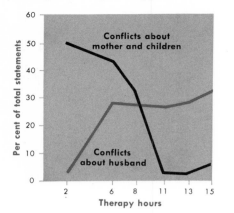

Coding responses permits a study of changes during therapy. In the brief psychotherapy of one patient, Mrs. B., who was treated according to psychoanalytic principles, discussion of conflicts about her mother and her children was gradually replaced by discussion of conflicts about her husband (Murray, Auld, and White, 1954). Compare this with the changes occurring in client-centered counseling as shown in Fig. 19-3, p. **534.**

As therapy proceeds, a person becomes able to talk about intimate matters that were at first embarrassing, with a decreasing show of emotion, as registered by the GSR. (Data from study by Dittes, 1957)

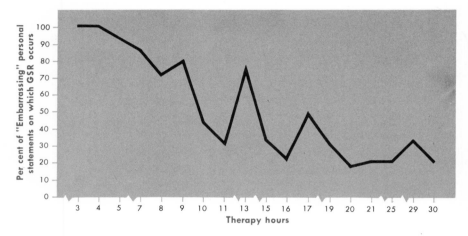

After the interview is over, the detailed study of the records begins. First the interview is transcribed by a typist. A sample portion is shown in Figure 19-6. This is a portion of an interview with a 33-year-old father of one child. Note that the patient's every sound and every pause are faithfully recorded by the typist. Part of the process of the study consists in numbering the sentences, so that they can be identified and scored; each 5-second pause is also numbered.

The next step is to code the interview, according to a system that the investigators have worked out. In this particular code, a sample of which is found in Figure 19-7,

capital letters stand for conscious expression, lower-case letters for inferred unconscious processes. Thus *H-A* means that the coder interprets statement 101 as hostile (*H*), with conscious expression of anxiety (*A*). He interprets statement 115 as hostile (*H*) with unconscious anxiety (*a*). *Res 5* indicates a silence interpreted as resistance; it is used for any silence of 5 seconds. (Note the pause of three-quarters of a minute between statement 101 and the next utterance, 111.) *H-Circ. Mgr.* indicates that by his statement the patient expressed hostility toward the circulation manager. Coding the verbal responses, and coordinating them with the GSR records, is but a first step in the analysis. The next step is to seek common patterns of change in the patient that can tell the investigator more about the process of psychotherapy. Specimens of such patterns revealed by a patient are shown in Figure 19-8.

Another approach to psychotherapy conceives of the process as a communication system between the therapist and the patient, and analyzes this system according to the methods used in the study of communications in small groups.

In one investigation using this approach (Lennard and Bernstein, 1960) four therapists carried two patients each through eight months of psychotherapy, obtaining a tape recording of each session. Since the sessions occurred on the average twice a week, some 500 sessions were involved in the study. The investigators were able to determine the changes in the kinds of communications made over long periods, as well as typical changes within the session. Various kinds of comparisons could be made, such as that of Table 19-2, in which some consequences of greater or lesser activity on the part of the therapist are indicated. It appears that within the limits of this study patients preferred the more active therapists, as indicated by their more frequent willingness to remain in therapy when the research was over (and the period of reduced fees therefore ended), by the frequency of broken appointments, and by signs of strain that were indicated within sessions.

Much remains to be learned about the roots of psychological disturbances and their improvement under therapy. The social problems of mental illness are so great that they deserve increasing investment of manpower and money.

TABLE 19-2
Degree of therapist's activity and indications of strain in interaction between patient and therapist

	More active therapists		Less active therapists	
	A	B	C	D
Number of propositions offered by therapist per session	142	106	58	48
Kinds of propositions:				
Evaluative-prescriptive	32%	46%	18%	29%
High information specificity	47%	44%	24%	32%
Low information specificity	15%	4%	26%	27%
Unclassified	6%	6%	32%	12%
Total propositions	100%	100%	100%	100%
Signs of Strain:				
Patients who discontinued treatment although invited to continue at end of research	1	0	2	2
Broken appointments during first 25 sessions	0	0	3	7
Patients' complaints about strain	few	few	many	many

SOURCE: Lennard and Bernstein, 1960, Table 15, p. 115. Each therapist treated two patients.

19-9

Psychodrama

Psychodrama is the technique of having the patient act out his problems on a stage in closely supervised situations. Above, an audience of patients and doctors watches patient-actors unfold a domestic situation on the stage.

J. R. Black

CRITICAL DISCUSSION

The therapist as person vs. the therapist as technician

Freud once compared the problem of learning psychotherapy with a chess game, in the following words:

> Anyone who hopes to learn the noble game of chess from books will soon discover that only the openings and end-games admit of an exhaustive systematic presentation and that the infinite variety of moves which develop after the opening defy any such description. The gap in instruction can only be filled by a diligent study of games fought out by masters. The rules which can be laid down for the practice of psychoanalytic treatment are subject to similar limitations.[8]

What Freud was saying, in essence, was that formal study of psychotherapy might get at some features of it, but that therapy, as an art, had to be acquired through a kind of apprenticeship with master therapists. In commenting on these issues, Strupp (1960) points out that research on psychotherapy tends to stress either subtle features of human understanding or matters of technique, the former approach to a study of psychotherapy gaining in intuitive richness but being less precise, the latter approach to research being more precise, verifiable, and communicable, but in danger of sacrificing something that is of the essence of the clinical relationship. He believes that the difficulty of being at once profound and clear is not insurmountable.

The studies by Wolpe (1958), Dollard and Auld (1959), and Lennard and Bernstein (1960) would be classified largely as studies of technique, in that they label what the patient is doing and try to see what happens when the therapist responds in certain ways.

Other studies have been concerned more directly with the therapist as a person. Thus Rogers (1961) stresses the therapist's attitudes, and says that techniques are relatively unimportant. Bandura (1956) showed that therapists with high anxiety levels were rated as less successful in psychotherapy. The way in which the therapist reacts to the hostility of the patient has been found to modify the expression of hostility by the patient (Bandura, Lipsher, and Miller, 1960). The general attitude of faith or hope engendered by the therapist is thought to be important (Frank, 1959). The question of the sources of the therapist's attitudes has been discussed by Strupp (1959).

---

[8] Freud (1913); translated in Freud (1958), p. 123.

The most extreme form of antinatural-science approach to psychotherapy is taken by the existentialists (e.g., May, Angel, and Ellenberger, 1958). By their emphasis on the uniqueness of each person's individual existence, which excludes all comparisons with other persons or with social standards of value, they virtually deny any possibility of scientific knowledge about the person or the therapeutic process.

The problem of making a science of psychotherapy is not easily solved, and the search for quantifiable and experimental approaches must not be permitted to obscure the subtlety of personal interactions in the therapeutic situation. However, personal interactions can be subjected to study also, and there is no necessary reason why something as important as psychotherapy should be inaccessible to the methods of natural science.

Psychoanalysis

Psychoanalysis is a method for the treatment of psychoneuroses developed by Sigmund Freud (1856-1939). Psychoanalysis is not a large profession. There are some 750 members of the American Psychoanalytic Association, the recognized organization for the fully accredited psychoanalysts in this country. But the influence of psychoanalysis is much more pervasive than the small group of practitioners suggests.

Along with a method of treatment, Freud proposed a body of psychological theory that has, in one form or another, influenced much of modern thinking—in drama and literature as well as in psychology, medicine, and social science. While we shall be concerned chiefly with the nature of psychoanalytic therapy, it should be kept in mind that the observations made within this technique represent the basic data upon which Freud's theories rest.

Free association

The psychoanalyst ordinarily sees a patient for 50 minutes a visit several times a week for periods of from one to several years. Psychoanalytic therapy, in its original form, is thus not only intensive but extensive. The introductory session is similar to an ordinary counseling session. The patient gives a description of his symptoms. He recounts relevant facts from his personal biography. Then he is prepared to enter upon *free association,* one of the foundations of the psychoanalytic method.

The patient is taught the "basic rule" that he is to say everything that enters his mind without selection, without editing. This basic rule is a very difficult one to follow. The patient's lifetime has been spent in learning self-control, in learning to hold his tongue, in learning to think before speaking. Even the patient who tries conscientiously to follow the basic rule finds that he fails to tell many things. Some passing thoughts seem to be too unimportant to mention, some too stupid, others too indiscreet.

The purpose of free association is to bring to awareness and to put into words repressed thoughts and feelings of which the patient is unaware or which ordinarily go unacknowledged if they come to awareness.

Suppose, for example, that a person's freedom is being hampered by the presence in his household of an invalid for whose care he is responsible. Under such circumstances, he may unconsciously wish for the relief that death of the invalid might bring. But he would disapprove of such a death wish as a violation of his loyalty to the sick person. Actually a death wish of this kind may be very near to awareness, but the habits of a lifetime make the patient deny the wish even to himself. He may show in his fantasies or in other ways a preoccupation with death; possibly he hums tunes that are played at funerals. By acknowledging these fleeting thoughts and feelings instead of repressing them, he becomes aware, first of all, of previously unrecognized ideas and feelings close to awareness. With practice, he gradually brings to consciousness ideas and feelings that he has more deeply repressed.

Interpretation

A person represses certain thoughts and feelings because he fears that to acknowledge them will threaten or degrade him. And he therefore resists their recall. These *resistances* must be overcome before he can associate freely. One of the tasks of the therapist is to aid the patient to overcome his resistances. Sometimes a patient has a free flow of associations until he comes to something that blocks him. Then his mind seems to go blank, and he can think of nothing to say. This blankness is interpreted as resistance to the recall of something effectively repressed. Sometimes, after a particularly revealing session, the patient may forget his next appointment, another indication of resistance to revealing what is hidden. Because resistances are unconscious, they mean that the patient is unable to cooperate fully even though he consciously wishes to do so.

The psychoanalyst attempts to overcome resistance and to lead the patient to fuller self-understanding through *interpretation*. The interpretation is likely to take two forms. First, the analyst calls the attention of the patient to his resistances. The patient often learns something about himself when he discovers that a train of associations is suddenly blocked, that he forgets his appointment, that he wants to change the subject, and so on. Second, the analyst may privately deduce the general nature of what lies behind the patient's statements, and by imparting a hint may facilitate further associations. The patient may say something that seems trivial to him and half-apologize for its unimportance. Here the analyst may point out that what seems trivial may in fact allude to something important. This hint may lead, if the interpretation is appropriately timed, to significant associations. It should be noted that the analyst is careful not to suggest *just what it is* that is important to the patient; this the patient must discover for himself.

The analyst gives somewhat different interpretations in the early and late stages of the analysis. Early in the analysis, he is likely to give interpretations that help the patient to understand resistance. He may encourage free association by pointing out the importance of the seemingly trivial or by noting connections in the patient's associations between thoughts that at first seemed totally unrelated. But as the analysis moves on, the analyst gives more complex interpretations of the content of the patient's associations. If the patient reports a dream, as he usually does, the analyst may encourage him to give associations to the dream in order to aid in its interpretation. Sooner or later the analyst himself figures in the patient's dreams or associations. The relationship between patient and analyst then becomes an occasion for interpretation. The patient's emotionalized attitudes toward the analyst are known as tranference, a process that we need to discuss further.

Transference

Any counseling relationship is social, involving a relationship between the client and the counselor. In psychoanalytical treatment the attitudes of the patient toward the analyst become important in determining his progress. Sooner or later the patient in analysis develops strong emotional responses toward the psychoanalyst, perhaps admiring him greatly in one session only to despise him in the next. This tendency of the patient to make the therapist the object of emotional response is known as *transference,* and the interpretation of transference, although a controversial topic, is one of the foundations of psychoanalytic therapy. According to the theory, the patient sees the therapist as possessing attitudes like his parents', or like his brothers' and sisters', though the therapist may actually be very unlike those for whom he substitutes.

To cite one example: A young woman being treated by a woman psychoanalyst remarked one day as she entered the analyst's office, "I'm glad you're not wearing those lace collars you wore the last several times I was here. I don't like them on you." During the hour, the analyst was able to point out that she had not in fact worn any lace collars. During the preceding sessions the patient had assigned the analyst the role of the patient's mother and had falsely pictured the analyst as dressing as the patient's mother had dressed when the patient was a child undergoing the emotionally disturbing experiences now being discussed in the analytic hours. The patient, while surprised, accepted the interpretation and thereby gained understanding of transference.

Transference does not always involve false perceptions; often the patient simply expresses feelings toward the analyst which he had felt toward figures important earlier in his life. On the basis of these expressed feelings, the analyst is able to interpret the nature of the impulses that have been displaced in his direction. For example, a patient who has always admired an older brother detects something in the analyst's attitude that reminds him of the brother. An angry attack upon the analyst may lead to the uncovering of hostile feelings toward his brother that the patient heretofore had never acknowledged. The analyst, by studying how the patient feels toward him, helps the patient to understand better his conduct in relation to others.

Abreaction, insight, and working through

The course of improvement during psychoanalytic therapy is commonly attributed to three main experiences: abreaction, gradual insight into one's difficulties, and the patient's repeated working through of his conflicts and his reactions to them.

Abreaction means a free expression of repressed emotion, a living again of an intense emotional experience. The process is also called catharsis, as though it were a kind of emotional cleansing. We have already met this aspect of treatment in release therapy. Such free expression may bring some relief, but by itself it does not eliminate the causes of conflict.

Insight refers to the understanding of the roots of the conflict. Sometimes insight comes upon the recovery of the memory of a repressed experience, but the popular notion that a psychoanalytic cure typically results from the sudden recall of a single dramatic episode is mistaken. The patient's troubles seldom have a single source, and insight comes through a gradual increase in self-knowledge. Insight and abreaction must work together: the patient must understand his feelings and feel what he understands. The reorientation is never simply intellectual.

Even while on the road to recovery, the patient goes through a lengthy process of re-education and problem-solving known as *working through*. By facing the same conflicts over and over again, the patient learns to react in more mature and problem-solving ways, to face rather than to deny reality, with the support of the analyst in the permissive situation of the interview. By working through, the patient becomes strong enough to face the threat of the full original conflict situation without distortion and to react without undue anxiety to it.

The end result claimed for a successful psychoanalysis is a deep-seated modification of the personality which will make it possible for the patient to cope with his problems on a realistic basis, without the recurrence of the symptoms that brought him to treatment, and leading to a more comfortable and richer life.

Research on psychoanalysis

Many of the subordinate features of psychoanalytic theory have been subjected to investigation, for example, slips of speech and other manifestations of unconscious influences, dream symbols, studies of projection and other defense mechanisms (Sears, 1943; Hilgard, 1952). The problems of psychoanalysis as a method of therapy are more difficult to investigate; most of what has passed for investigation are simply case studies, in which the interpretation of sequences of events is made plausible by psychoanalytic theory. Investigations within the clinical setting are not easy, but they can be made, and some of them are being carried out.

One study of free association, for example, was directed to the influence of the presence of the analyst (Colby, 1960). It was found that male subjects who were taught to give free associations into a tape-recorder while alone in a room, and to continue to free-associate when an analyst (who remained silent) was present, modified their free associations markedly when the listener was present. The rate at which associations flowed was relatively unchanged, but their content reflected awareness of the listener through many more references to male persons in these associations. Thus some features of transference are open to investigation.

Another study attempted to find the movement that took place in successive psychoanalytic sessions (Bellak and Smith, 1956). Although analysts reviewing recorded sessions could agree quite well as to the major conflicts being expressed within the period, there was little evidence that these main themes were being altered in sessions covering several months. Ideally, such studies should point not only to alterations but to the kinds of interpretations that led to them.

The general plausibility of much that is claimed for psychoanalysis suggests the importance of having its claims established on a firmer basis. This will come about only through imaginative and careful research.

Relative Success of Therapeutic Techniques

No attempt will be made here to evaluate the relative success of the methods of psychotherapy that we have discussed: traditional counseling, client-centered counseling, group therapy, child therapy, and psychoanalysis. Scientists will ultimately learn what kind of method will work best with what kind of client and what kind of therapist, but the problem is extremely complex.

In the first place, it is very difficult to determine how severe a person's problems are at the time he comes for treatment and how well he would get along without treatment. Even patients with severe mental illness sometimes recover spontaneously, that is, without any clear therapy and with no striking environmental change.

In the second place, the criteria of benefit from treatment are very difficult to establish. Can we trust the client's statement that he feels better or that he is pleased with his counselor? Can we trust his family's statement that he is easier to live with? Sometimes a person who has become relieved from his burdens of conflict may seem even harder to live with, for he now fights back against the people who originally caused some of his troubles.

Finally, the classification of success according to method of treatment cannot take into account the role of the individual therapist. We are dealing with subtle human relationships, and the sensitivity and understanding of the counselor or therapist are very important; no formal technique can make up for a lack of appropriate human qualities in the therapist.

These difficulties in appraising therapy do not leave us helpless. Experiments using before-and-after tests and recorded interviews have been performed chiefly by client-centered therapists (Rogers and Dymond, 1954) but also, as we have seen, by therapists using other methods. It is too early to assign relative values to the different approaches.

The most clearly demonstrable therapeutic successes up to the present time have been with the somatotherapies rather than with the psychotherapies. Thus vitamin treatment has reduced the prevalence of mental disturbances associated with pellagra;

antibiotics, through curing syphilis, have reduced the once prevalent organic psychosis known as general paresis; barbiturates have alleviated the symptoms of epilepsy. Electroconvulsive shock has helped greatly in overcoming depressive states. There are hopeful signs with the new tranquilizing drugs such as reserpine and chlorpromazine.

The successes of drug and other somatic therapies by no means exclude the importance of psychotherapy, alone or in combination. The fact that some drugs reduce the distress of patients suffering from mental illness does not excuse us from working upon prevention by trying to discover the underlying causes.

A few years ago much discussion was provoked by a review of research in which Eysenck (1952) concluded that mental patients with little or no treatment were quite as likely to recover as patients with extensive treatment. Eysenck's report has been seriously criticized, however, and the final answers on the effectiveness of psychotherapy are not yet in (Luborsky, 1954; S. Rosenzweig, 1954). Some psychiatrists have collected evidence of substantial success in psychotherapy (Wolpe, 1961).

Practices Enhancing Mental Health

Mental health is essentially a public health problem; that is, the ideal is to create circumstances for healthful living rather than to become preoccupied with the problems of disease. It is better to eliminate mosquitoes than to have to treat malaria, and to guard the water and milk supply rather than to have to treat typhoid fever. Similarly, it is better to provide for normal emotional development than to be concerned primarily with the therapy of neuroses.

Useful work

Absorption in useful work keeps an individual in touch with reality and enhances self-esteem, provided that he accepts the work as dignified and that it is suited to his abilities and interests.

Experience during the depression of the early '30's showed the demoralizing effects of idleness and unemployment. Initially the unemployed were placed on a dole, because it is the cheapest kind of relief to administer. But experience taught the importance of work-relief instead, for without work the individual tended to disintegrate (Bakke, 1940; Watson, 1942). It is increasingly accepted that the right to work is as fundamental as other human rights and as necessary for maintaining the integrity of the individual. Work is not only a matter of livelihood; it provides in itself an important satisfaction and is usually essential to self-esteem. Then, too, many people find satisfaction outside the job in working at hobbies such as stamp collecting or coin collecting, handicrafts, or gardening. These projects, because they are self-initiated and self-regulated, enhance the feeling of being a creative person.

Social participation

Man is a social animal and suffers when isolated from his fellows. The circumstances of modern life tend to produce loneliness for many people. As people move—and they move about a great deal these days—they lose contact with friends and relatives. Modern apartment dwellers often do not know those who live across the hall; the child often has difficulty finding playmates. Social correctives have to be introduced, not as newfangled ideas but as a return to earlier social arrangements. For example, the nursery school substitutes for the large family and for association with neighborhood children; the community center takes the place of the neighborhood barn dance. Such substitutes must be found for people of all ages. Similar problems emerge also, as we saw in Chapter 4, even for older people as they become an increasing proportion of the population.

An illustration of the importance of the social group is provided by studies of alcohol addiction. Alcoholism is a symptom of maladjustment very difficult to cure by ordinary psychotherapeutic methods. Some success has been achieved, however, by Alcoholics Anonymous, a club of ex-alcoholics who help each other to resist the temptation of alcohol. One interpretation of their success is that Alcoholics Anonymous provides the sociability that otherwise was found only at the bar and the support of understanding people who have faced similar problems (Bales, 1944).

Self-understanding

To what extent may a person better his own mental health through self-understanding? This is a difficult question, because a preoccupation with personal problems may be worse than ignoring them and going about the business of living. A few helpful suggestions, nevertheless, emerge out of the experiences of counselors:

1. *A person can learn to accept his feelings as something natural and normal.* Sometimes the desire to face situations unemotionally leads to a false kind of detachment and imperturbability that has destructive consequences. The person begins to suspect emotion and loses the ability to accept as valid the joys and sorrows of the interplay with other people. In many emotion-arousing situations the disturbing emotion is in part a result of his feeling that he does not come up to expectations or that he falls short of his ideal. Even to experience such emotions is frightening; so he tries to escape them by denial. Actually there are many situations in which one can accept unpleasant emotion as perfectly normal and not belittling. It is not necessary to be ashamed of being homesick, or of being afraid of a spirited horse one does not know how to ride, or of being angry at someone who has been a disappointment. These emotions are natural; civilized life permits them,

and it is more wholesome to give them free play than to deny them. To be anxious about one's emotions often leads to a vicious circle. You are afraid that you will be afraid. You then discover that you are in fact mildly afraid. The discovery confirms your suspicions about yourself and then exaggerates the fear. It is better to be willing to accept the naturalness of your emotions as they arise.

2. *If blocked by circumstances from free emotional expression, a person can seek permissible outlets.* Civilized life puts restraints upon free emotional expression. A person may not be permitted to tell his boss or his mother just what his feelings are, but he may accept his own feelings as justified and still withhold their direct expression. But on the principle that such unexpressed feelings tend to persist as tensions, some indirect outlet is desirable. Sometimes an equivalent can be found in violent exercise, expressing hostility with an ax upon a woodpile. Who hasn't taken a rapid walk and eventually found both his pace and his emotion slowing down? Sometimes it helps to acknowledge felt emotion to a sympathetic person not involved in the crisis situation. If a person accepts his right to feel emotion, he may give expression to it in indirect or substituted ways if the direct channels of expression are blocked.

3. *By discovering the occasions which provoke emotional overreaction, a person can learn to guard against it.* Most people find some kinds of situations in which they tend to be more emotional than do other people. It may be that some small failures cause them undue chagrin; it may be that they find certain people excessively annoying. By learning to detect the situations which lead to emotional distortion, they sometimes learn to see the situations in new ways so that they no longer cause this undue emotion. It occasionally happens that our exaggerated awareness of some shortcoming makes us unduly sensitive to criti-

cism. This is one form that projection takes. If my work is so heavy that I have to return to the office at nights, I may get the feeling that I am neglecting my wife or family. If, however, my wife so much as mentions my return to the office, I may get angry—sure that she is accusing me of neglect. Then I will insist that my family makes too many demands upon me. If I can recognize my wife's remark for what it is, an expression of sympathy because I am so busy, then I should feel no anger at her.

Limitations of self-help

The person overwrought by emotional problems does well to seek the counsel of a psychiatrist, a clinical psychologist, or other trained counselor. The mechanisms of self-deception are so pervasive, and unconscious motivation so real, that it is difficult to solve a long-standing personal problem without help. The willingness to seek help is a sign of emotional maturity, not of weakness. The counselor should not be thought of only as the court of last appeal. We do not wait until our teeth are falling out before we go to the dentist. Obtaining psychological help when we need it can become as accepted a practice as going to the dentist. To have emotional or personality disturbances is no more reprehensible than to have a cavity in a tooth.

SUMMARY

1. *Mental health,* like physical health, requires more than the absence of signs of disease. The mentally healthful person has made a satisfactory adjustment to the environment of things and of other people, he has a productive outlook on life, and he lives with zest.

2. The main classes of functional mental disorders (those with no clear organic basis) are the *psychoneurotic reactions* (anxiety reaction, conversion reaction, phobic reaction, obsessive-compulsive reaction) and the *psychotic reactions* (affective reaction, schizophrenic reaction, and paranoid reaction). There are also mental disorders associated with definite organic causes (alcoholism, physical disease, and injury), and the illnesses called *psychosomatic* in which there are physiological changes (such as ulcers) which accompany psychological (psychogenic) conditions.

3. Mental disorders constitute a serious social problem. It is estimated that 1 out of 10 babies born today will spend some time in a mental hospital; community studies have shown as many as 30 per cent of the population as having clinical symptoms of personality disturbance sufficient to interfere with their daily efficiency.

4. *Psychotherapy* is treatment of personality disturbance by psychological means. Among the several methods, that of *social readjustment* recognizes the social nature of the individual and tries to improve his mental health through changing the environment or through giving him the social skills that will increase his acceptability with others. Other methods include *traditional counseling, client-centered counseling, group therapy,* and therapy with children, often in the form of *play therapy.*

5. *Psychoanalysis* is an extended type of psychotherapy. One important method in psychoanalysis is that of *free association,* by which repressed thoughts and feelings are brought to awareness. By *interpreting* the patient's associations, the analyst helps him to see the roots of his disturb-

ance. Through the process of *transference* the patient uses the analyst as a substitute for other people as the object of many of his neurotic reactions. The analyst, in turn, attempts through the understanding of transference to use it as an aid to therapy. Through the processes of *abreaction, insight,* and *working through,* the neurosis may eventually be cured.

6. Research on the various methods of psychotherapy, including psychoanalysis, is concerned both with the therapeutic *process* (i.e., how the patient changes as a result of what goes on within the therapeutic sessions) and with *outcome* (i.e., what percentage of patients were more or less permanently helped by treatment). Present evidence is ambiguous in evaluating the relative advantages of the different methods of treatment; thus far the *somatotherapies* (physical treatment of the body by drugs, electric shock, etc.) have yielded more substantial results than the psychotherapies, but this must not be permitted to reduce emphasis upon the need for better understanding and more appropriate use of psychotherapy.

7. Mental health is a public health problem. It is desirable to place emphasis upon the *prevention* of maladjustment. Both useful work and satisfactory social participation are important in maintaining mental health. The individual can help himself through appropriate self-evaluation, by accepting his own emotions as natural, by finding channels for emotional expression, and by getting such understanding as he can of the occasions on which he overreacts. There are genuine limitations to self-help, however, and it is not a sign of weakness to seek professional help.

SUGGESTIONS FOR FURTHER READING

For general treatments of mental disorders there are the textbooks in psychiatry, such as Noyes and Kolb, *Modern clinical psychology* (5th Ed., 1958), and those in abnormal psychology, such as Coleman, *Abnormal psychology and modern life* (2nd Ed., 1956), or White, *The abnormal personality* (2nd Ed., 1956). Arieti, *American handbook of psychiatry* (2 vols., 1959) is a useful reference source.

For a great variety of systems, see Harper, *Psychoanalysis and psychotherapy* (1959), and Stein, *Contemporary psychotherapies* (1961). For environmental treatment, a good source is Rogers, *The clinical treatment of the problem child* (1939). On counseling as it concerns personal problems not classified as neurotic or psychotic, see Bordin, *Psychological counseling* (1955). On client-centered therapy, see Rogers and Dymond (Eds.), *Psychotherapy and personality change* (1954), and Rogers, *On becoming a person: a therapist's view of psychotherapy* (1961). Dollard and Miller, *Personality and psychotherapy* (1950) draws upon both psychoanalysis and learning theory.

Psychoanalytic therapy is a complex matter with a large literature. Useful introductions are Kubie, *Practical and theoretical aspects of psychoanalysis* (1950), and Menninger, *Theory of psychoanalytic technique* (1958). For the use of what has been learned in psychoanalysis for shorter psychotherapeutic treatment, see Alexander and French (Eds.), *Psychoanalytic therapy* (1946).

Problems of personal adjustment, especially as faced by college students, are treated in such books as Heyns, *The psychology of personal adjustment* (1958), Lindgren, *Psychology of personal and social adjustment* (2nd Ed., 1959), McKinney, *Psychology of personal adjustment* (3rd Ed., 1960), Shaffer and Shoben, *The psychology of adjustment* (2nd Ed., 1956).

Social Behavior

The behavior of animals in groups (pairs, herds, flocks) is as surely an evolutionary product as their bodily forms. Man's life is inescapably social, and human psychology necessarily concerns itself with the relations between the individual and the group. Social psychology is that branch of psychology concerned especially with the problems that arise in the interactions among individuals: person perception, interpersonal relations of various kinds, attitudes and opinions and their change. Among the applications of psychology to human affairs lie many within the field of social behavior: solving problems of vocational choice and of employee selection, meeting the problems created by industrial civilization. Psychology offers no panaceas for social problems, but its developing research methods, joining forces with those of other behavioral sciences, give promise of great social usefulness.

CHAPTER 20

Social Psychology

Individual behavior is always influenced by the social context in which it occurs. This is true for lower animals as well as for man, but man is pre-eminently social; he is born dependent upon other human beings, and his life is spent largely in interaction with other men. Other people are both stimuli for him and the occasions for his responses; their responses to him determine many of the things that he does and he feels.

All of the chapters of psychology can be written around the social theme: the *development* of social behavior, social *motives,* the *learning* of social behavior, the *perception* of people. An adequate account of general psychology is impossible without social references, and we have already met much that is social in earlier chapters. Social considerations figured particularly when behavior was viewed from the *developmental* point of view, as when we saw how early experiences lead to the socialization of the child, the acquiring of language, and the other requisites for social life. In this chapter we shall be somewhat more concerned with social behavior from the *interactive* point of view, that is, how the person behaves in the presence of others and is influenced by them.

Perception of Other Persons

If other people are to become stimuli for our behavior, we need to note the ways in which we perceive them. The attraction of people toward each other determines to a large degree how effective the groups in which people find themselves will be. This attraction among group members, producing cohesiveness within the group, depends upon how the individuals perceive each other and upon their perception of others not affiliated with them. While the ways in which people perceive each other have long been known to be important, for example in relation to prejudice, only within the last decade has person perception become one of the guiding ideas in social psychology (Tagiuri and Petrullo, 1958).

Many of the principles that apply to the perception of impersonal objects apply also to the perception of persons; we learned in Chapter 7 that needs and expectations may affect the perception of impersonal objects, and it is not surprising that perceptual distortion may occur in person perception. We turn now to a consideration of a few of the principles that have emerged from the study of the perception of other people.

Person perception and object perception

The perception of persons follows many of the same rules as the perception of impersonal objects.

Familiarity and Affective Preference. A subject wearing distorting lenses will see a familiar person (e.g., his marital partner) as less visually distorted than a stranger (Wittreich, 1952). If a photograph of a liked person is placed in an apparatus with ambiguous cues to distance, it will be judged to be at a significantly different distance from that of the same-sized photograph of a disliked person (Ittleson and Slack, 1958). If familiarity and preference can distort such perceptual judgments as those of size and distance, then the perception of social attributes will also be subject to distortion.

Principles of Grouping: Figure-Ground Structuring. The perception of individuals as belonging to a common group is achieved according to some of the principles made familiar by Gestalt psychology: similarity, proximity, good continuation, closure, etc. That is, we group together those of similar appearance, clothing, or mannerisms, assuming more congeniality, perhaps, than the similarity assures; we tend to see those who live near together or who associate together as sharing common values or beliefs (including "guilt by association"); we structure the social environment into figure and ground as we do the impersonal environment. When a figure appears, the boundaries are sharpened, and the distinction between what belongs to the figure and what belongs to the ground becomes clear; we may thus structure the world into the "free world" and the "Communist world," ignoring many of the other differences between nations and governments.

The Physical Stimulus. When perceptual distortion occurs, it does not mean that the physical stimulus is not attended to; rather, the stimulus alone does not determine the response because the response is modified by past experiences and present expectations. Careful studies of judgments of individuals from photographs show that these judgments are indeed based upon features of the presented face (Secord, 1958), but that some important distortions enter in. Secord lists five of these:

1. *Temporal extension.* An expression that happened to appear in the momentary photograph is assumed to be a characteristic one. Thus a person who smiled when his picture was taken is assumed to have a continuously happy disposition.

2. *Generalization from significant person.* If a picture reminds the viewer of a significant person in his background (even though he is unaware of this similarity), he is likely to attribute to the person photographed the traits of the earlier known significant person.

3. *Categorization.* This is a tendency to choose some one feature (perhaps the fact that the photograph is of a Negro) to place the person into a category including many traits assumed to hold for the members of that category. This, as we shall see later, is known as stereotyping.

4. *Functional inference.* Having identified a certain characteristic (e.g., age), some inferences are made depending upon the traits associated with that characteristic. This is somewhat similar to categorization, but may not "pigeon-hole" the individual quite as sharply.

5. *Metaphorical generalization.* Features of the face can suggest features of the personality through the association of coarseness of features with roughness or crudeness, fine features with delicacy and sensitivity— a generalization that may go far beyond the actual correlation.

The perceiver's influence upon person perception

Whenever there is any ambiguity in the stimuli that are present, the perceiving person supplements what is given to the senses. When one perceives the social characteristics of a person through observing him, there are acts of judgment involved in which the characteristics of the perceiver become particularly influential.

Perception of Self and of Others. In one study subjects were made fearful by having occasional electric shocks. When they were themselves afraid, they tended to judge the photographs of others as fearful (supplementary projection) or as aggressive (complementary projection).[1] Which direction the perceptual distortion took depended in part upon the judge's expectations about the behavior of the person being judged (Feshbach and Singer, 1957).

People who view themselves as having desirable traits tend to assign these characteristics to others whom they like more than

[1] We have met the concept of projection in Chapters 16 and 18.

to others whom they dislike or to whom they feel neutral. Thus for those who judged masculinity as a desirable characteristic, and felt themselves high in it, other liked men were judged as more highly masculine than other disliked men or men toward whom the judges felt indifferent (Lundy, 1958).

Selective Perception Based on Valued Traits. If one values personal appearance, this may become a key characteristic according to which other people are perceived; if strength, energy, sense of humor, or any other trait has high priority, this may enter to distort the general perception of the person. Evidence along these lines was obtained in a summer camp in which the children were asked to describe other children. The categories or traits that they used tended to be limited to a few for each child as a perceiver, but any one child used the same traits as a basis for classifying those children whom he knew. Thus he might judge all the boys on how good they were at games, or on how sociable (or isolated) they were (Hastorf, Richardson, and Dornbusch, 1958).

Interaction of Two People Perceived Together. If two people are perceived simultaneously, the way in which we perceive either one of them will depend in part on how we perceive the other. This has been pointed out by Peak (1958) in a study concerned only with differences in the degree to which the perceiver likes the two persons. She came to the following three conclusions:

1. If the two persons are liked to the same degree, each will be liked *more* when they are perceived simultaneously.
2. If one is liked a moderate amount more than the other, when they are seen together the degree of liking tends to be *equalized,* that is, the more liked loses a little in favor and the less liked gains a little.

3. When one is liked and the other is disliked, seeing the two together produces a *contrast* effect, leading to a greater liking of the one already liked and a greater disliking of the one previously disliked.

It is evident that effects such as this can be applied to dimensions other than liking and will also be found for groups greater than two people at a time. We do not perceive people in a social vacuum.

Cognitive Balancing. When a person perceives two other persons simultaneously, he also tends to perceive some sort of relation between them. That is, if he likes them both, he expects them to like each other; if he likes one and not the other, he expects them to dislike each other. A theoretical formulation has been given to such expectations by Heider (1958) in his theory of balanced states. A *balanced state,* according to Heider, is one in which the perceived relationships are harmonious and internally consistent. For example, if *A* likes *B*, and perceives that *B* also likes him, and *A* also likes *C*, then *A*'s perception will be in balance if he finds that *B* and *C* also like each other, but his perception will be imbalanced if he notes that *B* and *C* dislike each other. The tendency is for one's perception to move in the direction of balance; thus imbalance leads to motivation to change in the direction of cognitive balancing.

Kogan and Tagiuri (1958) made a test of Heider's theory. They began by asking a number of enlisted naval men first to indicate three members with whom they would choose to go on liberty, and then to guess which three men each of the other three would choose in turn. Some were also asked to indicate which three they would least like to go with on liberty. Now it is possible to assemble eight basic triangular situations involving the perceiver and *two* other persons, based on mutual like and dislike (see Figure 20-1). Four of these are balanced (either

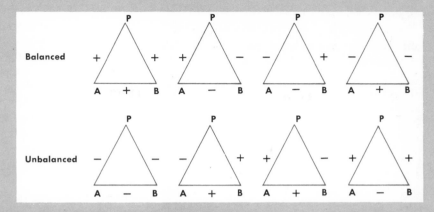

Balanced

Unbalanced

The states refer to the perceptions (cognitions) of the perceiver (P) as he observes the two persons A and B. A plus (+) sign means that the persons connected by the line are perceived to like each other; a minus (—) sign means that they dislike each other. The top four triangles represent balanced states, the bottom four unbalanced ones, according to the theory of Heider (1958).

three positive relations or one positive and two negative) and four are unbalanced (three negative relations or one negative and two positive relations). Kogan and Tagiuri predicted that their subjects would perceive balanced relations more often than unbalanced ones, and more often than the actual facts allowed. Thus if they liked two persons, they would expect them to like each other; if they liked one and disliked the other, they would expect the other two to dislike each other. The results came out as expected. The authors further observed that imbalanced social units are in fact rather rare.

The tendency to balance leads to an overestimation of the popularity of persons the perceiver likes, because he expects others whom he likes to like each other. But a somewhat curious finding also emerges: a perceiver tends to estimate the popularity of those whom he dislikes as higher than the popularity of those he fails to mention in his choices of liking and disliking (Tagiuri, 1958). This is, however, also predicted by Heider's theory, for a situation comes into balance if two people whom the perceiver dislikes happen to like each other.

The study of person perception relates the problems of social psychology to those of general psychology, but with a content that bears upon the interactions among people. We are now ready to turn to some studies of these interpersonal relations.

Interpersonal Relations

Just as the ways in which other people's reactions to each other are perceived differently depending upon the context in which these people appear (e.g., whether alone or together), so an individual's behavior depends also upon the presence or absence of other persons and upon the nature of the reactions of these other persons. We shall note this first in relation to conforming behavior, and then consider some other problems of group behavior.

Conformity to social influences

How much pressure does a group put upon its members to conform to the ideas of the majority? We all know the appeal of the expression, "When in Rome, do as the Romans do." Conformity is not only a good

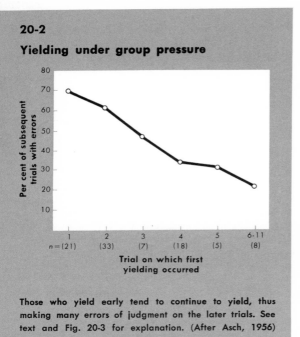

20-2

Yielding under group pressure

Per cent of subsequent trials with errors (y-axis: 10–80)

Trial on which first yielding occurred
n = (21) (33) (7) (18) (5) (8)
1 2 3 4 5 6-11

Those who yield early tend to continue to yield, thus making many errors of judgment on the later trials. See text and Fig. 20-3 for explanation. (After Asch, 1956)

way to get along, it is also for most people a congenial way. The question remains whether group pressures operate in ways beyond mere congeniality in order to influence a person's judgment.

In an experiment designed to study the effect of majority opinion, even when it is contrary to fact, small groups of subjects observed a standard straight line, and then judged which of three other lines equaled it in length. One of the other lines was longer, one shorter, one equal to the standard; the differences were great enough that threshold judgments were not involved. All but one member of each group had been instructed to agree upon a wrong answer for a majority of the trials. The experimental subject was thus pitted against a majority, and his problem was whether to report what he would have reported if he had been alone, and hence to disagree with the majority, or to doubt his own judgment and agree. Many subjects refused to change, and continued to hold to their independent appraisals. But a substantial number yielded under pressure

from the others' apparent judgments. The amount of yielding depended upon (1) the clarity of conditions (lack of clarity led to conformity to majority opinion), (2) individual differences, and (3) the size and unanimity of the opposition. With the opposition of only one other person there was very little yielding; with two against one the amount of yielding became pronounced; and a majority of three was nearly as effective as larger majorities against the lone dissenter.

The importance of some factor within the individual is suggested by the ease of yielding. Those who yielded early in the experiment showed greater willingness to conform than those who yielded late (Figure 20-2).

Questioning of the subjects showed that for the most part they respected the genuineness of the judgments expressed by the majority and that they had great doubt about their own judgments when they disagreed with the majority. In other words, the subject did not hold to his original belief and agree merely for the sake of agreement. Many thought there was some sort of optical illusion involved or that they were having some previously unsuspected trouble with their eyes (Asch, 1956).

Thus the mere assertion of majority opinion, without any effort to persuade, may lead susceptible individuals to agree with the majority even on a matter of fact on which individual judgment would lead to opposite conclusions.

Resistance to Change. Social behavior often shows a resistance to changing conditions. Perhaps this resistance comes about because the majority influences the beliefs of all group members. The minority who might be ready for change, instead of enlisting others, may often be drawn back into the position of the majority. But when change is desirable, the influence of group members upon each other can be used to help bring it about. The study of the use of such group processes to achieve desirable

William Vandivert from *Scientific American*

20-3

Conflict caused by resistance to yielding

Six of the seven subjects have been instructed to give uniformly wrong answers on 12 of the 18 pairs; the seventh, who has been told he is participating in an experiment in visual judgment, thus finds himself a lone dissenter when he gives the correct answers.

Subject leans forward anxiously to look at a pair of cards.

He shows the strain of repeated disagreement with the majority.

After 12 trials, he persists in his opinion, saying that "he has to call them as he sees them."

social changes has come to be called *action research*. The following illustration of action research was concerned with a problem that arose in a pajama factory in which workers were resistant to change, and when forced to change against their wishes lowered their production and often quit their jobs.

The factory in which the experiment on resistance to change took place employed 500 women and 100 men, working on a piece-rate basis. They thus knew what they could earn at a familiar job, but felt uncertain about what they might earn on a new assignment. In general they were resistant to changing assignments. Analysis of work records showed that most operators dropped off considerably when placed on a new job, and recovered their old work level very slowly. These facts set the background for the experiment.

On the assumption that group forces were interfering with change, it was decided to experiment with different methods of group interaction in order to change attitudes toward new assignments. One group was allowed no participation in planning the change (i.e., transfer to a new job); another was allowed participation through representation; the third was allowed total participation. The results showed the benefit of the total-participation method in producing readiness for change (Figure 20-4). The participation-through-representation group fell between the no-participation and the total-participation groups, starting low after transfer to the new jobs, but then gradually improving (Coch and French, 1948).

The main reasons for the success of the preferred group methods were that the need for the changes became clearly understood, and the workers themselves helped to plan the changes. As a consequence, group support was gained for the changes, and individual doubts were resolved.

Circumstances Favoring Compliance. A great deal of social behavior is regulated by group "norms" to which the group members are expected to comply. Thus closely knit groups come to share common attitudes and opinions on many topics. When a member is assimilated into a group, his perceptions tend to change to conform to the group norms. Studies have shown that the more strongly a member is attracted to a group, the more he tends to conform to the group norms (Kelley and Volkart, 1952). Moreover, a member who is not fully acceptable to a group tends to be more sensitive to majority group opinion than fully accepted members, who are freer to deviate and to hold opinions of their own (Jackson and Saltzstein, 1958).

While for the most part these changes of opinion in conformity to group pressure take place without great strain, sometimes compliance is forced. A study by Festinger and Carlsmith (1959) bears on the consequences of forced compliance. Subjects placed in a boring situation were offered various amounts of money to persuade prospective subjects for the same experiment that the experience had been interesting and exciting. According to the authors' theories, two results should occur on the basis of the following principles:

1. When a person is forced to do or say something discordant with his privately held opinion, there will be a tendency for that opinion to change in such a way as to make it correspond more closely to the act performed.
2. The greater the pressure used to induce the discordant act, the *smaller* will be the tendency to change the original opinion.

The first effect follows directly from Festinger's concept of *dissonance reduction* (i.e., the reduction of incongruity between opinion and action), a concept somewhat similar to Heider's strain toward balance. This result was found: subjects who complied in telling others that the task was interesting changed their own reports on how interesting the task had been.

The second effect is not so obvious, al-

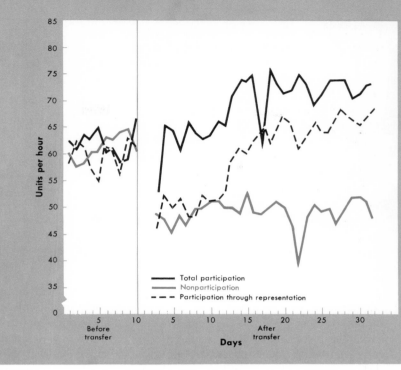

20-4

Overcoming resistance to change

Where group processes (total participation and participation through representation) are used, there is more rapid recovery from the work loss following transfer. (After Coch and French, 1948)

though it is also predicted from the theory. If one yields to a great pressure, the dissonance is reduced by the pressure, so that there is less incongruity in telling a fib for a large sum than for a small one. One doesn't tell a fib for a small sum; one changes one's opinions. The experimental results confirmed this prediction.

A person's behavior in any situation is often very much influenced by what someone else has just done. For example, Helson, Blake, and Mouton (1958) found that they could influence the number of signatures on a petition both by the strength of the request made to sign and by the reaction of others, for example, by the number of signatures already on the petition when it was circulated.

In a related experiment (Freed and others, 1955) the circumstances were studied under which students would violate a sign prohibiting entry of a building. Signs had three degrees of "strength," the stronger signs pointing to alternatives:

Strongest: "Absolutely No Admittance—Use Another Entrance."
Next: "You Are Requested to Enter by Another Entrance."
Weakest: "Absolutely No Admittance."

The subjects of the experiment were those who approached the entrance in the normal course of their lives; in other words, they did not know they were participating in an experiment. Accomplices, when they saw someone approaching, walked up to the door and read the sign; half the time the accomplice obeyed the instruction, half the time he disobeyed and entered. In the control condition, no accomplice was present.

Results were in the predicted direction. The highest conformity was found with the strongest sign and a compliant social model; the lowest conformity (greatest violation of the prohibition) with the weakest sign and a nonconforming model. Interviews with the inadvertent subjects showed that they were usually unaware of the background that determined their conformity or nonconformity.

Sabine Weiss

20-5

Fads and group pressure

Clothing fads reveal group pressure to conform.

Social conformity and independence of judgment are obviously both essential to the smooth running of social life and to progress. The foregoing studies, while dealing with small-scale social processes, are relevant to social behavior of broader significance.

Intergroup tensions and prejudice

Identification with groups has the desirable consequence of creating satisfying relationships among individuals. At the same time the very attitudes of identification may lead some people to reject those who are not within the group. The problem of antagonism among groups is of major concern because it is a threat to harmonious social living.

In-Groups and Out-Groups. We noted earlier the relevance to social perception of the figure-ground relationship (p. 552). A similar perceptual structuring occurs in group identification, so that the group in which membership is held becomes a figure with fairly definite contours. The group to which a person belongs and with which he identifies himself is known as an *in-group.* Other people are identified as members of *out-groups.* The boundaries are further sharpened if the interests of groups conflict

so that the in-group and the out-group come into competition. Feuds between family groups and political battles between the party in power and the party seeking power represent in-group–out-group conflicts. Caste and class distinctions are, of course, fundamentally based on in- and out-grouping.

The boundaries between groups are not all alike. Some boundaries are more permeable than others; that is, individuals can cross them and come into or go out of the group. On college and university campuses many clubs and societies are open to all or nearly all students who care to join them, and there is little coercion to remain in the group if interest lags. In other organizations, such as fraternities, admission is by way of special invitation and initiation, and the pressure is very strong against breaking group ties once they are established. The boundaries of fraternity membership are less permeable than those of the other clubs.

Assigning oneself to a group leads one also to assign others to groups—even though the "others" may have group feelings entirely different from the groups to which one assigns them. One kind of arbitrary group classification leads to *stereotyping,* in which people attribute to an individual characteristics which they believe typical of the group to which they assign him.

An illustration of stereotyping is given in a study by Secord, Bevan, and Katz (1956), in which subjects whose attitudes toward Negroes were known were asked to rate a number of pictures according to 25 traits. The pictures included 10 Negro faces and 5 white faces, with the Negro faces selected to reflect a wide range of Negroid features. The traits listed were 10 physiognomic traits characteristic of Negroes, and 15 personality traits widely regarded as part of the stereotype of the Negro. Once a subject selected a picture as that of a Negro, he tended to assign categorically the personality traits characteristic of the Negro as he conceived them, paying no attention whatever to the individual differences in the pictures. The results held for the less prejudiced individuals as well as for the more prejudiced ones. Thus there is a strong tendency to assign traits to an individual on the basis of his group membership, even though individuals vary in the extent to which they show the characteristics of the group.

We wish now to examine some of the ways in which in-group and out-group feelings create intergroup problems.

Scapegoating. The notion of a scapegoat derives from an ancient practice reported in the Old Testament. Periodically the sins of a tribe were with appropriate ceremonies transferred to a goat, which was then driven off into the wilderness. The innocent goat was made to suffer for the sins of the people.

The practice of finding a victim upon whom to place the blame for our troubles, and hence to make the object of our aggressions, is a familiar one. The child may retaliate against a pet when frustrated by parents or playmates; Hitler found it convenient to blame the Jews for Germany's plight; industrialists blame labor unions for rising prices; labor unions blame capitalists for causing depressions; farmers blame politicians for hard times connected with crop failures. We have already discussed scapegoating as the mechanism of displaced aggression.

How do group phenomena enter into the selection of objects for scapegoating? In an analysis of scapegoating, G. W. Allport (1944) pointed out the following four characteristics which make some people easy victims.

1. Members of the group to receive the aggression must be easily identifiable. The dark skin color of the Negroes makes them much more vulnerable to attack than if they looked like whites. A perceptible difference is enough to favor the separation of figure and ground, and to serve as a reminder of the possibility of difference between in-group and out-group. Sometimes identifiability is enforced, as when Hitler required Jews to wear special insignia.

2. Members of the out-group must be accessible. The mechanism of displacement requires that we substitute for the inaccessible target an accessible one (see p. 507). When Hitler had to find an enemy to attack before Germany rearmed, he turned to the Jews within Germany. In the South, when times are hard, the preferred targets of blame might be Northern industrialists rather than Negroes; but it is harder to give vent to feeling against the absent industrialists than against the accessible group at home.

3. Those selected as scapegoats must be unable to retaliate. If aggression is in danger of punishment, it swerves away and finds a victim unable to strike back. In an authoritarian situation—that is, one in which there is a strong leader—the leader may be responsible for much of the frustration of group members. But the leader is in a protected and powerful position. Hence the aggression is taken out on some lesser individual or individuals.

4. The scapegoats usually will have been scapegoats before. People and nations usually manage to justify their aggressions self-righteously. The current inciting incident is often too trivial or the responsibility of the

scapegoat too remote to justify the extent of the aggression except on the basis of previous antagonism. A very small incident is often the excuse for new aggression, because an undercurrent of hostility persists from the past. The Turk may attack the Armenian in his midst, the Japanese the Korean, partly because they have attacked these people before.

If a community wants to protect a group habitually chosen as scapegoats, in addition to invoking the usual sanctions that protect individual liberty it is necessary to counteract the four conditions that have been outlined above. The changes are a matter of degree. Racial characteristics which make some members of a group identifiable cannot be erased. But habits of dress and gesture which make ethnic groups different from others can be modified so that the minority group conforms more nearly to the practices of the dominant group, with a consequent reduction in social distance.

The accessibility of the target groups is lessened when segregation is lessened. Race riots in the North have occurred almost exclusively in cities in which a high degree of segregation exists, as in Chicago, where a mob can find a Negro community to attack. Boundary phenomena are enhanced when the boundaries are visible geographically.

The law must increase the retaliatory strength of the victims of aggression. We can check the displacement mechanism only by making aggression toward the out-group punishable in the same way as in-group aggression.

The fourth condition can be met chiefly through education. The more people become aware of the irrationality of group action and of past injustices in the blame assigned to minority groups, the more they will resist future abuses.

Racial Prejudice. By "racial prejudice" we mean expressions of disapproval toward members of given ethnic groups, whether racial in a biological sense or merely of the same cultural or national origins. Such prejudices in America are commonly expressed against Negroes, Jews, Irish, Italians, Mexicans, and other groups considered more or less "foreign," even though, like the American Indians, they are frequently as native as the groups showing the prejudice.

One study of women college students showed an excessive amount of racial prejudice (especially prejudice against Jews) among those who were members of sororities, those of upper income levels, and those who were politically conservative. While sororities often communicate race prejudice through their procedures of selecting members, the anti-Semitic attitudes did not follow simply from the group identifications of these girls. More careful study revealed many basic personality needs which were finding disguised expression in hostile feelings toward Jews.

A test designed to discover the degree of anti-Semitism was administered to a group of University of California women. Those with extreme anti-Semitic scores were interviewed and tested more intensively to determine what, if any, qualities they had in common. It was found that most of those high in anti-Semitism showed high conformity on socially acceptable characteristics such as respect for parents, neatness, self-control, and lack of sensuality. When the girls were studied with such devices as the Thematic Apperception Test, however, a great deal of repressed hostility was detected. It was inferred that many of their natural impulses to express their likes and dislikes directly were being repressed. Through the distortions of the defense mechanisms, especially projection, they were attributing bad qualities and impulses to minority groups, thereby justifying their feelings of antipathy (Frenkel-Brunswik and Sanford, 1945; Adorno and others, 1950).

Three methods of attacking the problem of race prejudice are possible. One is to try to improve the mental health of children as they grow up so that they do not need, in maintaining status or excusing their inadequacies, to indulge in scapegoating. The second is to reduce the social supports given to prejudice by community arrangements, such as segregation in residence or in the office, factory, or military camp. And, finally, it is possible to reduce the teaching of prejudice which goes on subtly through the stereotypes of comic strips, radio programs, and motion pictures.

The problem will not be fully solved until adults become aware of the degree to which they pass on to their children their own attitudes, often without intended malice. Probably the unintentional transmission of prejudice through casual remarks, anecdotes, and innuendoes accounts for more prejudice than direct efforts of agencies promoting hatred.

CRITICAL DISCUSSION
Values in social psychology

The limits of responsibility of the social psychologist in the study of value-laden fields, such as prejudice, are not entirely clear.

As a research scientist he must of course remain objective in his study of the facts as they exist, not selecting or distorting the phenomena in accordance with his own preferences. He can study prejudice exactly as he studies sensory thresholds or the learning curves of laboratory rats. On this much of his task there is agreement (Marquis, 1948).

The social scientist can also remain objective in evaluating programs whose policy direction is in the hands of someone else. Thus if a school system has decided to try to reduce prejudice among its pupils, he can arrange the before-and-after tests to see how well the program has worked. Here, too, his role can be detached, though now the temptation is strong for him to offer suggestions to correct obvious defects in the program. As soon as he does that, his personal values are being joined with those of the policy-makers, even though the advice he gives comes out of his scientific background.

It is almost inevitable that in our society the social scientist, in some of his roles at least, will use his techniques and knowledge

to influence policy. Thus he will fight for the right to be as rational as possible in the study of irrational social processes—a right that would be denied him in authoritarian countries. When he tries to influence policy, he is perhaps exercising his rights as a citizen rather than as a scientist, but these two functions are not always clearly distinguishable. We would not think well of an electrical engineer who was willing to take orders from a town council to install a direct-current system if he knew that an alternating-current system was better adapted to the community's needs. We would expect him to use his expertness to influence relevant policies. So, too, if the social psychologist were sure that one kind of treatment of offenders was better than another in reducing juvenile delinquency, we would expect him to advocate it. In these illustrations there is no conflict over the values: the community wants an efficient electrical system and wants to reduce delinquency. Therefore the scientist's advice on policy is acceptable. When the values are themselves the subject of debate, however, the role of the scientist is more difficult. Perhaps in these situations we can distinguish between his two roles, that of *investigator* and that of *advocate*, permitting both roles but not confusing the two (Allport, 1954b, pp. 515-19).

Attitudes, Opinions, and Their Change

In ordinary social interchange the attitudes, preferences, and prejudices that sway people affect the satisfactions of living together. They are part of the fabric of social motives; they provide occasions for conflict and for aroused emotion (p. 171). In a political democracy, sensitive to the wishes of the people, the molding and expressing of public opinion are of the essence of the political process. In an international situation in which the sensitivities of peoples are easily injured and antagonisms aroused, the understanding of attitudes and opinions may mean the difference between war and peace. Hence attitudes and opinions—who holds them and how they change—are legitimate topics for serious study.

Attitudes

A precise definition of attitude is difficult because attitudes overlap with other kinds of psychological preparation for response. We may accept the following definition, recognizing that it will become clearer when placed in the context of the following studies: An *attitude* represents both an *orientation* toward or away from some object, concept, or situation, and a *readiness to respond* in a predetermined manner to these or *related* objects, concepts, or situations.[2] Both orientation and readiness to respond have emotional, motivational, and intellectual aspects. They may be in part unconscious ("I do not like thee, Dr. Fell, the reason why I cannot tell . . .").

Enduring attitudes develop through many learning experiences related to other people. Allport (1935) has suggested four common conditions for the formation of attitudes:

1. The accretion and integration of responses learned in the course of growing up. For example, being raised in a home in which the father is deferred to and the sons are valued above the daughters will affect general attitudes regarding male supremacy.

2. The individuation, differentiation, or segregation of experiences. Experiences do not merely accumulate; they become sharpened and patterned, so that some attitudes become more specific as the individual grows up.

3. The influence of some dramatic experience or trauma. Sometimes a single experience may have a lasting influence and may generalize to related stimuli. Nausea following the eating of a strange food may generalize to a distaste for all related dishes. A bad experience with a single member of some ethnic group may lead to a distrust of all members of that group.

4. The adoption of ready-made attitudes.

[2] The definition combines features of Allport's definition (1954*a*), p. 43, and that of Hovland, Janis, and Kelley (1953), p. 7.

Sometimes attitudes are picked up through imitation of the attitudes of parents or others.

Because attitudes are so interwoven with affective and highly motivated experiences, they become abiding personality characteristics. On the other hand, attitudes as components of personality cannot be separated from the objects or events in the social context to which they refer. Thus a "conforming" person is not necessarily socially conservative: if he happens to be a member of a left-wing group, his conforming tendencies may lead him to go along with his group. An extended study of 10 men by Smith, Bruner, and White (1956) showed a good deal of correspondence between their individual life histories and their attitudes toward Russia, but the relationships were by no means one-to-one. It was clear, however, that their attitudes toward Russia were dictated only in part by the facts as they saw them; the attitudes were also expressions of other aspects of the individual personalities. For example, men who were more likely to blame others than themselves when things went wrong in their personal lives were also more likely to place the burden of blame on Russia for the worsening of United States-Soviet relations.

Attitude Scales. Attitude scales can be constructed in a manner similar to personality inventories. The questions, instead of dealing with personal problems and troubles, deal with preferences and beliefs about social issues. Such scales attempt to measure attitudes toward political parties, religion, Negroes, labor unions, international organizations. Once a satisfactory scale has been prepared, those who take it as a test can be scored for the degree to which they hold a favorable or unfavorable attitude, and changes in attitudes will show up in their scores on repeated tests.

One of the very early uses of such attitude scales was in testing the effect of a motion picture on changing the attitudes of school children. A large group of high school students took an attitude test to determine how favorable or unfavorable their attitudes were toward the Chinese. Then they witnessed a motion picture giving a sympathetic portrayal of Chinese life. When they took the attitude test the following day, scores showed a distinct shift in the favorable direction. Some of the students took the test again 5 months later, and others 19 months later. Results showed that 62 per cent of the students retained the improved attitude as long as a year and a half after they had seen the picture (Peterson and Thurstone, 1932).

Social psychologists have given a great deal of attention to constructing attitude scales and to developing theories about attitude measurement.

Many investigators, among them those who conducted the study described above, have made use of Thurstone's method (Thurstone and Chave, 1929). Thurstone constructed his attitude scales by assembling a large number of statements concerning a topic, some mildly favorable and mildly unfavorable, others strongly favorable and strongly unfavorable. A hundred or more judges sorted these statements into a number of piles, indicating their judgments as to the degree to which the statement was favorable or unfavorable. For example, a judge, whether personally pro- or anti-union, would sort the following statement as extremely favorable to unions: "All industrial workers should belong to unions." Similarly, he would sort the following as unfavorable: "Labor unions should be forbidden by law." He might have more trouble knowing just where to put statements such as: "Labor leaders do not represent rank-and-file membership," or "Workers have a right to organize, but the closed shop, in which all workers have to belong to the union, should be prohibited"; but studies have shown that judges who differ greatly in their own attitudes agree quite well in their estimation of the degree of favorableness or unfavorableness of individual items (Hinckley, 1932). Those who use Thurstone's method then construct the scale to be used as a test by selecting items upon which the judges are in substantial agreement. These will represent fairly equal intervals along the scale from favorable to unfavorable. Each item receives a number to indicate its scale position. When a subject takes the test, he indicates which statements he can endorse. His score corresponds to the average scale position of the items he endorses.

Another method, that of Likert (1932), eliminates the use of judges by having each subject give his answers along a 5-point scale: *strongly approve, approve, undecided, disapprove, strongly disapprove*. Although there are some differences, the results of the Thurstone and Likert methods agree rather well in discriminating between those with favorable and unfavorable attitudes on a given issue.

The quantitative techniques of Thurstone, Likert, and others have made it possible to study changes in attitudes through various influences and to study the persistence of changes through time.

CRITICAL DISCUSSION

Technical developments in attitude measurement

Technical developments in attitude appraisal during and since World War II deserve more than the passing mention they have received thus far, even though an introductory discussion cannot do justice to them because they are complex and involve advanced statistical and mathematical assumptions.

Guttman's *scalogram* method seeks to find "pure" scales along a single dimension, so that a subject who answers any one question favorably will answer favorably *all* items to which a favorable reply is more commonly given. We can imagine a table of favorable ($+$) and unfavorable ($-$) responses as follows, question 1 being the easiest answer in a favorable direction (and therefore the "least" favorable), question 6 being most extreme, that is, requiring the most favorable attitude possible in order to yield an agreeing answer:

Sub-ject	Least					Most
	1	2	3	4	5	6
A	+	+	+	+	+	+
B	+	+	+	+	+	−
C	+	+	+	+	−	−
D	+	+	+	−	−	−
E	+	+	−	−	−	−
F	+	−	−	−	−	−
G	−	−	−	−	−	−

With a scale that worked this way we would be sure that Subject *A* was the most favorable in attitude toward the given object or situation, and Subject *G* the least favorable. Note that one who has an in-between attitude, such as Subject *D*, expresses his attitude not merely as "favorable on three of the six questions" but "favorable on *only* the three questions that are most commonly answered in the direction of a favorable attitude." If the scale worked according to theory, the responses of Subject *D* would be the only kind of response pattern with three favorable answers out of six. The scale thus seeks an ideal of internal consistency. But this ideal is not actually found, and statistical devices have to be developed to determine how close the actual scale comes to it.

For instance, in scaling 12 questions on attitudes toward the Army, the question that was most easily answered in the favorable direction, and which therefore fell at the *least* favorable end of the scale, was: "In general, how interested do you think the Army is in your welfare?" (A series of possible replies was included for checking.)

The question at the *most* favorable extreme of the scale, which according to expectations would be answered favorably only if all other answers were favorable, was: "On the whole, do you think the Army gives a man a chance to show what he can do?"

The test of the scale comes when one determines how consistent with the ideal the replies actually are. This particular scale had a "coefficient of reproducibility" of $r = .89$ (a perfect scale would yield $r = 1.00$), so that it was moderately successful in meeting the criteria set us (Guttman, 1950).

Attitudes, Affects, and Beliefs. Attitudes commonly show a certain consistency among the feelings, beliefs, and overt actions called forth by the objects of these attitudes. That is, if the object of an attitude (e.g., the United Nations) evokes pleasant feelings, it is also likely to elicit beliefs about its effectiveness in promoting value (e.g., world peace), and to lead to actions consonant with the belief (e.g., contributing to the citizens' association that supports the United Nations).

What happens to an attitude when feelings (affective responses) change? Do the beliefs (cognitions) also change? Because the affective and cognitive components are correlated, it is plausible to expect change in one to produce a change in the other, but the matter has actually been put to test.

Rosenberg (1960*a*, 1960*b*) proposed that a strong and irreversible alteration of attitudinal affect would result in a reorganization of the person's associated cognitions. His subjects (22 graduate and professional students at Yale University) first indicated their affective responses to certain related propositions, and then their interest level in the topic, for seven issues: labor's right to strike, the city-manager plan, the United States being more conciliatory to Russia, the provision of comprehensive Federal medical insurance, living in Los Angeles, Negroes moving into white neighborhoods, and the United States and Canada uniting to form a single nation. The experiment was concerned with modifying the subjects' attitudes in one high-interest and one low-interest area through a change in only the affective component of the attitude.

For half the subjects (11 who were selected because of their high hypnotic susceptibility), affect was changed a week or two later through suggestion under hypnosis that their affective responses would change in a stated way, but that they would forget upon arousal from hypnosis that they had been given the suggestion. The 11 other subjects were treated similarly, but without hypnosis. The change in affect could be either from negative to positive or from positive to negative. Thus a subject who asserted labor's right to strike might receive the suggestion that the thought of a strike by labor would always

TABLE 20-1

Affect change and associated cognitive changes under post-hypnotic suggestion: high-interest attitude objects

	Difference between means of experimental and control groups * (N = 11 each)	p (experimental exceeds control in all comparisons)
Affect Change (result of suggestion within hypnosis)	3.30	.001
Associated Cognitive Change		
1. General cognitive reorganization	2.62	.01
2. Change in importance of associated values	3.15	.002
3. Change in importance as means to attain values	3.80	.0002
Control: Change in affect scores for attitude objects not manipulated	.07	.90

SOURCE: Rosenberg (1960b).

* The change scores are summarized through the application of a special statistical procedure known as the Mann-Whitney Rank Sum Test, the details of which need not concern us; the values reported are Mann-Whitney z's.

make him feel depressed, while a subject who had some hesitation about Negroes moving into a white neighborhood might be told under hypnosis that the mere idea of Negroes moving into white areas would give him a happy, exhilarated feeling. For 6 of the experimental subjects the affective manipulation was from negative to positive, while for the other 5 it was from positive to negative. Note that the subject was told that he would *feel* differently; nothing was said about changing any of his related beliefs.

The results for attitudes upon issues in which the subject expressed high interest are shown in Table 20-1. Note that in all comparisons the experimental subjects changed their associated cognitive attitudes more than the control subjects, whether the change was judged by the general amount of cognitive reorganization, by the change in value of the issue as a source of satisfaction to the subject, or by a change in estimation of the proposals as a means of attaining the value in question. For attitude areas in which there

was no manipulation, the experimental subjects changed no more than the control ones, showing that the change was not a consequence of the hypnotic experience as such. While only the high-interest attitudes are represented in the table, the results for low-interest areas were similar.

The results of Table 20-1 represented changes before and after a single half-hour hypnotic session, after which the original attitudes were restored. When, in a later experiment, the changed affect (in this case one on the foreign aid program of the United States) was permitted to remain for a week, with testing on the third, fifth, and eighth days before amnesia was removed, there was some residual effect of the changed attitude which persisted for at least 10 days after removal of the amnesia. These persistent changes were apparently due to a kind of "self-convincing" that went on in arguing for the new attitude while under the influence of the post-hypnotic suggestion.

It should be noted that the changes made were usually quite consistent with the general belief and attitude patterns of the subject, but modified in ways that made the changed attitude acceptable. For example, a subject who believed that abandoning economic aid to a country was bad for its economic growth might decide (if told under hypnosis to become less favorable to such aid) that the bad effect would be temporary, but the long range effect good. One favorable to desegregation might move from an impatient position to one favoring gradualism, thus preserving his general value system while actually altering the attitude to correspond to the new affect.[3]

Opinions and their measurement

Attitudes grade into opinions, and there is no sharp difference between them. We may attempt, however, to hold to a difference proposed by Hovland, Janis, and Kelley (1953). An attitude, as indicated earlier (p. 564), represents an orientation or preference and may be in part unconscious. An *opinion,* according to the above authors, always involves some kind of *expectation* or *prediction* (not merely a preference) and can always be put into words. The subject may avoid putting his opinions into words, or what he says may not express his true opinion, but according to this definition an opinion *can* always be *verbalized.*

No matter how we separate attitudes and opinions by definition, they are closely related. If you hate a person (expressing an *attitude* of hatred), you are likely to expect bad behavior of him (expressing an *opinion* about his behavior). If he behaves better than predicted (thus changing your *opinion*), you may like him better (thus also changing your *attitude*).

[3] The possibility that hypnosis can be used to produce drastic changes in attitude, as in brainwashing (p. 576), is remote, but some effect on attitudes for highly hypnotizable subjects cannot be ruled out. Other persuasive methods, without hypnosis, might prove equally effective; the control groups in the reported experiments were not intended to see what could be achieved without hypnosis, but only to show that changes had taken place under hypnosis.

Another rather practical distinction between attitude measurement and opinion measurement can be made: Attitude measurement tends to deal primarily with the *individual* (where he stands on a scale of favorable or unfavorable attitudes), while opinion measurement tends to deal with *subgroups* (e.g., the fraction of the population most likely to vote in a school bond issue). These differences bear some relation to the Hovland, Janis, and Kelley definitions because opinion studies, more often than attitude studies, deal with predicted action. The distinction is of some interest because investigators tend to be concerned with *private* attitude but with *public* opinion.

The public opinion poll first attained national interest with the presidential election of 1936. Using the then-accepted "straw-vote" technique, the *Literary Digest* incorrectly predicted the election of Landon over Roosevelt, while the better-designed polls, of which the Gallup poll is the best known, predicted Roosevelt's re-election. The success of the public opinion polls brought them into prominence.

The Public Opinion Survey. The public opinion survey is not to be identified only with the election poll, for many surveys have purposes other than predicting election outcomes. It is true, however, that newspaper and magazine polls grew out of the election prediction polls, so that the public opinion "ballot" tended at first to be modeled largely after an election ballot. People were asked to state what side of an issue they were on, and the percentage of answers was then reported.

We now know that the simple "yes-no" answer to a question about a public issue is likely to be very misleading. For one thing, the form of the question may produce a great variation in the number answering one way or the other.

Here are two questions asked of a sample of the public early in 1945: [4]

[4] Quoted by Cartwright (1946).

"After the war would you like to see the United States join some kind of world organization, or would you like to see us stay out?" (National Opinion Research Center, January, 1945)

Join	64%
Stay out	26
Undecided	10
	————
	100%

"Do you think the United States should join a world organization with police power to maintain world peace?" (American Institute of Public Opinion, April, 1945)

Yes	81%
No	11
No opinion	8
	————
	100%

There is no reason to suppose that the difference between 64 per cent and 81 per cent is a reflection of any change in international attitudes between January and April. The phrase "to maintain world peace" in the second question no doubt raised the percentage of affirmative answers.

One of the chief difficulties with the opinion ballot is that it is hard to know how firmly the respondent holds his convictions, a problem met also in attitude scaling. The answers to "yes-no" questions may be given as casually as they sometimes are to the questions in a college "true-false" examination. The vagueness or firmness of answers is partly dependent on the extent to which public opinion has crystallized on an issue. Often people are asked to give opinions about highly technical matters, such as the influence of atomic energy on the future of civilization. In response to such questions there is often a high percentage of "no opinion." Interpretations of the opinions offered then have to be made with extreme caution.

Even though the ballot form is used, many refinements in questioning are possible. One device is to use a number of fixed alternatives instead of a mere "yes-no" reply. Often a printed card with four or more possible replies is handed to the person being interviewed. He is asked to select the one which most nearly represents his own opinion. Another device is that of the "filter" question, used to determine what question should be asked next. The following illustration [5] shows

[5] American Institute of Public Opinion, November, 1940. Quoted by Cantril (1944), p. 22.

how a stereotyped reply can be broken down by asking a second question of those who answer in a conventional manner:

Do you believe in freedom of speech?

Yes	97%
No	1
Don't know	2
	————
	100%

If "Yes": Do you believe in it to the extent of allowing Fascists and Communists to hold meetings and express their views in this community?

Yes	23%
No	72
No opinion	5
	————
	100%

Because answers depend on the context in which the questions are asked, and because they depend so much upon both the form and the wording of the question, a single percentage can never be interpreted unambiguously. Successive polls repeating identical questions do indicate trends, however, and these are often very revealing.

The alternative to the ballot form of question is that known as the *free-answer* or *open* question, that is, a question to which the respondent must reply in his own words. This method has genuine advantages, although it requires somewhat more skilled interviewers (who are asked to record answers as nearly verbatim as possible), and it makes statistical analysis more difficult. For one thing, the free answer makes it easier to interpret the meaning of the question to the respondent. It also makes possible an understanding of the meaning of the reply. "Yes-no" answers often conceal meaning.

Many public opinion surveys now make use of both free-answer and fixed-alternative questions. One suggestion is that the free-answer question should be used in the pre-test to determine what answers are desirable as fixed alternatives in the main study. Then the findings of the main survey should again be studied through more detailed interviewing (Lazarsfeld, 1944).

The Problem of Sampling. A properly conducted public opinion survey is like any other scientific investigation. It has to be carefully designed in order to yield unambiguous results. We have considered some of the pitfalls in the form of the poll question. It is important that we know what the respondent understands by our questions, how thoughtful and informed his opinion is, with what conviction he states his answer, and what he intends by it. But it is also important that we ask our questions of the right people. The selection of those whose replies we seek constitutes the problem of *sampling.* While we have made great advances in selecting a sample, our sampling methods are still not foolproof.

The logic of sampling is fundamentally very simple. Once the total group to be sampled has been defined (e.g., registered voters, males of draft age, owners of motor vehicles), the ideal is so to design the sample that each person in the group has an equal chance of being represented.[6] If we could give every person in the country a number chosen at random, and then make our sample by drawing, say, every thousandth person, we would have a simple random sample. The cost of doing this would, of course, be prohibitive, so that methods have to be devised of achieving a compromise that lies near this ideal.

Let us examine two methods commonly used. The first is that of *quota control.* In the recent past this has been the method most widely used by the commercial polls, but it is a method that has led them into error. On the basis of census data, pollsters choose communities to represent the nation; within these communities they assign each

interviewer a quota of persons to be interviewed. These quotas, when added up, should represent the population of the country in miniature. The quota is developed not only according to the number of people from each community but according to certain characteristics or controls. These ordinarily include sex, age, and economic level, with separate quotas for whites and Negroes. While the intended sample may be fairly representative according to these characteristics, the actual sample tends to be unrepresentative. Because the interviewer selects the interviewees who meet the quota requirements, his personal biases inevitably enter. Many interviewers are middle-class housewives who hesitate to go into dingy houses on dirty streets. The sample thus tends to be short of the lowest economic groups, with the better-educated groups too well represented. One analysis of two polling samples showed 20 per cent more people polled in the better-educated group than there should have been according to U.S. Census reports (Cantril, 1944).

In order to avoid the bias introduced by the method of quota control, an alternative method known as *area sampling* has been developed. The main contrast with the quota method in practice is that no choice is left up to the interviewer. In the method of area sampling, when applied on a national or regional basis, interview assignments are usually made according to residence units. The interviewer is told exactly where to go and whom to interview. No substitutions are allowed, for the person hard to reach may be the very one needed to assure the representativeness of the sample. Not all desired respondents will be reached, but with this method the number not reached can be ascertained, and something about them can be known from the neighborhoods in which they live.

Area sampling is really only one variation of the broader method of *probability sampling,* in which the probability that each member of the population is included in the

[6] Instead of *equal chance* of being represented, it would be more accurate to say *known probability* of being represented. Thus we could sample 1 in 100 in a large city and 1 in 10 in a small city, and still arrive at an unbiased estimate for the whole population represented; in order to do so, the results would of course have to be weighted according to the number of persons each reply represented.

sample is determined in advance, so that sampling statistics can be accurately applied. There are other ways of obtaining the specific assignments required by probability sampling. In a wartime study of small manufacturing plants, for example, a representative sample was drawn from the social security files, and assignments were made by name and address of the plant.

Surprising accuracy can be achieved with small samples if they are carefully designed. The confidence limits can be determined by appropriate statistical formulas, so that the degree of accuracy can be known in advance, and the sample size determined in accordance with the needed accuracy for the purposes at hand.

The study of voting behavior

The study of elections has served well as a testing ground for public opinion measurement. Elections are important in a democracy, the issues and candidates are widely publicized, and accurate records are kept. The initial interest in studying voting behavior—predicting election outcomes—has come to be supplemented by many other interests related to the sources of political affiliation, the effects of income, education, and social class upon loyalty to a party, the nature of those who switch allegiance, and so on.

The fact that a poll result does not agree perfectly with the election result does not necessarily mean that the poll is a poor method of studying voter behavior. Several influences are at work which the poll cannot control. One of these is that voters change their minds. Even though they answer honestly about how they plan to vote, they may hear a speech or have a talk with friends and decide to vote differently. Then, too, not all of those interviewed will vote, so that the interview sample may not represent the voting sample. In states which discourage voting by Negroes, a representative sample of Negroes and whites would not be a good election sample. Bad weather may affect the farm and urban vote differently, since farmers find it harder than city people to get to the election booths in bad weather. Also, the system of electoral votes means that the polls predicting national elections have to work state by state, lest slight errors in borderline states with large electoral votes throw off the prediction much farther than if election were by direct popular vote. The test of predicting national elections is more severe than any other test to which the polls are put. The presidential election of 1960 made the difficulties abundantly clear; even the modern computing machines, fed all the information from prior elections, were unable to make satisfactory predictions from the votes as they came in on election night.

The study of political behavior, as represented by voting, calls for much more than a tabulation of voting and a noting of success or failure in prediction. Many serious studies are now conducted before and after each of the major elections in order to arrive at an understanding of the behavior of the voter. New circumstances, such as the TV debates between Mr. Kennedy and Mr. Nixon in the 1960 campaign, and the issue concerning Mr. Kennedy's membership in the Roman Catholic Church, provided important material for study, even though they made advance prediction perilous. The debates forced viewers and listeners to pay attention to both candidates, although earlier studies had made it clear that people tended to listen predominantly to candidates with whom they already agreed.

Some voters have no trouble at all in making up their minds how they will vote: their party affiliations, their social class or economic group interests, their liking for the party's candidate—all are in harmony. But other voters are in conflict: they like the candidate, but do not like the party's policies; they like the domestic policy, but are out of sympathy with the foreign policy. They then have trouble in making up their minds and often decide late. Thus in the elections of

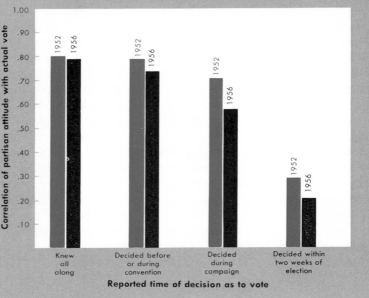

20-6

Unpredictability of late deciders

Within two elections it was found that the decisions of those who made up their minds late could not be predicted as well from their partisan attitudes as the decisions of those who made up their minds early. This is interpreted as due to conflict. (After Campbell and others, 1960, p. 79)

Correlation of partisan attitude with actual vote

1.00 .90 .80 .70 .60 .50 .40 .30 .20 .10

1952 1956 — Knew all along

1952 1956 — Decided before or during convention

1952 1956 — Decided during campaign

1952 1956 — Decided within two weeks of election

Reported time of decision as to vote

both 1952 and 1956, partisan attitudes readily predicted how those would vote who decided early, but did not predict for the later deciders (Figure 20-6) (Campbell and others, 1960). When their conflicting attitudes were studied, it was found that those with more conflicts were indeed the ones who represented the highest proportion of late deciders (Figure 20-7).

The shift in issues and alignments from one election to another reflects many changes associated with the age of the voters (which affects their memories of depression, war, etc.), with the present economic circumstances, and with the general outlook at the time. For example, with the generally upward rise in incomes and opportunities, there has been a lessening of voting along class or economic lines in this country; such cleavages have been lower among the younger people within the last several elections, and very slight among any group by the election of 1956 (Figure 20-8). Thus the study of elections tells us something about what is happening in the nation generally; these findings are probably more significant than predicting election outcomes.

The effectiveness of communications

How are people influenced to change their attitudes, opinions, and beliefs? The answer lies in part through ordinary learning experiences, through the rewards and punishments the individual receives from the culture. Attempts to influence people in large numbers come mainly by way of the channels of communication: through the spoken word over the radio, through the printed word in newspapers, books, and magazines, audio-visually through motion pictures and television, and through presentations before audiences. We turn now to a consideration of the effectiveness of some of these many varieties of communication.

The Mass Media. The mass media of communication are those whose messages reach millions of people: newspapers and magazines, motion pictures, radio, television. Many studies are concerned with the type and size of audience reached and with the influence upon such audiences. Only a few selected examples can be given here.

While the newspaper is not as important as it once was because of other sources of news reports, it has many features (in addition to news coverage) that make it an important part of the daily lives of a great many people. A 17-day newspaper strike in New York City provided the occasion for a study of what "missing the newspaper" meant to people (Berelson, 1954). People felt that they did not know as well what was going on in the world because they did not have the paper, but they also reported satisfaction in the act of reading, without primary concern in some cases for the content being read. The paper was a source of security, providing an indirect social contact with important people and a feeling of intimacy, and serving satisfying "ritualistic" values.

A striking case of the influence of the radio occurred some years ago in a broadcast of an "invasion from Mars." What happened was

20-7

Conflict and delayed voting decision

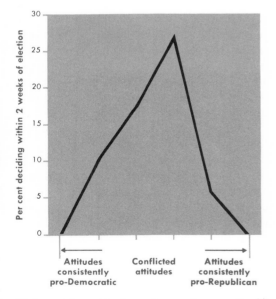

Of those with consistently pro-Democratic or pro-Republican attitudes, none waited until two weeks before the election to decide how to vote. For other voters, the more conflict in attitude, the greater the delay in deciding how to vote. Based on a scale of five partisan attitudes, election of 1956. (After Campbell and others, 1960, p. 82)

20-8

Occupational status and voting

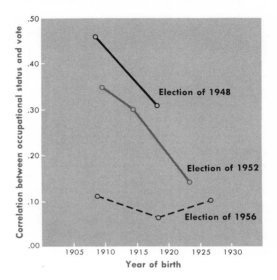

In the election of 1948, those born around 1910 showed the highest correspondence between their occupational status and their voting behavior. These voters reached their young adulthood in the depression period following 1929, and their memories of this period may have had something to do with their awareness of status and its political significance. In any case, the correlation between voting behavior and status decreased in each election from 1948 to 1956, as shown by the lower position of each successive curve on the chart. Note that in the two earlier elections the younger voters showed less correspondence between status and voting than the older ones. (Modified from Campbell and others, 1960, p. 358)

the subject of a study by Cantril, Gaudet, and Hertzog (1940). Some 6 million people listened to a radio play on the evening of October 30, 1938. Orson Welles as "Professor Richard Pierson" reported what purported to be an invasion by men from Mars, an invasion that threatened our whole civilization. So skillfully was the dramatization done that at least a million of the listeners were frightened or disturbed. Most of these thought they were listening to a news broadcast.

Before the broadcast ended, people were packing their belongings, driving their cars into the country at high speeds, crying, pray-

TABLE 20-2

Shifts in voting decisions following the viewing of the
Kennedy-Nixon television debates in the campaign of 1960:
a panel of 95 New Yorkers

	Decided for Kennedy	*Undecided*	*Decided for Nixon*
Before first debate	37	27	31
After first debate	47	20	28
After fourth debate	52	12	31

SOURCE: Lang and Lang (1961).

ing, seeking to rescue their loved ones. Later, detailed interviews were conducted with 135 persons, of whom over 100 were known to have been upset by the broadcast. The purpose of the interviews was to get at the psychological bases for the widespread panic that the broadcast caused.

It was found that the people had great faith in radio commentators. That faith made the people who thought they were listening to a news broadcast completely credulous. They were confirmed in their fears when they found their neighbors as disturbed as they and saw the congestion of traffic in the streets. The fear spread; the people coalesced into a panic-stricken mob, for there was nothing they could do to stem the power of these invaders from another world.

Although a relative newcomer on the scene, television since World War II has become widespread and is now a major channel reaching a mass audience. A dramatic illustration of its impact was provided by the Kennedy-Nixon debates in the election of 1960.

One study of the debates was based on interviews with 95 New Yorkers before the first debate, immediately after, and again after the fourth (and last) debate. While the sample is not generally representative of voters, the results confirmed the findings of a wider sample, as reported in the Gallup Poll release of October 12, 1960. According to the national poll, about twice as many thought Kennedy did better in the debates than thought Nixon did better; the results in the small sample showed a switch to Kennedy by 10 of the 95 voters and a loss of 3 Nixon voters after the first debate. More careful analysis, however, showed that Kennedy's gain in favorable impression was more pronounced than his gain in votes; most of the shifts came from undecided voters who already were leaning in the direction of a vote for Kennedy. After the fourth debate, Nixon had held his original supporters, while Kennedy had gained solely from the undecided group (Table 20-2) (Lang and Lang, 1961). In any case, there was some impact from the televised debates, and in an election so close any influence can be significant.

The importance of TV in the lives of contemporary school children is brought out strikingly by some studies reported by Schramm (1960). Of a sample of 508 fifth- and sixth-grade San Francisco children, 74 per cent viewed TV on any one day, with the average viewing time being 2½ hours, about the same as the amount of time spent in free play. Very little of the viewing was of educational programs.

A large-scale study in England (Himmelweit, Oppenheim, and Vince, 1958) showed slightly less viewing by English children than by American children. Viewing was negatively correlated with intelligence: the higher a child's intelligence, the less time he spent before the TV screen. While children can learn from TV, there appears to be no net gain, because TV replaces other experiences, such as reading. Television does not appear to lead to action; for example, few children proceeded to make anything even though a model for so doing was shown on television.

Influencing Opinion in Experimental Audiences. Some suggestions were made earlier about social conformity (pp. 555-60). We are here concerned with the influences received by a member of a particular kind of group, an *audience.* An audience receives some kind of *communication* from a speaker or other leader around whom the audience is *polarized,* i.e., to whom the members of the group pay more or less continuous attention. To illustrate many studies of experimental audiences, we shall examine three specimens.

1. *One-sided vs. two-sided arguments.* A study by Hovland, Lumsdaine, and Sheffield (1949) was arranged to establish which method of presentation was more effective: giving only one side of an argument, or giving both sides while favoring one. The study was done near the end of World War II, in which the desire was to prevent the American soldier from expecting the war with Japan to be over shortly after the war ended in Europe.

Radio transcriptions were prepared in two forms. The first program presented only the arguments indicating why the war in the Pacific would be long drawn out. The second program presented "both sides"; that is, in addition to arguments for a long war, it pointed out factors which might give the United States the advantage, especially if it could concentrate upon the Japanese when the war in Europe drew to a close.

In a preliminary survey, troops were first given a chance to estimate the probable length of the war, so that their changes in opinions and estimates could be appraised later after they had listened to the radio programs in orientation sessions.

The programs succeeded in doing what they attempted. The percentage of soldiers who expected the war to last at least a year and a half longer increased from 37 per cent before the programs to 59 per cent after them. A control group showed little change over the same period of time, thus proving the programs to have been effective. While the two programs appeared about equally effective, further analysis showed a curious difference in their effects upon men holding different views before hearing them.

Men who originally thought the war would be short showed a greater net change from hearing the "both sides" program; those who originally thought that the war would be long showed a greater net change from hearing the "one side" program.

The investigators suggest, plausibly enough, that the men who are unfavorably disposed to the basic message of the program (that is, that the war would be long) already knew the arguments on their side (favoring a short war). By rehearing the arguments they already believed, they gained confidence in the speaker and were ready to listen to opposed arguments.

2. *Credibility of the source.* Whether or not an opinion will be changed by a communication depends in part on the confidence the listener has in the speaker. In one experiment, three groups of high school students, who had been invited to a studio, were addressed on juvenile delinquency by a guest speaker who favored extreme leniency in the treatment of delinquents. The speaker was introduced to each group in a different way:

Positive: As an authority; a judge of a juvenile court.
Neutral: As an unidentified member of the studio audience.
Negative: As a member of the studio audience who had been a delinquent and was now out on bail after an arrest on a charge of dope peddling.

The opinions on leniency of treatment of juvenile offenders which resulted from the talk varied according to the order of credibility of the speaker, the "positive" speaker

Effect of credibility of speaker upon opinion change

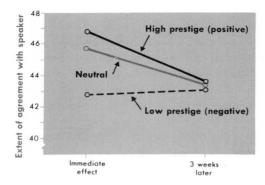

The high-prestige speaker caused more immediate changes in opinions than did the other two. After three weeks, however, the results were quite different. The three-weeks effect for the neutral source is inferred from the report. (After Kelman and Hovland, 1953)

having most effect, the "negative" speaker least. The differences between the group who heard the positive speaker and those who heard the negative were significant, with P less than .001 (Kelman and Hovland, 1953).

A retest three weeks later produced an important finding: Those exposed to the communication from a low prestige source showed more opinion change in the direction of the content of the communication than immediately after the communication, while those exposed to the high prestige source showed a reduced effect after three weeks (Figure 20-9). The communicator and the message apparently became dissociated, the people remembering what was said without thinking about who said it.

3. *Effect of fear arousal.* The appeal to fear is familiar in persuasive communications, whether in lectures on health, in religious revivals, or in political campaigns. How effective are such appeals? One experiment dealt with several degrees of appeal to fear in an illustrated lecture on dental hygiene participated in by all the members of a freshman class in a Connecticut high school (Janis and Feshbach, 1953).

Results showed that the communications were fear-arousing, as intended. The change in conformity to the recommended dental practices was, however, in an order *inversely* related to the amount of fear appeal (Table 20-3).

The conclusion from the experiment is that a nonfrightening appeal is more likely to lead to conformity than a frightening one, at least if the threats are not relieved by reassurances contained in the communication. If unrelieved, the audience becomes motivated to ignore or minimize the importance of the threats. This interpretation relates the results to the mechanism of repression (p. 516).

These three illustrations (one side vs. two sides, credibility of the source, effect of fear arousal) suffice to indicate the possibilities inherent in laboratory studies of the effects of communications on opinions.

Coercive persuasion: brainwashing

The term "brainwashing" was introduced by Hunter (1951) as a translation of a Chinese term meaning "cleansing of the mind," used in reference to ridding the Chinese of

TABLE **20-3**

Conformity to recommended dental hygiene practices after illustrated lecture

Nature of appeal used in lecture	Net change in direction of conformity *
Minimum fear appeal ($N = 50$)	+36%
Moderate fear appeal ($N = 50$)	+22%
Strong fear appeal ($N = 50$)	+ 8%
Control (other lecture)($N = 50$)	0%

SOURCE: Janis and Feshbach (1953).

* Net change is the total number who changed toward conformity less those who changed in the opposite direction. For the difference between the minimum fear appeal and the strong fear appeal, $P = .03$; for the difference between the minimal appeal and control, P less than .01. Other differences, P greater than .05.

old beliefs in order to become re-educated for life in a Communist state. The word has come to be applied to various efforts to change the outlook of prisoners, both military and civilian, through various persuasive techniques used while the authorities have control over the lives of the prisoners and hence can use coercive measures. The expression "coercive persuasion" is favored by Schein and others (1961).

The possibility of controlling men's minds came strongly to attention in the purge trials in the Soviet Union, in which former leaders in the Communist movement confessed their crimes publicly before they were executed. The confessions seemed so out of character that the Western world assumed that some special psychological methods (or perhaps drugs) had been used to produce the confessions. Later examination of the evidence (e.g., Leites and Bernaut, 1954) shows a complex set of historical and situational as well as psychological factors to be involved. Smith (1954) found some parallels in English treason trials in the sixteenth century and interpreted the confessions to mean that in some strange way the prisoners confessed in order to prove that the regime was more important than their own lives. The Russian methods traditionally isolated the prisoner from others, and through repeated interrogation a confession was finally extracted. As we shall see, the Chinese methods tend to be quite different, with the objective being to make the individual a useful member of the Communist community rather than to liquidate him.

Detailed information on Chinese methods of "thought reform" have come through two main sets of interviews, the first with American war prisoners who were returned from Chinese prisons during the exchange of prisoners following the cessation of the Korean fighting in 1953 (Lifton, 1954; Schein, 1956), the second with civilians who were returned from Chinese prisons to Hong Kong (Lifton, 1956). In the exchange of military prisoners it was found that a few

Americans had collaborated with the Chinese Communists, and 21 refused repatriation; in view of the very great number of prisoners held by the Western forces who refused repatriation, this was not a very significant validation of the Chinese indoctrination methods. The civilians actually proved in some ways more interesting, because of those who showed definite signs of change as a result of their experiences. Their number included doctors, missionaries, students, and businessmen. Two books (Lifton, 1961; Schein and others, 1961) give the reflections of those who have done the most to try to understand what happened.

One unique feature of the Chinese method was the absence of any use of torture to extract confessions. There were discomforts, some arising out of such inevitabilities as Westerners' dislike of Chinese prison food, and there were some manacles and chains, although these were used more for psychological effect than for their production of pain. That is, manacles were used to show that the crimes which the person was about to confess were severe ones, and they made his cellmates suspicious of him. A second feature was the use of the group pressures of cellmates to enhance the indoctrination program. Cellmates farther along in their sympathies with the Communist regime were used to persuade their lagging cellmates to come along also, and they reported on their progress to the interrogator. There were repeated lectures and, of course, individual interrogation, with various rewards for good behavior and deprivation of privileges for nonconformity.

The aim of the prison "reform" was to obtain a confession of past transgressions, and then to produce "conversion" to Communist ideals and programs. This, according to Schein and others (1961), took place in three major steps: *unfreezing, changing,* and *refreezing.* The unfreezing consists in beginning to doubt one's past standards to the point of desire to change or abandon that belief.

Lifton (1956) quotes a European priest, describing how he saw things at this stage in his "reform":

And now, like a monster out of the abyss, the most fearful realization dawns: You, the missionary, the herald of the gospel, are not you a messenger of the imperialist conquerors, their pioneer, on account of your ethnological and industrial reports on your missionland? And after the occupation of your missionland you go on rendering the conquerors many different services. And take your mission as a whole: Does it not now prove as a big, long and heavy sin? And the question whether your mission activity has been of more harm or good to the people answers itself. But because you grew up in imperialistic ideologies, it has never until now occurred to you how much you have been of help in the enslaving and the exploitation of a people which formerly enjoyed liberty . . .

The *unfreezing,* which ended in the confession of capitalistic sins against the people, was not permitted to come easily. Fabricated confessions, designed to ease the pressures of prison life, were detected and punished; one of the frustrating features of the experience was that the prisoner knew that he had to confess something but he did not know what he was to confess, and if he tried to guess he was detected. In the end, he had to find something that was plausible to him, as in the priest's statement just quoted.

The process of *changing* came about as the prisoner began to see merit in the points of view of those who were teaching him about Communism, as he began to learn from his cellmates and to adopt some of their positions to replace those of his own he had now distrusted and discarded. Finally, the *refreezing* consisted in consolidating the new position in such a way as to find it congenial. That is, others were pleased with the subject because of the views he held; he could see himself as an upright, sensitive, and forward-looking person, whose new beliefs fitted into his own conception of his love for his fellow-man. If this phase was successful, he would be a changed person when released to the non-Communist world.

The study of the released civilians in Hong Kong showed that the process was not very successful, if by success is meant the turning out of devoted Communists. Some showed no discernible effects at all, as illustrated in the case report of Father Phillips (Becker, 1958); some complied under duress, but they were in no sense "broken men" and had not fundamentally changed their attitudes; others who complied showed various degrees of attitude change accompanying their behavioral compliance. Among the more striking changes were those who felt a strong "sense of commitment," as though they had not previously cared enough about the plight of man; such a case is reported by Rickett and Rickett (1957). According to Schein and others (1961), such committed people felt some sympathy for the plight of the Chinese, but were not, in fact, committed Communists.

A number of theories have been proposed to account psychologically for the changes that take place under these circumstances. Some theories consider physiological stress along with the psychology of learning. One of these, for example, shows how "debility, dependency, and dread" could be used, according to what we know about learning, to produce the kinds of changes found (Farber and others, 1957); others suggest that psychoanalytic mechanisms can account for the change, especially various aspects of guilt, dependency, identification, and identity struggles (Moloney, 1955). Still others make use of the concepts familiar in the social psychology of attitude change (Kelman, 1958). While it is possible to interpret the results in these ways, it is widely conceded that those responsible for the indoctrination programs in the prisons of China were probably little influenced by any academic theory, basing their methods much more on such Confucian concepts as "sincerity," "self-cultivation," "harmony," combined with the practices and theories of Marxist-Leninist doctrine (Lifton, 1961).

SUMMARY   1. Studies of how we form impressions of others show that many *principles of object perception* apply: familiarity, grouping and figure-ground structuring, sensitivity to the physical characteristics of the stimulus.

2. The principles of object-perception are supplemented, however, by *the perceiver's influence* upon what he perceives. Thus his perception of himself affects his perception of others; he classifies people according to traits that he values; his likes and dislikes affect how he is impressed by two people perceived simultaneously, and how he expects them to perceive each other. When his perceptions are incongruous, there is a strain in the direction of *cognitive balance*.

3. Individual behavior tends to be influenced by the group of which the individual is a member. Resistance to change can be overcome by *group process,* in which participation by members of the group is used to make the change acceptable. The degree to which the individual is attracted to the group, how cohesive the group is, may affect the amount of conforming behavior. The behavior of others provides a kind of standard or *norm* for us; studies of petition-signing and of violation of prohibitions show that the strength of the invitation or the prohibition is but one determiner of conduct, the other what someone else has done in the situation.

4. Intergroup tensions arise because of boundaries between *in-groups* and *out-groups*. Racial prejudice is an illustration of the ways in which *scapegoating* and *stereotyping* operate.

5. An *attitude* can be described as an *orientation* favorable or unfavorable to some object, concept, or situation, and a *readiness to respond* in some predetermined manner to these or related objects, concepts, or events. Attitudes can be *scaled* by several methods, of which those of Thurstone and Likert are representative.

6. *Opinions* deal with *expectations* or *predictions* about the consequences of certain courses of action; while attitudes may in some cases be unconscious, opinions are always conscious and can be put into words.

7. The public opinion survey has found many uses in government and in industry beyond the prediction of election results.

8. One problem in conducting surveys is the use of *fixed-alternative* versus *free-answer* questions. The free-answer questions have the advantage of revealing how the respondent interprets the question and what he intends by his answers, but the difficulties of interviewing are increased.

9. Another problem is that of obtaining the *sample*. The choice lies between the *quota-control* method and the *area* method, a form of the method *probability sampling,* favored because it eliminates interviewer bias.

10. The study of voting behavior is now aimed at understanding characteristics of the voter and considerations affecting his choices, with the prediction of election outcomes a secondary matter. It is found, for example, that conflicts over issues delay the voter's decision. Recent elections have shown a decline in voting according to class or economic status.

11. The mass media (newspapers and magazines, motion pictures, radio, television) affect the attitudes, opinions, and beliefs of a large audience. Some representative studies of radio and television indicate how influential appeals over these media can become. Television is being studied also for its more specific role in educating the young.

12. Studies of the effects of communications on experimental audiences give partial answers to three questions, chosen as representative of other questions asked in such studies: (1) Is a one-sided or a two-sided argument more persuasive? (2) What is the influence of credibility of the source of the communication? (3) How effective is an appeal to fear in changing behavior?

13. *Coercive persuasion* ("brainwashing") refers to the efforts to convert the thinking of prisoners (both civilian and military) to a point of view favorable to the regime of the captors by coercive techniques that include environmental control (physical and social), deprivation, reward, confession—techniques ordinarily not considered "educational" because of the extreme uses of the power residing in the hands of those attempting to produce the changes. The steps of change can be described as *unfreezing* of familiar attitudes, beliefs, and values, *changing* these attitudes, beliefs and values, and then *refreezing,* or consolidating the new position.

SUGGESTIONS FOR FURTHER READING

For a general orientation to social psychology, Maccoby, Newcomb, and Hartley (Eds.), *Readings in social psychology* (3rd Ed., 1958) provides a well-selected collection of studies. For looking up special topics, Lindzey (Ed.), *Handbook of social psychology* (2 vols., 1954) is a good resource.

On the perception of others, the best survey is Tagiuri and Petrullo (Eds.), *Person perception and interpersonal behavior* (1958). Interpersonal behavior is dealt with more fully in Cartwright and Zander (Eds.), *Group dynamics* (2nd Ed., 1960). For responses to group pressure, see Berg and Bass, *Conformity and deviation* (1961). On prejudice see Allport, *The nature of prejudice* (1954).

For various systematic approaches to the understanding of attitudes and their change, see Rosenberg, Hovland, McGuire, Abelson, and Brehm, *Attitude organization and change* (1960).

The public opinion literature bulks large. For an introduction to methods by which surveys are conducted, see Hyman, *Survey design and analysis* (1955). Results of surveys, and other issues in connection with public opinion, are found in Katz, Cartwright, Eldersveld, and Lee (Eds.), *Public opinion and propaganda* (1954). On election studies there is a book of readings, Burdick and Brodbeck (Eds.), *American voting behavior* (1959), and a careful restudy of the attitudes and other characteristics that determined the presidential vote in 1956, Campbell and others, *The American voter* (1960). See also Schramm (Ed.), *The process and effects of mass communication* (1954).

Two recent books on "brainwashing" are Lifton, *Thought reform and the psychology of totalism* (1961), and Schein and others, *Coercive persuasion* (1961). See also Biderman and Zimmer (Eds.), *The manipulation of human behavior* (1961).

CHAPTER 21

Vocational and Professional Applications of Psychology

Science is essentially a technique for solving problems by way of understanding. In its pure science aspects, any science stresses the search for general principles and laws that yield this understanding; in its applied aspects, it seeks to use the understanding that has been achieved in order to solve practical problems. Many pure and applied sciences can be thought of in pairs: astronomy and navigation, physics and engineering, biology and agriculture, biochemistry and pharmacology, anatomy and surgery: both members of the pair have important problems of their own to solve, and the task of the applied scientist is not merely that of a broker or middleman advising the practical consumer how to use the products of pure science. The navigator, the engineer, the agriculturist, the pharmacologist, and the surgeon have to develop techniques and instruments of their own, and conduct their own researches in the same scientific spirit as that of the scientist working on the more abstract or purer problems.

The same considerations apply within psychology. Some of its search for general principles of development and interaction is clearly in the spirit of pure science; yet its efforts to solve problems of child rearing, of the management of learning, or of psychotherapy are applications to practical problems. While the earlier chapters have emphasized the pure-science aspects of psychology, applications have not been overlooked, especially when studies in the field of application have also enriched the knowledge of general psychology—as is often the case. Thus essentially practical studies in the testing of school children have led to a better understanding of individuality, and efforts to overcome resistance to change in a factory have contributed to our understanding of group process generally. The usefulness of a scientific experiment is determined not by the substance on which it works, or the practical significance of the problems it attacks, but by the precision of its methods and the relevance of its results to theory; applied science can serve pure science, just as pure science also serves the applied field.

In this chapter we shall consider some of the efforts of psychology to deal with social problems that have not been considered in previous chapters, especially those having to do with the work life of the individual as he faces his career and with the problems of an industrial society. Because the applications of a field of science tend to become professionalized, that is, to bring into existence practitioners who make the services of the applied science available to others, we shall then turn to some of the problems of psychology as a profession, concluding with a look into psychology's future.

Vocational Choice

Occupational choice may be looked at from the point of view either of the person seeking to find his vocation or of the employer trying to find someone to fit into a job opening. The problems are obviously different. The individual faces the choice among some 20,000 different occupations, and, if he is to plan ahead, he must make the choice early enough to prepare himself through appropriate training. The employer presumably knows what kind of worker he wants and has the somewhat simpler job of selecting from a limited number of applicants

21-1

Dissatisfaction with vocational choice

Field majored in	Per cent who wish they had done otherwise	Field most frequently mentioned as a better choice
Premedical	9%	A different profession
Pre-law	14%	Medicine
Home economics	14%	The humanities
Predental	18%	A different profession
Engineering	19%	A different branch of engineering
Fine arts, music	22%	The social sciences
Philosophy, religion	24%	The social sciences
Sciences, mathematics	24%	A different branch of sciences
Average for all graduates	25%	
Agricultural, forestry	27%	Medicine
Education	28%	Business administration
Social sciences	30%	Business administration
Business administration	30%	Engineering
History, literature, languages, etc.	33%	Medicine
Pharmacy	33%	Medicine

One-fourth of the more than 9000 college graduates surveyed in one study wish they had prepared for a different occupation. (After Havemann and West, 1952)

those most suitable to his opening. In the end, however, there are some basic similarities between the aims of employer and employee. Work satisfaction, and hence higher work morale and reduced turnover, will come about if the individual finds an appropriate place for himself and if the employer finds workers who can be satisfied with the jobs in which he places them.

Satisfaction in work as a social problem

Because satisfying work is essential to self-respect, congenial work opportunities are among the requisites of a satisfactory social order. The conditions of industrial life have tended to reduce satisfaction in work for a great many people. The rewards of craftsmanship, which come through planning and carrying work to completion, are denied most factory workers, whose tasks are simple and repetitive. Conditions of work are often not congenial because of noise or temperature or speed or lack of social relations with fellow workers. The need to commute to offices in large cities wastes

many good hours and reduces work satisfaction for many white-collar workers. The problem of finding satisfying work is one which pervades our culture.

Conditions of small-town life are apparently more conducive to job satisfaction than industrial life in metropolitan communities. An early study done in a Pennsylvania community of about 1000 people found 76 per cent of the employed adults satisfied with their jobs, even though many of them were engaged in menial tasks (Hoppock, 1935). But different results were obtained from a cross section of factory workers in industrial communities in a later survey (*Fortune*, June, 1947). The workers were asked: "If you could go back to the age of fifteen and start life over again, would you choose a different trade or occupation?" Slightly over half (57 per cent) answered "yes," indicating dissatisfaction with what they were then doing. A third (31 per cent) said "no," indicating that they liked their jobs as well as might be expected. The rest were undecided.

The range of choices open to those with college educations is great, and it ought to be possible for college graduates to find congenial work. But many college graduates are not satisfied with the positions in which they find themselves. A study of Northwestern University alumni found that three-fourths of those who replied were "completely satisfied" or "well-satisfied" with their work, while only 1 in 20 was dissatisfied (Inlow, 1951). But another study (Figure 21-1) finds 25 per cent of college graduates wishing they had studied something else in college (Havemann and West, 1952).

Because favored social status is associated only with certain occupations, people sometimes have social reasons for being dissatisfied with work that they otherwise like. For example, of a group of clerks and manual workers, 47 per cent reported that they were interested in their work. But of these same workers, only 17 per cent said that they would enter their present occupations if they had a choice. The largest proportion would have preferred to enter occupations of higher social status (Form, 1946).

The stability of the social status of occupations has been shown in several studies. When 25 occupations were ranked by students in 1946, the ranks corresponded very closely to ranks obtained in 1925 (Deeg and Paterson, 1947). For 22 of the 25 occupations, the shift in rank over 20 years was two or less steps. The three occupations that shifted more steps (farmer, traveling salesman, insurance agent) were all in middle ranks, where prestige is less well defined.

It is of interest that approximately the same social prestige rating is made by those in the lower prestige ranks as by those in the higher ranks. In Table 21-1 are given the ranks for 26 occupations as they were assigned by a group of graduate students and by a group of laborers. The correspondence is very close. One interesting discrepancy is that of the position of foreman, placed six ranks higher by the laborers than by the students. The gap between the

TABLE 21-1
Social status of occupations

| Occupation | As ranked by: | |
	Graduate students	La-borers
Physicians	1	2.5
Bankers, stock and loan brokers	2	2.5
Superintendents of state institutions	3	5
Officers in Army or Navy	4	4
Managers of business	5	1
Hotelkeepers	6	7
Grade school teachers	7	10
Real estate and insurance agents	8	14
Retail traders	9	9
Commercial travelers	10	8
Bookkeepers, cashiers, and accountants	11	11
Foremen	12	6
Farm proprietors	13	16
Clerks and stenographers	14	12
Policemen	15	13
Skilled factory workers	16	15
Salespeople and clerks	17	17
Train, bus, and streetcar drivers	18	18
Waiters and domestic servants	19	20
Janitors	20	19
Laundry workers	21	24
Unskilled factory workers	22	23
Farm laborers	23	21
Casual laborers	24	25
Coal miners	25	22
Unemployed	26	26

SOURCE: Cattell (1942).

foreman and manual workers is the result of foreman prestige as judged by those who work under a foreman.

Occupational mobility

Because of the importance of occupational level as a source of satisfaction, and because it is possible to gain an education and make choices for oneself, many individuals attempt to improve their status. America has long prided itself upon being a land of opportunity; this means, in the language of sociology, that status is not fixed but that people are *upwardly mobile,* that is, they are free to move from a less favored to a more favored social class position. This mobility is relative only, and the opportunity for downward mobility is present along with the opportunity for upward movement. There is a fairly sharp distinction between manual work and white-collar work, the latter tending to have the greater prestige; a study showed that of those at present in white-collar work only 20 per cent had ever worked full time at a manual job, while of those now in manual jobs only 11 per cent had ever worked full time in a nonmanual position. While there is thus some overlap, a large fraction of the nonmanual workers were always that, and a large fraction of manual workers never held any other kind of job (Lipset and Bendix, 1952).

The same study showed that there are some channels for change of status; many manual workers find it possible to go into sales jobs or to establish businesses of their own, although they are less likely to end up in business executive or upper white-collar positions (Table 21-2).

For those who have the ability, a college education is a source of upward mobility. There is a substantial correlation between occupational success and education in America; the U.S. Census (1958) reports a median income in 1956 of $6980 for those with 4 years or more of college, compared with $4887 for those with four years of high school, and $4035 for those of eight years of elementary school. It is difficult to unravel cause and effect here, for the more promising tend to continue their education; in any case, there are clear advantages for those who can, for whatever reasons, continue with their education. Is this because those who continue come from more favorable economic backgrounds to begin with? Generally speaking, yes; but it is of some interest to study the careers of those who have worked their way through college compared with those who were supported by their parents or had other subsidies. The argument is that if the advantage of opportunity were already established by the home, then those who worked their way should not do as well as those who had all the advantages to begin with. Table 21-3 shows some results of a survey made in

TABLE 21-2

Present occupational groups classified by major occupational group of first job

First job	Present job		
	Own business (per cent)	Lower white-collar and sales (per cent)	Business executive and upper white-collar (per cent)
Professional, semiprofessional, business owners, and executives	9	1	10
All white-collar and sales	34	49	63
All manual (including farm)	57	50	27
	——	——	——
	100	100	100
	$N = 111$	$N = 154$	$N = 97$

SOURCE: Lipset and Bendix (1952).

TABLE **21-3**

Earnings of self-help and supported students after reaching age 40

Earned income (1947)	Professional men		Businessmen	
	Supported as students (per cent)	Self-help students (per cent)	Supported as students (per cent)	Self-help students (per cent)
$7500 and over	37	32	53	41
$5000 to $7500	19	22	19	27
$3000 to $5000	26	34	20	25
Under $3000	18	12	8	7
	——	——	——	——
	100	100	100	100
	N = 152	N = 770	N = 182	N = 770

SOURCE: West (1953).

1947; while the incomes would be higher for a similar study carried on today, there is little reason to expect the relative positions to have changed. The table shows that the supported students were a little better off at age 40 or over than the self-help students, the difference being greater in business than in the professions. If we dare to generalize from these data, we could say that the professions provide a somewhat better avenue of equal opportunity, based on individual merit, than do business careers. The formerly popular theory that business rewards energy and ambition regardless of lowly origins does not appear to be as widely true today.

Ability tests in guidance

Because success in college courses is essential to securing the training necessary to enter the higher occupations, tests predictive of scholarship are indirectly also tests of vocational fitness. But differential tests designed specifically to measure vocational aptitudes are desirable, and much effort is now going into their development.

Very often we can gain a good deal of information at the college level from such tests, closely related to the subject matter of college courses. The profile charted in Figure 21-2 shows the test scores for a Yale freshman who was undecided as to the choice of career. His aptitudes in technological studies were clearly indicated. He entered the engineering school and attained high honors.

Two directions of development in differential tests are of interest. One consists in assembling appropriate tests into a battery and then establishing norms for a specific occupation. We have, for example, such batteries for engineering and science, for medicine, for law, for nursing, and for teaching. While somewhat promising, they do not as yet add very much to predictions made from college grades or appropriate intelligence tests.

For example, the Association of American Medical Colleges has had an admission-testing program for many years. The Moss Medical Aptitude Test, after having been accepted for a long time, was found to predict medical school grades less well than grades earned in college prior to admission. In one study (Moon, 1938) the correlation between the medical aptitude test and medi-

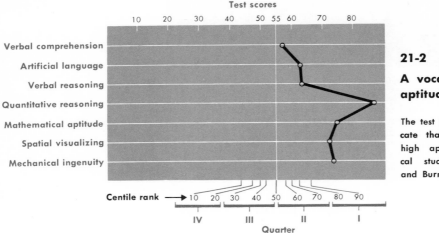

Test scores

| | 10 | 20 | 30 | 40 | 50 | 55 | 60 | 70 | 80 |

Verbal comprehension
Artificial language
Verbal reasoning
Quantitative reasoning
Mathematical aptitude
Spatial visualizing
Mechanical ingenuity

21-2

A vocational aptitude profile

The test results shown here indicate that this student had a high aptitude for technological studies. (After Crawford and Burnham, 1946)

Centile rank ⟶ 10 20   30 40 50   60 70   80 90

IV   III   II   I

Quarter

cal school success was .42, while liberal arts grades correlated .49; in another study (Stuit, 1941) the Moss test yielded correlations with first-year medical grades of .23 and .32 on two samples, while previously earned college grades correlated .45 and .46. If the Moss test was combined with college grades in a way to yield the maximum combined correlation, known as a multiple correlation, the raised correlation was only .49, a very small gain attributable to the test. Other custom-built tests, such as the Minnesota Medical Aptitude Test, have not fared any better.

The second direction of development for differential tests is to find a standard battery of tests appropriate to the whole range of occupations with norms for the separate occupations. The advantages for vocational guidance are obvious. A student who was uncertain about his abilities would have to take only one test battery; then he could find out how well his abilities suited the several occupations in which he was interested.

Such a battery of tests for high school guidance, named the Differential Aptitude Tests, has been developed by the Psychological Corporation. The tests include verbal reasoning, numerical ability, abstract reasoning, space relations, mechanical reason-

ing, clerical speed and accuracy, and two tests of language usage (Bennett, 1955).

How can a counselor help a student interpret his scores on this battery of tests? Obviously he can show the student a test profile and help him to understand what centile scores mean. But the student needs more information than this. On the basis of appropriate tables it is possible to determine the kinds of individuals with whom a student is likely to compete. For example, from existing information we can make assertions such as the following:

Premedical students: A superior group on all the tests; especially high in verbal reasoning, numerical ability, spelling, and sentences.

Engineering students: Superior in numerical ability, and outstanding as compared with all other groups in space relations and mechanical reasoning.

Employees in mechanical, electrical, and building trades: Above average in mechanical reasoning, average in space relations, poor in verbal skills (sentences and verbal reasoning).

Experience tables based on the uses of ability tests help a student to see himself in relation to others. But abilities are not all that count in vocational fitness.

Mapping a student's vocational interests

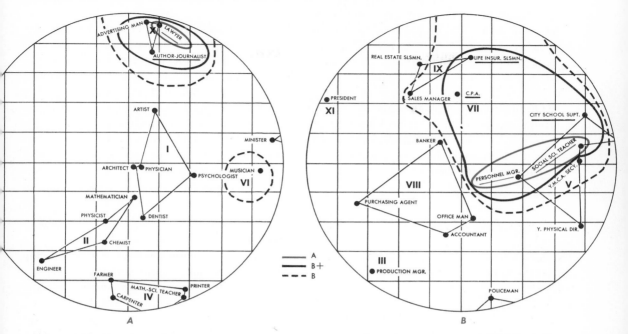

The charts are to be considered as two sides of a transparent globe, viewed from the front. The left chart is then the front of the globe, the right chart the back, with engineer and production manager close to each other, and minister and city school superintendent close to each other. The nearer any two occupations are, the greater the correlation between their interests; the farther apart, the less the correlation. Group scores are available for the occupations joined by light lines and labeled with Roman numerals.

Individual scores can be plotted on this surface to provide a kind of map of the individual's interests. The case shown is that of a psychology major tested in his senior year. His interests emphasize "verbal" and "uplift" activities, and are not typical of psychologists. (From Cronbach, 1960, p. 411; chart copyright © 1945, Stanford University Press)

Interest tests in guidance

Among the devices found most useful in vocational guidance at the college level is the vocational interest test. Two widely used tests are the Strong Vocational Interest Test and the Kuder Preference Record. Because the former has had the most extensive validation, the discussion will be directed chiefly toward the results from its use.

The Strong Vocational Interest Test consists of 400 items, most of which are answered by circling one of the three letters *L, I,* and *D* that appear with the item, *L* for like, *I* for indifferent, and *D* for dislike.

The items include, in the men's blank: 100 occupations, 36 school subjects, 49 amusements and hobbies, 48 miscellaneous activities, 47 peculiarities of people, 40 activities to be ranked by groups of 10 according to their order of preference, 40 paired items between which a choice is to be made, and 40 items consisting of self-ratings of abilities and personal characteristics.

The test has been given to large groups of men and women engaged in representative occupations. An individual who takes the test is scored according to the resemblance of his answers to those of people successfully employed in the given occupation. Thus, if he answers in the manner typical of life insurance salesmen, he is scored high in life insurance interest; if he answers in the manner typical of engineers, he is scored high in engineering interest. Separate scoring keys are available for a large number of occupations. The individual gets a separate score for each of the occupations for which the test is scored.

Occupational interests tend to run in groups, so that some simplification is obtained by scoring for occupational groups instead of for individual occupations.

The groups for men are:

GROUP I. Artist, psychologist, architect, physician, dentist.
GROUP II. Mathematician, physicist, engineer, chemist.
GROUP III. Production manager.
GROUP IV. Aviator, farmer, carpenter, mathematics-physical science teacher, printer, policeman, forest service.
GROUP V. YMCA secretary and physical director, personnel manager, city school superintendent, minister, social science teacher.
GROUP VI. Musician.
GROUP VII. Certified public accountant.
GROUP VIII. Purchasing agent, office worker, accountant, banker.
GROUP IX. Real estate salesman, life insurance salesman, sales manager.
GROUP X. Lawyer, author-journalist, advertising man.
GROUP XI. President of manufacturing concern.

Using the principles of factor analysis, Strong has been able to develop a kind of "map" to represent the interrelations of the interest scores on the different operations. The groups are numbered on the maps, which may be considered to be the two "hemispheres" of a globe (Figure 21-3). Individual scores, plotted on this map, aid in vocational guidance.

If a vocational interest test is to fulfill its function, it ought to reveal the similarity between a person's interests and the requirements of the occupation in which he is likely to be satisfied *before* he enters that occupation. In order to find out whether or not interests are sufficiently stable to make such predictions possible, persons tested while in college have been followed up by retesting them a number of years after they were out of college. In this way it was possible to find whether the occupation entered upon, and continued in, corresponded to that on which highest interest scores were obtained in college, or, if a person changed occupations, whether he changed to one on which his interest scores were already high when tested many years before the change. Occupational data from 663 college men who took the test in college and again 18 years after they were out of college showed that the following four propositions were confirmed in most comparisons:

1. Men who continued in an occupation made higher average scores for that occupation while in college than for *any other occupation.*
2. Men who continued in an occupation obtained higher average scores for that occupation while in college than the men *entering other* occupations.
3. Men who continued in an occupation obtained higher average scores for that occupation while in college than those who entered that occupation and then *changed to another occupation.*
4. Men changing from one occupation to another scored as high for the *second* occupation while in college as for the one first entered upon (Strong, 1955).

These results show that the vocational interest test has genuine predictive significance. They do not mean that interests are the only basis upon which vocational choice and vocational success rest, but they do mean that measured interests are important.

The Vocational Interest Test is somewhat less appropriate for purposes of employee selection than for purposes of guidance, because a job seeker may be less honest in answering the test than one seeking

TABLE 21-4

Annual sales of life insurance as related to scores on Strong Vocational Interest Test

Average annual sales	Number of agents	Per cent of agents with stated interest test scores who sold indicated amount of insurance		
		A	B+ and B	B− and C
$400,000 and up	6	3 ⎫	4 ⎫	0 ⎫
$200,000 to $399,000	47	31 ⎬ 56	13 ⎬ 29	5 ⎬ 14
$150,000 to $199,000	37	22 ⎭	12 ⎭	9 ⎭
$100,000 to $149,000	31	19	9	18
$50,000 to $99,000	52	16 ⎱ 25	38 ⎱ 62	23 ⎱ 68
Below $50,000	38	9 ⎰	24 ⎰	45 ⎰
Total		100	100	100
Number of agents	211	121	67	23

SOURCE: Strong (1943), p. 492.

help for himself. Despite this limitation, the interest test has been useful in some spheres of employee selection, especially in the selection of life insurance salesmen (Table 21-4). Comparison of test scores with annual sales shows that the amount of insurance sold corresponds to scores on the test. While two-thirds of those with B and C scores sold less than $100,000 of insurance per year, and only one in seven sold more than $150,000, the figures are reversed for the A group. Of those with A scores, more than half sold insurance in excess of $150,000, while only one in four fell below $100,000.

In commenting on similar results obtained for casualty insurance agents with the Aetna Life Affiliated Companies, their psychologist says: "In general, a man scoring high has three times the chance of success that a man has scoring low" (Bills, 1950, p. 214).

Vocational counseling

When an individual chooses his vocation, he is solving an important personal problem. If he is to choose wisely, he must work out for himself a balance among his goals and values, his interests, his abilities, and the opportunities that he faces for training and for employment. The vocational counselor, if he is to be of maximum help, must first of all be sensitive to the personal problems of the individual and skilled in psychotherapeutic techniques (Chapter 19). Second, he must be fully informed about special vocational requirements and opportunities and about the special tests useful for appraising individual ability and interest. These two roles (personal counselor and vocational expert) occasionally conflict, and some friendly arguments go on among experts as to the appropriate balance between them. The conventional opinion is that diagnostic tests save the time of the counselor. Hence a client who comes for vocational guidance is tested first and counseled later. But some counselors, impressed by the intrusion of personality problems in vocational choice, believe that personal counseling should come first, with tests introduced only when the client feels the need for them and is ready to profit from them (Barahal, Brammer, and Shostrom, 1950).

Students seldom make vocational choices in a dispassionate, rational manner. Because the choice involves the individual's self-estimation, level of aspiration, and status with his fellows, anxieties are aroused. Anxiety-reducing mechanisms are, as we have learned, often self-deceptive. Hence, a person who is selecting his vocation and formulating plans for training needs to be on his guard lest he make costly errors by blinding himself to realities. Distortions of judgment about himself and about the opportunities before him may arise out of earlier experiences he does not completely understand. These distortions are highly individual, but they fall into several recognizable classes:

1. *Lack of realism with respect to abilities and interests.* Many students continue to train for occupations for which they are unsuited, with a disproportionate number seeking to enter the professions.

2. *Lack of knowledge of the variety of occupational opportunities and training requirements.* Because of limited personal experience students are inclined to consider only a few well-established occupations or professions, although some of the newer or less familiar ones may be better suited to the individual's pattern of abilities and interests.

3. *Romanticism with regard to work.* Choice of an occupation merely because it has a high-sounding name or high social prestige will not assure satisfaction in it. Similarly, an idealistic choice of occupation because it seems to provide unusual opportunities for serving mankind may lead to difficulties.

4. *The influence of parental pressure.* The relationships between children and parents are subtle. Well-meaning parents, with sound plans for their children, may find their plans sabotaged because their children resent parental authority. Other children accept goals set by their parents, only to find that the goals are too high for them to reach.

To illustrate how parental influence may become an obstacle to vocational choice,

let us consider three cases of the vocational problems of only sons.

Case 1. "I want my son to follow in my footsteps." Raymond's father had built a wholesale grocery business of which he was justly proud. The trademark of the product had come to be a sign of quality. It was natural for the father to wish Raymond to carry on the family business. The father was so proud of having started from the bottom and built the business for himself that the son had a strong desire to build something for himself. The father could not see that for Raymond following in his father's footsteps meant that he could not be satisfied to take over an established business built by his father.

For a son to follow his father's vocation is an age-old practice, and there is much to commend it. The son has been raised in the social context of that enterprise and knows what it "feels like" to be a contractor or a lawyer or doctor. He may be suited to the vocation by inheritance and attitudinal training. Yet, as with Raymond, the resemblance between father and son may be more subtle than a predisposition to do the same kind of work.

Case 2. "I want my boy to be a professional man." Paul was the son of a contractor in Detroit. His father was successful, and they lived in an exclusive neighborhood. Paul had spent his vacations working on his father's projects, and wanted more than anything else to become a contractor himself. His father, who had not had the benefit of a college education, wanted his son to have a professional training and insisted that he prepare himself to become a lawyer. Despite Paul's high intellectual ability, he failed his work in law school and came to a psychological counselor very puzzled about himself. He felt that he was trying hard and could not understand why his work was not better. It soon emerged that he was in fact defying his father through failure, despite his conscious wish to obey and conform to his father's wishes. When his father was persuaded to accept his training in a graduate school of business as a worthy choice, Paul transferred and did work of good quality. Finally he became a contractor like his father.

The professional goal of becoming a lawyer was not Paul's own, and so he did not succeed in reaching it. The plan was artificial from his point of view; his own goal was realistic and to reach it was satisfying.

Case 3. Mother and Father disagree. Arthur's father was a musician, happy and successful in what he did. But Arthur's mother was never reconciled to having married a musician and she repeatedly disparaged music as a career. Arthur showed musical talent and was attracted to music as an occupation through identification with his father. But he struggled with a business course because of his mother's pressure upon him and had difficulty resolving his vocational conflict.

These three cases suffice to show some of the many forms parental pressure can take. The problem is especially acute among college students for two reasons. First, college permits vocational choices of high prestige value, satisfying to parental ambitions. Second, the college student often remains financially dependent upon his parents during his years of training for his vocation. The first of these considerations whets the parental appetite for domination, and the second reduces the son's or daughter's resistance.

For people like Raymond, Paul, and Arthur the vocational counselor must provide guidance which will help them clear up self-deceptions or conflicts with parents. For other individuals, whose personal adjustments are satisfactory, the choice of vocation is primarily a matter of finding an appropriate social outlet for their abilities.

Industrial Psychology

The development of the machine is a central fact of modern civilization. The machine has accelerated the urbanization of life, increased the destructiveness of military weapons, occasioned new forms of interclass strife, and in a thousand and one ways affected the daily lives of everyone. It has brought with it great conveniences, increased the supplies of goods, and speeded up communication and travel. All of these consequences of the recent development of the machine have created problems which psychology can be called upon to help solve.

The psychologist can approach the problems of industrial civilization on either of two levels. Because he is concerned with human relations on a large scale, he has an interest in broader problems of policy insofar as economic arrangements affect human dignity and satisfaction in living. The industrial problem, at this first and deeper level, has to be studied in the context of other social problems. What have factories done to the community, to home life, to personal security? What changes can be proposed to further personal growth and to improve group relationships according to democratic ideals?

At the second level, the psychologist is interested in man as a factor in production. Here the psychologist is engaged in *human factors research,* because he works to improve industrial efficiency through evolving better employment practices, finding methods of preventing accidents, fitting the man to the machine, adapting the machine to the man, and discovering the most favorable working environment.

At the present time, more of the service of the psychologist is at the second level— facilitating the production and distribution of goods. The psychologist is just beginning to find methods for dealing with broad problems of policy. Actually the two levels of activity are not completely distinct. When the psychologist finds, for example, condi-

TABLE 21-5

Success in employee selection by test *

Per cent of applicants being selected from those who take the test	Per cent who will be successful (body of table)					
	Correlation between test and criterion of success on the job					
	$r = .00$	.20	.40	.60	.80	1.00
10	30	43	58	74	90	100
30	30	38	47	58	70	100
50	30	36	41	47	54	60
70	30	33	37	40	42	43
90	30	31	32	33	33	33

SOURCE: Taylor and Russell (1939).

* Assumes that without the test 30 per cent of the employees will be satisfactory. Another table would have to be used if experience had shown a different percentage successful without the test.

tions of work and methods of supervision that lead to high (or low) morale in local factories, he is gaining information that bears upon larger aspects of economic policy concerned with human relations and human welfare.

Employee selection and training

When one deals with a practical problem, the total circumstances always affect how one can most appropriately use scientific findings. For example, when there is a plentiful supply of manpower, the industrial employer can select employees according to their successful prior work experiences and thereby save the costs of training. On the other hand, when there is a shortage of trained people, he selects as best he can on the basis of aptitude and then must provide the necessary on-the-job training. Industrial psychologists can help both in selection and training. Which area they are called upon to emphasize may depend upon economic conditions.

The success of selection devices will depend upon the fraction of applicants that must be employed. A test whose scores correlate with the criterion of ultimate job efficiency will be more satisfactory if only the

very high scorers rather than a larger fraction can be chosen. Tables have been prepared showing the predictive value of a coefficient of correlation between a selective test and satisfactory work under two conditions: (1) the proportion of workers who turn out satisfactorily when the test is not used, and (2) the proportion of the applicants that must be chosen. An example of such a table is presented in Table 21-5.

Table 21-5 helps to show the complexity of prediction in practical situations. Offhand it seems that a perfect test ought to yield perfect prediction: it will indeed lead to such prediction under favorable circumstances, but if the pool of workers does not contain enough capable of succeeding on the job, some will have to be selected whom the testers would prefer not to hire. Thus if only 30 per cent of workers are successful without the test, perfect results can be achieved with a perfect test only if no more than 30 per cent are hired; if 50 per cent are hired, this 30 per cent will be 30/50, or 60 per cent, of the hired workers, and the rest will fail. Tests are, of course, not perfect, but even a fallible test will be more successful if only the best bets among the applicants are selected.

Selection and training are related because well-selected workers are more easily trained. The correlations between initial performance on the job and performance after training will vary, of course, with the nature of the work. For example, in one study of power sewing-machine operators, the investigators found that for two jobs (trimming and hemming) initial performance and ultimate proficiency correlated .68 and .66, but for a third job (covering) the correlation was insignificant. Apparently the workers did not bring to the job any skills that transferred immediately to the task called covering; hence initial abilities could not be predictive. For all three jobs the speed of learning in the first few trials correlated with ultimate proficiency from .52 to .74 (Blankenship and Taylor, 1938).

The principles of learning and teaching apply also within industry. For example, the instructors themselves require training. In one study the units of work performed by beginners went up markedly after their instructors had first been trained in better teaching methods (Table 21-6).

Work methods and wage incentives

The efficient use of labor is essential for economical output. Two ways to increase efficiency at work are to adopt methods of work that get the most done with a minimum of waste motion, and to adopt methods of pay that reward the productive worker.

A pioneer in the study of productive efficiency, Frederick W. Taylor (1911) saw the possibility of what later became known as *motion and time study*. Taylor encouraged the worker to make full effort by paying him on the basis of what he accomplished. He taught the worker more efficient methods so that he could accomplish more in the same time. The result was that the worker earned more—and the employer's costs per unit were reduced.

While engineering results of motion and time study are excellent, the social-psychological results often are not because of the

TABLE 21-6

Effect of training of instructors on output of beginning workers trained by them

Days of training of workers	Units of work performed by beginning trainees	
	Untrained instructors	Trained instructors
5	18	27
10	24	33
12	25	38

SOURCE: Maier (1946), pp. 225-28.

worker's resentment. Taylor himself was aware of the psychological problems that his system introduced, but he did not understand psychology well enough to make the necessary corrections.

One reason for the resentment is that men in our culture want freedom to do things in their own way; they value individuality and resist regimentation. Given a choice of ten working conditions that might make for satisfaction in their jobs, those who take the Strong Vocational Interest Test pick more often than any other this condition: "Freedom in working out one's own methods of doing the work" (Strong, 1938, p. 543).

Beyond an individual's dislike of being treated as a tool, there are other threats—real or imagined—in management which is based upon motion and time study. Among the worker's objections are:

1. The fear that the number of jobs will be reduced.
2. The fear that the high pace of work will do him physical harm.
3. The fear of economic exploitation, e.g., that the new system will benefit the company more than the worker, with productivity going up faster than pay.

The consequence of these fears is a tendency for the worker to restrict output to

21-4

Workers' attitudes toward productivity

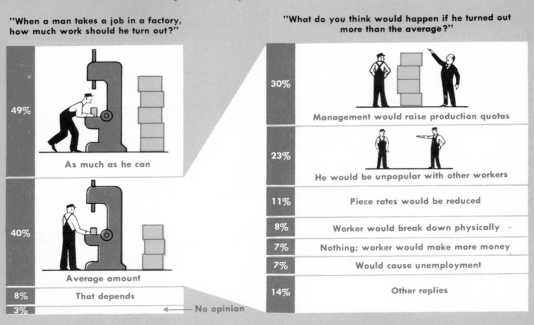

"When a man takes a job in a factory, how much work should he turn out?"

49% — As much as he can

40% — Average amount

8% — That depends

3% — No opinion

"What do you think would happen if he turned out more than the average?"

30% — Management would raise production quotas

23% — He would be unpopular with other workers

11% — Piece rates would be reduced

8% — Worker would break down physically

7% — Nothing; worker would make more money

7% — Would cause unemployment

14% — Other replies

Many workers fear an increase in productivity. (Data from Miller and Form, 1951, after *Factory Management and Maintenance*, January, 1946)

something less than he is capable of producing. The reasons for such restriction have been reported in a survey, the results of which are shown in Figure 21-4. These results support the statements made above about the worker's fears of exploitation and loss of job; in addition, they indicate the importance of fear of loss of face with fellow workers—another illustration of group pressure toward conformity (p. 555). If the worker's objections are to be met, there has to be very clear understanding about the incentive system being used (Shimmin, 1958).

These considerations mean that the problem of efficient work methods is not merely the mechanical one of determining the best way of doing a job with a minimum of effort; it is also a social-psychological problem of securing the worker's cooperation.

Human factors research

World War II saw the development of many complex instruments, such as radar devices used for aircraft detection and sonar devices for submarine detection. The airplane cockpit became a mass of instrument dials, almost too many for one man to keep track of. All of these instruments require reading and understanding by human operators. If the operator misreads a dial or fails to detect a signal on the radar screen, the dial or signal is useless. Designers recognized that machines must take into account the human operator, and a number of research laboratories were set up to work specifically upon the problem of better machine design in relation to the men who were to use the machine. Such research has continued; it has come to be known as *human*

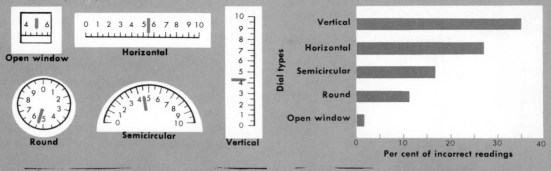

Left: Five dial shapes used in a study of errors in dial reading. *Right:* Per cent of incorrect readings for each of the dials. (After Sleight, 1948)

factors research,[1] and its problems are shared by the engineer familiar with the machinery and by the psychologist familiar with the human operator.

One illustration is provided by the study of errors in reading dials of different shapes. Dial shape proved very important in determining the number of errors (Figure 21-5). It is not always easy, however, to obtain adoption of new devices in the face of tradition. Thus a great many studies have been made of the best method of representing on an instrument the position of the aircraft relative to the horizon. The standard method is inside-out; that is, it shows a moving horizon and a fixed aircraft. However, studies invariably show the superiority of the outside-in arrangement, with a fixed horizon and a moving representation of the aircraft (Melton and Briggs, 1960). Yet equipment designers have been slow to follow the recommendations of research.

Human factors studies confirm precisely what we have known all along—that performance depends upon the cooperation between man and machine. If the machine is

[1] It has also been called *human engineering* and *applied experimental psychology,* but the term *human factors* has recently become the preferred one.

carefully designed to suit the capacities, physical sizes, and foibles of men, the job will be better done.

A report from the System Development Corporation (1959) shows that "human factors professional personnel" numbered 666 people in 55 employing organizations; of these, 453 (68 per cent) were psychologists. Since this area of employment was virtually nonexistent a few years ago, these figures indicate something of the manner in which the field is growing.

Space technology

The great interest in manned space travel has led to a careful consideration of the psychological problems involved. A man traveling in a projectile must not only be able to survive, but must be able to carry out the necessary operations to make his presence in the space ship scientifically useful. He therefore has to be protected from both excessive physical stress and the psychological stress of confinement, isolation, and a gravityless environment. The problems have already been discussed in the psychological literature, with reports on human factors in the operation of manned space vehicles, on the human factor in ballistic missile systems, and on human control

21-6

An application of psychological research

The complex instrument panel of this simulated space capsule has been carefully designed to accommodate the abilities and perceptions of the operator, so that even under stress of space travel he will be able to operate the instruments.

dynamics in air and space craft (e.g., Sells and Berry, 1961). In noting these studies as well as the tasks that lie ahead, Melton and Briggs (1960) state:

Indeed, the space age should be both a challenge and a source of satisfaction to engineering psychologists. Since the space vehicle will have radically different control characteristics and requirements, as compared to present-day aircraft, there should be considerably less resistance to instru-

mentation which conforms to human requirements more than to tradition.

The year 1961 saw what had been fantastic plans actually beginning to be realized, with the initial space flight of the Russian cosmonaut Gagarin and the later suborbital flights of the American astronauts Shepard and Grissom. The premature opening of the escape hatch in Grissom's flight capsule, which led to its loss at sea, illustrates the combined physical and psychological problem. It was necessary for the human operator to use the controls properly, and it was necessary for the controls to respond properly: a failure by either one could lead to loss, as in this case.

Industrial conflict and harmony

With the coming of the Industrial Revolution, workers lost the ownership of the tools of production to the owner-manager group. There followed a period of degradation of the worker, with extremely bad working conditions in the mines, textile mills, and other industries. Eventually the workers formed into trade unions, thereby banding together to fight for better working conditions. Now that more enlightened employment practices are the rule, with many labor laws governing working conditions, we are inclined to forget the conditions that originally gave rise to the labor movement. But some of the bitterness of the labor unions toward employers (and the resistance of the employers to the unions) remains.

One result of the conflict in interests between labor and management is a misperception by each side of the attitudes of the other. One study showed management representatives displaying more understanding of the union's position than vice versa, although both groups occasionally expected the opposing group to hold more extreme positions on controversial issues than it actually did hold (Libo, 1948). In a later study, using Guttman-type scales (see p. 565), Stagner, Chalmers, and Derber

(1958) found management's attitude toward the union uncorrelated with the union's attitude toward management.

Another investigator of union-management attitudes showed identical pictures, sometimes labeled "manager" and at other times "union official," to industrial relations men (representatives of management) and local labor leaders. When showing the pictures, the investigator read a standard description of the two men. In the responses of the union and management officials, the perception of the same men, described in the same words, was very different if he was thought to be a labor leader than if he was thought to be a manager. On the whole, he was viewed as more trustworthy if he represented the same side of the management-union division as the viewing subject (Haire, 1955).

Various suggestions have been made from time to time for arrangements leading to greater cooperation between workers and management in solving their mutual problems. During World War II, for example, some 5000 labor-management committees were registered with the War Production Board, representing some 7 million workers. However, by 1948 only 5 per cent of these were continuing (De Schweinitz, 1949). A later questionnaire sent to 1000 manufacturing companies led to 226 replies concerning the kind and amount of cooperation between labor and management (Table 21-7). The greatest success comes in an economically noncontroversial field (safety); cooper-

TABLE 21-7

Types of postwar labor-management cooperation among 226 firms practicing cooperation

Topics dealt with	Employee-management cooperation	Union-management cooperation	Total reporting this topic
Safety	22	14	36
Waste	27	6	33
Understanding of company policies	25	7	32
Regular attendance	24	4	28
Employee insurance	20	7	27
Quality control	21	5	26
Tools	23	2	25
Employee health	18	6	24
Job evaluation	14	9	23
Lateness	20	2	22
Training and apprenticeship	16	5	21
Methods improvement	18	3	21
Incentive systems	15	4	19
Labor turnover	18	1	19
Working conditions	15	3	18
Discipline	14	2	16
Production planning	14	1	15
Technological changes	11	2	13
Setting output standards	11	2	13
Utilization of machinery	12	0	12
Employment stabilization	10	2	12
Promotional programs	8	3	11

SOURCE: Dale (1954), p. 364.

Membership in the American Psychological Association

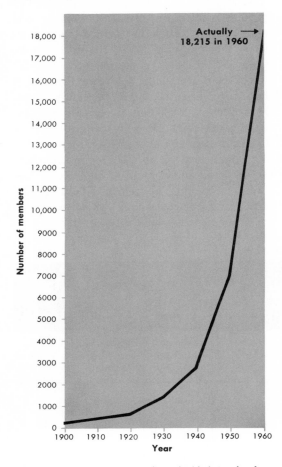

APA membership has more than doubled in the last decade.

Psychology as a Profession

The many applications of psychology suggest that psychologists have gone beyond their teaching and research positions in universities to become of service in a variety of fields. Psychology as a profession has grown up within the span of a single lifetime. Hence the public generally has a very hazy notion about what psychologists do; some 40 per cent of the respondents in one interview sample not many years ago reported that they would feel ill at ease talking with a psychologist (Guest, 1948). They associated psychology mostly with interest in the abnormal.

Fields of specialization within psychology

Psychology has been growing by leaps and bounds, as shown by the increase in membership of the national association of psychologists, the American Psychological Association (Figure 21-7). This acceleration has come about in part because of the increasing employment of psychologists outside colleges and universities. At present the academic positions (teaching, research, and administration in colleges and universities) account for barely half the psychologists. Next in order come governmental agencies, with the federal government employing as many as state and local governments combined. Next come private agencies: business, industry, clinics, and guidance centers. The number of psychologists who practice privately, offering their services to the public for a fee, is small. A summary of employment of psychologists, based on a sample from the 1948 directory of the American Psychological Association, is given in Table 21-8. Women are listed separately from men. The table shows that universities and colleges employ a larger proportion of men, with state and local governments providing relatively more frequent opportunities for women. But women as psychologists are employed in substantial numbers by all types of employers.

ation concerning production or economic problems is much less frequent.

With unionization and collective bargaining now established within our major industries, the problems of reducing conflict and friction and of promoting harmony become major tasks of industrial psychology.

These four specimen topics (selection and training, wage incentives, human factors research, and industrial conflict) merely suggest the variety of problems with which industrial psychologists deal.

TABLE 21-8

Psychologists classified according to agency employing them

Source of employment	Men	Women	Total
Colleges and universities Teaching, administration, personnel, etc.	55%	38%	50%
Federal government Veterans Administration, armed services, other agencies	14	7	12
State and city government School systems, hospitals and clinics, other agencies	7	24	12
Private organizations Business and industry, clinics and guidance centers, schools	11	14	12
Self-employed Private practice of psychology	2	3	2
Miscellaneous Student, retired, non-psychological occupation	11	14	12
Total	100	100	100
Number of cases in sample	598	265	863

SOURCE: Wolfle (1948). Based on a sample of the membership of the American Psychological Association.

TABLE 21-9

Fields of specialization within psychology

Specialty	Males	Females	Total	Per cent
Clinical	2912	1312	4,224	38.1
Counseling	1056	269	1,325	12.0
Developmental	181	199	380	3.4
Educational	635	218	853	7.7
School	113	162	275	2.5
Experimental, comparative, and physiological	957	135	1,092	9.9
Human engineering	149	6	155	1.4
Industrial	266	21	287	2.6
Personnel	766	70	836	7.5
Personality	306	51	357	3.2
Social	468	71	539	4.9
Quantitative (statistics, tests and measurements)	332	65	397	3.6
General and non-specialized	151	61	212	1.9
Nonpsychological	113	24	137	1.2
Totals	8405	2664	11,069	99.9

SOURCE: Ogg (1955), p. 5. Based on the replies of 11,069 psychologists to a questionnaire from the National Science Foundation.

What a psychologist does is not, of course, determined solely by who pays his salary. A psychologist working in a government laboratory may be doing exactly the same sort of work that he would do in a university. A psychologist at work in a Veterans Administration clinic may be doing just what he would do if he were working privately with a group of professional colleagues. One answer to what kinds of psychologists there are, and how many there are of each, is provided by a study conducted by the National Science Foundation (Table 21-9). (An analysis relating the type of employer to the field of specialization is given later in Table 21-10.)

Experimental Psychologists. The traditional field of general psychology, which is devoted to research in the principles of psychology as they apply to men in general or to organisms in general, is best supported by our institutions of higher learning, where the bulk of research in the "pure" problems of psychology goes on. Most university psychologists are also teachers of psychology, although, with funds for research increasingly available, some psychologists are devoting themselves to full-time research. Since World War II experimental psychologists have been increasingly drawn into applied experimental research, in which their training in sensory psychology is brought to bear on problems of communication, dial reading, and the development of detection devices. Laboratory studies of learning are used in developing training aids for the armed services and selection devices for duties requiring a high order of motor skill. For those who are drawn to psychology as a laboratory science, who like to use apparatus and find satisfaction in precise measurement, experimental psychology offers many opportunities.

Clinical and Counseling Psychologists. The largest single interest among professional psychologists is now in *clinical psychology*. The typical clinical psychologist works in an agency giving care or treatment —a mental hospital, an institution for the mentally subnormal, a prison, a juvenile court, a mental health clinic, a college or university health service, or a child guidance clinic. His affiliations with the medical profession are close, especially with psychiatry, as we learned in Chapter 19.

After the clinical psychologist has had sufficient experience, he is eligible upon examination to qualify for a diploma in Clinical Psychology awarded by the American Board of Examiners in Professional Psychology, a body created by psychologists to certify the competence of psychologists working at high levels of professional responsibility.

The close affiliation of the clinical psychologist with psychiatric problems draws him largely into hospitals and clinics, where disturbed patients come. This leaves an enormous amount of psychological work for guidance centers handling normal people whose problems are typically those of vocational and educational guidance and of social adjustment not severe enough to be considered psychiatric problems. Advisement and guidance workers, who have come to think of themselves as *counseling psychologists* rather than as clinical psychologists, secure a thorough training of a somewhat different kind from that of the clinical psychologist. They need to know much more than the clinical psychologist about occupations, about requirements for admission to professional schools and other training institutions, and about aids to study. They are not primarily concerned with the treatment of people so severely disturbed that they have to be hospitalized. The differences between the counselor and the clinical psychologist are, of course, not sharp, for the counselor has to be alert to the person who seems merely upset about a superficial problem but who is really deeply disturbed. The counselor refers such a person to clinical services, confining himself to problems not classifiable as illness. A diploma is provided by the American Board of Examiners in Professional Psychology for psychologists with top qualifications in counseling and guidance.

Clinical and counseling psychologists together account for half the psychologists in the National Science Foundation survey (Table 21-9).

Social Psychologists. Social psychologists are best known for their work in public opinion surveys, audience measurement, and market research. The survey method is now widely used for a variety of purposes by newspapers, magazines, radio and television networks, advertising agencies, and manufacturers, as well as by agencies of the government, such as the Census Bureau, Department of Labor, Department of Agriculture, Treasury Department, Federal Reserve System, and the armed forces. The technical skills required are sampling, interviewing, questionnaire construction, and the interpretation of survey data.

In view of continuing international tensions and the efforts to meet them by propaganda and counterpropaganda, propaganda analysis is important for social psychologists. More generally, all problems of psychological warfare fall within the province of social psychology; we considered, for example, some aspects of coercive persuasion (Chapter 20).

New developments in methods for studying small groups and for modification of group attitudes have brought social psychologists more actively into community work where they attempt, for example, to modify attitudes that produce intergroup tensions. Thus a kind of clinical social psychology is developing which may do for communities what clinical psychology now does for the individual.

Social psychology has both its pure-science and its applied-science aspects. (As a pure science it is concerned with such problems as the influence of the culture upon personality development, social motives, language and communication, the influence of the group upon individual performance, problems of identification, imitation, and role-playing.) We have treated these topics as part of general psychology, where indeed they belong. As an applied science social psychology is concerned with studying existing attitudes and preferences and how they are influenced. A division of the American Psychological Association, known as the Society for the Psychological Study of Social Issues, is especially interested in the possible services of social psychology in the solution of pressing public problems.

Statisticians. A knowledge of statistics is essential to all psychologists, but some specialize in statistical methods and the application of statistics to test construction.

Tests are important tools for the research psychologist generally, as well as for the clinical psychologist, the counselor, the educational psychologist, the industrial psychologist, and the social psychologist. Hence whenever any large-scale research enterprise is undertaken, at least one statistical expert is needed.

While statisticians in psychology have heretofore been associated largely with test construction and the interpretation of test results, their duties now are much wider. They are called upon as experts in sampling to design samples for public opinion or attitude or market surveys. They are called upon as experts in experimental design to help the experimental psychologist or other research psychologist arrange his procedures for gathering and analyzing data in the most economical manner.

Other Specialties. Other specialties named in Table 21-9 are self-explanatory in view of the consideration already given these topics.

CRITICAL DISCUSSION
Psychologists survey their profession

Because of the rapid growth of psychology as a profession, and the moving of its members into many new fields of activity, the American Psychological Association, with a grant from the National Science Foundation, recently began a self-study of psychology both as a science and as a profession. The scientific aspects are being reported in a series of volumes being edited by Sigmund Koch (Koch, 1959a, 1959b, 1959c). The professional aspects, having to do with personnel and training, were reported in a volume by Kenneth E. Clark, chairman of the committee in charge of that part of the survey (Clark, 1957). The following remarks have to do with Clark's findings.

One aspect of the study dealt with the background, training, and careers of psychologists who, in the eyes of their colleagues and by other measures, were designated as "significant contributors" to psychology. By comparison with others who received the Ph.D. degree during the same years, the significant contributors were found to have emerged as promising early in their careers, to have come from graduate departments that stand high in research training, to have been employed after receiving their doctoral degrees in positions that had sufficient freedom and facilities for them to make early scientific contributions. Their status in the profession was enhanced by their election to offices in professional associations and by their frequent citation in the experimental literature.

The study also concerned itself with differences among the various psychological specialties. Thus the areas of specialization in 1954 were found to vary with the type of employment, as shown in Table 21-10 (compare with Table 21-8). Another study shows two value clusters to stand out among the differing psy-

TABLE 21-10

Type of employer in 1954 of psychologists within various specialties who received their doctoral degrees from 1930 to 1944

Employer	Specialization within psychology					
	General	Exper. & Physiol.	Pers. & Social	Clinical	Educ. & Develop.	Industrial
College or university	71%	83%	73%	48%	83%	35%
Other educational institution	3	2	—	5	8	—
Federal government	11	8	8	18	7	9
Private industry, self-employed	1	1	1	11	—	8
Private industry, employee	5	2	7	—	—	37
Nonprofit organizations, including hospitals	4	4	10	10	1	11
State and local government	5	—	1	8	1	—
	100%	100%	100%	100%	100%	100%
	N = 77	N = 158	N = 101	N = 276	N = 177	N = 97

SOURCE: Clark (1957).

chological specialties (Thorndike, 1954): experimental psychologists show a peak of values in laboratory research, while clinical psychologists show a peak of interest in working with individuals.

Other aspects of the professional self-study included a survey of psychological services in several metropolitan areas (Milwaukee, Providence, Los Angeles, Atlanta), and a study of students entering graduate work in psychology.

Psychology and other professions

It is characteristic of applied problems that they belong to more than one field of inquiry. The social problems with which psychologists are concerned are usually problems within medicine, education, law, political science, sociology, and social welfare. Hence as psychology begins to offer professional services, there are many opportunities for collaboration with other professions.

Psychology and the Law. Legal psychology—the application of psychology to problems of lawmaking, law enforcement, the examination of witnesses, and the treatment of the delinquent and criminal—offers much promise for the future.

The study of *testimony* and *evidence* is one field of interest, opened up in the earliest application of psychology to the law in a book by Hugo Münsterberg entitled *On the Witness Stand* (1908). The heavy dependence in criminal trials upon the testimony of eyewitnesses may lead to miscarriages of justice; experimental evidence shows how fallible human perception and memory are, even when witnesses are seeking to report honestly. One law professor, noting the abuses of testimony, collected a whole volume of cases in which innocent people were convicted, largely on the basis of testimonial evidence (Borchard, 1932). An empirical study of 154 rules of evidence, participated in by both lawyers and psychologists, suggested that a number of these rules should be revised or discarded (Britt, 1940).

Another psychological problem is that of the *individual offender*. Who is likely to commit crimes? What are the chances of restitution to society? One question that arises is the relationship between intelligence and criminality. While it is frequently found that lower I.Q.'s are associated with crimes of violence (homicide, assault, and sex crimes), and higher I.Q.'s with crimes such as forgery and embezzlement, interpretation is difficult. Perhaps, with respect to crimes of violence, the more intelligent criminals escape detection or are more likely to receive suspended sentences; only the more intelligent members of the population are exposed to the temptations of embezzlement. Studies of juvenile delinquency show that intellectual deficiency cannot be the primary cause for delinquency, for the range of intelligence is wide and overlaps greatly with the intelligence distribution of a control population. Other psychological contributors to delinquency were considered earlier (Chapter 4).

Finally, there are many psychological problems within the *broader aspects of the law,* aspects having nothing to do with crime and punishment as we ordinarily think of them. Many problems coming before lawyers have psychological aspects: patent and trademark disputes, divorce, taxation, and social legislation. Social scientists are occasionally called upon as expert witnesses to determine the consequences of certain social practices. Thus in the hearings on desegregation leading to the Supreme Court decision, a brief was prepared by psychologists and other social scientists and was accepted in evidence by the Supreme Court (Clark, 1953).

Only a few of the fields of possible interaction between psychology and the law have thus far been developed. Law schools, unlike medical schools, have not made a practice of adding psychologists to their faculties. Thus the area is one in which developments may be expected in the future.

Psychology and Education. General psychology and educational psychology are closely related, partly because of the magnitude of the task confronting educators: providing appropriate learning experiences for all children—rural and urban, bright and dull—and extending learning opportunities upward into the adult years. The central topics within educational psychology (individual differences, learning and memory, motivation, group behavior, mental health, and personality) are merely the topics of general psychology placed in the context of the schools. In this context the topics become *applied:* when to begin the teaching of reading or arithmetic and how best to go about it; how to meet the problems of the slow and fast learner; which activities are best carried out individually, which in groups, how to train teachers, and so on. To some extent education has become the major technological outlet for psychology. The relationship of education to experimental psychology is conceivably similar to that between engineering and physics.

As a scientific specialty *educational psychology* is concerned with psychological research applied to any and all aspects of educational practices. Educational psychologists have their places on the faculties of universities and teachers colleges, and play a part in the training of teachers. The psychologists employed by the schools are more likely to be called school psychologists (instead of educational psychologists), for they have specific tasks: giving psychological tests, making special provisions for the handicapped or for children in need of remedial work, dealing with special guidance problems that require relationships with child guidance clinics or community social agencies. Because we have already discussed the central topics of educational psychology, and because we have seen some educational applications in the earlier chapters, we shall not here go further into the special problems of educational and school psychologists.

Psychology and Medicine. Clinical psychologists work closely with psychiatrists, social workers, psychiatric nurses, and others, particularly in child guidance clinics, mental health services of various kinds, and in hospitals for the mentally ill. We have seen how psychology bears on these problems in several chapters.

The psychologist's interest in child-rearing practices makes his work bear also on the practices of *pediatricians,* the medical doctors concerned with the diseases of childhood and with the healthy development of infants (Rubin-Rabson, 1950).

While psychology is itself a nonmedical science, its connections with medicine are very close, as are those of other basic sciences such as biochemistry and physiology. Medical science is interested in health as well as in disease; psychology's concern with the growth and development of the total functioning individual brings it into relationship with the health emphasis within medicine. As a behavioral science the ramifications of psychology are, of course, much broader than those of medicine.

The psychologist's role in society

Because so many personal and public problems are at the root psychological, the role of the psychologist in society is likely to become increasingly important. One of the present difficulties is that psychology has not yet developed sufficiently, nor are there enough men and women in it, to assume some of the responsibilities already asked of psychologists. A science can handle only problems that have become manageable. To have people seek the advice of a psychologist on problems for which his instruments are inadequate may be flattering to the psychologist, but it is also embarrassing to him. He must restrict himself to what he can do lest the public become disappointed in his answers. While the psychologist is wisely modest about what has been achieved thus far, he need not blind himself to the importance that his work may achieve if he builds soundly.

Where Psychology Is Going

At any one period in its history there are always centers of excitement in a science, where new problems are being worked upon and older issues reformulated in ways that revitalize them. In order to see the present and future in perspective, it is worthwhile to note some of the changes in emphasis that have taken place in psychology in the past.

Psychology broke off from philosophy by establishing itself as an experimental science in the latter part of the nineteenth century. As noted earlier, the first chair in psychology in America was established in 1888 at the University of Pennsylvania for J. McKeen Cattell, who had received his Ph.D. under Wundt at Leipzig. His laboratories, and the many others that were established at about that time, were concerned chiefly with sensory thresholds, reaction time, emotion, and memory. Their importance was that they proved that a laboratory science of psychology was possible.

World War I broadened psychology by drawing the most vigorous psychologists into the war effort, where, called upon to develop tests and to validate various devices, many of them learned statistics for the first time. The public acceptance of the intelligence test was very important, and individual differences became a respectable topic within the core of psychology. After World War I there came a flurry of tests and test theories, including the developments within factor analysis.

World War II gave a second forward boost to psychology. If World War I may be said to have launched ability testing, World War II promoted clinical and social psychology, on the one hand, and human factors research, on the other. Within clinical psychology there came the development of interest in projective tests, personality assessment, psychodynamics, and psychotherapy. The Veterans Administration and the National Institute of Mental Health seized upon these developments and encouraged them in the postwar years by subsidizing psychological training centers and by granting financial aid to those who wished to become trained as clinical psychologists. The best-known of the social-psychological developments during World War II were those in the survey field (consumer surveys, attitude-opinion studies, propaganda analysis) and studies of group dynamics, including small-group behavior and the study of experimental audiences. Human factors research drew psychologists from the fields of sensory psychology and learning—the pure-science fields that had remained largely confined to the laboratory and aloof from applications. These psychologists preferred the expression "applied experimental psychology" to the older "applied psychology"; the older industrial psychology had fitted man to the machine, while the newer approach required the machine to be designed with the human operator in mind. Soon these psychologists were at work in studies of specialized training, in designing dials, headphones, radar screens, and in studying "trouble-shooting" (diagnosing and repairing defective equipment).

All of this took a little settling down after World War II. The record was written down (19 volumes on psychology in the air forces, four volumes on the social-psychological studies in the army, and a number of others); some of the new material came to be used in the textbooks for instructional purposes. Some disillusionment set in; things that had seemed very exciting and promising in the heat of war no longer seemed quite as profound, and some of the leads turned out not to hold up very well when carefully tested. Much of the substance remains, however, and now, in the 1960's, the settling down has taken place, and new ways of looking at things have begun to emerge. It is always hard to identify the important developments that are taking place in the present, for while many possible lines of investigation are opened up, only a few

catch on; the historian's task is much easier than the prophet's. It is possible, however, to note some of the problems that represent the growing edge of psychology today, recognizing that other less dramatic features are also being investigated and may at any time produce some new forward thrust. Psychology is a complex field, as its history has shown, and its trends are more likely to be divergent than convergent.

Comparative psychology and evolutionary theory

Although the evolutionary interests of psychologists have always been strong, and animal laboratories have been a standard part of a department of psychology, the investigations of the animal laboratory have tended to focus on topical questions (aspects of learning and discrimination, the effects of drugs, the role of portions of the brain), and the experiments have tended to be carried out on a limited number of species, with considerable emphasis upon the white rat. There are two ways in which animal studies can be of use. The first, and in the past the more usual kind, is the kind of study in which lower animals are used to throw light on problems arising in human psychology, much as animals are used in the medical school in the study of treatments intended later to be used on man. The second is that in which the psychologist studies animals in their own right in order to comprehend their behavior and the interrelationships between species, recognizing what Frank Beach calls "the equality of organisms," that is, the equal significance of the worm, the octopus, the spider, and the porpoise for purposes of comparative behavior study. This second kind of comparative psychology is having a forward surge, partly through the influence of the European ethologists who showed how much was overlooked unless animals were carefully studied in their natural habitats. Their naturalistic studies and related studies in the laboratory contribute to the study of evolution by producing behavioral evidence of species relationships that supplement the morphological (i.e., structural) comparisons that have thus far been the chief sources of evidence for evolutionary theory.

The brain in behavior and experience

For a time, especially in the 1930's, there was a kind of declaration of psychology's independence from physiology, as there had been earlier from philosophy. This came about because of the discovery that many previously held notions of brain action were in fact faulty, that there was much less localization of function in the brain than had previously been thought, and that we knew virtually nothing about the action of the brain in relation to higher mental processes. It was argued that it did not matter whether the brain acts like a telephone switchboard or as a complex field of forces; in either case habits will still be acquired as they are now acquired, sensory thresholds will be what they are, and memory functions will remain as we know them. The position was that psychologists could set the problems for the physiologists to solve, that psychology was sounder in its facts than students of brain physiology were in theirs, and that psychology could not wait for the physiologist but had to go ahead on its own. This position has its merits even today, for there always is enough independence of one science from another for each to go its own way, even though there may be interconnections that will facilitate the advance of both.

This attitude began to change about 1950. Hebb's influential book on *The organization of behavior* appeared in 1949; while highly speculative, it made a good deal of sense and proposed a kind of neuropsychology that offered promise. Concurrently a number of exciting developments had taken place in neurophysiology itself. A new hormone, noradrenalin, had again made interesting the differences between fear and anger. The whole vegetative brain, responsible for

drive and affective behavior, was being re-studied, using such concepts as the "limbic system." The "general adaptation syndrome" called attention to widespread responses under stress. The knowledge of the arousal mechanism, operating via the reticular formation, led to new interpretations of sleep, waking, and energetic action. The knowledge that some efferent fibers could modulate afferent processes brought renewed interest to the physiology of sensory processes and of attention. The discovery of a "pleasure center" in the brain fitted in with an emerging neo-hedonism, or emphasis on the importance of pleasure in motivation. The brain enzymes began to be related to adaptive behavior; the discovery of new types of responses in the dendrites and an interest in the glia cells opened further possibilities.

Psychologists are now participating in all of these developments, and the prospects are better than they ever were for solution to some of our age-old problems on the relation between mind and body. Here is a dramatic illustration of the interrelationships of science: modern electronics and modern chemistry combined with anatomy, physiology, and psychology to make possible what no one could do alone.

Mathematical and computer models

There have been many attempts in the past to use mathematics in biology and social sciences, but here, too, recent forward strides make the present different from the past. With a background of the theory-of-games model of the economists, the decision-theory model of the political scientists, and the information-theory model of the communications theorists and cyberneticists, psychologists have gone forward with their own mathematical model-building, the most advanced work being done in probabilistic models concerned with the learning process. The high-speed computer provides a tool that supplements the mathematical model, although the mathematical model and the computer are essentially one, in that the program that is fed into the computer is itself some kind of mathematical model. The most exciting development of computer models is in the simulation of cognitive processes, i.e., of problem-solving and creative thinking. Computers are more than elaborate playthings, and there is a serious interaction that goes both ways: careful studies of human learning and thinking help in the design of the machines, but once the machine is built and we find what it can (or cannot) do, then we are likely, through correcting the instructions to the machine, to gain a better understanding of what the human being does. No one can yet tell just where all of this activity is leading, but a young psychologist who wants to know what is happening to his field will be excluded from much of it if he cannot read the literature using the nomenclature of probability and of the modern mathematics known as set theory and matrix algebra.

Learning, motivation, and the technology of instruction

The psychology of learning has been an ascendant field of interest in psychology ever since William James gave prominence to the concept of habit, but more particularly following the work of Thorndike and Watson early in this century and the influence of Pavlov's studies of the conditioned reflex. The careful systematic formulations of Hull, with exciting controversies stirred up by Tolman, Lashley, Köhler and others, gave this topic unusual prominence over the last three decades. Interest in learning, as a theoretical and experimental topic, continues unabated, although the complexities that have turned up have reduced psychologists' confidence in most of the general formulations and have diverted interest to motivation and other related topics.

While motivation has always interested some psychologists, the approach to the topic shifts; as it shifts, psychologists of different background and persuasion pick it up. For a time, early in the century, the problems of *instinct* were studied; later, *drives* induced by deprivation (especially hunger, thirst, sex) came under study; the psychoanalysts contributed *anxiety* and *guilt* as motivating forces. The newer developments, chiefly over the last decade, have emphasized such topics as the group of drives formerly neglected (exploration, curiosity, manipulation, frustration-induced drives); the influence of needs and values on perception; perceptual defense; the expression of motives in fantasy (e.g., achievement and affiliation motives); and how motives are expressed in values and value-systems. The topic of motivation has become so broad that many psychologists have become uneasy about it; this very uneasiness is a sign that the subject matter is being taken seriously, but that there are many unsolved problems.

A burst of criticism of the public schools, following the Russian launching of the satellite Sputnik, has challenged psychologists to apply whatever principles they have discovered in their laboratory investigations of learning and motivation to problems of improving actual instruction. For historical reasons that would take too much space to recount here, an earlier rapport between psychology and education, especially in the fields of learning and memory, was all but lost during the last two or three decades.[2] The laboratory had moved farther and farther away from relevant content, choosing its materials for the study of learning chiefly on the basis of convenience in relation to theoretical issues. Thus the laboratory drifted away from the problems of instruction, and the school found it increasingly difficult to make any use of the results of learning experiments.

The immediate response to the new challenge has come in the form of *programed*

[2] The schools continued to use the technical services of psychologists in the fields of testing and counseling, but curriculum and instruction made little or no use of psychological services.

learning and the teaching machine. This new development has brought the attention and services of many very well-trained experimental psychologists to education. Because of the nature of the programing technique, it has forced attention to the problems of organization of knowledge and has led the experimenter on learning to deal with subject matter relevant to schooling. But programed learning is only one illustration of emphasis upon the content of learning studies. The motivational side of learning is not being neglected, and studies of anxiety in school children, for example, consider the actual test situations to which the child is exposed in school. This renewed interest in the applied problems of learning and motivation, coming at a time when there is also a renewed interest in cognitive processes generally, is likely to have an important feedback to the psychology of learning and motivation. That is, when attention is paid to relevant learning content, features such as the organization of knowledge come to the fore and add dimensions that may have been neglected in laboratory studies in which meaning was a more artificial variable.

Behaviorism vs. subjective phenomena

At the height of behaviorism not many years ago, many psychologists developed a "you mustn't say" attitude toward subjective experiences of all kinds (pleasures, pains, percepts, images, ideas); when it was essential that reference be made to these "states" or "experiences," they had to be translated into "discriminatory responses" or "verbal responses" and thus be made behaviorally respectable. This attitude made a useful contribution to scientific methodology by constantly calling attention to the need for objectivity in science, for making observations reproducible, for keeping science communicable; but the contribution was at a price. In a subtle way the more "subjective" problems, such as those raised by dreams and hallucinations, tended to be neg-

lected because "you mustn't say" became generalized into "you mustn't study." This was not a necessary consequence of the behaviorist position, but it was an inadvertent by-product; fortunately this era is now passing, and there is now much freer use of perceptual concepts (and perceptual and cognitive language) than earlier.

There are less extreme and more extreme forms of this new interest in phenomena, with corresponding attitudes toward behaviorism. The less extreme form does not reject behaviorism as a general methodology, but adds *perceptual responses* to the muscular and glandular responses that were once the only legitimate substance of a strict S-R behaviorism. If perceptual responses are accepted as *central responses* (Sheffield, 1962), then the peripheralism of classical behaviorism is rejected. Sheffield is willing to say, for example, that a watchmaker looking at the outside of a familiar watch "sees" the works inside as a learned perceptual response; this is a genuine central response, and not merely a form of talking to himself about the works. Such a position leaves the principles of S-R learning theory intact, but allows great freedom in the discussion of perceptual content. It becomes easy, for example, to distinguish between the several responses that happen if you hammer your finger: feeling the pain, saying "ouch," and withdrawing the finger.

The more extreme form of rejection of behaviorism is found in various forms of phenomenology, existentialism, and humanistic psychology. For example, the experimental phenomenology of Fritz Heider (1958) is called by him a "naïve" psychology; it takes things as one finds them and does not attempt to reduce them to another level of analysis. That is, one stays close to the phenomena in talking about them; it is not necessary to reduce them to physiology or chemistry to "explain" them. Existentialism and humanistic psychology tend to reject the biological approach that has been characteristic of American psychology, seeing the problems of psychology rather in terms of human values, human concerns, individual uniqueness, and the individual meaning of life and destiny.

The main stream of psychology in the years ahead is more likely to be influenced by the moderate alteration of the behaviorist position than by the extreme forms of phenomenology. The less extreme position permits a freer interest in cognitive processes of all kinds, in dreams, in hypnotic phenomena, in intention, in problems of self-perception, planfulness, and "will," without thereby rejecting the search for lawfulness in behavior, for objectivity in experimentation, and for clarity in scientific communication. Phenomenology in the past has often served a useful critical function by warning against triviality and the neglect of important issues, and the present developments may again serve in this way. However, one cannot make a science of human behavior merely by standing in awe of it and marveling at it; such a position drifts into a more and more obscure account of the nature of man. But as soon as phenomenal description becomes at all clear and systematic, it partakes of the very science that phenomenology opposes and, in fact, becomes assimilated to it. To the extent that the phenomenologists call attention to the whole man in his environment, they provide the same sort of corrective that the ethologists have provided for comparative psychology: they see that the right questions are asked, whether or not we approve of the answers that they give.

One of the genuine problems that the humanistic psychologists pose is the need for a better understanding between a biological psychology and the position of the humanistic disciplines, a conflict which in other spheres has led to the distinction between our two cultures, scientific and nonscientific (Snow, 1959). Psychology has probably kept its distance from the humanities in part because of its eagerness to establish itself as a science, and in part because of its still-too-recent divorce from philosophy. Nevertheless psychologists study esthetics, language (psycholinguistics, communication), values, and meanings. We can hope that understanding between psychology and the humanities will increase—to their mutual advantage.

Behavior genetics, child development, and mental health

Nowhere do the problems of pure science and of applied science overlap more than in the study of human development, for adults are responsible for the decisions that are made in the course of a child's development, and if these decisions are guided by scientific knowledge they are illustrations of applied science. These are old problems, but new knowledge and techniques will affect the course of psychology in obtaining answers to the familiar problems.

Some new developments lie in the field of genetics, which occupies one side of the nature-nurture problem. The new techniques which permit the study of the chromosome structure of the individual have opened up many new possibilities that are only now being explored, such as defining the chromosomal background of mongolism. Behavior genetics, as applied to man, can advance our knowledge of the inheritance of human characteristics of many kinds, including aspects of intelligence, personality, and mental illness.

The older longitudinal studies of the past (following a group from birth onward) tended to bog down in data; because the time span is so great, observations that are recognized as needed today were not made when the studies were begun, and the answering of today's questions with data collected yesterday has not proved very satisfactory. Undoubtedly new longitudinal studies will use methods of group overlap, so that data covering a span of years can be collected more quickly. With modern sampling methods it is possible to study several age groups simultaneously; for example, by studying the age groups from birth through 5, 5 through 10, 10 through 15, and 15 through 20 at the same time, thereby doing the equivalent of 20 years' observations in five years.

One practical reason for proposing methods of child rearing is to achieve good mental health outcomes, that is, to bring up children who can cope with their problems and can face crises without breakdown. This is one facet of the general problem of personality development, from the point of view of its social significance; clinical psychology must concern itself with the prevention of mental illness, as well as with its diagnosis and treatment.

The research tasks before a developmental psychology include the study of normal development and the factors that affect it, given the raw materials provided by heredity and prenatal development; the prediction of outcomes (successful adjustment, delinquency, personality disturbances); diagnostic procedures along the way; and remedial practices, including psychotherapy. This is a large order, and much remains to be done.

A comprehensive social psychology

Nothing is more pressing than an understanding of human social life and institutions that will permit more rational solutions to the problems of human civilization than those we now attempt. War as an instrument of policy is recognized on all sides as stupid and dangerous to human survival; the armaments race has no equilibrium point and hence must run eventually to destructive encounter, unless some other policy intervenes. These are sober facts of human social behavior, about which we somehow feel helpless because we have not yet been able to accept scientific processes in the control of human affairs. It is a paradox that the highest developments of science are used in weapon development, but that the makers of these advanced weapons do not know how to control their use or even their reduction.

A comprehensive social psychology must deal with group behavior at all levels, including the international level; this does not mean that social psychology now has the answers to the problems that international issues create. Where does it now stand?

Systematic social psychology has tended to go back to the individual and to small groups to discover the forms of social perception and social interaction that are at the root of larger social institutions; even larger social decisions (e.g., the declaration of war by a nation's cabinet) can be simulated by a "game" in which the relevant information is given to the participants and they are then set the task of arriving at a decision. Decisions by leaders are, after all, the decisions of individual human beings.

To what extent the social institution acts like an organism is an old question, to which the answer is not entirely clear. There are kinds of "institution morality" that appear different from individual morality; thus nations are "insulted" and retaliate with a violence that would not characterize individual reactions; the people of two nations may declare their liking for each other and yet fight over national issues that are largely ceremonial in character.

It is the task of social psychology of the future to understand the rational and irrational in human social behavior and institutions. This understanding, if it can be applied in such a way as to make human relations more humane, could turn out to be science's greatest contribution to mankind.

SUMMARY   1. *Work satisfaction* is an important social problem. The conditions of modern life, with division of labor and occupational mobility, make it difficult to provide work satisfaction for all. A college education is clearly one avenue of upward occupational mobility.

2. Tests have proved helpful in vocational counseling. At the college level, both *ability* tests and *interest* tests are serviceable. Tests do not stand alone, however, and the process of vocational counseling involves more than the giving and interpreting of tests. Very often a student's vocational problems cannot be solved without first settling his problems of personal adjustment.

3. Many college students are undecided about their vocational futures, and some who have made definite choices have made them unwisely. The obstacles to satisfactory choice include lack of realism with respect to abilities and interests, lack of knowledge of the variety of occupational opportunities and of the demand for training, romanticism with regard to work, and unfortunate parental pressures.

4. Psychology finds ready application in the selection and training of workers within industry. Psychological tests are widely used.

5. Improvements in work methods and the use of incentive pay often meet with worker objections because men object to being treated as machines. Their fear of management may lead to work restriction lest pay rates be changed, workers displaced from jobs, or health injured.

6. *Human factors research* studies the relation between man and machine and tries to have machines designed to conform to the capacities of the operator. Space travel opens new challenges to psychology.

7. Union-management differences are a source of conflict. The achievement of greater understanding between management and union leaders may reduce the amount of strife between the factions. Reductions of labor-management tension is an important task of social psychology.

8. Psychology began as a small profession within the lifetime of some still living. It surged ahead after the two world wars, until by 1960 it numbered over 18,000 members in its national society, the American Psychological Association, and its rapid growth is continuing.

9. Colleges and universities are still the largest employers of psychologists; many members of the profession now work for government agencies or private organizations. Relatively few engage in private practice.

10. Of the numerous specializations within psychology, *clinical psychology* is now the largest; the two specialties of *clinical* and *counseling* psychology account for half the professional psychologists. Other specialties include *experimental psychology, social psychology,* and *statistics.*

11. Psychology is also applied within other professions, such as law, education, and medicine. *Legal psychology* has dealt with testimony and evidence, the examination of witnesses, study of the individual delinquent and criminal, and with some broader problems of the law. *Educational psychology* deals with the applications of principles of learning, motivation, personality, and group behavior to the schools, while the school psychologist has special functions within the school system. The relationships

with *medicine* are close, through clinical psychology and through the psychologist's interest in early childhood and in developmental problems.

12. In attempting to see where the problems of psychology lie in the years ahead, it is possible to note important developments in such areas as: *comparative psychology,* particularly in relation to evolutionary theory; *brain study,* in relation to both behavior and experience; *mathematical and computer models,* in learning and the simulation of cognitive processes; learning, motivation, and the technology of instruction, with an emphasis on the *content* of learning; a freer study of perceptual, cognitive, and other *subjective phenomena* through a lessening of the influence of a narrow behaviorism; behavior genetics, child development, and mental health; and a comprehensive social psychology. These developments in both pure and applied science make possible a very significant contribution of psychology to human understanding and to human welfare.

SUGGESTIONS FOR FURTHER READING

The historical background of special topics in applied psychology can be found in Fryer and Henry (Eds.), *Handbook of applied psychology* (1950).

On vocational problems, see Roe, *The psychology of occupations* (1956), and Super, *The psychology of careers* (1957).

The standard work on vocational interest tests is Strong, *Vocational interests of men and women* (1943), brought to a more recent date by Strong, *Vocational interests 18 years after college* (1955), and Darley and Hagenah, *Vocational interest measurement: theory and practice* (1955).

There are a number of textbooks in industrial psychology, of which Ghiselli and Brown, *Personnel and industrial psychology* (2nd Ed., 1955), and Harrell, *Industrial psychology* (2nd Ed., 1958), are representative. The shift from personnel selection and training to managerial problems is reflected in Haire, *Psychology in management* (1956), Leavitt, *Managerial psychology* (1958), and Likert, *New patterns of management* (1961).

Human factors research is summarized in Chapanis, *Research techniques in human engineering* (1959), and in McCormick, *Human engineering* (1957). Space technology, from the psychologist's viewpoint, is summarized in Flaherty, *Psychophysiological aspects of space flight* (1961), and Sells and Berry (Eds.), *Human factors in jet and space travel* (1961).

For industrial conflict, see Kornhauser, Dubin, and Ross (Eds.), *Industrial conflict* (1954), and Stagner, *Psychology of industrial conflict* (1956).

For psychology as a profession, see Clark, *America's psychologists: a survey of a growing profession* (1957), and Daniel and Louttit, *Professional problems in psychology* (1953). The beginning student who may be interested in psychology as a career will find the following pamphlets helpful: Ogg, *Psychologists in action* (1955), Super, *Opportunities in psychology* (1955), and Watson, *Psychology as a profession* (1954). For psychology in relation to other professions, see Gray, *Psychology applied to human affairs* (2nd Ed., 1954), and Guilford (Ed.), *Fields of psychology* (2nd Ed., 1950).

For a picture of contemporary psychology as a science with the best available guesses as to where it is going, the following volumes provide the thinking of recognized experts, written not for beginners but for other psychologists: Koch (Ed.), *Psychology: a study of a science.* (This work is eventually to be in seven volumes, the first three of which appeared in 1959.)

Glossary

The glossary defines technical words appearing in the text and some common words when they are used in psychology with special meanings. No attempt is made to give the range of variations of meaning beyond those used in the text. For fuller definitions and other shades of meaning, consult any standard dictionary of psychology, such as English and English, *A comprehensive dictionary of psychological and psychoanalytical terms* (1958).

ability. Demonstrable knowledge or skill. Ability includes aptitude and achievement (cf. *aptitude, achievement*).

abnormal fixation. A stereotyped habit very resistant to change (cf. *stereotypy*).

abreaction. In psychoanalysis, the process of reducing emotional tension by reliving (in speech or action or both) the experience which caused the tension (syn. *catharsis;* cf. *release therapy*).

absolute threshold. The intensity or frequency at which a stimulus becomes effective or ceases to become effective, as measured under experimental conditions (cf. *threshold, difference threshold*).

achievement. Acquired ability, e.g., school attainment in spelling (cf. *aptitude*).

achievement motive. The social motive to accomplish something of value or importance, to meet standards of excellence in what one does.

achromatic colors. Black, white, and gray (cf. *chromatic colors*).

acquiescence. A biasing variable in personality inventories, leading some subjects to reply more frequently in the affirmative, regardless of the content of the test item (cf. *social desirability variable*).

adaptive behavior. Behavior that brings the organism into adjustment with its variable environment (cf. *behavior*).

additive mixture. The mixture of lights; two spotlights focused on the same spot yield additive mixture; colored sectors of paper rotated on a color wheel also yield additive mixture (cf. *subtractive mixture*).

adolescence. In human beings, the period from puberty to maturity, roughly the early teens to the early twenties (cf. *puberty, prepuberal phase, puberal phase, postpuberal phase, late adolescent phase*).

adrenal gland. One of a pair of endocrine glands located above the kidneys. The medulla of the gland secretes the hormones adrenalin and noradrenalin. The cortex of the gland secretes a number of hormones, collectively called the adrenocortical hor-

mones, which include cortisone (cf. *endocrine gland*).

adrenalin. One of the hormones secreted by the adrenal medulla, active in emotional excitement (syn. *epinephrine;* cf. *noradrenalin*).

affective-arousal theory. A theory of motivation that accounts for the tendency for behavior to be directed according to anticipated pleasure or pain (McClelland).

affective experience. An emotional experience, whether pleasant or unpleasant, mild or intense (cf. *emotional state*).

affective psychotic reaction. Cf. *manic-depressive reaction, psychotic-depressive reaction.*

afferent nerve. A bundle of nerve fibers transmitting impulses into the central nervous system from the periphery. Receptors connect directly with afferent nerves (usually synonymous with *sensory nerve;* cf. *efferent nerve*).

affiliative motive. In man, the tendency to depend upon another person or persons, to associate with them, to form friendships or other attachments (syn. *dependency motive*).

afterimage. The sensory experience that remains when a stimulus is withdrawn. Usually refers to visual experience, e.g., the negative afterimage of a picture, or the train of colored images that results after staring at the sun.

age-mates. Other children of the same age with whom a child associates and from whom he commonly derives some of his standards (syn. *peer group*).

aggression. (1) Destructive activity of any sort. (2) Activity undertaken in order to do harm to another person either through actual physical injury or through some kind of belittling or malicious ridicule (this is the usual text usage).

agoraphobia. Fear of open places (cf. *phobic reaction*).

algorithm. A fixed routine for finding a mathematical solution, an exact procedure, as in extracting square root. A computer commonly uses algorithmic methods, but may use other methods (cf. *heuristic method*).

ambivalence. Simultaneous liking and disliking of an object or person; the conflict caused by an incentive that is at once positive and negative (cf. *conflict*).

amnesia. The partial or total loss of memory for past experiences. The memories lost in amnesia have not been completely destroyed, for the forgotten events may again be remembered without relearning when the person recovers from his amnesia (cf. *repression*).

anal stage. The second stage according to the psychoanalytic theory of psychosexual development, following the oral stage. The sources of gratification and conflict have to do with the expulsion and retention of feces (cf. *psychosexual development*).

androgen. The collective name for male sex hormones, of which testosterone, secreted by the testes, is best known (cf. *sex glands, estrogen*).

antagonistic muscles. Muscles arranged in pairs, so that when one contracts the other stretches, e.g., the biceps and triceps muscles of the upper arm (cf. *reciprocal innervation*).

anthropology. The science that studies chiefly nonliterate ("primitive") societies. Its main divisions are archaeology (the study of the physical monuments and remains from earlier civilizations), physical anthropology (concerned with the anatomical differences among men and their evolutionary origins), and social anthropology (concerned with language, social institutions, and behavior) (cf. *behavioral sciences*).

anticipation method. A method of rote memorization, appropriate to either serial memorization or paired-associates learning, in which the subject learns to respond to a stimulus item with the response item next to appear in the aperture of the memory drum. The method permits scoring successes and failures throughout memorization.

anxiety. A state of apprehension or uneasiness, related to fear. The object of anxiety (e.g., a vague danger or foreboding) is ordinarily less specific than the object of fear (e.g., a vicious animal).

anxiety reaction. A form of psychoneurotic reaction characterized by a diffuse dread, often accompanied by tenseness, palpitation, sweating, nausea (cf. *psychoneurotic reaction*).

apathy. Listlessness, indifference; one of the consequences of frustration (cf. *frustration*).

aphasia. Impairment or loss of ability to articulate words or to comprehend speech. Henry Head distinguished four classes: *verbal defect, syntactical defect, nominal defect,* and *semantic defect* (q.v.).

appetitive behavior. Seeking behavior (cf. *aversive behavior*).

aptitude. The capacity to learn, e.g., typing aptitude prior to practice on a typewriter. Aptitude tests are designed to predict the outcome of training, hence to predict future ability on the basis of present ability (cf. *achievement*).

area sampling. A method used in making surveys of attitudes and opinions, the respondents being selected according to their place of residence; one form of probability sampling (cf. *quota control, probability sampling*).

aroused motive. A motive that is inferred from behavior actually occurring (cf. *motivational disposition*).

assimilating. The tendency to distort memory in the direction of familiar objects and experiences, e.g., reproducing a geometrical form so that the reproduction looks more like a familiar object than the original did (syn. *normalizing;* cf. *systematic distortion*).

association areas. Portions of the cerebral hemispheres other than the projection areas. Because their function is unknown, the assumption is made that these areas serve some sort of integrative ("association") function (cf. *intrinsic cortex*).

association psychology. A pre-experimental psychology, whose basic explanatory principle was the association of ideas (cf. *faculty psychology*).

associative thinking. Relatively uncontrolled and undirected thinking as in free association, reverie, and dreams (cf. *directed thinking*).

asthenic type. A major body type, according to Kretschmer, characterized by a tall, thin body and associated (in the extreme) with schizophrenic psychosis (cf. *type theory, pyknic type*).

attention. The focusing of perception leading to heightened awareness of a limited range of stimuli.

attitude. An orientation toward or away from some object, concept, or situation; a readiness to respond in a predetermined manner to the object, concept, or situation (cf. *attitude scale, complex, opinion, prejudice*).

attitude scale. A scale for the quantitative appraisal of attitudes (cf. *scalogram*).

authoritarian personality. A personality syndrome said to be common to those whose attitudes are authoritarian instead of democratic. The syndrome is characterized by highly conventional behavior, concern over sex, superstitiousness, destructiveness, and cynicism (cf. *personality syndrome*).

autistic thinking. A form of associative thinking, controlled more by the thinker's needs or desires than by reality; wishful thinking (cf. *daydreaming, rationalization*).

autonomic nervous system. A system of nerve cells and nerve fibers regulating smooth muscle and glandular activities. While the system is closely integrated with the brain and spinal cord, it has some cell bodies and synapses lying outside the brain and spinal cord (syn. *vegetative nervous system;* cf. *parasympathetic division, sympathetic division*).

average. A value representative of a frequency distribution, around which other values are dispersed, e.g., the mean, median, or mode of a distribution of scores (syn., but somewhat obsolete, *measure of central tendency*).

aversive behavior. Avoidance behavior (cf. *appetitive behavior*).

avoidance learning. A form of learning controlled by the threat of punishment. The learning is motivated by the anxiety raised by the threat and the reduction of anxiety when the puishment is avoided (cf. *escape learning*).

axon. That portion of a neuron that transmits impulses to other neurons (cf. *neuron, dendrite*).

basal mental age. In individual tests of the Binet type, the highest age level at which, and below which, all tests are passed (cf. *mental age*).

basilar membrane. A membrane of the ear within the coils of the cochlea, supporting the organ of Corti. Movements of the basilar membrane stimulate the hair cells of the organ of Corti, producing the neural effects of auditory stimulation (cf. *cochlea, organ of Corti*).

behavior. Those activities of an organism that can be observed by another organism or by an experimenter's instruments. Included within behavior are verbal reports made about subjective, conscious experiences (cf. *conscious processes*).

behavioral sciences. The sciences concerned in one way or another with the behavior of man and lower organisms; especially social anthropology, psychology, and sociology, but including some aspects of biology, economics, political science, history, philosophy, and other fields of study (cf. *anthropology, psychology, sociology*).

behaviorism. A school or system of psychology associated with the name of John B. Watson; it defined psychology as the study of behavior and limited the data of psychology to observable activities. In its classical form it was more restrictive than the contemporary objective (behavioral) viewpoint in psychology (cf. *school of psychology*).

bimodal distribution. A frequency distribution with two points at which there are a high number of cases, hence two modes (cf. *mode*).

binocular cues. Cf. *distance cues*.

bit. A unit in information measurement; the amount of information that reduces by one-half the number of alternatives that may prove to be correct (cf. *information measurement, uncertainty*).

blood pressure. The pressure of the blood against the walls of the blood vessels. Changes in blood pressure following stimulation serve as one indicator of emotion (cf. *emotional indicator*).

blood volume. The volume of the blood in a bodily member (e.g., hand, finger) due to dilation or constriction of blood vessels. Changes in volume serve as one indicator of emotion (cf. *emotional indicator*).

body-sense area. A projection area of the cerebral cortex lying behind the fissure of Rolando. Electrical stimulation of the area commonly results in the report of sensory experiences, e.g., "It feels as though

I am moving my finger" (syn. *somesthetic area;* cf. *motor area*).

brain stem. The structures lying near the core of the brain; essentially all of the brain with the exception of the cerebral cortex and the cerebellum and their dependent parts.

brainwashing. Cf. *coercive persuasion.*

brightness. The dimension of color that describes its nearness in brilliance to white (as contrasted with black). A bright color reflects more light than a dark one (cf. *hue, saturation*).

brightness constancy. The tendency to see a familiar object as of the same brightness, regardless of light and shadow that change its stimulus properties (cf. *color constancy, object constancy*).

Broca's speech area. A portion of the left cerebral hemisphere said to control motor speech.

cardiac muscle. A special kind of muscle found only in the heart (cf. *smooth muscle, striate muscle*).

cardinal disposition. An outstanding disposition that dominates an individual personality, often making that person a "reference personality" according to which others are judged, e.g., a Beau Brummell or Don Juan (Allport) (cf. *central disposition, secondary disposition*).

case history. A biography obtained for scientific purposes; the material is sometimes supplied by interview, sometimes collected over the years.

caste. Social stratification in which boundaries are sharply defined and not to be crossed (cf. *class*).

castration. Surgical removal of the gonads; in the male, removal of the testes; in the female, removal of the ovaries.

center. A place within the nervous system where impulses in activated neurons can produce impulses in other neurons across synapses. A center contains numerous cell bodies of neurons; while most centers are within the brain and spinal cord, some lie outside (syn. *central processes;* cf. *ganglion*).

centile scale. A scale of ranked scores ranging between 0 and 100 (syn., but somewhat obsolete, *percentile scale*).

central nervous system. In vertebrates, the brain and spinal cord, as distinct from the nerve trunks and their peripheral connections (cf. *autonomic nervous system*).

central disposition. One of a few dispositions sometimes sufficient to characterize an individual (Allport) (cf. *cardinal disposition, secondary disposition*).

centralist position. A theoretical position held by certain psychologists who believe that thinking can best be explained as processes going on inside the brain or nervous system, with muscular movements as mere accompaniments or facilitators of the central processes (cf. *peripheralist position*).

cerebral cortex. The surface layer of the cerebral hemispheres in higher animals, including man. It is commonly called gray matter because its many cell bodies give it a gray appearance in cross section, in contrast with the nerve fibers that make up the white matter.

cerebral hemispheres. Two large masses of nerve cells and fibers constituting the bulk of the brain in man and other higher animals. The hemispheres are separated by a deep fissure, but connected by a broad band of fibers, the corpus callosum (syn. *cerebrum;* cf. *cerebral cortex*).

chemical integration. Bodily organization for harmonious or unified action through chemical substances transmitted via the bodily fluids, especially the hormones (cf. *hormones, mechanical integration, neural integration*).

childhood. The total life period from birth up to but not including adolescence (cf. *adolescence*).

chlorpromazine. Cf. *tranquilizer.*

chromatic colors. All colors other than black, white, and gray, e.g., red, yellow, blue (cf. *achromatic colors*).

chromosome. Small particles found in pairs in all the cells of the body, carrying the genetic determiners (genes) which are transmitted from parent to offspring. A human cell has 46 chromosomes, arranged in 23 pairs, one member of each pair deriving from the mother, one from the father (cf. *gene*).

chronological age (C.A.). Age from birth; calendar age (cf. *mental age*).

clairvoyance. A form of extrasensory perception in which the perceiver is said to identify a stimulus that is influencing neither his own sense organs nor those of another person (cf. *extrasensory perception, telepathy, precognition*).

class. A level of social stratification, e.g., upper, middle, and lower class, but without the rigid boundaries characterizing caste, so that mobility between classes is possible (cf. *caste*).

class interval. In statistics, a small section of a scale according to which scores of a frequency distribution are grouped, e.g., heights grouped into class intervals of a half inch (cf. *frequency distribution*).

classical conditioning. Conditioned-response experiments conforming to the pattern of Pavlov's experiment. The main feature is that the originally neutral conditioned stimulus, through repeated pairing with the unconditioned one, acquires the response originally given to the unconditioned stimulus (syn. *stimulus substitution;* cf. *operant conditioning*).

claustrophobia. Fear of closed places (cf. *phobic reaction*).

cleanliness training. A euphemism for teaching the infant to control urination and defecation.

client. A synonym for *patient,* the term used by counselors who wish to avoid the medical connotations of the patient-physician relationship (cf. *client-centered counseling*).

client-centered counseling. A method of psychological counseling designed to let the client learn to take responsibility for his own actions and to use his own resourcefulness in solving his problems (syn. *nondirective counseling;* cf. *traditional counseling*).

clinical psychologist. A psychologist, usually with a Ph.D. or Ed.D. degree, whose training includes hospital or clinic experience, so that he is prepared to work in a collaborative relationship with physicians although not himself medically trained. His techniques include testing, diagnosis, interviewing, psychotherapy, and the designing and conducting of research (cf. *counseling psychologist, psychiatrist*).

clique. A small exclusive group, usually reluctant to admit outsiders and often snobbish toward them.

cluster analysis. An analysis of trait (or item) intercorrelations, based on grouping together those traits (or items) that show similar patterns of inter-item correlation. The method is more superficial than factor analysis, for which it sometimes substitutes (cf. *factor analysis; surface trait*).

cochlea. The portion of the inner ear containing the receptors for hearing (cf. *basilar membrane, organ of Corti*).

coefficient of correlation. A numerical index used to indicate the degree of correspondence between two sets of paired measurements. The most common kind is the product-moment coefficient designated by *r*.

coercive persuasion. Influencing the thought patterns of prisoners whose lives are completely under the control of those seeking to influence them, thereby permitting kinds of influence not ordinarily possible (syn. *brainwashing*).

cognitive dissonance. The condition when one has beliefs or knowledge that disagree with each other or with behavioral tendencies; when such cognitive dissonance arises, the subject is motivated to reduce the dissonance through changes in behavior or cognition (Festinger).

cognitive theory. A point of view contrasted with stimulus-response (S-R) theory, more concerned with "knowing" and "perceiving" than with "movement-responses" (cf. *stimulus-response psychology*).

color blindness. Defective discrimination of chromatic colors (cf. *monochromatism, dichromatism, red-green color blindness*).

color circle. An arrangement of chromatic colors around the circumference of a circle in the order in which they appear in the spectrum, but with the addition of nonspectral reds and purples. The colors are so arranged that those opposite each other are complementaries in additive mixture.

color constancy. The tendency to see a familiar object as of the same color, regardless of changes in illumination on it which alter its stimulus properties (cf. *object constancy*).

color-mixing primaries. Three hues chosen to produce the total range of hues by their additive mixture. A spectral red, green, and blue are usually selected (cf. *psychological primaries*).

common trait. An aspect of personality in respect to which most people within a culture can be profitably compared (Allport) (cf. *disposition*).

comparative psychology. The study of the behavior of lower organisms in their interrelationships with each other and with man.

compensation. A form of defense mechanism by which one attempts to cover up or balance failure in, or lack of talent for, one activity by a strenuous effort to excel in either a different or an allied activity (cf. *substitution, sublimation, overcompensation*).

complementary hues. Two hues which in additive mixture yield either a gray or an unsaturated color of the hue of the stronger component.

complex. An attitude accompanied by excessive emotion, often causing neurotic responses (cf. *attitude*).

compulsive movements. Repetitive actions which a person feels driven to make and which he is unable to resist; ritualistic behavior; a form of dissociation (cf. *dissociation*).

compulsive personality. A personality syndrome characterized by cleanliness, orderliness, and obstinacy. In the extreme, behavior becomes repetitive and ritualistic (syn. *anal character;* cf. *personality syndrome*).

concept. The properties or relationships common to a class of objects or ideas. Concepts may be of concrete things, e.g., the concept "poodle dog" referring to a given variety of dog, or of abstract ideas, e.g., equality, justice, number, implying relationships common to many different kinds of objects or ideas.

concurrent validity. Validity determined by the internal consistency of the parts of a test, all scores obtained at the same testing (cf. *construct validity, content validity, predictive validity*).

conditioned emotion. An emotional response acquired by conditioning, i.e., one aroused by a stimulus that did not originally evoke it (cf. *conditioning*).

conditioned response. The learned or acquired response to a conditioned stimulus, i.e., to a stimulus that did not evoke the response originally (cf. *classical conditioning, unconditioned response*).

conditioning. The process by which conditioned responses are learned (cf. *classical conditioning, operant conditioning*).

cone. In the eye, an element of the retina found predominantly in the fovea and more sparsely throughout the retina. The cones mediate both chromatic and achromatic sensations (cf. *retina, rod, fovea*).

confidence limits. In statistics, upper and lower limits derived from a sample, used in making inferences about a population; e.g., from the mean of a sample and its standard error one can determine limits which permit a statement that the probability is 95 in 100 that the population mean falls within these limits (cf. *statistical inference, statistical significance*).

conflict. The simultaneous presence of opposing or mutually exclusive impulses, desires, or tendencies.

conjunctive concept. A type of concept in which all objects of a class share common characteristics; e.g., all rubies are hard, translucent, and red (cf. *disjunctive concept, relational concept*).

connotative meaning. The suggestions and emotional meanings of a word or symbol, beyond its denotative meaning. Thus naked and nude both refer to an unclothed body (denotative meaning), but they have somewhat different connotations (cf. *denotative meaning, semantic differential*).

conscience. An internal recognition of standards of right and wrong by which the individual judges his own conduct (cf. *superego*).

conscious processes. Events such as perceptions, afterimages, private thoughts, and dreams of which only the person himself is aware. They are accessible to others through verbal report or by way of inference from other behavior (syn. *experience, awareness;* cf. *unconscious processes*).

construct validity. Validity determined by a process of inference more complex than that involved in predicting a specific criterion. The inference is usually in hypothetical form; e.g., if this is a good measure of achievement motivation, it should relate to scores on a learning task, even though that task is not itself a measure of achievement motivation (cf. *concurrent validity, content validity, predictive validity*).

control group. In an experimental design contrasting two groups, that group not given the treatment whose effect is under study (cf. *experimental group*).

consummatory behavior. Cf. *goal activity.*

controlled association. The process in word-association experiments in which the subject is instructed to give a specific kind of associated word, e.g., one opposite to that of the stimulus word (cf. *free association*).

conversion reaction. A form of psychoneurotic reaction in which the symptoms are paralysis of the limbs, insensitive areas of the body (anesthesias), uncontrolled emotional outbursts, or related bodily symptoms. The presumption is that anxiety has been "converted" into a tangible symptom (syn. *hysteria;* cf. *psychoneurotic reaction*).

corpus callosum. A large band of fibers (white matter) connecting the two cerebral hemispheres.

correlation. Cf. *coefficient of correlation.*

counseling psychologist. A trained psychologist, usually with a Ph.D. or Ed.D. degree, dealing with personal problems not classified as illness, such as academic, social, or vocational problems of students. His skills are similar to those of the clinical psychologist, but his work is usually in a nonmedical setting (cf. *clinical psychologist*).

creative thinking. A form of directed thinking in which the subject seeks to discover new relationships, to achieve new solutions to problems, to invent methods or devices, or to produce new artistic objects or forms (cf. *critical thinking*).

criterion. (1) A set of scores or other records against which the success of a predictive test is verified. (2) A standard selected as the goal to be achieved in a learning task, e.g., the number of runs through a maze to be made without error as an indication that the maze has been mastered.

critical flicker frequency. If the rate of alternation between light and dark phases of stimuli is increased, there comes a point at which flicker disappears and a steady light is perceived; this fusion rate is known as the critical flicker frequency (syn. *critical fusion frequency*).

critical ratio. A mean, mean difference, or coefficient of correlation, divided by its standard error. Used in tests of significance (cf. *statistical significance*).

critical scores. Scores based on experience with tests used for a given purpose, so that persons scoring below the critical level are rejected as unlikely to succeed; e.g., a critical score on a scholastic aptitude test for college students is one below which no candidate is accepted for admission.

critical thinking. A form of directed thinking in which the subject seeks to arrive at judgments of truth or value (cf. *creative thinking*).

cues to distance. Cf. *distance cues*.

cue-stimulus theory. A theory of motivation that gets along without the concept of drive by assuming that behavior comes exclusively under the control of stimuli (cf. *drive*).

culture-fair test. A type of intelligence test that has been so constructed as to minimize bias due to the differing experiences of children raised in a rural rather than an urban culture or in a lower-class rather than in a middle-class or upper-class culture (syn. *culture-free test*).

cybernetics. The study of regulatory mechanisms, such as thermostats and governors. One of the several models used in theory construction (cf. *model*).

cyclothyme. A type of temperament associated, according to Kretschmer, with the pyknic body type and characterized by mood fluctuations, resembling in less extreme form the characteristics of manic-depressive psychosis (cf. *pyknic type, schizothyme*).

dark adaptation. The increased sensitivity to light when the subject has been continuously in the dark or under conditions of reduced illumination (cf. *light adaptation*).

daydreaming. Reverie; free play of thought or imagination. Because of self-reference, usually a form of autistic thinking (cf. *autistic thinking*).

decibel. A unit for measuring sound intensity, which has a logarithmic relation to the amplitude.

defense mechanism. An adjustment made, often unconsciously, either through action or the avoidance of action in order to escape recognition by oneself of personal qualities or motives which might lower self-esteem or heighten anxiety (cf. *rational problem-solving*).

delayed-response experiment. An experiment used with both subhuman animals and man as a test of memory. The subject observes the experimenter place an incentive under one of two or more containers. Then a shield is placed between the subject and the containers for a period of delay before the subject chooses the proper container. Accuracy of his choice tests his memory for the placing of the incentive.

delusion. False beliefs characteristic of some forms of psychotic disorder. They often take the form of de-

lusions of grandeur or delusions of persecution (cf. *paranoid reactions*).

dendrite. The specialized portion of the neuron which (together with the cell body) receives impulses from other neurons (cf. *axon*).

denial. Cf. *self-deception*.

denotative meaning. The primary meaning of a symbol, something specific to which the symbol refers or points; e.g., my street address is denotative; whether or not I live in a desirable neighborhood is a connotative meaning secondary to the address itself (cf. *connotative meaning*).

dependency motive. A motive based on the need to be taken care of by someone, to gain support through affiliation (syn. *affiliative motive*).

dependent variable. The variable whose measured changes are attributed to (or correspond to) changes in the independent variable. In psychological experiments, the dependent variable is often a response to a measured stimulus (cf. *independent variable*).

depth perception. The perception of the distance of an object from the observer or the distance from front to back of a solid object (cf. *distance cues*).

descriptive statistics. Simplifying or summarizing statements about measurements made on a population. Strictly speaking, descriptive statistics should apply solely to populations, rather than to samples, but the term is used loosely for summarizing statements about samples when they are treated as populations (cf. *statistical inference*).

detection of signals. A type of threshold measurement that contrasts with classical psychophysics by beginning with the basic assumption that any stimulus is detected against a background of interference ("noise") (cf. *threshold, psychophysical methods*).

developmental explanation. An explanation of behavior that stresses the historical roots of present activity, focusing on accumulating experience as the individual grows and learns (cf. *interactive explanation*).

deviation I.Q. An intelligence quotient (I.Q.) computed as a standard score with a mean of 100 and a standard deviation of 15 (Wechsler) or 16 (Stanford-Binet), to correspond approximately to traditional intelligence quotient (cf. *intelligence quotient*).

dichromatism. Color blindness in which either the red-green or the blue-yellow system is lacking. The red-green form is relatively common; the blue-yellow form is the rarest of all forms of color blindness (cf. *monochromatism, red-green color blindness*).

difference equation. An equation used in probabilistic treatments of learning to express the change in probability of response from one trial to the next (syn. *linear operator*).

difference threshold. The minimum difference between a pair of stimuli that can be perceived under experimental conditions (cf. *threshold, absolute threshold, just-noticeable-difference*).

dimension. A scale from one extreme to another along which orderly variations occur, e.g., pitch as a dimension of tone, brightness as a dimension of light, length as a size dimension, the degree of favorableness as a dimension of attitude (cf. *scale*).

direct aggression. Aggression against the person or object producing frustration (cf. *aggression, displaced aggression*).

directed thinking. Thinking directed toward a goal or toward the solution of a problem (cf. *creative thinking, critical thinking, associative thinking*).

discrimination. (1) In perception, the detection of differences between stimuli. (2) In conditioning, the differential response to the positive (reinforced) stimulus and to the negative (nonreinforced) stimulus (cf. *generalization*). (3) In social psychology, prejudicial treatment, as in racial discrimination.

discriminatory stimulus. A stimulus that becomes an occasion for an operant response, e.g., the knock that leads one to open the door. The stimulus does not elicit the operant response in the same sense that a stimulus elicits respondent behavior (cf. *operant behavior*).

disguise. Cf. *self-deception*.

disjunctive concept. A type of concept in which two members belong to the same class because of possessing either one of two quite different characteristics, e.g., two kinds of "strikes" in baseball (cf. *conjunctive concept, relational concept*).

aisplaced aggression. Aggression against a person or object other than that which was (or is) the source of frustration (cf. *direct aggression*).

displacement. In psychoanalysis, the substitution of one object for another as a source of gratification.

disposition. A personal trait to be distinguished from a common trait because of its uniqueness (Allport) (cf. *common trait*).

dissociation. A defense mechanism in which there is splitting of aspects of behavior or experience which normally would occur together. Thus dissociated movements occur without their appropriate emotional accompaniments, or dissociated thoughts occur without appropriate action (cf. *compulsive movements, defense mechanism, multiple personality*).

dissonance. (1) In music, an inharmonious combination of sounds; contrasted with consonance. (2) In social psychology, Festinger's term for a perceived inconsistency between one's own attitudes and one's behavior (cf. *cognitive dissonance*).

distance cues. (1) In vision, the monocular cues according to which the distance of objects is perceived—such as superposition of objects, perspective, light and shadow, and relative movement—and the binocular cues used in stereoscopic vision (cf. *stereoscopic vision*). (2) In audition, the corresponding cues governing perception of distance and direction, such as intensity and time differences of sound reaching the two ears (cf. *stereophonic hearing*).

distributed practice. An arrangement of learning trials in a task in which there is time intervening between trials, as opposed to immediately consecutive trials (syn. *spaced practice;* cf. *massed practice*).

dominance. The higher status position when social rank is organized according to a dominance-submission hierarchy; commonly found in human societies and in certain subhuman animal groups.

dominant gene. A member of a gene pair, which, if present, determines that the individual will show the trait controlled by the gene, whether or not the other member of the pair is the same or different, that is, recessive (cf. *recessive gene*).

drive. (1) An aroused condition of the organism based upon deprivation or noxious stimulation, including tissue needs, drug or hormonal conditions, and specified internal or external stimuli, as in pain (text usage). (2) Loosely, any motive (cf. *motive*).

drive-reduction principle. The principle that a motivated sequence of behavior can be best explained as moving from an aversive state of heightened tension (i.e., drive) to a goal state in which the drive is reduced. The goal of the sequence, in other words, is drive reduction.

duct gland. A gland, such as the tear gland or salivary gland, that secretes its product on the surface of the body or into the body cavities but not directly into the blood stream (cf. *endocrine gland*).

dynamometer. An instrument used in measuring strength of grip.

eardrum. The membrane at the inner end of the auditory canal, leading to the middle ear (cf. *middle ear*).

ectomorphic component. The third of the three components of physique in Sheldon's type theory. It comprises delicacy of skin, fine hair, and ultrasensitive nervous system (cf. *endomorphic component, mesomorphic component, type theory*).

educational psychologist. A psychologist whose research interest lies in the application of psychological principles to the education of children and adults in schools (cf. *school psychologist*).

EEG. Cf. *electroencephalogram*.

effector. A bodily organ activated by motor nerves; a muscle or gland (cf. *receptor*).

efferent nerve. A bundle of nerve fibers transmitting impulses from the central nervous system in the direction of the peripheral organs. Efferent nerve tracts commonly end in muscles or glands (usually synonymous with *motor nerve;* cf. *afferent nerve*).

ego. In Freud's tripartite division of the personality, that part corresponding most nearly to the perceived self, the controlling self which holds back the impulsiveness of the id in the effort to delay gratification until it can be found in socially approved ways (cf. *id, superego*).

ego-integrative motive. A motive built around the self, such as achievement and mastery, self-fulfilment (cf. *social motive, survival motive*).

ego involvement. Commitment to and absorption in a task so that success in it becomes important to self-esteem and failure leads to chagrin (cf. *level of aspiration*).

ego theory. The theory in psychoanalysis that stresses functions of the ego, as against almost exclusive preoccupation with libido (cf. *ego, libido theory*).

electroconvulsive shock therapy. A form of shock treatment for mental illness in which high-voltage current is passed briefly through the head, producing temporary unconsciousness and convulsions, with the intention of alleviating depression or other symptoms (cf. *shock therapy*).

electroencephalogram (EEG). A record obtained by attaching electrodes to the scalp (or occasionally to the exposed brain) and amplifying the spontaneous electrical activity of the brain. The EEG is useful in studying some forms of mental disturbance (e.g., epilepsy) and in research on brain function.

emergency reactions. The physiological accompaniments of intense emotional excitement interpreted (by Cannon and others) as a method of preparing the organism to meet emergencies.

emotional indicator. A sign or symptom of the activity going on in an emotional state. Physiological indicators that can be continuously recorded are commonly selected for experimental purposes.

emotional state. The condition of the organism during affectively toned experience, whether mild or intense (cf. *affective experience*).

endocrine gland. A ductless gland, or gland of internal secretion, that discharges its products directly into the blood stream. The hormones secreted by the endocrine glands are important chemical integrators of bodily activity (cf. *duct gland, hormones*).

endomorphic component. The first of three components of physique in Sheldon's type theory. It comprises prominence of intestines and other visceral organs, including a prominent abdomen, as in the obese individual (cf. *mesomorphic component, ectomorphic component, type theory*).

envy. The emotional and motivational consequence of rivalry with another person, based on some desired characteristic or possession of that person (cf. *jealousy*).

equilibratory senses. The senses which give discrimination of the position of the body in space and of the movement of the body as a whole (cf. *kinesthesis, semicircular canals, vestibular sacs*).

errors of measurement. That part of the variation in a distribution of scores, or in statistics derived from them, attributable to the fallibility of the measuring instrument, errors in observation, etc. (cf. *sampling errors*).

escape learning. A form of learning controlled by actual painful stimulation. Escape from the punishment brings an end to the unpleasant or painful situation and is therefore rewarding (cf. *avoidance learning*).

estrogen. The collective name for female sex hormones secreted within the ovary (syn. *ovarian hormones;* cf. *sex glands, androgen*).

estrus. The sexually receptive state in female mammals. It is a cyclical state, related to menstruation in the primates and man (syn. *heat;* cf. *menstruation*).

ethologist. One of a group of zoologists and naturalists particularly interested in kinds of behavior that are specific to a species. More of their work has been on insects, birds, and fishes than on mammals (cf. *instinct*).

expectation. An anticipation or prediction of future events based on past experience and present stimuli (cf. *sign learning*).

expectation-value theory. A theory of motivation and decision-making that accounts for choices on the basis of values (or utility) and the risks involved, e.g., the probability that such values will be attained.

experimental design. A plan for collecting and treating the data of a proposed experiment. The design is evolved after preliminary exploration, with the aims of economy, precision, and control, so that appropriate inferences and decisions can be made from the data.

experimental group. In an experimental design contrasting two groups, that group of subjects given the treatment whose effect is under investigation (cf. *control group*).

experimental psychologist. A psychologist whose research interest is in the laboratory study of general psychological principles as revealed in the behavior of lower organisms and man.

explicit movements. Movements easily observed and measured; overt movements (cf. *implicit movements*).

exploratory behavior. Behavior leading to inferences concerning the curiosity motive (cf. *investigatory response, locomotor response, orientation response*).

extinction. (1) The experimental procedure, following either classical or operant conditioning, of presenting the conditioned stimulus without the usual reinforcement. (2) The reduction in response that results from this procedure (cf. *reinforcement*).

extrasensory perception (ESP). A controversial category of experience consisting of perception not mediated by sense-organ stimulation (cf. *clairvoyance, precognition, telepathy, psychokinesis*).

extrinsic motivation. The motivational control of behavior through the possibility of reward or punishment external to whatever satisfactions or annoyances reside in the behavior itself, e.g., working for a prize rather than the satisfactions in the task (cf. *intrinsic motivation*).

extrovert. One of the psychological types proposed by Jung. The extrovert is more preoccupied with social life and the external world than with his inward experience (cf. *introvert, type theory*).

factor analysis. A statistical method used in test construction and in interpreting scores from batteries of tests. The method enables the investigator to compute the minimum number of determiners (factors) required to account for the intercorrelations among the scores on the tests making up the battery.

factors of advantage. The bases for favoring one stimulus pattern over another in attention. They include factors in the perceiving person (set, interest, habit) and factors in the stimuli (size, intensity, frequency, vividness) (cf. *attention, selectivity*).

faculty psychology. A pre-experimental psychology that viewed the mind as composed of a number of separate powers or faculties, including intellect, feeling, will, and many others (cf. *association psychology*).

fantasy. Daydreaming, "wool gathering," imagination; sometimes a consequence of frustration. It is used as a personality indicator in projective tests (cf. *projective tests*).

feedback. The returning to a control center of the information regarding events under its control; in psychology, the sensory return from the periphery used in the control of movement and analogous processes (cf. *cybernetics*).

feeling tone. The pleasantness or unpleasantness of an affective experience (cf. *affective experience*).

field dependency. A characteristic according to which individuals differ in maintaining their orientation in space. By contrast with field-independent subjects, a field-dependent one orients more on the basis of external visual cues than upon gravitational cues from his own body (Witkin).

field properties. In Gestalt psychology, the properties of organized wholes that influence the interpretation or action of the parts. The term derives by analogy to fields of force in physics (cf. *Gestalt psychology*).

field theory. That form of Gestalt psychology associated particularly with Kurt Lewin (cf. *Gestalt psychology*).

figure-ground perception. Perceiving a pattern as foreground against a background. Patterns are commonly perceived this way even when the stimuli are ambiguous and the foreground-background relationships are reversible.

fissure of Rolando. The central fissure of each cerebral hemisphere, lying between the frontal and parietal lobes (syn. *central fissure*).

fissure of Sylvius. A deep fissure at the side of each cerebral hemisphere, below which lies the temporal lobe.

fixation. In psychoanalysis, arrested development through failure to pass beyond one of the earlier stages or to change the objects of attachment (e.g., fixated at the oral stage, or fixated upon the mother).

fixed-alternative question. A question asked on a test, an examination, or a survey, requiring the answer to be selected from alternatives provided by the questioner (syn. *multiple-choice question;* cf. *free-answer question*).

forebrain. The portion of the brain evolved from the foremost of the three enlargements of the neural tube, consisting of the cerebrum, thalamus, hypothalamus, and related structures (cf. *hindbrain, midbrain*).

formal discipline. An older interpretation of transfer of training, justifying the study of a subject not for its own sake but for the training it supposedly gives the mental faculties, e.g., studying Latin not to learn Latin but to improve judgment and reasoning (cf. *faculty psychology, transfer of training*).

fovea. In the eye, a small area in the central part of the retina, packed with cones; in daylight, the most sensitive part of the retina for detail vision and color vision (cf. *retina, cone*).

fraternal twins. Twins developed from separate eggs. They are no more alike genetically than ordinary brothers and sisters, and can be of the same or different sexes (cf. *identical twins*).

free-answer question. A question asked on an examination or in a survey, requiring a reply in the form of a comment, sentence, or longer discourse (syn. *open question;* cf. *fixed-alternative question*).

free association. (1) The form of word-association experiment in which the subject gives any word he thinks of in response to the stimulus word (cf. *controlled association*). (2) In psychoanalysis, the effort to report without modification everything that comes into awareness.

frequency distribution. A set of scores assembled according to size and grouped into class intervals (cf. *class interval, normal distribution*).

frequency theory. A theory of hearing that assumes that neural impulses arising in the organ of Corti are activated by the basilar membrane of the ear in accordance with the frequency of its vibration rather than with the place of movement (cf. *place theory, traveling wave theory, volley theory*).

frontal lobe. A portion of each cerebral hemisphere, in front of the central fissure (cf. *occipital lobe, parietal lobe, temporal lobe*).

frustration. (1) As an event, the thwarting circumstances that block or interfere with goal-directed activity. (This is the usage in the text.) (2) As a state, the annoyance, confusion, or anger engendered by being thwarted, disappointed, defeated.

functional autonomy. The theory that motives may become independent of their origins, e.g., the miser may come to value money for its own sake rather than for the motive-satisfying things that originally gave it reinforcing value.

functional fixedness. The entrenchment of meaning which comes about through using a tool or object in a familiar way, so that the user finds it difficult to employ that tool or object in novel ways.

functional psychosis. A psychotic disorder of psychogenic origin without clearly defined structural change (cf. *organic psychosis*).

functionalism. Cf. *stimulus-response psychology*.

galvanic skin response (GSR). Changes in electrical conductivity of, or activity in, the skin, detected by a sensitive galvanometer. The reactions are commonly used as an emotional indicator (cf. *emotional indicator*).

ganglion (pl. **ganglia**). A collection of nerve cell bodies and synapses, constituting a center lying outside the brain and spinal cord, as in the sympathetic ganglia (cf. *center*).

gastrointestinal motility. Movements of parts of the digestive tract caused by contraction of smooth muscle; one form of emotional indicator (cf. *emotional indicator*).

gene. The unit of hereditary transmission, localized within the chromosomes. Each chromosome contains many genes. Genes are typically in pairs, one member of the pair being found in the chromosome from the father, the other in the corresponding chromosome from the mother (cf. *chromosome, dominant gene, recessive gene*).

general adaptation syndrome. Selye's term for the typical sequence of events when the body is subjected to severe stress, moving from the alarm reaction through resistance, to exhaustion.

generalization. (1) In concept formation, problem-solving, and transfer of training, the detection by the learner of a characteristic or principle common to a class of objects, events, or problems. (2) In conditioning, the principle that once a conditioned response has been established to a given stimulus, other similar stimuli will also evoke that response (cf. *gradient of generalization, discrimination*).

general aptitude. The aptitude for acquiring proficiency in many activities rather than in a special set of activities. An intelligence test is designed to measure general aptitude; a typing test is designed to measure special aptitude (cf. *special aptitude*).

general factor. (1) A general ability underlying test scores, especially in tests of intelligence, as distinct from special abilities unique to each test (Spearman). (2) A general ability with which each of the primary factors correlates (Thurstone) (cf. *factor analysis*).

genetics. That branch of biology concerned with heredity and the means by which hereditary characteristics are transmitted (cf. *population genetics*).

genital stage. In classical psychoanalysis, the final stage of psychosexual development, culminating in sexual union with a member of the opposite sex (cf. *psychosexual development*).

genotype. In genetics, the characteristics that an individual has inherited and will transmit to his descendants, whether or not he manifests these characteristics (cf. *phenotype*).

Gestalt psychology. A system of psychological theory emphasizing pattern, organization, wholes, and field properties. It permits a form of introspection known as phenomenology (cf. *behaviorism, field properties, phenomenology*).

glia cells. Supporting cells (not neurons) composing a substantial portion of brain tissue; recent speculation suggests that they may play a role in the storage of memory.

goal. (1) An end state or condition toward which the motivated behavior sequence is directed and by which the sequence is completed. (2) Loosely, the incentive (cf. *incentive*).

goal activity. The activity in the presence of the incentive that reduces the drive or in other ways completes the motivated sequence of behavior (syn. *consummatory behavior;* cf. *preparatory activity*).

gradient. (1) Any regular change correlated with a change in some dimension such as distance; often plotted as a curve (cf. *gradient of texture*). (2) A change in the tendency to respond in relation to a systematic change in distance, time interval, or other dimension of stimulation (cf. *gradient of approach, gradient of avoidance, gradient of generalization*).

gradient of approach. The increase in the strength of the tendency to move toward a positive incentive the nearer the subject is to the incentive (cf. *gradient of avoidance*).

gradient of avoidance. The increase in the strength of the tendency to withdraw from a negative incentive the nearer the subject is to the incentive (cf. *gradient of approach*).

gradient of generalization. The orderly decrease in strength of the generalized conditioned response with decreasing similarity of the stimuli used in testing to the original stimulus used in conditioning; often plotted as a curve (cf. *gradient, generalization*).

gradient of texture. If a surface is perceived visually as having substantial texture (hard, soft, smooth, rough, etc.) and if the texture has a noticeable grain, it becomes finer as the surface recedes from the viewing person, producing a gradient of texture which is important in judgments of slant and of distance (cf. *distance cues*).

graphic rating scale. One of several kinds of scale used when one person rates another. The rater records his judgment by placing a mark at some point along a printed line, one end of which indicates the lowest degree of the trait, and the other, the highest degree (cf. *rating scale*).

group test. A test administered to several people at once by a single tester. A college examination is usually a group test (cf. *individual test*).

group therapy. A group discussion or other group activity with a therapeutic purpose participated in by more than one client or patient at a time (cf. *psychotherapy*).

GSR. Cf. *galvanic skin response.*

guilt culture. A culture relying largely on the individual conscience as a means of social control. In such a culture honor means living up to one's own self-image (cf. *shame culture*).

habit. A learned stimulus-response sequence (cf. *conditioned response, sensorimotor task*).

hallucination. A sense experience in the absence of appropriate external stimuli; a misinterpretation of imaginary experiences as actual perceptions (cf. *illusion, schizophrenic reaction*).

hedonism. The theory that man seeks pleasure and avoids pain; an extreme form of the theory (in philosophy) is that pleasure or happiness is the highest good.

heterosexuality. Interest in or attachment to a member of the opposite sex; the normal adult outcome of psychosexual development.

heuristic method. A nonrigorous method for discovering the correct solution to a problem through obtaining approximations to the correct answer, through using analogies and other methods of search, without the painstaking exploration of all possibilities. Computing machines can be programed to use such methods (cf. *algorithm*).

hindbrain. The portion of the brain evolved from the final one of the three enlargements of the primitive neural tube, consisting of the cerebellum, the medulla, and related structures (cf. *forebrain, midbrain*).

homeostasis. An optimal level of organic function, maintained by regulatory mechanisms known as homeostatic mechanisms, e.g., the mechanisms maintaining a uniform body temperature (cf. *homeostat*).

homeostat. A particular portion of the brain that regulates the equilibrium point of some bodily system, similar to the regulation of temperature by a thermostat (cf. *homeostasis*).

homosexuality. (1) In psychoanalytic theory, a normal stage of psychosexual development, in which attachment is to members of one's own sex. (2) The adoption in adult life of the cultural role appropriate to a member of the opposite sex. (3) Engaging in sexual relations with a member of the same sex.

hormones. The internal secretions of the endocrine glands which are distributed via the blood stream and affect behavior (cf. *chemical integration, endocrine gland*).

hue. The dimension of color from which the major color names are derived (red, yellow, green, etc.), corresponding to wave length of light (cf. *brightness, saturation*).

human factors research. An applied science participated in jointly by engineers and psychologists, concerned with the design of equipment and the arrangement of work conditions to provide the most effective combination of man and machine (syn. *applied experimental psychology, biomechanics, human engineering*).

hunger drive. A drive based on food deprivation (cf. *drive, hunger pangs, specific hunger*).

hunger pangs. The twinges of pain experienced during stomach contractions.

hyperurbanism. Overcorrection of one's speech in an attempt to speak like the educated city dweller, e.g., "between you and I."

hypnotic trance. The dreamlike state of heightened suggestibility induced in a subject by a hypnotist (cf. *post-hypnotic suggestion*).

hypnotism. The process of inducing the hypnotic trance (syn. *hypnosis*).

hypothalamus. One of the structures at the base of the brain, portions of which are significant in sleep and in emotional and motivational behavior.

hypothetical construct. One form of inferred intermediate mechanism. The construct is conceived of as having properties of its own, other than those specifically required for the explanation, e.g., the memory trace, which is inferred to explain the retention curve, is assumed to have electrochemical properties, localization in the nervous system, etc. (cf. *intervening variable*).

id. In Freud's tripartite division of the personality, that part reflecting unorganized, instinctual impulses. If unbridled, it seeks immediate gratification of primitive needs (cf. *ego, superego*).

identical components theory. A theory of transfer of training which proposes that a new task is learned more easily the more it consists of the same components as tasks already mastered (E. L. Thorndike) (cf. *transfer of training*).

identical twins. Twins developed from a single egg. They are always of the same sex and commonly very much alike in appearance, although some characteristics may be in mirror-image, e.g., one right-handed, the other left-handed (syn. *uniovular twins;* cf. *fraternal twins*).

identification. (1) The normal process of acquiring appropriate social roles in childhood through copying, in part unconsciously, the behavior of significant adults, e.g., the child's identification with his like-sexed parent. (2) A defense mechanism by which an individual enhances self-esteem through behaving, in fantasy or in actual conduct, as if he were another person—the one with whom he identifies himself (cf. *imitation*). (3) Close affiliation with others of like interest, e.g., identifying with a group.

identification figures. Adult models copied, partly unconsciously, by the child, especially the child's parents (cf. *identification*).

identity formation. The process of achieving adult personality integration, as an outgrowth of earlier identifications and other influences (cf. *identification, role diffusion*).

idiot savant. A mentally subnormal individual (of any grade, but usually not classifiable as an idiot) who has unusual ability in one or more specialized activities.

illumination. The third of the four stages in creative thought proposed by Wallas, in which the solution suddenly appears or previously disconnected aspects suddenly are seen in relationship (cf. *preparation, incubation, verification*).

illusion. In perception, a misinterpretation of the relationships among presented stimuli, so that what is perceived does not correspond to physical reality; especially, but not exclusively, an optical or visual illusion (cf. *delusion, hallucination*).

imitation. Behavior that is modeled upon or copies that of another (cf. *identification*).

immediate memory span. The number of items (digits, letters, words, etc.) that can be repeated after a single presentation.

implicit movements. Movements that can be detected only with sensitive measuring instruments; covert movements (cf. *explicit movements*).

imprinting. A term used by ethologists for a species-specific type of learning that occurs within a limited period of time early in the life of the organism and is relatively unmodifiable thereafter; e.g., young ducklings learn to follow one adult female (usually the mother) within 11 to 18 hours after birth. But whatever object they are given to follow at this time they will thereafter continue to follow (cf. *ethologist*).

incentive. (1) A tangible goal object which provides the stimuli that lead to goal activity. (2) Loosely, any goal (cf. *goal*).

incubation. The second of the four stages in creative thought proposed by Wallas, during which, by a process not fully understood, the preparation leads to the emergence of the creative thought (cf. *preparation, illumination, verification*).

independent variable. The variable under experimental control with which the changes studied in the experiment are correlated. In psychological experiments, the independent variable is often a stimulus, responses to which are the dependent variables under investigation (cf. *dependent variable*).

individual differences. Relatively persistent unlikenesses in structure or behavior between persons or members of the same species.

individual test. A test designed to be administered to one person at a time. Binet intelligence tests are individual tests (cf. *group test*).

infancy. The period of helplessness and dependency in man or other organisms; in man, roughly the first two years (cf. *childhood, adolescence*).

infant debility. A condition of retarded development found among some institutionalized infants, attributed to the lack of affectionate care.

information measurement. A method derived from communication theory for dealing with the quantity of information in a particular communication (cf. *bit, uncertainty*).

in-group. A group to which a person belongs and with which he identifies himself (cf. *out-group*).

inner ear. The internal portion of the ear containing, in addition to the cochlea, the vestibular sacs and the semicircular canals (cf. *cochlea, semicircular canals, vestibular sacs*).

insight. (1) In problem-solving experiments, the perception of relationships leading to solution. Such a solution can be repeated promptly when the problem is again confronted. (2) In psychotherapy, the discovery by the subject of dynamic connections between earlier and later events, so that he comes to recognize the roots of his conflicts.

instinct. The name given to unlearned, patterned, goal-directed behavior, which is species-specific, as illustrated by nest building in birds or by the migration of salmon.

insulin. The hormone secreted by the pancreas (cf. *hormones, insulin shock*).

insulin shock. A state of coma resulting from reduced blood sugar when insulin is present in excessive amounts. Insulin shock is used as one form of shock therapy in treating mental illness (cf. *shock therapy*).

integration. The organization of parts into a harmoniously operating whole, as in the expression "integrated personality" (cf. *chemical integration, mechanical integration, neural integration*).

intelligence. (1) That which a properly standardized intelligence test measures. (2) According to Binet, the characteristics of an individual's thought processes that enable him to take and maintain a direction without becoming distracted, to adapt means to ends, and to criticize his own attempts at problem solution (cf. *mental age*).

intelligence quotient (I.Q.). A scale unit used in reporting intelligence test scores, based on the ratio between mental age and chronological age. The decimal point is omitted, so that the average I.Q. for children of any one chronological age is set at 100 (cf. *chronological age, mental age, deviation I.Q.*).

intensity. One of the dimensions of sensory experience; a quantitative measure of strength or degree, e.g., a bright light has a high intensity, a soft tone a low intensity. A change in intensity is distinguished from a change in quality, which is a change in kind (cf. *dimension, quality, quantity*).

interactive explanation. An explanation of behavior that deals with the arousal and control of behavior in the present, according to stimuli that are currently responded to, motives that are active, and possibilities of response that are open; nonhistorical explanation (cf. *developmental explanation*).

interest. A persisting tendency to pay attention to and to enjoy some activity or content, especially a vocational interest.

intermittent reinforcement. In either classical or operant conditioning, the procedure of presenting the unconditioned or reinforcing stimulus on some fraction of the trials rather than on every trial (syn. *partial reinforcement;* cf. *reinforcement*).

interpretation. In psychoanalysis, the analyst's calling attention to the patient's resistances in order to facilitate the flow of associations; also his explanation of symbols, as in dream interpretation (cf. *resistance*).

interpretive therapy. A form of psychotherapy, used with children as well as with adults, in which the therapist helps the subject to put his conflicts into words, to understand their symbolic meanings, and through this process to solve his problems (cf. *psychotherapy, release therapy, relationship therapy*).

interval scale. A scale with equal units but an arbitrary zero, e.g., the Fahrenheit temperature scale (cf. *ordinal scale, ratio scale*).

intervening variable. A process inferred to occur between stimulus and response, thus accounting for one response rather than another to the same stimulus. The intervening variable may be inferred without further specification, or it may be given concrete properties and become an object of investigation.

interview. A conversation between an investigator (the interviewer) and a subject (the respondent) used for gathering pertinent data either for the subject's benefit (as in the psychotherapeutic interview) or for information gathering (as in a sample survey).

intracerebral processes. Inferred processes in the brain used to account for response classes including perceptions, images, and thoughts that are incompletely specified in terms of movement (cf. *intervening variable*).

intrinsic cortex. Term used by Pribram for the so-called association areas, on the assumption that they have integrative functions in handling complex activities but that this handling does not necessarily involve learned associative links (cf. *association areas*).

intrinsic motivation. Motivation in which the action and the ends served by the action are organically or inherently related, as distinct from action motivated by promise of reward or threat of punishment, e.g., assembling a model airplane in order to fly it, composing a sonnet to give expression to a mood (cf. *extrinsic motivation*).

introspection. (1) A specified form of introspection (trained introspection) describing mental content only, without the intrusion of meanings or interpretations. (2) Any form of reporting on subjective (conscious) events or experiences (cf. *phenomenology*).

introvert. One of the psychological types proposed by Jung, referring to the individual who, especially in time of emotional stress, tends to withdraw into himself and to avoid other people (cf. *extrovert, type theory*).

investigatory response. The form of exploratory behavior which involves the manipulation of an unfamiliar object, picking it up, tearing it apart, etc. (Berlyne) (cf. *exploratory behavior, locomotor exploration, orientation response*).

item. Any single unit of test or experimental materials, e.g., a single question in a test composed of many questions or a single nonsense syllable in a list of syllables to be memorized (cf. *test, test battery*).

James-Lange theory. A classical theory of emotion, named for the two men who independently proposed it. The theory states that the stimulus first leads to motor responses, and then the awareness of these responses constitutes the experience of emotion.

J-curve. A distribution curve of the behavior of individuals, in the form of an inverted J. It appears when social controls are placed upon behavior, e.g., at an intersection when traffic is regulated by a stop sign.

jealousy. A special form of anxiety arising from fear of loss of a loved one's affection to a rival, with both emotional and motivational consequences (cf. *envy*).

just-noticeable difference (j.n.d.). A barely perceptible physical change in a stimulus; a measure of the difference threshold. The term is used also as a unit for scaling the steps of sensation corresponding to increase in the magnitude of stimulation (cf. *difference threshold*).

kinesthesis. The muscle, tendon, and joint senses, yielding discrimination of position and movement of parts of the body (cf. *equilabratory senses*).

late adolescent phase. A period of low-rate development of the individual as adult status is achieved, lasting two or more years. In males, it marks attainment of shoulder width, adult strength, wider distribution of pigmented hair on chest and thighs (cf. *adolescence*).

latency. (1) A measure of response, referring to the delay between the occurrence of the stimulus and the onset of the response. (2) In psychoanalysis, a period in middle childhood, roughly the years from six to twelve, when both sexual and aggressive impulses are said to be in a somewhat subdued state, so that the child's attention is directed outward, and his curiosity about the environment makes him ready to learn (cf. *psychosexual development*).

latent content. The underlying significance of a dream, e.g., the motives or wishes being expressed by it, as interpreted from the manifest content (cf. *interpretation, manifest content*).

latent learning experiment. A type of experiment in which opportunity for learning spatial relationships is given under conditions of inappropriate drive or absent incentive; e.g., a rat is permitted to explore a maze without food in the goal box. The learning is later tested under changed drive-incentive conditions. The experiment, when successful, is used to support the sign learning theory (cf. *sign learning*).

law of effect. Thorndike's principle that the consequences of an activity determine whether or not it will be learned. In its later forms stress was placed on the influence of reward. Hence learning under the law of effect is virtually synonymous with operant conditioning (q.v.).

learning. The persisting changes as a result of practice; the process by which new or altered behavior comes about as a result of prior response, provided the changes cannot be attributed to growth or to temporary changes in the state of the organism (as in fatigue or under drugs).

learning curve. A graph plotting the course of learning, in which the vertical axis (ordinate) plots a measure of proficiency (amount per unit time, time per unit amount, errors made, etc.), while the horizontal axis (abscissa) represents some measure of practice (trials, time, etc.).

level of aspiration. A goal that the individual sets as something he expects to achieve or strives to achieve. Reaching the goal is interpreted by him as success, falling short as failure (cf. *achievement motive*).

leveling. The systematic distortion in recall which leads toward greater symmetry, toward smoothing out irregularities or incongruities, e.g., reproducing a geometrical figure as regular and complete, although as presented it may have been irregular with one or more gaps (cf. *sharpening, systematic distortion*).

libido theory. The theory within psychoanalysis that human development and motivation are best understood by studying the manifestations of the libido—the energy of the sexual instinct—which throughout life becomes attached to new objects and expressed through various types of motivated behavior (cf. *ego theory, neo-Freudian theory*).

lie detector. An apparatus using one or more of the emotional indicators in order to determine guilt of a subject through his emotional responses while answering questions in a false or unintentionally revealing manner (cf. *emotional indicator*).

light adaptation. The decreased sensitivity of the eye to light when the subject has been continuously exposed to high levels of illumination (cf. *dark adaptation*).

limbic system. A set of structures in and around the midbrain, forming a functional unit regulating motivational-emotional types of behavior such as waking and sleeping, excitement and quiescence, feeding, and mating.

linear operator. Cf. *difference equation*.

linguistics. The investigation of problems of language; linguistics has been a branch of social anthropology, but psychologists have been participating increasingly in studies of language (syn. *psycholinguistics*).

localized functions. Behavior controlled by known areas

of the brain; e.g., vision is localized in the occipital lobes (cf. *projection area*).

location constancy. The tendency to perceive the place at which a resting object is located as remaining the same even though the relationship to the observer has changed (cf. *object constancy*).

locomotor exploration. That form of exploratory behavior which consists in running about, inspecting the environment (Berlyne) (cf. *exploratory behavior, investigatory response, orientation response*).

loudness. An intensity dimension of hearing correlated with the amplitude of the sound waves that constitute the stimulus. Greater amplitudes yield greater loudnesses (cf. *pitch, timbre*).

LSD-25. Cf. *lysergic acid derivatives*.

lysergic acid derivatives. Chemical substances derived from lysergic acid, the most important of which is LSD-25. When taken by a normal person, it produces symptoms similar in some respects to those of the schizophrenic reaction (cf. *schizophrenic reaction*).

manic-depressive reaction. An affective psychotic reaction characterized by mood swings from the normal in the direction either of excitement and elation (manic phase) or of fatigue, despondency, and sadness (depressive phase). Many patients do not show the whole cycle (cf. *psychotic-depressive reaction*).

manifest content. The remembered content of a dream, the characters and their actions, as distinguished from the inferred latent content (cf. *latent content*).

masochism. A pathological desire to inflict pain upon oneself or to suffer pain at the hands of others (cf. *sadism*).

mass media. The instruments of communication which reach large numbers of people simultaneously, including the press, radio, television, and motion pictures.

massed practice. Practice in which trials are continuous or closely spaced (cf. *distributed practice*).

maternal drive. The drive, particularly in subhuman animals, induced in the female through bearing and nursing young, leading to nest building, retrieving, and other forms of care (cf. *drive*).

maturation. Growth processes in the individual that result in orderly changes in behavior, whose timing and patterning are relatively independent of exercise or experience though they may require a normal environment (cf. *training*).

maze. A device commonly used in the study of animal and human learning, consisting of a correct path and blind alleys.

mean. The arithmetical average; the sum of all scores divided by their number (cf. *average*).

mean deviation. The average amount by which each score departs from the mean of all the scores (cf. *measure of variation*).

measure of central tendency. Cf. *average*.

measure of response. A quantitative index of response strength, such as amplitude, latency, probability, and rate of response.

measure of variation. A measure of the dispersion or spread of scores in a frequency distribution, e.g., the range, the mean deviation, the standard deviation (q.v.).

mechanical integration. Bodily organization for harmonious action through the mechanical arrangements of bones, joints, and muscles (cf. *chemical integration, neural integration*).

median. The score of the middle case when cases are arranged in order of size of score (cf. *average*).

membership group. A social group to which an individual belongs (cf. *reference group*).

memory trace. The inferred change in the nervous system which persists between the time that something is learned and the time that it is recalled.

menarche. The first menstrual period, indicative of sexual maturation in a girl (cf. *menstruation*).

menstruation. The approximately monthly discharge from the uterus (cf. *menarche*).

mental age (M.A.). A scale unit proposed by Binet for use in intelligence testing. If an intelligence test is properly standardized, a representative group of children of age 6 should earn an average mental age of 6, those of age 7, a mental age of 7, etc. A child whose M.A. is above his chronological age (C.A.) is advanced; one whose M.A. lags behind is retarded (cf. *chronological age, intelligence quotient*).

mental health. Absence of mental illness; more positively, a state characterized by adjustment, a productive orientation, and zest (cf. *mental illness*).

mental illness. Emotional, motivational, and social maladjustment severe enough to interfere with the ordinary conduct of life (cf. *mental health, psychoneurotic reaction, psychotic disorder*).

mentally defective. A descriptive term applied to a mentally subnormal individual whose deficiency is based on some sort of brain damage or organic defect (cf. *mentally retarded*).

mentally gifted. An individual with an unusually high level of intelligence, commonly an I.Q. of 140 or above.

mentally retarded. A mentally subnormal individual whose problems lie in a learning disability with no evident organic damage (cf. *mentally defective*).

mentally subnormal. An individual whose intelligence is below that necessary for adjustment to ordinary schooling; the more intelligent among the subnormal are classified as *educable* in special classes, the next level as *trainable,* while the lowest group classifies as more severely retarded (syn., but now obsolete, *feeble-minded;* cf. *mentally defective, mentally retarded*).

mesomorphic component. The second of three components of physique in Sheldon's type theory. Refers to the prominence of bone and muscle, as in the typical athlete (cf. *endomorphic component, ectomorphic component, type theory*).

method of approximations. A variation of operant conditioning in which the desired performance is encouraged by reinforcing "approach" responses, i.e., responses approximating the correct performance (cf. *operant conditioning, shaping of behavior*).

midbrain. The second of the three enlargements of the neural tube, upon which later structures of the brain have evolved. The midbrain in the fish consists chiefly of the optic lobes ("eye brain"); in man this portion has not been greatly increased in relative size, the most pronounced evolutionary changes having taken place in the forebrain (cf. *forebrain, hindbrain*).

middle ear. The portion of the ear containing the hammer, anvil, and stirrup bones, which connect the eardrum to the oval window of the inner ear.

miniature system. A set of interconnected laws and principles designed to account for a limited sphere of psychological activities, e.g., a theory of rote learning, a theory of hearing.

mirror drawing. A laboratory learning task in which the skill under study is that of tracing the contour of a star or other figure while viewing it in a mirror.

modality. A separate sense or sensory department, e.g., vision, audition. Experiences within a single modality can be arranged along continuous dimensions, with intermediate values. There is no simple way of moving across from one modality to another, e.g., to find the experience lying midway between a given odor and a given color.

mode. The most frequent score in a distribution, or the class interval in which the greatest number of cases fall (cf. *average*).

model. Miniature systems are often constructed according to a logical, mathematical, or physical model. That is, the principles according to which data are organized and made understandable parallel those of the model; e.g., the piano keyboard is a model for understanding the basilar membrane; the speed-regulating governor is a model for the feedback principle of cybernetics (cf. *miniature system*).

monochromatism. Total color blindness, the visual system being achromatic. A rare disorder (cf. *dichromatism*).

monocular cues. Cf. *distance cues*.

mood. A state of emotional susceptibility, enduring for some minutes or hours, in which most of the person's emotional responses tend to be similar, e.g., cheerful mood, morose mood (cf. *temperament*).

motion and time study. (1) Study designed to increase work efficiency by analysis of the actual movements involved and their time relationships. (2) A method used in the determination of rates of pay in wage-incentive plans (cf. *wage-incentive plan*).

motivated forgetting. The theory that forgetting can be explained according to the motives of the learner (cf. *repression, tension to complete*).

motivation. A general term referring to the regulation of need-satisfying and goal-seeking behavior (cf. *motive*).

motivational disposition. A persistent tendency to the arousal of a specific motive; the tendency exists even though the motive is not being expressed. Most classifications of motives refer to motivational dispositions (cf. *aroused motive*).

motivational sequence. A sequence of behavior which begins with a motive, continues in preparatory or goal-directed activity, and ends in goal activity in the presence of an incentive.

motive. Any condition of the organism that affects its readiness to start upon or continue in a sequence of behavior (cf. *motivational sequence, physiological motive, social motive*).

motor area. A projection area in the brain lying in front of the fissure of Rolando. Electrical stimulation commonly results in motor responses (cf. *body-sense area*).

multimodal distribution. A distribution curve with more than one mode (cf. *mode*).

multiple personality. An extreme form of dissociation in which the individual's personality is split into separate personalities often alternating with each other. The memories of one of the split-off personalities commonly are not accessible to the other (cf. *dissociation*).

multiple-response learning. The acquiring of patterns or sequences of responses in mastering a task, e.g., in learning a skill or memorizing a poem (cf. *sensorimotor task, rote memorization*).

muscle. The effectors through which motion is produced. Muscles are of three types: smooth muscle, striate muscle, and cardiac muscle (q.v.).

muscle tone. A state of slight contraction that keeps muscle in a readiness to respond. A tense person may have an exaggeration of muscle tone (syn. *muscle tonus*).

myelin. The fatty sheath surrounding certain nerve fibers known as myelinated fibers. Impulses travel faster and with less energy expenditure in myelinated than in unmyelinated fibers.

narcissism. Self-love; in psychoanalytic theory, the normal expression of pregenital development (cf. *pregenital stages*).

naturalistic observation. Observation of events as they occur in nature, without experimental control of behavior, e.g., studying the nest building of birds or observing the sleeping postures of a newborn human infant.

nature-nurture issue. The problem of determining the relative importance of the hereditary component (nature) and the result of up-bringing in the particular environment (nurture) upon mature ability; such a determination is especially important in relation to intelligence.

negative incentive. An object or circumstance away from which behavior is directed when the object or circumstance is perceived or anticipated (cf. *positive incentive*).

negativism. A type of defiant behavior in which there is active refusal to carry out requests. Common in early childhood but met occasionally at all ages (syn. *negativistic behavior*).

neo-Freudian theory. The views of psychoanalytic theorists and practitioners which, while related to those of Freud, have departed from his in important ways. Most neo-Freudians in interpreting personality development give more weight than Freud did to the influence of the specific culture as contrasted with inherited instinctual tendencies (e.g., libido). Some prominent neo-Freudians are Fromm, Horney, Kardiner, and Sullivan (cf. *libido theory*).

nerve cell. Cf. *neuron*.

nerve net. A nervous system characteristic of lower organisms, in which impulses are transmitted in all directions from the point of stimulation (cf. *synaptic nervous system*).

neural integration. Bodily organization for harmonious or unified action through the brain and nervous system (cf. *chemical integration, mechanical integration*).

neuron. The nerve cell; the unit of a synaptic nervous system. Man's brain contains billions of neurons (cf. *polarized synaptic transmission*).

neurosis. Cf. *psychoneurotic reaction*.

nominal defect. One of Head's classes of aphasia in which the subject has difficulty in naming objects (cf. *aphasia*).

nonliterate society. A society or culture without written records, formerly called a primitive society (cf. *anthropology*).

nonparametric statistics. Statistics·computed without the assumption of an underlying distribution of known form. The formulas of nonparametric statistics commonly make use of ranked data, as in rank-difference correlation (syn. *distribution-free statistics*).

nonsense syllable. An item used in rote memorization experiments, usually consisting of two consonants with a vowel between, e.g., PUV, GEB. The combination of letters must not form a word in familiar languages.

noradrenalin. One of the hormones secreted by the adrenal medulla, whose action is in some, but not all, respects similar to adrenalin (syn. *norephinephrine;* cf. *adrenalin*).

norm. An average, common, or standard performance under specified conditions, e.g., the average achievement test score of nine-year-old children or the average birth weight of male children (cf. *test standardization*).

normal curve. The plotted form of the normal distribution (q.v.).

normal distribution. The standard symmetrical bell-shaped frequency distribution, whose properties are commonly used in making statistical inferences from measures derived from samples (cf. *normal curve*).

nystagmus. Involuntary eye movements characterized by slow and quick phases in opposite directions; one of the consequences of bodily rotation.

object achievement. Perceiving an object as enduring and permanent, e.g., when the subject recognizes the object he now sees as the same object he saw before (cf. *object constancy*).

object constancy. The tendency to see objects as relatively unchanged under widely altered conditions of illumination, distance, and position (cf. *color constancy, location constancy, shape constancy, size constancy*).

object size. The size of an object as determined from measurement at its surface. When size constancy holds, the observer perceives a distant object as near its object size (cf. *perspective size, size constancy*).

objective science. A science whose data are open to observation by any competent observer, as in the physical and biological sciences. Behaviorism sought to eliminate subjectivity from psychology, hence to make it an objective science (cf. *subjective science*).

objective scoring. Scoring done according to a code so that all competent scorers arrive at the same score for the same test, e.g., the scoring of fixed-alternative (multiple-choice) questions (cf. *subjective scoring*).

obsessive-compulsive reaction. A psychoneurotic reaction taking one of three forms: (1) recurrent thoughts, often disturbing and unwelcome (obsessions); (2) irresistible urges to repeat stereotyped or ritualistic acts (compulsions); (3) both of these in combination (cf. *psychoneurotic reaction*).

occipital lobe. A portion of the cerebral hemisphere, behind the parietal and temporal lobes (cf. *frontal lobe, parietal lobe, temporal lobe*).

occupational therapy. A form of help to a patient suffering from personality maladjustment or mental illness, whereby he is kept busy in constructive work.

Oedipal stage. In psychoanalysis, an alternative designation of the phallic stage of psychosexual development, because it is at this stage that the Oedipus complex arises (cf. *psychosexual development, Oedipus complex*).

Oedipus complex. In psychoanalytic theory, sexual attachment to the parent of the opposite sex, originating as the normal culmination of the infantile period of development.

operant behavior. Behavior defined by the stimulus to which it leads rather than by the stimulus that elicits it, such as behavior leading to reward (syn. *emitted behavior, instrumental behavior;* cf. *respondent behavior, voluntary action*).

operant conditioning. The strengthening of an operant response by presenting a reinforcing stimulus if, and only if, the response occurs (syn. *instrumental conditioning, reward learning;* cf. *classical conditioning*).

opinion. A judgment or belief involving an expectation or prediction about behavior or events (cf. *attitude*).

oral behavior. Behavior deriving from the infant's need to suck or, more generally, to be fed through the mouth.

oral stage. In psychoanalysis, the first of the stages of psychosexual development, in which pleasure is derived from the lips and mouth, as in sucking at the mother's breast (cf. *psychosexual development*).

ordinal scale. A scale in which items are placed in order of size but without equal units or a true (absolute) zero. Most psychological scales are of this kind, e.g., scores on an intelligence test (cf. *interval scale, ratio scale*).

organ of Corti. In the ear, the actual receptor for hearing, lying on the basilar membrane in the cochlea and containing the hair cells where the fibers of the auditory nerve originate (cf. *basilar membrane, cochlea*).

organic motive. Cf. *physiological motive*.

organic psychosis. A psychotic disorder caused by disease, injury, drugs, or other definable structural change (cf. *functional psychosis, psychotic disorder*).

organism. In biology, any form of plant or animal life. In psychology, the word is used to refer to the living individual animal, whether human or subhuman.

orientation response. The form of exploratory behavior evoked by a novel or striking stimulus, consisting in prompt changes in posture and in sense-organ adjustment (cf. *exploratory behavior, investigatory response, locomotor exploration*).

otoliths. "Ear stones" (cf. *vestibular sacs*).

out-group. Persons outside the in-group, especially if they belong to a group with which the in-group is in conflict (cf. *in-group*).

ovarian hormones. Cf. *estrogen*.

overcompensation. A form of compensation in which extreme effort is made to overcome feelings of weakness or inferiority by excelling where one is weakest. Thus a sickly youngster may try to become an athlete or a professional dancer (cf. *compensation*).

overlearning. Any learning beyond bare mastery.

overtone. A higher frequency tone, a multiple of the fundamental frequency, which occurs when a tone is sounded by a musical instrument (cf. *timbre*).

pacing. The principle that tasks to be learned can be presented to the learner in an order of difficulty corresponding to his natural developmental rate (cf. *maturation, readiness to learn*).

pain drive. The drive aroused by noxious stimulation, revealed by agitated behavior or behavior directed toward removing or escaping from the painful stimulus (cf. *drive*).

paired-associates learning. That form of rote memorization in which items are learned in pairs, one item serving as the stimulus or cue for its associated item (cf. *serial memorization*).

pancreas. A bodily organ situated near the stomach. As a duct gland it secretes pancreatic juice into the intestines, but some specialized cells function as an endocrine gland, secreting the hormone insulin into the blood stream (cf. *endocrine gland*).

paranoid reaction. A form of functional psychotic reaction characterized by persistent systematized delusions. Because his personality in other respects remains intact, an occasional person with paranoid reactions may manage very well outside a hospital (cf. *delusion*).

parasympathetic division. A division of the autonomic nervous system, nerve fibers of which originate in the cranial and sacral portions of the spinal cord. Active in relaxed or quiescent states of the body, and to some extent antagonistic to the sympathetic division (q.v.).

parathyroid glands. Endocrine glands adjacent to the thyroid gland in the neck, whose hormones regulate calcium metabolism, thus maintaining the normal excitability of the nervous system. Parathyroid in-

adequacy leads to tetany (cf. *endocrine gland, tetany*).

parietal lobe. A portion of the cerebral hemisphere, behind the central fissure and between the frontal and occipital lobes (cf. *frontal lobe, occipital lobe, temporal lobe*).

part learning. Learning a multiple-response task in piecemeal fashion, then combining the acquired parts (cf. *whole learning*).

passive decay. A theory of forgetting which implies that the memory trace fades with disuse (cf. *memory trace*).

percentile scale. Cf. *centile scale*.

perception. The process of becoming aware of objects, qualities, or relations by way of the sense organs. While sensory content is always present in perception, what is perceived is influenced by set and prior experience, so that perception is more than a passive registration of stimuli impinging on the sense organs.

perceptual patterning. The tendency to perceive stimuli according to principles such as proximity, similarity, continuity, and closure. Emphasized by Gestalt psychologists (cf. *figure-ground perception*).

performance. Overt behavior, as distinguished from knowledge or information not translated into action. The distinction is important in theories of learning.

peripheralist position. A view held by some psychologists that all thinking goes on in action (in speech or other movements) (cf. *centralist position*).

personal disposition. Cf. *disposition*.

personality. The individual characteristics and ways of behaving which, in their organization or patterning, account for an individual's unique adjustments to his total environment (syn. *individuality*).

personality assessment. (1) Generally, appraisal of personality by any method. (2) More specifically, personality appraisal through complex observations and judgments, usually based in part upon behavior in contrived social situations.

personality dynamics. Theories of personality that stress personality dynamics are concerned with the interactive aspects of behavior (as in conflict resolution), with value hierarchies, with the permeability of boundaries between differentiated aspects of personality, etc. Contrasted with developmental theories, though not incompatible with them (cf. *interactive explanation*).

personality inventory. An inventory for self-appraisal, consisting of many statements or questions about personal characteristics and behavior which the person judges to apply or not to apply to him (cf. *projective test*).

personality structure. The inferred unifying pattern underlying individual ways of behaving, giving consistency to otherwise contradictory traits and meaning to otherwise inexplicable mannerisms and eccentricities.

personality syndrome. An acquired personality type; a combination of characteristics which, though unique in its individual expression, bears a resemblance to the personality structures of others who have shared somewhat similar problems and have adopted somewhat similar solutions to their problems (cf. *compulsive personality, authoritarian personality*).

perspective size. The size of an object according to the geometry of perspective, i.e., its size diminishes directly in proportion to its distance (cf. *object size, size constancy*).

phallic stage. In psychoanalysis, that stage of psychosexual development in which gratification is associated with sex organ stimulation and the sexual attachment is to the parent of the opposite sex (cf. *Oedipal stage, psychosexual development*).

phenomenology. Naive report on conscious experience, as by a child, as contrasted with trained introspection; the study of unanalyzed experience (cf. *Gestalt psychology*).

phenotype. In genetics, the characteristics that are displayed by the individual organism, e.g., eye color, intelligence, as distinct from those traits which he may carry genetically but not display (cf. *genotype*).

phi phenomenon. Stroboscopic motion in its simpler form. Commonly produced by successively turning on and off two separated stationary light sources; as the first is turned off and the second turned on, the subject perceives a spot of light moving from the position of the first to that of the second (cf. *stroboscopic motion*).

phobic reaction. Excessive fear in the absence of real danger (cf. *agoraphobia, claustrophobia, psychoneurotic reaction*).

physical sciences. Those sciences, such as astronomy, chemistry, mineralogy, and physics, dealing chiefly with laws and relationships derived from study of the inanimate world, rather than with laws and relationships peculiar to living things.

physiological motive. A motive based upon an evident bodily need, such as the need for food or water (syn. *organic motive;* cf. *social motive*).

physiological psychology. That branch of experimental psychology concerned with the relationship between physiological functions and behavior.

physiology. That branch of biology concerned primarily with the functioning of organ systems within the body.

pilomotor response. The response of muscles in the skin in which the hairs stand on end, giving a roughened appearance to the skin known as "goose flesh" or "goose-pimples." May result either from cold or as part of an emotional state (cf. *emotional indicator*).

pitch. A qualitative dimension of hearing correlated with the frequency of the sound waves that constitute the stimulus. Higher frequencies yield higher pitches (cf. *loudness, timbre*).

pituitary gland. An endocrine gland located centrally in the head. It consists of two parts, the anterior pituitary and the posterior pituitary. The anterior pituitary is the more important part because of its regulation of growth and of other endocrine glands. One of its hormones, ACTH (adrenocorticotropic hormone), has become medically important (syn. *hypophysis;* cf. *endocrine gland*).

place-learning experiment. A variety of animal maze experiments designed to test whether or not what is learned is the location of the goal in space rather than the movements required to reach the goal (cf. *sign learning*).

place theory. A theory of hearing that associates pitch with the place on the basilar membrane where activation occurs (cf. *frequency theory, traveling wave theory, volley theory*).

plateau. In a learning curve a period of no improvement, preceded and followed by improvement (cf. *learning curve*).

play therapy. Using play activities as an aid in solving a child's adjustment problems (cf. *psychotherapy, release therapy, relationship therapy, interpretive therapy*).

polarized synaptic transmission. The transmission of nervous impulses across synapses in one direction only (from axon to dendrite or cell body); characteristic of higher nervous systems, beyond the stage of the nerve net.

population. The total universe of all possible cases from which a sample is selected. The usual statistical formulas for making inferences from samples apply when the population is appreciably larger than the sample, e.g., five to ten times larger than the sample (cf. *sample*).

population genetics. That branch of genetics concerned with the distribution of genetic determiners throughout the population (cf. *genetics*).

positive incentive. An object or circumstance toward which behavior is directed when the object or circumstance is perceived or anticipated (cf. *negative incentive*).

post-hypnotic suggestion. A suggestion made to a hypnotized subject that he will perform in a prescribed way after coming out of the trance. The activity is usually carried out without the subject's awareness of its origin in a specific suggestion (cf. *hypnotism*).

postpuberal phase. A one- to two-year period beyond the puberal phase in which most of the skeletal growth is completed (syn. *postpubescence;* cf. *puberal phase*).

precognition. A claimed form of extrasensory perception in which a future event is perceived (cf. *extrasensory perception, clairvoyance, telepathy*).

predictive efficiency of r. The per cent by which the standard error of estimate is reduced over what it would be if r were zero, when the values of estimated y are predicted from x on the basis of r_{xy}. For example, predicting from an r of .866 reduces the standard error of estimate by one-half, hence the predictive efficiency of an r of that size is 50 per cent.

predictive validity. Validity determined by how well a test predicts a criterion (cf. *concurrent validity, content validity, construct validity*).

pregenital stages. In psychoanalysis, the oral, anal, and phallic stages of psychosexual development (cf. *psychosexual development*).

prejudice. An attitude that is firmly fixed, not open to free and rational discussion, and resistant to change (cf. *attitude*).

preparation. The first of four stages of creative thinking proposed by Wallas. In the preparation stage, the thinker obtains appropriate information, skills, and techniques which later come to fruition in what he creates or invents (cf. *incubation, illumination, verification*).

preparatory activity. Goal-directed or goal-seeking activity aroused by a drive or by external stimuli when the drive is active.

preparatory set. Cf. *set*.

prepuberal phase. The transitional period between childhood and adolescence, from one to two years preceding the puberal phase (syn. *prepubescence;* cf. *puberal phase*).

primary abilities. The abilities, discovered by factor analysis, that underlie intelligence test performance (cf. *factor analysis*).

primary colors. Cf. *color-mixing primaries, psychological primaries*.

primary sex characteristics. The structural or physiological characteristics that make possible sexual union and reproduction (cf. *secondary sex characteristics*).

primitivation. Cf. *regression*.

primitive society. Cf. *nonliterate society*.

proactive inhibition. The interference of earlier learning with the learning and recall of new material (cf. *retroactive inhibition, transfer of training*).

probability sampling. A general method of sampling, applicable to attitude and opinion surveys, in which the probability that any one member of the population will be included in the sample is known. The actual selection of cases is random so that inferences based on sampling statistics can be made (cf. *area sampling*).

probability value. A probability statement associated with a statistical inference, e.g., "The probability (P) is .05 that a difference of this size between the sample means would have occurred even though the population means were the same" (cf. *statistical inference, statistical significance*).

product-moment correlation. Cf. *coefficient of correlation*.

programing. (1) Instructions fed into a computer to determine the order of events. (2) In connection with automated self-instruction, arranging materials to be learned in sequences of units, called frames, so that learning can proceed with a minimum of error. The program can be presented in book form, as well as in a form suitable for use with a teaching machine (cf. *teaching machine*).

projection. A defense mechanism by which a person protects himself from awareness of his own undesirable traits by attributing those traits excessively to others (cf. *defense mechanism*).

projection area. A place in the cerebral cortex where a function is localized; e.g., the visual protection area is in the occipital lobes.

projective test. A personality test in which the subject reveals ("projects") himself through his imaginative productions. The projective test gives much freer possibilities of response than the fixed-alternative personality inventory. Examples of projective tests are the Rorschach test (ink blots to be interpreted) and the Thematic Apperception Test (pictures that elicit stories) (cf. *personality inventory*).

prolactin. A pituitary hormone associated with the secretion of milk (cf. *hormones*).

psi. The special ability said to be possessed by the subject who performs successfully in experiments on extrasensory perception and psychokinesis (cf. *extrasensory perception, psychokinesis*).

psychiatric nurse. A nurse specially trained to deal with patients suffering from mental disorders.

psychiatric social worker. A social worker trained to work with patients and their families on problems of mental health and illness, usually in close relationship with psychiatrists and clinical psychologists (cf. *psychiatrist, clinical psychologist*).

psychiatrist. A medical doctor specializing in the treatment and prevention of mental disorders both mild and severe (cf. *psychoanalyst, clinical psychologist, psychological counselor*).

psychiatry. A branch of medicine concerned with mental health and mental illness (cf. *psychiatrist, psychoanalyst*).

psychoanalysis. (1) The method developed by Freud and extended by his followers for treating neuroses. (2) The system of psychological theory growing out of experiences with the psychoanalytic method.

psychoanalyst. A psychotherapist, now usually trained as a psychiatrist, who uses methods related to those originally proposed by Freud for treating neuroses and other mental disorders (cf. *psychiatrist, clinical psychologist, psychological counselor*).

psychodrama. A form of spontaneous play acting used in psychotherapy.

psychogenic. Caused by psychological factors (e.g., emotional conflict, faulty habits) rather than by disease, injury, or other somatic cause; functional rather than organic.

psychograph. Cf. *trait profile.*

psychokinesis (PK). A claimed form of mental operation said to affect a material body or an energy system without any evidence of more usual contact or energy transfer, e.g., affecting the number which comes up in the throw of dice by a machine through wishing for that number (cf. *extrasensory perception*).

psychological primaries. Hues that appear to be pure, i.e., not composed of other hues. Most authorities choose a particular red, yellow, green, and blue. (The red-green and blue-yellow pairs chosen in this way are not complementary colors) (cf. *color-mixing primaries*).

psychology. The science of the behavior of man and other animals (cf. *behavior*).

psychoneurotic reaction. A form of maladjustment in which the individual is unable to cope with his anxieties and conflicts and develops abnormal symptoms. The disturbance is not so severe as to produce a profound personality derangement, as with the psychotic reactions (syn. *psychoneurosis, neurosis;* cf. *anxiety reaction, conversion reaction, phobic reaction, obsessive-compulsive reaction*).

psychophysical methods. Experimental and statistical methods for determining absolute thresholds, difference thresholds, and scale values for stimuli that can be arranged along a physical continuum (cf. *threshold*).

psychophysics. A name used by Fechner for the science of the relationship between mental processes and the physical world. Now usually restricted to the study of the sensory consequences of controlled physical stimulation (cf. *psychophysical methods*).

psychosexual development. In psychoanalysis, the theory that development takes place through stages (oral, anal, phallic, latency, genital), each stage characterized by a zone of pleasurable stimulation and appropriate objects of sexual attachment, culminating in normal heterosexual mating (cf. *oral stage, anal stage, phallic stage, latency, genital stage, psychosocial crises*).

psychosocial crises. A modification by Erikson of the psychoanalytic theory of psychosexual development, giving more attention to the social and environmental problems associated with the various stages of development, and adding some adult stages beyond genital maturing (cf. *psychosexual development*).

psychosomatic disorders. Ailments with organic symptoms attributable to emotional or other psychological causes.

psychotherapy. Treatment of personality maladjustment or mental illness by psychological means, usually, but not exclusively, through personal consultation (cf. *somatotherapy*).

psychotic-depressive reaction. An affective psychotic reaction resembling the depressive phase of the manic-depressive reaction, but not cyclical. It may arise as a consequence of a severe personal crisis (cf. *manic-depressive reaction*).

psychotic disorder. Mental illness in which the patient shows severe change or disorganization of personality, often accompanied by depression, delusions, hallucinations; commonly requires hospitalization (syn. *psychosis,* pl. *psychoses;* cf. *functional psychosis, organic psychosis*).

puberal phase. The period of most rapid changes during adolescence. Precisely defined, it is that period during which the growth rate exceeds the average rate as measured within a five-year period around the peak of maximum growth (Stolz). It usually lasts from two to four years (cf. *adolescence*).

puberty. The age at which secondary sex characteristics appear and sex functioning begins to mature (syn. *pubescence;* cf. *adolescence, puberal phase*).

public opinion. Widely shared beliefs, including common plans for action, chiefly in respect to problems of governmental policy (cf. *attitude, opinion*).

punctiform distribution. The arrangement of sensitive areas of the skin; a distribution of sensitive spots with insensitive areas between them.

punishment. A negative incentive, capable of producing pain or annoyance (cf. *reward*).

pupillary response. The constriction or dilation of the pupil of the eye, brought about either by changes in illumination or as an emotional accompaniment (cf. *emotional indicator*).

purpose. A goal that can be stated in words and toward which action is directed (cf. *unconscious motive*).

pursuit learning. A laboratory task in which the subject learns to keep the point of a hinged stylus in contact with a small metal target mounted on a rotating phonograph-like turntable.

pyknic type. A major body type, according to Kretschmer, characterized by a short, rounded body, and associated (in the extreme) with manic-depressive psychosis (cf. *type theory, asthenic type*).

quality. A characteristic denoting differences in kind, rather than differences in intensity or amount; e.g., a light and a sound differ in quality; red and blue, and the notes A and B♭, differ in quality (cf. *quantity*).

quantity. Amount or intensity (cf. *quality*).

quota control. A sampling method used in attitude and opinion surveys, in which the interviewer is instructed to select respondents with certain defined characteristics, e.g., of stated age, sex, economic level (cf. *area sampling*).

range. The variation of scores in a frequency distribution from the lowest to the highest. A value that grows larger as the number of cases increases, hence to be used with extreme caution (cf. *measure of variation*).

rank-difference correlation (ρ). A correlation computed from ranked data. The coefficient is designated by the small Greek letter rho (ρ) to distinguish it from the product-moment correlation (r), of which it is an approximation (cf. *coefficient of correlation*).

rapport. (1) Comfortable relationship between the subject and the tester, insuring cooperation in replying to test questions. (2) Similar relationship between client and counselor. (3) A special relationship of hypnotic subject to hypnotist.

rating scale. A device by which a rater can record his judgment of another person (or of himself) on the traits defined by the scale (cf. *graphic rating scale*).

ratio scale. A scale of equal units with a true (absolute) zero, so that the numerical values can be used as ratios, e.g., a weight of six pounds is three times as heavy as one of two pounds (cf. *interval scale, ordinal scale*).

rational problem-solving. Arriving at a solution by sound reasoning on the basis of the best available evidence; realistic problem-solving (cf. *defense mechanism*).

rationalization. A defense mechanism in which self-esteem is maintained by assigning plausible and acceptable reasons for conduct entered upon impulsively or for less acceptable reasons (cf. *defense mechanism*).

reaction-formation. A defense mechanism in which a

subject denies a disapproved motive through giving strong expression to its opposite (cf. *defense mechanism*).

readiness to learn. The state of the learner that makes a given task an appropriate one for him to master because (1) he is sufficiently mature physiologically, (2) he has the appropriate preparatory training, and (3) he has an aroused interest or desire to learn (cf. *maturation, pacing*).

recall. The form of remembering in which the subject demonstrates retention by repeating what was earlier learned, e.g., demonstrating recall of a poem by reciting it (cf. *recognition, redintegrative memory, relearning*).

receptor. A specialized portion of the body sensitive to particular kinds of stimuli and connected with sensory nerves, e.g., the retina of the eye. Used more loosely, the organ containing these sensitive portions, e.g., the eye or the ear (cf. *effector*).

recessive gene. A member of a gene pair which determines the characteristic trait or appearance of the individual only if the other member of the pair is recessive. If the other member of the pair is dominant, the effect of the recessive gene is masked (cf. *dominant gene*).

reciprocal inhibition. (1) The relationship between muscles that are controlled through reciprocal innervation (Sherrington). (2) A variety of psychotherapy in which symptoms are decreased through presenting their occasion under circumstances in which response is inhibited (Wolpe).

reciprocal innervation. A form of neural integration in which one of a pair of antagonistic muscles is actively inhibited when the other member of the pair contracts (cf. *antagonistic muscles*).

recognition. That form of remembering indicated by a feeling of familiarity when something previously encountered is again perceived (cf. *recall, redintegrative memory, relearning*).

red-green color blindness. The commonest form of color blindness, a variety of dichromatism. In the two subvarieties, red-blindness and green-blindness, both red and green vision are lacking, but achromatic bands are seen at different parts of the spectrum (cf. *color blindness, dichromatism*).

redintegrative memory. Remembering the whole of an earlier experience on the basis of partial cues; recollection of events in the personal history of the subject, with their attendant circumstances (cf. *recall, recognition, relearning*).

reduction screen. A screen containing a small aperture so that a restricted area of a surface can be viewed through it. With a reduction screen brightness constancy (and other constancies) tends to be lessened (cf. *object constancy*).

reference group. The group with which an individual compares himself when he makes self-estimates of status. Most people have several reference groups. A reference group may or may not be a membership group (cf. *membership group*).

reflex action. A relatively simple response largely under the control of a specific stimulus, occurring rather mechanically, such as the pupillary response to light or the knee-jerk from a tap on the tendon below the knee. Other examples of reflex action are sneezing, perspiring, and the beating of the heart (cf. *respondent behavior*).

refractory phase. The period of temporary inactivity in a neuron after it has once fired.

regression. A return to more primitive or infantile modes of response, either (1) retrogression to behavior engaged in when younger, or (2) primitivation, i.e., more infantile or childlike behavior, but not necessarily that which occurred in the individual's earlier life.

reinforcement. (1) In classical conditioning the experimental procedure of following the conditioned stimulus by the unconditioned stimulus. (2) In operant conditioning the analogous procedure of following the occurrence of the operant response by the reinforcing stimulus. (3) The process which increases the strength of conditioning as a result of these arrangements (cf. *classical conditioning, operant conditioning, extinction*).

reinforcing stimulus. (1) In classical conditioning, the unconditioned stimulus. (2) In operant conditioning, the stimulus that reinforces the operant (typically, a reward).

relational concept. A type of concept in which the instances share common relationships rather than common characteristics; thus an isosceles triangle has two sides equal, but they may be of any length (cf. *conjunctive concept, disjunctive concept*).

relationship therapy. A psychotherapeutic technique in which the benefit to the client is said to come from the comfortable relationship established between the client (usually a child) and the therapist, this relationship leading to improved relations with people in daily life (cf. *psychotherapy, release therapy, interpretive therapy*).

relearning. That form of remembering in which the subject demonstrates memory for something previously learned through the saving in time or trials required for learning the material again (cf. *recall, recognition, redintegrative memory*).

release therapy. A psychotherapeutic technique involving the free expression of emotion, especially used with children, in which benefit to the client is said to come from providing an opportunity to give expression, especially to hostile and destructive impulses (cf. *psychotherapy, relationship therapy, interpretive therapy*).

releaser. A term used by ethologists for a stimulus that sets off a cycle of instinctive behavior (cf. *ethologist, instinct*).

reliability. The self-consistency of a test as a measuring instrument. Reliability is measured by a coefficient of correlation between scores on two halves of a test, alternate forms of the test, or retests with the same test, a high correlation signifying high consistency of scores for the population tested (cf. *validity*).

reminiscence. In psychology a term for the occasional rise in a curve of retention before it falls, e.g., when under some circumstances more may be retained after an interval than immediately upon completion of learning (cf. *retention curve*).

repression. (1) A defense mechanism in which an impulse or memory which might provoke feelings of guilt is denied by its disappearance from awareness (cf. *defense mechanism, suppression*). (2) A theory of forgetting (cf. *motivated forgetting*).

reserpine. Cf. *tranquilizer.*

resistance. In psychoanalysis, a blocking of free association; a psychological barrier against bringing unconscious impulses to the level of awareness. Resistance is part of the process of maintaining repression (cf. *repression, interpretation*).

respiration rate. The rate of breathing. When respiration rate is used in the study of emotion, an additional measure is commonly used, known as the inspiration-expiration ratio. This is computed as a ratio between the time spent in inspiration and the time spent in expiration (I/E) (cf. *emotional indicator*).

respondent. (1) One who responds; used chiefly to refer to those interviewed in public opinon surveys. (2) A class of responses (cf. *respondent behavior*).

respondent behavior. A type of behavior corresponding to reflex action, in that it is largely under the control of, and predictable from, the stimulus (syn. *elicited behavior;* cf. *operant behavior*).

response. (1) The behavioral result of stimulation in the form of a movement or glandular secretion. (2) Sometimes, any activity of the organism, including central responses (such as an image or fantasy), whether or not the stimulus is identified and whether or not identifiable movements occur. (3) Products of the organism's activity, such as words typed per minute.

retention curve. A curve plotted with some measure of remembering on the vertical axis and the elapsed time since learning on the horizontal axis. The curve tends to fall rapidly at first, then more slowly, though this is not invariable (cf. *reminiscence*).

reticular formation. A system of ill-defined nerve paths and connections within the brain stem, lying outside the well-defined nerve pathways, and important as an arousal mechanism.

retina. The portion of the eye sensitive to light, containing the rods and the cones (cf. *rod, cone*).

retroactive inhibition. (1) The interference in recall of something earlier learned by something subsequently learned. (2) The theory of forgetting which proposes that much, or most, forgetting is due to the interference by new learning with the recall of the old (cf. *proactive inhibition, transfer of training*).

retrogression. Cf. *regression.*

reverberating circuit. A loop of neurons that may continue to fire without external stimulation; one of the speculative mechanisms to account for the persistence of memories.

reward. A positive incentive capable of arousing pleasure or satisfying a drive; a reinforcing stimulus (cf. *punishment*).

reward expectancy experiment. A kind of experiment designed to determine whether or not the learner will respond differently if an unexpected incentive is substituted for the familiar expected one (cf. *sign learning*).

rhodopsin. Cf. *visual purple.*

rod. In the eye, an element of the retina mediating achromatic sensation only; particularly important in peripheral vision and night vision (cf. *retina, cone*).

role. By analogy with an actor's role, the kind of behavior expected of an individual because of his place within social arrangements, e.g., the male role, the mother's role, the lawyer's role. Any one person fulfills or adopts numerous roles on varied occasions.

role diffusion. A stage of development said by Erikson to characterize many adolescents (and others) in which various identifications with others have not been harmonized and integrated (cf. *identification, identity formation*).

role playing. A method for teaching principles affecting interpersonal relations by having the subject assume a part in a spontaneous play, whether in psychotherapy or in leadership training (cf. *psychodrama*).

rote memorization. Verbatim learning, as in learning a poem "by heart" (cf. *paired-associates learning, serial memorization, substance memorization*).

saccule. Cf. *vestibular sacs.*

sadism. A pathological motive that leads to inflicting pain upon another person (cf. *masochism*).

salivary secretion. Secretion of the salivary glands, elicited by food or chemical substance in the mouth or by conditioned stimuli, or occurring as an emotional accompaniment (cf. *emotional indicator*).

sample. A selection of scores from a total set of scores known as the "population." If selection is random, an unbiased sample results; if selection is nonrandom, the sample is biased and unrepresentative (cf. *population*).

sampling errors. The variation in a distribution of scores, or of statistics derived from them, to be attributed to the fact that measurements are made on a variable sample from a larger population. Thus sampling errors persist even though all measurements are accurate (cf. *errors of measurement, sample*).

saturation. The dimension of color that describes its purity; if highly saturated it appears to be pure hue and free of gray, but if of low saturation it appears to have a great deal of gray mixed with it (cf. *brightness, hue*).

scale. A set of ascending or descending values used to designate a position or an interval along a dimension. Thus a ruler may have a scale in inches, a test a scale in I.Q. units (cf. *interval scale, ordinal scale, ratio scale*).

scaling. Converting raw data into types of scores more readily interpreted, e.g., into ranks, centiles, standard scores (cf. *attitude scale*).

scalogram. A scale for measuring favorability or unfavorability of attitudes constructed according to Guttman's method. The intent is to arrive at a "pure" scale, so that a subject with a specified attitude who answers a certain question favorably will be favorable to all questions less extreme, and unfavorable to all questions more extreme (cf. *attitude scale*).

scapegoating. A form of displaced aggression in which an innocent but helpless victim is blamed or punished as the source of the scapegoater's frustration (cf. *displaced aggression*).

schizophrenic reaction. A functional psychotic disorder in which there is a lack of harmony or split between aspects of personality functioning, especially between emotion and conduct. Both delusions and hallucinations may be present (syn. *schizophrenia,* formerly *dementia praecox;* cf. *psychotic disorder*).

schizothyme. A type of temperament associated, according to Kretschmer, with the asthenic body type and characterized by inadequate or inappropriate emotional responses to stimuli, resembling in less extreme form the characteristics of schizophrenia (cf. *asthenic type; cyclothyme*).

school of psychology. An all-embracing system designed to encompass the data of psychology according to a limited set of principles and procedures. Such schools are not as prominent today as they once were (syn. *system of psychology;* cf. *behaviorism, Gestalt psychology, psychoanalysis, S-R psychology*).

school psychologist. A professional psychologist employed by a school or school system, with responsibility for testing, guidance, research, etc. (cf. *educational psychologist*).

secondary reinforcer. A stimulus that has become reinforcing through prior association with a reinforcing stimulus (cf. *reinforcing stimulus*).

secondary sex characteristics. The physical features distinguishing the mature male from the mature female, apart from the reproductive organs. In man, the deeper voice of the male and the growth of the beard are illustrative (cf. *primary sex characteristics*).

secondary disposition. A minor disposition, aroused by a narrow range of stimuli, and resulting in a narrow range of equivalent responses (Allport) (cf. *cardinal disposition, central disposition*).

second-order conditioning. Conditioning in which what was previously the conditioned stimulus now serves as the unconditioned or reinforcing stimulus (cf. *secondary reinforcer*).

selectivity. The perceptual response to parts of incoming stimuli and the ignoring of others (cf. *attention*).

self. The subject's personality as perceived by the subject (cf. *personality*).

self-consciousness. A form of heightened self-awareness when an individual is especially concerned about reactions of others to him.

self-deception. Behavior whose motives are unconscious or inadequately perceived by the person himself because of (1) denial of the true motives, or (2) disguise of these motives (cf. *defense mechanism*).

self-demand schedule. A flexible arrangement for feeding in which the time an infant is fed is determined according to his behavior. It replaces a four-hour or other rigid schedule (syn. *self-schedule, demand schedule*).

self-perception. The individual's awareness of himself; differs from self-consciousness because it may take the form of objective self-appraisal (cf. *self-consciousness*).

self-recitation. In memorization, the method of spending some fraction of the study time in attempted recall.

semantic defect. One of Head's classes of aphasia, in which the subject loses comprehension of meaning, especially of relationships, e.g., the rules of a game (cf. *aphasia*).

semantic differential. A method developed by Osgood for using rating scales and factor analysis in studying the connotative meanings of words (cf. *connotative meaning*).

semicircular canals. Three curved tubular canals, in three planes, which form part of the labyrinth of the inner ear and are concerned with equilibrium and motion.

sensorimotor task. A multiple-response task in which muscular movement is prominent, e.g., riding a bicycle, playing a piano. Laboratory sensorimotor tasks include mazes, mirror drawing, pursuit learning, etc. (cf. *multiple-response learning*).

sensory adaptation. The reduction in sensitivity (i.e., raised threshold) that comes about with prolonged stimulation as in vision, smell, taste, temperature sensitivity (cf. *dark adaptation, light adaptation*).

septal area. A portion of the brain deep in the central part, between the lateral ventricles, which when stimulated electrically (in the rat, at least) appears to yield a state akin to pleasure.

serial memorization. That form of rote memorization in which a list of items, or a passage of prose or poetry, is learned in sequence from beginning to end, so that each item or word is a cue to the one that follows it (cf. *paired-associates learning*).

serial position effect. The difficulty in memorization and recall resulting from position of items within a list to be learned and remembered. The point of maximum difficulty is just after the middle of the list.

set. (1) A preparatory adjustment or readiness for a particular kind of action or experience, usually as a result of instructions, e.g., the set to respond with a word opposite in meaning to the stimulus word in an experiment on controlled association. (2) A habitual tendency to respond in a particular manner.

sex gland. As duct glands, the sex glands are active in mating behavior, but as endocrine glands their hormones affect secondary sex characteristics as well as maintaining functional sexual activity. The male hormones are known as androgens, the female hormones as estrogens (syn. *gonads;* cf. *endocrine gland*).

sex-linked trait. A trait determined by a gene transmitted with the same chromosomes that determine sex, e.g., red-green color blindness (cf. *X-chromosome, Y-chromosome*).

shame culture. That form of social control in which a person's behavior is regulated by the ridicule or criticism of others (cf. *guilt culture*).

shape constancy. The tendency to see a familiar object as of the same shape regardless of the viewing angle (cf. *object constancy*).

shaping of behavior. Modifying operant behavior by reinforcing only those variations in response that deviate in a direction desired by the experimenter; the whole population of responses thus reinforced then drifts in the desired direction (Skinner) (syn. *method of approximations*).

sharpening. The tendency to distort memory in the direction that accentuates some distinguishing or dramatic characteristic of the thing remembered (cf. *leveling, systematic distortion*).

shock therapy. A form of treatment of mental illness, especially in the relief of depression (cf. *electroconvulsive shock therapy, insulin shock*).

sibling. A brother or a sister.

sibling rivalry. Jealousy between siblings, often based on their competition for parental affection.

sign learning. An acquired expectation that one stimulus (the sign) will be followed by another (the significate) provided a familiar behavior route is followed. This interpretation of learning, by Tolman, is considered by him an alternative to the interpretation of learning as habit formation (cf. *latent learning experiment, place-learning experiment, reward expectancy experiment*).

sine wave. A cyclical wave which when plotted corresponds to the plot of the trigonometric sine function. The sound waves of pure tones yield this function when plotted.

size-age confusion. The tendency to judge age by size, e.g., perceiving as awkward those adolescents who are large for their ages.

size constancy. The tendency to see a familiar object as of its actual size regardless of its distance (cf. *object constancy*).

skewed distribution. A frequency distribution that is not symmetrical. It is named for the direction in which the tail lies; e.g., if there are many small incomes and a few large ones, the distribution is skewed in the direction of the large incomes (cf. *frequency distribution, symmetrical distribution*).

smooth muscle. The type of muscle found in the digestive organs, blood vessels, and other internal organs. Controlled via the autonomic nervous system (cf. *cardiac muscle, striate muscle*).

social desirability variable. A biasing variable in personality inventories, leading some subjects to reply in the direction of socially approved responses, whether or not their answers are descriptive of themselves (cf. *acquiescence*).

social femininity. The tendency to answer questions on a masculinity-femininity test as women do rather than as men do.

social masculinity. The tendency to answer questions on

a masculinity-femininity test as men do rather than as women do.

social motive. A motive serving group life, involving particularly interactions with other organisms of the same species (cf. *ego-integrative motive, survival motive*).

social psychologist. A psychologist whose research interest lies in the behavior of the individual as he influences and is influenced by other individuals in a social environment (cf. *anthropologist, sociologist*).

socialization. The shaping of individual characteristics and behavior through the training that the social environment provides.

sociogram. A social map or diagram showing interactions, usually of mutual attraction or antagonism, among group members (cf. *sociometry*).

sociology. The behavioral or social science dealing with group life and social organization in literate societies (cf. *behavioral sciences*).

sociometry. A method of social mapping to indicate relationships of attraction and rejection among members of a social group. Each member expresses his choices for or against other members. The social map is constructed from the data provided by these choices (cf. *sociogram*).

somatotherapy. Treatment of personality maladjustment or mental illness by drugs, electric shock, surgery, or other methods directly affecting bodily processes (cf. *psychotherapy*).

source trait. A trait derived by the method of factor analysis; all traits loaded heavily on a common factor belong together (Cattell) (cf. *surface trait*).

spastic paralysis. A condition of excessive isotonic muscular contraction, commonly due to a brain injury at birth (syn. *cerebral palsy*).

special aptitude. The degree of aptitude to learn a specific activity, e.g., musical aptitude, clerical aptitude (cf. *general aptitude*).

specific hunger. Hunger for a specific food incentive, such as a craving for sweets (cf. *hunger drive*).

spontaneous recovery. The return in strength of a conditioned response after a lapse of time following extinction (cf. *extinction*).

S-R psychology. Cf. *stimulus-response psychology*.

standard deviation. The square root of the mean of the squares of the amount by which each case departs from the mean of all the cases (syn. *root mean square deviation;* cf. *measure of variation, standard error, standard score*).

standard error. The standard deviation of the sampling distribution of a mean and of certain other derived statistics. It can be interpreted as any other standard deviation (cf. *standard deviation*).

standard error of estimate. The standard error of the differences between predicted values and true values of some measure. Used, for example, in interpreting a coefficient of correlation (cf. *predictive efficiency of r*).

standard score. (1) A score that has been converted to a scale with a mean of zero and a standard deviation of 1.0, based on a distribution of scores used in calibration. (2) A score based on standard scores but converted to another scale for convenience, e.g., with a mean of 50 and a standard deviation of 10.

stanine score. A U.S. Air Forces type of standard score (originally, "standard nine"), with a mean of 5 and a standard deviation of 2. Scores range from 1 through 9 (cf. *standard score*).

statistical inference. A statement about a population or populations based on statistical measures derived from samples (cf. *descriptive statistics*).

statistical significance. The trustworthiness of an obtained statistical measure as a statement about reality, e.g., the probability that the population mean falls within the limits determined from a sample. The expression refers to the reality of the statistical finding and not to its importance (cf. *confidence limits, critical ratio, probability value*).

statistician. An applied mathematician; in psychology, one especially trained in the statistical tools useful in test construction and the interpretation of test data and in the design of experiments.

status motives. Motives related to one's established or desired position relative to others (cf. *dominance, achievement*).

stereophonic hearing. The binaural perception of the distance and direction of a sound source owing to the difference in reception by the two ears.

stereoscopic vision. (1) The binocular perception of depth and distance of an object owing to the overlapping fields of the two eyes. (2) The equivalent effect when slightly unlike pictures are presented individually to each eye in a stereoscope (cf. *distance cues*).

stereotype. A biased generalization, usually about a social or national group, according to which individuals are falsely assigned traits they do not possess. Thus a person may have a stereotyped conception of the Italians or Scots which distorts his perception of any individual Italian or Scot.

stereotypy. The continued repetition of behavior which appears to serve no realistic purpose and may, in fact, be punished. Inflexible behavior, which may be a consequence of frustration (cf. *frustration*).

steroids. Complex chemical substances, some of which are prominent in the secretions of the adrenal cortex and may be related to some forms of mental illness (cf. *adrenal gland*).

stimulus (pl. **stimuli**). (1) Some specific physical energy impinging upon a receptor sensitive to that kind of energy. (2) Any objectively describable situation or event (whether outside or inside the organism) that is the occasion for an organism's response (cf. *response*).

stimulus-response psychology. A psychological view that all behavior is in response to stimuli and that the appropriate tasks of psychological science are those identifying stimuli, the responses correlated with them, and the processes intervening between stimulus and response. There are several varieties of stimulus-response (S-R) theory, depending on the kind of intervening processes inferred (cf. *intervening variables*).

stimulus substitution. Cf. *classical conditioning*.

striate area. Cf. *visual area*.

striate muscle. Striped muscle; the characteristic muscles controlling the skeleton, as in the arms and legs. Activated by cerebro-spinal nervous system (cf. *cardiac muscle, smooth muscle*).

stroboscopic motion. An illusion of motion resulting from the successive presentation of discrete stimulus patterns arranged in a progression corresponding to movement, e.g., motion pictures (cf. *phi phenomenon*).

subjective science. A science limited to self-observation, so that its data are not public. Psychology based solely on introspection is subjective in that its raw data are limited to the observations of the subject on his own conscious processes. However, the report of these experiences provides objective data, so that introspection does not have to be excluded from objective psychology (cf. *objective science*).

subjective scoring. Test scoring requiring complex judgments by the scorer, as in the grading of essay examinations (cf. *objective scoring*).

sublimation. A form of the defense mechanism of substitution, whereby socially unacceptable motives find expression in socially acceptable forms; most commonly applied to the sublimation of sexual desires (cf. *substitution, compensation*).

submission. Cf. *dominance*.

substance memorization. The learning of the message, plot, or events in a passage in contrast to learning its exact words (cf. *rote memorization*).

substitution. A defense mechanism whereby the person maintains self-esteem by substituting approved goals for unapproved ones and activities that can be carried out successfully for activities doomed to failure (cf. *sublimation, compensation, overcompensation*).

subtractive mixture. Color mixture in which absorption occurs, so that results differ from additive mixture obtained by rotating colors on a color wheel or by mixing projected lights. Subtractive mixture occurs when transparent colored filters are placed one in front of the other, and when pigments are mixed (cf. *additive mixture*).

superego. In Freud's tripartite division of the personality, that part corresponding most nearly to conscience, controlling through moral scruples rather than by way of social expediency. The superego is said to be an uncompromising and punishing conscience (cf. *id, ego*).

suppression. A process of self-control in which impulses, tendencies to action, wishes to perform disapproved acts, etc., are in awareness, but not overtly revealed (cf. *repression*).

surface trait. A trait derived by the method of cluster analysis; all traits that intercorrelate above some predicted value (e.g., above $r = .60$) can be considered to have something in common (Cattell) (cf. *source trait*).

survival motive. A motive closely related to maintaining the life of the organism in its environment; thus motives related to bodily needs for food, water, air, moderate temperatures, etc. (cf. *ego-integrative motive, social motive*).

symmetrical distribution. A frequency distribution in which cases fall equally in the class intervals on either side of the middle; hence the mean, median, and mode fall together (cf. *frequency distribution, skewed distribution*).

sympathetic division. A division of the autonomic nervous system, characterized by a chain of ganglia on either side of the spinal cord, with nerve fibers originating in the thoracic and lumbar portions of the spinal cord. Active in emotional excitement and to some extent antagonistic to the parasympathetic division (q.v.).

synapse. Cf. *synaptic nervous system*.

synaptic nervous system. A nervous system characteristic of all higher organisms, in which nerve cells are distinct and conduction is polarized, that is, occurs only in one direction across the junction between nerve cells called a synapse (cf. *nerve net*).

syntactical defect. One of Head's classes of aphasia, in which the subject is unable to form intelligible sentences (cf. *aphasia*).

systematic distortion. A theory of forgetting which implies that memory is distorted through orderly changes in the memory trace other than fading or dropping out of details (cf. *assimilating, leveling, sharpening*).

taboo. Something strongly prohibited or banned within a culture, usually with severe penalties for violation.

tachistoscope. An instrument for the brief exposure of words, symbols, pictures, or other visually presented material.

taste deficiency. A trait used in the study of population genetics. Nontasting of certain substances, such as phenyl-thio-carbamide, is a recessive characteristic in man, while tasting is a dominant characteristic (cf. *dominant gene, recessive gene, population genetics*).

teaching machine. A device to provide self-instruction by means of a program proceeding in steps following each other at a rate determined by the learner; the machine is arranged to provide knowledge about the correctness or incorrectness of each reply (cf. *programing*).

telepathy. The claimed form of extrasensory perception in which what is perceived depends upon thought transference from one person to another (cf. *extrasensory perception, clairvoyance, precognition*).

temperament. That aspect of personality revealed in the tendency to experience moods or mood changes in characteristic ways; general level of reactivity and energy (cf. *mood*).

temporal lobe. A portion of the cerebral hemisphere, at the side below the fissure of Sylvius and in front of the occipital lobe (cf. *frontal lobe, occipital lobe, parietal lobe*).

tension to complete. The motive that persists when a task is interrupted before completion; used to explain the fact that under many circumstances incompleted tasks are better remembered than completed ones (cf. *motivated forgetting*).

test. A collection of items (questions, tasks, etc.) so arranged that replies or performances can be scored and the scores used in appraising individual differences (cf. *item, test battery*).

test battery. A collection of tests whose composite scores are used to appraise individual differences (cf. *item, test*).

test method. A method of psychological investigation. Its advantages are that it allows the psychologist to collect large quantities of useful data from many people, with a minimum of disturbance of their routines of existence and with a minimum of laboratory equipment (cf. *test, experimental method*).

test profile. A chart plotting scores from a number of tests given to the same individual (or group of individuals) in parallel rows on a common scale, with the scores connected by lines, so that high and low scores can be readily perceived (cf. *trait profile*).

test standardization. The establishment of norms for interpreting scores by giving a test to a representative population and by making appropriate studies of its reliability and validity (cf. *norm, reliability, validity*).

tetany. A physiologically disturbed state of the organism marked by widespread intermittent muscular contractions and muscular pain; may be caused by calcium deficiency as a consequence of defective parathyroid secretion (cf. *parathyroid glands*).

thinking. Behavior carried on in terms of ideas (representational or symbolic processes); ideational problem-solving as distinguished from perceptual solution or solution through overt manipulation (cf. *associative thinking, directed thinking*).

threshold. The transitional point at which an increasing stimulus or an increasing difference not previously perceived becomes perceptible (or at which a decreasing stimulus or previously perceived difference becomes imperceptible). The value obtained depends in part upon the methods used in determining it (cf.

absolute threshold, difference threshold, psychophysical methods).

thyroid gland. An endocrine gland located in the neck, whose hormone thyroxin is important in determining metabolic rate (cf. *endocrine gland*).

thyroxin. The hormone of the thyroid gland (cf. *thyroid gland*).

timbre. The quality distinguishing a tone of a given pitch sounded by one instrument from that sounded by another. The differences are due to overtones and other impurities (cf. *overtone*).

token learning. An arrangement within operant conditioning in which a token (e.g., a poker chip) as a secondary reinforcer can be exchanged for a primary reinforcing stimulus (e.g., food).

traditional counseling. Counseling based on the acknowledged expertness and responsibility of the counselor, who diagnoses difficulties and advises further steps (cf. *client-centered counseling*).

trained introspection. Cf. *introspection.*

training. Learning that is guided by another individual, such as a parent or teacher, or, as in self-training, learning that is deliberately undertaken to shape behavior in particular directions (cf. *maturation*).

trait. A persisting characteristic or dimension of personality according to which individuals can be rated or measured (cf. *trait profile, type theory*).

trait profile. A chart plotting the ratings of a number of traits of the same individual on a common scale in parallel rows, so that the pattern of traits can be visually perceived (syn. *psychograph;* cf. *trait, test profile*).

trait theory. The theory that human personality is most profitably characterized by the scores that an individual makes on a number of scales, each of which represents a trait or dimension of his personality (cf. *type theory*).

tranquilizer. A drug such as chlorpromazine or reserpine used to reduce anxiety and relieve depression; hence useful in the therapy of mental disorders.

transfer of training. The effect of prior learning on present learning. If learning a new task is facilitated, transfer is positive; if the new learning is interfered with, transfer is negative (cf. *formal discipline, proactive inhibition, retroactive inhibition*).

transfer through principles. A theory of transfer of training which proposes that new learning is facilitated by detecting the applicability of principles or generalizations discovered in prior learning (Judd) (cf. *transfer of training*).

transference. In psychoanalysis, the patient's unconsciously making the therapist the object of emotional response, thus transferring to him responses appropriate to other persons important in the life history of the patient.

traveling wave theory. A modification by Békésy of the place theory of hearing. The theory states that when a sound of given frequency enters the ear, a wave travels along the basilar membrane and displaces it a maximum amount at a certain point, the point depending on its frequency (cf. *basilar membrane, frequency theory, place theory, volley theory*).

trial-and-error learning. An expression characterizing multiple-response learning, in which the proper response is selected out of varied behavior through the influence of reward and punishment. Variously described as approximation and correction, fumble and success, etc. (cf. *multiple-response learning, operant conditioning*).

trichromatism. Normal color vision, based on the classification of color vision according to three color systems: black-white, blue-yellow, and red-green. The normal eye sees all three; the color-blind eye is defective in one or two of the three systems (cf. *dichromatism, monochromatism*).

type theory. The theory that human subjects can profitably be classified into a small number of classes or types, each class or type having characteristics in common which set its members apart from other classes or types (cf. *trait theory*).

uncertainty. In information measurement, the amount of information about alternatives that is not yet known. The task of transmitting information is to reduce uncertainty by reducing the alternatives remaining (cf. *information measurement*).

unconditioned response. The response given originally to the unconditioned stimulus used as the basis for establishing a conditioned response to a previously neutral stimulus (cf. *conditioned response*).

unconscious motive. A motive of which the subject is unaware, or aware of in distorted form. Because there is no sharp dividing line between conscious and unconscious, many motives have both conscious and unconscious aspects.

unconscious processes. (1) Processes, such as wishes or fears, that might be conscious but of which the subject is unaware. (2) Less commonly, physiological processes of the body (circulation, metabolism, etc.) that go on outside of awareness (cf. *consciousness*).

utricle. Cf. *vestibular sacs.*

validity. The predictive significance of a test for its intended purposes. Validity can be measured by a coefficient of correlation between scores on the test and the scores which the test seeks to predict, i.e., scores on some criterion (cf. *criterion, reliability*).

variable. One of the stimulus, response, or background items undergoing study in an experiment (cf. *dependent variable, independent variable*).

variance. The square of a standard deviation or standard error.

variation. Cf. *measure of variation.*

verbal defect. One of Head's classes of aphasia, involving the defective forming of words, e.g., speaking one number for another without awareness of the error (cf. *aphasia*).

verbal report. A statement in words by a subject; often an account of his subjective, conscious experiences, thus making them accessible for study (cf. *behavior*).

verification. The final step in creative thought proposed by Wallas. For the mathematician or scientist, verification is in the form of logical or experimental proof. For the artist, verification consists in a review, to determine whether or not the artistic creation expresses what is intended (cf. *preparation, incubation, illumination*).

vestibular sacs. Two sacs in the labyrinth of the inner ear, called the saccule and utricle, which contain the otoliths ("ear stones"). Pressure of the otoliths on the hair cells in the gelatinous material of the utricle and saccule gives us the sense of upright position or departure from it (cf. *equilibratory senses*).

visual area. A projection area lying in the occipital lobe. In man, partial damage to this area produces blindness in portions of the visual field corresponding to the amount and location of the damage (syn. *striate area*).

visual field. The total visual stimuli acting upon the eye when it is directed toward a fixation point.

visual purple. A light-sensitive substance contained in the rods of the eye (syn. *rhodopsin*).

volley theory. A modified frequency theory of hearing proposed by Wever and Bray which suggests that the frequency of the stimulus may be represented in bundles of fibers in the auditory nerve responding somewhat independently, so that the frequency is represented by the composite volley, even though no single fiber carries impulses at that rate (cf. *frequency theory, place theory, traveling wave theory*).

voluntary action. Self-initiated action (cf. *operant behavior*).

wage-incentive plan. A plan for increasing output per worker by paying a bonus for added output. A form of piece-rate pay.

weighted items. If one item (or a single test in a battery of tests) has been found to predict better than another, it is assigned a higher weight, so that it will influence a composite score more than the item (or test) of lower predictive value.

whole learning. Learning a multiple-response task as a unit, e.g., memorizing a long poem from beginning to end without separate practice of the parts (cf. *part learning*).

word-association experiment. An experiment designed for studying associative processes in which the subject responds to a stimulus-word by saying as promptly as possible the first word that he thinks of (cf. *free association, controlled association*).

working through. In psychoanalytic therapy, the process of reeducation by having the patient face the same conflicts over and over again in the consultation room, until he can independently face and master the conflicts in ordinary life.

work inhibition. A psychoneurotic reaction whereby a person is unable to work at his occupation although able to carry on other usual activities (cf. *psychoneurotic reaction*).

X-chromosome. A chromosome which, if paired with another X-chromosome, determines that the individual will be a female. If it is combined with a Y-chromosome, the individual will be a male. The X-chromosome transmits sex-linked traits (cf. *chromosome, sex-linked trait, Y-chromosome*).

Y-chromosome. The chromosome which, combined with an X-chromosome, determines maleness. Its role in sex-linked traits is as though it carried only recessive genes (cf. *chromosome, sex-linked trait, X-chromosome*).

zest. In mental health, the ability to take a hearty interest in living, to seek out opportunities for useful activity, recreation, good fellowship; to be distinguished, however, from frenzied overactivity (cf. *mental health*).

References and Index to Authors of Works Cited

The numbers in **bold face** following each reference give the text pages on which the paper or book is cited. Abbreviations of journal titles are given in accordance with the conventions of the journals of the American Psychological Association. Citations in the text are made by author and date of publication.

ABELSON, R. P., *see* Rosenberg and others (1960).

ABORN, M. (1953) The influence of experimentally induced failure on the retention of material acquired through set and incidental learning. *J. exp. Psychol.*, 45:225-31. – **302, 304, 517**

ABRAMSON, H. A. and EVANS, L. T. (1954) Lysergic acid diethylamide (LSD25): II. Psychobiological effects on the Siamese fighting fish. *Science,* 120: 990-1. – **140**

ABT, L. E. and BELLAK, L. (Eds.) (1950) *Projective psychology.* N. Y.: Knopf. – **467**

ADAMS, J. A., *see* Reynolds and Adams (1953).

ADAMSON, R. E. (1952) Functional fixedness as related to problem solving: a repetition of three experiments. *J. exp. Psychol.*, 44:288-91. – **357**

ADAMSON, R. E., and TAYLOR, D. W. (1954) Functional fixedness as related to elapsed time and set. *J. exp. Psychol.*, 47:122-26. – **357**

ADLER, A. (1917) *Study of organ inferiority and its psychical compensation.* Washington: Nervous and Mental Disease Publishing Co. – **518**

ADOLPH, E. F. (1939) Measurements of water drinking in dogs. *Amer. J. Physiol.*, 125:75-86. – **130**

ADOLPH, E. F. (1941) The internal environment and behavior: water content. *Amer. J. Psychiat.*, 97: 1365-373. – **131**

ADORNO, T. W., FRENKEL-BRUNSWIK, E., LEVINSON, D. J., and SANFORD, R. N. (1950) *The authoritarian personality.* N. Y.: Harper. – **480, 562**

AINSWORTH, M. D., *see* Klopfer and others (1954).

ALDRICH, C. A., and NORVAL, M. A. (1946) A developmental graph for the first year of life. *J. Pediat.*, 29:304-08. – **71**

ALEXANDER, F. (1948) *Fundamentals of psychoanalysis.* N. Y.: Norton. – **340**

ALEXANDER, F., and FRENCH, T. M. (Eds.) (1946) *Psychoanalytic therapy.* N. Y.: Ronald. – **550**

ALLEE, W. C., COLLIAS, N., and LUTHERMAN, C. Z. (1939) Modification of the social order in flocks of hens by the injection of testosterone propionate. *Physiol. Zool.*, 12:412-40. – **139**

ALLEN, F. H. (1942) *Psychotherapy with children.* N. Y.: Norton. – **536**

ALLEN, R. M. (1958) *Personality assessment procedures.* N. Y.: McGraw-Hill. – **467**

ALLPORT, F. H. (1955) *Theories of perception and the concept of structure.* N. Y.: Wiley. – **222**

ALLPORT, G. W. (1935) Attitudes. In Murchison, C. (Ed.) *Handbook of social psychology.* Worcester, Mass.: Clark Univ. Press, 798-844. – **564**

ALLPORT, G. W. (1937) *Personality.* N. Y.: Holt. – **449, 450, 472**

ALLPORT, G. W. (1944) *ABC's of scapegoating.* Chicago: Central Y.M.C.A. College. – **561**

ALLPORT, G. W. (1954a) The historical background of modern social psychology. In Lindzey, G. (Ed.) *Handbook of social psychology.* Reading, Mass.: Addison-Wesley, 3-56. – **564**

ALLPORT, G. W. (1954b) *The nature of prejudice.* Reading, Mass.: Addison-Wesley. – **563, 580**

ALLPORT, G. W. (1955) *Becoming.* New Haven, Conn.: Yale Univ. Press. – **495**

ALLPORT, G. W. (1960) *Personality and social encounter.* Boston: Beacon Press. – **473, 495**

ALLPORT, G. W. (1961) *Pattern and growth in personality.* N. Y.: Holt, Rinehart and Winston. – **472, 495**

ALLPORT, G. W., and ODBERT, H. S. (1936) Trait-names: a psycho-lexical study. *Psychol. Monogr.*, No. 211. – **473**

ALLPORT, G. W., VERNON, P. E., and LINDZEY, G. (1960) *A study of values: a scale for measuring the dominant interests in personality* (3rd Ed.). Boston: Houghton Mifflin. – **364, 472**

ALPER, T. G., and BORING, E. G. (1944) Intelligence test scores of northern and southern white and Negro recruits in 1918. *J. abnorm. soc. Psychol.*, 39:471-74. – **443**

AMERICAN PSYCHIATRIC ASSOCIATION (1952) *Diagnostic and statistical manual of mental disorders.* Washington, D. C. – **524**

AMES, A., JR. (1951) Visual perception and the rotating trapezoidal window. *Psychol. Monogr.*, 65, No. 324. – **190**

ANASTASI, A., and FOLEY, J. P., JR. (1958). *Differential psychology* (3rd Ed.). N. Y.: Macmillan. – **422, 446**

ANDERSON, E. E. (1941) The externalization of drive. I. Theoretical considerations. *Psychol. Rev.*, 48: 204-24. – **15**

ANDERSON, G. L., *see* Anderson, H. H., and Anderson, G. L. (1951).

ANDERSON, H. H. (Ed.) (1959) *Creativity and its cultivation.* N. Y.: Harper. – **367**

ANDERSON, H. H., and ANDERSON, G. L. (Eds.) (1951) *An introduction to projective techniques.* N. Y.: Prentice-Hall. – **467**

ANDERSSON, B. (1953) The effect of injections and hypertonic solutions in parts of the hypothalamus of goats. *Acta Physiol. Scand.*, 28:188-201. – **131**

ANDREAS, B. G. (1960) *Experimental psychology.* N. Y.: Wiley. – **29**

ANDREWS, T. G. (Ed.) (1948) *Methods of psychology.* N. Y.: Wiley. – **29**

ANGEL, E., *see* May, Angel, and Ellenberger (1958).

ANGELL, G. W. (1949) The effect of immediate knowledge of quiz results on final examination scores in freshman chemistry. *J. educ. Res.*, 42:391-94. – **316**

ANGYAL, A. (1941) *Foundations for a science of personality.* N. Y.: Commonwealth Fund. – **144**

ANKLES, T. M. (1939) *A study of jealousy as differentiated from envy.* Boston: Bruce Humphries. – **174**

ANSBACHER, H. L., and ANSBACHER, R. R. (Eds.) (1956) *The individual psychology of Alfred Adler.* N. Y.: Basic Books. – **518**

ANSBACHER, R. R., *see* Ansbacher, H. L., and Ansbacher, R. R. (1956).

ARIETI, S. (Ed.) (1959) *American handbook of psychiatry.* (2 vols.) N. Y.: Basic Books. – **550**

ARNOLD, M. (1949) A demonstrational analysis of the TAT in a clinical setting. *J. abnorm. soc. Psychol.,* 44:97-111. – **458**

ARNOLD, M., *see also* Kuhlen and Arnold (1944).

ASCH, S. E. (1956) Studies of independence and submission to group pressure: 1. A minority of one against a unanimous majority. *Psychol. Monogr.,* 70, No. 416. – **556**

ATKINSON, J. W. (1953) The achievement motive and recall of interrupted and completed tasks. *J. exp. Psychol.,* 46:381-90. – **146, 304**

ATKINSON, J. W. (1957) Motivational determinants of risk-taking behavior. *Psychol. Rev.,* 64:359-72. – **153**

ATKINSON, J. W. (Ed.) (1958) *Motives in fantasy, action, and society.* Princeton, N. J.: Van Nostrand. – **157**

ATKINSON, J. W., *see also* McClelland and Atkinson (1948).

ATKINSON, R., *see* Suppes and Atkinson (1960).

ATTNEAVE, F. (1959) *Applications of information theory to psychology.* N. Y.: Holt. – **354**

AULD, F., JR., *see* Dollard and Auld (1959); Murray, Auld, and White (1954).

AUSTIN, G. A., *see* Bruner, Goodnow, and Austin (1956).

AUSTIN, G. A., BRUNER, J. S., and SEYMOUR, R. V. (1953) Fixed-choice strategies in concept attainment. *Amer. Psychologist,* 8, 314 (abstract). – **352**

AUSUBEL, D. P. (1954) *Theory and problems of adolescent development.* N. Y.: Grune and Stratton. – **102**

AX, A. F. (1953) The physiological differentiation between fear and anger in humans. *Psychosom. Med.,* 15:433-42. – **160, 163, 164**

BAILEY, L. L., *see* Marquart and Bailey (1955).

BAKKE, E. W. (1940) *Citizens without work: a study of the effects of unemployment upon the workers' social relations and practices.* New Haven, Conn.: Yale Univ. Press. – **547**

BALES, R. F. (1944) The therapeutic role of Alcoholics Anonymous as seen by a sociologist. *Quart. J. Stud. Alcohol,* 5:267-78. – **548**

BALL, E. S., *see* Bossard and Ball (1955).

BANDURA, A. (1956) Psychotherapists' anxiety level, self-insight, and psychotherapeutic competence. *J. abnorm. soc. Psychol.,* 22:349-56. – **542**

BANDURA, A., LIPSHER, D. H., and MILLER, P. E. (1960) Psychotherapists' approach-avoidance reactions to patients' expressions of hostility. *J. consult. Psychol.,* 24:1-8. – **542**

BANDURA, A., ROSS, D., and ROSS, S. A. (1961) Imitation of film-mediated aggressive models. (Unpublished manuscript) – **88**

BANDURA, A., and WALTERS, R. H. (1959) *Adolescent aggression.* N. Y.: Ronald Press. – **95**

BARAHAL, G. D., BRAMMER, L. M., and SHOSTROM, E. L. (1950) A client-centered approach to vocational counseling. *J. consult. Psychol.,* 14:256-60. – **589**

BARKER, C. H., *see* Schein, Schneier, and Barker (1961).

BARKER, R. G. (1942) An experimental study in the resolution of conflict by children. In McNemar, Q., and Merrill, M. A. (Eds.) *Studies in personality.* N. Y.: McGraw-Hill, 13-34. – **499, 500**

BARKER, R. G., *see also* Stone and Barker (1937).

BARKER, R. G., DEMBO, T., and LEWIN, K. (1941) Frustration and regression: an experiment with young children. *Univ. Ia. Stud. Child Welf.,* 18, No. 386. – **505, 511**

BARKER, R. G., WRIGHT, B. A., MEYERSON, L., and GONICK, M. R. (1953) Adjustment to physical handicap and illness. N. Y.: Soc. Sci. Res. Coun. *Bull.* 55 (Revised). – **99, 102**

BARKER, R. G., and WRIGHT, H. F. (1954) *Midwest and its children.* Evanston, Ill.: Row, Peterson. – **486**

BARRON, R. (1954) Personal soundness in university graduate students. Berkeley: Univ. of California Press. – **456**

BARTLETT, F. C. (1932) *Remembering.* Cambridge: Cambridge Univ. Press. – **296, 297, 310**

BARTLEY, S. H. (1941) *Vision: a study of its basis.* N. Y.: Van Nostrand. – **250**

BASS, B. M., *see* Berg and Bass (1961).

BATEMAN, D. E., *see* Lacey, Bateman, and Van Lehn (1952).

BATEMAN, F., *see* Soal and Bateman (1954).

BAYLEY, N. (1932) A study of the crying of infants during mental and physical tests. *J. genet. Psychol.,* 40:306-29. – **169**

BAYLEY, N. (1933) Mental growth during the first three years. *Genet. Psychol. Monogr.,* 14:1-92. – **429**

BAYLEY, N. (1940a) Mental growth in young children. *Yearb. nat. Soc. Stud. Educ.,* 39(II):11-47. – **429**

BAYLEY, N. (1940b) Factors influencing the growth of intelligence in young children. *Yearb. nat. Soc. Stud. Educ.,* 39(II):49-79. – **429**

BAYLEY, N. (1946) Tables for predicting adult height from skeletal age and present height. *J. Pediat.,* 28:49-64. – **100**

BAYLEY, N. (1949) Consistency and variability in the growth of intelligence from birth to eighteen years. *J. genet. Psychol.,* 75:165-96. – **429, 430**

BAYLEY, N. (1954) Some increasing parent-child similarities during the growth of children. *J. educ. Psychol.,* 45:1-21. – **100**

BAYLEY, N., and TUDDENHAM, R. D. (1944) Adolescent changes in body build. *Yearb. nat. Soc. Stud. Educ.,* 43:33-55. – **100**

BEACH, F. A. (1944) Relative effects of androgen upon the mating behavior of male rats subjected to prebrain injury or castration. *J. exp. Zool.,* 97:249-85. – **136**

BEACH, F. A. (1956) Characteristics of masculine "sex drive." In Jones, M. (Ed.) *Nebraska symposium on motivation.* Lincoln: Univ. of Nebraska Press, 1-32. – **136**

BEACH, F. A. (1960) Experimental investigations of species-specific behavior. *Amer. Psychologist,* 15, 1-18. – **6**

BEACH, F. A., *see also* Ford and Beach (1951).

BEARDSLEE, D. C., and WERTHEIMER, M. (Eds.) (1958) *Readings in perception.* Princeton, N. J.: Van Nostrand. – **222**

BECK, L. F. (1936) Hypnotic identification of an amnesia victim. *Brit. J. med. Psychol.,* 16:36-42. – **517**

BECK, L. H. (1950) Osmics: theory and problems related to the initial events in olfaction. In Glaser, O. (Ed.) *Medical physics.* Chicago: Year Book Publishers, II:658-64. – **241**

BECKER, K. (1958) *I met a traveller: the triumph of Father Phillips.* N. Y.: Farrar, Strauss, and Cudahy. – **578**

BÉKÉSY, G. V. (1960) *Experiments in hearing.* N. Y.: McGraw-Hill. – **239, 250**

BELL, H. M. (1950) Retention of pursuit rotor skill after one year. *J. exp. Psychol.*, 40:648-49. – **270**

BELLAK, L., and SMITH, M. B. (1956) An experimental exploration of the psychoanalytic process: exemplification of a method. *Psychoanal. Quart.*, 25:385-414. – **546**

BELLAK, L., *see also* Abt and Bellak (1950).

BENDIG, A. W. (1953) Twenty questions: an information analysis. *J. exp. Psychol.*, 46:345-48. – **353**

BENDIX, R., *see* Lipset and Bendix (1952).

BENEDICT, R. (1946) *The chrysanthemum and the sword.* Boston: Houghton Mifflin. – **517**

BENNETT, G. K. (1955) The D.A.T.—a seven-year follow-up. *Test Service Bull.*, No. 49. N. Y.: Psychological Corporation. – **586**

BENNETT, E. L., *see* Rosenzweig, Krech, and Bennett (1960).

BENSLEY, M., *see* Heidbreder, Bensley, and Ivy. (1948).

BENZINGER, T. H. The human thermostat. *Scient. Amer.*, 1961, 204, 134-47. – **41, 42**

BERELSON, B. (1954) What "missing the newspaper" means. In Schramm, W. (Ed.) *The process and effects of mass communication.* Urbana, Ill.: Univ. of Illinois Press, 36-47. – **573**

BERG, I. A. (1959) The unimportance of test content. In Bass, B. M., and Berg, I. A. *Objective approaches to personality assessment.* Princeton, N. J.: Van Nostrand, 83-9. – **457**

BERG, I. A., and BASS, B. M. (Eds.) (1961) *Conformity and deviation.* N. Y.: Harper. – **580**

BERLYNE, D. (1955) The arousal and satiation of perceptual curiosity in the rat. *J. comp. physiol. Psychol.*, 48:328-46. – **132**

BERLYNE, D. E. (1958) The influence of the albedo and complexity of stimuli on visual fixation in the human infant. *Brit. J. Psychol.*, 49:315-18. – **132, 134**

BERLYNE, D. E. (1960) *Conflict, arousal, and curiosity.* N. Y.: McGraw-Hill. – **132, 134, 157**

BERLYNE, D. E., and SLATER, J. (1957) Perceptual curiosity, exploratory behavior and maze learning. *J. comp. physiol. Psychol.*, 50:228-32. – **132**

BERNAUT, E., *see* Leites and Bernaut (1954).

BERNSTEIN, A. (1955) Some relations between techniques of feeding and training during infancy and certain behavior in childhood. *Genet. Psychol. Monogr.*, 51:3-44. – **76**

BERNSTEIN, A., *see* Lennard and Bernstein (1960).

BERRY, C. A., *see* Sells and Berry (1961).

BERRY, P. C., *see* Taylor, Berry, and Block (1958).

BERSH, P. J. (1951) The influence of two variables upon the establishment of a secondary reinforcer for operant responses. *J. exp. Psychol.*, 41:62-73. – **261**

BERYL, F. (1926) Über die Grössenauffassung bei Kindern. *Z. Psychol.*, 100:344-71. – **192**

BEST, C. H., and TAYLOR, N. B. (1955) *The physiological basis of medical practice.* Baltimore: Williams & Wilkins. – **49**

BEVAN, W., *see* Secord, Bevan, and Katz (1956).

BEXTON, W. H., HERON, W., and SCOTT, T. H. (1954) Effects of decreased variation in the environment. *Canad. J. Psychol.*, 8:70-6. – **56**

BIDDULPH, R., *see* Shower and Biddulph (1931).

BIDERMAN, A. D., and ZIMMER, H. (Eds.) (1961) *The manipulation of human behavior.* N. Y.: Wiley. – **580**

BILLS, M. A. (1950) Field salesmen. In Fryer, D. H., and Henry, E. R. (Eds.) *Handbook of applied psychology.* N. Y.: Rinehart, 212-15. – **589**

BINDRA, D. (1959) *Motivation, a systematic reinterpretation.* N. Y.: Ronald Press. – **157**

BINET, A., and SIMON, T. (1905) Sur la nécessité d'établir un diagnostic scientifique des états inférieurs de l'intelligence. *Année psychol.*, 11:163-90. – **401**

BIRCH, H. G., and RABINOWITZ, H. S. (1951) The negative effect of previous experience on productive thinking. *J. exp. Psychol.*, 41:121-25. – **356**

BIRNEY, R. C., and TEEVAN, R. C. (Eds.) (1961a) *Instinct.* Princeton, N. J.: Van Nostrand. – **94**

BIRNEY, R. C., and TEEVAN, R. C. (Eds.) (1961b) *Reinforcement.* Princeton, N. J.: Van Nostrand. – **287**

BISHOP, G. H., and CLARE, M. H. (1952). Sites of origin of electric potentials in striate cortex. *J. Neurophysiol.*, 15:201-20. – **53**

BLAKE, R. R., *see* Freed and others (1955); Helson, Blake, and Mouton (1958).

BLANCHARD, M. B., *see* Jones, Conrad, and Blanchard (1932).

BLANCHARD, P. (1946) Cases illustrating psychoanalytic contributions to the problems of reading disabilities. *Psychoanal. Stud. Child,* 2. – **332**

BLANKENSHIP, A. B., and TAYLOR, H. R. (1938) Prediction of vocational proficiency in three machine operations. *J. appl. Psychol.*, 22:518-26. – **593**

BLEWETT, D. B. (1954) An experimental study of the inheritance of intelligence. *J. ment. Sci.*, 100:922-33. – **435**

BLOCK, C. H., *see* Taylor, Berry, and Block (1958).

BLOCK, J. (1957) Studies in the phenomenology of emotions. *J. abnorm. soc. Psychol.*, 54:358-63. – **166**

BLOCK, J., and THOMAS, H. (1955) Is satisfaction with the self a measure of adjustment? *J. abnorm. soc. Psychol.*, 51:254-59. – **485**

BLOCK, J., PATTERSON, V., BLOCK, J., and JACKSON, D. D. (1958) A study of the parents of schizophrenic and neurotic children. *Psychiatry,* 21:387-97. – **528**

BLOOM, B. S., *see* Stern, Stein, and Bloom (1956).

BLUM, G. S. (1954) An experimental reunion of psychoanalytic theory with perceptual vigilance and defense. *J. abnorm. soc. Psychol.*, 49:94-98. – **485**

BLUMENTHAL, J. C. (1960) *English 2600.* N. Y.: Harcourt, Brace & World. – **325**

BORCHARD, E. M. (1932) *Convicting the innocent: 65 actual errors of criminal justice.* New Haven, Conn.: Yale Univ. Press. – **602**

BORDIN, E. S. (1955) *Psychological counseling.* N. Y.: Appleton-Century-Crofts. – **550**

BORING, E. G. (1950) *A history of experimental psychology* (2nd Ed.) N. Y.: Appleton-Century-Crofts. – **29**

BORING, E. G., *see also* Alper and Boring (1944); Holway and Boring (1940), (1941); Taylor and Boring (1942).

BOSSARD, J. H. S., and BALL, E. S. (1955) Personality roles in the large family. *Child Develpm.*, 26:71-8. – **90**

BOWER, G. H. (1961) Application of a model to paired-associate learning. *Psychometrika,* 26:255-80. – **266**

BOWLBY, J. (1958) The nature of the child's role to his mother. *Int. J. Psychoanal.*, 39:350-73. – **78**

BOWMAN, P. H., *see* Guetzkow and Bowman (1946).

BOYD, E. (1952) *An introduction to human biology and anatomy for first year medical students.* Denver: Child Research Council. – **97**

BOYD, W. C. (1950) *Genetics and the races of man.* Boston: Little, Brown. – **442**

BRADWAY, K. P. (1945) An experimental study of factors associated with Stanford-Binet I.Q. changes from the preschool to junior high school. *J. genet. Psychol.*, 66:107-28. – **430**

BRADY, J. V. (1948) Ulcers in "executive" monkeys. *Scient. Amer.*, 199:95-100. – **526, 527**

BRADY, J. V., PORTER, R. W., CONRAD, D. G., and MASON, J. W. (1958) Avoidance behavior and the development of gastroduodenal ulcers. *J. exp. Anal. Behav.*, 1:69-73. – **527**

BRAMMER, L. M., *see* Barahal, Brammer, and Shostrom (1950).

BRECKINRIDGE, E. L. (1953) *Effective use of older workers.* Chicago: Wilcox & Follett. – **120**

BREHM, J. W., *see* Rosenberg and others (1960).

BRELAND, K., and BRELAND, M. (1951) A field of applied animal psychology. *Amer. Psychologist*, 6:202-04. – **264**

BRELAND, M., *see* Breland, K., and Breland, M. (1951).

BRIDGES, K. M. B. (1932) Emotional development in early infancy. *Child Develpm.*, 3:324-34. – **168**

BRIGGS, G. E., *see* Melton and Briggs (1960).

BRIGGS, L. J., and REED, H. B. (1943) The curve of retention for substance material. *J. exp. Psychol.*, 32:513-17. – **315**

BRITT, S. H. (1940) The rules of evidence; an empirical study in psychology and law. *Cornell Law Quart.*, 25:556-80. – **602**

BRODBECK, A. J., *see* Burdick and Brodbeck (1959); Davis and others (1948).

BROSS, I. D. J. (1953) *Design for decision.* N. Y.: Macmillan. – **157, 392**

BROWN, C. W., *see* Ghiselli and Brown (1955).

BROWN, J. F., and VOTH, A. C. (1937) The path of seen movement as a function of the vector field. *Amer. J. Psychol.*, 49:543-63. – **203**

BROWN, J. S. (1942) The generalization of approach responses as a function of stimulus intensity and strength of motivation. *J. comp. Psychol.*, 33:209-26. – **501**

BROWN, J. S. (1948) Gradients of approach and avoidance responses and their relation to motivation. *J. comp. physiol. Psychol.*, 41:450-65. – **502**

BROWN, J. S. (1961) *The motivation of behavior.* N. Y.: McGraw-Hill. – **149, 157**

BROWN, R. W. (1958) *Words and things.* Glencoe, Ill.: Free Press. – **344, 345, 367**

BROWN, R. W., and LENNEBERG, E. H. (1954) A study in language and cognition. *J. abnorm. soc. Psychol.*, 49:454-62. – **349, 387**

BRUCE, R. W. (1933) Conditions of transfer of training. *J. exp. Psychol.*, 16:343-61. – **318**

BRUNER, J. S. (1957) Neural mechanisms in perception. *Psychol. Rev.*, 64:340-58. – **51**

BRUNER, J. S., *see also* Austin, Bruner, and Seymour (1953); Smith, Bruner, and White (1956).

BRUNER, J. S., BUSIEK, R. D., and MINTURN, A. L. (1952) Assimilation in the immediate reproduction of visually perceived figures. *J. exp. Psychol.*, 44:151-55. – **295**

BRUNER, J. S., and GOODMAN, C. C. (1947) Value and need as organizing factors in perception. *J. abnorm. soc. Psychol.*, 42:33-44. – **214**

BRUNER, J. S., GOODNOW, J. J., and AUSTIN, G. A. (1956) *A study of thinking.* N. Y.: Wiley. – **351, 352**

BRUNER, J. S., and POSTMAN, L. J. (1949) On the perception of incongruity: a paradigm. *J. Pers.*, 18:206-23. – **213**

BRUNER, J. S., POSTMAN, L. J., and RODRIGUES, J. (1951) Expectation and the perception of color. *Amer. J. Psychol.*, 64:216-27. – **189**

BRYAN, W. L., and HARTER, N. (1897) Studies in the physiology and psychology of the telegraphic language. *Psychol. Rev.*, 4:27-53. – **268**

BUGELSKI, B. R. (1956) *The psychology of learning.* N. Y.: Holt. – **287**

BUGELSKI, B. R., and CADWALLADER, T. (1956) A reappraisal of the transfer and retroaction surface. *J. exp. Psychol.*, 52:360-66. – **318**

BUHLER, C. (1933) The social behavior of children. In Murchison, C. (Ed.) *Handbook of child psychology.* Worcester, Mass.: Clark Univ. Press, 374-416. – **106**

BURCHARD, E. M. L. (1936) Physique and psychosis: an analysis of the postulated relationship between body constitution and mental disease syndrome. *Comp. Psychol. Monogr.*, 13, No. 1. – **469**

BURDICK, E., and BRODBECK, A. J. (Eds.) (1959) *American voting behavior.* Glencoe, Ill.: Free Press. – **580**

BURGESS, E. W., and COTTRELL, L. S. (1939) *Predicting success or failure in marriage.* Englewood Cliffs, N. J.: Prentice-Hall. – **114**

BURGESS, E. W., and WALLIN, P. (1953) *Engagement and marriage.* N. Y.: Lippincott. – **115**

BURKS, B. S. (1928) The relative influence of nature and nurture upon mental development: a comparative study of foster parent-child resemblance and true parent-child resemblance. *Yearb. nat. Soc. Stud. Educ.*, 27(I):219-316. – **430, 431, 432, 434**

BURLINGHAM, D., *see* Freud and Burlingham (1943) (1944).

BURNS, B. D. (1951) Some properties of isolated cerebral cortex in the unanesthetized cat. *J. Physiol.*, 112:156-75. – **54**

BURT, C. L., and HOWARD, M. (1957) The relative influence of heredity and environment on assessments of intelligence. *Brit. J. statist. Psychol.*, 10:99-104. – **444**

BURTT, H. E. (1941) An experimental study of early childhood memory. *J. genet. Psychol.*, 58:435-39. – **290**

BUSH, R. R., and ESTES, W. K. (Eds.) (1959) *Studies in mathematical learning theory.* Stanford, Calif.: Stanford Univ. Press. – **287**

BUSH, R. R., and MOSTELLER, F. (1955) *Stochastic models for learning.* N. Y.: Wiley. – **285**

BUSIEK, R. D., *see* Bruner, Busiek, and Minturn (1952).

BUTLER, R. A. (1953) Discrimination learning by rhesus monkeys to visual-exploration motivation. *J. comp. physiol. Psychol.*, 46:95-98. – **132**

BUXTON, C. E., and ROSS, H. V. (1949) Relationship between reminiscence and type of learning technique in serial anticipation learning. *J. exp. Psychol.*, 39:41-46. – **312**

CADWALLADER, T., *see* Bugelski and Cadwallader (1956).

CAHILL, H., and HOVLAND, C. I. (1960) The role of memory in the acquisition of concepts. *J. exp. Psychol.*, 59:137-44. – **359**

CAMPBELL, A. (1943) St. Thomas Negroes—a study of personality and culture. *Psychol. Monogr.*, 55, No. 5. – **82**

CAMPBELL, A., CONVERSE, P. E., MILLER, W. E., and STOKES, D. E. (1960) *The American voter.* N. Y.: Wiley. – **572, 573, 580**

CAMPBELL, B. A., and SHEFFIELD, F. D. (1953) Relation of random activity to food deprivation. *J. comp. physiol. Psychol.*, 46:320-22. – **134**

CAMPBELL, R. K., *see* Hilgard, Campbell, and Sears (1938).

CAMPBELL, V. N., *see* Goldbeck, Campbell, and Llewellyn (1960).

CANNON, W. B. (1929) *Bodily changes in pain, hunger, fear, and rage* (2nd Ed.). N. Y.: Appleton-Century-Crofts. – **183**

CANNON, W. B. (1934) Hunger and thirst. In Murchison, C. (Ed.) *Handbook of general experimental psychology*. Worcester, Mass.: Clark Univ. Press, 247-63. – **129**

CANNON, W. B. (1939) *The wisdom of the body* (Rev. Ed.). N. Y.: Norton. – **58**

CANNON, W. B. (1945) *The way of an investigator: a scientist's experiences in medical research*. N. Y.: Norton. – **360**

CANTRIL, H. (1944) *Gauging public opinion*. Princeton, N. J.: Princeton Univ. Press. – **569, 570**

CANTRIL, H., GAUDET, H., and HERZOG, H. (1940) *The invasion from Mars*. Princeton, N. J.: Princeton Univ. Press. – **573**

CAPA, C., and PINES, M. (1957) *Retarded children can be helped*. Great Neck, N. Y.: Channel. – **416**

CARLSMITH, J. M., *see* Festinger and Carlsmith (1959).

CARMICHAEL, L. (1926) The development of behavior in vertebrates experimentally removed from the influence of external stimulation. *Psychol. Rev.*, 33:51-58. – **242**

CARMICHAEL, L. (1954a) The onset and early development of behavior. In Carmichael, L. (Ed.) *Manual of child psychology* (2nd. Ed.) N. Y.: Wiley, 60-185. – **65**

CARMICHAEL, L. (Ed.) (1954b) *Manual of child psychology*. (2nd Ed.). N. Y.: Wiley. – **94**

CARMICHAEL, L., HOGAN, H. P., and WALTER, A. A. (1932) An experimental study of the effect of language on the reproduction of visually perceived form. *J. exp. Psychol.*, 15:73-86. – **296**

CARMICHAEL, L., ROBERTS, S. O., and WESSEL, N. Y. (1937) A study of the judgment of manual expressions as presented in still and motion pictures. *J. soc. Psychol.*, 8:115-42. – **166**

CARMICHAEL, L., and SMITH, M. F. (1939) Quantified pressure stimulation and generality of response in fetal life. *J. genet. Psychol.*, 54:425-34. – **65**

CARTER, L. F., and SCHOOLER, K. (1949) Value, need, and other factors in perception. *Psychol. Rev.*, 56: 200-07. – **214**

CARTWRIGHT, D. (1946) Public opinion polls and democratic leadership. *J. soc. Issues*, 2:23-32. – **568**

CARTWRIGHT, D., *see also* Katz and others (1954).

CARTWRIGHT, D., and ZANDER, A. (Eds.) (1960) *Group dynamics: research and theory* (2nd Ed.). Evanston, Ill.: Row, Peterson. – **580**

CATTELL, J. MC K. (1903) A statistical study of eminent men. *Pop. Sci. Mon.*, 62:359-77. – **112**

CATTELL, R. B. (1942) The concept of social status. *J. Soc. Psychol.*, 15:293-308. – **583**

CATTELL, R. B. (1946) *Description and measurement of personality*. Yonkers, N. Y.: World Book. – **474**

CATTELL, R. B. (1949) *The culture free intelligence test*. Champaign, Ill.: IPAT. – **402**

CATTELL, R. B. (1950) *Personality*. N. Y.: McGraw-Hill. – **475**

CATTELL, R. B. (1957a) *Personality and motivation structure and measurement*. Yonkers, N. Y.: World Book. – **467, 475, 484, 495**

CATTELL, R. B. (1957b) *The Sixteen Personality Factor Questionnaire* (Rev. Ed.) Champaign, Ill.: IPAT. – **455**

CATTELL, R. B. (1960) The multiple abstract variance analysis equations and solutions: for nature-nurture research on continuous variables. *Psychol. Rev.*, 67:353-72. – **444**

CATTELL, R. B., KRISTY, N. F., and STICE, G. F. (1957) A first approximation to nature-nurture ratios for eleven primary personality factors in objective tests. *J. abnorm. soc. Psychol.*, 54:143-59. – **444**

CHALMERS, W. E., *see* Stagner, Chalmers, and Derber (1958).

CHANDLER, P. J., *see* Freed and others (1955).

CHANG, J. J., *see* Hild, Chang, and Tasaki (1958).

CHAPANIS, A. (1959) *Research techniques in human engineering*. Baltimore, Md.: Johns Hopkins Univ. Press. – **612**

CHAPLIN, J. P., and KRAWIEC, T. S. (1960) *Systems and theories of psychology*. N. Y.: Holt, Rinehart and Winston. – **29**

CHAPMAN, D. W. (1932) Relative effects of determinate and indeterminate *Aufgaben*. *Amer. J. Psychol.*, 44:163-74. – **211**

CHAVE, E. J., *see* Thurstone and Chave (1929).

CHERNOFF, F., and MOSES, L. E. (1959) *Elementary decision theory*. N. Y.: Wiley. – **157**

CHILD, I. L. (1954) Personality. *Annu. Rev. Psychol.*, 5:149-70. – **332, 334**

CHILD, I. L., *see also* Whiting and Child (1953).

CHILD, I. L., STORM, T., and VEROFF, J. (1958) Achievement themes in folk tales related to socialization practice. In Atkinson, J. W. (Ed.) *Motives in fantasy, action, and society*. Princeton, N. J.: Van Nostrand, 479-94. – **145**

CHOW, K. L., *see* Nissen, Chow, and Semmes (1951).

CHRISTIE, R., and JAHODA, M. (Eds.) (1954) *Studies in the scope and method of "The authoritarian personality."* Glencoe, Ill.: Free Press. – **480**

CHURCH, J. (1961) *Language and the discovery of reality*. New York: Random House. – **94**

CLARE, M. H., *see* Bishop and Clare (1952).

CLARK, B., and GRAYBIEL, A. (1949) Linear acceleration and deceleration as factors influencing nonvisual orientation during flight. *J. Aviat. Med.*, 20: 92-101. – **248**

CLARK, K. B. (1953) Desegregation: an appraisal of the evidence. *J. soc. Issues*, 9:2-76. – **603**

CLARK, K. E. (1957) *America's psychologists*. Washington, D. C.: Amer. Psychol. Assn. – **601, 602, 612**

CLARK, L. L., LANSFORD, T. G., and DALLENBACH, K. M. (1960) Repetition and associative learning. *Amer. J. Psychol.*, 73:22-40. – **266**

CLARK, R. A., *see* McClelland and others (1953).

CLAUSEN, J. A., *see* Kohn and Clausen (1956).

CLECKLEY, H. M., *see* Thigpen and Cleckley (1954), (1957).

CLEVELAND, S. E., *see* Fisher and Cleveland (1958).

COCH, L., and FRENCH, J. R. P., JR. (1948) Overcoming resistance to change. *Hum. Relat.*, 1:512-32. – **558, 559**

COHEN, A. K. (1955) *Delinquent boys: the culture of the gang*. Glencoe, Ill.: Free Press. – **108**

COHEN, J., and OGDON, D. P. (1949) Taste blindness to phenyl-thio-carbamide and related compounds. *Psychol. Bull.*, 46:490-98. – **427**

COLBY, K. M. (1960) *An introduction to psychoanalytic research*. N. Y.: Basic Books. – **546**

COLEMAN, J. C. (1956) *Abnormal psychology in modern life* (2nd Ed.). Chicago: Scott, Foresman. – **550**

COLEMAN, W., and WARD, A. W. (1955) A comparison of Davis-Eells and Kuhlmann-Finch scores of children from high and low socioeconomic status. *J. educ. Psychol.*, 46:465-69. – **403**

COLLIAS, N., *see* Allee, Collias, and Lutherman (1939).

COMBS, A. W., and SNYGG, D. (1959) *Individual behavior* (Rev. Ed.). N. Y.: Harper. – **492**

CONGER, J. J., *see* Mussen and Conger (1956).

CONRAD, D. G., *see* Brady and others (1958).

CONRAD, H. S., *see* Jones and Conrad (1933); Jones, Conrad, and Blanchard (1932).

CONRAD, H. S., and JONES, H. E. (1940) A second study of familial resemblance in intelligence. *Yearb. nat. Soc. Stud. Educ.*, 39(II):97-141. – **430**

CONVERSE, P. E., *see* Campbell and others (1960).

COOK, T. W. (1934) Massed and distributed practice in puzzle solving. *Psychol. Rev.*, 41:330-55. – **313**

COOMBS, C. H., *see* Thrall and others (1954).

COOPER, M., *see* Lemkau, Tietze, and Cooper (1941).

COTTRELL, L. S., *see* Burgess and Cottrell (1939).

COUCH, A., and KENISTON, K. (1960) Yeasayers and naysayers: agreeing response set as a personality variable. *J. abnorm. Soc. Psychol.*, 60:151-74. – **457**

COULSON, J. E., and SILBERMAN, H. F. (1960) Results of an initial experiment in automated teaching. In Lumsdaine, A. A., and Glaser, R. (Eds.) *Teaching machines and programmed learning*, 452-68. – **325**

COURTS, F. A. (1939) Relations between experimentally induced muscular tension and memorization. *J. exp. Psychol.*, 25:235-56. – **10, 11, 178**

COWLES, J. T. (1937) Food-tokens as incentives for learning by chimpanzees. *Comp. Psychol. Monogr.*, 14, No. 71. – **262**

CRAIGHILL, P. G., *see* Sarason, Mandler, and Craighill (1952).

CRAWFORD, A. B., and BURNHAM, P. S. (1946) *Forecasting college achievement*, I. New Haven, Conn.: Yale Univ. Press. – **586**

CROCKER, E. C. (1945) *Flavor*. N. Y.: McGraw-Hill. – **241**

CRONBACH, L. J. (1942) Studies of acquiescence as a factor in the true-false test. *J. educ. Psychol.*, 33:401-15. – **457**

CRONBACH, L. J. (1956) Assessment of individual differences. *Annu. Rev. Psychol.*, 7:173-96. – **461**

CRONBACH, L. J. (1960) *Essentials of psychological testing* (2nd Ed.). N. Y.: Harper. – **399, 407, 422, 456, 464, 465, 467, 587**

CROTHERS, E. J., *see* Estes, Hopkins, and Crothers (1961).

CRUIKSHANK, R. M. (1941) The development of visual size constancy in early infancy. *J. genet. Psychol.*, 58:327-51. – **192**

CULLEN, C., *see* Li, Cullen, and Jasper (1956).

CULLER, E., and GIRDEN, E. (1951) The learning curve in relation to other psychometric functions. *Amer. J. Psychol.*, 64:327-49. – **271**

CURLE, A. (1947) Transitional communities and social reconnection, Part I. *Hum. Relations*, 1:45-68. – **482**

CURLE, A., and TRIST, E. L. (1947) Transitional communities and social reconnection, Part II. *Hum. Relations*, 1:240-88. – **483**

DAHLSTROM, W. G., *see* Welsh and Dahlstrom (1956).

DAHLSTROM, W. G., and WELSH, G. S. (1960) *An MMPI handbook: a guide to use in clinical practice and research*. Minneapolis, Minn.: Univ. of Minnesota Press. – **467**

DALE, E. (1954) Union-management cooperation. In Kornhauser, A., Dubin, R., and Ross, A. M. (Eds.) *Industrial conflict*. N. Y.: McGraw-Hill, 359-72. – **597**

DALLENBACH, K. M., *see* Clark, Lansford, and Dallenbach (1960); Minami and Dallenbach (1946).

DALTON, R. H. (1961) *Personality and social interaction*. Boston: Heath. – **495**

D'AMATO, M. R., and JAGODA, H. (1960) Effects of extinction trials on discrimination reversal. *J. exp. Psychol.*, 59:254-60. – **18**

DANIEL, R. S., and LOUTTIT, C. M. (1953) *Professional problems in psychology*. Englewood Cliffs, N. J.: Prentice-Hall. – **612**

DANZINGER, L., and FRANKL, L. (1934) Zum Problem der Funktionreifung. *Z. Kinderforsch.*, 43:219-54. – **80**

DARLEY, J. G., and HAGENAH, T. (1955) *Vocational interest measurement: theory and practice*. Minneapolis: Univ. of Minnesota Press. – **612**

DAVENPORT, C. B., and LOVE, A. G. (1921) *Army anthropology (Medical Department of U.S. Army in the World War*, Vol. XV: *Statistics*, Part I). Washington: U.S. Government Printing Office. – **377**

DAVID, H. P., and VON BRACKEN, H. (Eds.) (1957) *Perspectives in personality theory*. N. Y.: Basic Books. – **495**

DAVIDSON, K. S., *see* Sarason and others (1960).

DAVIS, A., *see* Eells and others (1951).

DAVIS, A., and DOLLARD, J. (1940) *Children of bondage*. Washington: Amer. Coun. Educ. – **141**

DAVIS, A., and EELLS, K. (1953) *Davis-Eells games*. Yonkers: World Book Co. – **402**

DAVIS, H. (Ed.) (1947) *Hearing and deafness*. N. Y.: Rinehart. – **250**

DAVIS, H. V., SEARS, R. R., MILLER, H. C., and BRODBECK, A. J. (1948) Effects of cup, bottle and breast feeding on oral activities of newborn infants. *Pediatrics*, 2:549-58. – **76**

DAVIS, R. L., *see* Thrall and others (1954).

DEEG, M. E., and PATERSON, D. G. (1947) Changes in social status of occupations. *Occupations*, 25:205-08. – **583**

DEESE, J. (1958) The psychology of learning (2nd Ed.). N. Y.: McGraw-Hill. – **287**

DEESE, L., *see* Peak and Deese (1937).

DELGADO, J. M. R., ROBERTS, W. W., and MILLER, N. E. (1954) Learning motivated by electrical stimulation of the brain. *Amer. J. Physiol.*, 179:587-93. – **3**

DE MARTINO, H. A., *see* Stacey and De Martino (1958).

DEMBER, W. N. (1960) *The psychology of perception*. N. Y.: Holt, Rinehart, and Winston. – **220**

DEMBO, T., *see* Barker, Dembo, and Lewin (1941).

DEMENT, W. (1960) The effect of dream deprivation. *Science*, 131:1705-07. – **341**

DEMENT, W., and KLEITMAN, N. (1957) The relation of eye movements during sleep to dream activity: an objective method for the study of dreaming. *J. exp. Psychol.*, 53:339-46. – **341, 350**

DENNIS, M. G., *see* Dennis, W., and Dennis, M. G. (1940).

DENNIS, W. (1935) The effect of restricted practice upon the reaching, sitting, and standing of two infants. *J. genet. Psychol.*, 47:17-32. – **70**

DENNIS, W. (1954a) Bibliographies of eminent scientists. *Sci. Mon., N. Y.*, 79:180-83. – **118**

DENNIS, W. (1954b) Predicting scientific productivity in later decades from records of earlier decades. *J. Gerontol.*, 9:465-67. – **119**

DENNIS, W. (1955) Variations in productivity among creative workers. *Sci. Mon., N. Y.*, 80:277-78. – **118**

DENNIS, W. (1958) The age decrement in outstanding scientific contributions: fact or artifact? *Amer. Psychologist*, 13:457-60. – **120**

DENNIS, W., and DENNIS, M. G. (1940) The effect of cradling practices upon the onset of walking in Hopi children. *J. genet. Psychol.*, 56:77-86. – **70**

DERBER, M., *see* Stagner, Chalmers, and Derber (1958).

DE SCHWEINITZ, D. (1949) *Labor and management in a common enterprise*. Cambridge, Mass.: Harvard Univ. Press. – **597**

DEUTSCH, J. A. (1960) *The structural basis of behavior*. Chicago: Univ. of Chicago Press. – **131**

DEUTSCH, J. A., and JONES, A. D. (1959) The water-salt receptor and preference in the rat. *Nature*, 183:1472. – **131**

DEWEY, J. (1910) *How we think*. Boston: Heath. – **363**

DIMOCK, H. S. (1937) *Rediscovering the adolescent*. N. Y.: Association Press. – **101, 102**

DITTES, J. E. (1957) Galvanic skin response as a measure of patient's reaction to therapist's permissiveness. *J. abnorm. soc. Psychol.*, 55:295-303. – **540**

DOANE, B. K., see Heron, Doane, and Scott (1956).

DOANE, B. K., MAHATOO, W., HERON, W., and SCOTT, T. H. (1959) Changes in perceptual function after isolation. *Canad. J. Psychol.*, 13:210-19. – **56**

DOLLARD, J., see Davis and Dollard (1940).

DOLLARD, J., and AULD, F., JR. (1959) *Scoring human motives: a manual*. New Haven, Conn.: Yale Univ. Press. – **537, 538, 542**

DOLLARD, J., and MILLER, N. E. (1950) *Personality and psychotherapy*. N. Y.: McGraw-Hill. – **481, 495, 538, 550**

DOLLARD, J., and others (1939) *Frustration and aggression*. New Haven, Conn.: Yale Univ. Press. – **140, 521**

DORÉ, L. R., and HILGARD, E. R. (1937) Spaced practice and the maturation hypothesis. *J. Psychol.*, 4:245-59. – **312**

DROLETTE, M. E., see Funkenstein, King, and Drolette (1957).

DUBIN, R., see Kornhauser, Dubin, and Ross (1954).

DU BOIS, P. H. (Ed.) (1947) The classification program. *AAF Aviat. Psychol. Program Res. Rep.*, No. 2. – **395, 398, 400**

DUFFY, E. (1951) The concept of energy-mobilization. *Psychol. Rev.*, 58:30-40. – **167**

DUFORT, R. H., see Kimble and Dufort (1956).

DUNBAR, F. (1954) *Emotions and bodily changes* (4th Ed.). N. Y.: Columbia Univ. Press. – **183**

DUNBAR, F. (1955) *Mind and body: psychosomatic medicine* (2nd Ed.). N. Y.: Random House. – **179**

DUNCKER, K. (1945) On problem-solving (Trans. by Lynne S. Lees). *Psychol. Monogr.*, 58, No. 270. – **356**

DUNN, W. L., JR. (1954) Visual discrimination of schizophrenic subjects as a function of stimulus meaning. *J. Pers.*, 23:48-64. – **334**

DUSENBURY, D., and KNOWER, F. H. (1939). Experimental studies of the symbolism of voice and action: II. A study of the specificity of meaning in abstract tonal symbols. *Quart. J. Speech*, 25:67-75. – **166**

DVORINE, I. (1953) *Dvorine Pseudo-Chromatic plates* (2nd Ed.). Baltimore: Scientific Publishing. – **228**

DYMOND, R. F., see Rogers and Dymond (1954).

EBBINGHAUS, H. (1885) *Memory* (Trans. H. A. Ruger and C. E. Bussenius). N. Y.: Teachers College (1913). – **272, 281, 292, 310**

ECCLES, J. C. (1953) *The neurophysiological basis of the mind; the principles of neurophysiology*. N. Y.: Oxford Univ. Press. – **61**

ECCLES, J. C. (1958) The physiology of imagination. *Scient. Amer.* 199, 135-46. – **40, 52**

EDWARDS, A. L. (1954) *Edwards Personal Preference Schedule* (Manual). N. Y.: Psychological Corporation. – **142, 455, 485**

EDWARDS, A. L. (1957) *The social desirability variable in personality assessment and research*. N. Y.: Dryden. – **457, 467**

EDWARDS, A. L. (1960) *Experimental design in psychological research* (Rev. Ed.). N. Y.: Holt, Rinehart and Winston. – **392**

EELLS, K., see Davis and Eells (1953).

EELLS, K., DAVIS, A., HAVIGHURST, R. J., HERRICK, V. E.,

and TYLER, R. W. (1951) *Intelligence and cultural differences*. Chicago: Univ. of Chicago Press. – **402**

EINDHOVEN, J. E., and VINACKE, W. E. (1952) Creative processes in painting. *J. gen. Psychol.*, 47:139-64. – **363**

EKMAN, G. (1951) On the number and definition of dimensions in Kretschmer's and Sheldon's constitutional systems. In *Essays in psychology dedicated to David Katz*. Uppsala: Almquist & Wiksells, 72-104. – **469**

ELDERSVELD, S., see Katz and others (1954).

ELKIN, F., and WESTLEY, W. A. (1955) The myth of adolescent culture. *Amer. Sociol. Rev.*, 20:680-84. – **95**

ELLEN, P. (1956) The compulsive nature of abnormal fixations. *J. comp. physiol. Psychol.*, 49:309-17. – **509**

ELLENBERGER, H. F., see May, Angel, and Ellenberger (1958).

ENGLISH, H. B. (1943) *The psychology of learning: a study guide* (mimeographed). Columbus, O.: Butler Letter Service. – **292**

ENGLISH, H. B., and ENGLISH, A. C. (1958) *A comprehensive dictionary of psychological and psychoanalytical terms*. N. Y.: Longmans, Green. – **613**

ERICKSEN, S. C. (1942) Variability in attack in massed and distributed practice. *J. exp. Psychol.*, 31:339-45. – **313**

ERIKSEN, C. W. (1960) Discrimination and learning without awareness: a methodological survey and evaluation. *Psychol. Rev.*, 67:279-300. – **224**

ERIKSON, E. H. (1950) *Childhood and society*. N. Y.: Norton. – **536**

ERIKSON, E. H. (1956) The problem of ego identity. *J. Amer. psychoanal. Assn.*, 4:56-121. – **451**

ERIKSON, E. H. (1959) Identity and the life cycle. *Psychol. Issues*, 1, No. 1. – **450, 478, 479**

ESPENSCHADE, A. (1940) Motor performance in adolescence. *Monogr. Soc. Res. Child Develpm.*, 5, No. 24. – **101**

ESTES, W. K. (1944) An experimental study of punishment. *Psychol. Monogr.*, 57, No. 263. – **328, 330**

ESTES, W. K. (1949) A study of motivating conditions necessary for secondary reinforcement. *J. exp. Psychol.*, 39:306-10. – **263**

ESTES, W. K. (1958) Stimulus-response theory of drive. In Jones, M. R. (Ed.) *Nebraska Symposium on motivation*. Lincoln, Nebr.: Univ. of Nebraska Press. – **150**

ESTES, W. K. (1959) *The statistical approach to learning theory*. In Koch, S. (Ed.) *Psychology: a study of a science*, Vol. 2. N. Y.: McGraw-Hill. – **282, 284, 285**

ESTES, W. K. (1960) Learning theory and the new "mental chemistry." *Psychol. Rev.*, 67:207-23. – **266, 306**

ESTES, W. K., see also Bush and Estes (1959).

ESTES, W. K., HOPKINS, B. L., and CROTHERS, E. J. (1960) All-or-none and conservation effects in the learning and retention of paired associates. *J. exp. Psychol.*, 60:329-39. – **266**

EVANS, J. L., GLASER, R., and HOMME, L. E. (1960) A preliminary investigation of variation in the properties of verbal learning sequences of the "teaching machine" type. In Lumsdaine, A. A., and Glaser, R. *Teaching machines and programmed learning*. Washington, D. C.: National Educ. Assn., 446-51. – **325**

EVANS, L. T., see Abramson and Evans (1954).

EVANS, R. M. (1948) *An introduction to color*. N. Y.: Wiley. – **228, 250**

EYSENCK, H. J. (1952) The effects of psychotherapy: an evaluation. *J. consult. Psychol.*, 16:319-24. – **547**

EYSENCK, H. J. (1959) *The structure of human personality*. London: Methuen. – **467**

FALSTEIN, E. I., *see* Johnson and others (1941).

FARBER, I. E. (1954) Anxiety as a drive state. In Jones, M. R. (Ed.). *Nebraska symposium on motivation*. Lincoln, Nebr.: Univ. of Nebraska Press, 1-46. – **333**

FARBER, I. E. (1955) The role of motivation in verbal learning and performance. *Psychol. Bull.*, 52:311-27. – **332**

FARBER, I. E., HARLOW, H. F., and WEST, L. J. (1957) Brainwashing, conditioning, and DDD. *Sociometry*, 20:271-85. – **578**

FAUST, W. L., *see* Taylor and Faust (1952).

FELEKY, A. (1922) *Feelings and emotions*. N. Y.: Pioneer Press. – **165**

FELIX, R. H., and KRAMER, M. (1953) Extent of the problem of mental disorders. *Ann. Amer. Acad. pol. soc. Sci.*, 286:5-14. – **528**

FENICHEL, O. (1945) *The psychoanalytic theory of neurosis*. N. Y.: Norton. – **523**

FERGUSON, L. W. (1952) *Personality measurement*. N. Y.: McGraw-Hill. – **467**

FESHBACH, S., *see* Janis and Feshbach (1953).

FESHBACH, S., and SINGER, R. (1957) The effects of fear arousal and suppression of fear upon social perception. *J. abnorm. soc. Psychol.*, 55:283-88. – **553**

FESTINGER, L. (1942) Wish, expectation, and group standards as affecting level of aspiration. *J. abnorm. soc. Psychol.*, 37:184-200. – **152**

FESTINGER, L. (1957) *A theory of cognitive dissonance*. Evanston, Ill.: Row, Peterson. – **152, 153, 157**

FESTINGER, L. (1961) The psychological effects of insufficient rewards. *Amer. Psychologist*, 16:1-11. – **152**

FESTINGER, L., and CARLSMITH, J. M. (1959) Cognitive consequences of forced compliance. *J. abnorm. soc. Psychol.*, 58:203-10. – **558**

FESTINGER, L., and KATZ, DANIEL (Eds.) (1953) *Research methods in the behavioral sciences*. N. Y.: Dryden. – **29**

FIELDS, V., *see* Lorr and Fields (1954).

FINDLAY, A. (1948) *A hundred years of chemistry* (2nd Ed.). London: Duckworth. – **361**

FISHER, C. (1954) Dreams and perception: the role of preconscious and primary modes of perception in dream formation. *J. Amer. psychoanal. Assn.*, 2:389-445. – **340**

FISHER, S., and CLEVELAND, S. E. (1958) *Body image and personality*. Princeton, N. J.: Van Nostrand. – **461, 493**

FISKE, D. W., *see* Vielley and Fiske (1951).

FISKE, D. W., and MADDI, S. R. (Eds.) (1961) *Functions of varied experience*. Homewood, Ill.: Dorsey Press. – **94**

FITCH, F. G., *see* Hull and others (1940).

FLAHERTY, B. E. (Ed.) (1961) *Psychophysiological aspects of space flight*. N. Y.: Columbia Univ. Press. – **612**

FOLEY, J. P., JR., *see* Anastasi and Foley (1958).

FOLLEY, J. D., JR., *see* Miller, Folley, and Smith (1953).

FOORD, E. N., *see* Hebb and Foord (1945).

FORD, C. E., JONES, K. W., MILLER, O. J., MITTWOCH, U., PENROSE, L. S., and RIDLER, M. (1959a) The chromosomes in a patient showing both Mongolism and the Klinefelter syndrome. *Lancet*, I, 709-10. – **425**

FORD, C. E., JONES, K. W., POLANI, P. E., DE AMEIDA, J. C., and BRIGGS, J. H. (1959b) A sex-chromosome anomaly in a case of gonadal dysgenesis (Turner's syndrome). *Lancet*, I, 711-13. – **425**

FORD, C. S., and BEACH, F. A. (1951) *Patterns of sexual behavior*, N. Y.: Harper. – **100**

FORD, E. C., *see* Hathaway and Ford (1960).

FORLANO, G. (1936) School learning with various methods of practice and rewards. *Teach. Coll. Contr. Educ.*, No. 688. – **306**

FORM, W. H. (1946) Toward an occupational social psychology. *J. soc. Psychol.*, 24:85-99. – **583**

FORM, W. H., *see also* Miller and Form (1951).

FRANCK, K., and ROSEN, E. (1949) A projective test of masculinity and femininity. *J. consult. Psychol.*, 13:247-56. – **114**

FRANK, J. D. (1959) The dynamics of the psychotherapeutic relationship. *Psychiatry*, 22:17-39. – **542**

FRANK, J. D., *see also* Powdermaker and Frank (1953).

FRANKL, L., *see* Danzinger and Frankl (1934).

FRANZ, S. I. (1933) *Persons one and three*. N. Y.: McGraw-Hill. – **489**

FRANZBLAU, R. N. (1935) Race differences in mental and physical traits studied in different environments. *Arch. Psychol.*, N. Y., No. 177. – **442**

FREDENBERG, N. C. (1956) Paired associates learning as a function of anxiety level and shock. *Diss. Abstr.*, 16, 1950. – **134**

FREED, A., CHANDLER, P. J., BLAKE, R. R., and MOUTON, J. S. (1955) Stimulus and background factors in sign violation. *J. Pers.*, 23:499. – **559**

FREEMAN, F. N., *see* Wood and Freeman (1932); Newman, Freeman, and Holzinger (1937).

FRENCH, E. G. (1958) Effects of the interaction of motivation and feedback on performance. In Atkinson, J. W. (ed.) *Motives in fantasy, action, and society*. N. Y.: Van Nostrand, 400-08. – **143**

FRENCH, J. R. P., JR., *see* Coch and French (1948).

FRENCH, T. M. (1952) *The integration of behavior*. Vol. 1. Chicago, Ill.: Univ. of Chicago Press. – **174**

FRENCH, T. M., *see also* Alexander and French (1946).

FRENKEL-BRUNSWIK, E. (1939) Mechanisms of self-deception. *J. soc. Psychol.*, 10:409-20. – **514**

FRENKEL-BRUNSWIK, E. (1942) Motivation and behavior. *Genet. Psychol. Monogr.*, 26:121-265. – **142**

FRENKEL-BRUNSWIK, E. (1949) Intolerance of ambiguity as an emotional and perceptual personality variable. *J. Pers.*, 18:108-43. – **214**

FRENKEL-BRUNSWIK, E., *see also* Adorno and others (1950).

FRENKEL-BRUNSWIK, E., and SANFORD, R. N. (1945) Some personality factors in anti-Semitism. *J. Psychol.*, 20:271-91. – **562**

FREUD, A. (1937) *The ego and the mechanisms of defense*. London: Hogarth Press. – **521**

FREUD, A., and BURLINGHAM, D. (1943) *War and children*. N. Y.: Internat. Univ. Press. – **80**

FREUD, A., and BURLINGHAM, D. (1944) *Infants without families*. N. Y.: Internat. Univ. Press. – **80**

FREUD, S. (1913) On the beginning of treatment. In Freud, S. (1958), 123-44. – **542**

FREUD, S. (1927) *The ego and the id*. London: Hogarth Press. – **484**

FREUD, S. (1938) *The basic writings of Sigmund Freud*. (Ed. A. A. Brill) N. Y.: Modern Library.

FREUD, S. (1958) The case of Schreber, papers on technique, and other works. *The standard edition of the complete psychological works of Sigmund Freud*, Vol. XII. London: Hogarth Press. – **542**

FRIEDMAN, G. A., *see* McClelland and Friedman (1953).

FROMM, E. (1947) *Man for himself*. N. Y.: Rinehart. – **523**

FROMM, E. (1949) The Oedipus myth. In Anshen, R. N. (Ed.) *The family*. N. Y.: Harper, 334-58. – **154**

FRYER, D. H., and HENRY, E. R. (Eds.) (1950) *Handbook of applied psychology* (2 vols.). N. Y.: Rinehart. – **462, 612**

FULLER, J. L., and THOMPSON, W. R. (1960) *Behavior genetics*. New York: Wiley. – **446**

FUNKENSTEIN, D. H. (1955) The physiology of fear and anger. *Sci. Amer.*, 192:74-80. – **165**

FUNKENSTEIN, D. H., KING, S. H., and DROLETTE, M. E. (1957) *Mastery of stress*. Cambridge, Mass.: Harvard Univ. Press. – **165**

GALAMBOS, R. (1961) A glia-neural theory of brain function. *Proc. nat. Acad. Sciences*, 47:129-36. – **55**

GALANTER, E. (Ed.) (1959) *Automatic teaching: the state of the art*. N. Y.: Wiley. – **320, 355**

GALANTER, E., see also Miller, Galanter, and Pribram (1960).

GALLOWAY, A., see Wallach and Galloway (1946).

GALTON, F. (1889) Natural inheritance. London: Macmillan. – **377**

GARDNER, E. (1958) *Fundamentals of neurology* (3rd Ed.). Philadelphia, Pa.: Saunders. – **61**

GARDNER, E. F., see Kelley and others (1953).

GARDNER, R. W. (1959) Cognitive control principles and perceptual behavior. *Bull. Menninger Clin.*, 23:241-48. – **489**

GARMEZY, N. (1952) Stimulus differentiation by schizophrenic and normal subjects under conditions of reward and punishment. *J. Pers.*, 20:253-76. – **334**

GARRETT, H. E. (1940) Variability in learning under massed and spaced practice. *J. exp. Psychol.*, 26:547-67. – **313**

GATES, A. I. (1917) Recitation as a factor in memorizing. *Arch. Psychol.*, N. Y., No. 40. – **305**

GATES, G. S. (1923) An experimental study of the growth of social perception. *J. educ. Psychol.*, 14:449-61. – **169**

GATES, G. S. (1926) An observational study of anger. *J. exp. Psychol.*, 9:325-36. – **177**

GAUDET, H., see Cantril, Gaudet, and Herzog (1940).

GAUTIER, M., see Lejeune, Gautier, and Turpin (1959).

GELDARD, F. A. (1953) *The human senses*. N. Y.: Wiley. – **250**

GERARD, R. W. (1953) What is memory? *Sci. Amer.*, 190:118-26. – **54, 297**

GESELL, A., and THOMPSON, H. (1941) Twins T and C from infancy to adolescence: a biogenetic study of individual differences by the method of co-twin control. *Genet. Psychol. Monogr.*, 24:3-122. – **72**

GHISELLI, E. E., and BROWN, C. W. (1955) *Personnel and industrial psychology* (2nd Ed.). N. Y.: McGraw-Hill. – **612**

GIBSON, E. J. (1940) A systematic application of the concepts of generalization and discrimination to verbal learning. *Psychol. Rev.*, 47:196-229. – **274**

GIBSON, E. J., and WALK, R. D. (1956) The effect of prolonged exposure to visually presented patterns on learning to discriminate them. *J. comp. physiol. Psychol.*, 49:239-42. – **24**

GIBSON, E. J., and WALK, R. D. (1960) The "visual cliff." *Sci. Amer.*, 202, No. 4, 64-71. – **209**

GIBSON, J. J. (1929) The reproduction of visually perceived forms. *J. exp. Psychol.*, 12:1-39. – **295**

GIBSON, J. J. (1959) Perception as a function of stimulation. In Koch, S. (Ed.) *Psychology: a study of a science*. Vol. 1. N. Y.: McGraw-Hill, 456-501. – **210**

GLADWYN, T., see Masland, Sarason, and Gladwyn (1958).

GLASER, N. M., see Maier, Glaser, and Klee (1940).

GLASER, R., see Evans, Glaser, and Homme (1959); Lumsdaine and Glaser (1960).

GLUECK, E. T. (1956) Status of Glueck prediction studies. *J. crim. Law, Criminol., police Sci.*, 47, No. 1. – **108**

GOLDBECK, R. A. (1960) *The effect of response mode and learning material difficulty on automated instruction*. Pittsburgh, Pa.: Amer. Inst. Res. (Mimeographed.) – **325**

GOLDBECK, R. A., CAMPBELL, V. N., and LLEWELLYN, J. E. (1960) *Further experimental evidence on response modes in automated instruction*. Pittsburgh, Pa.: Amer. Inst. Res. (Mimeographed.) – **325**

GOLDHAMER, H., and MARSHALL, A. W. (1953) *Psychosis and civilization*. Glencoe, Ill.: Free Press. – **529**

GOLDSTEIN, K. (1939) *The organism: a holistic approach to biology derived from pathological data in man*. N. Y.: American Book Co. – **144**

GOLDSTEIN, K., and SCHEERER, M. (1941) Abstract and concrete behavior: an experimental study with special tests. *Psychol. Monogr.*, 53, No. 239. – **350**

GONICK, M. R., see Barker and others (1953).

GOODENOUGH, F. (1931) Anger in young children. *Univ. Minn. Inst. Child Welf. Monogr. Ser.*, No. 9. – **179**

GOODENOUGH, F. (1932) Expression of the emotions in a blind-deaf child. *J. abnorm. soc. Psychol.*, 27: 328-33. – **168**

GOODMAN, C. C., see Bruner and Goodman (1947).

GOODNOW, J. J., see Bruner, Goodnow, and Austin (1956).

GOUGH, H. G. (1957) *California Psychological Inventory*. Palo Alto, Calif.: Consulting Psychologists Press. – **114, 365**

GRAHAM, C. H., and HSIA, Y. (1958) The discrimination of a normal and a color-blind eye in the same person. *Proc. Amer. Phil. Soc.*, 102:168-73. – **231**

GRANIT, R. (1947) *Sensory mechanisms of the retina*. N. Y.: Oxford Univ. Press. – **233**

GRANT, D. A. (1951) Perceptual vs. analytical responses to the number concept of a Weigl-type card sorting test. *J. exp. Psychol.*, 41: 23-9. – **346**

GRAY, H. (1948) Predictions of adult stature. *Child Developmt.*, 19:167-75. – **100**

GRAY, J. S. (1954) *Psychology applied to human affairs* (2nd Ed.). N. Y.: McGraw-Hill. – **612**

GRAYBIEL, A., see Clark and Graybiel (1949).

GREENSPOON, J. (1955) The reinforcing effect of two spoken sounds on the frequency of two responses. *Amer. J. Psychol.*, 68:409-16. – **316**

GUEST, L. (1948) The public's attitudes toward psychologists. *Amer. Psychologist*, 3:135-39. – **598**

GUETZKOW, H. (1951) An analysis of the operation of set in problem-solving behavior. *J. gen. Psychol.*, 45:219-44. – **355**

GUETZKOW, H., and BOWMAN, P. H. (1946) *Men and hunger*. Elgin, Ill.: Brethren Publishing House. – **508**

GUILFORD, J. P. (1940) An inventory of factors STDCR. Beverly Hills, Calif.: Sheridan Supply Co. – **471**

GUILFORD, J. P. (Ed.) (1950) *Fields of psychology* (2nd Ed.). N. Y.: Van Nostrand. – **612**

GUILFORD, J. P. (1954) *Psychometric methods* (2nd Ed.) N. Y.: McGraw-Hill. – **392**

GUILFORD, J. P. (1959a) *Personality*. N. Y.: McGraw-Hill. – **452, 467, 495**

GUILFORD, J. P. (1959b) Traits of creativity. In Anderson, H. H. (Ed.) *Creativity and its cultivation*. N. Y.: Harper, 142-61. – **364**

GUILFORD, J. P. (1961) Factorial angles to psychology. *Psychol. Rev.*, 68:1-20. – **410**

GUMP, P. V., and KOUNIN, J. S. (1959) Issues raised by ecological and "classical" research efforts. *Merrill-Palmer Q. Beh. Develop.*, 6:148-52. – **476**

GUTTMAN, L. (1950) The basis for scalogram analysis. In Stouffer, S. A., and others, *Measurement and prediction*. Princeton, N. J.: Princeton Univ. Press, 60-90. – **566**

HADAMARD, J. (1945) *The psychology of invention in the mathematical field*. Princeton, N. J.: Princeton Univ. Press. – **361**

HAGEN, E., *see* Thorndike and Hagen (1961).

HAGENAH, T., *see* Darley and Hagenah (1955).

HAIRE, M. (1955) Role-perceptions in labor-management relations: an experimental approach. *Industr. Labor Relat. Rev.*, 8:204-16. – **597**

HAIRE, M. (1956) *Psychology in management*. N. Y.: McGraw-Hill. – **612**

HALL, C. S. (1934) Emotional behavior in the rat: I. Defecation and urination as measures of individual differences in emotionality. *J. comp. Psychol.*, 18:385-403. – **162**

HALL, C. S. (1951) The genetics of behavior. In Stevens, S. S. (Ed.) *Handbook of experimental psychology*. N. Y.: Wiley, 304-29. – **426**

HALL, C. S. (1954) *A primer of Freudian psychology*. Cleveland: World Publ. Co. – **478, 495**

HALL, C. S., *see also* Witt and Hall (1949).

HALL, C. S., and LINDZEY, G. (1957) *Theories of personality*. N. Y.: Wiley. – **495**

HALL, J. F. (1961) *Psychology of motivation*. Chicago: Lippincott. – **157**

HALL, M., *see* Hull and others (1940).

HAMBURGER, V., *see* Willier and others (1955).

HAMILTON, M. A., *see* Laidlaw and Hamilton (1937).

HAMMOCK, J., *see* Holt and Hammock (1961).

HANLEY, C. (1961) Social desirability and response bias in the MMPI. *J. consult. Psychol.*, 25:13-20. – **457**

HARDY, M. (1934) Observations on the innervation of the macula sacculi in man. *Anat. Rec.*, 59:403-18. – **248**

HARLOW, H. F. (1949) The formation of learning sets. *Psychol. Rev.*, 56:51-65. – **277**

HARLOW, H. F. (1958) On the meaning of love. *Amer. Psychologist*, 13:673-85. – **77**

HARLOW, H. F. (1961) *The heterosexual affectional system*. Address, Amer. Psychological Assn., New York, Sept. 3. – **74**

HARLOW, H. F., *see also* Farber, Harlow, and West (1957).

HARLOW, H. F., HARLOW, M. K., and MEYER, D. R. (1950) Learning motivated by a manipulation drive. *J. exp. Psychol.*, 40:228-34. – **132**

HARLOW, H. F., and ZIMMERMAN, R. R. (1959) Affectional responses in the infant monkey. *Science*, 130:421-32. – **77**

HARLOW, M. K., *see* Harlow, H. F., Harlow, M. K., and Meyer (1950).

HARMS, E. (Ed.) (1960) Fundamentals of psychology: the psychology of thinking. *Ann. N. Y. Acad. Sci.*, 91:1-158. – **367**

HARPER, R. A. (1959) *Psychoanalysis and psychotherapy: 36 systems*. Englewood Cliffs, N. J.: Prentice-Hall. – **536, 550**

HARRELL, M. S., *see* Harrell, T. W., and Harrell, M. S. (1945).

HARRELL, T. W. (1958) *Industrial psychology* (2nd Ed.) N. Y.: Rinehart. – **612**

HARRELL, T. W., and HARRELL, M. S. (1945) Army General Classification Test scores for civilian occupations. *Educ. psychol. Meas.*, 5:229-39. – **439**

HARRIMAN, A. E., *see* Ross and Harriman (1949).

HARRIS, I. D. (1961) *Emotional blocks to learning*. N. Y.: Free Press of Glencoe. – **335**

HARTER, N., *see* Bryan and Harter (1897).

HARTLEY, E. L., *see* Maccoby, Newcomb, and Hartley (1958).

HARTMAN, T., *see* Leibowitz and Hartman (1959), (1960).

HARTMANN, H. (1958) *Ego psychology and the problem of adaptation*. N. Y.: Internat. Univ. Press. – **484**

HARVEY, E. N. (1922) Some recent experiments on the nature of the nervous impulse. *J. nerv. ment. Dis.*, 55:503-05. – **35**

HASKELL, R. I. (1923) *A statistical study of the comparative results produced by teaching derivation in the ninth-grade Latin classes and in the ninth-grade English classes of non-Latin pupils in four Philadelphia high schools*. (Ph.D. dissertation.) Philadelphia: Univ. of Pennsylvania. – **319**

HASTINGS, W. W. (1902) *A manual for physical measurements*. Springfield, Mass. – **97**

HASTORF, A. H., RICHARDSON, S. A., and DORNBUSCH, S. M. (1958) The problem of relevance in the study of person perception. In Tagiuri, R., and Petrullo, L. (Eds.) *Person perception and interpersonal behavior*. Stanford, Calif.: Stanford Univ. Press, 54-62. – **554**

HATHAWAY, M. L. (1957) Heights and weights of children and youth in the United States. *U.S. Dept. Agr. Home Econ. Res. Rpt. 2.* – **97, 100**

HATHAWAY, M. L. and FORD, E. D. (1960) Heights and weights of adults in the United States. Washington, D. C.: *U.S. Dept. of Agr., Home Economics Res. Rpt. 10.* – **100**

HAVEMANN, E., and WEST, P. S. (1952) *They went to college*. N. Y.: Harcourt, Brace & World. – **582, 583**

HAVIGHURST, R. J., *see* Eells and others (1951).

HAYES, C. (1951) *The ape in our house*. N. Y.: Harper. – **70**

HEAD, H. (1926) *Aphasia and kindred disorders of speech* (2 vols.). London: Cambridge Univ. Press. – **350**

HEATH, R. G. (1954) *Studies in schizophrenia*. Cambridge, Mass.: Harvard Univ. Press. – **528**

HEBB, D. O. (1946) On the nature of fear. *Psychol. Rev.*, 53:259-76. – **169**

HEBB, D. O. (1949) *The organization of behavior*. N. Y.: Wiley. – **61, 194, 210**

HEBB, D. O. (1955) Drives and the CNS (conceptual nervous system). *Psychol. Rev.*, 62:243-54. – **54**

HEBB, D. O. (1958) *A textbook of psychology*. Philadelphia, Pa.: Saunders. – **54, 55**

HEBB, D. O., and FOORD, E. N. (1945) Errors of visual recognition and the nature of the trace. *J. exp. Psychol.*, 35:335-48. – **295**

HECHT, S., and SHLAER, S. (1938) An adaptometer for measuring human dark adaptation. *J. opt. Soc. Amer.*, 28:269-75. – **228**

HECHT, S., SCHLAER, S., and PIRENNE, M. H. (1942) Energy, quanta, and vision. *J. gen. Physiol.*, 25:819-40. – **224**

HECHT, S., and WILLIAMS, R. E. (1922-23) The visibility of monochromatic radiation and the absorption spectrum of visual purple. *J. gen. Physiol.*, 5:1-34. – **232**

HEGGE, T. G. (1944) Occupational status of higher grade defectives in the present emergency. *Amer. J ment. Def.*, 49:86-98. – **416**

HEIDBREDER, E. (1933) *Seven psychologies*. N. Y.: Appleton-Century-Crofts. – **29**

HEIDBREDER, E., BENSLEY, M., and IVY, M. (1948) The attainment of concepts: IV. Regularities and levels. *J. Psychol.*, 25:299-329. – **346**

HEIDER, F. (1958) *The psychology of interpersonal relations*. N. Y.: Wiley. – **157, 554, 555, 608**

HEIDER, F., and SIMMEL, M. (1944) An experimental study of apparent behavior. *Amer. J. Psychol.*, 57: 243-59. – **216**

HELSON, H., BLAKE, R. R., and MOUTON, J. S. (1958) Petition-signing as adjustment to situational and personal factors. *J. soc. Psychol.*, 1958, 48:3-10. – **559**

HENDRICKSON, G., and SCHROEDER, W. H. (1941) Transfer of training in learning to hit a submerged target. *J. educ. Psychol.*, 32:205-13. – **317**

HENNEY, K. (1938) *Principles of radio* (3rd Ed.). N. Y.: Wiley. – **237**

HENRY, E. R., *see* Fryer and Henry (1950).

HENRY, N. B. (Ed.) (1944) Adolescence. *Yearb. nat. Soc. Stud. Educ.*, 43(I). – **122**

HENRY, W. E. (1956) *The analysis of fantasy*. N. Y.: Wiley. – **459, 467**

HERON, W., *see* Bexton, Heron, and Scott (1954); Doane and others (1959).

HERON, W., DOANE, B. K., and SCOTT, T. H. (1956) Visual disturbance after prolonged perceptual isolation. *Canad. J. Psychol.*, 10:13-16. – **56**

HERON, W. T. (1935) The inheritance of maze learning ability in rats. *J. comp. Psychol.*, 19:77-89. – **426**

HERON, W. T. (1941) The inheritance of brightness and dullness in maze learning ability in the rat. *J. genet. Psychol.*, 59:41-49. – **426**

HERRICK, V. E., *see* Eells and others (1951).

HERRON, E. W., *see* Holtzman and others (1961).

HERTZMAN, M., *see* Witkin and others (1954).

HERZOG, H., *see* Cantril, Gaudet, and Herzog (1940).

HESS, R. D. (1955) Controlling cultural influence in mental testing: an experimental test. *J. educ. Res.*, 49:53-58. – **403**

HESS, E. H. (1956) Space perception in the chick. *Scient. Amer.* 195:71-80. – **67**

HESS, E. H. (1959) Imprinting. *Science,* 130:133-141. – **67**

HESS, E. H., *see also* Ramsay and Hess (1954).

HEYNS, R. (1958) *The psychology of personal adjustment*. N. Y.: Holt. – **550**

HILD, W., CHANG, J. J., and TASAKI, I. (1958) Electrical responses of astrocytic glia from the mammalian central nervous system cultivated *in vitro*. *Experientia* 14:211-20. – **55**

HILGARD, E. R. (1952) Experimental approaches to psychoanalysis. In Pumpian-Mindlin, E. (Ed.) *Psychoanalysis as science*. Stanford, Calif.: Stanford Univ. Press, 3-45. – **545**

HILGARD, E. R. (1956) *Theories of learning* (2nd Ed.). N. Y.: Appleton-Century-Crofts. – **265, 287, 304**

HILGARD, E. R. (1961) Hypnosis and experimental psychodynamics. In Brosin, H. (Ed.) *Lectures on experimental psychiatry*. Pittsburgh, Pa.: Univ. of Pittsburgh Press, 193-212. – **27**

HILGARD, E. R., *see also* Doré and Hilgard (1937).

HILGARD, E. R., CAMPBELL, R. K., and SEARS, W. N. (1938) Conditioned discrimination: the effect of

knowledge of stimulus-relationships. *Amer. J. Psychol.*, 51:498-506. – **257**

HILGARD, E. R., JONES, L. V., and KAPLAN, S. J. (1951) Conditioned discrimination as related to anxiety. *J. exp. Psychol.*, 42:94-9. – **334**

HILGARD, E. R., and MARQUIS, D. G. (1940) *Conditioning and learning*. N. Y.: Appleton-Century-Crofts. – **267**

HILGARD, E. R., SAIT, E. M., and MAGARET, G. A. (1940) Level of aspiration as affected by relative standing in an experimental social group. *J. exp. Psychol.*, 27:411-21. – **151**

HILGARD, J. R. (1933) The effect of early and delayed practice on memory and motor performances studied by the method of co-twin control. *Genet. Psychol. Monogr.*, 14, No. 6. – **73, 74**

HILGARD, J. R. (1951) Sibling rivalry and social heredity. *Psychiatry*, 14:375-85. – **90**

HILGARD, J. R., and NEWMAN, M. F. (1959) Anniversaries in mental illness. *Psychiatry*, 22:113-21. – **528**

HILGARD, J. R., and NEWMAN, M. F. (1961) Evidence for functional genesis in mental illness: schizophrenia, depressive psychoses, and psychoneuroses. *J. nerv. ment. Dis.*, 132:3-16. – **528**

HILL, W. F. (1956) Activity as an autonomous drive. *J. comp. physiol. Psychol.*, 49:15-19. – **132**

HIMMELWEIT, H. T., OPPENHEIM, A. N., and VINCE, P. (1958) *Television and the child*. N. Y.: Oxford Univ. Press. – **574**

HINCKLEY, E. D. (1932) The influence of individual opinion on construction of an attitude scale. *J. soc. Psychol.*, 3:283-96. – **565**

HINDE, R. A. (1959) Some recent trends in ethology. In Koch, S. (Ed.) *Psychology, a study of a science*, vol. 2. N. Y.: McGraw-Hill, 561-610. – **67**

HIRSCH, N. D. M. (1926) A study of natio-racial mental differences. *Genet. Psychol. Monogr.*, 1:231-406. – **442**

HIRSCH, J., and BOUDREAU, J. C. (1958) Studies in experimental behavior genetics: I. The heritability of phototaxis in a population of *Drosophila melanogaster*. *J. comp. physiol. Psychol.*, 51:647-51. – **428**

HIRSH, I. J. (1952) *The measurement of hearing*. N. Y.: McGraw-Hill. – **250**

HOCH, P. H. (1955) Experimental psychiatry. *Amer. J. Psychiat.*, 111:787-90. – **528**

HOELZEL, F. (1927) Central factors in hunger. *Amer. J. Physiol.*, 82:665-71. – **128**

HOFFER, A., and OSMOND, H. (1959) The adrenochrome model and schizophrenia. *J. nerv. ment. Dis.*, 128:18-35. – **528**

HOGAN, H. P., *see* Carmichael, Hogan, and Walter (1932).

HOLMEN, M. G., KATTER, R. V., HONES, A. M., and RICHARDSON, I. F. (1956) An assessment program for OCS applicants. *Hum RRO tech. Rep. 26*. – **465**

HOLT, H. O., and HAMMOCK, J. (1961) Books as teaching machines: some data. Paper, Midwestern Psychol. Assn., Chicago, May 4-6. – **323**

HOLT, R. R. (1958) Clinical and statistical prediction: a reformulation and some new data. *J. abnorm. soc. Psychol.*, 56:1-12. – **466**

HOLT, R. R., *see* Klopfer and others (1954).

HOLT, R. R., and HAVEL, J. (1960) A method for assessing primary and secondary process in the Rorschach. In Rickers-Ovsiankina, Maria A. (Ed.) *Rorschach psychology*. N. Y.: Wiley, 263-315. – **485**

HOLT, R. R., and LUBORSKY, L. (1958) *Personality patterns of psychiatrists*. N. Y.: Basic Books. – **464**

HOLTZMAN, W. H., THORPE, J. S., SWARTZ, J. D., and HERROW, E. W. (1961) *Inkblot perception and personality*. Austin, Tex.: University of Texas Press. – **461, 467**

HOLWAY, A. H., and BORING, E. G. (1940) The moon illusion and the angle of regard. *Amer. J. Psychol.*, 53:109-16. – **199**

HOLWAY, A. H., and BORING, E. G. (1941) Determinants of apparent visual size with distance variant. *Amer. J. Psychol.*, 54:21-37. – **192**

HOLZINGER, K. J., *see* Newman, Freeman, and Holzinger (1937).

HOLZMAN, M. (1958) Theories of choice and conflict in psychology and economics. *Conflict Resolution*, 2:310-20. – **504**

HOMME, L. E., *see* Evans, Glaser, and Homme (1959).

HONZIK, C. H., *see* Tolman and Honzik (1930).

HOPKINS, B. L., *see* Estes and others (1960).

HOPPE, F. (1930) Erfolg und Misserfolg. *Psychol. Forsch.*, 14:1-62. – **151**

HOPPOCK, R. (1935) *Job satisfaction*. N. Y.: Harper. – **582**

HOSTELLER, R. C., *see* McGaugh and Hosteller (1961).

HOVLAND, C. I. (1937) The generalization of · conditioned responses: I. The sensory generalization of conditioned responses with varying frequencies of tone. *J. gen. Psychol.*, 17:125-48. – **256**

HOVLAND, C. I. (1939) Experimental studies in rote-learning theory: IV. Comparison of reminiscence in serial and paired associate learning. *J. exp. Psychol.*, 24:466-84. – **273**

HOVLAND, C. I., *see also* Cahill and Hovland (1960); Hull and others (1940); Hunt and Hovland (1960); Kelman and Hovland (1953); Rosenberg and others (1960); Sears and Hovland (1941).

HOVLAND, C. I., and HUNT, D. E. (1960) Computer simulation of concept attainment. *Behav. Sci.*, 5:265-7. – **359**

HOVLAND, C. I., JANIS, I. L., and KELLEY, H. H. (1953) *Communication and persuasion*. New Haven, Conn.: Yale Univ. Press. – **564, 568**

HOVLAND, C. I., and KURTZ, K. H. (1951) Experimental studies in rote-learning theory: IX. Influence of work-decrement factors on verbal learning. *J. exp. Psychol.*, 42:265-72. – **294**

HOVLAND, C. I., LUMSDAINE, A. A., and SHEFFIELD, F. C. (1949) *Experiments on mass communication*. Princeton, N. J.: Princeton Univ. Press. – **575**

HOWARD, M., *see* Burt and Howard (1957).

HSIA, Y., *see* Graham and Hsia (1958).

HSU, F. L. K. (1949) Suppression versus repression. *Psychiatry*, 12:223-42. – **516**

HUFF, D. (1954) *How to lie with statistics*. N. Y.: Norton. – **392**

HULL, C. L. (1931) Goal attraction and directing ideas conceived as habit phenomena. *Psychol. Rev.*, 38:487-506. – **350**

HULL, C. L. (1932) The goal gradient hypothesis and maze learning. *Psychol. Rev.*, 39, 25-43. – **266, 267**

HULL, C. L. (1943) *Principles of behavior*. N. Y.: Appleton-Century-Crofts. – **149, 283**

HULL, C. L. (1951) *Essentials of behavior*. New Haven, Conn.: Yale Univ. Press. – **281**

HULL, C. L. (1952) *A behavior system*. New Haven, Conn.: Yale Univ. Press. – **276, 282**

HULL, C. L., HOVLAND, C. I., ROSS, R. T., HALL, M., PERKINS, D. T., and FITCH, F. G. (1940) *Mathematico-deductive theory of rote learning*. New Haven, Conn.: Yale Univ. Press. – **274**

HUMPHREY, B. M., *see* Rhine and Humphrey (1944).

HUMPHREY, E. M., and ZANGWILL, L. O. (1952) Dysphasia in left-handed patients with unilateral brain lesions. *J. Neurol. Neurosurg. Psychiat.*, 15:184-93. – **45**

HUMPHREY, G. (1951) *Thinking, an introduction to its experimental psychology*. N. Y.: Wiley. – **345**

HUMPHREYS, L. G. (1957) Characteristics of type concepts with special reference to Sheldon's typology. *Psychol. Bull.*, 54:218-28. – **469**

HUNT, D. E., *see* Hovland and Hunt (1960).

HUNT, D. E., and HOVLAND, C. I. (1960) Order of consideration of different types of concepts. *J. exp. Psychol.*, 59:220-5. – **347**

HUNT, J. MC V. (1941) The effects of infant feeding-frustration upon adult hoarding behavior. *J. abnorm. soc. Psychol.*, 36:338-60. – **81**

HUNTER, E. (1951) *Brainwashing in Red China*. N. Y.: Vanguard. – **576**

HURVICH, L. M., and JAMESON, D. (1955) A quantitative theoretical account of color vision. *Trans. N. Y. Acad. Sci.*, 18:33-8. – **233**

HYDÉN, H. (1961) Satellite cells in the nervous system. *Scient. Amer.*, 205:62-70. – **55**

HYMAN, H. H. (1955) *Survey design and analysis*. Glencoe, Ill.: Free Press. – **580**

INBAU, F. E. (1942) *Lie detection and criminal investigation*. Baltimore: Williams & Wilkins. – **181**

INHELDER, B., and PIAGET, J. (1958) *The growth of logical thinking from childhood to adolescence*. N. Y.: Basic Books. – **367**

INKELES, A., and LEVINSON, D. J. (1954) National character: the study of modal personality and sociocultural systems. In Lindzey, G. (Ed.) *Handbook of social psychology*. Reading, Mass.: Addison-Wesley, 977-1020. – **449**

INLOW, G. M. (1951) Job satisfaction of liberal arts graduates. *J. appl. Psychol.*, 35:175-81. – **583**

IRION, A. L. (1949) Reminiscence in pursuit-rotor learning as a function of length of rest and amount of pre-rest practice. *J. exp. Psychol.*, 39:492-99. – **294**

ITTLESON, W. H., and SLACK, C. W. (1958) The perception of persons as visual objects. In Tagiuri, R., and Petrullo, L. (Eds.) *Person perception and interpersonal behavior*. Stanford, Calif.: Stanford Univ. Press, 210-28. – **558**

IVY, M., *see* Heidbreder, Bensley, and Ivy. (1948).

JACKSON, C. M. (1928) Some aspects of form and growth. In Robbins, W. J., and others. *Growth*. New Haven, Conn.: Yale Univ. Press. – **101**

JACKSON, D. D. (Ed.) (1960) *The etiology of schizophrenia*. N. Y.: Basic Books. – **528**

JACKSON, D. D., *see also* Block and others (1958).

JACKSON, D. N., *see* Messick and Jackson (1961).

JACKSON, J. M., and SALTZSTEIN, H. D. (1958) The effect of person-group relationships on conformity processes. *J. abnorm. soc. Psychol.*, 57:17-24. – **558**

JACKSON, T. A. (1942) Use of the stick as a tool by young chimpanzees. *J. comp. Psychol.*, 34:223-35. – **276**

JACOBS, P. A., and STRONG, J. A. (1959) A case of human intersexuality having a possibly XXY sex-determining mechanism. *Nature*, London, 183, 302. – **425**

JACOBSON, E. (1932) Electrophysiology of mental activities. *Amer. J. Psychol.*, 44:677-94. – **349, 350**

JAGODA, H., *see* D'Amato and Jagoda (1960).

JAMES, W. (1890) *Principles of psychology* (2 vols.). N. Y.: Holt. – **202**

JAMES, W. (1892) *Psychology: briefer course*. N. Y.: Holt. – **337**

JAMESON, D., *see* Hurvich and Jameson (1955).

JANIS, I. L., *see* Hovland, Janis, and Kelley (1953).

JANIS, I. L., and FESHBACH, S. (1953) Effects of fear-arousing communications. *J. abnorm. soc. Psychol.,* 48:78-92. – **576**

JASPER, H., *see* Li and others (1956); Penfield and Jasper (1954).

JASTROW, J. (1935) *Wish and wisdom.* N. Y.: Appleton-Century. – **218**

JENKINS, J. G., and DALLENBACH, K. M. (1924) Obliviscence during sleep and waking. *Amer. J. Psychol.,* 35:605-12. – **299**

JENKINS, M. D., *see* Witty and Jenkins (1934).

JENKINS, W. L. (1951) Somesthesis. In Stevens, S. S. (Ed.) *Handbook of experimental psychology.* N. Y.: Wiley, 1172-190. – **243**

JENNINGS, H. H. (1950) *Leadership and isolation* (2nd Ed.) N. Y.: Longmans, Green. – **464**

JERSILD, A. T. (1952) *In search of self.* New York: Teachers Coll., Columbia Univ. – **108**

JERSILD, A. T. (1957) *The psychology of adolescence.* N. Y.: Macmillan. – **122**

JOHNSON, A. M., FALSTEIN, E. I., SZUREK, S. A., and SVENDSEN, M. (1941) School phobia. *Amer. J. Orthopsychiat.,* 11:702-12. – **332**

JOHNSON, D. M. (1955) *The psychology of thought and judgment.* N. Y.: Harper. – **363, 367**

JONES, A. D., *see* Deutsch and Jones (1959).

JONES, A. M., *see* Holmen and others (1956).

JONES, A. W., *see* Pressey and Jones (1955).

JONES, E. (1957) How to tell your friends from geniuses. *Sat. Rev. Lit.,* 40:9-11, 39-40. – **365**

JONES, H. E. (1943) Development in adolescence. N. Y:. Appleton-Century-Croft. – **463**

JONES, H. E., and CONRAD, H. S. (1933) The growth and decline of intelligence. *Genet. Psychol. Monogr.,* 13, No. 3. – **412**

JONES, H. E., CONRAD, H. S., and BLANCHARD, M. B. (1932) Environmental handicap in mental test performance. *Univ. Calif. Publ. Psychol.,* 5:63-99. – **440**

JONES, L. V., *see* Hilgard, Jones, and Kaplan (1951).

JONES, M. H., *see* Jones, N. F. and Jones, M. H. (1953).

JONES, N. F., and JONES, M. H. (1953) Modern theories of olfaction: a critical review. *J. Psychol.,* 36:207-41. – **241**

JUDD, D. B. (1952) *Color in business, science, and industry.* N. Y.: Wiley. – **250**

JUNG, C. G. (1923) *Psychological types.* N. Y.: Harcourt, Brace & World. – **471**

KAGAN, J., and LESSER, G. S. (1961) *Contemporary issues in thematic apperceptive methods.* Springfield, Ill.: Charles C. Thomas. – **467**

KAHN, F. (1943) *Man in structure and function* (2 vols.). N. Y.: Knopf. – **207**

KALLMANN, F. J. (1953) *Heredity in health and mental disorder.* N. Y.: Norton. – **437, 528**

KALLMANN, F. J. (1959) The genetics of mental illness. In Arieti, S. (Ed.) *American handbook of psychiatry.* N. Y.: Basic Books, 175-96. – **528**

KALLMANN, F. J., and ROTH, B. (1956) Genetic aspects of preadolescent schizophrenia. *Amer. J. Psychiat.,* 112:599-606. – **437, 528**

KALLMANN, F. J., and SANDER, G. (1949) Twin studies on senescence. *Amer. J. Psychiat.* 106:29-36. – **436**

KALMUS, H. (1955) The discrimination by the nose of the dog of individual human odors and in particular of the odors of twins. *Brit. J. anim. Behav.,* 3:25-31. – **240**

KARDINER, A. (1939) *The individual and his society.* N. Y.: Columbia Univ. Press. – **449**

KATONA, G. (1940) *Organizing and memorizing.* N. Y.: Columbia Univ. Press. – **308, 310**

KATTER, R. V., *see* Holmen and others (1956).

KATZ, BERNARD (1952) The nerve impulse. *Scient. Amer.,* 185:55-64. – **53**

KATZ, BRENDA, *see* Secord, Bevan, and Katz (1956).

KATZ, D., *see* Festinger and Katz (1953).

KATZ, D., CARTWRIGHT, D., ELDERSVELD, S., and LEE, A. MC C. (Eds.) (1954) *Public opinion and propaganda.* N. Y.: Dryden. – **580**

KAUFMAN, L., and ROCK, I. (1960) The moon illusion: the problem re-opened. Paper, Eastern Psychol. Assn., Apr. 15-16. – **200**

KEELER, C. E., and KING, H. D. (1942) Multiple effect of coat color genes in the Norway rat, with special reference to temperament and domestication. *J. comp. Psychol.,* 34:241-50. – **426**

KELLEHER, R. T. (1958) Stimulus-producing responses in chimpanzees. *J. exp. Anal. Behav.,* 1:87-102. – **132**

KELLER, F. S., and SCHOENFELD, W. N. (1950) *Principles of psychology.* N. Y.: Appleton-Century-Crofts. – **262**

KELLEY, H. H., *see* Hovland, Janis, and Kelley (1953).

KELLEY, H. H., and VOLKART, E. H. (1952) The resistance to change of group-anchored attitudes. *Amer. sociol. Rev.,* 17:453-65. – **558**

KELLEY, T. L., MADDEN, R., GARDNER, E. F., TERMAN, L. M., and RUCH, G. M. (1953) *Stanford Achievement Test: Directions for administering.* Yonkers, N. Y.: World Book. – **396**

KELLOGG, L. A., *see* Kellogg, W. N., and Kellogg, L. A. (1933).

KELLOGG, W. N., and KELLOGG, L. A. (1933) *The ape and the child.* N. Y.: McGraw-Hill. – **69**

KELLY, E. L. (1939) Concerning the validity of Terman's weights for predicting marital happiness. *Psychol. Bull.,* 306:202-03. – **115**

KELLY, E. L., and FISKE, D. W. (1951) *The predictability of performance in clinical psychology.* Ann Arbor, Mich.: Univ. of Michigan Press. – **464**

KELMAN, H. C. (1958) Compliance, identification, and internalization: three processes of attitude change. *Conflict Resolution,* 2:51-60. – **578**

KELMAN, H. C., and HOVLAND, C. I. (1953) "Reinstatement" of the communicator in delayed measurement of opinion change. *J. abnorm. soc. Psychol.,* 48:327-35. – **576**

KENDERINE, M. (1931) Laughter in the preschool child. *Child Develpm.,* 2:228-30. – **176**

KENISTON, K., *see* Couch and Keniston (1960).

KESSEN, W., *see* Mandler and Kessen (1959).

KETY, S. (1959) Biochemical theories of schizophrenia. *Science,* 129:1528-32, 1590-96. – **528**

KIERKEGAARD, S. (1944) *The concept of dread.* (Trans. by W. Lowrie.) Princeton, N. J.: Princeton Univ. Press. – **174**

KILPATRICK, F. P. (Ed.) (1961) *Explorations in transactional psychology.* N. Y.: New York Univ. Press. – **222**

KIMBLE, G. A. (1955) Shock intensity and avoidance learning. *J. comp. physiol. Psychol.,* 48:281-84. – **24**

KIMBLE, G. A. (1961) *Hilgard and Marquis' Conditioning and learning* (2nd Ed.). N. Y.: Appleton-Century-Crofts. – **259, 287**

KIMBLE, G. A., and DUFORT, R. H. (1956) The associative factor in eyelid conditioning. *J. exp. Psychol.,* 52:386-91. – **266**

KING, H. D., *see* Keeler and King (1943).

KING, S. H., *see* Funkenstein, King, and Drolette (1957).

KINSEY, A. C., POMEROY, W. B., and MARTIN, C. E. (1948) *Sexual behavior in the human male.* Philadelphia: Saunders. – **104**

KIRK, S. A. (1948) An evaluation of the study by Bernardine G. Schmidt entitled "Changes in personal, social, and intellectual behavior of children originally classified as feeble-minded." *Psychol. Bull.,* 45:321-33. – **416**

KLEE, J. B., *see* Maier, Glaser, and Klee (1940).

KLEEMEIER, R. W. (Ed.) (1961) *Aging and leisure: a research perspective into the meaningful use of time.* N. Y.: Oxford Univ. Press. – **122**

KLEIN, G. S. (1954) Need and regulation. *Nebr. symposium on motivation,* vol. 2. Lincoln, Nebr.: Univ. of Nebraska Press, 224-74. – **485, 489**

KLEIN, G. S. (1958) Cognitive control and motivation. In Lindzey, G. (Ed.) *Assessment of human motives.* N. Y.: Rinehart. – **489**

KLEIN, G. S. (1959) On subliminal activation. *J. nerv. ment. Dis.,* 128:293-301. – **224**

KLEITMAN, N., *see* Dement and Kleitman (1957).

KLINEBERG, O. (1931) A study of psychological differences between "racial" and national groups in Europe. *Arch. Psychol.,* N. Y., No. 132. – **440**

KLINEBERG, O. (1935) *Negro intelligence and selective migration.* N. Y.: Columbia Univ. Press. – **443**

KLINEBERG, O. (1938) Emotional expression in Chinese literature. *J. abnorm. soc. Psychol.,* 33:517-20. – **168**

KLOPFER, B., AINSWORTH, M. D., KLOPFER, W. G., and HOLT, R. R. (1954) *Developments in the Rorschach technique.* Yonkers, N. Y.: World Book Co. – **467**

KLOPFER, W. G., *see* Klopfer, B., and others (1954).

KLUCKHOHN, C., *see* Leighton and Kluckhohn (1947).

KNIEF, L. M., and STROUD, J. B. (1959) Intercorrelations among various intelligence, achievement, and social class scores. *J. educ. Psychol.,* 50:117-20. – **403**

KNOWER, F. H., *see* Dusenbury and Knower (1939).

KOCH, S. (Ed.) (1959) *Psychology: a study of a science.* (Vol. I, 1959a; Vol. 2, 1959b; Vol. 3, 1959c; four more volumes in preparation.) N. Y.: McGraw-Hill. – **521, 601, 612**

KOGAN, N., and TAGIURI, R. (1958) Interpersonal preference and cognitive organization. *J. abnorm. soc. Psychol.,* 56:113-16. – **554**

KÖHLER, W. (1925) *The mentality of apes.* N. Y.: Harcourt, Brace & World. – **275, 287**

KOHLER, I. (1961) On the development and transformation of the perceptual world. *Psychol. Issues,* 2, No. 8. – **193**

KOHN, M. L., and CLAUSEN, J. A. (1956) Parental authority behavior and schizophrenia. *Amer. J. Orthopsychiat.,* 26:297-313. – **528**

KOLB, L. C. (1956) Psychiatry. *Annu. Rev. Med.,* 7:109-22. – **528**

KOLB, L. C., *see also* Noyes and Kolb (1958).

KORNHAUSER, A., DUBIN, R., and ROSS, A. M. (Eds.) (1954) *Industrial conflict.* N. Y.: McGraw-Hill. – **612**

KOUNIN, J. S. (1941) Experimental studies of rigidity. I. One measurement of rigidity in normal and feeble-minded persons. *Character and Pers.,* 9:251-72. – **486**

KOUNIN, J. S., *see also* Gump and Kounin (1959).

KRAELING, D., *see* Miller and Kraeling (1952).

KRAMER, M., *see* Felix and Kramer (1953).

KRASNER, L. (1958) Studies of the conditioning of verbal behavior. *Psychol. Bull.,* 55:148-70. – **265**

KRAWIEC, T. S., *see* Chaplin and Krawiec (1960).

KRECH, D., *see* Rosenzweig, Krech, and Bennett (1960).

KRETSCHMER, E. (1925) *Physique and character.* N. Y.: Harcourt, Brace & World. – **469**

KRIS, E. (1952) *Psychoanalytic explorations in art.* N. Y.: Internat. Univ. Press. – **364**

KRISTY, N. F., *see* Cattell and others (1957).

KROUT, M. H. (1954) An experimental attempt to determine the significance of unconscious manual symbolic movements. *J. gen. Psychol.,* 51:121-52. – **515**

KRUEGER, W. C. F. (1929) The effect of over-learning on retention. *J. exp. Psychol.,* 12:71-8. – **306, 307**

KUBIE, L. S. (1950) *Practical and theoretical aspects of psychoanalysis.* N. Y.: Internat. Univ. Press. – **550**

KUBIE, L. S. (1958) *Neurotic distortion of the creative process.* Lawrence, Kans.: Univ. of Kansas Press. – **364**

KUENNE, M. R. (1946) Experimental investigation of the relation of language to transposition behavior in young children. *J. exp. Psychol.,* 36:471-90. – **347, 348**

KUHLEN, R. G. (1945) Age differences in personality during adult years. *Psychol. Bull.,* 42:333-58. – **110**

KUHLEN, R. G., *see also* Pressey and Kuhlen (1957).

KUHLEN, R. G., and ARNOLD, M. (1944) Age differences in religious beliefs and problems during adolescence. *J. genet. Psychol.,* 63:291-300. – **110**

KURTZ, K. H., *see* Hovland and Kurtz (1951).

LACEY, J. I., BATEMAN, D. E., and VAN LEHN, R. (1952) Autonomic response specificity and Rorschach color responses. *Psychosom. Med.,* 14:256-60. – **470**

LACEY, J. I., and VAN LEHN, R. (1952) Differential emphasis in somatic response to stress. *Psychosom. Med.,* 14:71-81. – **470**

LAIDLAW, R. W., and HAMILTON, M. A. (1937) A study of thresholds in apperception of passive movement among normal control subjects. *Bull. Neurol. Inst., N. Y.,* 6:268-73. – **246**

LAMBERT, W. W., SOLOMON, R. L., and WATSON, P. D. (1949) Reinforcement and extinction as factors in size estimation. *J. exp. Psychol.,* 39:637-41. – **214**

LANCASTER, E. (1958) *The final face of Eve.* N. Y.: McGraw-Hill. – **489**

LAND, E. H. (1959) Color vision and the natural image. *Proc. natl. Acad. Sci.,* 45:115-29, 636-44. – **233**

LANDIS, C., ZUBIN, J., and METTLER, F. A. (1950) The functions of the human frontal lobe. *J. Psychol.,* 30:123-38. – **163**

LANDIS, J. T. (1942) What is the happiest period of life? *Sch. & Soc.,* 55:643-45. – **110, 111**

LANG, G. E., *see* Lang, K., and Lang, G. E. (1961).

LANG, K., and LANG, G. E. (1961) Ordeal by debate: viewer reactions. *Pub. Opin. Quart.,* 25:277-88. – **574**

LANSFORD, *see* Clark, Lansford, and Dallenbach (1960).

LANTZ, B. (1945) Some dynamic aspects of success and failure. *Psychol. Monogr.,* 59, No. 271. – **178**

LAWRENCE, M. (1949) *Studies in human behavior.* Princeton, N. J.: Princeton Univ. Press. – **207**

LAWSON, R. (1960) *Learning and behavior.* N. Y.: M cmillan. – **287**

LAZARSFELD, P. F. (1944) The controversy over detailed interviews: an offer for negotiation. *Publ. Opin. Quart.,* 8:36-60. – **569**

LEAHY, A. M. (1935) Nature-nurture and intelligence. *Genet. Psychol. Monogr.,* 17:235-308. – **430, 431, 432, 434**

LEAVITT, H. J. (1958) *Managerial psychology.* Chicago, Ill.: Univ. of Chicago Press. – **612**

LECKY, P. (1945) *Self-consistency.* N. Y.: Island Press. – **144**

LEDERBERG, J. (1960) A view of genetics. *Science,* 131:269-76. – **55**

LEE, A. MC C., *see* Katz and others (1954).

LEE, E. S. (1951) Negro intelligence and selective migration: a Philadelphia test of the Klineberg hypothesis. *Amer. sociol. Rev.,* 16:227-33. – **440, 441**

LEEPER, R. W. (1935) A study of a neglected portion of the field of learning: the development of sensory organization. *J. genet. Psychol.,* 46:41-75. – **197**

LEEPER, R. W., and MADISON, P. (1959) *Toward understanding human personalities.* N. Y.: Appleton-Century-Crofts. – **495**

LEHMAN, H. C. (1938) The most proficient years at sports and games. *Res. Quart. Amer. Assn. Hlth & phys. Educ.,* 9:3-19. – **116**

LEHMAN, H. C. (1953) *Age and achievement.* Princeton, N. J.: Princeton Univ. Press. – **112, 117, 118, 119, 122**

LEHMAN, H. C. (1960) The age decrement in outstanding scientific creativity. *Amer. Psychologist,* 15:128-34. – **120**

LEIBOWITZ, H., and HARTMAN, T. (1959) Magnitude of the moon illusion as a function of the age of the observer. *Science,* 130:569-70. – **200, 201**

LEIBOWITZ, H., and HARTMAN, T. (1960) The moon illusion. *Science,* 131, 694. – **200, 201**

LEIGHTON, D. C. (1955) The distribution of psychiatric symptoms in a small town. (Paper read at American Psychiatric Association, May, 1955; mimeographed.) – **529**

LEIGHTON, D. C., and KLUCKHOHN, C. (1947) *Children of the people.* Cambridge, Mass.: Harvard Univ. Press. – **82**

LEITES, N., and BERNAUT, E. (1954) *Ritual of liquidation.* Glencoe, Ill.: Free Press. – **577**

LEJEUNE, L., GAUTIER, M., and TURPIN, R. (1959) Les chromosomes humains en culture de tissus. *C. R. Acad. Sci.,* Paris, 248, 262. – **425**

LEMKAU, P., TIETZE, C., and COOPER, M. (1941) Mental hygiene problems in an urban district. *Ment. Hyg., N. Y.,* 25:624-46. – **529**

LENNARD, H. L., and BERNSTEIN, A. (1960) *The anatomy of psychotherapy.* N. Y.: Columbia Univ. Press. – **541, 542**

LENNEBERG, E. H., *see* Brown and Lenneberg (1954).

LEONARD, W. E. (1927) *The locomotive-god.* N. Y.: Century. – **173**

LERNER, I. M. (1950) *Population genetics and animal improvement.* Cambridge: Cambridge Univ. Press. – **444**

LEUBA, C. (1941) Tickling and laughter: two genetic studies. *J. genet. Psychol.,* 58:201-09. – **176**

LEVAN, A., *see* Tijo and Levan (1956).

LEVIN, H., *see* Sears, Maccoby, and Levin (1957).

LEVINE, S. (1958) Noxious stimulation in infant and adult rats and consummatory behavior. *J. comp. physiol. Psychol.,* 51:230-33. – **68**

LEVINSON, D. J., *see* Adorno and others (1950).

LEVY, L. H., and ORR, T. B. (1959) The social psychology of Rorschach validity research. *J. abnorm. soc. Psychol.,* 58:79-83. – **461**

LEWIN, K. (1935) *A dynamic theory of personality.* N. Y.: McGraw-Hill. – **485, 499, 521**

LEWIN, K. (1936) *Principles of topological psychology.* N. Y.: McGraw-Hill. – **485-86**

LEWIN, K. (1942) Field theory and learning. *Yearb. nat. Soc. Stud. Educ.,* 41(II):215-42. – **329**

LEWIN, K. (1946) Behavior and development as a function of the total situation. In Carmichael, L. (Ed.) *Manual of child psychology.* N. Y.: Wiley, 791-844. – **327**

LEWIN, K., *see also* Barker, Dembo, and Lewin (1941).

LEWIS, D. (1960) *Quantitative methods in psychology.* N. Y.: McGraw-Hill. – **392**

LEWIS, H. B., *see* Witkin and others (1954).

LEWIS, S. (1934) *Work of art.* N. Y.: Doubleday, Doran. – **450**

LI, C. L., CULLEN, C., and JASPER, H. H. (1956) Laminar microelectrode analysis of cortical unspecific recruiting response and spontaneous rhythms. *J. neurophysiol.,* 19:131-43. – **53**

LIBERMAN, A. M., *see* McClelland and Liberman (1949).

LIBO, L. M. (1948) Attitude prediction in labor relations: a test of "understanding." *Studies in Industrial Relations,* No. 10. Stanford University: Graduate School of Business. – **596**

LICKLIDER, J. C. R. (1959) Three auditory theories. In Koch, S. (Ed.) *Psychology: a study of a science.* Vol. 1. N. Y.: McGraw-Hill, 41-144. – **240**

LIFTON, R. J. (1954) Home by ship: reaction patterns of American prisoners of war repatriated from North Korea. *Amer. J. Psychiat.,* 110:732-39. – **577**

LIFTON, R. J. (1956) "Thought reform" of Western Civilians in Chinese Communist prisons. *Psychiatry,* 19:173-95. – **577, 578**

LIFTON, R. J. (1961) *Thought reform and the psychology of totalism.* N. Y.: Norton. – **577, 578, 580**

LIKERT, R. (1932) A technique for the measurement of attitudes. *Arch. Psychol., N. Y.,* 28, No. 194. – **565**

LIKERT, R. (1961) *New patterns of management.* N. Y.: McGraw-Hill. – **612**

LINDAHL, L. G. (1945) Movement analysis as an industrial training method. *J. appl. Psychol.,* 29:420-36. – **316**

LINDGREN, H. C. (1959) *Psychology of personal and social adjustment.* (2nd Ed.) N. Y.: American Book. – **551**

LINDSAY, K. J. (1959) *Transfer and retroaction as a function of response similarity, materials, and experimental design.* Ph.D. dissertation, Stanford Univ. – **318**

LINDSLEY, D. B. (1951) Emotion. In Stevens, S. S. (Ed.) *Handbook of experimental psychology.* N. Y.: Wiley, 473-516. – **167**

LINDZEY, G. (Ed.) (1958) *Assessment of human motives.* N. Y.: Rinehart. – **157, 495**

LINDZEY, G., *see also* Allport, Vernon, and Lindzey (1960).

LINTON, R. (1945) *The cultural background of personality.* N. Y.: Appleton-Century-Crofts. – **482**

LIPSET, S. M., and BENDIX, R. (1952) Social mobility and occupational career patterns. II. Social mobility. *Amer. J. Sociol.,* 57:494-504. – **584**

LIPSHER, D. H., *see* Bandura, Lipsher, and Miller (1960).

LIVINGSTON, R. B. (1958) Central control of afferent activity. In *Reticular formation of the brain* (Henry Ford International Symposium). Boston: Little, Brown, 177-86. – **52**

LLEWELLYN, J. E., *see* Goldbeck and others (1960).

LOEWENSTEIN, W. R. (1960) Biological transducers. *Scient. Amer.,* 203:98-108. – **50**

LOGAN, F. A. (1959) The Hull-Spence approach. In Koch, S. *Psychology: a study of a science.* Vol. 2. N. Y.: McGraw-Hill, 293-358. – **281**

LORR, M., and FIELDS, V. (1954) A factorial study of body types. *J. clin. Psychol.,* 10:182-85. – **469**

LORGE, I. (1930) Influence of regularly interpolated time intervals on subsequent learning. *Teach. Coll. Contr. Educ.,* No. 438. – **269**

LOUTTIT, C. M., *see* Daniel and Louttit (1953).

LOVE, A. G., *see* Davenport and Love (1921).

LOWE, C. M. (1961) The self-concept: fact or artifact? *Psychol. Bull.,* 58:325-36. – **492**

LOWELL, E. L. (1950) A methodological study of projectively measured achievement motivation. (Unpublished M. A. thesis.) Middletown, Conn.: Wesleyan Univ. – **145**

LOWELL, E. L., *see also* McClelland and others (1953).

LUBORSKY, L. (1954) A note on Eysenck's article "The effects of psychotherapy: an evaluation." *Brit. J. Psychol.*, 45:129-31. – **547**

LUBORSKY, L., *see also* Holt and Luborsky (1958).

LUCHINS, A. S. (1942) Mechanization in problem solving: the effect of *Einstellung*. *Psychol. Monogr.*, 54, No. 248. – **355**

LUCHINS, A. S., and LUCHINS, E. H. (1959) *Rigidity of behavior.* Eugene, Ore.: Univ. of Oregon Press. – **367**

LUCHINS, E. H., *see* Luchins, A. S., and Luchins, E. H. (1959).

LUH, C. W. (1922) The conditions of retention. *Psychol. Monogr.*, 31, No. 142. – **293**

LUMSDAINE, A. A. (1959) Teaching machines and self-instructional materials. *Audio-visual commun. Rev.*, 7:163-72. – **321, 324**

LUMSDAINE, A. A., *see also* Hovland, Lumsdaine, and Sheffield (1949).

LUMSDAINE, A. A., and GLASER, R. (Eds.) (1960) *Teaching machines and programmed learning.* Washington, D. C.: National Education Association. – **320, 323, 335**

LUNDY, R. M. (1958) Self-perceptions regarding masculinity-femininity and descriptions of same and opposite sex sociometric choices. *Sociometry,* 21: 238-46. – **554**

LURIA, Z., *see* Osgood and Luria (1954).

LURIE, M. H., *see* Stevens, Davis, and Lurie (1935).

LUTHERMAN, C. Z., *see* Allee, Collias, and Lutherman (1939).

LUTON, F. H., *see* Roth and Luton (1943).

MC ARTHUR, C. (1956) Personalities of first and second children. *Psychiatry,* 19:47-54. – **90**

MC CLELLAND, D. C. (1951) *Personality.* N. Y.: Sloane. – **145**

MC CLELLAND, D. C. (Ed.) (1955) *Studies in motivation.* N. Y.: Appleton-Century-Crofts. – **145, 150, 157**

MC CLELLAND, D. C. (1958) Risk taking in children with high and low need for achievement. In Atkinson, J. W. (Ed.) *Motives in fantasy, action, and society.* Princeton, N. J.: Van Nostrand. – **154**

MC CLELLAND, D. C. (1961) *The achieving society.* Princeton, N. J.: Van Nostrand. – **157**

MC CLELLAND, D. C., and ATKINSON, J. W. (1948) The projective expression of needs: I. The effect of different intensities of the hunger drive on perception. *J. Psychol.*, 25:205-22. – **213**

MC CLELLAND, D. C., ATKINSON, J. W., CLARK, R. A., and LOWELL, E. L. (1953) *The achievement motive.* N. Y.: Appleton-Century-Crofts. – **144, 157**

MC CLELLAND, D. C., and FRIEDMAN, G. A. (1952) A cross-cultural study of the relationship between child-training practices and achievement motivation appearing in folk tales. In Swanson, G. E., Newcomb, T. M., and Hartley, E. L. (Eds.) *Readings in social psychology.* N. Y.: Holt, 243-48. – **145**

MC CLELLAND, D. C., and LIBERMAN, A. M. (1949) The effect of need for achievement on recognition of need-related words. *J. Pers.*, 18:236-51. – **146**

MC CONNELL, R. A., *see* Schmeidler and McConnell (1958).

MC CONNELL, R. A., SNOWDON, R. J., and POWELL, K. F. (1955) Wishing with dice. *J. exp. Psychol.*, 50:269-75. – **218**

MC CORD, F. (1941) The effect of frustration on hoarding in rats. *J. comp. Psychol.*, 32:531-41.

MC CORD, J., *see* McCord, W., McCord, J., and Zola (1959).

MC CORD, W., MC CORD, J., and ZOLA, I. K. (1959) *Origins of crime.* N. Y.: Columbia Univ. Press. – **92**

MC CORMICK, E. J. (1957) *Human engineering.* N. Y.: McGraw-Hill. – **612**

MC CURDY, H. G. (1956) Coin perception studies and the concept of schemata. *Psychol. Rev.*, 63:160-68. – **216**

MC CURDY, H. G. (1957) The childhood pattern of genius. *J. Elisha Mitchell sci. Soc.*, 73:448-62. – **365**

MC CURDY, H. G. (1961) *The personal world: an introduction to the study of personality.* N. Y.: Harcourt, Brace & World. – **495**

MC DONALD, W. T., *see* McGeoch and McDonald (1931).

MC GAUGH, J. L., *see* Thiessen and McGaugh (1958).

MC GAUGH, J. L., and HOSTETTER, R. C. (1961) Retention as a function of the temporal position of sleep and activity following waking. (Unpublished manuscript.) – **312, 313**

MC GEOCH, J. A. (1930) The influence of associative value upon the difficulty of nonsense-syllable lists. *J. genet. Psychol.*, 37:421-26. – **315**

MC GEOCH, J. A., and IRION, A. L. (1952) *The psychology of human learning* (2nd Ed.). N. Y.: Longmans, Green. – **287, 301, 310, 314, 335**

MC GEOCH, J. A., and MC DONALD, W. T. (1931) Meaningful relation and retroactive inhibition. *Amer. J. Psychol.*, 43:579-88. – **299**

MC GRAW, M. B. (1940) Neural maturation as exemplified in achievement of bladder control. *J. Pediat.*, 16:580-90. – **73**

MC GRAW, M. B. (1943) *The neuromuscular maturation of the human infant.* N. Y.: Columbia Univ. Press. – **74**

MC GUIRE, W. J., *see* Rosenberg and others (1960).

MC KAY, H. D., *see* Shaw and others (1942).

MC KINNEY, F. (1960) *Psychology of personal adjustment* (3rd Ed.). N. Y.: Wiley. – **550**

MAC KINNON, D. W. (1958) An assessment of Air Force officers. Part V: Summary and applications. WADC Technical Report 58-91 (V). Wright Development Center. – **464**

MAC KINNON, D. W. (1960) What do we mean by talent and how do we test for it? In *The search for talent.* N. Y.: College Entrance Examination Board. – **364**

MC LEAN, H. V., *see* Miller and McLean (1941).

MC LEAN, P. D. (1950) Psychosomatic disease and the "visceral brain"; recent developments bearing on the Papez theory of emotion. *Psychosomat. Med.*, 11:338-53. – **42**

MAC LEOD, R. B. (1932) An experimental investigation of brightness constancy. *Arch. Psychol., N. Y.*, No. 135. – **189**

MAC LEOD, R. B. (1940) Brightness-constancy in unrecognized shadows. *J. exp. Psychol.*, 27:1-22. – **188**

MC NEMAR, O., *see* Taylor and McNemar (1955).

MC NEMAR, Q. (1938) Special review of Newman, Freeman, and Holzinger's *Twins: a study of heredity and environment. Psychol. Bull.*, 35:237-49. – **435**

MC NEMAR, Q. (1940) A critical examination of the University of Iowa studies of environmental influences upon the I.Q. *Psychol. Bull.*, 37:63-92. – **431, 438**

MC NEMAR, Q. (1942) *The revision of the Stanford-Binet scale.* Boston: Houghton Mifflin. – **403, 404, 435, 440**

MC NEMAR, Q. (1945) Note on Wellman's re-analysis of I.Q. changes of orphanage preschool children. *J. genet. Psychol.*, 67:215-19. – **438**

MC NEMAR, Q. (1960) At random: sense and nonsense. *Amer. Psychologist*, 15:295-300. – **387**

MC NEMAR, Q. (1962) *Psychological statistics* (3rd Ed.). N. Y.: Wiley. – **392**

MACCOBY, E. E., *see* Sears, Maccoby, and Levin (1957).

MACCOBY, E. E., NEWCOMB, T. M., and HARTLEY, E. L. (Eds.) (1958) *Readings in social psychology* (3rd Ed.). N. Y.: Holt. – **580**

MACHOVER, K., *see* Witkin and others (1954).

MADDEN, R., *see* Kelley and others (1953).

MADISON, P., *see* Leeper and Madison (1959).

MAGARET, A., *see* Hilgard, Sait, and Magaret (1940).

MAGOUN, H. W. (1958) *The waking brain.* Springfield, Ill.: Thomas. – **40**

MAHATOO, W., *see* Doane and others (1959).

MAIER, N. R. F. (1932) The effect of cerebral destruction on reasoning and learning in rats. *J. comp. Neurol.*, 54:45-75. – **279**

MAIER, N. R. F. (1946) *Psychology in industry.* Boston: Houghton Mifflin. – **593**

MAIER, N. R. F. (1949) *Frustration: a study of behavior without a goal.* N. Y.: McGraw-Hill. – **509, 521**

MAIER, N. R. F. (1956) Frustration theory: restatement and extension. *Psychol. Rev.*, 63:370-88. – **509**

MAIER, N. R. F., GLASER, N. M., and KLEE, J. B. (1940) Studies of abnormal behavior in the rat: III. The development of behavior fixations through frustration. *J. exp. Psychol.*, 26:521-46. – **509**

MAIER, N. R. F., and SCHNEIRLA, T. C. (1935) *Principles of animal psychology.* N. Y.: McGraw-Hill. – **278**

MALINOWSKI, B. (1929) *The sexual life of savages in northwestern Melanesia.* N. Y.: Liveright. – **104**

MANDLER, G., *see* Sarason, Mandler, and Craighill (1952).

MANDLER, G., and KESSEN, W. (1959) *The language of psychology.* N. Y.: Wiley. – **19**

MANDLER, G., and SARASON, S. B. (1952) A study of anxiety and learning. *J. abnorm. soc. Psychol.*, 47:166-73. – **333, 334**

MARQUART, D. I., and BAILEY, L. L. (1955) An evaluation of the culture free test of intelligence. *J. genet. Psychol.*, 86:353-58. – **403**

MARQUIS, D. G. (1948) Research planning at the frontiers of science. *Amer. Psychologist*, 3:430-38. – **563**

MARQUIS, D. G., *see also* Hilgard and Marquis (1940).

MARQUIS, D. P. (1941) Learning in the neonate: the modification of behavior under three feeding schedules. *J. exp. Psychol.*, 29:263-82. – **75**

MARROW, A. J. (1938) Goal tensions and recall. *J. gen. Psychol.*, 19:3-35, 37-64. – **304**

MARSHALL, A. W., *see* Goldhamer and Marshall (1953).

MARTIN, C. E., *see* Kinsey, Pomeroy, and Martin (1948).

MARTIN, W. E., and STENDLER, C. B. (1959) *Child development: the process of growing up in society* (2nd Ed.). N. Y.: Harcourt, Brace & World. – **94**

MASLAND, R. L., SARASON, S. B., and GLADWYN, T. (1958) *Mental subnormality.* N. Y.: Basic Books. – **413, 414, 422**

MASLOW, A. H. (1954) *Motivation and personality.* N. Y.: Harper. – **125, 144**

MASON, J. W., *see* Brady and others (1958).

MASON, W. A. (1960) The effects of social restriction on the behavior of rhesus monkeys: I. Free social behavior. *J. comp. physiol. Psychol.*, 53:582-89. – **88**

MAX, L. W. (1935) An experimental study of the motor theory of consciousness: III. Action-current responses in deaf-mutes during sleep, sensory stimulation, and dreams. *J. comp. Psychol.*, 19:469-86. – **350**

MAY, R. (1950) *The meaning of anxiety.* N. Y.: Ronald. – **174**

MAY, R., ANGEL, E., and ELLENBERGER, H. F., (Eds.) (1958) *Existence: a new dimension in psychiatry and psychology.* N. Y.: Basic Books. – **7, 543**

MEAD, M. (1935) *Sex and temperament in three primitive societies.* N. Y.: Morrow. – **104, 111**

MEAD, M. (1940) Character formation in two South Seas societies. *Proc. Amer. Neurol. Assn.*, 66:99-103. – **82**

MEAD, M. (1949) *Male and female.* N. Y.: Morrow. – **111, 122**

MEEHL, P. E. (1950) Configural scoring. *J. consult. Psychol.*, 14:165-71. – **476**

MEEHL, P. E. (1954) *Clinical vs. statistical prediction.* Minneapolis, Minn.: Univ. of Minnesota Press. – **465**

MEEHL, P. E. (1957) When shall we use our heads instead of the formula? *J. counsel. Psychol.*, 4:268-73. – **466**

MEISSNER, P. B., *see* Witkin and others (1954).

MELTON, A. W., and BRIGGS, G. E. (1960) Engineering psychology. *Annu. Rev. Psychol.*, 11:71-98. – **595, 596**

MELZACK, R., and SCOTT, T. H. (1957) The effects of early experience on the response to pain. *J. comp. physiol. Psychol.*, 50:155-61. – **68**

MENNINGER, K. (1958) *Theory of psychoanalytic technique.* N. Y.: Basic Books. – **550**

MERRILL, M. A. (1938) The significance of I.Q.'s on the revised Stanford-Binet scales. *J. educ. Psychol.*, 29:641-51. – **406**

MERRILL, M. A. (1947) *Problems of child delinquency.* Boston: Houghton Mifflin. – **531**

MERRILL, M. A., *see also* Terman and Merrill (1937), (1960).

MESSICK, S. (1960) Dimensions of social desirability. *J. consult. Psychol.*, 24:279-87. – **457**

MESSICK, S., *see also* Jackson and Messick (1958).

MESSICK, S., and JACKSON, D. N. (1961) Acquiescence and the factorial interpretation of the MMPI. *Psychol. Bull.*, 58:299-304. – **457**

METTLER, F. A., *see* Landis, Zubin, and Mettler (1950).

MEYER, D. R., *see* Harlow, H. F., Harlow, M. K., and Meyer (1950).

MEYER, M. M., and TOLMAN, R. S. (1955) Correspondence between attitudes and images of parental figures in TAT stories and in therapeutic interviews. *J. consult. Psychol.*, 19:79-82. – **459**

MEYERSON, L., *see* Barker and others (1953).

MICHOTTE, A. (1946) *La perception de la causalité.* Paris: Vrin. – **216**

MILES, C. C., *see* Terman and Miles (1936).

MILES, C. P. (1961) Human chromosome anomalies: recent advances in human cytogenetics. *Stanford med. Bull.*, 19:1-18. – **425**

MILLER, D. C., and FORM, W. H. (1951) *Industrial sociology.* N. Y.: Harper. – **594**

MILLER, D. R., and SWANSON, G. E. (1959) *Inner conflict and defense.* N. Y.: Holt-Dryden. – **114, 521**

MILLER, G. A. (1951) *Language and communication.* N. Y.: McGraw-Hill. – **367**

MILLER, G. A. (1953) What is information measurement? *Amer. Psychologist,* 8:3-11. – **354**

MILLER, G. A. (1956) The magical number seven, plus-or-minus two, or some limits on our capacity for processing information. *Psychol. Rev.,* 63:81-97. – **354**

MILLER, G. A., GALANTER, E., and PRIBRAM, K. H. (1960) *Plans and the structure of behavior.* N. Y.: Holt. – **146, 147**

MILLER, H. C., *see* Davis and others (1948).

MILLER, J. G. (1955) Toward a general theory of the behavioral sciences. *Amer. Psychologist,* 10:513-31. – **57**

MILLER, M. L., and MC LEAN, H. V. (1941) The status of the emotions in palpitation and extrasystoles with a note on the effort syndrome. *Psychoanal. Quart.,* 10:545-60. – **527**

MILLER, N. E. (1948a) Fear as an acquired drive. *J. exp. Psychol.,* 38:89-101. – **172**

MILLER, N. E. (1948b) Theory and experiment relating psychoanalytic displacement to stimulus-response generalization. *J. abnorm. soc. Psychol.,* 43:155-78. – **506**

MILLER, N. E. (1959) Liberalization of basic S-R concepts: extensions to conflict behavior, motivation, and social learning. In Koch, S. (Ed.) *Psychology: a study of a science,* Vol. 2. N. Y.: McGraw-Hill, 196-292. – **501, 502, 503, 521**

MILLER, N. E. (1961) Analytic studies of drive and reward. *Amer. Psychologist,* 16:739-54. – **134**

MILLER, N. E., *see also* Dollard and Miller (1950); Delgado, Roberts, and Miller (1954).

MILLER, N. E., and KRAELING, D. (1952) Displacement: greater generalization of approach than avoidance in a generalized approach-avoidance conflict. *J. exp. Psychol.,* 43:217-21. – **507**

MILLER, P. E., *see* Bandura, Lipsher, and Miller (1960).

MILLER, R. B., FOLLEY, J. D., JR., and SMITH, P. R. (1953) Systematic trouble shooting and the half-split technique. *USAF Hum. Resour. Cent., Tech. Rep.,* No. 53-21. – **353**

MILLER, W. E., *see* Campbell and others (1960).

MILNE, A. A. (1924) *When we were very young.* N. Y.: Dutton. – **516**

MILNER, B. (1958) Psychological defects produced by temporal lobe excision. In *The brain and human behavior.* Res. Publ. Assn. Nerv. Ment. Dis., 244-57. **42**

MILNER, P., *see also* Olds and Milner (1954).

MILTON, G. A. (1957) The effects of sex-role identification upon problem-solving skill. *J. abnorm. soc. Psychol.,* 55:208-12. – **364**

MILTON, O., and WEST, L. J. (1961) *Programed instruction: What it is and how it works.* N. Y.: Harcourt, Brace & World. – **322**

MINAMI, H., and DALLENBACH, K. M. (1946) The effect of activity upon learning and retention in the cockroach. *Amer. J. Psychol.,* 59:1-58. – **299**

MINTURN, A. L., *see* Bruner, Busiek, and Minturn (1952).

MOLONEY, J. C. (1955) Psychic self-abandon and extortion of confession. *Int. J. Psychoanal.,* 36:53-60. – **578**

MONTAGU, M. F. A. (1946) *Adolescent sterility.* Springfield, Ill.: Thomas. – **100**

MOON, C. R. (1938) Study of premedical and medical scholastic records of students in the University of Illinois College of Medicine. *J. Assn. Amer. med. Coll.,* 13:208-12. – **585**

MORGAN, C. D., and MURRAY, H. A. (1935) A method for investigating fantasies: the thematic apperception test. *Arch. Neurol. Psychiat.,* 34:289-306. – **458**

MORGAN, C. M. (1937) The attitudes and adjustments of recipients of old age assistance in upstate and metropolitan New York. *Arch. Psychol., N. Y.,* 30, No. 214. – **110**

MORGAN, C. T. (1947) The hoarding instinct. *Psychol. Rev.,* 54:335-41. – **81**

MORGAN, C. T., and MORGAN, J. D. (1940) Studies in hunger: II. The relation of gastric denervation and dietary sugar to the effect of insulin upon food-intake in the rat. *J. genet. Psychol.,* 57:153-63. – **129**

MORGAN, J. D., *see* Morgan, C. T., and Morgan, J. D. (1940).

MORGAN, R. L., and UNDERWOOD, B. J. (1950) Proactive inhibition as a function of response similarity. *J. exp. Psychol.,* 40:592-603. – **300**

MORGULIS, S., *see* Yerkes and Morgulis (1909).

MORRIS, C. (1946) *Signs, language, and behavior.* Englewood Cliffs, N. J.: Prentice-Hall. – **345**

MOSES, L. E. (1952) Non-parametric statistics for psychological research. *Psychol. Bull.,* 49:122-43. – **386**

MOSES, L. E., *see also* Chernoff and Moses (1959).

MOSTELLER, F., *see* Bush and Mosteller (1955).

MOUTON, J. S., *see* Freed and others (1955); Helson and others (1958).

MOWRER, O. H. (1940) An experimental analogue of "regression" with incidental observations on "reaction-formation." *J. abnorm. soc. Psychol.,* 35:56-87. – **510**

MOWRER, O. H. (1950) *Learning theory and personality dynamics.* N. Y.: Ronald. – **538**

MOWRER, O. H. (1960) *Learning theory and behavior.* N. Y.: Wiley. – **174**

MUENCH, G. A., and ROGERS, C. R. (1946) Counseling of emotional blocking in an aviator. *J. abnorm. soc. Psychol.,* 41:207-15. – **6**

MUNN, N. L. (1940) The effect of knowledge of the situation upon judgment of emotion from facial expressions. *J. abnorm. soc. Psychol.,* 35:324-38. – **166**

MUNROE, R. L. (1955) *Schools of psychoanalytic thought.* N. Y.: Dryden. – **478**

MUNSELL, A. H. (1941) *Color notation.* Baltimore: Munsell Color Co. – **228**

MÜNSTERBERG, H. (1908) *On the witness stand.* N. Y.: McClure. – **602**

MURDOCK, G. P. (1937) Comparative data on the division of labor by sex. *Social Forces,* 15:551-53. – **112**

MURPHY, G. (1949a) *Historical introduction to modern psychology* (Revised Ed.). N. Y.: Harcourt, Brace & World. – **29**

MURPHY, G. (1949b) The place of parapsychology among the sciences. *J. Parapsychol.,* 13:62-71. – **216**

MURPHY, G., *see also* Solley and Murphy (1960).

MURRAY, E. J., AULD, F., JR., and WHITE, A. M. (1954) A psychotherapy case showing progress but no decrease in the comfort-relief quotient. *J. consult. Psychol.,* 18:349-53. – **540**

MURRAY, H. A., and others (1938) *Explorations in personality.* N. Y.: Oxford Univ. Press. – **125, 126, 142, 455**

MURRAY, H. A., *see also* Morgan and Murray (1935).

MUSSEN, P. H. (Ed.) (1960) *Handbook of research methods in child development.* N. Y.: Wiley. – **94**

MUSSEN, P. H., and CONGER, J. J. (1956) *Child development and personality.* N. Y.: Harper. – **94**

MUSSEN, P. H., and NAYLOR, H. K. (1954) The relationships between overt and fantasy aggression. *J. abnorm. soc. Psychol.*, 49:235-40. – **459**

MYERS, G. C. (1928) The price of speed pressure. *Educ. Res. Bull.*, 7:265-68. – **74**

NAKAMURA, C. Y. (1958) Conformity and problem solving. *J. abnorm. soc. Psychol.*, 56:315-20. – **364**

NAYLOR, H. K., *see* Mussen and Naylor (1954).

NEWCOMB, T. M. (1950) *Social psychology.* N. Y.: Dryden. – **482, 495**

NEWCOMB, T. M., *see also* Maccoby, Newcomb, and Hartley (1958).

NEWELL, A. J., SHAW, J. C., and SIMON, H. A. (1958*a*) Elements of a theory of human problem solving. *Psychol. Rev.*, 65:151-66. – **359**

NEWELL, A. J., SHAW, J. C., and SIMON, H. A. (1958*b*) *The processes of creative thinking.* Paper P-1320. Santa Monica, Calif.: The Rand Corp. – **359**

NEWELL, A., and SIMON, H. A. (1961) Computer simulation of human thinking. *Science,* 134:2011-2017. – **359**

NEWMAN, E. B. (1939) Forgetting of meaningful material during sleep and waking. *Amer. J. Psychol.,* 52:65-71. – **298**

NEWMAN, H. H., FREEMAN, F. N., and HOLZINGER, K. H. (1937) *Twins: a study of heredity and environment.* Chicago: Univ. of Chicago Press. – **434, 435**

NEWMAN, M. F., *see* Hilgard and Newman (1959), (1961).

NEYMAN, C. A., and YACORZYNSKI, G. K. (1942) Studies of introversion-extroversion and conflict of motives in the psychoses. *J. gen. Psychol.,* 27:241-55. – **471**

NISSEN, H. W., CHOW, K. L., and SEMMES, J. (1951) Effects of restricted opportunity for tactual, kinesthetic, and manipulative experience on the behavior of a chimpanzee. *Amer. J. Psychol.,* 64:485-507. – **68**

NORRIS, E. B., *see* Spence and Norris (1950).

NORVAL, M. A., *see* Aldrich and Norval (1946).

NOWLIS, V. (1942) Sexual status and degree of hunger in chimpanzee competitive interaction. *J. comp. Psychol.,* 34:185-94. – **139**

NOWLIS, V., *see also* Sears and others (1953).

NOYES, A. P., and KOLB, L. C. (1958) *Modern clinical psychiatry* (5th Ed.) Philadelphia, Pa.: Saunders. – **550**

OAKES, W. F. (1956) Latent learning in the three-table apparatus. *J. exp. Psychol.,* 51:287-89. – **279**

ODBERT, H. S., *see* Allport and Odbert (1936).

ODEN, M. H., *see* Terman and Oden (1947).

OGDON, D. P., *see* Cohen and Ogdon (1949).

OGG, E. (1955) Psychologists in action. *Publ. Affairs Pamph.,* 229. N. Y.: Public Affairs Committee, Inc. – **599, 612**

OLDS, J., and MILNER, P. (1954) Positive reinforcement produced by electrical stimulation of septal area and other regions of rat brain. *J. comp. physiol. Psychol.,* 47:419-27. – **3**

OLSON, W. C. (1949) *Child development.* Boston: Heath. – **74**

OPPENHEIM, A. N., *see* Himmelweit, Oppenheim, and Vince (1958).

OPTICAL SOCIETY OF AMERICA (1953) *The science of color.* N. Y.: Crowell. – **250**

ORLANSKY, H. (1949) Infant care and personality. *Psychol. Bull.,* 46:1-48. – **84**

ORR, T. B., *see* Levy and Orr (1959).

OSBORN, A. F. (1953) *Applied imagination.* N. Y.: Scribner's. – **358**

OSGOOD, C. E. (1949) The similarity paradox in human learning: a resolution. *Psychol. Rev.,* 56:132-43. – **318**

OSGOOD, C. E. (1952) The nature and measurement of meaning. *Psychol. Bull.,* 49:197-237. – **166, 343, 344**

OSGOOD, C. E. (1953) *Method and theory in experimental psychology.* N. Y.: Oxford Univ. Press. – **196, 310, 344, 345**

OSGOOD, C. E. (Ed.) (1954) Psycholinguistics: a survey of theory and research problems. *J. abnorm. soc. Psychol.,* 49:4, Pt. 2, Suppl. – **343**

OSGOOD, C. E., and LURIA, Z. (1954) A blind analysis of a case of multiple personality using the semantic differential. *J. abnorm. soc. Psychol.,* 49:579-91. – **490**

OSGOOD, C. E., SUCI, G. J., and TANNENBAUM, P. H. (1957) *The measurement of meaning.* Urbana, Ill.: Univ. of Illinois Press. – **367**

OSMOND, H., *see* Hoffer and Osmond (1959).

OSS ASSESSMENT STAFF (1948) Assessment of men. N. Y.: Rinehart. – **464, 465, 467**

PANTIN, C. F. A. (1952) The elementary nervous system. *Proc. Roy. Soc.,* London, Series B, 140:147-68. – **36**

PATERSON, D. G., *see* Deeg and Paterson (1947).

PATRICK, C. (1935) Creative thought in poets. *Arch. Psychol., N. Y.,* 26, No. 178. – **363**

PATRICK, C. (1937) Creative thought in artists. *J. Psychol.,* 4:35-73. – **363**

PATTERSON, V., *see* Block and others (1958).

PATTON, H. D., and RUCH, T. C. (1946) Taste. In Fulton, J. F. (Ed.) *Howell's textbook of physiology.* Philadelphia: Saunders, 370-84. – **242**

PAVLOV, I. P. (1927) *Conditioned reflexes.* N. Y.: Oxford Univ. Press. – **256, 287**

PEAK, H. (1958) Psychological structure and psychological activity. *Psychol. Rev.,* 65:325-47. – **554**

PEAK, H., and DEESE, L. (1937) Experimental extinction of verbal material. *J. exp. Psychol.,* 20:244-61. – **273**

PENFIELD, W. (1958) *The excitable cortex in conscious man.* Liverpool, Eng.: Liverpool Univ. Press. – **45**

PENFIELD, W., and JASPER, H. (1954) *Epilepsy and the functional anatomy of the human brain.* Boston: Little, Brown. – **45**

PENFIELD, W., and RASMUSSEN, T. (1950) *The cerebral cortex of man.* N. Y.: Macmillan. – **44**

PENFIELD, W., and ROBERTS, L. (1959) *Speech and brain mechanisms.* Princeton, N. J.: Princeton Univ. Press. – **351**

PERIN, C. T. (1942) Behavior potentiality as a joint function of the amount of training and the degree of hunger at the time of extinction. *J. exp. Psychol.,* 30:93-113. – **282, 283**

PERKINS, D. T., *see* Hull and others (1940).

PETERSON, R. C., and THURSTONE, L. L. (1932) *The effect of motion pictures on the social attitudes of high school children.* Ann Arbor, Mich.: Edwards Bros. – **565**

PETRULLO, L., *see* Tagiuri and Petrullo (1958).

PFAFFMANN, C. (1951) Taste and smell. In Stevens, S. S. (Ed.) *Handbook of experimental psychology.* N. Y.: Wiley, 1143-171. – **84**

PFAFFMANN, C. (1959) The afferent code for sensory quality. *Amer. Psychologist,* 14:226-34. – **243, 244**

PIAGET, J. (1926) *The language and thought of the child.* N. Y.: Harcourt, Brace & World. – **94**

PIAGET, J. (1950) *The psychology of intelligence.* N. Y.: Harcourt, Brace & World. – **187**

PIAGET, J. (1952) *The origins of intelligence in children.* N. Y.: Internat. Univ. Press. – **133**

PIAGET, J., *see also* Inhelder and Piaget (1958).

PINES, M., *see* Capa and Pines (1957).

PIRENNE, M. H., *see* Hecht, Schlaer, and Pirenne (1941).

PITTENDRIGH, C. S., *see* Simpson, Pittendrigh, and Tiffany (1957).

POINCARÉ, H. (1913) *The foundations of science.* N. Y.: Science Press. – **361**

POLYA, G. (1945) *How to solve it.* Princeton, N. J.: Princeton Univ. Press. – **359**

POLYA, G. (1954) *Mathematics and plausible reasoning.* Princeton, N. J.: Princeton Univ. Press. – **359**

POLYAK, S. L. (1941) *The retina.* Chicago: Univ. of Chicago Press. – **227**

POMEROY, W. B., *see* Kinsey, Pomeroy, and Martin (1948).

PORTER, D. A. (1959) Some effects of year-long teaching machine instruction. In Galanter, E. H. (Ed.) *Automatic teaching: the state of the art.* N. Y.: Wiley, 85-90. – **4**

PORTER, R. W., *see* Brady and others (1958).

POSTMAN, L. J., *see* Bruner and Postman (1949); Bruner, Postman, and Rodrigues (1951).

POWDERMAKER, F. B., and FRANK, J. D. (1953) *Group psychotherapy.* Cambridge, Mass.: Harvard Univ. Press. – **534**

POWELL, K. F., *see* McConnell, Snowdon, and Powell (1955).

PRATT, J. G., *see* Rhine and Pratt (1957).

PRESSEY, S. L. (1926) A simple apparatus which gives tests and scores—and teaches. *Sch. and Soc.,* 23: 373-76. – **320**

PRESSEY, S. L. (1927) A machine for automatic teaching of drill material. *Sch. and Soc.,* 25:549-52. – **320**

PRESSEY, S. L., and JONES, A. W. (1955) Age changes in moral codes, anxieties, and interests, as shown by the "X-O" tests. *J. Psychol.,* 30:485-502. – **110**

PRESSEY, S. L., and KUHLEN, R. G. (1957) *Psychological development through the life span.* N. Y.: Harper. – **122**

PRIBRAM, K. H. (1958) Neocortical function in behavior. In Harlow, H. F., and Woolsey, C. N. (Eds.) *Biological and biochemical bases of behavior.* Madison, Wis.: Univ. of Wisconsin Press, 151-72. – **42**

PRIBRAM, K. H. (1960) A review of theory in physiological psychology. *Annu. Rev. Psychol.,* 1-40. – **39, 46, 61**

PRIBRAM, K. H., *see also* Miller, Galanter, and Pribram (1960).

PRINCE, M. (1906) *The dissociation of a personality.* N. Y.: Longmans, Green. – **489**

PRONKO, N. H., *see* Snyder and Pronko (1952).

RABINOWITZ, H. S., *see* Birch and Rabinowitz (1951).

RADLER, D. H., *see* Remmers and Radler (1957).

RAMSAY, O. A., and HESS, E. H. (1954) A laboratory approach to the study of imprinting. *Wilson Bull.,* 66:196-206. – **67**

RAND Corporation (1955) *A million random digits.* Glencoe, Ill.: Free Press. – **219**

RANKE, J. (1894) *Der Mensch.* Leipzig and Vienna: Bibliographisches Institut. – **225**

RAPAPORT, D. (1942) *Emotions and memory.* Baltimore: Williams & Wilkins. (Reprinted, 1950, N. Y.: Internat. Univ. Press.) – **310**

RAPAPORT, D. (Ed.) (1951) *Organization and pathology of thought.* N. Y.: Columbia Univ. Press. – **367**

RAPAPORT, D. (1959) The structure of psychoanalytic theory: a systematizing attempt. In Koch, S. *Psychology: a study of a science.* Vol. 3. N. Y.: McGraw-Hill, 55-183. – **484**

RASMUSSEN, T., *see* Penfield and Rasmussen (1950).

RATLIFF, F., and RIGGS, L. A. (1950) Involuntary motions of the eye during monocular fixation. *J. exp. Psychol.,* 40:687-701. – **226**

RAWCLIFFE, D. H. (1959) *Illusions and delusions of the supernatural and occult.* N. Y.: Dover. – **218**

RAYNER, R., *see* Watson and Rayner (1920).

REED, H. B. (1938) Meaning as a factor in learning. *J. educ. Psychol.,* 29:419-30. – **315**

REED, H. B., *see also* Briggs and Reed (1943).

REIFF, R., and SCHEERER, M. (1959) *Memory and hypnotic age regression.* N. Y.: Inter. Univ. Press. – **289, 291**

REMMERS, H. H., and RADLER, D. H. (1957) *The American teenager.* Indianapolis: Bobbs-Merrill. – **105, 109**

RENNIE, T. A. C. (1955) *Studies in urban mental health.* (Paper read at American Psychiatric Association, May, 1955; mimeographed.) – **529**

REYMERT, M. L. (Ed.) (1950) *Feelings and emotions.* N. Y.: McGraw-Hill. – **183**

REYNOLDS, B., and ADAMS, J. A. (1953) Motor performance as a function of click reinforcement. *J. exp. Psychol.,* 45:315-20. – **316**

REYNOLDS, M. M. (1928) Negativism of preschool children. *Teach. Coll. Contrib. Educ.,* No. 288.

RHINE, J. B. (1942) Evidence of precognition in the covariation of salience ratios. *J. Parapsychol.,* 6:111-43. – **219**

RHINE, J. B., and HUMPHREY, B. M. (1944) The PK effect: special evidence from hit patterns. I. Quarter distributions of the page. *J. Parapsychol.,* 8:18-60. – **218**

RHINE, J. B., and PRATT, J. G. (1957) *Parapsychology, frontier science of the mind.* Springfield, Ill.: Thomas. – **216, 219**

RIBBLE, M. A. (1943) *The rights of infants.* N. Y.: Columbia Univ. Press. – **76**

RICHARDSON, H. M. (1932) The growth of adaptive behavior in infants: an experimental study at seven age levels. *Genet. Psychol. Monogr.,* 12:195-359. – **276**

RICHARDSON, I. F., *see* Holmen and others (1956).

RICHARDSON, S. A., *see* Hastorf, Richardson and Dornbusch (1958).

RICHTER, C. P. (1943) The self-selection of diets. In *Essays in biology.* Berkeley: Univ. of California Press, 500-05. – **130**

RICKERS-OVSIANKINA, M. A. (Ed.) (1960) *Rorschach psychology.* N. Y.: Wiley. – **467**

RICKETT, A., and RICKETT, ADELE (1957) *Prisoners of liberation.* N. Y.: Cameron Associates. – **578**

RICKETT, ADELE, *see* Rickett and Rickett (1957).

RICKMAN, J. (Ed.) (1957) *A general selection from the works of Sigmund Freud.* N. Y.: Liveright. – **495**

RIESEN, A. H. (1951) Post-partum development of behavior. *Chicago Med. Sch. Quart.,* 13:17-24. – **68**

RIGGS, L. A., *see* Ratliff and Riggs (1950).

ROBERTS, H. V., *see* Wallis and Roberts (1956).

ROBERTS, S. O., *see* Carmichael, Roberts, and Wessel (1937).

ROBERTS, W. W., *see* Delgado, Roberts, and Miller (1954).

ROCK, I. (1957) The role of repetition in associative learning. *Amer. J. Psychol.,* 70:186-93. – **266**

ROCK, I., *see* Kaufman and Rock (1960).

RODRIGUES, J. A., *see* Bruner, Postman, and Rodrigues (1951).

ROE, A. (1952) *The making of a scientist.* N. Y.: Dodd, Mead. – **364**

ROE, A. (1956) *The psychology of occupations.* N. Y.: Wiley. – **612**

ROGERS, C. R. (1939) *The clinical treatment of the problem child.* Boston: Houghton Mifflin. – 550

ROGERS, C. R., (1951) *Client-centered therapy.* Boston: Houghton Mifflin. – 532, 533

ROGERS, C. R. (1961) *On becoming a person: a therapist's view of psychotherapy.* Boston: Houghton Mifflin. – 533

ROGERS, C. R., *see also* Muench and Rogers (1946).

ROGERS, C. R., and DYMOND, R. F. (Ed.) (1954) *Psychotherapy and personality change.* Chicago: Univ. of Chicago Press. – 533, 546, 550

ROHEIM, G. (1943) *The origin and function of culture.* N. Y.: Nervous and Mental Disease Publishing Co. – 82

ROKEACH, M. (1960) *The open and closed mind.* N. Y.: Basic Books. – 367, 486

RORSCHACH, H. (1942) *Psychodiagnostics.* Berne: Hans Huber. – 459

ROSENBERG, M. J. (1960a) Cognitive reorganization in response to the hypnotic reversal of attitudinal affect. *J. Pers.,* 28:39-63. – 566

ROSENBERG, M. J. (1960b) An analysis of affective-cognitive consistency. In Rosenberg and others. *Attitude organization and change.* New Haven, Conn.: Yale Univ. Press, 15-64. – 566, 567

ROSENBERG, M. J., HOVLAND, C. I., MC GUIRE, W. J., ABELSON, R. P., and BREHM, J. W. (1960) *Attitude organization and change.* New Haven, Conn.: Yale Univ. Press. – 580

ROSENBLITH, W. A. (Ed.) (1961) *Sensory communication.* N. Y.: Wiley. – 250

ROSENTHAL, D. (1959) Some factors associated with concordance and discordance with respect to schizophrenia in monozygotic twins. *J. nerv. ment. Dis.,* 129:1-10. – 437

ROSENZWEIG, M. R. (1954) Cortical correlates of auditory localization and of related perceptual phenomena. *J. comp. physiol. Psychol.,* 47:269-76. – 205

ROSENZWEIG, M. R., KRECH, D., and BENNETT, E. L. (1960) A search for relations between brain chemistry and behavior. *Psychol. Bull.,* 57:476-92. – 55

ROSENZWEIG, S. (1954) A transvaluation of psychotherapy: a reply to Hans Eysenck. *J. abnorm. soc. Psychol.,* 49:298-304. – 547

ROSS, A. M., *see* Kornhauser, Dubin, and Ross (1954).

ROSS, D., *see* Bandura, Ross, S., and Ross, S. A. (1961).

ROSS, H. V., *see* Buxton and Ross (1949).

ROSS, R. T., *see* Hull and others (1940).

ROSS, S., and HARRIMAN, A. E. (1949) A preliminary study of the Crocker-Henderson odor-classification system. *Amer. J. Psychol.,* 62:399-404. – 241, 243

ROSS, S. A., *see* Bandura, Ross, D., and Ross, S. A. (1961).

ROTH, B., *see* Kallmann and Roth (1956).

ROTH, W. F., JR., and LUTON, F. H. (1943) The mental health program in Tennessee. *Amer. J. Psychiat.,* 99:662-75. – 529

ROTTER, J. B. (1954) *Social learning and clinical psychology.* N. Y.: Prentice-Hall. – 538

ROTTER, J. B., and DYMOND, R. F., *see* Schroder and Rotter (1952).

RUBIN-RABSON, G. (1950) Medical practice with special reference to pediatrics. In Fryer, D. H., and Henry, E. R. *Handbook of applied psychology.* N. Y.: Rinehart, 625-30. – 604

RUCH, G. M., *see* Kelley and others (1953).

RUCH, T. C., *see* Patton and Ruch (1946).

RUEBUSH, B. K., *see* Sarason and others (1960).

RUGER, G. J., *see* Thorndike and Ruger (1923).

RUSK, R. R. (1940) The intelligence of Scottish children. *Yearb. nat. Soc. Stud. Educ.,* 39(II):269-73. – 440

RUSSELL, B., *see* Whitehead and Russell (1925).

RUSSELL, J. T., *see* Taylor and Russell (1939).

SABATTA, J. (1909) *Atlas and textbook of human anatomy.* N. Y.: Saunders. – 234

SAIT, E. M., *see* Hilgard, Margaret, and Sait (1940).

SALTZSTEIN, H. D., *see* Jackson and Saltzstein (1958).

SAMUELS, I. (1959) Reticular mechanisms and behavior. *Psychol. Bull.,* 56:1-25. – 40

SANDER, G., *see* Kallmann and Sander (1949).

SANDIFORD, P. (1938) *Foundations of educational psychology.* N. Y.: Longmans, Green. – 433

SANFORD, R. N., *see* Adorno and others (1950); Frenkel-Brunswik and Sanford (1945).

SANTOS, J., *see* Solley and Santos (1958).

SARASON, I. (1956) Effect of anxiety, motivational instructions, and failure on serial learning. *J. exp. Psychol.,* 51:253-60. – 333

SARASON, S. B., *see also* Mandler and Sarason (1952); Masland, Gladwyn, and Sarason (1958).

SARASON, S. B., MANDLER, G., and CRAIGHILL, P. G. (1952) The effect of differential instructions on anxiety and learning. *J. abnorm. soc. Psychol.,* 47:561-65. – 332, 333

SARASON, S. B., DAVIDSON, K. S., LIGHTHALL, F. K., WAITE, R. R., and RUEBUSH, B. K. (1960) *Anxiety in elementary school children.* N. Y.: Wiley. – 335

SCHACHTEL, E. G. (1959) *Metamorphosis.* N. Y.: Basic Books. – 289

SCHACHTER, S. (1959) *Psychology of affiliation.* Stanford, Calif.: Stanford Univ. Press. – 90, 138

SCHEERER, M., *see* Reiff and Scheerer (1960).

SCHEERER, M., *see also* Goldstein and Scheerer (1941).

SCHEIN, E. H. (1956) The Chinese indoctrination program for prisoners of war. *Psychiatry,* 19:149-72. – 577

SCHEIN, E. H., SCHNEIER, I., and BARKER, C. H. (1961) *Coercive persuasion.* N. Y.: Norton. – 577, 578, 581

SCHEINFELD, A. (1943) *Women and men.* N. Y.: Harcourt, Brace & World. – 122

SCHJELDERUP-EBBE, T. (1935) Social behavior of birds. In Murchison, C. (Ed.) *Handbook of social psychology.* Worcester, Mass.: Clark Univ. Press, 947-72. – 139

SCHLOSBERG, H. (1952) The description of facial expressions in terms of two dimensions. *J. exp. Psychol.,* 44:229-37. – 166

SCHLOSBERG, H. (1954) Three dimensions of emotion. *Psychol. Rev.,* 61:81-8. – 166, 167

SCHLOSBERG, H., *see also* Woodworth and Schlosberg (1954).

SCHMEIDLER, G. R., and MC CONNELL, R. A. (1958) *ESP and personality patterns.* New Haven, Conn.: Yale Univ. Press. – 218

SCHMIDT, H. O. (1945) Test profiles as a diagnostic aid: the Minnesota Multiphasic Inventory. *J. appl. Psychol.,* 29:115-31. – 455

SCHNEIER, I., *see* Schein, Schneier, and Barker (1961).

SCHNEIRLA, T. C., *see* Maier and Schneirla (1935).

SCHOENFELD, W. N., *see* Keller and Schoenfeld (1950).

SCHOOLER, K., *see* Carter and Schooler (1949).

SCHRAMM, W. (Ed.) (1954) *The process and effects of mass communication.* Urbana: Univ. of Illinois Press. – 580

SCHRAMM, W. (1960) Television in the life of the child: implications for the school. In Schramm, W. (Ed.) *New teaching aids for the American classroom.* Stanford, Calif.: Inst. for Comm. Res., 50-70. – 335, 574

SCHRODER, H. M., and ROTTER, J. B. (1952) Rigidity as learned behavior. *J. exp. Psychol.*, 44:141-50. – **357**

SCHROEDER, W. H., *see* Hendrickson and Schroeder (1941).

SCOTT, T. H., *see* Bexton, Heron, and Scott (1954); Doane and others (1959); Heron, Doane, and Scott (1956); Melzack and Scott (1957).

SEAGOE, M. V. (1936) The influence of degree of wholeness on whole-part learning. *J. exp. Psychol.*, 19:763-68. – **315**

SEARLE, L. V. (1949) The organization of hereditary maze-brightness and maze-dullness. *Genet. Psychol. Monogr.*, 39:279-325. – **426**

SEARS, P. S. (1940) Levels of aspiration in academically successful and unsuccessful children. *J. abnorm. soc. Psychol.*, 35:498-536. – **146**

SEARS, P. S., *see also* Sears, R. R., and others (1953).

SEARS, R. R. (1936) Experimental studies of projection: I. Attribution of traits. *J. soc. Psychol.*, 7:151-63. – **480, 513**

SEARS, R. R. (1943) Survey of objective studies of psychoanalytic concepts. *Soc. Sci. Res. Coun. Bull.*, 51. – **480, 545**

SEARS, R. R. (1961) Relation of early socialization experiences to aggression in middle childhood. *J. abnorm. soc. Psychol.*, 63:466-92. – **88, 141**

SEARS, R. R., *see also* Davis and others (1948).

SEARS, R. R., MACCOBY, E. E., and LEVIN, H. (1957) *Patterns of child rearing.* Evanston, Ill.: Row, Peterson. – **91, 92, 94, 137**

SEARS, R. R., WHITING, J. W. M., NOWLIS, V., and SEARS, P. S. (1953) Some child-rearing antecedents of aggression and dependency in young children. *Genet. Psychol. Monogr.*, 47:135-234. – **137, 140, 141**

SEARS, R. R., and WISE, G. W. (1950) Relation of cup feeding in infancy to thumb-sucking and the oral drive. *Amer. J. Orthopsychiat.*, 20:123-38. – **84**

SEARS, W. N., *see* Hilgard, Campbell, and Sears (1938).

SECORD, P. F. (1958) Facial features and inference processes in interpersonal perception. In Tagiuri, R., and Petrullo, L. (Eds.). *Person perception and interpersonal behavior.* Stanford, Calif.: Stanford Univ. Press, 300-15. – **553**

SECORD, P. F., BEVAN, W., and KATZ, B. (1956) Perceptual accentuation and the Negro stereotype. *J. abnorm. soc. Psychol.*, 53:78-83. – **561**

SEEMAN, J. (1949) A study of the process of nondirective therapy. *J. consult. Psychol.*, 13:157-68. – **534**

SEIBERT, L. C. (1932) A series of experiments on the learning of French vocabulary. *Johns Hopkins Univ. Stud. Educ.*, No. 18. – **306**

SELLS, S. B., *see* Woodworth and Sells (1935).

SELLS, S. B., and BERRY, C. A. (Eds.) (1961) *Human factors in jet and space travel: a medical-psychological analysis.* N. Y.: Ronald. – **596, 612**

SELYE, H. (1950) *The physiology and pathology of exposure to stress.* Montreal: ACTA Press. – **57**

SELYE, H. (1956) *The stress of life.* N. Y.: McGraw-Hill. – **57, 61**

SEMMES, J., *see* Nissen, Chow, and Semmes (1951).

SENDEN, M. V. (1932) *Raum- und Gestaltauffassung bei operierten Blindgeborenen vor und nach Operation.* Leipzig: Barth. – **194**

SETTLAGE, P. H., *see* Harlow and others (1952).

SEWARD, J. P. (1956) Reinforcement and expectancy: two theories in search of a controversy. *Psychol. Rev.*, 63:105-13. – **280**

SEYMOUR, R. V., *see* Austin, Bruner, and Seymour (1953).

SHAFER, R. (1954) *Psychoanalytic interpretation in Rorschach testing.* N. Y.: Grune and Stratton. – **485**

SHAFFER, L. F. (1947) Fear and courage in aerial combat. *J. consult. Psychol.*, 11:137-43. – **159**

SHAFFER, L. F., and SHOBEN, E. J., JR. (1956) *Psychology of adjustment* (2nd Ed.). Boston: Houghton Mifflin. – **55**

SHAW, C. R., MC KAY, H. D., and others (1942). *Juvenile delinquency in urban areas.* Chicago: Univ. of Chicago Press. – **531**

SHAW, J. C., *see* Newell, Shaw, and Simon (1958a), (1958b).

SHEER, D. (Ed.) (1961) *Electrical stimulation of the brain.* Austin, Tex.: Hogg Foundation and Univ. of Texas Press. – **61**

SHEFFIELD, F. D. (1961) Theoretical considerations in the learning of complex sequential tasks from demonstration and practice. In Lumsdaine, A. A. (Ed.) *Student response in programed instruction: a symposium.* Washington, D. C.: National Academy of Sciences–National Research Council. – **608**

SHEFFIELD, F. D., *see* Campbell and Sheffield (1953); Hovland, Lumsdaine, and Sheffield (1949).

SHELDON, W. H. (1954) *Atlas of men: a guide for somatotyping the adult male at all ages.* N. Y.: Harper. – **469**

SHELDON, W. H., and STEVENS, S. S. (1942) *The varieties of temperament.* N. Y.: Harper. – **469**

SHELDON, W. H., STEVENS, S. S., and TUCKER, W. B. (1940) *The varieties of human physique.* N. Y.: Harper. – **469**

SHIMMIN, S. (1958) Workers' understanding of incentive payment systems. *Occup. Psychol.*, 32:106-10. – **594**

SHLAER, S., *see* Hecht and Shlaer (1938); Hecht, Shlaer, and Pirenne (1941).

SHOBEN, E. J., *see* Shaffer and Shoben (1956).

SHOSTROM, E. L., *see* Barahal, Brammer, and Shostrom (1950).

SHOWER, E. G., and BIDDULPH, R. (1931) Differential pitch sensitivity of the ear. *J. acous. Soc. Amer.*, 3:275-87. – **239**

SHUTTLEWORTH, F. K. (1939) The physical and mental growth of girls and boys age six to nineteen in relation to age at maximum growth. *Monogr. Soc. Res. Child Develpm.*, 46, No. 210. – **98**

SIDMAN, M. (1960) *Tactics of scientific research.* N. Y.: Basic Books. – **29**

SIEGEL, S. (1956) *Nonparametric statistics.* N. Y.: McGraw-Hill. – **386, 392**

SIIPOLA, E. M. (1935) A study of some effects of preparatory set. *Psychol. Monogr.*, 46, No. 210. – **212**

SILBERMAN, H. F., *see* Coulson and Silberman (1959).

SIMMEL, M., *see* Heider and Simmel (1944).

SIMON, H. A., *see* Newell and Simon (1961); Newell, Shaw, and Simon (1958a), (1958b).

SIMON, T., *see* Binet and Simon (1905).

SIMPSON, G. G., PITTENDRIGH, C. S., and TIFFANY, L. H. (1957) *Life: an introduction to biology.* N. Y.: Harcourt, Brace & World. – **35, 36, 38**

SINGER, R., *see* Feshbach and Singer (1957).

SKEELS, H. M., *see* Skodak and Skeels (1949).

SKINNER, B. F. (1938) *The behavior of organisms.* N. Y.: Appleton-Century-Crofts. – **134, 259, 261, 287**

SKINNER, B. F. (1950) Are theories of learning necessary? *Psychol. Rev.*, 57:193-216. – **262, 265**

SKINNER, B. F. (1954) The science of learning and the art of teaching. *Harvard educ. Rev.*, 24:86-97. – **320**

SKINNER, B. F. (1958) Teaching machines. *Science,* 128:969-77.

SKODAK, M., and SKEELS, H. M. (1949) A final follow-up of one hundred adopted children. *J. genet. Psychol.,* 75:3-19. – **430, 431**

SLACK, C. W., *see* Ittleson and Slack (1958).

SLATER, E. (1953) *Psychotic and neurotic illnesses in twins.* London: Her Majesty's Stationery Office. – **437**

SLATER, J., *see* Berlyne and Slater (1957).

SLAVSON, S. R. (1950) *Analytic group psychotherapy with children, adolescents, and adults.* N. Y.: Columbia Univ. Press. – **534**

SLEIGHT, R. B. (1948) The effect of instrument dial shape on legibility. *J. appl. Psychol.,* 32:170-88. – **596**

SLOAN, L. L., and WOLLACH, L. (1948) A case of unilateral deuteranopia. *J. opt. Soc. Amer.,* 38:502-09. – **231**

SLOTKIN, J. S. (1952) *Personality development.* N. Y.: Harper. – **84**

SMITH, L. B. (1954) English treason trials and confessions in the sixteenth century. *J. Hist. Ideas,* 15: 471-98. – **577**

SMITH, M. B., *see* Bellak and Smith (1956).

SMITH, M. B., BRUNER, J. S., and WHITE, R. W. (1956) *Opinions and personality.* N. Y.: Wiley. – **564**

SMITH, M. E. (1926) An investigation of the development of the sentence and the extent of vocabulary in young children. *Univ. Ia. Stud. Child Welf.,* 3, No. 5. – **86**

SMITH, M. K. (1941) Measurement of the size of general English vocabulary through the elementary grades and high school. *Genet. Psychol. Monogr.,* 24:311-45. – **86**

SMITH, P. R., *see* Miller, Folley, and Smith (1953).

SMITH, S. (1942) Language and non-verbal test performance of racial groups in Honolulu before and after a 14-year interval. *J. gen. Psychol.,* 26:51-93. – **438**

SMITHIES, E. M. (1933) *Case studies of normal adolescent girls.* N. Y.: Appleton-Century-Crofts. – **81**

SNOW, C. P. (1959) *The two cultures and the scientific revolution.* N. Y.: Cambridge Univ. Press. – **609**

SNOWDON, R. J., *see* McConnell, Snowdon, and Powell (1955).

SNYDER, F. W., and PRONKO, N. H. (1952) *Vision with spatial inversion.* Wichita, Kans.: McCormich-Armstrong. – **193**

SNYDER, L. S. (1932) Studies in human inheritance: IX. The inheritance of taste deficiency in man. *Ohio J. Sci.,* 32:436-40. – **426**

SNYDER, W. U., and others (1947) *Casebook of non-directive counseling.* Boston: Houghton Mifflin. – **533**

SNYGG, D., *see* Combs and Snygg (1959).

SOAL, S. G., and BATEMAN, F. (1954) *Modern experiments in telepathy.* New Haven, Conn.: Yale Univ. Press. – **216, 217, 218**

SOKOLOV, E. N. (1960) Neuronal models and the orienting reflex. In Brazier, M. A. B. (Ed.) *The central nervous system and behavior.* N. Y.: Josiah Macy Jr. Foundation. – **132**

SOLLEY, C. M., and MURPHY, G. (1960) *Development of the perceptual world.* N. Y.: Basic Books. – **210, 222**

SOLLEY, C. M., and SANTOS, J. (1958) Perceptual learning with partial verbal reinforcement. *Percept. mot. skills,* 8:183-93. – **197, 198**

SOLOMON, P. (Ed., with others) (1961) *Sensory deprivation.* Cambridge, Mass.: Harvard Univ. Press. – **61**

SOLOMON, R. L., *see* Lambert, Solomon, and Watson (1949).

SONES, A. M., and STROUD, J. B. (1940) Review, with special reference to temporal position. *J. educ. Psychol.,* 31:665-76. – **307**

SPALTEHOLZ, W. (1918) *Handatlas der Anatomie des Menschen.* Leipzig: S. Hirzel. – **234**

SPEARMAN, C. (1904) "General intelligence" objectively determined and measured. *Amer. J. Psychol.,* 15:201-93. – **408**

SPENCE, K. W. (1954) Current interpretations of learning data and some recent developments in stimulus-response theory. In the Kentucky Symposium, *Learning theory, personality theory, and clinical research.* N. Y.: Wiley. – **333**

SPENCE, K. W. (1956) *Behavior theory and conditioning.* New Haven, Conn.: Yale Univ. Press. – **150, 282**

SPENCE, K. W., and NORRIS, E. B. (!950) Eyelid conditioning as a function of the inter-trial interval. *J. exp. Psychol.,* 40:716-20. – **311**

SPERRY, R. W. (1951) Mechanisms of neural maturation. In Stevens, S. S. (Ed.) *Handbook of experimental psychology.* N. Y.: Wiley, 236-80. – **245**

SPERRY, R. W. (1959) The growth of nerve circuits. *Scient. Amer.,* 200, Nov. – **65, 66**

SPITZ, R. A. (1946) The smiling response: a contribution to the ontogenesis of social relations. *Genet. Psychol. Monogr.,* 34:57-125. – **85**

SPITZER, H. F. (1939) Studies in retention. *J. educ. Psychol.,* 30:641-56. – **307**

STACEY, C. L., and DE MARTINO, M. F. (Eds.) (1958) *Understanding human motivation.* Cleveland, O.: Howard Allen. – **157**

STAFF, PERSONNEL RESEARCH SECTION, CLASSIFICATION AND REPLACEMENT BRANCH, ADJUTANT GENERAL'S OFFICE (1945) The Army General Classification Test. *Psychol. Bull.,* 42:760-68. – **438**

STAGNER, R. (1956) *Psychology of industrial conflict.* N. Y.: Wiley. – **612**

STAGNER, R. (1961) *Psychology of personality* (3rd Ed.). N. Y.: McGraw-Hill. – **495**

STAGNER, R., CHALMERS, W. E., and DERBER, M. (1958) Guttman-type scales for union and management attitudes toward each other. *J. appl. Psychol.,* 42: 293-300. – **596**

STEIN, M. I. (1955) *The Thematic Apperception Test* (Rev. Ed.). Reading, Mass.: Addison-Wesley. – **458**

STEIN, M. I. (Ed.) (1961) *Contemporary psychotherapies.* N. Y.: Free Press of Glencoe. – **500**

STEIN, M. I., *see also* Stern, Stein, and Bloom (1956).

STELLAR, E. (1954) The physiology of motivation. *Psychol. Rev.,* 61:5-22. – **162**

STENDLER, C. B., *see* Martin and Stendler (1959).

STEPHENSON, W. (1939) Methodological consideration of Jung's typology. *J. ment. Sci.,* 85:185-205. – **492, 493**

STEPHENSON, W. (1953) *The study of behavior: Q-technique and its methodology.* Chicago: Univ. of Chicago Press. – **492**

STERN, C. (1960) *Principles of human genetics* (2nd Ed.). San Francisco: Freeman. – **446**

STERN, G. G., STEIN, M. I., and BLOOM, B. S. (1956) *Methods in personality assessment.* Glencoe, Ill.: Free Press. – **467**

STEVENS, S. S. (Ed.) (1951) *Handbook of experimental psychology.* N. Y.: Wiley. – **250**

STEVENS, S. S. (1961) Is there a quantal threshold? In Rosenblith, W. A. (Ed.) *Sensory communication.* N. Y.: Wiley, 806-13. – **224**

STEVENS, S. S., *see also* Sheldon and Stevens (1942); Sheldon, Stevens, and Tucker (1940).

STEVENS, S. S., and DAVIS, H. (1938) *Hearing.* N. Y.: Wiley. – **238**

STEVENS, S. S., DAVIS, H., and LURIE, M. H. (1935) The localization of pitch perception on the basilar membrane. *J. gen. Psychol.,* 13:297-315. – **242**

STEWART, N. (1947) A.G.C.T. scores of army personnel grouped by occupations. *Occupations,* 26:5-41. – **439**

STICE, G. F., *see* Cattell, Kristy, and Stice (1957).

STOKES, D. E., *see* Campbell and others (1960).

STOLZ, H. R., and STOLZ, L. M. (1951) *Somatic development of adolescent boys.* N. Y.: Macmillan. – **96, 97, 98, 122**

STOLZ, L. M., *see* Stolz, H. R., and Stolz, L. M. (1951).

STONE, C. P., and BARKER, R. G. (1937) Aspects of personality and intelligence in postmenarcheal and premenarcheal girls of the same chronological age. *J. comp. Psychol.,* 23:439-55. – **104**

STONE, L. J. (1954) A critique of studies ˙of infant isolation. *Child Develpm.,* 25:9-20. – **84**

STORM, T., *see* Child, Storm and Veroff (1958).

STRANDSKOV, H. H. (1954) A twin study pertaining to the genetics of intelligence. *Caryologia Suppl., Att. 9th Internat. Cong. Genet.,* 811-13. (Cited by Fuller and Thompson, 1960, page 203.) – **435**

STRANG, R. (1957) *The adolescent views himself.* N. Y.: McGraw-Hill. – **122**

STRATTON, G. M. (1897) Vision without inversion of the retinal image. *Psychol. Rev.,* 4:341-60, 463-81. – **193**

STRAUSS, A. A., *see* Werner and Strauss (1941).

STREET, R. F. (1931) A Gestalt completion test. *Teach. Coll. Contr. Educ.,* No. 481. – **196**

STRONG, E. K., JR. (1938) *Psychological aspects of business.* N. Y.: McGraw-Hill. – **593**

STRONG, E. K., JR. (1943) *Vocational interests of men and women.* Stanford, Calif.: Stanford Univ. Press. – **589, 612**

STRONG, E. K., JR. (1955) *Vocational interests 18 years after college.* Minneapolis: Univ. of Minnesota Press. – **588, 612**

STRONG, J. A., *see* Jacobs and Strong (1959).

STROUD, J. B. (1942) Predictive value of obtained intelligence quotients of groups favored and unfavored in socio-economic status. *Elem. Sch. J.,* 43:97-104. – **403**

STROUD, J. B., *see also* Knief and Stroud (1959).

STRUPP, H. H. (1959) Toward an analysis of the therapist's contribution to the treatment process. *Psychiatry,* 22:349-62. – **542**

STRUPP, H. H. (1960) Some comments on the future of research in psychotherapy. *Behav. Sci.,* 5:60-71. – **542**

STUIT, D. B. (1941) The prediction of scholastic success in a college of medicine. *Educ. psychol. Meas.,* 1:77-84. – **586**

SUCI, G. J., *see* Osgood, Suci, and Tannenbaum (1957).

SULLIVAN, H. S. (1949) The theory of anxiety and the nature of psychotherapy. *Psychiatry,* 12:3-13. – **174**

SUPER, D. E. (1955) *Opportunities in psychology.* N. Y.: Vocational Guidance Manuals. – **612**

SUPER, D. E. (1957) *The psychology of careers.* N. Y.: Harper. – **612**

SUPPES, P., and ATKINSON, R. C. (1960) *Markov learning models for multiperson interactions.* Stanford, Calif.: Stanford Univ. Press. – **285**

SVENDSEN, M., *see* Johnson and others (1941).

SWANSON, C. E., *see* Miller and Swanson (1959).

SWARTZ, J. D., *see* Holtzman and others (1961).

SWEENEY, E. J. (1953) *Sex differences in problem solving.* Res. Rept. No. 1, ONR Contract 25125. Stanford, Calif.: Dept. of Psychology. – **364**

SWETS, J. A. (1961) Is there a sensory threshold? *Science,* 134:168-77. – **224**

SYMONDS, P. M. (1949) *Dynamic psychology.* N. Y.: Appleton-Century-Crofts. – **512, 521**

SYSTEM DEVELOPMENT CORPORATION (1959) *1959 salary survey of human factors professional personnel.* Santa Monica, Calif.: System Development Corp. – **595**

SZUREK, S. A., *see* Johnson and others (1941).

TAGIURI, R. (1958) Social preference and its perception. In Tagiuri, R., and Petrullo, L. (Eds.) *Person perception and interpersonal behavior.* Stanford, Calif.: Stanford Univ. Press, 316-36. – **555**

TAGIURI, R., *see also* Kogan and Tagiuri (1958).

TAGIURI, R., and PETRULLO, L. (Eds.) (1958) *Person perception and interpersonal behavior.* Stanford, Calif.: Stanford Univ. Press. – **216, 552, 580**

TANNENBAUM, P. H., *see* Osgood, Suci, and Tannenbaum (1957).

TANSER, H. A. (1939) *The settlement of Negroes in Kent County, Ontario.* Chatham, Ontario: Shephard Pub. Co. – **443**

TASAKI, I., *see* Hild, Chang, and Tasaki (1958).

TAYLOR, D. W. (1943) The learning of radio-telegraphic code. *Amer. J. Psychol.,* 56:319-53. – **315**

TAYLOR, D. W., *see also* Adamson and Taylor (1954).

TAYLOR, D. W., and BORING, E. G. (1942) Apparent size as a function of distance for monocular observers. *Amer. J. Psychol.,* 55:102-05. – **192, 199**

TAYLOR, D. W., and FAUST, W. L. (1952) Twenty questions: efficiency in problem solving as a function of size of group. *J. exp. Psychol.,* 44:360-68. – **357**

TAYLOR, D. W., and MC NEMAR, O. (1955) Problem solving and thinking. *Ann. Rev. Psychol.,* 6:455-82. – **357**

TAYLOR, D. W., BERRY, P. C., and BLOCK, C. H. (1958) Does group participation when using brainstorming facilitate or inhibit creative thinking? *Admin. Sci. Quart.,* 3:23-47. – **358**

TAYLOR, F. W. (1911) *The principles of scientific management.* N. Y.: Harper. – **593**

TAYLOR, H. C., and RUSSELL, J. T. (1939) The relationship of validity coefficients to the practical effectiveness of tests in selection: discussion and tables. *J. appl. Psychol.,* 23:565-78. – **592**

TAYLOR, H. R., *see* Blankenship and Taylor (1938).

TAYLOR, N. B., *see* Best and Taylor (1950).

TAYLOR, W. S. (1933) A critique of sublimation in males: a study of forty superior single men. *Genet. Psychol. Monogr.,* 13:1-115. – **518**

TEEVAN, R. C., and BIRNEY, R. C. (Eds.) (1961) *Color vision.* Princeton, N. J.: Van Nostrand. – **250**

TERMAN, L. M., *see* Kelley and others (1953).

TERMAN, L. M., and MERRILL, M. A. (1937) *Measuring intelligence.* Boston: Houghton Mifflin. – **405**

TERMAN, L. M., and MERRILL, M. A. (1960) *Stanford-Binet intelligence scale: Manual for the third revision, Form L-M.* Boston: Houghton Mifflin. – **442**

TERMAN, L. M., and MILES, C. C. (1936) *Sex and personality,* N. Y.: McGraw-Hill. – **112, 113**

TERMAN, L. M., and ODEN, M. H. (1947) *The gifted child grows up.* Stanford, Calif.: Stanford Univ. Press. – **418**

TERMAN, L. M., and ODEN, M. H. (1959) *The gifted group at mid-life.* Stanford, Calif.: Stanford Univ. Press. – **417, 419, 422**

TERMAN, L. M., and others (1938) *Psychological factors in marital happiness*. N. Y.: McGraw-Hill. – **114, 115**

THIESSEN, D. D., and MC GAUGH, J. L. (1958) Conflict and curiosity in the rat. Paper, Western Psychol. Assn., Monterey, Calif., Apr. 16-18. – **132**

THIGPEN, C. H., and CLECKLEY, H. M. (1954) A case of multiple personality. *J. abnorm. soc. Psychol.,* 49:135-51. – **489, 490**

THIGPEN, C. H., and CLECKLEY, H. M. (1957) *The three faces of Eve.* N. Y.: McGraw-Hill. – **489**

THOMAS, H., *see* Block and Thomas (1955).

THOMAS, W. I. (1923) *The unadjusted girl.* Boston: Little, Brown. – **125**

THOMPSON, H., *see* Gesell and Thompson (1941).

THOMPSON, W. R. (1954) The inheritance and development of intelligence. *Proc. Assn. Res. Nerv. Ment. Dis.,* 33:209-31. – **427**

THOMPSON, W. R., *see also* Fuller and Thompson (1960).

THOMSON, G. H. (1921) The Northumberland mental tests. *Brit. J. Psychol.,* 12:201-22. – **440**

THORNDIKE, E. L. (1911) *Animal intelligence.* N. Y.: Macmillan. – **265**

THORNDIKE, E. L. (1924) Mental discipline in high school studies. *J. educ. Psychol.,* 15:1-22, 83-98. – **317**

THORNDIKE, E. L. (1932) Reward and punishment in animal learning. *Comp. Psychol. Monogr.,* 8, No. 39. – **328**

THORNDIKE, E. L. (1935) *The psychology of wants, interests, and attitudes.* N. Y.: Appleton-Century-Crofts. – **328**

THORNDIKE, E. L., and RUGER, G. J. (1923) The effect of first-year Latin upon knowledge of English words of Latin derivation. *Sch. & Soc.,* 81:260-70, 417-18. – **317**

THORNDIKE, R. L. (1954) The psychological value systems of psychologists. *Amer. Psychologist,* 9:787-89. – **602**

THORNDIKE, R. L., and HAGEN, E. (1961) *Measurement and evaluation in psychology and education.* N. Y.: Wiley. – **422**

THORPE, J. S., *see* Holtzman and others (1961).

THOULESS, R. H. (1950) Thought transference and related phenomena. *Proc. Roy. Institution of Great Britain.* – **216**

THRALL, R. M., COOMBS, C. H., and DAVIS, R. L. (Eds.) (1954) *Decision processes.* N. Y.: Wiley. – **157**

THURSTONE, L. L. (1938) Primary mental abilities. *Psychometr. Monogr.,* No. 1. Chicago: Univ. of Chicago Press. – **409**

THURSTONE, L. L. (1947) *Multiple-factor analysis.* Chicago: Univ. of Chicago Press. – **409**

THURSTONE, L. L., *see also* Peterson and Thurstone (1932).

THURSTONE, L. L., and CHAVE, E. J. (1929) *The measurement of attitudes.* Chicago: Univ. of Chicago Press. – **565**

THURSTONE, L. L., and THURSTONE, T. G. (1941) Factorial studies of intelligence. *Psychometr. Monogr.,* No. 2. Chicago: Univ. of Chicago Press. – **401, 402, 409, 410**

THURSTONE, T. G., *see* Thurstone, L. L., and Thurstone, T. G. (1941).

TIETZE, C., *see* Lemkau, Tietze, and Cooper (1941).

TIETZE, T. (1949) A study of mothers of schizophrenic patients. *Psychiatry,* 12:55-65. – **528**

TIFFANY, L. H., *see* Simpson, Pittendrigh, and Tiffany (1957).

TIFFIN, J. (1959) Six merit rating systems. *Personnel J.,* 37:288-91. – **463**

TIGHE, T. J., *see* Walk, Gibson, and Tighe (1957).

TILLICH, P. (1952) *The courage to be.* New Haven, Conn.: Yale Univ. Press. – **174**

TINBERGEN, N. (1951) *The study of instinct.* London: Oxford Univ. Press. – **67**

TINKLEPAUGH, O. L. (1928) An experimental study of representative factors in monkeys. *J. comp. Psychol.,* 8:197-236. – **278**

TJIO, J. H., and LEVAN, A. (1956) The chromosome number of man. *Hereditas,* 42, 1. – **424**

TOLMAN, E. C. (1932) *Purposive behavior in animals and men.* N. Y.: Appleton-Century-Crofts. – **287**

TOLMAN, E. C. (1948) Cognitive maps in rats and men. *Psychol. Rev.,* 55:189-208. – **277**

TOLMAN, E. C., and HONZIK, C. H. (1930) Introduction and removal of reward, and maze performance in rats. *Univ. Calif. Publ. Psychol.,* 4:257-75. – **279**

TOLMAN, R. S., *see* Meyer and Tolman (1955).

TOMKINS, S. S. (1947) *The Thematic Apperception Test: the theory and technique of interpretation.* N. Y.: Grune and Stratton. – **467**

TRAGER, G. L. (1957) Language. In *Encyclopedia Britannica,* XIII:696-703. – **85**

TRIST, E. L., *see* Curle and Trist (1947).

TRYON, C. M. (1943) Evaluations of adolescent personality by adolescents. In Barker, R. G., Kounin, J. S., and Wright, H. F. (Eds.) *Child behavior and development.* N. Y.: McGraw-Hill, 545-66. – **107**

TRYON, R. C. (1940) Genetic differences in maze-learning ability in rats. *Yearb. nat. Soc. Stud. Educ.,* I:111-19. – **426**

TSAI, C. (1925) The relative strength of sex and hunger motives in the albino rat. *J. comp. Psychol.,* 5:407-15. – **135**

TSANG, Y. C. (1938) Hunger motivation in gastrectomized rats. *J. comp. Psychol.,* 26:1-17. – **128**

TUCKER, W. B., *see* Sheldon, Stevens, and Tucker (1940).

TUDDENHAM, R. D. (1948) Soldier intelligence in World Wars I and II. *Amer. Psychologist,* 3:54-56. – **439**

TUDDENHAM, R. D., *see also* Bayley and Tuddenham (1944).

TURPIN, R., *see* Lejeune, Gautier, and Turpin (1959).

TYLER, L. E. (1956) *The psychology of human differences* (2nd Ed.). N. Y.: Appleton-Century-Crofts. – **422, 446, 469**

TYLER, R. W. (1934) Some findings from studies in the field of college biology. *Sci. Educ.,* 18:133-42. – **309**

TYLER, R. W., *see also* Eells and others (1951).

UNDERWOOD, B. J. (1957a) Interference and forgetting. *Psychol. Rev.,* 64:49-60. – **300, 301**

UNDERWOOD, B. J. (1957b) *Psychological research.* N. Y.: Appleton-Century-Crofts. – **29**

UNDERWOOD, B. J. (1961) Ten years of massed practice on distributed practice. *Psychol. Rev.,* 68:229-47. – **313**

UNDERWOOD, B. J., *see also* Morgan and Underwood (1950).

VAN LEHN, R., *see* Lacey and Van Lehn (1952), Lacey, Bateman, and Van Lehn (1952).

VERNON, P. E. (1950) The validation of civil service selection board procedures. *Occup. Psychol.,* 24: 75-95. – **464**

VERNON, P. E., *see* Allport, Vernon, and Lindzey (1960).

VEROFF, J., *see* Child, Storm, and Veroff (1958).

VERPLANCK, W. S. (1955) The control of the content of conversation: reinforcement of statements of opinion. *J. abnorm. soc. Psychol.,* 51:668-76. – **265**

VINACKE, W. E. (1952) *The psychology of thinking.* N. Y.: McGraw-Hill. – **367**

VINACKE, W. E., *see also* Eindhoven and Vinacke (1952).

VINCE, P., *see* Himmelweit, Oppenheim, and Vince (1958).

VOEKS, V. W. (1955) Gradual strengthening of S-R connections or increasing number of S-R connections. *J. Psychol.,* 39:289-99. – **266**

VOGT, E. Z., and HYMAN, R. (1959) *Water witching U.S.A.* Chicago, Ill.: Univ. of Chicago Press. – **219**

VOLKART, E. H., *see* Kelley and Volkart (1952).

VON BRACKEN, H., *see* David and Von Bracken (1957).

WAITE, R. R., *see* Sarason and others (1960).

WALD, G. (1951) The photochemical basis of rod vision. *J. opt. Soc. Amer.,* 41:949-56. – **231**

WALD, G. (1954) The molecular basis of visual excitation. *Amer. Scientist,* 42:73-95. – **231**

WALK, R. D., GIBSON, E. J., and TIGHE, T. J. (1957) Behavior of light- and dark-reared rats on a visual cliff. *Science,* 126:80-1. – **210**

WALLACH, H. (1948) Brightness constancy and the nature of achromatic colors. *J. exp. Psychol.,* 38: 310-24. – **210**

WALLACH, H., and GALLOWAY, A. (1946) The constancy of colored objects in colored illumination. *J. exp. Psychol.,* 36:119-26. – **188**

WALLAS, G. (1921) *The art of thought.* N. Y.: Harcourt, Brace & World. – **360**

WALLIN, P., *see* Burgess and Wallin (1953).

WALLIS, W. A., and ROBERTS, H. V. (1956) *Statistics: a new approach.* Glencoe, Ill.: Free Press. – **392**

WALLS, G. L. (1960) "Land! Land!" *Psychol. Bull.,* 57:29-48. – **233**

WALTER, A. A., *see* Carmichael, Hogan, and Walter (1932).

WALTERS, R. H., *see* Bandura and Walters (1959).

WANG, G. H. (1923) The relation between "spontaneous" activity and oestrous cycle in the white rat. *Comp. Psychol. Monogr.,* 2, No. 6. – **136**

WAPNER, S., *see* Werner and Wapner (1955); Witkin and others (1954).

WARD, A. W., *see* Coleman and Ward (1955).

WARD, L. B. (1937) Reminiscence and rote learning. *Psychol. Monogr.,* 49, No. 220. – **293, 300, 315**

WARDEN, C. J. (1931) *Animal motivation.* N. Y.: Columbia Univ. Press. – **134**

WASHBURN, A. L., *see* Cannon and Washburn (1912).

WATSON, G. (1942) Morale during unemployment. In Watson, G. (Ed.) *Civilian morale.* Boston: Houghton Mifflin. – **547**

WATSON, J. B. (1913) Psychology as the behaviorist views it. *Psychol. Rev.,* 20:158-77. – **17**

WATSON, J. B. (1925) *Behaviorism* (Revised Ed., 1930). N. Y.: Norton. – **17**

WATSON, J. B., and RAYNER, R. (1920) Conditioned emotional reactions. *J. exp. Psychol.,* 3:1-14. – **170**

WATSON, P. D., *see* Lambert, Solomon, and Watson (1949).

WATSON, R. I. (1954) *Psychology as a profession.* Garden City, N. Y.: Doubleday. – **612**

WATTENBERG, W. W. (1955) *The adolescent years.* N. Y.: Harcourt, Brace & World. – **122**

WECHSLER, D. (1949) *Wechsler intelligence scale for children.* N. Y.: Psychological Corp. – **407**

WECHSLER, D. (1955) *The Wechsler Adult Intelligence Scale manual.* N. Y.: Psychological Corp. – **413**

WECHSLER, D. (1958) *The measurement and appraisal of adult intelligence.* (4th Ed.) Baltimore: Williams & Wilkins. – **407, 422**

WEISS, P. A., *see* Willier, Weiss, and Hamburger (1955).

WEISSMAN, P. (1957) Conscious and unconscious autobiographical dramas of Eugene O'Neill. *J. Amer. psychoanal. Assn.,* 5:432-60. – **364**

WELLINGTON, M., *see* Wenger and Wellington (1943).

WELLMAN, B. L. (1945) I.Q. changes of preschool and non-preschool groups during the preschool years: a summary of the literature. *J. Psychol.,* 20:347-68. – **438**

WELSH, G. S., and DAHLSTROM, W. G. (Eds.) (1956) *Basic readings on the MMPI in psychology and medicine.* Minneapolis: Univ. of Minnesota Press. – **454, 467**

WELSH, G. S., *see also* Dahlstrom and Welsh (1960).

WENDT, G. R. (1951) Vestibular functions. In Stevens, S. S. (Ed.) *Handbook of experimental psychology.* N. Y.: Wiley, 1191-223. – **247**

WERNER, H., and STRAUSS, A. A. (1941) Pathology of figure-ground relation in the child. *J. abnorm. soc. Psychol.,* 36:236-48. – **415**

WERNER, H., and WAPNER, S. (1955) The Innsbruck studies on distorted visual fields in relation to the organismic theory of perception. *Psychol. Rev.,* 62:130-38. – **193**

WENGER, M. A., and WELLINGTON, M. (1943) The measurement of autonomic balance in children: method and normative data. *Psychosom. Med.,* 5:241-53. – **470**

WERTHEIMER, MAX (1912) Experimentelle Studien über das Sehen von Bewegungen. *Z. Psychol.,* 61: 161-265. – **19**

WERTHEIMER, MAX (1923) Untersuchungen zur Lehre von der Gestalt. *Psychol. Forsch.,* 4:301-50; portions trans. in Ellis, W. D. (1938) *A source book of Gestalt psychology.* N. Y.: Harcourt, Brace & World. – **194**

WERTHEIMER, MAX (1959) *Productive thinking* (Rev. Ed.). N. Y.: Harper. – **362**

WERTHEIMER, MICHAEL, *see* Beardslee and Wertheimer (1958).

WESMAN, A. G., *see* Seashore, Wesman, and Doppelt (1950).

WESSEL, N. Y., *see* Carmichael, Roberts, and Wessel (1937).

WEST, L. J., *see* Farber, Harlow, and West (1957); Milton and West (1961).

WEST, P. S. (1953) Social mobility among college graduates. In Bendix, R., and Lipset, S. M. (Eds.) *Class, status, and power.* Glencoe, Ill.: Free Press, 465-80. – **585**

WEST, P. S., *see* Havemann and West (1952).

WESTLEY, W. A., *see* Elkin and Westley (1955).

WEVER, E. G. (1949) *Theory of hearing.* N. Y.: Wiley. – **239, 250**

WHEATLEY, M. D. (1944) The hypothalamus and affective behavior in cats. *Arch. Neurol. Psychiat.,* 52:298-316. – **162**

WHITE, A. N., *see* Murray, Auld, and White (1954).

WHITE, R. W. (1956) *The abnormal personality* (2nd Ed.). N. Y.: Ronald. – **550**

WHITE, R. W. (1959) Motivation reconsidered: the concept of competence. *Psychol. Rev.,* 66:297-333. – **144**

WHITE, R. W., *see also* Smith, Bruner, and White (1956).

WHITEHEAD, A. N., and RUSSELL, B. (1925) *Principia mathematica* (2nd Ed.). Cambridge, Eng.: Cambridge Univ. Press. – **359**

WHITING, J. W. M. (1954) The cross-cultural method. In Lindzey, G. (Ed.) *Handbook of social psychology.* Reading, Mass.: Addison-Wesley, II, 523-31. – **83, 84**

WHITING, J. W. M., *see also* Sears and others (1953).

WHITING, J. W. M., and CHILD, I. L. (1953) *Child training and personality: a cross-cultural study.* New Haven, Conn.: Yale Univ. Press. – **82, 84, 481**

WHITWELL, J. R. (1936) *Historical notes on psychiatry.* London: Lewis & Co. – **527**

WHORF, B. L. (1950) *Four articles on metalinguistics.* Washington: Foreign Service Institute. – **348**

WHORF, B. L. (1956) *Language, thought, and reality.* (J. B. Carroll, Ed.). N. Y.: Wiley. – **348**

WIGGINS, J. S. (1959) Interrelationships among MMPI measures of dissimulation under standard and social desirability instructions. *J. consult. Psychol.,* 23: 419-27. – **457**

WIGGINS, J. S. (1962) Strategic, method, and stylistic variance in the MMPI. *Psychol. Bull.,* 59 (in press). – **457**

WILCOXON, H. C. (1952) "Abnormal fixation" and learning. *J. exp. Psychol.,* 44:324-33. – **509**

WILLIAMS, R. J. (1956) Biochemical individuality. N. Y.: Wiley. – **470**

WILLIER, B. H., WEISS, P. A., and HAMBURGER, V. (1955) *Analysis of development.* Philadelphia: Saunders. – **66, 94**

WINTERBOTTOM, M. (1953) The sources of achievement motivation in mothers' attitudes toward independence training. In McClelland, D. C., and others, *The achievement motive.* N. Y.: Appleton-Century-Crofts, 297-304. – **145**

WISE, G. W., *see* Sears and Wise (1950).

WITKIN, H. A. (1959) The perception of the upright. *Scient. Amer.,* 200:50-56. – **196**

WITKIN, H. A. LEWIS, H. B., HERTZMAN, M., MACHOVER, K., MEISSNER, P. B., and WAPNER, S. (1954) *Personality through perception.* N. Y.: Harper. – **215**

WITT, G. M., and HALL, C. S. (1949) The genetics of audiogenic seizures in the house mouse. *J. comp. physiol. Psychol.,* 42:58-63. – **426**

WITTREICH, W. J. (1952) The Honi phenomenon: A case of selective perceptual distortion. *J. abnorm. soc. Psychol.* 47:705-12. – **552**

WITTY, P. A., and JENKINS, M. D. (1934) The educational achievement of gifted Negro children. *J. educ. Psychol.,* 25:585-97. – **444**

WOLF, S., and WOLFF, H. G. (1942) Evidence on the genesis of peptic ulcer in man. *J. Amer. Med. Assn.,* 120:670-75. – **167**

WOLFE, J. B. (1936) Effectiveness of token-rewards for chimpanzees. *Comp. Psychol. Monogr.,* 12, No. 60. – **262**

WOLFF, H. G., *see* Wolf and Wolff (1942).

WOLFLE, D. (1948) Annual report of the executive secretary: 1948. *Amer. Psychologist,* 3:503-10. – **599**

WOLFLE, D. (1954) *America's resources of specialized talent.* N. Y.: Harper. – **419**

WOLLACH, L., *see* Sloan and Wollach (1948).

WOLMAN, B. B. (1960) *Contemporary theories and systems in psychology.* N. Y.: Harper. – **29**

WOLPE, J. (1958) *Psychotherapy by reciprocal inhibition.* Stanford, Calif.: Stanford Univ. Press. – **536, 542**

WOLPE, J. (1961) The prognosis in unpsychoanalyzed recovery from neurosis. *Amer. J. Psychiat.,* 117: 35-39. – **547**

WOOD, B. D., and FREEMAN, F. N. (1932) *An experimental study of the educational influences of the typewriter in the elementary school classroom.* N. Y.: Macmillan. – **72**

WOODROW, H. (1927) The effect of type of training upon transference. *J. educ. Psychol.,* 18:159-72. – **319**

WOODWORTH, R. S. (1938) *Experimental psychology.* N. Y.: Holt. – **165**

WOODWORTH, R. S. (1941) *Heredity and environment: a critical survey of recently published material on twins and foster children.* N. Y.: Soc. Sci. Res. Coun. Bull., No. 47. – **444**

WOODWORTH, R. S. (1948) *Contemporary schools of psychology* (Revised Ed.). N. Y.: Ronald. – **29**

WOODWORTH, R. S., and SCHLOSBERG, H. (1954) *Experimental psychology* (Revised Ed.). N. Y.: Holt. – **183, 205, 310, 335**

WOODWORTH, R. S., and SELLS, S. B. (1935) An atmosphere effect in formal syllogistic reasoning. *J. exp. Psychol.,* 18:451-60. – **341**

WRIGHT, B. A., *see* Barker and others (1953).

WRIGHT, H. F., *see* Barker and Wright (1954).

WULF, F. (1922) Über die Veränderung von Vorstellungen (Gedächtnis und Gestalt). *Psychol. Forsch.,* 1:333-73. – **295**

YACORZYNSKI, G. K., *see* Neymann and Yacorzynski (1942).

YARROW, L. J. (1961) Maternal deprivation: toward an empirical and conceptual re-evaluation. *Psychol. Bull.,* 58:459-90. – **84**

YERKES, R. M. (Ed.) (1921) Psychological examining in the United States Army. *Memoirs of the National Academy of Sciences,* Vol. 15. Washington: U.S. Government Printing Office. – **411**

YERKES, R. M. (1940) Social behavior of chimpanzees: dominance between mates, in relation to sexual status. *J. comp. Psychol.,* 30:147-86. – **139**

YERKES, R. M., and MORGULIS, S. (1909) The method of Pavlov in animal psychology. *Psychol. Bull.,* 6:257-73. – **254**

YOUNG, P. T. (1937) Laughing and weeping, cheerfulness and depression: a study of moods among college students. *J. soc. Psychol.,* 8:311-34. – **176, 179**

YOUNG, P. T. (1961) *Motivation and emotion.* N. Y.: Wiley. – **157, 183**

ZANDER, A. F. (1944) A study of experimental frustration. *Psychol. Monogr.,* 56, No. 256. – **507**

ZANDER, A. F., *see also* Cartwright and Zander (1960).

ZANGWILL, L. O., *see* Humphrey and Zangwill (1952).

ZEIGARNIK, B. (1927) Das Behalten erledigter und unerledigter Handlungen. *Psychol. Forsch.,* 9:1-85. – **304**

ZIMMER, H., *see* Biderman and Zimmer (1961).

ZIMMERMAN, R. R., *see* Harlow and Zimmerman (1959).

ZOLA, I. K., *see* McCord, McCord, and Zola (1959).

ZUBIN, J. (1954) Failures of the Rorschach technique. *J. proj. Tech.,* 18:303-15. – **461**

ZUBIN, J., *see also* Landis, Zubin, and Mettler (1950).

Index

(Page numbers in italics refer to charts, maps, tabular matter, and illustrations.)

Ability, 613; *see also* Aptitude; Achievement; Performance
Abilities: primary, 409-10, 628; as relevant to personality, 453
Ability tests, 112, 393, 585-86
Abnormal fixation, 508, 613
Abreaction, 545, 613
Absolute threshold, 223, 613
Abstraction, 345, 346
Acetylcholine, 55
Achievement, 394
Achievement motive, *126,* 144-46, 613
Achievement tests, 393, 396-97, 398, 399
Achromatic colors, 227, 229, 613
Acquiescence, in personality inventory, 457, 613
Action research, 558
Activation theory of emotion, 167
Activity, as drive, 132
Adaptive behavior, 55, 613
Additive mixture, 229, 613
Adjustment, 4; failure of defense mechanisms to provide, 520; vs. maladjustment, 522-23; to personal problems, rationality and irrationality in, 518-20
Adler, Alfred, 518
Adolescence, 95-110, 613; acne in, 100; age-mate relationships in, 106-07; awkwardness during, 101-02; bodily changes during, 96-102; and emancipation from home, 104-06; growth patterns in, and height, *97, 98,* 99-100; ideals formed in, 108 *ff.;* metabolism in, 100; motor skills during, 101, *101,* 102; parental control resented in, 105-06; problems of, 102-10; psychosexual development in, 478; psychosocial crises in, 479; and puberty, 95, 96-98; self-consciousness during, 102, 632; self-evaluation in, 108, *108,* 109, 110; sexual development in, 103-04; size-age confusion during, 101, 102, 632; values formed in, 108 *ff.,* 613
Adrenal glands, 32, 33-34, 613
Adrenalin, 33, 48, 161, 165, 528, 613
Adrenocortical hormones, 33
Adulthood, 110-20; achievement records in, 418-19; feminine role in, 111, 112, 113, 114; gifted children grown into, 417-19; happiest years of, 110, 111; intelligence in, 411-12, *413,* 417-19; marital happiness in, 114-15; masculine role in, 111, 112, 113, 114; productive years in, 116-19; psychosocial crises in, 479; and retirement, 120
Affective-arousal theory, of motivation, 150, 613

Affective experience, 158-59, 613
Affective reactions, 525, 566, 613
Affective tone, 158
Affects, changed under post-hypnotic suggestion, 566-68
Afferent nerves, 51, 52, 613
Affiliative motive, *126,* 137-39, 613
Afterimage, 230, 232, 613
Age(s) of maximum growth rates, *98;* and winning of championships in sports, 116
Age-mates, 106-07, 613
Aggression, 87, 88, *89, 126,* 139-41, 155, 613; direct, 506; displaced, 506-07
Agoraphobia, 524, 613
Alcoholics Anonymous, 548
Alcoholism, 503, 548
Algorithm, 358, 359, 613
Allergy, 34
All-or-nothing principle, 53
Allport, Gordon W., personality theory, 472, 473
Allport-Vernon-Lindzey Test, 364, 472
Alpha waves, of brain, *40*
Ambivalence, 500, 501, *501,* 502, 503, 613
Ambivert, 471
American Board of Examiners in Professional Psychology, 600
American Journal of Psychology, 15
American Men of Science, 418, 419
American Psychiatric Association, 529
American Psychoanalytic Association, 543
American Psychological Association, 598, 601
Amnesia, 9, 291, 302, 512, 517, 613; childhood, 289; *see also* Forgetting
Amoeba, 35
Amplitude, of sound wave, 234, 235, 236, *239*
Anal stage, 477, *478, 479,* 480, 613
Androgen, 613; *see* Hormones
Anger, 163, 169, 177; impulses following, 177; in infancy, 168; physiological responses in, 164, 165, 167
Antagonistic muscles, 31, 613
Anthropology, 8, 613
Anticipation method, in paired-associates learning, 273, 613-14
Anti-Semitism, 562
Anxiety, 139, 141, 167, 173, 174, 175, 485, 607, 614; and learning, 332-33
Anxiety reactions, 524, 614
Apathy, 507-08, 614
Aphasia, 9, 45, 350, 351, 614
Apperception, 15
Appetite, 130
Appetitive behavior, 149, 614; *see also* Goal activity; Drive(s)
Approach-approach conflict, 499
Approach-avoidance conflict, 500-01
Approximations, method of, 263-64, *265,* 624
Aptitude, 394, 614
Aptitude tests, 393, 394-96, 585, 586
Aqueous humor, 225
Arapesh, 82, 111
Area sampling, 570, 613
Argument, one-sided vs. two-sided, 575
Argumentum ad hominem, 341
Aristotle, 13
Army Alpha test, 411, 438, 439, 443
Army Beta test, 411
Army General Classification Test, 438
Aroused motive, 124, *125,* 128, 135, 143-44, 614; emotion as, 172
Arthritis, 34
Arts, creative thinking in, 362-64

Aspiration, level of, 151-52
Assimilation, in memory, 295, *296*, 614
Association: controlled, 336-37; free, 21, 336, 543, 546
Association areas, 45-46, 614
Association of American Medical Colleges, 585
Association psychology, 14, 22, 614
Associative thinking, 336, 337-41, 614
Asthenic body type, 469, 614
Attention, 210-12, 614
Attitudes, 563-68, 614; ambivalent, 500, 501, *501*, 502, 503; formation of, 564; measurement of, 564-66; surveys of, 390; as tendencies to experience emotions, 171
Attitude scale, 564-66, 614
Audience, experimental, 575-76
Auditory area, 45
Auditory sense, 233-40; and cerebral cortex, 45; physiology of, 238-39; theories of, 238, 239-40; *see also* Ear
Authoritarian personality, 480, 480 *n.*, 614
Autistic thinking, 337, 614
Autonomic nervous system, 46, *47*, 48, 49, 162, 614
Average(s), 371-73, 614
Aversive behavior, 131-32, 149, 614; *see also* Goal activity; Drive(s)
Avicenna, 527
Avoidance-avoidance conflict, 500
Avoidance learning, 329-30, 614
Axons, 52, *52*, 53, 614

Baby, *see* Infancy
Bach family, and inheritance of musical talent, *433*
Balanced state, theory of, 554-55, *555*
Barrier score, in Rorschach test, 461
Basal mental age, 405, 614
Basilar membrane, 233, 238, 242, 614
Beat, musical, 237
Becquerel, A. H., 360
Behavior 3, 6, 614; adaptive, 55; aggressive, 87, 88, *89*, 140-42, 155; compulsive, 515-16, *516;* negativistic, 87, 105, 415; novelty in, 263; operant, 258, 259, 260; orderly patterns of, in maturation, 69-70; political, 571-72, *572*, 574; regressive, 88, 509-10; respondent, 258; retrogressive, 510; role, 482; species-specific, 67; unconscious processes included in, 8; verbal reports in study of, 7; voting, 571-72, *572*, 574
Behavior genetics, 423-28, 609
Behavioral sciences, 8, 614
Behaviorism, 17-18, 19, 20, 349, 608-09, 614
Belief, 566
Bell, Alexander Graham, 235
Bell Telephone Laboratories, 235
Berkeley Growth Study, 429
Biceps, 32
Bimodal distribution, 426, *427*, 614
Binary digit, 354
Binet, Alfred, 401, 404
Binocular cues, *see* Stereoscopic vision; Stereophonic hearing
Biology, 34; psychology related to, 8
Birth order and personality, 90-91
Bit, in information theory, 354, 614
Bladder control, training in, 72-73, 78
Blind spot, 226
Blood: and emotional excitement, 159, 161; pressure, 159-61, *160*, *164*, 614; sugar in, 161; volume, 159-61, *160*, *164*, 614
Body image, 493
Body-sense area, 44, 614-15
Body types, in personality theory, 468-69

Brace Motor Skills Test, 101
Brain, 3, *41*, 606; alpha waves of, *40;* electrical stimulation of, 38-39, *39;* evolution of, 36-37; extirpation experiments on, 6, 38, 46; hemispheres of, 43; injury to, 38, 415; lobes of, 43; memory traces in, 294; organization of, 37-42; study of, methods for, 37-39; surgery on, in animals, 6, 38; and thinking, 349-51; tumor of, 38; visceral, 42; *see also* Cerebral cortex
Brain stem, 40, 615
Brainstorming, 358
Brainwashing, 568 *n.*, 576-78, 615
Breast-feeding, 76, *76*
Brightness, 187-89, 229-30, 615
Brightness constancy, 187, 188, *188*, 189, 615
Brill, A. A., *20*
Broca's speech area, 45, 615

California First-Year Mental Scale, 429
California Pre-school Scale, 429
California Psychological Inventory, 114
Calorimeter, 41
Camouflage, 196
Cannon, Walter B., 58, 161, 162, 360, 360 *n.*
Cardiac muscles, 31, 615
Cardinal disposition, 472-73, 615
Case history, 13
Caste, 615
Castration, in sex drive of rat, 136, 615
Categorization (stereotyping), 553, 560-61
Catharsis, emotional, 181; *see also* Abreaction
Cattell, J. McKeen, 15
Cattell, Raymond B., 473, 474, 475
Cattell's 16 PF Questionnaire, 455
Cell body, of neuron, 52
Center (nerve), 51, 615
Centile scale, 379, 396, 615
Central disposition, 472-73, 615
Central nervous system, 3, 51, 162, 615
Centralist position, 349, 615
Cerebellum, of dogfish, 37, *37*
Cerebral cortex, 37, 39, 42-46, 615; association areas of, 45-46; and emotional expression, 162-63; localized functions of, 42; projection areas of, 43, *43*, 44-46; of shrew, *38*
Cerebral hemispheres, 43, *44*, 45, 615
Cerebrum, 42, 43, *44*; of dogfish, 37
Chance events, 377
Character-psychology, 7
Chemical integration, 32, 615
Chicks, experiments with, 328
Childhood (children), 615; aggressive behavior in, 87, 88, 89, 141-42; attitudes, influenced by television, 574-75; birth order in, and personality, 90-91; disciplinary practices in, 91-92; feeding problems in, 91; frustration in, 504-10; and heredity, 428-36; language learned in, 71, 85-87; language in thinking of, 347-48; laughter in, 175-76, 177; maturation and training in, 70-74; and mental subnormality, 412-17; and mentally gifted, 417; play activities in, 87; psychosexual development in, 478; psychosocial crises in, 479; retardation in, 412, 413-14, 416; school as influence in, 93; sex roles in, 87-88; sibling rivalry in, 88-90; social relationships in, outside home, 92-93; therapy in, 535-36; *see also* Adolescence; Infancy; Intelligence quotient; Intelligence tests
Chimpanzees: dominance-submission among, 139-40; fear in, study of, 169-70; in food experiments, 133; insight of, in problem-solving, 274-75; rate of development vs. rate of human infant, 69-70; reared in dark, 68; vending machine operated by, 262

Half-split technique, use of, in information theory, 352-54
Hall, G. Stanley, 15, *20*, 162
Hallucination, 9, 525, 621
Halo effect, in rating, 463
Hamster, as experimental animal, 54
Hand, evolution of, *34*
Harvard University, 15
Hearing, *see* Auditory sense; Ear
Heart rate, in emotion, 161
Hedonism, 175, 621
Height: annual increments in, 98; growth in, *97*, 98, 99-100; resemblance in, of children of same parents, 434, *434*
Helmholtz, Hermann von, 232, 233, 238
Hemispheres, cerebral, 43, *44*, 45
Heredity, 8, 34; in animal behavior, 426-28; and environment, 67, 423, 430 *ff.*, 434, 437-44; in human behavior, 428-37; and mental illness, 436-37, 528; and musical talent, *433;* in schizophrenia, 528; *see also* Genetics
Hering theory of color vision, 232, 233
Heterosexuality, 154, 621
Heuristic methods, 358, 359, 621
Hilgard, J. R., 79 *n.*, 90 *n.*
Hilprecht, Hermann, 361
Hindbrain, 36, 40, 621; of dogfish, 37, *37*
Hitler, Adolf, scapegoating by, 561
Hobbes, Thomas, 14
Homeostasis, 40, 55, 56, 58, 621
Homeostats, in body, 40, 41, 621
Homo sapiens, 34
Homosexuality, 154, 621
Hope, as counterpart to anxiety, 174, 175
Hopi Indians, 70, 80
Hormones, 32, 33, 136-37, 161, 621
Hue, 229, 621
Hull-Spence theory of learning, 281-82
Human factors research, 8, 223, 591, 594-95, *595*, 621
Humanistic psychology, 608, 609
Hume, David, 14
Hunger, 126, 127, 128-31, 621
Hunger drive, 128-31, 621
Hunger pangs, 128, 621
Hydra, nerve net in, *35*
Hyperurbanism, 86, 621
Hypnosis, 9, 16, 289, 513, 566-67, *567*, 568, 568 *n.*, 621
Hypothalamus, 3, 40, 41, 131, 162; of dogfish, 37, *37*, 621
Hypothetical construct, 297, 621
Hysteria, 524

Id, 484, 485, 621
Idea, as representational process, 336
Ideal self, 492
Ideals, adolescent, 108 *ff.*
Identical components theory, 317, 621
Identical twins, 72, 73, 434, 435, 436, 437, *437*, 528, 621
Identification, 514, 621
Identification figures, 87, 450, 621
Identity formation, 450-51, 621
Idiot savant, 621
Illumination, 360, 622
Illusions, perceptual, 198-201, 622
Image, 345
Imitation (similance), *126*, 622
Immediate memory span, 306, 622
Implicit language habits, 349
Implicit movements, 17, 622

Imprinting, 66-67, 622
Impulse, nerve, 52-53
Incentive, 149, 150, 153, 622
Incubation, 360, 361, 622
Independent variable, 10, 10 *n.*, 11, 24, 269, 622
Individual, and personality syndrome, 488-91
Individual differences, 15, 390, 393-420, 622; *see also* Intelligence; Heredity; Intelligence tests; Aptitude tests; Achievement tests
Individual test, 411, 622
Individuality, 4
Industrial psychology, 591-98
Infancy, 64, 622; breast-feeding in, 76, *76*; crying in, occasions for, 169; emotional responsiveness in, 167-68, 170, *170;* fear in, 163, 170, *170;* feeding in, 75-76; frustration in, 81, 138; insecurity in, aftereffects of, 78-84; measurement of psychological development in, 428-29; and mothering, 76-78, 79, 80; muscular activity in, 69, *70;* orderly behavior patterns in, 69-70; perception in, 187; psychosexual development in, 478; psychosocial crises in, 479; socialization in, 74-78; sucking needs in, 76; walking learned in, 72
Infant debility, 79, 622
Inference, 7, 7 *n.;* functional, 553; statistical, 633
Inferiority complex, 172
Information: coding of, 354; half-split technique in use of, 352-54; measurement of, 354, 622
In-group, 106, 560, 561, 622
Inhibition, 256; proactive, 298, 299-301, 628; reciprocal, 538, 630; retroactive, 298, 299, 631
Inner ear, 233, 246, 622
Innervation, reciprocal, 32, 630
Insecurity, 78-84, 174
Insight: in problem-solving, 274-77, *280*, 630; in psychoanalysis, 545, 630
Instinct, 607, 630; controversy on, 67
Insulin, *32*, 622
Insulin shock, *32*, 622
Institute for Personality Assessment Research, 364, 464
Integration: chemical, 32-34, 615; mechanical, 30, 624; neural, 34, 625; within organism, 30-34; of personality, 450
Intelligence, 4; adult, 411-12, *413*, 417-19; defined, 404, 622; and education, 438-39; and ethnic groups, 441, 442; extremes of, 412-19; hereditary component in, 428-36; national differences in, analysis of, 440, 441, 442; occupational level related to, 439-40; racial differences in, analysis of, 440, 441, 442-44; subnormal, 412-17; wisdom differentiated from, 412
Intelligence quotient, 405-06, 429, 430, 431, 622; in American children of foreign parentage, 442, *442;* in adult intelligence, 411, 412; of criminals, 603; of foster children, 430, 431, *431*, 432, *432;* in mentally gifted children, 417, 418; in mentally subnormal children, 414, 415, 416; and racial differences, *443*, 444
Intelligence tests, 4, 15, 178, 401-20; adult, 411-12, *413*, 417-19; culture-fair, 402-03, 617; diagnostic, 406-10; factor analysis in, 408-10, 420; item selection in, 401-02, 403-04; present status of, 419-20; rapport in, 441
Intensity (emotion), 158-59, 178, 622
Interaction of two people, in person perception, 554
Interactive explanation, 22, 23, 622
Interactive theories, *see* Personality dynamics, theories of
Interests: personality reflected in, 453; tests for, in vocational guidance, *587*, 587-89, *589*

Intergroup tension, 560-63
Intermittent reinforcement, 260-61, *262*, 622
International Intelligence Test, 442
Interpersonal relatedness factor, in emotion, 166
Interpersonal relations, 555-63
Interpretation, in psychoanalysis, 544, 622
Interpretive therapy, 536, 622
Interval scale, 381, 622
Intervening variable, 50, 622
Interview, 13, 622
Interview analysis, *539*, 540, *540*
Intracerebral process, 50, 623
Intrapsychic process, 477
Intrinsic cortex, 46, 623
Intrinsic motivation, 326-27, 623
"Intrinsic system" (Pribram), 46
Introspection, 13, 13 *n.*, 14, 17, 19, 623
Introversion, 470, 471, 623
Investigatory response, 133, 623
Iowa, University of, 430, 432
Iris, 225, *225*
Irrationality, in problem-solving, 518-20; *see also* Defense mechanisms
Isolation chamber, experimental, *56*
Item, 401-04, 623

James, William, 15, 163, 187, 336, 337, 337 *n.*, 358, 463, 473, 607
James-Lange theory of emotions, 163, 623
J-curve, 623
Jealousy, 174, 477, 478, 623
Jellyfish, nerve net in, 35, *35*
Johns Hopkins University, 15
Jones, Ernest, *20*
Jordan, David Starr, 298
Judd, Charles H., 317
Jung, Carl G., *20*, 470
Juvenile delinquency, 23, 95, 107-08, 531, *531*, 603
Just-noticeable difference, 623; *see* Difference threshold

Kekule, Friedrich, 361
Kierkegaard, S., 174
Kinesthesis, 245-46, 623
Klinefelter's syndrome, 424, 425
Knee jerk, 49
Koffka, Kurt, 19
Kohler, I., 193
Köhler, Wolfgang, 19, 274

Laboratory, psychological, 9-11, 14
Labor-management relations, 596-98
Lack, as cause of frustration, 498
Ladd-Franklin theory of color vision, 232
Land polaroid camera, 233
Language, 342 *ff.*, 609; in children's thinking, 347-48; and forms of thought, 348-49; learned in childhood, 71, 85-87; *see also* Problem-solving; Thinking; Learning
Language habits, implicit, 349
Late adolescent phase, 97-98, 623
Latency, 623
Latent content, of dreams, 338, 623
Latent learning, 279, *279*, 623
Laughter, 175-77
Law, and psychology, 602-03
Law of effect, Thorndike's, 265, 623
Lawrence, M., 207
Lay psychoanalyst, 530 *n.*
Learning, 3, 4, 14, 20, 22, 607, 608; as achievement of understanding, 274-80; and anxiety, 332-33; associative, 252-53, 265-66, 281; cognitive, 253; defined, 64, 252, 623; of emotional expression, 168-70; emotions as obstacles to, 331-33; Estes statistical model of, 282-85; food preferences distorted by, 130; Hull-Spence theory of, 281-82; irrelevant, 333-34; latent, 279, *279;* management of, 311-34; mathematical models of, 281-85; and maturation, 70-74; and meaningfulness, 315-16; motivational control of, 325-31; multiple-response, 253, 267-74; nature of, 252-85, 312-14; paired-associates, 272, 273; by parts and wholes, 314-15; and personality development, 480-81; and personality dynamics, 485; place, *278*, 278-79; plateau in, 270; programed, 4, 319-25, 607-08; punishment and reward in control of, 325-31; pursuit-rotor, *269*, 270, *270;* readiness for, through maturation, 72; reward and punishment in control of, 325-31; self-recitation method in, 305, 306; sign, 277-79; of skills, 268-72; statistical model of, 282-85; through stimulus substitution, 255, 263; and teaching machine, 324-25; tension as aid to, 178; theories of, 252-85, 312-14; token, 262; understanding achieved by, 274-80; by wholes and parts, 314-15; *see also* Insight; Training
Learning curves, 269-70, 271, *271*, 273, 623
Legal psychology, 602-03
Lens of eye, 225, *225*, 226
Leonard, William Ellery, 173
Level of activation factor, 166
Level of aspiration, 151-52, 623
Leveling, 295, 623
Lewin, Kurt, 19, 20; field theory of, 485-86
Lewis, Sinclair, 449
Libido, 154, 623
Lie detector, 180, *180*, 181, 623
Life-space, Lewin's theory of, 485-86
Light, mixture of, 229; and shadow, perception of, 206, *207; see also* Color
Light adaptation, 227-28, 623
Limbic system, 42, 46, 623
Linear operator, 623; *see* Difference equation
Lobster, equilibratory organ of, 247
Localized functions, 42-46, 623
Local signs, 245
Location constancy, 187, 192-93, 624
Locke, John, 14
Locomotive God, The, 173
Locomotor exploration, 133, 624
Lodge, Oliver, 218
Loudness, 235, 236, 238, *239*, 240, 624
Lysergic acid derivative (LSD-25), 528, 624

Maladjustment, 522-23
Malaise vs. zest, 523
Malebranche, N. de, 200
Manic-depressive psychosis, 468, 469, 624
Manic disturbance, 453
Manifest content, of dreams, 338, 340, 624
Manipulation, as drive, 132
Marriage, happiness in, 114-15
Masochism, 141, 624
Mass media of communication, 572-75
Massed practice, 269, 624; vs. distributed practice, 311-14
Masturbation, 104
Maternal drive, 135-36, 624
Matrix intercorrelation, in study of emotion, 167
Maturation, 3, 64, 67, 69-74, 624; as embryological development, 64-66; of emotional patterns, 167-68; and environment, 65-66; orderly behavior patterns

Maturation (Cont.)
  in, 69-70; postnatal, 69; and readiness for learning, 72; and training, 70-74; *see also* Growth
Maze, 624
Maze behavior, *18*, 267, *267*, 277, 427, *427*, 501
Mean, 371, *372*, 624
Mean deviation, 374, 624
Meaning: as behavioral disposition, 345; connotative, 343, 344; denotative, 343; learning affected by, 315-16; and symbols, 342-45
Measure of central tendency, 371 *n.; see* Average
Measure of response, 624
Measure of variation, 370, 373-75, 624
Measurement: activity, 134-35, *134;* of approach-and-avoidance gradient, *503*; of attitudes, 564-66; of motivational dispositions, 142-44; of opinions, 568-71; in psychology, 23-27; of self-perception, 492-93
Mechanical aptitude tests, 394
Mechanical integration, 30, 624
Median, 372, 624
Mediation process, as fractional response, 345
Medicine, psychology related to, 8-9, 16, 603-04
Medulla, adrenal, 33
Medusa, nerve ring of, 35, *35*
Membership group, 624
Memory, 20, 42, 151; distortion of, 295-98; logical, vs. rote learning, 307-09; physiology of, 53-55; redintegrative, 288-89, 291; rote, *see* Rote memorization; *see also* Remembering
Memory drum, 272, *272*
Memory trace, 294, 297-98, 624; distortion of, 295-98
Menarche, 98, 624
Menninger School of Psychiatry, 464
Menstruation, 98, 100, 104, 624
Mental age, 401, 405, 614; basal, 405, 614
Mental health, 4, 522-49 *passim*, 609, 624; emotions in, 548-49; practices enhancing, 547-49; and self-understanding, 548-49; useful work and, 547; *see also* Psychotherapy
Mental illness, 523-30, 624; and heredity, 436-37, 528; prevalence of, 528-30; prospect of cure of, 528-30; *see also* Psychotherapy
Mentally defective, 413, 414-15, 624
Mentally gifted, 417-19, 624
Mentally retarded, 413-14, *414*, 624
Mentally subnormal, 412-17, 624
Mesmer, Anton, 16
Mesomorphic compound, 469, 624
Mesomorphy, 469
Metabolism, in adolescence, 100
Metaphorical generalization, 553
Midbrain, 36, 40, 624; of dogfish, 37, *37*
Middle ear, 233, 624
Miniature systems, 21, 22, 624
Minnesota, University of, 430, 431, 432
Minnesota Medical Aptitude Test, 586
Minnesota Multiphasic Personality Inventory (MMPI), 454-55, 457
Mirror drawing, *268*, 268-69, *269*, 624
MMPI, *see* Minnesota Multiphasic Personality Inventory
Modality, 624
Modalities of traits, 452, *452*
Mode, 372, 625
Model(s), 625; Estes statistical, 282-85; mathematical, of learning, 281-85; scientific, 21-22
Mongolism, 425
Monkeys, experiments with, 74, 77, *77*, 132, *133*, *274*, 277, 278, *526*, 527
Monochromatism, 230, 232, 625

Monocular cues, 205-06
Mood, 179, 625
Moon illusion, 200, *201*
Moss Medical Aptitude Test, 585, 586
Mother complex, 172
Mothering, 76-78, 79, 80
Motion and time study, 593-94, 625
Motion sickness, 247
Motivated forgetting, 301-05, 625; *see also* Repression
Motivation (motives), 3, 124-55, 607, 608; achievement, 144-48; affiliative, within social grouping, 137-39; aroused, 124, 135, 153; ego-integrative, 128, 144-48; and emotions, 172-78; intrinsic, 326, *326;* social, 127, 135-44; survival, 128-35; theories of, 149-55; unconscious, 148; *see also* Drive(s)
Motivational disposition, 124-27, 136, 153, 453, 625; measuring, 141-44; sex as, 136; *see also* Aroused motive
Motivational sequence, 175-78, *176*, 625
Motor area, 44, 625
Multimodal distribution, 625; *see* Mode
Multiple personality, 489-91, 625
Multiple-response learning, 253, 267-74, 625
Mundugumor, 82, 111
Münsterberg, Hugo, 602
Murphy, Gardner, 210, 216
Muscles, 3, 625; kinds of, 30-32; tension in, 31, 161; tone of, 31, 625; tremor of, in emotion, 161
Musical aptitude tests, 394
Musical talent, inheritance of, *433*
Mutation, 34
Myelin sheath, 52, 53, 625

Narcissism, 154, 478, 625
National Academy of Sciences, 119
National Association for Retarded Children, 413
National groups, and intelligence, 441, 442
National Institute of Mental Health, 604
National Science Foundation, 599, 600, 601
Nativism vs. empiricism, in space perception, 208, 210
Naturalistic observation, 12-13, 625
Nature-nurture issue, 444, 625; *see also* Heredity; Environment
Navaho Indians, 80, 82
Necker cubes, 197, 198, *198*
Need-drive-incentive theory, 149-50
Needs: drives arising from, 149; perception influenced by, 213; psychogenic, 125, 126, *126*; and values, 213-16; viscerogenic, 125
Negative incentive, 449, 500, 502-03, 625; *see also* Goal(s); Drive(s)
Negativistic behavior, 87, 105, 415
Negroes, 82, 141, 440, 441, 443, 444, 561, 567
Neo-Freudian theory, 483, 625
Nerve(s): afferent, 51, 52; degeneration of, 38; efferent, 51, 52; and transmission of impulses, 52-53
Nerve cell, *see* Neuron(s)
Nerve impulse, 52-53
Nerve net, 35, *35*, 36, 625
Nervous system, 3, 625; autonomic, 46, *47*, 48, 49, 162; central, 3, 51, 162; evolution of, 34-46; operation of, 48-55; *see also* Synaptic nervous system
Neural integration, 34, 625
Neuron(s), 35, 36, 40, 46, 51, 52, *52*, 53, 54, 55, 625
Neuroses, *see* Psychoneuroses
Newspapers, 572-73
Newton, Isaac, 228, 365
Night vision, 227
Noise, as complex sound, 237-38
Nominal defect, 350, 625
Nonliterate society, 82, 95, 111-12, 625

Perspiration control, and temperature change, 41-42, *42*

Persuasion, 575-76; *see also* Public opinion

Phallic stage, 477, 478, *478, 479,* 627

Pharmacology, 8

Phenomenology, 7, 19, 19 *n.*, 608, 609, 627

Phenotypes, 423-24, 627; variance of, 444

Phi phenomenon, 19, 202, *203,* 627

Phobias, 173

Phobic reactions, 524, 627

Physical sciences, and psychology, 8

Physiological motives, 127-36, 627; *see also* Social motives; Survival motives

Physiology, 627; and body types, 470; psychology related to, 8, 627

Physique, and personality, 452, 468-69

Pig, operant conditioning of, 264

Pigeon: intermittent reinforcement in, 260-61; operant conditioning of, by method of approximations, 264, *265*

Pilomoter response, 161, 627

Pitch, 235, 236, 240, 627

Pitchentera, 82, 627

Pituitary gland, 32

PK, *see* Psychokinesis

Place learning, *278,* 278-79, 627

Place theory, of hearing, 238, 239

Plasticity, *65,* 66

Plateau in learning, 270, 627

Plato, 13, 289

Play therapy, 535, 627

Pleasure principle, 484

Poincaré, Henri, 361

Polarized synaptic transmission, 36, *36,* 52, 53-54, 627; *see also* Neuron

Political behavior, 571-72, *572,* 574

Poll, public opinion, 390, 568-69; *see also* Opinion

Polyps, nerve net in, 35

Population, in statistics, 376, 628

Population genetics, 425-26, 628

Positive incentive, 499, 500-03, 628; *see also* Goal(s); Drive(s)

Post-hypnotic suggestion, 513, 628

Postpubescence, 97, 628

Practice, in learning skills, 269, 270

Prepuberal phase, 97, 628

Precognition, 216, 217, 220, 628

Prediction: clinical, 465, 466; statistical, 465, 466; tests as basis of, 397, 399-400

Predictive efficiency of *r,* 388, *388,* 628

Predictive validity, 399, 628

Preferences, as tendencies to experience emotions, 171

Pregenital stages of sexual development, 477, 478, *478, 479,* 628

Prejudice, 171, 560, 628; racial, 562-63

Preparation, 360, 628

Preparatory activity, 628; *see* Goal activity; Drive(s)

Preparatory set, in perception, 212-13, 628

Prepubescence, 97, 628

Pressey, S. L., 110, 320

Prestige-seeking, 152

Primary abilities, 409-10, 628

Primary colors, 229, 628

Primary Mental Abilities, tests for, 409, 435

Primary sex characteristics, 96, 628

Primary taste qualities, 241

Primitivation, 510, 628

Primitive Society, *see* Nonliterate society

Proactive inhibition, 298, 299-301, 628

Probability sampling, 570-71, 628

Probability values, 385, 628

Problem-solving, 4, 20, 351-59; and emotion, 178; heuristic, 358-59; insight in, 274-77, *280;* limitations upon, 518-19; obstacles to, 354-57; strategies in, 351-52; *see also* Language; Thinking

Productivity vs. unproductivity, 523

Product-moment correlation, 385, 386, 387

Profile: of scores, 454; trait, 473, *474,* 476

Profile analysis, 476

Programing, 319-25, 628; *see also* Teaching machine

Projection, 513-14, 549, 553, 553 *n.*, 628

Projection area, 42-43, 44-45, 628

Projective tests, in personality appraisal, 457-63, 628

Prolactin, 136, 628

Proximity principle, 194, 195, *195*

Psi, 218, 220, 628

Psychiatric nurse, 530, 628

Psychiatric social worker, 530, 628

Psychiatrist (psychiatry), 7, 8, 16, 302, 530, 628

Psychoanalysis, 16, 20-21, 22, 23, 154-55, 289, 536, 543-46, 628; abreaction in, 545; free association in, 21, 336, 543, 546; insight in, 545; interpretation in, 544; personality development according to, 477-80, 481; research on, 545-46; as theory of personality dynamics, 484-85; transference in, 545-46; working-through process in, 545

Psychoanalyst, 530, 628

Psychodrama, *542,* 628

Psychogenic needs, 125, *126,* 628

Psychograph, 473, 629; *see also* Trait profile

Psychokinesis, 217, 218, 219, 220, 629

Psycholinguistics, 609

Psychological Corporation, 586

Psychological primaries (colors), 229, 629

Psychological types, 470-71

Psychology: applied, 2-3, 252, 629; association, 14, 22; as behavioral science, 2-29 *passim;* behavioristic, 17-18, 19, 20, 349, 608-09; biology related to, 8; case histories in, 13; clinical, 530, 600; comparative, 6, 15, 605-06; counseling, 600; educational, 603; and engineering, 8; European viewpoints in, 7; experimental, 9-11, 14, 599-600; faculty, 14; field theory in, 19, 20, 485-86; future of, 604-10; Gestalt, 19-20, 22-23, 194, 196, 197, 202, 486, 553; history of, 13-16; humanistic, 608, 609; industrial, 591-98; interview as tool of, 13; introspective, 13, 13 *n.*, 14, 17, 19; legal, 602-03; measurement in, 23-27; medicine related to, 8-9, 16, 603-04; miniature systems in, 21, 22; naturalistic observation in, 12-13; philosophic origins of, 13-14; and physical sciences, 8; physiology related to, 8; as profession, 598-604; professional and vocational applications of, 581-610; and psychiatry, 7, 8, 16; psychoanalytical, *see* Psychoanalysis; schools of, 16; social, 6, 552-78, 600-01, 610; specialization within, 598-602; statistics in, 25 *ff.*, 390, 601; stimulus-response, 17-18, 19, 20, 22, 23; theory in, role of, 16-23; vocational and professional applications of, 581-610

Psychoneuroses, 524, 529, 629

Psychophysical methods, in threshold measurements, 224, 629

Psychophysics, 629

Psychosexual development, 477-79, *478, 479,* 629; *see also* Psychoanalysis

Psychosis, 525-26; manic-depressive, 468, 469; paranoid, 525-26; schizophrenic, 525

Psychosocial crises, 478-79, *479,* 629

Psychosomatic disorders, 57-58, 179, 527, 629

Psychosomatic medicine, 8, 167

Psychotherapy, 181, 302, 529, 629; for children, 535-36; existentialist approach to, 543; group, 534-35; interpretive, 536; play, 535; relationship, 536; relative success of methods of, 546-47; release,

Trobriand Islanders, 104
Trouble-shooting, 352, 353, 354
Turner's syndrone, 425
Twins, 70, 72, 73, 434, 435, 436, 437, *437*, 528
Two-point threshold, 245, *246*
Type theories, 468-72, 488, 635
Types: body 468-69; psychological, 470-71

Uncertainty, 353-54, *353,* 635
Unconscious motive, 148, 635; *see* Psychoanalysis
Unconscious processes, 7-8, 21, 148, 361, 635
"Understanding"-psychology, 7
Union-management relations, 596-98
Unlearning, 301
Utricle, *248; see also* Vestibular sacs

Validity, 397-99, 635; coefficient of, 398; concurrent, 399, 616; construct, 399, 616; content, 399; predictive, 399, 628; of test scores, 397, 398, 399
Values: adolescent, 108 *ff.;* and needs, 213-16; perception influenced by, 214; personality reflected in, 453; in social psychology, 563
Variable(s): 9, 635; dependent, 10, 10 *n.,* 11, 24, 25, 269, 617; independent, 10, 10 *n.,* 11, 24, 269, 622; intervening, 18, 50, 622; measurement of, 23, 24, 25; social desirability, 457, 632; statistical investigation of, 25-27; and uniqueness, 452
Variance, 25 *n.,* 635; genetic, 444
Variation: concomitant, 24, 25; measures of, 370-75, 624
Verbal comprehension, 409
Verbal defect, 350, 635
Verbal report, 7, 20 *n.,* 635
Verbal scale, in intelligence tests, 407, 408
Verbal scores, in intelligence tests, 412
Verification, 360, 361-62, 635
Vestibular sacs, 247, 635
Visceral brain, 42
Viscerogenic needs, 125
Vision, 224-33; adaptation of, to illumination, 227-28; night, 227; physiology of, 231-32; stereoscopic, 203-04, 633; *see also* Color; Eye; Light
Visual area, 44-45, 46, 635
Visual field, 225-26, 635
Visual purple, 231, 635
Visual sense, *see* Vision

Vitreous humor, 225
Vocational choice, 581-91
Vocational guidance, 585-91; ability tests in, 585-86; interest tests in, *587,* 587-89, *589*
Volley theory of hearing, 239, 636
Voluntary action, 636; *see* Operant behavior
Voting behavior, study of, 571-72, *572,* 574

Wage incentive plan, 593, 636
Wage incentives, 593
War, 610
Waterfall illusion, 201
Watson, John B., and behaviorism, 17, 19
Wave lengths of light, 228
Weaning, 83, 84, 137
Wechsler Adult Intelligence Scale, 406, 407, 408, 411
Wechsler-Bellevue Test, 429
Wechsler Intelligence Scale for Children, 407, 408
Weeping, 169
Weighted items, 394, 636
Wertheimer, Max, 19
Whole learning, 314-15, 636
Wholist strategy, in problem-solving, 351, 352
Whorf, B. L., theory of language and thought, 348
Will, as term in psychology, 146, 147
Window, rotating trapezoidal, 190, *190*
Wisdom, differentiated from intelligence, 412
Wish-fulfillment, 484
Woodworth, Robert S., 18, 205, 317
Word association experiment, 636
Word fluency, 409
Work: efficiency in, 593, 594; satisfaction in, 582-83; useful, and mental health, 547
Work inhibition, 523, 636
Working-through, in psychoanalysis, 545, 636
World Health Organization, 413
Wundt, Wilhelm, 14, 15, *15*

X-chromosome, 424, 425, 636

Yale University, 15, 82, 281
Y-chromosome, 424, 425, 636
Young-Helmholtz theory of color vision, 232, 233

Zest, 523, 636
Zuni Indians, 349